PEARSON   ALWAYS LEARNING

John J. Macionis • S. Mikael Jansson • Cecilia M. Benoit
Jakub Burkowicz

Society
The Basics

Second Custom Edition for the University of British Columbia

Taken from:
Society: The Basics, Sixth Canadian Edition
by John J. Macionis, S. Mikael Jansson, Cecilia M. Benoit, and Jakub Burkowicz

Cover Art: Courtesy of Jules Selmes/Pearson Education Ltd and stockyimages/123rf.com and Michaelpuche, doglikehorse, Rob Marmion, Goodluz, arek_malang, Flashon Studio/Shutterstock.

Taken from:

Society: The Basics, Sixth Canadian Edition
by John J. Macionis, S. Mikael Jansson, Cecilia M. Benoit, and Jakub Burkowicz
Copyright © 2017 Pearson Canada Inc.
Toronto, Ontario

This special edition published in cooperation with Pearson Education, Inc.

Pearson Education, Inc., 330 Hudson Street, New York, New York 10013
A Pearson Education Company
www.pearsoned.com

Printed in the United States of America

000200010272128568

JC

ISBN 10: 1-323-80323-8
ISBN 13: 978-1-323-80323-3

Brief Contents

Contents

6   Sexuality and Society   162

7   Deviance   196

8   Social Stratification   234

9 Global Stratification   280

10 Gender Stratification   308

16 Social Change: Modern and Postmodern Societies   550

the Power of Society to encourage or discourage participation in social movements   551

Boxes

Maps

NATIONAL MAPS: *Seeing Ourselves*

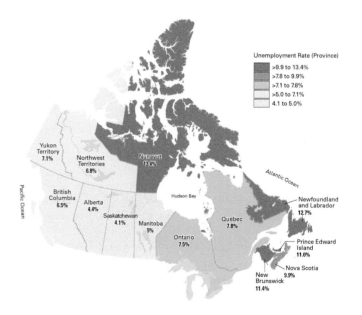

Preface

The world challenges us like never before. The economy is uncertain, not only in Canada, but also around the world. For decades, income inequality in our society has steadily increased, just as it is increasing for the world as a whole. There is a lot of anger about how our leaders in Ottawa are doing—or not doing—their jobs. Technological disasters of our own making threaten the natural environment, and patterns of extreme weather only add to the mounting evidence of global warming.

Perhaps no one should be surprised to read polls that tell us most people are anxious about their economic future, unhappy with our government and political system, and worried about the state of the planet. Many of us feel overwhelmed, as if we were up against forces we can barely understand—much less control.

That is where sociology comes in. For more than 150 years, sociologists have been working to better understand how society operates. We sociologists may not have all the answers, but we have learned quite a lot. A beginning course in sociology is your introduction to the fascinating and very useful study of the social world. After all, we all have a stake in understanding our world and doing all we can to improve it.

Society: The Basics, Sixth Canadian Edition, provides you with comprehensive understanding of how your social world works. You will find this book informative, engaging, and even entertaining. Before you have finished the first chapter, you will discover that sociology is not only useful—it is also a great deal of fun. *Sociology is a field of study that can change the way you see the world and open the door to many new opportunities.* What could be more exciting than that?

What's New in This Edition?

Here is a quick summary of the new material found throughout *Society: The Basics*, Sixth Canadian Edition.

- **Learning Objectives**. Each major section of every chapter begins with a specific Learning Objective. All Learning Objectives are listed at the beginning of each chapter and they organize the summary at the end of each chapter.

- **Power of Society figures**. If you could teach your students only one thing in the introductory course, what would it be? Probably, most instructors would answer, *"to understand the power of society to shape people's lives."* Each chapter now begins with a Power of Society figure that does exactly that—forcing students to give up some of their cultural common sense that points to the importance of "personal choice" in the face of evidence of how society shapes our major life decisions.

- A **new design** makes this edition of the text the cleanest and easiest ever to read. Also, the photo and art programs have been thoroughly reviewed and updated.

- **Updated statistics**. We live and breathe statistical data in our jobs as sociologists. Having current statistical information in the text is paramount. The Sixth Canadian Edition incorporates statistical data from the 2011 Census, and, where appropriate, the National Household Survey conducted by Statistics Canada, as well as other new and relevant sources.

- **New scholarship dealing with race, class, and gender**. For example, Chapter 3 ("Socialization") opens up by considering how race impacts the socialization of alcohol consumption. Chapter 6 ("Sexuality and Society") has expanded discussion of transgender issues. Chapter 10 ("Gender Stratification") has new discussions of global and multicultural feminism. Chapter 11 ("Race and Ethnicity") has expanded discussion of visible minorities, new discussion of white privilege, as well as a new discussion of the history of racism in Canada toward eastern and southern Europeans.

- Much more on **Aboriginal peoples**. Many chapters explicitly recognize Canada's history of colonialism and its impact on Aboriginal peoples. Chapter 2 ("Culture") has new discussion on changes in Canadian cultural values concerning Aboriginal peoples. Chapter 7 ("Deviance") includes an updated discussion of the over-representation of Aboriginal peoples in the criminal justice system, as well as a new discussion of Aboriginal community–based solutions to crime. Chapter 13 ("Family and Religion") features a new discussion on the various structures of Aboriginal families. Chapter 14 ("Education, Health, and Medicine") discusses the impact of underfunding on schooling in Aboriginal communities.

- Much more on **social media.** More than ever before, social life revolves around computer-based technology that shapes networks and social movements. Social media are discussed throughout the text and major sections on social media are found in Chapter 4 ("Social Interaction in Everyday Life") and Chapter 5 ("Groups and Organizations").

Here is a brief summary of some of the material that is new, chapter-by-chapter:

Chapter 1: Sociology: Perspective, Theory, and Method
The new Power of Society figure shows that our class background plays a role in how likely we are to marry. The revised chapter has updates on the suicide rate by gender and region in Canada; the number of children born to women in nations around the world; the number of high-income, middle-income, and low-income nations; and the changing share of racial minorities in major sports.

Chapter 2: Culture
The new Power of Society figure shows varying levels of support for access to abortion in high- and low-income nations. The chapter has updates on the number of languages spoken as a measure of this country's cultural diversity; the extent of global illiteracy; patterns of immigration, and the share of all webpages written in English. The chapter has added new data on the social views of drunk driving. There is a new box on the origins of hip-hop music. The discussion of Canadian multiculturalism has been expanded and an updated discussion of Canadian values is featured.

Chapter 3: Socialization: From Infancy to Old Age
The new Power of Society figure shows that race and ethnicity impact the patterns of alcohol consumption among youth. The chapter has revised the discussion on cultural capital and updated the Seeing Sociology in Everyday Life box. Erik H. Erikson's eight stages of development have been added. The discussion on resocialization has been expanded to include the distinction between voluntary and involuntary resocialization, as well as Ervin Goffman's five types of total institutions.

Chapter 4: Social Interaction in Everyday Life

The new Power of Society figure shows internet use by people of different age categories. The discussion of nonverbal communication highlights its importance to people with a physical disability. Find updates on the discussion on emotional labour and "put down" jokes. The discussion of body language and deception has been expanded. There is a new section on social media, pointing out how computer technology has changed patterns of social networking and reality construction.

Chapter 5: Groups and Organizations

The new Power of Society figure explores how social class shapes the odds of performing volunteer work. The revised chapter has updates on the size and scope of McDonalds. There is a new section on social media and networking.

Chapter 6: Sexuality and Society

The new Power of Society figure tracks the trend toward acceptance of same-sex marriage. Find updates on the size of the lesbian, gay, bisexual, and transgender (LGBT) community; the share of high school students who have had sexual intercourse; and the share of married people who engage in extramarital sex. Find discussion of Bill C-36, which has criminalized a number of activities related to sex work; a new section on transgenderism; the latest statistics on teen pregnancy and rape; new discussion of male power over women in terms of reproductive health; and new discussion (including a new Global Map) of global access to abortion.

Chapter 7: Deviance

The new Power of Society figure shows how race places some categories of the Canadian population at much higher risk of being incarcerated. Find the latest information on the number of serious crimes committed in recent years. There is analysis of patterns of arrest for "violent crimes" and "property crimes" for 2013. The chapter reports the number of police in Canada and the number of people in prison; provides an updated discussion of the highest risk for being an offender by considering age, gender, class, and race and ethnicity; and features an expanded discussion on corporate crime. The chapter also considers racism within the criminal justice system and protests against police brutality. Find new sections on fundamental justice and Aboriginal-based sentencing circles.

Chapter 8: Social Stratification

The new Power of Society figure shows how family status sets the odds in Canada for experiencing poverty. The chapter has updates on social inequality in Russia, China, and South Africa and the latest data for all measures of economic inequality in Canada, including income and wealth, the economic assets of the country's richest families, and the educational achievement of various categories of the population. New data show the poverty rate for visible minorities. There are 2011 data on the extent of poverty, the number of working poor, and how poverty interacts with age, race, ethnicity, gender, and family type; a new estimate of the hourly wage needed to support an urban worker above the poverty line; and new data on the extent of homelessness.

Chapter 9: Global Stratification

The new Power of Society figure shows how the nation into which a person is born sets the odds of surviving to the age of five. The chapter has updates on garment factory work in Bangladesh; the distribution of income and wealth and the number of people in the world who are poor; the average income for the world as a whole; the number and updated social profile of nations at different levels of development; the latest UN data on quality of life in various regions of the world; and the latest data on global debt. There is expanded discussion of the link between population increase and poverty. Recent data illuminate economic trends in various regions of the world and confirm the increasing economic gap between the highest- and lowest-income nations. There are updates on wealth and well-being in selected nations at each level of economic development.

Chapter 10: Gender Stratification

The new Power of Society figure shows the gender wage gap. Find updates on life expectancy for Canadian women and men; the share of degrees earned by each sex in various fields of study; the share of Canadian women and men in the labour force, the share working full time, and the share in many sex-typed occupations; the share of large corporations with women in leadership positions; unemployment rates for women and men; and the latest data on income and wealth by gender. There are the most recent statistics on women in political leadership positions and updated discussion of violence against women and men. A new section of women in the military is featured. The coverage of intersection theory reflects the most recent income data. There is a new discussion of multicultural and global feminism.

Chapter 11: Race and Ethnicity

The new Power of Society figure considers mixed-race unions in Canada. Find updates on the share and size of all racial and ethnic categories of the Canadian population; the share of Canadian marriages that are interracial; the population and distribution of Aboriginal peoples in Canada; the major visible minority populations; and the income levels and poverty rates for all major racial and ethnic categories of the Canadian population. Trends highlighted include the increase of Canadians who report multiple-ethnic origins and the increase in workers who participate in the Temporary Foreign Worker Program. Find new discussion on white privilege, racism in the Canadian labour market, and intersectionality.

Chapter 12: Economics and Politics

The new Power of Society figure demonstrates how race and ethnicity guide the type of work people do. Find updates on the share of the Canadian population by visible minority status in the labour force and the share of women and men who are self-employed. There is expanded discussion of the nature of work in Canada's post-industrial economy; the role of labour unions; and the effects of the U.S. recession on the Canadian economy. Find updated data on the Canadian unemployment rate. New discussion on "socialism of the twenty-first century" is featured.

The chapter has updates on the number of people employed in government; voter turnout and voter preferences—by class, race, gender, and religion—in the 2011 elections; the number of lobbyists and special interest groups; recent political trends involving college students; the latest data on the extent of terrorism; the latest data on civilian deaths in the Iraq War; the latest nuclear disarmament negotiations, recent changes in nuclear proliferation, and changing support for strategic defence initiative (SDI) as a peace-keeping policy; and the latest data on global and U.S. military spending. There is a new National Map showing regional results in the 2015 federal election. There is new discussion on voter abstention.

Chapter 13: Family and Religion

The new Power of Society figure shows how religious affiliation—or the lack of it—is linked to attitudes on sex and sexuality. There is expanded discussion of the importance of grandparents in childrearing and the experience of loneliness and families in later life. There is new discussion of the trend of cohabitation as an alternative to marriage. There is new discussion of singlehood. New historical data on Canadian trends in divorce and marriages are featured. The chapter has updates on Canadian family forms, including blended families and one-parent families. New information is provided on Aboriginal family forms; ethnically and racially mixed marriages; gay and lesbian families; and visible minority families. There is new discussion of the incidence of court-ordered child support and the frequency of non-payment; and the rate of family violence against women and children. Data for 2015 show the number of nations that permit same-sex marriage.

The latest data show the extent of religious belief in Canada as well as the share of people favouring various denominations. Data for 2011 document the numbers of self-identifying Catholics, Muslims, Hindus, Sikhs, Buddhists, and Jews. There is expanded discussion of a trend away from religious affiliation, and historical data are provided on the decline of religious attendance in Canada. There is expanded discussion of the secularization debate as well as more extensive application of feminist theory to religion. There is an expanded discussion of New Age spirituality, as well as a new discussion of Aboriginal spirituality and the history of black churches in Canada.

Chapter 14: Education, Health, and Medicine

The new Power of Society figure shows the importance of class for shaping educational experience. Find new global data that compare the academic performance of children in Canada with that of children in Japan, India, and the United States. New data identify the share of Canadian adults completing high school and college, how income affects access to higher education, and how higher education is linked to earnings later on. There are new data on educational attainment by province and territory. New data on high school teachers' salaries across Canada are provided and a new section on the teaching market has been added. Dropping out of high school and grade inflation in colleges and universities are discussed. New sections address the latest trends in charter and magnet schools in Canada, as well as homeschooling, adult education, and schooling people with disabilities. A box on Aboriginal education has been added.

The revised chapter has expanded discussion of prejudice against people based on body weight. There are updates on global patterns of health reflecting improvements in the well-being of young children; cigarette smoking and illnesses resulting from this practice; how gender shapes patterns involving eating disorders; patterns of AIDS and other sexually transmitted diseases; and euthanasia. The revised chapter considers how class and race shape the health outcomes of Canadians. New data document the prevalence of gonorrhea, chlamydia, and syphilis in the Canadian population. New data on HIV cases and race are featured. New information is provided for the Canadian health care system; comparisons are made to the U.S. system and other nations; and the nursing shortage is discussed.

Chapter 15: Population, Urbanization, and Environment

The new Power of Society figure shows that concern for environmental issues is typically greater in high-income nations. The chapter has the most recent data on the size of the Canadian population as well as fertility and mortality rates for Canada and for various world regions; new data for infant mortality and life expectancy; new global population projections; and updated coverage of trends in urbanization. Find expanded coverage of social life in rural places. A new section addresses neighbourhood gentrification in Canada. New discussions highlight urbanization in low-income regions of the world, changes in water consumption, and the declining size of the planet's rainforests.

Chapter 16: Social Change: Modern and Postmodern Societies

The new Power of Society figure shows in which nations people are more or less likely to engage in public demonstrations. The chapter has updates on life expectancy and other demographic changes. New data highlight population change between 2006 and 2011. There is an updated National Map showing the extent of residential growth and decline across Canada. There is discussion of collective behaviour, including new sections for crowds; mobs and riots; rumour; and fashion and fads. A new box on the history of jeans frames the discussion of the relationship of tradition

to modernity. There is new discussion of the Geechee people of Hog Hammock, whose rising property values threaten to displace this historic African-American community. Discussion of political economy and new social movement theory has been expanded.

Student Resources

REVEL™ Designed for the way today's students read, think, and learn, REVEL is a groundbreaking immersive learning experience. It is based on a simple premise: When students are engaged deeply, they learn more and get better results.

Built in collaboration with educators and students, REVEL brings course content to life with rich media and assessments—integrated directly within the authors' narrative—that provide opportunities for students to read, learn, and practise in one environment.

Learn more about REVEL
http://www.pearsonhighered.com/revel/

A Word About Language

This text has a commitment to describe the social diversity of Canada and the world. This promise carries with it the responsibility to use language thoughtfully. The book uses the terms "Aboriginal" and "First Nations" rather than the word "Indian." Similarly, we use the term "visible minority" to refer to people of non-white backgrounds. Most tables and figures refer to "visible minorities" as well, because this is the term Statistics Canada uses when collecting statistical data about our population.

Students should realize, however, that many individuals do not describe themselves using these terms. For example, in this text, the term "Aboriginal" refers to people whose ancestors lived here prior to the arrival of Europeans. Here again, however, most people in this broad category identify with their historical society, such as Ojibwe, Blackfoot, Tla-o-qui-aht, Haida, or Kwantlens and Iroquois. "First Nations" refers to Canada's Aboriginal peoples who are neither Inuit nor Metis. Likewise, across Canada, people of Spanish descent identify with a particular ancestral nation, whether it be Argentina, Mexico, some other Latin American country, or Spain or Portugal in Europe. The same holds for Asian Canadians. Although this term is a useful shorthand in sociological analysis, most people of Asian descent think of themselves in terms of a specific country of origin, say, Japan, the Philippines, Taiwan, or Vietnam.

On a global level, this text avoids the word "American"—which literally designates two continents—to refer to just the United States. For example, referring to the term "the U.S. economy" is more precise than "the American economy." This convention may seem a small point, but it implies the significant recognition that the Americas also include Canada.

Supplements for Instructors

Instructor supplements are available for download from a password-protected section of Pearson Canada's online catalogue (**www.pearsoncanada.ca/highered**). Navigate to your book's catalogue page to view a list of those supplements that are available. See your local sales representative for details and access.

INSTRUCTOR'S MANUAL This text offers an instructor's manual that will be of interest even to those who have never chosen to use one before. The manual provides the expected detailed chapter outlines and discussion questions and much more—summaries of important developments, recent articles from *Teaching Sociology* that are relevant to classroom discussions, suggestions for classroom activities, and supplemental lecture material for every chapter of the text.

TEST ITEM FILE This key author-created supplement reflects the material in the textbook—both in content and in language—far better than the testing file available with any other introductory sociology textbook. The file contains over 2000 items—more than 100 per chapter—in multiple-choice, true-false, and essay formats. All of the questions are identified by level of difficulty.

COMPUTERIZED TEST BANK Pearson's computerized test banks allow instructors to filter and select questions to create quizzes, tests, or homework. Instructors can revise questions or add their own, and may be able to choose print or online options. These questions are also available in Microsoft Word format.

POWERPOINT® SLIDES These PowerPoint slides combine graphics and text in a colourful format to help you convey sociological principles in a visual and exciting way. Each chapter of the textbook has approximately 15 to 25 slides that communicate the key concepts in that chapter.

PEERSCHOLAR Firmly grounded in published research, peerScholar is a powerful online pedagogical tool that helps develop your students' critical and creative thinking skills. peerScholar facilitates this through the process of creation, evaluation, and reflection. Working in stages, students begin by submitting a written assignment. peerScholar then circulates their work for others to review, a process that can be anonymous or not depending on your preference. Students receive peer feedback and evaluations immediately, reinforcing their learning and driving the development of higher-order thinking skills. Students can then re-submit revised work, again depending on your preference. Contact your Pearson representative to learn more about peerScholar and the research behind it.

MULTIMEDIA GUIDE This teaching guide that can accompany any Pearson introductory sociology text helps professors bring sociological concepts to life in the classroom with material to which students relate. Featuring 20 scenes from Hollywood feature films, documentaries, TV episodes, and over 30 songs, this guide provides

- A synopsis of the film or documentary and the relevant scene, the scene location on the DVD, and an explanation of how the selection relates to sociology
- The cultural context of album and song as well as an explanation of how the song relates to sociological issues
- 5 to 10 discussion questions plus 1 assignment follow each scene and song

NOTE: Pearson Canada does not provide the films, documentaries, television episodes, or songs.

LEARNING SOLUTIONS MANAGERS Pearson's Learning Solutions Managers work with faculty and campus course designers to ensure that Pearson technology products, assessment tools, and online course materials are tailored to meet your specific needs. This highly qualified team is dedicated to helping schools take full advantage of a wide range of educational resources, by assisting in the integration of a variety of instructional materials and media formats. Your local Pearson Canada sales representative can provide you with more details on this service program.

In Appreciation

I dedicate this Sixth Canadian Edition of *Society: The Basics* to the memory of my mother, May Johnston Macionis (1917–2013). Mom, the life lessons you passed along to me, especially the importance of reaching out to other members of the community—and to people in other communities—will remain within me always. May you find peace on your journey!

With best wishes to my colleagues and with love to all,

Jan J. Macionis

I would like to acknowledge my co-authors, John J. Macionis, S. Mikael Jansson, and Cecilia Benoit, whose work over the years has raised this textbook to a high standard—one that I am proud and delighted to be a part of. I am also grateful to the following peer reviewers who provided many helpful suggestions: Angela Aujla (Humber College); Deanna Behnke-Cook (University of Guelph); Deborah Boutilier (Niagara College); Irfan Chaudhry (MacEwan University); Pearl Crichton (Concordia University); Glenn Davis (Red River College); Melanie Marchand (Georgian College); and Miriam Melamed-Turkish (George Brown College), as well as to the people at Pearson whose skills helped to bring this book to fruition—among them, Matthew Christian, Acquisitions Editor; Charlotte Morrison-Reed, Developmental Editor; Sarah Gallagher, Project Manager; Tania Andrabi, Production Editor; Cat Haggert, Copyeditor; and Katie McWhirter, Sales and Editorial Representative.

This book also benefited from support given by a number of colleagues, friends, and mentors, many of whom generously provided feedback and suggestions whenever I requested such help. Gratitude is due to Wendy Chan (Simon Fraser University); Robert Menzies (Simon Fraser University); Dany Lacombe (Simon Fraser University); Robert Ratner (University of British Columbia); Sean Ashley (Capilano University); Efe Peker (Simon Fraser University/Université Paris 1 Panthéon-Sorbonne); Ann Travers (Simon Fraser University); Maureen Kihika (Simon Fraser University); Jennifer Thomas (Simon Fraser University); Ataman Avdan (Simon Fraser University); and Adam Barker (University of Leicester). I am also thankful to Shantala Robinson, who lent her artistic vision to this project.

Thanks is also due to Marni Westerman (Douglas College) and the Department of Humanities and Social Sciences at Douglas College, Adrian Lipsett and the support staff at Alexander College, as well as the department of Sociology and Anthropology at Simon Fraser University, for giving me the opportunity to test this book out in action (that is, in teaching). I am also indebted to all of my students who provided me with a new way of looking at textbooks and the task of teaching sociology. I am, furthermore, extremely grateful to Tracey Anbinder, Manager, Academic and Administrative Services; Lynn Wood, Program Assistant; and Rosaline Baik, Coordinator at the Faculty of Arts and Social Sciences at Simon Fraser University (Surrey campus). Their kind willingness to accommodate my writing needs has been of tremendous help.

Deep appreciation is also due to my wife, Taslim, who provided support throughout. Her dedication to our family has allowed me to do what I do best.

Lastly, I would like to dedicate this sixth edition of the book to three of the most imaginative and inquisitive people in my life—my sons Anjay, Alek, and Augustyn—with the hope that they find in sociology an answer and a challenge.

Jakub Burkowicz

About the Authors

John Macionis John J. Macionis (pronounced "ma-SHOW-nis") was born and raised in Philadelphia, Pennsylvania. He earned a bachelor's degree from Cornell University and a doctorate in sociology from the University of Pennsylvania.

His publications are wide-ranging, focusing on community life in the United States, interpersonal intimacy in families, effective teaching, humour, new information technology, and the importance of global education. In addition to authoring this best-seller, Macionis has also written *Sociology*, the best-selling hardback text in the field, now in its sixteenth edition. He collaborates on international editions of the texts: *Sociology: Canadian Edition; Society: The Basics, Canadian Edition;* and *Sociology: A Global Introduction. Sociology* is also available for high school students and in various foreign-language editions.

In addition, Macionis and Nijole V. Benokraitis have edited the best-selling anthology *Seeing Ourselves: Classic, Contemporary, and Cross-Cultural Readings in Sociology*, also available in a Canadian edition. Macionis and Vincent Parrillo have written the leading urban studies text, *Cities and Urban Life*. Macionis's most recent textbook is *Social Problems* (Pearson Prentice Hall), now in its fourth edition and the leading book in this field. The latest on all the Macionis textbooks, as well as information and dozens of internet links of interest to students and faculty in sociology, are found at the author's personal website: **www.macionis.com** or **www.TheSociologyPage.com**. Additional information, instructor resources, and online student study guides for the texts are found at the Pearson site: **www.pearsoncanada.ca**.

John Macionis is Professor and Distinguished Scholar of Sociology at Kenyon College in Gambier, Ohio, where he has taught for more than 30 years. During that time, he has chaired the Sociology Department, directed the college's multidisciplinary program in humane studies, presided over the campus senate and the college's faculty, and taught sociology to thousands of students.

In 2002, the American Sociological Association presented Macionis with the Award for Distinguished Contributions to Teaching, citing his innovative use of global material as well as the introduction of new teaching technology in his textbooks.

Professor Macionis has been active in academic programs in other countries, having travelled to some 50 nations. He writes, "I am an ambitious traveler, eager to learn and, through the texts, to share much of what I discover with students, many of whom know little about the rest of the world. For me, traveling and writing are all dimensions of teaching. First, and foremost, I am a teacher—a passion for teaching animates everything I do."

At Kenyon, Professor Macionis teaches a number of courses, but his favourite class is Introduction to Sociology, which he offers every semester. He enjoys extensive contact with students and invites everyone enrolled in each of his classes to enjoy a home-cooked meal.

The Macionis family—John, Amy, and children McLean and Whitney—live on a farm in rural Ohio. In his free time, Macionis enjoys tennis, swimming, hiking, and playing oldies rock-and-roll (he recently released his third CD). Macionis is an environmental activist, focusing on the Lake George region of New York's Adirondack Mountains, where he works with a number of organizations, including the Lake George Land Conservancy, where he serves as president of the board of trustees.

Professor Macionis welcomes (and responds to) comments and suggestions about this book from faculty and students. Write to him at the Sociology Department, Palme House, Kenyon College, Gambier, OH 43022, or send e-mail to **macionis@kenyon.edu**.

Mikael Jansson Mikael Jansson is a Scientist at the Centre for Addictions Research of BC, and an Adjunct Assistant Professor in the Department of Sociology at the University of Victoria. Having lived in Sweden, Canada, Mexico, and Finland, he moved 10 times before deciding to study migration at the University of Western Ontario where he received a doctorate in Social Demography in the department of Sociology. His work is currently focused primarily on research along with many guest and invited lectures in Canada and internationally.

Mikael is involved in several longitudinal research projects on changing lives and health over the life course. His research is focused on youth (including street-involved youth) and personal service workers such as food and beverage servers, hair stylists, and sex workers. He is just completing a five-year research project about people working in the sex industry. This cross-Canada study has several sub-projects and Mikael is focusing on the families of sex workers with the goal of understanding how partners support each other when at least one partner is working in the sex industry. He conducted in-person interviews with 30 couples across Canada for this project and has supervised or conducted in person interviews with close to 500 sex workers across Canada and the United States in the last decade.

He has published nine books (including the one you are reading now), almost 50 refereed articles, chapters and reports, and made more than a hundred invited presentations in Canada and many other countries. If you are interested you can access many of his articles by searching for him on Google Scholar. He is frequently sought out to review articles and grant proposals by Canadian and international publishers and funders.

He is an avid (but slow) bicyclist and rides more than 10 000 kilometres each year. Many of these kilometres are in other countries because he brings a bicycle with him whenever he travels. His most recent trip was from Turin, Italy, through Croatia, Bosnia and Herzegovina, Montenegro, and Albania on his way to Athens, Greece. He has ridden his bicycle more than 1000 kilometers on every continent except Australia/Oceania and Antarctica.

You can reach Mikael at **mjansson@uvic.ca**. He welcomes enquires from students interested in working with him in Victoria on his research projects.

Cecilia Benoit Cecilia Benoit was born and raised in Newfoundland, Canada. She earned Bachelor degrees in Education and Sociology, and a Masters in Sociology from Memorial University. Her doctorate degree is from the Department of Sociology at the University of Toronto.

She is a Professor in the Department of Sociology at the University of Victoria, Scientist at the Centre for Addictions Research of BC, and Fellow of both the Royal Society of Canada and the Canadian Academy of Health Sciences.

The courses she teaches include Introductory Sociology, Sociology of Health across the Life Course, and Population Health, Health Equity & Health Care. She has mentored 40 graduate students, many of whom now hold leadership roles in the public and nonprofit sectors or work as policy analysts for national organizations.

Apart from research focused on the occupation of midwifery and the organization of maternity care in Canada and internationally, Professor Benoit has been involved in a variety of projects that employ mixed methodologies to investigate the health of different vulnerable groups, including Aboriginal women in Vancouver's Downtown Eastside, young people confronting health stigmas linked to obesity and asthma, workers in lower-prestige service occupations, adults in the sex industry, pregnant and early parenting women dealing with addiction and other challenges and street-involved youth in transition to adulthood.

Professor Benoit is the author/coauthor/coeditor of a number of scholarly works, including *Midwives in Passage* (1991), *Women, Work and Social Rights* (2000), *Professional Identities in Transition* (1999), *Birth by Design* (2001), *Reconceiving Midwifery* (2004), *Ethical Issues in Community-based Research with Children and Youth* (2006), *Valuing Care Work* (2011) and *'I Feel like I've Really Grown Up': The Experience of Emerging Adulthood among Street-Involved Youth* (2016). She has also published over 150 peer-reviewed articles, book chapters, and government reports. Her articles have appeared in leading journals in sociology and the health sciences, including: *Social Science & Medicine, Sociology of Health & Illness, Social Forces, Qualitative Health Research, Current Sociology, International Journal for Equity in Health,* Canadian Journal of Public Health, and *Health Psychology*. Much of her work involves co-authorship with students and/or knowledge users.

You can find out about Professor Benoit's research by checking out her websites at **http://web.uvic.ca/~cbenoit/**, **http://www.understandingsexwork.com** or contact her at **cbenoit@uvic.ca**.

The Benoit-Jansson family (or should that be the Jansson-Benoit family?) live in a small house close to the University of Victoria. Together with their daughter, Annika, they enjoy the lakes and forests on Vancouver Island, spending their leisure time fly-fishing in the spring, swimming in the summer, and gathering wild mushrooms in the fall (these being the only three seasons in Victoria). They like to bike all year around.

Jakub Burkowicz Jakub Burkowicz (pronounced "Ya-koob Bur-ko-vitch") was born and partially raised in Poland. His family briefly resided in what was then known as West Germany before immigrating to Canada in 1989. He has called Vancouver home since the early 90s. Immigration has made him curious about how societies work, and he has devoted himself to the task of understanding (and changing) the social world.

Currently, Jakub is a PhD (ABD) Candidate at the Department of Sociology and Anthropology at Simon Fraser University. His doctoral research is a historical sociology that examines Canadian perceptions of Slavic immigrants, particularly by considering how this category of Eastern and Central Europeans was racialized from the 1880s to the 1960s. To document this, he has dug through a number of archives uncovering newspaper and magazine articles, encyclopedic entries, medical articles, novels, poems, police reports, academic research, political speeches, and debates in the House of Commons.

Jakub is also interested in the study of social movements. He has recently served as Guest Editor of a special topic issue of *Affinities: A Journal of Radical Theory, Culture, and Action*. The issue examines how an activist culture of prefigurative politics constructs antiracist spaces where colonialism, systemic racism, white supremacy, and fascism are challenged and dismantled. It also reflects Jakub's own commitment to community-based scholarly work, giving him a chance to invite and work on manuscripts submitted by academics, artists, and activists. He continues to write and research on this topic.

In addition, he has taught as a sessional instructor at Simon Fraser University, Douglas College, and Alexander College. Besides Introduction to Sociology, he currently teaches such courses as Sociological Theory, Social Movements, Sociology of Knowledge, and Canadian Society. You can learn more about Jakub's teaching and research by contacting him at **jmburkow@sfu.ca**.

When not committing sociology, Jakub spends his free time with his family, which includes his wife Taslim, and his sons Anjay, Alek, and Augustyn.

Society
The Basics

1 Sociology: Perspective, Theory, and Method

Darren Baker/Fotolia

LEARNING OBJECTIVES

1.1 Explain how the sociological perspective helps us understand that society shapes our individual lives.

1.2 State several reasons that a global perspective is important in today's world.

1.3 Identify the advantages of sociological thinking for developing public policy, for encouraging personal growth, and for advancing in a career.

1.4 Link the origins of sociology to historical social changes.

1.5 Summarize sociology's major theoretical approaches.

1.6 Describe sociology's three research orientations.

1.7 Identify the importance of gender in sociological research.

1.8 Discuss the importance of ethics to sociological research.

1.9 Explain why a researcher might choose each of sociology's research methods.

1.10 Recall the 10 important steps in carrying out sociological research.

the Power of Society

to guide our likelihood of getting married

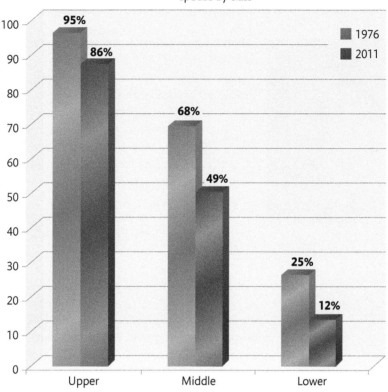

Proportion of families with one married or common-law spouse by class

Source: Cross & Mitchell (2014). Figure 4, p. 17, http://www.imfcanada.org/sites/default/files/event/CMD-FINAL.pdf. Reprinted with permission.

How likely are you to get married? You might be surprised to find that part of the answer depends on your social class. Research in Canada indicates a "marriage gap," with wealthy Canadians forming more wedding unions than poor Canadians. That gap has also widened over time: In 1976, 95 percent of upper class and 25 percent of lower class Canadians were married (a gap of 70 percent), while by 2011 the numbers were 86 and 12 percent, respectively (a gap of 74 percent). Although we tend to think of love and marriage as very personal matters, it is clear that society guides the process.

Chapter Overview

You are about to begin a course that could change your life. Sociology is a new and exciting way of understanding the world around you. It will change what you see, how you think about the world, and it may well change how you think about yourself. Chapter 1 of this text introduces the discipline of sociology. The most important skill to gain from this course is the ability to use what we call the *sociological perspective*. The chapter next introduces *sociological theory*, which helps us build understanding from what we see using the sociological perspective. The chapter continues by explaining how sociologists "do" sociology, describing three general approaches to conducting research and four specific methods of data collection.

PHOTOS.com/Thinkstock

From the moment he first saw Tonya step off the subway train, Duane knew she was "the one." As the two walked up the stairs to the street and entered the building where they were both taking classes, Duane tried to get Tonya to stop and talk. At first, she ignored him. But after class they met again, and she agreed to join him for coffee. That was three months ago. Today, they are engaged to be married.

If you were to ask people in Canada, "Why do couples like Tonya and Duane marry?" it is a safe bet that almost everyone would reply, "People marry because they fall in love." Most of us find it hard to imagine a happy marriage without love; for the same reason, when people fall in love we expect them to think about getting married.

But is the decision about whom to marry really just a matter of personal feelings? There is plenty of evidence to show that if love is the key to marriage, Cupid's arrow is carefully aimed by the society around us.

Society has many "rules" about whom we should and should not marry. Until recently, Canadian law ruled out marriage between members of the same sex, even if a couple was deeply in love. But there are other rules as well. Sociologists have found that people, especially when they are young, are very likely to marry someone close in age, and people of all ages typically marry someone of the same race, of similar social class background, of much the same level of education, and with the same degree of physical attractiveness (Chapter 13, "Family and Religion," provides details). People end up making choices about whom to marry, but society narrows the field long before they do.

When it comes to love, our decisions do not result simply from what philosophers call "free will." Sociology teaches us that our social world guides our life choices in much the same way that the seasons influence our choice of clothing.

The Sociological Perspective

1.1 Explain how the sociological perspective helps us understand that society shapes our individual lives.

Sociology is *the systematic study of human society*. At the heart of this discipline is a distinctive point of view called the *sociological perspective*.

Seeing the General in the Particular

sociology the systematic study of human society

sociological perspective the special point of view of sociology that sees general patterns of society in the lives of particular people

One good way to define the **sociological perspective** is *seeing the general in the particular* (Berger, 1963). This definition tells us that sociologists look for *general* patterns in the behaviour of *particular* people. Although every individual is unique, society shapes the lives of people in various *categories* (such as children and adults, women and men, the rich and the poor) very differently.

We begin to see the world sociologically by realizing how the general categories into which we fall shape our particular life experiences.

For example, the Power of Society figure on page 3 shows how the social world shapes the likelihood of marriage by class background. We know that a large majority of married couples are from middle and upper, rather than lower, class backgrounds. In looking for general patterns, sociologists also ask more fine-tuned questions, like how does social class position affect what women look for in a spouse? In a classic study of women's hopes for their marriages, Lillian Rubin (1976) found that higher-income women typically expected the men they married to be sensitive to others, to talk readily, and to share feelings and experiences. Lower-income women, she found, had very different expectations and were looking for men who did not drink too much, were not violent, and held steady jobs. Obviously, what women expect in a marriage partner has a lot to do with social class position.

This text explores the power of society to guide our actions, thoughts, and feelings. We may think that marriage results simply from the personal feeling of love. Yet the sociological perspective shows us that factors such as our sex, age, race, and social class guide our selection of a partner. It might be more accurate to think of love as a feeling we have for others who match up with what society teaches us to want in a mate.

Seeing the Strange in the Familiar

At first, using the sociological perspective may seem like *seeing the strange in the familiar*. Consider how you might react if someone were to say to you, "You fit all the right categories, which means you would make a wonderful spouse!" We are used to thinking that people fall in love and decide to marry based on personal feeling and the things that make us unique. But the sociological perspective reveals to us the initially strange idea that society shapes what we think and do in patterned ways.

Seeing Society in Our Everyday Lives

The society in which we live has a lot to do with our everyday choices in food, clothing, music, schooling, jobs, and just about everything else. Even the most "personal" decisions we make turn out to be shaped by society. To see how society shapes personal choices, consider the decision by women to bear children. Like the selection of a mate, the choice of having a child—or how many children to have—would seem to be very personal. Yet there are social patterns here as well. As shown in Global Map 1–1 on page 6, the average woman in Canada has just about two children during her lifetime. In Honduras, however, the "choice" is about three; in Kenya, about four; in Yemen, five; in Afghanistan, six; and in Niger, seven (Population Reference Bureau, 2012).

What accounts for these striking differences? Because poor countries provide women with less schooling and fewer economic opportunities, women's lives are centred in the home, and they are less likely to use contraception. The strange truth is that society has much to do with the familiar decisions that women and men make about childbearing.

Another example of the power of society to shape even our most private choices comes from the study of suicide. What could be more personal than the lonely decision to end your own life? Emile Durkheim (1858–1917), one of sociology's pioneers, showed that, even here, social forces are at work.

Examining official records in and around his native France, Durkheim (1966, orig. 1897) found that some categories of people were more likely than others to take their own lives. He found that men, Protestants, wealthy people, and the unmarried each had much higher suicide rates than women, Catholics and Jews, the poor, and married people. Durkheim explained these differences in terms of *social integration*: Categories of people with strong social ties had low suicide rates, and more individualistic people had high suicide rates.

In Durkheim's time, men had much more freedom than women. But despite its advantages, freedom weakens social ties and thus increases the risk of suicide. Likewise, more individualistic Protestants were more likely to commit suicide than more tradition-bound Catholics and Jews, whose rituals encourage stronger social ties. The wealthy have much more freedom than the poor—but once again, at the cost of a higher suicide rate.

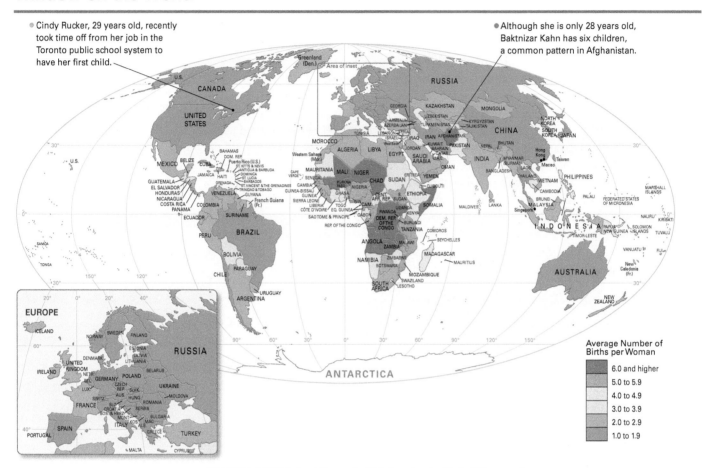

● Cindy Rucker, 29 years old, recently took time off from her job in the Toronto public school system to have her first child.

● Although she is only 28 years old, Baktnizar Kahn has six children, a common pattern in Afghanistan.

Average Number of Births per Woman

	6.0 and higher
	5.0 to 5.9
	4.0 to 4.9
	3.0 to 3.9
	2.0 to 2.9
	1.0 to 1.9

GLOBAL MAP 1–1 Women's Childbearing in Global Perspective

Is childbearing simply a matter of personal choice? A look around the world shows that it is not. In general, women living in poor countries have many more children than women in rich nations. Can you point to some of the reasons for this global disparity? In simple terms, such differences mean that if you had been born into another society (whether you are female or male), your life might be quite different from what it is now.

Source: Data from Population Reference Bureau (2012).

A century later, Durkheim's analysis still holds true. Figure 1–1 shows suicide rates for women and men in Canada between 1950 and 2009. While the suicide rate fluctuates over time, suicide remains three times as high for men than for women. In 2009, almost 3000 men and 900 women took their own lives. Applying Durkheim's logic, the higher suicide rate among men reflects their greater wealth and freedom. Conversely, the lower rate among women follows from their limited social choices. On first glance, it does not appear that Durkheim's theory fits the statistics on suicide among Canada's Aboriginal peoples: Even though Aboriginals are poorer and less independent than non-Aboriginals, the rate of suicide among Aboriginals is more than twice the Canadian rate. Yet Durkheim also identified instability and change as factors that inhibit social integration and thus potentially contribute to higher suicide rates. We would thus do well to consider the legacy of colonial oppression, the residential school system, and continuing racism and alienation experienced by many Aboriginal peoples in Canada (see Chapter 11, "Race and Ethnicity").

Seeing Sociologically: Marginality and Crisis

Anyone can learn to see the world using the sociological perspective. But two situations help people see clearly how society shapes individual lives: living on the margins of society and living through a social crisis.

Diversity Snapshot

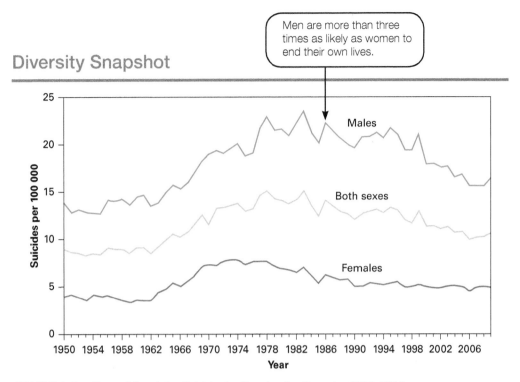

Men are more than three times as likely as women to end their own lives.

FIGURE 1–1 Rate of Death by Suicide, by Gender, for Canada, 1950–2009.

Suicide rates are consistently higher for men than for women. For both sexes, suicide rates rose between the 1960s and 1980s, peaking in 1983 at 15.1 per 100 000 and dropping to 10.7 per 100 000 by 2009.

Source: Adapted from http://www.statcan.gc.ca/pub/82-624-x/2012001/article/chart/11696-02-chart1-eng.htm. This does not constitute an endorsement by Statistics Canada of this product (2012a).

Living on the Edge

From time to time, everyone feels isolated, as if we are living on the edge. For some categories of people, however, being an *outsider*—not part of the dominant category— is an everyday experience. The greater people's social marginality, the better they are able to use the sociological perspective.

For example, no Black person grows up in the United States or Canada without understanding the importance of race in shaping people's lives. Songs by rap artists and groups like Lupe Fiasco, Talib Kweli, KRS-One, Dead Prez, the Coup, Mos Def, and Public Enemy express not only the experience of poverty but also the experience of losing many innocent lives to violence in a society of such wide racial disparities. The perspective of such artists, which are spread throughout the world by mass and social media, show that some people of colour in the United States—especially African Americans living in inner cities—feel as if their hopes and dreams are crushed by society. As noted above, Aboriginal people in Canada often feel the same way. But white Canadians and Americans, as the dominant majority, think less often about race and the privileges whiteness provides them with, believing that race affects only non-white people and not themselves as well. People at the margins of social life, including not only racial minorities but also women, Aboriginals, gays and lesbians, people with disabilities, and the very old, are aware of social patterns that others rarely think about.

Periods of Crisis

Periods of rapid change or crisis make everyone feel a little off balance, encouraging us to use the sociological perspective. The sociologist C. Wright Mills (1959) illustrated this idea using the Great Depression of the 1930s. As the unemployment rate in North America soared to 25 percent, people without jobs could not help but see general social forces at work in their particular lives. Rather than saying, "Something is wrong with

People with the greatest privileges tend to see individuals as responsible for their own lives. Those at the margins of society, by contrast, are quick to see how race, class, and gender can create disadvantages. The rap artist Lupe Fiasco has given voice to the frustration felt by many African Americans living in inner cities.

me; I can't find a job," they took a sociological approach and realized, "The economy has collapsed; there are no jobs to be found!" Mills believed that using what he called the "sociological imagination" in this way helps people understand their society and how it affects their own lives. The Seeing Sociology in Everyday Life box on page 9 takes a closer look.

The Importance of a Global Perspective

(1.2) State several reasons that a global perspective is important in today's world.

As new information technology draws even the farthest reaches of the planet closer together, many academic disciplines are taking a **global perspective**, *the study of the larger world and our society's place in it.* What is the importance of a global perspective for sociology?

First, global awareness is a logical extension of the sociological perspective. Sociology shows us that our place in society shapes our life experiences. It stands to reason, then, that the position of our society in the larger world system affects everyone in Canada.

The world's 195 nations can be divided into three broad categories according to their level of economic development (see Global Map 9–1 on page 286). **High-income countries** are the *nations with the highest overall standards of living.* The 74 countries in this category include Canada and the United States, Argentina, the nations of Western Europe, Israel, Saudi Arabia, Japan, and Australia. Taken together, these nations generate most of the world's goods and services, and the people who live in them own most of the planet's wealth. Economically speaking, people in these countries are better off, not because they are smarter or work harder than anyone else but because they were lucky enough to be born in, or to have immigrated to, a rich region of the world.

A second category is **middle-income countries**, *nations with a standard of living about average for the world as a whole.* People in any of these 72 nations—many of the countries of Eastern Europe, South Africa and some other African nations, and almost all of Latin America and Asia—are as likely to live in rural villages as in cities and to walk or ride tractors, scooters, bicycles, or animals as they are to drive automobiles. On average, they receive eight years of schooling. Most middle-income countries also have considerable social inequality within their own borders, meaning that some people are extremely rich (members of the business elite in nations across North Africa, for example) but many more lack safe housing and adequate nutrition (people living in the shanty settlements that surround Lima, Peru, or Mumbai, India).

The remaining 49 nations of the world are **low-income countries**, *nations with a low standard of living in which most people are poor.* Most of the poorest countries in the world are in Africa, and a few are in Asia. Here again, a few people are very rich, but the majority struggle to get by with poor housing, unsafe water, too little food, and perhaps most serious of all, little chance to improve their lives (United Nations, 2012; World Bank, 2012).

Chapter 9 ("Global Stratification") explains the causes and consequences of global wealth and poverty. But every chapter of this text makes comparisons between Canada and other nations for five reasons:

global perspective the study of the larger world and our society's place in it

high-income countries nations with the highest overall standards of living

middle-income countries nations with a standard of living about average for the world as a whole

low-income countries nations with a low standard of living in which most people are poor

1. **Where we live shapes the lives we lead.** As we saw in Global Map 1–1 on page 6, women living in rich and poor countries have very different lives, as suggested by the number of children they have. To understand ourselves and appreciate how others live, we must understand something about how countries differ, which is one good reason to pay attention to the global maps found throughout this text.

2. **Societies throughout the world are increasingly interconnected.** Historically, people in Canada took only passing note of the countries beyond our own borders. In recent decades, however, Canada and the rest of the world have become linked as never before. Electronic technology now transmits pictures, sounds, and written documents around the globe in seconds.

Seeing Sociology in Everyday Life

The Sociological Imagination: Turning Personal Problems into Public Issues

As Mike opened the envelope, he felt the tightness in his chest. The letter he dreaded was in his hands—his job was finished at the end of the day. After 11 years! Years in which he had worked hard, sure that he would move up in the company. All those hopes and dreams were now suddenly gone. Mike felt like a failure. Anger at himself—for not having worked even harder, for having wasted so many years of his life in what had turned out to be a dead-end job—swelled inside him.

But as he returned to his workstation to pack his things, Mike soon realized that he was not alone. Almost all his colleagues in the tech support group had received the same letter. Their jobs were moving to India, where the company was able to provide telephone tech support for less than half the cost of employing workers in Vancouver.

By the end of the weekend, Mike was sitting in his living room with a dozen other ex-employees. Comparing notes and sharing ideas, they now realized that they were simply a few of the victims of a massive outsourcing of jobs that is part of what analysts call the "globalization of the economy."

In good times and bad, the power of the sociological perspective lies in making sense of our individual lives. We see that many of our particular problems (and our successes, as well) are not unique to us but are the result of larger social trends. Half a century ago, the sociologist C. Wright Mills pointed to the power of what he called the *sociological imagination* to help us understand everyday events. As he saw it, society—not people's personal failings—is the main cause of poverty and other social problems. By turning personal problems into public issues, the sociological imagination also is the key to bringing people together to create needed change. In this excerpt,[*] Mills (1959:3–5) explains the need for a sociological imagination:

> When society becomes industrialized, a peasant becomes a worker; a feudal lord is liquidated or becomes a businessman. When classes rise or fall, a man is employed or unemployed; when the rate of investment goes up or down, a man takes new heart or goes broke. When wars happen, an insurance salesman becomes a rocket launcher; a store clerk, a radar man; a wife lives alone; a child grows up without a father. Neither the life of an individual nor the history of a society can be understood without understanding both.
>
> Yet men do not usually define the troubles they endure in terms of historical change…. The well-being they enjoy, they do not usually impute to the big ups and downs of the society in which they live. Seldom aware of the intricate connection between the patterns of their own lives and the course of world history, ordinary men do not usually know what this connection means for the kind of men they are becoming and for the kinds of history-making in which they might take part. They do not possess the quality of mind essential to grasp the interplay of men and society, of biography and history, of self and world….
>
> What they need … is a quality of mind that will help them [see] what is going on in the world and … what may be happening within themselves. It is this quality … [that] may be called the sociological imagination.[†]

What Do You Think?

1. As Mills sees it, how are personal troubles different from public issues? Explain this difference in terms of what happened to Mike in the story above.

2. Living in Canada, why do we often blame ourselves for the personal problems we face?

3. How can using the sociological imagination give us power to change the world?

[*]In this excerpt, Mills uses "man" and male pronouns to apply to all people. As far as gender is concerned, even this outspoken critic of society reflected the conventional writing practices of his time.
[†]Mills (1959: 3-5). Mills, C. Wright. The Sociological Imagination. New York: Oxford University Press, 1959. Reprinted with permission.

One effect of this new technology is that people all over the world now share many of the same tastes in food, clothing, movies, and music. Rich countries such as Canada and the United States influence other nations, whose people are ever more likely to gobble up fast food, dance to the latest hip-hop music, and speak English.

But the larger world also has an impact on us. We are likely to know the contributions of famous immigrants such as Adrienne Clarkson, governor general of Canada from 1999 to 2005 (who came to Canada as a refugee from Hong Kong), and Dionne Brand, poet, novelist, essayist, and professor (who was born in Trinidad). About 250 000 immigrants enter Canada each year, bringing their skills and talents, along with their fashions and foods, greatly increasing the racial and cultural diversity of this country.

3. **What happens in the rest of the world affects life here in Canada.** As trade has increased across national boundaries, the world has developed a global economy. Large corporations make and market goods worldwide. Stock traders in Toronto pay close attention to the financial markets in Tokyo and Hong Kong even as wheat farmers in

Saskatchewan watch the price of grain in the former Soviet republic of Georgia. Because most new Canadian jobs involve international trade, greater global understanding has never been more important.

In the last several decades, the power and wealth of North America has been challenged by what some analysts have called "the rise of the rest," meaning the increasing power and wealth of the rest of the world. As nations such as Brazil, Russia, India, and China have expanded their economic production, many of the manufacturing and office jobs that once supported a large share of the Canadian and U.S. labour force have moved overseas. One consequence of this trend is that, as the United States struggles to climb out of its recent 2008 recession, Canada is affected as well. The United States is Canada's largest trading partner, accounting for 75 percent of Canadian exports. A higher unemployment rate and decreased consumption in the United States have led to a slowdown in Canadian exports, particularly in the energy, industrial goods, and auto sectors. Although Canada has been relatively less affected by the recession, as many analysts see it, we now live in a new global economy that is reshaping societies all around the world (Cross, 2011).

4. **Many social problems that we face in Canada are far more serious elsewhere.** Poverty is a serious problem in Canada, but as Chapter 9 ("Global Stratification") explains, poverty in Latin America, Africa, and Asia is both more common and more serious. In the same way, although women have lower social standing than men in Canada, gender inequality is much greater in the world's poor countries.

5. **Thinking globally helps us learn more about ourselves**. We cannot walk the streets of a distant city without thinking about what it means to live in Canada. Comparing life in various settings often leads to unexpected lessons. For instance, were you to visit a squatter settlement in Chennai, India, you would likely find people thriving in the love and support of family members despite desperate poverty. Why, then, are so many poor

We can easily see the power of society over the individual by imagining how different our lives would be had we been born in place of any of these children from, respectively, Kenya, Ethiopia, Myanmar, Peru, South Korea, and India.

people in North America angry and alone? Are material things—so central to our definition of a "rich" life—the best way to measure human well-being?

In sum, in an increasingly interconnected world, we can understand our way of life and ourselves only to the extent that we understand others and the societies in which they live. Sociology is an invitation to learn a new way of looking at the world around us. But is this invitation worth accepting? What are the benefits of applying the sociological perspective?

Applying the Sociological Perspective

1.3 Identify the advantages of sociological thinking for developing public policy, for encouraging personal growth, and for advancing in a career.

Applying the sociological perspective is useful in many ways. First, sociology is at work guiding many of the laws and policies that shape our lives. Second, on an individual level, making use of the sociological perspective leads to important personal growth and expanded awareness. Third, studying sociology is excellent preparation for the world of work.

Sociology and Public Policy

Sociologists have helped shape public policy—the laws and regulations that guide how people in communities live and work—in countless ways, including health care, education, juvenile justice, divorce law, and social welfare. Canadian researcher Robin Bagley's (1984) work on sex offences against minors had a major impact on public policy, leading among other things to the 1988 enactment of section 212 of the Criminal Code, which prohibits attempts to purchase sex from persons under 18 years of age (Lowman, 1987).

Sociology and Personal Growth

By applying the sociological perspective, we are likely to become more active and aware and to think more critically in our everyday lives. Using sociology pays off in four ways:

1. **The sociological perspective helps us assess the truth of "common sense."** We all take many things for granted, but that does not make them true. One example is the idea that we are free individuals who are personally responsible for our own lives. If we think that we decide our own fate, we may be quick to praise successful people as superior and consider others with fewer achievements personally deficient. A sociological approach, by contrast, encourages us to ask whether common beliefs are really true and, to the extent that they are not, why they are so widely held.

2. **The sociological perspective helps us see the opportunities and constraints in our lives.** Sociological thinking leads us to see that in the game of life, we have a say in how to play our cards, but it is society that deals us the hand. The more we understand the game, the better players we will be. Sociology helps us learn more about the world so that we can pursue our goals more effectively.

3. **The sociological perspective empowers us to be active participants in our society.** The better we understand how society operates, the more effective citizens we become. As C. Wright Mills explained in the box on page 9, it is the sociological perspective that turns a private problem (such as being out of work) into a public issue (a lack of good jobs). As we come to see how society affects us, we may decide to support society as it is, or we may set out with others to change it.

4. **The sociological perspective helps us live in a diverse world.** North Americans represent just 5 percent of the world's population, and as the remaining chapters of this book explain, many of the other 95 percent live very differently than we do. Still, like people everywhere, we tend to view our own way of life as "right," "natural," and "better." The sociological perspective prompts us to think critically about the relative strengths and weaknesses of all ways of life, including our own.

Careers: The "Sociology Advantage"

Most students at colleges and universities today are very interested in getting a good job. A background in sociology is excellent preparation for the working world. Of course, completing a bachelor's degree in sociology is the right choice for people who decide they would like to go on to graduate work and eventually become a secondary school teacher, professor, or researcher in this field. Throughout Canada and the United States, tens of thousands of men and women teach sociology in universities and colleges. But just as many professional sociologists work as researchers for government agencies or private foundations and businesses, gathering important information on social behaviour and carrying out evaluation research. In today's cost-conscious world, agencies and companies want to be sure that the products, programs, and policies they create get the job done at the lowest cost. Sociologists, especially those with advanced research skills, are in high demand for this kind of work (Deutscher, 1999).

Just about every job in today's economy involves working with people. For this reason, studying sociology is good preparation for your future career. In what ways does having "people skills" help human resources specialists perform their job?

In addition, a smaller but increasing number of people work as clinical sociologists. These women and men work, much as clinical psychologists do, with the goal of improving the lives of troubled clients. A basic difference is that sociologists focus on difficulties not in the personality but in the individual's web of social relationships.

But sociology is not just for people who want to be sociologists. People who work in criminal justice—including jobs in police departments, probation offices, and correction facilities—also gain the "sociology advantage" by learning what categories of people are most at risk of becoming criminals or victims, how effective various policing policies and programs are at preventing crime, and why people turn to crime in the first place. Similarly, people who work in the health care field—including physicians, nurses, and technicians—gain a sociology advantage by learning about patterns of health and illness within the population, as well as how factors such as race, ethnicity, gender, and social class affect human well-being.

According to the Canadian Association of University Teachers, sociologists are hired for hundreds of jobs in fields such as advertising, banking, criminal justice, education, government, health care, public relations, and research. In almost any type of work, success depends on understanding how various categories of people differ in beliefs, family patterns, and other ways of life. Unless you have a job that never involves dealing with people, you should consider the workplace benefits of learning more sociology.

The Origins of Sociology

(1.4) Link the origins of sociology to historical social changes.

Like the "choices" people make, major historical events rarely just "happen." Even sociology itself is the result of powerful social forces.

Social Change and Sociology

Striking changes in Europe during the eighteenth and nineteenth centuries made people think more about society and their place in it, spurring the development of sociology. Three kinds of change were especially important in the development of sociology: the rise of a factory-based economy, the explosive growth of cities, and new ideas about democracy and political rights.

A New Industrial Economy

During the Middle Ages, most people in Europe plowed fields near their homes or engaged in small-scale *manufacturing* (a term derived from Latin words meaning "to make by hand").

By the end of the eighteenth century, inventors used new sources of energy—the power of moving water and then steam—to operate large machines in mills and factories. As a result, instead of labouring at home or in tightly knit groups, workers became part of a large and anonymous labour force, under the control of strangers who owned the factories. This change in the system of production took people away from their homes, weakening the traditions that had guided community life for centuries.

The Growth of Cities

Across Europe, landowners took part in what historians call the *enclosure movement*—they fenced off more and more farmland to create grazing areas for sheep, the source of wool for the thriving textile mills. Without land, countless tenant farmers had little choice but to head to the cities in search of work in the new factories.

As cities grew larger, these urban migrants faced many social problems, including pollution, crime, and homelessness. Moving through streets crowded with strangers, they faced a new, impersonal social world.

Political Change

Economic development and the growth of cities also brought new ways of thinking. In the writings of Thomas Hobbes (1588–1679), John Locke (1632–1704), and Adam Smith (1723–1790), we see a shift in focus from people's moral duties to God and king to the pursuit of self-interest. Philosophers now spoke of *personal liberty* and *individual rights*. Echoing these sentiments, the Canadian Charter of Rights and Freedoms clearly states that "every individual is equal before and under the law and has the right to the equal protection and equal benefit of the law without discrimination and, in particular, without discrimination based on race, national or ethnic origin, colour, religion, sex, age or mental or physical disability" (Department of Justice, 1982).

The French Revolution, which began in 1789, was an even greater break with political and social tradition. As the French social analyst Alexis de Tocqueville (1805–1859) declared, the change in society in the wake of the French Revolution amounted to "nothing short of the regeneration of the whole human race" (1955:13, orig. 1856).

A New Awareness of Society

Huge factories, exploding cities, and a new spirit of individualism—these changes combined to make people more aware of their surroundings. The new discipline of sociology was born in England, France, and Germany—precisely the countries where these changes were greatest.

Science and Sociology

Throughout history, the nature of society has fascinated people, including the brilliant philosopher K'ung Fu-tzu, or Confucius (551–479 BCE), in China and the Greek philosophers Plato (427–347 BCE) and Aristotle (384–322 BCE).[1] Later, the Roman emperor Marcus Aurelius (121–180 CE), the medieval thinkers Saint Thomas Aquinas (1225–1274 CE) and Christine de Pizan (1363–1431 CE), and the great English playwright William Shakespeare (1564–1616 CE) wrote about the workings of society.

Yet these thinkers were more interested in imagining the ideal society than they were in studying

What we see depends on our point of view. When gazing at the stars, lovers see romance, but scientists see thermal reactions. How does using the sociological perspective change what we see in the world around us?

Frank Zullo/Science Source/Getty Images

[1]The abbreviation BCE means "before the common era." We use this throughout the text instead of the traditional BC ("before Christ") to reflect the religious diversity of our society. Similarly, in place of the traditional AD (*anno Domini*, "in the year of our Lord") we use the abbreviation CE ("common era").

Comte's Three Stages of Society

Theological Stage	Metaphysical Stage	Scientific Stage
(the Church in the Middle Ages)	(the Enlightenment and the ideas of Hobbes, Locke, and Rousseau)	(modern physics, chemistry, sociology)

society as it really was. It was the French social thinker Auguste Comte (1798–1857) who coined the term *sociology* in 1838 to describe this new way of thinking. This makes sociology among the youngest of the academic disciplines—far newer than history, physics, or economics, for example.

Comte (1975, orig. 1851–54) saw sociology as the product of three stages of historical development. During the earliest *theological stage*, from the beginning of human history up to the end of the European Middle Ages about 1350 CE, people took the religious view that society expressed God's will.

With the dawn of the Renaissance in the fifteenth century, Comte explained, the theological stage gave way to a *metaphysical stage* in which people came to see society as a natural rather than a supernatural phenomenon. The English philosopher Thomas Hobbes (1588–1679), for example, suggested that society reflected not the perfection of God so much as the failings of a selfish human nature.

What Comte called the *scientific stage* began with the work of early scientists such as the Polish astronomer Copernicus (1473–1543), the Italian astronomer and physicist Galileo (1564–1642), and the English physicist and mathematician Isaac Newton (1642–1727). Comte's contribution came in applying the scientific approach—first used to study the physical world—to the study of society.[2]

positivism a scientific approach to knowledge based on "positive" facts as opposed to mere speculation

Comte's approach is called **positivism**, *a scientific approach to knowledge based on "positive" facts as opposed to mere speculation*. Comte thought that knowledge based on tradition or metaphysics was really only speculation. A positivist approach to knowledge, however, is based on *science*. As a positivist, Comte believed that society operates according to certain laws, just as the physical world operates according to gravity and other laws of nature. Comte believed that by using science, people could come to understand the laws not only of the physical world but of society as well.

By the beginning of the twentieth century, sociology had taken hold in the United States (two decades earlier than in Canada) and showed the influence of Comte's ideas. Today, most sociologists continue to consider science a crucial part of sociology, but we now realize that human behaviour is far more complex than the movement of planets. We are creatures of imagination and spontaneity, so human behaviour can never be explained by any rigid "laws of society." In addition, early sociologists such as Karl Marx (1818–1883) were troubled by the striking inequalities of industrial society. They hoped that the new discipline of sociology would not just help us understand society but also lead to change toward greater social justice.

Sociological Theory

(1.5) Summarize sociology's major theoretical approaches.

theory a statement of how and why specific facts are related

The desire to translate observations into understanding brings us to the important part of sociology known as *theory*. A **theory** is *a statement of how and why specific facts are related*. The job of sociological theory is to explain social behaviour in the real world. For example, recall Durkheim's theory that categories of people with low social integration (men, Protestants, the wealthy, and the unmarried) are at higher risk of suicide. Figure 1–2 on page 15 shows the suicide rates for each province and territory and gives you a chance to do some theorizing of your own.

In deciding which theory to use, sociologists face two basic questions: What issues should we study? And how should we connect the facts? Making a decision to use one theoretical approach over another, sociologists are choosing a "road map" to guide their thinking. In

---

[2]Illustrating Comte's stages, the ancient Greeks and Romans viewed the planets as gods; Renaissance metaphysical thinkers saw them as astral influences (giving rise to astrology); by the time of Galileo, scientists understood planets as natural objects moving according to natural laws.

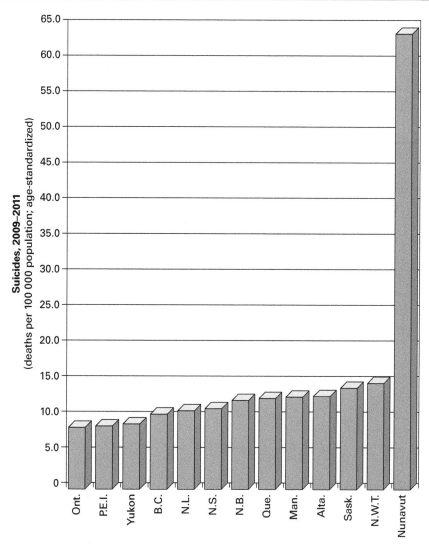

FIGURE 1–2 Suicide Rates Across Canada, 2009–2011

Suicide rates vary across Canada. Look for patterns. By and large, high suicide rates occur where people live far apart from one another. More densely populated provinces have low suicide rates. How do these data support or contradict Durkheim's theory of suicide?

Sources: Statistics Canada, http://www.statcan.gc.ca/pub/82-624-x/2012001/article/chart/11696-02-chart1-eng.htm. Reproduced and distributed on an "as is" basis with the permission of Statistics Canada.

other words, a **theoretical approach** is *a basic image of society that guides thinking and research.* Sociologists make use of three major theoretical approaches: the *structural-functional approach,* the *social-conflict approach,* and the *symbolic-interaction approach.*

The Structural-Functional Approach

The **structural-functional approach** is *a framework for building theory that sees society as a complex system whose parts work together to promote solidarity and stability.* As its name suggests, this approach points to **social structure**, *any relatively stable pattern of social behaviour.* Social structure gives our lives shape in families, the workplace, or the college classroom. This approach also looks for each structure's **social functions**, *the consequences of a social pattern for the operation of society as a whole.* All social patterns, from a simple handshake to complex religious rituals, function to tie people together and to keep society going, at least in its present form.

The structural-functional approach owes much to Auguste Comte, who pointed out the need to keep society unified when many traditions were breaking down. Emile Durkheim,

theoretical approach a basic image of society that guides thinking and research

structural-functional approach a framework for building theory that sees society as a complex system whose parts work together to promote solidarity and stability

social structure any relatively stable pattern of social behaviour

social functions the consequences of a social pattern for the operation of society as a whole

manifest functions the recognized and intended consequences of any social pattern

latent functions the unrecognized and unintended consequences of any social pattern

social dysfunction any social pattern that may disrupt the operation of society

who helped establish sociology in French universities, also based his work on this approach. A third structural-functional pioneer was the English sociologist Herbert Spencer (1820–1903). Spencer, employing an "organic analogy," compared society to the human body: Just as the structural parts of the human body—the skeleton, muscles, and internal organs—each carry out certain functions to help the entire organism survive, social structures work together to preserve society. The structural-functional approach, then, leads sociologists to identify various structures of society and to investigate their functions.

Sociologist Robert K. Merton (1910–2003) expanded our understanding of social function by pointing out that any social structure probably has many functions, some more obvious than others. He distinguished between **manifest functions**, *the recognized and intended consequences of any social pattern*, and **latent functions**, *the unrecognized and unintended consequences of any social pattern*. For example, the obvious function of this country's system of higher education is to give young people the information and skills they will need to hold jobs after graduation. Perhaps just as important, although less often acknowledged, is higher education's function as a "marriage broker," bringing together young people of similar social backgrounds. Another latent function of higher education is to limit unemployment by keeping millions of people out of the labour market, where many of them might not easily find jobs.

But Merton also recognized that not all the effects of social structure are good. Thus a **social dysfunction** is *any social pattern that may disrupt the operation of society*. Globalization of the economy, a rising flow of immigrants, and increasing inequality of income are all factors that—in the eyes of some people—disrupt existing social patterns. As these examples suggest, what is helpful and what is harmful for society is a matter about which people often disagree. In addition, what is functional for one category of people (say, a banking system that provides high profits for Bay Street executives) may well be dysfunctional for other categories of people (workers who lose pension funds invested in banks that fail or people who cannot pay their mortgages and end up losing their homes).

EVALUATE The main idea of the structural-functional approach is its vision of society as stable and orderly. The main goal of the sociologists who use this approach, then, is to figure out "what makes society tick."

In the mid-1900s, most sociologists favoured the structural-functional approach. In recent decades, however, its influence has declined. By focusing attention on social stability and unity, critics point out, structural-functionalism is not critical of inequalities based on social class, race, ethnicity, and gender, all of which cause tension and conflict. In general, its focus on stability at the expense of conflict makes this approach somewhat conservative. As a critical response, sociologists developed the social-conflict approach.

CHECK YOUR LEARNING How do manifest functions differ from latent functions? Give an example of a manifest function and a latent function of automobiles in Canada.

The Social-Conflict Approach

The **social-conflict approach** is *a framework for building theory that sees society as an arena of inequality that generates conflict and change*. Unlike the structural-functional emphasis on solidarity and stability, this approach highlights how factors such as class, race, ethnicity, gender, and age are linked to inequality in terms of money, power, education, and social prestige. A conflict analysis rejects the idea that social structure promotes the operation of society as a whole, focusing instead on how any social pattern benefits some people while hurting others.

Sociologists using the social-conflict approach look at ongoing conflict between dominant and disadvantaged categories of people—the rich in relation to the poor, white people in relation to visible minorities, and men in relation to women. Typically, people on top try to protect their privileges while the disadvantaged try to gain more for themselves.

A social-conflict analysis of our educational system shows how schooling reproduces class inequality from one generation to the next. For example, secondary schools assign students to either college preparatory or vocational training programs. From a structural-functional point of view such "tracking" benefits everyone by providing schooling that fits students' abilities. But conflict analysis argues that tracking often has less to do with talent than with social background, meaning that well-to-do students are placed in higher tracks, while poor children end up in lower tracks.

In this way, young people from privileged families get the best schooling, which leads them to college and university and later to high-income careers. The children of poor families, by contrast, are not prepared for higher education and, like their parents before them, typically get stuck in low-paying jobs. In both cases, the social standing of one generation is passed on to the next, with schools justifying the practice in terms of individual merit (Bowles & Gintis, 1976; Oakes, 1982, 1985).

Many sociologists use social-conflict theory not just to understand society but also as part of their efforts to reduce inequality. Karl Marx championed the cause of workers in what he saw as their battle against factory owners. In a well-known statement (inscribed on his monument in London's Highgate Cemetery), Marx declared, "The philosophers have only interpreted the world, in various ways; the point, however, is to change it."

The social-conflict approach points out patterns of inequality in everyday life. Generally, students tend to be members of a privileged class who regularly come into contact with those who face numerous disadvantages. In what way does participating in higher education depend on the work of those who cannot partake in it?

Feminism and Gender-Conflict Theory

One important social-conflict theory is **gender-conflict theory** (or **feminist theory**), *the study of society that focuses on inequality and conflict between women and men.* The gender-conflict approach is closely linked to **feminism**, *support of social equality for women and men.*

The importance of gender-conflict theory lies in making us aware of the many ways in which our society places men in positions of power over women, in the home (where men are usually considered "head of the household"), in the workplace (where men earn more income and hold most positions of power), and in the mass media (where, for instance, more men than women are hip-hop stars).

Another contribution of feminist theory is making us aware of the importance of women to the development of sociology. Harriet Martineau (1802–1876) is regarded as the first woman sociologist. Born to a wealthy English family, Martineau made her mark in 1853 by translating the writings of Auguste Comte from French into English. She later documented the evils of slavery and argued for laws to protect factory workers, defending workers' right to unionize. She was particularly concerned about the position of women in society and fought for changes in education policy so that women could look forward to more in life than being a wife and mother in the home.

In Canada, Nellie McClung (1873–1951) was a pioneer of women's rights who started school at age 10 and received a teaching certificate six years later. McClung was a supporter of suffrage for women and a well-known advocate for Prohibition, factory laws for women, formal compulsory education, reform in Canadian prisons, and equal representation for women in the political realm. While an elected Liberal MLA in Alberta, she became a member of the "Famous Five," who in 1927 petitioned the Government of Canada to include women in the definition of "person" in the *British North America Act*. The Famous Five's success in 1929 meant that women could be appointed to the Senate.

All chapters of this book consider the importance of gender and gender inequality. For an in-depth look at feminism and the social standing of women and men, see Chapter 10 ("Gender Stratification").

social-conflict approach a framework for building theory that sees society as an arena of inequality that generates conflict and change

gender-conflict theory (feminist theory) the study of society that focuses on inequality and conflict between women and men

race-conflict theory the study of society that focuses on inequality and conflict between people of different racial and ethnic categories

feminism support of social equality for women and men

Daniel Grafton Hill (1923–2003) is a well-known authority on Black history and was a Canadian sociologist, civil servant, and human rights specialist. Dorothy Smith (1926–) is a well-known and respected Canadian sociologist who was involved with establishing the first women's studies courses in Canada.

Race-Conflict Theory

Another important type of social-conflict theory is **race-conflict theory**, *the study of society that focuses on inequality and conflict between people of different racial and ethnic categories.* Just as men have power over women, white people have numerous social advantages over visible minorities and Aboriginal peoples, including, on average, higher incomes, more schooling, better health, and longer life expectancy.

Race-conflict theory also points out the contributions to the development of sociology made by racial minorities. Cecil Foster (1954–) grew up in a poor neighbourhood in Barbados when that country was still a colony of Britain. He became a reporter and columnist with a critical eye toward that nation's government. Finding himself a target of threats, Foster immigrated to Canada in 1978 where he has since worked as a journalist and sociologist. He continues to write and lecture about the Caribbean immigrant experience, racism, and multiculturalism in Canada.

An important contribution to understanding race was made by William Edward Burghardt Du Bois (1868–1963). Born to a poor Massachusetts family, Du Bois enrolled at Fisk University in Nashville, Tennessee, and then at Harvard University, where he earned the first doctorate awarded by that university to a person of colour. Du Bois then founded the Atlanta Sociological Laboratory, which was an important centre of sociological research in the early decades of the twentieth century. Like most people who follow the social-conflict approach (whether focusing on class, gender, or race), Du Bois believed that scholars should not simply learn about society's problems but also try to solve them. He therefore studied the Black communities across the United States, pointing to numerous social problems ranging from educational inequality, a political system that denied people their right to vote, and the terrorist practice of lynching. Du Bois spoke out against racial inequality and participated in the founding of the National Association for the Advancement of Colored People (NAACP) (E. Wright, 2002a, 2002b). The Thinking About Diversity box on page 19 takes a closer look at the ideas of W. E. B. Du Bois. An important contribution to understanding race in Canada was made by Daniel Grafton Hill (1923–2003), who is especially remembered for his sociological writings on Black history and human rights.

EVALUATE The various social-conflict theories have gained a large following in recent decades, but like other approaches, they have met with criticism. Because any social-conflict theory focuses on inequality, it largely ignores how shared values and interdependence can unify members of a society. In addition, say critics, to the extent that it pursues political goals, a social-conflict approach cannot claim scientific objectivity. Supporters of social-conflict theory respond that all theoretical approaches have political consequences.

A final criticism of both structural-functional and social-conflict theories is that they paint society in broad strokes—in terms of "family," "social class," "race," and so on. A third theoretical approach views society less in general terms and more as the specific, everyday experiences of individual people. The Applying Theory table on page 20 summarizes the contributions of each of these approaches.

CHECK YOUR LEARNING Why do you think sociologists characterize the social-conflict approach as "activist"? What is it actively trying to achieve?

Thinking About Diversity: Race, Class, and Gender

W.E.B. Du Bois: A Pioneer in Sociology

One of sociology's pioneers, William Edward Burghardt Du Bois saw sociology as a key to solving society's problems, especially racial inequality. Du Bois earned a Ph.D. in sociology from Harvard University and established the Atlanta Sociological Laboratory, one of the first centres of sociological research in the United States. He helped his colleagues in sociology—and people everywhere—see the deep racial divisions in his country. White people can simply be "Americans," Du Bois explained, but African Americans have a "double consciousness," reflecting their status as citizens who are never able to escape identification based on the colour of their skin.

In his sociological classic *The Philadelphia Negro: A Social Study* (1899), Du Bois explored Philadelphia's African American community, identifying both the strengths and the weaknesses of people wrestling with overwhelming social problems on a day-to-day basis. He challenged the belief—widespread at that time—that Blacks were inferior to whites, and he blamed white prejudice for the problems African Americans faced. He also criticized successful people of colour for being so eager to win white acceptance that they gave up all ties with the Black community, which needed their help.

Despite notable achievements, Du Bois gradually grew impatient with academic study, which he felt was too detached from the everyday struggles of people of colour. Du Bois wanted change. It was the hope of sparking public action against racial separation that led Du Bois, in 1909, to participate in the founding of the National Association for the Advancement of Colored People (NAACP), an organization that has been active in supporting racial equality for more than a century. As the editor of the organization's magazine, *Crisis*, Du Bois worked tirelessly to challenge laws and social customs that deprived African Americans of the rights and opportunities enjoyed by the white majority.

Du Bois described race as the major problem facing his country in the twentieth century. Early in his career, as a sociological researcher, he was hopeful about overcoming racial divisions. By the end of his life, however, he had grown bitter, claiming that little had changed. At the age of 93, Du Bois emigrated to Ghana, where he died two years later.

What Do You Think?

1. If he were alive today, do you think that Du Bois would still consider race a major problem in the twenty-first century? Why or why not?

2. How much do you think African Americans today experience "double consciousness"?

3. In what ways can sociology help us understand and reduce racial conflict?

Sources: Based on Baltzell (1967), Du Bois (1967, orig. 1899), E. Wright (2002a, 2002b), and personal communication with Earl Wright II.

Schomburg Center, NYPL/Art Resource, NY

The Symbolic-Interaction Approach

Both the structural-functional approach and the social–conflict approach share a **macro-level orientation**, meaning *a broad focus on social structures that shape society as a whole.* Macro-level sociology takes in the big picture, rather like observing a city from a helicopter and seeing how highways help people move from place to place or how housing differs from rich to poor neighbourhoods. Sociology also uses a **micro-level orientation**, *a close-up focus on social interaction in specific situations.* Exploring city life in this way occurs at street level, where you might watch how children invent games on a school playground or observe how pedestrians respond to homeless people they pass on the street. The **symbolic-interaction approach**, then, is *a framework for building theory that sees society as the product of the everyday interactions of individuals.*

How does "society" result from the ongoing experiences of tens of millions of people? One answer, detailed in Chapter 4 ("Social Interaction in Everyday Life"), is that society is nothing more than the reality that people construct for themselves as they interact with one another. That is, we human beings live in a world of symbols, and we attach meaning to virtually everything, from the words on

macro-level orientation a broad focus on social structures that shape society as a whole

micro-level orientation a close-up focus on social interaction in specific situations

symbolic-interaction approach a framework for building theory that sees society as the product of the everyday interactions of individuals

Sports: Playing the Theory Game

Sport is a popular pastime. Many children and teens play two or more organized sports. Adults who don't participate themselves follow their favourite teams or players on TV or on the internet. What can we learn by applying sociology's major theoretical approaches to this familiar element of life in Canada?

Structural-Functional Approach According to the structural-functional approach, the manifest functions of sports include recreation and getting in shape. Sports have important latent functions as well, from building social relationships to creating jobs. Perhaps the most important latent function of sports is to encourage competition, which is central to our society's way of life.

Of course, sports also have dysfunctional consequences. Colleges and universities sometimes recruit students for their athletic skill rather than their academic ability. This practice lowers a school's academic standards and shortchanges athletes, whose intense practice schedules often interfere with their studies (Upthegrove, Roscigno, & Charles, 1999).

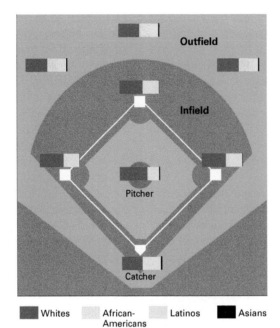

Whites · African-Americans · Latinos · Asians

"Stacking" in Professional Baseball

In professional baseball, white players are more likely to play the central positions in the infield, while people of colour are more likely to play in the outfield. What do you make of this pattern?

Source: Lapchick (2015a). Lapchick, Richard, with Alejandra Diaz-Cameron and Derek Mcmechan. "The 2015 Racial and Gender Report Card: Major League Baseball." Orlando: Institute for Diversity and Ethics in Sports. University of Central Florida, 2015. Used with permission.

Social-Conflict Approach A social-conflict analysis points out how sports are linked to social inequality. Some sports—tennis, swimming, golf, skiing—are expensive, so participation is largely limited to the well-to-do. Football, baseball, and basketball, however, are accessible to people at almost all income levels. Thus the games people play are not simply a matter of choice but also a reflection of their social standing (Zirin, 2008).

Gender-conflict or feminist theory leads us to recognize that, throughout history, men have dominated the world of sports. The first modern Olympic Games, held in 1896, excluded women from competition. Through most of the twentieth century in Canada, even hockey teams barred girls based on the traditional ideas that they lack the strength and the stamina to play sports and that they risk losing their femininity if they do. Even today, women still take a back seat to men, particularly in sports with the greatest earnings and social prestige (Travers, 2013).

Applying Theory

Major theoretical approaches

	Structural-Functional Approach	Social-Conflict, Gender-Conflict, and Race-Conflict Approaches	Symbolic-Interaction Approach
What is the level of analysis?	Macro-level	Macro-level	Micro-level
What image of society does the approach have?	Society is a system of interrelated parts that is relatively stable. Each part works to keep society operating in an orderly way. Members generally agree about what is morally right and morally wrong.	Society is a system of social inequalities based on class (Marx), gender (gender-conflict theory and feminism), and race (race-conflict theory). Society operates to benefit some categories of people and harm others. Social inequality causes conflict that leads to social change.	Society is an ongoing process. People interact in countless settings using symbolic communications. The reality people experience is variable and changing.
What core questions does the approach ask?	How is society held together? What are the major parts of society? How are these parts linked? What does each part do to help society work?	How does society divide a population? How do advantaged people protect their privileges? How do disadvantaged people challenge the system seeking change?	How do people experience society? How do people shape the reality they experience? How do behaviour and meaning change from person to person and from one situation to another?

Race-conflict theory reminds us that our society has long excluded visible minorities from professional sports. Even so, opportunities have expanded in recent decades. In 1947, Jackie Robinson broke through the "colour line" to become the first African American player in Major League Baseball, playing for the Brooklyn Dodgers. In 1958, Canadian-born William O'Ree made headlines as the first Black player to be recruited into the National Hockey League. In 2015, African Americans (13 percent of the U.S. population) accounted for 8.3 percent of Major League Baseball players, 68.7 percent of National Football League (NFL) players, and 74.4 percent of National Basketball Association (NBA) players (Lapchick, 2015a, 2015b, 2015c).

But racial discrimination still exists in professional sports. The figure shows the results of a 2014 study of racial "stacking" in Major League Baseball. White players are concentrated in the central "thinking" positions of pitcher (69 percent white) and catcher (51.6 percent white). African Americans represent only 3 percent of pitchers, and there were no Black catchers. But 7.9 percent of infielders are African Americans, as are 25.4 percent of outfielders (positions characterized as requiring "speed and reactive ability") (Lapchick, 2015a).

Who benefits most from professional sports? The vast profits that sports generate are controlled by a small number of people—predominantly white men. In sum, sports in our society are bound up with inequalities based on gender, race, and wealth.

All Olympic Games involve outstanding athletes. However, the sports that are central to the Summer Games, including track and field events, have a higher share of athletes who are visible minorities. By contrast, the Winter Olympics have fewer minorities and more well-to-do athletes. Can you explain why?

PCN Photography/Alamy Stock Photo

The Symbolic-Interaction Approach

At the micro-level, a sporting event is a complex, face-to-face interaction. In part, play is guided by the players' assigned positions and the rules of the game. But players are also spontaneous and unpredictable. Following the symbolic-interaction approach, we see sports less as a system and more as an ongoing process.

From this point of view, too, we would expect each player to understand the game a little differently. Some players enjoy stiff competition; for others, love of the game may be greater than the need to win. In addition, the behaviour of any single player is likely to change over time. A rookie may feel self-conscious during the first few games in the big leagues but go on to develop a comfortable sense of fitting in with the team. To fully appreciate the power of the sociological perspective, you should become familiar with all these approaches.

What Do You Think?

1. Describe how a macro-level approach to sports differs from a micro-level approach.

2. Make up three questions about sports that reflect the focus of each of the three theoretical approaches.

3. How might you apply the three approaches to other social patterns, such as the workplace or family life?

---

this page to the wink of an eye. We create "reality," therefore, as we define our surroundings, decide what we think of others, and shape our own identities.

Symbolic-interaction theory has roots in the thinking of Max Weber (1864–1920), a German sociologist who emphasized understanding a particular setting from the point of view of the people in it. Since Weber's time, sociologists have taken micro-level sociology in a number of directions. Chapter 3 ("Socialization: From Infancy to Old Age") discusses the ideas of George Herbert Mead (1863–1931), who explored how our personalities develop as a result of social experience. Chapter 4 ("Social Interaction in Everyday Life") presents the work of Canadian-born sociologist Erving Goffman (1922–1982), whose *dramaturgical analysis* describes how we resemble actors on a stage as we play out our various roles. Other contemporary sociologists, including George Homans and Peter Blau, have developed *social-exchange analysis*, the idea that interaction is guided by what each person stands to gain and lose from others. In the ritual of courtship, for example, people seek mates who offer at least as much—in terms of physical attractiveness, intelligence, and social background—as they offer in return. Social constructionist theory of knowledge, which maintains that humans generate knowledge and meaning from their experiences and not from an objective reality, is a late modern outgrowth of the symbolic–interaction tradition.

EVALUATE Without denying the existence of macro-level social structures such as the family and social class, symbolic-interaction theory reminds us that society basically amounts to people *interacting*. That is, micro-level sociology shows us how individuals construct and experience society. However, by emphasizing what is unique in each social scene, this approach risks overlooking the widespread influence of culture, as well as structural factors such as class, gender, and race.

CHECK YOUR LEARNING How does a micro-level analysis differ from a macro-level analysis? Provide an explanation of a social pattern at both levels.

Keep in mind that each of the major theoretical approaches leads you to recognize particular facts as important and to answer questions in particular ways. As the Seeing Sociology in Everyday Life box exploring social patterns in sports on pages 20–21 shows, the fullest understanding of society comes from using all the approaches.

Three Ways to Do Sociology

(1.6) Describe sociology's three research orientations.

Any sociologists want to learn about the social world. But just as some may prefer one theoretical approach to another, many sociologists favour one research orientation. The following sections describe three ways to do sociological research: positivist, interpretive, and critical sociology.

Positivist Sociology

positivist sociology the study of society based on scientific observation of social behaviour

science a logical system that develops knowledge from direct, systematic observation

empirical evidence information we can verify with our senses

One popular way to do sociological research is **positivist sociology**, which is *the study of society based on scientific observation of social behaviour*. As explained earlier, positivist research discovers facts through the use of **science**, *a logical system that develops knowledge from direct, systematic observation*. Positivist sociology is sometimes called empirical sociology because it is based on **empirical evidence**, which is *information we can verify with our senses*.

Scientific research often challenges what we accept as "common sense." Here are five examples of widely held beliefs that are not supported by scientific evidence:

1. **"Poor people are far more likely than rich people to break the law."** Not true. If you regularly watch television shows like *COPS*, you might think that police arrest only people from "bad" neighbourhoods. Chapter 7 ("Deviance") explains that poor people do stand out in the official arrest statistics. But research also shows that police and prosecutors are more likely to treat well-to-do people more leniently, as when a celebrity is accused of shoplifting or drunk driving. Some laws are even written in a way that criminalizes poor people more and affluent people less.

2. **"Canada is a middle-class society in which most people are more or less equal."** False. Data presented in Chapter 8 ("Social Stratification") show that the richest 20 percent of Canadian families control 67 percent of the nation's total wealth, but almost half of all families have scarcely any wealth at all. The gap between the richest people and average people in Canada has never been greater.

3. **"Most poor people don't want to work."** Wrong. Research described in Chapter 8 indicates that this statement is true of some but not most poor people. In fact, of the almost 5 million poor in Canada, a third are children, people with disabilities, and elderly people who are not expected to work.

4. **"Differences in the behaviour of females and males are just 'human nature.'"** Wrong again. Much of what we call "human nature" is constructed by the society in

which we live. Further, as Chapter 10 ("Gender Stratification") argues, some societies define "feminine" and "masculine" very differently than we do.

5. **"People marry because they are in love."** Not exactly. To members of our society, few statements are so obvious. Surprisingly, however, in many societies, marriage has little to do with love. Chapter 13 ("Family and Religion") explains why.

These examples confirm the old saying that "it's not what we *don't* know that gets us into trouble as much as the things we *do* know that *just aren't so*." The Seeing Sociology in Everyday Life box on page 24 explains why we also need to think critically about the "facts" we find in the popular media and on the internet.

We have all been brought up hearing many widely accepted "truths," being bombarded by "expert" advice in the popular media, and feeling pressure to accept the opinions of those around us. As adults, we need to evaluate more critically what we see, read, and hear. Sociology can help us do that. Sociologists (and everyone else) can use science to assess many kinds of information.

Concepts, Variables, and Measurement

Let's take a closer look at how science works. A basic element of science is the **concept**, *a mental construct that represents some part of the world in a simplified form*. Sociologists use concepts to label aspects of social life, including "the family" and "the economy," and to categorize people in terms of their "gender" or "social class."

A **variable** is *a concept whose value changes from case to case*. The familiar variable "height," for example, has a value that varies from person to person. The concept "social class" can describe people's social standing using the values "upper class," "middle class," "working class," and "lower class."

The use of variables depends on **measurement**, *a procedure for determining the value of a variable in a specific case*. Some variables are easy to measure, as when a nurse checks our blood pressure. But measuring sociological variables can be far more difficult, because the value of any variable in part depends on how it is defined.

Good research therefore requires that sociologists **operationalize a variable** by *specifying exactly what is to be measured before assigning a value to a variable*. Before measuring the concept of "social class," for example, you would have to decide exactly what you were going to measure—say, income level, years of schooling, or occupational prestige.

concept a mental construct that represents some part of the world in a simplified form

variable a concept whose value changes from case to case

measurement a procedure for determining the value of a variable in a specific case

operationalize a variable specify exactly what is to be measured before assigning a value to a variable

reliability consistency in measurement

validity actually measuring exactly what you intend to measure

Statistics

Sociologists also face the problem of dealing with large numbers of people. For example, how do you report income for thousands or even millions of individuals? Listing streams of numbers would carry little meaning and tells us nothing about the people as a whole. To solve this problem, sociologists use *descriptive statistics* to state the "average" for a large population. The most commonly used descriptive statistics are the *mean* (the arithmetic average of all measures, which you calculate by adding all the values and dividing by the number of cases), the *median* (the score at the halfway point in a listing of numbers from lowest to highest), and the *mode* (the score that occurs most often).

Reliability and Validity

For a measurement to be useful, it must be reliable and valid. **Reliability** refers to *consistency in measurement*. A measurement is reliable if repeated measurements give the same result time after time. But consistency does not guarantee **validity**, which is *actually measuring exactly what you intend to measure*. Valid measurement means more than hitting the same spot somewhere on a target again and again; it means hitting the exact target, the bull's-eye.

Say you want to know just how religious the students at your university or college are. You might ask students how often they attend religious services. But is going to a house of worship really the same thing as being religious? Maybe not, because people take part in religious rituals

Seeing Sociology in Everyday Life

Is What We Read in the Popular Press True? The Case of Extramarital Sex

Every day, we see stories in newspapers and magazines that tell us what people think and how they behave. But a lot of what you read turns out to be misleading or worse.

Take the issue of extramarital sex, meaning married or common-law people having sex with someone other than their spouse or partner. A look at the covers of the many "women's magazines" at the supermarket checkout or a quick reading of the advice column in your local newspaper might lead you to think that extramarital sex is a major issue.

The popular media seem full of stories about how to keep your spouse or partner from "cheating" or pointing out the clues that tip you off when he or she is having an affair. Most of the studies reported in the popular press, and on websites, suggest that more than half of people in intimate relationships—women as well as men—cheat.

But is extramarital sex really that widespread? No. Researchers who conduct sound sociological investigation have found that, in any given year, only 3 to 4 percent of married or common-law people have an extramarital relationship, and no more than 15 to 20 percent have ever done so. Why, then, do surveys in the popular media report rates of extramarital sex that are so much higher? We can answer this question by taking a look at who fills out pop surveys.

Gina Sanders/Fotolia

First, people with a personal interest in a topic are most likely to respond to an offer to complete a survey. For this reason, people who have some personal experience with extramarital sex (either their own behaviour or their partner's) are more likely to show up in these studies. In contrast, studies correctly conducted by trained sociologists carefully select subjects so that the results are representative of the entire population.

Second, because the readership of the magazines and online sources that conduct these surveys is, on average, young, their surveys end up attracting a high proportion of young respondents. And one thing we know about young people is that they are more likely to have sex outside of their primary romantic relationship. For example, the typical married or common-law person who is age 30 is more than twice as likely to have had an extramarital relationship than the typical married or common-law person over age 60.

Third, women are much more likely than men to read the popular magazines that feature sex surveys. Therefore, women are more likely to fill out these surveys. In recent decades, the share of women, especially younger women, who have had extramarital sex has gone up. Why are today's younger women more likely than women a generation or two earlier to have had extramarital sex? Probably because women today are working outside of the home and many are travelling as part of their job. In general, today's women have a wider social network that brings them into contact with others.

Chapter 6 ("Sexuality and Society") takes a close look at sexual patterns, including extramarital relationships. For now, just remember that a lot of what you read in the popular media and online may not be as true as some people think.

What Do You Think?

1. Can you think of other issues on which popular media surveys may give misleading information? What are they?

2. Explain why we should have more trust in the results of sound research carried out by skilled sociologists than in the surveys conducted by the popular media.

3. Do you think companies are likely to sell more magazines or newspapers if they publish "research" results that distort the truth? Explain.

Sources: T.W. Smith (2006); Black (2007); and Parker-Pope (2008).

---

for many reasons, some of them having little to do with religion; in addition, some strong believers avoid organized religion altogether. Thus even when a measurement yields consistent results (meaning that it is reliable), it can still miss the intended target (and therefore lack validity). Good sociological research depends on careful measurement, which is always a challenge to researchers.

Correlation and Cause

The real payoff in scientific research is determining how variables are related. **Correlation** means *a relationship in which two (or more) variables change together*. But sociologists want to know not just how variables change but which variable changes the other. The scientific ideal is to determine **cause and effect**, *a relationship in which change in one variable causes change in another*. As noted earlier, Emile Durkheim found that the degree of social integration (the cause) affected the suicide rate (the effect) among categories of people. Scientists refer to *the variable that causes the change* as the **independent variable** and *the variable that changes* (the effect) as the **dependent variable**. Understanding cause and effect is valuable because it allows researchers to *predict* how one pattern of behaviour will produce another.

correlation a relationship in which two (or more) variables change together

cause and effect a relationship in which change in one variable (the independent variable) causes change in another (the dependent variable)

independent variable the variable that causes the change

dependent variable the variable that changes

Just because two variables change together does not necessarily mean that they have a cause-and-effect relationship. For instance, the marriage rate in Canada falls to its lowest point in January, which also happens to be the month when the national death rate is highest. Does this mean that people drop dead because they don't marry or that they don't marry because they die? Of course not. More likely, it is the cold and often stormy weather across much of the country in January (perhaps combined with the post-holiday blues) that is responsible for both the low marriage rate and the high death rate.

When two variables change together but neither one causes the other, sociologists describe the relationship as a **spurious correlation**, *an apparent but false relationship between two (or more) variables that is caused by some other variable*. A spurious correlation between two variables usually results from some third factor. For example, delinquency rates are high where young people live in crowded housing, but this is not because crowded housing causes youngsters to "turn bad." Both crowded housing and delinquency result from a third factor: poverty. To be sure of a real cause-and-effect relationship, we must show that (1) variables are correlated, (2) the independent (causal) variable occurs before the dependent variable, and (3) there is no evidence that a third variable has been overlooked, causing a spurious correlation.

spurious correlation an apparent but false relationship between two (or more) variables that is caused by some other variable

The Ideal of Objectivity

A guiding principle of science is **objectivity**, or *personal neutrality in conducting research*. Ideally, objective research allows the facts to speak for themselves and not be influenced by the personal values and biases of the researcher. In reality, of course, achieving total neutrality is impossible for anyone. But carefully observing the rules of scientific research will maximize objectivity.

objectivity personal neutrality in conducting research

The German sociologist Max Weber noted that people usually choose *value-relevant* research topics—topics they care about. But once their work is under way, he cautioned, researchers should try to be *value-free*. That is, we must be dedicated to finding truth as it *is* rather than as we think it *should be*. For Weber, this difference sets science apart from politics. Researchers (unlike politicians) must stay open-minded and be willing to accept whatever results come from their work, whether they personally agree with them or not.

Weber's argument still carries much weight in sociology, although most researchers realize that we can never be completely value-free or even fully aware of our biases. In addition, keep in mind that sociologists are not "average" people: Most are highly educated white men and women who are more politically liberal than the population as a whole. Sociologists need to remember that they, too, are influenced by their social backgrounds.

One principle of scientific research is that sociologists should try to be objective in their work, so that their personal values and beliefs do not distort their findings. But such a detached attitude may discourage the connection needed for people to open up and share information. Thus sociologists have to decide how much to pursue objectivity and how much to show their own feelings.

Interpretive Sociology

Not all sociologists agree that science is the only way—or even the best way—to study human society. This is because, unlike planets or other elements of the natural world, humans are much more than objects moving around in ways that can be measured. Of course, we are active creatures, but our humanity lies in the fact that we attach *meaning* to our actions, and meaning is not easy to observe directly. Therefore, sociologists have developed a second research orientation known as **interpretive sociology**, *the study of society that focuses on discovering the meanings people attach to their social world*. Max Weber, the pioneer of this framework, argued that the proper focus of sociology is *interpretation*, or understanding the meanings people create in their everyday lives. Sociologists who use this approach may well measure behaviour, making use of the positivist approach, but their greater goal is discovering what people *mean* by what they do.

The Importance of Meaning

Interpretive sociology does not reject science completely, but it does change the focus of research. Interpretive sociology differs from positivist sociology in four ways. First, positivist sociology focuses on actions—on what people do—because that is what we can observe directly. Interpretive sociology, by contrast, focuses on people's understanding of their actions and their surroundings. Second, positivist sociology claims that objective reality exists "out there," but interpretive sociology counters that reality is subjective, constructed by people in the course of their everyday lives. Third, positivist sociology tends to favour *quantitative* data—numerical measurements of people's behaviour—while interpretive sociology favours *qualitative* data, or researchers' perceptions of how people understand their world. Fourth, the positivist orientation is best suited to research in a laboratory, where investigators conducting an experiment stand back and take careful measurements. On the other hand, the interpretive orientation claims that we learn more by interacting with people, focusing on subjective meaning, and learning how they make sense of their everyday lives. As the chapter will explain, this type of research often uses personal interviews or fieldwork and is best carried out in a natural or everyday setting.

Weber's Concept of *Verstehen*

Max Weber claimed that the key to interpretive sociology lies in *Verstehen* (pronounced "fair-SHTAY-in"), the German word for "understanding." It is the interpretive sociologist's job not just to observe *what* people do but also to share in their world of meaning, coming to appreciate *why* they act as they do. Subjective thoughts and feelings, which scientists tend to dismiss because they are difficult to measure, are the focus of the interpretive sociologist's attention.

Critical Sociology

Like the interpretive orientation, critical sociology developed in reaction to what many sociologists saw as the limitations of positivist sociology. In this case, however, the problem involves the central principle of scientific research: objectivity.

Positivist sociology holds that reality is "out there" and that the researcher's job is to study and document how society works. But Karl Marx, who founded the critical orientation, rejected the idea that society exists as a "natural" system. To assume that society is somehow "fixed," he claimed, is the same as saying that society cannot be changed. With a focus on society as it exists, positivist sociology, from this point of view, ends up supporting the status quo. **Critical sociology**, by contrast, is *the study of society that focuses on the need for social change*.

The Importance of Change

Critical sociology does not ignore "facts." Researchers using this approach may well make use of scientific methods to learn, for example, how much income inequality there is in the United States. But rather than asking the positivist question "How much inequality *is* there?" critical sociologists ask moral and political questions, such as "*Should* we have this much inequality?" or "*Should* society exist in its present form?"

Their answer, typically, is that it should not. So, critical sociology does not reject using science to learn about what's going on in the social world.

interpretive sociology the study of society that focuses on discovering the meanings people attach to their social world

critical sociology the study of society that focuses on the need for social change

But critical sociology does reject the scientific neutrality that requires researchers to try to be "objective" and limit their work to studying the status quo.

One recent account of the critical orientation, echoing Marx, claims that the point of this type of sociology is "not just to research the social world but to change it in the direction of democracy and social justice" (Feagin & Hernán, 2001:1). In making value judgments about how society should be improved, critical sociology rejects Weber's goal that sociology be a value-free science and emphasizes instead that sociologists should be activists in pursuit of greater social equality. Sociologists using the critical orientation seek to change not only society but also the character of research itself. They often identify personally with their research subjects and encourage them to help decide what to study and how to do the work. Often, researchers and subjects use their findings to provide a voice for less powerful people and to advance the political goal of a more equal society (Hess, 1999, 2001; Perrucci, 2001).

Sociology as Politics

Positivist sociologists object to researchers taking sides in this way. The positivist claim is that to the extent that critical sociology (whether feminist, Marxist, or of some other critical orientation) becomes political, it gives up scientific objectivity, and therefore cannot correct for its own biases. The critical sociology response is that *all* research is political in that either it calls for change or it does not. As critical sociology sees it, sociologists thus have no choice about their work being political, but they can choose *which* positions to support.

Critical sociology is an activist orientation that ties knowledge to action and seeks not just to understand the world as it exists but also to improve it. In general, positivist sociology tends to appeal to researchers who try to be non-political or who have more conservative political views; critical sociology appeals to those whose politics range from liberal to radical left.

Research Orientations and Theory

We have now considered various research orientations as well as various theoretical approaches. Is there a link between research orientations and sociological theory? The connection is not precise, but each of the three ways to do sociology—positivist, interpretive, and critical— does stand closer to one of the theoretical approaches presented earlier in this chapter. The positivist orientation is linked to the structural-functional approach, and this is because both are concerned with the scientific goal of understanding society as it is. The interpretive orientation is linked to the symbolic-interaction approach by the fact that both focus on the meanings people attach to their social world. Finally, the critical orientation is linked to the social-conflict approach because both are animated by the goal of reducing social inequality.

The Summing Up table provides a quick review of the differences among the three ways to do sociology. Many sociologists favour one orientation over another; however, because each provides useful insights, it is a good idea to become familiar with all three.

Summing Up

Three Research Orientations in Sociology

	Positivist Sociology	Interpretive Sociology	Critical Sociology
What is reality?	Society is an orderly system. There is an objective reality "out there."	Society is ongoing interaction. People construct reality as they attach meanings to their behaviour.	Society is patterns of inequality. Reality is that some categories of people dominate others.
How do we conduct research?	Using a scientific orientation, the researcher carefully observes behaviour, gathering empirical, ideally quantitative, data. Researcher tries to be a neutral observer.	Seeking to look "deeper" than outward behaviour, the researcher focuses on subjective meaning. The researcher gathers qualitative data, discovering the subjective sense people make of their world. Researcher is a participant.	Seeking to go beyond positivism's focus on studying the world as it is, the researcher is guided by politics and uses research as a strategy to bring about desired social change. Researcher is an activist.
Corresponding theoretical approach	Structural-functional approach	Symbolic-interaction approach	Social-conflict approach

Gender and Research

1.7 Identify the importance of gender in sociological research.

gender the personal traits and social positions that members of a society attach to being female or male

In recent years, sociologists have become aware that research is affected by **gender**, *the personal traits and social positions that members of a society attach to being female or male.* Margrit Eichler (1988) identifies five ways in which gender can shape research:

1. **Androcentricity.** *Androcentricity* (literally, "focus on the male") means approaching an issue from a male perspective. Sometimes researchers act as if only men's activities are important, ignoring what women do. For years, sociologists studying occupations focused on the paid labour of men and overlooked the housework and child care traditionally performed by women. Research that tries to explain human behaviour cannot ignore half of humanity.

   Gynocentricity—seeing the world from a female perspective—can also limit good sociological investigation. However, in our male-dominated society, this problem arises less often.

2. **Overgeneralizing.** This problem occurs when sociologists gather data only from men but then use that information to draw conclusions about all people. For example, a researcher might speak to a handful of male public officials and then form conclusions about an entire community.

3. **Gender blindness.** Failing to consider gender at all is called *gender blindness.* The lives of men and women differ in many ways. A study of growing old in Canada might suffer from gender blindness if it overlooked the fact that most elderly men live with spouses but elderly women generally live alone.

4. **Double standards.** Researchers must be careful not to judge men and women by different standards. For example, a family researcher who labels a couple "man and wife" may define the man as the "head of the household" and treat him as important while assuming that the woman simply engages in family "support work."

5. **Interference.** Another way gender can distort a study is if a subject reacts to the sex of the researcher, interfering with the research operation. While studying a small community in Sicily, for instance, Maureen Giovannini (1992) found that many men treated her as a *woman* rather than as a *researcher.* Some thought it inappropriate for an unmarried woman to speak privately with a man. Others denied Giovannini access to places they considered off-limits to women.

If you ask only male subjects about their attitudes or actions, you may be able to support conclusions about "men" but not more generally about "people." What would a researcher have to do to ensure that research data support conclusions about all of society?

There is nothing wrong with focusing research on people of one sex or the other. But all sociologists, as well as people who read their work, should be mindful of how gender can affect an investigation.

Research Ethics

1.8 Discuss the importance of ethics to sociological research.

Like all other scientific investigators, sociologists must be aware that their work can harm as well as help subjects or communities. For this reason, the Canadian Sociological Association (CSA) (2012)—the major professional association for sociologists in Canada—has established formal guidelines for conducting research.

Sociologists must try to be skilful and fair-minded in their work. They must disclose all research findings without omitting significant data. They should make their results available to other sociologists who may want to conduct a similar study.

Sociologists must also make sure that subjects taking part in a research project are not harmed, and they must stop their work right away if they suspect that any subject is at risk of

Thinking About Diversity: Race, Class, and Gender

Research with First Nations, Inuit, and Metis Peoples of Canada

In a society as racially, ethnically, and religiously diverse as Canada, sociological investigators will inevitably confront people who differ from themselves. Learning—in advance—how to conduct ethical research with people of diverse cultural backgrounds and histories can not only facilitate the research and ensure that no harm comes to the participants, but also keep avenues open for future collaborations.

Canada's national research funding agencies—the Canadian Institutes of Health Research (CIHR), the Natural Sciences and Engineering Research Council of Canada (NSERC), and the Social Sciences and Humanities Research Council of Canada (SSHRC)—and the First Nations, Inuit, and Metis peoples of Canada have worked together to produce consensus guidelines for conducting research that aims to meet the goals of all parties involved. In December 2014, CIHR, NSERC, and SSHRC jointly released the latest edition of the *Tri-Council Policy Statement: Ethical Conduct for Research Involving Humans*. Chapter 9, in this second edition of the policy statement, discusses the latest thinking about ethical research involving Canada's Aboriginal peoples. This chapter, developed with Aboriginal partners, emphasizes the need for equitable partnerships and provides safeguards specific to First Nations, Inuit, and Metis people.

Chapter 9 cautions researchers to be aware of the "apprehension or mistrust" of traditional research conducted *on* (not *with*) Canada's Aboriginal peoples. Such research was predominantly driven by the needs and concerns of researchers and often had little or no benefit to Aboriginal communities—and sometimes even resulted in harm. Some of the guidelines that researchers hoping to conduct research with First Nations, Inuit, and Metis peoples should follow include:

1. Researchers must meaningfully engage the Aboriginal community that their research is likely to affect, by, for example, inviting Elders to participate in research design.

2. First Nations, Inuit, and Metis representatives should be invited to join ethical review boards and to provide project oversight, where appropriate.

3. Researchers and ethical review boards should also include the voices of community members and knowledge holders who do not have a voice in formal leadership.

4. Researchers must ensure that the research is relevant to community priorities and that it has real benefits for—and that the results are widely distributed to—the participating community.

What Do You Think?

1. What are some likely consequences of researchers not being sensitive to the different histories and cultures of Canada's First Nations, Inuit, and Metis peoples?

2. What do researchers need to do to avoid these problems?

3. Discuss the research process with classmates from various cultural backgrounds. What similar or different concerns would be raised by these people when taking part in research?

Sources: CIHR (2007); CIHR, NSERC, and SSHRC (2014).

harm. Researchers are also required to protect the privacy of individuals involved in a research project, even if they come under pressure from authorities, such as the police or the courts, to release confidential information. Researchers must also get the *informed consent* of participants, which means that the subjects must fully understand their responsibilities and the risks that the research involves before agreeing to take part.

Another guideline concerns funding. Sociologists must include in their published results all sources of financial support. They must avoid accepting money from a source if there is any question of a conflict of interest. Researchers must never accept funding from any organization that seeks to influence the research results for its own purposes.

The federal government also plays a part in research ethics. Every Canadian college and university that seeks federal funding for research involving human subjects must have a Human Research Ethics Committee (HREC) to ensure that the proposed research adheres to the guidelines stated in the second edition of *Tri-Council Policy Statement: Ethical Conduct for Research Involving Humans* (CIHR, NSERC, and SSHRC, 2014).

Finally, there are global dimensions to research ethics. Before beginning work in another country, an investigator must become familiar enough with that society to understand what people *there* are likely to regard as a violation of privacy or a source of personal danger. In a diverse society such as our own, the same rule applies to studying people whose cultural background differs from that of the researcher. The Thinking About Diversity box offers tips on the sensitivity outsiders should apply when studying Aboriginal communities in Canada.

Research Methods

(1.9) Explain why a researcher might choose each of sociology's research methods.

research method a systematic plan for doing research

A **research method** is *a systematic plan for doing research*. Four commonly used methods of sociological investigation are experiments, surveys, participant observation, and the use of existing data. None is better or worse than any other. Rather, just as a carpenter chooses a particular tool for a particular job, researchers select a method according to whom they want to study and what they want to learn.

Testing a Hypothesis: The Experiment

experiment a research method for investigating cause and effect under highly controlled conditions

hypothesis a statement of a possible relationship between two (or more) variables

The **experiment** is *a research method for investigating cause and effect under highly controlled conditions*. Experiments closely follow the logic of science, testing a specific **hypothesis**, *a statement of a possible relationship between two (or more) variables*. A hypothesis is really an educated guess about how variables are linked, usually expressed as an *if–then* statement: *If* this particular thing were to happen, *then* that particular thing will result.

An experimenter gathers the evidence needed to reject or to not reject the hypothesis in four steps: (1) State which variable is the *independent variable* (the "cause" of the change) and which is the *dependent variable* (the "effect," the thing that is changed). (2) Measure the initial value of the dependent variable. (3) Expose the dependent variable to the independent variable (the "cause" or "treatment"). (4) Measure the dependent variable again to see what change, if any, took place. If the expected change took place, the experiment supports the hypothesis; if not, the hypothesis must be modified.

Successful experiments depend on careful control of all factors that might affect what the experiment is trying to measure. Control is easiest in a research laboratory, but experiments in an everyday location—"in the field," as sociologists say—have the advantage of letting researchers observe subjects in their natural settings.

Illustration of an Experiment: The "Stanford County Prison"

Prisons can be violent settings, but is this due simply to the "bad" people who end up there? Or, as Philip Zimbardo suspected, does prison itself somehow cause violent behaviour? To answer this question, Zimbardo devised a fascinating experiment that he called the "Stanford County Prison" (Zimbardo, 1972; Haney, Banks, & Zimbardo, 1973).

Zimbardo thought that once inside a prison, even emotionally healthy people are likely to engage in violence. So Zimbardo treated the *prison setting* as the independent variable capable of causing *violence*, the dependent variable.

To test this hypothesis, Zimbardo and his research team first constructed a realistic-looking "prison" in the basement of the psychology building on the campus of Stanford University in California. Then they placed an ad in a local newspaper, offering to pay young men to help with a two-week research project. To each of the 70 who responded they administered a series of physical and psychological tests and then selected the healthiest 24.

The next step was to assign randomly half of the men to be "prisoners" and half to be "guards." The plan called for the guards and prisoners to spend the next two weeks in the mock prison. The prisoners began their part of the experiment when real police officers "arrested" them at their homes. After searching and handcuffing the men, the police drove them to the local police station, where they were fingerprinted. Then police transported their captives to the Stanford prison, where the guards locked them up. Zimbardo started his video camera and watched to see what would happen next.

The experiment turned into more than anyone had bargained for. Both guards and prisoners soon became embittered and hostile toward one another. Guards humiliated the prisoners by assigning them to jobs such as cleaning toilets with their bare hands. The prisoners resisted and insulted the guards. Within four days, the researchers had removed five prisoners who displayed "extreme emotional depression, crying, rage and acute anxiety" (Haney, Banks,

& Zimbardo, 1973:81). Before the end of the first week, the situation had become so bad that the researchers had to end the experiment.

The events that unfolded at the "Stanford County Prison" supported Zimbardo's hypothesis that prison violence is rooted in the social character of the jails themselves, not in the personalities of individual guards and prisoners. This finding raises questions about prisons, suggesting the need for some basic reforms. Zimbardo's experiment also shows the potential of research to threaten the physical and mental well-being of subjects. Such dangers are not always as obvious as they were in this case. Therefore, researchers must carefully consider the potential harm to subjects at all stages of their work and halt any study, as Zimbardo did, if subjects suffer harm of any kind.

EVALUATE In carrying out the "Stanford County Prison" study, the researchers chose to do an experiment because they were interested in testing a hypothesis. In this case, Zimbardo and his colleagues wanted to find out if the prison setting itself (rather than the personalities of individual guards and prisoners) is the cause of prison violence. The fact that the "prison" erupted in violence—even when using guards and prisoners who had "healthy" profiles— supports their hypothesis.

CHECK YOUR LEARNING How might Zimbardo's findings help explain the abuse of a 16-year-old Somali boy in 1993 by two Canadian soldiers participating in the United Nations peacekeeping efforts in Somalia or the abuse of Iraqi prisoners by American soldiers after the 2003 invasion of Iraq?

Asking Questions: Survey Research

A **survey** is *a research method in which subjects respond to a series of statements or questions on a questionnaire or in an interview.* As the most widely used of all research methods, the survey is well suited to studying what cannot be observed directly, such as political attitudes or religious beliefs.

A survey targets some *population*, for example, unmarried mothers or adults living in rural Alberta. Sometimes every adult in the country is the survey population, as in polls taken during national political campaigns. Of course, contacting a vast number of people is all but impossible, so researchers usually study a *sample*, a much smaller number of subjects selected to represent the entire population. Surveys using samples of as few as 1500 people commonly give accurate estimates of public opinion for the entire country.

Beyond selecting subjects, the survey must have a specific plan for asking questions and recording answers. The most common way to do this is to give subjects a *questionnaire* with a series of written statements or questions. Often the researcher lets subjects choose possible responses to each item, as on a multiple-choice test. Sometimes, though, a researcher may want subjects to respond freely to permit all opinions to be expressed. Of course, this free-form approach means that the researcher later has to make sense out of what can be a bewildering array of answers.

In an *interview*, a researcher personally asks subjects a series of questions, thereby solving one problem common to the questionnaire method: the failure of some subjects to return the questionnaire to the researcher. A further difference is that interviews give participants freedom to respond as they wish. Researchers often ask follow-up questions to clarify an answer or to probe a bit more deeply. In doing this, however, a researcher must avoid influencing the subject even in subtle ways, such as by raising an eyebrow as the subject offers an answer.

survey a research method in which subjects respond to a series of statements or questions on a questionnaire or in an interview

Focus groups are a type of survey in which a small number of people representing a target population are asked for their opinions about some issue or product. Here a sociology professor asks students to evaluate textbooks for use in her introductory class.

Illustration of Survey Research: Longitudinal Studies of Hidden Populations

How do you contact and stay in touch with research participants who are not members of mainstream society? Some individuals cannot be reached through a straightforward survey because they belong to what academics call hard-to-reach or hidden populations (Spreen & Zwaagstra, 1994). Such populations share three main characteristics: (1) there is no known list of the members of the population; (2) acknowledgement of belonging to the group is threatening because membership involves fear of prosecution or of being the object of hate or scorn; and (3) members are distrustful of non-members, do whatever they can to avoid revealing their identities, and are likely to refuse to co-operate with outsiders or to give unreliable answers to questions about themselves and their networks. Intravenous drug users and those who trade sex for money are examples of two hidden populations. Yet the need for reliable research on the individuals who are members of these populations has become urgent, given public concern over high rates of sexually transmitted infections (STIs), hepatitis, HIV infections, HIV transmission, and generally poor health status among these groups (Heckathorn, 1997).

One of the more powerful ways to understand health changes over time is to use a *longitudinal research design* and collect data from individuals repeatedly for as long as possible. But this again is problematic for studies of hidden populations, because members are unlikely to freely give their real names and reliable contact information.

Cecilia Benoit and Mikael Jansson, two of the authors of this text, are leading a research project in British Columbia that adopts a longitudinal design to better understand the causal links between youth marginalization, street involvement, and health. Youth qualify for the project based on their weak attachment to parents or guardians and the school system and their strong association with the street economy. They are interviewed twice in the first month of contact and then every few months for as long as they are willing to participate in the study (to a maximum of four years). Because of particular characteristics of this hidden population, combined with distrust of academics and others in positions of authority, several sampling techniques are being used to increase the probability of obtaining a reliable sample. Four non-profit community organizations are helping to establish respondent contact strategies to advertise the study and access the various subgroups of marginalized youth. The study is also widely advertised in shelters, drop-in centres, and other places that marginalized youth concentrate.

A final method of recruiting research participants is a technique known as *respondent-driven sampling* (Heckathorn, 1997). The technique begins with a small number of research participants who serve as "seeds." The seeds are given three recruitment coupons to hand to peers they believe may want to come forward for an interview (based on the rationale that reclusive participants are more likely to respond to the appeals of their peers). The seeds are paid a nominal fee for each peer who comes forward for an interview (paid at the seed's third interview).

EVALUATE Cecilia Benoit and Mikael Jansson chose the survey as their method because they wanted to ask a lot of questions and gather information from their subjects. Certainly, some of the information they collected could have been obtained using a questionnaire. But they decided to carry out interviews because they are dealing with a complex and sensitive topic. Interacting with their subjects one on one for several hours, the researchers could put them at ease, discuss personal matters, and ask them follow-up questions.

CHECK YOUR LEARNING What strategies might researchers use to establish trust with populations that are skeptical of academics?

In the Field: Participant Observation

participant observation a research method in which investigators systematically observe people while joining them in their routine activities

Participant observation is *a research method in which investigators systematically observe people while joining them in their routine activities*. This method lets researchers study everyday social life in any natural setting, from a nightclub to a religious seminary. Cultural anthropologists use participant observation to study other societies, calling this method *fieldwork* and calling their research results an *ethnography*.

At the beginning of a field study, most researchers do not have a specific hypothesis in mind. In fact, they may not yet realize what the important questions will turn out to be. This makes most participant observation *exploratory* and *descriptive*, falling within interpretive sociology and producing mostly qualitative, rather than quantitative, data. Compared with experiments and surveys, participant observation has few hard-and-fast rules. But this flexibility allows investigators to explore the unfamiliar and adapt to the unexpected.

Participant observers try to gain entry into a setting without disturbing the routine behaviour of others. Their role is twofold: To gain an insider's viewpoint, they must become participants in the setting, "hanging out" for months or even years, trying to act, think, and even feel the same way as the people they are observing; at the same time, they must remain observers, standing back from the action and applying the sociological perspective to social patterns that others take for granted.

Because the personal impressions of a single researcher play such a central role, critics claim that participant observation falls short of scientific standards. Yet its personal approach is also its strength: Where a high-profile team of sociologists administering a formal survey might disrupt a setting, a sensitive participant observer often can gain important insight into people's behaviour.

Illustration of Participant Observation: Street Corner Society

Did you ever wonder what everyday life was like in an unfamiliar neighbourhood? In the late 1930s, a young graduate student at Harvard University named William Foote Whyte (1914–2000) set out to study social life in a rather rundown section of Boston. His curiosity led him to carry out four years of participant observation in this neighbourhood, which he called "Cornerville."

At the time, Cornerville was home to first- and second-generation Italian immigrants, many of whom were poor. Many Bostonians considered Cornerville a place to avoid: a slum inhabited by criminals. Wanting to learn the truth, Whyte set out to discover for himself exactly what life was like inside this community. His celebrated book, *Street Corner Society* (1981, orig. 1943), describes Cornerville as a community with its own code of values, complex social patterns, and particular social conflicts.

Participant observation is a method of sociological research that allows a researcher to investigate people as they go about their everyday lives in some "natural" setting. At its best, participant observation makes you a star in your own reality show; but living in what may be a strange setting far from home for months at a time is always challenging.

To start, Whyte considered a range of research methods. He could have taken questionnaires to one of Cornerville's community centres and asked local people to fill them out. Or he could have invited members of the community to come to his Harvard office for interviews. But it is easy to see that such formal strategies would have gained little co-operation from the local people and produced few insights. Whyte decided, therefore, to ease into Cornerville life and slowly build a personal understanding of this rather mysterious place.

Right away, Whyte discovered the challenges of even getting started in field research. As an upper-middle-class WASP graduate student from Harvard, he stood out on the streets of Cornerville. Even a friendly overture from such an outsider could seem pushy and rude. Early on, Whyte dropped in at a local bar, hoping to buy a woman a drink and encourage her to talk about Cornerville. Looking around the room, he could find no woman alone. He thought he might have an opportunity when he saw a man sit down with two women. He walked over and asked, "Pardon me. Would you mind if I joined you?" Instantly, Whyte realized his mistake:

> There was a moment of silence while the man stared at me. Then he offered to throw me down the stairs. I assured him that this would not be necessary, and demonstrated as much by walking right out of there without any assistance. (1981:289)

As this incident suggests, gaining entry to a community is the vital (and sometimes hazardous) first step in field research. "Breaking in" requires patience, ingenuity, and a little luck. Whyte's big break came in the form of a young man named "Doc," whom he met in a local social service agency. Whyte complained to Doc about how hard it was to make friends in Cornerville. Doc responded by taking Whyte under his wing and introducing him to others in the community. With Doc's help, Whyte soon became a neighbourhood regular.

Thinking About Diversity: Race, Class, and Gender

Youth Marginalization, Street Involvement, and Health: Using Tables in Research

A table provides a lot of information in a small amount of space, so learning to read tables can increase your reading efficiency. When you spot a table, look first at the title to see what information it contains. The title of the table to the right tells you that the table presents characteristics of a representative sample of all youth in Victoria, British Columbia, and also a group of street-involved youth in Victoria.

Across the top of the table, you will see that the first column lists the characteristics described in the middle column for the representative sample of all youth and in the third column for the street-involved youth. Reading down each column, note the categories within each variable; even though the percentages in each column add up to a number very close to 100, they do not total exactly 100 percent because of rounding errors.

Starting at the top left, we see that the youth in both samples are aged 14 through 18 and that the street-involved youth are a little older than the random sample since there are almost three times as many 18-year-olds (27 percent) as there are 14-year-olds (10 percent) in the street-involved youth sample. Moving down the table, we see that there are slightly more females than males in both samples.

The two groups of youth differ quite markedly in the remaining three characteristics displayed. First, there are many more youth in the street-involved youth sample who claim an Aboriginal background (31 percent) than do so in the random sample (2 percent). Second, the youth in the two groups have very different sexual orientation, since 59 percent of street-involved youth labelled themselves heterosexual compared to 88 percent of youth in the random sample.

But the biggest differences between these two groups of youth is found in the third remaining group of percentages that shows who the youth lived with while they were 12 years old. While 62 percent of youth in the random sample lived with both biological parents throughout that year, only 15 percent of street-involved youth did so. Remarkable also is the high number of street-involved youth who lived the whole year before they became teenagers with foster parents (7 percent).

What Do You Think?

1. Why are statistical data, such as those in this table, an efficient way to convey a lot of information?

2. Looking at the table, how do you think the future life course of these two groups of youth will differ? Explain.

3. Do you see any ways in which this group of street-involved youth in Victoria may differ from marginalized youth in other areas of Canada? If so, what are they?

Randomly Selected Youth Compared to Street-Involved Youth in Victoria, British Columbia, Selected Characteristics

	Random Sample	Street Youth
Age		
14	21%	10%
15	20%	17%
16	21%	17%
17	23%	28%
18	14%	27%
Total	99%	99%
Gender		
Male	49%	43%
Female	51%	57%
Total	100%	100%
Aboriginal Background		
Yes	2%	31%
No	98%	68%
Total	100%	99%
Sexual Orientation		
Heterosexual	88%	59%
Homosexual	2%	4%
Bisexual	5%	32%
Other	1%	3%
Missing	4%	2%
Total	100%	100%
Living Situation While 12 Years Old		
Both biological parents	62%	15%
Mother only	11%	21%
Mother and partner	9%	7%
Father only	1%	6%
Foster parents	0%	7%
Other	17%	43%
Total	100%	99%

Note: These percentages are calculated based on original data collected by Cecilia Benoit and Mikael Jansson in Victoria, British Columbia, from two groups of youth. The first is a group of 484 youth who were randomly selected and the second consists of 164 street-involved youth.

Whyte's friendship with Doc illustrates the importance of a *key informant* in field research. Such people not only introduce a researcher to a community but often remain a source of information and help. But using a key informant also has its risks. Because any person has a particular circle of friends, a key informant's guidance is certain to "spin" the study in one way or another. Moreover, in the eyes of others, the reputation of the key informant, for better or worse, usually rubs off on the investigator. So although a key informant is helpful early on, a participant observer must seek a broader range of contacts.

Having entered the Cornerville world, Whyte quickly learned another lesson: A field researcher needs to know when to speak and when to shut up. One evening, Whyte joined a group discussing neighbourhood gambling. Wanting to get the facts straight, he asked innocently, "I suppose the cops were all paid off?"

> The gambler's jaw dropped. He glared at me. Then he denied vehemently that any policeman had been paid off and immediately switched the conversation to another subject. For the rest of that evening I felt very uncomfortable. The next day, Doc offered some sound advice:
>
> "Go easy on that 'who,' 'what,' 'why,' 'when,' 'where' stuff, Bill. You ask those questions and people will clam up on you. If people accept you, you can just hang around, and you'll learn the answers in the long run without even having to ask the questions." (1981:303)

In the months and years that followed, Whyte became familiar with everyday life in Cornerville, married a local woman, and learned that the common stereotypes were wrong. In Cornerville, most people worked hard, many were quite successful, and some even boasted of sending children to college. Even today, Whyte's book makes for fascinating reading about the deeds, dreams, and disappointments of immigrants and their children living in one ethnic community, and it contains the rich detail that can only come from years of participant observation.

EVALUATE To study the community he called "Cornerville," William Whyte chose participant observation—a good choice because he did not have a specific hypothesis to test, nor did he know at the outset what questions he would ask. By living in the community for several years, Whyte was able to paint a complex picture of its social life.

CHECK YOUR LEARNING Give an example of topics for sociological research that would be best studied using (1) an experiment, (2) a survey, and (3) participant observation.

Using Available Data: Existing Sources

Not all research requires investigators to collect new data. Sometimes sociologists make **use of existing sources**, *a research method in which a researcher uses data already collected by others*.

Every five years, Statistics Canada conducts a census of all Canadian households, mailing forms to each address. While historically the response rate has been quite high (it was 93.5 percent for the 2006 Census), the rate fell to 69.3 percent in 2011. What might explain the drop? Many academics, library organizations, think tanks, and members of the business community agree that the change, which significantly lowers the validity of the data, has to do with the Conservative government's elimination of the mandatory long form census in 2010. The voluntary National Household Survey (NHS), which came to replace it, failed to include 1128 Canadian subdivisions. National Map 1–1 on page 36 provides a look at the share of census subdivisions that filled out and returned their information forms as part of the 2011 National Household Survey. With a defeat of the Conservatives in 2015 and a return to the mandatory long-form census, we can anticipate high response rates for the 2016 census.

use of existing sources a research method in which a researcher uses data already collected by others

---

research method a systematic plan for doing research

experiment a research method for investigating cause and effect under highly controlled conditions

survey a research method in which subjects respond to a series of statements or questions on a questionnaire or in an interview

participant observation a research method in which investigators systematically observe people while joining them in their routine activities

use of existing sources a research method in which a researcher uses data already collected by others

NATIONAL MAP 1–1 Suppressed and Included Subdivisions in the 2011 National Household Survey

As the above map shows, the non-response rate—the rate at which people do not participate in the survey—varied greatly. Under the 2006 Census, when the non-response rate for any geographic area was 25 percent or higher, the data was withheld. Under the 2011 Census, the standards were loosened: Data was suppressed if the non-response rate was 50 percent or more.

Source: Statistics Canada (2012b); Cain (2013).

Data about other nations in the world are found in various publications of the United Nations and the World Bank. In short, data about the whole world are as close as your library or the internet.

Using available information saves time and money. This method has special appeal to sociologists with low budgets. And in fact, government data are usually more extensive and more accurate than what most researchers could obtain on their own.

But using available data, as we noted above, has problems of its own. Data may not be available in the exact form that is needed. For example, you may be able to find the average salaries paid to professors at your school but not separate figures for the amounts paid to women and men. Further, there are always questions about how accurate the existing data are. In his nineteenth-century study of suicide, described earlier, Emile Durkheim used official records. But Durkheim had no way to know if a death classified as a suicide was really an accident or vice versa.

Illustration of the Use of Existing Sources: Studying Media Narratives

Media representations of human activity constitute an important source of data. Academic analysis of media's place in the production and reproduction of dominant ideas, meanings, and values has been greatly influenced by the work of sociologist Stuart Hall (1978) and other contributors to the field of cultural studies (Pateman, 1988; Sacks, 1996; Kitzinger, 2000; Watkins & Emerson, 2000). These approaches to media illustrate how the transmission of social knowledge changes over time.

Because media representations of key social categories such as gender, class, race, and sexuality are important loci of self and personal identity construction (Seale, 2003), unfavourable media stories can negatively affect a person's sense of self and emotional well-being, whether or not these stories are actually true. In addition, contemporary media create social understanding between spatially distanced or socially segregated groups. The standard images found in the media become taken as truth unless the audience has the empirical knowledge to reject them. Thus, in the absence of personal experience with, for example, members of ethnic and visible minorities (Ungerleider, 1991), media stories can serve as key cultural sites where negative labels are created and taken up by the majority of citizens.

Hallgrimsdottir, Phillips, and Benoit (2006) compared media stories of people who work in the sex industry with these individuals' self-reports of their personal backgrounds and experiences of what they do for a living. The authors aimed to describe the level of similarity between media depictions of sex workers and their own description of their lives. The authors relied on two different kinds of data. First, they analyzed the print media discussion of the sex industry in one metropolitan region of Canada, the capital metropolitan region of Victoria, British Columbia. In doing so, they focused on the years 1980 to 2004 in a single regional daily newspaper, the Victoria *Times Colonist*. Articles of newspaper coverage of sex industry–related work were located using both a computerized and a paper subject index. Each article was analyzed in terms of both explicit and embedded content to generate a long list of themes. These themes were subsequently collapsed into a series of narrative categories and, in a final reading of the data, each article was assigned once to a single category. Second, the authors compared these media narratives with the self-reported experiences of sex workers—their background and personal lives, work experiences, and health and well-being—in the same city and over a comparable time period (Benoit & Millar, 2001).

Not surprisingly, the researchers found that most media narratives of the sex industry were not reflected in the personal stories of sex workers themselves. The interview data showed instead that media narratives follow relatively rigid and standardized cultural scripts in which individuals in the sex industry are presented as having poor moral character and as breaking the law, causing social disruption, and spreading contagious diseases. These cultural scripts organized the media narratives by directing what was included as newsworthy and what was left out of news accounts. The researchers also found that the contents of these cultural scripts can be used to understand how stigma is reproduced in our society.

Summing Up

Four Research Methods

	Experiment	Survey	Participant Observation	Existing Sources
Application	For explanatory research that specifies relationships between variables Generates quantitative data	For gathering information about issues that cannot be directly observed, such as attitudes and values Useful for descriptive and explanatory research Generates quantitative or qualitative data	For exploratory and descriptive study of people in a "natural" setting Generates qualitative data	For exploratory, descriptive, or explanatory research whenever suitable data are available
Advantages	Provides the greatest opportunity to specify cause-and-effect relationships Replication of research is relatively easy	Sampling, using questionnaires, allows surveys of large populations. Interviews provide in-depth responses	Allows study of "natural" behaviour Usually inexpensive	Saves time and expense of data collection Makes historical research possible
Limitations	Laboratory settings have an artificial quality Unless the research environment is carefully controlled, results may be biased	Questionnaires must be carefully prepared and may yield a low return rate Interviews are expensive and time-consuming	Time-consuming Replication of research is difficult Researcher must balance roles of participant and observer	Researcher has no control over possible biases in data Data may only partially fit current research needs

EVALUATE The main reason why Hallgrimsdottir and colleagues chose to use existing media sources is that they provided a context for understanding the interview data. Using existing sources alone can sometimes be problematic because they were not created with the purpose of answering sociologists' questions. For this reason, using such documents requires a critical eye and a good deal of creative thinking.

CHECK YOUR LEARNING What other questions about the media and human activity might you wish to answer using existing sources?

Putting It All Together: Ten Steps in Sociological Research

(**1.10**) Recall the 10 important steps in carrying out sociological research.

The following 10 questions will guide you through a research project in sociology:

1. **What is your topic?** Being curious and using the sociological perspective can generate ideas for social research at any time and in any place. Pick a topic you find interesting and that you think is important to study.

2. **What have others already learned?** You are probably not the first person with an interest in some issue. Visit the library and search the internet to see what theories and methods other researchers have applied to your topic. In reviewing the existing research, note problems that have come up to avoid repeating past mistakes.

3. **What, exactly, are your questions?** Are you seeking to explore an unfamiliar social setting? To describe some category of people? To investigate cause and effect among variables? Clearly state the goals of your research, and operationalize all variables.

4. **What will you need to carry out research?** How much time and money are available to you? What special equipment or skills does the research require? Can you do all of the work yourself?

5. **Are there ethical concerns?** Might the research harm anyone? How can you minimize the chances for injury? Will you promise your subjects anonymity? If so, how will you ensure that anonymity will be maintained?

6. **What method will you use?** Consider all major research strategies and combinations of methods. The most suitable method will depend on the kinds of questions you are asking and the resources available to you.

7. **How will you record the data?** The research method you use guides your data collection. Be sure to record information accurately and in a way that will make sense to you later on (it may be months before you write up the results of your work). Watch out for any personal bias that may creep into your work.

8. **What do the data tell you?** Determine what the data say about your initial questions. If your study involves a specific hypothesis, you should be able to confirm, reject, or modify it on the basis of your findings. Keep in mind that there will be several ways to interpret your results, depending on the theoretical approach you apply, and you should consider them all.

9. **What are your conclusions?** Prepare a final report explaining what you have learned. Also, evaluate your own work. What problems arose during the research process? What questions were left unanswered?

10. **How can you share what you've learned?** Consider making a presentation to your class or maybe even to a meeting of professional sociologists. The point is to share what you have learned with others and to let them respond to your work.

Controversy & Debate

Is Sociology Nothing More Than Stereotypes?

Jena: (*raising her eyes from her notebook*) Today, in sociology class, we talked about stereotypes.

Marcia: (*trying to focus on her science lab*) Okay, here's one: Roommates don't like to be disturbed when they're studying.

Jena: Seriously, my studious friend, we all have stereotypes, even professors.

Marcia: (*becoming faintly interested*) Like what?

Jena: Professor Chandler said today in class that Protestants are most likely to kill themselves. And later Yannina—this girl from, I think, Ecuador—said something like "You Canadians are rich, but you don't take marriage seriously, and you love to divorce!"

Marcia: My brother said to me last week that "everybody knows you have to be Black to play professional basketball." Now there's a stereotype!

Students, like everyone else, are quick to make generalizations about people. As this chapter explains, sociologists, too, love to generalize by looking for social patterns in everyday life. However, beginning students of sociology may wonder if sociological generalizations aren't really the same thing as stereotypes. For example, are the statements reported by Jena and Marcia true generalizations or false stereotypes?

A **stereotype** is *a simplified description applied to every person in some category*. Each of the statements the students made is a stereotype that is false, for three reasons. First, rather than describing averages, each statement describes every person in some category in exactly the same way; second, even though many stereotypes often contain an element of truth, each of these three statements leaves out relevant facts and distorts reality; and third, each statement is motivated by bias, spoken more as a put-down than as a fair-minded observation.

A sociology classroom is a good place to examine common stereotypes.

Good sociology makes generalizations, but they must meet three conditions. First, sociologists do not carelessly apply any generalization to everyone in a category. Second, sociologists make sure that a generalization squares with all available facts. And third, sociologists make generalizations fair-mindedly, in the interest of getting at the truth.

Jena remembered her professor saying (although not in quite the same words) that the suicide rate among Protestants is higher than among Catholics or Jews. Based on information presented earlier in this chapter, that is a true statement. However, the way Jena incorrectly reported the classroom remark—"If you're a Protestant, you're likely to kill yourself"—is not good sociology. It is not a true generalization because the vast majority of Protestants do no such thing. It would be just as wrong to jump to the conclusion that a particular friend, because he is a Protestant male, is about to end his own life. (Imagine refusing to lend money to a roommate who happens to be an Anglican, explaining, "Well, given the way people like you commit suicide, I might never get paid back!")

Second, sociologists shape their generalizations to available facts. A more factual version of the statement Yannina made is that while by world standards the Canadian population has a very high standard of living, almost everyone in our society does marry at some point with every intention of staying married, with only few people taking pleasure in divorcing.

Third, sociologists try to be fair-minded and want to get at the truth. The statement made by Marcia's brother about African Americans and basketball is a stereotype and therefore not good sociology for two reasons. First, as stated it is simply not true, and second, it seems motivated by racial bias rather than truth-seeking.

The bottom line, then, is that good sociological generalizations are *not* the same as stereotyping. But a sociology course is an excellent setting for getting at the truths behind common stereotypes. The classroom encourages discussion and offers the factual information you need to decide whether a particular statement is a valid sociological generalization or a harmful or unfair stereotype.

What Do You Think?

1. Can you think of a common stereotype of sociologists? What is it? After reading this box, do you still think it is valid?
2. Do you think taking a sociology course can help correct people's stereotypes? Why or why not?
3. Can you think of a stereotype of your own that might be challenged by sociological analysis?

The Controversy & Debate box discusses the use of the sociological perspective and reviews many of the ideas presented in this chapter. This box will help you apply what you have learned to the important question of how the generalizations made by sociologists differ from the common stereotypes we hear every day.

stereotype a simplified description applied to every person in some category

Seeing Sociology in Everyday Life

CHAPTER 1 Sociology: Perspective, Theory, and Method

Why do couples marry?

We asked this question at the beginning of this chapter. The common sense answer is that people marry because they are in love. But as this chapter has explained, society guides our everyday lives, affecting what we do, think, and feel. Look at the three photographs, each showing a couple that, we can assume, is "in love." In each case, can you provide some of the rest of the story? By looking at the categories that the people involved represent, explain how society is at work in bringing the two people together.

Warren Toda/EPA/Newscom

In 2011, American actress Eva Mendes began dating her co-star, Canadian actor Ryan Gosling. Mendes gave birth to their first child in 2014. Looking at this common-law couple, what social patterns do you see?

In 1980, when she was 12 years old, singer Celine Dion met her manager, René Angélil, who is 26 years her senior. The couple married in 1994. What social patterns do you see in this relationship?

WENN Ltd/Alamy Stock Photo

In 1997, during the fourth season of her hit TV show, *Ellen*, Ellen DeGeneres "came out" as a lesbian, which put her on the cover of *Time* magazine. Since then, she has been an activist on behalf of gay and lesbian issues. Following California's brief legalization of same-sex marriage in 2008, she married her long-time girlfriend, Australian actress Portia de Rossi.

Mark Savage/Corbis

HINT Society is at work on many levels. Consider (1) rules about same-sex and other-sex marriage, (2) laws defining the categories of people whom one may marry, (3) the importance of race and ethnicity, (4) the importance of social class, (5) the importance of age, and (6) the importance of social exchange (what each partner offers the other). All societies enforce various rules that state who should or should not marry whom.

Seeing Sociology in *Your* Everyday Life

1. Analyze the marriages of your parents, other family members, and friends in terms of class, race, age, and other factors. What evidence can you find that society guides the feelings that we call "love"?

2. Go to www.sociologyinfocus.com to access the Sociology in Focus blog, where you can read the latest posts by a team of young sociologists who apply the sociological perspective to topics of popular culture.

3. As this chapter has explained, the time in human history when we are born, the society in which we are born, as well as our class position, race, and gender all shape the personal experiences we have throughout our lives. Does this mean we have no power over our own destiny? No, in fact, the more we understand how society works, the more power we have to shape our own lives.

Making the Grade

The Sociological Perspective

1.1 Explain how the sociological perspective helps us understand that society shapes our individual lives. (pages 4–8)

The **sociological perspective** reveals the power of society to shape individual lives.

- C. Wright Mills called this point of view the "sociological imagination," which transforms personal troubles into public issues.
- Being an outsider or experiencing a social crisis encourages the sociological perspective.

sociology the systematic study of human society
sociological perspective the special point of view of sociology that sees general patterns of society in the lives of particular people

The Importance of a Global Perspective

1.2 State several reasons that a global perspective is important in today's world. (pages 8–11)

Global awareness is an important part of the sociological perspective because

- where we live shapes the lives we lead.
- societies throughout the world are increasingly interconnected.
- what happens in the rest of the world affects life here in Canada.
- many social problems that we face in Canada are far more serious elsewhere.
- thinking globally helps us learn more about ourselves.

global perspective the study of the larger world and our society's place in it
high-income countries the nations with the highest overall standards of living
middle-income countries nations with a standard of living about average for the world as a whole
low-income countries nations with a low standard of living, in which most people are poor

Applying the Sociological Perspective

1.3 Identify the advantages of sociological thinking for developing public policy, for encouraging personal growth, and for advancing in a career. (pages 11–12)

The sociological perspective

- is used by government agencies when developing laws and regulations that guide how people in communities live and work.

- helps us understand the barriers and opportunities in our lives.
- is an advantage in many fields of work that involve working with people.

The Origins of Sociology

1.4 Link the origins of sociology to historical social changes. (pages 12–14)

Rapid social change helped trigger the development of sociology:

- rise of an industrial economy
- explosive growth of cities
- new political ideas.

Auguste Comte named the discipline of sociology in 1838.

- Early philosophers had tried to describe the ideal society, but Comte wanted to understand society as it really is.
- Karl Marx and many later sociologists used sociology to try to make society better.

positivism a scientific approach to knowledge based on "positive" facts as opposed to mere speculation

Sociological Theory

1.5 Summarize sociology's major theoretical approaches. (pages 14–22)

macro-level The **structural-functional approach** explores how social structures work together to help society operate.

- Auguste Comte, Emile Durkheim, and Herbert Spencer helped develop the structural-functional approach.

The **social-conflict approach** shows how inequality creates conflict and causes change.

- Two important types of conflict analysis are **gender-conflict theory**, which is also called **feminist theory**, and **race-conflict theory**.

theory a statement of how and why specific facts are related
theoretical approach a basic image of society that guides thinking and research
structural-functional approach a framework for building theory that sees society as a complex system whose parts work together to promote solidarity and stability
social structure any relatively stable pattern of social behaviour
social functions the consequences of a social pattern for the operation of society as a whole
manifest functions the recognized and intended consequences of any social pattern
latent functions the unrecognized and unintended consequences of any social pattern
social dysfunction any social pattern that may disrupt the operation of society

- Karl Marx helped develop the social-conflict approach.

 micro-level The **symbolic-interaction approach** studies how people, in everyday interaction, construct reality.

- Max Weber and George Herbert Mead helped develop the social-interaction approach.

social-conflict approach a framework for building theory that sees society as an arena of inequality that generates conflict and change
gender-conflict theory (feminist theory) the study of society that focuses on inequality and conflict between women and men
feminism support of social equality for women and men
race-conflict theory the study of society that focuses on inequality and conflict between people of different racial and ethnic categories
macro-level orientation a broad focus on social structures that shape society as a whole
micro-level orientation a close-up focus on social interaction in specific situations
symbolic-interaction approach a framework for building theory that sees society as the product of the everyday interactions of individuals

Three Ways to Do Sociology

1.6 Describe sociology's three research orientations. (pages 22–27)

Positivist sociology uses the logic of science.
- tries to establish cause and effect
- demands that researchers try to be objective
- is loosely linked to structural-functional theory

Interpretive sociology focuses on the meanings people attach to behaviour.
- People construct reality in their everyday lives.
- Weber's *Verstehen* is learning how people understand their world.
- is linked to symbolic-interaction theory

Critical sociology uses research to bring about social change.
- focuses on inequality
- rejects the principle of objectivity, claiming that all research is political
- is linked to social-conflict theory

positivist sociology the study of society based on scientific observation of social behaviour
science a logical system that bases knowledge on direct, systematic observation
empirical evidence information we can verify with our senses
concept a mental construct that represents some aspect of the world in a simplified form
variable a concept whose value changes from case to case
measurement a procedure for determining the value of a variable in a specific case
operationalize a variable specifying exactly what is to be measured before assigning a value to a variable
reliability consistency in measurement
validity actually measuring exactly what you intend to measure
correlation a relationship in which two (or more) variables change together
cause and effect a relationship in which change in one variable (the independent variable) causes change in another (the dependent variable)
independent variable the variable that causes the change
dependent variable the variable that changes
spurious correlation an apparent but false relationship between two (or more) variables that is caused by some other variable
objectivity or personal neutrality in conducting research
interpretive sociology the study of society that focuses on the meanings people attach to their social world
critical sociology the study of society that focuses on the need for social change

Gender and Research

1.7 Identify the importance of gender in sociological research. (page 28)
- Gender can affect sociological research if a researcher fails to avoid problems of androcentricity, overgeneralizing, gender blindness, double standards, or interference.

gender the personal traits and social positions that members of a society attach to being female or male

Research Ethics

1.8 Discuss the importance of ethics to sociological research. (pages 28–29)
- Sociologists must ensure that subjects in a research project are not harmed, and include in their published results all sources of financial support.

Research Methods

1.9 Explain why a researcher might choose each of sociology's research methods. (pages 30–38)
- The **experiment** allows researchers to study cause and effect between two or more variables in a controlled setting.
- **Survey** research uses questionnaires or interviews to gather subjects' responses to a series of questions.
- Through **participant observation**, researchers join with people in a social setting for an extended period of time.
- Researchers use data collected by others from **existing sources** to save time and money.

research method a systematic plan for doing research
experiment a research method for investigating cause and effect under highly controlled conditions
hypothesis a statement of a possible relationship between two (or more) variables.
survey a research method in which subjects respond to a series of statements or questions on a questionnaire or in an interview
participant observation a research method in which investigators systematically observe people while joining them in their routine activities
use of existing sources a research method in which a researcher uses data already collected by others

Putting It All Together: Ten Steps in Sociological Research

1.10 Recall the 10 important steps in carrying out sociological research. (pages 38–39)

stereotype a simplified description applied to every person in some category

2 Culture

LEARNING OBJECTIVES

2.1 Explain the development of culture as a human strategy for survival.

2.2 Identify the elements of culture.

2.3 Analyze how a society's level of technology shapes its culture.

2.4 Discuss the components of cultural diversity.

2.5 Apply sociology's macro-level theories to gain greater understanding of culture.

2.6 Critique culture as limiting or expanding human freedom.

the Power of Society

to guide our attitudes on social issues such as abortion

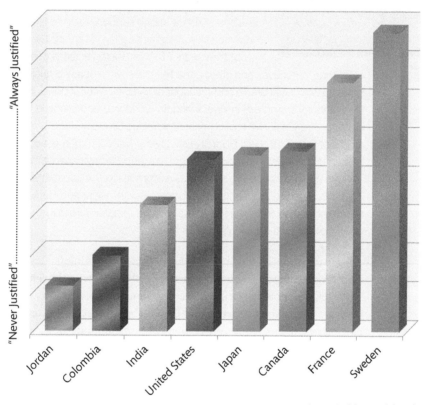

Survey Question: "Please tell me whether you think abortion can always be justified, never be justified, or something in between."

"Always Justified"

"Never Justified"

Jordan Colombia India United States Japan Canada France Sweden

Source: Inglehart et al. (2012).

Is how we feel about abortion as "personal" an opinion as we may think? If we compare the attitudes of people around the world, we see remarkable variation from country to country. People living in Sweden, for example, claim that abortion is almost always justified; people living in Jordan, by contrast, almost never support this procedure. For people living in Canada, abortion is an issue on which public opinion is fairly evenly divided. By making such global comparisons, we see that society guides people's attitudes on various issues, which is part of the way of life we call culture.

Chapter Overview

This chapter focuses on the concept of "culture," which refers to a society's entire way of life. Notice that the root of the word *culture* is the same as that of the word *cultivate*, suggesting that people living together actually "grow" their way of life over time.

Paul Bradbury/OJO Images/Getty Images

Ernst & Young (E&Y), one of Canada's largest corporate finance firms, pays a lot of attention to cultural diversity these days. The company employs more than 3000 full-time people at 14 offices across Canada, with just less than half of its employees located at its headquarters in the hub of Toronto's financial district. With a population of almost 5 million, Toronto is the fifth largest and most ethnically diverse city in North America. Vancouver is equally diverse. Nearly 40 percent of Vancouver's current population is of visible minority background, with immigrants of Chinese, Indian, and Filipino origin making up the three most numerous groups. Given these population statistics, it is no wonder that E&Y offices in these two cities are strong supporters of the firm's diversity initiatives. Driven by a corporate value statement calling for an "inclusive and flexible environment," over the past few years E&Y has hosted a series of ethnic diversity networking events in Toronto, Vancouver, and other Canadian cities where it has branch offices. The company has a full-time director of leadership and manager of diversity with responsibilities ranging from benchmarking the company's progress in diversifying its workforce and clientele to changing corporate culture to creating a truly inclusive environment (Workplace Diversity Update, 2004). In 2011, E&Y was selected as one of Canada's "Best Diversity Employers," with 30.6 percent of its employees and 28 percent of its managers of visible minority background (http://www.canadastop100.com/diversity/).

What has been the result of this diversity initiative? A substantial increase in its share of business is with local ethnic groups. Italian, Chinese, South Asian, and Portuguese native-language speakers spend more than $25.1 million annually in the Greater Toronto Area alone. Any company would do well to follow Ernst & Young's lead.

Canada prides itself on being a *multicultural* nation. Cultural diversity reflects this country's long history of receiving immigrants from all over the world. The ways of life found around the world differ not only in terms of languages and forms of dress but also in terms of preferred foods, musical tastes, family patterns, and beliefs about right and wrong. Some of the world's people have many children, while others have few; some honour the elderly, while others seem to glorify youth. Some societies are peaceful and others are warlike, and they embrace thousands of different religious beliefs and ideas about what is polite and rude, beautiful and ugly, pleasant and repulsive. This amazing human capacity for so many different ways of life is a matter of human culture.

What Is Culture?

2.1 Explain the development of culture as a human strategy for survival.

Anatomically modern humans appeared 200 000 to 100 000 years ago. Evidence suggests that what we call "culture," however, first appeared in the Middle Stone Age about 40 000 years ago. **Culture** is *the ways of thinking, the ways of acting, and the material objects that together form a people's way of life*. Culture includes what we think, how we act, and what we own. Culture is both our link to the past and our guide to the future.

To understand all that culture is, we must consider both thoughts and things. **Nonmaterial culture** is *the ideas created by members of a society*, ideas that range from art to Zen. **Material culture**, by contrast, is *the physical things created by members of a society*, everything from armchairs to zippers.

Culture shapes not only what we do but also what we think and how we feel—elements of what we commonly, but wrongly, describe as

culture the ways of thinking, the ways of acting, and the material objects that together form a people's way of life

nonmaterial culture the ideas created by members of a society

material culture the physical things created by members of a society

Thinking Globally

Confronting the Yąnomamö: The Experience of Culture Shock

A small aluminum motorboat chugged steadily along the muddy Orinoco River, deep within South America's vast tropical rain forest. The anthropologist Napoleon Chagnon was nearing the end of a three-day journey to the home territory of the Yąnomamö, one of the most technologically simple societies on Earth.

Some 12 000 Yąnomamö live in villages scattered along the border of Venezuela and Brazil. Their way of life could not be more different from our own. The Yąnomamö wear little clothing and live without electricity, automobiles, cell phones, or other conveniences most people in Canada take for granted. Their traditional weapon, used for hunting and warfare, is the bow and arrow. Since most of the Yąnomamö knew little about the outside world, Chagnon would be as strange to them as they would be to him.

By 2:00 in the afternoon, Chagnon had almost reached his destination. The heat and humidity were becoming unbearable. He was soaked with perspiration, and his face and hands swelled from the bites of gnats swarming around him. But he hardly noticed, so excited was he that in just a few moments, he would be face to face with people unlike any he had ever known.

Herve Collart/Sygma/Corbis

Chagnon's heart pounded as the boat slid onto the riverbank. He and his guide climbed from the boat and headed toward the sounds of a nearby village, pushing their way through the dense undergrowth. Chagnon describes what happened next:

I looked up and gasped when I saw a dozen burly, naked, sweaty, hideous men staring at us down the shafts of their drawn arrows! Immense wads of green tobacco were stuck between their lower teeth and lips, making them look even more hideous, and strands of dark green slime dripped or hung from their nostrils—strands so long that they clung to their [chests] or drizzled down their chins.

My next discovery was that there were a dozen or so vicious, underfed dogs snapping at my legs, circling me as if I were to be their next meal. I just stood there holding my notebook, helpless, and pathetic. Then the stench of the decaying vegetation and filth hit me and I almost got sick. I was horrified. What kind of welcome was this for the person who came here to live with you and learn your way of life, to become friends with you? (Chagnon, 1992:11–12)

Fortunately for Chagnon, the Yąnomamö villagers recognized his guide and lowered their weapons. Though reassured that he would survive the afternoon, Chagnon was still shaken by his inability to make any sense of the people surrounding him.

What Do You Think?

1. Can you think of an experience of your own similar to the one described here? Explain what happened.

2. Do you think you ever caused culture shock in others? What did you learn from this experience?

3. Why is it difficult for people who live within different cultural systems to interact without discomfort? At the same time, are there benefits gained from doing so?

"human nature." The warlike Yąnomamö of the Brazilian rain forest have been described by Western anthropologists as "aggressive," while halfway around the world the Semai of Malaysia have been depicted as "peaceful." The cultures of Canada and Japan both stress achievement and hard work, but many members of Canadian society value individualism more than the Japanese, who value collective harmony.

Given the extent of cultural differences in the world and people's tendency to view their own way of life as "natural," it is no wonder that travellers often find themselves feeling uneasy as they enter an unfamiliar culture. This uneasiness is **culture shock**, *personal disorientation when experiencing an unfamiliar way of life*. People can experience culture shock right here in Canada when, say, Jamaican Canadians explore an Iranian neighbourhood in Montreal, university students from Kingston venture into the Mennonite countryside in Southern Ontario, or Vancouverites travel through a small native community in Northern British Columbia. But culture shock is most intense when we travel abroad: The Thinking Globally box featured above tells the story of a researcher making his first visit to the home of the Yąnomamö living in the Amazon region of South America.

culture shock personal disorientation when experiencing an unfamiliar way of life

Human beings around the globe create diverse ways of life. Such differences begin with outward appearance: Contrast the women shown here from Ethiopia, India, and Canada and the men from Republic of China, Ecuador, and Papua New Guinea. Less obvious but of even greater importance are internal differences, since culture also shapes our goals in life, our sense of justice, and even our innermost personal feelings.

January 2, high in the Andes Mountains of Peru. Here in the rural highlands, people are poor and depend on one another. The culture is built on co-operation among family members and neighbours who have lived nearby for many generations. Today, we spent an hour watching a new house being constructed. A young couple had invited their families and many friends, who arrived at about 6:30 in the morning, and right away they began building. By midafternoon, most of the work was finished, and the couple then provided a large meal, drinks, and music that continued for the rest of the day.

All societies contain cultural differences that can provoke a mild case of culture shock. This woman travelling on a British subway is not sure what to make of the woman sitting next to her, who is wearing the Muslim full-face veil known as the *niqab*.

No particular way of life is "natural" to humanity, even though most people around the world view their own behaviour that way. The co-operative spirit that comes naturally in small communities high in the Andes Mountains of Peru is very different from the competitive living that comes naturally to many people in, say, Regina or Halifax. Such variations come from the fact that as human beings, we join together to create our own way of life. Every other animal, from ants to zebras, behaves very much the same all around the world because behaviour is guided by *instincts*, biological programming over which the species has no control. A few animals—notably chimpanzees and related primates—have the capacity for limited culture, as researchers have noted by observing them using tools and teaching simple skills to their offspring. But the creative power of humans is far greater than that of any other form of life and has resulted in countless ways of "being human." In short, *only humans rely on culture rather than instinct to create a way of life and ensure our survival* (Harris, 1987; Morell, 2008). To understand how human culture came to be, we need to look back at the history of our species.

Culture and Human Intelligence

Scientists tell us that our planet is 4.5 billion years old. Life appeared about 1 billion years later. Fast-forward another 2 to 3 billion years, and we find dinosaurs ruling Earth. It was after these giant creatures disappeared, some 65 million years ago, that our history took a crucial turn with the appearance of the animals we call primates.

The importance of primates is that they have the largest brains relative to body size of all living creatures. About 12 million years ago, primates began to evolve along two different lines, setting humans apart from the great apes, our closest relatives. Some 5 million years ago, our distant human ancestors climbed down from the trees of Central Africa to move about in the tall grasses. There, walking upright, they learned the advantages of hunting in groups and made use of fire, tools, and weapons; built simple shelters; and fashioned basic clothing. These Stone Age achievements may seem modest, but they mark the point at which our ancestors set off on a distinct evolutionary course, making culture their primary strategy for survival. By about 250 000 years ago, our species, *Homo sapiens* (Latin for "intelligent person"), had finally emerged. Humans continued to evolve so that by about 40 000 years ago, people who looked more or less like us roamed the planet. With larger brains, these "modern" *Homo sapiens* developed culture rapidly, as the wide range of tools and cave art that have survived from this period suggests.

About 12 000 years ago, the founding of permanent settlements and the creation of specialized occupations in the Middle East (today's Iraq and Egypt) marked the "birth of civilization." About this point, the biological forces we call instincts had mostly disappeared, replaced by a more efficient survival scheme: *fashioning the natural environment for ourselves*. Ever since, humans have made and remade their world in countless ways, resulting in today's fascinating cultural diversity.

Culture, Nation, and Society

The term "culture" calls to mind other similar terms, such as "nation" and "society," although each has a slightly different meaning. *Culture* refers to a shared way of life. A *nation* is a political entity, a territory with designated borders, such as Canada, Japan, Peru, or Zimbabwe. **Society** refers to *people who interact in a defined territory and share a culture.*

Canada, then, is both a nation and a society. But many nations, including Canada, are *multicultural;* that is, their people follow various ways of life that blend (and sometimes clash).

society people who interact in a defined territory and share a culture

How Many Cultures?

How many cultures are there in Canada? One indicator of culture is language; the Canada 2011 Census lists more than 200 nonofficial mother tongues spoken in this country, most of which were brought by immigrants from nations around the world (Statistics Canada, 2012a). The census also recorded 60 Aboriginal languages, with the most popular being Cree languages, Ojibway, Innu/Montagnais, and Oji-Cree (Statistics Canada, 2012b).

Globally, experts document almost 7000 languages, suggesting the existence of as many distinct cultures. Yet with the number of languages spoken around the world declining, roughly half of those 7000 languages now are spoken by fewer than 10 000 people. Experts expect that the coming decades may see the disappearance of hundreds of these languages, and perhaps half the world's languages may even disappear before the end of this century (Crystal, 2010). Languages on the endangered list include Han (spoken in northwestern Canada), Gullah, Pennsylvania German, and Pawnee (all spoken in the United States), Oro (spoken in the Amazon region of Brazil), Sardinian (spoken on the European island of Sardinia), Aramaic (in the Middle East), Nu Shu (a language spoken in southern China that is the only one known to be used exclusively by women), and Wakka Wakka as well as several other Aboriginal tongues spoken in Australia. As you might expect, when a language is becoming extinct, the last people to speak it are the oldest members of a society. What accounts for the worldwide decline in the number of spoken languages? The main reason is globalization itself, including high-technology communication, increasing international migration, and the expanding worldwide economy (UNESCO, 2001; Barovick, 2002; Hayden, 2003; Lewis, 2009).

The Elements of Culture

2.2 Identify the elements of culture.

Although cultures vary greatly, they all have common elements, including symbols, language, values, and norms. We begin our discussion with the one that is the basis for all the others: symbols.

Symbols

symbol anything that carries a particular meaning recognized by people who share a culture

Like all creatures, humans use their senses to experience the surrounding world, but unlike others, we also try to give the world *meaning*. Humans transform the elements of the world into *symbols*. A **symbol** is *anything that carries a particular meaning recognized by people who share a culture*. A word, a whistle, a wall covered with graffiti, a flashing red light, a raised fist—all serve as symbols. We can see the human capacity to create and manipulate symbols reflected in the very different meanings associated with the simple act of winking an eye, which can convey interest, understanding, or insult.

Societies create new symbols all the time. "Cyber-symbols," such as emoticons for example, have developed along with our increasing use of computers for communication.

We are so dependent on our culture's symbols that we take them for granted. However, we become keenly aware of the importance of a symbol when someone uses it in an unconventional way, as when a person burns, or turns upside down, a Canadian flag during a political demonstration. Entering an unfamiliar culture also reminds us of the power of symbols; culture shock is really the inability to "read" meaning in strange surroundings. Not understanding the symbols of a culture leaves a person feeling lost and isolated, unsure of how to act, and sometimes frightened.

Culture shock is a two-way process. On one hand, travellers *experience* culture shock when encountering people whose way of life is different. For example, North Americans who consider dogs beloved household pets might be put off by the Masai of eastern Africa, who ignore dogs and never feed them. The same travellers might be horrified to find that in parts of Indonesia and the People's Republic of China, people roast dogs for dinner.

On the other hand, a traveller may *inflict* culture shock on local people by acting in ways that offend them. A Canadian who asks for steak in an Indian restaurant may unknowingly offend Hindus, who consider cows sacred and never to be eaten. Global travel provides almost endless opportunities for this kind of misunderstanding.

Symbolic meanings also vary within a single society. To some people in Canada, a fur coat represents a prized symbol of success, but to others it represents the inhumane treatment of animals. By ordering all Canadian flags to be removed from provincial government buildings in Newfoundland and Labrador in 2004, the then premier, Danny Williams, gained support from some people who saw the flag as a symbol of federal oppression rather than national pride.

Language

An illness in infancy left Helen Keller (1880–1968) blind and deaf. Without these two senses, she was cut off from the symbolic world, and her social development was greatly limited. Only when her teacher, Anne Mansfield Sullivan, broke through Keller's isolation using sign language did Helen Keller begin to realize her human potential. This remarkable woman, who later became a famous educator herself, recalls the moment she first understood the concept of language:

Keren Su/China Span/Alamy Stock Photo

People throughout the world communicate not just with spoken words but also with bodily gestures. Because gestures vary from culture to culture, they can occasionally be the cause of misunderstandings. For instance, the commonplace "thumbs up" gesture we use to express "Good job!" can get a person from Canada into trouble in Greece, Iran, and a number of other countries, where people take it to mean "Up yours!"

We walked down the path to the well-house, attracted by the smell of honeysuckle with which it was covered. Someone was drawing water, and my teacher placed my hand under the spout. As the cool stream gushed over one hand, she spelled into the other the word *water*, first slowly, then rapidly. I stood still, my whole attention fixed upon the motions of her fingers. Suddenly I felt a misty consciousness as of something forgotten—a thrill of returning thought; and somehow the mystery of language was revealed to me. I knew then that "w-a-t-e-r" meant the wonderful cool something that was flowing over my hand. That living word awakened my soul; gave it light, hope, joy, set it free! (Keller, 1903:24)

FIGURE 2–1   Human Languages: A Variety of Symbols

Here the English word *read* is written in 12 of the hundreds of languages humans use to communicate with one another.

Language, the key to the world of culture, is *a system of symbols that allows people to communicate with one another*. Humans have created many alphabets to express the hundreds of languages we speak. Several examples are shown in Figure 2–1. Even rules for writing differ: Most people in Western societies write from left to right, but people in northern Africa and western Asia write from right to left, and people in eastern Asia write from top to bottom. Global Map 2–1 on page 52 shows where we find the three most widely spoken languages: English, Chinese, and Spanish.

Language not only allows communication but is also the key to **cultural transmission**, *the process by which one generation passes culture to the next*. Just as our bodies contain the genes of our ancestors, our culture contains countless symbols of those who came before us. Language is the key that unlocks centuries of accumulated wisdom.

Throughout human history, every society has transmitted culture by using speech, a process sociologists call the "oral cultural tradition." Some 5000 years ago, humans invented writing, although at that time only a privileged few learned to read and write. Not until the twentieth century did high-income nations boast of nearly universal literacy. Still, by some estimates about 1 in 6 Canadian adults are functionally illiterate, unable to read and write on a level that is required to meet regular needs. In low-income countries of the world, at least one-third of adults are illiterate (Bailey, Tuinman, & Jones, 2012; World Bank, 2012).

Language skills may link us with the past, but they also spark the human imagination to connect symbols in new ways, creating an almost limitless range of future possibilities. Language sets humans apart as the only creatures who are self-conscious, aware of our limitations and ultimate mortality, yet able to dream and to hope for a future better than the present.

Does Language Shape Reality?

Does someone who speaks Cree, the language spoken by Aboriginal people who originated from the James Bay area of Canada, experience the world differently from other Canadians who think in, say, English or French? Edward Sapir and Benjamin Whorf claimed that the answer is yes, since each language has its own distinctive symbols that serve as the building blocks of reality (Sapir, 1929, 1949; Whorf, 1956, orig. 1941). Further, they noted that each language has words or expressions not found in any other symbolic system. Finally, all languages fuse symbols with distinctive emotions so that, as multilingual people know, a single idea may "feel" different when spoken in Hindi rather than in Persian or Dutch.

Formally, the **Sapir-Whorf thesis** holds that *people see and understand the world through the cultural lens of language*. In the decades since Sapir and Whorf published their work, however, scholars have taken issue with this proposition. Some critics argue that although we do fashion reality out of our symbols, evidence does not support the notion that language *determines* reality in the

language a system of symbols that allows people to communicate with one another

cultural transmission the process by which one generation passes culture to the next

Sapir-Whorf thesis the idea that people see and understand the world through the cultural lens of language

GLOBAL MAP 2–1 Language in Global Perspective

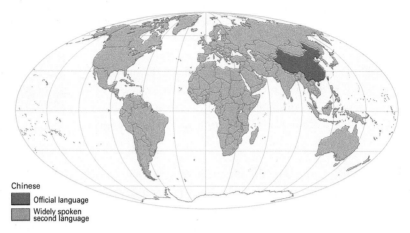

Chinese (including Mandarin, Cantonese, and dozens of other dialects) is the native tongue of one-fifth of the world's people, almost all of whom live in Asia. Although all Chinese people read and write with the same characters, they use several dozen dialects. The "official" dialect, taught in schools throughout the People's Republic of China and the Republic of Taiwan, is Mandarin (the dialect of Beijing, China's capital). Cantonese, the language of Canton, is the second most common Chinese dialect; it differs in sound from Mandarin roughly the way French differs from Spanish.

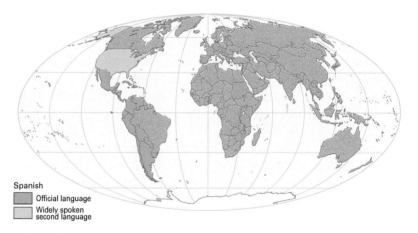

Spanish is the native language of about 6 percent of humanity. The largest concentration of Spanish speakers is in Latin America and, of course, Spain. Spanish is also the second most widely spoken language in the world and in the United States.

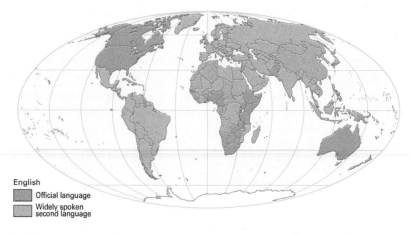

English is the native tongue or official language in several world regions, spoken by approximately 5 percent of humanity, and has become the third most popular language in the world.

Sources: Lewis (2009); European Union (2012); Lewis, Simons, & Fennig (2015)

way Sapir and Whorf claimed. For example, we know that children understand the idea of "family" long before they learn that word; similarly, adults can imagine new ideas or things before naming them (Kay & Kempton, 1984; Pinker, 1994).

Values and Beliefs

While in urban centres throughout Canada middle-class parents teach their children values such as hard work, competition, and respect for authority, First Nations families who live in remote communities teach traditional activities like hunting and trapping, sharing, and respect for elders (Sawchuck, 2011). In applauding such characteristics, we are supporting certain **values**, *culturally defined standards that people use to decide what is desirable, good, and beautiful and that serve as broad guidelines for social living*. People who share a culture use values to make choices about how to live.

Values are broad principles that support **beliefs**, *specific thoughts or ideas that people hold to be true*. In other words, values are abstract standards of goodness, and beliefs are particular matters that people accept as true or false. For example, surveys show that most Canadian adults agree that their country should provide equal opportunities to all groups, including women and men (Adams, 1997). Yet, in reality, the proportion of women in the House of Commons was only 22.1 percent in 2011, though this number has been increasing ever so slowly in the last decade (Inter-Parliamentary Union, 2011).

values culturally defined standards that people use to decide what is desirable, good, and beautiful and that serve as broad guidelines for social living

beliefs specific thoughts or ideas that people hold to be true

Key Values of Canadian Culture

Canada is a country of native peoples and immigrants from many different countries. Its complex demographic makeup and vast geography mean that few values command the support of everyone. Even so, a number of dominant values have emerged. Surveys conducted by social researchers (Nanos, 2007; Environics Research Group, 2011a; Environics Research Group, 2011b) identify a number of them.

1. **Democracy and human rights.** Canadians believe that all citizens ought to enjoy democratic rights.
2. **Health care and the social safety net.** People in Canada value social programs and services. Many feel that Canada has one of the best health care systems in the world, and that it should continue to be available equally to all.
3. **Support for the environment.** The environment is part of Canada's national identity. Across the country, people express support for actions that address climate change, with 74 percent of Canadians favouring government setting limits on carbon dioxide emissions.
4. **Importance of gender and racial equality.** The Canadian Charter of Rights and Freedoms enshrines gender and racial equality, while Canadians continue to see themselves as a multicultural nation in terms of policy, demographics, and ideals.
5. **Value of immigration.** It is often said that Canada is "a country of immigrants." While this is not true for the Indigenous people who have resided here for at least 12 000 years, Canadians today recognize the positive role that immigration plays in the country's economic and social life.

WENN Ltd/Alamy Stock Photo

How does the popularity of the television show *Canadian Idol* illustrate some of the key values of Canadian culture listed here?

6. **Support for diversity.** Support for the country's many diversities—religious, linguistic, sexual, and ethnic—is a central value. In 2005 Canada became the first country in the Americas (and fourth in the world) to legalize gay marriage. Currently, 62 percent of Canadians back the inclusion of gay rights in the Charter of Rights and Freedoms.

7. **Free market and property rights.** At the same time as they value social programs, Canadians also profess a respect for property and for the capitalist system. Individual success is often measured in terms of material comfort and wealth. Competition and individualism are championed as the basis of prosperity.

Values: Often in Harmony, Sometimes in Conflict

Looking over the list above, we see that these dominant cultural values are often difficult to realize. For example, recent federal governments have tended to present an image of Canada as "one" nation bound together by shared values, traditions, and beliefs, yet simultaneously promote fiscal responsibility over public funding of social programs. Results of a 2013 study by the Broadbent Institute indicate that many Canadians do not necessarily agree with this government sentiment. Over two-thirds (70 percent) of Canadians polled "said they'd prefer a government that is more robust in the services," and 60 percent stated that they "would be 'willing' or 'very willing' to pay higher taxes if it meant that the money would go to fund social programs such as health care" (Broadbent Institute, 2013).

Such conflicts in values inevitably cause strain, leading to awkward balancing acts in the beliefs and actions of many Canadians. Some may decide that one value is more important than another, while others may simply learn to live with inconsistencies. While Canadians appear to be more liberal overall in their attitudes about moral issues, there remain notable differences, including along regional lines (Angus Reid Public Opinion, 2007). This was confirmed in a 2011 survey showing that British Columbia has the lowest percentage of people in Canada—just 17 percent compared to 36 percent in the rest of western Canada—who believe that all the poor have to do to improve their lives is "pull themselves up by their own bootstraps" (Todd, 2011).

Values: Change Over Time

Like all elements of culture, values change over time. A century ago, people in Canada openly valued colonialism, industry, white immigration, male leadership, and hard work. Today, however, we question the legacy these values have had on Indigenous people, the environment, racial minorities, women, and workers. While patterns of Canada's colonial past persist—as is evident in the reservation system and treaty negotiations—the establishment of a Truth and Reconciliation Commission, in 2008, signals some willingness to re-evaluate what was once a deeply entrenched support for colonialism. Changing Canadians' cultural values of colonialism is not, however, a straightforward process: Amid calls for respect for Aboriginal title, equitable partnerships with Aboriginal people in resource and energy projects, and greater protection for Aboriginal languages and culture, a number of Canadians still harbour anti-Aboriginal sentiments. The Canadian government, although expressing a need to re-establish the relationship between the Crown and Aboriginal peoples, continues a non-consultative and, what some observers describe as, antagonistic approach (APTN National News, 2012; Bennett, 2013).

Values: A Global Perspective

Values vary from culture to culture around the world. In general, the values that are important in higher-income countries differ somewhat from those common in lower-income countries.

Because lower-income nations contain populations that are vulnerable, people in these countries develop cultures that value survival. This means that people place a great deal of importance on physical safety and economic security. They worry about having enough to eat and a safe place to sleep at night. Lower-income nations also tend to be traditional, with values that celebrate the past and emphasize the importance of family and religious beliefs. These nations, in which men have most of the power, typically discourage or forbid practices such as divorce and abortion.

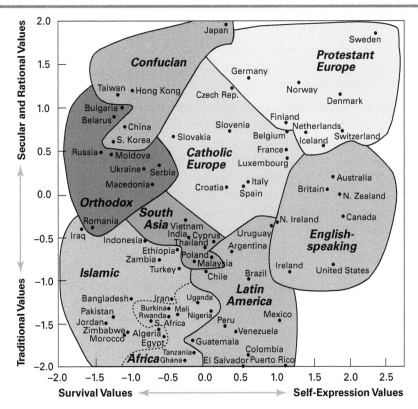

FIGURE 2–2 Cultural Values of Selected Countries

A general global pattern is that rich countries tend to be secular and rational and favour self-expression. By contrast, the cultures of poor countries tend to be more traditional and concerned with economic survival. Each region of the world has distinctive cultural patterns, including religious traditions, that affect values. Looking at the figure, what patterns can you see? How does Canada compare to Great Britain, Denmark, and other high-income countries?

Source: Inglehart, Ronald and Christian Welzel. "The WVS Cultural Map of the World." 2010. Available at http://www.worldvaluessurvey .org/wvs/articles/folder_published/article_base_54. Used with permission.

People in higher-income countries develop cultures that value individualism and self-expression. These countries are rich enough that most of their people take survival for granted, focusing their attention instead on which "lifestyle" they prefer and how to achieve the greatest personal happiness. In addition, these countries tend to be secular-rational, placing less emphasis on family ties and religious beliefs and more emphasis on people thinking for themselves and being tolerant of others who differ from them. In higher-income countries, too, women have social standing more equal to men and there is widespread support for practices such as divorce and abortion (Inglehart et al., 2012). Figure 2–2 shows how selected countries of the world compare in terms of their cultural values.

Norms

Middle-class Canadians are reluctant to reveal to others the size of their paycheque, while people in China tend to share such "personal" information eagerly. Both patterns illustrate the operation of **norms**, *rules and expectations by which a society guides the behaviour of its members*. In everyday life, people respond to each other with *sanctions*, rewards or punishments that encourage conformity to cultural norms.

Folkways, Mores, and Laws

People pay less attention to **folkways**, *norms for routine or casual interaction*. Examples include ideas about appropriate greetings and proper dress. A man who does not wear a tie to a formal dinner party may raise eyebrows for violating folkways or "etiquette." If, however, he were to arrive at the dinner party wearing *only* a tie, he would violate cultural mores and invite a more serious response.

Sociologist William Graham Sumner (1959, orig. 1906) coined the term **mores** (pronounced "MORE-ayz") to refer to *norms that are widely observed and have great moral significance.* In short, folkways draw a line between polite and rude behaviour, and mores distinguish between right and wrong. Certain mores include *taboos*, such as our society's insistence that adults not engage in sexual relations with children.

Finally, other kinds of norms are **laws**, *systems of rules recognized and enforced by governing institutions.* In complex societies, laws are associated with formal legal systems, such as the Criminal Code of Canada. Because they are codified, laws are the most well-defined norms. Laws, however, can also exist in stateless Aboriginal cultures, which without writing anything down maintain laws on the basis of custom and tradition.

Social Control

Folkways, mores, and laws are the basic rules of everyday life. Although we sometimes resist pressure to conform, we can see that norms make our dealings with others more orderly and predictable. Observing or breaking the rules of social life prompts a response from others in the form of either reward or punishment. Sanctions—whether an approving smile or a raised eyebrow—operate as a system of **social control**, *attempts by society to regulate people's thoughts and behaviour.*

As we learn cultural norms, we gain the capacity to evaluate our own behaviour. Doing wrong (say, downloading a term paper from the internet) can cause both *shame* (the painful sense that others disapprove of our actions) and *guilt* (a negative judgment we make of ourselves). Of all living things, only cultural creatures can experience shame and guilt. This is probably what Mark Twain had in mind when he remarked that people "are the only animals that blush—or need to."

Ideal and Real Culture

Values and norms do not describe actual behaviour so much as they suggest how we should behave. We must remember that ideal culture always differs from real culture, which is what actually occurs in everyday life. To illustrate, the Canadian Automobile Association's Traffic Safety Culture survey reveals that 98 percent of Canadians find drinking and driving "socially unacceptable" (2010). This is not surprising given strong advocacy campaigns that alert us to the dangers of driving under the influence. However, while condemning drunk driving, 27 percent of those questioned admitted to driving while under the influence "at least once" in the past year (Canadian Automobile Association, 2010). But a culture's moral standards are important all the same, calling to mind the old saying, "Do as I say, not as I do."

Technology and Culture

(2.3) Analyze how a society's level of technology shapes its culture.

In addition to symbolic elements such as values and norms, every culture includes a wide range of physical human creations called *artifacts*. The Chinese eat with chopsticks rather than knives and forks, the Japanese place mats rather than rugs on the floor, and many men and women in India prefer flowing robes to the close-fitting clothing common in Canada. The material culture of a people can seem as strange to outsiders as their language, values, and norms.

A society's artifacts partly reflect underlying cultural values. The warlike Yąnomamö carefully craft their weapons and prize the poison tips on their arrows. By contrast, our society's emphasis on individualism and independence helps explain our high regard for the automobile: In 2009, Canadians owned about 560 cars per 1000 residents—near the top per capita of any country. Even in an age of high gasoline prices, many of these automobiles are the large sport utility vehicles that we might expect rugged, individualistic people to choose.

In addition to expressing values, material culture also reflects a society's level of **technology**, *knowledge that people use to make a way of life in their surroundings*. The more complex a society's technology, the easier it is for members of that society to shape the world for themselves.

Gerhard Lenski argued that a society's level of technology is crucial in determining what cultural ideas and artifacts emerge or are even possible (Nolan & Lenski, 2010). He pointed to the importance of *socio-cultural evolution*—the historical changes in culture brought about by new technology—which unfolds in terms of four major levels of development: hunting and gathering, horticulture and pastoralism, agriculture, and industry.

Standards of beauty—including the colour and design of everyday surroundings—vary significantly from one culture to another. This Ndebele couple in South Africa dresses in the same bright colours they use to decorate their home. Members of North American and European societies, by contrast, make far less use of bright colours and intricate detail, so their housing and clothing appear much more subdued.

Hunting and Gathering

The oldest and most basic way of living is **hunting and gathering**, *the use of simple tools to hunt animals and gather vegetation for food*. From the time of our earliest ancestors 3 million years ago until about 1800, most people in the world lived as hunters and gatherers. Today, however, this technology supports only a few societies, including the Kaska Aboriginals of northwestern Canada, the Pygmies of Central Africa, the Khoisan of southwestern Africa, the Aborigines of Australia, and the Semai of Malaysia. Typically, hunters and gatherers spend most of their time searching for game and edible plants. Their societies are small, generally with several dozen people living in a nomadic, family-like group, moving on as they deplete an area's vegetation or follow migratory animals.

Everyone helps search for food, with the very young and the very old doing what they can. Women usually gather vegetation—the primary food source for these peoples—while men do most of the hunting. Because the tasks they perform are of equal value, the two sexes are regarded as having about the same social importance (Leacock, 1978).

Hunters and gatherers do not have formal leaders. They may look to one person as a *shaman*, or priest, but holding such a position does not excuse the person from the daily work of finding food. Overall, hunting and gathering is a simple and egalitarian way of life.

Limited technology leaves hunters and gatherers vulnerable to the forces of nature. Storms and droughts can easily destroy their food supply, and they have few effective ways to respond to accidents or disease. Looking back at these societies, we see that many died in childhood, and only half lived to the age of 20.

What would it be like to live in a society with simple technology? That's the premise of the television show *Survivor*. What advantages do societies with simple technology afford their members? What disadvantages do you see?

As people with powerful technology steadily close in on them, hunting and gathering societies are vanishing. Fortunately, studying their way of life has provided us with valuable information about our socio-cultural history and our fundamental ties to the natural environment.

Horticulture and Pastoralism

Horticulture, *the use of hand tools to raise crops*, appeared around 10 000 years ago. The hoe and the digging stick (used to punch holes in the ground for planting seeds) first turned up in fertile regions of the Middle East and Southeast Asia, and by 6000 years ago, these tools were in use from Western Europe to China. Central and South Americans also learned to cultivate plants, but rocky soil and mountainous land forced members of many societies to continue to hunt and gather even as they adopted this new technology (Fisher, 1979; Chagnon, 1992).

In especially dry regions, societies turned not to raising crops but to **pastoralism**, *the domestication of animals*. Throughout the Americas, Africa, the Middle East, and Asia, many societies combine horticulture and pastoralism.

Growing plants and raising animals allows societies to feed hundreds of members. Pastoral peoples remain nomadic, but horticulturalists make permanent settlements. In a horticultural society, a material surplus means that not everyone has to produce food; some people are free to make crafts, become traders, or serve as full-time priests. Compared with hunters and gatherers, pastoral and horticultural societies are more unequal, with some families operating as a ruling elite and men increasing their power at the expense of women.

Because hunters and gatherers have little control over nature, they generally believe that the world is inhabited by spirits. As they gain the power to raise plants and animals, however, people come to believe in one God as the creator of the world. The pastoral roots of Judaism and Christianity are evident in the term "pastor" and the common view of God as a "shepherd" who stands watch over all.

Agriculture

Around 5000 years ago, technological advances led to **agriculture**, *large-scale cultivation using plows harnessed to animals or more powerful energy sources*. Agrarian technology first appeared in the Middle East and gradually spread throughout the world. The invention of the animal-drawn plow, the wheel, writing, numbers, and new metals changed societies so much that historians call this era the "dawn of civilization."

By turning the soil, plows allow land to be farmed for centuries, so agrarian people can live in permanent settlements. With large food surpluses that can be transported by animal-powered wagons, populations grow into the millions. As members of agrarian societies become more and more specialized in their work, credit, and later on money, is used as a form of common exchange, replacing the earlier system of barter. Although the development of agrarian technology expands human choices and fuels urban growth, it also makes social life more individualistic and impersonal.

Agriculture also brings about a dramatic increase in social inequality. Most people live as serfs or slaves, but a few elites are freed from labour to cultivate a "refined" way of life based on the study of philosophy, art, and literature. At all levels, men gain pronounced power over women.

People with only simple technology live much the same the world over, with minor differences caused by regional variations in climate. But agrarian technology gives people enough control over the world that cultural diversity dramatically increases (Nolan & Lenski, 2010).

Industry

Industrialization occurred as societies replaced the muscles of animals and humans with new forms of power. Formally, **industry** is *the production of goods using advanced sources of energy to drive large machinery*. The introduction of steam power, starting in England about 1775, greatly boosted productivity and transformed culture in the process.

technology knowledge that people use to make a way of life in their surroundings

| hunting and gathering the use of simple tools to hunt animals and gather vegetation for food | horticulture the use of hand tools to raise crops **pastoralism** the domestication of animals | agriculture large-scale cultivation using plows harnessed to animals or more powerful energy sources | industry the production of goods using advanced sources of energy to drive large machinery | post-industrialism the production of information using computer technology |

Agrarian people work in or near their homes, but most people in industrial societies work in large factories under the supervision of strangers. In this way, industrialization pushes aside the traditional cultural values that guided family-centred agrarian life for centuries.

Industry also made the world seem smaller. In the nineteenth century, railroads and steamships carried people across land and sea faster and farther than ever before. In the twentieth century, this process continued with the invention of the automobile, the airplane, radio, television, and computers.

Industrial technology also raises living standards and extends the human life span. Schooling becomes the rule because industrial jobs demand more and more skills. In addition, industrial societies reduce economic inequality and steadily extend political rights.

It is easy to see industrial societies as "more advanced" than those relying on simpler technology. After all, industry raises living standards and stretches life expectancy to the seventies and beyond—about twice that of the Yąnomamö. But as industry intensifies individualism and expands personal freedom, it weakens human community. Industry also has led people to abuse the natural environment, which threatens us all. And although advanced technology gives us labour-saving machines and miraculous forms of medical treatment, it also contributes to unhealthy levels of stress and has created weapons capable of destroying in a flash everything that our species has achieved.

Post-industrial Information Technology

Going beyond the four categories discussed by Lenski, we see that many industrial societies, including Canada, have now entered a post-industrial era in which more and more economic production makes use of *new information technology*. **Post-industrialism** refers to *the production of information using computer technology*. Production in industrial societies centres on factories that make *things*, but post-industrial production centres on computers and other electronic devices that create, process, store, and apply *ideas and information*.

The emergence of an information economy changes the skills that define a way of life. No longer are mechanical abilities the only key to success. People find that they must learn to work with symbols by speaking, writing, computing, and creating images and sounds. One result of this change is that our society now has the capacity to create symbolic culture on an unprecedented scale as people work with computers to generate new words, music, and images.

Cultural Diversity: Many Ways of Life in One World

(**2.4**) Discuss the components of cultural diversity.

Take a stroll down Queen Street in Toronto or through Vancouver's Gastown and it will soon become obvious to you that Canada is a culturally diverse society. Compared to a country like Japan, whose historic isolation makes it the most *monocultural* of all high-income nations, immigration over the past century and a half has turned Canada into one of the most *multicultural* of all high-income countries.

In 1901, 12.8 percent of the population were born outside of Canada. More than 75 percent of these people were born in Europe and almost 60 percent came from the United Kingdom. By

Sitcoms are based on popular culture rather than high culture. *Trailer Park Boys* follows the misadventures of two petty felons who live in a fictional trailer park in Dartmouth, Nova Scotia. While some critics object to the show as "low-brow," others applaud it as a skilfully executed mockumentary.

2001, the percentage of the population born outside of Canada had increased to 18.4 percent and more than half of these people were born outside of Europe. By 2006, there was a further increase to just under 20 percent. This diverging immigration is also reflected in the much greater diversity in the background of Canadians today (see Table 11–1 in Chapter 11 for details of the ethnic diversity in Canada in 2006). Statistics Canada predicts that if this trend continues, between 25 and 28 percent of the Canadian population could be foreign-born by 2031 (Statistics Canada, 2011). To understand the reality of life in Canada, we must move beyond shared cultural patterns to consider the importance of cultural diversity.

High Culture and Popular Culture

Cultural diversity involves not just immigration but also social class. In fact, in everyday talk, we usually use the term "culture" to mean art forms such as classical literature, music, dance, and painting. We describe people who regularly attend the opera or the theatre as "cultured," because we think that they appreciate the "finer things in life."

We speak less kindly of ordinary people, assuming that everyday culture is somehow less worthy. We are tempted to judge the music of Handel as "more cultured" than hip-hop, couscous as better than cornbread, horse polo as more polished than hockey.

These differences arise because many cultural patterns are readily available to only some members of a society. Sociologists use the term **high culture** to refer to *cultural patterns that distinguish a society's elite* and **popular culture** to designate *cultural patterns that are widespread among a society's population.*

Common sense may suggest that high culture is superior to popular culture, but sociologists are uneasy with such judgments for two reasons. First, neither elites nor ordinary people share all of the same tastes and interests; people in both categories differ in many ways. Second, do we praise high culture because it is inherently better than popular culture or simply because its supporters have more money, power, and prestige? For example, there is no difference at all between a violin and a fiddle; however, we name the instrument a violin when it is used to produce classical music typically enjoyed by a person of higher position and we call it a fiddle when the musician plays country, folk, or bluegrass tunes appreciated by people with lower social standing.

We should also remember that Canadian culture is made up of the life patterns of *all* people who reside here. What's more, this national culture is being created all the time—not just by people whose names are familiar to all of us, but also by countless people including those living in some of the most disadvantaged neighbourhoods in the country. The Thinking About Diversity box on page 62 provides a case in point.

high culture cultural patterns that distinguish a society's elite

popular culture cultural patterns that are widespread among a society's population

Subculture

subculture cultural patterns that set apart some segment of a society's population

The term **subculture** refers to *cultural patterns that set apart some segment of a society's population.* People who ride "chopper" motorcycles, people who enjoy hip-hop music and fashion, Vancouver Eastside drug users, jazz musicians, Calgary cowboys, skateboarders, and West Coast wilderness campers—all display subcultural patterns.

It is easy but often inaccurate to place people in some subcultural category because almost everyone participates in many subcultures without necessarily having much commitment to any one of them. In some cases, however, cultural differences can set people apart from one another with tragic results. Consider the former nation of Yugoslavia in southeastern Europe. The 1990s civil war there was fuelled by those who emphasized extreme ethnic and national differences. This *one* small country made use of *two* alphabets, embraced *three* major religions, spoke *four* major languages, was home to *five* major nationalities, was divided into *six* separate political republics, and absorbed the cultural influences of *seven* surrounding countries. The cultural conflict that plunged this nation into civil war shows that subcultures are a source not only of pleasing variety but also of tension and even violence.

A generation ago, most people regarded tattoos as a mark of low social status. Today, this cultural pattern is gaining popularity among people at all social class levels.

Many people view Canada as a "mosaic" in which many nationalities make up the Canadian cultural identity. But how accurate is this image? Some authors writing on the country's two dominant groups, English-speaking and French-speaking, maintain that Canadians make up "two solitudes" (Rocher, 1990), as is evident in the lack of formal and informal interaction among the French-speaking and English-speaking intellectual elites within the Royal Society of Canada (Ogmundson & McLaughlin, 1994).

Others argue that subcultures involve not just *difference* but also *hierarchy*. Too often what we view as "dominant" or "mainstream" culture are patterns favoured by powerful segments of the population, while what we view as "subculture" are, in fact, the patterns of less-advantaged people, such as high school dropouts (Tanner, Krahn, & Hartnagel, 1995) or youth who belong to the electronic dance music culture, which includes raving, clubbing, and partying (Riley, Griffin, & Morey, 2010). Hence, sociologist John Porter (1965) characterized Canada as a "vertical mosaic," in which a privileged male elite consists overwhelmingly of people of British origin (Bell & Tepperman, 1979; Reitz, 1980). While researchers disagree on the extent to which Canada is a closed society that has marginalized some groups at the expense of others (Curtis, Grab, & Guppy, 1999; Beaman & Beyer, 2008), why is it that the cultural patterns of rich skiers in Whistler, for example, tend to seem like less of a "subculture" than the cultural patterns of street youth in the urban core of our cities (Baron, 2004; Benoit, Jansson, Hallgrimsdottir, & Roth, 2008)? Why do those who alter their bodies through cosmetic surgery seem like less of a subculture than those who tattoo themselves (Atkinson, 2003; Yamada, 2008)? Some sociologists therefore prefer to level the playing field of society by emphasizing multiculturalism.

Multiculturalism

Multiculturalism is *a perspective recognizing the cultural diversity of Canada and promoting equal standing for all cultural traditions.* Multiculturalism represents a sharp change from the past, when our society did not recognize the cultural mosaic. Today, we spiritedly debate how to balance a celebration of cultural differences with our shared value of equality.

Multiculturalists point out that, from the outset, the European immigrants to the so-called New World (of course, "new" only to those who came from abroad) exploited the various Aboriginal cultures; some First Nations peoples were decimated, while others were severely reduced in numbers and marginalized on reserves (Dickason, 1992). After Confederation in 1867, people of British origin gained the top political positions in the country,

Thinking About Diversity: Race, Class, and Gender

Popular Culture Born in the Inner City: The DJ Scene and Hip-Hop Music

Aaron Jerald (AJ) O'Bryant probably never thought he would help change American and, relatedly, Canadian culture. In 1960, he was born into a social world where the odds were stacked against him. His family, living in the United States, resided in a low-income, African-American neighbourhood on the Lower East Side of Manhattan. Orphaned at 13, he moved in with his grandmother, who lived in the South Bronx, close to an intersection that was a known gathering point for local gang members.

In the 1970s, the South Bronx was brewing with social problems. As factories closed, the area lost thousands of good-paying manufacturing jobs, and unemployment and poverty were on the rise. Drug use, crime, and violence became part of everyday life.

Not surprisingly, AJ entered his teenage years thinking that violence was the way to express his frustration. He got into fights on the streets and at school, to the point of being expelled for throwing another student through a window. His grandmother enrolled him at a local school for "at-risk" young people, but he found little to like in the classroom. Within a few years, he dropped out of school and began selling drugs, which earned him fast cash as he tried to stay one step ahead of the police.

Like young people everywhere, AJ wanted to earn the respect of others. He also had a love for music. As the new "DJ" scene emerged in New York City in the mid-1970s, AJ was captivated by Afrika Bambaataa, Grandmaster Flowers, and Pete "DJ" Jones. Perhaps most of all, he idolized a young DJ named Kool Herc. AJ remembers the first time he saw Herc. "People in the Bronx were saying 'Yo, there's this dude named Herc, and this dude is *crazy*.' He was at the park on Sedgewick Avenue. So the next thing is I'm sitting there watching this dude and he's drawing a crowd." AJ was hooked on this music scene and wanted to be part of it.

AJ didn't know the first thing about DJing, but he hung out with other DJs. They became skilled at operating a turntable and playing records, figuring out *which* records to play and *what part* of records people wanted to hear, and they developed a whole set of rules and conventions that would define the new DJ scene.

In the summer of 1977, AJ did his first public performance in the local park. Although people from around New York had come to see the main act, a well-known DJ named Lovebug Star Ski, there were also many people from AJ's community who showed up to see *him*. He knew he was starting to make it as a DJ, and as his reputation spread, AJ lost interest in drug dealing. He was becoming a local hero. AJ explains, "The guys who own the stores close by the park would bring me beer or whatever I wanted for doing my music because it attracted lots of people and made money for them."

AJ's reputation grew as he took part in "battles," competitions between DJs not unlike the competitions for respect in gang culture. In a battle, DJs would each play for an hour, switching back and forth. The DJ who succeeded in working the crowd into a frenzy was the winner.

AJ's big break came as the result of a challenge to battle a DJ named Flash, the star of the South Bronx DJ scene, and to do it in Flash's territory. At first, AJ refused, thinking he could never hope to sway Flash's own neighbourhood crowd. But his mentor, Lovebug Star Ski, insisted, and AJ agreed.

The night of the battle, more than 500 people packed the Dixie Club in Flash's neighbourhood. Even before the competition started, there were rowdy cheers for Flash. Seeing Flash haul in some new and expensive equipment further intimidated AJ as he began his set. He started with "Groove to Get Down" by T-Connection, "Catch a Groove" by Juice, and "Funky Granny" by Kool & The Gang—rhythms that were funky and new to most of the audience. As he moved from one record to the next, the crowd began to groove with him. Then AJ pulled off a wild moment when Lovebug Star Ski jumped up onto the stage to rhyme with AJ's music. The crowd lost their minds.

Flash followed with his own set and he did his usual amazing work. The crowd cheered for their local DJ, but everyone knew that *both* men had put on very impressive performances. AJ had made it in the larger South Bronx DJ scene, a feat that would lead to opportunities that no doubt saved him from the dangerous social world of drugs and gangs that surrounded him.

AJ and many other young people like him did not make headlines in the New York papers. But they created a style of musical performance—DJing—that is now popular on campuses across Canada and the United States. And the musical style that emerged from that movement—hip-hop or rap music—has become the most popular type of music among this country's young people.

What Do You Think?

1. Is the DJ scene part of popular culture or high culture? Why?
2. What does this story tell us about who creates new cultural patterns?
3. Can you think of other cultural patterns that were born among low-income people?

Source: Ewoodzie (forthcoming).

Janine Wiedel Photolibrary/Alamy Stock Photo

viewing those of other backgrounds (Aboriginal peoples, the French, Southern and Eastern Europeans, the Chinese, and so on) as being of "lower stock." As Porter (1965:62) states,

> After all, Canada was a British creation, though indifferently conceived by British statesmen of the day. In the first decades of Canada's existence, who would have doubted that the British were destined to an uninterrupted epoch of imperial splendour? Although the French participated in Confederation, Canada's political and economic leaders were British and were prepared to create a British North America. Born British subjects, they intended to die as such.

As a result of this hierarchy, Canadian historians have tended to focus on the descendants of the English and other Northern Europeans, describing historical events from their point of view. And historians have tended to push to the margins the perspectives and accomplishments of Aboriginals and Canadians of African, Asian, and Latin American descent. Multiculturalists condemn this singular pattern as **Eurocentrism**, *the dominance of European (especially English) cultural patterns*. Molefi Kete Asante, a leading advocate of multiculturalism, argues that like "the 15th-century Europeans who could not cease believing that the Earth was the centre of the universe, many today find it difficult to cease viewing European culture as the centre of the social universe" (1988:7).

multiculturalism a perspective recognizing the cultural diversity of Canada and promoting equal standing for all cultural traditions

Eurocentrism the dominance of European (especially English) cultural patterns

Few Canadians would deny that our way of life has wide-ranging roots. But multiculturalism is controversial because it asks us to rethink norms and values that form the core of the dominant culture. One currently contested issue surrounds language. In 1969, the Official Languages Act made both French and English the official languages of Canada—and so the country became officially bilingual. However, many tensions remain over the actual implementation of Canada's language policy.

Another controversy centres on how Canadian schools should teach culture. Proponents defend multiculturalism, first, as a strategy to present a more accurate picture of Canada's past. Proposed educational reforms seek, for example, to tone down the simplistic praise commonly directed at Christopher Columbus and other European explorers by acknowledging the tragic impact of the European conquest on the Aboriginal peoples of this hemisphere. Moreover, a multicultural approach recognizes the achievements of many women and men whose cultural backgrounds have, up till now, confined them to the sidelines of history.

Second, proponents claim, multiculturalism enables students to grasp Canada's even more diverse present. The 2011 census shows that in Toronto immigrants make up a great proportion of the total population (46 percent) (Statistics Canada, 2013), leading the United Nations to call it "one of the world's most diverse cities" (UNESCO, 2014). Notably, other Canadian cities with substantial immigrant populations are Vancouver (40 percent), Calgary (26.2 percent), and Montreal (22.6 percent) (Statistics Canada, 2013).

Third, proponents assert, multiculturalism can strengthen the academic achievement of Canada's Aboriginal and visible minority children, who may find little personal relevance in Eurocentric education (Adams, 2007; Banting, Courchene, & Seidle, 2007; Ghosh, 1996). National Map 2–1 on page 64 takes a closer look at language diversity in different parts of Canada.

Fourth and finally, proponents of multiculturalism consider it needed preparation for living in a world in which nations are increasingly interdependent. Multiculturalism, in short, teaches global connectedness.

Although multiculturalism has found favour in recent years, it has drawn criticism too. It is worth noting that such criticism is not unified and that conservative as well as radical voices identify various flaws in multiculturalism. Conservative critics of multiculturalism point to its tendency to encourage divisiveness rather than unity by encouraging people to identify with only their own category rather than the nation as a whole. As William Gairdner sees it, the multicultural act "was the first step, not toward, but away from Canadian unity in a name of a self-contradictory policy that has made us a more race-conscious, race-sensitive, and culturally divided people than ever before" (2010).

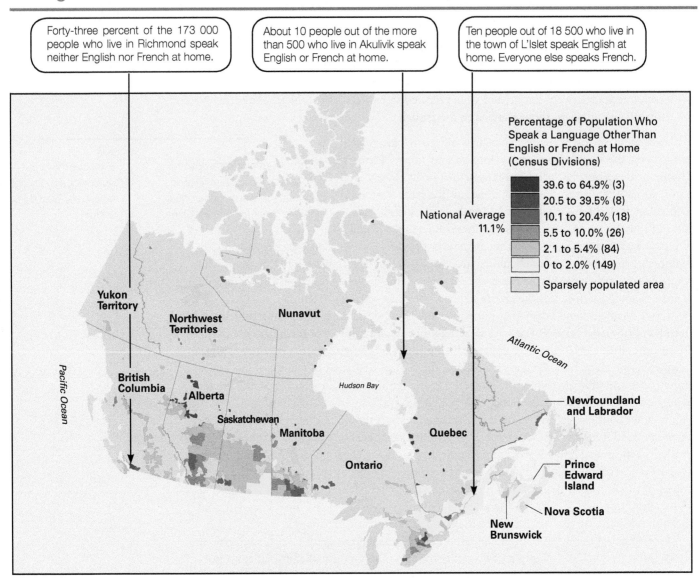

Forty-three percent of the 173 000 people who live in Richmond speak neither English nor French at home.

About 10 people out of the more than 500 who live in Akulivik speak English or French at home.

Ten people out of 18 500 who live in the town of L'Islet speak English at home. Everyone else speaks French.

Percentage of Population Who Speak a Language Other Than English or French at Home (Census Divisions)

39.6 to 64.9% (3)
20.5 to 39.5% (8)
10.1 to 20.4% (18)
5.5 to 10.0% (26)
2.1 to 5.4% (84)
0 to 2.0% (149)

Sparsely populated area

National Average 11.1%

NATIONAL MAP 2–1 Nonofficial Home Languages across Canada, 2006

The map shows that the percentage of households that speak nonofficial languages at home varies greatly across Canada. The largest number of Canadians who speak a language other than French or English live in Toronto, Montreal, and Vancouver, with Toronto the leader. Somewhat surprising is the level of relative language homogeneity in large parts of southern Quebec. What is the cause of this? What other trends do you see?

Source: Calculated based on Statistics Canada (2007).

Moreover, conservative critics contend that multiculturalism erodes any claim of universal truth by evaluating ideas according to the race of those who present them. Our common humanity, in other words, dissolves into an "Aboriginal experience," "Chinese experience," "European experience," and so on. Weary of such divisiveness, these critics decry Toronto's new Africentric and Aboriginal educational programs—programs in which some students complete Ontario's regular curriculum while integrating lessons from either African or Aboriginal cultures—for promoting segregation.

On the other hand, some of those who employ a gender and race-conflict perspective doubt that multiculturalism actually benefits minorities. The feminist sociologist Sarita Srivastava observes that multiculturalism produces and reproduces stereotypes. She argues that multiculturalism prefers to take the *3-D approach* of celebrating "dance, dress, and dining" while "[failing] to take account [of] the multiple dimensions of racial and social inequality" (Srivastava, 2007).

Rather than eliminating racism, multiculturalism turns culture into caricature as it portrays "non-Europeans the world over into pre-modern, traditional, or even downright savage peoples, while equating Europeans with modernity, progress, and civilization" (Bannerji, 2000).

For these critics, multiculturalism de-politicizes the problem of racism by taking attention away from capitalism, colonialism, and patriarchy, and approaching racism instead as a problem of intolerant individual attitudes that can be remedied with more folk festivals. The policy of multiculturalism is therefore not so much an expression of goodwill guided by the value of racial equality as it is an attempt by Anglo-Canada to create and manage different identities while preserving its dominant institutions and way of life (Day, 2000).

Counterculture

Cultural diversity also includes outright rejection of conventional ideas or behaviour. **Counterculture** refers to *cultural patterns that strongly oppose those widely accepted within a society*.

During the 1960s, for example, a youth-oriented counterculture rejected mainstream culture as overly competitive, self-centred, and materialistic. Instead, hippies and other counterculturalists favoured a collective and co-operative lifestyle in which "being" was more important than "doing" and the capacity for personal growth—or "expanded consciousness"—was prized over material possessions like homes and cars. Such differences led some people to "drop out" of the larger society and join countercultural communities.

Countercultures are still flourishing. The Occupy movement, which emerged with the occupation of New York City's financial district in 2011, shares many countercultural features. Just as the '60s hippy counterculture was based on the social unrest of the civil rights, women's, and anti-war movements, so too does the Occupy movement exist as a movement of movements, growing into, as sociologist Heather Gautney notes, such "localized acts of occupation, like Occupy our Homes, Occupy Colleges, or Occupy High (schools)" (2010). Decrying the influence of corporations on political life, the growing income gap between the "1 percent" and "99 percent," rising tuition fees, lack of affordable housing, and police brutality, the Occupy movement seems to be questioning the desirability of the American Dream itself. And it is doing so through the clever countercultural use of slogans, visual arts, and social media, as well as a leaderless brand of activism that favours a collective decision-making method known as General Assemblies.

Cultural Change

Perhaps the most basic human truth of this world is that "all things shall pass." Even the dinosaurs, which thrived on this planet for 160 million years, exist today only as fossils. Will humanity survive for millions of years to come? All we can say with certainty is that given our reliance on culture, for as long as we survive, the human record will show continuous change.

Figure 2–3 on page 66 shows that the living arrangements of young Canadian adults aged 18 to 34 have changed in the few years between 1981 and 2001 (Clark, 2007). These changes are remarkable: Only half as many people in this age group were married and had children in 2001 as compared to 1981. Conversely, there was a 30 percent increase in the proportion who were living with their parents. Some attitudes have changed only slightly: Today, as a generation ago, most women and men look forward to raising a family. Yet raising a family today is an experience quite different from raising one in earlier times. The important point is that change in one dimension of a cultural system usually sparks changes in other dimensions. For example, women's rising participation in post-secondary education and the labour force has paralleled changing family patterns, including first marriage at a later age, a rising divorce rate, increased cohabitation, and a growing number of children being raised in single-parent households (Balakrishnan, Lapierre-Adamcyk, & Krotki, 1993; Wu, 1999; Benoit & Hallgrimsdottir, 2011). Such connections illustrate the principle of **cultural integration**, *the close relationships among various elements of a cultural system*.

Some elements of culture change faster than others. William Ogburn (1964) observed that technology moves quickly, generating new elements of material culture (such as test-tube babies) faster than nonmaterial culture (such as ideas about parenthood) can keep up with them. Ogburn

counterculture cultural patterns that strongly oppose those widely accepted within a society

cultural integration the close relationships among various elements of a cultural system

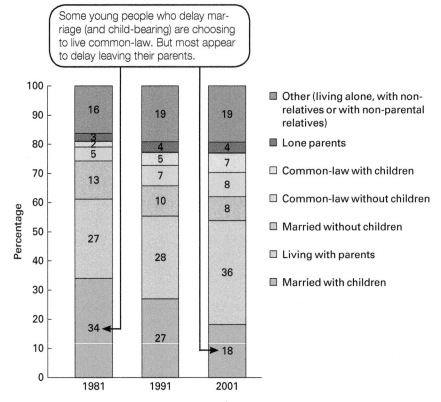

FIGURE 2–3 Living Arrangements of People in Canada, Ages 18 to 34, 1981, 1991, 2001

Some of the decline in the married population is explained by the increase in common-law relationships. Nevertheless, there is a sharp increase in the proportion of young Canadians who live with their parents. What do you think are the causes for these changes?

Source: Clark, Warren. "Delayed transitions of young adults," Canadian Social Trends, Winter No.84, Catalogue no.11-008, 2007, p.19, http://dsp-psd .pwgsc.gc.ca/collection_2007/statcan/11-008-X/11-008-XIE2007007.pdf. This does not constitute an endorsement by Statistics Canada of this product.

cultural lag the fact that some cultural elements change more quickly than others, disrupting a cultural system

called this inconsistency **cultural lag**, *the fact that some cultural elements change more quickly than others, disrupting a cultural system*. For example, in a world in which it is possible for a woman to give birth to a child by using another woman's egg, which has been fertilized in a laboratory with the sperm of a total stranger, how are we to apply traditional ideas about motherhood and fatherhood?

Causes of Cultural Change

Cultural changes are set in motion in three ways. The first is *invention*, the process of creating new cultural elements. Invention has given us the telephone (1876), the airplane (1903), and the computer (late 1940s); each of these elements of material culture has had a tremendous impact on our way of life. The same is true of the minimum wage and women's shelters, each an important element of nonmaterial culture. The process of invention goes on constantly, as indicated by the thousands of applications submitted every year to the Canadian Intellectual Property Office.

Discovery, a second cause of cultural change, involves recognizing and understanding more fully something already in existence—perhaps a distant star or the foods of another culture or women's athletic ability. Many discoveries result from painstaking scientific research, and others happen by a stroke of luck, as in 1898, when Marie Curie unintentionally left a rock on a piece of photographic paper, noticed that emissions from the rock had exposed the paper, and thus discovered radium.

The third cause of cultural change is *diffusion*, the spread of cultural traits from one society to another. Because new information technology sends information around the globe in seconds, cultural diffusion has never been greater than it is today.

Certainly, Canadian society has contributed many significant cultural elements to the world, including the renowned classical music of pianist Glenn Gould and the popular novels of Margaret Atwood, who was awarded the 2000 Booker Prize for her acclaimed novel *The Blind Assassin*. Sometimes, though, we forget that diffusion works the other way, so that much of what we assume is "Canadian" actually comes from elsewhere. Most clothing, furniture, clocks, newspapers, money, and even the English language are derived from other cultures around the world (Linton, 1937).

It is certainly correct to talk about "Canadian culture," especially when we are comparing our way of life to the culture of some other society. But this discussion of cultural change shows us that culture is always complex and always changing. The Thinking About Diversity box on page 68 offers a good example of the diverse and dynamic character of culture with a brief look at the history of rock-and-roll music.

Ethnocentrism and Cultural Relativism

December 10, a small village in Morocco. Watching many of our fellow travellers browsing through a tiny ceramics factory, we have little doubt that North Americans are among the world's greatest shoppers. We delight in surveying hand-woven carpets in China or India, inspecting finely crafted metals in Turkey, or collecting the beautifully coloured porcelain tiles we find here in Morocco. Of course, all these items are wonderful bargains. But one major reason for the low prices is unsettling: Many products from the world's low- and middle-income countries are produced by children—some as young as five or six—who work long days for pennies per hour.

We in Canada think of childhood as a time of innocence and freedom from adult burdens like regular work. In poor countries throughout the world, however, families depend on income earned by children. So what people in one society think of as right and natural, people elsewhere find puzzling and even immoral. Perhaps the Chinese philosopher Confucius had it right when he noted that "all people are the same; it's only their habits that are different."

Just about every imaginable idea or behaviour is commonplace somewhere in the world, and this variation from culture to culture causes travellers both excitement and, at times, distress. The Australians flip light switches down to turn them on; North Americans flip them up. The British drive on the left side of the road; North Americans drive on the right side. The Japanese name city blocks; North Americans name streets. Egyptians stand very close to others in conversation; North Americans are used to maintaining several feet of "personal space." Bathrooms lack toilet paper in much of rural Morocco, causing considerable discomfort for North Americans, who recoil at the thought of using the left hand for bathroom hygiene, as the Moroccans do.

Given that a particular culture is the basis for each person's reality, it is no wonder that people everywhere exhibit **ethnocentrism**, *the practice of judging another culture by the standards of one's own culture*. Some degree of ethnocentrism is necessary for people to be emotionally attached to their way of life. But ethnocentrism also generates misunderstanding and sometimes even leads to conflict. Take the annual dog meat festival in Yulin, China, which has seen international opposition to its summer solstice celebration. A petition against the festival, which was started in Elliot Lake, Ontario, has reached over 4.2 million signatures as of July 2015. As residents of Yulin, however, point out, how is the eating of dog meat any different than the Western practice of eating the flesh of cows, chickens, or pigs (Qin, 2015)? Is it not a measure of ethnocentrism to object to crispy skin dog meat but not rare cow steak?

Members of every cultural system tend to prefer what they know and are wary about what is different. The ancient Romans took this view of difference to an

In the world's low-income countries, most children must work to provide their families with needed income. These young girls work long hours in a brick factory in the Kathmandu Valley, Nepal. Is it ethnocentric for people living in high-income nations to condemn the practice of child labour because we think youngsters belong in school? Why or why not?

Thinking About Diversity: Race, Class, and Gender

Early Rock-and-Roll: Race, Class, and Cultural Change

In the 1950s, rock-and-roll emerged as a major part of North American popular culture. Before then, mainstream "pop" music was aimed at white adults. Songs were written by professional composers, recorded by long-established record labels, and performed by well-known artists such as Perry Como, Eddie Fisher, Doris Day, and Patti Page. Just about every big-name performer was white.

At that time, the United States was rigidly segregated racially, which created differences in the cultures of white people and black people. In the subcultural world of African Americans, music had sounds and rhythms reflecting jazz, gospel singing, and rhythm and blues. These musical styles were created by African-American composers and performers working with black-owned record companies broadcast on radio to an almost entirely black audience.

Class, too, divided the musical world of the 1950s, even among whites. A second musical subculture was country and western, a musical style popular among poorer whites, especially people living in the South. Like rhythm and blues, country and western music had its own composers and performers, its own record labels, and its own radio stations.

"Crossover" music was rare, meaning that very few performers or songs moved from one musical world to gain popularity in another. But this musical segregation began to break down about 1955 with the birth of rock-and-roll. Rock was a new mix of older musical patterns, blending mainstream pop with country and western and, especially, rhythm and blues.

As rock-and-roll drew together musical traditions, it soon divided society in a new way—by age. Rock was the first music clearly linked to the emergence of a youth culture—rock was all the rage among teenagers but was little appreciated by their parents. Rockers took a rebellious stand against "adult" culture, looked like what parents might have called "juvenile delinquents," and claimed to be "cool," an idea that most parents did not even understand.

Young people idolized performers sporting sideburns, turned-up collars, and black leather jackets. By 1956, the unquestioned star of rock-and-roll was a poor white southern boy from Tupelo, Mississippi, named Elvis Aron Presley. With rural roots, Elvis Presley knew country and western music, and after moving to Memphis, Tennessee, he learned black gospel and rhythm and blues.

Presley became the first superstar of rock-and-roll not just because he had talent but also because he had great crossover power. With early hits including "Hound Dog" (a rhythm and blues song originally recorded by Big Mama Thornton) and "Blue Suede Shoes" (written by country and western star Carl Perkins), Presley broke down many of the musical walls based on race and class.

By the end of the 1950s, popular music developed in many new directions, creating soft rock (Ricky Nelson, Pat Boone), rockabilly (Johnny Cash), and dozens of doo-wop groups, both black and white. By the 1960s rock-and-roll became an international phenomenon, including a substantial following in Canada, but until the 1960s and the development of rock music

nearly all of its stars were from the United States. Certain Canadian pop performers of the 1950s and early 1960s—among them the Crew-Cuts, Paul Anka, and Ronnie Hawkins—were seen as "rock-and-roll" stars. Rock music also expanded further, including folk music (the Kingston Trio; Peter, Paul, and Mary; Bob Dylan), surf music (the Beach Boys, Jan and Dean), and the "British invasion" led by the Beatles.

Starting on the clean-cut, pop side of rock, the Beatles soon shared the spotlight with another British band proud of its "delinquent" clothing and street fighter looks—the Rolling Stones. By now, music was a huge business. The first Canadian rock band to reach international fame, The Guess Who, released the song "American Woman" in 1970. Also, "folk rock" became a niche with bands like the Byrds, the Mamas and the Papas, Simon and Garfunkel, and Crosby, Stills, and Nash. In addition, "Motown" (named after the "motor city," Detroit) and "soul" music launched the careers of dozens of African-American stars, including James Brown, Aretha Franklin, the Four Tops, the Temptations, and Diana Ross and the Supremes.

On the West Coast, San Francisco developed political rock music performed by Jefferson Airplane, the Grateful Dead, and Janis Joplin. West Coast spin-off styles included "acid rock," influenced by drug use, performed by the Doors and Jimi Hendrix. The jazz influence returned as "jazz rock" and was played by U.S.-based groups such as Chicago and Blood, Sweat, and Tears, and the Canadian band Lighthouse.

This brief look at the birth of rock-and-roll shows the power of race and class to shape subcultural patterns. It also shows that the production of culture became a megabusiness. Most of all, it shows us that culture does not stand still but is a living process, changing, adapting, and reinventing itself over time.

What Do You Think?

1. The American way of life shaped rock-and-roll. In what ways did the emergence of rock-and-roll change Canadian culture?

2. Throughout this period of musical change, most musical performers were men. What does this tell us about gender and music? Is today's popular music still dominated by men?

3. Can you carry on the story of musical change to the present? (Think of disco, heavy metal, punk rock, rap, and hip-hop.)

Source: Based on Stuessy and Lipscomb (2008) and Encyclopedia of Music in Canada (2011).

Carlos Rene Perez/AP Images   Bettmann/Corbis   John Kennedy/Splash News/Newscom

Elvis Presley (*centre*) drew together the music of rhythm and blues singers, such as Big Mama Thornton (*left*), and influenced later acts like The Guess Who (*right*). The development of rock-and-roll illustrates the ever-changing character of American and Canadian culture.

extreme, using the same word for both "stranger" and "enemy." Even language is culturally biased. Centuries ago, people in Europe and North America referred to China as the "Far East." But this term, unknown to the Chinese, is an ethnocentric expression for a region that is far to the east *of us.* The Chinese name for their country translates as "Central Kingdom," suggesting that they, like us, see their own society as the centre of the world. The map shown on the right challenges the ethnocentrism of many Canadians by presenting a "down under" view of the Western Hemisphere.

The alternative to ethnocentrism is **cultural relativism**, *the practice of judging a culture by its own standards.* Cultural relativism can be difficult for travellers to adopt: It requires not only openness to unfamiliar values and norms but also the ability to put aside cultural standards we have known all our lives. Even so, as people of the world come into increasing contact with one another, the importance of understanding other cultures becomes ever greater.

As the opening to this chapter explained, businesses in Canada are learning the value of marketing to a culturally diverse population. Similarly, businesses are learning that success in the global economy depends on awareness of cultural patterns around the world. IBM, for example, now provides technical support for its products using websites in 33 languages (IBM, 2012).

This trend is a change from the past, when many corporations used marketing strategies that lacked sensitivity to cultural diversity. Coors's phrase "Turn It Loose" startled Spanish-speaking customers by proclaiming that the beer would cause diarrhea. Braniff Airlines translated its slogan "Fly in Leather" so carelessly into Spanish that it read "Fly Naked." Similarly, Eastern Airlines' slogan "We Earn Our Wings Every Day" became "We Fly Daily to Heaven" (Helin, 1992).

But cultural relativism introduces problems of its own. If almost any kind of behaviour is the norm *somewhere* in the world, does that mean everything is equally right? Does the fact that some Indian and Moroccan families benefit from having their children work long hours justify child labour? Enlightenment philosophers thought that since we are all members of a single species, surely there must be some universal standards of proper conduct. But what are they? And in trying to develop them, how can we avoid imposing our own standards on others? There are no simple answers to these questions. But when confronting an unfamiliar cultural practice, it is best to resist making judgments before grasping what people in that culture understand the issue to be. Remember also to think about your own way of life as others might see it. After all, what we gain most from studying others is better insight into ourselves.

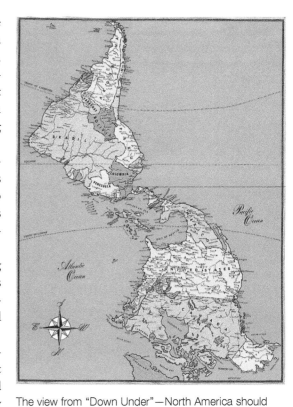

The view from "Down Under"—North America should be "up" and South America "down," or so we think. But because we live on a globe, "up" and "down" have no meaning at all. The reason this map of the Western Hemisphere looks wrong to us is not because it is geographically inaccurate; it simply violates the ethnocentric assumption that Canada should be "above" the rest of the Americas.

ethnocentrism the practice of judging another culture by the standards of one's own culture

cultural relativism the practice of judging a culture by its own standards

A Global Culture?

Today more than ever, we can observe many of the same cultural practices the world over. Walking the streets of Seoul, South Korea; Kuala Lumpur, Malaysia; Chennai, India; Cairo, Egypt; or Casablanca, Morocco, we see people wearing jeans, hear familiar music, and read ads for many of the same products we use at home. Are we witnessing the birth of a single global culture?

Societies now have more contact with one another than ever before, thanks to the flow of goods, information, and people:

1. **Global economy: The flow of goods.** International trade has never been greater. The global economy has spread many of the same consumer goods—from cars and TV shows to music and fashions—throughout the world.

2. **Global communications: The flow of information.** The internet and satellite-assisted communications enable people to experience events taking place thousands of miles away, often as they happen. Cell phone communication instantly links people all around the world, just as new technology enables text messages written in one language

to be delivered in another. In addition, although less than one-third of internet users speak English as their first language, most of the world's Web pages are written in English. This fact helps explain why, as we saw in Global Map 2–1 on page 52, English is rapidly emerging as the preferred second language around the world.

3. **Global migration: The flow of people.** Knowing about the rest of the world motivates people to move to where they imagine life will be better. In addition, today's transportation technology, especially air travel, makes relocating easier than ever before. As a result, in most countries, significant numbers of people were born elsewhere, including, as Chapter 15 ("Population, Urbanization, and Environment") shows, 20.6 percent of Canada's population.

These global links help make the cultures of the world more similar. Even so, there are three important limitations to the global culture thesis. First, the flow of information, goods, and people is uneven in different parts of the world. Generally speaking, urban areas (centres of commerce, communication, and people) have stronger ties to one another, while many rural villages remain isolated. In addition, the greater economic and military power of North America and Western Europe means that these regions influence the rest of the world more than the rest of the world influences them.

Second, the global culture thesis assumes that people everywhere are able to *afford* various new goods and services. As Chapter 9 ("Global Stratification") explains, in reality, desperate poverty in much of the world deprives people of even the basic necessities of a safe and secure life.

Third, although many cultural practices are now found in countries throughout the world, people everywhere do not attach the same meanings to them. Do children in Tokyo draw the same lessons from reading the Harry Potter books as children in Calgary or Winnipeg do? Similarly, we enjoy foods from around the world while knowing little about the lives of the people who created them. In short, people everywhere still see the world through their own cultural lenses.

Theoretical Analysis of Culture

(**2.5**) Apply sociology's macro-level theories to gain greater understanding of culture.

Sociologists investigate how culture helps us make sense of ourselves and the surrounding world. Here we will examine several macro-level theoretical approaches to understanding culture. A micro-level approach to the personal experience of culture, which emphasizes how individuals not only conform to cultural patterns but also create new patterns in their everyday lives, is the focus of Chapter 4 ("Social Interaction in Everyday Life").

The Functions of Culture: Structural-Functional Theory

The structural-functional approach explains culture as a complex strategy for meeting human needs. Borrowing from the philosophical doctrine of *idealism*, this approach considers values the core of a culture (Parsons, 1966; Williams, 1970). In other words, cultural values direct our lives, give meaning to what we do, and bind people together. Countless other cultural traits have various functions that support the operation of society.

Thinking functionally helps us to understand unfamiliar ways of life. Consider the Old Order Mennonite farmer in Southern Ontario plowing hundreds of acres with a team of horses. His farming methods may violate the Canadian cultural value of efficiency, but from the Amish point of view, hard work functions to develop the discipline necessary for a highly religious way of life. Long days of working together not only make the Amish self-sufficient but also strengthen family ties and unify local communities.

Of course, Amish practices have dysfunctions as well. The hard work and strict religious discipline are too demanding for some, who end up leaving the community. Then, too, strong religious beliefs sometimes prevent compromise; slight differences in religious practices have caused the Amish to divide into different communities (Kraybill, 1989, 1994). This is not unlike the situation found in tightly controlled Mennonite communities in Manitoba, as Miriam Toews chronicled in her award-winning novel *A Complicated Kindness* (Toews, 2005).

If cultures are strategies for meeting human needs, we would expect to find many common patterns around the world. **Cultural universals** are *traits that are part of every known culture*. Comparing hundreds of cultures, George Murdock (1945) identified dozens of cultural universals. One common element is the family, which functions everywhere to control sexual reproduction and to oversee the care of children. Funeral rites, too, are found everywhere, because all human communities cope with the reality of death. Jokes are another cultural universal, serving as a safe means of releasing social tensions.

cultural universals traits that are part of every known culture

EVALUATE The strength of structural-functional theory is that it shows how culture operates to meet human needs. Yet by emphasizing a society's dominant cultural patterns, this approach largely ignores the cultural diversity that exists in many societies, including our own. Also, because this approach emphasizes cultural stability, it downplays the importance of change. In short, cultural systems are not as stable or a matter of as much agreement as structural-functional theory leads us to believe. The Applying Theory table below summarizes this theoretical approach's main lessons about culture and contrasts this information with what we learn from two other approaches that we consider next.

CHECK YOUR LEARNING In Canada, what are some of the functions of sports, Canada Day celebrations, and Thanksgiving?

Inequality and Culture: Social-Conflict Theory

The social-conflict approach stresses the link between culture and inequality. Any cultural trait, from this point of view, benefits some members of society at the expense of others.

Why do certain values dominate a society in the first place? Many conflict theorists, especially Marxists, argue that culture is shaped by a society's system of economic production. "It is not the consciousness of men that determines their being," Karl Marx proclaimed; "it is their social being that determines their consciousness" (Marx & Engels, 1978:4, orig. 1859). Social-conflict theory, then, is rooted in the philosophical doctrine of *materialism*, which holds that a society's system of material production (such as Canada's own capitalist economy) has a powerful effect on the rest of a culture. This materialist approach contrasts with the idealist leanings of structural functionalism.

Social-conflict analysis ties Canada's dominant cultural values of competitiveness and material success to the country's capitalist economy, which serves the interests of the nation's wealthy elite. The culture of capitalism teaches us to think that rich and powerful people work harder or longer than others and therefore deserve their wealth and privileges. It also encourages us to view capitalism as somehow "natural," discouraging us from trying to reduce economic inequality.

Eventually, however, the strains of inequality erupt into movements for social change. Two historical examples are the civil rights movement and the women's movement. A more recent example is the Occupy Wall Street movement, which has focused on our society's increasing economic inequality. All these movements seek greater equality, and all have encountered opposition from defenders of the status quo.

Applying Theory

	Structural-Functional Theory	Social-Conflict and Feminist Theories
What is the level of analysis?	Macro-level	Macro-level
What is culture?	Culture is a system of behaviour by which members of societies co-operate to meet their needs.	Culture is a system that benefits some people and disadvantages others.
What is the foundation of culture?	Cultural patterns are rooted in a society's core values and beliefs.	Marx claimed that cultural patterns are rooted in a society's system of economic production.
		Feminist theory says cultural conflict is rooted in gender.
What core questions does the approach ask?	How does a cultural pattern help society operate?	How does a cultural pattern benefit some people and harm others?
	What cultural patterns are found in all societies?	How does a cultural pattern support social inequality?

Gender and Culture: Feminist Theory

As Marx saw it, culture is rooted in economic production. Therefore, our society's culture largely reflects the capitalist economic system. Feminists agree with Marx's claim that culture is an arena of conflict, but they see this conflict as being rooted in gender.

gender the personal traits and social positions that members of a society attach to being female or male

Gender refers to *the personal traits and social positions that members of a society attach to being female or male.* From a feminist point of view, gender is a crucial dimension of social inequality, a topic that Chapter 10 ("Gender Stratification") examines in detail. As that chapter explains, men have greater access to the workforce than women do and so men earn more income. Men also have greater power in our national political system; for example, no woman has yet been elected as a prime minister of Canada. In addition, on the level of everyday experience, men exercise the most power in the typical household.

Feminists claim that our culture is "gendered." This means that our way of life reflects the ways in which our society defines what is male as more important than what is female. This inequality is evident in the language we use. We tend to say "man and wife," a phrase used in traditional wedding vows; we almost never hear the phrase "woman and husband." Similarly, the masculine word *king* conveys power and prestige, with a meaning that is almost entirely positive. The comparable feminine word *queen* has a range of meanings, some of which are negative.

Not only does our culture define what is masculine as dominant in relation to what is feminine, but also our way of life defines this male domination as "natural." Such a system of beliefs serves to justify gender inequality by claiming it cannot be changed.

In short, cultural patterns reflect and support gender inequality. Cultural patterns also perpetuate this inequality to the extent that they carry it forward into the future.

EVALUATE The social-conflict approach suggests that cultural systems do not address human needs equally, allowing some people to dominate others. Marx focused on economic inequality and analyzed culture as an expression of capitalism. Feminists focus on gender and understand culture as a reflection of male domination. All these dimensions of inequality are "built into" our way of life. At the same time, such inequality also generates pressure toward change. Yet by stressing the divisiveness of culture, this approach understates ways in which cultural patterns integrate members of a society. Thus we should consider both social-conflict and structural-functional insights for a fuller understanding of culture.

CHECK YOUR LEARNING How might a social-conflict analysis of university and college fraternities and sororities differ from a structural-functional analysis?

Culture and Human Freedom

2.6 Critique culture as limiting or expanding human freedom.

This chapter leads us to ask an important question: To what extent are human beings, as cultural creatures, free? Does culture bind us to each other and to the past? Or does culture enhance our capacity for individual thought and independent choice?

Culture as Constraint

As symbolic creatures, humans cannot live without culture. But the capacity for culture does have some drawbacks. We may be the only animal to name ourselves, but living in a symbolic world means that we are also the only creatures who experience alienation. In addition, culture is largely a matter of habit, which limits our choices and drives us to repeat troubling patterns, such as racial prejudice and sex discrimination, in each new generation.

Our society's emphasis on competitive achievement urges us toward excellence, yet this same pattern also isolates us from one another. Material things comfort us in some ways but divert us from the security and satisfaction that come from close relationships and spiritual strength.

Culture as Freedom

For better or worse, human beings are cultural creatures, just as ants and elephants are prisoners of their biology. But there is a crucial difference. Biological instincts create a ready-made world; culture forces us to make choices as we make and remake a world for ourselves. No better evidence of this freedom exists than the cultural diversity of our own society and the even greater human diversity found around the world.

Learning more about this cultural diversity is one goal shared by sociologists. The Thinking Globally box offers some contrasts between the cultures of Canada and the United States. Wherever we may live, the better we understand the workings of the surrounding culture, the better prepared we are to use the freedom it offers us.

Thinking Globally

Canada and the United States: Two National Cultures or One?

Canada and the United States are two of the largest high-income nations in the world, and they share a common border of about 6400 kilometres. But do they share the same culture?

One important point to make right away is that both nations are *multicultural*. Not only do both countries have hundreds of Aboriginal societies, but immigration has also brought people from all over the world to both Canada and the United States. In both countries, most early immigrants came from Europe, but in recent years most immigrants have come from nations in Asia and Latin America. Vancouver, for example, has a Chinese community about the same size as the Latino community in Los Angeles.

Canada differs from the United States in one important respect—historically, Canada has had *two* dominant cultures: French (about 16 percent of the population) and British (roughly 36 percent). Almost one-third of people in Quebec (where French is the official language) and New Brunswick (which is officially bilingual) claim some French ancestry.

Are the dominant values of Canada much the same as those of the United States? Seymour Martin Lipset (1985) finds that they differ to some degree. The United States declared its independence from

Great Britain in 1776; Canada did not formally separate from Great Britain until 1982, and the British monarch is still Canada's official head of state. Thus, Lipset continues, the dominant culture of Canada lies between the culture of the United States and that of Great Britain.

The culture of the United States is more individualistic, and Canada's is more collective. In the United States, individualism is seen in the historical importance of the cowboy, a self-sufficient loner, and even outlaws such as Jesse James and Billy the Kid are regarded as heroes because they challenged authority. In Canada, it is the Mountie—Canada's well-known police officer on horseback—who is looked on with great respect. Canada's greater emphasis on collective life is also evident in stronger labour unions: Canadian workers are almost three times as likely to be members of a union as workers in the United States (Steyn, 2008).

Politically, people in the United States tend to think that individuals should do things for themselves. In Canada, much as in Great Britain, there is a strong sense that government should look after the interests of everyone. The U.S. Constitution emphasizes the importance of "life, liberty, and the pursuit of happiness" (words that place importance on the individual), while Canadian society is based on "peace, order, and good government" (words that place importance on the government) (Steyn, 2008). One clear result of this difference today is that Canada has a much broader social welfare system (including universal health care) than the United States (which has only recently introduced a limited system of public health care). It also helps explain the fact that about one-third of all households in the United States own one or more guns, and the idea that individuals are entitled to own a gun, although controversial, is widespread. In Canada, by contrast, few households have a gun and the government restricts gun ownership, as in Great Britain.

What Do You Think?

1. Why do you think some Canadians feel that their way of life is overshadowed by that of the United States?

2. Ask your American friends to name Canada's capital city. Are you surprised by how few know the answer? Why or why not?

3. Why do many people in the United States not know very much about either Canada or Mexico, countries with which they share long borders?

The individuals that a society celebrates as heroic are a good indication of that society's cultural values. In the United States, outlaws such as Jesse James (and later, Bonnie and Clyde) were regarded as heroes because they represented the individual standing strong against authority. In Canada, by contrast, people have tended to look up to the Mountie, who symbolizes society's authority over the individual.

Seeing Sociology in Everyday Life

What clues do we have to a society's cultural values?

The values of any society—that is, what that society thinks is important—are reflected in various aspects of everyday life, including the things people have and the ways they behave. An interesting way to "read" a culture's values is to look at the "superheroes" who are celebrated. Take a look at the characters in the two photos shown here; in each case, describe what makes the character special and what each character represents in cultural terms.

Melissa Moseley/Corbis

A long-time superhero important to North American culture is Spider-Man. In all three *Spider-Man* movies, Peter Parker (who transforms into Spider-Man when he confronts evil) is secretly in love with Mary Jane Watson, but—in true superhero style—he does not allow himself to follow his heart.

Captain Canuck Inc./Chapterhouse Comics

Captain Canuck is a Canadian comic book superhero who first appeared in the mid-1970s. The original story featured Canadian secret agent Tim Evans, who had special powers because of his contact with extraterrestrials and controlled the world from his location in Canada. Later appearances by Captain Canuck saw him fighting a global conspiracy and taking on the biker gang Unholy Avengers.

HINT Superman (as well as Spider-Man and Captain Canuck) defines North American society as good; after all, Superman and Captain Canuck fight for "truth, justice, and the North American way." Many superheroes have stories that draw on popular figures in Western cultural history, including religious figures such as Moses and Jesus: They have mysterious origins (we never really know their true families), they are "tested" through great moral challenges, and they finally succeed in overcoming all obstacles. (Today's superheroes, however, are likely to win the day using force and often violence.) Having a "secret identity" means that superheroes can lead ordinary lives (and means that we ordinary people can imagine being superheroes). But to keep their focus on fighting evil, superheroes must place their work ahead of any romantic interests ("Work comes first!").

Seeing Sociology in *Your* Everyday Life

1. What traits define popular culture "heroes" such as Sylvester Stallone's film characters Rocky, Rambo, and Barney Ross; Robert Downey, Jr.'s film character Iron Man; and Vin Diesel's film character Dominic Toretto?

2. Go to www.sociologyinfocus.com to access the Sociology in Focus blog, where you can read the latest posts by a team of young sociologists who apply the sociological perspective to topics of popular culture.

3. Do you know someone on your campus who has lived in another country or a cultural setting different from what is familiar to you? Try to engage in conversation with someone whose way of life is significantly different from your own. Try to discover something that you accept or take for granted in one way that the other person sees in a different way and try to understand why.

Jochem Wijnands/Horizons WWP/
Alamy Stock Photo

Making the Grade

What Is Culture?

2.1 Explain the development of culture as a human strategy for survival. (pages 46–50)

Culture is a **way of life**.
- Culture is shared by members of a society.
- Culture shapes how we act, think, and feel.

Culture is a **human trait**.
- Although several species display a limited capacity for culture, only human beings rely on culture for survival.

Culture is a **product of evolution**.
- As the human brain evolved, culture replaced biological instincts as our species' primary strategy for survival.

We experience **culture shock** when we enter an unfamiliar culture and are not able to "read" meaning in our new surroundings. We create culture shock for others when we act in ways they do not understand.

> **culture** the ways of thinking, the ways of acting, and the material objects that together form a people's way of life
>
> **nonmaterial culture** the ideas created by members of a society
>
> **material culture** the physical things created by members of a society
>
> **culture shock** personal disorientation when experiencing an unfamiliar way of life
>
> **society** people who interact in a defined territory and share a culture

The Elements of Culture

2.2 Identify the elements of culture. (pages 50–56)

Culture relies on **symbols** in the form of words, gestures, and actions to express meaning.
- The fact that different meanings can come to be associated with the same symbol (for example, a wink of an eye) shows the human capacity to create and manipulate symbols.
- Societies create new symbols all the time (for example, new computer technology has sparked the creation of new cyber-symbols).

Language is the symbolic system by which people in a culture communicate with one another.
- People use language—both spoken and written—to transmit culture from one generation to the next.
- Because every culture is different, each language has words or expressions not found in any other language.

Values are abstract standards of what *ought* to be (for example, equality of opportunity).
- Values can sometimes be in conflict with one another.
- Lower-income countries have cultures that value survival; higher-income countries have cultures that value individualism and self-expression.

Beliefs are specific statements that people who share a culture hold to be true (for example, "A qualified woman could be elected prime minister").

Norms, rules that guide human behaviour, are of two types:
- **mores** (e.g., sexual taboos), which have great moral significance
- **folkways** (e.g., greetings or dining etiquette), which are matters of everyday politeness

> **symbol** anything that carries a particular meaning recognized by people who share a culture
>
> **language** a system of symbols that allows people to communicate with one another
>
> **cultural transmission** the process by which one generation passes culture to the next
>
> **Sapir-Whorf thesis** the idea that people see and understand the world through the cultural lens of language
>
> **values** culturally defined standards that people use to decide what is desirable, good, and beautiful and that serve as broad guidelines for social living
>
> **beliefs** specific thoughts or ideas that people hold to be true
>
> **norms** rules and expectations by which a society guides the behaviour of its members
>
> **folkways** norms for routine or casual interaction
>
> **mores** norms that are widely observed and have great moral significance
>
> **laws** systems of rules recognized and enforced by governing institutions
>
> **social control** attempts by society to regulate people's thoughts and behaviour

Technology and Culture

 2.3 Analyze how a society's level of technology shapes its culture (pages 56–59)

Culture is shaped by **technology**. We understand technological development in terms of stages of **socio-cultural evolution**:

- hunting and gathering
- horticulture and pastoralism
- agriculture
- industry
- post-industrial information technology

technology knowledge that people use to make a way of life in their surroundings

hunting and gathering the use of simple tools to hunt animals and gather vegetation for food

horticulture the use of hand tools to raise crops

pastoralism the domestication of animals

agriculture large-scale cultivation using plows harnessed to animals or more powerful energy sources

industry the production of goods using advanced sources of energy to drive large machinery

post-industrialism the production of information using computer technology

Cultural Diversity

 2.4 Discuss the components of cultural diversity. (pages 59–70)

We live in a **culturally diverse society.**

- This diversity is due to Canada's history of immigration.
- Diversity reflects regional differences, and also differences in social class that set off **high culture** (available only to elites) from **popular culture** (available to average people).

Subculture is based on differences in interests and life experiences.
- Hip-hop fans and jocks are two examples of youth subcultures in Canada.

Multiculturalism is an effort to enhance appreciation of cultural diversity.
- Multiculturalism developed in reaction to the "melting pot" idea, which was thought to result in minorities losing their identity as they adopted mainstream cultural patterns.

Counterculture is strongly at odds with conventional ways of life.
- The Occupy movement, which questions the influence and desirability of corporations, is an example of a counterculture.

Cultural change results from
- **invention** (e.g., the telephone and the computer)
- **discovery** (e.g., the recognition that women are capable of political leadership)
- **diffusion** (e.g., the growing popularity of various ethnic foods and musical styles)

Cultural lag results when some parts of a cultural system change faster than others.

Ethnocentrism links people to their society but can cause misunderstanding and conflict between societies.

Cultural relativism is increasingly important as people of the world come into more contact with each other.

high culture cultural patterns that distinguish a society's elite

popular culture cultural patterns that are widespread among a society's population

subculture cultural patterns that set apart some segment of a society's population

counterculture cultural patterns that strongly oppose those widely accepted within a society

multiculturalism a perspective recognizing the cultural diversity of Canada and promoting equal standing for all cultural traditions

Eurocentrism the dominance of European (especially English) cultural patterns

counterculture cultural patterns that strongly oppose those widely accepted within a society

cultural integration the close relationships among various elements of a cultural system

cultural lag the fact that some cultural elements change more quickly than others, disrupting a cultural system

ethnocentrism the practice of judging another culture by the standards of one's own culture

cultural relativism the practice of judging a culture by its own standards

Theoretical Analysis of Culture

 2.5 Apply sociology's macro-level theories to gain greater understanding of culture. (pages 70–72)

Structural-functional theory views culture as a relatively stable system built on core values. All cultural patterns play some part in the ongoing operation of society.

Social-conflict theory sees culture as a dynamic arena of inequality and conflict. Cultural patterns benefit some categories of people more than others.

Feminist theory highlights how culture is "gendered," dividing activities between the sexes in ways that give men greater power and privileges than women have.

cultural universals traits that are part of every known culture

gender the personal traits and social positions that members of a society attach to being female or male

Culture and Human Freedom

2.6 Critique culture as limiting or expanding human freedom. (pages 72–73)
- Culture can limit the choices we make.
- As cultural creatures, we have the capacity to shape and reshape our world to meet our needs and pursue our dreams.

3 Socialization: From Infancy to Old Age

LEARNING OBJECTIVES

3.1 Describe how social interaction is the foundation of personality.

3.2 Explain six major theories of socialization.

3.3 Analyze how the family, school, peer groups, and the mass media guide the socialization process.

3.4 Discuss how our society organizes human experience into distinctive stages of life.

3.5 Characterize the operation of total institutions.

the Power of Society

to shape alcohol use among youth

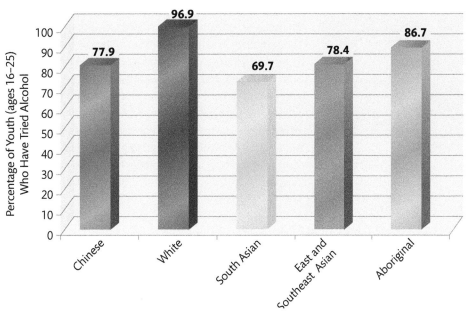

Source: Duff, Puri, and Chow (2011).

How conscious are youth of their decision to consume alcohol? Canadian-born youth report a higher likelihood of alcohol use than youth born overseas. Moreover, white youth report higher levels of recent alcohol use than youth in every other ethnic and racial category. Although we tend to think we make choices about alcohol consumption (as well as our use of other drugs), society guides our behaviour in this respect as it does in so many others.

Chapter Overview

Having completed a macro-level look at culture in Chapter 2, we turn now to a micro-level look at how individuals become members of society through the process of socialization.

Terry Vine/Blend Images/Alamy Stock Photo

On a cold winter day in 1938, a social worker walked quickly to the door of a rural Pennsylvania farmhouse. Investigating a case of possible child abuse, the social worker entered the home and soon discovered a five-year-old girl hidden in a second-floor storage room. The child, whose name was Anna, was wedged into an old chair with her arms tied securely above her head so that she couldn't move. She was wearing filthy clothes, and her arms and legs were as thin as matchsticks (Davis, 1940).

Anna's situation can only be described as tragic. She had been born in 1932 to an unmarried and mentally impaired woman of 26 who lived with her strict father. Angry about his daughter's "illegitimate" motherhood, the grandfather did not even want the child in his house, so for the first six months of her life, Anna was passed among several welfare agencies. But her mother could not afford to pay for her care, and Anna was returned to the hostile home of her grandfather.

To lessen the grandfather's anger, Anna's mother kept Anna in the storage room and gave her just enough milk to keep her alive. There she stayed—day after day, month after month, with almost no human contact—for five long years.

Learning about Anna's rescue, the sociologist Kingsley Davis immediately went to see the child. He found her with local officials at a county home. Davis was stunned by the emaciated girl, who could not laugh, speak, or even smile. Anna was completely unresponsive, as if alone in an empty world.

Social Experience: The Key to Our Humanity

3.1 Describe how social interaction is the foundation of personality.

Socialization is so basic to human development that we sometimes overlook its importance. But here, in the terrible case of an isolated child, we can see what humans would be like without social contact. Although physically alive, Anna hardly seems to have been human. We can see that without social experience, a child is not able to act or communicate in a meaningful way and seems to be as much an object as a person.

Sociologists use the term **socialization** to refer to *the lifelong social experience by which people develop their human potential and learn culture*. Unlike other species, whose behaviour is mostly or entirely set by biology, humans need social experience to learn their culture and to survive. Social experience is also the foundation of **personality**, *a person's fairly consistent patterns of acting, thinking, and feeling*. We build a personality by internalizing—taking in—our surroundings. But without social experience, as Anna's case shows, personality hardly develops at all.

Human Development: Nature and Nurture

Anna's case makes clear that humans depend on others to provide the care needed not only for physical growth but also for personality to develop. A century ago, however, people mistakenly believed that humans were born with instincts that determined their personality and behaviour.

The Biological Sciences: The Role of Nature

Charles Darwin's groundbreaking study of evolution led people to think that human behaviour was instinctive, simply our "nature." Such ideas led to claims that our economic system

socialization the lifelong social experience by which people develop their human potential and learn culture

personality a person's fairly consistent patterns of acting, thinking, and feeling

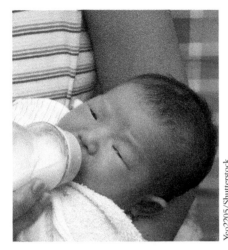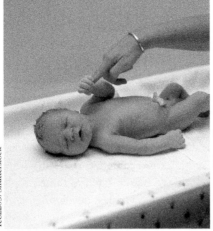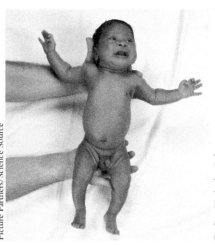

Human infants display various *reflexes*—biologically based behaviour patterns that enhance survival. The sucking reflex, which actually begins before birth, enables the infant to obtain nourishment. The grasping reflex, triggered by placing a finger on the infant's palm, causing the hand to close, helps the infant to maintain contact with a parent and, later on, to grasp objects. The Moro reflex, activated by startling the infant, has the infant swinging both arms outward and then bringing them together across the chest. This action, which disappears after several months of life, probably developed among our evolutionary ancestors so that a falling infant could grasp the body hair of a parent.

reflects "instinctive human competitiveness," that some people are "born criminals," or that women are "naturally" emotional while men are "naturally" rational.

People trying to understand cultural diversity also misunderstood Darwin's thinking. Centuries of world exploration had taught Western Europeans that people behaved quite differently from one society to another. But Europeans linked these differences to biology rather than culture. It was an easy, although incorrect and very damaging, step to claim that members of technologically simple societies were biologically less evolved and therefore "less human." This ethnocentric view helped justify colonialism: Why not take advantage of others if they seem not to be human in the same sense that you are? This was the experience for Canada's Aboriginal peoples, who were viewed by Canada's former colonial powers as "savages" and "barbarians" (Dickason, 1992; Francis, 1998).

The Social Sciences: The Role of Nurture

In the twentieth century, biological explanations of human behaviour came under fire. The psychologist John B. Watson (1878–1958) developed a theory called *behaviourism*, which holds that behaviour is not instinctive but learned. Thus people everywhere are equally human, differing only in their cultural patterns. In short, Watson rooted human behaviour not in nature but in *nurture*.

Today, social scientists are cautious about describing *any* human behaviour as instinctive. This does not mean that biology plays no part in human behaviour. Human life, after all, depends on the functioning of the body. We also know that children often share biological traits (like height and hair colour) with their parents and that heredity plays a part in intelligence, musical and artistic talent, and personality (such as how you react to frustration). However, whether you develop your inherited potential depends on how you are raised. For example, unless children use their brain early in life, the brain does not fully develop (Goldsmith, 1983; Begley, 1995).

Without denying the importance of nature, then, we can correctly say that nurture matters more in shaping human behaviour. More precisely, *nurture is our nature.*

Social Isolation

As the story of Anna shows, being cut off from the social world is very harmful to human beings. For ethical reasons, researchers can never place people in total isolation to study what happens. But in the past, they have studied the effects of social isolation on non-human primates.

Research with Monkeys

In a classic study, the psychologists Harry and Margaret Harlow (1962) placed rhesus monkeys—whose behaviour is in some ways surprisingly similar to human behaviour—in various conditions of social isolation. They found that complete isolation (with adequate nutrition) for even six months seriously disturbed the monkeys' development. When returned to their group, these monkeys were passive, anxious, and fearful.

The Harlows then placed infant rhesus monkeys in cages with an artificial "mother" made of wire mesh with a wooden head and the nipple of a feeding tube where the breast would be. These monkeys also survived but were unable to interact with others when placed in a group.

But monkeys in a third category, isolated with an artificial wire mesh "mother" covered with soft terry cloth, did better. Each of these monkeys would cling to the "mother" closely. Because these monkeys showed less developmental damage than earlier groups, the Harlows concluded that the monkeys benefited from this closeness. The experiment confirmed how important it is that adults cradle infants affectionately.

Finally, the Harlows discovered that infant monkeys could recover from about three months of isolation. But by about six months, isolation caused irreversible emotional and behavioural damage.

Studies of Isolated Children

Tragic cases of children isolated by abusive family members show the damage caused by depriving human beings of social experience. We will review three such cases.

Anna: The Rest of the Story The rest of Anna's story validates the Harlows' findings. After her discovery, Anna received extensive medical attention and soon showed improvement. When Kingsley Davis (1940) visited her after 10 days, he found her more alert and even smiling (perhaps for the first time in her life). Over the next year, Anna made slow but steady progress, showing more interest in other people and gradually learning to walk. After a year and a half, she could feed herself and play with toys.

But as the Harlows might have predicted, five long years of social isolation had caused permanent damage. At age eight, Anna's mental development was less than that of a two-year-old. Not until she was almost 10 did she begin to use words. Because Anna's mother had a mental disability, perhaps Anna was also affected. The riddle was never solved, however, because Anna died at age 10 of a blood disorder, possibly related to the years of abuse she suffered (Davis, 1940, 1947).

The personalities we develop depend largely on the environment in which we live. When a child's world is shredded by violence, the damage (including losing the ability to trust) can be profound and lasting. This drawing was made by a child living through the daily violence of the civil war in Syria. What are the likely effects of such experiences on a young person's self-confidence and capacity to form trusting ties?

Another Case: Isabelle A second case involves another girl found at about the same time as Anna and under similar circumstances. After more than six years of virtual isolation, this girl, named Isabelle, displayed the same lack of responsiveness as Anna. But Isabelle had the benefit of an intensive learning program directed by psychologists. Within a week, Isabelle was trying to speak, and a year and a half later, she knew some 2000 words. The psychologists concluded that intensive effort had pushed Isabelle through six years of normal development in only two years. By the time she was 14, Isabelle was attending grade 6 classes, damaged by her early ordeal but on her way to a relatively normal life (Davis, 1947).

A Third Case: Genie A more recent case of childhood isolation involves a California girl abused by her parents (Curtiss, 1977; Rymer, 1994). From the time she was two, Genie was tied to a potty chair in a dark garage. In 1970, when she was rescued at age 13, Genie weighed only 27 kilograms (59 pounds) and had the mental development of a one-year-old. With intensive treatment, she became physically healthy, but her language ability remains that of a young child. Today, Genie lives in a home for developmentally disabled adults.

EVALUATE All evidence points to the crucial role of social experience in forming personality. Human beings can sometimes recover from abuse and short-term isolation. But there is a point—exactly when is unclear from the small number of cases studied—at which isolation in infancy causes permanent developmental damage.

CHECK YOUR LEARNING What do studies of isolated children teach us about the importance of social experience?

Understanding Socialization

(3.2) Explain six major theories of socialization.

Socialization is a complex, lifelong process. The following discussion highlights the work of six social scientists spanning the disciplines of psychology and sociology—Sigmund Freud, Jean Piaget, Lawrence Kohlberg, Carol Gilligan, George Herbert Mead, and Erik H. Erikson—who made lasting contributions to our understanding of human development.

Sigmund Freud's Elements of Personality

Sigmund Freud (1856–1939) lived in Vienna at a time when most Europeans considered human behaviour to be biologically fixed. Trained as a physician, Freud gradually turned to the study of personality and eventually developed the celebrated theory of psychoanalysis.

Basic Human Needs

Freud claimed that biology plays a major part in human development, although not in terms of specific instincts, as is the case in other species. Rather, he theorized that humans have two basic needs or drives that are present at birth. First is a need for sexual and emotional bonding, which he called the "life instinct," or *eros* (named after the Greek god of love). Second, we share an aggressive drive he called the "death instinct," or *thanatos* (the Greek word for "death"). These opposing forces, operating at an unconscious level, create deep inner tension.

Freud's Model of Personality

Freud combined basic needs and the influence of society into a model of personality with three parts: id, ego, and superego. The **id** (Latin for "it") represents *the human being's basic drives*, which are unconscious and demand immediate satisfaction. Rooted in biology, the id is present at birth, making a newborn a bundle of demands for attention, touching, and food. But society opposes the self-centred id, which is why one of the first words a child typically learns is "no."

To avoid frustration, a child must learn to approach the world realistically. This is done through the **ego** (Latin for "I"), which is *a person's conscious efforts to balance innate pleasure-seeking drives with the demands of society*. The ego arises as we become aware of our distinct existence and face the fact that we cannot have everything we want.

In the human personality, the **superego** (Latin for "above or beyond the ego") is *the cultural values and norms internalized by an individual*. The superego operates as our conscience, telling us *why* we cannot have everything we want. The superego begins to form as a child becomes aware of parental demands and matures as the child comes to understand that everyone's behaviour should take account of cultural norms.

Freud's Model of Personality

id the human being's basic drives

ego a person's conscious efforts to balance innate pleasure-seeking drives with the demands of society

superego the cultural values and norms internalized by an individual

Personality Development

To the id-centred child, the world is a bewildering assortment of physical sensations that bring either pleasure or pain. As the superego develops, however, the child learns the moral concepts of right and wrong. Initially, in other words, children can feel good only in a physical way (such as by being held and cuddled), but after three or four years, they feel good or bad according to how they judge their behaviour against cultural norms (doing "the right thing").

The id and the superego remain in conflict, but in a well-adjusted person, the ego manages these opposing forces. If conflicts are not resolved during childhood, Freud claimed, they may surface as personality disorders later on.

Culture, in the form of the superego, *represses* selfish demands, forcing people to look beyond their own desires. Often the competing demands of self and society result in a compromise that Freud called *sublimation*, which changes selfish drives into socially acceptable behaviour. For example, marriage makes the satisfaction of sexual urges socially acceptable, and competitive sports are an outlet for aggression.

EVALUATE In Freud's time, few people were ready to accept sex as a basic human drive. More recent critics have charged that Freud's work presents humans in male terms and devalues women (Donovan & Littenberg, 1982). Others argue that his model of personality justifies a repressive and authoritarian view of society (Deleuze & Guattari, 1983). Freud's theories are also difficult to test scientifically. But Freud influenced everyone who later studied human personality. Of special importance to sociology are his ideas that we internalize social norms and that childhood experiences have a lasting impact on personality.

CHECK YOUR LEARNING What are the three elements in Freud's model of personality? Explain how each one operates.

Jean Piaget's Theory of Cognitive Development

The Swiss psychologist Jean Piaget (1896–1980) studied human *cognition*, how people think and understand. As Piaget watched his own three children grow, he wondered not just what they knew but also how they made sense of the world. Piaget went on to identify four stages of cognitive development.

The Sensorimotor Stage

Stage one is the **sensorimotor stage**, *the level of human development at which individuals experience the world only through their senses*. For about the first two years of life, the infant knows the world only by touching, tasting, smelling, looking, and listening. "Knowing" to young children amounts to what their senses tell them.

The Preoperational Stage

About age two, children enter the **preoperational stage**, *the level of human development at which individuals first use language and other symbols*. Now children begin to think about the world mentally and use imagination. But "pre-op" children between about ages two and six still attach meaning only to specific experiences and objects. They can identify a toy as their "favourite" but cannot explain what *types* of toys they like.

Lacking abstract concepts, a child also cannot judge size, weight, or volume. In one of his best-known experiments, Piaget placed two identical glasses containing equal amounts of water on a table. He asked several children aged five and six if the amount in each glass was the same. They nodded that it was. The children then watched Piaget take one of the glasses and pour its contents into a taller, narrower glass so that the level of the water in the glass was higher. He asked again if each glass held the same amount. The typical five- or six-year-old now insisted that the taller glass held more water. By about age seven, children are able to think more abstractly and realize that the amount of water stays the same.

sensorimotor stage the level of human development at which individuals experience the world only through their senses

preoperational stage the level of human development at which individuals first use language and other symbols

concrete operational stage the level of human development at which individuals first see causal connections in their surroundings

formal operational stage the level of human development at which individuals think abstractly and critically

The Concrete Operational Stage

Next comes the **concrete operational stage**, *the level of human development at which individuals first see causal connections in their surroundings.* Between the ages of 7 and 11, children focus on how and why things happen. In addition, children now attach more than one symbol to a particular event or object. If, for example, you say to a child of five, "Today is Wednesday," she may respond, "No, it's my birthday!"—indicating that she can use just one symbol at a time. But a 10-year-old at the concrete operational stage would be able to respond, "Yes, and it's also my birthday."

The Formal Operational Stage

The last stage in Piaget's model is the **formal operational stage**, *the level of human development at which individuals think abstractly and critically.* At about age 12, young people begin to reason abstractly rather than thinking only of concrete situations. For example, if you ask a child of seven, "What would you like to be when you grow up?" you might receive a concrete response such as "a teacher." But most teenagers can think more abstractly and might reply, "I would like a job that helps others." As they gain the capacity for abstract thought, young people also learn to understand metaphors. Hearing the phrase "A penny for your thoughts" might lead a child to ask for a coin, but a teenager will recognize a gentle invitation to intimacy.

EVALUATE Freud saw human beings torn by opposing forces of biology and culture. Piaget saw the mind as active and creative. He saw an ability to engage the world unfolding in stages as the result of both biological maturation and social experience.

But do people in all societies pass through all four of Piaget's stages? Living in a traditional society that changes slowly probably limits a person's capacity for abstract and critical thought. Even in North America, perhaps 30 percent of people never reach the formal operational stage (Kohlberg & Gilligan, 1971).

CHECK YOUR LEARNING What are Piaget's four stages of cognitive development? What does his theory teach us about socialization?

Lawrence Kohlberg's Theory of Moral Development

Lawrence Kohlberg (1981) built on Piaget's work to study *moral reasoning,* how people come to judge situations as right or wrong. Here again, development occurs in stages.

Young children who experience the world in terms of pain and pleasure (Piaget's sensorimotor stage) are at the *preconventional* level of moral development. At this stage of reasoning actions are justified on the basis of the kind of consequences that it produces for the person carrying it out. Rightness amounts to "what feels good to me" and wrongness to "getting into trouble."

The *conventional* level, Kohlberg's second stage, appears by the teen years (corresponding to Piaget's final, formal operational stage). At this point, young people lose some of their selfishness as they learn to define right and wrong in terms of what pleases parents and conforms to cultural norms. Accordingly, actions are justified on the basis of what others would think of the person carrying them out. At this stage, individuals also become aware of not just action but also intention. They may realize, for example, that stealing food for hungry children is not the same as stealing an iPod to sell for pocket change.

In Kohlberg's final stage of moral development, the *postconventional* level, people move beyond their society's norms to consider abstract ethical principles. As they think about ideas such as liberty, freedom, or justice, they may argue that what is lawful still may not be right. When the South African civil rights activist Nelson Mandela challenged white rule in the mid-1960s (the apartheid system of government at the time), he violated his country's segregation laws to call attention to the injustice of those laws.

EVALUATE Like the work of Piaget, Kohlberg's model explains moral development in terms of distinct stages. But whether this model applies to people in all societies remains unclear. Further, many people in Canada apparently never reach the postconventional level of moral reasoning, although exactly why is still an open question.

Another problem with Kohlberg's research is that his subjects were all boys. He committed a common research error, described in Chapter 1 ("Sociology: Perspective, Theory, and Method"), by generalizing the results of male subjects to all people. This problem led a colleague, Carol Gilligan, to investigate how gender affects moral reasoning.

CHECK YOUR LEARNING What are Kohlberg's three stages of moral development? What does his theory teach us about socialization?

Carol Gilligan's Theory of Gender and Moral Development

Carol Gilligan compared the moral development of girls and boys and concluded that the two sexes use different standards of rightness.

Boys, Gilligan (1982, 1990) claims, have a *justice perspective*, relying on formal rules to define right and wrong. Girls, by contrast, have a *care and responsibility perspective*, judging a situation with an eye toward personal relationships and loyalties. For example, as boys see it, stealing is wrong because it breaks the law. Girls are more likely to wonder why a person would steal and to be sympathetic toward someone who steals, say, to feed her family.

Kohlberg treats rule-based male reasoning as superior to the person-based female approach. Gilligan notes that impersonal rules dominate men's lives in the workplace, but personal relationships are more relevant to women's lives as mothers and caregivers. Why, then, Gilligan asks, should we set up male standards as the norms by which to judge everyone?

EVALUATE Gilligan's work sharpens our understanding of both human development and gender issues in research. Yet the question remains, does nature or nurture account for the differences between females and males? In Gilligan's view, cultural conditioning is at work, a view that finds support in other research. For example, sociologist Nancy Chodorow (1994) claims that children grow up in homes in which, typically, mothers do much more nurturing than fathers. As girls identify with mothers, they become more concerned with care and responsibility to others. By contrast, boys become more like fathers, who are often detached from the home, and develop the same formal and detached personalities. Perhaps the moral reasoning of females and males will become more similar as more women organize their lives around the workplace.

CHECK YOUR LEARNING According to Gilligan, how do boys and girls differ in their approach to understanding right and wrong?

George Herbert Mead's Theory of the Social Self

George Herbert Mead (1863–1931) developed the theory of *social behaviourism* to explain how social experience develops an individual's personality (1962, orig. 1934).

The Self

Mead's central concept is the **self**, *the part of an individual's personality composed of self-awareness and self-image.* Mead's genius was in seeing the self as the product of social experience.

First, said Mead, *the self is not there at birth; it develops.* The self is not part of the body, and it does not exist at birth. Mead rejected the idea that personality is guided by biological drives (as Freud asserted) or biological maturation (as Piaget claimed).

Second, *the self develops only with social experience,* as the individual interacts with others. Without interaction, as we see from cases of isolated children, the body grows, but no self emerges.

Third, Mead continued, *social experience is the exchange of symbols.* Only people use words, a wave of the hand, or a smile to create meaning. We can train a dog using reward and punishment, but the dog attaches no meaning to its actions. Human beings, by contrast, find meaning in almost every action.

Fourth, Mead stated that *seeking meaning leads people to imagine other people's intentions.* In short, we draw conclusions from people's actions, imagining their underlying intentions. A dog responds to *what you do;* a human responds to *what you have in mind* as you do it. You can train a dog to go to the hallway and bring back an umbrella, which is handy on a rainy day. But because the dog doesn't understand intention, if the dog cannot find the umbrella, it is incapable of the *human* response: to look for a raincoat instead.

Fifth, Mead explained that *understanding intention requires imagining the situation from the other's point of view.* Using symbols, we imagine ourselves "in another person's shoes" and see ourselves as that person does. We can therefore anticipate how others will respond to us even before we act. A simple toss of a ball requires stepping outside ourselves to imagine how another will catch our throw. All social interaction involves seeing ourselves as others see us—a process that Mead termed *taking the role of the other.*

The Looking-Glass Self

As we interact with others, the people around us become a mirror (an object that people used to call a "looking glass") in which we can see ourselves. What we think of ourselves, then, depends on how we think others see us. For example, if we think others see us as clever, we will think of ourselves in the same way. But if we feel they think of us as clumsy, then that is how we will see ourselves. Charles Horton Cooley (1864–1929) used the phrase **looking-glass self** to mean *a self-image based on how we think others see us* (1964, orig. 1902).

The I and the Me

Mead's sixth point is that *by taking the role of the other, we become self-aware.* Another way of saying this is that the self has two parts. One part of the self operates as the subject, being active and spontaneous. Mead called the active side of the self the "I" (the subjective form of the personal pronoun). The other part of the self works as an object, that is, the way we imagine others see us. Mead called the objective side of the self the "me" (the objective form of the personal pronoun). All social experience has both components: We initiate an action (the I-phase, or subject side, of the self) and then we continue the action based on how others respond to us (the me-phase, or object side, of the self).

Development of the Self

According to Mead, the key to developing the self is learning to take the role of the other. Because of their limited social experience, infants can do this only through *imitation*. They mimic behaviour without understanding underlying intentions, and so at this point they have no self.

As children learn to use language and other symbols, the self emerges in the form of *play*. Play involves assuming roles modelled on **significant others**, *people, such as parents, who*

Childhood is a time to learn principles of right and wrong. According to Carol Gilligan, however, boys and girls define what is "right" in different ways. After reading about Gilligan's theory, can you suggest what these two children might be arguing about?

self George Herbert Mead's term for the part of an individual's personality composed of self-awareness and self-image

looking-glass self Cooley's term for a self-image based on how we think others see us

significant others people, such as parents, who have special importance for socialization

The self is able simultaneously to take the role of:	*no one* (no ability to take the role of the other)	*one* other in *one* situation	*many* others in *one* situation	*many* others in *many* situations
when:	engaging in imitation	engaging in play	engaging in games	recognizing the generalized other

FIGURE 3–1 Building on Social Experience

George Herbert Mead described the development of the self as a process of gaining social experience. That is, the self develops as we expand our capacity to take the role of the other.

George Herbert Mead wrote, "No hard-and-fast line can be drawn between our own selves and the selves of others." This statement helps to explain the immense importance of "significant others" in our lives. How does this father affect the self emerging in his son?

generalized other widespread cultural norms and values we use as references in evaluating ourselves

have special importance for socialization. Playing "mommy" or "daddy" is an important activity that helps young children imagine the world from a parent's point of view.

Gradually, children learn to take the roles of several others at once. This skill lets them move from simple play (say, playing catch) with one other to complex *games* (such as baseball) involving many others. By about age seven, most children have the social experience needed to engage in team sports.

Figure 3–1 charts the progression from imitation to play to games. But there is a final stage in the development of the self. A game involves taking the role of specific people in just one situation. Everyday life demands that we see ourselves in terms of cultural norms as *any* member of our society might. Mead used the **generalized other** to refer to *widespread cultural norms and values we use as references in evaluating ourselves.*

As life goes on, the self continues to change along with our social experiences. But no matter how much the world shapes us, we always remain creative beings able to react to the world around us. Thus, Mead concluded, we play a key role in our own socialization.

EVALUATE Mead's work explores the character of social experience itself. In the symbolic interaction of human beings, he believed he had found the root of both self and society.

Mead's view is completely social, allowing no biological element at all. This is a problem for critics who stand with Freud (who said our general drives are rooted in the body) and Piaget (whose stages of development are tied to biological maturity).

Be careful not to confuse Mead's concepts of the I and the me with Freud's id and superego. For Freud, the id originates in our biology, but Mead rejected any biological element of the self (although he never clearly spelled out the origin of the I). In addition, the id and the superego are locked in continual combat, but the I and the me work cooperatively together (Meltzer, 1978).

CHECK YOUR LEARNING Explain the meaning and importance of Mead's concepts of the I and the me. What did Mead mean by "taking the role of the other"? Why is this process so important to socialization?

Erik H. Erikson's Eight Stages of Development

Although some analysts (including Freud) point to childhood as the crucial time when personality takes shape, Erik H. Erikson (1902–1994) took a broader view of socialization. He explained that we face challenges throughout the life course (1963, orig. 1950).

Stage 1: Infancy—the challenge of trust (versus mistrust). Between birth and about 18 months, infants face the first of life's challenges: to establish a sense of trust that their world is a safe place. Family members play a key part in how any infant meets this challenge.

Stage 2: Toddlerhood—the challenge of autonomy (versus doubt and shame). The next challenge, up to age three, is to learn skills to cope with the world in a confident way. Failing to gain self-control leads children to doubt their abilities.

Stage 3: Preschool—the challenge of initiative (versus guilt). Four- and five-year-olds must learn to engage their surroundings—including people outside the family—or experience guilt at failing to meet the expectations of parents and others.

Stage 4: Preadolescence—the challenge of industriousness (versus inferiority). Between ages six and thirteen, children enter school, make friends, and strike out on their own more and more. They either feel proud of their accomplishments or fear that they do not measure up.

Stage 5: Adolescence—the challenge of gaining identity (versus confusion). During the teen years, young people struggle to establish their own identity. In part, teenagers identify with others, but they also want to be unique. Almost all teens experience some confusion as they struggle to establish an identity.

Stage 6: Young adulthood—the challenge of intimacy (versus isolation). The challenge for young adults is to form and maintain intimate relationships with others. Making close friends (and especially falling in love) involves balancing the need to bond with the need to have a separate identity.

Stage 7: Middle adulthood—the challenge of making a difference (versus self-absorption). The challenge of middle age is contributing to the lives of others in the family, at work, and in the larger world. Failing at this, people become self-centred, caught up in their own limited concerns.

Stage 8: Old age—the challenge of integrity (versus despair). As the end of life approaches, people hope to look back on what they have accomplished with a sense of integrity and satisfaction. For those who have been self-absorbed, old age brings only a sense of despair over missed opportunities.

EVALUATE Erikson's theory views personality formation as a lifelong process, with success at one stage (say, as an infant gaining trust) preparing us to meet the next challenge. However, not everyone faces these challenges in the exact order presented by Erikson. Nor is it clear that failure to meet the challenge of one stage of life means that a person is doomed to fail later on. A broader question, raised earlier in our discussion of Piaget's ideas, is whether people in other cultures and in other times in history would define a successful life in Erikson's terms.

In sum, Erikson's model points out that many factors, including the family and school, shape our personalities. In the next section, we take a close look at these important agents of socialization.

CHECK YOUR LEARNING In what ways does Erikson take a broader view of socialization than other thinkers presented in this chapter?

Agents of Socialization

3.3 Analyze how the family, school, peer groups, and the mass media guide the socialization process.

Every social experience we have affects us in at least a small way. However, several familiar settings have special importance in the socialization process. These include the family, the school, the peer group, and the mass media.

The Family

The family affects socialization in many ways. For most people, in fact, the family may be the most important socialization agent of all.

Nurture in Early Childhood

Infants are totally dependent on others for care. The responsibility for providing a safe and caring environment typically falls on parents and other family members. For several years—at least until children begin school—the family also has the job of teaching children skills, values, and beliefs. Overall, research suggests, nothing is more likely to produce a happy, well-adjusted child than a loving family (Gibbs, 2001).

Not all family learning results from intentional teaching by parents. Children also learn from the type of environment adults create for them. Whether children learn to see themselves as strong or weak, smart or stupid, loved or simply tolerated—and as Canadian researcher Clyde Hertzman (2010) suggests, whether they see the world as trustworthy or dangerous—depends largely on the quality of the surroundings provided by parents and other caregivers. Hertzman and colleagues (2001) have gathered a wide range of scientific evidence to support the idea that what happens to children during their early years is important to lifelong health and well-being. Research suggests that this is also the case for many street-involved youth (Benoit, Jansson, & Anderson, 2007; Ensign & Bell, 2004).

Race, Ethnicity, and Class

The family also gives children a social identity and, in part, social identity involves race and ethnicity. Racial and ethnic identity is complex because, as Chapter 11 ("Race and Ethnicity") explains, societies define these concepts in different ways. Approximately 2 percent of the population of Canada, 2.4 percent in the United States, and 0.6 percent in Britain now self-identify as mixed race, and inter-ethnic unions are increasing (Aspinall, 2003). In addition, in the 2011 Canadian census, 13.8 million people (42 percent) said that they consider themselves to be in two or more ethnic categories, and 5.8 million chose *Canadian* as their single ethnic origin (Statistics Canada, 2013a). Table 11–1 on page 347 shows the most frequently listed ethnic categories in Canada.

Social class, like race, plays a large part in shaping a child's personality. Whether born into families of high or low social position, children gradually come to realize that their family's social standing affects how others see them and, in time, how they come to see themselves.

In addition, research shows that class position affects not just how much money parents have to spend on their children, but also what parents expect of them (Ellison, Bartkowski, & Segal, 1996). When people were asked to pick from a list of traits they thought most desirable in a child, people at all social class levels chose hard work and helping others as the most important personal qualities. However, people with lower class standing were nearly twice as likely as people in the upper classes to say that obedience and popularity are important personal traits. Similarly, people of higher social class position are more likely to encourage imagination and creativity in their children (NORC, 2011). Canadian children from the lowest social class are twice as likely to have conduct disorders as children from the highest social class, although the reason for this is not well understood (Stevenson, 1999).

What might account for the difference? Melvin Kohn (1977) explains that people of lower social standing usually have limited education and perform routine jobs under close supervision. Expecting that their children will hold similar positions, they encourage obedience and may even use physical punishment like spanking to get it. Because well-off parents have had more schooling, they usually have jobs that demand independence, imagination, and creativity, so they try to inspire the same qualities in their children. Consciously or not, all parents act in ways that encourage their children to follow in their footsteps.

Wealthier parents are more likely to push their children to achieve, and they also typically provide their daughters and sons with an extensive program of leisure activities, including sports, travel, and music lessons. These enrichment activities—far less available to

Wealthy parents give their children advantages that go beyond money. Research shows that they talk more to their children, enhancing their intellectual development (Fernald, Marchman, & Weisleder, 2013). All parents can help their children simply by engaging them in conversation.

children growing up in low-income families—build **cultural capital**, which refers to *material objects, values, and knowledge acquired by members of the elite culture* (Bourdieu, 1986). Thus, wealthy parents will pass on to their children financial wealth as well as non-financial social assets that may include certain hobbies, tastes in food and art, and styles of speech and dress. Such cultural capital advances learning and creates a sense of confidence in these children that they will be successful throughout their lives (Lareau, 2002).

There is, however, no conclusive evidence that poverty or affluence is directly related to the quality of parenting that children receive. Research shows that neither rich nor poor Canadians have a monopoly on child-rearing skills. Rather, children with behaviour problems and low academic achievement come from different economic backgrounds, as do children who perform well socially and academically (Bertrand, McCain, Mustard, & Williams, 1999). Regardless of class background, Bernd Baldus and Verna Tribe (1992) argue that by grade 6 (average age 11 years) most children use social inequality as a criterion to order the world around them. Further, grade 6 students have by this age learned to acquire cognitive and affective predispositions causing them to think that less economically advantaged persons are likely to be unsuccessful in life or to engage in morally questionable behaviour.

Social class also affects how long the process of growing up takes, as the Seeing Sociology in Everyday Life box on page 92 explains.

cultural capital material objects, values, and knowledge acquired by members of the elite culture

The School

Schooling enlarges children's social world to include people with backgrounds different from their own. It is only as they encounter people who differ from themselves that children come to understand the importance of factors such as race and social position. As they do, they are likely to cluster in playgroups made up of one class, race, and gender.

Gender

Schools join with families in socializing children into gender roles. Studies show that at school, boys engage in more physical activities and spend more time outdoors, and girls are more likely to help teachers with various housekeeping chores. Boys also engage in more aggressive behaviour in the classroom, while girls are typically quieter and better behaved (Best, 1983; Jordan & Cowan, 1995).

What Children Learn

Schooling is not the same for children living in rich and poor communities. As Chapter 14 ("Education, Health, and Medicine") explains, children from well-off families typically have a far better experience in school than those whose families are poor.

What children learn in school goes beyond the formally planned lessons. Schools also informally teach many things, which sociologists call the *hidden curriculum*. Activities such as spelling bees, for example, teach children not only how to spell words but also how society divides the population into "winners" and "losers." Organized sports help students develop their strength and skills while also teaching children to value competition. And learning to regulate bathroom breaks according to class schedule, or asking for special permission to do so, prepares students to discipline their bodily needs in workplaces.

For most children, school is also the first experience with bureaucracy. The school day is based on impersonal rules and a strict time schedule. Not surprisingly, these are also the traits of the large organizations that will employ young people later in life.

The Peer Group

By the time they enter school, children have discovered the **peer group**, *a social group whose members have interests, social position, and age in common.* Unlike the family and the school, the peer group lets children escape the direct supervision of adults. Among their peers, children learn how to form relationships on their own. Peer groups also offer the chance to discuss interests that adults may not share with their children (such as clothing and popular music) or permit (such as drugs and sex).

peer group a social group whose members have interests, social position, and age in common

Seeing Sociology in Everyday Life

Are We Grown Up Yet? Defining Adulthood

Solly: (*seeing several friends walking down the dorm hallway, just returned from dinner*) Yo, guys! Jeremy's 18 today. We're going down to Celebrities to party.

Matt: (*shaking his head*) Dunno, dude. I got a lab to finish up. It's just another birthday.

Solly: Not just any birthday, my friend. He's 18—an *adult!*

Matt: (*sarcastically*) If turning 18 would make me an adult, I wouldn't still be clueless about what I want to do with my life!

Are you an adult or still an adolescent? Does turning 18 make you a "grown-up"? According to the sociologist Tom Smith (2003), in our society, no one factor announces the onset of adulthood. In fact, the results of his survey—using a representative sample of 1398 people over the age of 18—suggest that many factors play a part in our decision to consider a young person as "grown up."

According to the survey, the single most important transition in claiming adult standing in North America today is the completion of schooling. But other factors are also important: Smith's respondents linked adult standing to taking on a full-time job, gaining the ability to support a family financially, no longer living with parents, and finally marrying and becoming a parent. In other words, almost everyone in Canada thinks that a person who has done *all* of these things is fully "grown up."

The age of leaving the parental home is rising in Canada. In 1986, only 16 percent of those aged 25 to 29 lived with their parents. In 2006, this number was 26 percent—one out of four. (See Figure 3–2.) And as Barbara Mitchell (2006) notes, not only are young adults delaying their departure, many are also likely to "boomerang" home at least once before making it on their own.

Given these patterns, at what age is the transition to adulthood likely to be completed? On average, somewhere between ages 25 and 27. But such an average masks important differences based on factors related to social class. People who do not attend college or university (more common among people growing up in

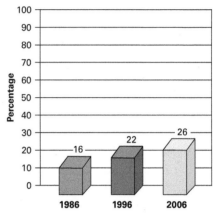

FIGURE 3–2 Percentage of 25- to 29-Year-Olds Living in Parental Home, Canada

Source: Statistics Canada (2011).

lower-income families) typically finish school before age 20, and a full-time job, independent living, marriage, and parenthood may follow within a year or two. Those from more privileged backgrounds are likely to attend college or university and may go on to graduate or professional school, delaying the process of becoming an adult for as long as 10 years, past the age of 30.

What Do You Think?

1. Do you consider yourself an adult? At what age did your adulthood begin? If not, when do you anticipate it will start?

2. Consider a woman whose children are grown, who has recently divorced, and who is now going to university to earn a degree so she can find a job. Is she likely to feel that she is suddenly not quite "grown up" now that she is back in school? Why or why not?

3. How does the research described in this box show that adulthood is a socially defined concept rather than a biological stage of life?

It is not surprising, then, that parents often express concern about who their children's friends are. In a rapidly changing society, peer groups have great influence, and the attitudes of young and old may differ because of a "generation gap." The importance of peer groups typically peaks during adolescence, when young people begin to break away from their families and think of themselves as adults. Relentless teasing by peers—girls as well as boys—can result in brutal beatings and even murder (such as in the 1997 case of 14-year-old Reena Virk of Victoria, British Columbia) or in the suicide of affected youths who are unable to withstand the taunting and other forms of abuse (White & Kral, 2014). The problem is that there is no single cause of bullying at our nation's schools. In addition, youth tend to condone bullying and even to join in, rather than to speak out against it (Artz, 1998; Moretti, Jackson, & Odgers, 2004; Hymel, Rocke Henderson, & Bonanno, 2005).

Even during adolescence, however, parental influence on children remains strong. Peers may affect short-term interests such as music or films, but parents have greater influence on long-term goals, such as going to college or university (Davies & Kandel, 1981). Research shows that parents continue to have an influence on adolescents' physical activity, and efforts to increase physical activity among teens should focus on increasing levels of family cohesion, parental engagement, parent–child communication, and adolescent self-esteem (Ornelas, Perreira, & Ayala, 2007).

Finally, any neighbourhood or school is made up of many peer groups. As Chapter 5 ("Groups and Organizations") explains, individuals tend to view their own group in positive terms and put down other groups. In addition, people are influenced by peer groups they would like to join, a process sociologists call **anticipatory socialization**, *learning that helps a person achieve a desired position*. In school, for example, young people may copy the styles and slang of a group they hope will accept them. Later in life, a young lawyer who hopes to become a partner in the law firm may conform to the attitudes and behaviour of the firm's partners in order to be accepted.

anticipatory socialization learning that helps a person achieve a desired position

The Mass Media

August 30, Isle of Coll, off the west coast of Scotland. The last time we visited this remote island, there was no electricity and most of the people spoke the ancient Gaelic language. Now that a power cable comes from the mainland, homes have electric lights, modern appliances, television, and computers that access the internet. Today, most of the islanders have cell phones and routinely text others all over Britain and around the world. Technology and the new social media have pushed this remote place into a vastly larger, more connected world. It is no surprise that traces of the island's own culture have all but disappeared, with only rare performances of its traditional dancing or music. Today, most of the population consists of mainlanders who ferry over with their cars to spend time in their vacation homes. And everyone now speaks English.

The **mass media** are *the means for delivering impersonal communications to a vast audience.* The term *media* (plural of *medium*) comes from the Latin word for "middle," suggesting that the media connect people. *Mass* media resulted as communications technology (first newspapers and then radio, television, films, and the internet) spread information on a massive scale. The mass media are important not only because they are so powerful but also because their influence is likely to differ from that of the family, the local school, and the peer group. In short, the mass media introduce people to ideas and images that reflect the larger society and the entire world.

mass media the means for delivering impersonal communications to a vast audience

In North America, television, introduced in the 1930s, quickly became the dominant medium after World War II. Today, 99 percent of Canadian households have at least one TV set, and a majority have three or more. As Figure 3–3 indicates, Canada has one of the highest rates of television ownership in the world.

The Extent of Mass Media Exposure

Just how "glued to the tube" are we? Some categories of people watch television more than others, of course. Generally, minorities, older people, and people with lower incomes spend the most time watching TV.

The latest statistics show that Canadian adult viewers watched television an average of 29.4 hours each week in 2013. Virtually everyone in Canada watches television, but not equally: Women, French-speaking Quebecers, and residents of the Atlantic provinces watched more television than other Canadians. Years before children learn to read, television watching is a regular routine. Children aged 2 to 11 watch more than 20 hours each week. This is so despite research that suggests that television makes children more passive and less likely to use their imagination (Singer & Singer, 1983; American Psychological

Global Snapshot

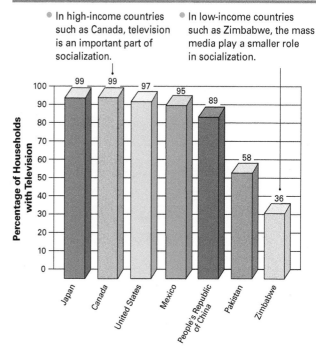

- In high-income countries such as Canada, television is an important part of socialization.
- In low-income countries such as Zimbabwe, the mass media play a smaller role in socialization.

FIGURE 3–3 Television Ownership in Global Perspective

Television is popular in high- and middle-income countries, where almost every household owns at least one TV set.

Source: International Telecommunication Union (2012); TVB (2012).

Association, 1993; Fellman, 1995). Teens aged 12 to 17 also spent over 20 hours a week in front of the TV in 2004, almost six hours more than in 2004 (Television Bureau of Canada, 2013). Access to the internet is also on the rise, with 83 percent of all Canadian households claiming it in 2012 compared to 79 percent in 2010 (Statistics Canada, 2013b). Given the rising popularity of smartphones, computers, tablets, and televisions that provide internet access, Canadians also report rising rates of internet TV viewing. The typical adult user watched over one and a half hours of internet TV a week in 2007 and over three hours in 2012 (Canadian Radio-television and Telecommunications Commission, 2013).

Television and Politics

The comedian Fred Allen once quipped that we call television a "medium" because it is "rarely well done." For a number of reasons, television (as well as other mass media) provokes plenty of criticism. Some liberal critics argue that for most of television's history, racial and ethnic minorities have not been visible or have been included only in stereotypical roles (such as minorities playing servants or Southeast Asians playing new immigrants). In recent years, however, minorities have moved closer to centre stage on television. There are now far more ethnic minority actors on prime-time North American television than there were a generation ago, and they play a far larger range of characters (Lichter & Amundson, 1997; Fetto, 2003).

Some argue that the number of people from minority groups who appear in the mass media has increased mainly because advertisers recognize the marketing advantages of appealing to these large segments of North American society (Wilson & Gutiérrez, 1985). In Canada, the popularity of such shows as *This Hour Has 22 Minutes* is a case in point, placing at centre stage representatives from this country's poorest province to poke fun at Canadian national quirks.

From another perspective, conservative critics charge that the television and film industries are dominated by a liberal "cultural elite." In recent years, they claim, "politically correct" media have advanced liberal causes, including feminism and gay rights (Rothman, Powers, & Rothman, 1993; B. Goldberg, 2002). But not everyone agrees, and some counter that the popularity of Fox News, home to Sean Hannity, Bill O'Reilly, and other conservative commentators, suggests that television programming offers "spin" from both sides of the political spectrum.

Television and Violence

In 1996, the American Medical Association (AMA) issued the startling statement that violence in television and films had reached such a high level that it posed a hazard to our health. Surveys confirm that three-fourths of North American adults say they have either walked out of a movie or turned off television because of too much violence. There may be reason for this concern: Almost two-thirds of television programs contain violence, and in most such scenes, characters engaging in violence show no remorse (Rideout, 2007).

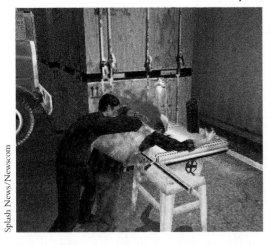

Concern with violence and the mass media extends to the world of video games, especially those popular with young boys. Among the most controversial games, which include high levels of violence, is *The Sopranos: Road to Respect*. Do you think the current rating codes are sufficient to guide parents and children who buy video games, or would you support greater restrictions on game content?

Like the American television industry, the Canadian industry has moved to control television viewing of violent programming, especially by children. Both countries have adopted a rating system for programs. The Canadian Association of Broadcasters has a "violence code," which it uses to evaluate particular programs for violent content. The voluntary code bans the broadcast of shows containing gratuitous violence of any type or shows that condone, encourage, or glamorize violence. The code establishes that shows containing such scenes can only be aired during the "watershed period" between 9:00 P.M. and 6:00 A.M.

Back in 1997, the television industry adopted a rating system for programs. In addition, televisions manufactured after 2000 have a "V-chip" that allows parents to block programming that they do not wish their children to watch. But we are left to wonder whether watching violent programming is itself the cause of harm to young people or whether, for example, children who receive little attention from parents or who suffer from other risk factors end up watching more television. In any case, we might well ask why the mass media contain so much violence in the first place?

Splash News/Newscom

Television and the other mass media enrich our lives with entertaining and educational programming. The media also increase our exposure to diverse cultures and provoke discussion of current issues. At the same time, however, the power of the media—especially television—to shape how we think remains highly controversial.

EVALUATE This section shows that socialization is complex, with many different factors shaping our personalities as we grow. In addition, these factors do not always work together. For instance, children learn certain things from peer groups and the mass media that may conflict with what they learn at home.

Beyond family, school, peer group, and the media, other spheres of life also play a part in social learning. For many people in Canada, these include the workplace, religious organizations, the military, and social clubs. In the end, socialization proves to be not just a simple matter of learning but also a complex balancing act as we absorb information from a variety of sources. In the process of sorting and weighing all of the information we receive, we form our own distinctive personalities.

CHECK YOUR LEARNING Identify all the major agents of socialization discussed in this section of the chapter. What are some of the unique ways that each of these helps us develop our individual personalities?

Socialization and the Life Course

(3.4) Discuss how our society organizes human experience into distinctive stages of life.

Although childhood has special importance in the socialization process, learning continues throughout our lives. An overview of the life course reveals that our society organizes human experience according to age—namely, the stages of life we know as childhood, adolescence, adulthood, and old age.

Childhood

The next time you go shopping for athletic shoes, check where the shoes on display are made. Most brands are manufactured in countries such as Taiwan and Indonesia where wages are far lower than they are in Canada. What is not stated anywhere on the shoes is that many are made by children who spend their days working in factories instead of going to school. About 215 million of the world's children work, with 60 percent of working children labouring in agriculture. Half of the world's working children live in Asia, while another quarter live in Africa. About half of the working children labour full time, and one-half of these boys and girls do work that is dangerous to their physical and mental health. For their efforts, they earn very little—typically, about 50 cents an hour (Human Rights Watch, 2006; Thrupkaew, 2010; International Labour Organization, 2011; U.S. Department of Labor, 2012). As Global Map 3–1 on page 96 shows, child labour is most common in Africa and Asia.

The idea of children working long days in factories may be disturbing to people who live in high-income nations because we think of *childhood*—roughly the first 12 years of life—as a carefree time of learning and play. Yet, as the historian Philippe Ariès (1965) explains, the whole idea of "childhood" is fairly new. During the Middle Ages, children of four or five were treated like adults and expected to fend for themselves.

We defend our idea of childhood by pointing out that youngsters are biologically immature. But a look back in time and around the world shows that the concept of childhood is grounded not in biology but in culture (LaRossa & Reitzes, 2001). In rich countries, not everyone has to work, so childhood can be extended to allow time for young people to learn the skills they will need in a high-technology workplace.

Because childhood in Canada lasts such a long time, some people worry when children seem to be growing up too fast. In part, this "hurried child" syndrome results from changes in the family—including high divorce rates and both parents in the labour force—that leave

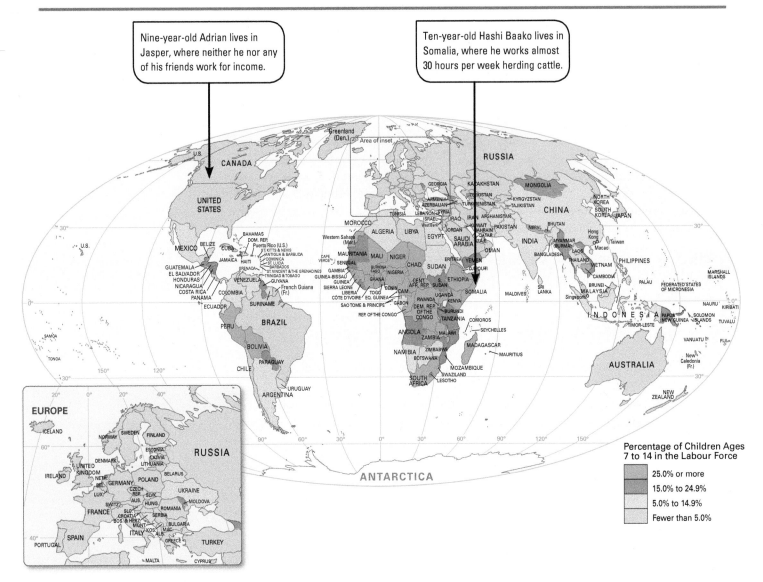

Nine-year-old Adrian lives in Jasper, where neither he nor any of his friends work for income.

Ten-year-old Hashi Baako lives in Somalia, where he works almost 30 hours per week herding cattle.

Percentage of Children Ages 7 to 14 in the Labour Force

- 25.0% or more
- 15.0% to 24.9%
- 5.0% to 14.9%
- Fewer than 5.0%

GLOBAL MAP 3–1 Child Labour in Global Perspective

Because industrialization extends childhood and discourages children from working and taking part in other activities considered suitable only for adults, child labour is uncommon in Canada and other high-income countries. In less economically developed nations of the world, however, children are a vital economic asset, and they typically begin working as soon as they are able. How would childhood in, say, the African nation of Chad or Ghana differ from that in Canada or the United States?

Source: UNICEF (2012).

children with less supervision. In addition, "adult" programming on television (not to mention in films and on the internet) carries grown-up concerns such as sex, drugs, and violence into young people's lives. Today's 10- to 12-year-olds, says one executive of a children's television channel, have about the same interests and experiences typical of 12- to 14-year-olds a generation ago. Perhaps this is why today's children, compared to kids 50 years ago, have higher levels of stress and anxiety (Hymowitz, 1998; Gorman, 2000; Hoffman, 2010).

Adolescence

At the same time that industrialization created childhood as a distinct stage of life, adolescence emerged as a buffer between childhood and adulthood. We generally link *adolescence*, or the teenage years, with emotional and social turmoil as young people struggle to develop their own identities. Again, we are tempted to attribute teenage rebelliousness and confusion to the biological changes of puberty. But it is in fact the result of cultural inconsistency. For example, the mass media glorify sex and schools hand out condoms, even as parents urge restraint. Consider, too, that an 18-year-old may face the adult duty of going to war but lacks the adult right to drink a beer. In short, adolescence is a time of social contradictions, when people are no longer children but not yet adults. As is true of all life stages, adolescence varies according to social background. Most young people from working-class families move directly from high school into the adult world of work and parenting. Such men and women are typically considered adults by the time they reach age 20 (Tanner, Krahn, & Hartnagel, 1995). Wealthier teens, however, have the resources to attend college or university and perhaps graduate school, stretching their adolescent years into the late twenties and even the thirties (Smith, 2003). The Thinking About Diversity box on page 100 provides an example of how class, age, and gender shape the life course transitions of Canadian youth.

Adulthood

If stages of the life course were based on biological changes, it would be easy to define *adulthood*. Regardless of exactly when it begins, adulthood is the time when most of life's accomplishments take place, including pursuing a career and raising a family. Personalities are largely formed by then, although marked changes in a person's environment—such as unemployment, divorce, or serious illness—can cause significant changes to the self.

Early Adulthood

During early adulthood—until about age 40—young adults learn to manage day-to-day affairs for themselves, often juggling conflicting priorities: partner, children, schooling, work, and parents. During this stage of life, many women try to "do it all," a pattern that reflects the fact that our culture gives them the major responsibility for child rearing and housework even if they have demanding jobs outside the home.

Women in Canada find themselves occupied by an unending series of "family shifts" (Eichler, 1997) that results in little leisure and in chronic sleep deprivation. It should be noted, however, that the participation of partners in sharing home responsibilities and whether women have access to public services such as quality child care (available in France and Sweden, for example) have been shown to significantly reduce women's second shift of unpaid caring work in the home (Baker, 1995; Benoit & Hallgrimsdottir, 2011).

Middle Adulthood

In middle adulthood—ages 40 to 65—people sense that their life circumstances are pretty well set. They also become more aware of the fragility of health, which the young typically take for granted (Kobayashi, 2010). Women who have spent many years raising a family can find middle adulthood emotionally trying. Children grow up and require less attention, and husbands become absorbed in their careers, leaving some women with spaces in their lives that are difficult to fill. Many women who divorce during middle adulthood also face serious financial problems (Weitzman, 1985, 1996) and social isolation (Kobayashi, Cloutier-Fisher, & Roth, 2009). For all these reasons, an increasing number of women in middle adulthood decide to return to school and seek new careers.

For everyone, growing older means experiencing physical decline, a prospect our culture makes especially challenging for women. Because good looks are considered more important for women, the appearance of wrinkles and greying hair can be traumatic. Men have their own particular difficulties as they get older. Some must admit that they are never going to reach earlier career goals. Others realize that the price of career success has been neglect of family or personal health. Social isolation is also a major concern for some (Kobayashi et al., 2009).

Many of us experienced adolescence as a difficult stage of life. The popular Canadian television show *Degrassi: The Next Generation* follows a group of students with challenging lives, including low self-esteem, early history of abuse and neglect, peer difficulties, and experimentation with sex and drugs.

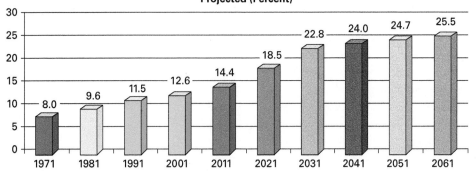

Population 65 years and over, Canada, Historical and Projected (Percent)

FIGURE 3–4 The Greying of the Canadian Population

Source: Statistics Canada (2010), http://www4.hrsdc.gc.ca/.3ndic.1t.4r@-eng.jsp?iid=33#foot_1. This does not constitute an endorsement by Statistics Canada of this product.

Old Age

Old age—the later years of adulthood and the final stage of life—begins around the mid-sixties. With people living longer, the elderly population is growing nearly as fast as the Canadian population as a whole. As Figure 3–4 shows, 5 million people, or one person in seven, is over age 65, and the elderly now outnumber teenagers. The number of seniors will double by 2036, reaching 10.4 million, and will grow to one in four people, or 24.1 million, by 2051.

We can only begin to imagine the full consequences of the "greying of Canada" (see National Map 3–1). As more and more people retire from the labour force, the share of non-working adults—already 10 times greater than in 1900—will go up, increasing demand for health care and other social products and services.

Seeing Ourselves

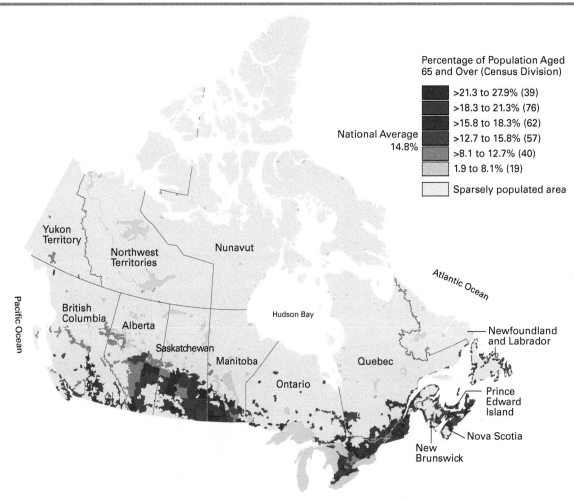

NATIONAL MAP 3–1 Aging across Canada, 2011

The aging of the population is largely a southern phenomenon. Even though we associate Victoria, British Columbia, with the phrase *newlyweds and nearly deads*, the map shows that the concentration of those over age 65 is also high in the Prairies and north of Toronto. Which social forces do you think primarily determine this pattern?

Source: Statistics Canada (2012a).

But perhaps most important, elderly people will be more visible in everyday life. As the twenty-first century goes on, the young and the old will interact more and more.

The aging of the Canadian population is the focus of **gerontology** (*geron* in Greek means "old person"), *the study of aging and the elderly*. Gerontologists study both the physical and the social dimensions of growing old.

gerontology the study of aging and the elderly

Aging and Biology

For most of our population, grey hair, wrinkles, and declining energy begin in middle age. After about age 50, bones become more brittle, injuries take longer to heal, and the risks of chronic illnesses (such as arthritis and diabetes) and life-threatening conditions (such as heart disease and cancer) rise steadily. Sensory abilities—taste, sight, touch, smell, and especially hearing—become less sharp with age (Treas, 1995; Metz & Miner, 1998).

Even so, most older people are neither disabled nor discouraged by their physical condition (Chappell, MacDonald, & Stones, 2005). According to the 2009 Canadian Community Health Survey, 44 percent of Canadian seniors perceived their health to be excellent or very good. On average, the health of Canadian seniors is steadily improving (Chappell, 2009; Public Health Agency of Canada, 2009). Good health likely plays a part in making *centenarians*, seniors 100 years or over in age, the second most rapidly growing age category in Canada (60- to 64-year-olds are the first most rapidly growing category) (Statistics Canada, 2012b).

Aging and Culture

Culture shapes how we understand growing old. In low-income countries, old age gives people great influence and respect because elders control the most land and have wisdom gained over the course of a lifetime. For these reasons, a preindustrial society usually takes the form of a **gerontocracy**, *a form of social organization in which the elderly have the most wealth, power, and prestige.*

gerontocracy a form of social organization in which the elderly have the most wealth, power, and prestige

Industrialization lessens the social standing of the elderly, giving more wealth, power, and prestige to younger people. This trend seems to be continuing: The average age of today's corporate executives, which was 59 in 1980, was just 54 in 2008 (Spencer Stuart, 2008). In an industrial society, older people typically live apart from their grown children, and rapid social change makes much of what seniors know obsolete, at least from the point of view of younger people. A problem common to industrial societies, then, is **ageism**, *prejudice and discrimination on the basis of age.*

ageism prejudice and discrimination on the basis of age.

November 1, approaching Kandy, Sri Lanka. Our little van struggles up the steep mountain incline. Breaks in the lush vegetation offer spectacular views that interrupt our conversation about growing old. "Then there are no old-age homes in your country?" I ask. "In Colombo and other cities, I am sure," our driver responds, "but not many. We are not like you Americans." "And how is that?" I ask, stiffening a bit. His eyes remain fixed on the road: "We would not leave our fathers and mothers to live alone."

Not surprisingly, growing old in Canada is challenging. When we're young, becoming older means taking on new roles and responsibilities. In old age, the opposite happens as people leave behind roles that have given them identity, pleasure, and prestige. When people retire from familiar work routines, some find restful recreation or new activities, but others lose their sense of self-worth and suffer outright boredom.

Aging and Income

Reaching old age means living with less income. But today, the Canadian elderly population is doing better than ever. The rate of poverty among the elderly, as measured by Statistics Canada's low income cut-off, has declined from about 21 percent in 1980 to 5.3 percent in 2010 (Citizens for Public Justice, 2012). A generation ago, old age carried the highest risk of poverty; today, that is true of young people under 18.

What changed? An increasing share of older couples earned double incomes during their working years, which helped them save more. In addition, better health allows older people

Thinking About Diversity: Age, Class, and Gender

Street Youth: A Fast Track to Adulthood

If you went to a public high school in Canada with a few hundred students or more, there was likely someone in your school who did not have a home to go to every night. How do you think this homeless individual's life differed from your own and that of your other classmates, other than not having a regular bed to sleep in? Cecilia Benoit and Mikael Jansson, two of the authors of this book, have conducted studies with street-involved youth in Victoria, British Columbia, for almost a decade and find that the behaviours that many see as the exuberance of university students, including experimenting with drugs, jobs, partners, and living situations, are normative for street-involved youth of a younger age. Why might this be?

When considering the characteristics of these two groups of young people, we notice important differences in regard to access to resources. For example, street-involved youth tend to come from families that are less well off, grant less social support to young people, and experience more change in family structure. These differences have important consequences because they mean that street-involved youth experiment with a less secure safety net and therefore the consequences of making a mistake are much worse for them. It is also more difficult for them to phone home when they need a place to stay, when they've broken up with a partner, or when they've misused drugs.

Street-involved youth enter adulthood faster than other youth in the general population, but without supports and resources. When we consider solutions for these young people, we need to think about their needs as similar to those of youth who enter adulthood at a later age. Both groups need social support, consistency, and access to financial resources. Focusing on only one element, such as homelessness or addiction, is not enough.

The needs of street-involved youth must be met at their non-normative stage, as if they are older than their chronological age, and they need an environment that respects their individuality and talents and willingly grants them access to crucial services.

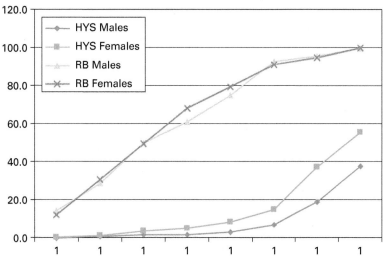

Percentage of Youth Having Lived Alone for a Month or Longer, by Gender and Study

- HYS Males
- HYS Females
- RB Males
- RB Females

Note: HYS (Healthy Youth Survey) is a random sample of youth. RB (Risky Business?) is a sample of street-involved youth.

What Do You Think?

1. Can you construct a formal definition of "homeless" and "street-involved"? What might researchers look for as features indicating homelessness? How would these features differ from street involvement?

2. According to this definition, have you ever been homeless? How many street-involved people do you know?

3. How do you think we can reduce the number of street-involved youth in Canada?

Sources: Nelson and Barry (2005); Schulenberg, Merline, Johnston, O'Malley, and Bachman (2005); Arnett (2005, 2006); Benoit, Jansson, Hallgrimsdottir, and Roth (2008).

---

to continue to work for income. Government programs have become more generous, so that almost half of all government spending now goes to programs that assist the elderly even as spending on children has remained more or less flat. But the recent economic downturn has cancelled out many of these advantages as people have lost some of the pension income they were counting on and more of today's workers are not receiving pension benefits at all. Many retirees live with fixed incomes, so inflation tends to affect them more severely than it does younger working people. Women and visible minorities are especially likely to find that growing old means growing poorer (Milligan, 2007; Statistics Canada, 2000).

If many seniors are struggling, they are doing better than many younger people. From 1980 to 2005, senior Canadian men living alone increased their income by 64 percent, while senior women living alone increased theirs by 46 percent, which was many times higher than people under age 35 (Statistics Canada, 2008a). A reasonable question, then, is whether we should continue to favour the oldest members of our society and risk slighting younger members, who now suffer most from poverty.

Death and Dying

Throughout most of human history, low living standards and limited medical technology meant that death from accident or disease could come at any stage of life. Today, however, men have a life expectancy of 78.8 years while women are expected to live 83.3 years, a mere 4.5 years difference, the lowest since the end of World War II (Statistics Canada, 2012c).

After observing many people as they were dying, the psychiatrist Elisabeth Kübler-Ross (1969) described death as an orderly transition involving five distinct stages. Typically, a person first faces death with *denial*, perhaps out of fear and perhaps because our culture tends to ignore the reality of death. The second phase is *anger*, when a person facing death sees it as a gross injustice. Third, anger gives way to *negotiation* as the person imagines the possibility of avoiding death by striking a bargain with a supreme or divine being. The fourth response, *resignation*, is often accompanied by psychological depression. Finally, a complete adjustment to death requires *acceptance*. At this point, no longer paralyzed by fear and anxiety, the person whose life is ending sets out to find peace and makes the most of whatever time remains.

More recent research has shown that Kübler-Ross simplified the process of dying—not everyone passes through these stages or does so in the order in which she presents them (Konigsberg, 2011). At the same time, this research has helped draw attention to death and dying. As the share of women and men in old age increases, we can expect our culture to become more comfortable with the idea of death. In recent years, people in Canada have started talking about death more openly, and the trend is toward viewing dying as preferable to prolonged suffering. More couples now prepare for death with legal and financial planning. This openness may ease somewhat the pain of the surviving spouse, a consideration for women, who, more often than not, outlive their husbands.

The Life Course: Patterns and Variations

This brief look at the life course points to two major conclusions. First, although each stage of life is linked to the biological process of aging, the life course is largely a social construction. For this reason, people in other societies may experience a stage of life quite differently or, for that matter, not at all. Second, in any society, the stages of the life course present certain problems and transitions that involve learning something new and, in many cases, unlearning familiar routines.

Societies organize the life course according to age, but other forces, such as class, race, ethnicity, and gender also shape people's lives. This means that the general patterns described in this chapter apply somewhat differently to various categories of people.

People's life experiences also vary, depending on when, in the history of the society, they were born. A **cohort** is *a category of people with something in common, usually their age*. Because members of a particular age cohort are generally influenced by the same economic and cultural trends, they tend to have similar attitudes and values. Women and men born in the late 1940s and 1950s, for example, grew up during a period of economic expansion that gave them a sense of optimism. Today's college and university students, who have grown up in an age of economic uncertainty, are less confident about the future.

A cohort is a category of similar-age people who share common life experiences. Just as these university graduates in the 1960s were mainly young people, so many of them today are the same people, now over age 60.

cohort a category of people with something in common, usually their age

Resocialization: Total Institutions

(**3.5**) Characterize the operation of total institutions.

A final type of socialization, experienced by more than 163 000 people in Canada's correctional system, involves being confined—usually against their will—in prisons (Dauvergne, 2012). This is the special world of the **total institution**, *a setting in which people are isolated from the rest of society and controlled by an administrative staff.*

total institution a setting in which people are isolated from the rest of society and controlled by an administrative staff

According to Erving Goffman (1961), total institutions, of which prisons are just one type, have a number of distinct characteristics. Staff members typically supervise all aspects of daily life, including where residents (often called "inmates") eat, sleep, and work. Life in a total institution is controlled and standardized, with the same food, uniforms, and activities for everyone. And formal rules dictate when, where, and how inmates perform their daily routines. Considering these indicators, Goffman came to recognize five types of total institutions:

1. **Institutions that care for "incapable" or "harmless" members.** Retirement homes and orphanages provide care for those who cannot care for themselves. While providing care, such total institutions also subject their members to a world of rules and regulations.

2. **Institutions that care for those who pose an unintended threat to the community.** Patients confined to psychiatric wards or leprosariums may pose a threat to others and are incapable of looking after themselves.

3. **Institutions that protect the community against those who intent to threaten it.** Jails, P.O.W camps, and concentration camps have all been justified on the basis of offering social protection.

4. **Institutions that pursue instrumental tasks.** Boarding schools, work camps, and army barracks may have voluntary members who remain cut off from the rest of society and who stick to routines imposed by administrative staff.

5. **Institutions that pursue normative tasks.** Religious monasteries and convents act as "retreats from the world" that segregate and discipline their members.

resocialization radically changing an inmate's personality by carefully controlling the environment

The purpose of such rigid routines is **resocialization**, *radically changing an inmate's personality by carefully controlling the environment*. Often total institutions are places in which *involuntary resocialization* takes place. This occurs when inmates do not consent to the experience of being resocialized. Prisons and mental hospitals, for example, physically isolate inmates behind fences, barred windows, and locked doors and control their access to the telephone, computers, mail, and visitors. The institution becomes their entire world, making it easier for the staff to bring about personality change—or at least obedience—in the inmate. Total institutions can also, however, be places in which *voluntary resocialization* occurs. This happens whenever people choose to participate, for example, by joining the army or seeking rehabilitation for substance abuse. Much voluntary resocialization also takes place outside of total institutions, when we embark on a new career, become parents, or participate in anticipatory socialization (see page 93).

In total institutions resocialization is a two-part process. First, the staff breaks down a new inmate's existing identity. For example, an inmate must give up personal possessions, including clothing and grooming articles used to maintain a distinctive appearance. Instead, the staff provides standard-issue clothes so that everyone looks alike. The staff subjects new inmates to "mortifications of self," which can include searches, head shaving, medical examinations, fingerprinting, and assignment of a serial number. Once inside the walls, individuals also give up their privacy as guards routinely inspect their living quarters.

In the second part of the resocialization process, the staff tries to build a new self in the inmate through a system of rewards and punishments. Having a book to read, watching television, or making a telephone call may seem like minor pleasures to the outsider, but in the rigid environment of the total institution, gaining such simple privileges as these can be a powerful motivation to conform. The length of confinement typically depends on how well the inmate co-operates with the staff.

Andrew Vaughan/The Canadian Press

Prisons are one example of a total institution in which inmates undergo supervision and control by institutional staff. What do we expect prison to do to young people convicted of crimes? How well do you think prisons do what people expect them to?

Controversy & Debate

Are We Free Within Society?

Mike: Sociology is a good course. Since my professor started telling us to look at our lives with a sociological eye, I'm realizing that a lot of who, what, and where I am is because of society.

Kim: (*teasingly*) Oh, so society is responsible for making you so smart and witty and handsome?

Mike: No, that's all me. But I'm seeing that being at university and playing hockey is maybe not all me. I mean, it's at least also about social class and gender. What people are and the society around them can never be completely separated.

What do you think? How free are we, really? Throughout this chapter, we have stressed one key theme: Society—through its agents (family, school, peers, and the mass media)—shapes how we think, feel, and act. As the sociological perspective points out, human beings are like puppets in that we, too, respond to backstage forces. Society, after all, gives us a culture and also shapes our lives according to class, race, and gender. If this is so, then in what sense are we free?

James Porto/The Image Bank/Getty Images

Does understanding more about how society shapes our lives give us greater power to "cut the strings" and choose for ourselves how to live?

Sociologists speak with many voices when addressing this question. The politically liberal response is that individuals are *not* free of society—in fact, as social creatures, we never could be. But if we are condemned to live in a society with power over us, it is important to do what we can to make our home as socially just as possible. That is, we should try to lessen inequality, working to reduce class differences and other barriers to opportunity for visible minorities and women.

A more conservative response is that we are free because society can never dictate our dreams. North American history—right from early settlement to the present—is one story after another of individuals pursuing personal goals in spite of great challenges. This argument says that individual efforts rather than progressive government social policies result in the greatest freedom for citizens. This sentiment is much stronger in the United States than Canada but even here many people believe that we can change our lives around or achieve great things if we just work hard enough.

All of these arguments can be found in George Herbert Mead's analysis of socialization. Mead recognized that society makes demands on us, sometimes limiting our options. But he also reminded us that human beings are spontaneous and creative, capable of continually acting on society both with acceptance and with efforts to bring about change. Mead noted the power of society while still affirming the human capacity to evaluate, to criticize, and ultimately to choose and change.

In the end, then, we may seem like puppets, but this impression is correct only on the surface. A crucial difference is that we have the ability to stop, look up at the "strings" that make us move, decide what we think about them, and even yank on the strings defiantly (Berger, 1963:176). If our pull is strong enough, we can accomplish more than we might think. As Margaret Mead once remarked, "Never doubt that a small group of thoughtful, committed citizens can change the world. Indeed, it is the only thing that ever has."

What Do You Think?

1. Do you think that our society gives more freedom to males than to females? Why or why not?

2. Do you think that most people in our society feel that they have some control over their lives or not? Why?

3. Has learning about socialization increased or decreased your feeling of freedom? Why?

Total institutions affect people in different ways. Some inmates may end up "rehabilitated" or "recovered," but others may change little, and still others may become hostile and bitter. Over a long period of time, living in a rigidly controlled environment can leave some people *institutionalized*, without the capacity for independent living.

But what about the rest of us? Does socialization crush our individuality or empower us to reach our creative potential? The Controversy & Debate box above takes a closer look at this question.

Seeing Sociology in Everyday Life

Anders Ryman/Corbis

When do we grow up and become adults?

As this chapter explains, many factors come into play in the process of moving from one stage of the life course to another. In global perspective, what makes our society unusual is that there is no one event that clearly tells everyone (and us, too) that the milestone of adulthood has been reached. We have important events that say, for example, when someone completes high school (graduation ceremony) or gets married (wedding ceremony). Look at the photos shown here. In each case, what do we learn about how the society defines the transition from one stage of life to another?

Among the Hamer people in the Omo Valley of Ethiopia, young boys must undergo a test to mark their transition to manhood. Usually the event is triggered by the boy's expressing a desire to marry. In this ritual, witnessed by everyone in his society, the boy must jump over a line of bulls selected by the girl's family. If he succeeds in doing this three times, he is declared a man and the wedding can take place (marking the girl's transition to womanhood). Does our society have any ceremony or event similar to this to mark the transition to adulthood?

On the San Carlos Reservation in Arizona, young Apache girls perform the Sunrise Dance to mark their transition to adulthood. Carefully painted by an elder according to Apache tradition, each girl holds a special staff, which symbolizes her hope for a long and healthy life and spiritual happiness. Many of the world's societies time these coming-of-age rituals to correspond to a girl's first menstrual cycle. Why do you think this is so?

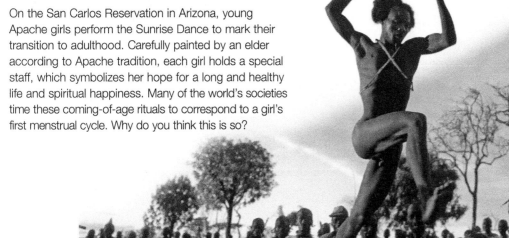

Remi Benali/Terra/Corbis

Societies differ in how they structure the life course, including which stages of life are defined as important, which years of life various stages correspond to, and how clearly movement from one stage to another is marked. Given our cultural emphasis on individual choice and freedom, many people tend to say "You're only as old as you feel" and let people decide these things for themselves. When it comes to reaching adulthood, our society is not very clear—the Seeing Sociology in Everyday Life box on page 92 points out many factors that figure into becoming an adult. So there is no widespread "adult ritual" as we see in these photos. Keep in mind that, for us, class matters a lot in this process, with young people from more affluent families staying in school and delaying full adulthood until well into their twenties or even their thirties. Finally, in these tough economic times, the share of young people in their twenties living with parents goes way up, which can delay adulthood for an entire cohort.

Chung Sung-Jun/Getty Images

These young men and women in Seoul, South Korea, are participating in a Confucian ceremony to mark their becoming adults. This ritual, which takes place on the twentieth birthday, defines young people as full members of the community and also reminds them of all the responsibilities they are now expected to fulfill. If we had such a ritual in Canada, at what age would it take place? Would a person's social class affect the timing of this ritual?

Seeing Sociology in *Your* Everyday Life

1. Across Canada, many families plan elaborate parties to celebrate a daughter's or son's graduation from high school. In what respect is this a ritual that marks reaching adulthood? How does social class affect whether people define this event as the beginning of adulthood?

2. Go to www.sociologyinfocus.com to access the Sociology in Focus blog, where you can read the latest posts by a team of young sociologists who apply the sociological perspective to topics of popular culture.

3. In what sense are human beings free? After reading through this chapter, develop a personal statement of the extent to which you think you are able to guide your own life. Notice that some of the thinkers discussed in this chapter (such as Sigmund Freud) argued that there are sharp limits on our ability to act freely; by contrast, others (especially George Herbert Mead) claimed that human beings have significant ability to be creative. What is your personal statement about the extent of human freedom?

Terry Vine/Spaces Images/Alamy
Stock Photo

Social Experience: The Key to Our Humanity

(3.1) Describe how social interaction is the foundation of personality. (pages 80–83)

Socialization is a **lifelong process.**

- Socialization develops our humanity as well as our particular personalities.
- The importance of socialization is seen in the fact that extended periods of social isolation result in permanent damage (cases of Anna, Isabelle, and Genie).

Socialization is a matter of **nurture** rather than **nature**.

- A century ago, most people thought human behaviour resulted from biological instinct.
- For us as human beings, it is our nature to nurture.

socialization the lifelong social experience by which people develop their human potential and learn culture

personality a person's fairly consistent patterns of acting, thinking, and feeling

Understanding Socialization

(3.2) Explain six major theories of socialization. (pages 83–89)

Sigmund Freud's model of the human personality has three parts:

- **id:** innate, pleasure-seeking human drives
- **superego:** the demands of society in the form of internalized values and norms
- **ego:** our efforts to balance innate, pleasure-seeking drives and the demands of society

Jean Piaget believed that human development involves both biological maturation and gaining social experience. He identified four stages of cognitive development:

- The **sensorimotor stage** involves knowing the world only through the senses.
- The **preoperational stage** involves starting to use language and other symbols.
- The **concrete operational stage** allows individuals to understand causal connections.
- The **formal operational stage** involves abstract and critical thought.

Lawrence Kohlberg applied Piaget's approach to stages of moral development:

- We first judge rightness in **preconventional** terms, according to our individual needs.
- Next, **conventional** moral reasoning takes account of parental attitudes and cultural norms.
- Finally, **postconventional** reasoning allows us to criticize society itself.

Carol Gilligan found that gender plays an important part in moral development, with males relying more on abstract standards of rightness and females relying more on the effects of actions on relationships.

To **George Herbert Mead:**

- The **self** is part of our personality and includes self-awareness and self-image.
- The self develops only as a result of social experience.
- Social experience involves the exchange of symbols.
- Social interaction depends on understanding the intention of another, which requires taking the role of the other.
- Human action is partly spontaneous (the I) and partly in response to others (the me).
- We gain social experience through imitation, play, games, and understanding the **generalized other.**

Horton Cooley used the term **looking-glass self** to explain that we see ourselves as we imagine others see us.

Erik H. Erikson identified challenges that individuals face at each stage of life from infancy to old age.

id Freud's term for the human being's basic drives

ego Freud's term for a person's conscious efforts to balance innate pleasure-seeking drives with the demands of society

superego Freud's term for the cultural values and norms internalized by an individual

sensorimotor stage Piaget's term for the level of human development at which individuals experience the world only through their senses

preoperational stage Piaget's term for the level of human development at which individuals first use language and other symbols

concrete operational stage Piaget's term for the level of human development at which individuals first see causal connections in their surroundings

formal operational stage Piaget's term for the level of human development at which individuals think abstractly and critically

self George Herbert Mead's term for the part of an individual's personality composed of self-awareness and self-image

looking-glass self Cooley's term for a self-image based on how we think others see us

significant others people, such as parents, who have special importance for socialization

generalized other George Herbert Mead's term for widespread cultural norms and values we use as references in evaluating ourselves

Agents of Socialization

 Analyze how the family, school, peer groups, and the mass media guide the socialization process. (pages 89–95)

The **family** is usually the first setting of socialization.
- Family has the greatest impact on attitudes and behaviour.
- A family's social position, including race and social class, shapes a child's personality.
- Ideas about race, gender, and social class are learned first in the family.

Schools give most children their first experience with bureaucracy and impersonal evaluation.
- Schools teach knowledge and skills needed for later life.
- Schools expose children to greater social diversity.
- Schools reinforce ideas about gender.

The **peer group** helps shape attitudes and behaviour.
- The peer group takes on great importance during adolescence.
- The peer group frees young people from adult supervision.

The **mass media** have a huge impact on socialization in modern, high-income societies.
- The average Canadian child spends as much time watching television and videos as attending school and interacting with parents.
- The mass media often reinforce stereotypes about gender and race.
- The mass media expose people to a great deal of violence.

cultural capital material objects, values, and knowledge acquired by members of the elite culture

peer group a social group whose members have interests, social position, and age in common

anticipatory socialization learning that helps a person achieve a desired position

mass media the means for delivering impersonal communications to a vast audience

Socialization and the Life Course

3.4 Discuss how our society organizes human experience into distinctive stages of life. (pages 95–101)

The concept of **childhood** is grounded not in biology but in culture. In high-income countries, childhood is extended.

The emotional and social turmoil of **adolescence** results from cultural inconsistency in defining people who are not children but not yet adults. Adolescence varies by social class.

Adulthood is the stage of life when most accomplishments take place. Although personality is now formed, it continues to change with new life experiences.

Old age is defined as much by culture as biology.
- Traditional societies give power and respect to elders.
- Industrial societies define elders as unimportant and out of touch.
- The "greying of Canada" means that the average age of our nation's population is going up.

Acceptance of **death and dying** is part of socialization for the elderly. This process typically involves five stages: denial, anger, negotiation, resignation, and acceptance.

gerontology the study of aging and the elderly

gerontocracy a form of social organization in which the elderly have the most wealth, power, and prestige

ageism prejudice and discrimination on the basis of age.

cohort a category of people with something in common, usually their age

Resocialization: Total Institutions

3.5 Characterize the operation of total institutions. (pages 101–103)

Total institutions include orphanages, psychiatric wards, prisons, boarding schools, and monasteries.
- Staff members supervise all aspects of life.
- Life is standardized, with all inmates following set rules and routines.

Resocialization is a two-part process:
- breaking down inmates' existing identity
- building a new self through a system of rewards and punishments

total institution a setting in which people are isolated from the rest of society and manipulated by an administrative staff

resocialization radically changing an inmate's personality by carefully controlling the environment

4 Social Interaction in Everyday Life

LEARNING OBJECTIVES

4.1 Explain how social structure helps us to make sense of everyday situations.

4.2 State the importance of status to social organization.

4.3 State the importance of role to social organization.

4.4 Describe how we socially construct reality.

4.5 Apply Goffman's analysis to several familiar situations.

4.6 Construct a sociological analysis of three aspects of everyday life: emotions, language, and humour.

the Power of Society

to guide the way we surf the internet

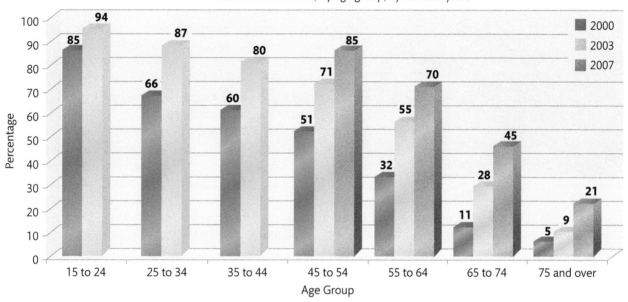

Rates of internet use, by age group, by selected years

Source: Statistics Canada, http://www.statcan.gc.ca/pub/11-008-x/2009002/c-g/10910/c-g001-eng.htm. This does not constitute an endorsement by Statistics Canada of this product.

Is our use of the internet as much of a personal choice as we may think? In 2000, 51 percent of Canadian adults aged 45 to 54 surfed the web. By 2007, 85 percent of 45- to 54-year-olds (and only 21 percent of people aged 75 or over) did so. It turns out that age is a powerful predictor of our online habits (Veenhof & Timusk, 2009).

Chapter Overview

This chapter takes a micro-level look at society, examining patterns of everyday social interaction. First, the chapter identifies important social structures, including status and role, which guide our behaviour in the presence of others. Then it explains how we construct reality in social interaction. Finally, the chapter applies the lessons learned to three everyday experiences: emotion, language, and humour.

Ingram Publishing/Superstock

Harold and Sybil are on their way to another couple's home in an unfamiliar area of their city. For the last 20 minutes, as Sybil sees it, they have been driving in circles, searching in vain for Mortimer Street.

"Look, Harold," says Sybil. "There are some people up ahead. Let's ask for directions." Harold, gripping the wheel ever more tightly, begins muttering under his breath. "I know where I am. I don't want to waste time talking to strangers. Just let me get us there." "I'm sure you know where you are, Harold," Sybil responds, looking straight ahead. "But I don't think you know where you're going."

Harold and Sybil are lost in more ways than one: Not only can't they find where their friends live, but they also cannot understand why they are growing angrier with each other with each passing minute.

What's going on? Like most men, Harold cannot stand getting lost. The longer he drives around, the more incompetent he feels. Sybil can't understand why Harold doesn't pull over to ask someone the way to Mortimer Street. If she were driving, she thinks to herself, they would already be comfortably settled in with their friends.

Why don't many men like to ask for directions? Because men are so eager to claim competence and independence, they are uncomfortable asking for any type of help and are reluctant to accept it. In addition, to ask another person for assistance is the same as saying, "You know something I don't know." If it takes Harold a few more minutes to find Mortimer Street on his own—and to keep his sense of being in control—he thinks that's the way to go.

Women are socialized to be more in tune with others and strive for connectedness. From Sybil's point of view, asking for help is right because sharing information builds social bonds and at the same time gets the job done. Asking for directions seems as natural to her as searching on his own is to Harold. Obviously, getting lost is sure to create conflict for Harold and Sybil as long as neither one of them understands the other's point of view.

social interaction the process by which people act and react in relation to others

Such everyday social patterns are the focus of this chapter. The central concept is **social interaction**, *the process by which people act and react in relation to others.* We begin by presenting the rules and building blocks of everyday experience and then explore the almost magical way in which face-to-face interaction creates the reality in which we live.

Social Structure: A Guide to Everyday Living

(4.1) Explain how social structure helps us to make sense of everyday situations.

September 8, Åbo, Finland. It is shortly before 8:00 A.M. when we arrive at Folkhälsans Daghem (daycare centre) for the first time. We help our daughter discard her outside wear and change from sneakers to slippers at the space already labelled with her name. The other children are washing their hands—part of the arrival routine—and, eager to fit into her new environment, our daughter follows suit. Seated at two

small, square tables are a dozen or so children aged three to six, peacefully eating their breakfast with their non-parental caregivers. As Canadians, we used to attend to our daughter's dietary needs at daycare ourselves—packed lunches and a snack. The communal arrangement seems very strange (and appealing) to us. We are all the more amazed to learn that Finnish law requires that all daycare children be given a daily breakfast, hot lunch, and afternoon snack free of charge! When we pick our daughter up at the end of the day, we notice that she is the last one there at 4:30 P.M. Eager to fit in ourselves, we soon adjust our daily schedule and start to pick our daughter up around 4:00 P.M., as the other parents do.

Members of every society rely on social structure to make sense of everyday situations. As our family's introduction to the daycare system in Finland suggests, the world can be confusing, even frightening, when society's rules are unclear. Let's take a closer look at the ways in which societies organize everyday life.

Status

4.2 State the importance of status to social organization.

We celebrate athletes such as Brian McKeever not only because in 2010 he became the first Canadian athlete to be named to both Paralympic and Olympic teams and went on to win three golds at the 2010 Paralympics, but also because of challenges in his life resulting from legal blindness.

In every society, people build their everyday lives using the idea of **status**, *a social position that a person holds.* In everyday use, the word *status* generally means "prestige," as when we say that a university president has more "status" than a newly hired assistant professor. But sociologically speaking, both "president" and "professor" are two statuses, or positions, within the university organization.

Status is part of our social identity and helps define our relationship to others. As Georg Simmel (1950:307, orig. 1902), one of the founders of sociology, once pointed out, before we can deal with anyone, we need to know who the person is.

Status Set

Each of us holds many statuses at once. The term **status set** refers to *all the statuses a person holds at a given time.* A teenage girl may be a daughter to her parents, a sister to her brother, a student at her school, and a goalie on her soccer team.

Status sets change over the life course. A child grows up to become a parent, a student graduates to become a lawyer, and a single person marries to become a partner, sometimes becoming single again as a result of death or divorce. Joining an organization or finding a job enlarges our status set; withdrawing from activities makes it smaller. Over a lifetime, people gain and lose dozens of statuses.

status a social position that a person holds

ascribed status a social position a person receives at birth or takes on involuntarily later in life

achieved status a social position a person takes on voluntarily that reflects personal ability and effort

Ascribed and Achieved Status

Sociologists classify statuses in terms of how people attain them. An **ascribed status** is *a social position a person receives at birth or takes on involuntarily later in life.* Examples of ascribed statuses include being a daughter, a Cuban, an Aboriginal, or a widower. Ascribed statuses are matters about which we have little or no choice.

By contrast, an **achieved status** refers to *a social position a person takes on voluntarily that reflects personal ability and effort.* Achieved statuses in Canada include being an honour student, NHL hockey player, nurse, software writer, or drug dealer.

In the real world, of course, most statuses involve a combination of ascription and achievement. That is, people's ascribed statuses influence the statuses they achieve. People who achieve the status of lawyer, for example, are likely to share the ascribed benefit of being born into relatively

Thinking About Diversity: Race, Class, and Gender

Physical Disability as a Master Status

Physical disability works in much the same ways as class, gender, or race in defining people in the eyes of others. In the following interviews, two women explain how a physical disability can become a master status—a trait that overshadows everything else about them. The first voice is that of 29-year-old Donna Finch, who lives with her husband and son and holds a master's degree in social work. She is also blind.

Most people don't expect handicapped people to grow up; they are always supposed to be children. . . . You aren't supposed to date, you aren't supposed to have a job, somehow you're just supposed to disappear. I'm not saying this is true of anyone else, but in my own case I think I was more intellectually mature than most children, and more emotionally immature. I'd say that not until the last four or five years have I felt really whole.

Modern technology means that most soldiers who lose limbs in war now survive. How do you think the loss of an arm or a leg affects a person's social identity and sense of self?

Michael Hanson/Getty Images

Rose Helman is an elderly woman who has recently retired. She suffers from spinal meningitis and is also blind.

You ask me if people are really different today than in the '20s and '30s. Not too much. They are still fearful of the handicapped. I don't know if fearful is the right word, but uncomfortable at least. But I can understand it somewhat; it happened to me. I once asked a man to tell me which staircase to use to get from the subway out to the street. He started giving me directions that were confusing, and I said, "Do you mind taking me?" He said, "Not at all." He grabbed me on the side with my dog on it, so I asked him to take my other arm. And he said, "I'm sorry, I have no other arm." And I said, "That's all right, I'll hold onto the jacket." It felt funny hanging onto the sleeve without the arm in it.

Some stigmatized individuals manage their identity through acts of resistance; that is, they "artfully dodge or constructively challenge stigmatizing processes" (Link & Phelan, 2001:378). The Canadian Federation of the Blind, a voluntary organization whose members work to fight the social and economic inequality of blind people in Canada, has developed a variety of strategies to educate the general public and employers about the societal barriers to attaining meaningful employment for legally blind adults and to assist governments to develop social policies to rectify the problem (McCreath, 2011).

What Do You Think?

1. Have you ever had an illness or disability that became a master status? If so, how did others react?

2. How might such a master status affect someone's personality?

3. Can being very fat or very thin serve as a master status? Why or why not?

4. What are some factors that may increase success in resisting a negative master status?

Source: Based on Orlansky and Heward (1981).

well-off families. By the same token, many less desirable statuses, such as homeless person, drug addict, or unemployed worker, are more easily achieved by people who were born into poverty.

Master Status

Some statuses matter more than others. A **master status** is *a status that has special importance for social identity, often shaping a person's entire life*. For most people, a job is a master status because it reveals a great deal about a person's social background, education, and income. In a few cases, a person's name is a master status; being an Eaton, a Trudeau, or a Bronfman is enough by itself to push an individual into the Canadian limelight.

A master status can be negative as well as positive. Take, for example, serious illness. Sometimes people, even long-time friends, avoid cancer patients or people with AIDS because of their illnesses (Nancarrow Clarke & Nancarrow Clarke, 1999; Flowers et al., 2006). As another example, the fact that all societies limit the opportunities of women makes gender a master status, especially when it intersects with sexual transmitted infections and other chronic illnesses (Nack, 2002).

Sometimes a physical disability serves as a master status to the point where we dehumanize people by seeing them only in terms of their disability (Darling & Bryant, 2001; Nosek, Hughes, Swedlund, Taylor, & Swank, 2003; Taub, McLorg, & Fanflik, 2004). The Thinking About Diversity box shows how.

status set all the statuses a person holds at a given time

master status a status that has special importance for social identity, often shaping a person's entire life

Role

(**4.3**) State the importance of role to social organization.

A second important social structure is **role**, *behaviour expected of someone who holds a particular status*. A person *holds* a status and *performs* a role (Linton, 1937). For example, holding the status of student leads you to perform the role of attending classes.

Both statuses and roles vary by culture. In Canada, the status of "uncle" refers to the brother of a mother or a father; in Vietnam and Sweden, however, the word for "uncle" is different on the mother's and father's sides of the family, and the two men have different responsibilities. In every society, actual role performance varies with an individual's unique personality, and some societies, such as Canada, permit more individual expression of a role than others.

role behaviour expected of someone who holds a particular status

role set a number of roles attached to a single status

Role Set

Because we hold many statuses at once in our status set, and because a single status generates multiple roles, everyday life is a mix of many roles. Robert Merton (1968) introduced the term **role set** to identify *a number of roles attached to a single status*. Consider, for example, how the status of a student consists of a specific role set. As a student you attend classes, but chances are you also carry out research to complete assignments, take part in study groups, and possibly participate in student organized social events.

Figure 4–1 shows four statuses of one person, each status linked to a different role set. First, as a professor, this woman interacts with students (the teacher role) and with other academics (the colleague role). Second, in her work as a researcher, she gathers and analyzes data (the fieldwork role) that she uses in her publications (the author role). Third, the woman occupies the status of "wife," with a marital role (such as confidante and sexual partner) toward her spouse, with whom she shares household duties (domestic role). Fourth, she holds the status of "mother," with routine responsibilities for her children (the maternal role), as well as toward their school and other organizations in her community (the civic role).

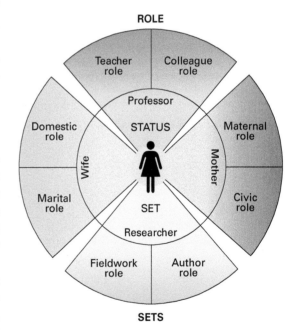

FIGURE 4–1 Status Set and Role Sets

A status set includes all the statuses a person holds at a given time. The status set defines *who we are* in society. The many roles linked to each status define *what we do*.

Source: North Wind Picture Archives.

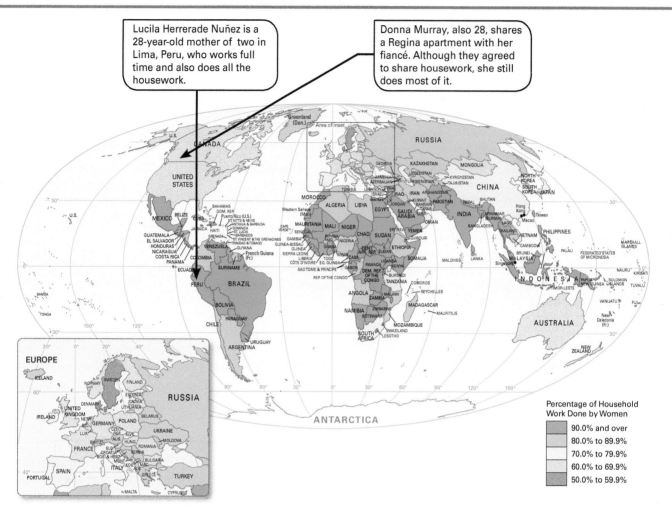

Lucila Herrerade Nuñez is a 28-year-old mother of two in Lima, Peru, who works full time and also does all the housework.

Donna Murray, also 28, shares a Regina apartment with her fiancé. Although they agreed to share housework, she still does most of it.

Percentage of Household Work Done by Women

- 90.0% and over
- 80.0% to 89.9%
- 70.0% to 79.9%
- 60.0% to 69.9%
- 50.0% to 59.9%

GLOBAL MAP 4–1   Housework in Global Perspective

Throughout the world, housework is a major part of women's routines and identities. This is especially true in low- and middle-income societies of Latin America, Africa, and Asia, where women's work does not generally bring in a wage or salary. But our society also defines housework and child care as "feminine" activities, even though a majority of Canadian women work in the paid economy.

Source: United Nations (2010).

A global perspective shows that the roles people use to define their lives differ from society to society. In low-income countries, people spend fewer years as students, and family roles are often very important to social identity. In high-income nations, people spend more years as students, and family roles are typically less important to social identity. Another dimension of difference involves housework. As Global Map 4–1 shows, especially in poor countries, housework falls heavily on women.

Role Conflict and Role Strain

People in modern, high-income nations juggle many responsibilities demanded by their various statuses and roles. As most new parents can testify, the combination of parenting and working outside the home is physically and emotionally draining (Fox, 2009). Sociologists thus recognize **role conflict** as *conflict among the roles connected to two or more statuses.*

We experience role conflict when we find ourselves pulled in various directions as we try to respond to the many statuses we hold. One response to role conflict is deciding that "something has to go." More than one politician, for example, has decided not to run for office because of the conflicting demands of a hectic campaign schedule and family life. In other cases, people put off having children in order to stay on the "fast track" for career success.

role conflict conflict among the roles connected to two or more statuses

role strain tension among the roles connected to a single status

Even roles linked to a single status may make competing demands on us. **Role strain** refers to *tension among the roles connected to a single status.* A university professor may enjoy being friendly with students. At the same time, however, the professor must maintain the personal distance needed to evaluate students fairly. In short, performing the various roles attached to even one single status can be something of a balancing act.

One strategy for minimizing role conflict is separating parts of our lives so that we perform roles for one status at one time and place and carry out roles connected to another status in a completely different setting (Nippert-Eng, 1995). A familiar example of this is deciding to "leave the job at work" before heading home to the family or, perhaps more relevant for Canadian women these days, "leaving the family at home" while at their job (McDaniel, 2002).

Current research (Wallace, 2013) suggests that when it comes to practising law in Western Canada, role strain encountered in interactions with other members of the profession is the strongest predictor of lawyers' well-being and career commitment.

Role Exit

After she left the life of a Catholic nun to become a university sociologist, Helen Rose Fuchs Ebaugh began to study her own experience of *role exit*, the process by which people disengage from important social roles. Studying a range of "exes," including ex-nuns, ex-doctors, ex-husbands, and ex-alcoholics, Ebaugh identified elements common to the process of becoming an "ex."

According to Ebaugh (1988), the process begins as people come to doubt their ability to continue in a certain role. As they imagine alternative roles, they ultimately reach a tipping point when they decide to pursue a new life. Even as they were moving on, however, a past role can continue to influence their lives. Exes carry with them a self-image shaped by an earlier role, which can interfere with building a new sense of self. For example, an ex-nun may hesitate to wear stylish clothing and makeup.

Exes must also rebuild relationships with people who knew them in their earlier life. Learning new social skills is another challenge. For example, Ebaugh reports, ex-nuns who enter the dating scene after decades in the church are often surprised to learn that sexual norms are very different from those they knew when they were teenagers. Exiting a role is made more complicated if that role is seen by society as deviant, such as the role of sex worker. Saunders (2007) argues that national policies that reinforce "exiting" through compulsory rehabilitation and the criminalization of sex work make leaving the role very difficult for those involved.

The Social Construction of Reality

(4.4) Describe how we socially construct reality.

In 1917, the Italian playwright Luigi Pirandello wrote a play called *The Pleasure of Honesty* about a character named Angelo Baldovino, a brilliant man with a checkered past. Baldovino enters the fashionable home of the Renni family and introduces himself in a peculiar way:

> Inevitably we construct ourselves. Let me explain. I enter this house and immediately I become what I have to become, what I can become: I construct myself. That is, I present myself to you in a form suitable to the relationship I wish to achieve with you. And, of course, you do the same with me. (1962:157–58)

Baldovino suggests that although behaviour is guided by status and role, we have the ability to shape who we are and to guide what happens from moment to moment. In other words, "reality" is not as fixed as we may think.

The **social construction of reality** is *the process by which people creatively shape reality through social interaction.* This idea—introduced by sociologists Peter L. Berger and Thomas Luckmann—is the foundation of the symbolic-interaction approach, described in Chapter 1 ("Sociology: Perspective, Theory, and Method"). As Baldovino's remark suggests, quite a bit of "reality" remains unclear in everyone's mind, especially in unfamiliar situations. So we present ourselves in terms that suit the setting and our purposes, we try to guide what happens next, and as others do the same, reality takes shape. Social interaction, then, is a complex negotiation that builds reality (Berger & Luckmann, 1966). Most everyday situations involve at least some agreement about what's going on. But how people see events depends on their different backgrounds, interests, and intentions. One example of changing patterns in everyday interaction involves greeting another person.

"Street Smarts"

What people commonly call "street smarts" is actually a form of constructing reality. In his autobiography *Down These Mean Streets,* Piri Thomas recalls moving to an apartment in Spanish Harlem. Returning home one evening, young Piri found himself cut off by Waneko, the leader of the local street gang, who was flanked by a dozen others.

Flirting is an everyday experience in reality construction. Each person offers information to the other and hints at romantic interest. Yet the interaction proceeds with a tentative and often humorous air so that either individual can withdraw at any time without further obligation.

Goodshoot/Thinkstock/Getty Images

"Whatta ya say, Mr. Johnny Gringo," drawled Waneko.

Think man, I told myself, think your way out of a stomping. . . "I hear you 104th Street coolies are supposed to have heart," I said. "I don't know this for sure. You know there's a lot of streets where a whole 'click' is made out of punks who can't fight one guy unless they all jump him for the stomp." I hoped this would push Waneko into giving me a fair one. . .

"Maybe we don't look at it that way."

Crazy, man, I cheer inwardly. . . "I wasn't talking to you," I said. "Where I come from, the pres is president 'cause he got heart when it comes to dealing."

Waneko was starting to look uneasy. He had bit on my worm and felt like a sucker fish. His boys were now light on me. They were no longer so much interested in stomping me as seeing the outcome between Waneko and me. "Yeah," was his reply. . . .

I knew I'd won. Sure, I'd have to fight; but one guy, not ten or fifteen. . . I took care of this with my next sentence. "I don't know you or your boys," I said, "but they look cool to me. They don't feature as punks."

I had left him out purposely when I said "they." Now his boys were in a separate class. I had cut him off. . . He got away from the stoop and asked, "Fair one, Gringo?" (1967:56–57)

This situation reveals the drama—sometimes subtle, sometimes savage—by which human beings creatively build everyday reality. But, of course, not everyone enters a situation with equal standing. If a police officer had happened to drive by when Piri and Waneko were fighting, both young men might have ended up in jail.

The Thomas Theorem

By displaying his wits and fighting with Waneko until they both tired, Piri Thomas won acceptance by the gang. What took place that evening in Spanish Harlem is an example of the **Thomas theorem**, named after W. I. Thomas and Dorothy Thomas (1928; Thomas, 1966:301, orig. 1931): *Situations that are defined as real are real in their consequences.*

Applied to social interaction, the Thomas theorem means that although reality is initially "soft" as it is being shaped, it can become "hard" in its effects. In the case just described, local gang members saw Piri Thomas act in a worthy way, so in their eyes, he *became* worthy.

Ethnomethodology

Most of the time, we take social reality for granted. To become more aware of the social world we help create, Harold Garfinkel (1967) devised **ethnomethodology**, *the study of the way people make sense of their everyday surroundings.* This approach begins by pointing out that

People build reality from their surrounding culture. Yet because cultural systems are marked by diversity and even outright conflict, reality construction always involves tensions and choices. Turkey is a nation with a mostly Muslim population, but it has also embraced Western culture. Here, women confront starkly different definitions of what is "feminine."

everyday behaviour rests on a number of assumptions. When you ask someone the simple question "How are you?" you usually want to know how the person is doing in general, but you might really be wondering how the person is dealing with a specific physical, mental, spiritual, or financial challenge. In Canada, however, people tend to assume that others are not really interested in the details about these things. Upon arrival in Canada from Sweden, one of the authors soon learned that Canadians asked "How are you?" out of politeness, not because they wanted to listen to an honest answer of how he was feeling.

One good way to try to uncover the assumptions we make about everyday reality is to break the rules. For example, the next time someone greets you by saying, "How are you?" offer details from your last physical examination or explain all of the good and bad things that have happened since you woke up that morning and see how the person reacts.

The results are predictable, because we all have some idea of the "rules" of everyday interaction. The person will most likely become confused or irritated by your unexpected behaviour—a reaction that helps us see not only what the rules are but also how important they are to everyday reality.

Reality Building: Class and Culture

People do not build everyday experience out of thin air. In part, how we act or what we see in our surroundings depends on our interests. Gazing at the sky on a starry night, for example, lovers discover romance, and scientists see hydrogen atoms fusing into helium. Social background also affects what we see, which is why residents of Hull, Quebec, experience the world somewhat differently than people living across the river in Ottawa, Ontario.

With a global perspective reality construction varies even more. Consider these everyday situations: People waiting for a bus in London typically "queue up" in a straight line; people in Winnipeg, on the other hand, are rarely so orderly. The law in Saudi Arabia forbids women to drive cars, a ban unheard of in Canada. In this country, people assume that "a short walk" means a few blocks or a few minutes; in the Andes Mountains of Peru, this same phrase means travelling a few miles.

The point is that people build reality from the surrounding culture. Chapter 2 ("Culture") explains how people the world over find different meanings in specific gestures, so inexperienced travellers can find themselves building an unexpected and unwelcome reality. Similarly, in a study of popular culture, JoEllen Shively (1992) screened westerns—films set in the American West—to men of European descent and to Aboriginal men. The men in both categories claimed to enjoy the films, but for very different reasons. White men interpreted the films as praising rugged people striking out for the frontier and conquering the forces

In 2012, the Chinese government decided to require all students to take "patriotism" classes supporting the Chinese Communist Party. In an age of social media, the reaction was immediate as millions of students, linked by smartphone technology, mobilized against a plan they denounced as "brainwashing." Have you ever used social networking sites to engage in political action?

of nature. Aboriginal men saw in the same films a celebration of land and nature. Given their different cultures, it is as if people in the two categories saw two different films.

Films also have an effect on the reality we all experience. The 2010 film *My Name is Khan*, for example, about a Muslim man with Asperger syndrome, is one in a series of recent films that have changed people's awareness of the struggle of coping with mental disorders.

The Increasing Importance of Social Media

The social construction of reality has always involved face-to-face social interaction. In recent years, however, this process has also been aided by computer technology. The concept of **social media** refers to *technology that links people in social activity.* Although newspapers and other print media are older examples of social media, more recent computer technology is much more powerful because it connects a far larger number of people. In addition, computer-based technology is interactive, allowing individuals not only to receive messages but also to send information to others.

In the past, when people came together to form communities based on a common interest, they gathered in a single location. Even a generation ago, few people imagined the dramatic changes that computer technology would bring to the landscape of social interaction. Today, of course, most people in Canada and nations around the world participate in various online communities with countless others who share some interest. Participants may be anywhere in physical space, and they are people whom we may or may not ever meet in person.

The expansion of social media can be seen in the explosive increase in the public's use of social networking sites. Facebook, which began formal operation in 2004, now has some 1 billion members worldwide. Similarly, Twitter was launched in 2006 as a social networking and micro-blogging system that allows users to send and receive short text messages called "tweets." It now boasts some 175 million registered users.

Some sociologists have argued that the rise of social media has connected people in new ways but weakened social ties among people who share physical space. Take the case of two college roommates, each of whom might be interacting with thousands of other people while sitting just a few feet apart in the same dorm room, barely paying attention to each other. Much the same argument was made about the spread of telephone technology more than a century ago.

Like every major change in society, the rise of social media will spark controversy and debate. But there is little doubt that this trend is reshaping all aspects of everyday life from the way people engage in social movements to the way they look for romance (Farrell, 2012; Turkle, 2012).

social media technology that links people in social activity

Dramaturgical Analysis: The "Presentation of Self"

(4.5) Apply Goffman's analysis to several familiar situations.

dramaturgical analysis Erving Goffman's term for the study of social interaction in terms of theatrical performance

Erving Goffman (1922–1982) was another sociologist who analyzed social interaction, explaining that people live their lives much like actors performing on a stage. If we imagine ourselves as directors observing what goes on in the theatre of everyday life, we are doing what Goffman called **dramaturgical analysis**, *the study of social interaction in terms of theatrical performance.*

Dramaturgical analysis offers a fresh look at the concepts of status and role. A status is like a part in a play, and a role serves as a script, supplying dialogue and action for the characters. Goffman described each individual's "performance" as the **presentation of self**, *a person's efforts to create specific impressions in the minds of others.* This process, sometimes called *impression management*, begins with the idea of personal performance (Goffman, 1959, 1967).

presentation of self Erving Goffman's term for a person's efforts to create specific impressions in the minds of others

Performances

As we present ourselves in everyday situations, we reveal information to others both consciously and unconsciously. Our performance includes how we dress (in theatrical terms, our costume), the objects we carry (props), and our tone of voice and gestures (our demeanour). In addition, we vary our performance according to where we are (the set). We may joke loudly in a restaurant, for example, but lower our voice when entering a synagogue, mosque, or church. People design settings, such as homes, offices, and corner pubs, to bring about desired reactions in others.

An Application: The Doctor's Office

Consider how physicians set up their offices to convey particular information to an audience of patients. The fact that medical doctors enjoy high prestige and power in Canada is clear upon entering a doctor's office. First, the doctor is nowhere to be seen. Instead, in what Goffman describes as the "front region" of the setting, the patient encounters a receptionist, or gatekeeper, who decides whether and when the patient can meet the doctor. A simple glance around the doctor's waiting room, with patients (often impatiently) waiting to be invited into the inner sanctum, leaves little doubt that the doctor and the staff are in charge.

The "back region" is composed of the examination rooms plus the doctor's private office. Once inside the office, the patient can see a wide range of props, such as medical books and framed degrees, that give the impression that the doctor has the specialized knowledge necessary to call the shots. The doctor is usually seated behind a desk—the larger the desk, the greater the statement of power—and the patient is given only a chair.

The doctor's appearance and manner offer still more information. The white lab coat (costume) may have the practical function of keeping clothes from becoming dirty, but its social function is to let others know at a glance the physician's status. A stethoscope around the neck and a medical chart in hand (more props) have the same purpose. A doctor uses highly technical language that is often mystifying to the patient, again emphasizing that the doctor is in charge. Finally, patients use the title "doctor," but they, in turn, are often addressed by their first names, which further shows the doctor's dominant position. The overall message of a doctor's performance is clear: "I will help you, but you must allow me to take charge."

Nonverbal Communication

The novelist William Sansom describes a fictional Mr. Preedy, an English vacationer on a beach in Spain:

> He took care to avoid catching anyone's eye. First, he had to make it clear to those potential companions of his holiday that they were of no concern to him whatsoever. He stared through them, round them, over them—eyes lost in space. The beach might have been empty. If by chance a ball was thrown his way, he looked surprised; then let a smile of amusement light his face (Kindly Preedy), looked around dazed to see that there were people on the beach, tossed it back with a smile to himself and not a smile *at* the people. . . .
>
> [He] then gathered together his beach-wrap and bag into a neat sand-resistant pile (Methodical and Sensible Preedy), rose slowly to stretch his huge frame (Big-Cat Preedy), and tossed aside his sandals (Carefree Preedy, after all). (1956:230–31)

Without saying a single word, Mr. Preedy offers a great deal of information about himself to anyone watching him. This is the process of **nonverbal communication**, *communication using body movements, gestures, and facial expressions rather than speech.*

nonverbal communication communication using body movements, gestures, and facial expressions rather than speech

People use many parts of the body to convey information through *body language*. Facial expressions are the most important type of body language. Smiling, for instance, shows pleasure, although we distinguish among the deliberate smile of Kindly Preedy on the beach, a spontaneous smile of joy at seeing a friend, a pained smile of embarrassment after spilling a cup of coffee, and the full, unrestrained smile of self-satisfaction that we often associate with winning some important contest.

Eye contact is another key element of nonverbal communication. Generally, we use eye contact to invite social interaction. Someone across the room "catches our eye," sparking a conversation. Avoiding another's eyes, by contrast, discourages communication. Hands, too, speak for us. Common hand gestures in our society convey, among other things, an insult, a request for a ride, an invitation for someone to join us, or a demand that others stop in their tracks. Gestures also supplement spoken words. For example, pointing at someone in a threatening way gives greater emphasis to a word of warning, just as shrugging the shoulders adds an air of indifference to the phrase "I don't know" and rapidly waving the arms adds urgency to the single word "Hurry!"

In everyday interaction, body language is an important way in which we transmit information to an audience as well as "read" information in the behaviour of others. To people who have limited skills in the spoken language used by those around them, body language takes on special importance. Similarly, to people who have a physical impairment—perhaps older people who have lost some of their ability to hear—"reading" body language can enhance understanding (Stepanikova et al., 2011).

Body Language and Deception

As any actor knows, it is very difficult to pull off a perfect performance in front of others. In everyday interaction, unintended body language can contradict our planned meaning: A teenage boy offers an explanation for getting home late, for example, but his mother begins to doubt his words because he avoids looking her in the eye. The teenage celebrity on a television talk show claims that her recent musical flop is "no big deal," but the nervous swing of her leg suggests otherwise. Because nonverbal communication is hard to control, it offers clues to deception in much the same way that changes in breathing, pulse rate, perspiration, and blood pressure recorded on a lie detector indicate that a person is lying.

Recognizing dishonest performances is difficult because no single bodily gesture tells us for sure that someone is lying. But because any performance involves so much body language, few people can engage in deception (especially when they feel a strong emotion) without some slip-up or "leaking" information that raises the suspicions of a careful observer. The key to detecting lies is to view the whole performance with an eye for inconsistencies.

 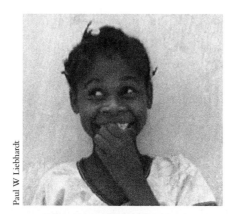 

Paul W Liebhardt

Hand gestures vary widely from one culture to another. Yet people everywhere chuckle, grin, or smirk to indicate that they don't take another person's performance seriously. Therefore, the world over, people who cannot restrain their mirth tactfully cover their faces.

Gender and Performances

Compared to men, women are more likely to be socialized to respond to others, and thus they tend to be more sensitive than men to nonverbal communication (Butler, 1997; van Sterkenburg & Knoppers, 2004). Research suggests that women "read" men better than men "read" women (Farris et al., 2008). Gender is also one of the key elements in the presentation of self, as the following sections explain.

Demeanour

Demeanour—the way we act and carry ourselves—is a clue to social power. Simply put, powerful people enjoy more personal freedom in how they act. At the office, off-colour remarks, swearing, or putting your feet on the desk may be acceptable for the boss but rarely, if ever, for employees. Similarly, powerful people can interrupt others; but less powerful people are expected to show respect through silence (Smith-Lovin & Brody, 1989; Henley, Hamilton, & Thorne, 1992; C. Johnson, 1994).

Because women generally occupy positions of lesser power, demeanour is a gender issue as well. As Chapter 10 ("Gender Stratification") explains, more than 50 percent of all employed women in Canada are employed in a small number of "feminine" occupations— teaching, nursing, health-related occupations, and clerical service work—all of which are under the control of supervisors (in many cases, males). Women, then, learn to craft their personal performances more carefully than men and defer to men more often in everyday interaction.

Use of Space

How much space does a personal performance require? Our culture has traditionally measured femininity by how *little* space women occupy—the standard of "daintiness"—and masculinity by how *much* territory a man controls—the standard of "turf" (Henley, Hamilton, & Thorne, 1992). The next time you use public transportation or are at a movie, observe how men and women are sitting. Males typically spread their legs while sitting or casually stretch out an arm over the back of the seat, while females are more likely to cross their legs and keep their arms close to their bodies. Why? Power plays a key role here; the more power you have, the more space you use. Compared with men, women are more likely to craft their personal performances during leisure time as well as while performing their jobs.

For both sexes, the concept of **personal space** refers to *the surrounding area over which a person makes some claim to privacy*. In Canada and the United States, people typically position themselves about a metre apart when speaking; throughout the Middle East, by contrast, people stand much closer. Just about everywhere, men (with their greater social power) often intrude into women's personal space. If a woman moves into a man's personal space, however, he is likely to take it as a sign of sexual interest.

personal space the surrounding area over which a person makes some claim to privacy

Staring, Smiling, and Touching

Eye contact encourages interaction. In conversations, women hold eye contact more than men. But men have their own brand of eye contact: staring. When men stare at women, they are claiming social dominance and defining women as sexual objects.

Although it often shows pleasure, smiling can also be a sign of trying to please someone or of submission. In a male-dominated world, it is not surprising that women smile more than men (Henley, Hamilton, & Thorne, 1992).

Finally, mutual touching suggests intimacy and caring. Apart from close relationships, touching is generally something men do to women (but less often, in our culture, to other men, though this may be changing). A male physician touches the shoulder of his female nurse as they examine a report, a young man touches the back of his woman friend as he guides her across the street, or a male tennis instructor touches the arms of young women as he teaches them to hit a serve. In such examples, the intent of the touching may be harmless and may bring little response, but it amounts to a subtle ritual by which men claim dominance over women.

Idealization

People behave the way they do for many, often complex reasons. Even so, Goffman suggests, we construct performances to *idealize* our intentions. That is, we try to convince others (and perhaps ourselves) that what we do reflects ideal cultural standards rather than selfish motives.

Idealization is easily illustrated by returning to the world of doctors and patients. In a hospital, doctors engage in a performance commonly described as "making rounds." Entering the room of a patient, the doctor often stops at the foot of the bed and silently reads the patient's chart. Afterwards, doctor and patient talk briefly. In ideal terms, this routine involves a doctor making a personal visit to check on a patient's condition.

In reality, the picture is not so perfect. A doctor may see several dozen patients a day and remember little about many of them. Reading the chart is a chance to recall the patient's name and medical problems, but revealing the impersonality of medical care would undermine the cultural ideal of the doctor as deeply concerned about the welfare of others.

Doctors, professors, and other professionals typically idealize their motives for entering their chosen careers. They describe their work as "making a contribution to science," "helping others," "serving the community," and even "answering a call from God." Rarely do they admit the more common, less honourable motives: the income, power, prestige, and leisure time that these occupations provide.

We all use idealization to some degree. When was the last time you smiled and spoke politely to someone you do not like? Have you acted interested in a class that you found boring? Such little lies in our performances help us get through everyday life. Even when we suspect that others are putting on an act, we are unlikely to challenge their performances for reasons that we shall examine next.

Embarrassment and Tact

The famous speaker giving a campus lecture keeps mispronouncing the university's name; the head coach rises to speak at the team's end-of-season banquet unaware of the napkin still tucked in her dress; the student enters the lecture hall late and soaking wet, attracting the gaze of hundreds of classmates. As carefully as individuals may try to craft their performances, slip-ups of all kinds occur. The result is *embarrassment*, or discomfort following a spoiled performance. Goffman describes embarrassment as "losing face."

Embarrassment is an ever-present danger because idealized performances usually contain some deception. In addition, most performances involve juggling so many elements that one thoughtless moment can shatter the intended impression.

A curious fact is that an audience often overlooks flaws in a performance, allowing the actor to avoid embarrassment. If we do point out a misstep ("Excuse me, but your fly is open"), we do it quietly and only to help someone avoid even greater loss of face. In Hans Christian Andersen's classic fable "The Emperor's New Clothes," the child who blurts out the truth, that the emperor is parading about naked, is scolded for being rude.

Often members of an audience actually help the performer recover from a flawed performance. *Tact* is helping someone "save face." After hearing a supposed expert make an

To most people in Canada, these expressions convey anger, fear, disgust, happiness, surprise, and sadness. But do people elsewhere in the world define them in the same way? Research suggests that all human beings experience the same basic emotions and display them to others in the same basic ways. But culture plays a part by specifying the situations that trigger one emotion or another.

embarrassingly inaccurate remark, for example, tactful people may ignore the comment, as if it had never been spoken, or react with mild laughter, treating what was said as a joke. Or they may simply respond, "I'm sure you didn't mean that," an indication that someone heard the statement but will not allow it to destroy the actor's performance.

Why is tact so common? Because embarrassment creates discomfort not just for the actor but also for everyone else as well. Just as a theatre audience feels uneasy when an actor forgets a line, people who observe the awkward behaviour are reminded of how fragile their own performances often are. Socially constructed reality thus functions like a dam holding back a sea of chaos. When one person's performance springs a leak, others tactfully help make repairs. Everyone lends a hand in building reality, and no one wants it suddenly swept away.

In sum, Goffman's research shows that although behaviour is spontaneous in some respects, it is more patterned than we like to think. Four centuries ago, William Shakespeare captured this idea in lines that still ring true:

> All the world's a stage,
> And all the men and women merely players:
> They have their exits and their entrances;
> And one man in his time plays many parts.
> (*As You Like It*, act 2, scene 7)

Interaction in Everyday Life: Three Applications

4.6 Construct a sociological analysis of three aspects of everyday life: emotions, language, and humour.

The final sections of this chapter illustrate the major elements of social interaction by focusing on three dimensions of everyday life: emotions, language, and humour.

Emotions: The Social Construction of Feeling

Emotions, more commonly called *feelings*, are an important element of human social life. Indeed, what we *do* often matters less than how we *feel* about it. Emotions seem very personal because they are "inside." Even so, just as society guides our behaviour, it guides our emotional life.

The Biological Side of Emotions

Studying people all over the world, Paul Ekman (1980a, 1980b) reports that people everywhere express six basic emotions: happiness, sadness, anger, fear, disgust, and surprise. In addition, Ekman found that people in every society use much the same facial expressions to show these emotions. Ekman believes that some emotional responses are "wired" into human beings; that is, they are biologically programmed in our facial features, muscles, and central nervous system.

Why might this be so? Over centuries of evolution, emotions developed in the human species because they serve a social purpose: supporting group life. Emotions are powerful forces that allow us to overcome our self-centredness and build connections with others. Thus the capacity for emotion arose in our ancestors along with the capacity for culture (Turner, 2000).

The Cultural Side of Emotions

But culture does play an important role in guiding human emotions. First, Ekman explains, culture defines *what triggers* an emotion. Whether people define the departure of an old friend as joyous (causing happiness), insulting (arousing anger), a loss (producing sadness), or mystical (provoking surprise and awe) has a lot to do with the culture. Second, culture provides rules for the *display* of emotions. For example, most people in Canada express emotions more freely with

Controversy & Debate

Managing Feelings: Women's Abortion Experiences

Liz: I just *can't* be pregnant! I'm going to see my doctor tomorrow about an abortion. There's no way I can deal with a baby at this point in my life!

Jen: I can't believe you'd do that, Liz! How are you going to feel a few years from now when you think about what that *child* would be doing if you'd let it live?

Few issues today generate as much emotion as abortion. In a study of women's abortion experiences, the sociologist Jennifer Keys (2010) discovered emotional scripts or "feeling rules" that guided how women feel about ending a pregnancy.

Keys explains that different emotional scripts arise from the political controversy surrounding abortion. The anti-abortion movement defines abortion as a personal tragedy, the "killing of an unborn child." Given this definition, women who terminate a pregnancy through abortion are doing something morally wrong and can expect to feel grief, guilt, and regret. So intense are these feelings, according to supporters of this position, that such women often suffer from "post-abortion syndrome."

Those who take the pro-choice position have an opposing view of abortion. From this point of view, the woman's problem is the *unwanted pregnancy*; abortion is an acceptable medical solution. Therefore, the emotion common to women who terminate a pregnancy should be not guilt but relief.

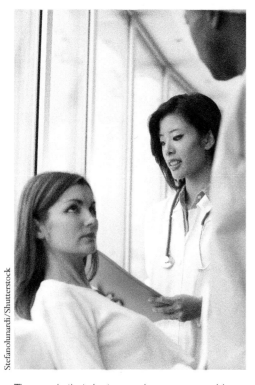

The words that doctors and nurses use guide whether a woman having an abortion defines the experience in positive or negative terms.

In her research, Keys conducted in-depth interviews with 40 women who had recently had abortions and found that all of them used such scripts to "frame" their situation in an anti-abortion or pro-choice manner. In part, this construction of reality reflects the woman's own attitude about abortion. In addition, however, women's partners and friends typically encouraged specific feelings about the event. Ivy, one young woman in the study, had a close friend who was also pregnant. "Congratulations!" she exclaimed when she learned of Ivy's condition. "We're going to be having babies together!" Such a statement established one "feeling rule"—having a baby is *good*—which sent the message to Ivy that her planned abortion should trigger guilt. Working in the other direction, Jo's partner was horrified by the news that she was pregnant. Doubting his own ability to be a father, he blurted out, "I would rather put a gun to my head than have this baby!" His panic not only defined having the child as a mistake but alarmed Jo as well. Clearly, her partner's reaction made the decision to end the pregnancy a matter of relief from a terrible problem.

Medical personnel also play a part in this process of reality construction by using specific terms. Nurses and doctors who talk about "the baby" encourage the anti-abortion framing of abortion and provoke grief and guilt. On the other hand, those who use language such as "pregnancy tissue," "fetus," or "the contents of the uterus" encourage the pro-choice framing of abortion as a fairly routine medical procedure leading to relief. Olivia began using the phrase "products of conception," which she picked up from her doctor. Denise spoke of her procedure as "taking the extra cells out of my body. Yeah, I did feel some guilt when I thought that this was the beginning of life, but my body is full of life—you have lots of cells in you."

After undergoing the procedure, most women reported actively trying to manage their feelings. Explained Ivy, "I never used the word 'baby.' I kept saying to myself that it was not formed yet. There was nothing there yet. I kept that in my mind." On the other hand, Keys found that all of the women in her study who leaned toward the anti-abortion position did use the term "baby." Gina explained, "I do think of it as a baby. The truth is that I ended my baby's life.... Thinking that makes me feel guilty. But—considering what I did—maybe I *should* feel guilty." Believing that what she had done was wrong, in other words, Gina actively called out the feeling of guilt—in part, Keys concluded, to punish herself.

What Do You Think?

1. In your own words, explain "emotional scripts" or "feeling rules."

2. Can you apply the idea of "feeling rules" to the experience of getting married?

3. In light of this discussion, how accurate is it to say that our feelings are not as personal as we may think they are?

Source: Keys (2010).

family members than with colleagues in the workplace. Similarly, we expect children to express emotions to parents, but parents tend to hide their emotions from their children. Third, culture guides how we *value* emotions. Some societies encourage the expression of emotion; others expect members to control their feelings and maintain a "stiff upper lip." Gender also plays a part; traditionally, at least, many cultures expect women to show emotions, but they discourage emotional expression by men as a sign of weakness. In some cultures, of course, this pattern is less pronounced or even reversed (Brody, 1999; Lee, 1999).

Emotions on the Job

In Canada, most people are freer to express their feelings at home than on the job. The reason, as sociologist Arlie Russell Hochschild (1979, 1983) explains, is that the typical corporation or other place of business does indeed try to control not only the behaviour of its employees but also their emotions. Hochschild used the term **emotional labour** to refer to *suppressed or induced feelings produced by an employee in accordance with the rules of an organization*. Take the case of an airline flight attendant who offers passengers a drink, a snack, and a smile. Do you think that this smile might convey real pleasure at serving the customer? It may. But Hochschild's study of flight attendants points to a different conclusion: The smile is a form of emotional labour demanded by the airline as the right way to do the job. Therefore, from Hochschild's research we see an added dimension of the "presentation of self" described by Erving Goffman. Not only do our everyday life presentations to others involve surface acting but they also involve the "deep acting" of emotions.

With these patterns in mind, it is easy to see that we socially construct our emotions as part of our everyday reality, a process sociologists call *emotion management*. The Controversy & Debate box on page 124 links the emotions displayed by women who decide to have an abortion to their political views and to their personal view of terminating a pregnancy.

Digital Vision/Thinkstock/Getty Images

Many of us think emotions are simply part of our biological makeup. While there is a biological foundation to human emotion, sociologists have demonstrated that what triggers an emotion—as well as when, where, and to whom the emotion is displayed—is shaped by culture. For example, many occupations not only regulate a worker's on-the-job behaviour but also expect workers to display a particular emotion, as in the case of the always-smiling airline flight attendant. Can you think of other jobs that regulate emotions in this way?

emotional labour suppressed or induced feelings produced by an employee in accordance with the rules of an organization

Language: The Social Construction of Gender

As Chapter 2 ("Culture") explains, language is the thread that weaves members of a society in the symbolic web we call culture. Language communicates not only a surface reality but also deeper levels of meaning. One such level involves gender. Language defines men and women differently in terms of both power and value (Thorne, Kramarae, & Henley, 1983; Henley, Hamilton, & Thorne, 1992).

Language and Power

A young man proudly rides his new motorcycle up his friend's driveway and boasts, "Isn't she a beauty?" On the surface, the question has little to do with gender. Yet why does he use the pronoun *she* instead of *he* or *it* to refer to his prized possession?

The answer is that language helps men establish control over their surroundings. A man attaches a female pronoun to a motorcycle (or car, boat, or other object) because it reflects the power of *ownership*. Perhaps this is also why, in Canada and elsewhere, a woman who marries traditionally takes the last name of her husband. But many women today are asserting their independence by keeping their own name or combining the two family names. Thus, language and power shape, and are in turn shaped by, the social context (Bourdieu, 1993).

Language and Value

Typically, the English language treats as masculine whatever has greater value, force, or significance. For instance, the adjective *virtuous*, meaning "morally worthy" or "excellent," comes

Most of us have had the unpleasant experience of being "chewed out" at work for doing something that displeased the boss. Do you think women and men in positions of power can show anger with the same response from an audience? In other words, do we tolerate more of this type of emotional expression from managers of one sex than the other?

from the Latin word *vir*, meaning "man." On the other hand, the adjective *hysterical*, meaning "emotionally out of control," comes from the Greek word *hystera*, meaning "uterus."

In many familiar ways, language also confers different value on the two sexes. Traditional masculine terms such as *king* and *lord* have a positive meaning, while comparable terms, such as *queen*, *madam*, or *dame*, can have negative meanings. Similarly, use of the suffixes *-ess* and *-ette* to denote femininity usually devalues the words to which they are added. For example, a *major* has higher standing than a *majorette*, as does a *host* in relation to a *hostess* or a *master* in relation to a *mistress*. Language both mirrors social attitudes and helps perpetuate them.

Given the importance of gender in everyday life, perhaps we should not be surprised that women and men sometimes have trouble communicating with each other. In fact, some people comment, with more than a little seriousness, that the two sexes often seem to be speaking different languages.

Because humour involves challenging established social conventions, comedians have typically been "outsiders" of some sort. Rick Mercer, originally from "The Rock" (Newfoundland and Labrador), is among the many comics starring on radio and television who use their cultural roots to poke fun at themselves and their audiences. Mercer's *Talking to Americans* shows that some people have a need to speak even when they don't understand the question.

Reality Play: The Social Construction of Humour

Humour plays an important part in everyday life. Everyone laughs at a joke, but few people think about what makes something funny.

We can apply many of the ideas developed in this chapter to explain how, when we use humour, we "play with reality" (Macionis, 1987).

The Foundation of Humour

Humour is produced by the social construction of reality; it arises as people create and contrast two different realities. Generally, one reality is *conventional*, that is, what culture leads people to expect in a specific situation. The other reality is *unconventional*, an unexpected violation of cultural patterns. Humour arises from the contradictions, ambiguities, and double meanings found in differing definitions of the same situation.

Note how this principle works in one of Woody Allen's lines: "I'm not afraid to die; I just don't want to be there when it happens." Or take the old Slavic folk saying: "All mushrooms are edible—but some only once." In these examples, the first thought represents a conventional notion; the second half, however, interjects an unconventional—even absurd—meaning that collides with what we are led to expect.

This same pattern holds true for virtually all humour. Rick Mercer's New Year's resolution to "not stop drinking altogether but to explore light beer as a lunchtime beverage" ends up being not much of a resolution after all.

There are countless ways to mix realities and generate humour. Reality play can be found in single statements that contradict themselves, such as "Nostalgia is not what it used to be"; statements that repeat themselves, such as Yogi Berra's line "It's *déjà vu* all over again"; or statements that mix up words, such as Oscar Wilde's line "Work is the curse of the drinking class." Even switching around syllables does the trick, as in the case of the country song "I'd Rather Have a Bottle in Front of Me than a Frontal Lobotomy."

You can also build a joke the other way around, leading the audience to expect an unconventional answer and then delivering a very ordinary one. When a reporter asked the famous gangster Willy Sutton why he continued to rob banks, for example, he replied dryly, "Because that's where the money is." Regardless of how a joke is constructed, the greater the opposition or difference that is created between the two definitions of reality, the greater is the humour that results.

The Dynamics of Humour: "Getting It"

After hearing a joke, did you ever say, "I don't get it"? To "get" humour, members of an audience must understand both the conventional and the unconventional realities involved well enough to appreciate their difference. A comedian may make getting a joke harder by leaving out some important information. In such cases, listeners must pay attention to the *stated* elements of the joke and then fill in the missing pieces on their own. As a simple case, consider Rick Mercer's comment on the New Democratic Party (NDP) in Canada: "I wanted to work in a political campaign and went with them because, essentially, they'd take anyone." Here, "getting" the joke depends on realizing that the NDP had a marginal status in Canada and was therefore not attractive to many volunteers. Or take one of W.C. Fields's lines: "Some weasel took the cork out of my lunch!" "What a lunch!" we think to ourselves to "finish" the joke.

Here is an even more complex joke: What do you get if you cross an insomniac, an agnostic, and a dyslexic? Answer: A person who stays up all night wondering if there is a dog. To get this one, you need a good bit of information: You must know that insomnia is an inability to sleep, that an agnostic doubts the existence of God, and that dyslexia causes a person to reverse the letters in words.

Why would a comedian want the audience to make this sort of effort to understand a joke? Our enjoyment of a joke is increased by the pleasure of figuring out for ourselves all the pieces needed to "get it." In addition, getting the joke makes you an "insider" compared to those who don't get it. We have all experienced the frustration of not getting a joke: fear of being judged stupid, along with a sense of being excluded from a pleasure shared by others. Sometimes someone may tactfully explain the joke so that the other person doesn't feel left out. But as the old saying goes, if a joke has to be explained, it isn't very funny.

The Topics of Humour

All over the world, people smile and laugh, making humour a universal element of human culture. But because the world's people live in different cultures, humour rarely travels well.

 October 1, Kobe, Japan. Is it possible to share a joke with people who live halfway around the world? At dinner, I ask two Japanese college women to tell me a joke. "You know 'crayon'?" Asako asks. I nod. "How do you ask for a crayon in Japanese?" I respond that I have no idea. She laughs out loud as she says what sounds like "crayon crayon." Her companion

Mayumi laughs too. My wife and I sit awkwardly, with a quizzical look on our faces. Asako relieves some of our embarrassment by explaining that the Japanese word for "give me" is kureyo, which sounds like "crayon." I force a smile.

What is humorous to the Japanese may be lost on the Finns, Iraqis, or Canadians. Even the social diversity in our society means that different types of people will find humour in different situations. People in Atlantic Canada and the Prairies have their own brands of humour, as do the French and English, 15- and 40-year-olds, investment bankers and construction workers. Aboriginal people and those from visible minority groups also make jokes that get back at people in more advantaged positions.

But for everyone, topics that lend themselves to double meanings or controversy generate humour. In Canada, the first jokes many of us learned as children concerned bodily functions kids are not supposed to talk about. The mere mention of "unmentionable acts" or even certain parts of the body can dissolve young faces in laughter.

Are there jokes that do break through the culture barrier? Yes, but they must touch on universal human experiences such as, say, turning on a friend:

I think of a number of jokes, but none seems likely to work. Understanding jokes is difficult for people who know little of our culture. Is there something more universal? Inspiration: "Two fellows are walking in the woods and come upon a huge bear. One guy leans over and tightens up the laces on his running shoes. 'Jake,' says the other, 'what are you doing? You can't outrun that bear!' 'I don't have to outrun the bear,' responds Jake. 'All I have to do is outrun you!'" Smiles all around.

Humour often walks a fine line between what is funny and what is "sick" or offensive. During the Middle Ages, people used the word *humours* (derived from the Latin *humidus*, meaning "moist") to refer to the various bodily fluids believed to regulate a person's health. Researchers today document the power of humour to reduce stress and improve health. One recent study of cancer patients, for example, found that the greater people's sense of humour, the greater the odds of surviving the disease. Such findings confirm the old saying that "laughter is the best medicine" (Bakalar, 2005; Sven Svebak, cited in M. Elias, 2007). At the extreme, however, people who always take conventional reality lightly risk being defined as deviant or even mentally ill (a common stereotype shows insane people laughing uncontrollably, and for a long time mental hospitals were known as "funny farms").

Then, too, every social group considers certain topics too sensitive for humorous treatment, and joking about them risks criticism for having a "sick" sense of humour (and being labelled "sick" yourself). People's religious beliefs, tragic accidents, or appalling crimes are some of the topics of sick jokes or no jokes at all.

The Functions of Humour

Humour is found everywhere because it works as a safety valve for potentially disruptive statements. Put another way, humour provides an acceptable way to discuss a sensitive topic without appearing to be serious or offending anyone. Having said something controversial, people often use humour to defuse the situation by simply stating, "I didn't mean anything by what I said—it was just a joke!"

People also use humour to relieve tension in uncomfortable situations. One study of medical examinations found that most patients try to joke with doctors to ease their own nervousness (Baker et al., 1997).

Dave Thomas and Rick Moranis portrayed the stereotypical Canadian hosers Bob and Doug McKenzie in a skit that premiered on *SCTV* in 1980. The comedy is based in making fun of ourselves. But do you think that we would find the same skit funny if it was on an American show with American actors? When people in a category (especially those who have historically been dominant) make fun of people in another category, their humour can easily seem like a "put-down."

Humour and Conflict

Humour may be a source of pleasure, but it can also be used to put down other people. Men who tell jokes about women, for example, are typically expressing some measure of hostility toward them (Powell & Paton, 1988; Benokraitis & Feagin, 1995). Similarly, jokes about gay people reveal tensions about sexual orientation. Real conflict can be masked by humour in situations where one or both parties choose not to bring the conflict out into the open (Primeggia & Varacalli, 1990).

"Put-down" jokes make one category of people feel good at the expense of another. After collecting and analyzing jokes from many societies, Christie Davies (1990) confirmed that ethnic conflict is one driving force behind humour in most of the world. The typical ethnic joke makes fun of some disadvantaged category of people, at the same time making the joke teller feel superior. Given the Anglo-Saxon traditions of Canadian society, Ukrainians and other ethnic and racial minorities have long been the butt of jokes, as have the Irish in England, Sikhs in India, Turks in Germany, Hausas in Nigeria, Tasmanians in Australia, and Kurds in Iraq. Besides making the joke teller feel superior, put-down jokes also impede assimilation. In her study of anti-Slavic prejudice in the United States, sociologist Josephine Wtulich (1994) observed that Polish put-down jokes maintained social divisions by appearing just as the Poles began to experience upward social mobility.

Disadvantaged people also make fun of the powerful, although usually with some concern about who might be listening. Canadian women have long joked about Canadian men, just as French Canadians portray Anglos in humorous ways and poor people poke fun at the rich. Throughout the world, people also target their leaders with humour, and officials in some countries take such jokes seriously enough to arrest those who do not show proper respect (Speier, 1998).

In sum, humour is much more important than we may think. It is a means of mental escape from a conventional world that is never entirely to our liking (Flaherty, 1984, 1990; Yoels & Clair, 1995). This fact helps explain why so many North American comedians are from the ranks of historically marginalized peoples, including Jews and African Americans. As long as we maintain a sense of humour, we assert our freedom and are never prisoners of reality. By putting a smile on our faces, we can change ourselves and the world just a little and for the better.

Seeing Sociology in Everyday Life

How do we construct the reality we experience?

This chapter suggests that Shakespeare may have had it right when he said: "All the world's a stage." And, if so, the internet may be the latest and greatest stage so far. When we use social media websites, as Goffman explains, we present ourselves as we want others to see us. Everything we write about ourselves as well as how we arrange our page creates an impression in the mind of anyone interested in "checking us out." Take a look at the page shown below, paying careful attention to all of the details. What is the young man explicitly saying about himself? What can you read "between the lines"? That is, what information can you identify that he may be trying to conceal or at least purposely not be mentioning? How honest do you think his "presentation of self" is? Why? Do a similar analysis of the young woman's profile shown on the right.

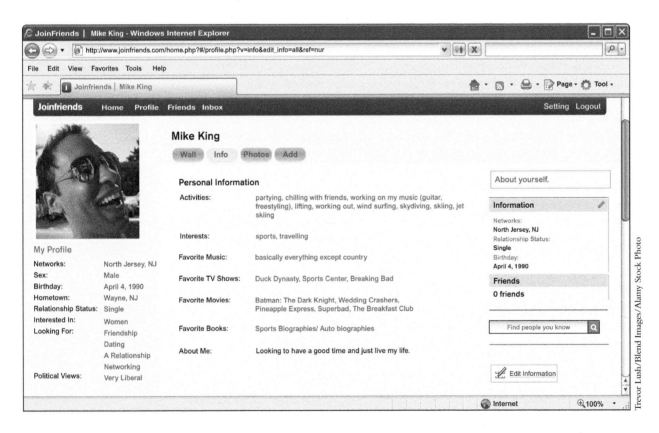

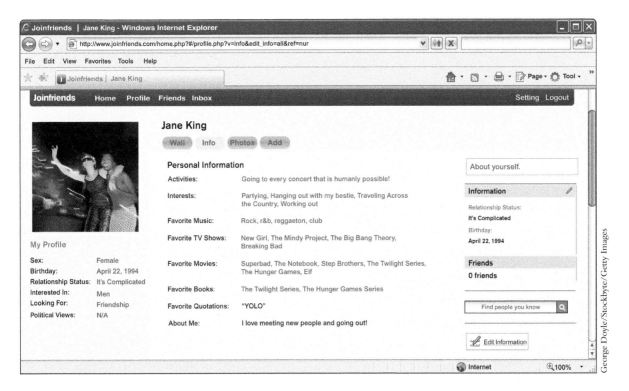

George Doyle/Stockbyte/Getty Images

HINT Just about every element of a presentation conveys information about us to others, so all information found on a website like this one is significant. Some information is intentional—for example, what people write about themselves and the photos they choose to post. Other information may be unintentional but is nevertheless picked up by the careful viewer, who may be noting the following things:

- The length and tone of the person's profile. Is it a long-winded list of talents and accomplishments or humorous and modest?
- The language used. Poor grammar may be a clue to educational level.
- What hour of the day or night the person wrote the material. A person creating his or her profile at 11:00 p.m. on a Saturday may not be quite the party person he or she describes himself or herself to be.

Seeing Sociology in *Your* Everyday Life

1. Identify five important ways in which you present yourself to others, including, for example, the way you decorate your dorm room, apartment, or house; the way you dress; and the way you behave in the classroom. In each case, think about what you are trying to say about yourself. Do you present a different self to various others, such as friends, professors, and parents?

If so, how do you account for the differences?

2. Go to www.sociologyinfocus.com to access the Sociology in Focus blog, where you can read the latest posts by a team of young sociologists who apply the sociological perspective to topics of popular culture.

3. This chapter has explained that we all engage in a process called

the social construction of reality. What that means is that each of us plays a part in shaping the reality we experience. Let's apply this idea to the issue of personal freedom. To what extent does the material presented in this chapter support a claim that humans are free to shape their own lives?

Goodshoot/Thinkstock/Getty Images

Making the Grade

Social Structure: A Guide to Everyday Living

(4.1) Explain how social structure helps us to make sense of everyday situations. (pages 110–111)

Social structure refers to social patterns that guide our behaviour in everyday life. The building blocks of social structure are status and role.

> **social interaction** the process by which people act and react in relation to others

Status

(4.2) State the importance of status to social organization. (pages 111–113)

Status is a social position that is part of our social identity and that defines our relationships to others. A status can be either an

- **ascribed status**, which is involuntary (for example, being a teenager, an orphan, or a French Canadian), or an
- **ascribed status**, which is earned (for example, being an honours student, a pilot, or a thief).

A master status, which can be either ascribed or achieved, has special importance for a person's identity (for example, being blind, a doctor, or a Trudeau).

> **status** a social position that a person holds
> **status set** all the statuses a person holds at a given time
> **ascribed status** a social position a person receives at birth or takes on involuntarily later in life
> **achieved status** a social position a person takes on voluntarily that reflects personal ability and effort
> **master status** a status that has special importance for social identity, often shaping a person's entire life

Role

(4.3) State the importance of role to social organization. (pages 113–115)

Role is behaviour expected of someone who holds a particular status.

Role conflict results from tension among roles linked to two or more statuses (for example, a woman who juggles her responsibilities as a mother and a corporate CEO).

Role strain results from tension among roles linked to a single status (for example, the professor who enjoys personal interaction with students but at the same time knows that social distance is necessary in order to evaluate students fairly).

> **role** behaviour expected of someone who holds a particular status
> **role set** a number of roles attached to a single status
> **role conflict** conflict among the roles connected to two or more statuses
> **role strain** tension among the roles connected to a single status

The Social Construction of Reality

(4.4) Describe how we socially construct reality. (pages 115–118)

Through **social interaction**, we construct the reality we experience.
- For example, two people interacting both try to shape the reality of their situation.

The **Thomas theorem** says that the reality people construct in their interaction has real consequences for the future.
- For example, a teacher who believes a certain student to be intellectually gifted may well encourage exceptional academic performance.

Ethnomethodology is a strategy to reveal the assumptions people have about their social world.
- We can expose these assumptions by intentionally breaking the "rules" of social interaction and observing the reactions of other people.

Both **culture** and **social class** shape the reality people construct.
- For example, a "short walk" for a Torontonian is a few city blocks, but for a peasant in Latin America, it could be a few miles.

The expansion of **social media** has dramatically changed how people interact.
- The social construction of reality no longer requires people to have face-to-face interaction.

> **social construction of reality** the process by which people creatively shape reality through social interaction
> **Thomas theorem** W. I. Thomas's claim that situations defined as real are real in their consequences
> **ethnomethodology** Harold Garfinkel's term for the study of the way people make sense of their everyday surroundings
> **social media** technology that links people in social activity

Dramaturgical Analysis: The "Presentation of Self"

(4.5) Apply Goffman's analysis to several familiar situations. (pages 118–123)

Dramaturgical analysis explores social interaction in terms of theatrical performance: A status operates as a part in a play, and a role is a script.

Performances are the way we present ourselves to others.

- Performances are both conscious (intentional action) and unconscious (nonverbal communication).
- Performances include costume (the way we dress), props (objects we carry), and demeanour (tone of voice and the way we carry ourselves).

Gender affects performances because men typically have greater social power than women. Gender differences involve *demeanour, use of space,* and *smiling, staring,* and *touching.*

- **Demeanour**—With greater social power, men have more freedom in how they act.
- **Use of space**—Men typically command more space than women.
- **Staring** and **touching** are generally done by men to women.
- **Smiling,** as a way to please another, is more commonly done by women.

Idealization of performances means we try to convince others that our actions reflect ideal culture rather than selfish motives.

Embarrassment is the "loss of face" in a performance. People use **tact** to help others "save face."

dramaturgical analysis Erving Goffman's term for the study of social interaction in terms of theatrical performance

presentation of self Erving Goffman's term for a person's efforts to create specific impressions in the minds of others

nonverbal communication communication using body movements, gestures, and facial expressions rather than speech

personal space the surrounding area over which a person makes some claim to privacy

Interaction in Everyday Life: Three Applications

(4.6) Construct a sociological analysis of three aspects of everyday life: emotions, language, and humour. (pages 123–129)

Emotions: The Social Construction of **Feeling**

The same basic emotions are biologically programmed into all human beings, but culture guides what triggers emotions, how people display emotions, and how people value emotions. In everyday life, the presentation of self involves managing emotions as well as behaviour.

Language: The Social Construction of **Gender**

Gender is an important element of everyday interaction. Language defines women and men as different types of people, reflecting the fact that society attaches greater power and value to what is viewed as masculine.

Reality Play: The Social Construction of **Humour**

Humour results from the difference between conventional and unconventional definitions of a situation. Because humour is a part of culture, people around the world find different situations funny.

emotional labour suppressed or induced feelings produced by an employee in accordance with the rules of an organization

5 Groups and Organizations

LEARNING OBJECTIVES

5.1 Explain the importance of various types of groups to social life.

5.2 Describe the operation of large, formal organizations.

5.3 Summarize the changes to formal organizations over the course of the last century.

5.4 Assess the consequences of modern social organization for social life.

the Power of Society

to link people into groups

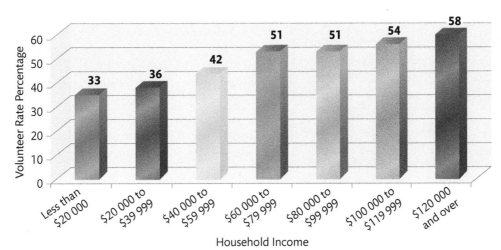

Source: Statistics Canada, http://www.statcan.gc.ca/pub/
11-008-x/2012001/article/11638-eng.pdf. This does not
constitute an endorsement by Statistics Canada of this product.

Does your income influence your likelihood to perform volunteer work? In 2010, 13.3 million people, or 47 percent of the population, volunteered in Canada by doing such things as coaching children, counselling, delivering meals, and advocating for social causes. Charities and non-profits attract people from various income levels; however, our likelihood to volunteer depends on our income. Look at how income affects membership in volunteer organizations—people with the highest incomes ($120 000 and over) are more likely to volunteer than other income earners. Membership in voluntary groups and organizations is not simply a matter of choice; it is also a reflection of the way society is organized.

Chapter Overview

We spend much of our lives within the collectivities that sociologists call social groups and formal organizations. This chapter analyzes social groups, both small and large, highlighting the differences between them. Then the focus shifts to formal organizations that carry out various tasks in our modern society and provide most of us with jobs.

Everett Collection Historical/Alamy Stock Photo

With the workday over, Rey and Flor pushed through the doors of the local McDonald's restaurant. "Man, am I hungry," announced Rey, heading right into line. "Look at all the meat I'm gonna eat." But Flor, a recent immigrant from a small village in the Philippines, is surveying the room with a sociological eye. "There is much more than food to see here. This place is all about Canada!"

And so it is, as we shall see. But back in 1948, when the story of McDonald's began, people in Pasadena, California, paid little attention to the opening of a new restaurant by brothers Maurice and Richard McDonald. The McDonald brothers' basic concept, which was soon called "fast food," was to serve meals quickly and cheaply to large numbers of people. The brothers trained employees to do highly specialized jobs: One person grilled hamburgers while others "dressed" them, made french fries, whipped up milkshakes, and handed the food to the customers in assembly-line fashion.

As the years went by, the McDonald brothers prospered, and they opened several more restaurants, including one in San Bernardino. It was there, in 1954, that Ray Kroc, a travelling blender and mixer salesman, paid them a visit.

Kroc was fascinated by the efficiency of the McDonald brothers' system and saw the potential for expanding into a nationwide chain of fast-food restaurants. The three launched the plan as partners. Soon Kroc bought out the McDonalds (who returned to running their original restaurant) and went on to become one of the greatest success stories of all time. Today, McDonald's is one of the mostly widely known brand names in the world, with 33 500 restaurants serving 69 million people daily throughout Canada and in 118 other countries (McDonald's, 2012).

The success of McDonald's points to more than just the popularity of hamburgers and french fries. The organizational principles that guide this company are coming to dominate social life in Canada and elsewhere. As Flor correctly observed, this one small business not only transformed the restaurant industry but also changed our way of life.

We begin this chapter by looking at *social groups*, the clusters of people with whom we interact in our daily lives. As you will learn, the scope of group life expanded greatly during the twentieth century. From a world of families, local neighbourhoods, and small businesses, our society now relies on the operation of huge corporations and other bureaucracies that sociologists describe as *formal organizations*. Understanding this expansion of social life and appreciating what it means for us as individuals are the main objectives of this chapter.

Social Groups

(**5.1**) Explain the importance of various types of groups to social life.

Almost everyone wants a sense of belonging, which is the essence of group life. A **social group** is *two or more people who identify with and interact with one another.* Human beings come together as couples, families, circles of friends, sport teams, churches, clubs, businesses, neighbourhoods, and corporations. Whatever the form, groups contain people with shared experiences, loyalties, and interests. While keeping their individuality, members of social groups also think of themselves as a special "we."

Not every collection of individuals forms a group. People with a status in common, such as "punk rocker," "civil servant," "East Asian," or "Nova Scotian," are not a group but a *category*. Though they know that others hold the same status, most are strangers to one another. Similarly, students sitting in a large lecture hall interact to a very limited extent. Such a loosely formed collection of people in one place is a *crowd* rather than a group.

However, the right circumstances can quickly turn a crowd into a group. Events from terrorist attacks to a policeman at Osgoode Law School in Toronto saying that "women should avoid dressing like sluts in order not to be victimized"[1] can make people bond quickly with strangers.

social group two or more people who identify with and interact with one another

primary group a small social group whose members share personal and lasting relationships

secondary group a large and impersonal social group whose members pursue a specific goal or activity

Primary and Secondary Groups

People often greet one another with a smile and a simple "Hi! How are you?" The response is usually "Fine, thanks. How about you?" This answer is often more scripted than sincere. Explaining how you are *really* doing might make people feel so awkward that they would beat a hasty retreat.

Social groups are of two types, based on their members' degree of genuine personal concern for one another. According to sociologist Charles Horton Cooley (introduced in Chapter 3, p. 87), a **primary group** is *a small social group whose members share personal and lasting relationships*. Joined by *primary relationships*, people spend a great deal of time together, engage in a wide range of activities, and feel that they know one another pretty well. In short, they show real concern for one another. Cooley called personal and tightly integrated groups "primary" because they are among the first groups we experience in life. In addition, family and friends have primary importance in the socialization process, shaping our attitudes, behaviour, and social identity.

Members of primary groups help one another in many ways, but they generally think of their group as an end in itself rather than as a means to other ends. In other words, we tend to think that family and friendship link people who "belong together." Members of a primary group also tend to view each other as unique and irreplaceable. Especially in the family, we are bound to others by emotion and loyalty. Brothers and sisters may not always get along, but they always remain "family."

In contrast to the primary group, the **secondary group** is *a large and impersonal social group whose members pursue a specific goal or activity*. In most respects, secondary groups have characteristics opposite those of primary groups. *Secondary relationships* involve weak emotional ties and little personal knowledge of one another. Many secondary groups exist for only a short time, beginning and ending without particular significance. Students enrolled in the same course at a large university or people walking together as part of a social movement—people who may or may not see one another after the semester or the walk ends—are examples of secondary groups.

Secondary groups include many more people than primary groups. For example, dozens or even

Kablonk/Golden Pixels LLC/Alamy Stock Photo

As human beings, we live our lives as members of groups. Such groups may be large or small, temporary or long-lasting, and can be based on kinship, cultural heritage, or some shared interest.

[1]A social movement began in Toronto after a male police officer told a group of female university students to stop "dressing like sluts" if they didn't want to be raped. The movement caused women to take to the streets and spread to cities around the world, demonstrating their anger with being treated as sexual objects and intimidated into sexual conformity.

hundreds of people may work for the same company, yet most of them pay only passing attention to one another. Sometimes the passage of time transforms a group from secondary to primary, as with co-workers who share an office for many years and develop closer relationships. But generally, members of a secondary group do not think of themselves as "we." Secondary ties need not be hostile or cold, of course. Interactions among students, co-workers, sports team members, and business associates are often quite pleasant even if they are impersonal.

Unlike members of primary groups, who display a *personal orientation*, people in secondary groups have a *goal orientation*. Primary group members define each other according to *who* they are in terms of family ties or personal qualities, but people in secondary groups look to one another for *what* they are—that is, what they can do for each other. In secondary groups, we tend to "keep score," aware of what we give others and what we receive in return. This goal orientation means that secondary group members usually remain formal and polite. It is in a secondary relationship, therefore, that we ask the question "How are you?" without expecting a truthful answer.

The Summing Up table below reviews the characteristics of primary and secondary groups. Keep in mind that these traits define two types of groups in ideal terms; most real groups contain elements of both. For example, a women's group on a university campus may be quite large (and therefore secondary), but its members may identify strongly with one another and provide a lot of mutual support (making it seem primary).

Are some regions of Canada more primary in character than others? Many people think that small towns and rural areas emphasize primary relationships and that large cities are characterized by secondary ties. This generalization holds some truth, but some urban neighbourhoods, especially those populated by people of a single ethnic or religious category, can be very tightly knit.

Group Leadership

How do groups operate? One important element of group dynamics is leadership. Although a small circle of friends may have no leader at all, most large secondary groups place leaders in a formal chain of command.

Two Leadership Roles

instrumental leadership group leadership that focuses on the completion of tasks

expressive leadership group leadership that focuses on the group's well-being

Groups typically benefit from two kinds of leadership. **Instrumental leadership** refers to *group leadership that focuses on the completion of tasks.* Members look to instrumental leaders to make plans, give orders, and get things done. **Expressive leadership**, by contrast, is *group leadership that focuses on the group's well-being.* Expressive leaders take less of an interest in achieving goals and focus on promoting the well-being of members and minimizing tension and conflict among members.

Because they concentrate on performance, instrumental leaders usually have formal, secondary relationships with other members. These leaders give orders and reward or punish people according to how much they contribute to the group's efforts. Expressive leaders build more personal, primary ties. They offer sympathy to members going through tough times, keep the group united, and lighten serious moments with humour. Typically, successful instrumental leaders enjoy more *respect* from members and expressive leaders generally receive more personal *affection*.

Summing Up

Primary Groups and Secondary Groups		
	Primary Group	Secondary Group
Quality of relationships	Personal orientation	Goal orientation
Duration of relationships	Usually long-term	Variable; often short-term
Breadth of relationships	Broad; usually involving many activities	Narrow; usually involving few activities
Perception of relationships	Ends in themselves	Means to an end
Examples	Families, circles of friends	Co-workers, political organizations

Three Leadership Styles

Sociologists also describe leadership in terms of its decision-making style. *Authoritarian leadership* focuses on instrumental concerns, takes personal charge of decision making, and demands that group members obey orders. Although this leadership style may win little affection from the group, a fast-acting authoritarian leader is appreciated in a crisis.

Democratic leadership is more expressive, making a point of including everyone in the decision-making process. Although less successful in a crisis situation, when there is little time for discussion, democratic leaders generally draw on the ideas of all members to develop creative solutions to problems.

Laissez-faire leadership allows the group to function more or less on its own (*laissez-faire* in French means "leave it alone"). This style is typically the least effective in promoting group goals in hierarchical organizations (White & Lippitt, 1953; Ridgeway, 1983; Eagly, Johannesen-Schmidt, & van Engen, 2003). It is, however, well suited to groups with members who are knowledgeable, passionate, and capable of working independently (Goodnight, 2004).

In the earliest types of societies, the same person combined several elements of leadership. In patriarchal societies, such as nineteenth- and early twentieth-century Canada, conventional cultural norms bestowed authoritarian leadership on men. As family "breadwinners" and "heads," men assumed primary responsibility for bringing in family income, made major decisions, and disciplined children, a responsibility that was strongly endorsed by the Canadian government of the time (Benoit, 2000; Christie, 2000). Women were assigned a democratic leadership role, with the expectation that they would lend family members emotional support and maintain peaceful family relationships. Greater equality between men and women has blended the gender-based distinction between authoritarian and democratic leadership. Yet recent research shows that women's leadership styles still tend to be more democratic than men's, which is possibly due to female leaders' continuing struggle for legitimacy if they attempt to lead in an authoritarian manner (Eagly & Johannesen-Schmidt, 2001).

Group Conformity

Groups influence the behaviour of their members, often promoting conformity. "Fitting in" provides a secure feeling of belonging, but at the extreme, group pressure can be unpleasant and even dangerous. Interestingly, as experiments by Solomon Asch and Stanley Milgram showed, even strangers can encourage group conformity.

Asch's Research

Solomon Asch (1952) recruited students for what he told them was a study of visual perception. Before the experiment began, he explained to all but one member of a small group that their real purpose was to put pressure on the remaining person. Placing six to eight students around a table, Asch showed them a "standard" line, as drawn on Card 1 in Figure 5–1, and asked them to match it to one of the three lines on Card 2.

Anyone with normal vision can see that the line marked "A" on Card 2 is the correct choice. Initially, as planned, everyone made the matches correctly. But then Asch's secret accomplices began answering incorrectly, leaving the uninformed student (seated at the table so as to answer next to last) bewildered and uncomfortable.

What happened? Asch found that one-third of all subjects chose to conform by answering incorrectly. Apparently, many of us are willing to compromise our own judgment to avoid the discomfort of being different, even from people we do not know.

Milgram's Research

Stanley Milgram, a former student of Solomon Asch's, conducted conformity experiments of his own. In Milgram's controversial study (1963, 1965; Miller, 1986), a researcher explained to male recruits that they would be taking part in

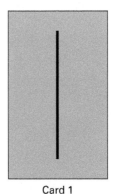
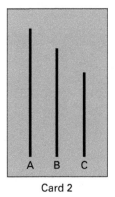

Card 1   Card 2

FIGURE 5–1 Cards Used in Asch's Experiment in Group Conformity

In Asch's experiment, subjects were asked to match the line on Card 1 to one of the lines on Card 2. Many subjects agreed with the wrong answers given by others in their group.

Source: Asch (1952). Asch, Solomon. Social Psychology. Englewood Cliffs, NJ: Prentice Hall, 1952. Courtesy of Solomon Asch Center for Study of Ethnopolitical Conflict.

a study of how punishment affects learning. One by one, he assigned subjects to the role of teacher and placed another person—actually an accomplice of Milgram's—in a connecting room to pose as a learner.

The teacher watched as the learner was seated in what looked like an electric chair. The researcher applied electrode paste to one of the learner's wrists, explaining that this would "prevent blisters and burns." The researcher then attached an electrode to the wrist and secured the leather straps, explaining that these would "prevent excessive movement while the learner was being shocked." The researcher assured the teacher that although the shocks would be painful, they would cause "no permanent tissue damage."

The researcher then led the teacher back to the next room, explaining that the "electric chair" was connected to a "shock generator," actually a phony but realistic-looking piece of equipment with a label that read "Shock Generator, Type ZLB, Dyson Instrument Company, Waltham, Mass." On the front was a dial that appeared to regulate electric shock from 15 volts (labelled "Slight Shock") to 300 volts (marked "Intense Shock") to 450 volts (marked "Danger: Severe Shock").

Seated in front of the "shock generator," the teacher was told to read aloud pairs of words. Then the teacher was to repeat the first word of each pair and wait for the learner to recall the second word. Whenever the learner failed to answer correctly, the teacher was told to apply an electric shock.

The researcher directed the teacher to begin at the lowest level (15 volts) and to increase the shock by another 15 volts every time the learner made a mistake. And so the teacher did. At 75, 90, and 105 volts, the teacher heard moans from the learner; at 120 volts, shouts of pain; at 270 volts, screams; at 315 volts, pounding on the wall; after that, dead silence. None of the 40 subjects assigned to the role of teacher during the initial research even questioned the procedure before reaching 300 volts, and 26 of the subjects—almost two-thirds—went all the way to 450 volts. Even Milgram was surprised at how readily people obeyed authority figures.

Milgram (1964) then modified his research to see if groups of ordinary people—not authority figures—could pressure people to administer electrical shocks, as Asch's groups had pressured individuals to match lines incorrectly.

This time, Milgram formed a group of three teachers, two of whom were his accomplices. Each of the three teachers was to suggest a shock level when the learner made an error; the rule was that the group would then administer the *lowest* of the three suggested levels. This arrangement gave the person not "in" on the experiment the power to deliver a lesser shock regardless of what the others said.

Darren Calabrese/The Canadian Press

A perceived security threat from demonstrators led to police groupthink behaviour during the G20 meeting in Toronto in 2010.

The accomplices suggested increasing the shock level with each error, putting pressure on the third member to do the same. The subjects in these groups applied voltages three to four times higher than the levels applied by subjects acting alone. In this way, Milgram showed that people are likely to follow the lead not only of legitimate authority figures but also of groups of ordinary individuals, even when it means harming another person.

Janis's "Groupthink"

Experts also cave in to group pressure, says Irving L. Janis (1972, 1989). Janis argues that a number of U.S. foreign policy errors, including the failure to foresee Japan's attack on Pearl Harbor during World War II and the country's ill-fated involvement in the Vietnam War, resulted from group conformity among the highest-ranking U.S. political leaders. A Canadian example of group conformity among political leaders happened in December 2010, when provincial and federal politicians spent millions, allegedly for the G20 meeting in Toronto even though the expenditures were totally unrelated.

Common sense tells us that group discussion improves decision making. Janis counters that group members often seek agreement that closes off other points of view. Janis called this process **groupthink**, *the tendency of group members to conform, resulting in a narrow view of some issue.*

A classic example of groupthink led to the failed U.S. invasion of the Bay of Pigs in Cuba in 1961. Looking back, Arthur Schlesinger Jr., an adviser to President John F. Kennedy, confessed feeling guilty for "having kept so quiet during those crucial discussions in the Cabinet Room," adding that the group discouraged anyone from challenging what, in hindsight, Schlesinger considered "nonsense" (quoted in Janis, 1972:30, 40). Groupthink may also have been a factor in the U.S. invasion of Iraq in 2003, when U.S. leaders were led to believe—erroneously—that Iraq had stockpiles of weapons of mass destruction. Interestingly, many of the United States' foreign allies, including Canada, did not support either of these two decisions.

groupthink the tendency of group members to conform, resulting in a narrow view of some issue

Reference Groups

How do we assess our own attitudes and behaviour? Frequently, we use a **reference group**, *a social group that serves as a point of reference in making evaluations and decisions.*

A young man who imagines his family's response to a woman he is dating is using his family as a reference group. A supervisor who tries to predict her employees' reaction to a new vacation policy is using them in the same way. As these examples suggest, reference groups can be primary or secondary. In either case, our need to conform shows how others' attitudes affect us.

We also use groups that we do *not* belong to for reference. Being well prepared for a job interview means showing up dressed the way people in that company dress for work. Conforming to groups we do not belong to is a strategy to win acceptance and illustrates the process of *anticipatory socialization*, described in Chapter 3 ("Socialization: From Infancy to Old Age").

reference group a social group that serves as a point of reference in making evaluations and decisions

Stouffer's Research

Samuel Stouffer and his colleagues (1949) conducted a classic study of reference group dynamics during World War II. Researchers asked soldiers to rate their own, or any competent soldier's, chances of promotion in their army unit. You might guess that soldiers serving in outfits with high promotion rates would be optimistic about advancement. Yet Stouffer's research pointed to the opposite conclusion: Soldiers in army units with low promotion rates were actually more positive about their chances to move ahead.

The key to understanding Stouffer's results lies in the groups against which soldiers measured themselves. Those assigned to units with lower promotion rates looked around them and saw people making no more headway than they were. Although they had not been promoted, neither had many others, so they did not feel deprived. However, soldiers in units with higher promotion rates could think of many people who had been promoted sooner or more often than they had. With such people in mind, even soldiers who had been promoted themselves were likely to feel shortchanged.

The point is that we do not make judgments about ourselves in isolation, nor do we compare ourselves with just anyone. Regardless of our situation in *absolute* terms, we form a subjective sense of our well-being by looking at ourselves *relative* to specific reference groups.

In-Groups and Out-Groups

Each of us favours some groups over others, based on political outlook, social prestige, or even just manner of dress. On some university campuses, for example, left-leaning student activists may look down on fraternity members, whom they view as conservative; fraternity members, in turn, may snub the "nerds" who they feel work too hard. People in just about every social setting make similar positive and negative evaluations of members of other groups.

in-group a social group toward which a member feels respect and loyalty

out-group a social group toward which a person feels a sense of competition or opposition

Such judgments illustrate another key element of group dynamics: the opposition of in-groups and out-groups. An **in-group** is *a social group toward which a member feels respect and loyalty*. An in-group exists in relation to an **out-group**, *a social group toward which a person feels a sense of competition or opposition*. In-groups and out-groups are based on the idea that "we" have valued traits that "they" lack.

Tensions between groups sharpen the groups' boundaries and give people a clearer social identity. However, members of in-groups generally hold overly positive views of themselves and unfairly negative views of various out-groups.

Power also plays a part in intergroup relations. A powerful in-group can define others as a lower-status out-group. Historically, settler colonial populations in countries such as Canada and Australia viewed the original Aboriginal inhabitants as an out-group and subordinated them socially, politically, and economically (Barker, 2014). Internalizing these negative attitudes, Aboriginal peoples have struggled to overcome negative self-images (Kaplan-Myrth, 2005). In this way, in-groups and out-groups foster loyalty but also generate conflict (Tajfel, 1982; Bobo & Hutchings, 1996).

Group Size

The next time you go to a small party or gathering, try to arrive first. If you do, you will be able to observe some fascinating group dynamics. Until about six people enter the room, every person who arrives usually joins in a single conversation. As more people arrive, the group divides into two or more clusters, and it divides again and again as the party grows. This process shows that group size plays a crucial role in how group members interact.

dyad a social group with two members

triad a social group with three members

To understand why, note the mathematical number of relationships possible among two to seven people. As shown in Figure 5–2, two people form a single relationship; adding a third person results in three relationships; adding a fourth person yields six. Increasing the number of people one at a time, then, expands the number of relationships much more rapidly since every new individual can interact with everyone already there. Thus by the time seven people join one conversation, 21 "channels" connect them. With so many open channels, at this point the group usually divides into smaller conversation groups.

The Dyad

The German sociologist Georg Simmel (1858–1918) studied social dynamics in the smallest social groups. Simmel (1950, orig. 1902) used the term **dyad** (Greek for "pair") to designate *a social group with two members*. Simmel explained that social interaction in a dyad is usually more intense than in larger groups because neither member shares the other's attention with anyone else. In Canada, love affairs, marriages, and the closest friendships are typically dyadic.

But like a stool with only two legs, dyads are unstable. Both members of a dyad must work to keep the relationship going; if either withdraws, the group collapses. To make marriage more stable, society supports the marital dyad with legal, economic, and often religious ties.

The Triad

Simmel also studied the **triad**, *a social group with three members*, which contains three relationships, each uniting two of the three people. A triad is more stable than a dyad because one member can act as a mediator if relations between the other two become strained. Such group dynamics help explain why members of a dyad (say, intimate partners having conflict) often seek out a third person (such as a therapist) to discuss tensions between them.

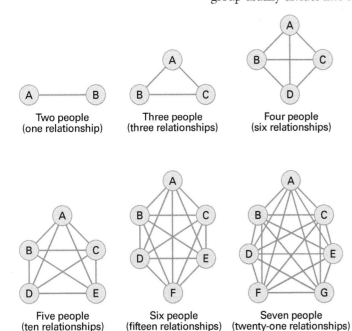

FIGURE 5–2   Group Size and Relationships

As the number of people in a group increases, the number of relationships that link them increases much faster. By the time six or seven people share a conversation, the group usually divides into two. Why are relationships in smaller groups typically more intense?

On the other hand, two of the three can pair up at times to press their views on the third, or two may intensify their relationship, leaving the other feeling left out. For example, when two of the three develop a romantic interest in each other, they will come to understand the meaning of the old saying, "Two's company, three's a crowd."

As groups grow beyond three people, they become more stable and capable of withstanding the loss of one or more members. At the same time, increases in group size reduce the intense personal interaction possible only in the smallest groups. This is why larger groups are based less on personal attachment and more on formal rules and regulations.

Social Diversity: Race, Class, and Gender

Race, ethnicity, class, and gender each play a part in group dynamics. Peter Blau (1977; Blau, Blum, & Schwartz, 1982; South & Messner, 1986) points out three ways in which social diversity influences intergroup contact:

The triad, illustrated by Shantala Robinson's painting *Three by the Ocean*, includes three people. A triad is more stable than a dyad because conflict between any two persons can be mediated by the third member. Even so, should the relationship between any two become more intense in a positive sense, those two are likely to exclude the third.

1. **Large groups turn inward.** Blau explains that the larger a group is, the more likely its members are to have relationships just among themselves. Say a college is trying to enhance social diversity by increasing the number of international students. These students may add a dimension of difference, but as the number of students from a particular nation increases, they become more likely to form their own social group. Thus efforts to promote social diversity may have the unintended effect of promoting separatism.

2. **Heterogeneous groups turn outward.** If you look at the various ethnic groups in your community, you are likely to find that those with a longer history in Canada are more heterogeneous and more likely to interact with others than are recent arrivals. Immigrants to Canada tend to settle in major cities. This is one reason that residents of Montreal and Vancouver have more intergroup contact than residents of small towns and outports, which comprise people of only one or a few types.

3. **Physical boundaries create social boundaries.** To the extent that a social group is physically segregated from others (by having its own dorm or dining area, for example), its members are less likely to interact with other people. Military families in Canada and elsewhere serve as an example. As Deborah Harrison and Lucie Laliberté (1994:21) point out, "[T]he military is a portable total institution that isolates its members from civilians. … As in the case of other total institutions, isolation from civilians facilitates control." One result has been concealment of abuse and violence by dominant members of the in-group against those with less power (Harrison, 2006).

Networks

A **network** is *a web of weak social ties.* Think of a network as a "fuzzy" group containing people who come into occasional contact but who lack a sense of boundaries and belonging. If you think of a *group* as a "circle of friends," think of a *network* as a "social web" expanding outward, often reaching great distances and including large numbers of people.

network a web of weak social ties

The largest network of all is the World Wide Web. But the internet has expanded much more in some global regions than in others. Global Map 5–1 on page 144 shows that internet use is high in high-income countries such as Canada and far less common in low-income nations in Africa and Southeast Asia.

Closer to home, some networks come close to being groups, as in the case of university friends who stay in touch years after graduation by email and telephone. More commonly, however, a network includes people we know of or who know of us but with whom we

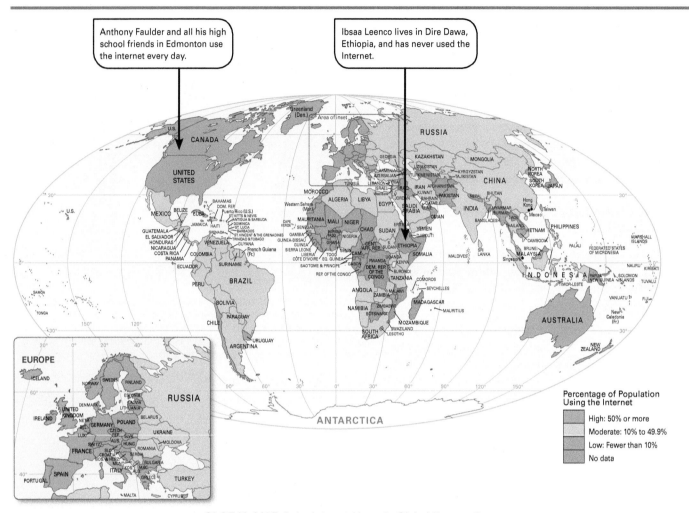

Anthony Faulder and all his high school friends in Edmonton use the internet every day.

Ibsaa Leenco lives in Dire Dawa, Ethiopia, and has never used the Internet.

Percentage of Population Using the Internet

High: 50% or more
Moderate: 10% to 49.9%
Low: Fewer than 10%
No data

GLOBAL MAP 5–1   Internet Users in Global Perspective

This map shows how the Information Revolution has affected countries around the world. In most high-income nations, at least one-half of the population uses the internet. By contrast, only a small share of people in low-income nations does so. What effect does this pattern have on people's access to information? What does this mean for the future in terms of global inequality?

Source: International Telecommunication Union (2012).

interact rarely, if at all. As one woman known as a community organizer explains, "I get calls at home, [and] someone says, 'Are you Roseann Navarro? Somebody told me to call you. I have this problem … '" (quoted in Kaminer, 1984:94).

Network ties often give us the sense that we live in a "small world." In a classic experiment, Stanley Milgram (1967; Watts, 1999) gave letters to subjects in Kansas and Nebraska intended for a few specific people in Boston who were unknown to the original subjects. No addresses were supplied, and the subjects in the study were told to send the letters to others they knew personally who might know the target people. Milgram found that the target people received the letters with, on average, six subjects passing them on. This result led Milgram to conclude that just about everyone is connected to everyone else by "six degrees of separation." Later research, however, has cast doubt on Milgram's conclusions. Examining Milgram's original data, Judith Kleinfeld noted that most of Milgram's letters (240 out of 300) never arrived at their destinations (Wildavsky, 2002). Those that did were typically given to people who were wealthy, a fact that led Kleinfeld to conclude that rich people are far better connected across the country than ordinary men and women.

Network ties may be weak, but they can be a powerful resource. For immigrants who are trying to become established in a new community, business people seeking to expand their operations, or new university and college graduates looking for a job, *who* you know often is just as important as *what* you know (Hagan, 1998; Petersen, Saporta, & Seidel, 2000).

Networks are based on people's educational institutions, clubs, neighbourhoods, political parties, religious organizations, and personal interests. Obviously, some networks contain people with considerable more wealth, power, and prestige than others; that explains the importance of being "well connected." The networks of more privileged categories of people—such as the members of the prestigious Royal Society of Canada—are a valuable form of "social capital," which can lead people in these categories to higher-paying jobs (Green, Tigges, & Diaz, 1999; Lin, Cook, & Burt, 2001).

Some people also have denser networks than others; that is, they are connected to more people. Typically, the largest social networks include people who are affluent, young, well educated, and living in large cities. Networks are also dynamic. Typically, about half of the individuals in a person's social network change over a period of about seven years (Fernandez & Weinberg, 1997; Podolny & Baron, 1997). Some researchers go further; rather than studying geographical communities, such as neighbourhoods, they study social networks or ties that members use to gain resources, and call these "communities" (Wellman, 1999; Chen & Wellman, 2009).

Gender also shapes networks. Although the networks of men and women are typically of the same size, women include more relatives (and more women) in their networks, and men include more co-workers (and more men). Research suggests that women's ties do not carry quite the same clout as the "old-boy" networks that men often rely on for career and social advancement. Even so, research suggests that as gender equality increases, the networks of women and men are becoming more alike (Reskin & McBrier, 2000; Torres & Huffman, 2002).

Social Media and Networking

Networks have long operated as webs of weak social ties involving dozens, hundreds, and for the very "well connected," even thousands of people. In recent decades, networks have become far larger along with the development of social media based on computer technology. Recall from Chapter 4 ("Social Interaction in Everyday Life") that social media refers to technology that links people in social activity.

Computer-based social media have exploded in popularity over the past decade. Consider the case of Facebook, which began when a Harvard University sophomore named Mark Zuckerberg developed a simple interactive website for part of his campus in 2003. This site quickly evolved into an early form of what we know today and, within a month, half the campus was using it. Facebook expanded to other campuses, invited high school students to join, and by 2006 was open to anyone over age 13 with computer access and an email account. By 2011, 600 million people were involved in Facebook networks—17 times the population of Canada—and by the end of 2012, the number had passed 1 billion. Today, Facebook, Twitter, and other social networking sites connect people all over the world.

Formal Organizations

(**5.2**) Describe the operation of large, formal organizations.

A century ago, most people lived in small groups of family, friends, and neighbours. Today, our lives revolve more and more around **formal organizations**, *large secondary groups organized to achieve their goals efficiently.* Formal organizations such as business corporations and government agencies differ from small primary groups in their impersonality and their formally planned atmosphere.

formal organizations large secondary groups organized to achieve their goals efficiently

When you think about it, organizing the more than 35 million members of Canadian society is truly remarkable, whether it involves paving roads, collecting taxes, schooling children, or delivering the mail. To carry out most of these tasks, we rely on large, formal organizations.

Global Snapshot

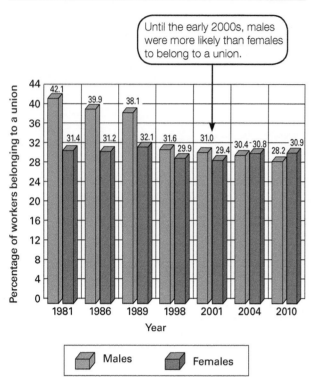

Until the early 2000s, males were more likely than females to belong to a union.

FIGURE 5–3 Union Membership, Canada, 1981–2010

Source: Morrisette, Schellenberg, & Johnson (2005); Uppal (2010).

Types of Formal Organizations

Amitai Etzioni (1975) identified three types of formal organizations, distinguished by the reasons people participate in them: utilitarian organizations, normative organizations, and coercive organizations.

Utilitarian Organizations

Just about everyone who works for income belongs to a *utilitarian organization*, one that pays people for their efforts. Becoming part of a utilitarian organization—a business, government agency, or school system, for example—is usually a matter of individual choice, although most people must join one or another such organization to make a living. Figure 5–3 shows that union membership declined by almost 30 percent for Canadian males between 1981 (42.1 percent) and 2010 (28.2 percent), while union membership remained relatively constant for females.

Normative Organizations

People join *normative organizations* not for income but to pursue some goal they think is morally worthwhile. Sometimes called *voluntary associations*, these include community service groups (such as the Parent Advisory Council [PAC], Canadian International Development Agency [CIDA], the Lions Club, the Status of Women Canada, the Red Cross, or the Sea Shepherd Conservation Society), as well as political parties and religious organizations. In global perspective, people in Canada and other high-income countries with relatively democratic political systems are most likely to join voluntary associations. A recent Canadian survey found that young people (aged 15 to 24) had the highest participation in volunteering (58 percent compared to, for example, those aged 55 to 64 who had a volunteer rate of 41 percent) (Vézina & Crompton, 2012).

Coercive Organizations

Membership in *coercive organizations* is involuntary. People are forced to join these organizations as a form of punishment (prisons) or treatment (some psychiatric hospitals). Coercive organizations have special physical features, such as locked doors and barred windows, and are supervised by security personnel. They isolate people, whom they label "inmates" or "patients," for a period of time to radically change their attitudes and behaviour. Recall from Chapter 3 ("Socialization: From Infancy to Old Age") the power of a total institution to change a person's sense of self.

It is possible for a single organization to fall into *all* of these categories from the point of view of different individuals. For example, a mental hospital serves as a coercive organization for a patient, a utilitarian organization for a psychiatrist, and a normative organization for a hospital volunteer.

Origins of Formal Organizations

Formal organizations date back thousands of years. Elites who controlled early empires relied on government officials to collect taxes, undertake military campaigns, and build monumental structures, from the Great Wall of China to the pyramids of Egypt.

However, early organizations had two limitations. First, they lacked the technology to let people travel over large distances, to communicate quickly, and to gather and store information. Second, the preindustrial societies they were trying to rule had traditional cultures. **Tradition**, according to German sociologist Max Weber, consists of *behaviour, values, and beliefs passed from generation to generation*. Tradition makes a society conservative, Weber explained, because it limits an organization's productive efficiency and ability to change.

By contrast, Weber described the modern worldview as based on **rationality**, *a way of thinking that emphasizes deliberate, matter-of-fact calculation of the most efficient way to accomplish a particular task*. A rational worldview pays little attention to the past and encourages productive efficiency because is open to any changes that might get the job done better or more quickly.

rationalization of society the historical change from tradition to rationality as the main type of human thought

tradition behaviour, values, and beliefs passed from generation to generation

rationality a way of thinking that emphasizes deliberate, matter-of-fact calculation of the most efficient way to accomplish a particular task

The rise of the modern world rests on what Weber called the **rationalization of society**, *the historical change from tradition to rationality as the main type of human thought*. Modern society, he claimed, becomes "disenchanted" as sentimental ties give way to a rational focus on science, complex technology, and the organizational structure called "bureaucracy."

Characteristics of Bureaucracy

Bureaucracy is *an organizational model rationally designed to perform tasks efficiently*. Bureaucratic officials regularly create and revise policy to increase efficiency. To appreciate the power and scope of bureaucratic organization, consider that a phone in the 56 percent of Canadian households that have a traditional land line plus the cellphone owned by 83 percent of Canadian households can connect you within seconds to any other phone in a home, a business, an automobile, or even a hiker's backpack on a remote trail in the Rocky Mountains (Statistics Canada, 2014). Such instant communication was beyond the imagination of people who lived in the ancient world.

bureaucracy an organizational model rationally designed to perform tasks efficiently

Our telephone system depends on technology such as electricity, fibre optics, and computers. But the system could not exist without the bureaucracy that keeps track of every telephone call—noting which phone calls which other phone, when, and for how long—and presents the relevant information to millions of telephone users in the form of a monthly bill.

What specific traits promote organizational efficiency? Max Weber (1978, orig. 1921) identified six key elements of the ideal bureaucratic organization:

1. **Specialization.** Our ancestors spent most of their time performing the general task of looking for food and shelter. Bureaucracy, by contrast, assigns individuals highly specialized jobs.

2. **Hierarchy of positions.** Bureaucracies arrange workers in a vertical ranking. Each person is thus supervised by someone "higher up" in the organization while in turn supervising others in lower positions. Usually, with few people at the top and many at the bottom, bureaucratic organizations take the form of a pyramid.

3. **Rules and regulations.** Cultural tradition counts for little in a bureaucracy. Instead, rationally enacted rules and regulations guide a bureaucracy's operation. Ideally, a bureaucracy operates in a completely predictable way.

4. **Technical competence.** Bureaucratic officials have the technical competence to carry out their duties. Bureaucracies typically hire new members according to set standards and then monitor their performance. Such impersonal evaluation contrasts with the ancient custom of favouring relatives, whatever their talents, over strangers.

5. **Impersonality.** Bureaucracy puts rules ahead of personal whim so that both clients and workers are all treated in the same way. From this impersonal approach comes the commonplace image of the "faceless bureaucrat."

6. **Formal, written communications.** It is said that the heart of bureaucracy is not people but paperwork. Instead of the casual, face-to-face talk that characterizes interaction within small groups, bureaucracy depends on formal, written memos and reports, which accumulate in vast files.

Weber described the operation of the ideal bureaucracy as rational and highly efficient. In real life, actual large organizations often operate very differently from Weber's model, as can be seen on the television show *The Mindy Project*.

Jordin Althaus/Fox/Everett Collection

Summing Up

Small Groups and Formal Organizations

	Small Groups	Formal Organizations
Activities	Much the same for all members	Distinct and highly specialized
Hierarchy	Often informal or non-existent	Clearly defined according to position
Norms	General norms, informally applied	Clearly defined rules and regulations
Membership criteria	Variable; often based on personal affection or kinship	Technical competence to carry out assigned tasks
Relationships	Variable and typically primary	Typically secondary, with selective primary ties
Communications	Typically casual and face to face	Typically formal and in writing
Focus	Person oriented	Task oriented

Bureaucratic organization promotes efficiency by carefully hiring workers and limiting the unpredictable effects of personal taste and opinion. The Summing Up table reviews the differences between small social groups and large formal organizations.

Organizational Environment

organizational environment
factors outside an organization that affect its operation

No organization operates in a vacuum. The performance of any organization depends not only on its own goals and policies but also on the **organizational environment**, *factors outside an organization that affect its operation*. These factors include technology, economic and political trends, current events, the available workforce, population patterns, and other organizations.

Modern organizations are shaped by *technology*, including copiers, fax machines, telephones, and computers This technology gives employees access to more information and more people than ever before. At the same time, modern technology allows managers to monitor worker activities much more closely than in the past (Kiss & Mosco, 2005; Ball, 2010).

Economic and political trends affect organizations. All organizations are helped or hurt by periodic economic growth or recession. Most industries also face competition from abroad as well as changes in laws—such as new environmental standards—at home.

Population patterns also affect organizations. The average age, typical level of education, social diversity, and size of a local community determine the available workforce and sometimes the market for an organization's products or services.

Current events can have significant effects on organizations that are far removed from the location of the events themselves. Events such as the sweeping political revolutions in the Middle East in 2011 and the 2011 federal election that gave majority power to Stephen Harper and the Conservative Party affect the operation of both government agencies and business organizations.

Other organizations also contribute to the organizational environment. To be competitive, a hospital in Canada must keep open lines of communication with provincial medical, nursing, and allied workers' professional associations and unions, abide by federal laws governing the health care system, and work with regional health boards attempting to balance increasing public demands for quality health services and limited annual budgets (Armstrong & Armstrong, 1996, 2002; Segall & Fries, 2011).

The Informal Side of Bureaucracy

Weber's ideal bureaucracy deliberately regulates every activity. In actual organizations, however, human beings are creative (and stubborn) enough to resist bureaucratic regulation. Informality may simply amount to cutting corners on the job at times, but it can also provide the flexibility needed for an organization to adapt and be successful.

In part, informality comes from the personalities of organizational leaders. Studies of Canadian and U.S. corporations document that the qualities and quirks of individuals—including personal charisma, interpersonal skills, and willingness to recognize problems—can have a great effect on organizational outcomes (Halberstam, 1986; Baron, Hannan, & Burton, 1999).

Authoritarian, democratic, and laissez-faire types of leadership (described earlier in this chapter) reflect individual personality as much as any organizational plan. In the "real world" of organizations, leaders sometimes seek to benefit personally by abusing organizational power. Many of the corporate leaders of banks and insurance companies that collapsed during the North American financial meltdown of 2008 walked away with multimillion-dollar "golden parachutes." Throughout the business world, leaders take credit for the efforts of the people who work for them, at least when things go well. In addition, the importance of many secretaries and other front-line service workers to how well a boss performs is often much greater than most people think (and greater than their official job titles and salaries suggest) (Drew, Mills, & Gassaway, 2007).

Communication offers another example of organizational informality. Memos and other written communications are the formal way to spread information throughout an organization. Typically, however, people also create informal networks, or "grapevines," that spread information quickly, if not always accurately. Grapevines, using both word of mouth and email, are particularly important to rank-and-file workers because higher-ups often try to keep important information from them.

The spread of email has "flattened" organizations somewhat, allowing even the lowest-ranking employee to bypass immediate superiors and communicate directly with the organization's leader or all fellow employees at once. Some organizations object to such "open-channel" communication and limit the use of email. Microsoft Corporation (whose founder, Bill Gates, has an unlisted email address that helps him limit his mail to a few hundred messages a day) pioneered the development of screens that filter out messages from everyone except certain approved people (Gwynne & Dickerson, 1997).

Using new information technology as well as age-old human ingenuity, members of organizations often try to break free of rigid rules in order to personalize procedures and surroundings. Such efforts suggest that we should take a closer look at some of the problems of bureaucracy.

Problems of Bureaucracy

We rely on bureaucracy to manage everyday life efficiently, but many people are uneasy about large organizations. Bureaucracy can dehumanize and manipulate us, and some say it poses a threat to political democracy. These dangers are discussed in the following sections.

Bureaucratic Alienation

Max Weber held up bureaucracy as a model of productivity. However, Weber was keenly aware of bureaucracy's ability to *dehumanize* the people it is supposed to serve. The same impersonality that fosters efficiency also keeps officials and clients from responding to another's unique personal needs. Typically, officials at large government and corporate agencies must treat each client impersonally as a standard "case." Sometimes the tendency toward dehumanization goes too far, as in 2008 when the U.S. Army accidentally sent letters to family members of soldiers killed in Iraq and Afghanistan, addressing the recipients as "John Doe" ("Army Apologizes," 2009).

Formal organizations create *alienation*, according to Weber, by reducing the human being to "a small cog in a ceaselessly moving mechanism" (1978:988, orig. 1921). Although formal organizations are designed to benefit people, Weber feared that people might well end up serving formal organizations.

Bureaucratic Inefficiency and Ritualism

Inefficiency, the failure of a formal organization to carry out the work it exists to perform, is a familiar problem. Anyone who has ever tried to complain to Canada Post about a lost or damaged package, to obtain a refund for a coupon attached to a purchased item, or to convince a librarian that an overdue book has already been returned knows that bureaucracies sometimes can be maddeningly unresponsive. According to one report, government agencies

George Tooker's painting *Government Bureau* is a powerful statement about the human costs of bureaucracy. The artist paints members of the public in a drab sameness—reduced from human beings to mere "cases" to be disposed of as quickly as possible. Set apart from others by their positions, officials are "faceless bureaucrats" concerned more with numbers than with providing genuine assistance (notice that the artist places the fingers of the officials on calculators).

responsible for buying equipment for staff can take up to three years to process a request for a new computer. As a result of such inefficiency, by the time the computer arrives, it is already out of date (Gwynne & Dickerson, 1997). While, as noted above, new technology has greatly expanded networking in today's world, especially among younger people who typically make use of Facebook, Twitter, LinkedIn, Pinterest, Instagram, and other popular social networking websites, things may be less effective once in cyberspace. Information we post may end up being seen by almost anyone, which can cause some serious problems, especially if it is partial or, worse, inaccurate.

People sometimes describe inefficiency by saying that an organization has too much "red tape," meaning that important work does not get done. The term *red tape* is derived from the ribbon used by slow-working eighteenth-century English administrators to wrap official parcels and records (Shipley, 1985).

To Robert Merton (1968), red tape amounts to a new twist on the already familiar concept of group con-

bureaucratic ritualism a focus on rules and regulations to the point of undermining an organization's goals

formity. He coined the term **bureaucratic ritualism** to describe *a focus on rules and regulations to the point of undermining an organization's goals*. For example, welfare agencies require people living with chronic disabilities to prove every three or six months that they are eligible for health-related funding. Yet, such ritualism, which requires filling out voluminous paperwork, functions as a barrier to providing welfare, as many of those who need it have difficulties finding doctors who are willing to fill out their forms (Welch, 2014). In short, rules and regulations should be a means to an end, not an end in themselves that takes the focus away from the organization's stated goals.

Bureaucratic Inertia

If bureaucrats sometimes have little reason to work very hard, they have every reason to protect their jobs. Officials typically work to keep an organization going even after its original goal has been realized. As Max Weber put it, "Once fully established, bureaucracy is among the social structures which are hardest to destroy" (1978:987, orig. 1921).

bureaucratic inertia the tendency of bureaucratic organizations to perpetuate themselves

Bureaucratic inertia refers to *the tendency of bureaucratic organizations to perpetuate themselves*. Formal organizations tend to take on a life of their own beyond their formal objectives. For example, the North Atlantic Treaty Organization (NATO), founded in order to counter to the military power of the Soviet Union and its member states collectively known as the Warsaw Pact (WP), now focuses on peacekeeping and humanitarian missions. In addition, NATO now includes the Czech Republic, Hungary, and Poland as member nations rather than as the foes that the organization was originally created to defend against.

Oligarchy

oligarchy the rule of the many by the few

Early in the twentieth century, Robert Michels (1876–1936) pointed out the link between bureaucracy and political **oligarchy**, *the rule of the many by the few* (1949, orig. 1911). According to what Michels called the "iron law of oligarchy," the pyramid shape of bureaucracy places a few leaders in charge of the resources of the entire organization.

Weber believed that a strict hierarchy of responsibility resulted in high organizational efficiency. But Michels countered that this hierarchical structure also concentrates power and thus threatens democracy because officials can and often do use their access to information, resources, and the media to promote their own personal interests.

The Metropolitan Museum of Art/Art Resource, NY

Furthermore, bureaucracy helps distance officials from the public, as in the case of the corporate president or public official who is "unavailable for comment" to the local press or when the Prime Minister's Office withholds documents from Parliament claiming "executive privilege." Oligarchy, then, thrives in the hierarchical structure of bureaucracy and reduces the accountability of leaders to the people (Tolson, 1995).

Political competition, term limits, a system of checks and balances, and the law prevent the Canadian government from becoming an out-and-out oligarchy. Even so, in Canadian political races, incumbents, who generally have more visibility, power, and money than their challengers, enjoy a significant advantage. To illustrate, consider Canada's 2011 federal election. Even with spending limits and a non-partisan system for drawing districts, the system still favoured incumbents, as 83 percent were re-elected. The situation is even worse in the United States, where in recent congressional elections, 90 percent of congressional officeholders on the ballot were able to win re-election.

The Evolution of Formal Organizations

(5.3) Summarize the changes to formal organizations over the course of the last century.

The problems of bureaucracy—especially the alienation it produces and its tendency toward oligarchy—stem from two organizational traits: hierarchy and rigidity. To Weber, bureaucracy was a top-down system: Rules and regulations made at the top guide every facet of people's lives down the chain of command. A century ago in North America, Weber's ideas took hold in an organizational model called *scientific management*. We take a look at this model and then examine three challenges over the course of the twentieth century that gradually led to a new model: the *flexible organization*.

Scientific Management

Frederick Winslow Taylor (1911) had a simple message: Most businesses were sadly inefficient. Managers had little idea of how to increase their business's output, and workers relied on the same tired skills of earlier generations. To increase efficiency, Taylor explained, business should apply the principles of science. **Scientific management** is thus *the application of scientific principles to the operation of a business or other large organization.*

Scientific management involves three steps. First, managers carefully observe the job performed by each worker, identifying all operations involved and measuring the time needed for each. Second, managers analyze their data, trying to discover ways for workers to perform each job more efficiently. For example, managers might decide to give workers different tools or to reposition various work operations within the factory. Third, management provides guidance and incentives for workers to do their jobs more efficiently. If a factory worker moves 20 tonnes of pig iron in one day, for example, management would show the worker how to do the job more efficiently and then provide higher wages as the worker's productivity rises. Taylor concluded that if scientific principles were applied to all steps of the production process, companies would become more profitable, workers would earn higher wages, and consumers would benefit by paying lower prices.

A century ago, auto pioneer Henry Ford put it this way: "Save ten steps a day for each of 12 000 employees, and you will have saved fifty miles of wasted motion and misspent energy" (Allen & Hyman, 1999:209). In the early 1900s, the Ford Motor Company and many other businesses followed Taylor's lead and made improvements in efficiency. Today, corporations carefully review every aspect of their operation in a never-ending effort to increase efficiency.

The principles of scientific management suggested that workplace power should reside with the owners and executives, who have historically paid little attention to the ideas of their workers. Formal organizations have also faced important challenges, involving race and

scientific management the application of scientific principles to the operation of a business or other large organization

gender, rising competition from abroad, and the changing nature of work. We now take a brief look at each of these challenges.

The First Challenge: Race and Gender

In the 1960s, critics charged that big businesses and other organizations engaged in unfair hiring practices. Rather than hiring on the basis of competence, as Weber had proposed, organizations routinely excluded women and other minorities, especially from positions of power. As a result, in the early 1960s, the vast majority of managers—just under 90 percent—were white men (Benoit, 2000).

Patterns of Privilege and Exclusion

By 1987, 30 percent of managerial positions in Canada were held by women, and by 2009 the figure had risen to 37 percent. Therefore, even today, Canadian men still hold 63 percent of managerial jobs across the country. Moreover, all of this growth in women's presence in management occurred in the early part of this period. Further, women who hold managerial positions tend to be clustered in lower-level managerial positions. As Figure 5–4 shows, in 2009 women comprised only 32 percent of senior managers (Statistics Canada, 2011). The 2012 Catalyst Census: Financial Post 500 Women Senior Officers and Top Earners does not show much improvement. According to the report, only 18.1 percent of senior posts in Financial Post 500 companies were held by women, a minor increase from 17.7 percent in 2010. Additionally, women corporate officers had increased their percentage of the top earner positions in 2012 to 6.9 percent from 6.2 percent in 2010. Meanwhile, more than one in three (35.9 percent) of companies had zero women among their senior officers (Mulligan-Ferry, Malordy, & Peter, 2013).

Rosabeth Moss Kanter (1977; Kanter & Stein, 1979) claims that excluding women and minorities from the workplace ignores the talents of more than half of the population. Furthermore, underrepresented people in an organization often feel like socially isolated outgroups—uncomfortably visible, taken less seriously, and given fewer chances for promotion. Sometimes what passes for "merit" or good work in an organization is simply being of the right social category (Castilla, 2008).

Opening up an organization so that change and advancement happen more often, Kanter claims, improves everyone's on-the-job performance by motivating employees to become "fast-trackers" who work harder and are more committed to the company. By contrast, an organization with many dead-end jobs turns workers into less productive "zombies" who are never asked for their opinion on anything. An open organization encourages leaders to seek out the input of all employees, which usually improves decision making.

The "Female Advantage"

Some organizational researchers argue that women bring special management skills that strengthen an organization. According to Deborah Tannen (1994), women have a greater "information focus" and more readily ask questions in order to understand an issue. Men, by contrast, have an "image focus" that makes them wonder how asking questions in a particular situation will affect their reputation.

In another study of women executives, Sally Helgesen (1990) found three other gender-linked patterns. First, women place greater value on communication skills and share information more than men do. Second, women are more flexible leaders who typically give their employees greater freedom. Third, compared to men, women tend to emphasize the interconnectedness of all organizational operations. These patterns, which Helgesen dubbed the *female advantage*, help make companies more flexible and democratic.

In sum, one challenge to conventional bureaucracy is to become more open and flexible in order to take advantage of the experience, ideas, and creativity of everyone, regardless of race or gender. The result goes right to the bottom line: greater profits.

Diversity Snapshot

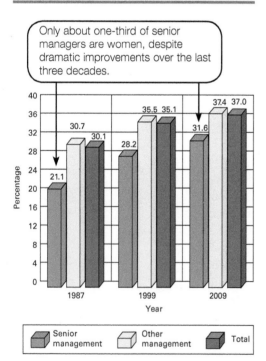

Only about one-third of senior managers are women, despite dramatic improvements over the last three decades.

FIGURE 5–4 Women as a Percentage of Total Canadians Employed in Management Positions
Source: Data from Statistics Canada (2011).

The Second Challenge: The Japanese Work Organization

In 1980, the corporate world in North America was shaken to discover that the most popular automobile model sold was not a Chevrolet, Ford, or Plymouth but the Honda Accord, made in Japan. Recently, the Japanese corporation Toyota passed General Motors to become the largest carmaker in the world (Meier, 2012). This is quite a change. As late as the 1950s, the label "Made in Japan" generally indicated that a product was cheap and poorly made. But times have changed. The success of the Japanese auto industry, as well as companies making electronics, cameras, and many other products, drew attention to the "Japanese work organization." How was so small a country able to challenge the world's economic powerhouse?

December 9, Kyoto (8:05 A.M.). After five minutes of collective warmup, the 25 workers on the construction project next to our hotel stand in four lines. For five minutes they stand listening to something. What is it? Are they listening to the work plan for today or are they listening to an inspirational speaker? So many things are different here, even as most things are familiar.

Japanese organizations reflect that nation's strong collective spirit. In contrast to the Canadian emphasis on rugged individualism, the Japanese value co-operation. In effect, formal organizations in Japan are more like large primary groups. A generation ago, William Ouchi (1981) highlighted differences between formal organizations in Japan and North America. First, Japanese companies hired new workers in groups, giving everyone the same salary and responsibilities. Second, many Japanese companies hired workers for life, fostering a strong sense of loyalty. Third, with the idea that employees would spend their entire careers there, many Japanese companies trained workers in all phases of their operations. Fourth, although Japanese corporate leaders took final responsibility for their organization's performance, they involved workers in "quality circles" to discuss decisions that affected them. Fifth, Japanese companies played a large role in the lives of workers, providing home mortgages, sponsoring recreational activities, and scheduling social events. Together, such policies encourage much more loyalty among members of Japanese organizations than is typically the case in their North American counterparts.

Not everything worked out well for Japan's corporations. About 1990, the Japanese economy entered a recession that lasted for two decades. During this downturn, many Japanese companies changed their policies, no longer offering workers jobs for life or many of the other benefits noted by Ouchi. But the long-term outlook for Japan's business organizations remains bright.

In recent years, the widely admired Toyota corporation has also seen challenges. After expanding its operations to become the world's largest carmaker, Toyota was forced to recall millions of automobiles due to mechanical problems, suggesting that one consequence of the company's rapid growth was losing focus on what had been the key to its success all along—quality (Saporito, 2010).

The Third Challenge: The Changing Nature of Work

Beyond rising global competition and the need to provide equal opportunity for all, pressure to modify conventional organizations is also coming from changes in the nature of work itself. Chapter 2 ("Culture") described the shift from industrial to post-industrial production. Rather than working in factories using heavy machinery to make *things*, more and more people today are using computers and other electronic technology to create or process *information*. The post-industrial society, then, is characterized by information-based organizations.

Frederick Taylor developed his concept of scientific management at a time when most jobs involved tasks that, though often backbreaking, were routine and repetitive. Workers shovelled coal, poured liquid iron into moulds, welded body panels to automobiles on an assembly line, or shot hot rivets into steel girders to build skyscrapers. In addition, many of the industrial workers in Taylor's day were immigrants, most of whom had little schooling and many of whom knew little English. The routine nature of industrial jobs, coupled with the limited skills of the labour force, led Taylor to treat work as a series of fixed tasks set down by management and followed by employees.

Many of today's information-age jobs are very different: The work of designers, artists, consultants, writers, editors, composers, programmers, business owners, and others now demands individual creativity and imagination. Here are several ways in which today's organizations differ from those of a century ago:

1. **Creative freedom.** As one Hewlett-Packard executive put it, "From their first day of work here, people are given important responsibilities and are encouraged to grow" (cited in Brooks, 2000:128). Today's organizations now treat employees with information-age skills as a vital resource. Executives can set production goals but cannot dictate how workers are to accomplish tasks that require imagination and discovery. This gives highly skilled workers *creative freedom*, which means they are subject to less day-to-day supervision as long as they generate good results in the long run.

2. **Competitive work teams.** Organizations typically give several groups of employees the freedom to work on a problem, offering the greatest rewards to those who come up with the best solution. Competitive work teams, a strategy first used by Japanese organizations, draw out the creative contributions of everyone and at the same time reduce the alienation often found in conventional organizations (Maddox, 1994; Yeatts, 1994).

3. **A flatter organization.** By spreading responsibility for creative problem solving throughout the workforce, organizations take on a flatter shape. That is, the pyramid shape of conventional bureaucracy is replaced by an organizational form with fewer levels in the chain of command, as shown in Figure 5–5.

4. **Greater flexibility.** The typical industrial-age organization was a rigid structure guided from the top. Such organizations may accomplish a large amount of work, but they are not especially creative or able to respond quickly to changes in the larger environment. The ideal model in the information age is a more open, *flexible* organization that both generates new ideas and adapts quickly to the rapidly changing global marketplace.

What does all this mean for formal organizations? As David Brooks puts it, "The machine is no longer held up as the standard that healthy organizations should emulate. Now it's the ecosystem" (2000:128). Today's "smart" companies seek out intelligent, creative people (AOL's main building is called "Creative Centre 1") and nurture the growth of their talents.

Keep in mind, however, that many of today's jobs do not involve creative work at all. More correctly, the post-industrial economy has created two very different types of work: high-skill creative work and low-skill service work. Work in the fast-food industry, for example, is routine and highly supervised and thus has much more in common with the factory work of a century ago than with the creative teamwork typical of today's information organizations. Therefore, at the same time that some organizations have taken on a flexible, flatter form, others continue to use the rigid chain of command.

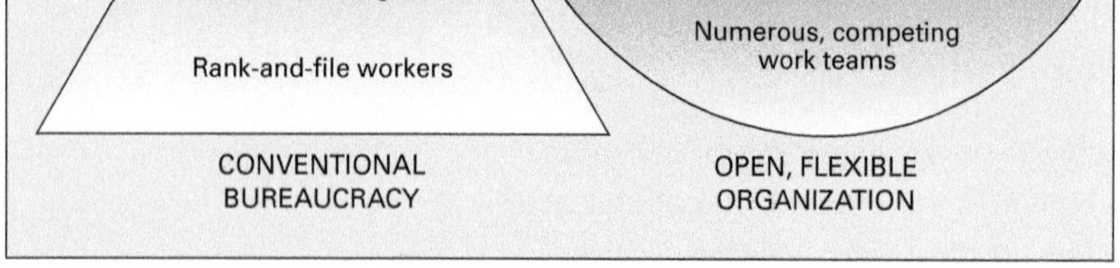

FIGURE 5–5 Two Organizational Models

The conventional model of bureaucratic organizations has a pyramid shape, with a clear chain of command. Orders flow from the top down, and reports of performance flow from the bottom up. Such organizations have extensive rules and regulations, and their workers have highly specialized jobs. More open and flexible organizations have a flatter shape, more like a football. With fewer levels in the hierarchy, responsibility for generating ideas and making decisions is shared throughout the organization. Many workers do their jobs in teams and have a broad knowledge of the entire organization's operation.

The "McDonaldization" of Society

As noted in the opening to this chapter, McDonald's has enjoyed enormous success, now operating more than 33 500 restaurants in Canada and around the world. Japan has more than 3300 Golden Arches; Europe has 7100 restaurants, and McDonald's prepared for the 2012 Olympics in London by building a giant restaurant that employed 500 people and seated 1500 customers.

McDonald's is far more than a restaurant chain; it is a cultural symbol. People around the world associate McDonald's with North America. One poll found that 98 percent of U.S. schoolchildren could identify Ronald McDonald, making him as well known as Santa Claus.

Even more important, the organizational principles that underlie McDonald's are coming to dominate our entire society. Our culture is becoming "McDonaldized," an awkward way of saying that we model many aspects of life on this restaurant chain: Parents buy toys at worldwide chain stores all carrying identical merchandise; we drop in for a 10-minute oil change while running errands; face-to-face communication is being replaced more and more by email, voice mail, and texting; more vacations take the form of resorts and tour packages; television packages the news in the form of 10-second sound bites; university admissions officers size up applicants they have never met by glancing at their GPAs; and professors assign ghostwritten textbooks[2] and evaluate students with tests mass-produced for them by publishing companies. The list goes on and on.

Four Principles

What do all these developments have in common? According to George Ritzer (1993), the McDonaldization of society rests on four organizational principles:

1. **Efficiency.** Ray Kroc, the marketing genius behind the expansion of McDonald's back in the 1950s, set out to serve a hamburger, french fries, and a milkshake to a customer in exactly 50 seconds. Today, one of the company's most popular menu items is the Egg McMuffin, an entire breakfast in a single sandwich. In the restaurant, customers pick up their meals at a counter, dispose of their own trash, and stack their own trays as they walk out the door or, better still, drive away from the pickup window taking whatever mess they make with them. Such efficiency is now central to our way of life. We tend to think that anything done quickly is, for that reason alone, good.

2. **Predictability.** An efficient organization wants to make everything it does as predictable as possible. McDonald's prepares all food using set formulas. Company policies guide the performance of every job.

3. **Uniformity.** The first McDonald's operating manual set the weight of a regular raw hamburger at 1.6 ounces, its size at 3.875 inches across, and its fat content at 19 percent. A slice of cheese weighs exactly half an ounce, and fries are cut precisely 9/32 of an inch thick.

   Think about how many of the objects around your home, the workplace, and the campus are designed and mass-produced uniformly according to a standard plan. Not just our environment but also our everyday life experiences—from travelling the nation's highways to sitting at home viewing television—are more standardized than ever before.

   Almost anywhere in the world, a person can walk into a McDonald's restaurant and buy the same sandwiches, drinks, and desserts prepared in the same way.[3] Uniformity results from a highly rational system that specifies every action and leaves nothing to chance.

4. **Control.** The most unreliable element in the McDonald's system is the human beings who work there. After all, people have their good and bad days, and they sometimes let their minds wander, or simply decide to do something in a different way. To minimize the unpredictable human element, McDonald's has automated its equipment to cook food at a fixed temperature for a set length of time. Even the cash register at McDonald's is keyed to pictures of the menu items so that ringing up a customer's order is as simple as possible.

Similarly, automatic teller machines are replacing bank tellers, highly automated bakeries now produce bread while people stand back and watch, and chickens and eggs (or is it

---

[2] A number of popular sociology textbooks were not written by the people whose names appear on the cover. This book is not one of them.

[3] As McDonald's has "gone global," a few products have been added or changed according to local tastes. For example, in Uruguay, customers enjoy the McHuevo (a hamburger with a poached egg on top); Norwegians can buy McLaks (grilled salmon sandwiches); the Dutch favour the Groenteburger (vegetable burger); in Thailand, McDonald's serves Samurai pork burgers (pork burgers with teriyaki sauce); the Japanese can purchase a Chicken Tatsuta Sandwich (chicken seasoned with soy and ginger); Filipinos eat McSpaghetti (spaghetti with tomato sauce and bits of hot dog); and in India, where Hindus eat no beef, McDonald's sells a vegetarian Maharaja Mac (Sullivan, 1995).

Controversy & Debate

Computer Technology, Large Organizations, and the Assault on Privacy

Jake completes a page on Facebook, which includes his name and college, email address, photo, biography, and current personal interests. It can be accessed by billions of people around the world.

Late for a meeting with a new client, Sarah drives her car through a yellow light as it turns red at a main intersection. A computer linked to a pair of cameras notes the violation and takes one picture of her licence plate and another of her sitting in the driver's seat. Seven days later, she receives a summons to appear in traffic court.

Julio looks through his mail and finds a letter from a Toronto data services company telling him that he is one of about 145 000 people whose name, address, social insurance number, and credit file have recently been sold to criminals posing as business people. With this information, other people can obtain credit cards or take out loans in his name.

These cases show that today's organizations—which know more about us than ever before and more than most of us even realize—pose a growing threat to personal privacy. Large organizations are necessary for today's society to operate. In some cases, organizations using or selling information about us may actually be helpful. But cases of identity theft are on the rise, and personal privacy is on the decline.

In the past, small-town life gave people little privacy. But at least if people knew something about you, you were just as likely to know something about them. Today, unknown people "out there" can access information about each of us all the time without our learning about it.

In part, the loss of privacy is a result of more and more complex computer technology. Are you aware that every email you send and every website you visit leaves a record in one or more computers? These records can be retrieved by people you don't know as well as by employers and other public officials.

Another part of today's loss of privacy reflects the number and size of formal organizations. As explained in this chapter, large organizations tend to treat people impersonally, and they have a huge appetite for information. Mix large organizations with ever more complex computer technology, and it is no wonder that most people in Canada are concerned about who knows what about them and what people are doing with this information.

For decades, the level of personal privacy in our country has been declining. When the government first began issuing driver's licences, for example, they generated files for every licensed driver. Today, officials can send this information at the touch of a button not only to the police but also to many other organizations. Similarly, Canada Revenue Agency and federal and provincial social services agencies collect extensive information.

Business organizations now do much the same thing, although, as these examples show, people may not be aware that their choices and activities end up in a company's database. Most people find credit cards a great convenience—in Canada, more than 90 percent of adults have access to at least one credit card (Canadian Bankers Association, 2014)—but few people stop to think that credit card purchases automatically generate records that can end up almost anywhere.

Then there are the small cameras found not only at traffic intersections but also in stores, public buildings, and parking garages and across university and college campuses. So-called security cameras may increase public safety—say, by discouraging a mugger or even a terrorist—at the cost of the little privacy we have left (Walby, 2005; Hier, 2010). In the United Kingdom, the typical resident of London appears on closed-circuit television about 300 times every day, and all this "tracking" is stored in computer files. In the United States, New York City already has 4000 surveillance cameras in the streets and subway system, which city officials claim might well have prevented an attack such as the 2013 Boston Marathon bombing (Rossen & Connor, 2013).

Of course, some legal protections remain. Under the Access to Information Act, citizens and groups can exercise their rights to examine and correct records kept on them by federal government bodies such as the RCMP, the Canada Border Services Agency, or the Canadian Security Intelligence Service (CSIS). The government also limits the collection, use, and disclosure of personal information between agencies, but the fact is that many private as well as public organizations now have information about us. Experts estimate that 90 percent of U.S. households are profiled in databases somewhere, and estimates for Canadian households are likely to be similar. In both countries there is public concern that current laws simply do not address the extent of the privacy problem. In 2015, in the name of fighting terrorism, the Canadian government passed bill C-51—a bill designed to enhance the capacity of government agencies, like CSIS, to share private information with domestic and foreign bodies. Can current laws ensure that privacy will remain part of our way of life?

What Do You Think?

1. Do you think that the use of surveillance cameras in public places enhances or reduces personal security? Explain.

2. Do you use websites such as Facebook? Why do you think so many young people are eager to spread personal information in this way?

3. Do you think laws will ensure that some privacy remains, or are we on a road to the elimination of personal privacy?

Sources: "Online Privacy" (2000), Heymann (2002), O'Harrow (2005), Walby (2005), Tingwall (2008), Werth (2008), Hier (2010), Hui (2010), Stein (2011), and Canadian Bankers Association (2014).

eggs and chickens?) emerge from automated hatcheries. In supermarkets, laser scanners at self-checkouts are phasing out human checkers. We do most of our shopping in malls, where everything from temperature and humidity to the kinds of stores and products sold are subject to continuous control and supervision (Ide & Cordell, 1994).

Can Rationality Be Irrational?

There is no doubt about the popularity or efficiency of McDonald's. But there is another side to the story.

Max Weber was alarmed at the increasing rationalization of the world, fearing that formal organizations would cage our imaginations and crush the human spirit. As Weber saw it, rational systems were efficient but dehumanizing. McDonaldization bears him out. Each of the four principles just discussed limits human creativity, choice, and freedom. Echoing Weber, Ritzer states that "the ultimate irrationality of McDonaldization is that people could lose control over the system and it would come to control us" (1993:145). Perhaps even McDonald's understands this—the company has now expanded its offerings of more upscale foods, such as premium roasted coffee and salad selections that are more sophisticated, fresh, and healthful (Philadelphia, 2002).

The Future of Organizations: Opposing Trends

Assess the consequences of modern social organization for social life.

The best of today's information-age jobs—including working at Google, the popular search engine website—allow people a lot of personal freedom as long as they produce good ideas. At the same time, many other jobs, such as working the counter at McDonald's, involve the same routines and strict supervision found in factories a century ago.

Early in the twentieth century, ever-larger organizations arose in Canada, most taking on the bureaucratic form described by Max Weber. In many respects, these organizations resembled armies led by powerful generals who issued orders to their captains and lieutenants. Foot soldiers, working in the factories, did what they were told.

With the emergence of the post-industrial economy around 1950, as well as rising competition from abroad, many organizations evolved toward a flatter, more flexible model that prizes communication and creativity. Such "intelligent organizations" (Pinchot & Pinchot, 1993; Brooks, 2000) have become more productive than ever. Just as important, for highly skilled people who now enjoy creative freedom, these organizations cause less of the alienation that so worried Weber.

But this is only half the story. Although the post-industrial economy has created many highly skilled jobs over the past half-century, it has created even more routine service jobs, such as those offered by McDonald's. Fast-food companies now represent the largest pool of low-wage labour, aside from migrant workers (Schlosser, 2002). Work of this kind, which Ritzer terms "McJobs," offers few of the benefits that today's highly skilled workers enjoy. On the contrary, the automated routines that define work in the fast-food industry, telemarketing, and similar fields are very much the same as those that Frederick Taylor described a century ago.

Today, organizational flexibility gives better-off workers more freedom but often means the threat of "downsizing" and job loss for many rank-and-file employees. Organizations facing global competition seek out creative employees, but they are also eager to cut costs by eliminating as many routine jobs as possible. The net result is that some people are better off than ever while others worry about holding their jobs and struggle to make ends meet—a trend that Chapter 8 ("Social Stratification") explores in detail.

Canadian organizations are the envy of the world for their productive efficiency. Indeed, there are few places on Earth where the mail arrives as quickly and dependably as it does in this country. But we should remember that the future is far brighter for some workers than for others. In addition, as the Controversy & Debate box explains, organizations pose an increasing threat to our privacy—something to keep in mind as we envision our organizational future.

Seeing Sociology in Everyday Life

CHAPTER 5 Groups and Organizations

What have we learned about the way modern society is organized?

This chapter explains that since the opening of the first McDonald's restaurant in 1948, the principles that underlie the fast-food industry—efficiency, predictability, uniformity, and control—have spread to many aspects of our everyday lives. Here is a chance to identify aspects of McDonaldization in several familiar routines. In each of the two photos on page 159, can you identify specific elements of McDonaldization? That is, in what ways does the organizational pattern or the technology involved increase efficiency, predictability, uniformity, and control? In the photo below, what elements do you see that are clearly not McDonaldization? Why?

Small, privately owned stores like this one were once the rule in Canada. But the number of "mom and pop" businesses is declining as "big box" discount stores and fast-food chains expand. Why are small stores disappearing? What social qualities of these stores are we losing in the process?

Corepics VOF/Shutterstock

Automated teller machines became common in Canada in the early 1970s. A customer with an electronic identification card can complete certain banking operations (such as withdrawing cash) without having to deal with a human bank teller. What makes the ATM one example of McDonaldization? Do you like using ATMs? Why or why not?

At checkout counters in many supermarkets, customers lift each product through a laser scanner linked to a computer to identify what the product is and what it costs. The customer then inserts a credit or debit card to pay for the purchase and proceeds to bag the items.

HINT This process, which is described as the "McDonaldization of society," has made our lives easier in some ways, but it has also made our society ever more impersonal, gradually diminishing our range of human contact. Also, although this organizational pattern is intended to serve human needs, it may end up doing the opposite by forcing people to live according to the demands of machines. Max Weber feared that our future would be an overly rational world in which we all might lose much of our humanity.

Seeing Sociology in *Your* Everyday Life

1. Have colleges and universities been affected by the process called McDonaldization? Do large, anonymous lecture courses qualify as an example? Why? What other examples of McDonaldization can you identify on your campus?

2. Go to www.sociologyinfocus.com to access the Sociology in Focus blog, where you can read the latest posts by a team of young sociologists who apply the sociological perspective to topics of popular culture.

3. What experiences do you have that are similar to using an ATM or a self-checkout at a discount store? Identify several examples and explain ways that you benefit from using them. In what ways might you be harmed by using these devices?

Making the Grade

Kablonk/Golden Pixels
LLC/Alamy Stock Photo

**Chapter 5
Groups and
Organizations**

Social Groups

(**5.1**) Explain the importance of various types of groups to social life. (pages 136–145)

Social groups are two or more people who identify with and interact with one another.

- **A primary group** is small, personal, and lasting (examples include family and close friends).
- **A secondary group** is large, impersonal, goal-oriented, and often of shorter duration (examples include a college class or a corporation).

Elements of Group Dynamics

Group leadership

- *Instrumental leadership* focuses on completing tasks.
- *Expressive leadership* focuses on a group's well-being.
- *Authoritarian leadership* is a "take charge" style that demands obedience; *democratic leadership* includes everyone in decision making; *laissez-faire leadership* lets the group function mostly on its own.

Group conformity

- The Asch, Milgram, and Janis research shows that group members often seek agreement and may pressure one another toward conformity.
- Individuals use **reference groups**—including both **in-groups** and **out-groups**—to form attitudes and make evaluations.

Group size and diversity

- Georg Simmel described the **dyad** as intense but unstable; the **triad**, he said, is more stable but can dissolve into a dyad by excluding one member.
- Peter Blau claimed that larger groups turn inward, socially diverse groups turn outward, and physically segregated groups turn inward.

Networks are relational webs that link people with little common identity and limited interaction. Being "well connected" in networks is a valuable type of social capital.

- **Social media** based on computer technology have involved people in more and more social networks that now extend around the world

social group two or more people who identify with and interact with one another

primary group a small social group whose members share personal and lasting relationships

secondary group a large and impersonal social group whose members pursue a specific goal or activity

instrumental leadership group leadership that focuses on the completion of tasks

expressive leadership group leadership that focuses on the group's well-being

groupthink the tendency of group members to conform, resulting in a narrow view of some issue

reference group a social group that serves as a point of reference in making evaluations and decisions

in-group a social group toward which a member feels respect and loyalty

out-group a social group toward which a person feels a sense of competition or opposition

dyad a social group with two members

triad a social group with three members

network a web of weak social ties

Formal Organizations

(**5.2**) Describe the operation of large, formal organizations. (pages 145–151)

Formal organizations are large secondary groups organized to achieve their goals efficiently.

- **Utilitarian organizations** pay people for their efforts (examples include a business or government agency).
- **Normative organizations** have goals people consider worthwhile (examples include voluntary associations such as Lions Clubs International).
- **Coercive organizations** are organizations people are forced to join (examples include prisons and mental hospitals).

All formal organizations operate in an **organizational environment**, which is influenced by

- technology
- political and economic trends
- current events
- population patterns
- other organizations

formal organization a large secondary group organized to achieve its goals efficiently

tradition behaviour, values, and beliefs passed from generation to generation

rationality a way of thinking that emphasizes deliberate, matter-of-fact calculation of the most efficient way to accomplish a particular task

rationalization of society the historical change from tradition to rationality as the main type of human thought

organizational environment factors outside an organization that affect its operation

Modern Formal Organizations: Bureaucracy

Bureaucracy, which Max Weber saw as the dominant type of organization in modern societies, is based on

- specialization
- hierarchy of positions
- rules and regulations
- technical competence
- impersonality
- formal, written communications

Problems of bureaucracy include

- bureaucratic alienation
- bureaucratic inefficiency and ritualism
- bureaucratic inertia
- oligarchy

bureaucracy an organizational model rationally designed to perform tasks efficiently

bureaucratic ritualism a focus on rules and regulations to the point of undermining an organization's goals

bureaucratic inertia the tendency of bureaucratic organizations to perpetuate themselves

oligarchy the rule of the many by the few

The Evolution of Formal Organizations

5.3 Summarize the changes to formal organizations over the course of the last century. (pages 151–157)

scientific management Frederick Taylor's term for the application of scientific principles to the operation of a business or other large organization

Conventional Bureaucracy

- In the early 1900s, Frederick Taylor's **scientific management** applied scientific principles to increase productivity.

More Open, Flexible Organizations

- In the 1960s, Rosabeth Moss Kanter proposed that opening up organizations for all employees, especially women and other minorities, increased organizational efficiency.
- In the 1980s, global competition drew attention to the Japanese work organization's collective orientation.

The Changing Nature of Work

Recently, the rise of a post-industrial economy has created two very different types of work:

- highly skilled and creative work (examples include designers, consultants, programmers, and executives)
- low-skilled service work associated with the "McDonaldization" of society, based on efficiency, uniformity, and control (examples include jobs in fast-food restaurants and telemarketing)

The Future of Organizations: Opposing Trends

5.4 Assess the consequences of modern social organization for social life. (page 157)

- In our post-industrial society, many organizations are evolving toward a "flatter," more flexible model that encourages worker creativity.
- At the same time, other organizations that provide services require more workers to perform "McJobs," which describes low-wage, routine work.

6 Sexuality and Society

Rob Melnychuk/Getty Images

LEARNING OBJECTIVES

6.1 Describe how sexuality is both a biological and a cultural issue.

6.2 Explain changes in sexual attitudes in Canada.

6.3 Analyze factors that shape sexual orientation.

6.4 Discuss several current controversies involving sexuality.

6.5 Apply sociology's major theories to the topic of sexuality.

the Power of Society

to shape our attitudes on social issues involving sexuality

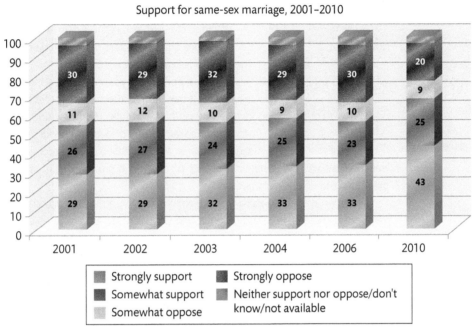

Support for same-sex marriage, 2001–2010

	Strongly support	Strongly oppose
	Somewhat support	Neither support nor oppose/don't know/not available
	Somewhat oppose	

Source: Courtesy of Focus Canada 2010, Environics Institute for Survey Research. Used with permission.

Does society shape our opinions on issues involving sexuality? In 2001, 41 percent of Canadian adults objected to sexual relations between two people of the same sex. By about 2010, however, this attitude declined to 29 percent of the population. Nationwide, Canada legalized same-sex marriage in 2005. Today, same-sex marriage is supported by 68 percent of Canadians. Although we tend to think of our attitudes as personal choices, larger social trends are also at work; disapproval rates are highest among older Canadians, men, individuals with low incomes, Albertans, and Conservative party supporters.

Chapter Overview

Sex. No one can doubt that it is an important dimension of our lives. But, as this chapter explains, sex is not simply a biological process linked to reproduction. It is society, including culture and patterns of inequality, that shapes patterns of sexual behaviour and gives meaning to sexuality in our everyday lives.

Ariel Skelley/Blend Images/Alamy Stock Photo

Pam Goodman walks along the hallway with her friends Jennifer Delosier and Cindy Thomas. The three young women are high school students in a small prairie town.

"What's happening after school?" Pam asks.

"Dunno," replies Jennifer. "Maybe Todd is coming over."

"Got the picture," adds Cindy. "We're so gone."

"Shut up!" Pam stammers, smiling. "I hardly know Todd." "OK, but ..." The three girls break into laughter.

It is no surprise that young people spend a lot of time thinking and talking about sex. And as the sociologist Peter Bearman discovered, sex involves more than just talk. Bearman and two colleagues (Bearman, Moody, & Stovel, 2004) conducted confidential interviews with 832 high school students, learning that 573 (69 percent of the students) had had at least one "sexual and romantic relationship" during the previous 18 months. So most, but not all, of these students are sexually active.

Bearman wanted to learn about sexual activity in order to understand the problem of sexually transmitted diseases (STDs) among young people. Why are the rates of STDs so high? And what can account for the sudden "outbreaks" of disease that involve dozens of young people in a community?

To find the answers to these questions, Bearman asked the students to identify their sexual partners (promising, of course, not to reveal any confidential information). This allowed him to trace connections between individual students in terms of sexual activity, which revealed a surprising pattern: Sexually active students were linked to each other through networks of common partners much more than anyone might have expected. In all, common partners linked half of the sexually active students, as shown in the diagram.

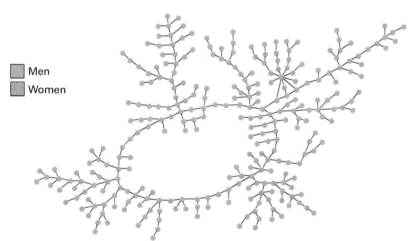

□ Men
□ Women

Other relationships
(If a pattern was observed more than once, numeral indicates frequency.)

Source: Bearman, Moody, and Stovel (2004).

Awareness of the connections among people can help us understand how STDs spread from one infected person to another in a short period of time. Bearman's study also shows that research can teach us a great deal about human sexuality, which is an important dimension of social life. You will also see that sexual attitudes and behaviour have changed dramatically over the past century in Canada.

Understanding Sexuality

(6.1) Describe how sexuality is both a biological and a cultural issue.

How much of your thoughts and actions every day involve sexuality? If you are like most people, the answer is "quite a lot," because sexuality is about much more than having sex. Sexuality is a theme found almost everywhere—in sports, on campus,

We claim that beauty is in the eye of the beholder, which suggests the importance of culture in setting standards of attractiveness. All of the people pictured here—from Kenya, Arizona, Saudi Arabia, Thailand, Ethiopia, and Ecuador—are considered beautiful by members of their own society.

in the workplace, and especially in the mass media. There is also a sex industry that includes pornography and prostitution, both of which are multibillion-dollar businesses in this country. The bottom line is that sexuality is an important part of how we think about ourselves as well as how others think about us. For this reason, there are few areas of social life in which sexuality does not play some part.

Although sex is a big part of everyday life, Canadian culture has long treated sex as taboo; even today, many people avoid talking about it. As a result, although sex can produce much pleasure, it also causes confusion, anxiety, and sometimes outright fear. Even scientists long considered sex off limits as a topic of research. Not until the middle of the twentieth century did researchers turn their attention to this vital dimension of social life. Since then, as this chapter explains, we have discovered a great deal about human sexuality.

Sex: A Biological Issue

Sex refers to *the biological distinction between females and males*. From a biological point of view, sex is the way the human species reproduces. A female ovum and a male sperm, each containing 23 chromosomes (biological codes that guide physical development), combine to form an embryo. To one of these pairs of chromosomes—the pair that determines the child's sex—the mother contributes an X chromosome and the father contributes either an X or a Y. Should the father contribute an X chromosome, a female (XX) embryo results; a Y from the father produces a male (XY) embryo. A child's sex is thereby determined biologically at the moment of conception.

sex the biological distinction between females and males

The sex of an embryo guides its development. If the embryo is male, the growth of testicular tissue starts to produce large amounts of testosterone, a hormone that triggers the development of male genitals (sex organs). If little testosterone is present, the embryo develops female genitals.

Sex and the Body

Some differences in the body set males and females apart. Right from birth, the two sexes have different **primary sex characteristics**, namely, *the genitals, organs used for reproduction*. At puberty, as people reach sexual maturity, additional sex differentiation takes place. At this point, people develop **secondary sex characteristics**, *bodily development, apart from the genitals, that distinguishes biologically mature females and males*. Mature females have wider hips for giving birth, milk-producing breasts for nurturing infants, and deposits of soft, fatty tissue that provide a reserve supply of nutrition during pregnancy and breastfeeding. Mature males typically develop more muscle in the upper body, more extensive body hair, and deeper voices. Of course, these are general differences; some males are smaller and have less body hair and higher voices than some females.

Keep in mind that sex is not the same thing as gender. *Gender* is an element of culture and refers to the personal traits and patterns of behaviour (including responsibilities, opportunities, and privileges) that a culture attaches to being female or male. Chapter 10 ("Gender Stratification") explains that gender is an important dimension of social inequality.

Intersexual People

Sex is not always as clear-cut as has been just described. The term **intersexual people** refers to *people whose bodies (including genitals) have both female and male characteristics*. Intersexuality is both natural and very rare, involving well below 1 percent of a society's population. An older term for intersexual people is *hermaphrodite* (a word derived from Hermaphroditus, the child of the mythological Greek gods Hermes and Aphrodite, who embodied both sexes). A true hermaphrodite has both a female ovarian and male testicular tissues.

However, our culture demands that sex be clear-cut, a fact evident in the requirement that parents record the sex of their new child at birth as either female or male. In Canada, some people respond to intersexual people with confusion or even disgust. But attitudes in other societies can be quite different: The Pokot of eastern Africa, for example, pay little attention to what they consider a rare biological error, and the Navajo look on intersexual people with awe, seeing in them the full potential of both the female and the male (Geertz, 1975).

Transsexuals

Transsexuals are *people who feel they are one sex even though biologically they are the other*. Estimates suggest that 1 or 2 of every 1000 people who are born experience the feeling of being trapped in a body of the wrong sex and have a desire to be the other sex.

Some people respond to this feeling by undergoing *gender reassignment*, surgical alteration of their genitals and breasts, usually accompanied by hormone treatments. This medical process is complex and takes months or even years, but it helps many people gain a joyful sense of finally becoming on the outside the person that they feel they are on the inside (Gagné, Tewksbury, & McGaughey, 1997; Olyslager & Conway, 2007).

Sex: A Cultural Issue

Sexuality has a biological foundation. But like all aspects of human behaviour, sexuality is also very much a cultural issue. Biology may explain some animals' mating rituals, but humans have no similar biological program. Although there is a biological "sex drive" in the sense that people find sex pleasurable and may want to engage in sexual activity, our biology does not dictate any specific ways of being sexual any more than our desire to eat dictates any particular foods or table manners.

Gregg DeGuire/PictureGroup/The Canadian Press

Chaz Bono, on the left, is the only child of entertainers Sonny Bono and Cher. Born Chastity Sun Bono, at age 18 Bono "came out" as a lesbian and became a gay rights advocate. In 2010, Bono legally changed his name to Chaz after completing a female-to-male gender transition.

primary sex characteristics the genitals, organs used for reproduction

intersexual people people whose bodies (including genitals) have both female and male characteristics

secondary sex characteristics bodily development, apart from the genitals, that distinguishes biologically mature females and males

transsexuals people who feel they are one sex even though biologically they are the other

Cultural Variation

Almost every sexual practice shows considerable variation from one society to another. In his pioneering study of human sexuality in North America, Alfred Kinsey and his colleagues (1948) found that most heterosexual couples reported having intercourse in a single position—face to face, with the woman on the bottom and the man on top. Halfway around the world, however, on islands in the South Seas, most couples *never* have sex in this way. In fact, when the people of the South Seas learned of this practice from Western missionaries, they poked fun at it as the strange "missionary position."

Even the simple practice of showing affection varies from society to society. Most people in Canada kiss in public, but the Chinese kiss only in private. The French kiss publicly, often twice (once on each cheek), and the Belgians kiss three times (starting on either cheek). The Maori of New Zealand rub noses, and most people in Nigeria don't kiss at all.

Modesty, too, is culturally variable. If a woman stepping into a bath is disturbed by someone entering the room, what body part do you think she would cover? Helen Colton (1983) reports that an Islamic woman covers her face, a Laotian woman covers her breasts, a Samoan woman covers her navel, a Sumatran woman covers her knees, and a European woman covers her breasts with one hand and her genital area with the other.

Around the world, some societies restrict sexuality, and others are more permissive. In China, for example, norms closely regulate sexuality so that few people have sexual intercourse before their wedding day. In Canada, at least in recent decades, intercourse prior to marriage has become the norm, and some people choose to have sex outside of marriage. Over the last 50 years, married couples have been declining. In 1961, married couples made up 96.1 percent of Canadian families; by 2011, they accounted for 67 percent (Statistics Canada, 2012a). The decrease in married couples is taking place at the same time as common-law couples are growing. Common-law couples have increased from 5.6 percent of all families in 1981 to 16.7 percent in 2011. As National Map 6–1 on page 168 indicates, common-law couples with children are also on the rise, with such families becoming more common in certain parts of Canada.

The Incest Taboo

When it comes to sex, do all societies agree on anything? The answer is yes. One cultural universal—an element that is found in every society the world over—is the **incest taboo**, *a norm forbidding sexual relations or marriage between certain relatives*. In Canada, both law and cultural mores prohibit close relatives (including brothers and sisters, parents and children) from having sex or marrying. But in another example of cultural variation, exactly which family

incest taboo a norm forbidding sexual relations or marriage between certain relatives

Over the course of the past century, social attitudes in North America have become more accepting of most aspects of human sexuality. What do you see as some of the benefits of this greater openness? What are some of the negative consequences?

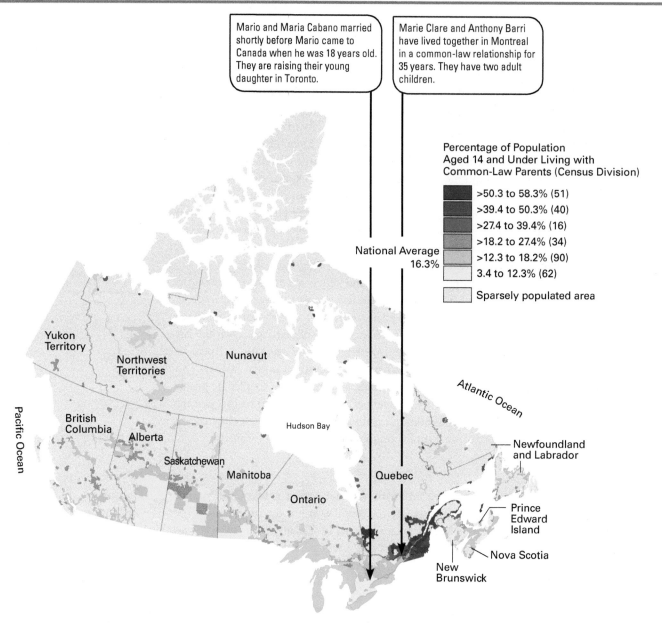

Mario and Maria Cabano married shortly before Mario came to Canada when he was 18 years old. They are raising their young daughter in Toronto.

Marie Clare and Anthony Barri have lived together in Montreal in a common-law relationship for 35 years. They have two adult children.

Percentage of Population Aged 14 and Under Living with Common-Law Parents (Census Division)

>50.3 to 58.3% (51)
>39.4 to 50.3% (40)
>27.4 to 39.4% (16)
>18.2 to 27.4% (34)
>12.3 to 18.2% (90)
3.4 to 12.3% (62)

Sparsely populated area

National Average 16.3%

NATIONAL MAP 6-1   Percentage of Population Aged 14 and Under Living with Common-Law Parents in 2011

About 7.3 percent of families in Canada are common-law couples with children. There are marked differences across the country, primarily by rural or urban status, but there are also marked differences between Quebec and the other provinces.

Source: Statistics Canada (2012b).

members are included in a society's incest taboo varies. It is legal throughout Canada, Mexico, and Europe to marry your cousin but about half of the states in the United States outlaw marriage between first cousins and the other half do not; a few permit this practice but with restrictions (National Conference of State Legislatures, 2012).

Some societies (such as the North American Navajo) apply incest taboos only to the mother and others on her side of the family. Throughout history, in a number of countries members of the nobility intermarried with relatives. There are even societies on record (including ancient Peru and Egypt) in which noble families formed brother-sister marriages. This pattern was a strategy to keep power within a single family (Murdock, 1965, orig. 1949).

Why does at least some form of incest taboo exist in every society around the world? Part of the reason is rooted in biology: Reproduction between close relatives of any species increases the odds of producing offspring with genetic diseases. But why, of all living species, do only humans observe an incest taboo? This fact suggests that controlling sexuality among close relatives is a necessary element of *social* organization. For one thing, the incest taboo limits sexual competition in families by restricting sex to spouses (ruling out, for example, a sexual relationship between parent and child). Second, because family ties define people's rights and obligations toward one another, reproduction between close relatives would hopelessly confuse kinship lines: If a mother and son had a daughter, would the child consider the male a father or a brother? Third, by requiring people to marry outside their immediate families, the incest taboo serves to integrate the larger society as people look beyond their close kin when seeking to form new families.

The incest taboo has long been a sexual norm in Canada and throughout the world. But many other sexual norms have changed over time. In the twentieth century, as the next section explains, our society experienced both a sexual revolution and a sexual counter-revolution.

Sexual Attitudes in Canada

(6.2) Explain changes in sexual attitudes in Canada.

What do people in Canada think about sex? Our cultural attitudes about sexuality have always been somewhat contradictory. Early immigrants demanded strict conformity in attitudes and behaviour, and they imposed severe punishment for any sexual misconduct, even if it took place in the privacy of the home. Later on, most European immigrants arrived with rigid ideas about "correct" sexuality, typically limiting sex to reproduction within marriage. Some regulation of sexual activity has continued ever since. Until 1969, for example, section 179 of the Criminal Code of Canada stated the following: "Everyone is guilty of an indictable offence and liable to two years' imprisonment who knowingly, without lawful excuse or justification, offers to sell, advertises, publishes an advertisement of or has for sale or disposal any medicine, drug or article intended or represented as a means of preventing conception or causing abortion" (quoted in McLaren & McLaren, 1986:19). Today, section 159(1) of the Criminal Code states that "every person who engages in an act of anal intercourse is guilty of an indictable offence and liable to imprisonment for a term not exceeding ten years or is guilty of an offence punishable on summary conviction." It wasn't until 1969 that an exception clause was written into the latter law, stating that the subsection does not apply to acts that take place in private—defined as there being only two people present in a private space—between consenting adults.

But this is just one side of the story. As Chapter 2 ("Culture") explains, Canadian culture is individualistic—many of us believe that people should be free to do pretty much as they wish as long as they cause no direct harm to others. The idea that what people do in the privacy of their own homes is no one else's business makes sex a matter of individual freedom and personal choice. One of Canada's former prime ministers, the late Pierre Elliott Trudeau, while still serving as the minister of justice, said as much in what is perhaps his most famous statement while in public office: "[T]he state has no business in the bedrooms of the nation."

When it comes to sexuality, is Canada restrictive or permissive? The answer is both. On one hand, many people in Canada still view holding oneself back sexually to be an important indicator of personal morality (for women even more than for men). On the other hand, sex is more and more a part of popular culture carried by the mass media. One recent study concluded that young people feel that most of the television shows they watch and the music they listen to has sexual themes. Furthermore, researchers claim that the number of scenes in television shows with sexual content has been increasing over time (Kunkel et al., 2005;

DeAngellis, 2011). Within this complex framework, we now turn to changes in sexual attitudes and behaviour that have occurred over the course of the past century.

The Sexual Revolution

Over the past century, Canada witnessed profound changes in sexual attitudes and practices. The first indications of this change came with industrialization in the 1920s as thousands of people migrated from farms and small towns to rapidly growing cities. There, living apart from their families and meeting new people in the workplace, young men and women enjoyed considerable sexual freedom, one reason that decade became known as the "Roaring Twenties."

In the 1930s and 1940s, the Great Depression and World War II slowed the rate of change. But in the postwar period, after 1945, a researcher named Alfred Kinsey set the stage for what later came to be known as the *sexual revolution*. In 1948, Kinsey and his colleagues published their first study of sexuality in the United States, and it raised eyebrows there as well as in Canada and Europe. The uproar resulted not so much from what he said as from the fact that scientists were actually studying sex, a topic many people were uneasy talking about even in the privacy of their homes.

Kinsey also had some very interesting things to say. His two books (Kinsey, Pomeroy, & Martin, 1948; Kinsey et al., 1953) became bestsellers partly because they revealed that people, on average, were far less conventional in sexual matters than most had thought. These books encouraged a new openness toward sexuality, which helped set the sexual revolution in motion.

In the late 1960s, the sexual revolution truly came of age. Youth culture dominated public life, and expressions such as "sex, drugs, and rock-and-roll" and "if it feels good, do it!" summed up a new, freer attitude toward sex. The baby boom generation, born between 1946 and 1964, became the first cohort in Canadian history to grow up with the idea that sex was part of people's lives, whether they were married or not.

New technology also played a part in the sexual revolution. The birth control pill, introduced in 1960, not only prevented pregnancy but also made "protected" sex more convenient. Unlike a condom or a diaphragm, which must be applied at the time of intercourse, the pill could be taken like a daily vitamin supplement. Now women as well as men could engage in sex spontaneously without any special preparation.

Because women were historically subject to greater sexual regulation than men, the sexual revolution had special significance for them. Society's traditional "double standard" allows (and even encourages) men to be sexually active but expects women to be virgins until marriage and faithful to their husbands afterwards. Canadian surveys since the mid-1990s show that females aged 15 to 24 are considerably less likely than their male counterparts to have had multiple sex partners in the last year, as shown in Figure 6–1(A). While in previous years females and males in this age group were equally likely to have had sex before age 17, as Figure 6–1(B) shows, males slightly surpassed

Diversity Snapshot

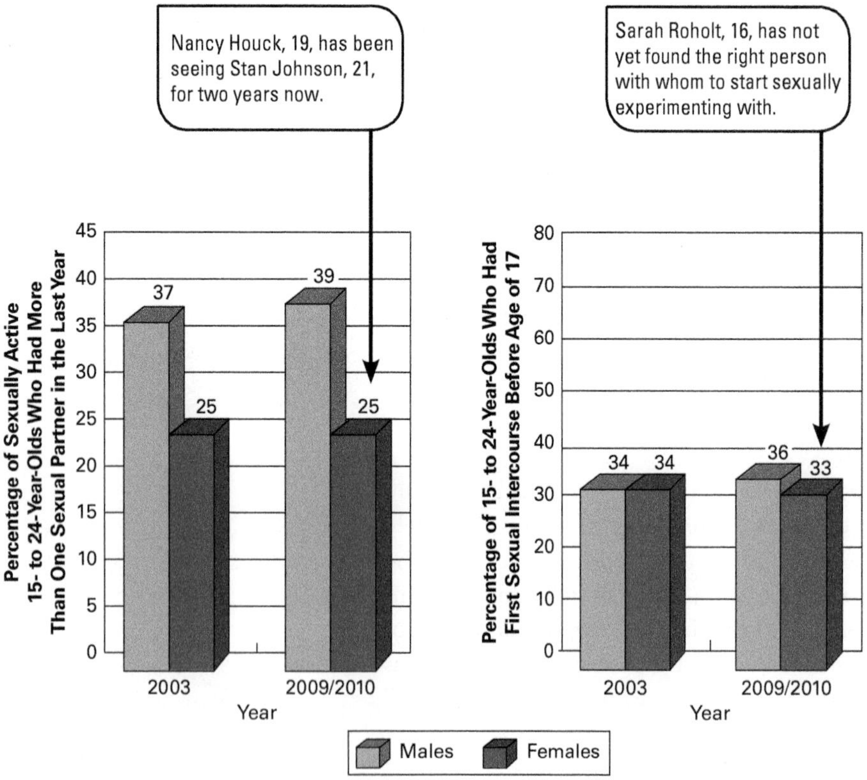

Nancy Houck, 19, has been seeing Stan Johnson, 21, for two years now.

Sarah Roholt, 16, has not yet found the right person with whom to start sexually experimenting with.

Males   Females

FIGURE 6–1 (A) Multiple Sexual Partners in the Last Year, (B) Sex before the Age of 17

Some sexual behaviour among teenagers appears to become similar for males and females. Keep in mind that other factors, such as age differences between dating partners, have an impact on sexual behaviour.

Source: Rotermann (2012).

females in 2009/2010. The reasons for this are unclear but what is clear from other studies is that young males and females are delaying having sex today as compared to 1996, when 11 percent of males and 13 percent of females had sex before age 15. By 2009/2010, 10 percent of males and 8 percent of females said they had had sex before turning 15 (Rotermann, 2008, 2012).

Greater openness about sexuality develops as societies become richer and the opportunities for women increase. With these facts in mind, look for a pattern in the global use of birth control shown in Global Map 6–1.

The Sexual Counter-Revolution

The sexual revolution made sex a topic of everyday discussion and sexual activity more a matter of individual choice. However, by 1980, the climate of sexual freedom that had marked

Window on the World

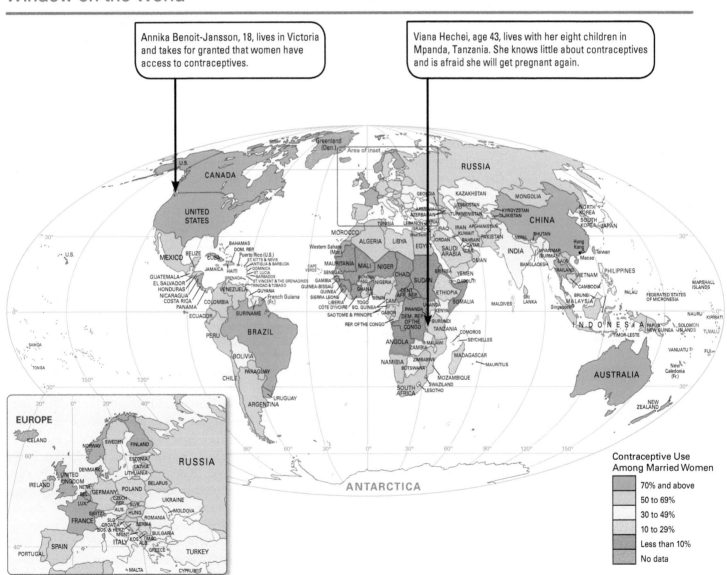

GLOBAL MAP 6–1 Contraceptive Use in Global Perspective

The map shows the percentage of married women using modern contraception methods (such as barrier methods, contraceptive pill, implants, injectables, intrauterine devices, or sterilization). In general, how do high-income nations differ from low-income nations? Can you explain this difference?

Sources: Data from United Nations (2008) and Population Reference Bureau (2011).

the late 1960s and 1970s was criticized by some people as evidence of moral decline, and the *sexual counter-revolution* began.

Politically speaking, the sexual counter-revolution was a conservative call for a return to "family values" and a change from sexual freedom back toward what critics saw as the sexual responsibility valued by earlier generations. Critics of the sexual revolution objected not just to the idea of "free love" but also to trends such as cohabitation (heterosexual couples living together without being married) and unmarried couples having children.

Looking back, the sexual counter-revolution did not greatly change the idea that people should decide for themselves when and with whom to have a sexual relationship. But whether for moral reasons or concerns about sexually transmitted diseases, more people began limiting their number of sexual partners or choosing not to have sex at all.

Is the sexual revolution over? It is true that many people are making more careful decisions about sexuality. But as the rest of this chapter explains, the ongoing sexual revolution is evident in the fact that there is now greater acceptance of premarital sex as well as increasing respect for various sexual orientations.

Premarital Sex

In light of the sexual revolution and the sexual counter-revolution, how much has sexual behaviour in Canada really changed? One interesting trend involves premarital sex—sexual intercourse before marriage—among young people.

Consider first what North Americans *say* about premarital intercourse. Public opinion in North America is far more accepting of premarital sex today than was the case a generation ago, but American society clearly remains more divided on this issue than does Canadian society. While in a recent poll only about 59 percent of people in the United States say sexual relations between unmarried women and men are "morally acceptable," some 83 percent of Canadians surveyed had no qualms about it (Angus Reid, 2013). As shown in Table 6–1, Canadians find many social behaviours morally acceptable, including contraception, divorce, abortion, and having a baby outside of marriage.

Now let's look at what young people actually *do*. For women, there has been a marked change over time. The Kinsey studies reported that among people born in the early 1900s, about 50 percent of men but just 6 percent of women had had premarital sexual intercourse before age 19. Studies of baby boomers, born after World War II, show a slight increase in premarital intercourse among men and a large increase—to about one-third—among women. The most recent studies show that by the time they are seniors in high school, about one-third of young men and women have had premarital sexual intercourse. In addition, sexual experience among high school students who are sexually active is limited—only 15 percent of students report four or more sexual partners. Over the last 20 years, the statistics tracking sexual activity among high school students have shown a gradual trend downward (Laumann et al., 1994; Martinez, Copen, & Abma, 2011; Centers for Disease Control and Prevention, 2012). In fact, as shown in Figure 6–1 on page 170, Canadian teens appear to be initiating sexual intercourse a bit later than the generation before and there is a small drop in the number of sex partners teens are reporting compared to a decade and a half ago (Boyce et al., 2003; Boyce, 2004; Maticka-Tyndale, 2008; Rotermann, 2008, 2012). Recent research shows that romantic love between young people can help fill the emotional gaps during the transition to adulthood, and it may act as a barrier to delinquent behaviour, including involvement in crime (McCarthy & Casey, 2008).

A common belief is that an even larger share of young people engages in oral sex. This choice reflects the fact that this practice avoids the risk of pregnancy; in addition, many young people see oral sex as something less than "going all the way." Recent research suggests that the share of young people between the ages of 15 and 19 who have had oral sex is 48 percent for boys and 46 percent for girls, which is only

TABLE 6–1 How Canadians View Sex and Relationships

"For each issue, respondents were asked whether this is morally acceptable, morally unacceptable, or not a moral issue."

	Morally Unacceptable
Sexual relations between unmarried adults	15%
Using contraceptives	4%
Divorce	9%
Abortion	26%
Homosexuality	15%
Married people having an affair	76%

Source: Pew Research Center (2014).

slightly larger than the share who have had intercourse (Centers for Disease Control and Prevention, 2012). Therefore, mass media claims of an "oral sex epidemic" are almost certainly exaggerated.

Finally, a significant minority of young people choose abstinence (not having sexual intercourse). Many also choose not to have oral sex, which, like intercourse, can transmit disease. Even so, research confirms the fact that premarital sex is widely accepted among young people today

Sex Between Adults

Judging from the mass media, Canadians are very active sexually. But do popular images reflect reality? According to a poll by the Angus Reid Group (1998a), the frequency of sexual activity varies widely in the Canadian population. In response to the question "How many times a month do you have sex?" the pattern breaks down like this: while, on average, Canadians have sex 6.2 times per month—or slightly more than once a week—the average is 7.5 times for Atlantic Canadians, 8.9 times for adults aged 18 to 34, 12.0 times for those living with a partner, and 7.3 times for high-income Canadians (defined as those with household incomes over $55 000). In short, no single pattern accurately describes sexual activity in Canada today.

We also know that sexual activity among Canadian adults is lower today (64 percent) than it was in 1984 (75 percent) (Angus Reid Group, 1998a). The Global Erectile Dysfunction Poll indicates that Canadians aged 46 to 60, while in line with the national average of having sex slightly more than once a week, are less likely to do so spontaneously than are people in other countries. Also, in this age category, 40 percent of Canadians admitted to coming up with excuses in order to avoid having sex (SKIM Healthcare, 2011).

And yet, despite the widespread image of "swinging singles" promoted on television shows such as *Sex and the City*, it is married people who have sex with partners the most. In addition, married people report the highest level of satisfaction—both physical and emotional—with their partners (Laumann et al., 1994).

Extramarital Sex

What about married people having sex outside of marriage? This practice, commonly called "adultery" (sociologists prefer the more neutral term *extramarital sex*), is widely condemned. Table 6–1 shows that 76 percent of Canadians think that "married people having an affair" is morally unacceptable. Likewise, 90 percent of U.S. adults consider a married person's having sex with someone other than the marital partner to be "always wrong" or "almost always wrong" (NORC, 2013). The norm of sexual fidelity within marriage has been and remains a strong element of North American culture.

But, of course, actual behaviour falls short of the cultural ideal. A national Canadian survey shows that 12 percent of married, common-law, or living in a relationship Canadians stated that they have had an affair while in their current relationship (a similar proportion—11 percent—preferred not to answer) (Forum Research, 2012a). Researchers also report that this share is higher among men (14 percent) than among women (10 percent) (with once again a similar proportion preferring not to answer). Stating this the other way around, a vast majority of men (73 percent) and women (82 percent) remain sexually committed to their partners. Research also indicates that 59 percent of men and women who engage in extramarital sex have done so more than once. The incidence of extramarital sex is highest in Ontario and the Prairies (both at 14 percent) and lowest in Atlantic Canada (5 percent), and is higher among 55 to 64 year olds (14 percent) and lowest among Canadians aged 35 to 54 and 65 and over (both at 10 percent) (Forum Research, 2012a).

Sex over the Life Course

Patterns of sexual activity change with age. In Canada, most young women and men become sexually active between ages 16 and 21. By the time they reach their mid-twenties, about 90 percent of both women and men report being sexually active with a partner at least once during the past year (Boyce, 2004; McCreary Centre Society, 2004; Rotermann, 2008).

Overall, adults report having sexual intercourse about 62 times a year, which is slightly more often than once a week. Young adults report the highest frequency of sexual intercourse at 84 times per year. This number falls to 64 times for adults in their forties and declines further to about 10 times per year for adults in their seventies.

From another angle, by about age 60, less than half of adults (54 percent of men and 42 percent of women) say they have had sexual intercourse one or more times during the past year. By age 70, just 43 percent of men and 22 percent of women report the same behaviour (Smith, 2006; Reece et al., 2010).

Sexual Orientation

6.3 Analyze factors that shape sexual orientation.

Sexual orientation is *a person's romantic and emotional attraction to another person.* **Heterosexuality** (*hetero* is Greek for "the other of two") means *sexual attraction to someone of the other sex* whereas **homosexuality** (*homo* is Greek for "the same") means *sexual attraction to someone of the same sex.* Keep in mind that people do not necessarily fall into just one of these categories; they may have varying degrees of attraction to both sexes.

The idea that sexual orientation is not clear-cut is confirmed by the existence of **bisexuality**, *sexual attraction to people of both sexes.* Some bisexual people are equally attracted to males and females; many others are more attracted to one sex than the other. Finally, **asexuality** refers to *a lack of sexual attraction to people of either sex.* Figure 6–2 shows each of these sexual orientations in relation to the others.

It is important to remember that sexual *attraction* is not the same thing as sexual *behaviour.* Many people, perhaps even most people, have experienced attraction to someone of the same sex, but far fewer ever actually engage in same-sex behaviour. This is in large part because our culture discourages such actions.

While heterosexuality is the norm almost everywhere, most societies tolerate homosexuality. Among the ancient Greeks, upper-class men considered homosexuality the highest form of relationship, partly because they looked down on women as intellectually inferior. As men saw it, heterosexuality was necessary only so they could have children, and "real" men preferred homosexual relations (Kluckhohn, 1948; Ford & Beach, 1951; Greenberg, 1988).

Diversity Snapshot

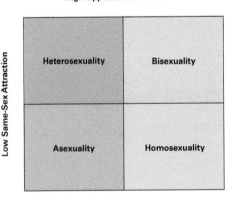

High Opposite-Sex Attraction

Heterosexuality	Bisexuality
Asexuality	Homosexuality

Low Same-Sex Attraction — High Same-Sex Attraction

Low Opposite-Sex Attraction

FIGURE 6–2 Four Sexual Orientations

A person's levels of same-sex attraction and opposite-sex attraction are two distinct dimensions that combine in various ways to produce four major sexual orientations.

Source: Adapted from Storms (1980).

What Gives Us a Sexual Orientation?

The question of how people come to have a particular sexual orientation is strongly debated. The arguments cluster into two general positions: sexual orientation as a product of society and sexual orientation as a product of biology.

Sexual Orientation: A Product of Society

This approach argues that people in any society attach meanings to sexual activity, and these meanings differ from place to place and over time. As Michel Foucault (1990, orig. 1978) points out, for example, there was no distinct category of people called "homosexuals" until a century ago, when scientists and eventually the public as a whole began defining people that way. Throughout history, many people no doubt had what we would call "homosexual experiences," but neither they nor others saw in this behaviour the basis for any special identity.

Anthropological studies show that patterns of homosexuality differ from one society to another. In Siberia, for example, the Chukchee Eskimo have a practice in which one man dresses as a woman and does a woman's work. The Sambia, who dwell in the Eastern Highlands of New Guinea, have a ritual in which young boys perform oral sex on older men in the belief that eating semen will make them more masculine. In southeastern Mexico, a region in which ancient religions recognize gods who are both female and male, the local culture defines

sexual orientation a person's romantic and emotional attraction to another person

| heterosexuality sexual attraction to someone of the other sex | homosexuality sexual attraction to someone of the same sex | bisexuality sexual attraction to people of both sexes | asexuality a lack of sexual attraction to people of either sex |

people not only as female and male but also as *muxes* (MOO-shays), a third sexual category. *Muxes* are men who dress and act as women, some only on ritual occasions, some all the time. The Thinking About Diversity box on page 176 takes a closer look. Such diversity around the world shows that sexual expression is not fixed by human biology but is socially constructed (Murray & Roscoe, 1998; Blackwood & Wieringa, 1999; Rosenberg, 2008).

Sexual Orientation: A Product of Biology

A growing body of evidence suggests that sexual orientation is innate, or rooted in human biology, in much the same way that people are born right-handed or left-handed. Arguing this position, Simon LeVay (1993) links sexual orientation to the structure of a person's brain. LeVay studied the brains of both homosexual and heterosexual men and found a small but important difference in the size of the hypothalamus, a part of the brain that regulates hormones. Such an anatomical difference, he claims, plays a part in shaping a person's sexual orientation.

Genetics may also influence sexual orientation. One study of 44 pairs of brothers, all homosexual, found that 33 pairs had a distinctive genetic pattern involving the X chromosome. The gay brothers also had an unusually high number of gay male relatives—but only on their mother's side. Such evidence leads some researchers to think there may be a "gay gene" located on the X chromosome (Hamer & Copeland, 1994).

EVALUATE Mounting evidence supports the conclusion that sexual orientation is rooted in biology, although the best guess at present is that both nature and nurture play a part. Remember that sexual orientation is not a matter of neat categories. Most people who think of themselves as homosexual have had heterosexual experiences, just as many people who think of themselves as heterosexual have had homosexual experiences. Explaining sexual orientation, then, is not easy.

There is also a political issue here with great importance for gay men and lesbians. To the extent that sexual orientation is based in biology, homosexuals have no more choice about their sexual orientation than they do about their skin colour. If this is so, shouldn't gay men and lesbians expect the same legal protection from discrimination as, for example, visible minorities?

CHECK YOUR LEARNING What evidence supports the position that sexual behaviour is constructed by society? That sexual orientation is rooted in biology?

How Many Gay People Are There?

What share of our population is gay? This is a difficult question to answer because, as noted earlier, sexual orientation is not a matter of neat categories. In addition, not all people are willing to reveal their sexuality to strangers or even to family members. Kinsey estimated that about 4 percent of males and 2 percent of females have an exclusively same-sex orientation, although he pointed out that most people experience same-sex attraction at some point in their lives.

The results of research surveys show that how homosexuality is defined makes a big difference in the size of the homosexual population. Some social scientists put the gay share of the population at 10 percent This is about the share of people who say that they have *ever* felt any sexual attraction to a person of the same sex. But feeling some sexual attraction and acting on

Thinking About Diversity: Race, Class, and Gender

A Third Gender: The *Muxes* of Mexico

Alejandro Taledo, 16 years old, stands on a street corner in Juchitán, a small town in the state of Oaxaca, in southeastern Mexico. Called Alex by her friends, she has finished a day of selling flowers with her mother and now waits for a bus to ride home for dinner.

As you may know, Alejandro is commonly a boy's name. In fact, this young Mexican was born an anatomical male. But several years ago, Alex decided that, whatever her sex, she felt she was a girl and she decided to live according to her own feelings.

In this community, she is not alone. Juchitán and the surrounding region are well known not only for beautiful black pottery and delicious food but also for the large number of gays, lesbians, and transgender people who live there. At first glance, this fact may surprise people who think of Mexico as a traditional country, especially when it comes to gender and sexuality. In Mexico, the stereotype goes, men control the lives of women, especially their sexuality. But like all stereotypes, this one misses some important facts. Nationally, Mexico has become more tolerant of diverse sexual expression. In 2009, Mexico City, the nation's capital, began recognizing same-sex marriages. And nowhere is acceptance for sexual orientation greater than it is in the region around Juchitán.

There, transgender people are called *muxes* (MOO-shays), which is based on the Spanish word *mujer*, meaning "woman." *Muxes* are considered neither male nor female but of a third gender. Some *muxes* wear women's clothing and act almost entirely in a feminine way. Others adopt a feminine look and behaviour

only on special occasions. One of the most popular events is the region's grand celebration, which is held every November and is attended by more than 2000 *muxes* and their families. A highlight of this event is a competition for the title of "transvestite of the year."

The acceptance of transgender people in central Mexico has its roots in the culture that existed before the Spanish arrived. At that time, anyone with ambiguous gender was viewed as especially wise and talented. The region's history includes accounts of Aztec priests and Mayan gods who cross-dressed or were considered to be both male and female. In the sixteenth century, the coming of the Spanish colonists and the influence of the Catholic Church undermined many of these transgender roles. But acceptance of mixed sexual identity continues today in this region, where many people hold so tightly to their traditions that they speak only their ancient Zapotec language rather than Spanish.

And so it is in Juchitán that *muxes* are respected, accepted, and even celebrated. *Muxes* are successful in business and take leadership roles in the church and in politics. Most important, they are commonly accepted by friends and family alike. Alejandro lives with her parents and five siblings and helps her mother both selling flowers on the streets and at home. Her father, Victor Martinez Jimenez, is a local construction worker who speaks only Zapotec. He still refers to Alex as "him" but says "it was God who sent him, and why would I reject him? He helps his mother very much. Why would I get mad?" Alex's mother, Rosa Taledo Vicente, adds, "Every family considers it a blessing to have one gay son. While daughters marry and leave home, a *muxe* cares for his parents in their old age."

What Do You Think?

1. Do you think that Canadian society is tolerant of people wishing to combine masculine and feminine dress and behaviour? Why or why not?

2. *Muxes* are people who were born biologically male. How do you think the local people in this story would feel about women who wanted to dress and act like men? Would you expect equal treatment of such people? Why or why not?

3. How do you personally feel about the existence of a third category of sexual identity? Explain your views.

Sources: Gave (2005), Lacey (2008), and Rosenberg (2008).

Shaul Schwarz/Getty Images

it are two different issues. In one U.S. study, just 6 percent of men and 11 percent of women between the ages of 15 and 44 reported engaging in homosexual activity *at some time in their lives*. At the same time, just 2.3 percent of men and 1.3 percent of women defined themselves as "partly" or "entirely" homosexual (Laumann et al., 1994).

In recent U.S. surveys, about 1.1 percent of men and 3.5 percent of women described themselves as bisexual. But bisexual experiences appear to be fairly common among younger people, especially on college and university campuses (Laumann et al., 1994; Leland, 1995;

Reece et al., 2010; Chandra et al., 2011). Many bisexuals do not think of themselves as either gay or straight, and their behaviour reflects aspects of both gay and straight living.

Canadian studies on the number of gay and bisexual people indicate similar results. One survey of those aged 18 and over showed that 5.3 percent of Canadians identify themselves as lesbian, gay, bisexual, or transgendered (Forum Research, 2012b). A total of 45 300 couples in the 2006 Census of Canada belonged to a same-sex family, which is 0.6 percent of all marital and common-law unions in the country. The 2011 Census enumerated 64 575 same-sex couples, representing an increase of 42.4 percent from 2006 (Statistics Canada, 2012b). Figure 6–3 shows the number of same-sex and opposite-sex Canadian families.

The Gay Rights Movement

In 2003, the Ontario Court of Appeal issued the first certificate of marriage to a gay couple in Canada. Since this historic moment, it is estimated that more than 20 000 marriage licences have been issued to same-sex couples in Canada.

In recent decades, public opinion about sexual orientation has shown a remarkable change. In Canada and in much of the world, public attitudes toward homosexuality have been moving toward greater acceptance. As shown in the Power of Society figure at the beginning of this chapter, 68 percent of Canadians support same-sex marriage. This is an increase in support from previous polls. Among

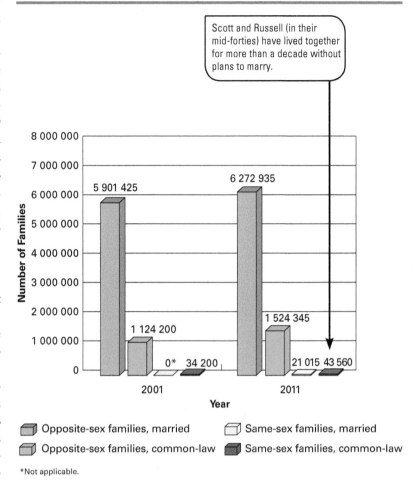

Scott and Russell (in their mid-forties) have lived together for more than a decade without plans to marry.

Legend:
- Opposite-sex families, married
- Opposite-sex families, common-law
- Same-sex families, married
- Same-sex families, common-law

*Not applicable.

FIGURE 6–3 Distribution of Couples by Conjugal Status, Canada, 2011
Source: Statistics Canada (2012b).

Gay parades are now a common feature in most Canadian cities despite resistance in the past by some elected officials in places like Fredericton, Hamilton, and Kelowna.

Student Snapshot

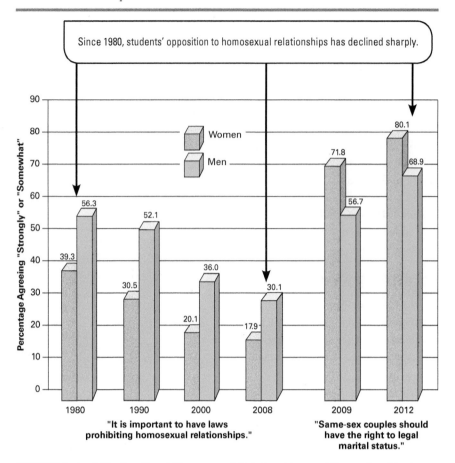

Since 1980, students' opposition to homosexual relationships has declined sharply.

FIGURE 6–4 Attitudes About Homosexual Relationships and Same-Sex Marriage Among First-Year College Students, 1980–2012

The historical trend among university and college students is toward respect of homosexual relationships, a view held by a large majority.

Sources: Astin et al. (2002) and Pryor et al. (2010).

college students, who are typically more tolerant of homosexuality than the general population, we see a similar trend toward acceptance. In 1980, as Figure 6–4 shows, about half of college students supported laws prohibiting homosexual relationships; in the following decades, that share declined dramatically. The most recent surveys on this issue asked students whether they supported same-sex couples having the legal right to marry; by 2012, as the figure shows, three-quarters of college students claimed to support legal same-sex marriage (Astin et al., 2002; Pryor et al., 2013).

In large measure, this change was brought about by the gay rights movement, which began in the middle of the twentieth century. Up to that time, most people in this country did not discuss homosexuality, and it was common for employers (including the federal government and the armed forces) to fire anyone who was gay or lesbian (or was even *accused* of being gay). Mental health professionals, too, took a hard line, describing homosexual people as "sick" and sometimes placing them in mental hospitals where, it was hoped, they might be "cured."

Facing such prejudice, it is no surprise that most lesbians and gay men remained "in the closet," closely guarding the secret of their sexual orientation. But the gay rights movement gained strength during the 1960s. One early milestone occurred in 1973, when the American Psychiatric Association (APA) declared that it would no longer define homosexuality as an illness; the organization stated that it was nothing more than "a form of sexual behavior." In

2009, the APA went a step further and condemned the use of psychological therapy in an effort to make gay people straight (Cracy, 2009).

The gay rights movement also began using the term **homophobia** to describe *discomfort over close personal interaction with people thought to be gay, lesbian, or bisexual* (Weinberg, 1973). Concepts such as homophobia (literally, "fear of sameness"), and more recently "heterosexism" and "heteronormativity," turn the tables on society: Instead of asking "What's wrong with gay people?" the question becomes "What's wrong with people who can't accept a different sexual orientation?"

As another indication of the growing acceptance of same-sex relationships, in recent years an increasing number of high schools have had requests from gay and lesbian students that they be allowed to bring a same-sex date to the senior prom.

Transgender

As the gay rights movement has gained acceptance for gay, lesbian, and bisexual people, there has also been greater acceptance of people who challenge conventional gender patterns. **Transgender** is a broad concept that refers to *appearing or behaving in ways that challenge conventional cultural norms concerning how females and males should look and act*. People in the transgender community do not think of themselves or express their sexuality according to conventional standards. In other words, transgender people disregard conventional ideas about femininity or masculinity in favour of combining feminine and masculine traits or perhaps embodying something entirely different.

Transgender is not a sexual orientation. Transgender people may think of themselves as gay or lesbian, heterosexual, bisexual, asexual, as some combination of these categories, or in entirely different terms. To be transgender is also not always the same as to be transsexual. Although overlap may exist between the two categories, there are important differences as well. Suzanne Kessler and Wendy McKenna (2000) propose three ways of conceptualizing the "trans" prefix in respect to sex and gender: 1) transgender as synonymous with transsexual, where change from one sex to another is sought (male to female or vice versa); 2) transgender as distinct from transsexual, involving movement between genders (masculine to feminine or vice versa) without a change in primary or secondary sex characteristics; 3) transgender as distinct from transsexual, involving the leaving behind of the binary gender system (neither masculine nor feminine).

Researchers estimate that about 3 in every 1000 adults in North America have a transgender identity (Gates, 2011). It is becoming common to speak about the lesbian, gay, bisexual, and transgender (LGBT) population. Because someone may identify with more than one of these categories, no exact number can be placed on the size of the LGBT population. But estimates suggest that over 5 percent of the Canadian adult population is within the LGBT community.

homophobia discomfort over close personal interaction with people thought to be gay, lesbian, or bisexual

transgender appearing or behaving in ways that challenge conventional cultural norms concerning how females and males should look and act

Sexual Issues and Controversies

(**6.4**) Discuss several current controversies involving sexuality.

Sexuality lies at the heart of a number of controversies in Canada today. Here we take a look at four key issues: teen pregnancy, pornography, prostitution, and sexual violence.

Teen Pregnancy

Because being sexually active carries the risk of pregnancy, this behaviour demands a high level of personal responsibility. Teenagers may be biologically mature enough to conceive, but many are not emotionally mature enough to appreciate the consequences of their actions.

In 2001, the annual teenage pregnancy rate in Canada fell to 35.4 pregnancies for every 1000 women under the age of 20. The teen pregnancy rate in Canada has continued to fall, and is in fact dropping faster than in the United States and England. Between 2001 and 2010,

Canada's teen pregnancy rate fell by 20.3 percent, resulting, in 2010, in a teenage pregnancy rate that was 28.2 pregnancies for every 1000 women (McKay, 2012). These outcomes are an indication of a greater awareness among Canadian youth about how to prevent pregnancy and delay parenting, as well as their ready access to contraception and abortion (McKay & Barrett, 2010). However, research shows that inequities persist in our country, including among rural and very young teens who have less access to sexual and reproductive health care (Shoveller et al., 2007). Furthermore, access to abortion remains limited or out of reach in some regions of the country (Maticka-Tyndale, 2008).

The situation is much different in the United States. Surveys show that there are almost 768 000 teen pregnancies in the United States each year, most of them unplanned. The rate of births to teenage women in the United States is higher than that of most other high-income countries and is twice the rate in Canada (Alan Guttmacher Institute, 2012; Ventura et al., 2012).

Did the sexual revolution raise the level of teenage pregnancy? Perhaps surprisingly, the answer is no. The rate of pregnancy among teens in 1950 was higher than it is today, partly because people back then married at a younger age. Because abortion was against the law, many pregnancies led to quick marriages. As a result, there were many pregnant teenagers, but most were married. Figure 6–5 shows that the number of pregnant teens today has fallen, but the vast majority of these women are unmarried.

Pornography

pornography sexually explicit material intended to cause sexual arousal

Pornography is *sexually explicit material intended to cause sexual arousal*. But what is or is not pornographic has long been a matter of debate. Recognizing that different people view the portrayals of sexuality differently, the Supreme Court of Canada gives local communities the power to decide for themselves what violates "community standards" of decency and lacks any "redeeming social value."

Child pornography is a very different matter, however. Section 163.1 of the Criminal Code states that "every person who possesses any child pornography is guilty of either a) an indictable offence and liable to imprisonment for a term not exceeding five years; or b) an

Student Snapshot

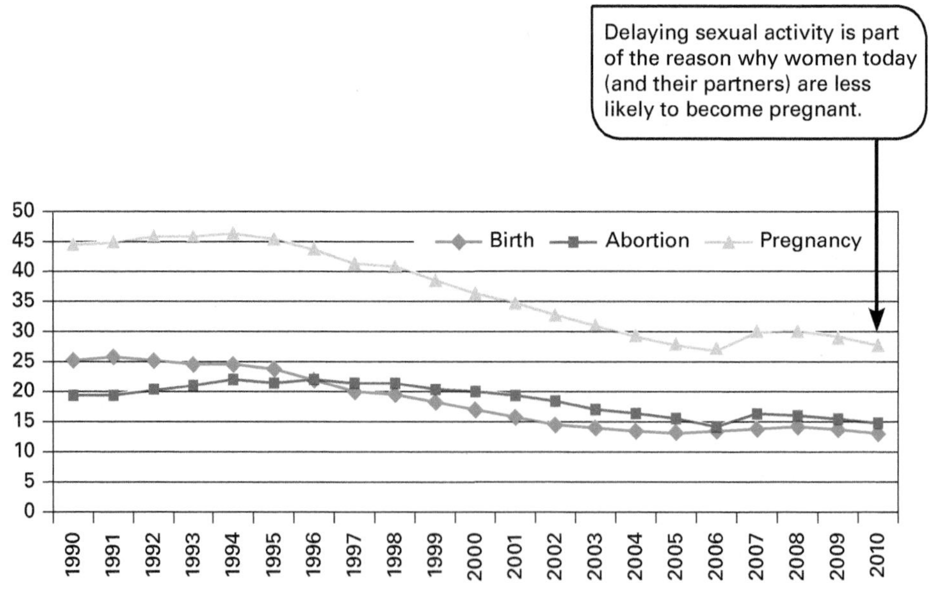

Delaying sexual activity is part of the reason why women today (and their partners) are less likely to become pregnant.

FIGURE 6–5 Teenage Pregnancies, Abortions, Live Births, Canada, 1990–2010

Source: P. 167 (graph) from McKay, Alexander. "Trends in Canadian National and Provincial/Territorial Teen Pregnancy Rates: 2001-201." The Canadian Journal of Human Sexuality, Volume 21, No. 3&4. Used with permission.

offence punishable on summary conviction." Yet enforcement of even this law has proven to be difficult. In 1999, the British Columbia Court of Appeal struck down subsection 4 of section 163.1 of the Criminal Code, which makes the possession of child pornography a criminal offence, because the subsection contravened the Charter of Rights and Freedoms. In January 2000, the Supreme Court of Canada heard arguments in an appeal of this B.C. court decision. During a retrial in March 2002, the presiding judge concluded that the written document of the accused, which consisted of 17 short stories describing man-boy and boy-boy sex—including sadism, masochism, and fellatio—contained "artistic merit" and was therefore not in violation of the child pornography law. However, the accused was found guilty of the lesser offence of possessing sexually explicit photographs of children. The accused was given a minimal sentence of house arrest for four months that included internet restrictions and the prohibition from interacting with anyone under the age of 18.

Supreme Court decisions aside, pornography is very popular in Canada: sexually explicit videos, movies, and magazines; telephone "sex lines"; and thousands of internet websites make up a thriving industry that takes in approximately $10 billion each year. In a recent study, 35 percent of Canadians report viewing or purchasing pornography at least once a week, while another 15 percent preferred not to answer. Users tend to be young, male, and wealthy, and are more likely to reside in Atlantic Canada or British Columbia (Forum Research, 2014).

Yet pornography has its critics. Traditionally, people have criticized pornography on *moral* grounds. As national surveys confirm, 50 percent of adults are concerned that pornography is harmful to Canadian society (Forum Research, 2014). Today, however, pornography is also seen as a *power* issue because it endorses the cultural ideal of men as the legitimate controllers of both sexuality and women (MacKinnon, 1987). While it is difficult to prove a scientific cause-and-effect relationship between what people view and how they act, the public shares a concern about pornography and violence, with almost half of adults holding the opinion that pornography encourages people to commit rape (NORC, 2013).

Prostitution

Prostitution is *the selling of sexual services*. Often called "the world's oldest profession," prostitution has been widespread throughout recorded history. One Canadian survey found that 4 percent of male respondents admitted to having paid for sexual favours one or more times (Peat Marwick, 1984). Sociologist Chris Atchison points out that no recent data on the subject exist but that, when compared to research on countries like New Zealand, Australia, and Britain, the number of Canadians who have purchased sex is likely to be between 4 and 7 percent (Paris, 2014). To the extent that people think of sex as an expression of interpersonal intimacy, they find the idea of sex for money disturbing. Even in this regard, however, there are no cross-cultural universals and there is no clear agreement on the issue in Canada. As one study revealed, gender plays a role in shaping how Canadians view prostitution. While 62 percent of men believe that selling sex should be legal, a smaller amount, 40 percent, of women echo this sentiment. And while 55 percent of women believe that purchasing sex should be illegal, only 35 percent of men support this view (Angus Reid Global, 2014).

Prostitution is actually not illegal in Canada. Rather, sex workers in Canada are arrested, prosecuted, and sometimes convicted not because they sell sex for money but because they "communicate" in a public place for the purpose of engaging in prostitution (Shaver, 1993; Hackler, 1999). Meanwhile, in Sweden, a 1999 law makes it legal for sex workers to sell sex but illegal for "johns" (customers) to purchase it (Boethus, 1999). The common belief in Canada is that "sex workers" or "sex industry workers" (less stigmatizing terms than *prostitutes*) are almost always female rather than male and are more culpable and blameworthy than their customers. In 2014, the Canadian government passed a similar law to Sweden's. Known as Bill C-36, it attempts to criminalize the buyers of sex. Its critics—sex workers among them—point out that, although the law is presented as something that will "protect" sex

prostitution the selling of sexual services

industry workers, it actually criminalizes the kind of work that they do. Some of the proposed changes that the law makes is to prohibit sellers from advertising as well as communicating with clients in public, thus driving the sex trade industry further underground. Consequently, as it is socially constructed and legally enforced, prostitution in Canada remains biased against women and in favour of men (Shaver, 1993; Boritch, 1997).

Around the world, prostitution shows tremendous variation: sex workers in the Netherlands and Germany not only have legal rights to work but also pay taxes and collect social benefits that accompany most legitimate jobs. In Queensland and Victoria, Australia, brothels may operate legally if their owners and operators are licensed by state-level government and if the town approves the brothel premises under town planning guidelines. The Prostitution Reform Act 2003 was passed in New Zealand with the main aim of decriminalizing most aspects of sex industry work at the national level and enhancing the working conditions and health and safety of legal adult residents working in the sex industry (Abel, Fitzgerald, & Healy, 2010). On the other hand, in low-income countries where patriarchy is strong and traditional cultural norms limit women's ability to earn a living, prostitution may be the only option available to women in terms of providing for their own and their children's survival.

Types of Prostitution

Most sex workers are women (estimates range from 70 to 80 percent), and they fall into different categories. Call girls (and, more rarely, call boys) are elite sex workers who are typically young, attractive, and well educated and who arrange their own "dates" with clients by texting or telephone. The classified pages of any large city newspaper contain numerous ads for "escort services," by which women (and sometimes men) offer both companionship and sex for a fee.

In the middle category are prostitutes who are employed in "massage parlours" or brothels under the control of managers. These sex workers have less choice about their clients, receive less money for their services, and get to keep no more than half of the money they earn.

At the bottom of the hierarchy are streetwalkers, women and men who "work the streets" of large cities. Some female streetwalkers are under the control of male pimps who take most of their earnings. Many others are people with a substance addiction who sell sex in order to buy drugs. Both types of people are at high risk of becoming the victims of violence (Davidson, 1998; Estes, 2001).

Canadian research shows that sex workers located in off-street "escort agencies" tend to enjoy safer, more stable, and more lucrative work conditions than do their counterparts working on the street (Lowman & Fraser, 1995; Brock, 1998; Lewis & Maticka-Tyndale, 1999). Other research on off-street and on-street sex work supports this general finding but also shows that, in the absence of even minimum work standards, workers in escort agencies and massage parlours and other indoor employment venues have no legal avenue to protect themselves when subject to exploitation by their employers (Benoit & Millar, 2001; Phillips & Benoit, 2005).

Most sex workers offer heterosexual services. However, gay male sex workers also trade sex for money. Researchers report that many gay sex workers have suffered rejection by family and friends because of their sexual orientation (Weisberg, 1985; Boyer, 1989; Kruks, 1991). Research on transgender sex workers in San Francisco's Tenderloin area suggests that they face a similar situation of discrimination and rejection because of their sexual orientation (Weinberg, Shaver, & Williams, 2000).

A Victimless Crime?

Prostitution is against the law in many countries, but many people consider it a victimless crime. Consequently, instead of enforcing prostitution laws all the time, police stage only occasional crackdowns. This policy reflects a desire to control prostitution while also recognizing that it is impossible to eliminate it entirely.

Is selling sex a victimless crime that hurts no one? Certainly, many people take this position, arguing that prostitution should be viewed as an occupation, as simply a way to make a living (Scambler & Scambler, 1997; Elias, Bullough, Elias, & Elders, 1998). Further, because of difficulties in getting jobs that provide a decent wage for marginalized people, in particular working-class female single parents, sex work represents a viable choice from their perspective (Chapkis, 1997). However, because prostitution is a semi-illegal and illegitimate occupation in Canada, it is very difficult for sex workers to receive the same benefits and rights as other workers, such as sick leave, health insurance, social insurance, or workers' compensation (Shaver, 1993; Lowman & Fraser, 1995; Lewis & Maticka-Tyndale, 1999).

The issue of violence among sex workers has recently gained media attention after the multiple murders of women involved in street-based sex work in Vancouver's Downtown Eastside. Subsequently, on September 28, 2010, Ontario Superior Court Justice Susan Himel found three crucial sections of the Criminal Code of Canada unconstitutional and struck them down because "the law as it stands is currently contributing to danger faced by prostitutes."[1] See the Controversy & Debate box on page 184 for a discussion of this issue. An Angus Reid (2009) survey conducted following this court case asked a representative sample of Canadian adults how strongly they supported or opposed allowing sex workers to work indoors or in brothels. Overall, 60 percent of respondents gave moderate or strong support to allowing indoor sex work, while 30 percent were opposed. Seventy-one percent of men would allow sex work indoors or in brothels, compared to 50 percent of women, and respondents become more liberal in their attitudes the further west they live. These results show that Canadians are less supportive of criminalization of prostitution but that significant gender and regional differences remain.

Sexual Violence: Rape and Date Rape

Ideally, sexual activity occurs within a loving relationship between consenting adults. In reality, however, sex can be twisted by hate and violence. Here we consider two types of sexual violence: rape and date rape.

Rape

Although some people think rape is motivated only by a desire for sex, it is actually an expression of power—a violent act that uses sex to hurt, humiliate, or control another person. Data from the Canadian Centre for Justice Statistics indicate that 6 percent of females who reported being victims of a violent crime in Canada in 2008 were victims of sexual assault, and that 92 percent of the victims of sexual violence were women (Vaillancourt, 2010). Keep in mind that these crime statistics reflect only the reported cases; it is estimated that 91 percent of sexual assaults in Canada are not reported (Brennan & Taylor-Butts, 2008). The actual incidence of sexual assault is therefore much higher. *Sexual assault* is a comprehensive term referring to non-consensual sexual activity ranging from sexual touching, kissing, and sexual intercourse to sexual violence against a person's will. While men constitute 15 percent of sexual assault victims, women and children make up a disproportionate share. In 2007, 58 percent of all victims of sexual assault reported to the police in Canada were children and youth under 18 years of age, with children under the age of 12 making up 25 percent (Brennan & Taylor-Butts, 2008).

Date Rape

A common myth is that rape involves strangers. In reality, however, only about 30 percent of all rapes fit this pattern. About 70 percent of known cases of rape involve people who know one another—more often than not, pretty well—and these crimes usually take place in familiar surroundings, such as the home or a college or university campus. For this reason, the terms

---

[1] *Bedford v. Canada*, 07-CV-329807 PD1 ONSC 4264 (2010, p. 130). Retrieved from http://www.canlii.org/en/on/onsc/doc/2010/2010onsc4264/2010onsc4264.html

Controversy & Debate

Challenging the Prostitution Laws in Canada

Canadians place a premium on the importance of personal safety and health. To this end, a universal health care system and a variety of social, legal, and economic policies have been designed to ensure the health and safety of all members of Canadian society. Sadly, members of some of Canada's most stigmatized and vulnerable populations have fallen through this safety net. Many women, men, and transgender individuals working in the most unregulated and impoverished environments of the sex industry not only suffer from comparatively poor physical, emotional, and mental health but also experience an elevated risk of violence, victimization, and premature death. Violence against people working in the sex industry has become an even more salient social problem in light of the sentencing of Robert Pickton in 2007 for the multiple murders of Vancouver's Downtown Eastside "missing women"—the majority of whom have been identified as Aboriginal and all of whom were involved in sex work. While research shows that street-based sex workers are at greatest risk of sexual assault and homicide (Lowman, 1998; Du Mont & McGregor, 2004; Farley, Lynne, & Cotton, 2005), other forms of

Darren Calabrese/The Canadian Press

systematic racial, sexual, and gender-based violence are embedded in the structural organization of many other segments of the sex industry. These range from emotional abuse to dangerous working conditions and are exacerbated by social and legal stigma (Church & Henderson, 2001; Watts & Zimmerman, 2002; Lewis et al., 2005).

Canadian federal prostitution laws have long been seen by many academics, sex worker rights advocates, and health and social service providers as one of the most significant contributing factors in the violence and victimization experienced by sex workers (Lowman, 1998; Benoit & Shaver, 2006). The September 2010 landmark ruling by Ontario Superior Court Justice Susan Himel struck down three laws for endangering the lives of sex workers. While Himel called for no new prostitution laws, in 2014 the Conservative government introduced Bill C-36, which, according to critics, makes sex work once again more dangerous by reintroducing some of the laws Himel overturned. The deeper sociological question is what forms of policy and legislation will be most effective in helping to prevent violence and victimization and in supporting the diverse health and safety needs of people involved in this industry. Should Canada change its prostitution laws and legalize off-street sex work, as is currently the case in European countries such as the Netherlands and Germany, or should Canada follow the "Nordic model" of countries like Sweden and Norway and restrict sex work by decriminalizing the selling of sex while criminalizing the buying of sex, as per Bill C-36?

What Do You Think?

1. Does Bill C-36 harm those working in the sex industry?
2. Should Canada change its prostitution laws?
3. Apart from legal changes, what else should be done to reduce violence and victimization of people in the sex industry?

Sources: Lowman (1998); Church and Henderson (2001); Watts and Zimmerman (2002); Du Mont and McGregor (2004); Surratt, Inciardi, Kurtz, and Kiley (2004); Farley, Lynne, and Cotton (2005); Lewis, Maticka-Tyndale, Shaver, and Schramm (2005); Benoit and Shaver (2006); and Globe and Mail (2010, September 28).

"date rape" and "acquaintance rape" refer to forcible sexual violence against women by men they know (Laumann et al., 1994; Brennan & Taylor-Butts, 2008).

A second myth, often linked to date rape, is that the woman must have done something to encourage the man and made him think she wanted to have sex. Perhaps the victim agreed to go out with the offender. Maybe she even invited him into her room. But, of course, doing so no more justifies rape than it would any other type of physical assault.

Although rape is a physical attack, it often leaves emotional and psychological scars. Beyond the brutality of being physically violated, rape by an acquaintance also undermines a victim's sense of trust. Psychological scars are especially serious among the two-thirds of sexual assault victims who are under age 18 and even more so among the one-third who are under age 12. The home is no refuge from rape: One-third of all victims under age 18 are attacked by their own fathers or stepfathers (Snyder, 2000).

Experts agree that one factor that contributes to the problem of sexual violence on the college campus is the widespread use of alcoholic beverages. What policies are in force on your campus to discourage the kind of drinking that leads to one person imposing sex on another?

How common is date rape? One study in the United States found that about 9 percent of a sample of high school students reported being the victim of sexual or physical violence inflicted by the boys they were dating. About 12 percent of high school girls and 5 percent of high school boys reported being forced into having sexual intercourse against their will. The risk of abuse is especially high among girls who become sexually active before reaching the age of 15 (Dickinson, 2001; Centers for Disease Control and Prevention, 2012).

Nowhere has the issue of date rape been more widely discussed in recent years than on university and college campuses, where the danger of date rape is high. The collegiate environment promotes easy friendships and encourages trust among young people who still have much to learn about relationships and about themselves. As the Seeing Sociology in Everyday Life box on page 186 explains, the same campus environment that encourages communication provides few social norms to help guide young people's sexual experiences. To counter the problem, many schools now actively address myths about rape through on-campus workshops. In addition, greater attention is now focused on the abuse of alcohol, which increases the likelihood of sexual violence.

The control of women's sexuality is a common theme in human history. A product of the nineteenth century, the "chastity belt" was devised to lock about a woman's groin in order to prevent the "dangers" of masturbation. While such devices are all but unknown today, the social control of sexuality continues. Can you point to examples?

Theories of Sexuality

6.5 Apply sociology's major theories to the topic of sexuality.

Applying sociology's various theoretical approaches gives us a better understanding of human sexuality. The following sections discuss the three major approaches, and the Applying Theory table on page 187 highlights the key insights of each approach.

Seeing Sociology in Everyday Life

When Sex Is Only Sex: The Campus Culture of "Hooking Up"

Brynne: My mom told me once that she didn't have sex with my dad until after they were engaged.

Katy: I guess times really have changed!

Have you ever been in a sexual situation and not been sure of the right thing to do? Most colleges and universities highlight two important rules. First, sexual activity must take place only when both participants have given consent. The consent principle is what makes "having sex" different from date rape. Second, no one should knowingly expose another person to a sexually transmitted disease, especially when the partner is unaware of the danger.

These rules are very important, but they say little about the larger issue of what sex *means*. For example, when is it "right" to have a sexual relationship? How well do you have to know the other person? If you do have sex, are you obligated to see the person again?

Two generations ago, there were informal rules for campus sex. Dating was part of the courtship process. That is, "going out" was the way in which women and men evaluated each other as possible marriage partners while they sharpened their own sense of what they wanted in a mate. Because, on average, marriage took place in the early twenties, many college and university students became engaged and married while they were still completing their post-secondary education. In this cultural climate, sex was viewed by students as part of a relationship that carried a commitment—a serious interest in the other person as a possible marriage partner.

Today, partly because people now marry or cohabit much later, the culture of courtship has declined dramatically. About three-fourths of women in a recent national survey point to a relatively new campus pattern, the culture of "hooking up." What exactly is "hooking up"? Most describe it in words like these: "When a girl and a guy get together for a physical encounter—anything from kissing to having sex—and don't necessarily expect anything further."

Student responses to the survey suggest that hookups have three characteristics. First, most couples who hook up know little about each other. Second, a typical hookup involves people who have been drinking alcohol, usually at a campus party. Third, most women are critical of the culture of hooking up and express little satisfaction with these encounters. Certainly, some women (and men) who hook up simply walk away, happy to have enjoyed a sexual experience free of further obligation. But given the emotions that sex can unleash, hooking up often leaves someone wondering what to expect next: "Will you call me tomorrow?" "Will I see you again?"

The survey asked women who had experienced a recent hookup to report how they felt about the experience a day later. A majority of respondents said they felt "awkward," about half felt "disappointed" and "confused," and one in four felt "exploited." Clearly, for many people, sex is more than a physical encounter. In addition, because today's campus climate is very sensitive to charges of sexual exploitation, there is a need for clearer standards of fair play.

What Do You Think?

1. How extensive is the pattern of hooking up on your campus?

2. What do you see as the advantages of sex without commitment? What are the disadvantages of this kind of relationship?

3. Do you think men and women are likely to answer the preceding questions differently? Explain.

Source: Based in part on Marquardt and Glenn (2001).

Structural-Functional Analysis

The structural-functional approach highlights the contribution of any social pattern to the overall operation of society. Because sexuality can have such important consequences, society regulates this type of behaviour.

The Need to Regulate Sexuality

From a biological point of view, sex allows our species to reproduce. But culture and social institutions regulate *with whom* and *when* people reproduce. For example, most societies condemn a married person for having sex with someone other than his or her spouse. To allow the forces of sexual passion to go unchecked would threaten family life, especially the raising of children.

The fact that the incest taboo exists everywhere shows that no society permits completely free choice in sexual partners. Reproduction by family members other than married partners would break down the system of kinship and hopelessly confuse human relationships.

Applying Theory

Sexuality			
	Structural-Functional Theory	Symbolic-Interaction Theory	Social-Conflict and Feminist Theories
What is the level of analysis?	Macro level	Micro level	Macro level
What is the importance of sexuality for society?	Society depends on sexuality for reproduction. Society uses the incest taboo and other norms to control sexuality in order to maintain social order.	Sexual practices vary among the many cultures of the world. Some societies allow individuals more freedom than others in matters of sexual behaviour.	Sexuality is linked to social inequality. Canadian society regulates women's sexuality more than men's, which is part of the larger pattern of men dominating women.
Has sexuality changed over time? How?	Yes. As advances in birth control technology separate sex from reproduction, societies relax some controls on sexuality.	Yes. The meanings people attach to virginity and other sexual matters are all socially constructed and subject to change.	Yes and no. Some sexual standards have relaxed over time, but society still defines women in sexual terms, just as homosexual people are harmed by society's heterosexual bias.

Historically, the social control of sexuality was strong, mostly because sex often led to childbirth. We see these controls at work in the traditional distinction between "legitimate" reproduction (within marriage) and "illegitimate" reproduction (outside marriage). But once a society develops the technology to control births, its sexual norms become more permissive. In Canada and other high-income countries, over the course of the twentieth century, sex moved beyond its basic reproductive function and became accepted as a form of intimacy and even recreation (Giddens, 1992).

Latent Functions: The Case of Prostitution

Previously we saw why critics see prostitution as harmful. But does it have latent functions that help explain why this institution is so widespread? According to Kingsley Davis (1971), prostitution performs several useful functions. It is one way to meet the sexual needs of a large number of people who may not have ready access to sex, including soldiers, travellers, disabled people, and those who are not physically attractive enough or are too poor to attract a romantic partner (Lowman & Atchison, 2006). Some people favour prostitution because they want sex without the "hassle" of a relationship. As a number of analysts have pointed out, "Men don't pay for *sex*; they pay so they can *leave*" (Miracle, Miracle, & Baumeister, 2003).

EVALUATE The structural-functional approach helps us see the important part sexuality plays in the organization of society. The incest taboo and other cultural norms also suggest that society has always paid attention to who has sex with whom and, especially, who reproduces with whom.

Functionalist analysis sometimes ignores gender; when Kingsley Davis wrote of the benefits of prostitution for society, he was really talking about the benefits to *men*. In addition, the fact that sexual patterns change over time, just as they differ in remarkable ways around the world, is ignored by this perspective. To appreciate the varied and changeable character of sexuality, we now turn to the symbolic-interaction approach.

CHECK YOUR LEARNING Compared to traditional societies, why do modern societies give people more choice about matters involving sexuality?

Symbolic-Interaction Analysis

The symbolic-interaction approach highlights how as people interact, they construct everyday reality. As Chapter 4 ("Social Interaction in Everyday Life") explains, people sometimes construct very different realities, so the views of one group or society may well differ from those of another. In the same way, our understanding of sexuality can and does change over time, just as it differs from one society to another.

The Social Construction of Sexuality

Almost all social patterns involving sexuality saw considerable change over the course of the twentieth century. One good illustration is the changing importance of virginity. A century ago, our society's norm—for women, at least—was virginity before marriage. This norm was strong because there was no effective means of birth control, and virginity was the only guarantee a man had that his bride-to-be was not carrying another man's child. Today, because we have gone a long way toward separating sex from reproduction, the virginity norm has weakened considerably.

Today, in a society that uses birth control to separate sex from reproduction, people define sexual activity differently. Attitudes toward sex became more permissive and, as a result, the virginity norm has weakened considerably. Of course, among some categories of the population, the virginity norm is defined as more important; in others, it is less so.

In the same way, the rule that priests in the Catholic Church should be celibate is officially defended as a means to ensure that, by giving up marriage and children, a priest will have greater commitment to the work of the Church. Yet, the Catholic Church did not enact this rule until the twelfth century—more than a thousand years after Christ. Clearly, whether members of the clergy should be celibate is a matter of disagreement from one religious organization to another (Deluca, 2013).

A final example of our society's construction of sexuality involves young people. A century ago, childhood was a time of innocence in sexual matters. In recent decades, however, thinking has changed. Although few people encourage sexual activity between children, most people believe that children should be educated about sex by the time they are teenagers so that they can make intelligent choices about their behaviour as they grow older.

Global Comparisons

Around the world, different societies attach different meanings to sexuality. For example, the anthropologist Ruth Benedict (1938), who spent years learning the ways of life of the Melanesian people of southeastern New Guinea, reported that adults paid little attention when young children engaged in sexual experimentation with one another. Parents in Melanesia shrugged off such activity because, before puberty, sex cannot lead to reproduction. Is it likely that most parents in Canada would respond the same way?

Sexual practices also vary from culture to culture. Circumcision of infant boys (the practice of removing all or part of the foreskin of the penis) is common in Canada and the United States but rare in most other parts of the world, including European countries. A practice sometimes referred to incorrectly as female circumcision (removal of the clitoris) is rare in Canada and the United States but common in parts of Africa and the Middle East (Crossette, 1995; Huffman, 2000). (For more about this practice, more accurately called "female genital mutilation," see the Thinking About Diversity box on page 327).

EVALUATE The strength of the symbolic-interaction approach lies in revealing the socially constructed character of familiar social patterns. Understanding that people "construct" sexuality, we can better appreciate the variety of sexual attitudes and practices found over the course of history and around the world.

One limitation of this approach, however, is that not all sexual practices are so variable. Men everywhere have always been more likely to see women in sexual terms than the other way around. Some broader social structure must be at work in a pattern that is this widespread, as we shall see in the following section on the social-conflict approach.

CHECK YOUR LEARNING What evidence can you provide showing that human sexuality is socially constructed?

Social-Conflict and Feminist Analysis

As you have seen in earlier chapters, the social-conflict approach (particularly the gender-conflict or feminist approach) highlights dimensions of inequality. This approach shows how sexuality both reflects patterns of social inequality and helps perpetuate them. Feminism, a social-conflict approach focusing on gender inequality, links sexuality to the domination of women by men.

Sexuality: Reflecting Social Inequality

Recall our discussion of prostitution, a practice about which Canadians are deeply divided. Enforcement of prostitution laws is uneven at best, especially when it comes to who is and is not likely to be arrested. Gender bias is evident here: Although two people are involved, the record shows that police are far more likely to arrest (less powerful) female sex workers than (more powerful) male clients. Class inequality, too, is involved: It is street-level sex workers—those usually with the least income and most likely to be Aboriginals—who face the highest risk of arrest (Lowman, 2000; Saint James & Alexander, 2004). A feminist approach also leads us to ask whether as many women would be involved in prostitution if they had the economic opportunities equal to those of men.

More generally, which categories of people in Canadian society are most likely to be defined in terms of their sexuality? The answer, once again, is those with less power: women compared to men, visible minorities compared to whites, and gays and lesbians compared to heterosexuals. In this way, sexuality, a natural part of human life, is used by this society to define some categories of people as less worthy.

Sexuality: Creating Social Inequality

Social-conflict theorists, especially feminists, point to sexuality as the root of inequality between women and men. Defining women in sexual terms amounts to devaluing them from full human beings into objects of men's interest and attention. Is it any wonder that the word *pornography* comes from the Greek word *porne*, meaning "harlot" or "prostitute"?

If men define women in sexual terms, it is easy to see pornography—almost all of which is consumed by males—as a power issue. Because pornography typically shows women focused on pleasing men, it supports the idea that men have power over women.

Men have power over women in the world of reproductive health care as well. During 2012, more than 400 laws were introduced in U.S. state legislatures to limit the right of a woman and her doctor to make decisions about abortion. In Canada, abortion has been fully decriminalized since 1988, yet challenges by the pro-choice movement to its legal status persist. While Stephen Harper promised not to reopen the debate on abortion, during his tenure as prime minister eight private members' bills—all aiming to challenge access to abortion—were introduced. Conservative MP Stephen Woodworth submitted a motion that would require a special committee to study the Criminal Code in order to determine when a fetus can be legally considered a legal person (Mugyenyi, 2013). Woodworth's motion, as well as every legal challenge to decriminalization, has so far been defeated. Yet such efforts illustrate the efforts of a largely male cohort of politicians to limit reproductive rights for women.

Richard Lord/The Image Works

From a social-conflict point of view, sexuality is not so much a "natural" part of our humanity as it is a socially constructed pattern of behaviour. Sexuality plays an important part in social inequality: By defining women in sexual terms, men devalue them as objects. Would you consider the behaviour shown here to be "natural" or socially directed? Why?

Some radical critics doubt that the element of power can ever be removed from heterosexual relations (Dworkin, 1987). Most social-conflict theorists do not object to heterosexuality, but they do agree that sexuality can and does degrade women. Our culture often describes sexuality in terms of sport (men "scoring" with women) and violence ("slamming," "banging," and "hitting on," for example, are verbs used for both fighting and sex).

Another recent development by visible minority feminists and Indigenous people centres on the concept of *reproductive justice*. While many women and men have debated whether or not women should be able to obtain abortions or otherwise control their own bodies, the reproductive justice movement indicates that many women are disadvantaged to the point that they really are not able to make choices about their own lives. Currently, as reproductive justice activists point out, abortion is legal but access to it varies across the country. It is much more available in cities than in rural and remote areas. Prince Edward Island is without any abortion facilities at all, while New Brunswick is the only Canadian province that requires women to provide two referrals from physicians (Mugyenyi, 2013). Furthermore, abortion is the only medical procedure that is not covered by the Reciprocal Billing Agreement—meaning that women, in order to have the procedure covered, must obtain it in their home province (McCargar, 2014). As reproductive justice advocates remind us, only when such barriers are eliminated and when women and girls have social, economic, and political equality in Canada will there be reproductive justice.

Queer Theory

queer theory a body of research findings that challenges the heterosexual bias in Canadian society

heterosexism prejudice or discrimination against non-heterosexuals

Social-conflict theory has taken aim not only at men dominating women but also at heterosexuals dominating homosexuals. In recent years, as lesbians and gay men have sought public acceptance, a gay voice has arisen in sociology. The term **queer theory** refers to *a body of research findings that challenges the heterosexual bias in Canadian society*.

Queer theory begins with the claim that our society is characterized by **heterosexism**, *prejudice or discrimination against non-heterosexuals*. Our heterosexual culture victimizes a wide range of people, including gay men, lesbians, bisexuals, intersexuals, transsexuals, and even asexual people. Although most people agree that bias against women (sexism) and people of colour (racism) is wrong, heterosexism is widely tolerated and sometimes well within the law. For example, U.S. military forces cannot legally discharge a female soldier simply for "acting like a woman" because this would be a clear case of gender discrimination. But, until the law changed at the end of 2010, the military forces could and did discharge women and men for homosexuality if they were sexually active.

Heterosexism is also part of everyday culture (Land & Kitzinger, 2005; Travers, 2013). When we describe something as "sexy," for example, don't we really mean that it's attractive to *heterosexuals*?

EVALUATE The social-conflict approach shows that sexuality is both a cause and an effect of inequality. In particular, it helps us understand men's power over women and heterosexual people's domination of homosexual people.

At the same time, this approach overlooks the fact that many people do not see sexuality as a power issue. On the contrary, many couples enjoy a vital sexual relationship that deepens their commitment to one another. In addition, the social-conflict approach pays little attention to steps Canadian society has taken toward reducing inequality. Today's men are less likely to describe women as sex objects than they were a few decades ago. One of the most important issues in the workplace today is ensuring that all employees remain free from sexual harassment. Rising public concern (see Chapter 10, "Gender Stratification") has reduced the abuse of sexuality in the workplace. Likewise, there is ample evidence that the gay rights movement has secured greater opportunities and social acceptance for gay people.

CHECK YOUR LEARNING How does sexuality play a part in creating social inequality?

Window on the World

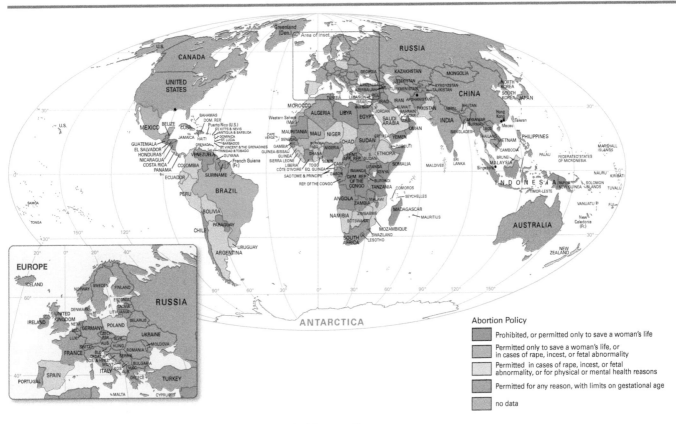

GLOBAL MAP 6–2 Women's Access to Abortion in Global Perspective

In global perspective, just 68 nations permit a woman to obtain an abortion for a wide variety of reasons. Generally, these are high-income nations, including many countries in Europe and North America. What pattern do you see involving countries that place the greatest restriction on abortion?

Source: Population Reference Bureau (2012).

This chapter closes with a look at what is perhaps the most divisive issue involving sexuality: **abortion**, *the deliberate termination of a pregnancy*. According to global research carried out in 2008, about one in five of all pregnancies ended in abortion. In addition, researchers concluded that half of all abortions performed during that year were "unsafe." For any nation, the level of economic development is closely linked to the abortion rate. Around the world, 86 percent of all abortions took place in less economically developed countries, as did 98 percent of the "unsafe" abortions (Alan Guttmacher Institute, 2012; Sedgh et al., 2012). A major reason for the high rate of unsafe procedures is that, as Global Map 6–2 shows, most nations either prohibit or place substantial restrictions on a woman's ability to have an abortion.

In Canada, the Supreme Court has supported a woman's legal access to abortion since 1988. But the debate over this procedure—which some see as a moral issue and others see as the foundation of social equality between the sexes—goes on. There seems to be no middle ground in the debate over this controversial issue.

abortion the deliberate termination of a pregnancy

Seeing Sociology in Everyday Life

How do the mass media play into our society's views of human sexuality?

Far from it being a "natural" or simply "biological" concept, cultures around the world attach all sorts of meanings to human sexuality. The magazine covers presented here show how the mass media reflect our own culture's ideas about sexuality. In each case, can you "decode" the magazine cover and explain its messages? To what extent do you think the messages are true?

Magazines like this one are found at the checkout lines of just about every supermarket and discount store in Canada. Looking just at the cover, what can you conclude about women's sexuality in our society?

Bill Aron/PhotoEdit, Inc.

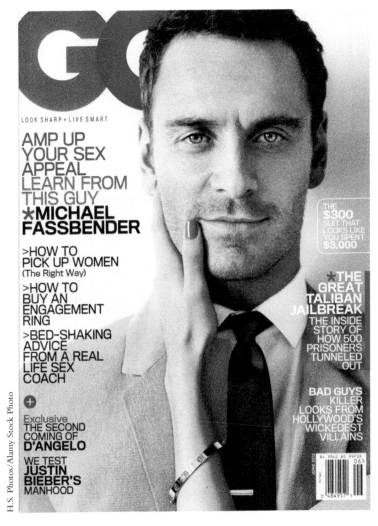

H.S. Photos/Alamy Stock Photo

Messages about sexuality are directed to men as well as to women. Here is a recent issue of *GQ*. What messages about masculinity can you find? Do you see any evidence of heterosexual bias?

HINT The messages we get from mass media sources like these not only tell us about sexuality but also tell us about what sort of people we ought to be. There is a lot of importance attached to sexuality for women, placing pressure on women to look good to men and to define life success in terms of attracting men with their sexuality. Similarly, being masculine means being successful, sophisticated, in charge, and able to attract desirable women. When the mass media endorse sexuality, it is almost always according to the norm of heterosexuality.

Seeing Sociology in *Your* Everyday Life

1. Looking at the *Cosmopolitan* cover, what evidence of heterosexual bias do you see? Explain.

2. Go to www.sociologyinfocus.com to access the Sociology in Focus blog, where you can read the latest posts by a team of young sociologists who apply the sociological perspective to topics of popular culture.

3. Based on what you have read in this chapter, what evidence supports the argument that sexuality is constructed by society?

Sexuality and Society **CHAPTER 6** **193**

Richard Lord/The Image Works

Making the Grade

Sexuality and Society

Understanding Sexuality

(6.1) Describe how sexuality is both a biological and a cultural issue. (pages 164–169)

Sex is biological, referring to bodily differences between females and males.

Gender is cultural, referring to behaviour, power, and privileges a society attaches to being female or male.

Sexuality is a **biological issue**.

- Sex is determined at conception as a male sperm joins a female ovum.
- Males and females have different genitals (*primary sex characteristics*) and bodily development (*secondary sex characteristics*).
- *Intersexual people* (*hermaphrodites*) have some combination of male and female genitalia.
- *Transsexual people* feel they are one sex although biologically they are the other.

Sexuality is a **cultural issue.**

- For humans, sex is a matter of cultural meaning and personal choice rather than biological programming.
- Sexual practices vary considerably from one society to another (examples include kissing, ideas about modesty, and standards of beauty).
- The *incest taboo* exists in all societies because regulating sexuality, especially reproduction, is a necessary element of social organization. Specific taboos vary from one society to another.

sex the biological distinction between females and males

primary sex characteristics the genitals, organs used for reproduction

secondary sex characteristics bodily development, apart from the genitals, that distinguishes biologically mature females and males

intersexual people people whose bodies (including genitals) have both female and male characteristics

transsexuals people who feel they are one sex even though biologically they are the other

incest taboo a norm forbidding sexual relations or marriage between certain relatives

Sexual Attitudes in Canada

(6.2) Explain changes in sexual attitudes in Canada. (pages 169–174)

The **sexual revolution**, which peaked in the 1960s and 1970s, drew sexuality into the open. Baby boomers were the first generation to grow up with the idea that sex was a normal part of social life.

The **sexual counter-revolution**, which was evident by 1980, aimed criticism at "permissiveness" and urged a return to more traditional "family values."

Beginning with the work of Alfred Kinsey, researchers have studied sexual behaviour and reached many interesting conclusions:

- Premarital sexual intercourse became more common during the twentieth century.
- The majority of young men and women in Canada have intercourse after the age of 17.
- Canadians have sex slightly more than once a week, but the rate varies across age groups and geographical regions.
- Extramarital sex is widely condemned; 76 percent of Canadians agree that married men or women having an affair is morally unacceptable.

Sexual Orientation

(6.3) Analyze factors that shape sexual orientation. (pages 174–179)

Sexual orientation is a person's romantic or emotional attraction to another person. Four sexual orientations are

- heterosexuality
- homosexuality
- bisexuality
- asexuality

The 2011 Census of Canada enumerated 64 575 same-sex couples.

Most research supports the claim that sexual orientation is rooted in biology in much the same way as is being right-handed or left-handed.

sexual orientation a person's romantic and emotional attraction to another person

heterosexuality sexual attraction to someone of the other sex

homosexuality sexual attraction to someone of the same sex

bisexuality sexual attraction to people of both sexes

asexuality a lack of sexual attraction to people of either sex

194   **CHAPTER 6**   Sexuality and Society

Sexual orientation is not a matter of neat categories because many people who think of themselves as heterosexual have homosexual experiences; the reverse is also true.

The gay rights movement helped change public attitudes toward greater acceptance of homosexuality The number of Canadian adults who say homosexuality is morally unacceptable continues to decline, standing currently at 15 percent.

Transgender refers not to a sexual orientation, but to appearing or behaving in ways that challenge conventional cultural norms about how females and males should look and act.

homophobia discomfort over close personal interaction with people thought to be gay, lesbian, or bisexual

transgender appearing or behaving in ways that challenge conventional cultural norms concerning how females and males should look and act

Sexual Issues and Controversies

6.4 Discuss several current controversies involving sexuality. (pages 179–186)

Teen Pregnancy Between 2001 and 2010, Canada's teen pregnancy rate fell by 20.3 percent, indicating a greater awareness among Canadian youth about how to prevent pregnancy and delay parenting, as well as their ready access to contraception and abortion.

Pornography The law allows local communities to set standards of decency. Conservatives condemn pornography on moral grounds; liberals view pornography as a power issue, condemning it as demeaning to women.

Prostitution The selling of sexual services is illegal almost everywhere in the United States but not in Canada, and its legality varies greatly across the globe. Many people view prostitution as a victimless crime, while others view it as an alternative for economically disadvantaged people and thus believe it should be decriminalized.

Sexual Violence Rapes are violent crimes in which victims and offenders typically know one another. According to research, the vast majority, 92 percent, of victims of sexual violence are women. As victims of sexual assault, they make up 6 percent of those who reported being victims of a violent crime in Canada in 2008.

Abortion Opposition to anti-abortion laws rose during the 1960s, and in 1988, the Supreme Court of Canada declared these laws unconstitutional. Pro-life activists continue to mount challenges to the legal access to abortion, while reproductive justice advocates continue to fight to increase women's access to it.

pornography sexually explicit material intended to cause sexual arousal

prostitution the selling of sexual services

abortion the deliberate termination of a pregnancy

Theories of Sexuality

6.5 Apply sociology's major theories to the topic of sexuality. (pages 186–191)

Structural-functional theory highlights society's need to regulate sexual activity and especially reproduction. One universal norm is the incest taboo, which keeps family relations clear.

Symbolic-interaction theory emphasizes the various meanings people attach to sexuality. The social construction of sexuality can be seen in sexual differences between societies and in changing sexual patterns over time.

Social-conflict theory links sexuality to social inequality. **Feminist theory** claims that men dominate women by devaluing them to the level of sexual objects. **Queer theory** claims that our society has a heterosexual bias.

queer theory a body of research findings that challenges the heterosexual bias in Canadian society

heterosexism prejudice or discrimination against non-heterosexuals

7 Deviance

LEARNING OBJECTIVES

7.1 Explain how sociology addresses limitations of a biological or psychological approach to deviance.

7.2 Apply structural-functional theories to the topic of deviance.

7.3 Apply symbolic-interaction theories to the topic of deviance.

7.4 Apply social-conflict theories to the topic of deviance.

7.5 Apply race-conflict and feminist theories to the topic of deviance.

7.6 Identify patterns of crime in Canada and around the world.

7.7 Analyze the operation of the criminal justice system.

the Power of Society

to affect the odds of being incarcerated

Incarcerated

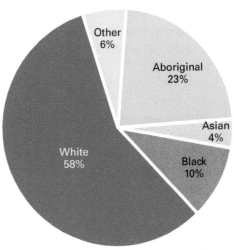

Source: Figure 5. The Federal Incarcerated and Conditional Release Populations by Aboriginal and Race available here: http://pbc-clcc.gc.ca/rprts/pmr/pmr_2013_2014/index-eng.shtml#f28. Used with permission of Public Works and Government Services Canada.

Does everyone—regardless of race—run the same risk of being sent to prison? Blacks account for almost 3 percent of the Canadian population but make up 10 percent of the inmate population, while Aboriginals account for 4 percent of the Canadian population but make up 23 percent of the inmate population. Countering this trend are Asians, who account for 15 percent of the Canadian population and only 4 percent of the inmate population, and whites, who account for 77 percent of the Canadian population and only 58 percent of the inmate population. Clearly, when it comes to the Canadian criminal justice system, race and racism play a role in the over-representation of Blacks and Aboriginals and the underrepresentation of Asians and whites.

Chapter Overview

Common sense may suggest that some things are simply "right" and some things are simply "wrong." We also tend to think—or hope—that most of us, at least most of the time, know the difference. But the line between "good" and "bad" is constructed by society in a way that is far from simple. This chapter investigates how and why society encourages both conformity and deviance. This chapter also introduces the concept of crime and surveys the operation of the criminal justice system.

Hechtenberg/Agencja Fotograficzna Caro/Alamy Stock Photo

"I was like the guy lost in another dimension, a stranger in town, not knowing which way to go." With these words, Bruce Glover recalls the day he returned to his hometown, after being away for 26 years—a long stretch in prison. Glover was a young man of 30 when he was arrested for running a call girl ring. Found guilty at trial, he was given a stiff jail sentence.

Now 56, he shakes his head as he says, "My mother passed while I was gone. I lost everything." On the day he walked out of prison, he had nowhere to go and no way to get there. He had no driver's licence or other valid identification, which our society requires of people who are looking for a job and a place to live. Glover had no money to buy the clothes he needed to go out and begin his life all over again. He turned to a prison official and asked for help. Only with the assistance of a state agency was he finally able to get some money and locate temporary housing (Jones, 2007).

This chapter explores issues involving crime and criminals, asking why some categories of people are at higher risk of being offenders—and victims—than others. In addition, the chapter explains how our criminal justice system handles offenders and also how it tackles the broader question of why societies develop standards of right and wrong in the first place. As you will see, law is simply one part of a complex system of social control: Society teaches us all to conform to countless rules, at least most of the time. We begin our investigation by defining several basic concepts.

What Is Deviance?

(7.1) Explain how sociology addresses limitations of a biological or psychological approach to deviance.

Deviance is *the recognized violation of cultural norms.* Norms guide almost all human activities, so the concept of deviance is quite broad. One category of deviance is **crime**, *the violation of a society's formally enacted criminal law.* Even criminal deviance spans a wide range, from minor traffic violations to drug use, sexual assault, and murder.

Most familiar examples of nonconformity are negative instances of rule breaking, such as stealing from a campus bookstore, assaulting a fellow student, or driving a car while intoxicated. But we also define especially righteous people—students who speak up too much in class or people who are overly enthusiastic about new computer technology—as deviant, even if we give them a measure of respect. Furthermore, sometimes those entrusted with making or defending the law behave in ways we define as deviant. Popular protests against police brutality, and public disapproval of politicians who engage in fraud and bribery, demonstrate that deviance can be committed by those in positions of power. What all deviant actions or attitudes, whether negative or positive, have in common is some element of *difference* that causes us to think of another person as an "outsider" (Becker, 1966).

Not all deviance involves action or even choice. The very *existence* of some categories of people can

deviance the recognized violation of cultural norms

crime the violation of a society's formally enacted criminal law

be troublesome to others. Able-bodied people often view people with disabilities as an out-group, just as rich people may shun the poor for falling short of their high-class standards.

social control attempts by society to regulate people's thoughts and behaviour

criminal justice system the organizations—police, courts, and prison officials—that respond to alleged violations of the law

Social Control

All of us are subject to **social control**, *attempts by society to regulate people's thoughts and behaviour.* Often this process is informal, as when parents praise or scold their children or when friends make fun of our choice of music or style of dress. Cases of serious deviance, however, may involve the **criminal justice system**, *the organizations—police, courts, and prison officials—that respond to alleged violations of the law.*

How a society defines deviance, *who* is branded as deviant, and *what* people decide to do about deviance all have to do with the way society is organized. Only gradually, however, have people recognized that the roots of deviance are deep in society, as the chapter now explains.

The Biological Context

Chapter 3 ("Socialization: From Infancy to Old Age") explained that a century ago, most people assumed—incorrectly, as it turns out—that human behaviour was the result of biological instincts. Early interest in criminality therefore focused on biological causes. In 1876, Cesare Lombroso (1835–1909), an Italian physician who worked in prisons, theorized that criminals stand out physically, with low foreheads, prominent jaws and cheekbones, protruding ears, hairiness, and unusually long arms. In other words, Lombroso claimed that criminals look like our apelike ancestors.

Had Lombroso looked more carefully, he would have found the physical features he linked to criminality throughout the entire population. We now know that no physical traits distinguish criminals from non-criminals.

In the middle of the twentieth century, William Sheldon took a different approach, suggesting that general body structure might predict criminality (Sheldon, Hartl, & McDermott, 1949). He cross-checked hundreds of young men for body type and criminal history and concluded that criminality was most likely among boys with muscular, athletic builds. Sheldon Glueck and Eleanor Glueck (1950) confirmed Sheldon's conclusion but cautioned that a powerful build does not necessarily *cause* or even *predict* criminality. Parents, they suggested, tend to be somewhat distant from powerfully built sons, who in turn grow up to show less sensitivity toward others. Moreover, in a self-fulfilling prophecy, people who expect muscular boys to be bullies may act in ways that bring about the aggressive behaviour they expect.

Today, researchers in the field of genetics are cautiously investigating possible links between biology and crime. Some research already suggests that such a link may exist. In 2003, scientists at the University of Wisconsin reported results of a 25-year study of crime among 400 boys. The researchers collected DNA samples from each boy and noted any history of trouble with the law. The researchers concluded that genetic factors (especially defective genes that, say, make too much of an enzyme) together with environmental factors (especially abuse early in life) were strong predictors of adult crime and violence. They noted, too, that these factors together were a better predictor of crime than either one alone (Lemonick, 2003; Pinker, 2003; Cohen, 2011; Shanks, 2011).

Melissa Moore/The Image Works

Deviance is always a matter of difference. Deviance emerges in everyday life as we encounter people whose appearance or behaviour differs from what we consider "normal." Who is the "deviant" in this photograph? From whose point of view?

EVALUATE Biological theories offer a limited explanation of crime. The best guess at present is that biological traits in combination with environmental factors explain some serious crime. Or, put another way, learning more about human genetics may help social researchers better direct their attention to specific aspects of the social environment that may encourage or discourage criminal behaviour. But the biggest problem with a purely biological approach to understanding crime is that most of the actions we define as deviant are carried out by people who are biologically quite normal.

In addition, because a biological approach looks at the individual, it offers no insight into how some kinds of behaviours come to be defined as deviant in the first place. Therefore, although there is much to be learned about how human biology may affect behaviour, research currently puts far greater emphasis on social influences.

CHECK YOUR LEARNING What does biological research add to our understanding of crime? What are the limitations of this approach?

Personality Factors

Like biological theories, psychological explanations of deviance focus on abnormality in the individual personality. Some personality traits are inherited, but most psychologists think that personality is shaped primarily by social experience. Deviance, then, is viewed as the result of "unsuccessful" socialization.

Classic research by Walter Reckless and Simon Dinitz (1967) illustrates the psychological approach. Reckless and Dinitz began by asking a number of teachers to categorize 12-year-old male students as either likely or unlikely to get into trouble with the law. They then interviewed both the boys and their mothers to assess each boy's self-concept and how he related to others. Analyzing their results, Reckless and Dinitz found that the "good boys" displayed a strong conscience (what Freud called superego), could handle frustration, and identified with conventional cultural norms and values. The "bad boys," by contrast, had a weaker conscience, displayed little tolerance for frustration, and felt out of step with conventional culture.

As we might expect, the "good boys" went on to have fewer run-ins with the police than the "bad boys." Because all the boys lived in an area where delinquency was widespread, the investigators attributed staying out of trouble to a personality that controlled deviant impulses. Based on this conclusion, Reckless and Dinitz called their analysis *containment theory*.

In a more recent study, researchers followed 500 non-identical twin boys from birth until they reached the age of 32. Twins were used so that researchers could compare each of the twins to his brother controlling for social class and family environment. Observing the boys when they were young, parents, teachers, and the researchers assessed their level of self-control, ability to withstand frustration, and ability to delay gratification. Echoing the earlier conclusions of Reckless and Dinitz, the researchers found that the brother who had lower scores on these measures in childhood almost always went on to get into more trouble, including criminal activity (Moffitt et al., 2011).

EVALUATE Psychologists have shown that personality patterns have some connection to deviance. Some serious criminals are psychopaths who do not feel guilt or shame, have no fear of punishment, and have little or no sympathy for the people they harm (Herpertz & Sass, 2000). More generally, the capacity for self-control and the ability to withstand frustration do seem to be skills that promote conformity. However, as noted in the case of the biological approach, most serious crimes are committed by people whose psychological profiles are normal.

Both the biological and psychological approaches view deviance as a trait of individuals. The reason that these approaches have had limited value in explaining deviance is that wrongdoing has more to do with the organization of society. We now turn to a sociological approach, which explores where ideas of right and wrong come from, why people define some rule breakers but not others as deviant, and what role power plays in this process.

CHECK YOUR LEARNING Why do biological and psychological analyses fail to explain deviance very well?

The Social Foundations of Deviance

Although we tend to view deviance as the free choice or personal failings of individuals, all behaviour—deviance as well as conformity—is shaped by society. Three social foundations of deviance identified here will be detailed later in this chapter:

1. **Deviance varies according to cultural norms.** No thought or action is inherently deviant; it becomes deviant only in relation to particular norms. Because norms vary from place to place, deviance also varies. In Saskatchewan, for example, strip clubs have been recently banned. In most cities across Canada stripping with a "no touch" rule takes place, while in Montreal "full contact" stripping is allowed. Moreover, in some cities it is legal to play music on the sidewalk and to beg for money, while street musicians and panhandlers in other cities risk being fined or imprisoned. The Criminal Code of Canada lays out what types of gaming activities are illegal in Canada, and the provinces are assigned responsibility to operate, licence, and regulate legal forms of gaming, including internet casinos. In Kahnawake, Quebec, the Mohawk community hosts numerous casino sites. The Mohawks of Kahnawake requested that the federal government designate them as an internet gaming jurisdiction (Heydary Hamilton PC, 2006), while recently the provincial government indicated that it may block sites that are not run by its own Lotto Quebec corporation (Fennario, 2015). Currently, e-cigarettes have been gaining in popularity as an alternative to smoke-producing cigarettes. As they are being debated by law makers, new legislation drafted across Canada varies from province to province. The government of Nova Scotia is proposing to prohibit "vaping" in vehicles with children under age 19, while the government of Ontario proposes the same the ban for cars containing passengers under age 16 (Canadian Press, 2015).

   Further, Killarney, Manitoba, has a curfew for people under the age of 15, who can be fined $250 if they are in a public space later than 1 A.M. Many cities and towns have different bylaws about activities such as operating escort agencies, camping in downtown parks, panhandling, vehicle parking, and public nudity.

   Around the world, deviance is even more diverse. Albania outlaws any public display of religious faith, such as the Catholic practice of "crossing" oneself; Cuba regulates private ownership of personal computers and limits access to the internet; Vietnam can prosecute citizens for meeting with foreigners; Malaysia does not allow women to wear tight-fitting jeans; Saudi Arabia bans the sale of red flowers on Valentine's Day; and Iran bans wearing makeup by women and forbids anyone from playing rap music (Chopra, 2008).

2. **People become deviant as others define them that way.** Everyone violates cultural norms at one time or another. Have you ever walked around talking to yourself or "borrowed" a pen from your workplace? Whether such behaviour defines us as mentally ill or criminal depends on how others perceive, define, and respond to it.

Why is it that street-corner gambling like this is usually against the law but playing the same games in a fancy casino is not?

3. **How societies set norms and how they define rule breaking both involve social power.** The law, declared Karl Marx, is the means by which powerful people protect their interests. A homeless person who stands on a street corner speaking out against the government risks arrest for disturbing the peace; a mayoral candidate during an election campaign who does exactly the same thing gets police protection. In short, norms and how we apply them reflect social inequality.

The Functions of Deviance: Structural-Functional Analysis

7.2 Apply structural-functional theories to the topic of deviance.

The key insight of the structural-functional approach is that deviance is a necessary part of social organization. This point was made a century ago by Emile Durkheim.

Durkheim's Basic Insight

In his pioneering study of deviance, Emile Durkheim (1964a, orig. 1893; 1964b, orig. 1895) made the surprising claim that there is nothing abnormal about deviance. In fact, it performs four essential functions:

1. **Responding to deviance clarifies moral boundaries.** By defining some individuals as deviant, people draw a boundary between right and wrong. For example, colleges and universities mark the line between academic honesty and cheating by disciplining students who cheat on exams.

2. **Deviance affirms cultural values and norms.** As moral creatures, people must prefer some attitudes and behaviours to others. But any definition of virtue rests on an opposing idea of vice: There can be no good without bad and no fairness without injustice. Deviance is needed to define and support morality.

3. **Responding to deviance brings people together.** People typically react to serious deviance—including on occasions when it is committed by those entrusted with enforcing the law—with shared outrage. In doing so, Durkheim explained, they reaffirm the moral ties that bind them. For example, after the 2007 police killing of Polish immigrant

Durkheim claimed that deviance is a necessary element of social organization, serving several important functions. The RCMP killing of Polish immigrant Robert Dziekański in 2007 and the death of Mexican immigrant Lucia Vega Jimenez, who committed suicide in a Canada Border Services Agency holding cell in 2013, brought people together across the country to affirm their community ties as they sought to understand how such actions could occur. Has any event where you live caused a similar community reaction?

Robert Dziekański at the Vancouver airport, people across Canada were joined by a common desire to control this type of senseless violence and to demand police accountability.

4. **Deviance encourages social change.** Deviance pushes a society's moral boundaries, suggesting alternatives to the status quo and encouraging change. Today's deviance, declared Durkheim, can become tomorrow's morality (1964b:71, orig. 1895). For example, rock-and-roll, condemned as immoral in the 1950s, became a multibillion-dollar industry just a few years later. In recent years, hip-hop music has followed the same path toward respectability.

An Illustration: The Puritans of Massachusetts Bay

Kai Erikson's classic study of the Puritans of Massachusetts Bay brings Durkheim's theory to life. Erikson (2005, orig. 1966) shows that even the Puritans, a disciplined and highly religious group, created deviance to clarify their moral boundaries. In fact, Durkheim might well have had the Puritans in mind when he wrote this:

> Imagine a society of saints, a perfect cloister of exemplary individuals. Crimes, properly so called, will there be unknown; but faults which appear [insignificant] to the layman will create there the same scandal that the ordinary offense does in ordinary consciousness. . . . For the same reason, the perfect and upright man judges his smallest failings with a severity that the majority reserve for acts more truly in the nature of an offense. (1964b:68–69, orig. 1895)

Deviance is thus not a matter of a few "bad apples" but a necessary condition of "good" social living.

Deviance may be found in every society, but the *kind* of deviance people generate depends on the moral issues they seek to clarify. The Puritans, for example, experienced a number of "crime waves," including the well-known outbreak of witchcraft in 1692. With each response, the Puritans answered questions about the range of proper beliefs by celebrating some of their members and condemning others as deviant.

Erikson discovered that even though the offences changed, the proportion of people the Puritans defined as deviant remained steady over time. This stability, he concluded, confirms Durkheim's claim that society creates deviants to mark its changing moral boundaries. In other words, by constantly defining a small number of people as deviant, the Puritans maintained the moral shape of their society.

Merton's Strain Theory

Some deviance may be necessary for a society to function, but Robert Merton (1938, 1968) argued that too much deviance results from particular social arrangements. Specifically, the extent and type of deviance people engage in depend on whether a society provides the *means* (such as schooling and job opportunities) to achieve cultural *goals* (such as financial success). Merton's strain theory is illustrated in Figure 7–1.

Conformity lies in pursuing cultural goals through approved means. Therefore, the Canadian "success story" is someone who gains wealth and prestige through talent, schooling, and hard work. But not everyone who wants conventional success has the opportunity to attain it. For example, people raised in poverty may have little hope of becoming successful if they play by the rules. According to Merton, the strain between our culture's emphasis on wealth and the lack of opportunities to get rich may encourage some people, especially the poor, to engage in stealing, drug dealing, and other forms of street crime. Merton called this type of deviance *innovation*—using unconventional means (street crime) rather than conventional means (hard work at a "straight" job) to achieve a culturally approved goal (wealth).

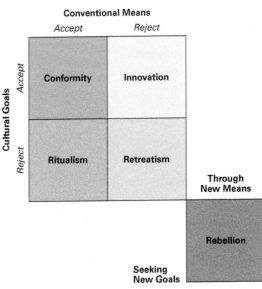

FIGURE 7–1 Merton's Strain Theory of Deviance

Combining a person's view of cultural goals and the conventional means to obtain them allowed Robert Merton to identify various types of deviance.

Source: Merton (1968).

The inability to reach a cultural goal may also prompt another type of deviance that Merton calls *ritualism*. For example, many people may not care much about becoming rich but rigidly stick to the rules (the conventional means) anyway in order to at least feel respectable.

A third response to the inability to succeed is *retreatism*: rejecting both cultural goals and conventional means so that a person in effect "drops out." Some alcoholics, drug addicts, and street people can be described as retreatists. The deviance of retreatists lies in their unconventional lifestyle and also in what seems to be their willingness to live this way.

The fourth response to failure is *rebellion*. Like retreatists, rebels such as radical environmentalists, Aboriginal activists, and anarchists reject both the cultural definition of success and the conventional means of achieving it, but they go one step further by forming a counterculture supporting alternatives to the existing social order.

Deviant Subcultures

Richard Cloward and Lloyd Ohlin (1966) extended Merton's theory, proposing that crime results not simply from limited legitimate (legal) opportunity but also from readily accessible illegitimate (illegal) opportunity. In short, deviance or conformity arises from the *relative opportunity structure* that frames a person's life.

The life of Al Capone, a notorious gangster, illustrates Cloward and Ohlin's theory. As the son of poor immigrants, Capone faced barriers of poverty and ethnic prejudice, which lowered his odds of achieving success in conventional terms. Yet as a young man during Prohibition (when alcoholic beverages were banned in Canada, the United States, and a number of European countries), Capone found in his neighbourhood people who could teach him how to sell alcohol illegally—a source of illegitimate opportunity. Where the structure of opportunity favours criminal activity, Cloward and Ohlin predict the development of *criminal subcultures*, such as Capone's criminal organization or today's inner-city street gangs.

But what happens when people are unable to find *any* opportunity, legal or illegal? Then deviance may take one of two forms. One is *conflict subcultures*, such as armed street gangs that engage in violence out of frustration and a desire for respect. Another possible outcome is the development of *retreatist subcultures*, in which deviants drop out and abuse alcohol or other drugs.

Albert Cohen (1971, orig. 1955) suggests that delinquency is most common among lower-class youths because they have the least opportunity to achieve conventional success. Neglected by society, they seek self-respect by creating a delinquent subculture that defines as worthy the traits these youths do have. Being feared on the street may not win many points with society as a whole, but it may satisfy a young person's desire to "be somebody" in the local neighbourhood.

Walter Miller (1970, orig. 1958) adds that delinquent subcultures are characterized by 1) *trouble*, arising from frequent conflict with teachers and police; 2) *toughness*, the value placed on physical size and strength, especially among males; 3) *smartness*, the ability to succeed on the streets, to outsmart or "con" others, and to avoid being similarly taken advantage of; 4) *a need for excitement*, the search for thrills or danger; 5) *a belief in fate*, a sense that people lack control over their own lives; and 6) *a desire for freedom*, often expressed as anger toward authority figures.

Finally, Elijah Anderson (1994, 2002; Kubrin, 2005) explains that in poor urban neighbourhoods, most people manage to conform to conventional or "decent" values. Yet faced with neighbourhood

Young people cut off from legitimate opportunity often form subcultures that many people view as deviant. Gang subcultures are one way young people gain the sense of belonging and respect denied to them by the larger culture.

A. Ramey/PhotoEdit, Inc.

crime and violence, indifference or even hostility from police, and sometimes neglect by their own parents, some young men decide to live by the "street code." To show that they can survive on the street, a young man displays "nerve," a willingness to stand up to any threat. Following this street code, the young man believes that even a violent death is better than being "dissed" (disrespected) by others. Some manage to escape the dangers, but the risk of ending up in jail—or worse—is very high for these young men, who have been pushed to the margins of our society.

EVALUATE Durkheim made an important contribution by pointing out the functions of deviance. However, there is evidence that a community does not always come together in reaction to crime; sometimes fear of crime causes people to withdraw from public life (Liska & Warner, 1991; Warr & Ellison, 2000).

Merton's strain theory has been criticized for explaining some kinds of deviance (stealing, for example) better than others (such as crimes of passion or mental illness). Also, not everyone seeks success in the conventional terms of wealth, as strain theory suggests.

The general argument of Cloward and Ohlin, Cohen, Miller, and Anderson—that deviance reflects the opportunity structure of society—has been confirmed by subsequent research (Allan & Steffensmeier, 1989; Uggen, 1999). However, these theories fall short by assuming that everyone shares the same cultural standards for judging right and wrong. In addition, if we define crime to include not only burglary and auto theft but also fraud and other crimes carried out by corporate executives and Wall Street tycoons, then more high-income people will be counted as criminals. There is evidence that people of all social backgrounds have become more casual about breaking the rules, as the Seeing Sociology in Everyday Life box on page 206 explains.

Finally, all structural-functional theories suggest that everyone who breaks important rules will be labelled deviant. However, becoming deviant is actually a highly complex process, as the next section explains.

CHECK YOUR LEARNING Why do you think many of the theories just discussed seem to say that crime is more common among people with lower social standing?

Labelling Deviance: Symbolic-Interaction Analysis

(**7.3**) Apply symbolic-interaction theories to the topic of deviance.

The symbolic-interaction approach explains how people define deviance in everyday situations. From this point of view, definitions of deviance and conformity are surprisingly flexible.

Labelling Theory

The main contribution of symbolic-interaction analysis is **labelling theory**, *the idea that deviance and conformity result not so much from what people do as from how others respond to those actions*. Labelling theory stresses the relativity of deviance, meaning that people may define the same behaviour in any number of ways.

Consider these situations: A college student takes a sweater off the back of a roommate's chair and packs it for a weekend trip, a married woman at a convention in a distant city has sex with an old boyfriend, and a city mayor gives a big contract to a major campaign contributor. We might define the first situation as carelessness, borrowing, or theft. The consequences of the second case depend largely on whether the woman's behaviour becomes known back

Seeing Sociology in Everyday Life

Deviant (Sub)Culture: Has It Become Okay to Do Wrong?

It's been a bad few years for the idea of playing by the rules. First Auditor General Sheila Fraser reported that senior civil servants broke rules when they awarded advertising contracts to Montreal advertising agencies. Then we learned that the executives of not just one but many corporations were guilty of fraud and outright stealing. The Roman Catholic Church, which many hold up as a model of moral behaviour, became embroiled in a scandal of its own. In this case, hundreds of priests across Canada, the United States, Europe, and Latin America are said to have sexually abused parishioners (most of them teens and children) over many decades while church officials busied themselves covering up the crimes.

Hundreds of priests have been removed from their duties pending investigations of abuse.

Plenty of people are offering explanations for this widespread pattern of wrongdoing. Some suggest that the pressure to win in the highly competitive corporate world—by whatever means necessary—can be overwhelming. As one analyst put it, "You can get away with your embezzlements and your lies, but you can never get away with *failing*."

Such thinking helps explain the wrongdoing among many CEOs in the corporate world, but it offers little insight into the problem of abusive priests. In some ways, at least, wrongdoing seems to have become a way of life for just about everybody. For example, the Auditor General has estimated that Canadians are more and more willing to evade taxes by engaging in the underground economy, particularly in the construction industry. The music industry claims that it has lost a vast amount of money because of illegal piracy of recordings, a practice especially common among young people. And surveys of high school students reveal that 75 percent admit to having cheated on a test at least once during the past year.

Emile Durkheim considered society to be a moral system, built on a set of rules about what people should and should not do. Years earlier, another French thinker named Blaise Pascal made the opposite claim that "cheating is the foundation of society." Today, which of the two statements is closer to the truth?

What Do You Think?

1. In your opinion, how widespread is wrongdoing in Canadian society today?

2. Do you think the people whose actions are described in this box consider what they are doing as wrong? Why or why not?

3. What are the reasons for this apparent increase in dishonesty?

Digital Vision/Photodisc/Getty Images

Do you consider cheating in school to be wrong? Would you turn in someone you saw cheat? Why or why not?

Source: Based on "Our Cheating Hearts" (2002).

---

home. In the third situation, is the official choosing the best contractor or paying off a political debt? The social construction of reality is a highly variable process of detection, definition, and response.

Primary and Secondary Deviance

Edwin Lemert (1951, 1972) observed that some norm violations—say, skipping school or underage drinking—provoke slight reaction from others and have little effect on a person's self-concept. Lemert calls such passing episodes *primary deviance*.

But what happens if people take notice of someone's deviance and really make something of it? After an audience has defined some action as primary deviance, the individual may begin to change, taking on a deviant identity by talking, acting, or dressing in a different way; rejecting the people who are critical; and repeatedly breaking the rules. Lemert (1951:77) calls this change of self-concept *secondary deviance*. He explains that "when a person begins to employ . . . deviant behavior as a means of defense, attack, or adjustment to the . . . problems created by societal reaction," deviance becomes secondary. For example, say that people have begun describing a young man as an "alcohol abuser," which establishes primary deviance. These people may then exclude him from their friendship network. His response may be to become bitter toward them, start drinking even more, and seek the company of others who approve of his drinking. These actions mark the beginning of secondary deviance, a deeper deviant identity.

Stigma

Secondary deviance marks the start of what Canadian sociologist Erving Goffman (1963) calls a *deviant career*. As people develop a stronger commitment to their deviant behaviour, they typically acquire a **stigma**, *a powerfully negative label that greatly changes a person's self-concept and social identity.*

A stigma operates as a master status (see Chapter 4, "Social Interaction in Everyday Life"), overpowering other aspects of social identity so that a person is discredited in the minds of others and becomes socially isolated. Often a person gains a stigma informally as others begin to see the individual in deviant terms. Sometimes, however, an entire community formally stigmatizes an individual through what Harold Garfinkel (1956) calls a *degradation ceremony*. A criminal trial is one example, operating much like a high school graduation ceremony in reverse: A person stands before the community and is labelled in negative rather than positive terms.

Retrospective and Projective Labelling

Once people stigmatize an individual, they may engage in *retrospective labelling*, interpreting someone's past in light of some present deviance (Scheff, 1984). For example, after discovering that a priest has sexually molested a child, others rethink his past, perhaps musing, "He always did want to be around young children." Retrospective labelling, which distorts a person's biography by being highly selective, typically deepens a deviant identity.

Similarly, people may engage in *projective labelling* of a stigmatized person, using a deviant identity to predict the person's future actions. Regarding the priest, people might say, "He's going to keep at it until he's caught." The more people in someone's social world think such things, the more these definitions affect the individual's self-concept, increasing the chance that they will come true.

Labelling Difference as Deviance

Is a homeless man who refuses to allow police to take him to a city shelter on a cold night behaving independently or "insanely"? Behaviour that irritates or threatens is labelled not just as "different" but as deviance or mental illness.

The psychiatrist Thomas Szasz (1961, 1970, 2003, 2004) charges that people are too quick to apply the label of mental illness to conditions that simply amount to difference we do not like. The only way to avoid this troubling practice, Szasz continues, is to abandon the idea of mental illness entirely. The world is full of people who think or act differently in ways that may irritate us, but such differences are not grounds for defining someone as mentally ill. Such labelling, Szasz claims, simply enforces conformity to the standards of people powerful enough to impose their will on others.

Most mental health care professionals reject the idea that mental illness does not exist. But they agree that it is important to think critically about how we define "difference." First, people who are mentally ill are no more

In 2010, Amy Bishop, a biology professor with a Harvard Ph.D., was denied tenure by her colleagues at her university. Soon after, she took a gun to a campus faculty meeting and killed three colleagues, wounding three others. What effect does the social standing of the offender have in our assessment of her as "crazy" or "sick" as opposed to simply "evil"?

labelling theory the idea that deviance and conformity result not so much from what people do as from how others respond to those actions

stigma a powerfully negative label that greatly changes a person's self-concept and social identity

medicalization of deviance the transformation of moral and legal deviance into a medical condition

to blame for their condition than people who suffer from cancer or some other physical problem. Therefore, having a mental or physical illness is not grounds for a person being labelled "deviant." Second, ordinary people without the medical knowledge to diagnose mental illness should avoid using such labels just to make people conform to their own standards of behaviour.

The Medicalization of Deviance

Labelling theory, particularly the ideas of Szasz and Goffman, helps explain an important shift in the way our society understands deviance. Over the past 50 or 60 years, the growing influence of psychiatry and medicine has led to the **medicalization of deviance**, *the transformation of moral and legal deviance into a medical condition.*

Medicalization amounts to swapping one set of labels for another. In moral terms, we evaluate people or their behaviour as "bad" or "good." However, the scientific objectivity of medicine passes no moral judgment, instead using clinical diagnoses such as "sick" or "well."

To illustrate, until the mid-twentieth century, people generally viewed alcoholics as morally weak people easily tempted by the pleasure of drink. Gradually, however, medical specialists redefined alcoholism so that most people now consider it a disease, rendering people "sick" rather than "bad." In the same way, obesity, drug addiction, child abuse, sexual promiscuity, and other behaviours that used to be strictly moral matters are widely defined today as illnesses for which people need help rather than punishment.

Similarly, behaviours that used to be defined as criminal—such as smoking marijuana—are more likely today to be seen as a form of treatment. In Canada, possession of any quantity of marijuana continues to be illegal; however, the current *Marihuana for Medical Purposes Regulations*, established in July 2013, permit the medical use of marijuana (Health Canada, 2014).

The Difference Labels Make

Whether we define deviance as a moral or a medical issue has three consequences. First, it affects *who responds* to deviance. An offence against common morality usually brings about a reaction from members of the community or the police. A medical label, however, places the situation under the control of clinical specialists, including counsellors, psychiatrists, and physicians.

A second issue is *how people respond* to deviance. A moral approach defines deviants as offenders subject to punishment. Medically, however, they are patients who need treatment. Punishment is designed to fit the crime, but treatment programs are tailored to the patient and may involve virtually any therapy that a specialist thinks might prevent future illness.

Third, and most important, the two labels differ on the *personal competence of the deviant person.* From a moral standpoint, whether we are right or wrong, at least we take responsibility for our own behaviour. Once we are defined as sick, however, we are seen as unable to control (or if "mentally ill," even to understand) our actions. People who are labelled incompetent are in turn subjected to treatment, often against their will. For this reason alone, attempts to define deviance in medical terms should be made with extreme caution.

Sutherland's Differential Association Theory

Learning any behavioural pattern, whether conventional or deviant, is a process that takes place in groups. According to Edwin Sutherland (1940), a person's tendency toward conformity or deviance depends on the amount of contact with others who encourage or reject conventional behaviour. This is Sutherland's theory of *differential association.*

A number of research studies confirm the idea that young people are more likely to engage in delinquency if they believe that members of their peer groups encourage such activity (Akers et al., 1979; Miller & Matthews, 2001). One investigation focused on sexual activity among grade 8 students. Two strong predictors of such behaviour for young girls was having a boyfriend who encouraged sexual relations and having girlfriends they believed would approve of such activity. Similarly, boys were encouraged to become sexually active by friends who rewarded them with high status in their peer group (Little & Rankin, 2001).

Hirschi's Control Theory

The sociologist Travis Hirschi (1969; Gottfredson & Hirschi, 1995) developed *control theory*, which states that social control depends on people anticipating the consequences of their behaviour. Hirschi assumes that everyone finds at least some deviance tempting. But the thought of a ruined career keeps most people from breaking the rules; for some, just imagining the reactions of family and friends is enough. On the other hand, individuals who feel they have little to lose by deviance are likely to become rule breakers.

All social groups teach their members skills and attitudes that encourage certain behaviour. In recent years, discussion on university and college campuses has focused on the dangers of binge drinking, which results in several deaths each year among young people in Canada. How much of a problem is binge drinking on your campus?

Joe Koshellek/MCT/Newscom

Specifically, Hirschi links conformity to four different types of social control:

1. **Attachment.** Strong social attachments encourage conformity. Weak family, peer, and school relationships leave people freer to engage in deviance.

2. **Opportunity.** The greater a person's access to legitimate opportunity, the greater the advantages of conformity. By contrast, someone with little confidence in future success is more likely to drift toward deviance.

3. **Involvement.** Extensive involvement in legitimate activities—such as holding a job, going to school, or playing sports—inhibits deviance (Langbein & Bess, 2002). By contrast, people who simply "hang out" waiting for something to happen have time and energy to engage in deviant activity.

4. **Belief.** Strong beliefs in conventional morality and respect for authority figures restrain tendencies toward deviance. People who have a weak conscience (and who are left unsupervised) are more open to temptation (Stack, Wasserman, & Kern, 2004).

Hirschi's analysis combines a number of earlier ideas about the causes of deviant behaviour. Note that a person's relative social privilege as well as family and community environment is likely to affect the risk of deviant behaviour (Hope, Grasmick, & Pointon, 2003).

EVALUATE The various symbolic-interaction theories all see deviance as a reality that may emerge within the process of interaction. Labelling theory links deviance not to the action but to the *reaction* of others. Thus some people are defined as deviant but others who think or behave in the same way are not. The concepts of secondary deviance, deviant career, and stigma show how being labelled deviant can become a lasting self-concept.

Yet labelling theory has several limitations. First, because labelling theory takes a highly relative view of deviance, it ignores the fact that some kinds of behaviour—such as murder—are condemned just about everywhere. Therefore, labelling theory is most usefully applied to less serious issues, such as sexual promiscuity or mental illness. Second, research on the consequences of deviant labelling does not clearly show whether deviant labelling produces further deviance or discourages it (Smith & Gartin, 1989; Sherman & Smith, 1992). Third, not everyone resists being labelled as deviant; some people actively seek it out (Vold & Bernard, 1986). For example, people take part in civil disobedience and willingly subject themselves to arrest in order to call attention to social injustice.

Sociologists consider Sutherland's differential association theory and Hirschi's control theory important contributions to our understanding of deviance. But why do society's norms and laws define certain kinds of activities as deviant in the first place? This question is addressed by social-conflict analysis, the focus of the next section.

CHECK YOUR LEARNING Clearly define primary deviance, secondary deviance, deviant career, and stigma.

Deviance and Inequality: Social-Conflict Analysis

(**7.4**) Apply social-conflict theories to the topic of deviance.

The social-conflict approach, as summarized in the Applying Theory table, links deviance to social inequality. That is, who or what is labelled "deviant" depends on which categories of people hold power in a society.

Deviance and Power

Alexander Liazos (1972) points out that the people we tend to define as deviants—the ones we dismiss as "nuts" and "sluts"—are typically not as bad or harmful as much as they are *powerless*. Bag ladies and unemployed men on street corners, not corporate polluters or international arms dealers, carry the stigma of deviance.

Social-conflict theory explains this pattern in three ways. First, all norms—especially the laws of any society—generally reflect the interests of the rich and powerful. People who threaten the wealthy are likely to be labelled deviant, either for taking people's property ("common thieves") or for advocating a more egalitarian society ("political radicals"). Karl Marx, a major architect of the social-conflict approach, argued that the law and all other social institutions support the interests of the rich. Or as Richard Quinney puts it, "Capitalist justice is by the capitalist class, for the capitalist class, and against the working class" (1977:3).

Second, even if their behaviour is called into question, the powerful have the resources to resist deviant labels. The majority of executives involved in recent corporate scandals have yet to be arrested; only a few have gone to jail.

Third, the widespread belief that norms and laws are natural and good masks their political character. For this reason, although we may condemn the unequal application of the law, we give little thought to whether the laws themselves are really fair or not.

Applying Theory

Deviance				
	Structural-Functional Theory	Symbolic-Interaction Theory	Social-Conflict Theory	Race-Conflict and Feminist Theories
What is the level of analysis?	Macro-level	Micro-level	Macro-level	Macro-level
What is deviance? What part does it play in society?	Deviance is a basic part of social organization. By defining deviance, society sets its moral boundaries.	Deviance is part of socially constructed reality that emerges in interaction. Deviance comes into being as individuals label something deviant.	Deviance results from social inequality. Norms, including laws, reflect the interests of powerful members of society.	Deviance reflects racial and gender inequality. Deviant labels are more readily applied to women and racial minorities.
What is important about deviance?	Deviance is universal: It exists in all societies.	Deviance is variable: Any act or person may or may not be labelled deviant.	Deviance is political: People with little power are at high risk of being labelled deviant.	Deviance is a means of control: Dominant categories of people discredit others as a means to dominate them.

Deviance and Capitalism

In the Marxist tradition, Steven Spitzer (1980) argues that deviant labels are applied to people who interfere with the operation of capitalism. First, because capitalism is based on private control of property, people who threaten the property of others—especially the poor who steal from the rich—are prime candidates for being labelled deviant. On the other hand, the rich who take advantage of the poor are less likely to be labelled deviant. For example, landlords who charge poor tenants high rents and evict anyone who cannot pay are not considered criminals; they are simply "doing business."

Second, because capitalism depends on productive labour, people who cannot or will not work risk being labelled deviant. Many members of our society think people who are out of work, even through no fault of their own, are somehow deviant.

Third, capitalism depends on respect for authority figures, causing people who resist authority to be labelled deviant. Examples are children who skip school or talk back to parents and teachers and adults who do not co-operate with employers or police.

Canadian media are calling it the "Senate expenses scandal." Beginning in 2012, Senators Mike Duffy, Mac Harb, Pamela Wallin, and Patrick Brazeau made improper housing allowance and travel expense claims. Trial dates have been set, starting in 2015. In June 2015, the Auditor General identified 30 more senators who have wrongfully filed expenses, 9 of whom will be investigated by the RCMP. Do you think that the courts will treat the senators fairly? Why or why not?

Fourth, anyone who directly challenges the capitalist status quo is likely to be defined as deviant. Such has been the case with labour organizers, radical environmentalists, civil rights and antiwar activists, and anarchists.

On the other side of the coin, society positively labels whatever supports the operation of capitalism. For example, winning athletes enjoy celebrity status because they express the values of individual achievement and competition, both vital to capitalism. Also, Spitzer notes, we condemn using drugs of escape (marijuana, psychedelics, heroin, and crack) as deviant but encourage drugs (such as alcohol and caffeine) that promote adjustment to the status quo.

The capitalist system also tries to control people who are not economically productive. The elderly, people with mental or physical disabilities, and Robert Merton's retreatists (people addicted to alcohol or other drugs) are a "costly yet relatively harmless burden" on society. Such people, claims Spitzer, are subject to control by social welfare agencies. But people who openly challenge the capitalist system, including the inner-city underclass and revolutionaries—Merton's innovators and rebels—are controlled by the criminal justice system and, in times of crisis such as the 1970 Front de libération du Québec crisis, the 1990 Oka Crisis in Quebec, the 1997 APEC summit in Vancouver, and the 2010 G20 summit in Toronto, by military forces.

Note that both the social welfare and the criminal justice systems blame individuals, not the system, for social problems. Welfare recipients are considered unworthy freeloaders, poor people who express rage at their plight are labelled rioters, anyone who actively challenges the government is branded a radical or a communist, and those who try to gain illegally what they will never get legally are rounded up as common criminals.

White-Collar Crime

St. Paul, Alberta, was known in the mid-1990s as the town of Bre-X millionaires because of the proportionately large number of people there who had invested in the gold company. It turned out, however, that Bre-X was a fraud. Many of those who had been wealthy on paper lost all of the money they had invested when it was discovered that the $6 billion company had become so valuable based only on some mining ore samples that had been tampered with.

Bre-X's management engaged in **white-collar crime**, defined by Edwin Sutherland (1940) as *crime committed by people of high social position in the course of their occupations.* White-collar criminals use their powerful offices illegally to enrich themselves and others, often causing significant public harm in the process. Rarely, however, do the actions of white-collar criminals result in police converging on a scene with guns drawn. For this reason, sociologists sometimes call white-collar offences that occur in government offices and corporate boardrooms "crime in the suites" as opposed to "crime in the streets."

The most common white-collar crimes are bank embezzlement, business fraud, bribery, and antitrust violations. Sutherland (1940) explains that such white-collar offences typically end up in a civil hearing rather than in a criminal courtroom. *Civil law* regulates business dealings between private parties, and *criminal law* defines an individual's moral responsibilities to society. In practice, then, someone who loses a civil case pays for damage or injury but is not labelled a criminal. Corporate officials are also protected by the fact that most charges of white-collar crime target the organization rather than individuals.

When white-collar criminals are charged and convicted, they usually escape punishment. Advertising executive Paul Coffin pleaded guilty to defrauding the government of about $1.5 million as his part of the Liberal party sponsorship scandal. In 2005, he received a sentence of two years' house arrest, although this sentence was later overturned on appeal and replaced by a jail sentence of 18 months. Nobody has been convicted in relation to the Bre-X affair.

As some analysts see it, until courts impose more prison terms, we should expect white-collar crime to remain widespread (Shover & Hochstetler, 2006).

Corporate Crime

Sometimes whole companies, not just individuals, break the law. **Corporate crime** signifies *the illegal actions of a corporation or people acting on its behalf.*

Corporate crime ranges from knowingly selling faulty or dangerous products to deliberately polluting the environment (Derber, 2004). Sociologist Laureen Snider (2015) identifies three categories of corporate crime: financial, safety, and environmental. An example of *financial crime* is the collapse of a number of corporations in recent years, linked to criminal conduct on the part of company officials, resulting in job and pension losses for tens of thousands of people. Other financial crimes include stock market fraud and dishonest accounting. Even more seriously, companies also commit *safety crimes*, resulting in injury or death of workers, or in the sale of unsafe goods. In May 2011, the operators of a mushroom farm outside Vancouver pleaded guilty in the deaths of three farm workers who died in a small shed when they were overcome by the toxic fumes from a broken pipe. In July 2013, a train loaded with crude oil derailed and exploded, resulting in the death of 47 people and the destruction of the entire downtown area of Lac Megantic, Quebec. Lastly, *environmental crimes* occur whenever corporations violate environmental laws and engage in environmentally destructive behaviour. In 2010, Canada's largest independent oil and gas company, Canadian Natural Resources Ltd., released 6000 litres of crude oil into fish habitat. The corporation pleaded guilty and was sentenced, in May 2015 in Alberta Provincial Court, to pay $125 000 (Environment Canada, 2015; Snider, 2015).

As Snider notes, "[c]orporate crimes are infinitely more harmful than the offences we usually think of as crimes. Corporate crimes cause thousands more injuries and deaths per year than the assaults and homicides that preoccupy the mass media" (2015:9). Consider that in 2013, the death toll for all job-related hazards in Canada was 902, or 2.5 workers for every workday (Association of Workers' Compensation Boards of Canada, 2013). This was significantly higher than the 2013 homicide rate of 505 (Statistics Canada, 2014b). Also, as social researchers point out, hundreds more workers likely die from underreported illnesses that can be related to their work. Corporations thus not only commit more grievous crimes than do individuals but many of the social harms they cause are not seen as crimes.

---

white-collar crime crime committed by people of high social position in the course of their occupations

corporate crime the illegal actions of a corporation or people acting on its behalf

organized crime a business supplying illegal goods or services

Organized Crime

Organized crime is *a business supplying illegal goods or services.* Sometimes criminal organizations force people to do business with them, as when a gang extorts money from shopkeepers for "protection." In most cases, however, organized crime involves the sale of illegal goods and services—often sex, drugs, and gambling—to willing buyers.

Organized crime has flourished in Canada and other high-income countries for more than a century. The scope of its operations expanded among immigrants, who found that this society was not willing to share its opportunities with them. Some ambitious individuals (such as Al Capone, mentioned earlier) made their own success, especially during Prohibition, when the government banned the production and sale of alcohol.

The Italian Mafia is a well-known example of organized crime. But other criminal organizations involve Blacks, Chinese, Colombians, Cubans, Haitians, Nigerians, and Russians, as well as others of almost every racial and ethnic category. Today, organized crime involves a wide range of activities, from selling illegal drugs to sex trafficking to credit card fraud to selling false identification papers to illegal immigrants (Valdez, 1997).

In Canada, the vicious scope of organized crime garnered public attention in spring of 2006 when eight members of the Bandidos motorcycle gang were murdered by other members of the gang, apparently for wanting to join the Hells Angels motorcycle gang. In the late 1990s, some 150 people died as a result of fighting between these archrival motorcycle gangs (Beltrame & Branswell, 2000; Canadian Press Newswire, 2000).

The television series *Boardwalk Empire* offers an inside look at the lives of gangsters in American history. How accurately do you think the mass media portray organized crime? Explain.

EVALUATE According to social-conflict theory, a capitalist society's inequality in wealth and power shapes its laws and how they are applied. The criminal justice and social welfare systems thus act as political agents, controlling categories of people who are a threat to the capitalist system.

Like other approaches to deviance, social-conflict theory has its critics. First, this approach implies that laws and other cultural norms are created directly by the rich and powerful. At the very least, this is an oversimplification, as laws also protect workers, consumers, and the environment, sometimes opposing the interests of corporations and the rich.

Second, social-conflict analysis argues that criminality springs up only to the extent that a society treats its members unequally. However, as Durkheim noted, deviance exists in all societies, whatever their economic system and their degree of inequality.

CHECK YOUR LEARNING Define white-collar crime, corporate crime, and organized crime.

Deviance, Race, and Gender

7.5 Apply race-conflict and feminist theories to the topic of deviance.

What people consider deviant reflects the relative power and privilege of different categories of people. The following sections offer two examples: how racial and ethnic hostility motivates hate crimes and how gender is linked to deviance.

Race-Conflict Theory: Hate Crimes

A **hate crime** is *a criminal act against a person or a person's property by an offender motivated by racial or other bias.* A hate crime may express hostility toward someone based on race, ethnicity,

hate crime a criminal act against a person or a person's property by an offender motivated by racial or other bias

Thinking About Diversity: Race, Class, and Gender

Hate Crime Laws: Do They Punish Actions or Attitudes?

Just after 2:00 A.M. on November 17, 2001, in a corner of Vancouver's Stanley Park where gays commonly meet, local resident Aaron Webster was brutally killed. His assailants were a group of five young males, also from the city, who told reporters that they "wanted to get into a fight."

Three years later, 22-year-old Ryan Cran, who was considered to be the ringleader of the group, was found guilty of manslaughter in Webster's beating death. In Cran's sentencing in February 2005, British Columbia Supreme Court Justice Mary Humphries said the attack on Webster was "random, cowardly, and terrifying" but an individual act—not a hate crime. The gay community and members of Webster's family argued otherwise, categorizing the murder as caused by hatred of gay people and pointing out the need for a stiffer sentence.

As this case illustrates, hate crime laws punish a crime more severely if the offender is motivated by bias against some category of people. Supporters make three arguments in favour of hate crime legislation. First, the offender's intentions are always important in weighing criminal responsibility, so considering hatred as an intention is nothing new. Second, victims of hate crimes typically suffer more serious injuries than victims of crimes with other motives. Third, a crime motivated by bias against homosexuals, or other groups who experience discrimination, inflames the public mood more than a crime carried out, say, for money.

Critics counter that while some hate crime cases involve hard-core homophobia or racism, most are impulsive acts by young people. Even more important, critics maintain, hate crime laws are a threat to guarantees of free speech in section 2(b) of the Canadian Charter of Rights and Freedoms. Hate crime laws allow courts to sentence offenders not just for their actions but also for their attitudes. As Harvard University law professor Alan Dershowitz cautions, "As much as I hate bigotry, I fear much more the Court attempting to control the minds of its citizens." In short, according to critics, hate crime laws open the door to punishing beliefs rather than behaviour.

In the case of Aaron Webster, the British Columbia Supreme Court decided against the hate crime ruling and instead punished Cran for his actual behaviour rather than his beliefs about homosexuals.

What Do You Think?

1. Do you think that crimes motivated by hate are more harmful than those motivated by, say, greed? Why or why not?

2. Do you think minorities, such as gays and lesbians, should be subject to the same hate crime laws as heterosexuals? Why or why not?

3. Do you favour or oppose hate crime laws? Why?

Sources: Terry (1993), Sullivan (2002), and Hartocollis (2007).

religion, ancestry, sexual orientation, or mental or physical disability. The Canadian government recorded 1414 hate crimes in 2012 (Statistics Canada, 2014a).

In 2010, two brothers from Nova Scotia erected a large cross (2.5 metres tall) on the front lawn of an interracial couple in their neighbourhood and then set the cross on fire. The case was brought to court and became a benchmark for hate crimes involving cross burning (CTV News, 2011). Race and ethnicity are the most common motivation for hate crimes, accounting for 704 incidents, or about half of all hate crimes, in 2012. Black, Asian, Arab, and Aboriginal populations make up the majority of victims in these cases. Religiously motivated hate crimes made up 419 incidents, or 30 percent of all hate crimes (Statistics Canada, 2014a). People who contend with multiple stigmas, such as visible minority gay men, are especially likely to be victims.

Anti-hate laws place restrictions on the freedom of expression guaranteed by the Canadian Charter of Rights and Freedoms. Many Canadians support such limits; however, opponents charge that such laws, which increase penalties based on the attitudes of the offender, punish "politically incorrect" thoughts. In 2013, section 13 of the Canadian Human Rights Act, which designated telephone and internet hate speech as discriminatory, was struck down. Hate speech remains a crime in Canada, but with the repeal of section 13, its regulation falls from human rights tribunals to criminal courts. The Thinking About Diversity box takes a closer look at the issue of hate crime laws.

Feminist Theory: Deviance and Gender

In 2009, several women in Sudan were convicted of "dressing indecently." The punishment was imprisonment and, in several cases, 10 lashes. The crime was wearing trousers (BBC, 2009).

This is an exceptional case, but the fact is that virtually every society in the world places stricter controls on women than on men. Historically, our own society has centred women's lives around the home. In Canada, even today, women's opportunities in the workplace, in politics, in athletics, and in the military are more limited than men's.

Elsewhere in the world, as the preceding example suggests, the constraints on women are greater still. In Saudi Arabia, women cannot vote or legally operate motor vehicles; in Iran, women who dare to expose their hair or wear makeup in public can be whipped; and not long ago, a Nigerian court convicted a divorced woman of bearing a child out of wedlock and sentenced her to death by stoning; her life was later spared out of concern for her child (Eboh, 2002).

Gender also figures in the theories of deviance you read about earlier in the chapter. Robert Merton's strain theory, for example, defines cultural goals in terms of financial success. Traditionally, at least, this goal has had more to do with the lives of men because women have been taught to define success in terms of relationships, particularly marriage and motherhood (Leonard, 1982). A more woman-focused theory might recognize the "strain" that results from the cultural ideal of equality clashing with the reality of gender-based inequality.

According to labelling theory, gender influences how we define deviance because people commonly use different standards to judge the behaviour of females and males. Further, because society puts men in positions of power over women, men often escape direct responsibility for actions that victimize women. In the past, at least, men who sexually harassed or assaulted women were labelled only mildly deviant and sometimes escaped punishment entirely.

By contrast, women who are victimized may have to convince others—even members of a jury—that they were not to blame for their own sexual harassment or assault. The ruling by the Ontario Court of Justice in favour of "Jane Doe," who sued Toronto Police Services for negligence in their handling of a serial rape case, illustrates this point. Ms. Doe alleged that the police should have done more to warn women in her neighbourhood about the rapist. It took 12 years before the court finally ruled that Ms. Doe's rights under the Canadian Charter of Rights and Freedoms had been violated because the police failed to give her equal protection under the law. This example confirms what research tells us: Whether people define a situation as deviance—and, if so, who the deviant is—depends on the gender of both the audience and the actors (King & Clayson, 1988).

Finally, despite its focus on social inequality, much social-conflict analysis does not address the issue of gender. If economic disadvantage is a primary cause of crime, as conflict theory suggests, why do women (whose economic position is much worse than men's) commit far *fewer* crimes than men?

Crime

7.6 Identify patterns of crime in Canada and around the world.

Crime is the violation of criminal laws enacted by a locality, province or territory, or the federal government. All crimes are composed of two elements: the *act* itself (or in some cases, the failure to do what the law requires) and *criminal intent* (in legal terminology, *mens rea*, or "guilty mind"). Intent is a matter of degree, ranging from wilful conduct to negligence. Someone who is negligent does not set out deliberately to hurt anyone but acts (or fails to act) in a way that results in harm. Prosecutors weigh the degree of intent in deciding whether, for example, to charge someone with first-degree murder, second-degree murder, or negligent manslaughter. Alternatively, they may consider a killing justifiable, as in self-defence.

Types of Crime

In Canada, there are a number of surveys that gather crime-related data. Two popular surveys are the Uniform Crime Reporting (UCR) survey and the General Social Survey (GSS) on

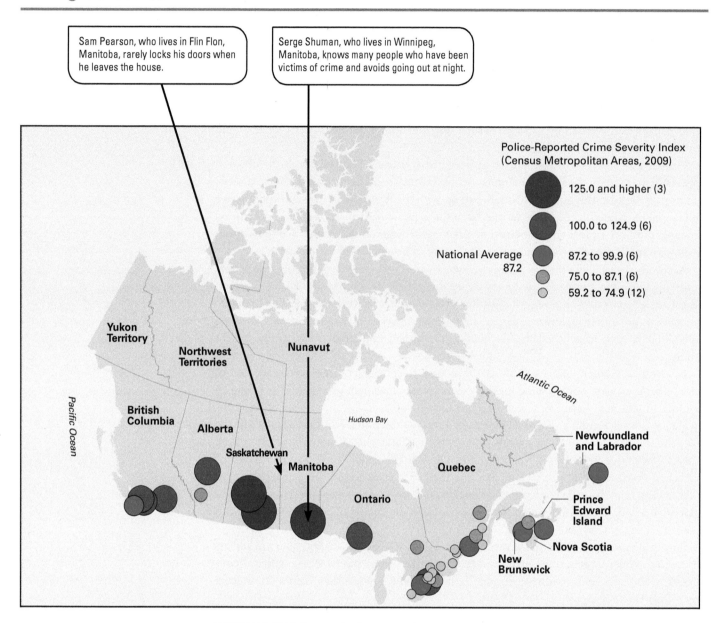

Sam Pearson, who lives in Flin Flon, Manitoba, rarely locks his doors when he leaves the house.

Serge Shuman, who lives in Winnipeg, Manitoba, knows many people who have been victims of crime and avoids going out at night.

NATIONAL MAP 7–1   The Severity of Crime Across Canada

The crime severity index is based on the volume of crime and the severity of the crime reported to the police. The severity of the crime is estimated based on the sentence assigned by the courts for various crimes. This means that the impact of a murder on the index is greater than that of the theft of a bicycle, even though both would have the same impact on the total crime rate.

Source: Dauvergne and Turner, 2010. Dauvergne, M., and S. Turner. "Police-Reported Crime Statistics in Canada, 2009." Juristat. Vol. 20, No. 2 (2010). Catalogue no. 85-002-X. [Online] www.statcan.gc.ca/pub/85-002-x/2010002/article/11292-eng.pdf. Reproduced and distributed on an "as is" basis with the permission of Statistics Canada.

Victimization. Implemented in 1962, the UCR survey gathers crime statistics reported by police departments across the country. The GSS survey was first conducted in 1988, and it collects information on the experience of being a victim of crime, as well as on the perception of crime and the criminal justice system. Both surveys treat violent crime and property crime as separate categories. National Map 7–1 shows the severity and volume of crime reported to police across Canada.

Crimes against the person, also called *violent crimes*, are *crimes that direct violence or the threat of violence against others.* Violent crimes include murder and manslaughter (legally defined as "the willful killing of one human being by another"), aggravated assault ("an unlawful attack by one person upon another for the purpose of inflicting severe or aggravated bodily injury"), sexual assault (includes unwanted sexual touching, sexual attack with or without a weapon, etc.), and robbery ("taking or attempting to take anything of value from the care, custody, or control of a person or persons, by force or threat of force or violence and/or putting the victim in fear").

Crimes against property, also called *property crimes*, are *crimes that involve theft of money or property belonging to others.* Property crimes include burglary ("the unlawful entry of a structure to commit a [serious crime] or a theft"), larceny-theft ("the unlawful taking, carrying, leading, or riding away of property from the possession of another"), auto theft ("the theft or attempted theft of a motor vehicle"), and arson ("any willful or malicious burning or attempt to burn the personal property of another").

A third category of offences include **victimless crimes**, *violations of law in which there are no obvious victims.* Also called *crimes without complaint*, they include illegal drug use, prostitution, and gambling. The term "victimless crime" is misleading, however. How victimless is a crime when a young homeless youth is persuaded into sex work? What about a pregnant woman who, by smoking crack, permanently harms her fetus? Perhaps it is more correct to say that people who commit such crimes are both offenders and victims.

Because public views of victimless crimes vary greatly, laws differ from place to place. For example, prostitution—the exchange of money for sex—is not illegal in Canada (see Chapter 6, "Sexuality and Society"). Nonetheless, a person can be charged who "in a public place . . . communicates . . . for the purpose of engaging in prostitution. . . . " This law is often more heavily enforced when residents of a neighbourhood complain about prostitution (Statistics Canada, 1997; HIV/AIDS Legal Network, 2005).

Criminal Statistics

Statistics gathered by police show crime rates rising from the early 1960s to 1991, but declining over the past two decades. Even so, police tallied nearly 1.8 million crimes in 2013, about 132 000 fewer than in 2012 (Boyce, Cotter, & Perreault, 2014). Figure 7–2 shows the crime rates for violent crimes and property crimes in Canada from 1962 to 2013.

Always read crime statistics with caution, because they include only crimes known to the police. Almost all homicides are reported, but assaults—especially among people who know one another—often are not. Police records include an even smaller share of the property crimes that occur, especially when the crime involves losses that are small.

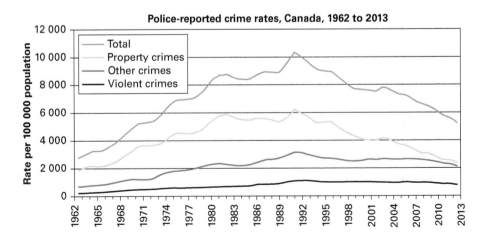

FIGURE 7–2 Crime Rates in Canada, 1962–2013

The graphs show that crime has been decreasing in Canada since the early 1990s.

Source: Canadian Centre for Justice Statistics, Uniform Crime Reporting Survey, http://www.statcan.gc.ca/pub/85-002-x/2014001/article/14040-eng.htm. Reproduced and distributed on an "as is" basis with the permission of Statistics Canada.

Researchers check official crime statistics by using *victimization surveys*, in which they ask a representative sample of people if they have had any experience with crime. The 2009 General Social Survey on Victimization, carried out in 2009, showed that about one-third (31 percent) of incidents had been reported to the police (Perreault & Brennan, 2010).

The Street Criminal: A Profile

Using various government crime reports, we can gain a general description of the categories of people most likely to be arrested for violent and property crimes.

Age

Official crime rates rise sharply during adolescence, peak in the late teens, and then fall as people get older. Age-specific rates for those accused of crime were highest among 15- to 22-year-olds, with the peak age at 17 years (Statistics Canada, 2010). While approximately 104 000 youth (aged 12 to 17 years) were accused of a crime in 2013, the youth crime rate has declined by 16 percent from 2012 and 39 percent from the previous decade (Boyce, Cotter, & Perreault, 2014).

Gender

Although each sex makes up roughly half of the country's population, police charge males more often than females: In 2009, about 233 000 females and 776 000 males were accused of a crime. While the proportion of females charged with a crime has risen over the last three decades, women currently account for only one-fifth of all adults charged with an offence (Mahony, 2011). This gender crime rate difference occurred across all crime categories.

How do we account for the dramatic difference? It may be that some law enforcement officials are reluctant to define women as criminals. In fact, all over the world, the greatest gender differences in crime rates occur in societies that most severely limit the opportunities of women. In Canada, however, the difference in arrest rates for women and men is narrowing, which probably indicates increasing sexual equality in our society. Since the early 1990s, women's rates for violent crime have doubled, shrinking the gap between the number of men and women charged (Mahony, 2011).

Social Class

Canadian police do not assess the social class of arrested persons, so no statistical data of the kind given for age and gender are available. But research has long indicated that street crime is more widespread among people of lower social position (Thornberry & Farnsworth, 1982; Wolfgang, Thornberry, & Figlio, 1987).

Yet the link between class and crime is more complicated than it appears on the surface. For one thing, many people look on the poor as less worthy than the rich, whose wealth and power confer "respectability" (Tittle, Villemez, & Smith, 1978; Elias, 1986). And although crime—especially violent crime—is a serious problem in the poorest inner-city communities of Canada and other countries, most of these crimes are committed by a few repeat offenders. The majority of people who live in poor communities have no criminal record at all (Wolfgang, Figlio, & Sellin, 1972; Elliott & Ageton, 1980; Harries, 1990).

The connection between social standing and criminality also depends on the type of crime. If we expand our definition

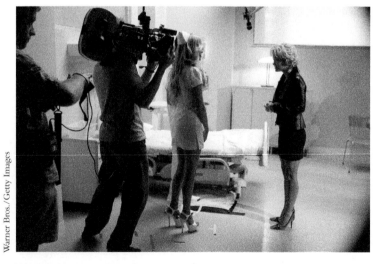

Warner Bros./Getty Images

What actions a society allows or outlaws sometimes seem curious. For example, in Canada prostitution is legal while almost everything associated with it—communicating with the intent of selling sex, advertising services, and purchasing sex—is outlawed. Yet, it's perfectly legal for film producers to pay people to have sex in front of a camera. Why do you think this might be the case?

of crime beyond street offences to include white-collar crime and corporate crime, the "common criminal" suddenly looks much more affluent and may live in a $100 million home.

Race and Ethnicity

In multicultural societies such as Canada, both race and ethnicity are strongly correlated to crime rates, although the reasons are many and complex. Official U.S. statistics show that 69.2 percent of arrests for FBI index crimes in 2011 involved white people. However, the African American arrest rate was higher than the rate for whites in proportion to their representation in the general population. African Americans make up 13.1 percent of the American population but account for 29.5 percent of the arrests for property crimes (versus 68.1 percent for whites) and 38.3 percent of arrests for violent crimes (versus 59.4 percent for whites) (U.S. Department of Justice, Federal Bureau of Investigation, 2012).

Firm conclusions about Canada are not as easy to come by because, unlike in the United States or Great Britain, the majority of Canadian police agencies do not collect data on race and ethnicity, a situation that researchers have criticized (Wortley & Marshall, 2005; Closs & McKenna, 2006; Millar & Owusu-Bempah, 2011; Chan & Chunn, 2014). However, the available evidence points to two conclusions. First, visible minorities tend to be underrepresented in arrest data and prison populations. Second, Aboriginals and Black people constitute two exceptions and are over-represented.

Aboriginals are dramatically over-represented in Canada's correctional facilities: In 1998–1999, Aboriginal persons made up 17 percent of admissions to provincial or territorial sentenced custody, even though they account for only 2 percent of the Canadian population (Thomas, 2000). By 2014, the percentage had risen to 23 percent.

Similarly, research on the total number of traffic stops made by the police in Kingston, Ontario, showed that the Black male residents of Kingston between the ages of 15 and 24 were three times more likely to be stopped and questioned by the police than people from other racial backgrounds (Wortley & Marshall, 2005). A more recent study in Metropolitan Toronto on self-declared "Black," "white," and "Chinese" male residents shows that Black males were over three times as likely as white or Asian males to experience multiple stops by the police (Wortley & Owusu-Bempah, 2011).

There are several reasons for the disproportionate number of arrests among Aboriginals and Blacks in Canada. First, race in Canada closely relates to social standing, which, as already explained, affects the likelihood of engaging in street crimes. Many poor people turn to crime in order to survive or to escape poverty (Blau & Blau, 1982; Martinez, 1996; Millar & Owusu-Bempah, 2011).

Second, crime is racialized. Canadian sociologists Wendy Chan and Dorothy Chunn point out that crimes committed by visible minorities are *over-emphasized*. Within media depictions of crime, for example, "Black suspects are more likely to be represented as superpredators." Crime is also racialized by the use of *encoded terms*, "which, on the surface, appear neutral, but when examined more closely refer to specific racial groups" (Chan & Chunn, 2014:13). Thus, terms like "illegal immigrants," "gangs," and "terrorists" implicate certain racial categories without explicitly naming them. The over-emphasis of non-white criminals and use of encoded terms by media and government agencies create a climate of prejudice that prompts police to arrest Black and Aboriginal people more readily. It also leads citizens to report on these categories more willingly. As a result, these visible minorities are overly criminalized (Chiricos, McEntire, & Gertz, 2001; Quillian & Pager, 2001; Demuth & Steffensmeier, 2004; Chan & Chunn, 2014).

Keep in mind, too, that categories of people with high arrest rates are also at higher risk of being victims of crime. In the United States, for example, African Americans are six times as likely as white people to die as a result of homicide (Rogers et al., 2001; Kochanek et al., 2011). In Canada, Aboriginal people are more likely than non-Aboriginal people to report being victimized. In 2009, 37 percent of Aboriginal people self-reported being the victim of a crime, compared to 26 percent of non-Aboriginals (Perreault, 2011).

"You look like this sketch of someone who's thinking about committing a crime."
David Sipress/The Cartoon Bank

Finally, some categories of the population have unusually low rates of arrest. People of Asian descent, who account for 15 percent of the Canadian population, represent only 4 percent of federal inmates. As Chapter 11 ("Race and Ethnicity") explains, Asian Canadians enjoy higher than average educational achievement and income. Also, Asian immigrant culture emphasizes family solidarity and discipline, both of which keep criminality down.

Crime in Global Perspective

By world standards, the crime rate in Canada is not very high, including when compared to the United States. Although recent crime trends are downward in the United States as well as in Canada, there were 14 612 murders in the United States in 2011, which amounts to one every 36 minutes around the clock. In large cities such as New York, rarely does a day go by without someone being killed as a result of criminal violence.

The rates of violent crime and also property crime in the United States are several times higher than in Europe. The contrast is even greater when the U.S. rate is compared to those in the nations of Asia, especially Japan, where rates of violent and property crime rates are among the lowest in the world.

Elliott Currie (1985) suggests that crime stems from a cultural emphasis on individual economic success, frequently at the expense of strong families and neighbourhoods. The United States also has extraordinary cultural diversity—a result of centuries of immigration—that can lead to conflict. In addition, economic inequality is higher in that country than in most other high-income nations. U.S. society's relatively weak social fabric, combined with considerable frustration among the poor, increases the level of criminal behaviour.

Another factor contributing to violence in the United States is extensive private ownership of guns. About two-thirds of murder victims in the United States die from shootings. The U.S. rate of handgun homicides is about seven times higher than in Canada, where strict limits to handgun ownership prevail (Goodwin, 2012; Cotter, 2014).

Across all regions of the United States, the trend in gun ownership is down. In the 1970s, half of U.S. households had at least one gun. This share fell to about 40 percent by the mid-1990s. Surveys conducted in 2012 suggest that one or more guns are found in just about one-third of all U.S. households. But even at that level, there are more guns (about 285 million) than adults in the United States, and 40 percent of these weapons are handguns, the weapons commonly used in violent crimes. In large part, gun ownership reflects people's fear of crime, yet the easy availability of guns in that country makes crime more deadly (Brady Campaign, 2012; NORC, 2013).

Supporters of gun control in the United States claim that restricting gun ownership would reduce the number of murders. They point out that the number of murders each year in Canada (543 in 2012), where the law prevents most people from owning guns, is comparable to the number of killings in just the city of Chicago alone (500 in 2012). But as critics of gun control point out, laws regulating gun ownership do not keep guns out of the hands of criminals, who almost always obtain guns illegally. They also claim that gun control is no magic bullet in the war on crime: The number of people in the United States killed each year by knives alone is almost three times the number of Canadians killed by weapons of all kinds (J. D. Wright, 1995; Munroe, 2007; U.S. Department of Justice, Federal Bureau of Investigation, 2012; Boyce & Cotter, 2013; Wilson, 2013).

The U.S. population remains evenly divided over the issue of gun control, with 46 percent of people saying it is more important to protect the personal right to own a gun and 47 percent saying it is more important to control gun ownership. But the momentum in this debate may be shifting in the wake of the fatal shooting of 20 children and 6 adults at the Sandy Hook Elementary School in Connecticut in 2012. This tragic mass killing stunned the nation and rallied the forces seeking greater gun control (Pew Research Center, 2012).

Crime rates are high in some of the largest cities of the world, including Lima, Peru; São Paulo, Brazil; and Manila, Philippines—all of which have rapid population growth and millions of desperately poor people. Outside of big cities, however, the traditional character of low-income societies allows local communities to control crime informally.

Some types of crime have always been multinational, such as terrorism, espionage, and arms dealing (Martin & Romano, 1992). But today, the globalization we are experiencing on many fronts also extends to crime. A recent case in point is the illegal drug trade. In part, the problem of illegal drugs in countries such

When economic activity such as selling illegal drugs takes place outside of the law, people turn to violence rather than courts to settle disagreements. In Central America, drug violence has pushed the homicide rate to the highest level in the world.

as Canada is a *demand* issue. That is, the demand for cocaine and other drugs is strong, and many people risk arrest or even a violent death for a chance to get rich in the drug trade. But the *supply* side of the issue is just as important. The South American nation of Colombia has long looked to cocaine production as a significant part of its national economy. Not only is cocaine Colombia's most profitable export, but it outsells all other exports combined, including coffee. Clearly, then, drug dealing and many other crimes are closely related to social conditions both in this country and elsewhere.

Different countries have different strategies for dealing with crime. The use of capital punishment (the death penalty) is one example. According to Amnesty International (2012), China executes more people than the rest of the world combined—probably in the thousands—but does not divulge its numbers. Of the 680 documented executions in 2011, 87 percent were in Iran, Saudi Arabia, Iraq, Yemen, and the United States. Global Map 7–1 on page 222 shows which countries currently use capital punishment. The global trend is toward abolishing the death penalty: Amnesty International (2012) reports that since 1985, 67 nations have ended this practice.

The Canadian Criminal Justice System

7.7 Analyze the operation of the criminal justice system.

The criminal justice system is a society's formal system of social control. We shall briefly examine the key elements of the Canadian criminal justice system: police, courts, and the system of punishment and corrections. First, however, we must understand an important principle that underlies the entire system, the idea of due process.

Fundamental Justice

Fundamental justice is the principle that the criminal justice system must guarantee procedural fairness and operate according to law. This idea was introduced in 1960 in the Canadian Bill of Rights and was constitutionalized in 1982 in the Canadian Charter of Rights and Freedoms. The Charter offers various protections to any person charged with a crime. Among these are the right to counsel, the right to be presumed innocent until proven guilty, the right not to be denied reasonable bail, freedom from being tried twice for the same crime, and freedom

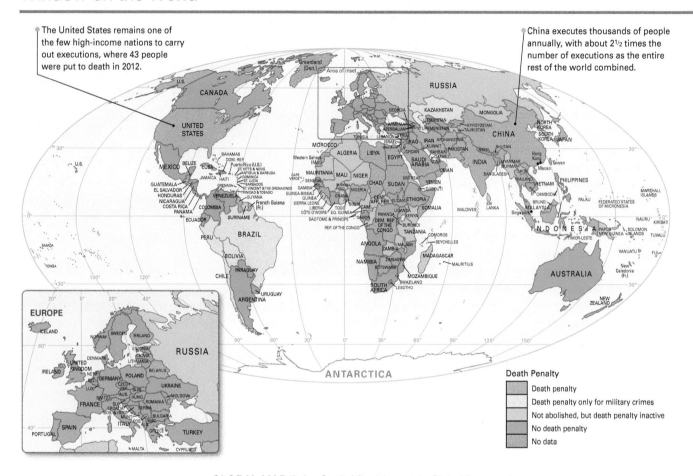

The United States remains one of the few high-income nations to carry out executions, where 43 people were put to death in 2012.

China executes thousands of people annually, with about 2½ times the number of executions as the entire rest of the world combined.

Death Penalty

Death penalty

Death penalty only for military crimes

Not abolished, but death penalty inactive

No death penalty

No data

GLOBAL MAP 7–1   Capital Punishment in Global Perspective

The map identifies 58 countries in which the law allows the death penalty for ordinary crimes; in 8 more, the death penalty is reserved for exceptional crimes under military law or during times of war. The death penalty does not exist in 97 countries; in 35 more, although the death penalty remains in law, no execution has taken place in more than 10 years. Compare rich and poor nations: What general pattern do you see? In what way are the United States and Japan exceptions to this pattern?

Source: Amnesty International (2012).

from unreasonable search or seizure. Furthermore, the Charter gives all people the right to a speedy and public trial by jury and from "cruel and unusual" punishment.

In general terms, the concept of fundamental justice means that anyone charged with a crime must receive 1) fair notice of legal proceedings; 2) the opportunity to present a defence during a hearing on the charges, which must be conducted according to law; and 3) a judge or jury that weighs evidence impartially (Inciardi, 2000). Furthermore, fundamental justice also guarantees that laws themselves must not be vague, arbitrary, or disproportionate (Stewart, 2012).

Fundamental justice limits the power of government, with an eye toward this nation's cultural support of individual rights and freedoms. Deciding exactly how far government can go is an ongoing process that makes up much of the work of the judicial system, especially the Supreme Court of Canada.

Police

The police generally serve as the primary point of contact between a society's population and the criminal justice system. In principle, the police maintain public order by enforcing the law. Because the 69 272 full-time police officers across Canada (Hutchins, 2014) cannot effectively

Police are allowed discretion in handling many different situations they face every day. At the same time, the police are required to treat people fairly. Here we see police deciding to make an arrest during the Occupy movement in Toronto in 2011. What factors do you think enter into this decision?

monitor the activities of 35 million people, the police use considerable personal judgment in deciding which situations warrant their attention and how to handle them.

How do police officers carry out their duties? In a study of police behaviour in five cities, Douglas Smith and Christy Visher (1981; Smith, 1987) concluded that because they must act swiftly, police quickly size up situations in terms of six factors. First, the more serious they think the situation is, the more likely they are to make an arrest. Second, police take account of the victim's wishes in deciding whether or not to make an arrest. Third, the odds of arrest go up the more uncooperative a suspect is. Fourth, police are more likely to take into custody someone they have arrested before, presumably because this suggests guilt. Fifth, the presence of observers increases the chances of arrest. According to Smith and Visher, the presence of observers prompts police to take stronger control of a situation, if only to move the encounter from the street (the suspect's turf) to the police department (where law officers have the edge). Sixth, all else being equal, police are more likely to arrest Aboriginals and Blacks, perceiving them as either more dangerous or more likely to be guilty.

Courts

After arrest, a court determines a suspect's guilt or innocence. In principle, Canadian courts rely on an adversarial process involving lawyers—one representing the defendant and another representing the state—in the presence of a judge, who monitors legal procedures.

In practice, however, about 90 percent of criminal convictions result from the process of **plea bargaining**, *a legal negotiation in which a prosecutor reduces a charge in exchange for a defendant's guilty plea.* Without ever going to trial, for example, the Crown may offer a defendant charged with burglary a lesser charge, perhaps possession of burglary tools, in exchange for a guilty plea (Canada, Department of Justice, 2015).

Plea bargaining is widespread because it spares the system the time and expense of trials. A trial is usually unnecessary if there is little disagreement over the facts of the case. In addition, because of the high number of cases entering the system, prosecutors could not possibly bring

plea bargaining a legal negotiation in which a prosecutor reduces a charge in exchange for a defendant's guilty plea

Television shows like *Suits* suggest that the criminal justice system carefully weighs the guilt and innocence of defendants. But as explained here, only 10 percent of criminal cases are actually resolved through a formal trial.

every case to trial even if they wanted to. By quickly resolving most of their work, then, the courts channel their resources into the most important cases.

But a system of plea bargaining pressures defendants (who are presumed innocent) to plead guilty. A person can exercise the right to a trial, but only at the risk of receiving a more severe sentence if found guilty at trial. Furthermore, low-income defendants must often rely on a crown attorney—typically an overworked and underpaid lawyer who may devote little time to even the most serious cases. Although plea bargaining may be efficient, it can compromise fundamental justice by undercutting both the adversarial process and the rights of defendants to effective legal representation.

Punishment

Hierarchically stratified societies resort to punishment as a means of social control. Wherever pronounced differences in power exist, punishment is used by authorities to instill discipline. Punishment is employed by everyone from teachers, who rely on detentions and time-outs, to the criminal justice system, which employs fines and incarceration.

Radical criminologists, restorative justice and prison abolitionist activists, and scholars like Angela Davis and Michel Foucault have called for the elimination of prisons and legal punishment on the grounds that these are unethical and ineffective means of dealing with social problems. Nonetheless, many people support punishment, and our society continues to utilize it. What is the argument for the punishment of wrongdoers? Scholars answer with four basic reasons: retribution, deterrence, rehabilitation, and societal protection.

Retribution

The oldest justification for punishment is to satisfy people's need for **retribution**, *an act of moral vengeance by which society makes the offender suffer as much as the suffering caused by the crime.* Retribution rests on a view of society as a moral balance. When criminality upsets this balance, punishment in equal measure restores the moral order, as suggested in the ancient code calling for "an eye for an eye, a tooth for a tooth."

In the Middle Ages, most Europeans viewed crime as sin—an offence against God as well as society that required a harsh response. Today, although critics point out that retribution does little to reform the offender, many people consider vengeance reason enough for punishment.

Summing Up

Four Justifications for Punishment	
Retribution	The oldest justification for punishment.
	Punishment is society's revenge for a moral wrong.
	In principle, punishment should be equal in severity to the crime itself.
Deterrence	An early modern approach.
	Crime is considered social disruption, which society acts to control.
	People are viewed as rational and self-interested; deterrence may work if people perceive that the pain of punishment outweighs the pleasure of crime.
Rehabilitation	A modern strategy linked to the development of social sciences.
	Crime and other deviance are viewed as the result of social problems (such as poverty) or personal problems (such as mental illness).
	Social conditions need to be improved; treatment should be tailored to the offender's condition.
Societal protection	A modern approach easier to carry out than rehabilitation.
	Even if society is unable or unwilling to rehabilitate offenders or reform social conditions, people may be protected by the imprisonment or execution of the offender.

Deterrence

A second justification for punishment is **deterrence**, *the attempt to discourage criminality through the use of punishment.* Deterrence is based on the eighteenth-century Enlightenment idea that humans, as calculating and rational creatures, will not break the law if they think that the pain of punishment will outweigh the pleasure of the crime.

Deterrence emerged as a reform measure in response to the harsh punishments based on retribution. Why put someone to death for stealing if theft can be discouraged with a prison sentence? As the concept of deterrence gained acceptance in industrial nations, the execution and physical mutilation of criminals in most high-income societies were replaced by milder forms of punishment such as imprisonment.

Punishment may deter crime in two ways. *Specific deterrence* is used to convince an individual offender that crime does not pay. Through *general deterrence*, the punishment of one person serves as an example to others.

Rehabilitation

The third justification for punishment is **rehabilitation**, *a program for reforming the offender to prevent later offences.* Rehabilitation arose along with the social sciences in the nineteenth century. Since then, sociologists have claimed that crime and other deviance spring from a social environment marked by poverty or a lack of parental supervision. Logically, then, if offenders learn to be deviant, they can also learn to obey the rules; the key is controlling the environment. *Reformatories* or *houses of correction* provided controlled settings where people could learn proper behaviour (recall the description of total institutions in Chapter 3, "Socialization: From Infancy to Old Age").

Like deterrence, rehabilitation motivates the offender to conform. In contrast to deterrence and retribution, which simply make the offender suffer, rehabilitation encourages

Four Justifications for Punishment

retribution an act of moral vengeance by which society makes the offender suffer as much as the suffering caused by the crime

deterrence the attempt to discourage criminality through the use of punishment

rehabilitation a program for reforming the offender to prevent later offences

societal protection rendering an offender incapable of further offences temporarily through imprisonment or permanently by execution

constructive improvement. Unlike retribution, which demands that the punishment fit the crime, rehabilitation tailors treatment to each offender. Thus identical crimes would prompt similar acts of retribution but different rehabilitation programs.

Societal Protection

A final justification for punishment is **societal protection**, *rendering an offender incapable of further offences temporarily through imprisonment or permanently by execution*. Like deterrence, societal protection is a rational approach to punishment intended to protect society from crime.

The reason why there are more than 38 000 adults in Canadian prisons is partly a reflection of the widespread attitude that we should "get criminals off the streets." Remember that this number represents a smaller fraction of the total number under the supervision of the correctional system—another 125 000 adults are on probation, serve a conditional sentence, or are on conditional release (Dauvergne, 2012).

EVALUATE The Summing Up table on page 225 reviews the four justifications for punishment. However, an accurate assessment of the consequences of punishment is no simple task.

The value of retribution lies in Durkheim's claim that punishing the deviant person increases society's moral awareness. For this reason, punishment was traditionally a public event. Although the last public execution in Canada is believed to have taken place in 1902 in Hull, Quebec, today's mass media ensure public awareness of executions carried out inside prison walls (Kittrie, 1971).

Does punishment deter crime? Despite our extensive use of punishment, our society has a high rate of **criminal recidivism**, *later offences by people previously convicted of crimes*. Numerous studies show that a substantial amount of people released from prison are rearrested within a few years. So, does punishment really deter crime? Only about one-third of all crimes are known to police and, of these, only about one in five results in an arrest. Most crimes, therefore, go unpunished, so the old saying that "crime doesn't pay" rings hollow.

Prisons provide short-term societal protection by keeping offenders off the streets, but they do little to reshape attitudes or behaviour in the long term (Carlson, 1976; R. Wright, 1994). Perhaps rehabilitation is an unrealistic expectation, because according to Sutherland's theory of differential association, locking up criminals together for years probably strengthens criminal attitudes and skills. Imprisonment also stigmatizes prisoners, making it harder for them to find legitimate employment later on (Griffiths, Dandurand, & Murdoch, 2007). Finally, prison breaks the social ties inmates may have in the outside world, which, following Hirschi's control theory, makes inmates more likely to commit new crimes upon release.

CHECK YOUR LEARNING What are society's four justifications for punishment? Does sending offenders to prison accomplish each of them? Why?

The Death Penalty

Perhaps the most controversial issue involving punishment is the death penalty. From 1993 to 2013, more than 7500 people were sentenced to death in U.S. courts; 1320 executions were carried out.

In 36 U.S. states, the law allows the state to execute offenders convicted of very serious crimes such as first-degree murder. But although a majority of states do permit capital punishment, only a few states are likely to carry out executions. Across the United States, half of the 3170 people on death row in April 2012 were in just four states: California, Texas, Florida, and Pennsylvania (U.S. Department of Justice, Bureau of Justice Statistics, 2011; Death Penalty Information Center, 2012).

Opponents of capital punishment point to research suggesting that the death penalty has limited value as a crime deterrent. Countries such as Canada, where the death penalty has been abolished, have not seen a rise in the number of murders. Critics also point out that the United

criminal recidivism later offences by people previously convicted of crimes

To increase the power of punishment to deter crime, capital punishment was long carried out in public. The 1902 hanging in Hull, Quebec, of Stanislaus Lacroix, a logger who killed his wife and a neighbour, is believed to be the last public execution in Canada. Now that the mass media report the story of executions across the United States, states carry out capital punishment behind closed doors.

States is the only Western, high-income nation that routinely executes offenders. As public concern about the death penalty increased, the use of capital punishment declined, falling from 85 executions in 2000 to 43 in 2012.

Public opinion surveys reveal that the share of U.S. adults who claim to support the death penalty as a punishment for murder remains high (60 percent) and has been fairly stable over time (NORC, 2013:253). American college students hold about the same attitudes as everyone else, with about two-thirds of first-year students expressing support for the death penalty (Pryor et al., 2008). Canadian surveys find our population more divided. According to an EKOS poll conducted in March 2010, Canadians are about evenly split on the issue of whether to revive the death penalty: 46 percent of those surveyed were opposed to bringing back capital punishment while 40 percent thought such a move was a good idea. These results were similar to those from a poll conducted in June 2000, when there was an almost even split on the issue (CBC News, 2010).

But judges, criminal prosecutors, and members of trial juries are less and less likely to call for the death penalty. One reason is that because the crime rate has come down in recent years, the public now has less fear of crime and is less interested in applying the most severe punishment.

A second reason is public concern that the death penalty may be applied unjustly. The analysis of DNA evidence—a recent advance—from old crime scenes has shown that many people were wrongly convicted of a crime. Across the United States, between 1975 and 2013, 141 people who had been sentenced to death were released from death row, including 18 in which new DNA evidence demonstrated their innocence. Such findings were one reason that, in 2011, the governor of Oregon declared a moratorium on executions, claiming that he could no longer support what he characterized as a "compromised and inequitable system" (State of Oregon, 2011).

A third reason for the decline in the use of the death penalty is that judges and juries in Canada and most other countries, and including those in many U.S. states, are now permitted to sentence serious offenders to life in prison without the possibility of parole. Such punishment offers to protect society from dangerous criminals who can be "put away" forever without requiring an execution.

Fourth and finally, prosecuting capital cases is very costly. Death penalty cases require more legal work and demand superior defence lawyers, often at public expense. In addition, such cases commonly include testimony by various paid "experts," including physicians and psychiatrists, which also runs up the costs of trial. Then there is the cost of many appeals that almost always follow a conviction leading to the sentence of death. When all these factors are put together, the cost of a death penalty case typically exceeds the cost of sending an offender to prison for life. So it is easy to see why many U.S. states often choose not to seek the death penalty (Dwyer, 2011).

Community-Based Corrections

Prisons certainly keep convicted criminals off the streets, but the evidence suggests that they do little to rehabilitate most offenders. Furthermore, prisons are expensive to operate due to the high costs associated with building the facilities and supporting each inmate.

One alternative to the traditional prison that has been adopted in many parts of Canada is **community-based corrections**, *correctional programs operating within society at large rather than behind prison walls.* Community-based corrections have three main advantages: They reduce costs, reduce overcrowding in prisons, and allow for supervision of convicts while eliminating the hardships of prison life and the stigma that accompanies going to jail. In general, the idea of community-based corrections is not so much to punish as to reform; such programs are therefore usually offered to individuals who have committed less serious offences and appear to be good prospects for avoiding future criminal violations (Inciardi, 2000).

Probation

One form of community-based corrections is *probation*, a policy permitting a convicted offender to remain in the community under conditions imposed by a court, including regular supervision. Courts may require that a probationer receive counselling, attend a drug treatment program, hold a job, avoid associating with "known criminals," or anything else a judge thinks is appropriate. Typically, a probationer must check in with an officer of the court (the probation officer) on a regular schedule to make sure the guidelines are being followed. Should the probationer fail to live up to the conditions set by the court or commit a new offence, the court may revoke probation and send the offender to jail.

Parole

Parole is a policy of releasing inmates from prison to serve the remainder of their sentences in the local community under the supervision of a parole officer. Although some sentences specifically deny the possibility of parole, most inmates become eligible for parole after serving a certain portion of their sentences behind bars. At that time, a parole board evaluates the risks and benefits of the inmate's early release from prison. If parole is granted, the parole board then monitors the offender's conduct until the sentence is completed. Should the offender not comply with the conditions of parole or be arrested for another crime, the board can revoke parole and return the offender to prison to complete the original sentence.

Sentencing Circles

A uniquely Canadian experiment allows Aboriginal offenders to choose to partake in a *sentencing circle*. In this form of community-based corrections, the offender, victim, elders, and community members work through a process in which the emphasis is on remedying the harm done and preventing it from occurring in the future. The sentencing circle attempts to heal community relations and to have all parties reach an understanding of the underlying causes of the harmful behaviour. Once an agreement has been reached between all parties, possible outcomes may include specialized counselling; restitution to the victim; a potlatch ceremony or other traditional remedies; or having the offender publicly speak out against the harmful behaviour they engaged in (Justice Education Society, 2015).

community-based corrections correctional programs operating within society at large rather than behind prison walls

Controversy & Debate

Crime Is Down—But Why?

Ryan: I'm a criminal justice major, and I want to be a police officer. Crime is a huge problem in Canada, and police keep the crime rate low.

Sandy: I'm a sociology major. As for combating crime, I'm not sure it's quite that simple. . . .

During the 1980s, crime rates shot upward and there seemed to be no solution to the problem. In the 1990s, serious crime rates began to fall until, by 2000, they were at levels not seen in more than a generation. Why? Researchers point to several reasons:

1. **A reduction in the youth population.** It was noted earlier that young people (particularly males) are responsible for much violent crime. During the 1990s, the population aged 15 to 24 dropped significantly, as the aging population increased.

2. **Changes in policing.** Much of the drop in crime (as well as the earlier rise in crime) took place in large cities. Many cities have adopted a policy of community policing, which means that police attempt to get to know the areas they patrol. In Toronto, for example, numerous Community Police Liaison Committees and Community Consultative Committees invite broader community involvement. In addition, the number of civilians assisting the police is increasing. Across Canada, civilian positions such as dispatcher, special constable, and security guard, are playing a greater role in policing. During the 1960s, the ratio was about 4.1 to 4.6 police officers for every civilian personnel. The ratio was 2.8 in 2003. In 2013, there were 69 272 officers and 27 872 civilians employed by policing services, for a 2.5 ratio.

3. **A better economy.** The Canadian economy boomed during the 1990s. Unemployment was down, reducing the likelihood that some people would turn to crime out of economic desperation. The logic here is simple: More jobs equal fewer crimes. Government data show that since 1991 the crime rate has continued to decrease steadily.

4. **Declining drug use and changing attitudes.** Marijuana use, for example, may have remained constant over time, while police are likely choosing to be more lenient about enforcing cannabis laws. Relatedly, some drug use has decreased. The Urban Health Research Initiative (UHRI) and the B.C. Centre for Excellence in HIV/AIDS report a decline in daily heroin use from 27.7 percent in 1996 to 14 percent in 2011. Improved harm reduction measures, like the introduction of a supervised injection site in Vancouver, may have contributed to the turnaround in crime.

The current picture looks better relative to what it was a decade or two ago. But one researcher cautions: "It looks better, but only because the early 1990s were so bad. So let's not fool ourselves into thinking everything is resolved. It's not."

What Do You Think?

1. Do you support the policy of community policing? Why or why not?

2. All across Canada new prisons are being built. How do you think prison expansion will affect the crime rate?

3. Which of the factors mentioned here do you think is the most important in crime control? Which is least important? Why?

Sources: Stastna (2013), Webb (2013), Hutchins (2014), and Statistics Canada (2015).

EVALUATE Researchers have carefully studied both probation and parole to see how well these programs work. Evaluations of both these policies are mixed. There is little question that probation and parole are much less expensive than conventional imprisonment; they also free up room in prisons for people who commit more serious crimes. Yet research suggests that, although probation seems to work for some people, it does not significantly reduce recidivism. Parole is also useful to prison officials as a means to encourage good behaviour among inmates. To date, the effectiveness of sentencing circles is unknown, as very little research has been conducted on this community-based correction.

CHECK YOUR LEARNING What are three types of community-based corrections? What are their advantages? What are their limitations?

Such evaluations point to a sobering truth: The criminal justice system—operating on its own—cannot eliminate crime. As the Controversy & Debate box explains, although police, courts, and prisons do have an effect on crime rates, crime and other forms of deviance are not just the acts of "bad people" but reflect the operation of society itself.

Seeing Sociology in Everyday Life

CHAPTER 7 Deviance

Why do most of us—at least most of the time—obey the rules?

As this chapter has explained, every society is a system of social control that encourages conformity to certain norms and discourages deviance or norm breaking. One way society does this is through the construction of heroes and villains. Heroes, of course, are people we are supposed to "look up to" and use as role models. Villains are people whom we look "down on" and reject their example, allowing them to become "anti-heroes" who point us in the opposite direction. Organizations of all types create heroes and villains that serve as guides to everyday behaviour. In each case that follows, who is being made into a hero? Why? What are the values or behaviours we are encouraged to copy in our own lives?

Universities and business organizations create heroes in various ways. Here we see Jeremy Pearce, a Simon Fraser University student, being awarded the Surrey Board of Trade's annual 25 under 25 Award. This award recognizes the criminology and sociology student as a role model for community-mindedness. Among 24 other recipients, Pearce is acknowledged for creating the Transit Watch program, which aims to decrease crime and improve safety for transit users. What is heroic in this case? What about villains—how do universities and business organizations create them, too?

Courtesy of Jeremy Pearce and Simon Fraser University

Religious organizations, too, use heroes to encourage certain behaviour and beliefs. The Roman Catholic Church has defined the Virgin Mary and more than 10 000 other men and women as "saints." For what reasons might someone be honoured in this way? What do saints do for the rest of us?

Miguel Angel Morenatti/AP Images

Most sports have a "hall of fame." A larger-than-life-size statue of the legendary slugger Babe Ruth attracts these children on their visit to the Baseball Hall of Fame. What are the qualities that make an athlete "legendary"? Isn't it more than just how far someone hits a ball?

Bill Greenblatt/UPI/Landow

HINT A society without heroes and villains would be one in which no one cared what people thought or how they acted. Societies create heroes as role models that are supposed to inspire us to be more like them. Societies create heroes by emphasizing one aspect of someone's life and ignoring other things. For example, Babe Ruth was a great ball player, but his private life was sometimes less than inspiring. Perhaps this is why the Catholic Church never considers anyone a candidate for sainthood until after—usually long after—the person has died.

Seeing Sociology in *Your* Everyday Life

1. Do athletic teams, fraternities and sororities, and even people in a university classroom create heroes and villains? Explain how and why.

2. Go to www.sociologyinfocus.com to access the Sociology in Focus blog, where you can read the latest posts by a team of young sociologists who apply the sociological perspective to topics of popular culture.

3. Based on the material presented in this chapter, we might say that "Deviance is a difference that makes a difference." That is, deviance is constructed as part of social life because, as Emile Durkheim argued, it is a necessary part of society. Make a (private) list of 10 negative traits that have been directed at you (or that you have directed at yourself). Then look at your list and try to determine what it says about the society we live in. Why, in other words, do these differences make a difference to members of our society?

Joe Koshollek/Newscom

Making the Grade

What Is Deviance?

7.1 Explain how sociology addresses limitations of a biological or psychological approach to deviance. (pages 198–202)

Deviance refers to norm violations ranging from minor infractions, such as bad manners, to major infractions, such as serious violence.

Biological theories focus on individual abnormality and explain human behaviour as the result of biological instincts.

Psychological theories focus on individual abnormality and see deviance as the result of "unsuccessful socialization."

Sociological theories view all behaviour—deviance as well as conformity—as products of society. Sociologists point out that

- what is deviant varies from place to place according to cultural norms
- behaviour and individuals become deviant as others define them that way
- what and who a society defines as deviant reflect who has and does not have social power

deviance the recognized violation of cultural norms
crime the violation of a society's formally enacted criminal law
social control attempts by society to regulate people's thoughts and behaviour
criminal justice system the organizations—police, courts, and prison officials—that respond to alleged violations of the law

The Functions of Deviance: Structural-Functional Analysis

7.2 Apply structural-functional theories to the topic of deviance. (pages 202–205)

Durkheim claimed that deviance is a normal element of society that clarifies moral boundaries, affirms cultural norms and values, brings people together, and encourages social change.

Merton's **strain theory** explains deviance in terms of a society's cultural goals and the means available to achieve them.

Deviant subcultures are discussed by Cloward and Ohlin, Cohen, Miller, and Anderson.

Labelling Deviance: Symbolic-Interaction Analysis

7.3 Apply symbolic-interaction theories to the topic of deviance. (pages 205–210)

Labelling theory claims that deviance depends less on what someone does than on how others react to that behaviour. If people respond to primary deviance by stigmatizing a person, secondary deviance and a deviant career may result.

The **medicalization of deviance** is the transformation of moral and legal deviance into a medical condition. In practice, this means a change in labels, replacing "good" and "bad" with "sick" and "well."

Sutherland's **differential association theory** links deviance to how much others encourage or discourage such behaviour.

Hirschi's **control theory** states that imagining the possible consequences of deviance often discourages such behaviour. People who are well integrated into society are less likely to engage in deviant behaviour.

labelling theory the idea that deviance and conformity result not so much from what people do as from how others respond to those actions
stigma a powerfully negative label that greatly changes a person's self-concept and social identity
medicalization of deviance the transformation of moral and legal deviance into a medical condition

Deviance and Inequality: Social-Conflict Analysis

7.4 Apply social-conflict theories to the topic of deviance. (pages 210–213)

Based on Karl Marx's ideas, social-conflict theory holds that laws and other norms operate to protect the interests of powerful members of any society. In a capitalist society, law operates to support the capitalist economy.

- **White-collar offences** are committed by people of high social position as part of their jobs. Sutherland claimed that such offences are rarely prosecuted and are most likely to end up in civil rather than criminal court.

white-collar crime crime committed by people of high social position in the course of their occupations
corporate crime the illegal actions of a corporation or people acting on its behalf
organized crime a business supplying illegal goods or services

- **Corporate crime** refers to illegal actions by a corporation or people acting on its behalf. Although corporate crimes cause considerable public harm, most cases of corporate crime go unpunished.
- **Organized crime** has a long history in Canada, especially among categories of people with few legitimate opportunities.

Deviance, Race, and Gender

7.5 Apply race-conflict and feminist theories to the topic of deviance. (pages 213–215)

- Race-conflict theory and feminist theory explain that what people consider deviant reflects the relative power and privilege of different categories of people.
- **Hate crimes** are crimes motivated by racial or other bias; they target people who are already disadvantaged based on race, gender, or sexual orientation.
- In Canada and elsewhere, societies control the behaviour of women more closely than that of men.

hate crime a criminal act against a person or a person's property by an offender motivated by racial or other bias

Crime

7.6 Identify patterns of crime in Canada and around the world. (pages 215–221)

Crimes against the person (violent crime) include murder, aggravated assault, and forcible rape.

Crimes against property (property crime) include burglary, larceny-theft, and arson.

- Four-fifths of people arrested for property and violent crimes are male.
- Street crime is more common among people of lower social position. Including white-collar and corporate crime makes class differences in criminality smaller.
- More whites than any other racial category are arrested for street crimes. However, Aboriginals and Blacks are arrested more often than whites in relation to their population size. Asians have a lower-than-average rate of arrest.

crimes against the person crimes that direct violence or the threat of violence against others; also known as *violent crimes*

crimes against property crimes that involve theft of property belonging to others; also known as *property crimes*

victimless crimes violations of law in which there are no obvious victims

The Canadian Criminal Justice System

7.7 Analyze the operation of the criminal justice system. (pages 221–229)

The **police** are the primary point of contact between a society's population and the criminal justice system.

- Police use personal discretion in deciding whether and how to handle a situation.
- Research suggests that police are more likely to make an arrest if the offence is serious, if bystanders are present, or if the suspect is Black or Aboriginal.

Courts rely on an adversarial process in which attorneys—one representing the defendant and one representing the state—present their cases in the presence of a judge who monitors legal procedures.

- In practice, Canadian courts resolve most cases through plea bargaining. Though efficient, this method puts less powerful people at a disadvantage.

Four justifications are offered for **punishment**: retribution, deterrence, rehabilitation, and societal protection.

- The **death penalty** remains controversial in the United States, the only high-income Western nation that routinely executes serious offenders. The trend is toward fewer executions.
- **Community-based corrections** include probation, parole, and sentencing circles. These programs lower the cost of supervising people convicted of crimes and reduce prison overcrowding. Probation and parole have not been shown to reduce recidivism, and the outcomes of sentencing circles are unknown.

plea bargaining a legal negotiation in which a prosecutor reduces a charge in exchange for a defendant's guilty plea

retribution an act of moral vengeance by which society makes the offender suffer as much as the suffering caused by the crime

deterrence the attempt to discourage criminality through the use of punishment

rehabilitation a program for reforming the offender to prevent later offences

societal protection rendering an offender incapable of further offences temporarily through imprisonment or permanently by execution

criminal recidivism later offences by people previously convicted of crimes

community-based corrections correctional programs operating within society at large rather than behind prison walls

8 Social Stratification

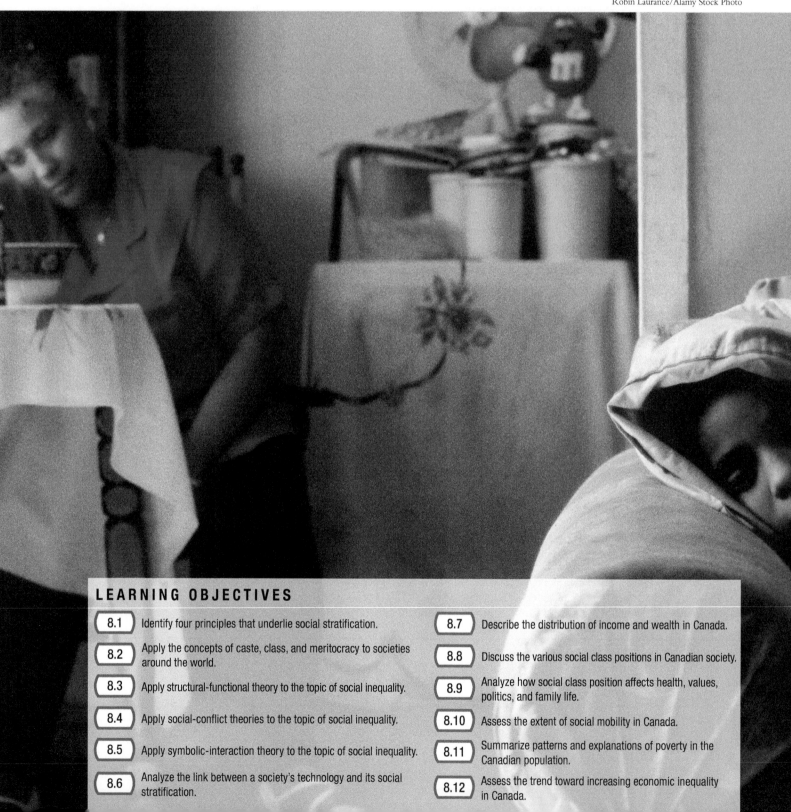

Robin Laurance/Alamy Stock Photo

LEARNING OBJECTIVES

8.1 Identify four principles that underlie social stratification.

8.2 Apply the concepts of caste, class, and meritocracy to societies around the world.

8.3 Apply structural-functional theory to the topic of social inequality.

8.4 Apply social-conflict theories to the topic of social inequality.

8.5 Apply symbolic-interaction theory to the topic of social inequality.

8.6 Analyze the link between a society's technology and its social stratification.

8.7 Describe the distribution of income and wealth in Canada.

8.8 Discuss the various social class positions in Canadian society.

8.9 Analyze how social class position affects health, values, politics, and family life.

8.10 Assess the extent of social mobility in Canada.

8.11 Summarize patterns and explanations of poverty in the Canadian population.

8.12 Assess the trend toward increasing economic inequality in Canada.

the Power of Society

to shape our chances of living in poverty

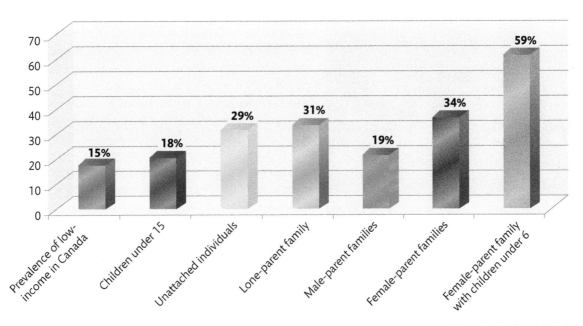

Source: Statistics Canada (2011a).

What are a person's odds of experiencing poverty? Our social position reflects factors such as our age and family status. In Canada, 15 percent of the population is considered low-income. However, 29 percent of unattached individuals are low-income, as are 18 percent of children under age 15. One of the most affected categories is lone-parent families, 31 percent of whom are low-income. By contrast, 19 percent of male-parent families and 34 percent of female-parent families are low-income. The rate spikes dramatically to 59 percent for female-parent families with children under the age of 6.

Chapter Overview

This chapter introduces the concept of social stratification, which is important because our social standing affects almost everything about our lives. This chapter defines social stratification, surveys systems of inequality through history and in various societies today, and then takes a close-up look at inequality in Canada. You will see that the extent of social inequality in Canada is greater than most people imagine.

AF archive/Alamy Stock Photo

On April 10, 1912, the ocean liner *Titanic* slipped away from the docks of Southampton, England, on its first voyage across the North Atlantic to New York. A proud symbol of the new industrial age, the towering ship carried 2300 men, women, and children. Some of the passengers were enjoying more luxury than most travellers today could imagine. By contrast, poor passengers crowded the lower decks, journeying to what they hoped would be a better life in North America.

Two days out, the crew received radio warnings of icebergs in the area but paid little notice. Then, near midnight, as the ship steamed swiftly westward, a stunned lookout reported a massive shape rising out of the dark ocean directly ahead. The ship steered hard to port, but moments later, the *Titanic* collided with a huge iceberg, as tall as the ship itself, and the impact split open its side as if the grand vessel were a giant tin can.

Seawater exploded into the ship's lower levels, pulling the ship down by the bow. Within 25 minutes of impact, alarms had sounded and people were rushing for the lifeboats. By 2:00 A.M., the bow was completely submerged, and the stern rose high above the water. Minutes later, all the ship's lights went out. Clinging to the deck, quietly observed by those huddled in lifeboats, hundreds of helpless passengers and crew solemnly passed their final minutes before the ship split in two and disappeared into the frigid Atlantic (Lord, 1976).

The tragic loss of more than 1600 lives made the sinking of the *Titanic* headline news around the world. Looking back on this terrible event with a sociological eye, we see that some categories of passengers had much better odds of survival than others. In keeping with that era's traditional ideas about gender, women and children boarded the lifeboats first, with the result that 80 percent of the people who died were men. Class was also a factor in who survived and who did not. More than 60 percent of the passengers travelling on first-class tickets were saved because they were on the upper decks, where warnings were sounded first and lifeboats were accessible. Only 36 percent of the second-class passengers survived, and of the third-class passengers on the lower decks, only 24 percent escaped drowning. On board the *Titanic*, class meant more than the quality of accommodations; it was a matter of life or death.

The fate of the passengers on the *Titanic* dramatically illustrates how social inequality affects the way people live—and sometimes whether they live at all. This chapter explores the important concept of social stratification and examines social inequality in Canada.

What Is Social Stratification?

8.1 Identify four principles that underlie social stratification.

Every society is marked by inequality, with some people having significantly more money, schooling, health, and power than others. **Social stratification**, defined as *a system by which a society ranks categories of people in a hierarchy*, is based on four important principles:

social stratification a system by which a society ranks categories of people in a hierarchy

1. **Social stratification is a trait of society, not simply a reflection of individual differences.** Many of us think of social standing in terms of personal talent and effort, and as a result, we often exaggerate the extent to which we control our own fate. Did a higher percentage of the first-class passengers on the *Titanic* survive because they were better swimmers than second- and third-class passengers? No. They did better because of their privileged position on the ship. Similarly, children born into wealthy families are more likely than children born into poverty to enjoy good health, do well in school, succeed in a career, and live a long life. Neither the rich nor the poor created social stratification, yet this system shapes the lives of us all.

2. **Social stratification carries over from generation to generation.** We have only to look at how parents pass their social position on to their children to see that stratification is a trait of societies rather than individuals. Some people, especially in industrial societies, do experience **social mobility**, *a change in position within the social hierarchy.* Social mobility may be upward or downward. We celebrate the achievements of rare individuals such as Gisele Bundchen (from Brazil) and actor Jim Carrey (Canada), neither of whom ever finished high school but both of whom nevertheless managed to rise to fame and fortune. Some people move downward in the social hierarchy because of business failures, illness, divorce, or economic recession and rising unemployment. More often people move *horizontally*; they switch one job for another at about the same social level. The social standing of most people remains much the same over their lifetimes.

3. **Social stratification is universal but variable.** Social stratification is found everywhere. Yet *what* is unequal and *how* unequal it is vary from one society to another. In some societies, inequality is mostly a matter of prestige; in others, wealth or power is the key element of difference. In addition, some societies contain more inequality than others.

4. **Social stratification involves not just inequality but beliefs as well.** Any system of inequality not only gives some people more than others but also defines these arrangements as fair. Like the *what* of social inequality, the explanations of *why* people should be unequal differ from society to society.

Liang Sen/Xinhua News Agency/Newscom

The personal experience of poverty is clear in this photograph of mealtime in a homeless shelter. The main sociological insight is that although we feel the effects of social stratification personally, our social standing is largely the result of the way society (or a world of societies) structures opportunity and reward. To the core of our being, we are all products of social stratification.

social mobility a change in position within the social hierarchy

Caste and Class Systems

8.2 Apply the concepts of caste, class, and meritocracy to societies around the world.

When comparing societies in terms of inequality, sociologists distinguish between *closed systems*, which allow little change in social position, and *open systems*, which permit much more social mobility. Closed systems are called *caste systems*, and more open systems are called *class systems*.

The Caste System

A **caste system** is *social stratification based on ascription, or birth.* A pure caste system is closed because birth alone determines a person's entire future, with little or no social mobility based on individual effort. People live out their lives in the rigid categories into which they were born, without the possibility for change for the better or worse.

In rural India, the traditional caste system still shapes people's lives. This girl in the photograph on the left is a member of the "untouchables," a category below the four basic castes. She and her family are clothes washers, people who clean material "polluted" by blood or human waste. Such work is defined as unclean for people of higher caste position. In the cities, by contrast, caste has given way to a class system where achievement plays a greater part in social ranking and income and consumption are keys to social standing.

An Illustration: India

Many of the world's agrarian societies are caste systems. Although India's economy is growing rapidly, much of the population still lives in traditional villages, where the caste system is part of everyday life. The traditional Indian system includes four major castes (or *varnas*, from a Sanskrit word that means "colour"): Brahmin, Kshatriya, Vaishya, and Sudra. On the local level, however, each of these is composed of hundreds of subcaste groups (*jatis*).

From birth, caste position determines the direction of a person's life. First, with the exception of farming, which is open to everyone, families in each caste perform one type of work, as priests, soldiers, barbers, leather workers, street sweepers, and so on.

Second, a caste system demands that people marry others of the same ranking. If people were to have "mixed" marriages with members of other castes, what rank would their children hold? Sociologists call this pattern of marrying within a social category *endogamous* marriage (*endo-* stems from the Greek word for "within"). According to tradition—this practice is now rare and found only in remote rural areas—Indian parents select their children's future marriage partners, often before the children reach their teens.

Third, caste guides everyday life by keeping people in the company of "their own kind." Norms reinforce this practice by teaching, for example, that a "purer" person of a higher caste position is "polluted" by contact with someone of lower standing.

Fourth, caste systems rest on powerful cultural beliefs. Indian culture is built on the Hindu tradition that doing the caste's life work and accepting an arranged marriage are moral duties.

Caste and Agrarian Life

Caste systems are typical of agrarian societies because agriculture demands a lifelong routine of hard work. By teaching a sense of moral duty, a caste system ensures that people are disciplined for a lifetime of work and are willing to perform the same jobs as their parents. Thus the caste system has hung on in rural India more than 70 years after being formally outlawed. People living in the industrial cities of India have many more choices about work and marriage partners than people in rural areas.

Another country long dominated by caste is South Africa, although the racial system of *apartheid* is no longer legal and is now in decline. The Thinking Globally box on page 239 takes a closer look.

caste system social stratification based on ascription, or birth

class system social stratification based on both birth and individual achievement

meritocracy social stratification based on personal merit

Thinking Globally

Race as Caste: A Report from South Africa

Don: I've been reading about racial caste in South Africa. I'm glad that's over.

Mike: But racial inequality is far from over. . . .

At the southern tip of the African continent lies South Africa, a country a little bit larger than Ontario but smaller than Quebec, with a population of about 51 million. For 300 years, the native Africans who lived there were ruled by white people, first by the Dutch traders and farmers who settled there in the mid-seventeenth century and then by the British, who colonized the area early in the nineteenth century. By the early 1900s, the British had taken over the entire country, naming it the Union of South Africa.

In 1961, the nation declared its independence from Britain, calling itself the Republic of South Africa, but freedom for the black majority was still decades away. To ensure their political control over the black population, whites instituted the policy of *apartheid*, or racial separation. Apartheid, written into law in 1948, denied blacks national citizenship, ownership of land, and any voice in the nation's government. As a lower caste, blacks received little schooling and performed menial, low-paying jobs. White people with even average wealth had at least one black household servant.

The members of the white minority claimed that apartheid protected their cultural traditions from the influence of people they considered inferior. When blacks resisted apartheid, whites used brutal military repression to maintain their power. Even so, steady resistance—especially from younger blacks, who demanded a political voice and economic opportunity—gradually forced the country to change. Criticism from other industrial nations added

to the pressure. By the mid-1980s, the tide began to turn as the South African government granted limited political rights to people of mixed race and Asian ancestry. Next, all people gained the right to form labour unions, to enter occupations once limited to whites, and to own property. Officials also repealed apartheid laws that separated the races in public places.

The pace of change increased in 1990 with the release from prison of Nelson Mandela, who led the fight against apartheid. In 1994, the first national election open to all races made Mandela president, ending centuries of white minority rule.

Despite this dramatic political change, social stratification in South Africa is still based on race. Even with the right to own property, one-fourth of black South Africans have no work, and one-fourth of the population lives below the poverty line. The worst off are some 7 million *ukuhleleleka*, which means "marginal people" in the Xhosa language. Soweto-by-the-Sea may sound like a summer getaway, but it is a shantytown, home to hundreds of thousands of people crammed into shacks made of packing crates, corrugated metal, cardboard, and other discarded materials. Recent years have seen some signs of prosperity; some shopping centres have been built, and most streets are now paved. But the poverty rate stands at about 25 percent and some families still live without electricity for lights or refrigeration. Some also lack plumbing, forcing people to use buckets to haul sewage. In some communities, women line up to take a turn at a single water tap that serves as many as 1000 people. Jobs are hard to come by, with an unemployment rate of about 25 percent. For those who do find work, most feel lucky to earn $250 a month.

South Africa's current president, Jacob Zuma, who was elected in 2009, leads a nation still crippled by its history of racial caste. Tourism is up and holds the promise of an economic boom in years to come, but the economy is still dominated by the white minority. The country can break from the past only by providing real opportunity to all of its people.

What Do You Think?

1. How has race been a form of caste in South Africa?

2. Although apartheid is no longer law, why does racial inequality continue to shape South African society?

3. Does race operate as an element of caste in Canada? Explain your answer.

Sources: Mabry & Masland (1999), Murphy (2002), Perry (2009), McGroarty & Maylie (2012), and World Bank (2012).

Per Anders Pettersson/Getty Images

The Class System

Because a modern economy must attract people to work in many occupations other than farming, it depends on developing people's talents in diverse fields. This process of schooling and specialization gives rise to a **class system**, *social stratification based on both birth and individual achievement.*

Class systems are more open than caste systems, so people who gain schooling and skills may experience social mobility. As a result, class distinctions become blurred, and even blood relatives may have different social standings. Categorizing people according to their colour, sex, or social background comes to be seen as wrong in modern societies as all people gain political rights and, in principle, equal standing before the law. In addition, work is no longer fixed at birth but involves some personal choice. Greater individuality also translates into more freedom in selecting a marriage partner.

Meritocracy

The concept of **meritocracy** refers to *social stratification based on personal merit*. Because industrial societies need to develop a broad range of abilities beyond farming, stratification is based not just on the accident of birth but also on *merit* (from a Latin word meaning "earned"), which includes a person's knowledge, abilities, and effort. A rough measure of merit is the importance of a person's job and how well it is done. To increase meritocracy, industrial societies expand equality of opportunity and teach people to expect unequal rewards based on individual performance.

A pure meritocracy has never existed, but in such a system social position would depend entirely on a person's ability and effort. Such a system would have ongoing social mobility, blurring social categories as individuals continuously move up or down in the system, depending on their latest performance.

Caste societies define merit in different terms, emphasizing loyalty to the system—that is, dutifully performing whatever job comes with the social position a person has at birth. Because they assign jobs before anyone can know anything about a person's talents or interests, caste systems waste human potential. On the other hand, because caste systems clearly assign everyone a "place" in society and a general type of work, they are very stable and orderly. Even industrial and post-industrial societies keep some elements of caste—such as letting wealth pass from generation to generation—rather than becoming complete meritocracies. A pure meritocracy would have individuals moving up and down the social ranking all the time. Such extreme social mobility would pull apart families and other social groupings. After all, economic performance is not everything: Would we want to evaluate our friends or family members solely on how successful they are in their jobs outside of the home? Probably not. Class systems in industrial societies move toward meritocracy to promote productivity and efficiency; but at the same time, they keep caste elements, such as family, and by doing so maintain a certain type of order and social unity.

Status Consistency

status consistency the degree of uniformity in a person's social standing across various dimensions of social inequality

Status consistency is *the degree of uniformity in a person's social standing across various dimensions of social inequality*. A caste system has little social mobility and therefore has high status consistency. This means that, remaining in the same social category, the typical person has the same relative standing with regard to wealth, power, and prestige as everyone else in the caste category. However, the greater mobility of class systems moves people up and down and therefore produces less status consistency. In Canada, for example, most college and university professors with advanced degrees enjoy high social prestige but earn relatively modest incomes. Low status consistency means that it is more difficult to define people's social position. Therefore, the lines between *classes* are much harder to define than the lines that separate *castes*.

Caste and Class: The United Kingdom

The mix of caste and meritocracy in class systems is well illustrated by the United Kingdom (Great Britain—composed of England, Wales, and Scotland—and Northern Ireland), an industrial nation with a long agrarian history.

Aristocratic England

In the Middle Ages, England had a system of aristocracy that resembled a caste. The aristocracy included the leading members of the church, who were thought to speak with the authority of God. Some clergy were local priests, who were not members of the aristocracy and who lived simple lives. But the highest church officials lived in palaces and presided over an organization that owned much land, which was the major source of wealth. Church leaders, who were typically referred to as the *first estate* in France and other European countries, also had a great deal of power to shape the political events of the day.

The rest of the aristocracy, which in France and other European countries was called the *second estate*, was a hereditary nobility that made up barely 5 percent of the population. The royal family—the king and queen at the top of the power structure—as well as lesser nobles (including several hundred families headed by men titled as dukes, earls, and barons) together owned most of the nation's land. Most of the men and women within the aristocracy were wealthy due to their land, and they had many servants for their homes as well as ordinary farmers to work their fields. With all their work done for them by others, members of the aristocracy had no occupations and thought that engaging in any work for income was beneath them. They used their time to develop skills in horseback riding and warfare and to cultivate refined tastes in art, music, and literature.

To prevent their vast landholdings from being divided by heirs when they died, aristocrats devised the law of *primogeniture* (from the Latin meaning "firstborn"), which required that all property pass to the oldest son or other male relation. Younger sons had to find other means of support. Some of these men became leaders in the church, where they would live as well as they were used to, and helped tie together the church and the state by having members of the same families running both. Other younger sons within the aristocracy became military officers or judges or took up other professions considered honourable for gentlemen. In an age when no woman could inherit her father's property and few women had the opportunity to earn a living on their own, a noble daughter depended for her security on marrying well.

Below the high clergy and the rest of the aristocracy, the vast majority of men and women were called *commoners* or, in France and other European countries, the *third estate*. Most commoners were serfs working land owned by nobles or the church. Unlike members of the aristocracy, most commoners had little schooling and were illiterate.

As the Industrial Revolution expanded England's economy, some commoners living in cities made enough money to challenge the nobility. More emphasis on meritocracy, the growing importance of money, and the expansion of schooling and legal rights eventually blurred the differences between aristocrats and commoners and gave rise to a class system.

Perhaps it is a sign of the times that these days, traditional titles are put up for sale by aristocrats who need money. In 1996, for example, Earl Spencer—the brother of Princess Diana—sold one of his titles, Lord of Wimbledon, to raise the $300 000 he needed to redo the plumbing in one of his large homes (McKee, 1996).

The United Kingdom Today

The United Kingdom has a class system today, but caste elements from England's aristocratic past still play a part in social standing. A small number of British families continue to hold considerable inherited wealth and enjoy high prestige, receive schooling at excellent universities, and are members of social networks in which people have substantial political influence. A traditional monarch, Queen Elizabeth II, is the United Kingdom's head of state, and Parliament's House of Lords is composed of "peers," about half of whom are of noble birth. However, control of government has passed to the House of Commons, where the prime minister and other leaders typically reach

In 2011, Prince William, second in line to the British throne, married commoner Catherine Middleton, who then took the title "Her Royal Highness the Duchess of Cambridge." They now take their place as part of a royal family that traces its ancestry back more than a thousand years—an element of caste that remains in the British class system.

their positions by achievement—winning an election—rather than by birth. Another sign of a more open system is the fact that in 2011, Prince William, the queen's grandson, married Catherine Middleton, a woman who was a commoner (although from a relatively privileged family) and thus might be said to have "earned" her new position.

Lower in the class hierarchy, roughly one-fourth of the British people fall into the middle class. Some earn comfortable incomes from professions and businesses and are likely to have investments in the form of stocks and bonds. Below the middle class, perhaps half of all Britons consider themselves "working class," earning modest incomes through service work or manual labour. The remaining one-fourth of the British people make up the lower class, the poor who lack steady work or who work full time but are paid too little to live comfortably. Most lower-class Britons live in the nation's northern and western regions, which have been plagued by closings of mines and factories.

The British mix of caste elements and meritocracy has produced a highly stratified society with some opportunity to move upward or downward, much the same as exists in Canada (Corak, 2006a). Historically, British society has been somewhat more caste-like than is the case in Canada, a fact reflected in the importance attached to linguistic accent. Distinctive patterns of speech develop in any society when people are set off from one another over several generations. People in Canada treat accent as a clue to where a person lives or grew up (we can easily differentiate a person who has lived their whole life in an outport of Newfoundland from a Bay Street lawyer who has lived their whole life in Toronto). In the United Kingdom, however, accent is more a mark of social class (upper-class people speak "the King's English," but most people speak "like commoners"). So different are these two accents that the British seem to be, as the saying goes, "a single people divided by a common language."

Classless Societies? The Former Soviet Union

Nowhere in the world do we find a society without some degree of social inequality. Yet some nations have claimed to be classless.

The Russian Revolution

The Union of Soviet Socialist Republics (USSR), one of the two military superpowers in the mid- to late twentieth century, was born out of a revolution in Russia in 1917. The Russian Revolution ended the feudal estate system ruled by a hereditary nobility and transferred most farms, factories, and other productive property from private ownership to state control. In the span of a single generation, the USSR had become an industrial society that made a number of notable achievements, ranging from the near elimination of homelessness and unemployment to providing free education (including post-secondary) and universal health care to its people. Following the lead of Karl Marx, who believed that private ownership of property was the source of social stratification, Soviet leaders boasted of becoming a classless society.

Critics, however, pointed out that based on their jobs, the Soviet people were actually stratified into four unequal categories. At the top were high government officials, known as *apparatchiks*. Next came the Soviet intelligentsia, including lower government officials, professors, scientists, physicians, and engineers. Below them were manual workers and, at the lowest level, the rural peasantry.

In reality, the Soviet Union was not classless at all, and political power was concentrated in only a small percentage of the population. But putting factories, farms, colleges, and hospitals under state control did

One of the major events of the twentieth century was the socialist revolution in Russia, which led to the creation of the Soviet Union. Following the ideas of Karl Marx, the popular uprising overthrew a feudal aristocracy, as depicted in the 1920 painting *Bolshevik* by Boris Mikhailovich Kustodiev.

De Agostini Picture Library/Getty Images

create greater economic equality (although with sharp differences in power) than in capitalist societies such as Canada.

The Modern Russian Federation

In 1985, Mikhail Gorbachev came to power with a new economic program known as *perestroika* ("restructuring"). Gorbachev saw that although the Soviet system had significantly reduced economic inequality, overall living standards lagged behind those of other industrial nations. Gorbachev tried to generate economic growth by reducing the centralized control of the economy.

Gorbachev's economic reforms turned into one of the most dramatic social movements in history. People throughout Eastern Europe blamed their poverty and lack of basic freedoms on the repressive ruling class of Communist Party officials. Beginning in 1989, people throughout Eastern Europe toppled their socialist governments, and in 1991, the Soviet Union itself collapsed, with its largest republic remaking itself as the Russian Federation.

The Soviet Union's story shows that social inequality involves more than economic resources. Soviet society may not have had the extremes of wealth and poverty found in the United Kingdom and Canada, but an elite class existed all the same, based on political power rather than wealth.

What about social mobility in so-called classless societies? In the twentieth century, there was as much upward social mobility in the Soviet Union as in the United Kingdom or Canada. Rapidly expanding industry and government drew many poor rural peasants into factories and offices. This trend illustrates what sociologists call **structural social mobility**, *a shift in the social position of large numbers of people due more to changes in society itself than to individual efforts.*

structural social mobility a shift in the social position of large numbers of people due more to changes in society itself than to individual efforts

> November 24, Odessa, Ukraine. The first snow of our voyage flies over the decks as our ship docks at Odessa, the former Soviet Union's southern port on the Black Sea. Not far from the dock, we gaze up at the Potemkin Steps, the steep stairway up to the city, where the first shots of the Russian Revolution rang out. It has been six years since our last visit, and much has changed; indeed, the Soviet Union itself has collapsed. Has life improved? For some people, certainly. There are now chic boutiques in which well-dressed shoppers buy fine wines, designer clothes, and imported perfumes. But for most people, life seems much worse. Flea markets line the curbs as families sell their home furnishings. When meat sells for $4 a pound and the average person earns about $30 a month, people become desperate. Even the city has to save money by turning off streetlights after 8:00 p.m. The spirits of most people seem as dim as Odessa's streets.

During the 1990s, structural social mobility in the Russian Federation turned downward as that country experienced something similar to the Great Depression of the 1930s in Canada. One indicator is that the average life span for men dropped by 5 years and for women by 2 years. Many factors contributed to this decline, including Russia's poor health care system, but the Russian people clearly have suffered in the turbulent period of economic change that began in 1991 (Gerber & Hout, 1998; Mason, 2004; World Bank, 2012).

The hope of the Boris Yeltsin administration was that, in the long run, privatizing state industries would improve the nation's economic performance. It has been over 20 years since the Soviet system was dismantled. After 10 years of initial decline, the economy has since expanded, but many Russians continue to face hard times. Following the 2014 fall of the price of oil and sanctions imposed on Russia for its annexation of Crimea, the Russian ruble has collapsed and Russia has entered a financial crisis. In addition, there is widespread concern both inside and outside of Russia that the increasing concentration of power under the rule of President Putin is eroding political freedoms (Daniels, 2000; Zuckerman, 2006; World Bank, 2012).

China: Emerging Social Classes

Sweeping political and economic change has affected not just the Russian Federation but also the People's Republic of China. After the Communist revolution in 1949, the state took control of all farms, factories, and other productive property. Communist Party leader Mao Zedong declared all work to be equally important, so officially, social classes no longer existed.

The new program greatly reduced economic inequality. But as in the Soviet Union, social differences remained. The country was ruled by a political elite with enormous power and considerable privilege; below them were managers of large factories and skilled professionals; next came industrial workers; at the bottom were rural peasants, who were not even allowed to leave their villages to migrate to cities.

Further economic change came in 1978 when Mao died and Deng Xiaoping became China's leader. The state gradually loosened its hold on the economy, allowing a new class of business owners to emerge. In 2012, Xi Jinping assumed a position of leadership over the Chinese Communist Party, which continues to control the country. In recent years, many political leaders have prospered as they have joined the ranks of the small but wealthy elite who control new, privately run industries. China's economy has experienced years of rapid growth and only recently shows signs of slowing. The nation has now moved into the middle-income category. Much of this new prosperity has been concentrated in cities, especially in coastal areas, where living standards have soared far above those in China's rural interior. A sign of the times is that the luxury automobile producer Bentley now sells more of its cars in China than in its home nation, Great Britain (Richburg, 2011; United Nations, 2011; *New York Times*, 2012).

Since the late 1990s, the booming cities along China's coast have become home to many thousands of people made rich by the expanding economy. In addition, these cities have attracted more than 100 million young migrants from rural areas in search of better jobs and a better life. Many more have wanted to move to the booming cities, but the government still restricts movement, which has the effect of slowing upward social mobility. For those who have been able to move, the jobs that are available are generally better than the work that people knew before. But many of these new jobs are dangerous, and most pay wages that barely meet the higher costs of living in the city, so the majority of the migrants remain poor. But, in general, China's population has experienced structural upward mobility as the economy has expanded by about 10 percent annually over the past three decades. China is now the world's second largest economy (after the United States), reflecting in part how much of the world's manufacturing now takes place there (Wu & Treiman, 2007; Chang, 2008; Powell, 2008; World Bank, 2011a, 2011b).

One new category in China's social hierarchy consists of the *hai gui*, a term derived from words meaning "returned from overseas" or "sea turtles." The ranks of the "sea turtles" are increasing by tens of thousands each year as young women and men return from educations in other countries, in many cases from college and university campuses in the United States. These young people, most of whom were from privileged families to begin with, typically return to China to find many opportunities and soon become very influential (Liu & Hewitt, 2008).

The young members of rich and politically well-connected families have emerged as a new political and economic aristocracy with a say in how the country is run. To illustrate, Xi Jinping, the new Communist Party

Imaginechina/AP Images

China has the fastest-growing economy of all the major nations and currently manufactures more products than even the United States. With more and more money to spend, the Chinese are now a major consumer of automobiles—a fact that probably saved the Buick brand from extinction.

leader and since 2013 the nation's president, is himself the son of an early leader in the Chinese Communist Party. Sometimes called "princelings," these powerful people may feud among themselves as they seek to gain influence. But most observers of the current scene in China agree that they represent another force to be reckoned with (Beech, 2012; Johnson, 2012).

In China, a new class system is emerging, a mix of the old Party hierarchy, a new business hierarchy, and a new "aristocratic" class of well-connected people. Economic inequality in China has increased as members of the new business and political elites have become millionaires and even billionaires. As Figure 8–1 shows, economic inequality in China is now slightly greater than it is in the United Kingdom. With so much change in China, that country's social stratification is likely to remain dynamic for some time to come (Bian, 2002; Wines & Johnson, 2011; Johnson, 2012; World Bank, 2012).

Ideology: The Power Behind Stratification

How do societies persist without sharing their resources more equally? The highly stratified British aristocracy lasted for centuries, and for 2000 years people in India accepted the idea that they should be privileged or poor based on the accident of birth.

A major reason that social hierarchies endure is **ideology**, *cultural beliefs that justify particular social arrangements, including patterns of inequality.* A belief—for example, the idea that the rich are smart and the poor are lazy—is ideological to the extent that it supports inequality by defining it as fair.

Plato and Marx on Ideology

According to the ancient Greek philosopher Plato (427–347 BCE), every culture considers some type of inequality fair. Although Karl Marx understood this, he was far more critical of inequality than Plato. Marx criticized capitalist societies for defending wealth and power in the hands of a few as a "law of the marketplace." Capitalist law, he continued, defines the right to own property, which encourages money to remain within the same families from one generation to the next. In short, Marx concluded, culture and institutions combine to support a society's elite, which is why established hierarchies last such a long time.

Historical Patterns of Ideology

Ideology changes along with a society's economy and technology. Because agrarian societies depend on most of their people performing a lifetime of labour, they develop caste systems that make carrying out the duties of a person's social position or "station" a moral responsibility. With the rise of industrial capitalism, an ideology of meritocracy arises, defining wealth and power as prizes to be won by the individuals who perform the best. This change means that the poor—often given charity under feudalism—are looked down on as personally undeserving. This harsh view is linked to the ideas of Herbert Spencer, as explained in the Thinking About Diversity box on page 246.

History shows how difficult it is to change social stratification. However, challenges to the status quo always arise. Traditional ideas about "a woman's place in the home," for example, have given way to economic opportunity for women in societies today. The continuing progress toward racial equality in South Africa is another case of widespread rejection of the ideology of apartheid. The popular uprisings against political dictatorships across the Middle East that began in 2011 show us that this process of challenging particular patterns of inequality continues.

Global Snapshot

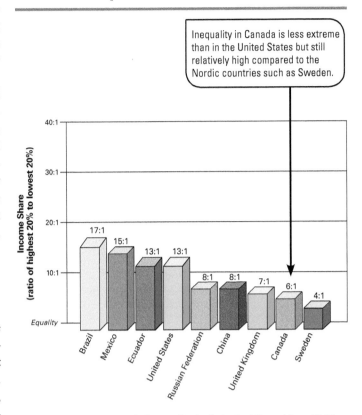

FIGURE 8–1   Economic Inequality in Selected Countries, 2012

Many low- and middle-income countries have greater economic inequality than Canada. But Canada has more economic inequality than many north European high-income nations.

Source: World Bank (2012).

ideology cultural beliefs that justify particular social arrangements, including patterns of inequality

Thinking About Diversity: Race, Class, and Gender

The Meaning of Class: Is Getting Rich "the Survival of the Fittest"?

Jake: My dad is amazing. He's really smart!

Frank: You mean he's rich. He owns I don't know how many businesses.

Jake: Do you think people get rich without being smart?

It's a question we all wonder about. How much is our social position a matter of intelligence? What about hard work? Being born to the "right family"? Even "dumb luck"?

More than in most societies, Canada and the United States link social standing to personal abilities, including intelligence. In 2010, *Time* magazine put Mark Zuckerberg on the cover and announced that he was "Person of the Year" for developing Facebook. For this achievement, and amassing a fortune of some $10 billion, it is easy to imagine that this Harvard dropout is a pretty smart guy (Grossman, 2010).

But the idea that social standing is linked to intelligence goes back a long time. We have all heard the words "the survival of the fittest," which describe our society as a competitive jungle in which the "best" survive and the rest fall behind. The phrase was coined by one of sociology's pioneers, Herbert Spencer (1820–1903), whose ideas about social inequality are still widespread today.

Spencer, who lived in England, eagerly followed the work of the natural scientist Charles Darwin (1809–1882). Darwin's theory of biological evolution held that a species changes physically over many generations as it adapts to the natural environment. Spencer incorrectly applied Darwin's theory to the operation of society, which does not operate according to biological principles. In Spencer's distorted view, society became the "jungle," with the "fittest" people rising to wealth and the "failures" sinking into miserable poverty.

It is no surprise that Spencer's views, as wrong as they were, were popular among the rising industrialists of the day. John D. Rockefeller (1839–1937), who made a vast fortune building the oil industry, recited Spencer's "social gospel" to young children in Sunday school. As Rockefeller saw it, the growth of giant corporations—and the astounding wealth of their owners—was merely the result of the survival of the fittest, a basic fact of nature. Neither Spencer nor Rockefeller had much sympathy for the poor, seeing poverty as evidence of individuals' failing to measure up in a competitive world. Spencer opposed social welfare programs because he thought they penalized society's "best" people (through taxes) and rewarded its "worst" members (through welfare benefits). By incorrectly using Darwin's theory, the rich could turn their backs on everyone else, assuming that the existing inequality was inevitable and somehow "natural."

Today, sociologists point out that our society is far from a meritocracy, as Spencer claimed. And it is not the case that companies or individuals who generate lots of money necessarily benefit society. The people who made hundreds of millions of dollars selling subprime mortgages in recent years certainly ended up hurting just about everyone. But Spencer's view that the "fittest" rise to the top remains widespread in our very unequal and individualistic culture.

What Do You Think?

1. How much do you think inequality in our society can correctly be described as "the survival of the fittest"? Why?

2. Why do you think Spencer's ideas are still popular in Canada today?

3. Is how much you earn a good measure of your importance to society? Why or why not?

The Functions of Social Stratification

(**8.3**) Apply structural-functional theory to the topic of social inequality.

Why does social stratification exist at all? According to the structural-functional approach, social stratification plays a vital part in the operation of society. This argument was presented many years ago by Kingsley Davis and Wilbert Moore (1945).

The Davis-Moore Thesis

Davis-Moore thesis the functional analysis claiming that social stratification has beneficial consequences for the operation of a society

The **Davis-Moore thesis** states that *social stratification has beneficial consequences for the operation of a society.* How else, ask Davis and Moore, can we explain the fact that some form of social stratification has been found in every society?

Davis and Moore note that modern societies have hundreds of occupational positions of varying importance. Certain jobs—say, washing cars or answering a telephone—are fairly easy and can be performed by almost anyone. Other jobs—such as designing a new generation of computers or transplanting human organs—are very difficult and demand the scarce talents of people with extensive and expensive training.

Therefore, Davis and Moore explain, the greater the functional importance of a position, the more rewards a society attaches to it. This strategy promotes productivity and efficiency because rewarding important work with income, prestige, power, or leisure encourages people to do these jobs and to work better, longer, and harder. In short, unequal rewards (the foundation of social stratification) benefit society as a whole.

Davis and Moore claim that any society could be egalitarian but only to the extent that people are willing to let *anyone* perform *any* job. Equality also demands that someone who performs a job poorly be rewarded just as much as someone who performs the job well. Such a system, they reason, clearly offers little incentive for people to try their best, reducing the society's productive efficiency.

The Davis-Moore thesis suggests the reason stratification exists; it does not state precisely what rewards a society should give to any occupational position or how unequal rewards should be. It merely points out that positions a society considers crucial must offer enough rewards to draw talented people away from less important work.

EVALUATE Although the Davis-Moore thesis is an important contribution to understanding social stratification, it has provoked criticism. Melvin Tumin (1953) wondered, first of all, how we assess the importance of a particular occupation. Perhaps the high rewards our society gives to physicians result partly from deliberate efforts by medical schools to limit the supply of physicians and thereby increase the demand for their services.

Furthermore, do rewards actually reflect the contribution someone makes to society? With income of about $14 million, hockey player Shea Weber, the highest-paid Canadian athlete in 2014–15, earned more in two days than a farmer will earn all year. Would anyone argue that the work of Shea Weber is more important than practising agriculture in order to produce food? And what about firefighters who risk their lives in order to protect the public in emergencies? Although they must be comfortable working in confined spaces and at dangerous heights, and are required to cope with physical and psychological stress while fulfilling a demanding work schedule, a new firefighter begins their career with an annual salary of $55 000 plus benefits. And we might also wonder about the heads of the big Wall Street financial firms that collapsed in 2008. It seems reasonable to conclude that these corporate leaders made some bad and harmful decisions, yet their salaries were astronomical. Even after finishing its worst year ever, with losses of $27 billion, Merrill Lynch paid bonuses of more than $1 million to each of more than 700 employees (Fox, 2009). Lloyd Blankfein, CEO of Goldman Sachs, paid himself a stock bonus worth $12.6 million (an amount it would take an average firefighter about 170 years to earn), despite his company's falling profits during 2010, a year in which salaries and benefits in the financial industry hit an all-time high. Increased government regulation and lacklustre performance led most Wall Street companies to trim salaries and bonuses in 2011 and 2012. Even so, as one analyst put it, "while payouts may be disappointing, they are still far higher than what most people will ever see" (Moore, 2012; *New York Times*, 2011; Roth, 2011; *Maclean's*, 2014; Service Canada, 2014). Do corporate executives deserve such megasalaries for their contributions to society?

Second, Tumin claimed that Davis and Moore ignore how the caste elements of social stratification can *prevent* the development of individual talent. Born to privilege, rich children have opportunities to develop their abilities, which is something many gifted poor children never have.

Third, living in a society that places so much emphasis on money, we tend to overestimate the importance of high-paying work; how much do stockbrokers or people who trade international currencies really contribute to the well-being of people in our society? For the same reason, it is difficult for us to see the value of any work not oriented toward making money, such as parenting, creative writing, playing in a symphony, or just being a good friend to someone in need (Packard, 2002).

Finally, by suggesting that social stratification benefits all of society, the Davis-Moore thesis ignores how social inequality can harm society and even promote conflict. Inequality,

Ben Rose/WireImage/Getty Images

Oprah Winfrey reported income of $165 million in 2011. Guided by the Davis-Moore thesis, why would societies reward some people with so much more fame and fortune than others? How would Karl Marx answer this question?

especially with limited upward mobility, can smother ambition and harden people's beliefs that they will never get ahead or even gain economic security. In this way, people come to see their society as fundamentally unjust, a belief that may encourage them to seek more radical change (Kaiser, 2010). This criticism leads to the social-conflict approach, which provides a very different explanation for social inequality.

CHECK YOUR LEARNING State the Davis-Moore thesis in your own words. What are Tumin's criticisms of this thesis?

Explaining Stratification: Social-Conflict Theories

8.4 Apply social-conflict theories to the topic of social inequality.

Social-conflict analysis argues that rather than benefiting society as a whole, social stratification benefits some people and disadvantages others. This analysis draws heavily on the ideas of Karl Marx, with contributions from Max Weber.

Karl Marx: Class Conflict

As Marx saw it, the Industrial Revolution promised humanity a society free from want. Yet during Marx's lifetime, the capitalist economy had done little to improve the lives of most people. Marx set out to explain a glaring contradiction: how, in a society so rich, so many could be so poor.

In Marx's view, social stratification is rooted in people's relationship to the means of production. People either own productive property (such as factories and businesses) or sell their labour to others. In feudal Europe, the aristocracy and the church owned the productive land; the peasants toiled as farmers. With the shift from feudalism to capitalism, the aristocracy was replaced by **capitalists** (sometimes called the *bourgeoisie*, a French word meaning "town dwellers"), *people who own and operate factories and other businesses in pursuit of profits*. Peasants became the **proletarians**, *people who sell their labour for wages*. Capitalists and proletarians have opposing interests and are separated by a vast gulf of wealth and power, making class conflict inevitable.

Marx lived during the nineteenth century, a time when a small number of industrialists in the United States were amassing great fortunes. The business tycoons who led the move into the industrial age included Andrew Carnegie (steel), J. P. Morgan (finance and steel), and John Jacob Astor (real estate; Astor was the richest passenger on the *Titanic* and one of the few very rich passengers to drown when the ship sank). All of them lived in fabulous mansions that

capitalists people who own and operate factories and other businesses in pursuit of profits

proletarians people who sell their labour for wages

Back in the Great Depression of the 1930s, "tent cities" that were home to desperately poor people could be found in much of Canada. The depression came to an end, but poverty persisted. The recent recession and the growing social inequality between classes in Canada have sparked a resurgence of tent cities in many Canadian cities, including this one—on the waterfront at the foot of Cherry St. in Toronto. How would structural-functional analysis explain such poverty? What about the social-conflict approach?

were filled with priceless works of art and staffed by dozens of servants. Even by today's standards, their incomes were staggering. For example, Carnegie earned more than $20 million in 1900 (more than $550 million in today's dollars), when the average worker earned roughly $500 a year (Baltzell, 1964; Williamson, 2012).

In time, Marx believed, the working majority would overthrow the capitalists once and for all. Capitalism would bring about its own downfall, Marx reasoned, because it makes workers poorer and poorer and gives them little control over what they make or how they make it. Under capitalism, work produces only **alienation**, *the experience of isolation and misery resulting from powerlessness.*

To replace capitalism, Marx proposed a *socialist* system that would meet the needs of all rather than just the needs of the elite few: "The proletarians have nothing to lose but their chains. They have a world to win" (Marx & Engels, 1972:362, orig. 1848).

alienation the experience of isolation and misery resulting from powerlessness

EVALUATE Marx has had enormous influence on sociological thinking. But his revolutionary ideas, calling for the overthrow of capitalist society, also make his work highly controversial.

One of the most popular criticisms of the Marxist approach is that it ignores a central idea of the Davis–Moore thesis: that a system of unequal rewards is needed to place people in the right jobs and to motivate people to work hard. Marx separated reward from performance; his egalitarian ideal was based on the principle "from each according to his ability, to each according to his needs" (Marx & Engels, 1972:388, orig. 1848). However, failure to reward individual performance may be what caused the declining productivity of the former Soviet Union and other socialist economies around the world. Defenders respond to such criticism by asking why we assume that humanity is inherently selfish rather than social; individual rewards are not the only way to motivate people to perform their social roles (Clark, 1991).

A second problem is that the revolutionary change Marx predicted has failed to happen, at least in advanced capitalist societies. The next section explains why.

CHECK YOUR LEARNING How does Marx's view of social stratification differ from the Davis–Moore thesis?

Why No Marxist Revolution?

Despite Marx's prediction, capitalism is still thriving. Why have industrial workers not overthrown capitalism? Ralf Dahrendorf (1959) suggested four reasons:

1. **Fragmentation of the capitalist class**. Today, tens of millions of stockholders, rather than single families, own most large companies. Day-to-day corporate operations are in the hands of a large class of managers, who may or may not be major stockholders. With stock widely held—about half of North American households own stocks—more and more people have a direct stake in the capitalist system (Federal Reserve Board, 2012).

2. **A higher standard of living**. As Chapter 12 ("Economics and Politics") explains, a century ago, most Canadian workers were in factories or on farms in **blue-collar occupations**, *lower-prestige jobs that involve mostly manual labour.* Today, most workers are in **white-collar occupations**, *higher-prestige jobs that involve mostly mental activity.* These jobs are in sales, customer support, management, and other service fields. Most of today's white-collar workers do not think of themselves as an "industrial proletariat." Just as important, the average income in Canada rose almost tenfold over the course of the twentieth century, even allowing for inflation. During this period, in addition, the number of hours in the workweek actually decreased. Therefore, despite recent tough times economically, the typical worker today is far better off than the typical worker was a century ago, an example of structural social mobility. One consequence of this rising standard of living is that more people support the status quo.

blue-collar occupations lower-prestige jobs that involve mostly manual labour

white-collar occupations higher-prestige jobs that involve mostly mental activity

3. **More worker organizations**. Workers today have the right to form labour unions and other organizations that make demands of management, backed by threats of work slowdowns and strikes. As a result, labour disputes are settled without threatening the capitalist system.

4. **Greater legal protections**. Over the past century, new laws made the workplace safer, and employment insurance, disability protection, and Old Age Security now provide workers with greater financial security.

A Counterpoint

These developments suggest that Canadian society has smoothed many of capitalism's rough edges. Yet some observers claim that Marx's analysis of capitalism is still largely valid (Domhoff, 1983; Hout, Brooks, & Manza, 1993; Raposa, 2015). First, wealth remains highly concentrated, with much of the privately owned property in the hands of a small proportion of our population. Second, many of today's white-collar jobs offer no more income, security, or satisfaction than factory work did a century ago (Reid, 1996; Lowe, 2000). Third, many, if not most, of today's workers feel squeezed by high unemployment, company downsizing, jobs moving overseas, and job benefits being cut to balance budgets. Fourth, the income and benefits that today's workers do enjoy came about through exactly the class conflict Marx described. In addition, as the conflicts between labour unions and private and public institutions across Canada show, workers still struggle to hold on to what they have. Fifth, although workers have gained some legal protections, ordinary people still face disadvantages that the law cannot overcome. Therefore, social-conflict theorists conclude, even without a socialist revolution in Canada, Marx was still mostly right about capitalism.

socio-economic status (SES) a composite ranking based on various dimensions of social inequality

The extent of social inequality in agrarian systems is greater than that found in industrial societies. One indication of the unchallenged power of rulers is the monumental structures built over years with the unpaid labour of common people. Although the Taj Mahal in India is among the world's most beautiful buildings, it was built as a tomb for a single individual.

Max Weber: Class, Status, and Power

Max Weber agreed with Karl Marx that social stratification causes social conflict, but he viewed Marx's two-class model as too simple. Instead, he claimed that social stratification involves three distinct dimensions of inequality.

The first dimension, economic inequality—the issue so important to Marx—Weber called *class* position. Weber did not think of classes as well-defined categories but as a continuum ranging from high to low. Weber's second dimension is *status*, or social prestige, and the third is *power*.

Weber's Socio-economic Status Hierarchy

Marx viewed social prestige and power as simple reflections of economic position and did not treat them as distinct dimensions of inequality. But Weber noted that status consistency in modern societies is often quite low: A local official might exercise great power yet have little wealth or social prestige.

Weber, then, characterizes social stratification in industrial societies as a multidimensional ranking rather than a hierarchy of clearly defined classes. In line with Weber's thinking, sociologists use the term **socio-economic status (SES)** to refer to *a composite ranking based on various dimensions of social inequality.*

Inequality in History

Weber observed that each of his three dimensions of social inequality stands out at a different time in the history of human societies. Status or social prestige is the main dimension of difference in agrarian societies, taking the form of honour. Members of these societies gain prestige by conforming to cultural norms that apply to their particular rank.

Industrialization and the development of capitalism eliminate traditional rankings based on birth but create striking financial inequality. Thus in an industrial society, the crucial difference between people is the economic dimension of class.

Over time, industrial societies witness the growth of a bureaucratic state. Bigger government and the spread of all types of other organizations make power more important in the stratification system. Especially in socialist societies, where government regulates many aspects of life, high-ranking officials become the new ruling elite.

This historical analysis points to a final difference between Weber and Marx. Marx thought societies could eliminate social stratification by abolishing private ownership of productive property. Weber doubted that overthrowing capitalism would significantly lessen social stratification. It might reduce economic differences, he reasoned, but socialism would increase inequality by expanding government and concentrating power in the hands of a political elite. The popular uprisings against socialist bureaucracies in Eastern Europe and the former Soviet Union show that discontent can be generated by socialist political elites and thus support Weber's position.

EVALUATE Weber's multidimensional view of social stratification greatly influenced sociologists and made the concept of socio-economic status hierarchy popular. But critics (particularly those who favour Marx's ideas) argue that although social class boundaries may have blurred, industrial and post-industrial societies still show striking patterns of social inequality.

As will be explained shortly, economic inequality has increased recently in Canada. Although some people favour Weber's multidimensional hierarchy, others think, in light of this trend, that Marx's view of the rich versus the poor is closer to the truth.

CHECK YOUR LEARNING What are Weber's three dimensions of social inequality? According to Weber, which of them would you expect to be most important in Canada? Why?

Explaining Stratification: Symbolic-Interaction Theory

(8.5) Apply symbolic-interaction theory to the topic of social inequality.

Because social stratification has to do with the way an entire society is organized, sociologists (Marx and Weber included) typically treat it as a macro-level issue. But a micro-level analysis of social stratification is also important because people's social standing affects their everyday interactions. The Applying Theory table on page 252 summarizes the contributions of the three theoretical approaches to social stratification.

In most communities, people interact primarily with others of about the same social standing. This pattern begins with the fact that due to social stratification, people tend to live with others like themselves. In larger public spaces, such as a large shopping mall, we often see couples or groups made up of individuals whose appearance and shopping habits are similar. At the same time, people with very different social standing commonly keep their distance from one another. Well-dressed people walking down the street on their way to an expensive restaurant, for example, might move across the sidewalk or even cross the street to avoid getting close to others they think are homeless people.

Finally, just about everyone realizes that the way we dress, the car we drive (or the bus we ride), and even the food and drink we order at the campus snack bar say something about our resources and personal tastes. Sociologists use the term **conspicuous consumption** to refer to *buying and using products because of the "statement" they make about social position.* Ignoring the water fountain in favour of paying for bottled water tells people that you have extra money to

conspicuous consumption
buying and using products because of the "statement" they make about social position

Applying Theory

	Structural-Functional Theory	Social-Conflict Theory	Symbolic-Interaction Theory
What is the level of analysis?	Macro-level	Macro-level	Micro-level
What is social stratification?	Stratification is a system of unequal rewards that benefits society as a whole.	Stratification is a division of a society's resources that benefits some people and harms others.	Stratification is a factor that guides people's interactions in everyday life.
What is the reason for our social position?	Social position reflects personal talents and abilities in a competitive economy.	Social position reflects the way society divides resources.	The products we consume all say something about social position.
Are unequal rewards fair?	Yes. Unequal rewards boost economic production by encouraging people to work harder and try new ideas. Linking greater rewards to more important work is widely accepted.	No. Unequal rewards only serve to divide society, creating "haves" and "have-nots." There is widespread opposition to social inequality.	Maybe. People may or may not define inequality as fair. People may view their social position as a measure of self-worth, justifying inequality in terms of personal differences.

spend. And no one needs a $100 000 automobile to get around, of course, but driving up in such a vehicle says "I have arrived" in more ways than one.

EVALUATE A micro-level analysis of social stratification helps us see patterns of social inequality in our everyday lives. At the same time, the limitation of this approach is that it has little to say about how and why broad patterns of social inequality exist, which was the focus of the structural-functional and social-conflict approaches.

CHECK YOUR LEARNING Point to several ways in which social stratification shapes the way people of different social positions behave in the course of a typical day.

Stratification and Technology: A Global Perspective

8.6 Analyze the link between a society's technology and its social stratification.

We can weave together a number of observations made in this chapter by considering the relationship between a society's technology and its type of social stratification. This analysis draws on Gerhard Lenski's model of socio-cultural evolution discussed in Chapter 2 ("Culture").

Hunting and Gathering Societies

With simple technology, hunters and gatherers produce only what is necessary for day-to-day living. Some people may produce more than others, but the group's survival depends on all sharing what they have. Thus no categories of people are better off than others.

Horticultural, Pastoral, and Agrarian Societies

As technological advances create a surplus, social inequality increases. In horticultural and pastoral societies, a small elite controls most of the surplus. Larger-scale agriculture is more productive still, and striking inequality—as great as at any time in history—places the nobility in an almost godlike position over the masses.

Industrial Societies

Industrialization pushes inequality downward. Prompted by the need to develop people's talents, meritocracy takes hold and weakens the power of traditional elites. Industrial productivity also raises the living standards of the historically poor majority. Specialized work demands schooling for all, sharply reducing illiteracy. A literate population demands a greater voice in political decision making, reducing social inequality and lessening men's domination of women.

Over time, even wealth becomes somewhat less concentrated (contradicting Marx's prediction). In the 1920s, the richest 1 percent of North American families owned about 40 percent of all wealth, a figure that fell to 30 percent by the 1980s as taxes—with higher rates for people with higher incomes—paid for new government programs benefiting the poor (Williamson & Lindert, 1980; Beeghley, 1989; U.S. House of Representatives, 1991). Such trends help explain why Marxist revolutions occurred in *agrarian* societies, such as Russia (1917), Cuba (1959), and Nicaragua (1979), where social inequality is most pronounced, rather than in *industrial* societies as Marx predicted. However, wealth inequality turned upward again after 1990 and is once again at about the same level as it was in the 1920s (Wolff, 2007). With the goal of reducing this trend, some governments have expressed their intention to raise federal income tax rates on high-income individuals.

The Kuznets Curve

In human history, then, technological advances first increase but then moderate the intensity of social stratification. Greater inequality is functional for agrarian societies, but industrial societies benefit from a more equal system. This historical trend, recognized by the Nobel Prize–winning economist Simon Kuznets (1955, 1966), is illustrated by the Kuznets curve, shown in Figure 8–2.

Social inequality around the world generally supports the Kuznets curve. Global Map 8–1 on page 254 shows that high-income nations that have passed through the industrial era (including Canada, the United States, and the nations of Western Europe) have somewhat less income inequality than nations in which a larger share of the labour force remains in farming (as is common in Latin America and Africa). At the same time, it is important to remember that income inequality reflects not just technological development but also a society's political and economic priorities. Income disparity in Canada may have declined during much of the last century, but this country still has more economic inequality than Japan and countries throughout Europe.

One criticism of the Kuznets curve is that it was developed by comparing societies at different levels of economic development (using what sociologists call "cross-sectional data"). Such data do not tell us about the future of any one society. In Canada, the recent trend showing increases in economic inequality suggests that the Kuznets curve may require serious revision—represented by the broken line in Figure 8–2 corresponding to the post-industrial era. The fact that Canadian society is now experiencing greater economic inequality suggests that the long-term trend may differ from what Kuznets projected half a century ago.

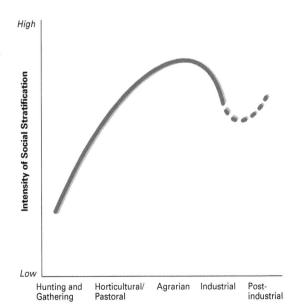

FIGURE 8–2 Social Stratification and Technological Development: The Kuznets Curve

The Kuznets curve shows that greater technological sophistication is generally accompanied by more pronounced social stratification. The trend reverses itself as industrial societies relax rigid, caste-like distinctions in favour of greater opportunity and equality under the law. Political rights are more widely extended, and there is even some levelling of economic differences. However, the emergence of post-industrial society has brought an upturn in economic inequality, as indicated by the broken line added by the authors.

Sources: Based on Kuznets (1955) and Lenski (1966).

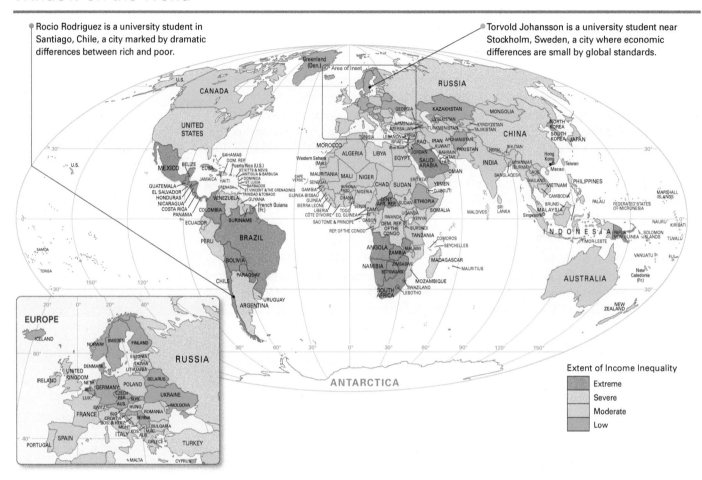

Rocio Rodriguez is a university student in Santiago, Chile, a city marked by dramatic differences between rich and poor.

Torvold Johansson is a university student near Stockholm, Sweden, a city where economic differences are small by global standards.

Extent of Income Inequality
- Extreme
- Severe
- Moderate
- Low

GLOBAL MAP 8–1 Income Inequality in Global Perspective

Societies throughout the world differ in the rigidity and extent of their social stratification and their overall standard of living. This map highlights income inequality. Generally speaking, the United States stands out among high-income nations, such as Canada, Great Britain, Sweden, Japan, and Australia, as having greater income inequality. The less economically developed countries of Latin America and Africa, including Colombia, Brazil, and the Central African Republic, as well as much of the Arab world, exhibit the most pronounced inequality of income. Is this pattern consistent with the Kuznets curve?

Source: Based on Gini coefficients obtained from Central Intelligence Agency (2012) and World Bank (2012).

Inequality in Canada

8.7 Describe the distribution of income and wealth in Canada.

Recently, there's been a lot of talk about economic inequality in Canada. The Occupy movement claims that 1 percent of the population is running away with the country while the remaining 99 percent of us are being left behind. The mass media provide almost daily accounts of increasing inequality. In addition, the 2015 Canadian federal election fuelled an intense debate over how to help average families find and keep jobs as the economy continues to stumble. This part of the chapter provides all the facts about the state of social inequality in Canada.

Historically, a widespread view has been that there are not class differences in Canada. Canada, like the United States, differs from most European nations and Japan in never having had a titled nobility. With the significant exception of our racial history, we have never known a caste system that rigidly ranks categories of people. Even so, Canadian society is highly stratified. Not only do the rich have most of the money, but they also receive the most schooling, enjoy the best health, and consume the most goods and services. Such privilege contrasts sharply with the poverty of millions of women and men who worry about finding next month's rent or paying a dentist's bill for their teenage son or daughter. Many people think of Canada as a "middle-class society" in which people are more or less alike. But is this really the case?

Income, Wealth, and Power

One important dimension of economic inequality is **income**, *earnings from work or investments.* Statistics Canada reports that the median Canadian after-tax family income was $71 700 in 2012. Table 8–1 takes a closer look at income by quintile. The richest 20 percent of Canadian families (earning a median income of $149 500 in 2012) received 43.6 percent of all income, and the bottom 20 percent (earning a median income of $14 700) received only 4.3 percent of all income (Uppal & LaRochelle-Côté, 2015). In short, while a small number of people have very high incomes, the majority make do with far less.

Income is only one part of a person's or family's **wealth**, *the total value of money and other assets, minus outstanding debts.* Wealth—including the total value of homes, cars, investments, insurance policies, retirement pensions, furniture, clothing, and all other personal property, minus a home mortgage and other debts—is distributed even more unequally than income.

The third pie chart of Figure 8–3 shows the distribution of wealth among all Canadian families for 2012.[1] The richest 20 percent of families (with a median family net worth of about $1 380 000) held 67.4 percent of all wealth. High up in this privileged category are the top 10 percent of families, the "very rich," who own 47.9 percent of all wealth. Richer still are the 1 percent of Canadians that qualify as "super-rich" (about 300 000 individuals) who claim $1 million in assets (not counting their principal residence) and possess a collective wealth of $979 billion (Flavelle, 2014; Statistics Canada, 2014a; World Wealth Report, 2015).

The wealth of the average Canadian family in 2012 was $243 800. Family wealth reflects the total value of homes, cars, investments, insurance policies, retirement pensions, furniture, clothing, and all other personal property, minus a home mortgage and other debts. The wealth of average people is not only less than that of the rich but also different in kind. Most people's

TABLE 8–1 Canadian Family Income

Quintile	Income Range
Richest 20%	$125 000 and up
Second 20%	$88 000–124 999
Middle 20%	$62 000–87 999
Fourth 20%	$38 500–61 999
Poorest 20%	$0–38 499

Source: Created by J. Burkowicz based on Ivanova (2011); Brown and Hodges (2014).

income earnings from work or investments

wealth the total value of money and other assets, minus outstanding debts

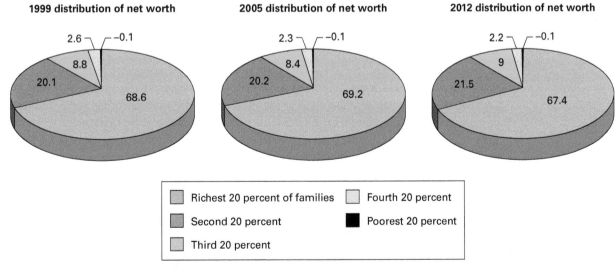

FIGURE 8–3 Distribution and Median Net Worth by Quintile, 1999, 2005, and 2012

Source: "Survey of Financial Security, 2012." The Daily (February 25, 2014a). http://www.statcan.gc.ca/daily-quotidien/140225/dq140225b-eng.htm?HP. This does not constitute an endorsement by Statistics Canada of this product.

---

[1]Statistics Canada reports both mean and median wealth for families (operationalized as "married couple with or without children, or a common-law couple with or without children, or a lone-parent family"). In 2012, mean family net worth was $554 100, higher than the median family net worth ($243 800) because high-income families pull up the mean but not the median.

wealth centres on a home and a car—property that generates no income—but the greater wealth of the rich is mostly in the form of stocks and other income-producing investments.

When financial assets are balanced against debts, the lowest-ranking 20 percent of families (with a median family net worth about $1100) held negative wealth amounting to −0.1 percent; that is, they actually live in debt. The negative percentage shown in Figure 8–3 has been constant since 1999.

In Canada, wealth is an important source of power. The small proportion of families that controls most of the country's wealth also has the ability to shape the agenda of the entire society. As explained in Chapter 12 ("Economics and Politics"), some sociologists argue that such concentrated wealth weakens democracy because the political system primarily serves the interests of the super-rich.

Occupational Prestige

In addition to generating income, work is also an important source of social prestige. We commonly evaluate each other according to the kind of work we do, giving greater respect to those who do what we consider to be more important work and less to others with more modest jobs.

Sociologists measure the relative social prestige of various occupations (Goyder, 2009). Table 8–2 shows that people give high prestige to occupations, such as medicine, law, and engineering, that require extensive training and generate high income. By contrast, less prestigious work—as a waitress or janitor, for example—not only pays less but requires less ability and schooling. We used to believe that occupational prestige rankings were much the same in all high-income nations (Lin & Xie, 1988) and relatively constant over time. In 2005, Canadian sociologist John Goyder replicated a study of occupational prestige conducted 40 years earlier and found that blue-collar occupations had gained the most prestige over the intervening years while many white-collar occupations had lost prestige. It is illustrative that child-care providers and firefighters gained the most prestige while members of Parliament, senators, Catholic priests, and lawyers lost the most.

In any society, high-prestige occupations go to privileged categories of people. In Table 8–2, for example, the highest-ranking occupations are dominated by men. Similarly, many of the lowest-prestige jobs are commonly performed by racial minorities.

Schooling

Industrial societies have expanded opportunities for schooling, but some people still receive much more than others. In 2011, although 89.1 percent of women and men aged 25 to 64 had completed high school, just 16.5 percent had completed a bachelor's degree. But we should note an important change in the recent decade with women taking more advantage of post-secondary schooling than men: Almost 60 percent of all degree holders aged 25 to 34 are women (Statistics Canada, 2013a; Conference Board of Canada, 2015a). Schooling affects both occupation and income because most (but not all) of the better-paying white-collar jobs shown in Table 8–2 require a college degree or other advanced study. Most blue-collar jobs, which bring lower income and social prestige, require less schooling.

Ancestry, Race, and Gender

A class system rewards individual talent and effort. But nothing affects social standing as much as birth into a particular family, which has a strong bearing on future schooling, occupation, and income. Research suggests that more than one-third of the richest individuals in the United States—those with hundreds of millions of dollars in wealth—derived their fortunes mostly from inheritance (Harford, 2007). The situation is much the same in Canada (Porter, 1965; Clement, 1975; Olsen, 1980; Brym & Fox, 1989; Bradbury et al., 2012). Inherited poverty shapes the future of tens of millions of others.

Also closely linked to social position in Canada is race. White people have a higher overall occupational standing than visible minorities. The median visible minority income of

TABLE 8–2 Occupational Prestige Scores for Selected Occupations, Canada, 2005

Occupation	Prestige Score	Occupation	Prestige Score
Physician	90.5	Power crane operator	57.6
University professor	84.3	Oil field worker	57.5
Registered nurse	81.6	Private in the army	57.5
Physicist	80.6	Construction labourer	57.4
High school teacher	80.3	Farm labourer	56.9
Police officer	78.6	Mail carrier	56.7
Chemist	77.7	Bricklayer	56.2
Architect	77.3	Catholic priest	56.1
Psychologist	76.7	Sculptor	55.9
Mathematician	74.8	Tractor-trailer driver	53.8
Lawyer	73.1	Bank teller	53
Sociologist	73	Quarry worker	53
Social worker	71.4	Butcher in a store	52.7
Bank manager	69	Supervisor of survey interviewers	52.4
Accountant	68.9	House painter	51.6
Economist	68.4	Logger	51.2
Electrician	67.9	Coal miner	50.7
Building contractor	67.2	Beauty salon operator	49
Dental hygienist	66.4	Flagperson on a road construction site	48.8
Child-care provider in a private home	65.1	Apprentice bricklayer	48.4
Professional forester	64.1	Waitress in a restaurant	48.3
Member of Canadian Senate	63.5	Garbage collector	47.9
Member of Canadian House of Commons	63.3	Cod fisherman	47.6
Librarian	63.2	Service station manager	47.5
Plumber	62.9	Sewing machine operator	45.3
Professionally trained librarian	62.3	Shipping clerk	43.7
Owner of a coffee shop	61.4	Lunchroom operator	43.3
House carpenter	61.1	Bartender	43.1
Funeral director	60.9	Taxicab driver	41.5
Tool and die maker	60.3	Stockroom attendant	40.4
Welder	60.2	Fruit packer in a cannery	40.1
Protestant minister	60.1	Bill collector	38.1
Automobile mechanic	59.8	Used car salesman	37.1
User support technician	58.9	Telemarketer	32.8
Cook in a restaurant	58.6	Someone who lives on social assistance	22.1
Survey research director	58.4		

Source: Goyder (2009).

full-year, full-time workers was $44 021 in 2010, or 87 percent of the $50 326 earned by non-visible minority individuals. Aboriginal people are even more disadvantaged, with a median income of $42 896 (Statistics Canada, 2011b). The larger proportion of young workers among visible minorities and Aboriginals accounts for some of this income disparity. Some of the racial difference in income results from the larger proportion of single-parent families among Aboriginal Canadians. Varying levels of education of these three populations can also be used to help us understand some of the disadvantage of Aboriginal workers. Visible minorities are more disadvantaged than these income data indicate because they tend to have a higher level of education than other Canadians, which should result in a higher income.

This difference in income makes a real difference in people's lives. Income gaps affect everything from home ownership rates to health status. Over time, this income difference builds into a huge wealth gap.

Social ranking involves ethnicity as well. People of English ancestry have enjoyed the most wealth and wielded the greatest power in Canadian society. Canadian-born Greek and Balkan men, however, earn 14.5 percent and 10.5 percent less than do men of British ancestry. Among immigrant men and women, those of Southern and Eastern European origins report lower incomes than immigrants of Western European origins (Pendakur & Pendakur, 1998, 2015). A detailed examination of how race and ethnicity affect social standing is presented in Chapter 11 ("Race and Ethnicity").

Of course, both men and women are found in families at every social level. Yet on average, women have less income, wealth, and occupational prestige than men. Among single-parent families, those headed by a woman are more than twice as likely to be poor as those headed by a man. Chapter 10 ("Gender Stratification") examines the link between gender and social stratification.

Social Classes in Canada

8.8 Discuss the various social class positions in Canadian society.

As noted earlier, rankings in a caste system are rigid and obvious to all. Defining social categories in a more fluid class system such as ours, however, is not so easy. Followers of Karl Marx see two major social classes: capitalists and proletarians. Other sociologists find as many as six classes (Warner & Lunt, 1941) or even seven (Coleman & Rainwater, 1978). Still others side with Max Weber, believing that people form not clear-cut classes but a multidimensional status hierarchy.

Defining classes in Canada is difficult because of the relatively low level of status consistency. Especially toward the middle of the hierarchy, people's social position on one dimension may not be the same as their standing on another. For example, a government official may have the power to administer a multimillion-dollar budget yet earn only a modest personal income. Similarly, many members of the clergy enjoy ample prestige but only moderate power and low pay. Or consider the casino poker player who wins little respect but makes a lot of money.

Finally, the social mobility characteristic of class systems—again, most pronounced around the middle—means that social position may change during a person's lifetime, further blurring class boundaries. With these issues in mind, we will examine four general rankings: the upper class, the middle class, the working class, and the lower class.

The Upper Class

Families in the upper class—the top 5 percent of the Canadian population—earn an income of at least $125 000. As a category, they possess 67.4 percent of all wealth in Canada. Many of them are what Karl Marx called "capitalists"—the owners of the means of production and thus of most of the nation's private wealth. Upper-class people work as top executives in large corporations and as senior government officials. Historically, though less so today, the upper class was comprised of white Anglo-Saxon Protestants (WASPs) (Porter, 1965; Clement, 1975).

Income is one way in which we can determine upper class membership. But more than the *size* of income is involved. Also important is the *source* of income. As a general rule, the more a family's income comes from inherited wealth in the form of shares of stock and bonds, real estate, and other investments, the stronger a family's claim to being upper class. The distinction between earning money and inheriting money brings us to the difference between "upper-uppers" and "lower-uppers."

Upper-Uppers

The *upper-upper class*, sometimes called "blue bloods" or simply "society," includes less than 1 percent of the Canadian population. Membership is almost always the result of birth, as suggested by the old remark that the easiest way to become an upper-upper is to be born one. Most of these families possess enormous wealth that is primarily inherited. For this reason, members of the upper-upper class are said to have "old money."

In 2011, about 270 000 people in Canada were classified as high-net-worth individuals (HNWI). They make up 1 percent of the Canadian population and reported incomes of at least $191 100, or about 10 percent of all income. Even further up the income hierarchy are the 0.1 percent of HNWI whose 2011 income was $685 000 and the 0.01 percent of HNWI who earned $2.57 million that year (CBC News, 2013; World Wealth Report, 2015). In 2015, *Forbes* listed 30 Canadian families or individuals worth more than US$1 billion (*Forbes*, 2015). David Thomson and family, of Thomson Reuters, topped the list of the richest persons in Canada and ranked as the twenty-fifth–richest in the world.

These women have appeared on the television program *Real Housewives of Vancouver*. Using the categories discussed in the pages that follow, within which social class category do you think they fall? Why?

Set apart by their wealth, upper-uppers live in exclusive neighbourhoods such as West-mount in Montreal, Forest Hill in Toronto, or the Uplands in Victoria. Their children typi-cally attend private schools with others of similar background and complete their formal education at high-prestige universities. In the historical pattern of European aristocrats, they study liberal arts rather than vocational skills.

Women of the upper-upper class often do volunteer work for charitable organizations. Such activities serve a dual purpose: They help the larger community, and they build networks that broaden this elite's power (Ostrander, 1980, 1984).

Lower-Uppers

Most upper-class people actually fall into the *lower-upper class.* And lower-uppers include some of the richest people in the world. The queen of England is in the upper-upper class based not only on her fortune of $500 million but on her family tree. J. K. Rowling, author of the Harry Potter books, is worth twice as much—more than $1 billion—but this woman (who was once on welfare) stands at the top of the lower-upper class. The major difference, in other words, is that members of the lower-upper class are the "working rich" who get their money mostly by earning it rather than through inheritance. These "new rich" families—who make up

People often distinguish between the "new rich" and families with "old money." Men and women who suddenly begin to earn high incomes tend to spend their money on status symbols because they enjoy the new thrill of high-roller living and they want others to know of their success. Those who grow up surrounded by wealth, by contrast, are used to a privileged way of life and are quieter about it. Thus the conspicuous consumption of the lower-upper class (*left*) can differ dramatically from the more private pursuits and understatement of the upper-upper class (*right*).

3 to 4 percent of the Canadian population—generally live in large homes in expensive neighbourhoods, own vacation homes near the water or in the mountains, and send their children to private schools and good colleges. Yet most do not gain entry into the clubs and associations of "old money" families.

The Middle Class

Made up of about 40 to 45 percent of the Canadian population, the large middle class has a tremendous influence on our culture. Television and movies usually show middle-class people, and most commercial advertising is directed at these average consumers. The middle class contains far more racial and ethnic diversity than the upper class.

Upper-Middles

People near the top of this category are called the *upper-middle class*, based on their above-average family income in the range of $88 000 to $125 000 a year (Brown & Hodges, 2014). Such income allows upper-middle-class families to own a comfortable house in a fairly expensive area, several automobiles, and investments. Most upper-middle-class children go on to university or college, and postgraduate degrees are common. Many go on to high-prestige occupations as physicians, engineers, lawyers, accountants, and business executives. Lacking the power of the richest people to influence national or international events, upper-middles often play an important role in local political affairs.

Average-Middles

The rest of the middle class falls close to the centre of the Canadian class structure. *Average-middles* typically work at less prestigious white-collar jobs as bank branch managers or high school teachers or in highly skilled blue-collar jobs such as electrical work and carpentry. Family income falls between $62 000 and $88 000 a year, which is roughly the national average.[2]

Middle-class people generally build up a small amount of wealth over the course of their working lives, mostly in the form of a house and a retirement account. In the past most average-middle-class men and women were likely to be high school graduates, but increasingly they are seeking post-secondary credentials.

What would you say about the social class standing of the Harrison family and their friend Chumlee, who star in the popular reality television show *Pawn Stars*? What about the work of running a family business? What about their dress and interests? What about the fact that they have recently made a lot of money from their television show? Does their situation not show that social class position is often complex and contradictory?

The Working Class

About one-third of the population falls within the working class (sometimes called the *lower-middle class*). In Marxist terms, the working class forms the core of the industrial proletariat. The blue-collar jobs held by members of the working class generally yield a family income of between $38 500 and $62 000 a year, somewhat below the national average. Working-class families have little or no wealth and are vulnerable to financial problems caused by unemployment or illness.

Many working-class jobs provide little personal satisfaction—requiring discipline but rarely imagination—and subject workers to continual supervision. These jobs also offer fewer benefits, such as medical insurance and pension plans. The data show that about half of working-class families own their own homes, which are typically in lower-cost neighbourhoods. College or university becomes a reality for only about one-quarter of working-class children.

[2]In some parts of Canada where the cost of living is very high (say, Ottawa), a family might need as much as $83 500 in annual income to reach the middle class, while in Montreal it would need about $59 000 (Brown & Hodges, 2014).

The Lower Class

The remaining 20 percent of our population make up the lower class. Low income makes their lives insecure and difficult. Many belong to the so-called "working poor." They are just slightly better off than unemployed people, holding low-prestige jobs that provide little satisfaction and minimal income. About 70 percent of lower-class children complete high school, and only about 15 percent ever complete a university degree.

Society segregates the lower class, especially when the poor are racial or ethnic minorities. Only some lower-class families own their own home, typically in the least desirable neighbourhoods. Although poor neighbourhoods are often found in inner cities, lower-class families also live in rural areas.

The Difference Class Makes

8.9 Analyze how social class position affects health, values, politics, and family life.

Social stratification affects nearly every dimension of our lives. In the following sections, we will briefly examine some of the ways social standing is linked to our health, values and attitudes, politics, and family life.

Health

Health is closely related to social standing. Children born into poor families are twice as likely to die from disease, neglect, accidents, or violence during their first year of life as children born into privileged families. Among adults, people with above-average incomes are almost twice as likely as low-income people to describe their health as excellent. In addition, on average, richer people live 3.5 years longer because they eat more nutritious food, live in safer and less stressful environments, and receive better medical care (Diderichsen et al., 2001; Wilkinson, 2005; Greenberg & Normandin, 2011).

Values and Attitudes

Some values and attitudes vary from class to class. The "old rich" have an unusually strong sense of family history because their position is based on wealth passed down from generation to generation. Secure in their birthright privileges, upper-uppers also favour understated manners and tastes; many "new rich" engage in *conspicuous consumption*, using homes, cars, and even airplanes as *status symbols* to make a statement about their social position.

Affluent people with greater education and financial security are also more respectful of homosexuality and tend to support gay rights. Working-class people, who grow up in an atmosphere of greater supervision and discipline and are less likely to attend college or university, tend to be more socially conservative (Lareau, 2002; NORC, 2011).

Social class has a great deal to do with an individual's self-concept. People with higher social standing experience more confidence in everyday interaction for the simple reason that others tend to view them as having greater importance. The Thinking About Diversity box on page 262 describes the challenges faced by one young woman from a poor family attending a university where most students are from elite families.

Politics

Do political attitudes follow class lines? The answer is yes, but the pattern is complex. A desire to protect their wealth prompts well-off people to take a more conservative approach to *economic* issues, favouring, for example, lower

Russell Lee/Corbis

Compared to the rich, poor and working-class people are half as likely to report good health and are more likely to report shorter life spans. In Canada, the highest income quintile has a life expectancy of 82 years; members of the lowest quintile can expect to live to about 78.5 years (Greenberg & Normandin, 2011). The toll of low income—played out in inadequate nutrition, little medical care, and high stress—is easy to see on the faces of the poor, who look old before their time.

Thinking About Diversity: Race, Class, and Gender

The Power of Class: A Low-Income Student Asks, "Am I as Good as You?"

Marcella grew up without the privileges that most other students on the campus of this private, liberal arts university take for granted. During her senior year, she and I talked at length about her university experiences and why social class presented a huge challenge to her. Marcella is not her real name; she wishes to remain anonymous. I have summarized what she has said about her university experience in the story that follows.

When I came here, I entered a new world. I found myself in a strange and dangerous place. All around me were people with habits and ideas I did not understand. A thousand times I thought to myself, I hope all of you will realize that there are other worlds out there and that I am from one of them. Will you accept me?

I am a child of poverty, a young woman raised in a world of want and violence. I am now on the campus of an elite university. I may have a new identity as a university student. But my old life is still going on in my head. I have not been able to change how I think of myself.

Do you want to find out more about me? Learn more about the power of social class to shape how we feel about ourselves? Here is what I want to say to you.

When I was growing up, I envied most of you. You lived in a middle-class bubble, a world that held you, protected you, and comforted you. Not me. While your parents were discussing current events, planning family trips, and looking out for you, my father and mother were screaming at each other. I will never be able to forget summer nights when I lay in my bed, sticky with sweat, biting my fingernails as a telephone crashed against the wall that separated my room from theirs. My father was drunk and out of control; my mother ducked just in time.

Your fathers and mothers work in office buildings. They have good jobs, as doctors, lawyers, and architects; they are corporate managers; they run small businesses. Your mothers and fathers are people who matter. My mom takes the bus to a hospital where she works for $10 an hour cleaning up after people. She spends her shift doing what she is told. My dad? Who knows. He was a

deadbeat, a drunk, a drug addict. I don't know if he still is or not. I haven't heard from him in eight years.

You grew up in a nice neighbourhood and probably lived for many years in one house. My family lived in low-cost rental housing. We moved a lot. When there was no money for rent, we packed up our stuff and moved to a new place. It seemed like we were always running away from something.

You grew up with books, with trips to the library, with parents who read to you. You learned how to speak well and have an impressive vocabulary. I never heard a bedtime story, and I had maybe one inspiring teacher. Most of what I know I had to learn on my own. Maybe that's why I always feel like I am trying to catch up to you.

You know how to use forks, knives, and spoons the right way. You know how to eat Chinese food and what to order at a Thai restaurant. You have favourite Italian dishes. You know how to order wine. You know about German beers, Danish cheeses, and French sauces. Me? I grew up having Thanksgiving dinner on paper plates, eating turkey served by social service volunteers. When you ask me to go with you to some special restaurant, I make some excuse and stay home. I can't afford it. More than that, I am afraid you will find out how little I know about things you take for granted.

How did I ever get to this university? I remember one of my teachers telling me that I "have promise." The university admissions office accepted me. But I am not sure why. I was given a scholarship that covers most of my tuition. That solved one big problem, and now I am here. But sometimes I am not sure I will stay. I have to study more than many of you to learn things you already know. I have to work two part-time jobs to make the money I needed to buy a used computer, clothes, and the occasional pizza at the corner place where many of you spend so much time.

It's amazing to me that I am here. I realize how lucky I am. But now that I am here, I realize that the road is so much longer than I thought it would be. Getting to this university was only part of the journey. The scholarship was only part of the answer. The biggest challenge for me is what goes on every day—the thousands of ways in which you live a life that I still don't really understand, the thousands of things that I won't know or that I will do wrong that will blow my cover, and show me up for the fraud I am.

What Do You Think?

1. How does this story show that social class involves much more than how much money a person has?

2. Why does Marcella worry that other people will think she is a "fraud"? If you could speak to her about this fear, what would you say?

3. Have you ever had similar feelings about being less important than—or better than—someone else based on social class position? Explain.

Penny Tweedie/Stone/Getty Images

taxes. But on *social* matters such as abortion and gay rights, highly educated, more affluent people are more liberal. People of lower social standing, by contrast, tend to be economic liberals, favouring government social programs that benefit them, but typically hold more conservative views on social issues (Angus Reid Group, 1996, 1998; Ipsos-Reid, 2003; NORC, 2011).

A clearer pattern emerges when it comes to political involvement. Higher-income people, who are better served by the system, are more likely to vote and to join political organizations than people with low incomes. In the 2011 federal election, 78 percent of adults with a university degree cast a vote, compared to 60 percent of adults with a high school education (Uppal & LaRochelle-Côté, 2012).

Family and Gender

Social class also shapes family life. Generally, lower-class families are somewhat larger than middle-class families because of earlier marriage and less use of birth control. Another family pattern is that working-class parents encourage children to conform to conventional norms and respect authority figures. Parents of higher social standing pass on a different "cultural capital" to their children, teaching them to express their individuality and imagination more freely (Kohn, 1977; McLeod, 1995; Lareau, 2002).

The more money a family has, the more opportunities parents have to develop their children's talents and abilities. According to some calculations, the cost of raising a child in Canada to age 18 is approximately $250 000 (Brown, 2015). Given the large amount of money involved, it stands to reason that only those families with the highest incomes can afford to pay for such luxuries as private schools. Privilege leads to privilege as family life reproduces the class structure in each generation.

Class also shapes our world of relationships. In a classic study of married life, Elizabeth Bott (1971, orig. 1957) found that most working-class couples divide their responsibilities according to traditional gender roles; middle-class couples, by contrast, are more egalitarian, sharing more activities and expressing greater intimacy. More recently, Karen Walker (1995) discovered that working-class friendships typically serve as sources of material assistance; middle-class friendships are likely to involve shared interests and leisure pursuits.

Social Mobility

(8.10) Assess the extent of social mobility in Canada.

Ours is a dynamic society marked by quite a bit of social movement. Earning a university or college degree, landing a higher-paying job, or marrying someone who earns a good income contributes to *upward social mobility*; dropping out of school, losing a job, or becoming divorced (especially for women) may result in *downward social mobility*.

Over the long term, though, social mobility is not so much a matter of individual changes as changes in society itself. In the first half of the twentieth century, for example, industrialization expanded the Canadian economy, pushing up living standards. Even people who were not good swimmers rode the rising tide of prosperity. More recently, the "outsourcing" of jobs and the closing of factories and other business operations have brought downward structural social mobility, dealing economic setbacks to many people in the United States and to a lesser extent in Canada. The economic downturn that hit hard at the end of 2007 reduced the income and economic opportunities of millions of people.

Sociologists distinguish between shorter- and longer-term changes in social position. **Intragenerational social mobility** is *a change in social position occurring during a person's lifetime* (*intra* is Latin for "within"). **Intergenerational social mobility**, *upward or downward social mobility of children in relation to their parents*, is important because it reveals long-term changes in society that affect everyone (*inter* is Latin for "between").

intragenerational social mobility a change in social position occurring during a person's lifetime

intergenerational social mobility upward or downward social mobility of children in relation to their parents

Thinking About Diversity: Race, Class, and Gender

Is Social Mobility the Exception or the Rule?

How likely are we to change our class position? What are the odds of going up or down the social hierarchy? What share of people, as adults, end up staying right where they started as children? To answer these questions, sociologist Lisa A. Keister used data from the National Longitudinal Survey of Youth (NLSY), a long-term study of 9500 men and women. These people were first studied in 1979 during their youth—when they were between 14 and 22 years old and living at home with one or both parents. The same people were studied again as adults in 2000, when they ranged in age from 35 to 43 years old. About 80 percent of the subjects were married and all had households of their own.

What Keister wanted to know was how the economic standing of the subjects may have changed over their lifetimes, which she measured by estimating (from NLSY data) their amount of wealth at two different times. In 1979, because the subjects were young and living at home, she measured the family wealth of the subjects' parents. Keister placed each subject's family in one of five wealth quintiles—from the richest 20 percent down to the poorest 20 percent—and these quintiles are shown in the vertical axis of the accompanying table. In 2000, she measured the wealth of the same people, who were now living in households of their own. Wealth rankings in 2000 are shown in the horizontal axis of the table.

So what did Keister learn? How much social mobility, in terms of household wealth, took place over the course of 21 years? Looking at the table, we can learn a great deal. The cell in the upper left corner shows us that, of the richest 20 percent of subjects in 1979, 55 percent of these young people went on to remain in the top wealth category in 2000. Obviously, because these people were starting out in the top category, there could be no upward movement (although some of the subjects were richer as adults than they were when they were young). Twenty-five percent of the richest subjects in 1979 had dropped one level to the second quintile.

That means that 80 percent of the richest people in 1979 were still quite well off in 2000; only 20 percent of the richest people were downwardly mobile across two or more categories (9 percent who fell two levels, 6 percent who fell three levels, and 5 percent who fell to the lowest wealth level).

A similar pattern is seen as we begin with the poorest subjects—those who were in the lowest wealth quintile in 1979. Obviously, again, because these people started out in the lowest category, they had nowhere to go but up. But 45 percent of these men and women remained in the lowest wealth category as adults (the bottom-right box), and 27 percent moved up one quintile. Another 28 percent of the poorest people moved up two or more quintiles as adults (11 percent who rose two levels, 9 percent who rose three levels, and 8 percent who rose to the richest level).

For subjects in the middle ranges, the data show that mobility was somewhat more pronounced. For those who started in the second richest quintile, just 33 percent ended up in the same place. The remaining 67 percent moved up or down at least one level, although the most common move was rising or falling one level. Of those in the third (or middle) quintile, 35 percent ended up in the same rank as adults, and 65 percent moved up or down at least one level. Again, most of those who moved shifted just one level. Similarly, of those who started out in the fourth quintile, 35 percent ended up in the same ranking as adults, and 65 percent moved in most cases one level up or down.

So what can we conclude about patterns of wealth mobility over a generation between 1979 and 2000? The first conclusion is that a majority of people did experience mobility, moving up or down one or more levels. So mobility was the rule rather than the exception. Second, movement downward was about as common as movement upward. Third, movement was somewhat more common among people closer to the middle of the wealth hierarchy—the largest share of people who "stayed put" (55 percent among those who started out at the top and 45 percent of those who started out at the bottom) were at one or the other extreme.

What Do You Think?

1. What about the results presented here surprises you? Explain.

2. Overall, how well do the results presented here square with what you imagine most people in this country think about mobility?

3. How do you think the recent economic recession has affected patterns of social mobility?

Childhood Standing, 1979	Adult Standing, 2000				
	Richest 20%	Second 20%	Third 20%	Fourth 20%	Poorest 20%
Richest 20% →	55	25	9	6	5
Second 20% →	25	33	23	11	8
Third 20% →	13	21	35	20	11
Fourth 20% →	7	14	20	35	24
Poorest 20% →	8	9	11	27	45

Myth Versus Reality

In few societies do people think about "getting ahead" as much as they do in Canada and the United States. But is there as much social mobility in our country as we like to think?

One recent American study of intergenerational mobility shows that about 32 percent of men had the same type of work as their fathers, 37 percent were upwardly mobile (for example, a son born to a father with a blue-collar job ends up doing white-collar work), and 32 percent were downwardly mobile (for example, the father has a white-collar job and the son does blue-collar work). Among women, 46 percent were upwardly mobile, 28 percent were downwardly mobile, and 27 percent showed no change compared to their fathers (Beller & Hout, 2006). The Thinking About Diversity box on page 264 provides the results of another study of long-term social mobility. Other countries fare better than the United States, including Canada. An OECD (2010) study of mobility in earnings, wages, and education across generations indicates that mobility is comparatively low in the United States, the United Kingdom, France, and southern European countries, and higher in Canada, Australia, and the Nordic countries.

Horizontal social mobility—changing jobs at the same class level—is even more common. Overall, about 80 percent of children show some type of social mobility in relation to their parents (Hout, 1998; Beller & Hout, 2006).

Research points to five general conclusions about social mobility in North America:

1. **Social mobility over the past century has been fairly high**. A high level of mobility is what we would expect in an industrial class system.

2. **Within a single generation, social mobility is usually small**. Most young families increase their income over time as they gain education and skills. A typical couple family headed by an adult under the age of 24 earned about $37 870 in 2013; a typical family headed by an adult aged 35–44 earned $94 770 (Statistics Canada, 2015a). Yet only a few people move "from rags to riches" (the way J. K. Rowling did) or lose a lot of money (a number of rock stars who made it big had little money left a few years later). Most social mobility involves small movement within one class level rather than large movement between classes.

3. **The long-term trend in social mobility has been upward**. Industrialization, which greatly expanded the Canadian economy, and the growth of white-collar work over the course of the twentieth century have raised living standards. In recent decades, however, mobility has been downward about as often as it has been upward (Keister, 2000).

4. **Since the 1970s, social mobility has been uneven**. Real income (adjusted for inflation) rose during the twentieth century until the 1970s. Since then, as shown in Figure 8–4, real income has risen and fallen, with overall smaller gains than was the case before 1970. Most recently, the economic recession that began in 2007 resulted in several years of declining incomes for most people.

5. **The short-term trend in social mobility has been downward**. Especially since the beginning of the recent recession in 2007, the middle class has become smaller as income and wealth have declined. As a result, 85 percent of people who identify themselves as "middle class" say that keeping the same standard of living has become more difficult (Pew Research Center, 2012).

Mobility by Income Level

The experience of social mobility depends on where in the social class system you happen to be. Figure 8–5 on page 266 shows how Canadian families at different income levels made out between 1976 and 2011. Well-to-do families (the highest 20 percent, but not all of the same families over the entire period) saw their incomes jump 58 percent, from an average of $126 100 in 1976 to $176 300 in 2011. People in the middle of the population saw almost no gains during these three decades. The 20 percent with the lowest income saw their incomes increase

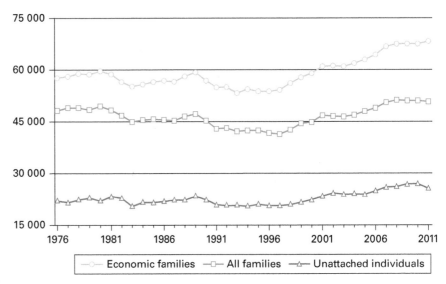

FIGURE 8–4 Median Annual Income, by Family Unit, 1976–2011

Average Canadian family income decreased in the early 1980s and 1990s and has grown since 1998 (in 2011 dollars, adjusted for inflation).

Source: Statistics Canada (2013b); Employment and Social Development Canada (2015a)

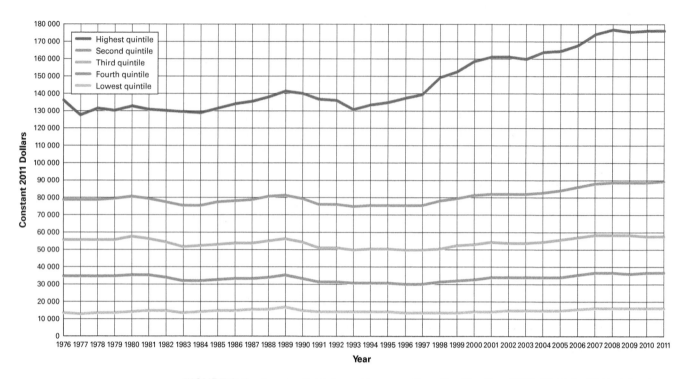

FIGURE 8–5 Average Total Annual Income, Canadian Families, 1976–2011 (in 2011 dollars)

The gap between high-income and low-income families is wider today than it was in 1976.

Source: Statistics Canada (2013c).

20 percent from $12 500 to $15 600 (adjusted for inflation). In addition to these changes over time, income varies regionally.

Mobility: Race, Ethnicity, and Gender

White people in Canada have always been in a more privileged position than people of Aboriginal and visible minority backgrounds. There was a slight decrease in the income gap percentage differences between Aboriginal and non-Aboriginal Canadians from 2000 to 2005, but the gap remains large and chronic unemployment persists among Aboriginal peoples (Statistics Canada, 2009a; Aboriginal Affairs and Northern Development Canada, 2013). Moreover, between 1980 and 2005, recent immigrants, who tend to be of visible minority backgrounds yet have a higher level of education than others in Canada, actually lost ground relative to their Canadian-born counterparts (Statistics Canada, 2008).

Feminists point out that historically, women have had less chance for upward mobility than men because most working women held clerical jobs (such as secretary) and service positions (such as food server) that offer few opportunities for advancement.

Over time, however, the median earnings gap between women and men has been narrowing. Women working full time in 1981 earned 77 percent of the hourly wages of men working full time; by 2011, women's median earnings were 87 percent as much (Morissette, Picot, & Lu, 2013).

Mobility and Marriage

Research points to the conclusion that marriage has an important effect on social standing. In a study of women and men in their forties, Jay Zagorsky (2006) found that people who marry and stay married accumulate about twice as much wealth as people who remain single or who divorce. Reasons for this difference include the fact that couples who live together typically enjoy double incomes and also pay only half the bills the two partners would have if they were single and living in separate households.

It is also likely that compared to single people, married men and women work harder in their jobs and save more money. Why? Primarily because they are working not just for themselves but also to support children and spouses who are counting on them.

Just as marriage pushes social standing upward, divorce usually makes social position go down. Couples who divorce take on the financial burden of supporting two households, which leaves them with less money for savings or other investment. After divorce, women are hurt more than men because typically the man earns more. Many women who divorce lose not only most of their income but also benefits such as health care and insurance coverage (Weitzman, 1996).

The Canadian Dream: Still a Reality?

The expectation of upward social mobility is deeply rooted in Canadian culture. Through much of our history, the economy has grown steadily, raising living standards. Today, at least for some people, this dream is alive and well. In 2006, more than half a million Canadians earned more than $100 000 and just over one-third earned more than $150 000. Looking at the data over time, 3.4 percent of full-time, full-year earners received $100 000 or more in 1980 (in 2005 constant dollars). This proportion had almost doubled to 6.5 percent in 2005 (Statistics Canada, 2009b). The trend over the last decade is that wealthy Canadians keep increasing their wealth. In 2012, the top two quintiles held 70 percent of all wealth, compared with 68 percent in 1999. And, during this period, those at the top quintile saw the most gains, with their wealth increasing by 107 percent (Uppal & LaRochelle-Côté, 2015). Yet not all indicators are so positive. Note these disturbing trends:

1. **For many workers, earnings have stalled**. Median earnings of Canadian workers remained stalled over the past 25 years, showing only a minor increase from $45 800 in 1976 to $48 300 in 2009 (in 2009 constant dollars). During this time period, median earnings among the poorest people in Canada (the bottom quintile) rose only from $12 400 to $14 500 (Conference Board of Canada, 2015b).

2. **More jobs offer little income**. The expanding global economy has moved many industrial jobs overseas, reducing the availability of high-paying factory jobs here in Canada. At the same time, the expansion of our service economy means that more of today's jobs—in fast-food restaurants or large discount stores—offer relatively low wages.

3. **Young people are remaining at home**. Currently, more than half of young people aged 18 to 24, unable to support a household, are living with their parents. Since 1975, the average age at first marriage has moved upward five years (to 26.6 years for women and 28.6 years for men).

Over the past generation, more people have become rich, and the rich have become richer. At the very top of the pile, the highest-paid corporate executives have enjoyed a runaway rise in their earnings. Yet the increasing share of low-paying jobs has brought downward mobility for many families, feeding the fear that the chance to enjoy a middle-class lifestyle is slipping away. As a glance back at Figure 8–4 on page 265 shows, median family income has increased for all; however, the increases have been modest for those at the bottom, and the gap between the rich and the poor continues to widen.

The Global Economy and the Canadian Structure

Underlying the shifts in the North American class structure over recent decades is global economic change. Much of the industrial production that gave Canadian workers high-paying jobs a generation ago has moved overseas, where wages are cheaper. With less industry at home, Canada now serves as a vast consumer market for industrial goods such as cars, stereos, cameras, and computers made in China, India, Japan, South Korea, Brazil, and elsewhere.

High-paying jobs in manufacturing are on a long-term decline. Between 2000 and 2007 alone, there was a decline of 278 000 jobs in manufacturing. Following the 2008–09 recession, a further 10 percent drop resulted in the loss of 188 000 manufacturing jobs (Statistics Canada, 2011c). In their place, the economy offers service work, which pays far less.

Traditionally high-paying corporations now employ fewer people than the expanding chains such as McDonald's, and fast-food clerks make only a fraction of what steelworkers earn.

The global reorganization of work has not been bad news for everyone. The global economy is driving upward social mobility for educated people who specialize in law, finance, marketing, and computer technology. Even allowing for the downturn that began at the end of 2007, the global economic expansion also helped push up the stock market more than thirteenfold between 1980 and 2013, reaping profits for families with money to invest.

But the same trend has hurt many average workers, who have lost their factory jobs and now perform low-wage service work. In addition, many companies (General Motors and Ford are recent examples) have downsized—cutting the ranks of their workforce—in an attempt to stay competitive in world markets. As a result, although 69 percent of all families today contain two or more people in the labour force—almost twice the share from 36 percent in 1976—many families are working harder than ever before simply to hold on to what they have (Nelson, 1998; Sennett, 1998; Statistics Canada, 2015b).

Poverty in Canada

8.11 Summarize patterns and explanations of poverty in the Canadian population.

Social stratification creates both "haves" and "have-nots." All systems of social inequality create poverty, or at least **relative poverty**, *the lack of resources of some people in relation to those who have more*. A more serious but preventable problem is **absolute poverty**, *a lack of resources that is life-threatening.*

As Chapter 9 ("Global Stratification") explains, about 1.3 billion human beings around the world—one person in five—are at risk of absolute poverty. Even in affluent Canada, families go hungry, sleep in parked cars or on the streets, and suffer from poor health simply because they are poor.

relative poverty the lack of resources of some people in relation to those who have more

absolute poverty a lack of resources that is life-threatening

The Extent of Poverty

Canada has no official way to assess the poverty rate. However, according to one popular measure known as the LICO, a family has an income below the *low income cut-off* if it spends more than 63 percent of its after-tax income on the necessities of food, clothing, and shelter, including corrections for different family sizes and the cost of living in particular communities. For example, in 2014, a family of four living in a large urban area (more than 500 000 people) with an income below $45 206 lived below the LICO (Employment and Social Development Canada, 2015b).

In 2011, the government classified about 4.7 million men, women, and children—almost 15 percent of the Canadian population—as poor (Statistics Canada, 2014b).[3]

Who Are the Poor?

Although no single description fits all poor people, poverty is greater among certain categories of the Canadian population. Where these categories overlap, the problem is especially serious.

Age

A generation ago, the elderly were at greatest risk for poverty. This was less true in the 2000s. From 21 percent in 1980, the poverty rate for seniors over the age of 65 plummeted to 4.8 percent in 2007 (Collin & Jensen, 2009). Recently, however, the poverty rate for seniors has been on the rise. Almost 605 000, or 13.4 percent of seniors, had a low income in 2010 and 7.2 percent live in poverty (Statistics Canada, 2011d; OECD, 2013).

The burden of poverty, however, falls most heavily on children. Despite the fact that in 1989 the Canadian Parliament unanimously vowed to eradicate child poverty by the year 2000, a UNICEF (2012) report indicated that 13.3 percent of children live in relative poverty. About

---

[3]These statistics refer to after-tax income. The proportion of the population living below LICO before taxes and transfers is considerably higher, as Figure 8–5 on page 266 shows.

965 250 children younger than age 15 (17.7 percent) lived in low-income families in 2010 (Statistics Canada, 2011d).

Race and Ethnicity

The majority of poor and low-income people are white. Data for 2006 show that across Canada, the 1.1 million visible minorities who lived in poverty accounted for 32 percent of all people living in poverty. However, the poverty rates for visible minorities are much higher than the national average, meaning that visible minorities have higher odds of being poor. In 2006, the 22 percent poverty rate for visible minority groups was twice that of the national average of 11 percent. And in major cities, visible minorities are represented among the poor in higher numbers than non-visible minorities: Visible minorities accounted for 58 percent of those living in poverty in Vancouver and 62 percent in Toronto (National Council of Welfare, 2012).

The 2011 census found that visible minorities had a low-income rate of 21.5 percent compared to 13.3 percent of non-visible minorities. The respective rates of low income vary from a low of 11.3 percent for Filipino Canadians and 14 percent for Japanese Canadians to a high of 34 percent for Arab Canadians and 36 percent for Korean Canadians (Statistics Canada, 2011d).

Pierre Puvis de Chavannes captured the humility and humanity of impoverished people in his painting *The Poor Fisherman*. This insight is important in a society that tends to define poor people as morally unworthy and deserving of their bitter plight.

Pierre Puvis de Chavannes (1824–1898), *The Poor Fisherman*.

The situation is even worse for Aboriginals, with a poverty rate of 31 percent, or almost one in three people (Statistics Canada, 2003a). Among Canadians of Aboriginal identity, 25.3 percent experienced low income in 2010. Aboriginal people in urban areas are more likely to experience low income (Collin & Jensen, 2009; Statistics Canada, 2011d).

Gender and Family Patterns

In 2010, the odds of being poor were 9.3 percent for women and 8.7 percent for men. Women who head households are at an even higher risk of poverty. The likelihood of being low-income is greater if the family is headed by a single woman (34.5 percent) than a single man (19.1 percent). Couple families, on the other hand, have below average poverty rates (9.6 percent) (Statistics Canada, 2011d; Citizens for Public Justice, 2012).

The term **feminization of poverty** describes *the trend of women making up an increasing proportion of the poor.* Analyzing differences between males and females, we notice that females have higher poverty rates than males in all age groups over 15 years of age (Statistics Canada, 2003b). In 2010, 15.8 percent of females were living on a low income compared to 13.9 percent for males, indicating a narrowing of the gap over the last few decades (Statistics Canada, 2011d). Once women have fallen into poverty, they also tend to remain poor for a longer period of time than men do. Between 2002 and 2007, 5.6 percent of females experienced poverty for four to six years, compared to 4.6 percent of males (Collin & Jensen, 2009).

feminization of poverty the trend of women making up an increasing proportion of the poor

The feminization of poverty is one result of a larger trend: the rapidly increasing number of households at all class levels headed by single women. This trend, coupled with the fact that households headed by women are at high risk of poverty, helps explain why women and their children make up an increasing share of the poor in Canada.

Urban and Rural Poverty

The 2006 census reported that the incidence of poverty is higher in urban areas than in rural areas, which is a phenomenon that has emerged in the last 20 years; before that time, the proportion living below the LICO was higher in rural areas (Statistics Canada, 2010).

Rural regions, however, do contain poverty, but it tends to be more "hidden." As researchers note, due to the isolation of many rural settings, poverty looks different there than it does in Canadian urban regions. Infrastructures that service the poor, such as soup kitchens or

Peter Horree/Alamy Stock Photo

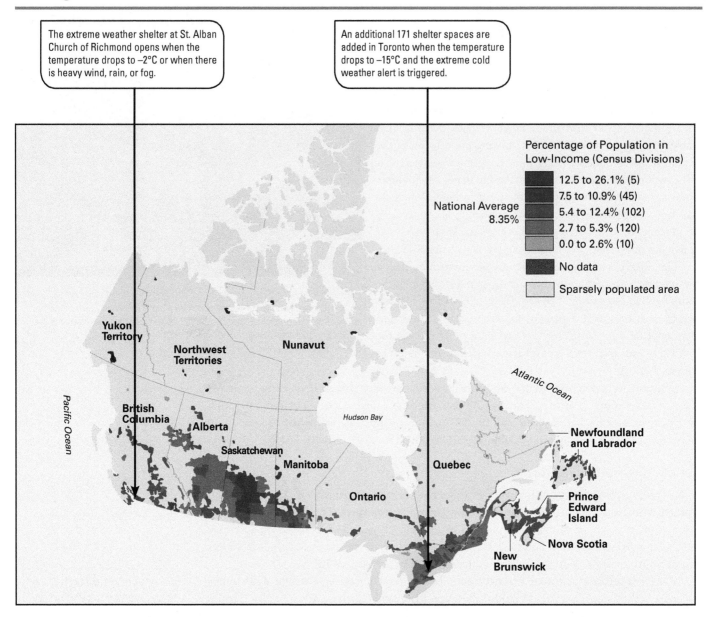

The extreme weather shelter at St. Alban Church of Richmond opens when the temperature drops to −2°C or when there is heavy wind, rain, or fog.

An additional 171 shelter spaces are added in Toronto when the temperature drops to −15°C and the extreme cold weather alert is triggered.

Percentage of Population in Low-Income (Census Divisions)

National Average 8.35%

- 12.5 to 26.1% (5)
- 7.5 to 10.9% (45)
- 5.4 to 12.4% (102)
- 2.7 to 5.3% (120)
- 0.0 to 2.6% (10)
- No data
- Sparsely populated area

NATIONAL MAP 8–1 Poverty Across Canada

The map shows the extent of poverty in different regions of Canada. There is a relatively high percentage in some of our largest urban centres but also in rural areas on the prairies and in eastern Canada. What is the poverty level where you live? Do you think that a high poverty level always coincides with a low median income level?

Source: Statistics Canada (2011e). Statistics Canada. Income Status after Tax and Economic Family Structure for the Economic Families in Private Households of Canada, Provinces, Census Divisions and Census Subdivisions, 2005–20% Sample Data. [Electronic Data File]. Catalogue no. 97-563-XCB2006040[1].IVT. 2011q. Reproduced and distributed on an "as is" basis with the permission of Statistics Canada.

drop-in centres, are not to be found in rural communities. Instead, rural poverty "tend[s] to be dispersed across unstable … forms of shelter in both built and natural environments" (Milbourne & Cloke, 2006; Halseth & Ryser, 2010:4).

National Map 8–1 provides a picture of the regional distribution of poverty in different parts of Canada.

Explaining Poverty

For one of the richest nations on Earth to contain millions of poor people raises serious questions. It is true, as some analysts remind us, that most poor people in Canada are far better off than the poor in other countries: For example, health care and education are publicly funded here. But there is little doubt that poverty harms the overall well-being of millions of people in this country.

Why is there poverty in the first place? We will examine two opposing explanations for poverty that lead to a lively and important political debate.

One View: Blame the Poor

One view holds that *the poor are mostly responsible for their own poverty*. Throughout this nation's history, people have placed a high cultural value on self-reliance, convinced that a person's social standing is mostly a matter of individual talent and effort. According to this view, society offers plenty of opportunities to anyone who is able and willing to take advantage of them, and the poor are people who cannot or will not work due to a lack of skills, schooling, or motivation.

In his study of poverty in Latin American cities, the anthropologist Oscar Lewis (1961) concluded that the poor become trapped in a *culture of poverty*, a lower-class subculture that can destroy people's ambition to improve their lives. Socialized in poor families, children become resigned to their situation, producing a self-perpetuating cycle of poverty.

Another View: Blame Society

A different position, argued by William Julius Wilson (1996a, 1996b; see also Mouw, 2000), holds that *society is primarily responsible for poverty*. Wilson points to the loss of jobs in our inner cities as the primary cause of poverty, claiming that there is simply not enough work to support families. Wilson sees any apparent lack of trying on the part of the poor as a result of little opportunity rather than as a cause of poverty. From Wilson's point of view, Lewis's analysis amounts to *blaming the victim*, that is, saying that victims are responsible for their own suffering.

To combat poverty and reduce the need for welfare, Wilson argues, the government must take the lead by investing in people and their communities. Such investments include funding jobs, providing affordable child care for low-income mothers and fathers, ensuring that schools teach both the language skills and the work skills that will prepare them for the types of jobs that will be available looking forward, and even expanding regional public transportation to help people get from where they live to the places where the jobs are.

The recent recession, along with increasing income inequality, has swelled the ranks of the poor to some 4.7 million people. As this section considered, especially vulnerable are children, the elderly, women, single-parent families, visible minorities, and Aboriginal people. Moreover, low income and the unemployment rate are closely associated. Such trends suggest that something more than people themselves—that is, traits of society—is at work (Foroohar, 2011; Yen, 2011).

EVALUATE The Canadian public is divided over whether the poor people or society is to be blamed for poverty. According to a Salvation Army study, about 50 percent of Canadians think that a family of four could get by on $10 000–$30 000 per year or less, and nearly half believe that "if poor people really want to work, they can always find a job." A minority, about 25 percent, stated that "people are poor because they are lazy and have lower moral values than average" (Salvation Army, 2011a).

Such opinions ignore that the *reasons* that people do not work are more in step with the "blame society" position. In other words, poverty stems from the structural features of our society, rather than from individual choices. Middle-class women may be able to combine working and child rearing, but this is much harder for poor women who cannot afford child care, and few employers provide child-care programs. As William Julius Wilson explains, many people are jobless not because they are avoiding work but because there are not enough jobs to go around. In short, the most effective way to reduce poverty is to ensure a greater supply of jobs as well as child care for parents who work (Wilson, 1996a; Bainbridge, Meyers, & Waldfogel, 2003).

CHECK YOUR LEARNING Explain the view that the poor should take responsibility for poverty and the view that society is responsible for poverty. Which is closer to your own view?

The Working Poor

Not all poor people are jobless, and the working poor command the sympathy and support of people on both sides of the poverty debate. In 2011, 6.4 percent of Canadians living in households where the main income recipient had 910 hours or more of paid work that year lived on a low income (Employment and Social Development Canada, 2015c). It is clear, then, that many poor families remained poor despite employment. A key cause for "working poverty" is that even two people working 40 hours per week, 52 weeks per year, cannot keep a family of four above the poverty line if they live in an urban area with a population of more than 500 000 and make only minimum wage, which in 2015 ranged from $10.20 per hour in Saskatchewan to $12.50 in Northwest Territories. In British Columbia, for example, a worker in metro Vancouver earning minimum wage ($10.45 per hour) and working full-year for 35 hours a week would earn $19 019—roughly $5500 less than what is needed for them to be above the poverty line (Ivanova, 2015). Currently, it would take an hourly wage of about $13.44 per hour to do that.

Individual ability and personal effort do play a part in shaping everyone's social position. However, the weight of sociological evidence points toward society, not individual character traits, as the primary source of poverty because more and more available jobs offer only low wages. Society must be at fault because the poor are categories of people—female heads of families, Aboriginal people, visible minorities, and people isolated from the larger society in inner-city neighbourhoods—who face special barriers and limited opportunities.

The Controversy & Debate box on page 273 takes a closer look at the current welfare debate. Understanding this important social issue can help us decide how our society should respond to the problem of poverty, as well as the problem of homelessness discussed next.

Homelessness

Many low-income people in Canada cannot afford even basic housing. There is no precise count of homeless people, but estimates suggest that in a year anywhere from 150 000 to 200 000 people access homeless services or sleep outside (Salvation Army, 2011b, 2013).

The familiar stereotypes of homeless people—men sleeping in doorways and women pushing rickety shopping carts containing everything they own—have been replaced by the "new homeless": people thrown out of work because of plant closings, women who take their children and leave home to escape domestic violence, women and men forced out of apartments by rent increases, children who run away from abusive families, and others unable to meet mortgage or rent payments because of low wages or no work at all. Today, no stereotype paints a complete picture of the homeless.

But virtually all homeless people have one thing in common: poverty. For that reason, the approaches already used in explaining poverty also apply to homelessness. One side of the debate places responsibility on personal traits of the homeless themselves. One-third of homeless people are substance abusers, and one-fourth have a serious mental illness. More broadly, a fraction of 1 percent of the population, for one reason or another, seems unable to cope with our complex and highly competitive society (Bassuk, 1984; Kaufman, 2004).

Others see homelessness resulting from societal factors, including discrimination, unemployment, stagnating incomes and low wages, and a lack of affordable housing. Supporters of this position point out that about 10 percent of families live below the LICO, and that children are the fastest-growing subcategory among the homeless. Others call attention to the myth that homeless people are "just like you and me." In fact, a 2009 survey of residents at Salvation Army shelters revealed that nearly 25 percent of the shelter population have jobs—but are still unable to make ends meet (Kozol, 1988; Bohannan, 1991; Casavant, 1999; Salvation Army, 2011b; Gaetz et al., 2013).

No one disputes that a large proportion of homeless people are personally impaired to some degree, although it is difficult to untangle how much is cause

Ryan Remiorz/The Canadian Press

Many young disadvantaged people are faced with little opportunity to improve their lives. Does this explain high substance abuse levels in some communities?

Controversy & Debate

The Welfare Dilemma: Canadian Perspectives

There is a remarkable consensus in this country regarding welfare: Nobody likes it. The political left criticizes it as an inadequate response to poverty, those on the right charge that it is hurting the people it allegedly helps and driving the country to bankruptcy, and the poor themselves find welfare to be a complex, confusing, and often degrading program.

Critics on the *political right* contend that welfare has actually worsened the problem of poverty for two reasons. First, it has eroded the traditional family by making it economically beneficial for women to have children outside of marriage and by contributing to the rapid rise in out-of-wedlock births among poor people. Second, government assistance undermines self-reliance among the poor and fosters dependency. Clearly, from the perspective of the right, welfare has strayed far from its original purpose of helping non-working women with children make the transition to self-sufficiency—typically, after divorce or the death of a husband. Instead, trapped in dependency, poor women raise children who will become poor adults.

The *political left* points to a double standard for assessing government social programs. Why, it asks, is there so much outrage at the thought of the government transferring money to poor mothers and children when most "welfare" goes to relatively rich people? From the perspective of the left, the amounts spent on welfare, while not negligible, pale in comparison with the tax writeoffs received by more affluent people for the registered retirement savings plans (RRSPs) they buy each year. And what about the billions of dollars in tax writeoffs for corporations, many of which are enjoying record profits? As the left sees it, "wealthfare" costs the country a great deal more than "welfare," even though public opinion supports the opposite view.

Critics claim that the political right—and much public opinion—distorts our understanding of the functions of social assistance. Images of irresponsible "welfare bums" mask the fact that most poor families who turn to public assistance are truly needy. Throughout Canada in recent years, the trend has been to slash welfare or social assistance rates as a deficit-reduction measure. Whatever the merits of social assistance, the political left faults it as a band-aid approach to the growing social problems of unemployment and poverty in Canada.

As for the charge that social assistance undermines families, the political left concedes that the proportion of single-parent families is rising, but disputes the argument that welfare is to blame. Rather, single parenting is a widespread cultural trend found at all class levels in most industrial societies. Therefore, leftist critics conclude, welfare or social assistance programs are not attacked because they have failed, but because they benefit poor people, a segment of the population long scorned as "undeserving." Our cultural tradition of equating wealth with virtue, and poverty with vice, allows rich people to display privilege as an indicator of ability—while poverty carries a negative stigma.

Many on the political right believe that welfare should be limited. Those on the left, in contrast, want to both improve and expand social assistance. Are there areas of common ground in this debate? In the mid-1990s, Conservative governments in Ontario and Alberta introduced reforms amounting to "workfare." Ontario's workfare program, called Ontario Works, still exists despite the fact that Liberals have formed the government since 2003. Is this an indicator of "common ground" between left and right?

What Do You Think?

1. Should provinces and territories slash their welfare budgets while allowing corporate tax writeoffs for the purchase of RRSPs?

2. Do you think welfare has become a way of life for many people?

3. Would an expanded welfare program lessen the extent of poverty in Canada? Why?

Source: Linda M. Gerber in Macionis and Gerber, *Sociology*, eighth Canadian edition (2014), p. 275. Used with permission.

---

and how much effect. But structural changes in the Canadian economy, the closing down of mental institutions in recent decades, and limited government support for lower-income people have all certainly contributed to homelessness.

Increasing Inequality, Increasing Controversy

8.12 Assess the trend toward increasing economic inequality in Canada.

There is a rising level of debate about income inequality in North America. The reason for the increasing controversy is simple—economic inequality has reached levels not seen in the United States since 1929, just before the Great Depression, and Canada since 1938, just before World War II. As shown in Figure 8–6 on page 274, the 1930s was

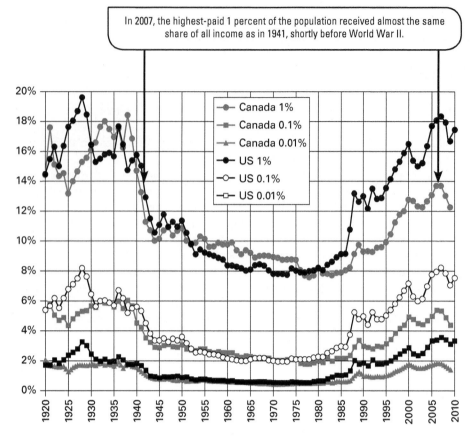

In 2007, the highest-paid 1 percent of the population received almost the same share of all income as in 1941, shortly before World War II.

FIGURE 8–6 Share of All Income Earned by the Richest 1, 0.1, and 0.01 percent, 1920–2010

In 1929, the richest 1 percent of the Canadian and U.S. population earned almost one-fourth of all income. This share declined in the decades that followed, dipping below 10 percent by the mid-1970s. In recent decades, however, the trend has been toward greater income inequality. In 2007, the highest-paid 1 percent of the population received almost the same share of all income as in 1941, during World War II.

Source: Veall (2012). Reprinted with permission of Canadian Journal of Economics.

a decade that saw steady gains in income for the highest-earning 1 percent of the population who, just before World War II, were receiving almost 20 percent of all income in Canada.

For several decades following World War II, the trend was toward greater income equality. By the 1970s, as the figure shows, the richest 1 percent received less than 10 percent of all income. During the last 30 years, however, the trend has reversed direction. In 2005, the highest-paid 1 percent of the population enjoyed about the same share of all income that the top earners received in 1925.

Canada has always been a nation in which most people expect some degree of economic inequality. This country's values of competitive individualism and personal responsibility support the idea that people should receive rewards in proportion to their talents, abilities, and efforts.

Even so, people are now losing confidence that this is, in fact, the case. In a recent survey, Canadian adults were presented with the statement "Income inequality is not an important public issue." In response, only 17 percent agreed while 73 percent disagreed (the remainder said that they neither agreed nor disagreed or that they did not know) (Graves, 2014). Other surveys find that a majority of people agree with the idea that "an excessive share of profits going to the wealthy" is a salient reason for economic stagnation (EKOS Research, 2013).

Are the Very Rich Worth the Money?

Such widespread concern about economic inequality suggests serious problems. First, in a society in which most think there is too much income inequality, people doubt that the highest-paid individuals are really worth the money they are paid. Certainly, there are some very smart, very talented, and very hardworking women and men in Canada who are rewarded with high incomes. People in the entertainment industry, like actress Rachel McAdams (net worth $14 million), television personality Howie Mandel (whose net worth is $40 million and who is paid about $70 000 for each episode of *America's Got Talent*), and comedian Russell Peters (net worth $40 million), earn more money than most of us may ever see. Even bigger stars like Mike Myers and Scott Speedman have a net worth of $175 million and $245 million, respectively. Such rewards are what we have come to expect very popular media stars to receive, and we may justify such pay because of the power these celebrities have to attract viewers and advertising money.

But we should be careful not to assume that income is directly related to talent, ability, and effort. In 2011, Alex Rodriguez of the New York Yankees took home the biggest paycheque among major league ballplayers, at $32 million. This amount almost equals the money paid that season to the entire Kansas City Royals team, whose players surely offer more talent, ability, and effort than even the single best player on the Yankees. Another Yankee—Babe Ruth—who was arguably the greatest ballplayer of all time, earned only

$80 000 (or $1.2 million in today's dollars) in his highest-paid seasons (1930 and 1931) with the Yankees.

Drawing inspiration from the Arab Spring movement, the Canadian-based anti-consumerist organization *Adbusters* created the hashtag #OCCUPYWALLSTREET on Twitter, thereby issuing the first call of the movement (*Adbusters*, 2011; Yardley, 2011). The Occupy movement gained support across Canada and the United States, and inspired citizen action around the world to criticize the very high pay that a small share of corporate leaders receives. In 2011, according to *Forbes* magazine, John Hammergren, CEO of McKesson Pharmaceuticals, was the highest-earning American CEO, receiving total compensation of $131 million in salary, bonus, stock options, and other perks; in Canada, it was Frank Stronach, who received $40.9 million. That year, Canada's 100 highest-paid CEOs, or the 0.01 percent, averaged just over $7 million each in earnings. Stated differently, by January 3, 2011, the top 100 Canadian CEOs each gained what it takes the average Canadian worker working full time till the end of the year to earn. Back in 1995, the compensation of the 50 highest-paid Canadian CEOs was about 85 times what the average company employee earned. In 2010, the top 50 CEOs earned about 255 times the company average, so the upward trend shows no sign of ending (Mackenzie, 2012; Tedesco, 2013; Tencer, 2013).

Defenders of such high pay claim that companies pay whatever it takes to attract the brightest and the most talented people to top leadership, which helps companies perform better. Critics counter that company performance is not clearly linked to CEO rewards—half of the companies paying top salaries to CEOs actually lost money in their most recent year (Helman, 2011; NORC, 2011).

In 2011, with economic inequality increasing, the Occupy movement emerged. This groundswell of anger and activism put much of the blame for the recent recession and growing inequality on the very rich.

Michael Hudson/The Canadian Press

Can the Rest of Us Get Ahead?

A second problem that accompanies increasing inequality is rising doubt that people who are willing to work hard can get ahead. The idea that those willing to make the effort can enjoy economic security and expect to improve social standing over time is at the heart of the Canadian dream. But, in recent decades, while people at the top of the income hierarchy have been generously rewarded, average people who work hard have been struggling to hang on to what they have. With good-paying jobs harder to find, it is not surprising that the share of people who say that they believe their children can surpass their parents' financial achievements has declined in the last decade. Relatedly, while over 60 percent of the U.S. and Canadian public identified themselves as middle class in 2002, by 2012 that number had dropped to 46 percent in the United States and 47 percent in Canada (Graves, 2014).

Today, the public's awareness of economic inequality is as high as it has been since the Great Depression of the 1930s. Should the trend toward greater economic inequality persist, and should the loss of confidence in our system of social inequality continue, the demands for basic change to our society are sure to intensify.

Finally, as we debate the shape of inequality here at home, we must remember that the drama of social stratification extends far beyond the borders of Canada. The most striking social inequality is found not by looking inside one country but by comparing living standards in various parts of the world. In Chapter 9, we broaden our focus by investigating global stratification.

Seeing Sociology in Everyday Life

CHAPTER 8 Social Stratification

How do we understand inequality in Canada?

This chapter sketches the class structure of Canada and how people end up in their positions in our system of social inequality. How accurately do you think the mass media reflect the reality of inequality in our society? Look at the three photos of television shows, one from back in the 1950s and the other two from today. What messages about social standing, and how we get there, does each show convey?

In *The Millionaire*, a popular television show that ran from 1955 until 1960, a very rich man (who was never fully shown on camera) had the curious hobby of giving away $1 million to other people he had never even met. Each week, he gave his personal assistant, Michael Anthony, a cheque to pass along to "the next millionaire." Anthony tracked down the person and handed over the money, and the story went on to reveal how such great wealth from out of nowhere changed someone's life for better (or sometimes for worse). What does this story line seem to suggest about social class position?

In the TV show *The Bachelor Canada*, first aired in 2012, a young bachelor works his way through a collection of 25 attractive young women, beginning with group dates, moving on to overnight visits with three "finalists," and (in most cases) proposing to his "final selection." Much of the interaction takes place in a lavish, 13 500-square-foot home located at a golf resort near Victoria, British Columbia. What does this show suggest is the key to social position? What message does this show promote about the importance of marriage for women?

Everett Collection

Brian Patterson/Corbis

Property Virgins, which began in 2006, follows first-time home buyers (i.e., "property virgins") as they learn to manoeuvre the housing market, their budgets, and their visions of a new dream home. What messages about social position and property does this show present to young people?

Aaron Harris/The Canadian Press

HINT In general, the mass media present social standing as a reflection of an individual's personal traits and sometimes sheer luck. In *The Millionaire*, wealth was visited on some people for no apparent reason at all. In *The Bachelor Canada*, women try to gain the approval of a man. In *Property Virgins,* the key to successful homeownership is learning to compromise expectations in order to match the reality of housing markets. But social structure is also involved in ways that we easily overlook. Is becoming a millionaire really a matter of luck? Is there any significance to the fact that (as of 2015) all the bachelors on that show have been white? Does everyone who learns to compromise have an equal chance to become a homeowner? Does social standing result from personal competition as much as television shows suggest?

Seeing Sociology in *Your* Everyday Life

1. During an evening of television viewing, assess the social class level of the characters you see on various shows. In each case, explain why you assign someone a particular social position. Do you find many clearly upper-class people? Middle-class people? Working-class people? Poor people? Describe the patterns you find.

2. Go to www.sociologyinfocus.com to access the Sociology in Focus blog, where you can read the latest posts by a team of young sociologists who apply the sociological perspective to topics of popular culture.

3. Social stratification involves how a society distributes resources. It also has a relational dimension—social inequality guides *with whom* we do and do not interact and also *how* we interact with people. Can you give examples of how social class differences guide social interaction in your everyday life?

Michael Hudson/The Canadian Press

Making the Grade

What Is Social Stratification?

8.1 Identify four principles that underlie social stratification. (pages 236–237)

- **Social stratification** is a trait of society, not simply a reflection of individual differences; carries over from one generation to the next; is supported by a system of cultural beliefs that defines certain kinds of inequality as just; takes two general forms: caste systems and class systems.

social stratification a system by which a society ranks categories of people in a hierarchy

social mobility a change in position within the social hierarchy

Caste and Class Systems

8.2 Apply the concepts of caste, class, and meritocracy to societies around the world. (pages 237–246)

- **Caste systems** are based on birth (ascription); permit little or no social mobility; shape a person's entire life, including occupation and marriage; are common in traditional, agrarian societies.
- **Class systems** are based on both birth (ascription) and **meritocracy** (individual achievement); permit some social mobility; are common in modern industrial and post-industrial societies.

caste system social stratification based on ascription, or birth

class system social stratification based on both birth and individual achievement

meritocracy social stratification based on personal merit

status consistency the degree of uniformity in a person's social standing across various dimensions of social inequality

structural social mobility a shift in the social position of large numbers of people due more to changes in society itself than to individual efforts

ideology cultural beliefs that justify particular social arrangements, including patterns of inequality

The Functions of Social Stratification

8.3 Apply structural-functional theory to the topic of social inequality. (pages 246–248)

Structural-functional theory points to ways social stratification helps society operate.

- The **Davis-Moore thesis** states that social stratification is universal because of its functional consequences.
- In caste systems, people are rewarded for performing the duties of their position at birth.
- In class systems, unequal rewards attract the ablest people to the most important jobs and encourage effort.

Davis-Moore thesis the functional analysis claiming that social stratification has beneficial consequences for the operation of society

Explaining Stratification: Social-Conflict Theories

8.4 Apply social-conflict theories to the topic of social inequality. (pages 248–251)

Social-conflict theory claims that stratification divides societies in classes, benefiting some categories of people at the expense of others and causing social conflict.

- Karl Marx claimed that capitalism places economic production under the ownership of capitalists, who exploit the proletarians, who sell their labour for wages.
- Max Weber identified three distinct dimensions of social stratification: economic class, social status or prestige, and power. Conflict exists between people at various positions on a multidimensional hierarchy of **socio-economic status (SES)**.

capitalists people who own and operate factories and other businesses in pursuit of profits

proletarians people who sell their labour for wages

alienation the experience of isolation and misery resulting from powerlessness

blue-collar occupations lower-prestige jobs that involve mostly manual labour

white-collar occupations higher-prestige jobs that involve mostly mental activity

socio-economic status (SES) a composite ranking based on various dimensions of social inequality

Explaining Stratification: Symbolic-Interaction Theory

8.5 Apply symbolic-interaction theory to the topic of social inequality. (pages 251–252)

Symbolic-interaction theory, a micro-level analysis that explores how inequality shapes everyday life, explains that we size people up by looking for clues to their social standing. **Conspicuous consumption** refers to buying and displaying products that make a "statement" about social class. Most people tend to socialize with others whose social standing is similar to their own.

conspicuous consumption buying and using products because of the "statement" they make about social position

Stratification and Technology: A Global Perspective

8.6 Analyze the link between a society's technology and its social stratification. (pages 252–254)

Hunting/Gathering ──→ Horticultural/Pastoral ──→ Agrarian ─────→ Industrial ─────→ Post-industrial

- Gerhard Lenski explains that advancing technology initially increases social stratification, which is most intense in agrarian societies.
- Industrialization reverses the trend, reducing social stratification.
- In post-industrial societies, social stratification again increases.

Inequality in Canada

(8.7) Describe the distribution of income and wealth in Canada. (pages 254–258)

> income earnings from work or investments
>
> wealth the total value of money and other assets, minus outstanding debts

Social stratification involves many dimensions:

- *Income*—Earnings from work and investments are unequal, with the richest 20 percent of families earning 43.6 percent of all income and the poorest 20 percent of families earning 4.3 percent.
- *Wealth*—The total value of all assets minus debts, wealth is distributed more unequally than income, with the richest 20 percent of families holding 67.4 percent of all wealth.
- *Power*—Income and wealth are important sources of power.
- *Occupational prestige*—White-collar jobs generally offer more income and prestige than blue-collar jobs. Many lower-prestige jobs are performed by women and people of colour.
- *Schooling*—Schooling affects occupation and income. Some categories of people have greater opportunities for schooling than others.
- *Family ancestry, race and ethnicity,* and *gender* all affect social standing.

Social Classes in Canada

(8.8) Discuss the various social class positions in Canadian society. (pages 258–261)

- **upper class**—5 percent of the population; earn family incomes above $125 000. Most in *upper-upper class* ("old rich") inherit wealth; *lower-upper class* ("new rich") work at high-paying jobs.
- **middle class**—40 to 45 percent of the population; average family income $62 000–$125 000. The *upper-middle class* has significant wealth; *average-middles* have less prestige, do white-collar work, and most attend college.
- **working class**—30 to 35 percent of the population; average family income $38 500–$62 000. People in the *lower-middle class* do blue-collar work; one-quarter of children attend college.
- **lower class**—20 percent of the population; average family income below $38 500. Most people lack financial security; many live below the poverty line; just 70 percent of children complete high school.

The Difference Class Makes

(8.9) Analyze how social class position affects health, values, politics, and family life. (pages 261–263)

- People with higher social standing generally have better health, hold certain values and political attitudes, and pass on advantages in the form of "cultural capital" to their children.

Social Mobility

(8.10) Assess the extent of social mobility in Canada. (pages 263–268)

> intragenerational social mobility a change in social position occurring during a person's lifetime
>
> intergenerational social mobility upward or downward social mobility of children in relation to their parents

- Social mobility is common in Canada, as it is in other high-income countries, but typically only small changes occur from one generation to the next.
- Due to the expansion of the global, post-industrial economy, the richest families now earn more than ever; families near the bottom of the class system have seen only small increases.

Poverty in Canada

(8.11) Summarize patterns and explanations of poverty in the Canadian population. (pages 268–273)

> relative poverty the lack of resources of some people in relation to those who have more
>
> absolute poverty a lack of resources that is life-threatening
>
> feminization of poverty the trend of women making up an increasing proportion of the poor

- The government classifies 4.7 million people—15 percent of the population—as poor.
- About 17.7 percent of the poor are under age 15.
- The majority of the poor are white, but in relation to their population, visible minorities and Aboriginal peoples are more likely to be poor.
- About 6.4 percent of Canadians live in poor households where the heads of families work at least part time.
- An estimated 150 000 to 200 000 people are homeless for some time during the course of a year.

Explanations of Poverty

- Blame individuals: The *culture of poverty* thesis states that poverty is caused by shortcomings in the poor themselves (Oscar Lewis).
- Blame society: Poverty is caused by society's unequal distribution of wealth and lack of good jobs (William Julius Wilson).
- The fact that almost half of the Canadian population is either poor or low-income (living with income at less than twice the poverty level) suggests that society more than individual traits is the main cause of poverty.

Increasing Inequality, Increasing Controversy

(8.12) Assess the trend toward increasing economic inequality in Canada. (pages 273–275)

- In recent decades, income inequality has increased, and surveys show most people think income differences are too large.

9 Global Stratification

LEARNING OBJECTIVES

9.1 Describe the division of the world into high-, middle-, and low-income countries.

9.2 Discuss patterns and explanations of poverty around the world.

9.3 Apply sociological theories to the topic of global inequality.

9.4 Evaluate trends in global inequality.

the Power of Society

to determine a child's chance of survival to age five

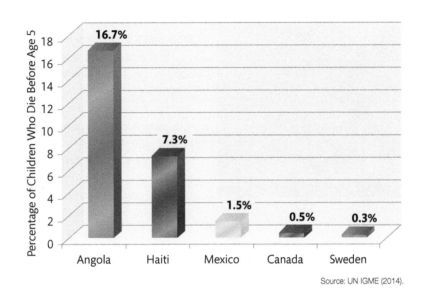

Source: UN IGME (2014).

In a world of unequal economic development, how does a child's country of birth affect the chances of survival? Of all children born in Angola, a low-income nation in southern Africa, 16.7 percent die before reaching the age of five. In Haiti, another low-income nation, 7.3 percent of children suffer this fate. In high-income nations, the share is much lower. In Canada, less than 1 percent of children will die so early in life. And in nations with more extensive social welfare systems, such as Sweden, the share is even lower.

Chapter Overview

Social stratification involves not just people within a single country; it is also a world-wide pattern of inequality among nations. This chapter shifts the focus from inequality within Canada to inequality in the world as a whole. The chapter begins by describing global inequality and then provides two theoretical models that explain global stratification.

x99/ZUMA Press/Newscom

More than 1000 workers were busily sewing together polo shirts on the fourth floor of the garment factory in Narsingdi, a small town about 50 kilometres northeast of Bangladesh's capital city of Dhaka. The thumping of hundreds of sewing machines produced a steady roar throughout the long working day.

But in an instant everything changed when an electric gun used to shoot spot remover onto stained fabric gave off a spark. Suddenly, a work table burst into flames. People rushed to smother the fire with shirts, but there was no stopping the blaze: In a room filled with combustible materials, the flames spread quickly.

The workers scrambled toward the narrow staircase that led to the street. At the bottom, however, the human wave pouring down the steep steps collided with a folding metal gate across the doorway that was kept locked to prevent workers from leaving during working hours. Panicked, the people turned, only to be pushed back by the hundreds behind them. In a single terrifying minute of screaming voices, thrusting legs, and pounding hearts, dozens were crushed and trampled. By the time the gates were opened and the fire put out, 52 garment workers lay dead.

Deadly fires such as this one occur regularly in Asian garment factories, where safety standards do not adequately protect workers. In recent years, almost 100 garment workers have perished annually in such fires in Bangladesh alone. Garment factories like this one are big business in this low-income nation, where clothing accounts for 78 percent of Bangladesh's total economic exports. One-quarter of these garments end up in stores in North America. The reason so much of the clothing we buy is made in poor countries like Bangladesh is simple economics: Bangladeshi garment workers, a large majority of whom are women, labour for close to 12 hours a day, typically six days a week, and yet rarely earn much more than that nation's minimum wage of $443 a month, a small fraction of what garment workers make in Canada.

Tanveer Chowdhury manages the garment factory owned by his family where this fire took place. Speaking to reporters, he complained bitterly about the tragedy. "This fire has cost me $586 373, and that does not include $70 000 for machinery and $20 000 for furniture. I made commitments to meet deadlines, and I still have the deadlines. I am now paying for air freight at $10 a dozen when I should be shipping by sea at 87 cents a dozen."

There was one other cost Chowdhury did not mention. To compensate families for the loss of their loved ones in the fire, he eventually agreed to pay $1952 per person. In Bangladesh, life—like labour—is cheap (based on Bearak, 2001; Hossain, 2011; Bangladesh Garment Manufacturers & Exporters Association, 2012; World Bank, 2012a).

G arment workers in Bangladesh are among the roughly 1.3 billion of the world's people who work hard every day and yet remain poor (Chen & Ravallion, 2012). As this chapter explains, although poverty is a reality in Canada and other nations, the greatest social inequality is not *within* nations but *between* them (Goesling, 2001). We can understand the full dimensions of poverty only by exploring **global stratification**, *patterns of social inequality in the world as a whole.*

global stratification patterns of social inequality in the world as a whole

Global Stratification: An Overview

9.1 Describe the division of the world into high-, middle-, and low-income countries.

Chapter 8 ("Social Stratification") described social inequality in Canada. Compared to social inequality in Canada, social stratification is far greater in global perspective. The pie chart at the left in Figure 9–1 divides the world's total income by quintiles (fifths) of the population. Recall from Chapter 8 that the richest 20 percent of the Canadian population with the highest incomes earns about 44 percent of the national income. The richest 20 percent of the global population, however, receives about 77 percent of world income. At the other extreme, the poorest 20 percent of the Canadian population earns about 4 percent of the national income; the poorest fifth of the world's people similarly struggles to survive on just 2 percent of global income. Remember that Chapter 8 ("Social Stratification") also shows the impact of progressive taxation and government support to low-income earners. Because of these policies, the 20 percent of the Canadian population with the lowest income earns a little more than 7 percent of the national income after transfer payment and taxes.

In terms of wealth, as the pie chart at the right in Figure 9–1 shows, global inequality is even greater. A rough estimate is that the richest 20 percent of the world's adults own about 94 percent of the planet's wealth. About half of all wealth is owned by about 1 percent of the world's adult population. On the other extreme, the poorest half of the world's adults own less than 1 percent of all global wealth. In terms of dollars, about half of the world's families have less than $3710 in total wealth, far less than the $243 800 in wealth for the typical Canadian family (Davies, Lluberas, & Shorrocks, 2012; Statistics Canada, 2014).

Because Canada is among the world's richest countries, even people in Canada with income below the government's poverty line live far better than the majority of people on the planet (Milanovic, 2011). The average person in a wealthy nation such as Canada is extremely well off by world standards. Any one of the world's richest *people* (in 2011, the world's three richest people—Carlos Slim Helú in Mexico, Bill Gates and Warren Buffett in the United States—were *each* worth more than $44 billion) has more personal wealth than the total economic output of more than 100 of the world's *countries* (Forbes, 2012; World Bank, 2012b).

A Word About Terminology

Classifying the 195 independent nations on Earth into categories ignores many striking differences. These nations have rich and varied histories, speak different languages, and take pride in their distinctive cultures. However, various models have been developed that help distinguish countries on the basis of global stratification.

One global model, developed after World War II, labelled the rich, industrial countries the "First World"; the less industrialized, socialist countries the "Second World"; and the non-industrialized, poor countries the "Third World." But the "three

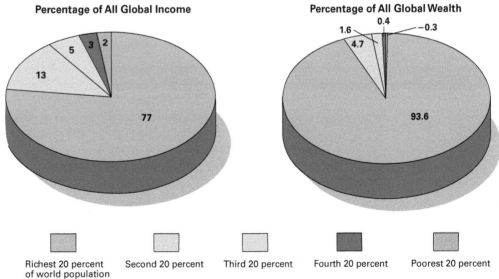

FIGURE 9–1 Distribution of Global Income and Wealth

Global income is very unequal, with the richest 20 percent of the world's people earning almost 40 times as much as the poorest 20 percent. Global wealth is even more unequally divided, with the richest 20 percent owning 94 percent of private wealth and the poorest half of the world's people having barely anything at all.

Sources: Milanovic (2009, 2011); Davies, Lluberas, and Shorrocks (2012).

Canada is among the world's high-income countries, in which industrial technology and economic expansion have produced material prosperity. The presence of market forces is evident in this view of downtown Toronto (*above, left*). India has recently become one of the world's middle-income countries (*above, right*). An increasing number of motor vehicles fill city streets. Afghanistan is among the world's low-income countries (*left*). As the photograph suggests, low-income countries have limited economic development and rapidly increasing populations. The result is widespread poverty.

worlds" model is less useful today. For one thing, it was a product of Cold War politics by which the capitalist West (the First World) faced off against the socialist East (the Second World) while other nations (the Third World) remained more or less on the sidelines. But the sweeping changes in Eastern Europe and the collapse of the former Soviet Union in the early 1990s mean that a distinctive Second World no longer exists.

Another problem is that the "three worlds" model lumped together more than 100 countries as the Third World. In reality, some relatively better-off nations of the Third World (such as Chile in South America) have 15 times the per-person productivity of the poorest countries of the world (such as Ethiopia in East Africa).

These facts call for a modestly revised system of classification. The 74 high-income countries are defined as the *nations with the highest overall standards of living*. These nations have a per capita gross national income (GNI) greater than $12 500. The world's 72 middle-income countries are not as rich; they are *nations with a standard of living about average for the world as a whole*. Their per capita GNI is less than $12 500 but greater than $2500. The remaining 49 low-income countries are *nations with a low standard of living in which most people are poor*. In these nations, per capita GNI is less than $2500 (United Nations Development Programme, 2012; World Bank, 2012b).

This model has two advantages over the older "three worlds" system. First, it focuses on economic development rather than political structure (capitalist or socialist). Second, it gives a better picture of the relative economic development of various countries because it does not lump together all less developed nations into a single "Third World."

When envisioning global stratification, keep in mind that there is social stratification within every nation. In Bangladesh, for example, members of the Chowdhury family, who own the garment factory described in the chapter-opening story, earn as much as $1 million per year, which is several thousand times more than their workers earn. The full extent

When natural disasters strike high-income nations, property damage may be great, but the loss of life is relatively low. For example, the 2010 earthquake in Chile (*left*) forced people from damaged homes but the death toll for the entire nation was about 400. By contrast, when another earthquake hit Haiti in 2010 (*right*), less well-built structures came tumbling down, resulting in more than 300 000 deaths.

of global inequality is even greater, because the wealthiest people in rich countries such as Canada live worlds apart from the poorest people in low-income nations such as Bangladesh, Haiti, and Sudan.

High-Income Countries

In nations where the Industrial Revolution first took place more than two centuries ago, productivity increased more than one hundredfold. To understand the power of industrial and computer technology, consider that South Korea—a small Asian nation about the size of Newfoundland—is as economically productive as the whole continent of Africa south of the Sahara, which has a land area more than twice the size of Canada.

Global Map 9–1 on page 286 shows that the high-income nations of the world include Canada, the United States, Mexico, Argentina, Chile, the nations of Western Europe, Israel, Saudi Arabia, Singapore, Hong Kong (part of the People's Republic of China), Japan, South Korea, the Russian Federation, Malaysia, Australia, and New Zealand.

These countries cover roughly 47 percent of Earth's land area, including parts of five continents, and they lie mostly in the Northern Hemisphere. In 2011, the population of these nations was about 1.6 billion, or about 23 percent of the world's people. About three-fourths of the people in high-income countries live in or near cities (Population Reference Bureau, 2012a; World Bank, 2012a).

Significant cultural differences exist among high-income countries; for example, the nations of Europe recognize more than 30 official languages. But these societies all produce enough economic goods and services to enable their people to lead comfortable lives. Per capita annual income (that is, average income per person per year) ranges from about $13 000 annually (in Venezuela, Bulgaria, and Lebanon) to more than $45 000 annually (in the United States, Norway, and Singapore). In fact, the people who live in high-income countries enjoy 64 percent of the world's total income.

In a high-income nation such as Canada, even the poor have a higher economic standard of living than about half the people in a middle-income nation such as Brazil and almost all of the people in a (less well-off) middle-income nation such as China (Milanovic, 2011). Even so, the populations of high-income countries include many low-income people. The Thinking About Diversity box on page 287 profiles the striking poverty that exists in *las colonias* along the southern border of the United States. Production in rich nations is capital-intensive; it is based on factories, big machinery, and advanced technology. Most of the largest corporations that design and market computers, as well as most computer users, are located in high-income countries. High-income countries control the world's financial markets, so daily events in

Window on the World

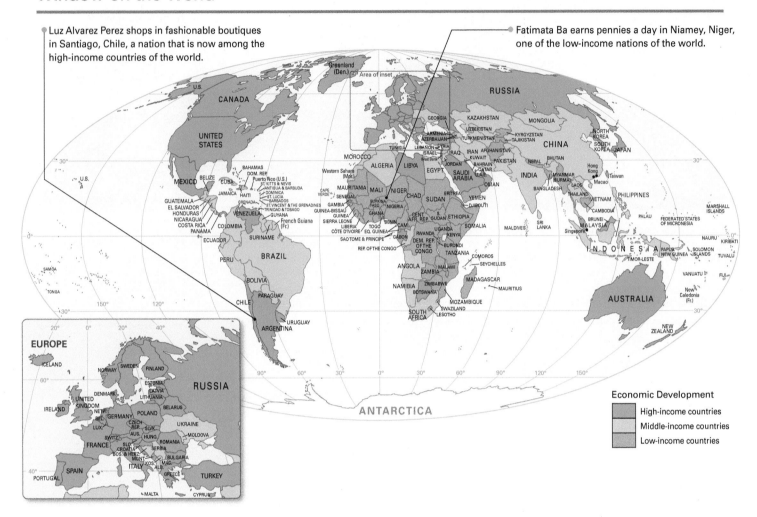

Luz Alvarez Perez shops in fashionable boutiques in Santiago, Chile, a nation that is now among the high-income countries of the world.

Fatimata Ba earns pennies a day in Niamey, Niger, one of the low-income nations of the world.

Economic Development

- High-income countries
- Middle-income countries
- Low-income countries

GLOBAL MAP 9–1 Economic Development in Global Perspective

In high-income countries—including Canada, the United States, Mexico, Chile, Argentina, the nations of Western Europe, Israel, Saudi Arabia, Singapore, Hong Kong, South Korea, Malaysia, Australia, the Russian Federation, Japan, and New Zealand—a highly productive economy provides people, on average, with material plenty. Middle-income countries—including most of South America and Asia— are less economically productive, with a standard of living about average for the world as a whole but far below that of Canada. These nations also have a significant share of poor people who are barely able to feed and house themselves. In the low-income countries of the world, poverty is severe and widespread. Although small numbers of elites live very well in the poorest nations, most people struggle to survive on a small fraction of the income common in Canada.

Note: Data for this map are provided by the United Nations and the World Bank. Each country's economic productivity is measured in terms of its gross national income (GNI), which is the total value of all the goods and services produced by a country's economy within its borders in a given year, plus net compensation and property income from abroad. Dividing each country's GNI by the country's population gives us the per capita (per person) GNI and allows us to compare the economic performance of countries of different population sizes. High-income countries have a per capita GNI of more than $12 500. Many are far richer than this, however; the figure for the United States exceeds $48 000. Middle-income countries have a per capita GNI ranging from $2500 to $12 500. Low-income countries have a per capita GNI of less than $2500. Figures used here reflect the World Bank's "purchasing power parities" (PPP) system, which is an estimate of what people can buy using their income in the local economy.

Source: Data from United Nations Development Programme (2012) and the World Bank (2012a).

the financial exchanges of Toronto, New York, London, Frankfurt, and Tokyo affect people throughout the world. In short, rich nations are very productive because of their advanced technology and also because they control the global economy.

Middle-Income Countries

Middle-income countries have per capita income of between $2500 and $12 500, close to the median (about $8350) for the world's nations. About 52 percent of the people in middle-income countries live in or near cities, and industrial jobs are common. The remaining

Thinking About Diversity: Race, Class, and Gender

Las Colonias: "America's Third World"

"We wanted to have something for ourselves," explains Olga Ruiz, who has lived in the border community of College Park, Texas, for 11 years. There is no college in College Park, nor does this dusty stretch of rural land have sewer lines or even running water. Yet this town is one of some 2300 settlements that have sprouted up in southern Texas along the 2000-kilometre border with Mexico that runs from El Paso to Brownsville. Together, they are home to roughly 500 000 people.

Many people speak of *las colonias* (Spanish for "the colonies") as "America's Third World" because these desperately poor communities look much like their counterparts in Mexico or in many other middle- or low-income nations. But almost all of the people living in the *colonias* are Mexican Americans; 85 percent of them are documented residents and more than half are U.S. citizens.

Anastacia Ledsema, now 72 years old, moved to a *colonia* called Sparks more than 40 years ago. Born in Mexico, Ledsema married a Texas man, and together they paid $200 for a quarter-acre lot in a new border community. For months, they camped out on their land. Step by step, however, they invested their labour and

Alison Wright/Corbis

their money to build a modest house. Not until 1995 did their small community get running water—a service that had been promised by developers years earlier. When the water line finally did arrive, however, things changed more than they had expected. "When we got water," recalls Ledsema, "that's when so many people came in." The population of Sparks quickly doubled to about 3000, overwhelming the water supply so that sometimes the faucet does not run at all.

The residents of all the *colonias* know that they are poor, and with annual per capita income of about $6000, they are. The U.S. Census Bureau has declared the county surrounding one border community to be the poorest in the United States. Concerned over the lack of basic services in so many of these communities, Texas officials have banned new settlements. But most of the people who move here—even those who start off sleeping in their cars or trucks—see these communities as the first step on the path to the American dream. Oscar Solis, a neighbourhood leader in Panorama Village, a community with a population of about 150, is proud to show visitors around the small but growing town. "All of this work we have done ourselves," he says with a smile, "to make our dream come true."

What Do You Think?

1. Are you surprised that such intense poverty exists in a rich country like the United States? Why or why not?

2. Does Canada have similar communities where poverty rates look much like communities in many middle- or low-income nations? What about Vancouver's Downtown Eastside and many Aboriginal communities?

3. To what extent do you think the people living in these communities will have their "dreams come true"? Explain your answer.

Source: Based on Schaffer (2002) and *The Economist* (2011).

48 percent of the people live in rural areas, where most are poor and lack access to schools, medical care, adequate housing, and even safe drinking water.

Looking at Global Map 9–1, we see that 72 of the world's nations fall into the middle-income category. At the high end are Costa Rica (Latin America), Serbia (Europe), and Kazakhstan (Asia), where annual income is about $11 000. At the low end are Nicaragua (Latin America), Cape Verde (Africa), and Vietnam (Asia), with roughly $3000 annually in per capita income.

One cluster of middle-income countries used to be part of the Second World. These countries, found in Eastern Europe and Western Asia, had mostly socialist economies until popular revolts between 1989 and 1991 swept their governments aside. Since then, these nations have introduced more free-market systems. These middle-income countries include Ukraine, Uzbekistan, Georgia, and Turkmenistan.

Other middle-income nations include Peru and Brazil in South America and Namibia and South Africa in Africa. Both India and the People's Republic of China have entered the middle-income category, which now includes most of Asia.

Taken together, middle-income countries span roughly 35 percent of the Earth's land area and are home to about 4.2 billion people, or about 60 percent of humanity. Some very large countries (such as China) are far less crowded than other small nations (such as El Salvador), but compared to high-income countries, these societies are densely populated.

Low-Income Countries

Low-income countries, where most people are very poor, are mostly agrarian societies with some industry. Forty-nine low-income countries, identified in Global Map 9–1 on page 286, are spread across Central and East Africa and Asia. Low-income countries cover 17 percent of the planet's land area and are home to about 1.2 billion people, or 17 percent of humanity. Population density is generally high, although it is greater in Asian countries (such as Bangladesh) than in Central African nations (such as Chad and the Democratic Republic of the Congo).

In poor countries, 35 percent of the people live in cities; most inhabit villages and farms as their ancestors have done for centuries. In fact, half the world's people are farmers, most of whom follow cultural traditions. With limited industrial technology, they cannot be very productive, one reason that many suffer severe poverty. Hunger, disease, and unsafe housing shape the lives of the world's poorest people.

Those of us who live in rich nations such as Canada find it hard to understand the scope of human need that exists in much of the world. From time to time, televised pictures of famine in very poor countries such as Ethiopia and Bangladesh give us shocking glimpses of the poverty that makes every day a life-and-death struggle for many people in low-income nations. Behind these images lie cultural, historical, and economic forces that we shall explore in the remainder of this chapter.

Global Wealth and Poverty

9.2 Discuss patterns and explanations of poverty around the world.

October 14, Manila, Philippines. What caught my eye was how clean she was—a girl no more than seven or eight years old. She was wearing a freshly laundered dress, and her hair was carefully combed. She stopped to watch us, following us with her eyes: Camera-toting North Americans stand out here, in one of the poorest neighbourhoods in the entire world.

Fed by methane from decomposing garbage, the fires never go out on Smokey Mountain, the vast garbage dump on the north side of Manila. Smoke covers the hills of refuse like a thick fog. But Smokey Mountain is more than a dump; it is a neighbourhood that is home to thousands of people. It is hard to imagine a setting more hostile to human life. Amid the smoke and the squalor, men and women do what they can to survive. They pick plastic bags from the garbage and wash them in the river, and they collect cardboard boxes or anything else they can sell. What chance do their children have, coming from families that earn only a few hundred dollars a year, with hardly any opportunity for schooling, breathing this foul air year after year? Against this backdrop of human tragedy, one lovely little girl has put on a fresh dress and gone out to play.

Now our taxi driver threads his way through heavy traffic as we head for the other side of Manila. The change is amazing: The smoke and smell of the dump give way to neighbourhoods that could be in Halifax or Victoria. A cluster of yachts floats on the bay in the distance. No more rutted streets; now we glide quietly along wide boulevards lined with trees and filled with expensive Japanese cars. We pass shopping plazas, upscale hotels, and high-rise office buildings. Every block or so we see the gated entrance to yet another exclusive residential community with security guards standing watch. Here, in large, air-conditioned homes, the rich of Manila live—and many of the poor work.

Low-income nations are home to some rich and many poor people. The fact that most people live on incomes of just a few hundred dollars a year means that the burden of poverty is far greater there than among the poor of Canada. This is not to suggest that Canadian poverty is a minor problem. In so rich a country, too little food, substandard housing, and tens of thousands who are homeless—many of whom are children—amount to a national tragedy (Hwang, 2001).

The Severity of Poverty

Poverty in poor countries is more severe than it is in rich countries. A key reason that the quality of life differs so much around the world is that economic productivity is lowest in precisely the regions where population growth is highest. Figure 9–2 shows the proportion of world population and global income for countries at each level of economic development. High-income countries are by far the most advantaged, with 64 percent of global income supporting just 23 percent of humanity. In middle-income nations, 60 percent of the world's people earn 33 percent of global income. This leaves 17 percent of the planet's population with just 3 percent of global income. In short, for every dollar received by individuals in a low-income country, someone in a high-income country takes home $14.

Table 9–1 on page 290 shows the extent of wealth and well-being in specific countries around the world. The first column of figures gives GNI for a number of high-, middle-, and low-income countries.[1] The United States, a large and highly productive nation, had a 2011 GNI of more than $15 trillion; Japan's GNI was $4.5 trillion; Canada's was $1.3 trillion. A comparison of GNI figures shows that the world's richest nations are thousands of times more productive than the poorest countries.

The second column of figures in Table 9–1 divides GNI by the entire population size to give an estimate of what people can buy with their income in the local economy. The per capita GNI for rich countries like Norway, Canada, and the United States is very high, exceeding $39 000. For middle-income countries the figures range from about $3600 in India to almost $12 000 in Costa Rica. In the world's low-income countries, per capita GNI is just one or two thousand dollars. In Niger or in Ethiopia, for example, a typical person labours all year to make what the average worker in Canada earns in a week.

The last column of Table 9–1 is a measure of quality of life in the various nations. This index, calculated by the United Nations (2011), is based on income, education (extent of adult literacy and average years of schooling), and longevity (how long people typically live). Index values are decimals that fall between extremes of 1 (highest) and 0 (lowest). By this calculation, Norwegians enjoy the highest quality of life (0.943), with residents of Canada close behind (0.908). At the other extreme, people in the Democratic Republic of the Congo in Africa have the lowest quality of life (0.286).

Relative versus Absolute Poverty

The distinction between relative and absolute poverty, made in Chapter 8 ("Social Stratification"), has an important application to global inequality. People living in rich countries generally focus on *relative poverty*, meaning that some people lack resources that are taken for granted by others. By definition, relative poverty exists in every society, rich or poor.

More important in global perspective, however, is *absolute poverty*, a lack of resources that is life-threatening. Human beings in absolute poverty lack the nutrition necessary for health and long-term survival. To be sure, some absolute poverty exists in Canada. But such immediately

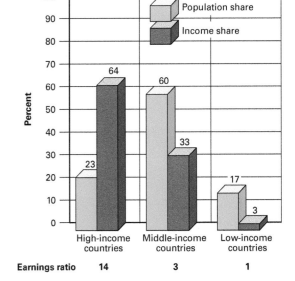

FIGURE 9–2 The Relative Share of Income and Population by Level of Economic Development

For every dollar earned by people in low-income countries, people in high-income countries earn $14.

Source: Based on Population Reference Bureau (2012a) and World Bank (2012b).

---

[1]Gross national income is the value of all the goods and services produced by a country's economy within its borders in a given year, plus all the income earned abroad by its people and companies.

TABLE 9–1 Wealth and Well-Being in Global Perspective, 2011

Country	Gross National Income ($ billions)	GNI per Capita (PPP US$)*	Quality of Life Index
High-Income			
Norway	311	62 970	0.943
Australia	812	34 431	0.929
United States	15 232	48 890	0.910
Canada	1 370	39 730	0.908
Sweden	399	42 200	0.904
Japan	4 541	35 530	0.901
South Korea	1 510	30 340	0.897
United Kingdom	2 251	35 940	0.863
Middle-Income			
Eastern Europe			
Serbia	85	11 640	0.766
Albania	29	8 900	0.739
Ukraine	324	7 080	0.729
Latin America			
Costa Rica	57	11 950	0.744
Ecuador	122	8 310	0.720
Brazil	2 261	11 500	0.718
Asia			
People's Republic of China	11 361	8 450	0.687
Thailand	583	8 390	0.682
India	4 491	3 620	0.547
Middle East			
Iran	833	10 164	0.707
Syria	104	4 243	0.632
Africa			
Algeria	301	8 370	0.698
Namibia	15	6 600	0.625
Low-Income			
Latin America			
Haiti	12	1 190	0.454
Asia			
Laos	16	2 600	0.524
Cambodia	32	2 260	0.523
Bangladesh	291	1 940	0.500
Africa			
Kenya	72	1 720	0.509
Ethiopia	94	1 110	0.363
Mali	17	1 050	0.359
Guinea	11	1 050	0.344
Democratic Republic of the Congo	23	350	0.286

*These data are purchasing power parity (PPP) calculations, which avoid currency rate distortion by showing the local purchasing power of each domestic currency.

Sources: United Nations Development Programme (2012); World Bank (2012a, 2012b).

life-threatening poverty strikes only a very small proportion of the Canadian population. In low-income countries, by contrast, almost one-half of the people live on about $1.25 a day and are in desperate need.

Because absolute poverty is deadly, people in low-income nations face an elevated risk of dying young. Global Map 9–2 on page 291 lets us explore this pattern by presenting the odds of living to the age of 65 that are typical for the nations of the world. In many rich societies, more than 85 percent of people reach this age; the figure for Canada is 88 percent. In the world's poorest countries, however, the odds of living to age 65 are less than one in three and two in ten children do not survive to the age of five (United Nations, 2011).

The Extent of Poverty

Poverty in poor countries is more widespread than it is in rich nations such as Canada and the United States In 2011, Statistics Canada classified 15 percent of the Canadian population as poor (see Chapter 8, "Social Stratification"). The same figure was reported by the U.S. Census Bureau for the American population. In low-income countries, however, most people live no better than the poor in Canada or the United States, and many are far worse off. As Global Map 9–2 shows, the low odds of living to the age of 65 in the countries of sub-Saharan Africa indicate that absolute poverty is greatest there, where more than one-fourth of the population is malnourished. In the world as a whole, at any given time, 12.5 percent of the people—about 868 million—suffer from chronic hunger, which leaves them less able to work and puts them at high risk of disease (United Nations Food and Agriculture Organization, 2012).

The typical adult in a rich nation such as Canada consumes about 3750 calories a day, an excess that contributes to widespread obesity and related health problems. The typical adult in a low-income country not only consumes just 2350 calories a day but also does more physical labour. Together, these factors result in undernourishment: too little food or not enough of the right kinds of food (United Nations Food and Agriculture Organization, 2012).

In the 10 minutes it takes to read this section of the chapter, about 100 people in the world who are sick and weakened from hunger will die. This number amounts to about 25 000 people a day, or 9 million people each year. Clearly, easing world hunger is one of the most serious responsibilities facing humanity today (United Nations World Food Programme, 2008).

Poverty and Children

Death comes early in poor societies, where families lack adequate food, safe water, secure housing, and access to medical care. In the world's low-income nations, one-quarter of all children do not receive enough nutrition to be healthy (World Bank, 2012a).

Poor children live in poor families, and many share in the struggle to get through each day. Organizations fighting child

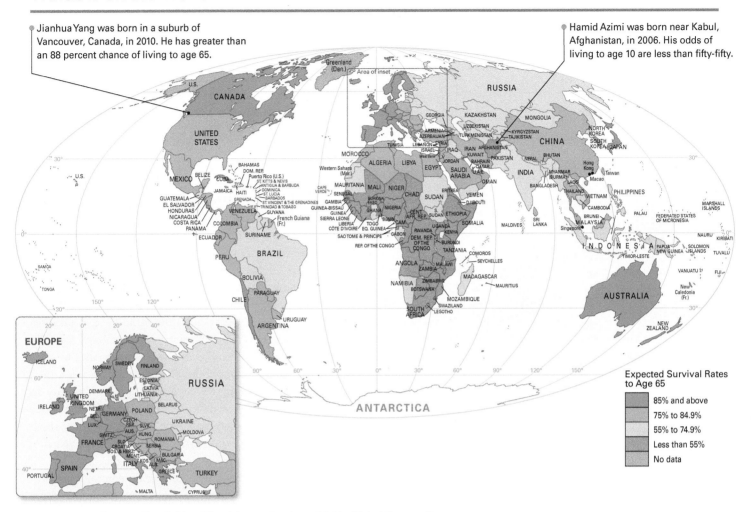

Jianhua Yang was born in a suburb of Vancouver, Canada, in 2010. He has greater than an 88 percent chance of living to age 65.

Hamid Azimi was born near Kabul, Afghanistan, in 2006. His odds of living to age 10 are less than fifty-fifty.

Expected Survival Rates to Age 65

- 85% and above
- 75% to 84.9%
- 55% to 74.9%
- Less than 55%
- No data

GLOBAL MAP 9–2 The Odds of Surviving to the Age of 65 in Global Perspective

This map identifies expected survival rates to the age of 65 for nations around the world. In 39 of the world's nations, including most high-income countries, more than 85 percent of people live to this age. In Canada, the share is 88 percent. But in low-income nations, death often comes early, with just one-third of people reaching the age of 65.

Source: United Nations (2011).

poverty estimate that as many as 100 million children living in cities in poor countries beg, steal, sell sex, or work for drug gangs to provide income for their families. Such a life almost always means dropping out of school and puts children at high risk of disease and violence. Many girls, with little or no access to medical assistance, become pregnant—a case of children who cannot support themselves having children of their own.

Analysts estimate that tens of millions of the world's children are orphaned or have left their families altogether, sleeping and living on the streets as best they can or perhaps trying to migrate to Canada and other high-income countries. Roughly half of all street children are found in Latin American cities such as Mexico City and Rio de Janeiro, where half

Sucheta Das/Reuters/Corbis

Tens of millions of children fend for themselves every day on the streets of poor cities where many fall victim to disease, drug abuse, and violence. What do you think must be done to ensure that children like these in Bangalore, India, receive adequate nutrition and a quality education?

Global Snapshot

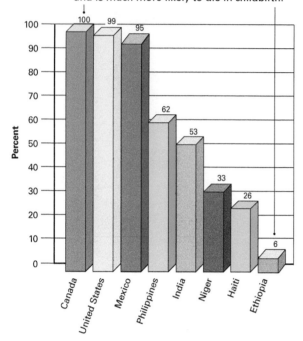

- Compared to a woman in Canada, an Ethiopian woman is far less likely to give birth with the help of medical professionals and is much more likely to die in childbirth.

FIGURE 9–3 Percentage of Births Attended by Skilled Health Staff

In Canada, most women give birth with the help of medical professionals or certified midwives and nurse practitioners, but this is usually not the case in low-income nations.

Source: World Bank (2012a).

of all children grow up in poverty. Many people in Canada know these cities as exotic travel destinations, but they are also home to thousands of street children living in makeshift huts, under bridges, or in alleyways (Leopold, 2007; Levinson & Bassett, 2007; Consortium for Street Children, 2011).

In cities around the world, officials engage in "urban cleansing," rounding up street children in an effort to make the city more attractive to visitors. These efforts are especially common when cities host major events such as the Olympics or the World Cup in soccer.

Poverty and Women

In rich societies, much of the work that women do is undervalued, underpaid, or overlooked entirely. In poor societies, women face even greater disadvantages. Most of the people who work in sweatshops (like the one described in the opening to this chapter) are women.

To make matters worse, tradition keeps women out of many jobs in low-income nations. In Bangladesh, for example, women work in garment factories because that society's conservative Muslim religious norms bar them from most other paid work and limit their opportunity for advanced schooling (Bearak, 2001). At the same time, traditional norms in poor societies also give women primary responsibility for child rearing and maintaining the household. Analysts estimate that in poor countries, although women produce about 70 percent of the food, men own 90 percent of the land. This is a far greater gender disparity in wealth than is found in high-income nations. It is likely, then, that about 70 percent of the world's roughly 1 billion people living at or near absolute poverty are women (World Bank, 2008; United Nations Statistics Division, 2010; Landsea Center for Women's Land Rights, 2011).

Finally, most women in poor countries receive little or no reproductive health care. Limited access to birth control keeps women at home with their children, keeps the birth rate high, and limits the economic production of the country. In addition, the world's poorest women typically give birth without help from trained health care personnel. Figure 9–3 illustrates a stark difference between low- and high-income countries in this regard.

Slavery

Poor societies have many problems in addition to hunger, including illiteracy, warfare, and slavery. In French and English Canada, slavery was legally practised until 1833 (Kihika, 2013); in the United States, slavery was legal until 1865. But slavery is still a reality for at least 20 million men, women, and children (International Labour Organization, 2012).

Anti-Slavery International describes five types of slavery. The first is *chattel slavery*, in which one person owns another. In spite of the fact that this practice is against the law almost everywhere in the world, several million people fall into this category. The buying and selling of slaves—generally people of one ethnic or caste group enslaving members of another—still takes place in many countries throughout Asia, the Middle East, and especially Africa. The Thinking Globally box on page 293 describes the reality of one slave's life in the African nation of Mauritania.

A second type of bondage is *slavery imposed by the state*. In this case, a government imposes forced labour on people convicted of criminal violations or on others simply because the government needs their labour. In China, for example, people who engage in prostitution or other crimes or who are addicted to drugs or engage in political dissent are subject to forced labour. In North Korea, the government sends common offenders, along with political prisoners, to "re-education" labour camps.

Thinking Globally

"God Made Me to Be a Slave"

Fatma Mint Mamadou is a young woman living in North Africa's Islamic Republic of Mauritania. Asked her age, she pauses, smiles, and shakes her head. She has no idea when she was born. Nor can she read or write. What she knows is tending camels, herding sheep, hauling bags of water, sweeping, and serving tea to her owners. This young woman is one of perhaps 50 000 slaves in Mauritania, which represents about 18 percent of that nation's population.

In the central region of this nation, having dark brown skin almost always means being a slave to an Arab owner. Fatma accepts her situation; she has known nothing else. She explains in a matter-of-fact voice that she is a slave like her mother before her and her grandmother before that. "Just as God created a camel to be a camel," she shrugs, "he created me to be a slave."

Fatma, her mother, and her brothers and sisters live in a squatter settlement on the edge of Nouakchott, Mauritania's capital city.

Human slavery continues to exist in the twenty-first century.

Their home is a 3-by-4-metre hut that they built from wood scraps and other materials found at construction sites. The roof is nothing more than a piece of cloth; there is no plumbing or furniture. The nearest water comes from a well a kilometre and a half down the road.

In this region, slavery began more than 500 years ago, about the time Columbus sailed west toward the Americas. As Arab and Berber tribes raided local villages, they made slaves of the people, and so it has been for dozens of generations ever since. In 1905, the French colonial rulers of Mauritania banned slavery. After the nation gained independence in 1961, the new government reaffirmed the ban. However, slavery was not officially abolished until 1981, and even then, it was not made a crime. In 2007, the nation passed legislation making the practice of slavery an offence punishable by up to 10 years in prison, and the government now provides monetary compensation to victims of slavery. But the new laws have done little to change strong traditions. The sad truth is that people like Fatma still have no conception of "freedom to choose."

The next question is more personal: "Are you and other girls ever raped?" Again, Fatma hesitates. With no hint of emotion, she responds, "Of course, in the night the men come to breed us. Is that what you mean by rape?"

What Do You Think?

1. How does tradition play a part in keeping people in slavery?
2. What might explain the fact that the world still tolerates slavery?
3. Explain the connection between slavery and poverty.

Source: Based on Burkett (1997); Fisher (2011); Anti-Slavery International (2012).

A third and more common form of bondage is *child slavery*, in which desperately poor families send their children out into the streets to beg or steal or do whatever they can to survive. Probably tens of millions of children—many in the poorest countries of Latin America and Africa—fall into this category. In addition, an estimated 10 million children are forced to labour daily in the production of tobacco, sugar cane, cotton, and coffee in more than 70 nations.

Fourth, *debt bondage* is the practice by which an employer pays wages to workers that are less than what the employer charges the workers for company-provided food and housing. Under such an arrangement, workers can never pay their debts so, for practical purposes, workers are enslaved. Many sweatshop workers in low-income nations fall into this category.

Fifth, *servile forms of marriage* may also amount to slavery. In India, Thailand, and some African nations, families marry off women against their will. Many end up as slaves working for their husband's family; some are forced into sex work.

An additional form of slavery is *human trafficking*, the moving of men, women, and children from one place to another for the purpose of performing forced labour. Women or

colonialism the process by which some nations enrich themselves through political and economic control of other nations

neocolonialism a new form of global power relationships that involves not direct political control but economic exploitation by multinational corporations

men are brought to a new country with the promise of a job and then forced to become prostitutes or farm labourers, or "parents" adopt children from another country and then force them to work in sweatshops. Such activity is big business: Next to trading in guns and drugs, trading in people brings the greatest profit to organized crime around the world (Orhant, 2002; Anti-Slavery International, 2012; International Labour Organization, 2012; U.S. Department of Labor, 2012).

In 1948, the United Nations issued its Universal Declaration of Human Rights, which states, "No one shall be held in slavery or servitude; slavery and the slave trade shall be prohibited in all their forms." Unfortunately, more than six decades later, this social problem still exists.

Explanations of Global Poverty

What accounts for severe and extensive poverty in so much of the world? The rest of this chapter provides various answers as to what makes some societies poor:

1. **Lack of technology.** About one-quarter of people in low-income countries farm the land using human muscle or animal power. With limited energy sources, economic production is modest.

2. **Population growth.** As Chapter 15 ("Population, Urbanization, and Environment") explains, the poorest countries have the world's highest birth rates. Despite the death toll from poverty, the populations of poor countries in Africa double every 25 years. In sub-Saharan Africa, 43 percent of the people are under the age of 15. With so many people entering their childbearing years, the wave of population increase will roll into the future. The result is more poverty. Why? The population of Uganda, for example, has swelled by about 5 percent annually in recent years; even with some economic development, living standards there have fallen. This is far from an isolated case. Globally, just about all future population increase will be in lower-income countries (Population Reference Bureau, 2012b).

3. **Cultural patterns.** Poor societies are usually traditional. Holding on to long-established ways of life means resisting change—even change that promises a richer material life.

4. **Social stratification.** Low-income societies distribute their wealth very unequally. Chapter 8 ("Social Stratification") explained that social inequality is greater in agrarian societies than in industrial societies. In Brazil, for example, 75 percent of all farmland is owned by just 4 percent of the people (Galano, 1998; IBGE, 2006; Frayssinet, 2009).

5. **Gender inequality.** Gender inequality in poor societies keeps women from holding jobs, which typically means that they have many children. An expanding population, in turn, slows economic development. Many analysts conclude that raising living standards in much of the world depends on improving the social standing of women.

6. **Global power relationships.** A final cause of global poverty lies in the relationships between the nations of the world. Historically, wealth flowed from poor societies to rich nations through **colonialism**, *the process by which some nations enrich themselves through political and economic control of other nations.* The countries of Western Europe colonized much of Latin America beginning just over five centuries ago. Such global exploitation allowed some nations to develop economically at the expense of other nations.

Although 130 former colonies gained their independence over the course of the twentieth century, exploitation continues through **neocolonialism** (*neo* is Greek for "new"), *a new form of global power relationships that involves not direct political control but economic exploitation by multinational corporations.* A **multinational corporation** is *a large business that operates in many countries.* Corporate leaders often impose their will on countries in which they do business to create favourable economic conditions for the operation of their corporations, just as colonizers did in the past (Bonanno, Constance, & Lorenz, 2000).

multinational corporation a large business that operates in many countries

Theories of Global Stratification

(**9.3**) Apply sociological theories to the topic of global inequality.

There are two major explanations for the unequal distribution of the world's wealth and power: *modernization theory* and *dependency theory*. Each theory suggests a different solution to the suffering of hungry people in much of the world.

Modernization Theory

Modernization theory is *a model of economic and social development that explains global inequality in terms of technological and cultural differences between nations*. Modernization theory, which follows the structural-functional approach, emerged in the 1950s, a time when U.S. society was fascinated by new developments in technology. To showcase the power of productive technology and also to counter the growing influence of the Soviet Union and socialism in much of the world, North American policy-makers drafted a market-based foreign policy that has been with us ever since (Rostow, 1960, 1978; Bauer, 1981; Berger, 1986; Firebaugh, 1996; Firebaugh & Sandu, 1998).

Historical Perspective

Modernization theory claims that until a few centuries ago, the entire world was poor. Because poverty is the norm throughout human history, modernization theory proposes that it is *affluence* that demands an explanation.

Affluence came within reach of a growing share of people in Western Europe during the late Middle Ages as world exploration and trade expanded. Soon after, the Industrial Revolution transformed first Western Europe and then North America. Industrial technology and the spirit of capitalism created new wealth as never before. At first, this new wealth benefited only a few individuals. But industrial technology was so productive that gradually the living standards of even the poorest people began to improve. Absolute poverty, which had plagued humanity throughout history, was finally in decline.

In high-income countries, where the Industrial Revolution began in the late 1700s or early 1800s, the standard of living jumped at least fourfold during the twentieth century. As middle-income nations in Asia and Latin America have industrialized, they too have become richer. But with limited industrial technology, low-income countries have changed much less.

The Importance of Culture

Why didn't the Industrial Revolution sweep away poverty throughout the world? Modernization theory points out that not every society wants to adopt new technology. Doing so requires a cultural environment that emphasizes the benefits of material wealth and new ideas.

Modernization theory identifies *tradition* as the greatest barrier to economic development. In some societies, strong family systems and a reverence for the past discourage people from adopting new technologies that would raise their living standards. Even today, many traditional people—from the Amish in North America to Islamic people in the Middle East to the Semai of Malaysia—oppose new technology as a threat to their family relationships, customs, and religious beliefs. Max Weber (1958, orig. 1904–05) found that at the end of the Middle Ages, Western Europe's cultural environment favoured change. As Chapter 13 ("Family and Religion") explains, the Protestant Reformation reshaped traditional Christian beliefs to generate a progress-oriented way of life. Wealth—looked on with suspicion by the Catholic Church—became a sign of personal virtue, and the growing importance of individualism steadily replaced the traditional emphasis on family and community. Taken together, these new cultural patterns nurtured the Industrial Revolution.

In rich nations such as Canada, most parents expect their children to enjoy years of childhood, largely free from the responsibilities of adult life. This is not the case in poor nations across Latin America, Africa, and Asia. Poor families depend on whatever income their children can earn, and many children as young as six or seven work full days weaving or performing other kinds of manual labour. Child labour lies behind the low prices of many products imported for sale in this country.

Rostow's Stages of Modernization

Modernization theory holds that the door to affluence is open to all. As technological advances spread around the world, all societies should gradually industrialize. According to Walt Rostow (1960, 1978), modernization occurs in four stages:

1. **Traditional stage.** Socialized to honour the past, people in traditional societies cannot easily imagine that life could or should be any different. They therefore build their lives around families and local communities, following well-worn paths that allow little individual freedom or change. Life is often spiritually rich but lacking in material goods.

   A century ago, much of the world was in this initial stage of economic development. Nations such as Bangladesh, Niger, and Somalia are still at the traditional stage and remain poor. Even in countries, such as India, that have recently joined the ranks of middle-income nations, certain elements of the population have remained highly traditional.

2. **Take-off stage.** As a society shakes off the grip of tradition, people start to use their talents and imagination, sparking economic growth. A market emerges as people produce goods not just for their own use but also to trade with others for profit. Greater individualism, a willingness to take risks, and a desire for material goods also take hold, often at the expense of family ties and time-honoured norms and values.

   Great Britain reached take-off by about 1800, the United States by 1820. Thailand, a middle-income country in eastern Asia, is now in this stage. Such development is typically speeded by help from rich nations, including foreign aid, the availability of advanced technology and investment capital, and opportunities for schooling abroad.

3. **Drive to technological maturity.** As this stage begins, "growth" is a widely accepted idea that fuels a society's pursuit of higher living standards. A diversified economy drives a population eager to enjoy the benefits of industrial technology. At the same time, however, people begin to realize (and sometimes regret) that industrialization is eroding traditional family and local community life. Great Britain reached this point by about 1840, the United States by 1860, and Canada in the early twentieth century. Today, Mexico, the U.S. territory of Puerto Rico, and Poland are among the nations driving to technological maturity.

   At this stage of development, absolute poverty is greatly reduced. Cities swell with people who leave rural villages in search of economic opportunity. Specialization creates the wide range of jobs that we find in our economy today. An increasing focus on work makes relationships less personal. Growing individualism generates social movements demanding greater political rights. Societies approaching technological maturity also provide basic schooling for all their people and advanced training for some. The newly educated consider tradition "backward" and push for further change. The social position of women steadily approaches that of men.

4. **High mass consumption.** Economic development steadily raises living standards as mass production stimulates mass consumption. Simply put, people soon learn to "need" the expanding array of goods that their society produces. The United States, Japan, Canada, Australia, and the nations of Western Europe moved into this stage by 1900. Now entering this level of economic development are two former British colonies that are prosperous small societies of eastern Asia: Hong Kong (part of the People's Republic of China since 1997) and Singapore (independent since 1965).

The Role of Rich Nations

Modernization theory claims that high-income countries play four important roles in global economic development:

1. **Controlling population.** Because population growth is greatest in the poorest societies, rising population can overtake economic advances. Rich nations can help limit population growth by exporting birth control technology and promoting its use. Once economic development is under way, birth rates should decline, as they have in industrialized nations, because children are no longer an economic asset.

2. **Increasing food production.** Rich nations can export high-tech farming methods to poor nations to increase agricultural yields. Such techniques, collectively referred to as the Green Revolution, include new hybrid seeds, modern irrigation methods, chemical fertilizers, and pesticides for insect control.

3. **Introducing industrial technology.** Rich nations can encourage economic growth in poor societies by introducing machinery and information technology, which raise productivity. Industrialization also shifts the labour force from farming to skilled industrial and service jobs.

4. **Providing foreign aid.** Investment capital from rich nations can boost the prospects of poor societies trying to reach Rostow's take-off stage. Foreign aid can raise farm output by helping poor countries buy more fertilizer and build irrigation projects. In the same way, financial and technical assistance can help build power plants and factories to improve industrial output. Each year, the United States provides more than US$35 billion in foreign aid to developing countries (U.S. Agency for International Development, 2012), while Canada gives about CAN$5 billion (Foreign Affairs, Trade and Development Canada, 2015). Keep in mind that these figures, while remarkable at first glance, are actually short of the 0.7 percent of GNI recommended by the United Nations. In 2014, the United States and Canada contributed only 0.19 and 0.24 of their GNI, respectively (Organisation for Economic Co-operation and Development, 2015).

EVALUATE Modernization theory has many influential supporters among social scientists (Parsons, 1966; Moore, 1977, 1979; Bauer, 1981; Berger, 1986; Firebaugh & Beck, 1994; Firebaugh, 1996; Firebaugh & Sandu, 1998). For decades, it has shaped the foreign policy of Canada, the United States, and other rich nations. Supporters point to rapid economic development in Asia—especially in South Korea, Taiwan, Singapore, and Hong Kong, as proof that the affluence achieved in Western Europe and North America is within the reach of all countries.

But modernization theory comes under fire from socialist countries (and left-leaning analysts in the West) as little more than a defence of capitalism. Its most serious flaw, according to critics, is that modernization simply has not occurred in many poor countries. Economic indicators reported by the United Nations show that living standards in a number of nations, including Haiti and Nicaragua in Latin America and Sudan, Ghana, and Rwanda in Africa, are little changed—and are in some cases worse—than in 1960 (United Nations Development Programme, 2008).

A second criticism of modernization theory is that it fails to recognize how rich nations, which benefit from the status quo, often block the path to development for poor countries. Centuries ago, critics charge, rich countries industrialized from a position of global strength. Can we expect poor countries today to do so from a position of global weakness?

Third, modernization theory treats rich and poor societies as separate worlds, ignoring the ways in which international relations have affected all nations. Many countries in Latin America and Asia are still struggling to overcome the harm caused by colonization, which boosted the fortunes of Europe.

Fourth, modernization theory holds up the world's most developed countries as the standard for judging the rest of humanity, revealing an ethnocentric bias. We should remember that our Western idea of "progress" has caused us to rush headlong into a competitive, materialistic way of life, which uses up the world's scarce resources and pollutes the natural environment.

Fifth and finally, modernization theory suggests that the causes of global poverty lie almost entirely in the poor societies themselves. Critics see this analysis as little more than blaming the victims for their own problems. Instead, they argue, an analysis of global inequality should focus just as much on the behaviour of rich nations as it does on the behaviour of poor ones and also on the global economic system. Concerns such as these reflect a second major approach to understanding global inequality, dependency theory.

CHECK YOUR LEARNING State the important ideas of modernization theory, including Rostow's four stages of economic development. Point to several strengths and weaknesses of this theory.

Dependency Theory

Dependency theory is *a model of economic and social development that explains global inequality in terms of the historical exploitation of poor nations by rich ones.* This analysis, which follows the social-conflict approach, puts the main responsibility for global poverty on rich nations, which for centuries have systematically impoverished low-income countries and made them dependent on the rich ones—a destructive process that continues today.

Modernization theory claims that corporations that build factories in low-income nations help people by providing them with jobs and higher wages than they had before; dependency theory views these factories as "sweatshops" that exploit workers. In response to the Olympic Games selling sports clothing produced by sweatshops, these women staged a protest in Athens, Greece; they are wearing white masks to symbolize the "faceless" workers who make much of what we wear. Is any of the clothing you wear made in sweatshop factories?

Historical Perspective

Everyone agrees that before the Industrial Revolution there was little affluence in the world. Dependency theory asserts, however, that people living in poor countries were actually better off economically in the past than their descendants are now. André Gunder Frank (1975), a noted supporter of this theory, argues that the colonial process that helped develop rich nations also *underdeveloped* poor societies.

Dependency theory is based on the idea that the economic positions of rich and poor nations of the world are linked and cannot be understood apart from each other. Poor nations are not simply lagging behind rich ones on the "path of progress"; rather, the prosperity of the most developed countries came largely at the expense of less developed ones. In short, some nations became rich only because others became poor. Both are products of the global commerce that began five centuries ago.

The Importance of Colonialism

Late in the fifteenth century, Europeans began exploring the Americas to the west, Africa to the south, and Asia to the east in order to establish colonies. They were so successful that a century ago, Great Britain controlled about one-fourth of the world's land, boasting that "the sun never sets on the British Empire." The United States, itself originally a collection of small British colonies on the eastern seaboard of North America, soon pushed across the continent, purchased Alaska, and gained control of Haiti, Puerto Rico, Guam, the Philippines, the Hawaiian Islands, part of Panama, and Guantanamo Bay in Cuba.

As colonialism spread, there emerged a brutal form of human exploitation—the international slave trade—beginning about 1500 and continuing until 1850. Even as the world was turning away from slavery, Europeans took control of most of the African continent, as Figure 9–4 shows, and dominated most of the continent until the early 1960s.

Formal colonialism has almost disappeared from the world. However, according to dependency theory, political liberation has not translated into economic independence. Far from it—the economic relationship between poor and rich nations continues the colonial pattern of domination. This *neocolonialism* is the heart of the capitalist world economy.

FIGURE 9–4 Africa's Colonial History

For more than a century, most of Africa was colonized by Western European nations, with France dominating in the northwestern region of the continent and Great Britain dominating in the east and south.

Wallerstein's Capitalist World Economy

Immanuel Wallerstein (1974, 1979, 1983, 1984) explains global stratification using a model of the "capitalist world economy." Wallerstein's term *world economy* suggests that the prosperity of some nations and the poverty and dependency of other countries result from a global economic system. He traces the roots of the global economy to the beginning of colonization more than 500 years ago, when Europeans began gathering wealth from the rest of the world. Because the world economy is based in high-income countries, it is capitalist in character.[2]

Wallerstein calls the rich nations the *core* of the world economy. Colonialism enriched this core by funnelling raw materials from around the world to Western Europe, where they fuelled the Industrial Revolution. Today, multinational corporations operate profitably worldwide, channelling wealth to North America, Western Europe, Australia, and Japan.

Low-income countries represent the *periphery* of the world economy. Drawn into the world economy by colonial exploitation, poor nations continue to support rich ones by providing inexpensive labour and a vast market for industrial products. The remaining countries are the *semi-periphery* of the world economy. They include middle-income countries like India and Brazil that have closer ties to the global economic core.

According to Wallerstein, the world economy benefits rich societies (by generating profits) and harms the rest of the world (by causing

modernization theory a model of economic and social development that explains global inequality in terms of technological and cultural differences between nations

dependency theory a model of economic and social development that explains global inequality in terms of the historical exploitation of poor nations by rich ones

---

[2]This discussion also draws on A.G. Frank (1980, 1981), Delacroix and Ragin (1981), Bergesen (1983), Dixon and Boswell (1996), and Kentor (1998).

poverty). The world economy thus makes poor nations dependent on rich ones. This dependency involves three factors:

1. **Narrow, export-oriented economies.** Poor nations produce only a few crops for export to rich countries. Examples include coffee and fruit from Latin American nations, oil from Nigeria, hardwoods from the Philippines, and palm oil from Malaysia. Today's multinational corporations purchase raw materials cheaply in poor societies and transport them to core nations, where factories process them for profitable sale. Thus poor nations develop few industries of their own.

2. **Lack of industrial capacity.** Without an industrial base, poor societies face a double bind: They count on rich nations to buy their inexpensive raw materials, and they must then try to buy from the rich nations the few expensive manufactured goods they can afford. In a classic example of this dependency, British colonialists encouraged the people of India to raise cotton but prevented them from weaving their own cloth. Instead, the British shipped Indian cotton to their own textile mills in Birmingham and Manchester, manufactured the cloth, and shipped finished goods back to India, where the very people who harvested the cotton bought the garments.

   Dependency theorists claim that the Green Revolution—widely praised by modernization theorists—works the same way. Poor countries sell cheap raw materials to rich nations and then must buy expensive fertilizers, pesticides, and machinery in return. Typically, rich countries profit from this exchange far more than poor nations do.

3. **Foreign debt.** Unequal trade patterns have plunged poor countries into debt. Collectively, the poor nations of the world owe rich countries some $4 trillion. Such staggering debt paralyzes a country, causing high unemployment and rampant inflation (World Bank, 2012b).

The Role of Rich Nations

Modernization theory and dependency theory assign very different roles to rich nations. Modernization theory holds that rich countries *produce wealth* through capital investment and new technology. Dependency theory views global inequality in terms of how countries *distribute wealth*, arguing that rich nations have *overdeveloped* themselves as they have *underdeveloped* the rest of the world.

Dependency theorists dismiss the idea that programs developed by rich countries to control population and boost agricultural and industrial output raise living standards in poor countries. Instead, they claim, such programs actually benefit rich nations and the ruling elites, not the poor majority, in low-income countries (Kentor, 2001).

The hunger activists Frances Moore Lappé and Joseph Collins (1986; Lappé, Collins, & Rosset, 1998) maintain that capitalist culture encourages people to think of poverty as somehow inevitable. In this line of reasoning, poverty results from "natural" processes, including having too many children, and natural disasters such as droughts. But global poverty is far from inevitable; in their view, it results from deliberate policies. Lappé and Collins point out that the world already produces enough food to allow every person on the planet to become quite fat. Moreover, India and most of Africa actually export food, even though many people there go hungry.

According to Lappé and Collins, the contradiction of poverty amid plenty stems from the rich-nation policy of producing food for profit, not people. That is, corporations in rich nations co-operate with elites in poor countries to grow and export profitable crops such as coffee, which means using land that could otherwise produce basics such as beans and corn for local families. Governments of poor countries support the practice of growing for export because they need food profits to repay foreign debt. According to Lappé and Collins, the capitalist corporate structure of the global economy is at the core of this vicious cycle.

EVALUATE The main idea of dependency theory is that no nation becomes rich or poor in isolation because a single global economy shapes the future of all nations. Pointing to continuing poverty in Latin America, Africa, and Asia, dependency theorists claim that development simply cannot proceed under the constraints now imposed by rich countries.

Rather, they call for radical reform of the entire world economy so that it operates in the interests of the majority of people.

Critics charge that dependency theory wrongly treats wealth as if no one gets richer without someone else getting poorer. Corporations, small business owners, and farmers can and do create new wealth through hard work and imaginative use of new technology. After all, they point out, the entire world's wealth has increased tenfold since 1950.

Second, dependency theory is wrong in blaming rich nations for global poverty because many of the world's poorest countries (such as Ethiopia) have had little contact with rich nations. On the contrary, a long history of trade with rich countries has dramatically improved the economies of nations, including Sri Lanka, Singapore, and Hong Kong (all former British colonies), as well as South Korea and Japan. In short, say the critics, most evidence shows that foreign investment encourages economic growth, as modernization theory claims, and not economic decline, as dependency theory holds (Vogel, 1991; Firebaugh, 1992).

Third, critics call dependency theory simplistic for pointing the finger at a single factor—the capitalist market system—as the cause of global inequality (Worsley, 1990). Dependency theory views poor societies as passive victims and ignores factors inside these countries that contribute to their economic problems. Sociologists have long recognized the vital role of culture in shaping people's willingness to embrace or resist change. Under the sway of an ultratraditional Buddhist culture, for example, the never-colonized Himalayan Kingdom of Bhutan has one of the smallest economies in the world. With successive kings urging suspicion of modernity (television was only introduced when a ban was lifted in 1999) and requiring the maintenance of "cultural roots," is it reasonable to blame capitalist societies for that country's stagnation?

Nor can rich societies be held responsible for the reckless behaviour of foreign leaders whose corruption and militarism impoverish their countries. Examples include the regimes of Ruhollah Khomeini in Iran, Idi Amin in Uganda, and Robert Mugabe in Zimbabwe. Some leaders even use food supplies as a weapon in internal political struggles, leaving the masses starving, as in the African nations of Ethiopia, Sudan, and Somalia. Likewise, many countries throughout the world have done little to improve the status of women or to control population growth.

Fourth, critics say that dependency theory is wrong to claim that global trade always makes rich nations richer and poor nations poorer. For example, in 2011, the United States had a trade deficit of $738 billion, meaning that it imported nearly three-quarters of a trillion dollars' more goods than it sells abroad. The single greatest debt ($296 billion) was owed to China, whose profitable trade has now pushed that country into the ranks of the world's middle-income nations (U.S. Census Bureau, 2012).

Fifth, critics fault dependency theory for offering only vague solutions to global poverty. Most dependency theorists urge poor nations to end all contact with rich countries, and some call for nationalizing foreign-owned industries. In other words, dependency theory is really an argument for some type of state managed socialism. In light of the difficulties that socialist societies (even better-off socialist countries such as Russia) have had in meeting the needs of their own people, critics ask, should we really expect such a system to rescue the entire world from poverty?

Although the world continues to grow richer, billions of people are being left behind. This shantytown in Cité Soleil, Haiti, is typical of many cities in low-income countries. What can you say about the quality of life in such a place?

Jan Sochor/Alamy Stock Photo

The Applying Theory table below summarizes the main arguments of modernization theory and dependency theory.

CHECK YOUR LEARNING State the main ideas of dependency theory. What are several of its strengths and weaknesses?

The Future of Global Stratification

(9.4) Evaluate trends in global inequality.

Among the most important trends in recent decades is the development of a global economy. In North America, rising production and sales abroad bring profits to many corporations and their stockholders, especially those who already have substantial wealth. At the same time, the global economy has moved manufacturing jobs abroad, closing factories in this country and hurting many average workers. The net result: greater economic inequality in countries such as Canada and the United States.

People who support the global economy claim that the expansion of trade results in benefits for all countries involved. For this reason, they endorse policies like the North American Free Trade Agreement (NAFTA) signed by Canada, the United States, and Mexico. Critics of expanding globalization make other claims: Manufacturing jobs are being lost in Canada and the United States, and more manufacturing now takes place abroad in factories where workers are paid little and few laws ensure workplace safety. In addition, other critics of expanding globalization point to the ever-greater stresses that our economy places on the natural environment.

But perhaps the greatest concern is the vast economic inequality that exists between the world's countries. The concentration of wealth in high-income countries, coupled with the grinding poverty in low-income nations, may well be the biggest problem facing humanity in the twenty-first century.

Both modernization theory and dependency theory offer some understanding of this urgent problem. In evaluating these theories, we must consider empirical evidence. Over the course of the twentieth century, living standards rose in most of the world. Even the economic output of the poorest 25 percent of the world's people almost tripled during those 100 years. As a result, the share of the world's population living on less than $1.25 a day fell from about 52 percent in 1981 to about 43 percent in 1990 and to about 22 percent in 2008 (Chen & Ravallion, 2012).

So far, the greatest reduction in poverty has taken place in Asia, a region generally regarded as an economic success story. Back in 1981, about 77 percent of the population of East Asia was living on less than $1.25 per day. By 2008, however, that share had declined dramatically to about 14 percent. Signalling this trend toward greater prosperity, in 2005,

Applying Theory

Global Poverty		
	Modernization Theory	**Dependency Theory**
Which theoretical approach is applied?	Structural-functional approach	Social-conflict approach
How did global poverty come about?	The whole world was poor until some countries developed industrial technology, which allowed mass production and created affluence.	Colonialism moved wealth from some countries to others, making some nations poor as it made other nations rich.
What are the main causes of global poverty today?	Traditional culture and a lack of productive technology.	Neocolonialism—the operation of multinational corporations in the global, capitalist economy.
Are rich countries part of the problem or part of the solution?	Rich countries are part of the solution, contributing new technology, advanced schooling, and foreign aid.	Rich countries are part of the problem, making poor countries economically dependent and in debt.

two very large Asian countries—India and China—joined the ranks of the middle-income nations (Sala-i-Martin, 2002; Bussollo et al., 2007; Davies et al., 2008; Chen & Ravallion, 2012).

During the 1970s, Latin America enjoyed significant economic growth, which pushed the share of its population living in $1.25-per-day poverty down to 12 percent by 1981. During the 1980s and 1990s, however, this number changed very little, with additional small gains after about 2005. By 2008, the share of people living in poverty was about 7 percent (Chen & Ravallion, 2012).

Sub-Saharan Africa represents the greatest challenge in humanity's efforts to reduce poverty. By 2008, for the first time, less than half the people (47 percent) of this global region were living at $1.25-per-day poverty or less. This poverty rate is still well above that of other world regions. Yet analysts are optimistic about Africa's future, pointing out that this region has enjoyed average economic growth of more than 5 percent a year over the past decade. In addition, six of the ten fastest developing countries in the world are now in southern Africa (Sala-i-Martin, 2002; Chen & Ravillion, 2012; Perry, 2012).

Looking at the world as a whole, the good news is that, in *absolute* terms, living standards are rising. Over the course of the last century, economic output has increased for both rich and poor nations. But the troubling trend is that living standards in rich and poor countries are not rising at the same rate. As a result, the *relative* gap between the rich and the poor in the world is increasing and, in 2011, this divide was more than five times larger than it was back in 1900. Figure 9–5 shows that the lower-income people in the world are being left behind.

Recent trends suggest the need to look critically at both modernization and dependency theories. The fact that governments have played a large role in the economic growth that has occurred in Asia and elsewhere challenges modernization theory and its free-market approach to development. On the other hand, since the upheavals in the former Soviet Union and Eastern Europe, a global re-evaluation of socialism has been taking place. Because socialist nations have a record of political repression, many low-income nations are unwilling to follow the advice of dependency theory and place economic development entirely under government control.

Although the world's future is uncertain, we have learned a great deal about global stratification. One insight, offered by modernization theory, is that poverty is partly a *problem of technology*. A higher standard of living for a surging world population depends on the ability of poor nations to raise their agricultural and industrial productivity. A second insight, derived from dependency theory, is that global inequality is also a *political issue*. Even with higher productivity, the human community must address crucial questions concerning how resources are distributed, both within societies and around the globe.

Although economic development raises living standards, it also places greater strains on the natural environment. As nations such as India and China—with a combined population of 2.6 billion—become more affluent, their people will consume more energy and other resources (China has recently passed Japan to become the second-largest consumer of oil, behind the United States, which is one reason that oil prices and supplies have been under pressure). Richer nations also produce more solid waste and create more pollution.

Finally, the vast gulf that separates the world's richest and poorest people puts everyone at greater risk of war and terrorism as the poorest people challenge the social arrangements that threaten their existence (Lindauer & Weerapana, 2002). In the long run, we can achieve peace on this planet only by ensuring that all people enjoy a significant measure of dignity and security.

Global Snapshot

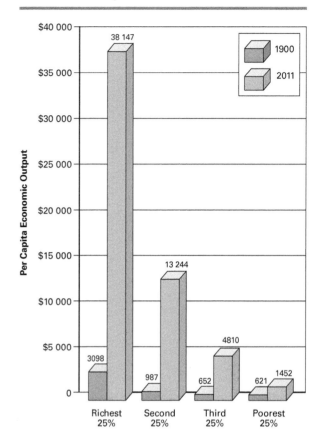

FIGURE 9–5 The World's Increasing Economic Inequality

The gap between the richest and poorest people in the world in 2011 was more than five times bigger than it was in 1900.

Source: World Bank (2012).

Seeing Sociology in Everyday Life

CHAPTER 9 Global Stratification

How much social inequality can we find if we look around the world?

This chapter explains that a global perspective reveals even more social stratification than we find here in Canada. Around the world, an increasing number of people in lower-income countries are travelling to higher-income nations in search of jobs. As "guest workers," they perform low-wage work that the country's own more well-off citizens do not wish to do. In such cases, the rich and poor truly live "worlds apart."

Rabih M'oghrabi/Newscom

Many guest workers come to Dubai from India to take jobs building this country's new high-rise hotels and business towers. With very little income, they often sleep six to a small room. How do you think living in a strange country, with few legal rights, affects these workers' ability to improve their working conditions?

Kamran Jebreili/AP Images

Guest workers in Dubai labour about 12 hours a day but earn only between $50 and $175 a month. Do you think the chance to take a job like this in a foreign country is an opportunity (income is typically twice what people can earn at home), or is it a form of exploitation?

Matt Shonfeld/Redux Pictures

Oil wealth has made some of the people of Dubai, in the United Arab Emirates, among the richest in the world. Dubai's wealthiest people can afford to ski on snow—in one of the hottest regions of the world—on enormous indoor ski slopes like this one. Is there anything about this picture that makes you uncomfortable? Explain your reaction.

HINT Dubai's recent building boom has been accomplished using the labour of about 1 million guest workers, who actually make up about 85 percent of the population of the United Arab Emirates. Recent years have seen a rising level of social unrest, including labour strikes, which has led to some improvements in working and living conditions and better health care. But guest workers have no legal rights to form labour unions, nor do they have any chance to gain citizenship.

Seeing Sociology in *Your* Everyday Life

1. What comparisons can you make between the pattern of guest workers coming to places such as Dubai in the Middle East and workers coming to Canada under the Temporary Foreign Worker program?

2. Go to www.sociologyinfocus.com to access the Sociology in Focus blog, where you can read the latest posts by a team of young sociologists who apply the sociological perspective to topics of popular culture.

3. Have you ever travelled in a low-income nation? Do you think people from a high-income nation such as Canada should feel guilty when seeing the daily struggles of the world's poorest people? Why or why not?

Sucheta Das/Reuters/Corbis

Making the Grade

Global Stratification: An Overview

9.1 Describe the division of the world into high-, middle-, and low-income countries. (pages 283–288)

High-Income Countries

- Contain 23 percent of the world's people
- Receive 64 percent of global income
- Have a high standard of living based on advanced technology
- Produce enough economic goods to enable their people to lead comfortable lives
- Include 74 nations, among them Canada, the United States, Mexico, Argentina, Chile, the nations of Western Europe, Israel, Saudi Arabia, the Russian Federation, Japan, South Korea, Malaysia, and Australia

Middle-Income Countries

- Contain 60 percent of the world's people
- Receive 33 percent of global income
- Have a standard of living about average for the world as a whole
- Include 72 nations, among them the nations of Eastern Europe, Peru, Brazil, Namibia, Egypt, Indonesia, India, and the People's Republic of China

Low-Income Countries

- Contain 17 percent of the world's people
- Receive 3 percent of global income
- Have a low standard of living due to limited industrial technology
- Include 49 nations, generally in Central and East Africa and Asia, among them Chad, the Democratic Republic of the Congo, Ethiopia, and Bangladesh

global stratification patterns of social inequality in the world as a whole

Global Wealth and Poverty

9.2 Discuss patterns and explanations of poverty around the world. (pages 288–294)

All societies contain **relative poverty**, but low-income nations face widespread **absolute poverty** that is life-threatening.

- Worldwide, about 868 million people are at risk due to poor nutrition.
- About 9 million people die each year from diseases caused by poverty.
- Throughout the world, women are more likely than men to be poor. Gender bias is strongest in poor societies.
- At least 20 million men, women, and children live in conditions that can be described as slavery.

Factors Causing Poverty

- Lack of technology limits production.
- High birth rates produce rapid population increase.
- Traditional cultural patterns make people resist change.
- Extreme social inequality distributes wealth very unequally.
- Extreme gender inequality limits the opportunities of women.
- Colonialism allowed some nations to exploit other nations; neocolonialism continues today.

colonialism the process by which some nations enrich themselves through political and economic control of other nations

neocolonialism a new form of global power relationships that involves not direct political control but economic exploitation by multinational corporations

multinational corporation a large business that operates in many countries

Theories of Global Stratification

9.3 Apply sociological theories to the topic of global inequality. (pages 295–302)

Modernization theory maintains that nations achieve affluence by developing advanced technology. This process depends on a culture that encourages innovation and change.

modernization theory a model of economic and social development that explains global inequality in terms of technological and cultural differences between nations

Walt Rostow identified four stages of development:

- *Traditional stage*—People's lives are built around families and local communities. (Example: Democratic Republic of the Congo)
- *Take-off stage*—A market emerges as people produce goods not just for their own use but also to trade with others for profit. (Example: Thailand)
- *Drive to technological maturity*—Economic growth and higher living standards are goals, schooling is widely available, and women's social standing improves. (Example: Mexico)
- *High mass consumption*—Advanced technology fuels mass production and mass consumption as people now "need" countless goods. (Example: Canada)

Modernization theory claims ...

- Rich nations can help poor nations by providing technology to control population size, increase food production, and expand industrial and information economy output and by providing foreign aid to pay for new economic development.
- Rapid economic development in Asia shows that affluence is within reach of other nations.

Critics claim ...

- Rich nations do little to help poor countries and benefit from the status quo. Low living standards in much of Africa and South America result from the policies of rich nations.
- Because rich nations, including Canada, control the global economy, many poor nations struggle to support their people and cannot follow the path to development taken by rich countries centuries ago.

Dependency theory maintains that global wealth and poverty were created by the colonial process beginning 500 years ago that developed rich nations and underdeveloped poor nations. This capitalist process continues today in the form of neocolonialism—economic exploitation of poor nations by multinational corporations.

Immanuel Wallerstein identified three categories of nations in a capitalist world economy:

- *Core*—the world's high-income countries, which are home to multinational corporations
- *Semi-periphery*—the world's middle-income countries, with ties to core nations
- *Periphery*—the world's low-income countries, which provide low-cost labour and a vast market for industrial products

Dependency theory claims ...

- Three key factors—export-oriented economies, a lack of industrial capacity, and foreign debt—make poor countries dependent on rich nations and prevent their economic development.
- Radical reform of the entire world economy is needed so that it operates in the interests of the majority of people.

Critics claim ...

- Dependency theory overlooks the tenfold increase in global wealth since 1950 and the fact that many of the world's developing nations benefit from strong ties to rich countries.
- Rich nations are not responsible for cultural patterns and political corruption that block economic development in many poor nations.

dependency theory a model of economic and social development that explains global inequality in terms of the historical exploitation of poor nations by rich ones

The Future of Global Stratification

9.4 Evaluate trends in global inequality. (pages 302–303)

- Global stratification is partly a matter of national differences in productive technology and partly a political matter involving how economic resources are distributed among nations and within nations.
- Although all regions of the world have made economic gains in absolute terms, the gap between rich and poor nations is more than five times larger than it was a century ago.

10 Gender Stratification

Cultura Creative/Alamy Stock Photo

LEARNING OBJECTIVES

10.1 Describe research that points to how society creates gender stratification.

10.2 Explain the importance of gender to socialization.

10.3 Analyze the extent of gender inequality in various social institutions.

10.4 Apply sociology's major theories to gender stratification.

10.5 Contrast liberal, radical, and socialist feminism.

the Power of Society

to impact our incomes

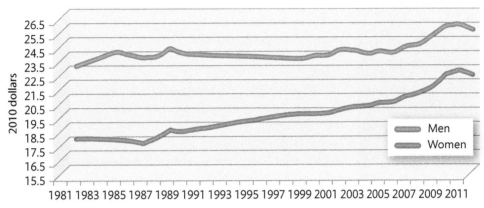

Source: Statistics Canada, http://www.statcan.gc.ca/pub/11f0019m/2013347/ct002-eng.htm.
Reproduced and distributed on an "as is" basis with the permission of Statistics Canada.

Does your gender influence your income? Research on the Canadian labour market indicates the existence of a gender wage gap. When it comes to hourly wages, women earn less than men. In 1981, among full-time workers, women earned 77 cents for every dollar that men earned. In 2011, women earned 87 cents for every dollar. As the figure above shows, while the gender wage gap has decreased, its existence demonstrates the power of gender to impact our lives.

Chapter Overview

We live in a world organized around not only the differences of social class, but also around the concepts of feminine and masculine, which sociologists call "gender." This chapter examines gender, explores the meaning societies attach to being female or male, and explains why gender is an important dimension of social stratification.

Library and Archives Canada

"We went to the Manitoba Legislature asking for plain, common justice, an old-fashioned square deal, and in reply to that we got hat-lifting. I felt that when a man offers hat-lifting when we ask for justice we should tell him to keep his hat right on. I will go further and say that we should tell him not only to keep his hat on but to pull it right down over his face."

So wrote Nellie McClung in her book *In These Times*, which tells the story of her struggle to gain equal rights for women in the public realm. Born in Ontario in 1873, McClung migrated west as a child with her family, first settling in Manitoba and later, as an adult, moving to Alberta and British Columbia. By the time she was 40, she had given birth to five children and had become a well-known public speaker for women's rights. Back then, in much of Canada, women could not own property or keep their wages if they were married; they could not draft a will; they were barred from filing lawsuits in a court, including seeking custody of their own children; they could not attend university; and they legally could be beaten by their husbands.

Nor could women express their disapproval of such conditions. In this "free country," many more decades would pass before all Canadian women gained the right to vote. At that time, most people considered such a proposal absurd and outrageous. Toronto journalist Goldwin Smith argued that giving women the right to vote would lead to "national emasculation." Smith also protested the right of women to enter universities (Prentice et al., 1996:221).

Much has changed in the 140 years since McClung's birth. Many of the proposals that she and other early feminists made are now accepted as matters of basic fairness. But as this chapter explains, women and men still lead different lives in Canada and elsewhere in the world; in most respects, men are still in charge. This chapter explores the importance of gender and explains that gender, like class position, is a major dimension of social stratification.

Gender and Inequality

10.1 Describe research that points to how society creates gender stratification.

Chapter 6 ("Sexuality and Society") explained that biological differences divide the human population into categories of female and male. Gender refers to the personal traits and social positions that members of a society attach to being female or male. Gender, then, is a dimension of social organization, shaping how we interact with others and even how we think about ourselves. More important, gender also involves *hierarchy*, placing men and women in different positions in terms of power, wealth, and other resources. This is why sociologists speak of **gender stratification**, *the unequal distribution of wealth, power, and privilege between men and women*. In short, gender affects the opportunities and constraints we face throughout our lives.

gender stratification the unequal distribution of wealth, power, and privilege between men and women

Male–Female Differences

Many people think there is something "natural" about gender distinctions, attributing them to the idea of the biological differences between males and females. But we must be careful not to think of social differences in biological terms. In 1848, for example, women were denied the vote because many people assumed that women did not have enough intelligence or any interest in politics. Such attitudes had nothing to do with biology; they reflected the *cultural patterns* of that time and place.

Another example is athletic performance. In 1925, most people—both women and men—believed that the best women runners could never compete with men in a marathon. Today, as Figure 10–1 shows, the gender gap has greatly narrowed, and the best women runners routinely post better times than the fastest men of decades past. Here again, most of the differences between men and women turn out to be socially created.

Differences in physical ability between the sexes do exist. On average, males are 10 percent taller than women, 20 percent heavier, and 30 percent stronger, especially in the upper body. On the other hand, women outperform men in the ultimate game of life itself: Life expectancy for men in 2013 was 80 years, while among women it was 84 years (Ehrenreich, 1999; World Health Organization, 2015).

In adolescence, males do a bit better in mathematics, and females show stronger verbal skills, leading many researchers to conclude that these differences reflect both biology and socialization (Lewin, 2008; College Board, 2012). Gender theorist Judith Butler, however, argues that the physical differences we observe are encouraged and produced by our social environments (2006).

Biologically, then, men and women differ in limited ways, with neither one naturally superior. Research does not point to any overall differences in intelligence between males and females. But culture can define the two sexes differently, as the global study of gender described in the next section shows.

Gender in Global Perspective

The best way to see how gender is based in culture is by comparing one society to another. Three important studies highlight just how different "masculine" and "feminine" can be.

The Israeli Kibbutz

In Israel, collective settlements are called *kibbutzim*. The *kibbutz* (the singular form of the word) has been an important setting for gender research because gender equality is one of its stated goals; men and women share in both work and decision making.

In recent decades, kibbutzim have become less collective and thus less distinctive organizations. But for much of their history, both sexes shared most everyday jobs. Many men joined women in taking care of children, and women joined men in repairing buildings and providing armed security. Both sexes made everyday decisions for the group. Girls and boys were raised in the same way; in many cases, young children were raised together in dormitories away from parents. Women and men in the kibbutzim achieved remarkable (although not complete) social equality, evidence that cultures define what is feminine and what is masculine.

Margaret Mead's Research

The anthropologist Margaret Mead carried out groundbreaking research on gender. If gender is based in the biological differences between men and women, she reasoned, people everywhere should define "feminine" and "masculine" in the same way; if gender is cultural, these concepts should vary.

Mead (1963, orig. 1935) studied three societies in New Guinea. In the mountainous home of the Arapesh, Mead observed men and women with remarkably similar attitudes and

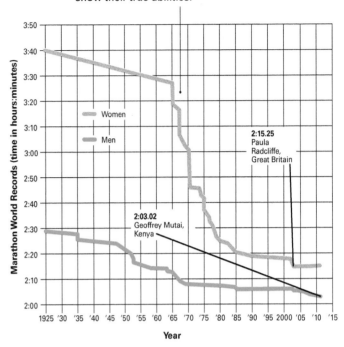

Diversity Snapshot

● The women's movement of the 1960s encouraged women to show their true abilities.

FIGURE 10–1 Men's and Women's Athletic Performance

Do men naturally outperform women in athletic competition? The answer is not obvious. Early in the twentieth century, men outpaced women by more than an hour in marathon races. But as opportunities for women in athletics have increased, women have been closing the performance gap. Only 12 minutes separate the current world marathon records for women (set in 2003) and for men (set in 2011).

Source: Marathonguide.com (2012).

In every society, people assume that certain jobs, patterns of behaviour, and ways of dressing are "naturally" feminine while others are just as obviously masculine. But in global perspective, we see remarkable variety in such social definitions. These men, Wodaabe pastoral nomads who live in the African nation of Niger, are proud to engage in a display of beauty most people in our society would consider feminine.

behaviour. Both sexes, she reported, were co-operative and sensitive to others—in short, what our culture would label "feminine."

Moving south, Mead studied the Mundugumor, whose headhunting and cannibalism stood in striking contrast to the gentle ways of the Arapesh. In this culture, both sexes were typically selfish and aggressive, traits we define as "masculine."

Finally, travelling west to the Tchambuli, Mead discovered a culture that, like our own, defined females and males differently. But, Mead reported, the Tchambuli *reversed* many of our ideas of gender: Females were dominant and rational, and males were submissive, emotional, and nurturing toward children. Based on her observations, Mead concluded that culture is the key to gender distinctions, because what one society defines as masculine another may see as feminine.

Some critics view Mead's findings as "too neat," as if she saw in these societies just the patterns she was looking for. Deborah Gewertz (1981) challenged what she called Mead's "reversal hypothesis," pointing out that Tchambuli males are really the more aggressive sex. Gewertz explains that Mead visited the Tchambuli (who themselves spell their name Chambri) during the 1930s, after they had lost much of their property in tribal wars, and observed men rebuilding their homes, a temporary role for Chambri men.

George Murdock's Research

In a broader study of more than 200 pre-industrial societies, George Murdock (1937) found some global agreement on which tasks are feminine and which are masculine. Hunting and warfare, Murdock observed, generally fall to men, and home-centred tasks such as cooking and child care tend to be women's work. With their simple technology, pre-industrial societies apparently assign roles reflecting men's and women's physical characteristics. With their greater size and strength, men hunt game and protect the group; because women bear children, they do most of the work in the home.

Beyond this general pattern, Murdock found much variety. Consider agriculture: Women did the farming in about the same number of societies as men; in most societies, the two sexes divided this work. When it came to many other tasks, from building shelters to tattooing the body, Murdock found that pre-industrial societies of the world were as likely to turn to one sex as the other.

EVALUATE Global comparisons show that, overall, societies do not consistently define tasks as feminine or masculine. With industrialization, the importance of muscle power declines, further reducing gender differences (Nolan & Lenski, 2010). In sum, gender is too variable to be a simple expression of biology; what it means to be female and male is mostly a creation of society.

CHECK YOUR LEARNING By comparing many cultures, what do we learn about the origin of gender differences?

Patriarchy and Sexism

Conceptions of gender vary, and there is evidence of societies in which women have greater power than men. One example is the Musuo, a very small society in southwestern China's

Yunnan province, in which women control most property, select their sexual partners, and make most decisions about everyday life. The Musuo appear to be a case of **matriarchy** ("rule by mothers"), *a form of social organization in which females dominate males*, which has only rarely been documented in human history.

The pattern found almost everywhere in the world is **patriarchy** ("rule by fathers"), *a form of social organization in which males dominate females*. Global Map 10–1 shows the great variation in the relative power and privilege of women that exists from country to country. According to the United Nations's Gender Inequality Index, Slovenia, Switzerland, Germany, Sweden, and Denmark give women the highest social standing; by contrast, women in Yemen, Niger, Dominican Republic, Afghanistan, and Mali have the lowest social standing compared with men. Of the world's 195 nations, Canada was ranked 23rd in terms of gender equality (United Nations Development Programme, 2014).

The justification for patriarchy is **sexism**, *the belief that one sex is innately superior to the other*. Sexism is not just a matter of individual attitudes; it is also built into the institutions of our society. *Institutional sexism* is found throughout the economy, with women highly concentrated in low-paying jobs. Similarly, the legal system has long excused violence against women, especially on the part of boyfriends, husbands, and fathers.

matriarchy a form of social organization in which females dominate males

patriarchy a form of social organization in which males dominate females

sexism the belief that one sex is innately superior to the other

Window on the World

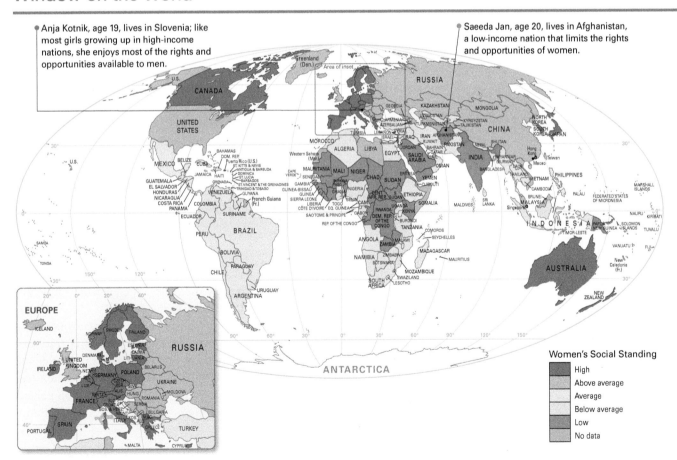

GLOBAL MAP 10–1 Women's Power in Global Perspective

Women's social standing in relation to men's varies around the world. In general, women live better in rich countries than in poor countries. Even so, some nations stand out: In Slovenia, Switzerland, Germany, Sweden, and Denmark, women come closest to social equality with men.

Source: United Nations Development Programme (2014).

The Costs of Sexism to Men

In patriarchal societies, sexism limits the talents and the ambitions of the half of the human population who are women. Although men benefit in many respects from sexism, their privilege comes with certain costs. Masculinity in our culture encourages men to engage in numerous high-risk behaviours: using tobacco and alcohol, playing dangerous sports, and even driving recklessly. As Marilyn French (1985) argues, patriarchy drives men to relentlessly seek control, not only of women but also of themselves and their world. Thus masculinity is linked not only to accidents but also to suicide, violence, and stress-related diseases. The *Type A personality*—marked by chronic impatience, driving ambition, competitiveness, and free-floating hostility—is one cause of heart disease and an almost perfect match with the behaviour our culture considers masculine (Ehrenreich, 1983).

Finally, as men seek control over others, they lose opportunities for intimacy and trust. As one analyst put it, competition is supposed to "separate the men from the boys." In practice, however, it separates men from men and from everyone else (Raphael, 1988).

Must Patriarchy Go On?

In pre-industrial societies, women have little control over pregnancy and childbirth, which limits the scope of their lives. In those same societies, men's greater height and physical strength are highly valued resources. But industrialization, including birth control technology, increases people's choices about how to live. In societies like our own, biological differences offer little justification for patriarchy.

But males are socially dominant in many areas of life in Canada and elsewhere. Does this mean that patriarchy is inevitable? Some researchers claim that biological factors such as differences in hormones and slight differences in brain structure "wire" the two sexes with different motivations and behaviours—especially aggressiveness in males—making patriarchy difficult or perhaps even impossible to change (Goldberg, 1974; Rossi, 1985; Popenoe, 1993; Udry, 2000). However, most sociologists believe that gender is socially constructed and *can* be changed. The fact that no society has completely eliminated patriarchy does not mean that we must remain prisoners of the past.

To understand why patriarchy continues today, we must examine how gender is rooted and reproduced in society, a process that begins in childhood and continues throughout our lives.

Gender and Socialization

10.2 Explain the importance of gender to socialization.

From birth until death, gender shapes human feelings, thoughts, and actions. Children quickly learn that their society considers females and males different kinds of people; by about age three, they begin to think of themselves in these terms.

In the past, many people in Canada traditionally described women using terms such as "emotional," "passive," and "co-operative." By contrast, men were described as "rational," "active," and "competitive." It is curious that we were taught for so long to think of gender in terms of one sex being opposite to the other, especially because women and men have so much in common and also because research suggests that most people develop personalities that are a mix of feminine and masculine traits (Bem, 1993; Krieger, 2003; Benoit et al., 2009).

gender roles (also known as **sex roles**) attitudes and activities that a society links to each sex

Just as gender affects how we think of ourselves, so it teaches us how to behave. **Gender roles** (also known as **sex roles**) are *attitudes and activities that a society links to each sex*. A culture that defines males as ambitious and competitive encourages them to seek out positions of leadership and play team sports. To the extent that females are defined as deferential and emotional, they are expected to be supportive helpers and quick to show their feelings (Johnson & Greaves, 2007).

Gender and the Family

The first question people usually ask about a newborn—"Is it a boy or a girl?"—has great importance because the answer involves not just sex but the likely direction of the child's life. In fact, gender is at work even before a child is born, especially in lower-income nations, because parents hope their firstborn will be a boy rather than a girl (Pappas, 2011).

Soon after birth, family members welcome infants into the "pink world" of girls or the "blue world" of boys (Bernard, 1981). People even send gender messages in the way they handle infants. One researcher at an English university presented an infant dressed as either a boy or a girl to a number of women; her subjects handled the "female" child tenderly, with frequent hugs and caresses, while treating the "male" child more aggressively, often lifting him up high in the air or bouncing him on a knee (Bonner, 1984; Tavris & Wade, 2001). The lesson is clear: The female world revolves around co-operation and emotion, and the male world puts a premium on independence and action.

Gender and the Peer Group

About the time they enter school, children begin to move outside the family and make friends with others of the same age. Considerable research points to the fact that young children tend to form single-sex play groups (Martin & Fabes, 2001).

Peer groups teach additional lessons about gender. After spending a year watching children at play, Janet Lever (1978) concluded that boys favour team sports with complex rules and clear objectives such as scoring runs or making touchdowns. Such games nearly always have winners and losers, reinforcing masculine traits of aggression and control.

Girls, too, play team sports. But, Lever explains, girls also play hopscotch, jump rope, or simply talk, sing, or dance. These activities have few rules, and rarely is victory the ultimate goal. Instead of teaching girls to be competitive, Lever explains, female peer groups promote the interpersonal skills of communication and co-operation, presumably the basis for girls' future roles as wives and mothers.

The games we play offer important lessons for our later lives. Lever's observations recall Carol Gilligan's gender-based theory of moral reasoning, discussed in Chapter 3 ("Socialization: From Infancy to Old Age"). Boys, Gilligan (1982) claims, reason according to abstract principles. For them, "rightness" amounts to "playing by the rules." By contrast, girls consider morality a matter of responsibility to others. Recent research on sports among adolescents and emergent adults extends these earlier findings.

Gender and Schooling

Gender shapes our interests and beliefs about our own abilities, guiding areas of study and, eventually, career choices (Correll, 2001). The types of courses people take in high school still reflect traditional gender patterns. For example, more girls than boys learn secretarial skills and take vocational classes such as cosmetology and food services. On the other hand, classes in woodworking and auto mechanics attract mostly young men.

In 2011, women accounted for 59 percent of adult's aged 25 to 34 with university degrees (Statistics Canada, 2013a). As such, it is no surprise that they are now represented in many fields of study that once excluded them, including mathematics, chemistry, and biology. But men still predominate in philosophy and STEM programs, which include sciences, technology, engineering, and mathematics, and women cluster in health and social science programs. Newer areas of study are also gender-typed: More men than women take computer science, and courses in gender studies enrol mostly women. This is a pattern for many high-income countries. Research in Italy largely confirms these findings: While the gender gap in the relational and economic fields has declined because of women's transfer to these areas, in the technical and scientific fields a substantial gender gap persists in recent cohorts (Triventi, 2010).

Biddiboo/The Image Bank/Getty Images

Sex is a biological distinction that develops prior to birth. Gender is the meaning that a society attaches to being female or male. Gender differences are a matter of power, because what is defined as masculine typically has more importance than what is defined as feminine. Infants begin to learn the importance of gender by the way parents treat them. Do you think this child is a girl or a boy? Why?

The Beauty Myth

Beth: I can't eat lunch. I need to be sure I can get into that black dress for tonight.

Sarah: Maybe eating is more important than looking good for Tom.

Beth: That's easy for you to say. You're a size 2, and Jake adores you!

The Duchess of Windsor once remarked, "A woman cannot be too rich or too thin." The first half of her observation might apply to men as well, but certainly not the second. After all, the vast majority of ads placed by the $11-billion-a-year North American cosmetics industry and the $60-billion diet industry target women.

One way our culture supports the beauty myth is through beauty pageants for women; over the years, contestants have become thinner and thinner.

According to Naomi Wolf (1990), certain cultural patterns add up to a "beauty myth" that is damaging to women. First, the foundation of the beauty myth is the notion, taught from an early age, that women should measure their worth in terms of physical appearance or, more specifically, how physically attractive they are *to men*. Of course, the standards of beauty embodied by the *Playboy* centrefold or the 100-pound fashion model are out of reach for most women.

Second, our society teaches women to prize relationships with men, whom they presumably attract with their beauty. Striving for beauty not only drives women to be extremely disciplined but also forces them to be highly attentive to and responsive to men. In short, beauty-minded women try to please men and avoid challenging male power.

Belief in the beauty myth is one reason that so many young women are focused on body image, particularly being as thin as possible, often to the point of endangering their health. During the past several decades, the share of young women who develop an eating disorder such as anorexia nervosa (dieting to the point of starvation) or bulimia (binge eating followed by vomiting) has risen dramatically.

The beauty myth, then, is the idea that striving to be physically attractive to men is the key to women's happiness. As Wolf sees it, however, such efforts are more likely to end up standing between women and their power and worthwhile accomplishments.

The beauty myth affects males as well: Men are told repeatedly that they should want to "possess" beautiful women. Such ideas about beauty reduce women to objects and motivate thinking about women as if they were dolls or status symbols rather than human beings.

There can be little doubt that the idea of beauty is important in everyday life. According to Wolf, the question is whether beauty is about how we look or how we act.

What Do You Think?

1. Is there a "money myth" that states that people's income is a simple reflection of their talent? Does it apply more to one sex than to the other?

2. Can you see a connection between the beauty myth and the rise of eating disorders among young women in North America?

3. Among people with physical disabilities, do you think that issues of "looking different" are more serious for women or for men? Why?

Gender and the Mass Media

Since television captured the public imagination in the early 1950s, white males have held centre stage; racial and ethnic minorities were all but absent from television until the early 1970s. Even when both sexes appeared on camera, men generally played the brilliant detectives, fearless explorers, and skilled surgeons. Women played the less capable characters, often unnecessary except for the sexual interest they added to the story.

Historically, advertisements have shown women in the home, cheerfully using cleaning products, serving food, trying out appliances, and modelling clothes. Men predominate in ads for cars, travel, banking services, industrial companies, and alcoholic beverages. The authoritative voiceover—the voice that describes a product on television and radio—is almost always male (Davis, 1993; Coltrane & Messineo, 2000; Messineo, 2008).

A careful study of gender in advertising reveals that men usually appear taller than women, implying male superiority. Women, by contrast, are more frequently presented lying down (on sofas and beds) or, like children, seated on the floor. Men's facial expressions and behaviour give off an air of competence and imply dominance; women often appear childlike, submissive, and sexual. Men focus on the products being advertised, and women often focus on the men (Goffman, 1979; Cortese, 1999).

Advertising also perpetuates what Naomi Wolf (1990) calls the "beauty myth." The Seeing Sociology in Everyday Life box on page 316 takes a closer look at how this myth affects both women and men.

Murray Close/Lionsgate/Everett Collection

In our society, the mass media have enormous influence on our attitudes and behaviour, and what we see shapes our view of gender. In the 2012 film *The Hunger Games*, we see Jennifer Lawrence playing Katniss Everdeen, a take-charge, female lead character. Such a portrayal is an exception to the conventional pattern by which active males play against more passive females. In your opinion, how much can the mass media change conventional ideas about gender? Why?

Gender and Social Stratification

10.3 Analyze the extent of gender inequality in various social institutions.

Gender involves more than how people think and act. It is also about how society is organized, how our lives are affected by social hierarchy. The reality of gender stratification can be seen in just about every aspect of our everyday lives. We look, first, to the world of working women and men.

Working Women and Men

In 1891, just 11.4 percent of females in Canada were engaged in paid employment. In 2014, 61 percent of women aged 15 and over worked for income, compared to 70 percent of men (Statistics Canada, 2015a). As the Power of Society figure at the beginning of this chapter points out, our society continues to encourage men more than women to work for income.

Among people in the labour force, women are more likely to do part-time and casual work, which is often lower-paid and with fewer benefits. In 2014, they accounted for nearly 70 percent of all part-time workers (Statistics Canada, 2015b). Men may still dominate the labour force, but the once common view that earning income is a man's role no longer holds true.

Factors that have contributed to a change in the Canadian labour force include the decline of farming, the growth of cities, a shrinking family size, and a rising divorce rate. In Canada, along with most other nations of the world, women working for income are the rule rather than the exception. In fact, 80 percent of Canadian women with a partner and a child under the age of 16 living at home are employed. In total, women represent 47.3 percent of all those employed in Canada (Statistics Canada, 2015b).

Gender and Occupations

Although women are closing the gap with men as far as working for income is concerned, the work done by the two sexes remains very different. The 2011 National Household Survey reports that less than half (47.3 percent) of the labour force is women. Among the various occupations, a high concentration of women exists in sales and service work, which draws

27.1 percent of all working women, most of whom are retail sales workers or administrative assistants. Another 24.6 percent of employed women are in business, finance, and administrative occupations. Table 10–1 shows the 20 most common occupations for women in Canada, which taken together represent 45.8 percent of all working women. Among the so-called "pink collar jobs," where women account for 9 out of 10 workers, are administrative assistant; registered nurse and registered psychiatric nurse; early childhood educator and assistant; and receptionist (Statistics Canada, 2013b).

Men dominate most other job categories, including the building trades, where over 95 percent of carpenters, welders, electricians, and machine operators are men. Likewise, men make up 98 percent of automotive service technicians, 96 percent of truck drivers, 77 percent of shippers and receivers, 76 percent of security guards, and 58 percent of retail and wholesale managers. As of May 2015, women were employed in 36 percent of all management positions and 28 percent of all senior management positions. According to a recent survey by the executive search firm Rosenzweig & Company, women hold only 8.5 percent of highest earning positions in Canada's top 100 companies. While that is an increase from 4.6 percent in 2006, 42 percent of Canadian corporations still have no women on their boards, and the majority of CEOs are men (OECD, 2012; Statistics Canada, 2013b, 2015c; CBC News, 2015a).

These findings parallel results from recent U.S. studies. Research indicates that just 19 of the *Fortune* 500 companies in the United States have a woman as their chief executive officer (CEO), and just 16 percent of the seats on corporate boards of directors are held by women. Of the 500 highest-paid corporate CEOs, just 17 are women. Such a gender imbalance leads many people to support increasing the leadership role of women in the business world.

TABLE 10–1 The 20 Most Common Occupations Among Women Aged 15 Years and Over and the Share of Women in the Total Workforce, 2011

Occupations Among Women	Number of Women	Percentage Distribution	Proportion of Women Among All (15 years and over)
All occupations	7 960 720	100.0	48.0
All of the 20 most common occupations	3 643 410	45.8	74.4
Retail salespersons	371 345	4.7	56.6
Administrative assistants	316 565	4.0	96.3
Registered nurses and registered psychiatric nurses	270 425	3.4	92.8
Cashiers	260 190	3.3	84.2
Elementary school and kindergarten teachers	227 810	2.9	84.0
Administrative officers	201 320	2.5	81.5
Food counter attendants, kitchen helpers, and related support occupations	200 695	2.5	64.2
General office support workers	184 720	2.3	84.4
Early childhood educators and assistants	181 705	2.3	96.8
Nurse aides, orderlies, and patient service associates	166 440	2.1	85.7
Retail and wholesale trade managers	151 605	1.9	41.7
Light duty cleaners	150 800	1.9	70.6
Receptionists	146 025	1.8	94.0
Food and beverage servers	142 400	1.8	78.8
Accounting and related clerks	121 160	1.5	85.1
Other customer and information services representatives	119 970	1.5	64.2
Accounting technician and bookkeepers	117 050	1.5	87.3
Financial auditors and accountants	112 300	1.4	55.2
Secondary school teachers	101 960	1.3	58.6
Social and community service workers	98 925	1.2	76.9

Source: Statistics Canada (2013b), http://www12.statcan.gc.ca/nhs-enm/2011/as-sa/99-012-x/2011002/tbl/tbl02-eng.cfm. Reproduced and distributed on an "as is" basis with the permission of Statistics Canada.

This claim is made not only as a matter of fairness but also because research into the earnings of this country's largest corporations shows that the companies with more women in leadership positions are more profitable (Graybow, 2007; Catalyst, 2012; *Forbes*, 2012; U.S. Department of Labor, 2012).

Overall, although more women now work for pay and some women have made significant inroads into traditionally male-dominated occupations, by and large they still remain segregated in the labour force in jobs at the middle and low end of the pay scale, usually supervised by men and with limited opportunity for advancement (Charles, 1992; Krahn & Lowe, 1998; Benoit, 2000a).

Gender stratification in everyday life is easy to see: Female nurses assist male physicians, female secretaries serve male executives, and female flight attendants are under the command of male airline pilots. In any field, the greater a job's income and prestige, the more likely it is to be held by a man. For example, about 750 000 people are employed as teachers and professors in Canada. Of these, 68 percent are women, but they are not distributed evenly in the teaching profession. In 2011, women accounted for 97 percent of early childhood educators and assistants, 84 percent of elementary and kindergarten teachers, and 59 percent of secondary school teachers. In 2005, women represented 40.5 percent of university teachers. In 2008, across Canada's 92 colleges and universities, only 15 percent had female presidents (Statistics Canada, 2006a; AUCC, 2008, 2014).

How are women kept out of certain jobs? By defining some kinds of work as "men's work," society defines women as less competent than men. In a study of coal miners, Suzanne Tallichet (2000) found that most men considered it "unnatural" for women to work in the mines. Women who did so were defined as deviant and subject to labelling as "sexually loose" or as lesbians. Such labelling made these women outcasts, presented a challenge to holding the job, and made advancement all but impossible.

In the corporate world, too, the higher in the company we look, the fewer women we find. You hardly ever hear anyone say out loud that women don't belong at the top levels of a company. But many people seem to feel this way, which can prevent women from being promoted. Sociologists describe this barrier as a *glass ceiling* that is not easy to see but blocks women's careers all the same.

Gender and Unemployment

The unemployment rates for women and men typically rise and fall together, with men having a slightly higher level of joblessness. By the end of 2014, the unemployment rate for women stood at 6.8 percent, just below the figure of 8 percent for men (Statistics Canada, 2015d). High unemployment among men reflects the fact that men's work is heavily in manufacturing, and many factory jobs have moved abroad.

Gender, Income, and Wealth

In 2011, the median annual earnings for women working full time were $47 300, and men working full time earned $65 700. This means that for every dollar earned by men, women earned about 72 cents (Statistics Canada, 2013c). These earnings differences are greatest among older workers because older working women typically have less education and seniority than older working men. Earning differences are smaller among younger workers because younger men and women tend to have similar schooling and work experience.

The gender wage gap also varies according to occupation. It is relatively low among judges, a profession in which women reported a median employment income of $225 220, earning 98.5 percent as much as men. The gap increases among social workers, a field in which women earned $51 381, or 90.3 percent as much as their male colleagues. Among chiropractors, however, the gap is much greater, with women earning $42 132, or 77.4 cents for every dollar earned by male chiropractors (Statistics Canada, 2011a).

The main reason women earn less is the *type* of work they do: largely clerical and service jobs. In effect, jobs and gender interact. People still perceive jobs with less clout as "women's work," just as people devalue certain work simply because it is performed by women (England, Hermsen, & Cotter, 2000; Cohen & Huffman, 2003).

In recent decades, supporters of gender equality have proposed a policy of "comparable worth," paying people not according to the historical double standard but according to the level of skill and responsibility involved in the work. As an example of the problem, consider the case of floral designers, the people who make attractive displays of flowers. These workers—most of whom are women—earn on average $14.16 an hour. At the same time, the people who drive the vans and other small trucks to deliver these flower arrangements—most of whom are men—earn about $16.80 an hour (PayScale, 2015a, 2015b). It is hard to see why floral arrangers would earn just 84 percent as much as van drivers. Is there a difference in the level of skill or training required? Or does the disparity reflect gender stratification?

In response to such patterns, several nations, including Canada, Great Britain, and Australia, have adopted comparable worth policies. Dedication to the pay equity principle was tested in the summer of 1998 when the Canadian Human Rights Tribunal determined that female federal workers were owed an estimated $5 billion. The federal government found itself torn between supporting the pay equity principle and dealing with the cost of doing so (Greenspoon, 1998). Finally, on October 29, 1999, the Public Service Alliance of Canada and the federal government came to an agreement to implement the Canadian Human Rights Tribunal's decision. Comparative worth policies have found limited acceptance in the United States. As a result, it is estimated that women in the United States lose as much as $1 billion in income annually.

A second cause of gender-based income disparity has to do with society's view of the family. Both men and women have children, of course, but our culture gives more of the responsibility of parenting to women. Pregnancy and raising small children keep many younger women out of the labour force at a time when their male peers are making significant career advancements. When women workers return to the labour force, they have less job experience and seniority than their male counterparts (Stier, 1996; Drolet, 2001; Sussman & Yssaad, 2005). Variation does exist across high-income countries, however. Countries with "women-friendly" parental leaves and benefits and publicly funded child-care programs lessen the cost of child-bearing for female workers (Benoit, 2000b; Leira, 2000; Beaujot, 2006). Canada's year-long parental and maternity leave policy moves the country closer to the Nordic norm of at least one year of paid leave for parents with their newborns.

In addition, women who choose to have children may be unable or unwilling to take on fast-paced jobs that tie up their evenings and weekends. To avoid role strain, they may take jobs that offer shorter commuting distances, more flexible hours, and employer-provided child-care services. For example, research shows that having babies alters the career paths of female academics (Mason & Goulden, 2004; Sussman & Yssaad, 2005). Women pursuing both a career and a family are torn between their dual responsibilities in ways that men are not. One study found that almost half of women in competitive jobs took time off to have children, compared to about 12 percent of men. Similarly, later in life, women are more likely than men to take time off from work to care for aging parents (Hewlett & Luce, 2005; Hewlett, 2010). Role conflict is also experienced by women on campus: Several studies confirm that young female professors with at least one child are less likely to have tenure than comparable men in the same field (Shea, 2002; Ceci & Williams, 2011).

The two factors noted so far—type of work and family responsibilities—account for about two-thirds of the earnings difference between women and men. A third factor—discrimination against women—accounts for most of the remainder (Fuller & Schoenberger, 1991). Drolet (2001) found that gender differences in the opportunity to supervise and perform certain tasks accounted for about 5 percent of the gender wage gap in Canada. Because overt discrimination is illegal, it is practised in subtle ways. Women on their way up the corporate ladder often run into the glass ceiling described earlier; company officials may deny its existence, but it effectively prevents many women from rising above middle management.

For all these reasons, women earn less than men in all major occupational categories. This disparity varies from job to job, but a significant gender wage gap remains.

Housework: Women's "Second Shift"

In Canada, housework has always presented a cultural contradiction: We claim that keeping a home is essential for family life, but people get little reward for doing it (Bernard, 1981). Here, as around the world, taking care of the home and children has been considered "women's work" (see Global Map 4–1 on page 114). As women have entered the labour force, the amount of housework women do has gone down, but the *share* done by women has stayed the same. Figure 10–2 shows that, overall, women average 13.8 hours a week of housework, compared to 8.3 hours for men. As the figure shows, women in all categories do significantly more housework than men.

Men do support the idea of women entering the paid labour force, and most count on the money women earn. But many men resist taking on an equal share of household duties (Heath & Bourne, 1995; Harpster & Monk-Turner, 1998; Stratton, 2001).

Gender and Education

In the past, our society considered schooling more necessary for men, who worked outside of the home, than for women, whose lives revolved around the home. By 1997, however, women earned 59 percent of all associate and bachelor's degrees and first professional degrees (Statistics Canada, 2000); this remained about the same in 2000 (Statistics Canada, 2003) and 2011 (Statistics Canada, 2013a).

In the mid-1990s, for the first time, women were earning half of postgraduate degrees, which are often a springboard to high-prestige jobs. For all areas of study in 1997, women earned 51 percent of master's degrees and 36 percent of all doctorates. In 2011, the proportions awarded to women at master's (58.1 percent) and doctoral levels (47.3 percent) were higher than ever before, and men outnumbered women only at the doctoral level (Statistics Canada, 2003, 2006b, 2013a).

College and university doors have opened to women, and differences in men's and women's majors are becoming smaller. In 1972–73, for example, women made up just 3 percent of students in engineering and applied sciences. In 2001–02, women received 24 percent of all degrees in these fields. Today, women's enrolment in STEM fields (science, technology, engineering, mathematics) has increased to 39 percent of all graduates. As of 2011, young women represent a majority of graduates with science and technology degrees (58.6 percent), almost two-thirds of biomedical degrees (64.2 percent), and a minority of physical science (41.3 percent), engineering (23.1 percent), and math degrees (30.4 percent) (Statistics Canada, 2000, 2003, 2006b, 2013a).

Figure 10–3 shows the post-secondary educational attainment by men and women aged 25 to 34 (recent

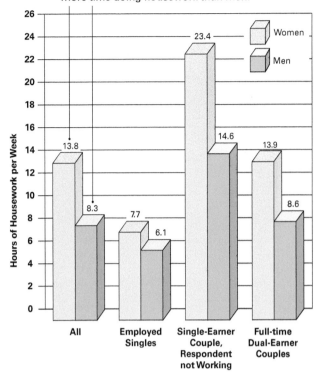

● On average, women spend considerably more time doing housework than men.

FIGURE 10–2 Time Spent on Household Domestic Work, by Working Arrangement, Canada, 2010

Regardless of employment or family status, women do more housework than men. What effect do you think the added burden of housework has on women's ability to advance in the workplace?

Source: Milan, Keown, and Urquijo (2011).

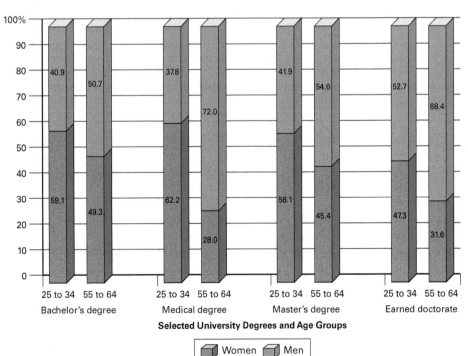

FIGURE 10–3 Proportion of Selected University Degrees as the Highest Level of Educational Attainment by Sex and Age Group, Canada, 2011

Source: Statistics Canada (2013a).

graduates) and those aged 55 to 64. The data reveal that, with the exception of doctorate degrees, recent graduate women are more likely to complete bachelor's, medical, and master's degree.

Based on the educational gains women have made, some analysts suggest that education is the one social institution where women rather than men predominate. More broadly, women's relative advantages in school performance have prompted a debate about whether men are in danger of "being left behind." While on the surface this may seem to be the case, we would do well to keep in mind that even when occupation and education are comparable, women still only earn 92 percent of men's wages (Morissette, Picot, & Lu, 2013). Educational strides have allowed women to close some of the wage gap, but the existence of glass ceilings and sexist attitudes toward women in general prevents women from earning greater incomes than men.

Gender and Politics

Before 1918, women were not allowed to vote in federal elections. Until 1919, they were not allowed to sit in the House of Commons. Agnes Macphail of Grey County, Ontario, was the first woman member of Parliament when, in 1921, she successful ran for the Progressive Party of Canada—a farmer-based political party. A decade later, in 1929, women were permitted to sit in the Canadian Senate (Prentice et al., 1996). By 1940, women could vote in all provincial elections, with Quebec being the last province to lift the ban. A number of racist measures prevented the extension of the franchise to all women. Japanese women, for example, were barred from voting until racial justifications for exclusion were repealed from the Dominion Elections Act in 1948. Doukhobor women won the right to vote in federal elections in 1955. It was not, however, until 1960 that women from all racial and ethnic backgrounds could vote in Canada, when the right was extended to Aboriginal women. Table 10–2 identifies milestones, as well as setbacks, in women's gradual movement into Canadian political life.

TABLE 10–2   Significant Advances and Setbacks for Woman in Canadian Politics

1883	First three suffrage bills are introduced by Sir John A. Macdonald. They are all defeated.
1887	In Manitoba, women property owners vote for the first time in municipal elections.
1906	Manitoba Legislation bars married women from municipal voting. The ban is lifted in 1907.
1916	Women in Alberta and Saskatchewan are given the provincial vote. The efforts of Nellie McClung and the Political Equality League help to win the provincial vote for women in Manitoba.
1917	Women with property are permitted to hold office in Saskatchewan. Nurses, under the Military Voters Act, are given the federal vote. Women in British Columbia are given the provincial vote. Women who are British subjects and have close relatives in the armed forces can vote, on behalf of their male relatives, in federal elections. In Alberta, Miss Robert McAdams and Mrs. Louise McKinney are first women to be elected to provincial legislatures.
1918	Women are given full federal franchise with the exception of Asian and Aboriginal women. Women are given the vote in Nova Scotia.
1919	Women are given the vote in New Brunswick.
1921	Mary Ellen Smith is appointed first woman Cabinet minister in British Columbia. Agnes McPhail is the first woman elected to the House of Commons.
1922	Women in Prince Edward Island are given the right to vote in provincial elections and to hold elected office.
1925	Women over the age of 25 can vote in Newfoundland.
1929	The Persons Case goes to the British Privy Council, overturning the decision of the Supreme Court of Canada. Women are deemed to be "persons" and can be appointed to the Senate.
1938	The Dominion Elections Act is revised. It retains the provision that disqualifies anyone who is already barred in provincial elections on racial grounds from voting in federal elections. This disenfranchises Japanese, Chinese, and "Hindu" (anyone from the Indian subcontinent) Canadians.
1940	Women gain the vote in Quebec provincial elections.
1948	Section of the Dominion Elections Act that makes race a ground for exclusion in federal franchise is repealed.
1955	Doukhobors win the right to vote in federal elections. Restrictions barring married women from the federal public service are removed.
1957	Ellen Fairclough is sworn in as the first woman federal Cabinet minister.
1960	Aboriginal people are no longer required to give up treaty rights or status in order to qualify to vote in federal elections.
1967	Royal Commission on the Status of Women is set up with Senator Florence Bird as chairperson.
1982	The Canadian Charter of Rights and Freedoms embeds into the Constitution the right of all citizens to vote.
1993	Kim Campbell appointed as Canada's first female prime minister.
2015	A record number of women are voted into the House of Commons; however, they continue to be underrepresented in government, occupying only 26 percent of the seats. No woman has yet to be elected as prime minister.

Source: Collated by J. Burkowicz from Manitoba Women's Directorate (1984); Canadian Human Rights Commission (2015); Nellie McClung Foundation (2015).

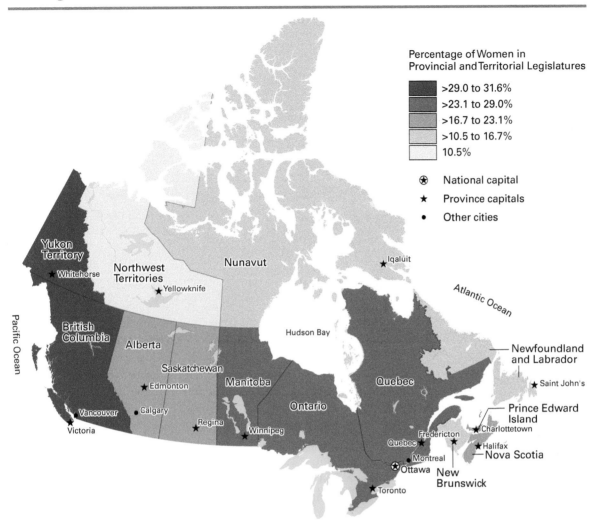

Percentage of Women in Provincial and Territorial Legislatures

- >29.0 to 31.6%
- >23.1 to 29.0%
- >16.7 to 23.1%
- >10.5 to 16.7%
- 10.5%

⊛ National capital
★ Province capitals
● Other cities

NATIONAL MAP 10–1   Representation of Women in Provincial and Territorial Legislatures, 2012

Although women make up half of Canadian adults, in 2012 just 20 percent of the seats in provincial and territorial legislatures were held by women. Look at the geographic variations in the map. In which regions of the country have women gained the greatest political power? What do you think accounts for this pattern?

Source: Library of Parliament (2012).

A small number of Canadian female politicians have achieved national prominence, as in the cases of Kim Campbell, who, in 1993, served as Canada's first female prime minister, and Alexa McDonough, who served as the national New Democratic Party leader from 1997 to 2003. Nevertheless, in 2006, Canada's provincial premiers and territorial leaders, as well as our prime minister, were a completely male cast. In 2011, two provinces were headed by women (Newfoundland and Labrador and British Columbia) and women occupied 76 of the 308 seats in the House of Commons. Green Party leader Elizabeth May made history in the May 2001 federal election by winning her party's first ever seat in the House of Commons. She is also the only female federal leader on Parliament Hill. The representation of women varies widely at the provincial and territorial levels. Women fill over 30 percent of the seats in Yukon and British Columbia, while managing to hold only 10.5 percent of the seats in Northwest Territories. National Map 10–1 shows the proportion of women in provincial and territorial legislatures across Canada.

Women make up half of Earth's population, but they hold just 20 percent of seats in the world's 190 parliamentary governments. This number is considerably higher than the

3 percent of seats women held 50 years ago. In part, this rise reflects the fact that almost 100 countries have adopted some form of gender quota (either constitutional, enacted into legislation, or a voluntary goal of political parties) that ensures women a greater political voice. Even so, only in 24 countries, among them Rwanda, Cuba, and Sweden, do women represent over one-third of the members of parliament (Paxton, Hughes, & Green, 2006; Inter-Parliamentary Union, 2012).

Finally, gender is linked to politics in another way—by shaping political attitudes. In general, women are somewhat more likely than men to favour liberal positions, such as expanding social programs that provide a "safety net" for people who are in need. On the other hand, men are somewhat more likely than women to favour conservative positions, such as building a stronger military. This difference in political attitudes is sometimes called the *gender gap* (Erickson & O'Neill, 2002). The gender gap was pronounced in the 2000 federal election, in which women were more likely to vote for the New Democratic Party and men for the Canadian Alliance. In 2004, however, the gap almost completely disappeared, leading to the success of the Conservative Party. The Tories captured 38 percent of female and 39 percent of male votes (Gidengil et al., 2006).

Gender and the Military

For the last 100 years, women have served in the Canadian Armed Forces. They served as nurses in the 1885 Northwest Rebellion, and in 1941 the Canadian government enrolled over 45 000 women for full-time military service. As of January 2014, women represented 14.8 percent of all Canadian troops as well as people serving in all capacities in the armed forces. Over 9400 women can be found in the Regular Force, and more than 4800 in the Primary Reserve.

Women make up a growing share of the Canadian military. Since 1989, the majority of combat roles have been opened to women, with the prohibition to serving on submarines being lifted in 2000. In 2006, Canada lost its first female soldier, Captain Nicola Goddard, who was killed in a battle with the Taliban near Kandahar (National Defence and the Canadian Armed Forces, 2014a, 2014b).

The debate on women's role in the military has been going on for centuries. Some people object to opening doors in this way, claiming that women lack the physical strength of men. Others point out that military women are better educated and score higher on intelligence tests than military men. But the heart of the issue is our society's deeply held view of women as *nurturers*—people who give life and help others—which clashes with the image of women trained to kill.

Whatever our views of women and men, the reality is that military women are in harm's way. In part, this reflects the fact that a soldier can be faced with violent combat at any time. Modern warfare technology also blurs the distinction between combat and noncombat personnel. A combat pilot can fire missiles at a distant target; by contrast, non-fighting medical evacuation teams must travel directly into the line of fire. Finally, for years women in the Canadian military have reported sexual harassment from their peers and commanding officers. Thus, they face harm not only from enemy combatants but also from within their own ranks. In 2015, a former Supreme Court justice issued a report into the military culture that found sexual harassment "endemic" within the organization, in part as a result of a culture of machismo that resists change (CBC News, 2015b).

Are Women a Minority?

minority any category of people distinguished by physical or cultural difference that a society sets apart and subordinates

A **minority** is *any category of people distinguished by physical or cultural difference that a society sets apart and subordinates.* Given the clear economic disadvantage of being a woman in our society, it seems reasonable to say that women are a minority in Canada even though they outnumber men.[1]

---

[1]Sociologists use the term "minority" instead of "minority group" because, as explained in Chapter 5 ("Groups and Organizations"), women make up a *category*, not a group. People in a category share a status or identity but generally do not know one another or interact.

Even so, most white women do not think of themselves in this way. This is partly because, unlike racial minorities (including Aboriginal Canadians) and ethnic minorities (say, Haitian Canadians), white women are better represented at all levels of the class structure, including the very top.

Bear in mind, however, that at every class level, women typically have less income, wealth, education, and power than men. Patriarchy makes women dependent on men—first their fathers and later their husbands—for their social standing (Bernard, 1981).

Violence Against Women

In the nineteenth century, men claimed the right to rule their households, even to the point of using physical discipline against their wives, and a great deal of "manly" violence is still directed against women. A Statistics Canada report estimates that about 173 600 women were victims of violent crime in 2011. This is 5 percent higher than the rate of violent crimes committed against men. Men are also more likely to be the perpetrators, being responsible for 83 percent of the violent crimes committed against women (Sinha, 2013).

While men also can be victims of sexual assault, 7 out of 10 victims are female, indicating a strong association between gender and this type of violent activity The rate of spousal assault also varies among women. The incidence of spousal assault against Aboriginal women is 2.5 times higher than that of spousal assault reported by non-Aboriginal women. Aboriginal women are also much more likely than non-Aboriginal women to report more harsh forms of violence, as well as higher likelihood of fearing for their lives (Sinha, 2013).

Violence toward women also occurs in casual relationships. As noted in Chapter 6 ("Sexuality and Society"), most rapes involve men known to and often trusted by their victims. Dianne Herman (2001) claims that abuse of women is built into our way of life. All forms of violence against women—from the catcalls that intimidate women on city streets to a pinch in a crowded subway to physical assaults that occur at home—express what she calls a "rape culture" of men trying to dominate women. Feminists explain that sexual violence is fundamentally about *power*, not sex, and therefore should be understood as a dimension of gender stratification. In global perspective, violence against women is built into other cultures in many different ways. One case in point is the practice of female genital mutilation, a painful and often dangerous surgical procedure that is performed in more than two dozen countries and is also known to occur in the United States, as shown in Global Map 10–2 on page 326. The practice is considered a form of child assault in Canada and prohibited under the Criminal Code. Some provincial and territorial colleges of physicians have also come out against the practice of female genital mutilation and made official statements advising physicians to refuse requests to perform the operation (Health Canada, 1999). However, this does not mean that the practice has ceased among some ethnic groups. The Thinking About Diversity box on page 327 describes an instance of female genital mutilation that took place in California and asks whether this practice, which some people defend as promoting "morality," amounts to a case of violence against women.

Violence Against Men

Our way of life also encourages violence against men. As noted in Chapter 7 ("Deviance"), the police accuse men of crimes at three times the rate for women. In addition, while women are more likely to be sexually victimized, stalked, and harassed by phone, men are more likely to be murdered, subject to serious physical assault, and robbed (Sinha, 2013).

Our culture tends to define masculinity in terms of aggression and violence. "Real men" work and play hard, speed on the highways, and let nothing stand in their way. A higher crime rate is one result, with a high number of male perpetrators. But even when no laws are broken, men's lives involve more stress and isolation than women's lives, which is one reason that the suicide rate for men is four times higher than for women (Centers for Disease Control and Prevention, 2012). In addition, as noted earlier, men live, on average, about five fewer years than women.

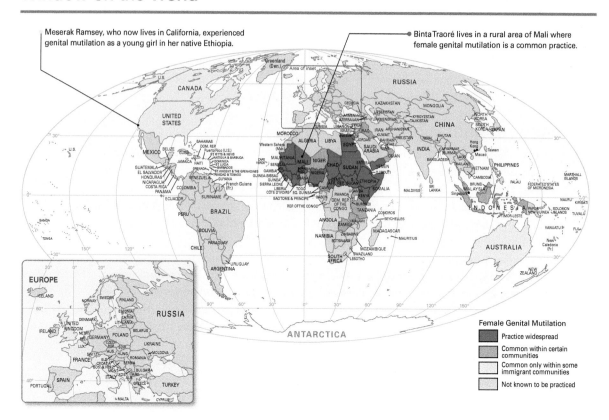

Meserak Ramsey, who now lives in California, experienced genital mutilation as a young girl in her native Ethiopia.

Binta Traoré lives in a rural area of Mali where female genital mutilation is a common practice.

Female Genital Mutilation

- Practice widespread
- Common within certain communities
- Common only within some immigrant communities
- Not known to be practiced

GLOBAL MAP 10–2   Female Genital Mutilation in Global Perspective

Female genital mutilation is known to be performed in at least 29 countries around the world. Across Africa, the practice is common and affects a majority of girls in the eastern African nations of Sudan, Ethiopia, and Somalia. In several Asian nations, the practice is limited to a few ethnic minorities. In the United States, Canada, several European nations, and Australia, there are reports of the practice among some immigrants.

Sources: Population Reference Bureau (2010) and World Health Organization (2012).

Violence is not simply a matter of choices made by individuals. It is cultural—that is, built into our very way of life, with resulting harm to both men and women. In short, the way any society constructs gender plays an important part in how violent or peaceful that society will be.

Sexual Harassment

sexual harassment comments, gestures, or physical contacts of a sexual nature that are deliberate, repeated, and unwelcome

Sexual harassment refers to *comments, gestures, or physical contacts of a sexual nature that are deliberate, repeated, and unwelcome.* During the 1990s, sexual harassment became an issue of national importance that rewrote the rules for workplace interaction between women and men.

Most (but not all) victims of sexual harassment are women. The reason is that, first, our culture encourages men to be sexually assertive and to view women in sexual terms. As a result, social interaction between men and women in the workplace, on campus, and elsewhere can easily take on sexual overtones. Second, most people in positions of power—including business executives, doctors, bureau chiefs, assembly line supervisors, professors, and military officers—are men who oversee the work of women. Surveys carried out in widely different work settings show that about 3 percent of women claim that they have been harassed on the job in the last year and about half of women say that they receive unwanted sexual attention (NORC, 2013:1486).

Sexual harassment is sometimes obvious and direct: A supervisor may ask for sexual favours from an employee and make threats if the advances are refused. Courts have declared

Thinking About Diversity: Race, Class, and Gender

Female Genital Mutilation: Violence in the Name of Morality

Meserak Ramsey, a woman born in Ethiopia and now working as a nurse in California, paid a visit to an old friend's home. Soon after arriving, she noticed her friend's 18-month-old daughter huddled in the corner of a room in obvious distress. "What's wrong with her?" she asked.

Ramsey was shocked when the woman said her daughter had recently had a clitoridectomy, the surgical removal of the clitoris. This type of female genital mutilation—performed by a midwife, a tribal practitioner, or a doctor and typically without anesthesia—is common in Nigeria, Sierra Leone, Senegal, Sudan, Ethiopia, Somalia, and Egypt and is known to be practised in certain cultural groups in other nations around the world. It is illegal in the United States as well as in Canada.

Among members of highly patriarchal societies, husbands demand that their wives be virgins at marriage and remain sexually faithful thereafter. The point of female genital mutilation is to eliminate sexual feeling, which, people assume, makes women less likely to violate sexual norms and thus be more desirable to men who seek to control them. In about one-fifth of all cases, an even more severe procedure, called infibulation, is performed, in which the entire external genital area is removed and the surfaces are stitched together, leaving only a small hole for urination and menstruation. Before marriage, a husband retains the right to open the wound and ensure himself of his bride's virginity.

Kuenzig/Laif/Aurora Photos

These young women have just undergone female genital mutilation. What do you think should be done about this practice?

How many women have undergone female genital mutilation? Worldwide, estimates suggest that at least 3 million girls (most live in Africa) undergo this procedure annually. Although the annual number is declining, globally, the number of women who have been cut in this way is at least 75 million and probably exceeds 100 million (Kristof & Wu Dunn, 2010; World Health Organization, 2012). In the United States, hundreds or even thousands of such procedures are performed every year. In most cases, immigrant mothers and grandmothers who have themselves been mutilated insist that young girls in their family follow their example. Indeed, many immigrant women demand the procedure *because* their daughters now live in the United States, where sexual mores are more lax. "I don't have to worry about her now," the girl's mother explained to Meserak Ramsey. "She'll be a good girl."

Medically, the consequences of genital mutilation include more than the loss of sexual pleasure. Pain is intense and can persist for years. There is also danger of infection, infertility, and even death. Ramsey knows the anguish all too well: She herself underwent genital mutilation as a young girl. She is one of the lucky ones who has had few medical problems since. But the extent of her suffering is suggested by this story: She invited a young couple to stay at her home. Late at night, she heard the woman's cries and burst into their room to investigate, only to learn that the couple was making love and the woman had just had an orgasm. "I didn't understand," Ramsey recalls. "I thought that there must be something wrong with American girls. But now I know that there is something wrong with me." Or with a system that inflicts such injury in the name of traditional morality.

What Do You Think?

1. Is female genital mutilation a medical procedure or a means of social control? Explain your answer.

2. Can you think of other examples of physical mutilation imposed on women? What are they?

3. What do you think should be done about female genital mutilation in places where it is widespread? Do you think respect for human rights should override respect for cultural differences in this case?

Sources: Crossette (1995); Boyle, Songora, and Foss (2001); and Sabatini (2011).

---

that such *quid pro quo* sexual harassment (the Latin phrase means "one thing in return for another") is a violation of civil rights.

More often, however, the problem of unwelcome sexual attention is a matter of subtle behaviour—sexual teasing, off-colour jokes, comments about someone's looks—that may or may not be intended to harass anyone. But based on the *effect* standard favoured by many feminists, such actions add up to creating a *hostile environment* for women in the workplace. Incidents

In recent decades, our society has recognized sexual harassment as an important problem. At least officially, unwelcome sexual attention is no longer tolerated in the workplace. The television show *Mad Men* gives us a window back to the early 1960s, before the more recent wave of feminism began.

of this kind are far more complex because they involve different perceptions of the same behaviour. For example, a man may think that repeatedly complimenting a co-worker on her appearance is simply being friendly. The co-worker, on the other hand, may believe that the man is thinking of her in sexual terms and is not taking her work seriously, an attitude that could harm her job performance and prospects for advancement.

Pornography

Chapter 6 ("Sexuality and Society") defined *pornography* as sexually explicit material that causes sexual arousal. However, people take different views of exactly what is and what is not pornographic; the law gives local communities the power to define whether sexually explicit material violates "community standards of decency" and lacks "any redeeming social value."

Traditionally, people have raised concerns about pornography as a *moral* issue. But pornography also plays a part in gender stratification. From this point of view, pornography is really a *power* issue because most pornography dehumanizes women, depicting them as the playthings of men.

In addition, there is widespread concern that some forms of pornography encourage violence against women by portraying them as weak and undeserving of respect. According to feminist Andrea Dworkin, pornography teaches men contempt for women (1987). A 2014 survey found that 50 percent of adults are concerned that pornography is harmful to Canadian society (Forum Research, 2014).

Like sexual harassment, pornography raises complex and sometimes conflicting concerns. Despite the fact that some material may offend just about everyone, many people, including "pro-sex" feminists (McElroy, 1995), defend the rights of free speech and artistic expression. Nevertheless, pressure to restrict pornography has increased in recent decades, reflecting both the long-standing concern that pornography weakens morality and the more recent concerns that it is demeaning and threatening to women.

Theories of Gender

10.4 Apply sociology's major theories to gender stratification.

Why does gender exist in all known societies? Sociology's macro-level approaches—the structural-functional and social-conflict approaches—address the central place of gender in social organization. In addition, the symbolic-interaction approach helps us see the importance of gender in everyday life. The Applying Theory table summarizes the important insights offered by each of these approaches.

Structural-Functional Theory

The structural-functional approach views society as a complex system of many separate but integrated parts. From this point of view, gender serves as a means to organize social life.

As Chapter 2 ("Culture") explained, the earliest hunting and gathering societies had little power over biology. Lacking effective birth control, women could do little to prevent pregnancy, and the responsibilities of child care kept them close to home. At the same time, men's greater strength made them better suited for warfare and hunting. Over the centuries,

Applying Theory

Gender			
	Structural-Functional Theory	**Symbolic-Interaction Theory**	**Social-Conflict and Intersection Theories**
What is the level of analysis?	Macro-level	Micro-level	Macro-level
What does gender mean?	Parsons described gender in terms of two complementary patterns of behaviour: masculine and feminine.	Numerous sociologists have shown that gender is part of the reality that guides social interaction in everyday situations.	Engels described gender in terms of the power of one sex over the other. Gender interacts with class, race, and ethnicity to create various levels of disadvantage.
Is gender helpful or harmful?	Helpful. Gender gives men and women distinctive roles and responsibilities that help society operate smoothly. Gender builds social unity as men and women come together to form families.	Hard to say; gender is both helpful and harmful. In everyday life, gender is one of the factors that help us relate to one another. At the same time, gender shapes human behaviour, placing men in control of social situations. Men tend to initiate most interactions, while women typically act in a more deferential manner.	Harmful. Gender limits people's personal development. Gender divides society by giving power to men to control the lives of women. Intersection theory explains that minority women face multiple disadvantages.

this sex-based division of labour became institutionalized and largely taken for granted (Lengermann & Wallace, 1985; Freedman, 2002).

Industrial technology opens up a much greater range of cultural possibilities. With human muscle power no longer the main energy source, the physical strength of men becomes less important. In addition, the ability to control reproduction gives women greater choices about how to live. Modern societies relax traditional gender roles as the societies become more meritocratic because rigid roles waste an enormous amount of human talent. Yet change comes slowly because gender is deeply rooted in culture.

Talcott Parsons: Gender and Complementarity

As Talcott Parsons (1942, 1951, 1954) observed, gender helps integrate society, at least in its traditional form. Gender forms a *complementary* set of roles that links women and men into family units and gives each sex responsibility for carrying out important tasks. Women take the lead in managing the day-to-day life of the household and raising children. Men connect the family to the larger world as they participate in the labour force.

FPG/Archive Photos/Getty Images

In the 1950s, Talcott Parsons proposed that sociologists interpret gender as a matter of *differences*. As he saw it, masculine men and feminine women formed strong families and made for an orderly society. In recent decades, however, social-conflict theory has reinterpreted gender as a matter of *inequality*. From this point of view, Canadian society places men in a position of dominance over women.

Thus gender plays an important part in socialization. Society teaches boys—presumably destined for the labour force—to be rational, self-assured, and competitive. Parsons called this complex of traits *instrumental* qualities. To prepare girls for child rearing, socialization stresses *expressive* qualities, such as emotional responsiveness and sensitivity to others.

Society encourages gender conformity by instilling in men and women a fear that straying too far from accepted standards of masculinity or femininity will cause rejection by the opposite sex. In simple terms, women learn to reject non-masculine men as sexually unattractive, and men learn to reject unfeminine women. In sum, gender integrates society both structurally (in terms of what we do) and morally (in terms of what we believe).

EVALUATE Influential in the 1950s, this approach has lost much of its standing today. First, structural-functionalism assumes a singular vision of society that is not shared by everyone. For example, historically, many women have worked outside the home because of economic necessity, a fact not reflected in Parsons's conventional, middle-class view of social life. Second, Parsons's analysis ignores the personal strains and social costs of rigid gender roles. Third, in the eyes of those seeking sexual equality, Parsons's gender "complementarity" amounts to little more than women submitting to male domination.

CHECK YOUR LEARNING In Parsons's analysis, what functions does gender perform for society?

Symbolic-Interaction Theory

The symbolic-interaction approach takes a micro-level view of society, focusing on face-to-face interaction in everyday life. As suggested in Chapter 4 ("Social Interaction in Everyday Life"), gender affects everyday interaction in a number of ways.

Gender and Everyday Life

If you watch women and men interacting, you will probably notice that women typically engage in more eye contact than men do. Why? Holding eye contact is a way of encouraging the conversation to continue; in addition, looking directly at someone clearly shows the other person that you are paying attention.

This pattern is an example of sex roles, defined earlier as the way a society defines how women and men should think and behave. To understand such patterns, consider the fact that people with more power tend to take charge of social encounters. When men and women engage one another, as they do in families and in the workplace, it is men who typically initiate the interaction. That is, men speak first, set the topics of discussion, and control the outcomes. With less power, women are expected to be more *deferential*, meaning that they show respect for others of higher social position. In many cases, this means that women (just like children or others with less power) spend more time being silent and also encouraging men (or others with more power) not just with eye contact but by smiling or nodding in agreement. As a technique to control a conversation, men often interrupt others, just as they typically feel less need to ask the opinions of other people, especially those with less power (Tannen, 1990; Henley, Hamilton, & Thorne, 1992, 1994; Ridgeway & Smith-Lovin, 1999).

Gender and Reality Construction

If a woman is planning to marry a man, should she take his last name or keep her own? This decision is about more than how she will sign a cheque: It also affects how employers will see her and even her future pay.

In the United States today, about 8 percent of women who marry men keep their own name. This is a decline from the 1990s, when the share peaked at about 23 percent. Research shows that women who marry in their thirties (after they have started a career) are much more likely to keep their own name than women who marry in their early twenties. Research also shows that subjects asked to assess women's personal traits typically perceive those who take their husband's last name as more caring, dependent, and emotional (traditional feminine qualities). By contrast, they assess women who keep their maiden names as more ambitious, talented, and capable (more competitive against others, including men). Data on salaries reveal a significant difference in pay: Married women who keep their own name end up earning about 40 percent more than those who adopt their husband's name (Shellenbarger, 2011).

Such patterns demonstrate how gender shapes the reality we experience in everyday life. They also suggest that women who face a decision about surnames when they marry may consider the choice they make will carry particular meaning to others and have important consequences.

EVALUATE The strength of the symbolic-interaction approach is helping us see how gender plays a part in shaping almost all our everyday experiences. Our society defines men (and everything we consider to be masculine) as having more value than women (and what is defined as feminine). For this reason, just about every familiar social encounter is "gendered" so that men and women interact in distinctive and unequal ways.

The symbolic-interaction approach suggests that individuals socially construct the reality they experience as they interact every day, using gender-linked traits such as clothing and demeanour (and, for women, also last name) as elements of their personal "performances" that shape ongoing reality.

Gender plays a part in the reality we experience. Yet, as a structural dimension of society, gender is at least largely beyond the immediate control of any of us as individuals as it gives some people power over others. In other words, patterns of everyday social interaction reflect our society's gender stratification. Everyday interaction also helps reinforce this inequality. For example, to the extent that fathers take the lead in dinner table discussions, the entire family learns to expect men to "display leadership" and "show their wisdom." As mothers do the laundry, children learn that women are expected to do household chores.

A limitation of the symbolic-interaction approach is that by focusing on situational social experience, it says little about the broad patterns of inequality that set the rules for our everyday lives. To understand the roots of gender stratification, we have to "kick it up a level" to see more closely how society makes men and women unequal. We will do this using the social-conflict approach.

CHECK YOUR LEARNING Point to several ways that gender shapes the everyday face-to-face interactions of individuals.

Social-Conflict Theory

From a social-conflict point of view, gender involves much more than differences in behaviour—gender is a structural system of *power* that provides privilege to some and disadvantage to others. Consider the striking similarity between the way traditional ideas about gender benefit men and harm women and the way ideas about race benefit men and disadvantage racial and ethnic minorities. Conventional ideas about gender do not make society operate smoothly, as a structural-functional analysis suggests. On the contrary, gender is a societal structure that creates division and tension, with men seeking to protect their privileges as women challenge the status quo.

As earlier chapters noted, the social-conflict approach draws heavily on the ideas of Karl Marx. Yet as far as gender is concerned, Marx was a product of his times, and his writings focused almost entirely on men. However, his friend and collaborator Friedrich Engels did develop a theory of gender stratification.

Gender and Class Inequality

Looking back through history, Engels saw that in hunting and gathering societies, the activities of women and men, though different, had equal importance. A successful hunt brought men great prestige, but the vegetation gathered by women provided most of a group's food supply.

As technological advances led to a productive surplus, social equality and communal sharing gave way to private property and ultimately a class hierarchy, and men gained significant power over women. With surplus wealth to pass on to heirs, upper-class men needed to be sure that their sons were their own, which led them to control the sexuality of women. The desire to control both women's sexuality and property brought about monogamous marriage and the family. Women were taught to remain virgins until marriage, to remain faithful to their husbands thereafter, and to build their lives around bearing and raising one man's children. Family law ensures that property is transmitted within families from one generation to the next, keeping the class system intact.

According to Engels (1902, orig. 1884), the rise of capitalism makes male domination even stronger. First, capitalism uses trade and industrial production to create more wealth, which gives greater power to men as income earners and owners of property. Second, an expanding capitalist economy depends on turning people, especially women, into consumers who seek personal fulfillment by buying and using products. Third, society assigns women the task of maintaining the home to free men to work in factories. The double exploitation of capitalism, as Engels saw it, lies in paying low wages for male labour and paying women no wages at all.

EVALUATE Social-conflict analysis is strongly critical of conventional ideas about gender, claiming that society would be better off if we minimized or even did away with this dimension of social structure. That is, this approach regards conventional families, which traditionalists consider personally and socially positive, as an oppressive instrument of the ruling class. A problem with social-conflict analysis, then, is that it minimizes the extent to which women and men live together co-operatively, and often happily, in families. A second problem lies in the assertion that capitalism is the basis of gender stratification. In fact, agrarian societies are typically more patriarchal than industrial-capitalist societies. In addition, although socialist nations, including the People's Republic of China and the former Soviet Union, did move women into the labour force, by and large they provided women with very low pay in sex-segregated jobs (Haney, 2002; Rosendahl, 1997).

CHECK YOUR LEARNING According to Engels, how does gender support social inequality in a capitalist class system?

Intersection Theory

In recent years, an additional social-conflict approach has gained great importance in sociology: intersection theory. The key insight of intersection theory is that there are multiple systems of stratification based on race, class, and gender, and these systems do not operate independently of one another. On the contrary, these dimensions of inequality intersect and interact. Formally, then, **intersection theory** is *analysis of the interplay of race, class, and gender, which often results in multiple dimensions of disadvantage*. Research shows that disadvantages linked to race and gender often combine to produce especially low social standing for some people (Davis, 1981; Crenshaw, 1991; Ovadia, 2001; McCall, 2005).

Income data confirm the basic claim of intersection theory. Looking first at race and ethnicity, the median income in 2010 for Aboriginal women working full time was $40 062, while non-Aboriginal women reported a median income of $44 534; Southeast Asian women earned $36 416. Looking at gender, Aboriginal women earned 85 percent as much as Aboriginal men, and Southeast Asian women earned 80 percent as much as Southeast Asian men.

To explore the "intersection" of these dimensions of inequality, we find that some categories of women experience greater disadvantages. Black women earned only 76 percent as much as non-visible minority men, and Filipino women earned just 68 percent as much (Statistics Canada, 2011b). These income differences reflect minority women's lower positions in the occupational and educational hierarchies.

intersection theory analysis of the interplay of race, class, and gender, which often results in multiple dimensions of disadvantage

The basic insight of intersection theory is that various dimensions of social stratification—including race and gender—can overlap and form great disadvantages for some categories of people, including women working as caregivers. Thus Filipino women confront a "double disadvantage," earning 84 cents for every dollar earned by non-visible minority women, and just 68 cents for every dollar earned by non-visible minority men. How would you explain the fact that some categories of people are much more likely to end up in low-paying jobs like this one?

Intersection theory helps us to see that although gender has a powerful effect on our lives, it does not operate alone. Class position, race and ethnicity, gender, and sexual orientation form a multilayered system that provides disadvantages for some and privileges for others (Saint Jean & Feagin, 1998).

Feminism

10.5 Contrast liberal, radical, and socialist feminism.

Feminism is support of social equality for women and men, in opposition to patriarchy and sexism. The first wave of feminism in North America began in the 1840s as women opposed to slavery, including Elizabeth Cady Stanton and Lucretia Mott, drew parallels between the oppression of black people and the oppression of women. Their main objective was obtaining the right to vote, which was finally achieved in 1918 by most women in Canada. But other disadvantages persisted, causing a second wave of feminism to arise in the 1960s that continues today.

Basic Feminist Ideas

Feminism views the everyday lives of women and men through the lens of gender. How we think of ourselves (gender identity), how we act (gender roles), and our social standing as women or men (gender stratification) are all rooted in the operation of society.

Although feminists disagree about many things, most support four general principles:

1. **Taking action to increase equality.** Feminist thinking is political; it links ideas to action. Feminism is critical of the status quo, pushing for change toward social equality for women and men. Feminism opposes laws and cultural norms that limit the education, income, and job opportunities of women. For this reason, feminists have long supported

In her recent book, Sheryl Sandberg, an executive at Facebook, describes the workplace barriers—including discrimination and sexual harassment—faced by women in our society. Sandberg also claims that to overcome these barriers, women must reject societal definitions of women as second-class citizens and "lean in" toward the goal of greater leadership positions. Critics suggest that the barriers to success faced by average women are far greater than those overcome by privileged women such as Sandberg.

Peter Foley/Bloomberg/Getty Images

the passage of the Canadian Human Rights Act, which prohibits discrimination based on sex, among other characteristics. Many feminists are also guided by intersection theory to seek equality based on race and class as well as gender.

2. **Expanding human choice.** Feminists argue that cultural ideas about gender divide the full range of human qualities into two opposing and limiting spheres: the female world of emotion and co-operation and the male world of rationality and competition. As an alternative, feminists propose a "reintegration of humanity" by which all individuals develop all human traits (French, 1985).

3. **Ending sexual violence.** Today's women's movement seeks to eliminate sexual violence. Feminists argue that patriarchy distorts the relationships between women and men, encouraging violence against women in the form of rape, domestic abuse, sexual harassment, and pornography (Dworkin, 1987; Freedman, 2002).

4. **Promoting sexual freedom.** Finally, feminism advocates women having control over their sexuality and reproduction. Feminists support the free availability of birth control information. As Figure 10–4 shows, all married Canadian women of child-bearing age use contraception; the use of contraceptives is far less common in many lower-income nations. Most feminists also support a woman's right to choose whether to have children or to end a pregnancy, rather than allowing men—husbands, physicians, and legislators—to control their reproduction. Many feminists also support gay people's efforts to end prejudice and discrimination in a largely heterosexual culture (Ferree & Hess, 1995; Armstrong, 2002).

Types of Feminism

Although feminists agree on the importance of gender equality, they disagree on how to achieve it: through liberal feminism, socialist feminism, or radical feminism (Stacey, 1983; Vogel, 1983; Ferree & Hess, 1995; Armstrong, 2002; Freedman, 2002). The Applying Theory table on page 336 highlights the key arguments made by each type of feminist thinking.

Liberal Feminism

Liberal feminism is rooted in classic liberal thinking that individuals should be free to develop their own talents and pursue their own interests. Liberal feminists accept the basic organization of our society but seek to expand the rights and opportunities of women. As they see it, gender should not operate as a form of caste, to the disadvantage of women. As an important step to achieving this goal, they support the passage of the Charter of Rights and Freedoms. Liberal feminists also support reproductive freedom for all women. They respect the family as a social institution but seek changes in society, including more widely available maternity and paternity leave and child care for parents who work.

Given their beliefs in the rights of individuals, liberal feminists think that women should advance according to their individual efforts and merit, rather than by working collectively for change. Both women and men, through personal achievement, are capable of improving their lives, as long as society removes legal and cultural barriers.

Global Snapshot

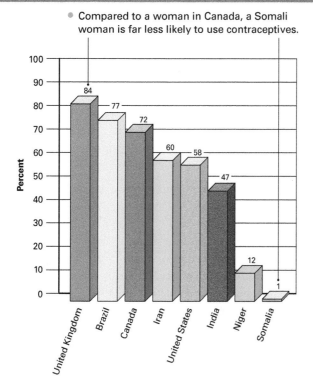

Compared to a woman in Canada, a Somali woman is far less likely to use contraceptives.

FIGURE 10–4 Use of Modern Contraceptive Methods by Married Women of Childbearing Age

In Canada, all married women of child-bearing age use contraception. In many lower-income countries, however, most women do not have the opportunity to make this choice.

Source: Population Reference Bureau (2015).

Socialist Feminism

Socialist feminism evolved from the ideas of Karl Marx and Friedrich Engels. From this point of view, capitalism increases patriarchy by concentrating wealth and power in the hands of a small number of men. Socialist feminists do not think the reforms supported by liberal feminists go far enough. They believe that the family form fostered by capitalism must change in order to replace "domestic slavery" with some collective means of carrying out housework and child care. Replacing the traditional family can come about only through a socialist revolution that creates a state-centred economy to meet the needs of all.

Radical Feminism

Like socialist feminism, *radical feminism* finds liberal feminism inadequate. Radical feminists believe that patriarchy is so firmly entrenched that even a socialist revolution would not end it. Instead, reaching the goal of gender equality means that society must eliminate gender itself.

One possible way to achieve this goal is to use new reproductive technology that has been developed by scientists in recent decades (see Chapter 13, "Family and Religion"). This technology has the ability to separate women's bodies from the process of child-bearing. With an end to motherhood, radical feminists reason, society could leave behind the entire family system, liberating women, men, and children from the oppression of family, gender, and sex itself (Dworkin, 1987). Radical feminism seeks an egalitarian and gender-free society, a revolution much more sweeping than that sought by Marx.

Multicultural and Global Feminism

The three types of feminism considered so far are strategies for change. They also tend to portray women as a single category of humanity, defined by their sex and subordinated by their

Applying Theory

Feminism			
	Liberal Feminism	**Socialist Feminism**	**Radical Feminism**
Does it accept the basic order of society?	Yes. Liberal feminism seeks change only to ensure equality of opportunity.	No. Socialist feminism supports an end to social classes and to family gender roles that encourage "domestic slavery."	No. Radical feminism supports an end to the family system.
How do women improve their social standing?	Individually, according to personal ability and effort.	Collectively, through socialist revolution.	Collectively, by working to eliminate gender itself.

society. In recent decades, however, new feminist perspectives have highlighted not only the common situation faced by all women but also their social and cultural differences (Collins, 2000; hooks, 2000; Tong, 2009).

Multicultural feminism draws on the insights provided by intersection theory. That is, while all women have a common position of oppression in relation to men, the life experiences of women differ according to their race, ethnicity, and class position. To put this differently, gender stratification cannot be completely understood without also taking account of racial oppression and class differences. In other words, systems of hierarchy are multidimensional, with various types of oppression that combine in their effects.

In the same way, global feminism attempts to recognize the common oppression in the lives of all the world's women, while also paying attention to their different positions within a world of nations set apart from one another by the system of global stratification. This simply means that the life experiences of women living in high-income nations are shaped by both oppression linked to gender and privilege linked to living in the core of the global capitalist economy. Similarly, the life experiences of women living in low-income nations reflect both gender stratification and their social location in an exploited region of the world.

Public Support for Feminism

Because all of the various types of feminism call for significant change, feminism has always been controversial. Today, about 31 percent of Canadian boys aged 12 to 17 support the idea that "a woman's most important role is to take care of her home and cook for her family" (Plan International, 2011). It is also true that only about 16 percent of Canadian adults claim that they are willing to identify themselves as feminists (Ipsos, 2014).

But, over time, the share of the population seeking opportunity and equality for women has steadily increased. The most dramatic changes took place in the early 1970s; later changes have been far smaller.

Most men and women who express criticism of feminism hold conventional ideas about gender. Some men oppose gender equality for the same reason that many white people have historically opposed social equality for racial minorities: They do not want to give up their privileges. Other men and women, including those who are neither rich nor powerful, distrust a social movement (especially its radical expressions) that attacks the traditional family and rejects social patterns that have guided male–female relations for centuries.

Men who have been socialized to value strength and dominance may feel uneasy about feminist ideals of men as gentle and warm (Doyle, 1983). Similarly, some women whose lives centre on their husbands and children may think that feminism does not value the social roles that give meaning to their lives. In general, opposition to feminism is greatest among women who have the least education and those who do not work outside the home (Marshall, 1985; Ferree & Hess, 1995; CBS News, 2005).

Support for feminism is strong and widely evident in academic circles. But this does not mean that feminism is accepted unequivocally. Some sociologists charge that feminism ignores a growing body of evidence that men and women think and act in somewhat different ways, and these differences may make complete gender equality impossible.

Furthermore, say critics, with its drive to increase women's presence in the workplace, feminism undervalues the crucial and unique contribution women make to the development of children, especially in the first years of life (Baydar & Brooks-Gunn, 1991; Popenoe, 1993; Gibbs, 2001).

Finally, there is the question of *how* women should go about improving their social standing. A large majority of adults in Canada think that women should have equal rights, but many also say that women should advance individually, according to their training and abilities.

For these reasons, most opposition to feminism is directed toward its socialist and radical forms, while support for liberal feminism is widespread. In addition, we are seeing an unmistakable trend toward gender equality, with more and more Canadian women participating in the labour force and an increasing number of male partners sharing responsibilities in the home. While gender equality in family and working life is more apparent in dual-career marriages of professional men and women (Hertz, 1986), pro-feminist men argue that their gender can be taught that both masculine and feminine identities are changing and that many of the choices open to them conflict with archaic masculine values (Morra & Smith, 1998).

Gender: Looking Ahead

Predictions about the future are no more than educated guesses. Just as economists disagree about the likely inflation rate a year from now, sociologists can offer only general observations about the likely future of gender and society.

Looking back, change has been remarkable. A century ago, women were second-class citizens, without access to many jobs, barred from public office, and with no right to vote. Although women remain socially disadvantaged, the movement toward equality has surged ahead. Two-thirds of people entering the workforce in the 1990s were women, and by 2000, for the first time, a majority of families had both husband and wife in the paid labour force. Today's economy depends a great deal on the earnings of women. In addition, the proportion of women in dual-earner families whose incomes were higher than their husband's rose from 11.9 percent in 1976 to 29.2 percent in 2008 (Williams, 2010).

Many factors have contributed to this long-term transformation. Perhaps most important, industrialization and advances in computer technology have shifted the nature of work from physically demanding tasks that favoured male strength to jobs that require thought and imagination. This change puts women and men on an even footing. Also, because birth control technology has given us greater control over reproduction, women's lives are less constrained by unwanted pregnancies.

Many women and men have deliberately pursued social equality. For example, sexual harassment complaints in the workplace are taken much more seriously today than they were a generation ago. Another important trend is the increasing share of college degrees that are earned by women. This trend, in turn, is likely to reduce the earnings gap in the years to come as more women assume positions of power in the corporate and political worlds (Foroohar, 2011). As these trends unfold, social change involving gender in the twenty-first century may turn out to be as great as those that have already taken place.

How much do you think conceptions of gender will change over your lifetime? Will there be more change in the lives of women or men? Why?

Seeing Sociology in Everyday Life

Can you spot "gender messages" in the world around you?

As this chapter makes clear, gender is one of the basic organizing principles of everyday life. Most of the places we go and most of the activities we engage in as part of our daily routines are "gendered," meaning that they are defined as either more masculine or more feminine. Understanding this fact, corporations keep gender in mind when they market products to the public. Take a look at the ads shown on this page and on page 339. In each case, can you explain how companies use gender to sell these products?

Image Courtesy of The Advertising Archives

GUCCI

There are a lot of gender dynamics going on in this ad. What do you see?

Generally, our society defines cosmetics as feminine because most cosmetics are marketed toward women. How and why is this ad different?

FACE

TIME FIGHTER

MENSGROOM

FACE CREAM
CRÈME POUR LE VISAGE

50mL 1.7 fl. oz.

What gender messages do you see in this ad?

DONNA KARAN
NEW YORK

HINT Looking for "gender messages" in ads is a process that involves several levels of analysis. Start on the surface by noting everything obvious in the ad, including the setting, the background, and especially the people. Then notice how the people are shown—what they are doing, how they are situated, their facial expressions, how they are dressed, and how they appear to relate to each other. Finally, state what you think is the message of the ad, based on both the ad itself and what you know about the surrounding society.

Seeing Sociology in *Your* Everyday Life

1. Look through some recent magazines and select three advertisements that involve gender. In each case, provide analysis of how gender is used in the ad.

2. Go to www.sociologyinfocus.com to access the Sociology in Focus blog, where you can read the latest posts by a team of young sociologists who apply the sociological perspective to topics of popular culture.

3. Do some research on the history of women's issues in your province or territory. When was the first woman sent to Parliament? What laws once existed that restricted the work women could do? Do any such laws exist today?

Carol Beckwith/Robert Estall photo
agency/Alamy Stock Photo

Making the Grade

Gender and Inequality

(10.1) Describe research that points to how society creates gender stratification. (pages 310–314)

Gender refers to the meaning a culture attaches to being female or male.

- Evidence that gender is rooted in culture includes global comparisons by Margaret Mead and others showing how societies define what is feminine and masculine in various ways.
- Gender is not only about difference: Because societies give more power and other resources to men than to women, gender is an important dimension of social stratification. **Sexism** is built into the operation of social institutions.
- Although some degree of **patriarchy** is found almost everywhere, it varies throughout history and from society to society.

gender stratification the unequal distribution of wealth, power, and privilege between men and women

matriarchy a form of social organization in which females dominate males

patriarchy a form of social organization in which males dominate females

sexism the belief that one sex is innately superior to the other

Gender and Socialization

(10.2) Explain the importance of gender to socialization. (pages 314–317)

Through the socialization process, gender becomes part of our personalities **(gender identity)** and our actions **(gender roles)**. All the major agents of socialization—family, peer groups, schools, and the mass media—reinforce cultural definitions of what is feminine and masculine.

gender roles (also known as sex roles) attitudes and activities that a society links to each sex

Gender and Social Stratification

(10.3) Analyze the extent of gender inequality in various social institutions. (pages 317–328)

Gender stratification shapes **the workplace**:

- Women account for 48 percent of the paid labour force, with 27.1 percent of all working women holding sales or service jobs.
- Comparing full-time Canadian workers, women annually earn 72 percent as much as men.

Gender stratification shapes **family life**:

- Most unpaid housework is performed by women, whether or not they hold jobs outside the home.
- Pregnancy and raising small children keep many women out of the labour force at a time when their male peers are making important career gains.

Gender stratification shapes **education**:

- Women now earn 59 percent of all bachelor's degrees.
- Women make up 62.2 percent of adults aged 25 to 34 with a medical degree and are an increasing share of graduates in professions traditionally dominated by men, including laboratory research and business administration.

Gender stratification shapes **politics**:

- Although the number of women in politics has increased significantly, the vast majority of elected officials, especially at the national level, are men.
- Women make up only about 14.8 percent of Canadian military personnel.

Violence against women and men is a widespread problem linked to how a society defines gender.

- **Sexual harassment** mostly victimizes women because our culture encourages men to be assertive and to see women in sexual terms.
- **Pornography** portrays women as sexual objects. Many see pornography as a moral issue; because some forms of pornography dehumanize women, it is also a power issue.

minority any category of people distinguished by physical or cultural difference that a society sets apart and subordinates

sexual harassment comments, gestures, or physical contacts of a sexual nature that are deliberate, repeated, and unwelcome

Theories of Gender

(**10.4**) Apply sociology's major theories to gender stratification. (pages 328–333)

Structural-functional theory suggests that

- in pre-industrial societies, distinctive roles for males and females reflect biological differences between the sexes.
- in industrial societies, marked gender inequality becomes dysfunctional and gradually decreases.

Talcott Parsons described gender differences in terms of complementary roles that promote the social integration of families and society as a whole.

Symbolic-interaction theory suggests that

- individuals use gender as one element of their personal performances as they socially construct reality through everyday interactions.
- gender plays a part in shaping almost all our everyday experiences.

Because our society defines men as having more value than women, the sex roles that define how women and men should behave place men in control of social situations; women play a more deferential role.

Social-conflict theory suggests that

- gender is an important dimension of social inequality and social conflict.
- gender inequality benefits men and disadvantages women.

Friedrich Engels tied gender stratification to the rise of private property and a class hierarchy. Marriage and the family are strategies by which men control their property through control of the sexuality of women. Capitalism exploits everyone by paying men low wages and assigning women the task of maintaining the home.

Intersection theory suggests that

- particular dimensions of difference in women's lives combine in a multi-layered system, creating unique disadvantage for various categories of women.
- visible minority women encounter greater social disadvantages than non-visible minority women and earn much less than non-visible minority men.

intersection theory analysis of the interplay of race, class, and gender, which often results in multiple dimensions of disadvantage

Feminism

(**10.5**) Contrast liberal, radical, and socialist feminism. (pages 333–337)

Feminism

- endorses the social equality of women and men and opposes patriarchy and sexism.
- seeks to eliminate violence against women.
- advocates giving women control over their reproduction.

There are three types of feminism:

- Liberal feminism seeks equal opportunity for both sexes within the existing society.
- Socialist feminism claims that gender equality will come about by replacing capitalism with socialism.
- Radical feminism seeks to eliminate the concept of gender itself and to create an egalitarian and gender-free society.

Multicultural feminism expands the focus on gender stratification to take into account the intersection of gender with race and ethnicity; global feminism points out that gender inequality also involves the varying positions of women around the world in the system of global stratification.

Today, support for social equality for women and men is widespread. Just 31 percent of Canadian boys say that women should stick to their traditional roles in society. Support for liberal feminism is widespread, with greater opposition directed toward socialist and radical feminism.

11 Race and Ethnicity

auremar/Fotolia

LEARNING OBJECTIVES

11.1 Explain the social construction of race and ethnicity.

11.2 Describe the extent and causes of prejudice.

11.3 Distinguish discrimination from prejudice.

11.4 Identify examples of pluralism, assimilation, segregation, and genocide.

11.5 Assess the social standing of racial and ethnic categories of Canadian society.

the Power of Society

to shape marriage

Couples by visible minority group, Canada, 2011

Visible minority groups	All Couples	Mixed Unions	Non-Mixed Unions
	number	percentage	
Japanese	32 820	78.7	21.3
Latin American	112 265	48.2	51.8
Black	167 950	40.2	59.8
Filipino	155 700	29.8	70.2
Arab	94 315	25.4	74.6
Korean	41 370	22.5	77.5
Southeast Asian	74 560	21.9	78.1
West Asian	51 300	19.5	80.5
Chinese	351 640	19.4	80.6
South Asian	407 510	13.0	87.0
Multiple visible minorities[1]	40 415	64.9	35.1
Visible minority, n.i.e.[2]	27 215	52.4	47.6

[1]This category includes respondents who reported more than one visible minority group by checking off two or more mark-in circles, e.g., "Black" and "South Asian."

[2]The abbreviation "n.i.e." means "not included elsewhere." This category includes respondents who reported a write-in response such as "Guyanese," "West Indian," "Tibetan," "Polynesian" or "Pacific Islander," etc.

Source: Statistics Canada (2014). http://www12.statcan.gc.ca/nhs-enm/2011/as-sa/99-010-x/99-010-x2011003_3-eng.pdf. This does not constitute an endorsement by Statistics Canada of this product.

Is love colour blind? While in the last 20 years their numbers have continued to gradually increase, mixed-race couples account for only 4.6 percent of all married and common-law couples in Canada. Most mixed-race unions are between one visible minority and one non-visible minority member. Significantly, not all categories mix to the same extent. Individuals who identify as Japanese form the highest rate (78.7 percent) of mixed unions while those identifying as South Asian form the lowest (13 percent).

Chapter Overview

This chapter explains how race and ethnicity are created by society. Canada is a nation that bases its identity on racial and ethnic diversity. Here and elsewhere, both race and ethnicity are not only matters of difference but also dimensions of social inequality.

Kablonk! RF/Golden Pixels LLC/Alamy
Stock Photo

On a cool November morning in Toronto, the instructor of a sociology class at York University is leading a small-group discussion of race and ethnicity. He explains that the meaning of both concepts is far less clear than most people think. Then he asks, "How do you describe yourself?"

Eva Rodriguez leans forward in her chair and is quick to respond. "Who am I? Or should I say what am I? This is hard for me to answer. Most people think of race as black and white. But it's not. I have both black and white ancestry in me, but you know what? I don't think of myself in that way. I don't think of myself in terms of race at all. It would be better to call me Puerto Rican or Hispanic. Personally, I prefer the term 'Latina.' Calling myself Latina says I have mixed racial heritage, and that's what I am. I wish more people understood that race is not clear-cut."

This chapter examines the meaning of race and ethnicity. There are now millions of people in Canada who, like Eva Rodriguez, do not think of themselves in terms of a single category but as having a mix of ancestry.

The Social Meaning of Race and Ethnicity

(**11.1**) Explain the social construction of race and ethnicity.

As the opening to this chapter suggests, people often confuse race and ethnicity. For this reason, we begin with some basic definitions.

Race

A **race** is *a socially constructed category of people who share biologically transmitted traits that members of a society consider important*. People may classify one another racially based on physical characteristics such as skin colour, facial features, hair texture, and body shape.

Racial diversity appeared among our human ancestors as the result of living in different geographic regions of the world. In regions of intense heat, for example, humans developed darker skin (from the natural pigment melanin), as protection from the sun; in regions with moderate climates, people developed lighter skin. Such differences are literally only skin deep because human beings the world over are members of a single biological species.

The striking variety of physical traits found today is also the product of migration; genetic characteristics once common to a single place (such as light skin or curly hair) are now found in many lands. Especially pronounced is the racial mix in the Middle East (that is, western Asia), historically a crossroads of migration. Greater physical uniformity characterizes more isolated people, such as the island-dwelling Japanese. But every population has some genetic mixture, and increasing contact among world's people ensures even more blending of physical characteristics in the future.

race a socially constructed category of people who share biologically transmitted traits that members of a society consider important

ethnicity a shared cultural heritage

The range of biological variation in human beings is far greater than any system of racial classification allows. This fact is made obvious by trying to place all of the people pictured here into simple racial categories.

Although we think of race in terms of biological elements, race is a socially constructed concept. It is true that human beings differ in any number of ways involving physical traits, but a "race" comes into being only when the members of a society decide that some particular physical trait (such as skin colour or eye shape) actually *matters.*

Because race involves social definitions, it is a highly variable concept. For example, the members of U.S. society consider racial differences more important than people of many other countries. They also tend to "see" three racial categories: typically, black, white, and Asian. Canadians commonly see Aboriginal, Asian, white, and black. Other societies identify many more categories. People in Brazil, for instance, distinguish between *branca* (white), *parda* (brown), *morena* (brunette), *mulata* (mulatto), *preta* (black), and *amarela* (yellow) (Inciardi, Surratt, & Telles, 2000).

In addition, race may be defined differently by various categories of people within a society. Research shows that white people in North America "see" black people as having darker skin colour than black people do (Hill, 2002).

The meanings and importance of race not only differ from place to place but also change over time. Back in 1900, for example, it was common in Canada to doubt the extent to which people of Irish, Italian, Jewish, or Slavic ancestry were "white" or to even consider them as "non-white." (Iacovetta, 1992; Satzewich, 2000). By 1950, however, this was no longer the case, and such people today are considered part of the "white" category (Loveman, 1999; Brodkin, 2007).

Today, Statistics Canada presents data on visible minorities rather than on race and allows people to describe themselves using more than one racial category, allowing one or more choices among more than 10 options and "other."

Racial Types

Scientists invented the concept of race more than a century ago as they tried to organize the world's physical diversity into three racial types. They called people with lighter skin and fine hair *Caucasoid*, people with darker skin and coarse hair *Negroid*, and people with yellow or brown skin and distinctive folds on the eyelids *Mongoloid*.

Sociologists consider such terms misleading at best and harmful at worst. For one thing, no society contains biologically "pure" people. The skin colour of people we might call "Caucasoid" (or "Indo-European," "Caucasian," or more commonly "white") ranges from very light (typical in Scandinavia) to very dark (in southern India). The same variation exists among so-called "Negroids" ("Africans" or more commonly "black" people) and "Mongoloids" ("Asians"). In fact, many "white" people (say, in southern India) actually have darker skin than many "black" people (the Aborigines of Australia). Overall, the three racial categories differ in just 6 percent of their genes, and there is actually more genetic variation *within* each category than *between* categories. This means that two people in the European nation of Sweden, randomly selected, are likely to have at least as much genetic difference as a Swede and a person in the African nation of Senegal (Harris & Sim, 2002; American Sociological Association, 2003; California Newsreel, 2003).

So how important is race? From a biological point of view, knowing people's racial category allows us to predict almost nothing about them. Why, then, do societies make so much of race? Such categories allow societies to rank people in a hierarchy, giving some people more money, power, and prestige than others and allowing some people to feel that they are inherently "better" than others. Because race may matter so much, societies may construct racial categories in extreme ways. Throughout much of the twentieth century, for example, many southern U.S. states labelled as "coloured" anyone with as little as one thirty-second African ancestry (that is, one African American great-great-great-grandparent). Today, the law allows parents to declare the race of a child (or not) as they wish. Even so, most members of U.S. society are still very sensitive to people's racial backgrounds.

A Trend Toward Mixture

The population of Canada is quite mixed. Over many generations and throughout the Americas, the genetic traits of Negroid Africans, Caucasoid Europeans, and Mongoloid Native Americans (whose ancestors came from Asia) have intermingled. Many "black" people therefore have a significant Caucasoid ancestry, just as many "white" people have some Negroid ancestry, and many "Aboriginals" have either or sometimes both. Whatever people may think, race is not a black-and-white issue.

The 2011 National Household Survey reveals that the Canadian population identifies with over 200 ethnic origins and that these categories are being increasingly combined. A trend toward mixture can be observed in the fact that while 81.5 percent of those who are first-generation children of immigrants to Canada identified primarily in terms of a single-ethnic origin (only 18.5 percent identified multiple-ethnic origins), the proportion of second-generation children of immigrants identified multiple-ethnic origins at a significantly higher rate of 45.4 percent. Third-generation children did so at an even higher rate of 49.6 percent (Statistics Canada, 2013a).

Ethnicity

Ethnicity is *a shared cultural heritage.* People define themselves—or others—as members of an *ethnic category* based on common ancestry, language, or religion that gives them a distinctive social identity. Canada is a multi-ethnic society in which English and French are the "official languages," yet many people speak other languages at home, including Mandarin, Cantonese, Hindi, Thai, Italian, German, Spanish, or Swedish. Keep in mind that race is constructed from *biological* traits and ethnicity is constructed from *cultural* traits. Of course, the two may go hand in hand. For example, Japanese Canadians have distinctive physical traits and, for those who maintain a traditional way of life, a distinctive culture as well. Table 11–1 presents the broad sweep of ethnic diversity in Canada, as recorded by the 2011 census.

With regard to religion, 22.1 million (67.3 percent) people identify as Roman Catholic or Protestant. The largest religious category is Catholic, accounting for 12.7 million (38.7 percent) of the population, followed by 2 million (6.1 percent) United Church adherents. The population of Muslim men and women is slightly over 1 million (3.2 percent) and is rapidly increasing due to both immigration and a high birthrate. Other religions include Hindus (1.5 percent), Sikhs (1.4 percent), Buddhists (1.1 percent), and Jews (1.0 percent) (Statistics Canada, 2013a).

Like race, the concept of "ethnicity" is socially constructed, becoming important only because society defines it that way. For example, Canadian society defines people of Spanish descent as "Latin," even though Italy has a more "Latin" culture than Spain. People of Italian descent are not viewed as Latin but as "European" and therefore less different from the point of view of the European majority (Camara, 2000; Brodkin, 2007). Like racial differences, the importance of ethnic differences can change over time. Ukrainians, for example, were not always called by that name in Canada, but were described variously as "Galicians" and "Ruthenians" (Burkowicz, 2013).

The relationship between race and ethnicity is a complex one. Sometimes racial identities can lose their distinct racial qualities and become regarded as ethnic categories. That is, identities can be redefined from racial to ethnic ones, and vice versa. A century ago, Eastern European Slavs were considered racially "different" in mostly Anglo and Franco Canada. This is much less true today as we are more likely to think of Eastern Europeans as ethnically differentiated, not racially homogenous, along such categories as Poles, Ukrainians (after some ethnic redefinition), Serbs (again, after a differentiation from "Yugoslav"), and Russians (Burkowicz, 2013).

On an individual level, people either play up or play down their ethnicity, depending on whether they want to fit in or stand apart from the surrounding society: Immigrants may drop their cultural traditions over time or, like many people of Aboriginal background in recent years, try to revive their heritage (Dickason, 1992; Nagel, 1994; Spencer, 1994). For most people, ethnicity is a more complex issue than race because they identify with several ethnic backgrounds. The Canadian rapper and television actor Drake, for example, was born to an African American Catholic father and a white Jewish Canadian mother. Drake explains, however, that "[a]t the end of the day, I consider myself a black man because I'm more immersed in black culture than any other. Being Jewish is kind of a cool twist. It makes me unique" (Biography.com, 2014).

TABLE 11–1 Ethnic Categories with 200 000 or More Members, Canada, 2011

Ethnic Group	Number of Responses	Single Response	One of Several Responses
Canadian	10 563 805	5 834 535	4 729 265
English	6 509 500	1 312 570	5 196 930
French	5 065 690	1 165 465	3 900 225
Scottish	4 714 970	544 440	4 170 530
Irish	4 544 870	506 445	4 038 425
German	3 203 330	608 520	2 594 805
Italian	1 488 425	700 845	787 580
Chinese	1 487 580	1 210 945	276 635
Ukrainian	1 251 170	276 055	975 110
East Indian	1 165 145	919 155	245 985
Dutch	1 067 245	297 885	769 355
Polish	1 010 705	255 135	755 565
Filipino	662 600	506 545	156 060
Russian	550 520	107 300	443 220
Welsh	458 705	28 785	429 915
Norwegian	452 705	44 075	408 630
Métis	447 655	68 205	379 445
Portuguese	429 850	250 320	179 530
American	372 575	32 935	339 640
Spanish	368 305	66 575	301 730
Swedish	341 845	26 080	315 770
Hungarian	316 765	80 540	236 220
Jewish	309 650	115 640	194 010
Jamaican	256 915	142 870	114 040
Greek	252 960	141 755	111 205
Vietnamese	220 425	157 450	62 970
Romanian	204 625	82 995	121 635
Danish	203 080	31 370	171 705
Total—Ethnic origins	32 852 320	19 036 295	13 816 025

Source: Compiled by J. Burkowicz from Statistics Canada (2013b).

Minorities

March 3, Toronto, Ontario. Spending several hours waiting at an airport in any major city in Canada presents a lesson in contrasts: The majority of the unionized airline staff are white; the majority of the employees who serve the food and clean are visible minorities.

As defined in Chapter 10 ("Gender Stratification"), a *minority* is any category of people distinguished by physical or cultural difference that a society sets apart and subordinates. Minority standing can be based on gender, race, ethnicity, class, or, as intersection theory reveals, on a combination of these and various other dimensions. Minorities have two

TABLE 11–2 Visible Minority Categories, Canada, 2011

Visible Minority Category	Number of People
Total visible minority population	6 264 750
South Asian	1 567 400
Chinese	1 324 745
Black	945 665
Filipino	619 310
Latin American	381 280
Arab	380 620
Southeast Asian	312 080
West Asian	206 840
Korean	161 130
Japanese	87 265
Visible minority, Other	106 475
Multiple visible minorities	171 935
Not a visible minority	26 587 575

Source: Statistics Canada (2013c).

important characteristics. First, they share a distinct identity, which may be based on physical or cultural traits. Second, minorities experience subordination. As the rest of this chapter shows, Canadian minorities typically have lower income and face discrimination in the labour market. Class, race, and ethnicity, as well as gender, are overlapping and reinforcing dimensions of social stratification.

According to intersectional theory, however, no one is purely in a position of privilege or disadvantage. We all occupy many statuses. As such, not all members of a minority category are disadvantaged in the same way. For example, some Aboriginal people are quite wealthy; other Aboriginal people are celebrated academic, professional, and artistic leaders. But even job success rarely allows individuals to escape their minority standing (Benjamin, 1991; Shields & Wheatley Price, 2000). As described in Chapter 4 ("Social Interaction in Everyday Life"), race or ethnicity often serves as a master status that overshadows personal accomplishments.

Minorities usually make up a small proportion of a society's population, but this is not always the case. Black South Africans are disadvantaged even though they are a numerical majority in their country. In Canada, women make up slightly more than half of the population but are still struggling for the opportunities and privileges enjoyed by men. This is because low social standing, not numbers, defines minorities.

In Canada, the term "visible minority" has been socially constructed by politicians, statisticians, scholars, and journalists. According to the 1995 Employment Equity Act, a **visible minority** describes *"persons, other than Aboriginal peoples, who are non-Caucasian in race or non-white in colour."* Based on this definition the following ethnic groups are designated as visible minorities in Canada: Chinese, South Asians, Blacks, Arabs, West Asians,

visible minority persons, other than Aboriginal peoples, who are non-Caucasian in race or non-white in colour

Filipinos, Southeast Asians, Latin Americans, Japanese, Koreans, and Pacific Islanders (see Table 11–2).

In the 2011 census, about one out of every five people, or 19.1 percent of the Canadian population, identified themselves as a visible minority (up from 16.2 percent in 2006) (Statistics Canada, 2013a). As shown in Figure 11–1, the share of visible minorities is expected to keep increasing. Statistics Canada projections anticipate a decline of immigration from Europe and increases in African and Asian immigration. Visible minorities made up 12.4 percent of the immigrants prior to 1971. Between 2006 and 2011, the number of visible minority immigrants increased to 78 percent (Statistics Canada, 2013a). Combine this immigration pattern with a slightly higher fertility rate among the visible minority population, and the number of visible minorities can be expected to reach 30.6 percent by 2031 (Statistics Canada, 2010).

The Thinking About Diversity box on page 349 describes the struggles of temporary foreign workers in Canada.

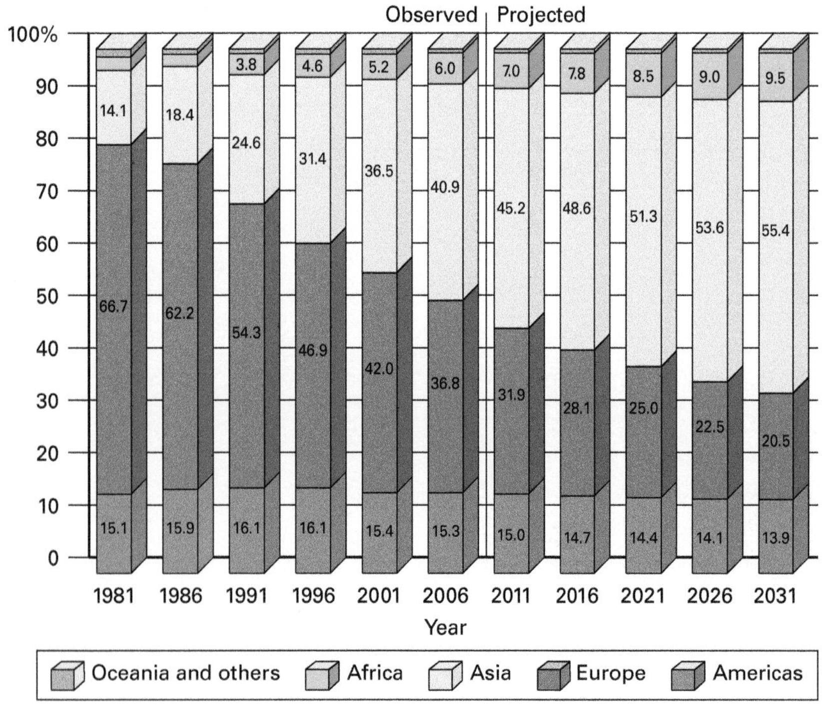

FIGURE 11–1 Distribution of the Foreign-Born Population by Continent of Birth, Canada, 1981 to 2031 (reference scenario)

Source: Statistics Canada (2010). http://www.statcan.gc.ca/pub/91-551-x/2010001/c-g/c-g002-eng.htm. This does not constitute an endorsement by Statistics Canada of this product.

Thinking About Diversity: Race, Class, and Gender

Hard Work: The Migrant Life in Canada

On June 20, 2014, Ministers Jason Kenney and Chris Alexander introduced a number of changes to the Temporary Foreign Worker Program. Their reforms set a limit as to the number of foreign low-wage workers that can be employed, raise the cost of the application fee, increase funding to the Canadian Border Services Agency, and allow for faster removal of migrant workers.

While appeasing those Canadians who would seek to "get rid" of migrant workers, such measures ignore the fact that Canada today is confronting a unique problem: It no longer has enough workers, especially those in construction and the trades. As the Canadian Council for Refugees points out, Canada has recently undergone a policy shift in order to address this lack. In 2006—for the first time in Canadian history—the government accepted more temporary migrant workers than permanent residents. From 2007 to 2012, the number of migrant workers increased by 70 percent.

Employers crying out for temporary workers argue that Canada should beef up its guest worker program and make it easier to recruit immigrants. On the other hand, critics (including trade unions) argue that guest workers depress wages for Canadian workers and worsen working conditions. At the same time, some Canadian unions have begun to support guest workers struggling to unionize.

The hard truth is that migrants do the jobs that no one else wants. They represent the bottom level of Canada's national economy, working in restaurants and hotels; on construction crews; and in private homes cooking, cleaning, and caring for children. Few migrants make much more than the minimum wage and—unless they gain landed immigrant or citizenship status—are unlikely to receive any health or pension benefits. Migrant workers thus pay into social services that they cannot access.

According to immigrant, refugee, and human rights activists, instead of challenging the abuse inherent in the Temporary Foreign Worker Program, the government's response places the blame on the victims themselves. Questioning the reforms, activist Harsha Walia observes that

> Migrant workers don't suppress wages; employers and the state do. Yet rhetoric such as "Canadians for Canadians jobs" alienates migrant workers and inhibits discussions about organizing to lift up the wage floor for *all* workers. Racism operates as a convenient buy-in for many citizen workers who pledge loyalty to nationalist protectionism rather than transnational solidarity. It also, not coincidentally, circumvents reflection on the causes of displacement and unemployment in the global South that compels the migration of workers.

Like the United States and Britain, Canada has not signed a UN Convention that protects the rights of migrant workers.

What Do You Think?

1. In what ways do you or members of your family depend on the low-paid labour of migrants?

2. Do you think there is anything wrong with paying someone the current minimum wage for hard work? Why or why not?

3. Do you think that guest workers to Canada should have the right to become permanent residents and eventually citizens?

Sources: Wong, Lloyd and Trumper, Ricardo. "Canada's Guestworkers: Racialized, Gendered and Flexible," 151–170, in *Race and Racism in 21st Century Canada: Continuity, Complexity, and Change*, Edited by Sean P. Hier and B. Singh Bolaria. University of Toronto Press, Higher Education Division © 2007. Reprinted with permission of the publisher; Canadian Council for Refugees (2012); Walia (2014).

Prejudice and Stereotypes

11.2 Describe the extent and causes of prejudice.

November 19, Jerusalem, Israel. We are driving along the outskirts of this historical city, a holy place to Jews, Christians, and Muslims— when Razi, our taxi driver, spots a small group of Falasha—Ethiopian Jews—on a street corner. "Those people over there," he points as he speaks, "they are different. They don't drive cars. They don't want to improve themselves. Even when our country offers them schooling, they don't take it." He shakes his head at the Ethiopians and drives on.

Prejudice is *a rigid and unfair generalization about an entire category of people.* Prejudice is unfair because *all* people in some category are described as the same, based on little or no direct evidence. Prejudice may target people of a particular social class, sex, sexual orientation, age, political affiliation, physical disability, race, or ethnicity.

prejudice a rigid and unfair generalization about an entire category of people

Prejudices are *prejudgments* that can be either positive or negative. Our positive prejudices tend to exaggerate the virtues of people like ourselves, and our negative prejudices condemn those who differ from us. Negative prejudice can be expressed as anything from mild dislike to outright hostility. Because such attitudes are rooted in culture, everyone has at least some prejudice.

Prejudice often takes the form of a *stereotype* (*stereo* is derived from a Greek word meaning "solid"), a simplified description applied to every person in some category. Many white people hold stereotypical views of minorities. Stereotyping is especially harmful to minorities in the workplace. If company officials see minority workers only in terms of a stereotype, they will make assumptions about their abilities, steering them toward certain jobs, and limiting their access to better opportunities (Kaufman, 2002).

Minorities, too, stereotype whites and other minorities (Smith, 1996; Cummings & Lambert, 1997). Surveys show, for example, that African Americans are more likely than whites to express the belief that Asians engage in unfair business practices and Asians are more likely than whites to criticize Hispanics for having too many children (Perlmutter, 2002). Furthermore, intersectional analysis reveals that white, working-class women are less likely to hold stereotypes than are white, working-class men (Bonilla-Silva, 2006).

Measuring Prejudice: The Social Distance Scale

One measure of prejudice is *social distance*, how closely people are willing to interact with members of some category. In the 1920s, Emory Bogardus developed the *social distance scale* shown in Figure 11–2 on page 351. Bogardus (1925) asked students at U.S. colleges and universities how closely they were willing to interact with people in 30 racial and ethnic categories. People express the greatest social distance (most negative prejudice) by declaring that a particular category of people should be barred from the country entirely (point 7); at the other extreme, people express the least social distance (most social acceptance) by saying they would accept members of a particular category into their family through marriage (point 1).

Bogardus (1925, 1967; Owen, Elsner, & McFaul, 1977) found that people felt much more social distance from some categories than from others. In general, students in his surveys expressed the most social distance from Hispanics, African Americans, Asians, and Turks, indicating that they would be willing to tolerate such people as co-workers but not as neighbours, close friends, or family members. Students expressed the least social distance from those from northern and western Europe, including English and Scottish people, and also Canadians, indicating that they were willing to include them in their families by marriage.

Student Snapshot

What patterns of social distance do we find among college and university students today? A recent study using the same social distance scale reported three major findings (Parrillo & Donoghue, 2005)[1]:

1. **Student opinion shows a trend toward greater social acceptance.** Today's students express less social distance from all minorities than students did several decades ago. Figure 11–2 shows that the mean (average) score on the social distance scale declined from 2.14 in 1925 to 1.93 in 1977 and to 1.44 in 2001. Respondents (81 percent of whom were white) showed notably greater acceptance of African Americans, a category that moved up from near the bottom in 1925 to the top one-third in 2001.

---

[1]Parrillo and Donoghue dropped seven of the categories used by Bogardus (Armenians, Czechs, Finns, Norwegians, Scots, Swedes, and Turks), claiming they were no longer visible minorities. They added nine new categories (Africans, Arabs, Cubans, Dominicans, Haitians, Jamaicans, Muslims, Puerto Ricans, and Vietnamese), claiming that these are visible minorities today. This change probably encouraged higher social distance scores, making the trend toward decreasing social distance all the more significant.

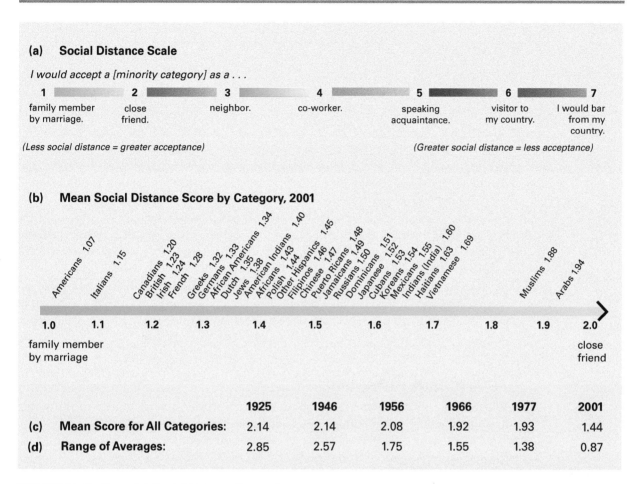

(a) **Social Distance Scale**

I would accept a [minority category] as a . . .

| 1 | 2 | 3 | 4 | 5 | 6 | 7 |

family member
by marriage.

close
friend.

neighbor.

co-worker.

speaking
acquaintance.

visitor to
my country.

I would bar
from my
country.

(Less social distance = greater acceptance) — *(Greater social distance = less acceptance)*

(b) **Mean Social Distance Score by Category, 2001**

Americans 1.07, Italians 1.15, Canadians 1.20, British 1.23, Irish 1.24, French 1.28, Greeks 1.32, Germans 1.33, African Americans 1.34, Dutch 1.35, Jews 1.38, American Indians 1.40, Polish 1.43, Other Hispanics 1.44, Filipinos 1.45, Chinese 1.46, Puerto Ricans 1.47, Jamaicans 1.48, Russians 1.49, Dominicans 1.50, Japanese 1.51, Cubans 1.52, Koreans 1.53, Mexicans 1.54, Indians (India) 1.55, Haitians 1.60, Vietnamese 1.63 1.69, Muslims 1.88, Arabs 1.94

| 1.0 | 1.1 | 1.2 | 1.3 | 1.4 | 1.5 | 1.6 | 1.7 | 1.8 | 1.9 | 2.0 |

family member
by marriage

close
friend

		1925	1946	1956	1966	1977	2001
(c)	**Mean Score for All Categories:**	2.14	2.14	2.08	1.92	1.93	1.44
(d)	**Range of Averages:**	2.85	2.57	1.75	1.55	1.38	0.87

FIGURE 11–2 Bogardus Social Distance Research

The social distance scale is a good way to measure prejudice. Part (a) illustrates the complete social distance scale, from least social distance at the far left to greatest social distance at the far right. Part (b) shows the mean (average) social distance score received by each category of people in 2001. Part (c) presents the overall mean score in specific years (the average of the scores received by all racial and ethnic categories). These scores have fallen from 2.14 in 1925 to 1.44 in 2001, showing that students express less social distance toward minorities today than they did in the past. Part (d) shows the range of averages, the difference between the highest and lowest scores in given years (in 2001, for instance, it was 0.87, the difference between the high score of 1.94 for Arabs and the low score of 1.07 for Americans). This figure has also become smaller since 1925, indicating that today's students tend to see fewer differences between various categories of people.

Source: Parrillo, Vincent, and Christopher Donoghue (2005). "Updating the Bogardus Social Distance Studies: A New National Survey." Social Science Journal. Vol. 42, No. 2 (April 2005): 257–71. Used with permission.

2. **People see less difference between various minorities.** The earliest studies found the difference between the highest- and lowest-ranked minorities (the range of averages) equal to almost three points on the scale. As the figure shows, the most recent research produced a range of averages of less than one point, indicating that today's students tend to see fewer differences between various categories of people.

3. **The terrorist attacks of September 11, 2001, may have reduced social acceptance of Arabs and Muslims.** The most recent study was conducted just a few weeks after September 11, 2001. Perhaps the fact that the 19 men who attacked the U.S. World Trade Center and the Pentagon were Arabs and Muslims is part of the reason that students ranked these categories last on the social distance scale. However, not a single student gave Arabs or Muslims a 7, indicating that they should be barred from the country. On the contrary, the 2001 mean scores (1.94 for Arabs and 1.88 for Muslims) show higher social acceptance than students in 1977 expressed toward 18 of the 30 categories of people studied.

Racism

racism the belief that one racial category is innately superior or inferior to another

A powerful and harmful form of prejudice, **racism** is *the belief that one racial category is innately superior or inferior to another.* Contrary to popular belief, racism is not as old as world history. While the ancient Greeks, the peoples of India, and the Chinese all considered people unlike themselves inferior, their prejudicial attitudes were not based on racial theories or categories. The Greeks did not regard themselves as "white," nor did they regard all Africans as "black." Historian George Fredrickson maintains that racism is a uniquely modern, European invention as "[n]o clear and unequivocal evidence of racism has been found in other cultures or in Europe before the Middle Ages" (2003). Scholars today generally agree that the categories of racial thought emerged during the European Renaissance and that it was only in the nineteenth century that racism emerged as a pseudo-scientific way of thinking about people (Malik, 1996).

We should not forget that Canada also has a long history of racial oppression. Slavery was practised in British North America prior to Canadian Confederation until 1833 (Brand, 1992; Ponting, 1994; Prentice et al., 1996; Kihika, 2013). More recently, evidence has been found of the interplay between racism, sexism, and immigration (Ng, 1993; Ng & Das Gupta, 1993; Iacovetta, 1995; Williams, Neighbors, & Jackson, 2003; Etowa et al., 2007).

Racism remains a serious social problem, as some people think that certain racial and ethnic categories are smarter than others. The Seeing Sociology in Everyday Life box on page 353 explains that these common-sense stereotypes fail to recognize that racial differences in mental abilities result from environment rather than from biology.

Theories of Prejudice

Where does prejudice come from? Social scientists provide several answers to this vexing question, focusing on frustration, personality, culture, and social conflict.

Scapegoat Theory

Scapegoat theory holds that prejudice springs from frustration among people who are themselves disadvantaged (Dollard et al., 1939). For instance, take the case of a white woman who is frustrated by her low-paying job in a textile factory. Directing her hostility at the powerful factory owners carries the obvious risk of being fired; therefore, she may blame her low pay on the presence of minority co-workers. Her prejudice does not improve her situation, but it is a relatively safe way to express anger, and it may give her the comforting feeling that at least she is superior to someone.

scapegoat a person or category of people, typically with little power, whom people unfairly blame for their own troubles

A **scapegoat**, then, is *a person or category of people, typically with little power, whom people unfairly blame for their own troubles.* Because they have little power and thus are usually "safe targets," minorities often are used as scapegoats.

Authoritarian Personality Theory

Theodor Adorno and colleagues (1950) considered extreme prejudice a personality trait of certain individuals. This conclusion is supported by research showing that people who show strong prejudice toward one minority are usually intolerant of all minorities. These *authoritarian personalities* rigidly conform to conventional cultural values and see moral issues as clear-cut matters of right and wrong. People with authoritarian personalities also view society as naturally competitive and hierarchical, with "better" people (like themselves) inevitably dominating those who are weaker (all minorities).

Adorno and his colleagues also found the opposite pattern to be true: People who express tolerance toward one minority are likely to be accepting of all. They tend to be more flexible in their moral judgments and treat all people as equals.

Adorno thought that people with little schooling and those raised by cold and demanding parents tend to develop authoritarian personalities. Filled with anger and anxiety as children, they grow into hostile, aggressive adults who seek out scapegoats.

Seeing Sociology in Everyday Life

Does Race Affect Intelligence?

As we go through an average day, we encounter people of various racial and ethnic categories. We also deal with people who are very intelligent as well as those whose abilities are more modest. But is there a connection between race or ethnicity and intelligence?

Are Asians smarter than white people? Is the typical white person more intelligent than the average black person? Throughout the history of Canada, we have painted one category of people as intellectually more gifted than another. Moreover, people have used such thinking to justify the privileges of the allegedly superior category and even to bar supposedly inferior people from entering this country.

So what do we know about intelligence? Scientists know that people, as individuals, differ in mental abilities. The distribution of human intelligence forms a "bell curve." A person's *intelligence quotient* (IQ) is calculated as the person's mental age in years, as measured by a test, divided by the person's actual age in years, with the result multiplied by 100. An eight-year-old who performs like a ten-year-old has an IQ of $10 \div 8 = 1.25 \times 100 = 125$. Average performance is defined as an IQ of 100.

In a controversial study of intelligence and social inequality, Richard Herrnstein and Charles Murray (1994) claim that race is related to measures of intelligence. More specifically, they say that the average IQ for people of European ancestry is 100, for people of East Asian ancestry is 103, and for people of African ancestry is 90.

Such assertions go against the democratic and egalitarian beliefs that no racial type is naturally better than another. Critics of Herrnstein and Murray's work argue that intelligence tests are not valid and even that the concept of intelligence has little real meaning.

Most social scientists believe that IQ tests do measure something important that we think of as intelligence, and they agree that *individuals* vary in intellectual aptitude. But they reject the idea that any *category* of people, on average, is naturally smarter than any other. So how do we explain the overall differences in IQ scores by race?

Thomas Sowell (1994, 1995) explains that most of this difference results not from biology but from environment. In some skilful sociological detective work, Sowell traced IQ scores for various racial and ethnic categories throughout the twentieth century. He found that, on average, early twentieth century immigrants from European nations such as Poland, Lithuania, Italy, and Greece, as well as from Asian countries including China and Japan, scored 10 to 15 points below the U.S. average. But by the end of the twentieth century, people in these same categories had IQ scores that were average or above average. Among Italian Americans, for example, average IQ jumped almost 10 points; among Polish Americans and Chinese Americans, the increase was almost 20 points.

Because genetic changes occur over thousands of years and most people in these categories marry others like themselves, biological factors cannot explain such a rapid rise in IQ scores. The only reasonable explanation is changing cultural patterns. The descendants of early immigrants improved their intellectual performance as their standard of living rose and their opportunity for schooling increased.

Sowell found that much the same was true of African Americans. Historically, the average IQ score of African Americans living in the North has been about 10 points higher than the average score of those living in the South. Among the descendants of African Americans who migrated from the South to the North after 1940, IQ scores went up, just as they did for descendants of European and Asian immigrants. Thus environmental factors appear to be critical in explaining differences in IQ among various categories of people.

According to Sowell, these test score differences tell us that *cultural patterns matter*. Asians who score high on tests are no smarter than other people, but they have been raised to value learning and pursue excellence. For their part, African Americans are no less intelligent than anyone else, but they carry a legacy of disadvantage that can undermine self-confidence and discourage achievement.

What Do You Think?

1. If IQ scores reflect people's environment, are they valid measures of intelligence? Could they be harmful?

2. According to Thomas Sowell, why do some racial and ethnic categories show dramatic short-term gains in average IQ scores?

3. Do you think that parents and schools influence a child's IQ score? If so, how?

Culture Theory

A third theory claims that although extreme prejudice may be found in some people, some prejudice is found in everyone. Why? Because prejudice is part of the culture in which we all live and learn. The Bogardus social distance studies help prove the point. Bogardus found that students across the country had much the same attitudes toward specific racial and ethnic categories, feeling closer to some and more distant from others.

More evidence that prejudice is rooted in culture is the fact that minorities express the same attitudes as white people toward categories other than their own. Such patterns suggest that individuals hold prejudices because we live in a "culture of prejudice" that has taught us to view certain categories of people as "better" or "worse" than others.

Do we live in a "culture of prejudice"? Minority job-seekers, especially those with good training, have reason to think that the answer may be yes.

Conflict Theory

A fourth explanation proposes that prejudice is used as a tool by powerful people not only to justify privilege for themselves but also to oppress others. Oil companies in northern Canada who look down on migrant and immigrant workers, for example, can get away with paying the immigrants low wages for long hours of hard work. Similarly, all elites benefit when prejudice divides workers along racial and ethnic lines and discourages them from working together to advance their common interests (Geschwender, 1978; Olzak, 1989). According to another conflict-based argument, a society based on *white privilege*, where whites routinely receive unearned advantages to the detriment of racial minorities, will incline white people toward racism. As numerous studies document, white people benefit from white privilege in that they do not have to worry that their race will negatively impact such things as job interviews, bank loans, encounters with the police, or attempts to secure a place of residence (Rothenberg, 2008). White people, therefore, do not have to be consciously racist to benefit from racism. In fact, many white people today claim to be "colour blind" as they continue to reap the rewards of a racially stratified social system. And in many cases, a challenge to white privilege by race-conscious minorities—such as the "Black Lives Matter" movement, which highlights the disproportionate amount of black people recently killed by the police—often sparks a backlash from whites (Steele, 1990; Bonilla-Silva, 2006; Burkowicz, 2015).

Discrimination

(**11.3**) Distinguish discrimination from prejudice.

Closely related to prejudice is **discrimination**, *unequal treatment of various categories of people.* Prejudice refers to *attitudes*, but discrimination is a matter of *action*. Like prejudice, discrimination can be either positive (providing special advantages) or negative (creating obstacles) and ranges from subtle to extreme.

Institutional Prejudice and Discrimination

We typically think of prejudice and discrimination as the hateful ideas or actions of specific people. But Stokely Carmichael and Charles Hamilton (1967) pointed out that far greater harm results from **institutional prejudice and discrimination**, *bias built into the operation of society's institutions*, including schools, hospitals, the police, and the workplace. For example, researchers have found that banks reject home mortgage applications from minorities at a higher rate—or charge higher rates for the same mortgage—compared to white applicants, even when income and quality of neighbourhood are held constant (Gotham, 1998; Blanton, 2007).

According to Carmichael and Hamilton, people are slow to condemn or even recognize institutional prejudice and discrimination because it often involves respected public officials and long-established traditions. One example of institutional discrimination in Canada was the Indian Act and its harsh rules toward Aboriginal people (Jamieson, 1986; Ponting & Kiely, 1997). The Act specifically discriminated against Aboriginal women. If a Status Indian woman married a non–Status Indian man, she lost her legal status

---

discrimination unequal treatment of various categories of people

institutional prejudice and discrimination bias built into the operation of society's institutions

and was denied rights and benefits under the Indian Act. This meant that many women and children of subsequent generations were culturally alienated from their traditional communities. According to Jeffries (1992:92–93),

> The government's treatment of women under the *Indian Act* was particularly devastating and tantamount to cultural genocide, because women were responsible for maintaining culture. If a woman chose to marry a non-Indian man, she was removed from the government's list of registered Indians . . . Upon marriage, the woman could no longer live in the community in which she was born, nor could she participate in any matters respecting the community. The final insult was upon death: neither she nor any of her children could be buried in a family plot on band land.

With the passage of Bill C-31 in 1985, this patriarchal principle was finally revoked. Yet Aboriginal women's access to land and housing remains problematic to this day (Benoit & Carroll, 1995). Since provincial divorce laws do not hold on reserves, Aboriginal women are at risk of losing all common property after separation or divorce.

Prejudice and Discrimination: The Vicious Circle

Prejudice and discrimination reinforce each other. The Thomas theorem, discussed in Chapter 4 ("Social Interaction in Everyday Life"), offers a simple explanation of this fact: *Situations that are defined as real become real in their consequences* (Thomas & Thomas, 1928; Thomas, 1966:301, orig. 1931).

Applying the Thomas theorem, we understand how stereotypes can become real to people who believe them and sometimes even to those who are victimized by them. Prejudice on the part of white people toward visible minority and Aboriginal peoples does not produce *innate* inferiority, but it can produce *social* inferiority, pushing minorities into low-paying jobs, inferior schools, and racially segregated housing or residential schools. Then, as white people interpret that social disadvantage as evidence that non-whites do not measure up, they unleash a new round of prejudice and discrimination, giving rise to a vicious circle in which each perpetuates the other, as shown in Figure 11–3.

The Black Lives Matter movement emerged as a response to the acquittal of the 2012 killing of 17-year-old Trayvon Martin by 28-year-old George Zimmerman. Calling out police brutality, the movement has since spread to Canada. The Black Lives Matter–Toronto Coalition protests racism within the Canadian criminal justice system. It draws our attention to such practices as carding, racial profiling, deportation, and incarceration that disproportionally affect black people.

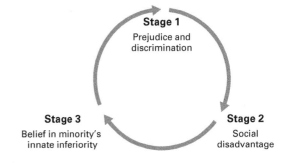

Stage 1: Prejudice and discrimination begin, often as an expression of ethnocentrism or an attempt to justify economic exploitation.

Stage 2: As a result of prejudice and discrimination, a minority is socially disadvantaged, occupying a low position in the system of social stratification.

Stage 3: This social disadvantage is then interpreted not as the result of earlier prejudice and discrimination but as evidence that the minority is innately inferior, unleashing renewed prejudice and discrimination by which the cycle repeats itself.

FIGURE 11–3 Prejudice and Discrimination: The Vicious Circle

Prejudice and discrimination can form a vicious circle, perpetuating themselves.

Majority and Minority: Patterns of Interaction

11.4 Identify examples of pluralism, assimilation, segregation, and genocide.

Sociologists describe patterns of interaction among racial and ethnic categories in a society in terms of four models: pluralism, assimilation, segregation, and genocide.

Pluralism

Pluralism is *a state in which people of all races and ethnicities are distinct but have equal social standing.* In other words, people who differ in appearance or social heritage all share resources roughly equally.

Patterns of Majority and Minority Interaction

Canada is pluralistic to the extent that all people have equal standing under the law. Also, many large cities contain "ethnic villages" where people proudly display the traditions of their immigrant ancestors. These include Chinatowns found in Victoria, Vancouver, and Toronto; the Jewish area around Avenue du Parc in Montreal; and the Portuguese neighbourhoods around Dundas Street West in Toronto (Zucchi, 2007).

But Canada is not truly pluralistic, for three reasons. First, although most people value their cultural heritage, few want to live exclusively with others exactly like themselves. Second, tolerance for social diversity goes only so far. One reaction to the growing proportion of minorities in Canada, for example, is the rise of white supremacist groups in many Canadian cities. Third, as you will see later in this chapter, it is simply a fact that people of various colours and cultures do not have equal social standing.

Assimilation

Many people traditionally have viewed Canada as a "mosaic" in which disparate cultural groups join together to create a tolerant and peaceful multicultural society. Rather than everyone joining as equals in some new cultural pattern, however, minorities typically adopt the traits of the dominant culture established by the earliest settlers. Why? Because doing so is both an avenue to upward social mobility and a way to escape the prejudice and discrimination directed at more visible minorities. Sociologists use the term **assimilation** to describe *the process by which minorities gradually adopt patterns of the dominant culture.* Assimilation can involve changing modes of dress, values, religion, language, and friends.

The amount of assimilation varies by category. For example, Swedes have assimilated more than Italians, the Dutch more than Dominicans, Germans more than the Japanese. Multiculturalists oppose making assimilation a goal because it suggests that minorities are a

Most Canadian cities today have distinct ethnic enclaves. Some people see this as a positive trend, arguing that it validates the uniqueness of ethnic cultures. Others argue the opposite, viewing ethnic enclaves as indicative of the ghettoization of marginalized groups in our society (Zucchi, 2007).

problem and it defines them (rather than majority people) as the ones who need to do all the changing.

Note that assimilation involves changes in ethnicity but not in race. For example, many descendants of Japanese immigrants discard their ethnic traditions but retain their racial identity. For racial traits to diminish over generations, **miscegenation**, or *biological reproduction by partners of different racial categories*, must occur. Interracial marriage is becoming more common. In 2011, about 360 045 couples in Canada were in mixed marriages or common-law relationships. While their numbers have grown to 4.6 percent of all couples in 2011 (up from 2.6 percent in 1991) (Statistics Canada, 2014), mixed-race couples are still rare in a country that prides itself on multiculturalism.

miscegenation biological reproduction by partners of different racial categories

Segregation

Segregation is *the physical and social separation of categories of people.* Some minorities, especially religious orders like the Amish, voluntarily segregate themselves. However, majorities usually segregate minorities by excluding them. Residential neighbourhoods, schools, occupations, hospitals, and even cemeteries may be segregated. Pluralism encourages cultural distinctiveness without disadvantage, but segregation enforces separation that harms a minority.

Racial segregation has a long history in Canada, as mentioned above, starting with the segregation of Aboriginal peoples on reserves. Apart from the internment of Ukrainian Canadians during World War I (Luciuk, 1988) and Japanese Canadians during World War II (Kogawa, 1981; Omatsu, 1992), *de jure* (Latin meaning "by law") discrimination in Canada has been relatively rare, in contrast with, for example, the United States. However, *de facto* ("in fact") segregation continues to this day.

Research by Balakrishnan and Hou (1995) has documented the concentration of different groups in Canada's urban centres. The authors found that visible minorities and Jewish people tend to live in specific areas of a city rather than being dispersed throughout. This contrasts with the British, Germans, and French, who are relatively evenly distributed (the British in Montreal are an exception to this general pattern).

Balakrishnan and Hou also documented the changing nature of residential segregation. First, even though the composition of the immigration stream to Canada has changed in recent decades—a larger proportion of today's immigrants are from Asia—the authors found that the distribution of Asians in urban areas is not changing. Balakrishnan and Hou attributed this to the fact that the selective nature of immigration policy has led to immigrants being highly skilled and therefore not choosing to live in the traditional low-income areas of our cities. Second, the authors pointed out, a certain amount of residential segregation comes from families and individuals choosing to live together rather than being forced into ethnic ghettos. The Jewish population is a case in point. Even though this population is above average in income and education—factors that historically imply freedom of choice—Jews are also among the most segregated ethnic groups in Canada.

Research from the United States shows that across the country, many whites (especially those with young children) continue to avoid neighbourhoods where African Americans live (Emerson, Yancey, & Chai, 2001; Krysan, 2002). At the extreme, Douglas Massey and Nancy Denton (1989) document the *hypersegregation* of poor African Americans in some inner cities. Hypersegregation means having little contact of any kind with people outside the local community. Hypersegregation is the daily experience of about 20 percent of poor African Americans and is a pattern found in about 25 large U.S. cities (Wilkes & Iceland, 2004; Iceland et al., 2010).

pluralism a state in which people of all races and ethnicities are distinct but have equal social standing

assimilation the process by which minorities gradually adopt patterns of the dominant culture

segregation the physical and social separation of categories of people

genocide the systematic killing of one category of people by another

Genocide

Genocide is *the systematic killing of one category of people by another.* This deadly form of racism and ethnocentrism violates nearly every recognized moral standard, yet it has occurred time and again in human history.

Genocide was common in the history of contact between Europeans and the original inhabitants of the Americas. From the sixteenth century on, the Spanish, Portuguese, English, French, and Dutch forcibly colonized vast empires. Although most native people died from diseases brought by Europeans, against which they had no natural defences, many who opposed the colonizers were killed deliberately (Matthiessen, 1984; Sale, 1990).

Genocide also occurred during the twentieth century. During World War I, at least 1 million Armenians in Eastern Europe perished under the rule of the Ottoman Empire. Soon after that, European Jews experienced a reign of terror known as the Holocaust during Adolf Hitler's rule in Germany. From about 1935 to 1945, the Nazis murdered more than 6 million Jews and another 5 million people including gay people, Roma (Gypsies), Eastern Europeans, and people with handicaps. Tragically, genocide continues in the modern world. Recent examples include Hutus killing Tutsis in the African nation of Rwanda, Serbs killing Bosnians in the Balkans of Eastern Europe, and the killing of hundreds of thousands of people in the Darfur region of Sudan in Africa.

These four patterns of minority-majority interaction have all been played out in Canada. Although many people proudly point to patterns of pluralism and assimilation, it is also important to recognize the degree to which Canadian society has been built on segregation from one end of the country to the other (black Canadians in Eastern Canada and Japanese Canadians in British Columbia) and genocide (of Aboriginal Canadians). The remainder of this chapter examines how these four patterns have shaped the history and present social standing of major racial and ethnic categories in Canada.

Race and Ethnicity in Canada

(11.5) Assess the social standing of racial and ethnic categories of Canadian society.

> Like all people who have nothing, I lived on dreams. I burned my way through stone walls to get to America.
> Nu, I got to America.
> Ten hours I pushed a machine in a shirtwaist factory, when I was yet lucky to get work. And always my head was drying up with saving and pinching and worrying to send home a little from the little I earned.
> Where are my dreams that were so real to me in the old country?

These words by Jewish immigrant Anzia Yezierska (quoted in Frager, 1992:10) capture the dreams and subsequent disappointments of many European immigrants who made the difficult journey across the Atlantic to find work in the emerging cities of the New World—including "Little York" (Toronto) in Upper Canada and "Ville-Marie" (Montreal) in Lower Canada. As the following history of Canada's racial and ethnic minorities reveals, our nation's golden door has opened more widely for some than for others.

Canada's Aboriginal Peoples

Some 15 000 years before Columbus landed in the Americas in 1492, migrating peoples crossed a land bridge from Asia to North America where the Bering Strait (off the coast of Alaska) lies today. Gradually, they spread throughout North and South America.

When the first Europeans arrived late in the fifteenth century, Native Americans numbered in the millions. But by the 1900s, after relentless subjugation and even acts of genocide, the "vanishing Americans" numbered just 250 000 (Dobyns, 1966; Tyler, 1973).

Columbus first referred to Native Americans that he encountered as "Indians" because he mistakenly thought he had reached the coast of India. Columbus found the indigenous people passive and peaceful, in stark contrast to the materialistic and competitive Europeans. Yet Europeans justified the seizure of Native American land by calling their victims thieves and murderers (Josephy, 1982; Matthiessen, 1984; Sale, 1990).

At the beginning of the eighteenth century there were about 10 Aboriginal people for every European settler in Canada; by 1881, there were about 40 Europeans for every Aboriginal person (Jaffe, 1992). This was not primarily because of a natural increase of European immigrants, however. Traders and later settlers to British North America and New France (later renamed Upper and Lower Canada) brought with them not only trade items but also racist attitudes toward the non-Christian "savages" who resided in the New World. The Europeans were even prepared to use their superior military power to subdue any Aboriginal peoples unwilling to be colonized.

Europeans also brought with them deadly diseases. Smallpox and other epidemic diseases (including measles, influenza, and tuberculosis) had killed many Europeans in the previous centuries. However, for the Aboriginal peoples of the New World, these contagions were "virgin soil epidemics," ravaging hitherto unexposed populations without any built-up immunity to soften the impact (Cohen, 1989). These "diseases of civilization," along with the ill effects of adulterated whisky, reduced the Aboriginal population of British Columbia, for example, by nearly two-thirds before the end of the 1800s (Jaffe, 1992). So marginalized were Canada's Aboriginal peoples that they were not entitled to vote alongside non-Aboriginal Canadian citizens until 1960.

In 2011, 1 400 685 Canadians identified themselves as Aboriginal persons: North American Indian (First Nations people), Métis, or Inuit. There has been a substantial increase in Canada's Aboriginal population in recent decades: Between 2006 and 2011, it grew by 20.1 percent, compared with 5.2 percent growth during the same period for non-Aboriginal Canadians (Statistics Canada, 2013d). Table 11–3 shows the geographic distribution of Canada's Aboriginal peoples.

David Rossiter/Lethbridge Herald/The Canadian Press

There has recently been a resurgence in Aboriginal peoples' pride in their heritage. Do you think that this resurgence is because of, or despite, being a minority group?

TABLE 11–3 Aboriginal Population, Canada, 2011

	Total Aboriginal Population	% of Population	% of Aboriginal People
Canada	1 400 685	100.0	4.3
Newfoundland and Labrador	35 800	2.6	7.1
Prince Edward Island	2 230	0.2	1.6
Nova Scotia	33 845	2.4	3.7
New Brunswick	22 615	1.6	3.1
Quebec	141 915	10.1	1.8
Ontario	301 425	21.5	2.4
Manitoba	195 900	14.0	16.7
Saskatchewan	157 740	11.3	15.6
Alberta	220 695	15.8	6.2
British Columbia	232 290	16.6	5.4
Yukon	7 705	0.6	23.1
Northwest Territories	21 160	1.5	51.9
Nunavut	27 360	2.0	86.3

Source: Statistics Canada (2013d).

Despite their growing number, Aboriginal peoples in Canada continue to earn far below the median average income for Canadians. Aboriginal peoples also are more likely to live in single-parent families, and they record higher rates of unemployment and have lower rates of school attendance. Their health status is also bleak when compared with that of the country's non-Aboriginal population. Aboriginal peoples have higher tuberculosis and suicide rates, and much shorter life expectancies, than their non-Aboriginal counterparts (Statistics Canada, 1995; Health Canada, 2009; Gionet & Roshanafshar, 2013).

Like other racial and ethnic minorities in Canada, Aboriginal peoples have recently reasserted pride in their cultural heritage. Some are finally resolving negotiations over territorial lands. Yet, as discussed in the Controversy & Debate box on page 361, not all Canadians are comfortable with special rights for Aboriginal groups, such as the Nisga'a of British Columbia.

British Canadians

British Canadians—sometimes referred to as White Anglo-Saxon Protestants (WASPs)—were not the first people to inhabit Canada, but they came to dominate this nation once European settlement began. Most British Canadians are of English descent, but this category also includes Scots, Irish, and Welsh. On the 2011 census, as shown in Table 11–1, among the most frequently cited British origins were English (6.5 million), Scottish (4.7 million), and Irish (4.5 million).

Historically, British immigrants were highly skilled and motivated by what we now call the "Protestant work ethic." Because of their number and power, British Canadians (with the possible exception of Irish Catholics) were not subject to the prejudice and discrimination experienced by other categories of immigrants. The historical dominance of British Canadians has been so great that, as noted earlier, others have sought to become more like them.

And the British cultural legacy still stands: English remained, until recent decades, Canada's only official language, and it still dominates the country's media and electronic communication systems. The Canadian legal and political systems, too, reflect their British origins.

French Canadians

The French explorers arrived in Canada in the sixteenth century, initially involving themselves in fishing and fur trading. Eventually, more French immigrated in search of a better life in "New France." By 1760, there were about 70 000 inhabitants of the colony, with approximately the same number of women as men (Prentice et al., 1996:37). When Acadia (now Nova Scotia) passed from French to British hands in 1713, men and women from that region were either deported to France or resettled in the northeastern regions of what was then "British North America." In the aftermath of the Seven Years' War (1756–1763), Canada fell under British colonial rule. Though the French retained some control over their own language, religion, and legal institutions, English Canada gained control over economic, political, and social matters.

To some extent, this remains the case even today. The historical legacy of the "two solitudes"—French and English—joined in an uneasy political union resulted in the so-called Quiet Revolution of the 1960s in Quebec. At its most intense, the Quiet Revolution involved the use of radical terrorism as a political weapon against the English (Rocher, 1990). And though the province has undergone substantial change in subsequent decades, in many respects French Quebec and English Canada can still be said to be "two nations warring in the bosom of the same state" (Guindon, 1990:30).

The Quebec language law—Bill 101—was upheld in April 2000, when the Quebec Superior Court ruled that French had to be the predominant language on commercial signs. A spray can quickly changes the familiar stop sign into a political message.

Controversy & Debate

Should Certain Groups in Canada Enjoy Special Rights?

"We are all governed by one law, the constitution, and that most fundamental of laws states that existing Aboriginal rights are recognized and affirmed . . . Critics . . . who oppose special rights per se oppose the constitution, and they should take their quarrel elsewhere."—Hamar Foster, Professor, University of Victoria, Victoria, British Columbia

Foster was commenting on final treaty negotiations among the federal government, the provincial government of British Columbia, and the Nisga'a people of the Nass Valley in the northwestern area of the province, which resulted in a number of benefits for this Aboriginal group, including an estimated $448 million. Other gains for the Nisga'a include the right to elect their own government, with authority to make laws in several key provincial jurisdictions, including those regarding land use, culture, and employment.

Such "special rights" accompanying the groundbreaking treaty (which, it is worth noting, had been pursued by the Nisga'a people for six generations) ignited a heated debate in the province, as well as across the country. People questioned whether any group—Aboriginal or otherwise—should have legal rights that are different from those of other Canadian citizens. Some critics of the deal argued that it entrenches inequality in Canadian society since the treaty gives the Nisga'a "special" rights based solely on race. Critics called for a province-wide referendum to let the public decide whether the treaty should become law. Others, sympathetic to the Nisga'a people's historical struggle, welcomed the agreement as a compromise that was finally acceptable to the Nisga'a. Such a compromise, argued proponents, would allow the Nisga'a to get on with tackling the high unemployment and other problems affecting their people. Supporters pointed out as well that the Nisga'a had given up other (similarly special) rights they previously held under the Indian Act.

Highlights of Nisga'a Treaty

Land. The Nisga'a receive 1930 square kilometres of Crown land and title to 62 square kilometres of land currently designated as Indian reserves. Nisga'a lands do not include private property held by non-Natives or agricultural leases. Provincial laws continue to apply to several parcels of land owned by non-Natives that will be surrounded by Nisga'a lands.

Self-government. Elections for a central Nisga'a government and four village governments must be held no later than six months after the treaty comes into force. Only Nisga'a can vote for the Nisga'a government, which has adopted a constitution recognizing the rights and freedoms of its citizens.

The Nisga'a government can make laws on Nisga'a citizenship, language, culture, property, public order, safety, employment, traffic, child and family services, health services, policing, and correctional and court services.

Non-Nisga'a Canadians can participate in elected bodies that directly affect them by making representations and seeking elections to public agencies such as the health board. Local laws affecting everything from traffic to garbage collection will apply to non-Nisga'a within Nisga'a lands, but most laws will apply only to Nisga'a citizens.

Nisga'a continue to be Aboriginal peoples under the Constitution and are entitled to the same rights as other Canadian citizens. The Charter of Rights and Freedoms and all federal and provincial laws continue to apply to Nisga'a people. However, Nisga'a people will no longer be exempt from sales and income taxes.

Resources. Ownership of all forests within Nisga'a lands, and all mineral, oil, and other subsurface resources, will be transferred to the Nisga'a, who can set conditions for their use. Current forest licences will remain in effect for five years. Nisga'a management standards must meet or exceed provincial standards.

Public access to Nisga'a lands for hunting, fishing, and recreation will be provided, although the Nisga'a government may make laws regulating public access for public safety or environmental reasons.

Nisga'a people will be guaranteed 26 percent of the Nass River allowable catch for salmon, and will be allowed to sell their salmon. Any federal commercial or recreational ban on fishing will also apply to the Nisga'a.

Key geographic features will be renamed with Nisga'a names and important cultural sites will be designated as heritage sites. The treaty states that it is the final settlement of Nisga'a Aboriginal rights.

Canadians continue to debate the treaty, asking what the outcome will be if Nisga'a treaty rights conflict with the rights of other Canadians. Indian and Northern Affairs Canada (2008) answers this way:

> Everyone on Nisga'a lands will continue to enjoy the same rights and freedoms under the Canadian Charter of Rights and Freedoms. Everyone will continue to be subject to the Criminal Code of Canada. The Treaty addresses the relationships of Nisga'a laws with the laws of Canada and B.C. and identifies the specific areas in which Nisga'a law will prevail. In addition, the Nisga'a government will be required to consult individuals who are not Nisga'a citizens living on Nisga'a lands about decisions that directly and significantly affect them. These people will also be able to participate in elected bodies that deal with issues that have a direct and significant effect on their lives. The means of participation can include opportunities to make representations, to vote for, or seek election to, Nisga'a public institutions and to have the same means of appeal as Nisga'a citizens.*

What Do You Think?

1. What is your interpretation of the Nisga'a treaty? Is it right that the treaty bestows special rights on a group of people?

2. Should other Aboriginal groups in Canada also be able to claim "special legal rights" to the land and resources of their forebears? Why or why not?

3. How can sociology play a part in understanding this and other debates over Aboriginal land claims?

*Indian and Northern Affairs Canada. Nisga'a Final Agreement—Issues and Responses. 2008. www.ainc-inac.gc.ca/al/ldc/ccl/fagr/nsga/nfa/snr-eng.asp. Used with permission.

Source: Adapted from Matas and McInnes (1998) and Indian and Northern Affairs Canada (2008).

Unlike the economy of earlier times when English merchants and traders were in control, the Quebec economy today is mainly under the control of francophone entrepreneurs. Politics has also changed significantly. During the 1990s, two French political parties controlled the majority of seats in the province, with the Parti Québécois holding power in the Quebec Legislature (the National Assembly) and a new separatist party—the Bloc Québécois—leading the separatist cause at the federal level for a while as the official opposition. The razor-thin defeat of the separatists in the Quebec referendum of 1995 (by a mere 1 percent of the vote) opened the eyes of other Canadians to the very real possibility of the breakup of the country. Since then, however, the separatist parties have suffered setbacks at both the provincial and the federal levels.

During Canada's forty-first general election held in 2011, the Bloc Québécois lost its official party status. Although in the previous 2006 elections it captured 51 of Quebec's 75 seats, in 2011 it managed to secure only 4 seats; a sizable group of Quebecers rode the "Orange Wave," offering support to the New Democratic Party (NDP) with 43 percent of the popular vote. The NDP made historic gains in Quebec, securing 59 seats in that province, and it went on to form the Official Opposition in Parliament. By the forty-second federal election held in 2015, the NDP would lose most of the ground it had gained in Quebec. The Bloc Québécois continued to remain without official party status, while the Liberals secured 40 of Quebec's 78 ridings. These results indicate a major change in the province regarding the important issues of the day: jobs, social security, and social justice rather than separation from Canada.

Canada's Other Immigrants

As previously noted, Canada is a country of Aboriginal peoples, as well as French and English colonial settlers. It is also a country of immigrants. Four distinct historical eras can be distinguished when investigating international migration to the country (Gee, 1990). The first wave was made up of the French, who were the original immigrants to the part of the New World that would later be called "Canada." The French immigrants eventually established the colony of New France between 1608 and 1760. During the nineteenth century, a new second wave of immigrants came, mainly from Britain, in two population flows: the United Empire Loyalists came from the American colonies, fleeing the American independence movement; and immigrants came directly from the British Isles. Smaller numbers of other Europeans also immigrated to Canada during this time, including Germans, Scandinavians, and Eastern Europeans.

The last decades of the nineteenth century and the first decades of the early twentieth century saw the arrival of the largest, third wave of immigrants to the country up to that point. Their numbers ranged from 3.7 to 4.6 million (Kalbach & McVey, 1979). The Canadian government considered the United States, England, and other North and Western European countries as "preferred" countries from which to accept immigrants. As immigration from these countries declined, Canada turned to immigration from "non-preferred" Eastern and Southern European countries (Rosenberg, 1993, orig. 1939).

Immigrants from these parts of Europe were initially viewed with apprehension, resentment, and even hostility. While today Italians, Poles, Ukrainians, Turks, Jews, and Hungarians are considered "white," this was not always the case. Today's *invisible minorities*—sometimes called "white ethnic minorities" (Chan & Chunn, 2014)—were not always so invisible or so white (Satzewich, 2000; Todorova, 2006; Burkowicz, 2013). The whiteness of these Europeans was widely contested by Canadian journalists, politicians, and intellectuals who equated their immigration with a threat to the racial makeup of Anglo and Franco Canada. Stereotypes of the "dirty," "backward," and "unassimilable" Italian and Slav immigrant prevailed. Many early twentieth-century Canadians shared the prejudice of historian John R. Commons, who believe that a line divided

> the continent of Europe from northeast to southwest ... [that] separates countries not only of distinct races but also of distinct civilizations. It separates Protestant Europe from Catholic Europe; it separates countries of representative institutions

and popular government from absolute monarchies; it separates lands where education is universal from lands where illiteracy predominates; it separates manufacturing countries, progressive agriculture, and skilled labor from primitive hand industries, backward agriculture, and unskilled labor; it separates an educated, thrifty peasantry from a peasantry scarcely a single generation removed from serfdom; it separates Teutonic races from Latin, Slav, Semitic, and Mongolian races (1907:69-70).

As racial minorities, some Europeans encountered discrimination either in exclusion from work or in having to accept arduous and unstable employment; in being classified as "enemy aliens" during World War I, which allowed for their internment (1914–1920) and disenfranchisement (1917); and in the breaking up of Polish and Ukrainian language schools, coupled with imprisonment of Doukhobors who engaged in the communal practice of nude parades, or who maintained their religiously inspired pacifism and opposition to military service. It was not until the middle of the twentieth century that racism against Eastern and Southern Europeans declined, coinciding with the arrival of greater numbers of non-Europeans to Canada.

The last, and fourth, wave of immigrants to Canada—more than 5 million of them—arrived in the post–World War II period. Many of these immigrants came from middle- and low-income countries around the globe. As the 1960s saw the abandonment of explicit racial and national immigration criteria, immigrants begun to arrive in greater numbers from non-European countries. Between 1979 and 2000, half of all immigrants to Canada came from Asia (Li, 2003).

The current regulations, which have ushered in the fourth wave, emphasize "economic immigration"—that is, the preferred immigrants ideally possess the particular skills and disposable capital to establish themselves economically after migration.

The 2011 census showed that 20.6 percent of the Canadian population (6.7 million people) were born outside Canada, up from 19.8 percent (6.2 million people) in 2006 (Statistics Canada, 2013a). Among the G8 countries, Canada has the highest proportion of immigrants. The composition of the immigration stream has changed substantially from the third wave. From 2006 to 2011, newcomers born in Asia (as well as in the Middle East) made up the largest proportion (56.9 percent). People from Europe made up the second largest group (13.7 percent) of new immigrants. An additional 12.3 percent originated from Central and South America and the Caribbean, and 12.5 percent of immigrants were born in Africa. The majority of the foreign-born population live in four provinces: Ontario, British Columbia, Quebec, and Alberta.

Visible Minorities

While their population increased significantly in the 1970s, non-European visible minorities have a longer history of Canadian immigration. Among the large number of late nineteenth century and early twentieth century immigrants were 15 000 Chinese who were permitted to come to Canada as a cheap source of labour for the construction of the transcontinental railroad. Between 1886 and 1923, Canada barred all Asians from settling permanently in the country and imposed a "head tax" on all Chinese wishing to immigrate. The initial head tax was $50, later $100, and finally, in 1904, $500, a very large sum at the time. The head tax on Chinese immigrants was not lifted until 1947. Everyone seemed to line up against the Chinese, as captured in a popular phrase of the time that a person "didn't have a Chinaman's chance" (Sung, 1967).

There were also numerous acts, regulations, and agreements that explicitly excluded other racialized immigrants. Two prominent ones are the Gentleman's Agreement of 1908, which compelled Japan to restrict the number of passports it issued to 400 a year, and the Continuous Journey Regulation of 1908, which restricted Indian immigration.

The head tax and generally racist attitude of many Canadians toward the Chinese created domestic hardship, because in Canada (and similarly in the United States) Chinese men

On December 7, 1941, Japan attacked Pearl Harbor and Hong Kong. Just weeks later, the Canadian federal government, under the War Measures Act, demanded the evacuation of all Japanese Canadians residing within about 160 kilometres of the Pacific Coast. Although apparently relocated for reasons of national security, no Japanese Canadian was ever charged with disloyalty to the country. In all, 20 000 men, women, and children of Japanese descent were forced to leave their homes for camps in the interior of British Columbia and farms in Alberta and Manitoba.

Source: William Lyon Mackenzie King Collection/National Archives of Canada/C-24452.

outnumbered Chinese women (Hsu, 1971; Lai, 1980; Prentice et al., 1996). For the relatively few Chinese women who managed to enter the country, the situation was far from friendly. Below, a woman of Chinese background recalls her life in Nanaimo, British Columbia, in the early decades of this century:

> When I went to school in Nanaimo in the 1920s we had to go to a segregated school. In those days there was still segregation for the "Others." We had to go to a special school because we were not white . . . We had to walk past the better schools, which were only for the white people or westerners, to go to this "ward" school that housed all the Indians, the ethnic people, or "Others" (quoted in Yee, 1992:235–6).

With the relaxation of Canadian immigration laws after 1947 and the more open immigration policies of recent decades, Chinese immigrants have received a warmer welcome. Anti-Asian racism, however, still continues to thrive in Canada (Gilmour et al., 2012).

As with the Chinese immigrants who immigrated a century earlier, Canada's visible minorities tend to live in the larger metropolitan areas (95.9 percent). In 2015, the majority of visible minorities resided in either Toronto, Montreal, or Vancouver.

It is clear that visible minorities continue to face racism in Canadian society. One way in which they do so is in the labour market, where they make up 18.2 percent of the labour force (Leitch, 2013). Toronto-based research demonstrates that visible minorities

TABLE 11–4 Income and Education, Aboriginal and Visible Minority Full-Time, Full-Year Workers, Canada, 2011

	All Canadians	Aboriginal Peoples	Visible Minorities
Average income	$ 60 526	$ 49 821	$ 53 504
Average income of those with a post-secondary certificate, diploma, or degree	$ 67 442	$ 56 691	$ 59 066

Source: Statistics Canada (2011b).

face discrimination when applying for work. Headed by Philip Oreopoulos, the research project sent out 13 000 job applications in response to various ads. Oreopoulos discovered that resumes with English-sounding names are 39 percent more likely to receive interview requests than are comparable resumes with Chinese, Indian, or Pakistani names (2011). Such discrimination likely contributes to the fact that visible minorities have higher rates of unemployment. In 2011, visible minorities were unemployed at a rate of 9.9 percent compared to 7.3 percent for non-visible minority workers (Jackson, 2013). Furthermore, even when visible minorities hold university degrees, they earn, on average, lower incomes than all Canadians, as shown in Table 11–4.

Race and Ethnicity: Looking Ahead

Canada has been, and will likely remain, a land of immigrants. Immigration has brought striking cultural diversity and tales of success, hope, and struggle told in hundreds of languages.

For those who came to this country during the third wave of immigration that peaked around 1910, the next generations brought gradual economic gains and at least some cultural assimilation. The government also recognized basic freedoms that it had earlier denied, including citizenship and the right to vote and hold public office.

The fourth wave of immigration began after World War II, and swelled as immigration laws were relaxed in the 1960s. Since 1990, more than 225 000 people have come to Canada each year on average, twice the number that arrived during the "Great Immigration" a century ago (although newcomers now enter a country with a much larger population). Most contemporary immigrants come not from Europe but from middle- and low-income countries.

Many of the immigrants who will arrive in the decades to come will face the same type of prejudice and discrimination experienced by those who came before them. Indeed, recent years have witnessed rising hostility toward foreigners (sometimes called *xenophobia*, a word with Greek roots meaning "fear of what is strange"). This is especially the case in the United States, where, in 1994, California voters passed Proposition 187, which stated that undocumented immigrants should be denied health care, social services, and public education; it was later overturned in federal court. The rise of neo-Nazi groups in the 1990s in Canada, and indeed across many high-income countries, as well as prejudice directed at Muslims in the post-9/11 climate, suggests that the United States is not alone in its fear of foreigners.

Even so, like Canada's Aboriginal peoples, who are enjoying a cultural revival, many new immigrants now try to join Canadian society while maintaining their traditional cultures. Some have also built racial and ethnic enclaves to keep their ethnic traditions and celebrations alive for the next generation. In addition, new arrivals still carry the traditional hope that their racial and ethnic identities can be a source of pride rather than a badge of inferiority.

Seeing Sociology in Everyday Life

CHAPTER 11 Race and Ethnicity

How does race interact with other forms of inequality in producing people's social standing?

This chapter explores the importance of race and ethnicity to social standing in Canada. You already know, for example, that visible minorities have higher rates of unemployment and that they earn on average less than all Canadians. But how does the interplay between racism, sexism, and immigration work to the economic benefit or detriment of various individuals? As you read in this chapter, intersection theory attempts to answer this question by considering how different dimensions of inequality intersect with race. Here's a chance to test your sociological thinking, and to put intersection theory to use, by answering several questions about how race and ethnicity, gender, education, and age affect social standing. Look at each of the statements below: Does the statement reflect reality or is it a myth?

Rido/Shutterstock

Q

1. In Canada, rich people are a diverse bunch made up fairly equally of men and women, and whites and non-whites. *Reality or myth?*
2. On average, white women make more money than all categories of visible minority women. *Reality or myth?*
3. University-educated women earn similar wages across all racial and ethnic groups. *Reality or myth?*
4. A bachelor's degree gives visible minority women an economic advantage over high school–educated white men. *Reality or myth?*

A.
1. *This is a myth.* While the median income for Canadians working full-year, full-time in 2010 was $49 351, white, university-educated, middle-aged men reported the highest median income of $91 162.

2. *Myth.* Canadian women earned a median income of $44 341. Japanese women, however, reported the highest median income of $47 545, Chinese women the second highest of $45 370, and white women the third highest of $44 994. Filipino, Korean, and Latin American women reported earning around $37 000.

3. *Myth.* While women with a bachelor's degree or higher reported a median income of $62 739, white women in this educational category earned the most, reporting a median income of $65 722. Meanwhile, Japanese women earned $58 641, black women $56 344, and South Asian women $51 201.

4. *For most visible minority women this is a reality.* But the advantage varies significantly by race and ethnicity. High school–educated white men reported a median income of $46 621. Arab women with a bachelor's degree or higher earned more at $50 814, while Latin American women earned only slightly more at $47 957. Meanwhile Korean and Filipino women with a bachelor's degree or higher earned around $42 000.

Source: Skelton (2013).

Seeing Sociology in *Your* Everyday Life

1. Give several of your friends or family members a quick quiz, asking them what share of the Canadian population is black, South Asian, Chinese, or not a visible minority (see Table 11–2 on page 348). Are any of these numbers exaggerated?

2. Go to www.sociologyinfocus.com to access the Sociology in Focus blog, where you can read the latest posts by a team of young sociologists who apply the sociological perspective to topics of popular culture.

3. Do you think people tend to see race in terms of biological traits or as categories constructed by society? What about you?

Melissa Renwick/ZUMA Press/
Newscom

Making the Grade

The Social Meaning of Race and Ethnicity

11.1 Explain the social construction of race and ethnicity. (pages 344–349)

Race refers to socially constructed categories based on biological traits that a society defines as important.

- The meaning and importance of race vary from place to place and over time.
- Societies use racial categories to rank people in a hierarchy, giving some people more money, power, and prestige than others.
- In the past, scientists created three broad categories—Caucasoids, Mongoloids, and Negroids—but there are no biologically pure races.

Ethnicity refers to socially constructed categories based on cultural traits that a society defines as important.

- Ethnicity reflects common ancestors, language, and religion.
- The importance of ethnicity varies from place to place and over time.
- People choose to play up or play down their ethnicity.
- Ethnicity intersects with various other statuses.

> **race** a socially constructed category of people who share biologically transmitted traits that members of a society consider important
>
> **ethnicity** a shared cultural heritage
>
> **visible minority** persons, other than Aboriginal peoples, who are non-Caucasian in race or non-white in colour

Prejudice and Stereotypes

11.2 Describe the extent and causes of prejudice. (pages 349–354)

Prejudice is a rigid and unfair generalization about a category of people.

- The social distance scale is one measure of prejudice.
- One type of prejudice is the **stereotype,** an exaggerated description applied to every person in some category.

There are four **theories of prejudice:**

- **Scapegoat theory** claims that prejudice results from frustration among people who are disadvantaged.
- **Authoritarian personality theory** (Adorno) claims that prejudice is a personality trait of certain individuals, especially those with little education and those raised by cold and demanding parents.
- **Culture theory** (Bogardus) claims that prejudice is rooted in culture; we learn to feel greater social distance from some categories of people.
- **Conflict theory** claims that prejudice is a tool used by powerful people to divide and control the population.

> **prejudice** a rigid and unfair generalization about an entire category of people
>
> **racism** the belief that one racial category is innately superior or inferior to another
>
> **scapegoat** a person or category of people, typically with little power, whom people unfairly blame for their own troubles

Discrimination

11.3 Distinguish discrimination from prejudice. (pages 354–355)

Discrimination refers to actions by which various categories of people are treated unequally.

- Prejudice refers to *attitudes*; discrimination involves *actions*.
- **Institutional prejudice and discrimination** are biases built into the operation of society's institutions, including schools, hospitals, the police, and the workplace.
- Prejudice and discrimination perpetuate themselves in a vicious circle, resulting in social disadvantage that fuels additional prejudice and discrimination.

> **discrimination** unequal treatment of various categories of people
>
> **institutional prejudice and discrimination** bias built into the operation of society's institutions

Majority and Minority: Patterns of Interaction

11.4 Identify examples of pluralism, assimilation, segregation, and genocide. (pages 355–358)

Pluralism means that racial and ethnic categories, although distinct, have roughly equal social standing.

- Canadian society is pluralistic in that all people in Canada, regardless of race or ethnicity, have equal standing under the law.
- Canadian society is not pluralistic in that all racial and ethnic categories do not have equal *social* standing.

> **pluralism** a state in which people of all races and ethnicities are distinct but have equal social standing
>
> **assimilation** the process by which minorities gradually adopt patterns of the dominant culture
>
> **miscegenation** biological reproduction by partners of different racial categories

Assimilation is the process by which minorities gradually adopt the patterns of the dominant culture.

- Assimilation involves changes in dress, language, religion, values, and friends.
- Assimilation is a strategy to escape prejudice and discrimination and to achieve upward social mobility.
- Some categories of people have assimilated more than others.

Segregation is the physical and social separation of categories of people.

- Although some segregation is voluntary (as by the Amish), majorities usually segregate minorities by excluding them from neighbourhoods, schools, and occupations.
- *De jure* segregation is segregation by law; *de facto* segregation describes settings that contain only people of one category.
- Hypersegregation means having little social contact with people beyond the local community.

Genocide is the systematic killing of one category of people by another.

- Historical examples of genocide include the extermination of Armenians by the Ottoman Empire and of Jews by the Nazis.
- Recent examples of genocide include Hutus killing Tutsis in the African nation of Rwanda, Serbs killing Bosnians in the Balkans of Eastern Europe, and the systematic killing in the Darfur region of Sudan.

segregation the physical and social separation of categories of people

genocide the systematic killing of one category of people by another

Race and Ethnicity in Canada

11.5 Assess the social standing of racial and ethnic categories of Canadian society. (pages 358–365)

Aboriginal peoples, the earliest human inhabitants of the Americas, have endured genocide, segregation, and forced assimilation. Today, the social standing of Aboriginal peoples is well below the national average.

British Canadians—sometimes referred to as White Anglo-Saxon Protestants (WASPs)—were among the original European settlers of Canada, and many continue to enjoy high social position today.

French Canadians were the other major European group to settle in Canada. Canada eventually fell under British colonial rule. Though the French retained some control over their own language, religion, and legal institutions, English Canada gained control over economic, political, and social matters. The historical legacy of the "two solitudes"—French and English—to some extent continues to this day.

Other Immigrants. Canada is also a country of immigrants from many other areas of the world. With the decline in British immigration, Canada sought immigrants from Eastern and Southern Europe. Regarded as a "non-preferred" class, these Europeans faced prejudice and discrimination. Canada also admitted smaller numbers of Asian immigrants whose immigration, unlike that of the Europeans, was discouraged. By the 1970s immigration shifted from European to Asian countries.

Visible Minorities. Today a majority of immigrants to Canada are visible minorities. In 2011, 19.1 percent of the Canadian population identified themselves as a visible minority. Visible minorities encounter racism by lacking white privilege and through labour market discrimination. The share of visible minorities is expected to keep increasing, reaching 30.6 percent by 2031.

12 Economics and Politics

CANADA: WE DON'T WANT YOUR DIRTY TARSANDS OIL

LEARNING OBJECTIVES

12.1 Summarize historical changes to the economy.	**12.6** Compare monarchy and democracy as well as authoritarian and totalitarian political systems.
12.2 Assess the operation of capitalist and socialist economies.	**12.7** Analyze economic and social issues using the political spectrum.
12.3 Analyze patterns of employment and unemployment in Canada.	**12.8** Apply the pluralist, power-elite, and Marxist models to the Canadian political system.
12.4 Discuss the importance of corporations to the Canadian economy.	**12.9** Describe causes of both revolution and terrorism.
12.5 Distinguish traditional, rational-legal, and charismatic authority.	**12.10** Identify factors encouraging war or peace.

the Power of Society

to shape our choices in jobs

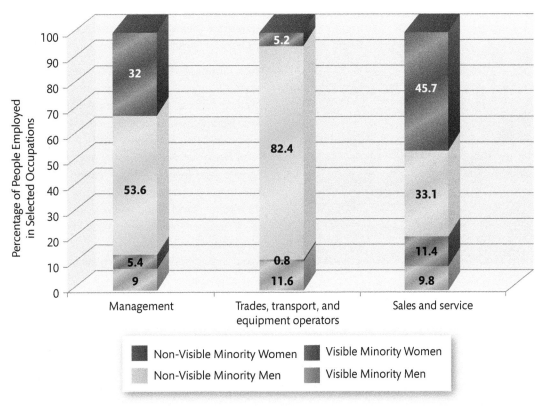

Source: Calculated by J. Burkowicz from Statistics Canada (2011h).

Will the jobs you take throughout your life reflect choices you make based on your personal abilities and interests? To some extent, yes. But the work we have has a lot to do with our position in a society that distributes opportunity unequally. Look at occupational fields such as management and trades, transport, and equipment operators—notice how these jobs are overwhelmingly filled by people born with the relative advantages that go with being white and male. By contrast, "low-prestige" service jobs are far more likely to be filled by women. Society has a lot to say about the type of work we all do.

Chapter Overview

This chapter begins a survey of the major social institutions. We begin with the economy, which is widely regarded as having the greatest impact on society as a whole. The chapter explores the operation of the economy and explains how changes in economic production have reshaped society. The chapter then continues by examining politics, a second major social institution, with attention to the character and causes of war and terrorism.

Carlos Barria/Reuters

Here's a quick quiz about the North American economy. (Hint: All six questions have the same correct answer.)

- Which business do 200 million people in the world visit each week?
- Which business sells the products of more than 100 000 companies?
- Which North American company, on average, opens three new stores somewhere in the world every day?
- Which North American company buys more than $25 billion worth of goods each year from China, making it a larger trading partner for China than the United Kingdom?
- Which North American company employs 2.2 million people worldwide, including approximately 94 000 in Canada and 1.4 million in the United States?
- Which single company actually grew in size during the recent economic downturn?

The answer, of course, is Walmart, the global discount chain founded by Sam Walton, who opened his first store in Arkansas in 1962. In 2012, Walmart announced revenues of $444 billion in annual sales through 395 stores in Canada, more than 4600 stores in the United States, and 5964 stores in other countries from Brazil to China, making it the second-largest corporation in North America.

But not everyone is pleased with the expansion of Walmart. Across North America, many people have joined a social movement to keep Walmart out of their local communities, fearing the loss of local businesses and, in some cases, local culture. Critics claim that the merchandising giant pays low wages, keeps out unions, and sells many products made in sweatshops abroad. In 2005, the Walmart store in Jonquière, Quebec, closed six months after the workers voted to have their interests represented by United Food and Commercial Workers union. In 2014, the Supreme Court of Canada found the chain guilty of violating Quebec's labour code and ordered the store to compensate the 190 employees it had put out of work. Since 2010, Walmart also has defended itself in the courts against claims of sex discrimination (Saporito, 2003; Walsh, 2007; Schell, 2011; Walmart, 2012, 2014; Shaw, 2014).

This chapter explores the economy and the closely related institution of politics. A number of very large corporations, including Walmart, are at the centre of the Canadian economy, raising questions about just how the economy operates, whose interests it ought to serve, and to what extent big business shapes the political life of Canada.

social institution a major sphere of social life, or societal subsystem, organized to meet human needs

Economics and politics are **social institutions,** *major spheres of social life, or societal subsystems, organized to meet human needs.* The two chapters that follow consider other social institutions: Chapter 13 focuses on family and religion, and Chapter 14 highlights education, health, and medicine. These discussions explain how social institutions have changed over the course of history, describe how they operate today, and point out controversies that are likely to shape them tomorrow.

The Economy: Historical Overview

12.1 Summarize historical changes to the economy.

As societies industrialize, a smaller share of the labour force works in agriculture. In Canada, much of the agricultural work that remains is performed by immigrants from lower-income nations. These farm workers from Mexico travel to Ontario to work on a temporary basis in agriculture.

The **economy** is *the social institution that organizes a society's production, distribution, and consumption of goods and services*. The economy operates, for better or worse, in a generally predictable manner. *Goods* are commodities ranging from necessities (such as food, clothing, and shelter) to luxury items (such as cars, swimming pools, and yachts). *Services* are activities that benefit people (including the work of priests, physicians, teachers, and computer software specialists). Three times in the past, technological revolutions reorganized the economy and, in the process, transformed social life.

The Agricultural Revolution

As Chapter 2 ("Culture") explained, the earliest societies were made up of hunters and gatherers living off the land. In these technologically simple societies, there was no distinct economy; producing and consuming were part of family life.

Harnessing animals to plows around 5000 years ago permitted the development of agriculture, which was 50 times more productive than hunting and gathering. The resulting surpluses meant that not everyone had to produce food, so many people took on other specialized work: making tools, raising animals, and building dwellings. Soon towns sprang up, linked by networks of traders dealing in food, animals, and other goods. These four factors—agricultural technology, specialized work, permanent settlements, and trade—made the economy a distinct social institution.

economy the social institution that organizes a society's production, distribution, and consumption of goods and services

The Industrial Revolution

By the mid-eighteenth century, a second technological revolution was under way, starting in England and spreading to Canada, the United States, and elsewhere. Industrialization changed the economy in five fundamental ways:

1. **New sources of energy.** Throughout history, "energy" had meant the muscle power of people or animals. Then, in 1765, the English inventor James Watt introduced the steam engine. One hundred times more powerful than animal muscles, early steam engines soon drove heavy machinery.

2. **Centralization of work in factories.** Steam-powered machinery moved work from homes to factories, centralized workplaces that housed the machines.

3. **Manufacturing and mass production.** Before the Industrial Revolution, most people grew or gathered raw materials such as grain, wood, or wool. In an industrial economy, the focus shifts so that most people turn raw materials into a wide range of finished products such as processed foods, furniture, and clothing.

4. **Specialization.** Centuries ago, people worked at home making products from start to finish. In the factory, a labourer repeats a single task over and over, making only a small contribution to the finished product.

5. **Wage labour.** Instead of working for themselves, factory workers became wage labourers working for strangers, who often cared less for them than for the machines they operated.

The Industrial Revolution gradually raised the standard of living as countless new products fuelled an expanding marketplace. Yet the benefits of industrial technology were shared very unequally, especially at the beginning. Some factory owners made huge fortunes, while the majority of industrial workers lived close to poverty. Children, too, worked in factories or in coal mines for pennies a day. Women working in factories were among the lowest paid, and their rigid supervision left them with little personal freedom. As time went on, workers formed

primary sector the part of the economy that draws raw materials from the natural environment

secondary sector the part of the economy that transforms raw materials into manufactured goods

tertiary sector the part of the economy that involves services rather than goods

labour unions to represent their interests collectively to factory owners. In the twentieth century, new laws banned child labour, set minimum wage levels, improved workplace safety, and extended schooling and political rights to a larger segment of the population.

The Information Revolution and Post-industrial Society

post-industrial economy a productive system based on service work and computer technology

By about 1950, the nature of production was changing once again. Canada was creating a **post-industrial economy**, *a productive system based on service work and computer technology*. Automated machinery (and later, robotics) reduced the role of human labour in factory production and expanded the ranks of clerical workers and managers. The post-industrial era is marked by a shift from industrial work to service work.

Driving this economic change is a third technological breakthrough: the computer. Just as the Industrial Revolution did two-and-a-half centuries ago, the Information Revolution has introduced new kinds of products and new forms of communication and has changed the character of work. There have been three significant changes:

1. **From tangible products to ideas.** The industrial era was defined by the production of goods; in the post-industrial era, people work with symbols. Computer programmers, writers, financial analysts, advertising executives, architects, editors, and various types of consultants make up more of the labour force in the information age.

2. **From mechanical skills to literacy skills.** The Industrial Revolution required mechanical skills, but the Information Revolution requires literacy skills: speaking and writing well and, of course, knowing how to use a computer. People able to communicate effectively are likely to do well; people without these skills face fewer opportunities.

3. **From factories to almost anywhere.** Industrial technology drew workers to factories located near power sources, but computer technology allows people to work almost anywhere. Laptop and wireless computers and cell phones now turn the home, car, or even an airplane into a "virtual office." What this means for everyday life is that new information technology blurs the line between our lives at work and at home.

Global Snapshot

● As countries become richer, the primary sector becomes a smaller part of the economy and the tertiary or service sector becomes larger.

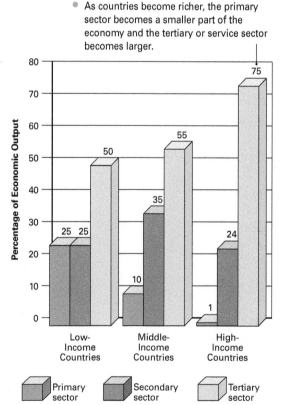

FIGURE 12–1 The Size of Economic Sectors, by Income Level of Country

Source: Estimates based on World Bank (2012).

Sectors of the Economy

The three revolutions just described reflect a shifting balance among the three sectors of a society's economy. The **primary sector** is *the part of the economy that draws raw materials from the natural environment*. The primary sector—agriculture, raising animals, fishing, forestry, and mining—is largest in low-income nations. Figure 12–1 shows that 25 percent of the economic output of low-income countries is in the primary sector, compared with 10 percent of economic activity among middle-income nations and just 1 percent in high-income countries such as Canada.

The **secondary sector** is *the part of the economy that transforms raw materials into manufactured goods*. This sector expands quickly as societies industrialize. It includes operations such as refining petroleum into gasoline and turning metals into tools and automobiles. The globalization of industry means that just about all the world's countries have a significant share of workers employed in the secondary sector. Figure 12–1 shows that the secondary sector now accounts for nearly the same share of economic output in low-income nations as it does in high-income countries.

The **tertiary sector** is *the part of the economy that involves services rather than goods*. The tertiary sector grows with industrialization, accounting for 50 percent of economic output in low-income countries, 55 percent in middle-income countries, and 75 percent in high-income countries. In 2014, 78 percent of the

Window on the World

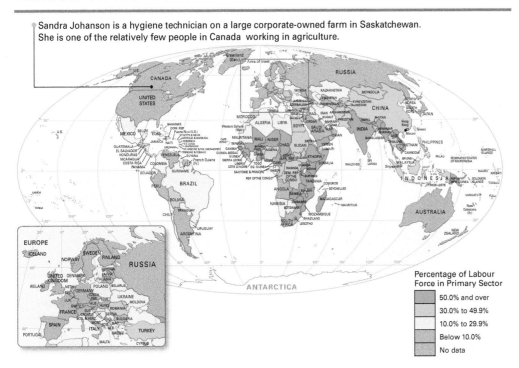

Sandra Johanson is a hygiene technician on a large corporate-owned farm in Saskatchewan. She is one of the relatively few people in Canada working in agriculture.

Percentage of Labour Force in Primary Sector

- 50.0% and over
- 30.0% to 49.9%
- 10.0% to 29.9%
- Below 10.0%
- No data

GLOBAL MAP 12–1 Agricultural Employment in Global Perspective

The primary sector of the economy is largest in the nations that are least developed. Thus, in the poor countries of Africa and Asia, up to half of all workers are farmers. This picture is altogether different in the world's most economically developed countries—including Canada, the United States, Great Britain, and Australia—which have only about 1 percent of their labour force in agriculture.

Source: Data from International Labour Organization (2014).

Canadian labour force was employed in service work, including secretarial and clerical jobs and work in food service, sales, law, health care, advertising, and teaching (Statistics Canada, 2015a).

The Global Economy

New information technology is drawing people around the world together and creating a **global economy**, *economic activity that crosses national borders*. The development of a global economy has five major consequences.

First, we see a global division of labour: Different regions of the world specialize in one sector of economic activity. As Global Map 12–1 shows, agriculture represents about half of the total economic output of the world's poorest countries. Global Map 12–2 on page 376 shows that most of the economic output of high-income countries, including Canada, is in the service sector. In short, the world's poorest nations specialize in producing raw materials, and the richest nations specialize in the production of services.

Second, an increasing number of products pass through more than one nation. Look no further than your morning coffee: The beans may have been grown in Colombia and transported to Halifax on a freighter that was registered in Liberia, made in a shipyard in Japan using steel from Korea, and fuelled by oil from Venezuela.

Third, national governments no longer control the economic activity that takes place within their borders. In fact, governments cannot even accurately regulate the value of their national currencies because dollars, euros, pounds sterling, and yen are traded around the clock in the financial markets of Toronto, New York, London, and Tokyo.

A fourth consequence of the global economy is that a small number of businesses operating internationally now control a vast share of the world's economic activity. Using the latest available data, the 1500 largest multinational companies (with sales of about $35 trillion) account for half the world's economic output (DeCarlo, 2012; World Bank, 2012a, 2012b).

global economy economic activity that crosses national borders

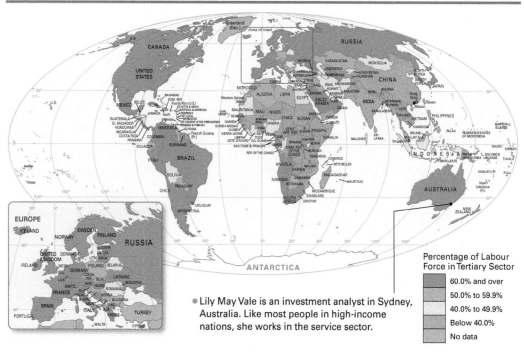

Percentage of Labour
Force in Tertiary Sector

- 60.0% and over
- 50.0% to 59.9%
- 40.0% to 49.9%
- Below 40.0%
- No data

● Lily May Vale is an investment analyst in Sydney, Australia. Like most people in high-income nations, she works in the service sector.

GLOBAL MAP 12–2 Service-Sector Employment in Global Perspective

The tertiary sector of the economy becomes ever larger as a nation's income level rises. In the United States, Canada, the countries of Western Europe, much of South America, Australia, and Japan, about two-thirds of the labour force performs service work.

Source: Data from International Labour Organization (2014).

Fifth and finally, the globalization of the economy raises concerns about the rights and opportunities of workers. Critics of this trend claim that Canada, the United States, and other high-income countries are losing jobs—especially factory jobs—to low-income nations. This means that workers here face lower wages and higher unemployment. At the same time, many workers abroad are paid extremely low wages. As a result, say critics, the global expansion of capitalism threatens the well-being of workers throughout the world.

The world is still divided into 195 politically distinct nations. But the rising level of international economic activity makes nationhood less significant than it was even a decade ago.

Economic Systems: Paths to Justice

12.2 Assess the operation of capitalist and socialist economies.

Every society's economic system makes a statement about justice by determining who is entitled to what. Two general economic models are capitalism and socialism. No nation anywhere in the world has an economy that is completely one or the other; rather, capitalism and socialism are two ends of a continuum along which all real-world economies can be located. We will look at each of these models in turn.

Capitalism

Capitalism is *an economic system in which natural resources and the means of producing goods and services are privately owned.* An ideal capitalist economy has three distinctive features:

1. **Private ownership of property.** In a capitalist economy, individuals can own almost anything. The more capitalist an economy is, the more private ownership there is of wealth-producing property such as factories, real estate, and natural resources.

2. **Pursuit of personal profit.** A capitalist society seeks to create profit and wealth. The profit motive is the reason people take new jobs, open new businesses, or try to improve products. Making money is considered the natural way of economic life. Just as important, the Scottish philosopher Adam Smith (1723–1790) claimed that as individuals pursue their self-interest, the entire society prospers (1937, orig. 1776).

3. **Competition and consumer choice.** A purely capitalist economy is a free-market system with no government interference (sometimes called a *laissez-faire economy*, from the French words meaning "leave it alone"). Adam Smith stated that a freely competitive economy regulates itself by the "invisible hand" of the law of supply and demand.

   Consumers regulate a market economy, Smith explained, by selecting the goods and services offering the greatest value. As producers compete for the customer's business, they provide the highest-quality goods at the lowest possible prices. In Smith's time-honoured phrase, from narrow self-interest comes "the greatest good for the greatest number of people." Government control of an economy, on the other hand, distorts market forces by reducing the quantity and quality of goods, shortchanging consumers in the process.

Justice in a capitalist system amounts to freedom of the marketplace, where anyone can produce, invest, buy, and sell according to individual self-interest. The increasing popularity of Walmart, described in the opening to this chapter, reflects a model of justice that combines competition and consumer choice with private property and profits.

Canada is considered a capitalist nation because most businesses are privately owned. However, it is not completely capitalist because the government plays a large role in the economy. Government itself owns—in part or completely—a number of productive organizations, including almost all of this country's schools, roads, parks, and museums; Crown corporations such as Canada Post and Via Rail; and the Canadian military. In addition, governments use taxation and other forms of regulation to influence what companies produce, to control the quality and cost of merchandise, to regulate what businesses import and export, and to motivate consumers to conserve natural resources.

Furthermore, the Canadian government also sets minimum wage levels, enforces workplace safety standards, regulates corporate mergers, provides farm price supports, taxes everyone on what they earn, and also supplements the income of a majority of people in Canada in the form of employment insurance, public pensions, student loans, child tax credits, and subsidies for child and elder care. Municipal, provincial, territorial, and federal governments combined are the nation's biggest employer, with 21.2 percent of the labour force on their payrolls in 2010 (École nationale d'administration publique, 2013).

Socialism

Socialism is *an economic system in which natural resources and the means of producing goods and services are collectively owned.* In its ideal form, a socialist economy rejects each of the three characteristics of capitalism just described in favour of three opposite features:

1. **Collective ownership of property.** A socialist economy limits private property, especially property used to generate profit, and establishes collective property. This can be achieved through government controls or through non-state, worker-run co-operatives. In a socialist economy, property is redistributed so that basic goods, such as housing and medicine, are made available to all, not just to the people with the most money.

2. **Pursuit of collective goals.** The individualistic pursuit of profit goes against the collective orientation of socialism. What capitalism celebrates as the "entrepreneurial spirit," socialism condemns as greed; individuals are urged to work for the common good of all. Commercial advertising thus plays little role in socialist economies.

3. **Equality and a social safety net.** Socialism rejects capitalism's laissez-faire approach in favour of an economy that meets the needs of all, especially a society's most vulnerable members. Eliminating inequality and poverty, providing tuition-free education, and establishing universal health care are popular socialist goals.

capitalism an economic system in which natural resources and the means of producing goods and services are privately owned

socialism an economic system in which natural resources and the means of producing goods and services are collectively owned

Capitalism thrives in Hong Kong (*left*), evident in streets choked with advertising and shoppers. In Bolivia's capital, Sucre (*right*), socialism is increasingly the rule, where a growing economy goes hand-in-hand with increased social spending.

Justice in a socialist context means not competing to gain wealth but meeting everyone's basic needs in a roughly equal manner. From a socialist point of view, the common capitalist practice of giving workers as little in wages and benefits as possible to boost company earnings is unjust because it puts profits before people.

Venezuela, Cuba, the People's Republic of China, and more than two dozen other nations in Asia, Africa, and Latin America model their economies on socialism, placing almost all wealth-generating property under state control (Miller, Holmes, & Feulner, 2012). The extent of world socialism declined during the 1990s as countries in Eastern Europe and the former Soviet Union geared their economies toward a market system. More recently, however, voters in Bolivia, Venezuela, Ecuador, and other nations in South America have elected leaders who are moving the national economies in a socialist direction.

Welfare Capitalism and State Capitalism

Most of the nations in Western Europe—especially Sweden, Denmark, and Italy—have market-based economies but also offer broad social welfare programs. Analysts call this third type of economic system **welfare capitalism**, *an economic and political system that combines a mostly market-based economy with extensive social welfare programs.*

Under welfare capitalism, the government owns some of the largest industries and services, such as transportation, the mass media, and health care. In Greece, France, and Sweden, almost half of economic production is "nationalized," or state-controlled. Most industry is left in private hands, although it is subject to extensive government regulation. High taxation (aimed especially at the rich) funds a wide range of social welfare programs, including universal health care and child care. In Sweden, for example, government-provided social services represent 28 percent of all economic output, much higher than the 19 percent share in the United States (OECD, 2012).

Another alternative is **state capitalism**, *an economic and political system in which companies are privately owned but co-operate closely with the government.* State capitalism is the rule in the nations along the Pacific Rim. Japan, South Korea, and Singapore are all capitalist countries, but their governments work in partnership with large companies, supplying financial assistance and controlling foreign imports to help their businesses compete in world markets (Gerlach, 1992).

welfare capitalism an economic and political system that combines a mostly market-based economy with extensive social welfare programs

state capitalism an economic and political system in which companies are privately owned but co-operate closely with the government

Relative Advantages of Capitalism and Socialism

Which economic system works best? Comparing economic models is difficult because all nations mix capitalism and socialism to varying degrees. In addition, nations differ in cultural attitudes toward work, access to natural resources, levels of technological development, and patterns of trade. Despite such complicating factors, some crude comparisons are revealing.

Economic Productivity

One key dimension of economic performance is productivity. A commonly used measure of economic output is *gross domestic product* (GDP), the total value of all goods and services produced within the nation's borders each year. Per capita (per person) GDP allows us to compare the economic performance of nations of different population sizes.

The output of mostly capitalist countries in the late 1980s—before the end of socialist economies in the Soviet Union and Eastern Europe—varied somewhat but averaged about $13 500 per person. The comparable figure for the mostly socialist former Soviet Union and nations of Eastern Europe was about $5000. This means that the capitalist countries outproduced the socialist nations by a ratio of 2.7 to 1 (United Nations Development Programme, 1990).

We must keep in mind, however, that countries that attempted to implement socialism in the twentieth century tended to start off further back in the race. In 1917, when Russia underwent a communist revolution, the country was semi-feudal and largely underdeveloped. From the 1950s to the early 1970s, the command economy of the Soviet Union experienced tremendous economic development, actually growing faster than the economy of the United States (Central Intelligence Agency, 1985). By the 1970s, an economic slowdown characterized the economies of the USSR and Eastern Bloc countries.

A recent comparison of socialist North Korea (per capita GDP of $1800) and capitalist South Korea ($22 424) provides an even sharper contrast (Central Intelligence Agency, 2012; World Bank, 2012a, 2012b).

North Korea

South Korea

National Geophysical Data Center

Directly comparing the economic performance of capitalism and socialism is difficult because nations differ in many ways. But a satellite image of socialist North Korea and capitalist South Korea at night shows the dramatically different electrical output of the two nations, one indication of economic activity.

Economic Equality

The distribution of resources within the population is another important measure of how well an economic system works. A comparative study of Europe in the mid-1970s, when that region was split between mostly capitalist and mostly socialist countries, compared the earnings of the richest 5 percent of the population and the poorest 5 percent (Wiles, 1977). Societies with mostly capitalist economies had an income ratio of about 10 to 1; the figure for socialist countries was 5 to 1. In other words, capitalist economies support a higher average economic output but with greater income inequality. Said another way, socialist economies create more economic equality but with a lower overall level of productivity.

Personal Freedom

One additional consideration in evaluating capitalism and socialism is the personal freedom each system gives its people. Capitalism emphasizes the *freedom to pursue self-interest* and depends on the ability of producers and consumers to interact with little interference by the state. Socialism, by contrast, emphasizes *freedom from basic want*. The goal of equality has often been attempted through state regulation of the economy, which in turn has tended to limit consumer choices and business opportunities.

Can a single society offer both political freedom and economic equality? In capitalist Canada, our political system offers many personal freedoms, but the economy generates a fair bit of inequality, and freedom is not worth as much to a poor person as to a rich one. By contrast, North Korea or Cuba has considerable economic equality, but people cannot speak out or travel freely within or outside of the country. Perhaps the closest any country comes to

Thinking Globally

Want Equality and Freedom? Try Denmark

Denmark is located in northwestern Europe, has about 5.5 million people, and is a little smaller than Nova Scotia. This country is a good example of the economic and political system called welfare capitalism, in which a market economy is mixed with broad government programs that provide for the welfare of all Danish people.

Most Danes consider life in their country to be very good. There is a high standard of living—Denmark and Canada both have a per-person GDP of about $37 800. However, Canada has almost 50 percent more income inequality than Denmark (the United States has almost twice as much). Denmark's unemployment rate for 2010 was 6 percent, lower than the 8.3 percent in Canada (OECD, 2011a).

Low inequality and low unemployment are largely the result of government regulation of the Danish economy. Taxes in Denmark are the highest in the world, with most people paying about 40 percent of their income in taxes and those earning over $70 000 paying more than 50 percent (people in Quebec pay close to 30 percent, while most people in Canada pay less than 25 percent at that income level). That's in addition to a sales tax of 25 percent on everything people buy. These high taxes increase economic equality (by taking more taxes from the rich and giving more benefits to the poor) and they also allow the government to fund social welfare programs that provide benefits to everyone. For example, every Danish citizen is entitled to government-funded college and university education and universal health care, and each worker receives at least five weeks of paid vacation leave each year. People who lose their jobs receive about 90 percent of their prior income from the government for up to four years.

Many people—especially the Danes themselves—feel that Denmark offers an ideal mix of political freedom (Danes have extensive political rights and elect their leaders) and economic security (all citizens benefit from extensive government services and programs).

What Do You Think?

1. What evidence of less income inequality might you expect to see in Denmark if you were to visit that country?

2. Would you be willing to pay most of your income in taxes if the government provided you with benefits such as schooling and health care? Why or why not?

3. Do you think most people in Canada would like to have our society become more like Denmark? Why or why not?

Sources: Fox (2007) and OECD (2011a, 2011b).

"having it all" is Denmark, where—as the Thinking Globally box takes a closer look—welfare capitalism combines a market economy with broad government programs that provide for the welfare of all citizens.

Changes in Socialist and Capitalist Countries

In 1989 and 1990, the nations of Eastern Europe, which had been seized by the former Soviet Union at the end of World War II, overthrew their socialist regimes. These nations—including the former German Democratic Republic (East Germany), the Czech Republic, Slovakia, Hungary, Romania, and Bulgaria—all moved toward capitalist market systems after decades of state-controlled economies. At the end of 1991, the Soviet Union itself formally dissolved, and many of its former republics introduced some free-market principles into their economies. Within a decade, three-fourths of former Soviet government enterprises were partly or entirely in private hands (Montaigne, 2001).

There were many reasons for these sweeping changes. First, the capitalist economies were by the 1970s more productive than their socialist counterparts. The socialist economies were successful in achieving economic equality, but living standards were low compared with those of Western Europe. Second, Soviet socialism was heavy-handed, rigidly controlling the media and restricting individual freedoms. In other words, socialism did away with *economic* elites, as Karl Marx predicted, but as Max Weber foresaw, socialism increased the power of *political* elites.

So far, the market reforms in Eastern Europe have proceeded unevenly. Some nations, such as Kazakhstan, Uzbekistan, and Turkmenistan, all with extensive reserves of oil and natural gas, did well even during the recent global recession. Other nations, including Lithuania, Latvia, and Azerbaijan, have seen their economies shrink and have faced rising unemployment. In just about every formerly socialist nation, the introduction of a market economy has brought with it an increase in economic inequality (Ignatius, 2007; Pew Research Center, 2011; World Bank, 2012a, 2012b).

A number of countries, primarily in South America, have recently been heading in a more socialist direction. In 2005, the people of Bolivia elected Evo Morales, a former farmer, union leader, and activist, as their new president, over a wealthy business leader who was educated in the United States. This election placed Bolivia in a group of South American nations—including Ecuador, Venezuela, Brazil, Chile, and Uruguay—that are moving toward what leaders of those countries call "socialism of the 21st century." Such a socialism combines democracy with a criticism of capitalism. The reasons for the shift toward socialism vary from country to country, but the common element is a desire to reduce economic inequality. In Bolivia, for example, the economy has grown in recent decades. Since Morales' socialist party won the elections, the Bolivian state has been the main driver of economic progress. It has pursued policies that have reduced poverty by 25 percent and increased the minimum wage and social spending (O'Hagan, 2014).

Work in the Post-industrial Canadian Economy

(**12.3**) Analyze patterns of employment and unemployment in Canada.

Economic change is occurring not just in the socialist world but also in Canada. The latest census for which data are available showed that, in 2011, there were approximately 17.99 million people in the labour force aged 15 years and over. Women now account for 48 percent of the Canadian workforce, up from 37 percent in 1976 (Ministry of Industry, 2007; Statistics Canada, 2013). As the Power of Society section at the beginning of the chapter illustrates, not everyone is equally represented throughout the various occupational fields. Nor does everyone participate in the labour market at the same rate. The Canadian unemployment rate in 2011 was 7.8 percent. Among visible minorities it was 9.9 percent and among non-visible minorities it was 7.3 percent. Among men, 9.8 percent of Latin Americans were unemployed, compared with 12.9 percent of blacks, and 7.8 percent of non-visible minorities. Among women, 11.2 percent of Latin Americans were unemployed, compared with 13 percent of blacks, and 6.7 percent of non-visible minorities (Statistics Canada, 2014).

The Changing Workplace

In 1911, 40 percent of Canadian workers had jobs in the primary sector. In 2010, just 4 percent were part of this economy. The family farm of yesterday has been replaced by *corporate agribusinesses*. Land is now more productive, but this change has caused painful adjustments across the country as a way of life is lost. A recent National Farmers Union report indicates that "farmer autonomy and local control of land and production, which are foundations of food sovereignty, are threatened by excessive farm debt loads, input financing, the conversion of farmland to non-farm uses such as industrial use, resource extraction and urbanization and by land grabbing" (Holtslander, 2015:4). Figure 12–2 on page 382 illustrates this trend by considering the shrinking role of the primary sector in the Canadian economy.

A century ago, industrialization swelled the ranks of workers in the manufacturing sector. By 1950, however, a white-collar revolution had moved most workers from factories into service occupations. Currently, more than 90 percent of new jobs are in the service sector, and close to 80 percent of the labour force perform service work.

As Chapter 8 ("Social Stratification") explained, much service work—including sales, clerical positions, and work in hospitals and restaurants—pays much less than older factory jobs. This means that many jobs in the post-industrial era provide only a modest standard of living. Women and other minorities, as well as many young people just starting their working careers, are the most likely to have jobs doing low-paying service work (Kalleberg, Reskin, & Hudson, 2000; Greenhouse, 2006).

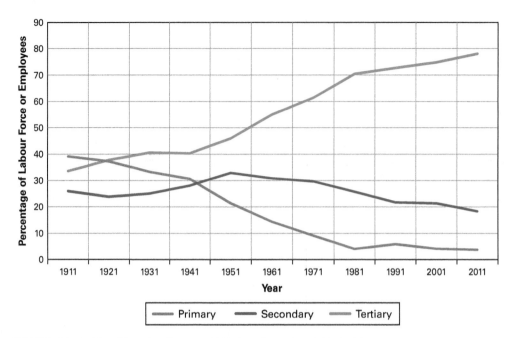

FIGURE 12–2 The Changing Pattern of Work in Canada, 1911–2011

Compared to a century ago, when the economy involved a larger share of factory and farm work, making a living in Canada now involves mostly white-collar service jobs.

Source: Estimated based on data in Leacy (1999); Bowlby (2001); and Statistics Canada (2011a, 2011b, 2011c, 2011d, 2011e, 2011f, 2011g).

Labour Unions

labour unions organizations that seek to improve wages and working conditions through various strategies, including negotiations and strikes

The changing Canadian economy has seen a decline in **labour unions**, *organizations that seek to improve wages and working conditions through various strategies, including negotiations and strikes.* During the Great Depression of the 1930s, Canadian union membership increased to more than one-third of non-farm workers by 1950. Then it fell slightly during the 1960s, but increased during the 1970s to return to the 1950 level, where it stabilized (Marshall, 2000). In 2013, the unionized rate for the total employed workforce in Canada was 27.2 percent (OECD, 2015).

Despite the historic decline, labour unions offer a number of advantages for workers. In June 2015, Canadian workers without union representation earned on average $23.41 per hour, while unionized workers earned $28.78 (Statistics Canada, 2015d). Furthermore, unionized workers tend to enjoy more benefits, security, and better working conditions. In addition, labour unions also impact culture and politics. Not only do they increase democracy in the workplace by giving workers a voice with which to counter the organized power of management, but there is also a positive relationship between unions and democracy itself. As Noam Chomsky observes, "unions are one of the few means by which ordinary people can enter the political arena" (1994). By inviting popular participation, unions are capable of changing social relations by, for example, fighting for social rights for minorities and protections for vulnerable members of Canadian society. Some scholars thus associate unions with democracy itself.

Canada has a middling position in regard to union rates. While unions in the United States (10.8 percent) and Japan (17.8 percent) claim a smaller share of workers than our society, union membership is between 15 and 40 percent in much of Europe, and it reaches a high of 67.7 percent in Sweden (OECD, 2015).

The widespread decline in union membership in countries such as Japan and the United States reflects the shrinking industrial sector of the economy. Newer service jobs—such as sales jobs at retailers like Walmart, described in the opening to this chapter—are usually not unionized. Citing low wages and worker complaints, unions are trying to organize Walmart employees, but the Walmart store in Jonquière, Quebec, closed six months after the workers voted to have their interests represented by the United Food and Commercial Workers union. The weak economy in Japan and the United States in the past few years has given unions a short-term boost. In the United States, the Obama administration is supporting new laws that may make it easier for workers to form unions. But long-term gains probably depend on the ability of unions, including those located in Canada, to adapt to the new global economy. Union members in Canada and elsewhere, accustomed to seeing foreign workers as "the enemy," will have to build new international alliances (McNally, 2006; Dalmia, 2008; Allen, 2009).

The strength of unions in the economy depends in large part on the laws that regulate how unions are formed. Over the course of this country's history, even when employees wanted to form a labour union, a company did not have to recognize the union as representing the workers. A common strategy used by unions to gain the right to represent workers was "card-check certification," which means that once the majority of workers at a particular company sign a card saying they wish to form a union, the certification process was complete; the company would have to recognize the union, all workers would pay union dues, and the union would represent all workers.

Union-busting policies by governments, however, undermine the ability of unions to represent workers. Take Bill C-525, which became law in 2015. The bill amends the Canada Labour Code, making it harder for federally regulated workers—spanning railway, postal, energy, airline, and telecommunication sectors—to form unions and easier to decertify them. One of the changes it introduces is to add to card-check certification a second step, consisting of a voting process. The new law will also count workers who abstain from voting to unionize as "no" votes (Canadian Union of Public Employees, 2013; Public Service Alliance of Canada, 2014).

On one side of the debate is the government which claims that the bill is needed because it protects workers' rights, defending them from what it sees as potential coercion during the card-check certification process. On the other side of the debate are unions claiming that the bill is anti-democratic and is specifically designed to bring down unionization rates.

Professions

Many kinds of jobs today are called *professional*; there are professional tennis players, professional housecleaners, and even professional exterminators. As distinct from an *amateur* (from the Latin for "lover," meaning one who acts out of love for the activity itself), a professional performs some task to earn a living. But what exactly is a profession?

A **profession** is *a prestigious white-collar occupation that requires extensive formal education.* People performing this kind of work make a *profession*, or public declaration, that they are able and willing to work according to certain performance standards and ethical principles. Professions include the ministry, medicine, law, and academia, and fields such as architecture, accountancy, and social work. An occupation is considered a profession to the extent that it demonstrates four basic characteristics (Goode, 1960; Ritzer & Walczak, 1990):

profession a prestigious white-collar occupation that requires extensive formal education

1. **Theoretical knowledge.** Professionals have a theoretical understanding of their field rather than mere technical training. Anyone can master first-aid skills, for example, but doctors have a theoretical understanding of human health. This means that tennis players, housecleaners, and exterminators do not really qualify as professionals according to the formal definition.

2. **Self-regulating practice.** The typical professional is self-employed, "in private practice" rather than working for a company. Professionals oversee their own work and observe a code of ethics.

3. **Authority over clients.** Because of their expertise, professionals are sought out by clients, who value their advice and follow their directions.

4. **Community orientation rather than self-interest.** The traditional professing of duty states an intention to serve the community rather than merely to seek income.

In almost all cases, professional work requires not just a university or college degree but a graduate degree as well. Not surprisingly, professions are well represented among the jobs beginning university and college students say they hope to get after graduation, as shown in Figure 12–3 on page 384.

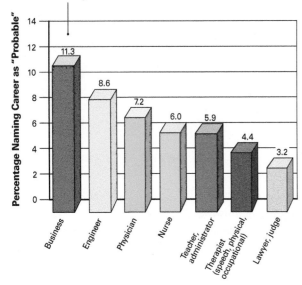

● In a society such as ours, with so many different types of work, no one career attracts the interest of more than a small share of today's students.

FIGURE 12–3 The Careers Most Commonly Named as "Probable" by First-Year University and College Students, 2012

Today's university and college students expect to enter careers that pay well and carry high prestige.

Source: Pryor et al. (2013).

Many occupations that do not qualify as true professions nonetheless seek to *professionalize* their services. Claiming professional standing usually begins by renaming the work to suggest special, theoretical knowledge, moving the field away from its original, lesser reputation. Stockroom workers become "inventory supply managers," exterminators are reborn as "insect control specialists," and cleanup workers describe themselves as "residential rehabilitation experts."

Interested parties may also form a professional association that certifies their skills. This organization then licenses its members, writes a code of ethics, and emphasizes the work's importance in the community. To win public acceptance, a professional association may also establish schools or other training facilities and perhaps start a professional journal. Not all occupations try to claim professional status. Some *paraprofessionals*, including paralegals and medical technicians, have specialized skills but lack the extensive theoretical education required of full professionals.

Self-Employment

Self-employment—earning a living without being on the payroll of a large organization—was once common in Canada. About 80 percent of the labour force was self-employed in 1800, compared with just 15 percent of workers in 2015 (Statistics Canada, 2015b). The relative decline has been steady in recent years as the number of self-employed Canadians has increased by 11 percent, compared to an increase of 17 percent for the overall labour force.

Lawyers, physicians, architects, and other professionals are well represented among the ranks of the self-employed in Canada. But most self-employed workers are small business owners, plumbers, farmers, carpenters, freelance writers and editors, artists, and long-distance truck drivers. In all, the self-employed are more likely to have blue-collar than white-collar jobs.

Women own one-third of this nation's small businesses, a share that increased steadily from 1976 (26 percent) to 1998 (36 percent) but has since levelled out (Industry Canada, 2011a). A 2004 survey showed that the degree of female ownership varied by industry, with accommodation and food services industries having the highest share. Yet in every industry the percentage of female-owned businesses lags behind that of male-owned businesses (Industry Canada, 2011b).

Unemployment and Underemployment

Every society has some level of unemployment. For one thing, few young people entering the labour force find a job right away; workers may leave their jobs to seek new work or to stay at home raising children; others may be on strike or suffer from long-term illnesses; and still others lack the skills to perform useful work.

But unemployment is not just an individual problem; it is also caused by the economy. Jobs disappear as occupations become obsolete and companies change the way they operate. Since 1980, the largest Canadian businesses and different levels of government have eliminated thousands of jobs in manufacturing and the public service.

Generally, companies downsize to become more competitive or close down entirely in the face of foreign competition or economic recession. During the recent recession in the United States, millions of jobs were lost in that country, with unemployment rising in just about every part of the economy. Not only blue-collar workers but also white-collar workers who had typically weathered downturns in the past have lost jobs during the last recession (U.S. Department of Labor, 2012). Canada fared relatively better than the United States, but the recession also impacted the unemployment rate here, which rose from 6.1 percent in August 2008 to 8.7 percent in August 2009 (Statistics Canada, 2015c).

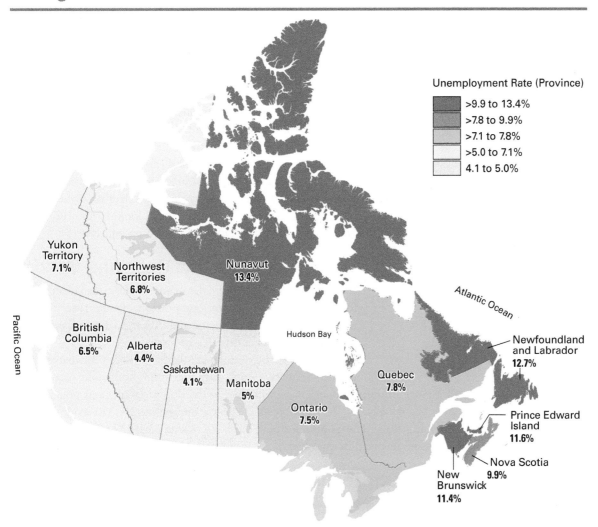

Unemployment Rate (Province)

- >9.9 to 13.4%
- >7.8 to 9.9%
- >7.1 to 7.8%
- >5.0 to 7.1%
- 4.1 to 5.0%

Yukon Territory 7.1%

Northwest Territories 6.8%

Nunavut 13.4%

Atlantic Ocean

Pacific Ocean

British Columbia 6.5%

Alberta 4.4%

Hudson Bay

Newfoundland and Labrador 12.7%

Saskatchewan 4.1%

Manitoba 5%

Quebec 7.8%

Ontario 7.5%

Prince Edward Island 11.6%

Nova Scotia 9.9%

New Brunswick 11.4%

NATIONAL MAP 12–1   Unemployment Rates Across Canada by Province, 2014

In 2014, the unemployment rate in Canada was 6.9 percent. While Nunavut has the highest level of unemployment in Canada, several census divisions in Newfoundland and Labrador had unemployment rates over 30 percent. Keep in mind that Statistics Canada calculates the unemployment rate as made up of those who are actively looking for work. This means that the unemployment rate does not take into account unwilling or unable individuals who have given up the job hunt, stay-at-home parents, full-time students, people who cannot participate for reasons of disability, or those who are underemployed. The depiction of the unemployment rate on this map makes us think of the structural causes and consequences of unemployment. Do you usually consider structural or personal factors when you try to understand the unemployment that exists where you live?

Source: Statistics Canada (2015c).

As National Map 12–1 shows, some regions of Canada, particularly the east coast, have high unemployment; in some places, the unemployment rate is more than three times the national rate (Statistics Canada, 2015c).

Figure 12–4 on page 386 shows that the unemployment rate in 2009 for Canadian men (9.4 percent) is substantially higher than for women (7.0 percent). In 2006, the rate for recent immigrants (12.3 percent) and the rate for Aboriginal people (14.8 percent) were higher than for other Canadians (Human Resources and Skills Development Canada, 2011).

Underemployment is also a problem for millions of workers. In an era of corporate bank-ruptcy, the failure of large banks, and downsizing by companies throughout the North American economy, millions of workers—the lucky ones who still have their jobs—have been left with lower salaries, fewer benefits such as health insurance, and disappearing pensions. Rising global competition, weaker worker organizations, and economic recession have combined to allow

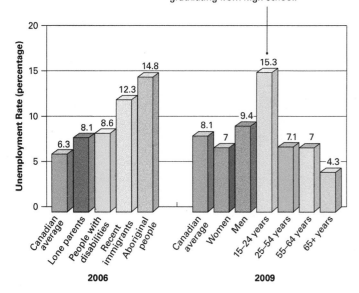

● Darlene Drako, 19, was laid off three months into her first job after graduating from high school.

2006

2009

FIGURE 12–4 Unemployment Rate for Various Categories of Adults, Canada, Various Years

Source: Human Resources and Skills Development Canada (2011).

many people to keep their jobs only by agreeing to cutbacks in pay or to the loss of other benefits (K. Clark, 2002; Gutierrez, 2007; McGeehan & Warren, 2009).

In addition, in 2010, 19.4 percent of employed Canadians worked part-time, defined as less than 35 hours a week; 27.4 percent of Canadian women in the paid workforce worked part-time at their main job, compared with 12.1 percent of employed men. Although most say they are satisfied with this arrangement, when viewed cross-nationally Canada has one of the highest shares of involuntary part-time workers (27.6 percent) as a percentage of part-time work (OECD, 2011c). As the North American economy struggles to climb out of the recent recession, it is likely that many workers are working less than what they desire. Many other adults are out of work and looking for a job or are "discouraged workers" who have given up entirely.

Workplace Diversity: Race and Gender

In the past, white men were the mainstay of the Canadian labour force. However, the nation's proportion of minorities is rising rapidly. The visible minority and Aboriginal populations are increasing faster than other Canadians.

Such dramatic changes are likely to affect Canadian society in countless ways. Not only will more and more workers be women and minorities, but the workplace will have to develop programs and policies that meet the needs of a socially diverse workforce and also encourage everyone to work together effectively and respectfully. The Thinking About Diversity box on page 387 takes a closer look at some of the issues involved in our changing workplace.

New Information Technology and Work

July 2, Edmonton, Alberta. The manager of the local hardware store scans the bar codes of a bagful of items. "The computer doesn't just total the costs," she explains. "It also keeps track of inventory, places orders with the warehouse, and decides which products to continue to sell and which to drop." "Sounds like what you used to do, Maureen," I respond with a smile. "Yep," she nods, with no smile at all.

Another workplace issue is the increasing role of computers and other new information technology. The Information Revolution is changing what people do in a number of ways (Rule & Brantley, 1992; Vallas & Beck, 1996):

1. **Computers are deskilling labour.** Just as industrial machines replaced the master craftsworkers of an earlier era, computers now threaten the skills of managers. More business operations are based not on executive decisions but on computer modelling. In other words, a machine decides whether to place an order, stock a dress in a certain size and colour, or approve a loan application.

2. **Computers are making work more abstract.** Most industrial workers have a hands-on relationship with their product. Post-industrial workers use symbols to perform abstract tasks, such as making a company more efficient, making software more user-friendly, or hiding risky assets inside financial "derivatives."

Reality television shows often follow a game show model where individuals compete over a prize, such as the hand of a bachelor (*The Bachelor Canada*), cash prizes (*Top Chef Canada, The Amazing Race Canada*, and *Big Brother Canada*), or fame (*Canadian Idol*). What do you think reality television says about the nature of work in the post-industrial Canadian economy? What do such shows teach us about individualism, hierarchy, teamwork, and competition?

Thinking About Diversity: Race, Class, and Gender

Diversity 2020: Changes Coming to the Workplace

An upward trend in the Canadian visible minority population is changing the workplace. The share of visible minorities employed in Canada increased from 4.7 percent in 1981 to 18.2 percent in 2011 (Leitch, 2013). As shown in Chapter 10 ("Gender Stratification"), over this time period, the proportion of women employed markedly increased, while a significantly lower proportion of men were employed than was the case 25 years before.

Welcoming social diversity means, first, recruiting talented workers of both sexes and all racial and cultural backgrounds. But developing the potential of all employees requires meeting the needs of women and other minorities, which may not be the same as those of white men. For example, child care at the workplace is a big issue for working mothers with small children.

Second, businesses must develop effective ways to deal with racism and xenophobia. They will have to work harder to ensure that workers are treated equally and respectfully, which means having zero tolerance for racial or sexual harassment.

Third, companies will have to rethink current promotion practices. At present, 75 percent of the directors of *Fortune* 100 companies are white men; 25 percent are women or other minorities (Alliance for Board Diversity, 2011). As noted in Chapter 11 ("Race and Ethnicity"), visible minorities, who in 2011 made up 15.3 percent of Canada's population, made up a greater percentage of the labour force at 18.2 percent. At the same time, visible minorities are underrepresented in managerial positions, where they make up 14.4 percent of the workforce. Aboriginal people are even less likely than women to have managerial jobs, especially at the top levels. In sum, "glass ceilings" that limit the advancement of skilled workers not only discourage effort but also deprive companies of their largest source of talent: women and other minorities.

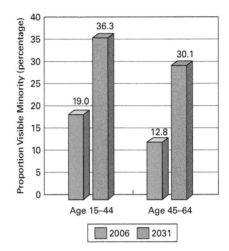

Proportion of Visible Minority Canadians, Aged 15 Through 64, 2006 and 2031

Looking ahead, the share of visible minorities in the Canadian labour force will more than double between 2006 and 2031.

Source: Statistics Canada (2010e). Projections of the Diversity of the Canadian Population. Catalogue no. 91-551-X. Ottawa: Minister of Industry, 2010. Reproduced and distributed on an "as is" basis with the permission of Statistics Canada.

What Do You Think?

1. What underlying factors are increasing the social diversity of the Canadian workplace?

2. In what specific ways do you think businesses should support minority workers?

3. In what other settings (such as schools) is social diversity becoming more important? Why?

---

3. **Computers limit workplace interaction.** Workers become isolated from one another because of the amount of time spent at computer terminals.

4. **Computers increase employers' control of workers.** Computers allow supervisors to check employees' output continuously, whether they work at keyboard terminals or on assembly lines.

5. **Computers allow companies to relocate work.** Because computer technology allows information to flow almost anywhere, instantly, the symbolic work in today's economy may not take place where we might think. We have all had the experience of calling a business (for instance, a hotel or bookstore) located in our own town only to find out that we are talking to a person at a computer workstation thousands of kilometres away. Computer technology provides the means to outsource many jobs—especially service work—to other places where wages may be lower.

Perhaps in the wake of widespread failures on Bay Street, there will be a trend away from allowing computers to manage risk, putting responsibility for business decisions back in the hands of people (Kivant, 2008). Or perhaps computers, people, and our economic system all have flaws that will always prevent us from living in a more harmonious world. But the rapidly increasing reliance on computers in business reminds us that new technology is never socially neutral. It changes the relationships between people in the workplace, shapes the way we

In today's corporate world, computers are changing the nature of work just as factories did more than a century ago. In what ways is computer-based work different from factory work? In what ways do you think it is very much the same?

work, and often alters the balance of power between employers and employees. Understandably, then, people welcome some aspects of the Information Revolution and oppose others.

Corporations

(**12.4**) Discuss the importance of corporations to the Canadian economy.

corporation an organization with a legal existence, including rights and liabilities, separate from that of its members

At the core of today's capitalist economy is the **corporation**, *an organization with a legal existence, including rights and liabilities, separate from that of its members*. We tend to think of corporations as recent phenomena; however, corporations have a long history dating to such seventeenth century entities as the Hudson's Bay Company, the British East India Company, and the Massachusetts Bay Company. Initially, they included powerful investors like court bankers and kings, and were themselves powerful formal organizations that established monopolies (see Chapter 5, "Groups and Organizations") over vast tracks of land and resources. Over time, corporations were restricted. The American Revolution was as much an uprising against the British monarchy as it was against British corporations. The Boston Tea Party demonstrated the deep suspicions colonists had about both. Early laws permitted corporations temporary licences, greatly restricting their power to act. Corporations were allowed to raise capital and to share profits with shareholders, but only in pursuit of specific projects that benefited the public. Furthermore, early corporations were prevented from influencing elections or public policy (Safina, 2012). In 1869, the Government of Great Britain forced the Hudson's Bay Company to reject the much more attractive U.S. government offer for its territory (known as Rupert's Land) and to sell off its monopoly to the Government of Canada.

Incorporating makes an organization a legal entity, able to enter into contracts and own property. Today, of the more than 30 million businesses in North America, about 5.8 million are incorporated (Internal Revenue Service, 2012). Incorporating protects the wealth of owners from lawsuits that result from business debts or harm to consumers; it can also mean a lower tax rate on the company's profits.

Economic Concentration

Most corporations are small, with assets of less than $500 000, so it is the largest corporations that dominate our nation's economy. In 2009, the U.S. government listed 2604 corporations with assets exceeding $2.5 billion, representing 81 percent of all corporate assets in that country (Internal Revenue Service, 2012). Similar trends have also been observed in Canada (Ministry of Industry, 2003).

America's largest corporation, measured in terms of sales, is Walmart, with 2012 revenue of more than $444 billion. Canada's largest corporation is the Royal Bank of Canada, reporting 2012 revenue of $34.5 billion.

Conglomerates and Corporate Linkages

Economic concentration creates **conglomerates**, *giant corporations composed of many smaller corporations*. Conglomerates form as corporations enter new markets, spin off new companies, or merge with other companies. For example, PepsiCo is a conglomerate that includes Pepsi-Cola, Frito-Lay, Gatorade, Tropicana, and Quaker.

conglomerates giant corporations composed of many smaller corporations

Many conglomerates are linked because they own each other's stock, the result being worldwide corporate alliances of staggering size. In 2012, for example, General Motors owned Opel (Germany), Vauxhall (Great Britain), Holden (Australia), and a share of Daewoo (South Korea) and had partnerships with Suzuki and Toyota (Japan) and several new brands in China.

Corporations are also linked through *interlocking directorates*, networks of people who serve as directors of many corporations (Weidenbaum, 1995; Kono et al., 1998). These boardroom connections provide access to valuable information about other companies' products and marketing strategies. While perfectly legal, such linkages encourage illegal activity, such as price fixing, as companies share information about their pricing policies.

Corporations: Are They Competitive?

According to the capitalist model, businesses operate independently in a competitive market. But in light of the extensive linkages that exist between them, it is obvious that large corporations do not operate independently. Also, a few large corporations dominate many markets, so they are not truly competitive.

The law forbids any company from establishing a **monopoly**, *the domination of a market by a single producer*, because with no competition, such a company could simply charge whatever it wanted for its products. But **oligopoly**, *the domination of a market by a few producers*, is both legal and common. Oligopoly arises because the huge investment needed to enter a major market, such as the auto industry, is beyond the reach of all but the biggest companies. In addition, competition means risk, which big business tries to avoid. Even so, we have recently seen that even the largest corporations are not immune to economic crisis, as shown by the 2009 bankruptcy of General Motors. They can also face rising competition, as the North American auto industry has seen from companies such as Kia and Hyundai.

Federal governments seek to regulate corporations in order to protect the public interest. Yet as corporate scandals have shown—most recently, involving the housing mortgage business and the collapse of so many banks—regulation is often too little too late, resulting in harm to millions of people. Government is also the corporate world's single biggest customer, and sometimes steps in to support many struggling corporations with multibillion-dollar bailout programs. Especially during tough economic times, the public tends to support a greater role for the government in the economy (Sachs, 2009).

Corporations and the Global Economy

Corporations have grown so large that they now account for most of the world's economic output. The biggest corporations are based in the United States, Japan, and Western Europe, but their marketplace is the entire world. Many large companies, such as McDonald's and the semiconductor chip maker Intel, earn most of their money outside North America. In 2011, General Motors sold almost three-fourths of its cars outside of the United States and Canada, especially in the "emerging markets" of Brazil, Russia, India, and China (General Motors, 2012).

Global corporations know that lower-income countries contain most of the world's people and resources. In addition, labour costs there are

monopoly the domination of a market by a single producer

oligopoly the domination of a market by a few producers

attractively low: A manufacturing worker in Mexico, who earns about $6.36 an hour, labours for almost a week to earn what a worker in Japan (who averages $35.34 an hour) or the United States ($35.67 an hour) or Canada ($36.59) earns in a single day (U.S. Department of Labor, 2013).

As Chapter 9 ("Global Stratification") explained, the impact of multinational corporations on low-income countries is controversial. Modernization theorists claim that multinational corporations, by unleashing the great productivity of capitalism, raise living standards in poor nations, offering tax revenues, capital investment, new jobs, and advanced technology that together accelerate economic growth (Berger, 1986; Firebaugh & Beck, 1994; Firebaugh & Sandu, 1998).

Dependency theorists respond that multinationals in fact make global inequality worse by blocking the development of local industries and by pushing poor countries to produce goods for export rather than food and other products for local people. From this standpoint, multinationals make poor nations increasingly dependent on rich nations (Wallerstein, 1979; Dixon & Boswell, 1996; Kentor, 1998).

In short, modernization theory praises the market as the key to progress and affluence for all of the world's people. Dependency theory takes a different position, calling for replacing markets with government-based economic policies.

The Economy: Looking Ahead

Social institutions are a society's way of meeting people's needs. But as we have seen, the Canadian economy only partly succeeds in this respect. As the years go by, our economy experiences alternating periods of expansion and recession. And in both good times and bad, our economy provides for some people much better than for others.

One important trend that underlies change in the economy is the Information Revolution. First, the share of the Canadian labour force engaged in manufacturing is one-third of what it was in 1960; service work, especially computer-related jobs, makes up the difference. For industrial workers, the post-industrial economy has brought unemployment and declining wages. Our society must face up to the challenge of providing millions of men and women with the language and computer skills they need to succeed in the modern economy.

A second transformation of recent years is the expansion of the global economy. Two centuries ago, the ups and downs people experienced reflected events and trends in their own town. One century ago, communities were economically linked so that one town's prosperity depended on producing goods demanded by people elsewhere in the country. Today, we have to look beyond the national economy because, for example, the historical rise in the cost of gasoline at our local gas station has as much to do with increasing demand for oil around the world, especially in China and India, as it does with local or national trends in Canada. As both producers and consumers, we are now subject to factors and forces that are both distant and unseen.

Finally, analysts around the world are rethinking conventional economic models. The global economy shows that socialism is less productive than capitalism, one important reason behind the collapse of socialist regimes in Eastern Europe and the Soviet Union. But capitalism has its own problems, as the Occupy movement has recently highlighted, including high levels of inequality and a steady stream of corporate scandal. These are two important reasons that the economy now operates with significant government regulation.

What will be the long-term effects of all these changes? Two conclusions seem certain. First, the economic future of Canada, the United States, and other nations will be played out in a global arena. The new post-industrial economy in Canada has emerged as more industrial production has moved to other nations. Second, it is imperative that we address the urgent issues of global inequality and population increase. Whether the world reduces or enlarges the gap between rich and poor societies may well steer our planet toward peace or war.

Power and Authority

(**12.5**) Distinguish traditional, rational-legal, and charismatic authority.

There is a close link between economics and **politics** (also known as the "polity"), *the social institution that distributes power, sets a society's goals, and makes decisions*. Early in the twentieth century, Max Weber (1978, orig. 1921) defined **power** as *the ability to achieve desired ends despite resistance from others*. The use of power is the business of **government**, *a formal organization that directs the political life of a society*. Governments typically claim to help people, but at the same time, governments demand that people obey the rules. Yet, as Weber noted, most governments do not openly threaten their people. Most of the time, people respect (or at least accept) their society's political system.

No government, Weber explained, is likely to keep its power for very long if compliance comes only from the threat of brute force, because there could never be enough police to watch everyone—and who would watch the police? Every government, therefore, tries to make itself seem legitimate in the eyes of the public.

This brings us to the concept of **authority**, *power that people perceive as legitimate rather than coercive*. A society's source of authority depends on its economy. According to Weber, preindustrial societies rely on **traditional authority**, *power legitimized by respect for long-established cultural patterns*. Woven into a society's collective memory, traditional authority may seem almost sacred. Chinese emperors in centuries past were legitimized by tradition, as were aristocratic rulers in medieval Europe. The power of tradition can be so strong that, for better or worse, people typically come to view traditional rulers as almost godlike.

Traditional authority declines as societies industrialize. For example, royal families still exist in 10 European nations, but the democratic cultures of countries such as the United Kingdom, Sweden, and Denmark have shifted power to commoners elected to office. Weber explained that the expansion of rational bureaucracy is the foundation of authority in modern societies. **Rational-legal authority** (sometimes called *bureaucratic authority*) is *power legitimized by legally enacted rules and regulations*.

Traditional authority is tied to family; rational-legal authority flows from offices in governments. A traditional monarch passes power on to heirs; a modern prime minister takes office and later on gives up power according to law.

Weber described one additional type of authority that has surfaced throughout history. **Charismatic authority** is *power legitimized by extraordinary personal abilities that inspire devotion and obedience*. Unlike its traditional and rational-legal counterparts, charismatic authority depends less on a person's ancestry or office and more on charisma, or personality. Followers see in charismatic leaders some special, perhaps even divine, power. Examples of charismatic leaders include Jesus of Nazareth; Nazi Germany's Adolf Hitler; India's liberator, Mahatma Gandhi; and civil rights leader Martin Luther King, Jr. All charismatic leaders aim to radically transform society, which explains why they are almost always controversial and why few of them die of old age.

Because charismatic authority flows from a single individual, the leader's death creates a crisis. The survival of a charismatic movement, Weber explained, requires the **routinization of charisma**, *the transformation of charismatic authority into some combination of traditional and bureaucratic authority*. After the death of Jesus, for example, followers institutionalized his teachings in a church, built on tradition and bureaucracy. Routinized in this way, Christianity has lasted 2000 years.

politics the social institution that distributes power, sets a society's goals, and makes decisions

power the ability to achieve desired ends despite resistance from others

government a formal organization that directs the political life of a society

authority power that people perceive as legitimate rather than coercive

traditional authority power legitimized by respect for long-established cultural patterns

rational-legal authority power legitimized by legally enacted rules and regulations (also known as *bureaucratic authority*)

charismatic authority power legitimized by extraordinary personal abilities that inspire devotion and obedience

routinization of charisma the transformation of charismatic authority into some combination of traditional and bureaucratic authority

Politics in Global Perspective

(12.6) Compare monarchy and democracy as well as authoritarian and totalitarian political systems.

The world's political systems differ in countless ways. Generally, however, they fall into four categories: monarchy, democracy, authoritarianism, and totalitarianism.

Monarchy

monarchy a political system in which a single family rules from generation to generation

Monarchy (with Latin and Greek roots meaning "one ruler") is *a political system in which a single family rules from generation to generation.* Monarchy is commonly found in agrarian societies. In Asia, Europe, and Africa, monarchies have for centuries coincided with agrarianism. In the world today, 26 nations have royal families[1]; most trace their ancestry back centuries. In Weber's analysis, then, monarchy is legitimized by tradition.

During the Middle Ages, *absolute monarchs* in much of the world claimed a monopoly of power based on divine right (or God's will). In some nations—including Oman, Saudi Arabia, and Swaziland—monarchs (not necessarily with divine support) still exercise virtually absolute control over their people.

Monarchy is typically found in societies that have yet to industrialize. The recent political unrest throughout the Middle East indicates growing resistance to this form of political system in today's world. Even so, King Salman and members of his royal family strengthen their control of Saudi Arabia through their support of Arabic heritage and culture.

---

[1]In Europe: Sweden, Norway, Denmark, Great Britain, the Netherlands, Liechtenstein, Luxembourg, Belgium, Spain, and Monaco; in the Middle East: Jordan, Saudi Arabia, Oman, Qatar, Bahrain, and Kuwait; in Africa: Lesotho, Swaziland, and Morocco; in Asia: Brunei, Tonga, Thailand, Malaysia, Cambodia, Bhutan, and Japan.

With industrialization, however, monarchs gradually pass from the scene in favour of elected officials. All the European societies with royal families today are *constitutional monarchies*, meaning that their monarchs are little more than symbolic heads of state; actual governing is the responsibility of elected officials, led by a prime minister and guided by a constitution. This is the case in Canada, which is a constitutional monarchy where Queen Elizabeth II personally embodies the Canadian Crown. Her day-to-day duties, however, are carried out by a Governor General at the federal level and Lieutenant Governors at the provincial level. In constitutional monarchies, nobility formally *reigns*, but elected officials actually *rule*.

Democracy

The historical trend throughout most of the world has been toward **democracy**, *a political system that derives its legitimacy from the people as a whole*. Because it is unrealistic to expect all citizens to be involved in governing, our system is in fact a *representative democracy*, which puts authority in the hands of leaders who from time to time compete for office in elections.

democracy a political system that derives its legitimacy from the people as a whole.

Most high-income countries of the world, including those that still have royal families, claim to be democratic. Industrialization and democracy go together because both require a literate populace. Also, with industrialization, the traditional legitimization of power in a monarchy gives way to rational-legal authority. Thus democracy and rational-legal authority are linked just like monarchy and traditional authority are.

Of course, some high-income nations, such as Saudi Arabia, do not give the population much political voice. More broadly, even countries such as Canada are not truly democratic, for two reasons. First, there is the problem of bureaucracy. The Canadian federal government has 419 542 employees. Add to this the 350 313 provincial and territorial personnel and 590 263 municipal and local government employees—1.3 million workers in all (Statistics Canada, 2012). Most of the officials who run the government are never elected by anyone and do not have to answer directly to the people.

The second problem involves economic inequality: Rich people have far more political power than poor people. Most of our political leaders have been wealthy men and women, and in politics, "money talks." Though many of Canada's elected leaders do not come from wealthy families, many have substantial personal wealth. Moreover, Canadian politicians are privileged by their education, with two-thirds of them having some background in law. The current prime minister, Justin Trudeau, has a Bachelor of Arts in literature and a Bachelor of Education. Given the even greater resources of billion-dollar corporations, how well does our "democratic" system listen to the voices of "average people"?

Still, democratic nations do provide many rights and freedoms. Global Map 12–3 on page 394 shows one assessment of political freedom around the world. According to Freedom House, an organization that tracks political trends, 90 of the world's nations (with 43 percent of the global population) were "free," respecting many civil liberties, in 2013. This represents a gain for democracy: Just 75 nations were considered free two decades earlier (Freedom House, 2013).

Democracy and Freedom: Capitalist and Socialist Approaches

Despite the problems just described, rich capitalist nations such as Canada claim to operate as democracies. Of course, socialist countries such as Cuba and the People's Republic of China make the same claim. This curious fact suggests that perhaps we need to look more closely at *political economy*, the interplay of politics and economics.

The political life of Canada, the United States, and the nations of Europe is largely shaped by the economic principles of capitalism, described earlier in this chapter. The pursuit of profit in a market system requires that "freedom" be defined in terms of people's right to act in their own self-interest. Thus the capitalist approach to political freedom translates into personal liberty, the freedom to act in whatever ways maximize profit or other personal advantage. From this point of view, political "democracy" means that individuals have the right to select their leaders from among those running for office.

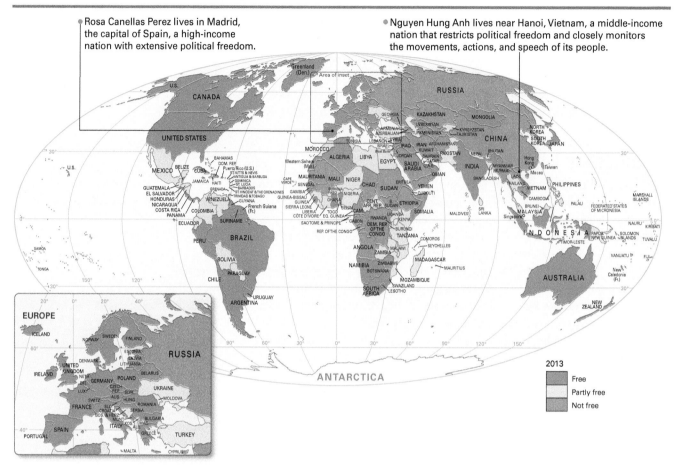

Rosa Canellas Perez lives in Madrid, the capital of Spain, a high-income nation with extensive political freedom.

Nguyen Hung Anh lives near Hanoi, Vietnam, a middle-income nation that restricts political freedom and closely monitors the movements, actions, and speech of its people.

2013
- Free
- Partly free
- Not free

GLOBAL MAP 12–3 Political Freedom in Global Perspective

In 2013, a total of 90 of the world's 195 nations, containing 43 percent of all people, were politically "free," that is, they offered their citizens extensive political rights and civil liberties. Another 58 countries, which included 23 percent of the world's people, were "partly free," with more limited rights and liberties. The remaining 47 nations, home to 34 percent of humanity, fall into the category of "not free." In these countries, government sharply restricts individual initiative. Between 1980 and 2013, democracy made significant gains, largely in Latin America and Eastern Europe.

Source: Freedom House (2013).

However, capitalist societies are marked by a striking inequality of income and wealth. If everyone acts according to self-interest, the inevitable result is that some people have much more power to get their way than others. In practice, a market system creates unequal wealth and transforms wealth into power. Critics of capitalism claim that a wealthy elite dominates the economic and political life of the society.

By contrast, socialist systems claim they are democratic because their economies meet everyone's basic needs for housing, schooling, work, and medical care. Despite being a much poorer country than the United States, for example, Cuba provides basic medical care to all its people regardless of their ability to pay.

But critics of socialism counter that the extensive government regulation of social life in these countries is oppressive. The socialist governments of China and Cuba, for example, do not allow their people to move freely across or even within their borders and tolerate no organized political opposition.

These contrasting approaches to democracy and freedom raise an important question: Can economic equality and political liberty go together? To foster economic equality, socialism limits the choices of individuals. Capitalism, on the other hand, provides broad political liberties, which in practice mean much more to the rich than to the poor.

Authoritarianism

Some governments prevent their people from having any voice in politics. **Authoritarianism** is *a political system that denies the people participation in government.* An authoritarian government is indifferent to people's needs and offers them no voice in selecting leaders. The absolute monarchies in Saudi Arabia and Oman are authoritarian, as is the military junta in Ethiopia. Sometimes, as the recent political movements in the Middle East illustrate, people stand up and oppose heavy-handed government. But not always. A largely peaceful system of "soft authoritarianism" thrives in the small Asian nation of Singapore, where political freedom is limited but people are secure and prosperous.

authoritarianism a political system that denies the people participation in government

totalitarianism a highly centralized political system that extensively regulates people's lives

Totalitarianism

October 30, Beijing, China. Several Canadian students are sitting around a computer in the lounge of a Chinese university dormitory. They are taking turns running internet searches on keywords such as "democracy" and "Amnesty International." They soon realize that China's government filters the results of internet searches, permitting only officially approved sites to appear. One Chinese student who is watching points out that things could be worse—in North Korea, she explains, most students have no access to computers at all.

The most intensely controlled political form is **totalitarianism**, *a highly centralized political system that extensively regulates people's lives.* Totalitarianism emerged in the twentieth century as governments gained the ability to rigidly control their populations. The Vietnamese government closely monitors the activities of all of its citizens. Similarly, the government of North Korea uses surveillance equipment and powerful computers to control its people by collecting and storing information about them.

Although some totalitarian governments claim to represent the will of the people, most seek to bend people to the will of the government. As the term "totalitarian" implies, such governments have a *total* concentration of power, allowing no organized opposition. Denying the people the right to assemble and controlling access to information, these governments create an atmosphere of isolation and fear. In the former Soviet Union, for example, most citizens had no access to telephone directories, copiers, fax machines, or accurate city maps. Only in the last few years has the Cuban government allowed ordinary citizens to own personal computers and cell phones.

Socialization in totalitarian societies is highly political, seeking obedience and commitment to the system. In North Korea, one of the world's strictest totalitarian states, pictures of leaders and political messages are everywhere, reminding citizens that they owe total allegiance to the state. Government-controlled schools and mass media present only official versions of events. When that nation's leader Kim Jong-il died in 2011, the official government news agency reported

KCNA/Xinhua/Landov

In totalitarian nations, government controls all aspects of people's lives. During the funeral of Kim Jong-il, absolute ruler of North Korea, people were told to line the route used for his public funeral and display appropriate anguish at his death. After the event, government officials examined photographs of the crowds and prosecuted those whose sorrow did not measure up to their demands.

the nation's people were in "utter despair" at the loss of the "Glorious Leader Who Descended from Heaven," but would find comfort in the "absolute surety that the leadership of [his son] Comrade Kim Jong-un will lead the great task of revolutionary enterprise." Three generations of the same family have tightly controlled this impoverished nation since 1948 (Chance & Kim, 2011; Rogers, 2011).

Totalitarian governments span the political spectrum from fascist (including Nazi Germany) to communist (such as North Korea). In all cases, however, one party claims total control of the society and permits no opposition. Some scholars have extended this notion to capitalist societies (for example, Canada or the United States), which they characterize as "totalitarian democracies" (Talmon, 1952; Engdahl, 2009). The Marxist scholar Marcuse (1966), for example, observed that while championing pluralism and not concentrating power in a single party, representative democracies can be totalitarian in the sense that they defend market values as a way of meeting our needs while preventing the emergence of an opposition to capitalism itself. Whether one accepts this as evidence of totalitarianism or not, it is difficult to deny that our society is one in which a handful of experts and administrators, in either public or private sectors, make many important choices for most of us, from what jobs we can pick to what products we can purchase.

A Global Political System?

Is globalization changing politics in the same way that it is changing the economy? On one level, the answer is no. Although most of today's economic activity is international, the world remains divided into nation-states, just as it has been for centuries. The United Nations (founded in 1945) was a small step toward global government, but its political role in world affairs has been limited.

On another level, however, politics has become a global process. For some analysts, multinational corporations represent a new political order because of their enormous power to shape events throughout the world. In other words, politics is dissolving into business as corporations grow larger than governments.

Also, the Information Revolution has moved national politics onto the world stage. Email, text messaging, and Twitter networks mean that few countries can conduct their political affairs in complete privacy. The recent "WikiLeaks" controversy shows that, in the age of computers and hacking, just about anyone can access information—even that guarded by governments—and make it available to anyone and everyone (Gellman, 2011).

Finally, several thousand *non-governmental organizations* (NGOs) seek to advance global issues, such as human rights (Amnesty International) and environmental protection (Greenpeace). NGOs will continue to play a key role in expanding the global political culture.

In sum, just as individual nations are losing control of their own economies, governments cannot fully manage the political events occurring within their borders.

Politics in Canada

(12.7) Analyze economic and social issues using the political spectrum.

In contrast to the United States' revolutionary break with Great Britain, Canada's political independence came about through a peaceful transition from monarchical rule to democratic decision making. This nation's political development reflects its distinctive history, capitalist economy, and cultural heritage.

Canadian Culture and the Rise of the Welfare State

Our cultural emphasis on individualism is reflected in the Canadian Human Rights Act and the Charter of Rights and Freedoms, both of which make explicit that all individuals have an equal right to make the lives for themselves that they are able to and wish to achieve. In making the best lives for themselves, some people in Canada—and many more in the United

Lower-income people have more pressing financial needs, and so they tend to focus on economic issues, such as job wages and benefits. Higher-income people, by contrast, provide support for many social issues, such as animal rights.

States, no doubt—share the sentiment of nineteenth-century philosopher and poet Ralph Waldo Emerson: "The government that governs best is the government that governs least." Yet many other Canadians view the government in a more positive light, agreeing to pay higher taxes to support quality public services.

What is clear is that our government has grown into a vast and complex **welfare state**, *a system of government agencies and programs that provide benefits to the population*. Government benefits begin even before birth (through prenatal nutrition programs, coverage of midwives' and physicians' fees, and patients' hospital stays) and continue into old age (through public pensions). Some programs are especially important to the poor, who are not well served by our capitalist economic system; but, students, farmers, homeowners, small business operators, veterans, performing artists, and even executives of giant corporations also get various subsidies and supports. In fact, virtually all Canadian adults look to the government to fund their health care services as well as public education programs for their children, and a majority of Canadian adults also look to government for at least part of our income.

Today's welfare state is the result of a gradual increase in the size and scope of government. At the time of Confederation in 1867, in most communities the presence of the federal government amounted to little more than a flag. Since then, the federal budget has steadily risen, reaching $290.3 billion in 2015–16.

As much as government has expanded in this country, the Canadian welfare state, though larger than that of our neighbour to the south, is still smaller than those of many other high-income nations. Figure 12–5 shows that government is larger in most of Europe, especially in France and the Scandinavian countries such as Denmark and Sweden.

> **welfare state** a system of government agencies and programs that provide benefits to the population

Global Snapshot

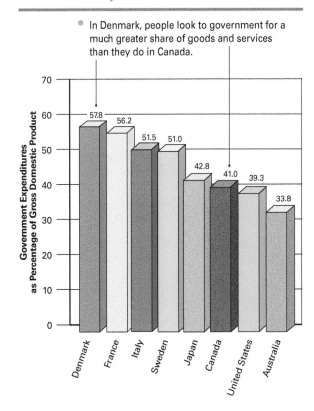

In Denmark, people look to government for a much greater share of goods and services than they do in Canada.

FIGURE 12–5 The Size of Government, 2013

Government activity accounts for a smaller share of economic output in Canada than in most other high-income countries.

Source: OECD (2013).

The Political Spectrum

Who supports a bigger welfare state? Who wants to cut it back? Answers to these questions reveal attitudes that form the *political spectrum*, beliefs that range from extremely liberal to extremely conservative. In a 2013 survey of U.S. adults, 27 percent said they were "liberal" (the political "left"), 32 percent described themselves as "conservative" (the political "right"), and 36 percent claimed to be political "moderates" (the political "middle") (NORC, 2013:218). In Canada, given the option of identifying as "liberal," "conservative," or "neither," one poll found that 48 percent of Canadians said that they are liberal, 25 percent chose conservative, and 22 percent proclaimed neither (EKOS Research, 2013).

The political spectrum helps us understand two types of issues: *Economic issues* focus on economic inequality; *social issues* involve moral questions about how people ought to live.

Economic Issues

Economic liberals support both extensive government regulation of the economy and a larger welfare state in order to reduce income inequality. The government can reduce inequality by taxing the rich more heavily and providing more benefits to the poor. Economic conservatives want to limit the hand of government in the economy and allow market forces more freedom, claiming that this produces more jobs and makes the economy more productive.

Social Issues

Social issues are moral questions about how people ought to live, ranging from abortion and the death penalty to gay rights and the treatment of minorities. Social liberals tend to support equal rights and opportunities for all categories of people, view abortion as a matter of individual choice, and oppose the death penalty because it has been unfairly applied to minorities. The "family values" agenda of social conservatives supports traditional gender roles and opposes gay marriage, affirmative action, and other "special programs" for minorities. At the same time, social conservatives condemn abortion as morally wrong and support the death penalty.

There are five major political parties in Canada: Liberals, Conservatives, New Democrats, Bloquistes, and Greens. Historically, Canada has tended to be governed by either liberal or conservative parties.

Canada's political spectrum has changed recently, with a number of newer political parties competing for the public's attention and, ultimately, their votes. These include the Green Party, as well as the provincial Parti Québécois, federal Bloc Québécois, and French parties based in Quebec.

In the 2015 federal election, major changes occurred for most parties. After winning the fewest seats in their history (34 seats in the 2011 elections), the Liberals, led by Justin Trudeau, won 184 seats and formed a majority government. After nine years in government, the Conservative Party became the official opposition (99 seats). And after winning the largest number of seats in their history in the 2011 election (103 seats), the New Democratic Party, led by Tom Mulcair, lost its Official Opposition status, coming in third in 2015 with 44 seats. The Bloc Québécois increased their popularity (to 10 seats) but the party was still short of the 12 seats needed to gain official party status. The Green Party lost 1 seat, winning a single seat in the party leader Elizabeth May's own riding.

Class, Race, Gender, and Religion

Most people hold a mix of conservative and liberal attitudes. Surveys show, for example, that many people favour security and safety (a conservative position) but also support legal abortion and government-funded health care (both liberal positions).

Class position helps explain political attitudes. With wealth to protect, well-to-do people tend to be conservative on economic issues, but their extensive schooling and secure social standing lead most to be social liberals. Low-income people display the opposite pattern, with most being liberal on economic issues but leaning in a more conservative direction on social issues (Kohut, 2012; EKOS Research, 2013).

While in 2011 the Progressive Conservative Party won 39.6 of the votes, its support among immigrants was 42 percent. In Toronto, immigrant supporters of the Conservatives were mainly Greek, Italian, and South Asian. Length of stay also seemed to shape the outcome: recent immigrants were more likely to vote for New Democrats (41 percent) while more established immigrants, who have been in the country more than 10 years, voted for the Conservatives (43 percent). Visible minorities, however, were only 31 percent likely to vote for the Conservatives. The majority of visible minorities, 38 percent, voted for the New Democratic Party in the 2011 election, which came in second with 30.6 percent of the popular vote (Ipsos-Reid, 2011).

Gender matters, too, because women tend to be somewhat more liberal than men. Among Canadian adults, more women lean toward the New Democrats, and more men vote for Conservative candidates. Before the 2015 federal election, for example, an opinion poll showed that most women voters, 35 percent, said that they intended to vote for the NDP, while among men the majority, also 35 percent, intended to vote for the Conservative Party (EKOS Research, 2015). This is consistent with previous voting patterns and is also reflected in voting patterns in the United States.

Finally, religion also plays a role in how Canadians vote. In the 2011 election, the majority of Protestants (55 percent) and Jews (52 percent) voted for the Conservatives, most Catholics (39 percent) chose the New Democrats, while the majority of Muslims (46 percent) sided with the Liberals. Most people who claimed no religious identity (42 percent) voted for the New Democrats (Ipsos-Reid, 2011).

Figure 12–6 shows the voting pattern over time among college students.

Party Identification

Surveys conducted when the 2015 election was first announced showed that about 33.5 percent favoured the New Democratic Party, 32 percent favoured the Conservative Party, 24.5 percent favoured the Liberal Party, 4.5 percent favoured the Bloc Québécois, and 4 percent favoured the Green Party (EKOS Research, 2015; Forum Research, 2015; Ipsos-Reid, 2015). But because many people hold mixed political attitudes, with liberal views on some issues and conservative stands on others, party identification in this country is not very strong. And as the 2015 election illustrates, in Canada party identification is subject to change, with support shifting from the NDP to the Liberals in the course of a few months. Relatively weak party identification is one reason that historically the liberal and the conservative parties have gained or lost power from election to election, and why the social democrats (like the NDP) have experienced only a short-lived rising popularity. Liberals won four consecutive elections forming a majority government from 1993 to 2000, and a minority government in 2004, and a majority government in 2015. Conservatives made gains thereafter, forming two minority governments in 2006 and 2008 and a majority in 2011.

There is also a regional divide in Canadian politics. In the last decade, people in Western and Prairie Provinces tended to vote conservative while Atlantic Provinces voted liberal (Anderson & Stephenson, 2010). Quebec has tended to vote for the Bloc Québécois but switched its support to the NDP in 2011, and to Liberals in 2015. In Ontario, Toronto is once again a liberal stronghold. National Map 12–2 shows the regional results for the 2015 federal election.

Student Snapshot

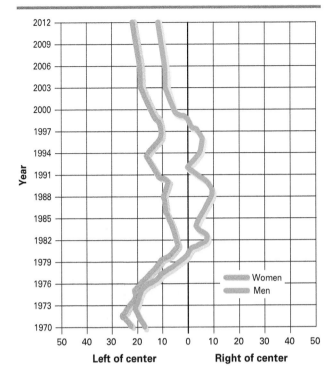

FIGURE 12–6 Left–Right Political Identification of College Students, 1970–2012

Student attitudes moved to the right after 1970 and shifted left in the late 1990s. College women tend to be more liberal than college men.

Sources: Astin et al. (2002), Sax et al. (2003), and Pryor et al. (2013).

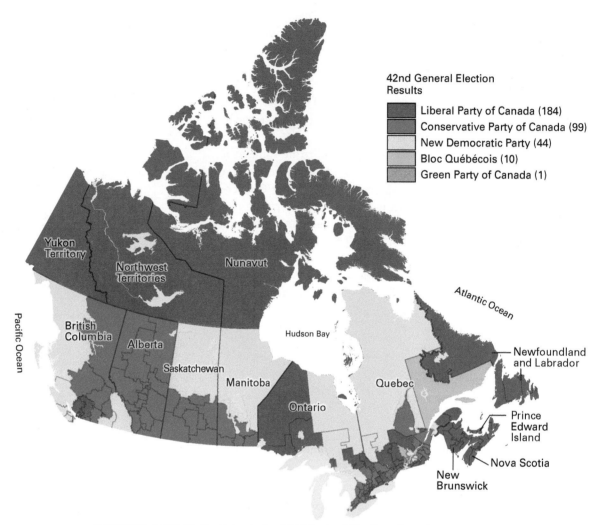

NATIONAL MAP 12–2   Votes in the 2015 Federal Election, Canada

The strong vote for the Liberal Party in the 2015 federal election is clear on this map. The Liberals captured all 32 ridings across Atlantic Canada, and won a total of 184 seats. They unseated the Conservatives, who lost 60 seats and secured 99 seats. The significant loss of seats for the increasingly centrist New Democratic Party in Quebec (a total loss of 42 in Quebec and 51 in Canada) is also apparent on this map. Why do you think there was such strong support for the Liberals and a decline in the strength of the NDP and Conservatives in the 2015 election?

Source: Adapted from Elections Canada (2015).

Special-Interest Groups

In the wake of events such as school shootings across North America, public support for gun control has been rising. In 1995, the Canadian government passed Bill C-68, which radically changed firearms legislation. The keystone of the law is universal firearms registration. The Canadian Association of Police Chiefs has been a strong supporter of the legislation, arguing that it will improve police safety across the country. Yet members of the National Firearms Association and its supporters have steadily worked in opposition to the legislation. In 2011, the majority Harper government introduced Bill C-19 to dismantle gun registration. Despite strong opposition across the country, especially in Quebec, this legislation passed and became law in 2012, as the opposition parties did not have enough members to defeat it in a vote.

Groups for and against the "gun lobby" are examples of **special-interest groups**, *people organized to address some economic or social issue*. Special-interest groups, which include associations of senior citizens, farmers, fireworks producers, and environmentalists, flourish in nations such as Canada, where loyalty to political parties tends to be low. Many special-interest groups employ lobbyists to support their goals. In Canada, over 5000 lobbyists are listed in the Registry of Lobbyists (Office of the Commissioner of Lobbying of Canada, 2011).

special-interest group people organized to address some economic or social issue

Voter Abstention

Canadian citizens are less likely to vote today than they were a century ago. Following World War II, voter turnout averaged 75 percent for a number of decades. Starting in the 1990s, it regularly dipped below the 70 percent mark. In the 2000 federal election, 64.1 percent of eligible voters showed up at the polls. In 2004, the percentage dropped even further, to 60.9 percent. More Canadian voters—64.7 percent—went to the ballot box in 2006. In the 2011 election, the voter turnout dropped again, to 61.1 percent, but returned to 68.5 percent in 2015—the highest turnout since the 1993 elections. Even with the recent increase, this turnout is generally lower than that in almost all other industrialized nations except for the United States.

Who is and is not likely to vote? Canadian women are less likely to cast a ballot than men. Seniors are more likely to vote than young people. White people are more likely to vote than are visible minorities, and Aboriginal people are the least likely of all to vote. Generally speaking, people with a bigger stake in society—parents with children at home, people with good jobs and extensive schooling—are most likely to vote. Class matters, too: people with employment are more likely to vote (66 percent) than those who are unemployed (57 percent). And homeowners were more likely to vote (71 percent) than non-homeowners (54 percent) (Uppal & LaRochelle-Côté, 2012).

The reasons why people do not vote are complex. They range from apathetic disinterest in the electoral process and simple forgetfulness to lack of access due to illness or disability and religious beliefs (Statistics Canada, 2011h). Registering and voting also depends on the ability to read and write, which discourages Canadian adults who have limited literacy skills. Some abstention is also due to politically principled—whether anarchist, Indigenist, or libertarian—opposition to state representation (Burkowicz, 2014). Electoral reforms made it possible for homeless people to vote in the 2000 federal election, a privilege that was previously denied them because they had no fixed address.

Conservatives suggest that abstention is really *indifference* to politics on the part of people who are content with their lives. Liberals and especially political radicals on the far left of the political spectrum counter that abstention reflects *alienation* from politics among people who are so deeply dissatisfied with society that they doubt that elections will make any real difference. The fact that it is the disadvantaged and powerless people who are least likely to vote suggests that the liberal explanation for abstention probably is closer to the truth.

Should Convicted Criminals Vote?

Although the right to vote is at the very foundation of our country's claim to being democratic, in the United States, all states except Vermont and Maine have laws that bar people in jail from voting. Overall, 5.85 million people (including 2.2 million African-American men) in the United States do not have the right to vote (Sentencing Project, 2012). Many other countries, including the United Kingdom, restrict people in prisons from voting in elections. Canada is an exception in this regard. In 2002, the Supreme Court of Canada ruled that prisoners should not be denied the right to vote. The federal election in 2004 was the first in which those in federal prison were permitted to cast a vote.

Should government take away people's political rights as a punishment for criminal acts? Critics point out that this practice may be politically motivated, because preventing convicted criminals from voting makes a difference in the way elections turn out because prisoners are more likely to be from the lower classes, which tend to support more left-leaning parties (Uggen & Manza, 2002).

Theoretical Analysis of Power in Society

(12.8) Apply the pluralist, power-elite, and Marxist models to the Canadian political system.

Sociologists have long debated how power is spread throughout the Canadian population. Power is a very difficult topic to study because decision making is complex and often takes place behind closed doors. Despite this difficulty, researchers have developed three competing models of power in Canada and other high-income countries. The Applying Theory table provides a summary of each.

The Pluralist Model: The People Rule

The **pluralist model**, closely linked to structural-functional theory, is *an analysis of politics that sees power as spread among many competing interest groups*. Pluralists claim, first, that politics is an arena of negotiation. No single organization can expect to achieve all of its goals. Organizations therefore operate as *veto groups*, realizing some goals but mostly keeping opponents from achieving all of theirs. The political process relies heavily on creating alliances and compromises among numerous interest groups so that policies gain wide support. In short, pluralists see power as spread widely throughout society, with all people having at least some voice in the political system (Dahl, 1961, 1982; Rothman & Black, 1998).

The Power-Elite Model: A Few People Rule

The **power-elite model**, based on social-conflict theory, is *an analysis of politics that sees power as concentrated among the rich*. The term "power elite" was coined by C. Wright Mills (1956), a social-conflict theorist who argued that the upper class holds most of society's wealth, prestige, and power.

Mills claimed that members of the power elite are in charge of the three major sectors of society: the economy, the government, and the military. The power elite is made up of the "super-rich" (corporate executives and major stockholders); top officials in Ottawa, and provincial capitals; and the highest-ranking officers in the Canadian military.

Further, Mills explained that these elites move from one sector to another, building power as they go. Wallace Clement (1975) argues this point about the Canadian elite, concluding that the corporate elite control both the economy and the mass media, and also have a major influence over politics. Cases in point are Canadian corporate giants that include Bell Canada, Rogers, Shaw Communications, and Vidéotron.

Power-elite theorists say that countries such as Canada and the United States are not democracies because our economic and political systems give a few people so much power

One of the most significant political forces to emerge in recent years is the Environmental Justice movement. Under the banner of "system change, not climate change," supporters engage in various activist projects. They claim that capitalism is the principal cause of climate change and that "green" solutions constitute a dead end. Campaigning against the Alberta Tar Sands and the Enbridge Pipeline in British Columbia, Environmental Justice activists include Aboriginal communities and anti-capitalist environmentalists. Do you see capitalism as an environmental problem the way many people on the left side of the political spectrum do? Or do you see it as potentially green the way many people on the right side of the political spectrum do? Why?

Applying Theory

Politics

	Pluralist Model	Power-Elite Model	Marxist Political-Economy Model
Which theoretical approach is applied?	Structural-functional approach	Social-conflict approach	Social-conflict approach
How is power spread throughout society?	Power is spread widely so that all groups have some voice.	Power is concentrated in the hands of top business, political, and military leaders.	Power is directed by the operation of the capitalist economy.
Is Canada a democracy?	Yes. Power is spread widely enough to make the country a democracy.	No. Power is too concentrated for the country to be a democracy.	No. The capitalist economy favours the few, so the country cannot be a democracy.

pluralist model an analysis of politics that sees power as spread among many competing interest groups

power-elite model an analysis of politics that sees power as concentrated among the rich

Marxist political-economy model an analysis that explains politics in terms of the operation of a society's economic system

that the average person's voice cannot be heard. They reject the pluralist idea that various centres of power serve as checks and balances on one another; according to the power-elite model, those at the top face no real opposition (Bartlett & Steele, 2000; Moore et al., 2002).

The Marxist Model: The System Is Biased

A third approach to understanding politics is the **Marxist political-economy model**, *an analysis that explains politics in terms of the operation of a society's economic system*. Like the power-elite model, the Marxist approach rejects the idea that Canada is a political democracy. But the power-elite model focuses on the enormous wealth and power of certain individuals; the Marxist model goes further and sees bias rooted in the nation's institutions, especially its economy. Karl Marx believed that a society's economic system (capitalist or socialist) shapes its political system. Therefore, power elites do not simply appear out of nowhere; they are creations of the capitalist economy.

From this point of view, reforming the political system—by, say, limiting the amount of money that rich people can contribute to political candidates—is unlikely to bring about true democracy. The problem does not lie in the people who exercise great power or the people who don't vote; the problem is the system itself—what Marxists call the "political economy of capitalism." In other words, as long as Canada has a predominantly capitalist economy, the majority of people will be shut out of politics, just as they are exploited in the workplace.

EVALUATE Which one of the three models is most accurate? Over the years, research has shown support for each one. In the end, of course, how you think our political system ought to work is as much a matter of political values as it is of scientific fact.

Classic research by Nelson Polsby (1959) supports pluralist theory. Polsby studied the politics of New Haven, Connecticut, where he found that key decisions involving urban renewal, choosing political candidates, and running the city's schools were made by different groups. Polsby concluded that in New Haven, no one group—not even the upper class—ruled all of the others.

Robert Lynd and Helen Lynd (1937) studied Muncie, Indiana (which they called "Middletown," to suggest that it was a typical city), and documented the fortune amassed by a single family, the Balls, from its business producing glass canning jars. Their findings support the power-elite position. The Lynds showed how the Ball family dominated the city's life, pointing to that family's name on a local bank, university, hospital, and department store. In Muncie, according to the Lynds, the power elite boiled down to more or less a single family. In Canada, such influence of wealth is observable in the province of New Brunswick, where the McCain and Irving families seem omnipotent.

From the Marxist perspective, the point is not which individuals make decisions. Rather, as Alexander Liazos (1982:13) explains, "The basic tenets of capitalist society shape everyone's life: the inequalities of social classes and the importance of profits over people." As long as the basic institutions of society are organized to meet the needs of the few rather than the many—in today's language, the 1 percent rather than the 99 percent—Liazos claims a democratic society is impossible.

Clearly, the political system in Canada gives almost everyone the right to participate in politics through elections. But as the power-elite and Marxist models point out, at the very least, the Canadian political system is far less democratic than most people think. Most citizens have the right to vote, but the major political parties and their candidates typically support only the positions that are acceptable to the most powerful segments of society and in tune with the operation of our capitalist economy.

Whatever the reasons, many people in Canada appear to be losing confidence in their leaders. Canadians want more government transparency and greater accountability (Pammet & LeDuc, 2003).

CHECK YOUR LEARNING What is the main argument of the pluralist model of power? What about the power-elite model? The Marxist political-economy model?

Power Beyond the Rules

(**12.9**) Describe causes of both revolution and terrorism.

Politics is always a matter of disagreement over a society's goals and the means to achieve them. A political system tries to settle controversy within a system of rules. But political activity sometimes breaks the rules or even tries to do away with the entire system.

Revolution

political revolution the overthrow of one political system in order to establish another

Political revolution is *the overthrow of one political system in order to establish another.* Revolution goes beyond *reform*, or change within a system, and even beyond a *coup d'état* (in French, literally, "blow to the state"), as when one leader topples another. Revolution involves change in the type of system itself.

No political system is immune to revolution, nor does revolution produce any one type of government. The U.S. Revolutionary War (1775–1776) replaced colonial rule by the British monarchy with a representative democracy. French revolutionaries in 1789 also overthrew a monarch, only to set the stage for the return of monarchy in the person of Napoleon. In 1917, the Russian Revolution replaced a monarchy with a socialist government built on the ideas of Karl Marx. In 1991, a second Russian revolution dismantled the socialist Soviet Union, and the nation was reborn as 15 independent republics, the largest of which—known as the Russian Federation—initially moved closer to a market system and a government offering greater political rights but has more recently become more tightly controlled by a central government. As a final example, the 2011 political uprising in Egypt forced that country's leader from office and led to a government dominated by the Muslim Brotherhood, an Islamic movement; in 2013, that nation's military forced the new president from office.

Despite their striking variety, revolutions share a number of traits (Tocqueville, 1955, orig. 1856; Skocpol, 1979; Tilly, 1986):

1. **Rising expectations.** Common sense suggests that revolution is more likely when people are severely deprived, but history shows that most revolutions occur when people's lives are improving. Rising expectations, rather than bitterness and despair, make revolution more likely. Driving the recent uprisings across the Middle East are young people who may be living better than their families did generations ago but not as well as they see people living in other parts of the world.

2. **Unresponsive government.** Revolution becomes more likely when a government is unwilling to reform itself, especially when demands for change being made by powerful segments of society are ignored. In Egypt, for example, the government led by Hosni Mubarak had done little to benefit many people or to reform its own corruption over many decades.

Khaled Elfiqi/epa european pressphoto agency b.v./Alamy Stock Photo

In 2011, as part of the popular movement that swept across northern Africa and the Middle East, Egyptians forced President Hosni Mubarak from office. In 2012, Mohamed Morsi was elected president. A year later, however, he too was forced from office by popular opposition, although many of his supporters continue to demand his return to power. Do you think the recent political changes in Egypt have been *revolutionary* or are they examples of *reform*? Why?

3. **Radical leadership by intellectuals.** The English philosopher Thomas Hobbes (1588–1679) claimed that intellectuals provide the justification for revolution, and universities are often at the centre of political change. Students played a key role in China's prodemocracy movement, the uprisings in Eastern Europe in the 1990s, and the recent uprisings across the Middle East.

4. **Establishing a new legitimacy.** Overthrowing a political system is not easy, but ensuring a revolution's long-term success is harder still. Some revolutionary movements are held together merely by hatred of the past regime and fall apart once new leaders are installed. This fact is one reason that it is difficult to predict the long-term outcome of recent political changes in the Middle East. Revolutionaries must also guard against counterrevolutionary drives led by overthrown leaders. This explains the speed and ruthlessness with which victorious revolutionaries typically dispose of former leaders.

Scientific analysis cannot declare that a revolution is good or bad. That judgment depends on the personal values of the citizenry, and the full consequences of such an upheaval become evident only after many years. For example, it is far from clear that the "prodemocracy" movement that has transformed parts of the Middle East will result in a long-term trend toward democracy. For one thing, polls show that just 60 percent of Egyptians, for example, claim that democracy is the best form of government. In addition, in the vacuum created by deposing an authoritarian ruler, many organizations—some more democratic than others—quickly compete for power (Bell, 2011).

Terrorism

The terrorist attacks on the United States on September 11, 2001, involving four commercial airliners, killed nearly 3000 people (from 68 nations, including Canada), injured many thousands more, destroyed the twin towers of the World Trade Center in New York City, and seriously damaged the Pentagon in Washington, D.C. Not since the attack on Pearl Harbor at the outbreak of World War II had the United States suffered such a blow. This event was the most serious terrorist act ever recorded in that country.

terrorism acts of violence or the threat of violence used as a political strategy by an individual or a group

Terrorism refers to *acts of violence or the threat of violence used as a political strategy by an individual or a group*. Like revolution, terrorism is a political act beyond the rules of established political systems. According to Paul Johnson (1981), terrorism has four distinguishing characteristics.

First, terrorists try to paint violence as a legitimate political tactic, despite the fact that such acts are condemned by virtually every nation. Terrorists also bypass (or are excluded from) established channels of political negotiation. Therefore, terrorism is a weak organization's strategy against a stronger enemy. The 1970 Front de libération du Québec kidnapping and subsequent murder of then Quebec labour minister Pierre Laporte was strongly condemned in all of Canada. At the same time, it served as a wake-up call for Canadians outside Quebec to the bitterness many Québécois feel about their position in Canada. Likewise, attacks against the U.S. embassies in Tanzania and Kenya in 1998 and the *U.S.S. Cole* in 2000 may have been morally wrong because they harmed innocent people, but they did raise the profile of organizations with grievances against the United States.

Second, terrorism is used not just by groups but also by governments against their own people. *State terrorism* is the use of violence, generally without support of law, by government officials. State terrorism is lawful in some authoritarian and totalitarian states, which survive

Terrorism is a complex political process typically involving parties with differing levels of global power. The television series *Homeland* illustrates that terrorism is also a matter of defining some parties as "good" and others as "evil" and sometimes never being sure which is which. How accurately do you think the mass media in Canada portray the global conflicts we call "terrorism"?

by creating widespread fear and intimidation. Saddam Hussein, for example, relied on secret police and state terror to protect his power in Iraq. More recently, Syrian president Bashar al-Assad has attempted to remain in power by using that country's military against a popular uprising that has turned into a bloody civil war.

Third, democratic societies reject terrorism in principle, but they are especially vulnerable to terrorists because they give broad civil liberties to their people and have less extensive police networks. In contrast, totalitarian regimes make widespread use of state terrorism, but their vast police power gives individuals few opportunities for acts of terror against the government.

Fourth and finally, terrorism is always a matter of definition. Governments claim the right to maintain order, even by force, and may label opposition groups who use violence as "terrorists." Political differences may explain why one person's "terrorist" is another's "freedom fighter" (Jenkins, 2003). Thus, U.S. and Canadian citizens may associate terrorism with organizations like ISIS, Boko Haram, and the Taliban. On the other hand, Cubans who have been living for over 50 years under a crippling U.S.-imposed embargo, in violation of the Charter of the United Nations and international law, may very well view the United States as a terrorist state. The same may be said for some citizens of Chile, who were forced from 1973 to 1990 to endure the CIA-backed dictator Augusto Pinochet.

Although hostage taking and outright killing provoke popular anger, taking action against terrorists is difficult. Most terrorist groups have no formal connection to any established state, so identifying the parties responsible may be all but impossible. In addition, a military response may risk confrontation with other governments—recall the heightened tensions with Pakistan in 2011 after U.S. soldiers entered the country in order to kill Osama bin Laden. Yet as the terrorism expert Brian Jenkins warns, a failure to respond "encourages other terrorist groups, who begin to realize that this can be a pretty cheap way to wage war" (quoted in Whitaker, 1985:29).

War and Peace

12.10 Identify factors encouraging war or peace.

war organized, armed conflict among the people of two or more nations, directed by their governments

Perhaps the most critical political issue is **war**, *organized, armed conflict among the people of two or more nations, directed by their governments*. War is as old as humanity, but understanding it is crucial today because we now have weapons that can destroy the entire planet.

At almost any moment during the twentieth century, nations somewhere in the world were engaged in violent conflict. In the "Great War" (World War I) alone, 56 500 Canadian soldiers lost their lives, and many more were injured. Other deadly conflicts since then took the lives of countless Canadians and people from all corners of the globe. To take another example, the United States has participated in 11 major wars. From the Revolutionary War to the War in Iraq, more than 1.3 million U.S. men and women have been killed in armed conflicts. As shown in Figure 12–7, many times that number of civilians have been killed. Domestic and international wars continue to be waged at this time around the world, eating up a substantial portion of national budgets that could otherwise be used for more constructive purposes.

The Causes of War

Wars occur so often that we might think that there is something natural about armed conflict. But there is no evidence that human beings must wage war under any particular circumstances. On the contrary, governments around the world usually have to force their people to go to war.

Like other forms of social behaviour, warfare is a product of society that is more common in some places than in others. The Semai of Malaysia, among the most peace-loving of the world's peoples, rarely resort to violence. In contrast, the Yąnomamö of South America (see the box on page 47) are quick to wage war.

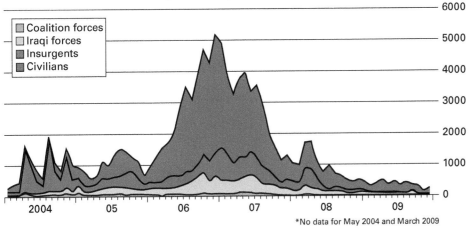

Iraq War Deaths, 2004–2009*

- Coalition forces
- Iraqi forces
- Insurgents
- Civilians

*No data for May 2004 and March 2009

FIGURE 12–7 Iraq War Deaths, 2004–2009

As this graph shows, the majority of deaths resulting from the U.S./U.K.-led invasion of Iraq were civilian deaths. The Iraq Body Count project estimates that from March 2003 to March 2013, 174 000 people were killed in Iraq, among them 134 100 civilians.

Sources: *The Economist* (2010); Iraq Body Count (2013).

If society holds the key to war or peace, under what circumstances do humans go to war? Quincy Wright (1987) cites five factors that promote war:

1. **Perceived threats.** Nations mobilize in response to a perceived threat to their people, territory, or culture. Leaders justified the U.S.-led military campaign against Iraq, for example, by stressing the threat that Saddam Hussein posed to neighbouring countries and also to the United States. However, Jean Chrétien, who was Canadian prime minister when the war started, decided not to support the U.S./U.K.-led campaign.

2. **Social problems.** When internal problems cause widespread frustration at home, a nation's leaders may try to divert public attention by attacking an external "enemy" as a form of scapegoating. Although U.S. leaders defended the 2003 invasion of Iraq as a matter of national security, the start of the war effectively shifted the nation's attention away from the struggling national economy and boosted the popularity of President George W. Bush.

3. **Political objectives.** Poor nations, such as Vietnam, have used wars to end foreign domination. Powerful countries such as the United States may benefit from periodic shows of force (recall the deployments of troops in Somalia, Haiti, Bosnia, and Afghanistan) to increase global political standing.

4. **Moral objectives.** Nations rarely claim that they are going to war to gain wealth and power. Instead, their leaders infuse military campaigns with moral urgency. By calling the 2003 invasion of Iraq "Operation Iraqi Freedom," U.S. leaders portrayed the mission as a morally justified war of liberation from an evil tyrant.

5. **The absence of alternatives.** A fifth factor promoting war is the lack of alternatives. Although the goal of the United Nations is to maintain international peace by finding alternatives to war, the organization has had limited success in preventing conflict between nations.

Social Class, Gender, and the Military

In World War II, three out of every four men in their late teens and twenties served in the military, either voluntarily or by being *drafted*—called to service. Only those who were ruled ineligible due to some physical or mental problem were freed from the obligation to service. Today, by contrast, there is no draft, and fighting is done by a volunteer military. But not every member of our society is equally likely to volunteer.

Since 2000, the Canadian Armed Forces has integrated women into all military combat positions. Do you see this as a step forward for women? Why or why not?

Gregory Holmgren/Alamy Stock Photo

One recent study concluded that the military has few young people who are rich and few who are very poor. Rather, working-class people, males in particular, look to the Canadian military for a job, to become eligible for money to use for higher education, or simply to get out of the small town where they grew up (Wait, 2002).

As Chapter 10 ("Gender Stratification") shows, throughout Canada's history, women have been a part of the military. In recent decades, however, women have taken on greater importance in the armed forces. For one thing, the share of women is on the rise, now standing at about 15 percent of the Canadian Forces.

Is Terrorism a New Kind of War?

People speak of terrorism as a new kind of war. War has historically followed certain patterns: It is played out according to basic rules, the warring parties are known to each other, and the objectives of the warring parties—which generally involve control of territory—are clearly stated.

Terrorism breaks from these patterns. The identity of terrorist organizations may not be known, those involved may deny their responsibility, and their goals may be unclear. The 2001 terrorist attacks against the United States were not attempts to defeat the nation militarily or to secure territory. They were carried out by people representing not a country but a cause, one not well understood in the United States. In short, they were expressions of anger and hate intended to create widespread fear.

Conventional warfare is symmetrical, with two nations sending armies into battle. By contrast, terrorism is a new kind of war: an asymmetrical conflict in which a small number of attackers—or sometimes a lone individual—use terror and a willingness to die as a means to level the playing field against a much more powerful enemy. Although the terrorists may be ruthless, the nation under attack must use caution in its response to terrorism because little may be known about the identity and location of the parties responsible.

One reason to pursue peace is the rising toll of death and mutilation caused by millions of land mines placed in the ground during wartime and left there afterwards. Civilians—many of them children—maimed by land mines receive treatment in this Kabul, Afghanistan, clinic.

The Costs and Causes of Militarism

The cost of armed conflict extends far beyond battlefield casualties. Together, the world's nations spend more than $1.7 trillion annually for military-related purposes. Spending this much diverts resources from the desperate struggle for survival by hundreds of millions of poor people.

Defence is the U.S. government's second biggest expenditure (after Social Security), accounting for about 19 percent of all federal spending, which amounted to more than $700 billion in the 2013 budget. The United States has emerged as the world's single military superpower, accounting for about 41 percent of the world's military spending. Put another way, the United States spends five times as much on its military than does China, the nation in second place, and nearly as much as the rest of the world's nations combined (Stockholm International Peace Research Institute, 2012; U.S. Office of Management and Budget, 2012).

For decades, military spending went up because of the *arms race* between the United States and the former Soviet Union, which dropped out of the race after its collapse in 1991. But some analysts (those who support power-elite theory) link high military spending to the domination of U.S. society by a **military-industrial complex**, *the close association of the federal government, the military, and defence industries.* The roots of militarism, then, lie not just in external threats but also in institutional structures at home (Marullo, 1987; Barnes, 2002).

military-industrial complex the close association of the federal government, the military, and defence industries

A final reason for continuing militarism is regional conflict. In the 1990s, localized wars broke out in Bosnia, Chechnya, and Zambia, and long-standing conflict continues in Israel-occupied territories of Palestine. Even limited wars have the potential to grow and involve other countries, including Canada's involvement in Afghanistan. India and Pakistan—both nuclear powers—moved to the brink of war in 2002 and then pulled back. In 2003, the announcement by North Korea that it, too, had nuclear weapons raised tensions in Asia.

Nuclear Weapons

The danger of catastrophic war increases with **nuclear proliferation**, *the acquisition of nuclear weapons technology by more and more nations*. Despite the easing of superpower tensions, the world still contains approximately 4000 operational nuclear warheads, representing a destructive power of several tonnes of TNT for every person on the planet. If even a small fraction of this stockpile is used in war, life as we know it would end. Albert Einstein, whose genius contributed to the development of nuclear weapons, reflected, "The unleashed power of the atom has changed everything save our modes of thinking and we thus drift toward unparalleled catastrophe." In short, nuclear weapons make unrestrained war unthinkable in a world not yet capable of peace.

nuclear proliferation the acquisition of nuclear weapons technology by more and more nations

The United States, the Russian Federation, Great Britain, France, the People's Republic of China, Israel, India, Pakistan, and North Korea all have nuclear weapons. A few nations stopped the development of nuclear weapons; Argentina and Brazil halted work in 1990, and South Africa dismantled its arsenal in 1991. In total, 191 countries have signed the Treaty on the Non-Proliferation of Nuclear Weapons. Four nations, however, possess nuclear weapons but have not joined the treaty: South Sudan, India, Israel, and Pakistan. Other nations may also develop nuclear capabilities. Such a trend makes any regional conflict very dangerous to the entire planet.

Mass Media and War

The 2003 U.S./U.K.-led invasion of Iraq was the first war in which television crews travelled with troops, reporting as the campaign unfolded. The mass media provided ongoing and detailed reports of events; cable television made available live coverage of the war 24 hours a day, 7 days a week.

Media outlets "frame" the news according to their own politics. Those media outlets that were critical of the war—especially the Arab news channel Al-Jazeera—tended to report the slow pace of the conflict, the casualties to the allied forces, and the deaths and injuries suffered by Iraqi civilians, all of which was information that would increase pressure to end the war. Media outlets that were supportive of the war—including most news organizations in the United States—tended to report the rapid pace of the war and the casualties to Iraqi forces and to downplay any harm to Iraqi civilians as minimal and unintended. In short, the power of the mass media to provide selective information to a worldwide audience means that television and other media are almost as important to the outcome of a conflict as the military forces who are doing the actual fighting.

Pursuing Peace

How can the world reduce the dangers of war? Here are the most recent approaches to peace:

1. **Deterrence.** The logic of the arms race holds that security comes from a "balance of terror" between the superpowers. The principle of *mutual assured destruction* (MAD) means that a nation launching a first strike against another will face greater retaliation. This deterrence policy kept the peace for almost 50 years during the Cold War. Yet it encouraged an enormous arms race and cannot control nuclear proliferation, which represents a growing threat to peace. Deterrence also does little to stop terrorism or to prevent wars that are started by a stronger nation (such as the United States) against a weaker foe (such as the Taliban government in Afghanistan or Saddam Hussein's Iraq).

Thinking Globally

Uprisings Across the Middle East: An End to the Islamic "Democracy Gap"?

The wave of popular political protest that swept across the Middle East in 2011 is the largest global political movement in the two decades since change swept through the former Soviet Union and the nations of Eastern Europe. What's going on? Why are so many nations in this part of the world erupting with political opposition?

Is there a "democracy gap" in the Middle East? Is there a lack of democracy in Islamic nations? Making any assessment of global democracy is more difficult than it may appear. For one thing, in a world marked by striking cultural diversity, can we assume that democracy and related ideas about political freedoms are the same everywhere? The answer cannot be a simple "yes," because with their various political histories, concepts such as "democracy" and "freedom" mean different things in different cultural settings.

What have researchers found? Freedom House is an organization that monitors political freedom around the world by tracking people's right to vote, to express ideas, and to move about without undue interference from government in nations around the world. Freedom House classifies nations in one of three categories: "not free," "partly free," and "free."

Freedom House reports that many of the nations that are classified as "not free" have populations that are largely Islamic. Around the world, 46 of the 195 nations had an Islamic-majority population in 2012. Just 10 (22 percent) of these 46 countries had democratic governments, and Freedom House rated only three (6.6 percent)—Indonesia, Senegal, and Sierra Leone—as "free." Of the remainder, 18 (39.1 percent) were considered to be "partly free" and 25 (54.3 percent) were classified as "not free." Of the 149 nations without a majority Islamic population, 108 (73 percent) had democratic governments, and 87 (58.4 percent) were rated as "free." When you put these facts together, countries without Islamic majorities were three times more likely to have democratic governments than countries with Islamic majorities. Freedom House concludes that countries with Islamic-majority populations display a "democracy gap."

This relative lack of democracy was found in all world regions that have Islamic-majority nations—in Africa, central Europe, the Middle East, and Asia. The pattern is especially strong among the 16 Islamic-majority states in the Middle East and North Africa that are ethnically Arabic: As of early 2013, only two, Tunisia and Libya, are electoral democracies.

What explains this "democracy gap"? Freedom House points to four factors. First, Islamic-majority countries are typically less developed economically with limited schooling for their people and widespread poverty. Second, these countries have cultural traditions that rigidly control the lives of women, limiting their economic, educational, and political opportunities. Third, although most countries limit the power of religious elites in government, and some (like the U.S., but not Canada) even recognize a "separation of church and state," Islamic-majority nations support a political role for Islamic leaders. In just two recent cases—Iran and Afghanistan under the Taliban—Islamic leaders have had formal control of government; more commonly, religious leaders do not hold office but exert considerable influence on political outcomes.

Fourth and finally, the enormous wealth that comes from Middle Eastern oil plays a part in preventing democratic government. In Iraq, Saudi Arabia, Kuwait, Qatar, the United Arab Emirates, and other nations, this resource has provided astounding riches to a small number of families, money they can use to shore up their political control. In addition, oil wealth permits elites to build airports and other modern facilities without encouraging broader economic development that raises the living standards of the majority.

For all these reasons, Freedom House concludes that the road to democracy for Islamic-majority nations is likely to be long. But today's patterns may not predict those of tomorrow. In 1950, very few Catholic-majority countries (mostly in Europe and Latin America) had democratic governments. Today, however, most of these nations are democratic. Keep in mind that 43 percent of the world's Muslims live in Nigeria, Turkey, Bangladesh, India, Indonesia, Germany, France, and the United States, where they already live under democratic governments. But perhaps the best indicator that change is now under way is the widespread demands for a political voice rising from people throughout the Middle East.

What Do You Think?

1. How do you think the political conflict in the Middle East will turn out? Will the cause of democracy be advanced? Explain your view.

2. Over the coming decades, do you think the Islamic "democracy gap" just described will disappear? Why or why not?

3. What role should Canada play in this process? Do you think Canada is a force that advances democracy? Why or why not?

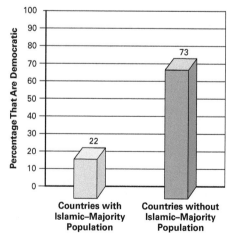

Democracy and Islam

Today, democratic government is much less common in countries with Islamic-majority populations.

Sources: Karatnycky (2002), Pew Research Center, Forum on Religion and Public Life (2012), and Freedom House (2013).

2. **High-technology defence.** If technology created the weapons, perhaps it can also protect us from them; such is the claim of the *strategic defence initiative* (SDI). Under SDI, satellites and ground installations would destroy enemy missiles soon after they were launched. In a survey shortly after the 2001 terrorist attacks, two-thirds of American adults supported SDI (Thompson & Waller, 2001; "Female Opinion," 2002). However, critics, many of them Canadians, claim that the system, which they refer to as "Star Wars," would be, at best, a leaky umbrella. Others worry that building such a system will spark another massive arms race. In 2015, the Obama administration has turned away from further development of SDI, signing, along with other world powers, a nuclear deal framework with Iran.

3. **Diplomacy and disarmament.** Some analysts believe that the best road to peace is diplomacy rather than technology (Dedrick & Yinger, 1990). Teams of diplomats working together can increase security by reducing, rather than building, weapons stockpiles, as the recent deal with Iran illustrates. But disarmament has limitations. No nation wants to be weakened by eliminating its defences. Successful diplomacy depends on everyone involved sharing responsibility for a common problem (Fisher & Ury, 1988). In 2010, the New Start treaty required the United States and Russia to reduce nuclear stockpiles to 1550 warheads within seven years; it also provided for a new system of monitoring compliance with this limitation. Even so, each nation will still have more than enough weapons to destroy the entire planet. In addition, the world now faces increasing threats from other nations.

4. **Resolving underlying conflict.** In the end, reducing the dangers of war may depend on resolving underlying conflicts by promoting a more just world. Poverty, hunger, and illiteracy are all root causes of war. Perhaps the world needs to reconsider the wisdom of spending thousands of times as much money on militarism as we do on efforts to find peaceful solutions (Sivard, 1988; Kaplan & Schaffer, 2001).

Politics: Looking Ahead

Just as economies are changing, so are political systems. Several problems and trends are likely to be important in the decades to come.

One troublesome problem, for many in Canada, is the inconsistency between democratic ideals and low turnout at the polls. Perhaps, as conservative pluralist theorists say, many people do not bother to vote because they are content with their lives. On the other hand, the liberal power-elite theorists may be right when they say that people withdraw from a system that concentrates so much wealth and power in the hands of a few people. Or perhaps, as anarchist critics claim, people find that our political system offers little real choice, limiting options and policies to those that support our capitalist economy. In any case, the 2015 federal election did witness a higher voter turnout than previous elections in the last two decades. Likely, high levels of distrust in Canada's former government, coupled with the activism of the Occupy and Idle No More movements, led to a widespread desire for political change.

A second issue is the global rethinking of political models. The Cold War between the United States and the Soviet Union encouraged people to think of politics in terms of two opposing models, capitalism and socialism. Today, however, people are more likely to consider a broader range of political systems that link government to the economy in various ways. Welfare capitalism, as found in Sweden and Denmark, or state capitalism, as found in South Korea and Japan, are just two possibilities. The Thinking Globally box takes a look at the debate over the chances for the emergence of democratic governments in the world's Islamic countries.

Third, we still face the danger of war in many parts of the world. Even as the United States and the Russian Federation dismantle some warheads, vast stockpiles of nuclear weapons remain, and nuclear technology continues to spread around the world. In addition, new superpowers are likely to arise (the People's Republic of China and India are well on their way), just as regional conflicts and terrorism are likely to continue. For our part, we can vote for leaders who will work toward finding nonviolent solutions to the age-old problems that provoke war, just as much as we can also create and join social movements that put us on the road to world peace.

Seeing Sociology in Everyday Life

How important are you to the political process?

This chapter explains that the economy is the social institution that organizes the production, distribution, and consumption of goods and services. It's no secret that we are living in tough economic times. Secure jobs are disappearing, earning a living wage is harder than it used to be, and public confidence in a secure future has taken a hit. As C. Wright Mills might have said, the problems we face as individuals are issues that are deeply rooted in the economy. Look at the three photos and ask yourself: What changes in today's economy create challenges for today's labour force?

Simon Dack/Alamy Stock Photo

Walk around a big-box store and examine products to see where they are made. It will not take long to see a pattern: What is it? As the share of manufactured goods made abroad rises, what happens to manufacturing jobs here in Canada?

Joerg Boethling/Alamy Stock Photo

Have you ever called an 800 support line and wondered where the person on the other end of the line was located? It is not only manufacturing jobs that have moved overseas. Lower wages have led corporations to relocate many service jobs—including many skilled office jobs—to places such as India, where service employment is skyrocketing. What are the long-term effects of the trend we call "outsourcing"?

Advancing technology makes our economy more productive, right? Generally, yes. But adopting new technology can make organizations more productive with fewer employees. Have you ever taken a "distance learning" class in which the professor was not in the classroom with you? How can computer technology enable colleges to teach more students using fewer faculty?

Ariel Skelley/Blend Images/Getty Images

HINT Industrial production has been moving from Canada to countries where wages are lower. In China, for example, industrial workers earn roughly 10 percent of what a worker is paid in this country. After the United States, China is the second-largest economy in the world (Canada ranks tenth). Since 2000, China's industrial production has increased, on average, about 10 percent a year. U.S. industrial production has actually declined during five years of this new century and, since 2000, has averaged less than a 1 percent annual increase. Economic activity is also expanding in India, a country that has seen striking growth in service jobs (Stevens, 2014), such as those shown in the photo of a call-centre in the city of Kolkata. In Canada and the United States, even highly skilled people such as college professors are facing challenges in today's economy. Computer technology is being used to allow professors to teach larger classes and also to allow a single faculty member to teach students in multiple classrooms in various places at the same time. In short, even when a corporation or organization becomes more productive, it does not always end up employing more people.

Seeing Sociology in *Your* Everyday Life

1. Visit a discount store such as Walmart or No Frills and do a little "fieldwork" in an area of the store that interests you. Pick 10 products, and see where each is made. Do the results support the existence of a global economy?

2. Go to www.sociologyinfocus.com to access the Sociology in Focus blog, where you can read the latest posts by a team of young sociologists who apply the sociological perspective to topics of popular culture.

3. Based on what you have read in this chapter, make three predictions about the nature of work and jobs 20 years from now. That is, what trends have you noted that seem likely to continue?

Chris Thomaidis/The Image Bank/
Getty Images

Making the Grade

The Economy: Historical Overview

(12.1) Summarize historical changes to the economy. (pages 373–376)

In technologically simple societies, economic activity is simply part of family life.

* The **agricultural revolution** (5000 years ago) made the economy a distinct social institution based on agricultural technology, specialized work, permanent settlements, and trade.
* The **Industrial Revolution** (beginning around 1750) expanded the economy based on new sources of energy and specialized work in factories that turned raw materials into finished products.
* The **post-industrial economy** is based on a shift from industrial work to service work and computer technology.
* The **primary sector** draws raw materials from the natural environment; it is of greatest importance (25 percent of the economy) in low-income nations.
* The **secondary sector** transforms raw materials into manufactured goods; it is a significant share (24 percent–35 percent) of the economy in low-, middle-, and high-income nations.
* The **tertiary sector** produces services rather than goods; it is the largest sector (50 percent–74 percent) in low-, middle-, and high-income countries

social institution a major sphere of social life, or societal subsystem, organized to meet human needs

economy the social institution that organizes a society's production, distribution, and consumption of goods and services

post-industrial economy a productive system based on service work and computer technology

primary sector the part of the economy that draws raw materials from the natural environment

secondary sector the part of the economy that transforms raw materials into manufactured goods

tertiary sector the part of the economy that involves services rather than goods

global economy economic activity that crosses national borders

Economic Systems: Paths to Justice

(12.2) Assess the operation of capitalist and socialist economies. (pages 376–381)

* **Capitalism** is based on private ownership of property and the pursuit of profit in a competitive marketplace. Capitalism results in
* greater income inequality
* freedom to act according to self-interest
* greater consumer choice

* **Socialism** is grounded in collective ownership of productive property through government or community control of the economy. Socialism results in
* less income inequality
* freedom from basic want
* greater social safety net

capitalism an economic system in which natural resources and the means of producing goods and services are privately owned

socialism an economic system in which natural resources and the means of producing goods and services are collectively owned

welfare capitalism an economic and political system that combines a mostly market-based economy with extensive social welfare programs

state capitalism an economic and political system in which companies are privately owned but co-operate closely with the government

Work in the Post-industrial Canadian Economy

(12.3) Analyze patterns of employment and unemployment in Canada. (pages 381–388)

* There are 17.99 million people in the Canadian labour force, 47 percent of whom are women.
* Agricultural work represents only 4 percent of jobs.
* Close to 80 percent of Canadian workers are employed in service work.
* Fifteen percent of Canadian workers are **self-employed**; many are professionals, but most self-employed have blue-collar jobs.
* In 2014, 6.9 percent of the country's labour force was unemployed. In addition, Canada has one of the highest shares of involuntary part-time workers (27.6 percent).

labour unions organizations of workers that seek to improve wages and working conditions through various strategies, including negotiations and strikes

profession a prestigious white-collar occupation that requires extensive formal education

Corporations

(12.4) Discuss the importance of corporations to the Canadian economy. (pages 388–390)

Corporations form the core of the Canadian economy.

* The largest corporations, which are conglomerates, account for most corporate assets and profits.
* Many large corporations operate as multinationals, producing and distributing products in nations around the world.

corporation an organization with a legal existence, including rights and liabilities, separate from that of its members

conglomerate a giant corporation composed of many smaller corporations

monopoly the domination of a market by a single producer

oligopoly the domination of a market by a few producers

Power and Authority

 12.5 Distinguish traditional, rational-legal, and charismatic authority. (page 391)

Max Weber claimed that

- Preindustrial societies rely on tradition to transform raw power into authority. **Traditional authority** is closely linked to kinship.
- As societies industrialize, tradition gives way to rationality. **Rational-legal authority** underlies the operation of bureaucratic offices as well as the law.
- At any time, some individuals transform power into authority through charisma. **Charismatic authority** is linked to extraordinary personal qualities.

politics the social institution that distributes power, sets a society's goals, and makes decisions
power the ability to achieve desired ends despite resistance from others
government a formal organization that directs the political life of a society
authority power that people perceive as legitimate rather than coercive
traditional authority power legitimized by respect for long-established cultural patterns
rational-legal authority power legitimized by legally enacted rules and regulations (also known as *bureaucratic authority*)
charismatic authority power legitimized by extraordinary personal abilities that inspire devotion and obedience
routinization of charisma the transformation of charismatic authority into some combination of traditional and bureaucratic authority

Politics in Global Perspective

12.6 Compare monarchy and democracy as well as authoritarian and totalitarian political systems. (pages 392–396)

- **Monarchy** is common in agrarian societies; leadership is based on kinship.
- **Democracy** is common in modern societies; leadership is linked to elective office.
- **Authoritarianism** is any political system that denies the people participation in government.
- **Totalitarianism** is a political system based on the extensive regulation of the lives of its citizens.

monarchy a political system in which a single family rules from generation to generation
democracy a political system that derives its legitimacy from the people as a whole
authoritarianism a political system that denies the people participation in government
totalitarianism a highly centralized political system that extensively regulates people's lives

Politics in Canada

12.7 Analyze economic and social issues using the political spectrum. (pages 396–401)

- The Canadian government has expanded over the past two centuries, with a **welfare state** that is slightly bigger than that of the United States and smaller than in most other high-income nations.
- The **political spectrum**, from the liberal left to the conservative right, involves attitudes on both economic issues and social issues.
- **Special-interest groups** advance the political aims of specific segments of the population.
- **Voter abstention** is high: 68.5 percent of eligible voters cast votes in the 2015 federal election.

welfare state a system of government agencies and programs that provides benefits to the population
special-interest group people organized to address some economic or social issue

Theoretical Analysis of Power in Society

12.8 Apply the pluralist, power-elite, and Marxist models to the Canadian political system. (pages 402–404)

- **The pluralist model** claims that political power is spread widely in Canada.
- **The power-elite model** claims that power is concentrated in a small, wealthy segment of the population.
- **The Marxist political-economy model** claims that our political agenda is determined by a capitalist economy, so true democracy is impossible.

pluralist model an analysis of politics that sees power as spread among many competing interest groups
power-elite model an analysis of politics that sees power as concentrated among the rich
Marxist political-economy model an analysis that explains politics in terms of the operation of a society's economic system

Power Beyond the Rules

12.9 Describe causes of both revolution and terrorism. (pages 404–406)

- **Revolution** radically transforms a political system.
- **Terrorism** employs violence in the pursuit of political goals and is used by a group against a much more powerful enemy.

political revolution the overthrow of one political system in order to establish another
terrorism refers to acts of violence or the threat of violence used as a political strategy by an individual or a group

War and Peace

12.10 Identify factors encouraging war or peace. (pages 406–411)

- The development and spread of nuclear weapons have increased the threat of global catastrophe.
- World peace ultimately depends on resolving the tensions and conflicts that fuel militarism.

war organized, armed conflict among the people of two or more nations, directed by their governments
military-industrial complex the close association of the federal government, the military, and defence industries
nuclear proliferation the acquisition of nuclear weapons technology by more and more nations

13 Family and Religion

Luca Barbieri/Alamy Stock Photo

LEARNING OBJECTIVES

13.1 Describe families and how they differ around the world.

13.2 Apply sociology's major theories to family life.

13.3 Analyze changes in the family over the life course.

13.4 Explain how class, race, and gender shape family life.

13.5 Analyze the effects of divorce, remarriage, and violence on family life.

13.6 Describe the diversity of family life in Canada.

13.7 Apply sociology's major theories to religion.

13.8 Analyze how religion encourages social change.

13.9 Distinguish among church, sect, and cult.

13.10 Contrast religious patterns in pre-industrial and industrial societies.

13.11 Analyze patterns of religiosity in Canada.

13.12 Discuss recent trends in religious life.

the Power of Society

to shape our values and beliefs

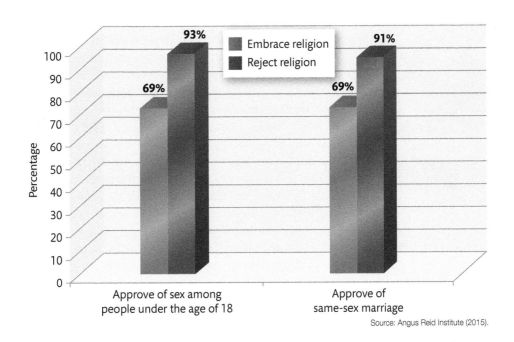

Source: Angus Reid Institute (2015).

Can a person's religious affiliation, or lack of it, give us any clues about that person's attitudes on sex and sexuality? In a recent survey of Canadian adults, 69 percent of those who described themselves as embracing religion and 93 percent of those who reject religion also said that they approve of sex among people under the age of 18. When it comes to same-sex marriage, 69 percent of those embracing religion and 91 percent of those rejecting it, approve. Clearly, people's values are not just a matter of personal choice; they also reflect people's social background, including their religious affiliation.

Chapter Overview

This chapter explores the meaning and importance of two major social institutions. First, the chapter identifies various forms of family life, explores the operations of families, and tracks changes in families over time. Then the chapter explains how religious belief differs from other types of knowledge, identifies types of religious organizations, and analyzes historical change in the importance of religion.

Andersen Ross/Blend Images/Getty Images

Rosa Yniguez is one of seven children who grew up in Jalisco, Mexico, in a world in which families worked hard, went to church regularly, and were proud of having many children. Rosa remembers friends of her parents who had a clock in their living room with a picture of each of their 12 children where the numbers on the clock face would be.

Now 35 years old, Rosa is living in San Francisco, attends a local Catholic church, and works as a cashier in a department store. In some respects, she has carried on her parents' traditions—but not in every way. Recalling her childhood, she says, "In Mexico, many of the families I knew had six, eight, ten children. Sometimes more. But I came to this country to get ahead. That is simply impossible with too many kids." As a result of her desire to keep her job and make a better life for her family, Rosa has decided to have no more than the three children she has now.

A tradition of having large families has helped make Hispanics the largest racial or ethnic minority in the United States and a substantial minority in Canada. The birth rate for immigrant women remains higher than for native-born women. But today, more and more Latinas are making the same decision as Rosa Yniguez and opting to have fewer children. Studies show that the birth rate for all immigrant women has been dropping for at least the past 10 years (Ubelacker, 2012; U.S. Census Bureau, 2012).

Families have been with us for a very long time. But as this story indicates, Canadian families are changing in response to a number of factors, including the desire of women to have more career options and to provide better lives for their children. It is probably true that the family is changing faster than any other social institution (Bianchi & Spain, 1996).

Religion is changing, too, as membership in long-established denominations is declining and new religious organizations are flourishing. This chapter examines family and religion, which are closely linked as society's *symbolic institutions*. Both the family and religion guide social life by setting standards of morality, maintaining traditions, and joining people together. With a focus on Canada, and making comparisons to other countries, we will examine why many people consider family and religion the foundations of society while others predict—and may even encourage—the decline of both institutions.

kinship a social bond based on common ancestry, marriage, or adoption

Family: Basic Concepts and Global Variations

(13.1) Describe families and how they differ around the world

family a social institution found in all societies that unites people in co-operative groups to care for one another, including any children

extended family a family composed of parents and children as well as other kin; also known as a *consanguine family*

nuclear family a family composed of one or two parents and their children; also known as a *conjugal family*

The **family** is *a social institution found in all societies that unites people in co-operative groups to care for one another, including any children.* Family ties also reflect **kinship**, *a social bond based on common ancestry, marriage, or adoption.* All societies contain families, but exactly who people call their kin has varied through history and varies today from one culture to another. Here and in other countries, families form around **marriage**, *a legal relationship, usually involving economic co-operation, sexual activity, and childbearing.*

marriage a legal relationship, usually involving economic co-operation, sexual activity, and childbearing

endogamy marriage between people of the same social category

exogamy marriage between people of different social categories

monogamy marriage that unites two partners

polygamy marriage that unites a person with two or more spouses

Today, some people object to defining only married couples or parents and children as families because it endorses a narrow standard of how to live. Because some business and government programs still use this conventional definition, many unmarried but committed partners of the same or opposite sex are excluded from family health care and other benefits. However, our society is gradually coming to recognize as families people with or without legal or blood ties who feel they belong together and define themselves as a family.

Like many European countries today, Canada has now joined the international trend toward acceptance of a wider definition of "family" (Beaujot, 2000; Fox & Luxton, 2001; Jenson, 2004), though this has not yet occurred south of the border where the U.S. Census Bureau uses the conventional definition of family. Statistics Canada no longer employs the traditional notion of family when collecting data on the Canadian "census family," which is currently defined to include "a married couple (with or without children of either or both spouses); a couple living common law (with or without children of either or both partners); a lone parent of any marital status, with at least one child living in the same dwelling" (Statistics Canada, 2011a). Until the 2001 census, when a question on "sexual orientation" was added, sociologists in Canada did not have access to accurate national data on gay families; the 2001 census was the first to provide data on same-sex partnerships. In 2001, a total of 34 200 couples—0.5 percent of all couples in Canada—identified themselves as same-sex common-law couples. The figure for 2006 was 45 300 same-sex couples and for 2011 it climbed to 64 575 (Statistics Canada, 2012).

How closely do people have to be related to consider themselves a "family"? In pre-industrial societies, people commonly recognize the **extended family**, *a family composed of parents and children as well as other kin*. This group is sometimes called the *consanguine family* because it includes everyone with "shared blood." With industrialization, however, increasing social mobility and geographic migration give rise to the **nuclear family**, *a family composed of one or two parents and their children*. The nuclear family is also called the *conjugal family*, meaning "based on marriage." Although many people in our society think of kinship in terms of extended families, most people carry out their everyday routines within a nuclear family.

Marriage Patterns

Cultural norms—and often laws—identify people as suitable or unsuitable marriage partners. Some marital norms promote **endogamy**, *marriage between people of the same social category*. Endogamy limits marriage prospects to others of the same age, village, race, ethnicity, religion, or social class. By contrast, **exogamy** is *marriage between people of different social categories*. In rural India, for example, a person is expected to marry someone from the same caste (endogamy) but from a different village (exogamy).

Bob D'Amico/ABC/Getty Images

What does the modern family look like? If we look to the mass media, this is a difficult question to answer. In the television series *Modern Family*, Jay Pritchett's family includes his much younger wife, his stepson Manny, his daughter Claire (who is married with three children), and his son Mitchell (who, with his gay partner, has an adopted Vietnamese daughter). How would you define the family?

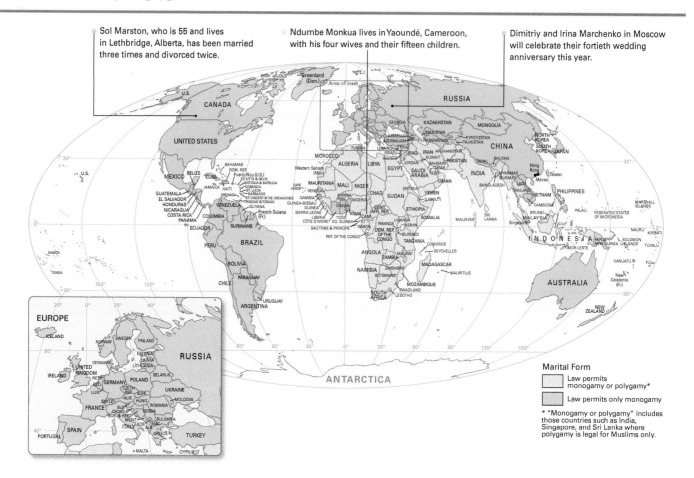

GLOBAL MAP 13–1   Marital Form in Global Perspective

Monogamy is the only legal form of marriage throughout the Western Hemisphere and in much of the rest of the world. In most African nations and in southern Asia, however, polygamy is permitted by law. In many cases, this practice reflects the influence of Islam, a religion that allows a man to have up to four wives. Even so, most marriages in these countries are monogamous, primarily for financial reasons.

Source: *Peters Atlas of the World* (1990), with updates by J.J. Macionis.

The reason for endogamy is that people of similar position pass along their standing to their children, clearly maintaining the traditional social hierarchy. Exogamy, on the other hand, links distant communities, builds alliances, and encourages the spread of culture.

In higher-income nations, laws permit only **monogamy** (from the Greek, meaning "one union"), *marriage that unites two partners.* Global Map 13–1 shows that monogamy is the rule throughout the Americas and Europe. But many lower-income countries, especially in Africa and southern Asia, permit **polygamy** (Greek, "many unions"), *marriage that unites a person with two or more spouses.* Polygamy has two forms. By far the more common is *polygyny* (Greek, "many women"), marriage that unites one man and two or more women. For example, Islamic nations in the Middle East and Africa permit men up to four wives. Even so, most Islamic families are monogamous because few men can afford to support several wives and even more children. *Polyandry* (Greek, "many men") unites one woman and two or more men. This extremely rare pattern exists in Tibet, a mountainous land where agriculture is difficult. There, polyandry discourages the division of land into parcels too small to support a family and divides the hard work of farming among many men.

Most of the world's societies at some time have permitted more than one marital pattern. Even so, most marriages have been monogamous (Murdock, 1965, orig. 1949). The historical preference for monogamy reflects two facts of life: Supporting several spouses is very expensive, and the number of men and women in most societies is roughly equal. Monogamy is also the dominant marriage pattern in Canada. However, there is a polygamist colony commune called "Bountiful," a community of approximately 1000 people just outside Creston in southeast British Columbia. This fundamentalist group broke away from the U.S.-based Mormon church or, officially, the Church of Jesus Christ of Latter-day Saints, in 1886 when the Mormon church disavowed polygamy. Polygamy is illegal in British Columbia, but until recently the government has adopted a hands-off approach to the community because of the guarantee of freedom of religion. In 2011, however, the Supreme Court of British Columbia upheld the polygamy ban, arguing that although such a ban infringed on constitutional rights and freedoms, the practice of polygamy was "inherently harmful." As Sean Ashley points out, the idea of "harm" was framed by the court in two ways: as harm to women who were cut off from their families, and moreover, as harm to society at large, in that polygamy may increase the number of single males who cannot find wives, leading potentially to other social problems (Ashley, 2014).

Residential Patterns

Just as societies regulate mate selection, they also designate where a couple should live. In pre-industrial societies, most newlyweds live with one set of parents who offer protection and assistance. Most common is the norm of *patrilocality* (Greek, "place of the father"), a residential pattern in which a married couple lives with or near the husband's family. But some societies, including the North American Iroquois, favour *matrilocality* ("place of the mother"), a residential pattern in which a married couple lives with or near the wife's family.

Industrial societies show yet another pattern. Finances permitting, they favour *neolocality* (Greek, "new place"), in which a married couple lives apart from both sets of parents.

Patterns of Descent

Descent refers to *the system by which members of a society trace kinship over generations.* Most pre-industrial societies trace kinship through either the father's side or the mother's side of the family. *Patrilineal descent*, the more common pattern, is a system tracing kinship through men. In this pattern, children are related to others only through their fathers. Tracing kinship through patrilineal descent ensures that fathers pass property on to their sons. Patrilineal descent characterizes most pastoral and agrarian societies, in which men produce the most valued resources. A less common pattern is *matrilineal descent,* a system tracing kinship through women. Matrilineal descent, in which mothers pass property to their daughters, is found in horticultural societies where women are the main food producers.

Industrial societies with greater gender equality recognize *bilateral descent* ("two-sided descent"), a system tracing kinship through both men and women. In this pattern, children include people on both the father's side and the mother's side among their relatives.

descent the system by which members of a society trace kinship over generations

Patterns of Authority

Worldwide, polygyny, patrilocality, and patrilineal descent are dominant and reflect the common global pattern of patriarchy. In industrial societies such as Canada, men are still typically heads of households, and most Canadian parents give children their father's last name. However, more egalitarian families are evolving, especially as the share of women in the labour force goes up. Nevertheless, while children now more commonly take both of their parents' last names, children very rarely use only their mother's last name when both parents are married and living together.

Theoretical Analysis of Families

(**13.2**) Apply sociology's major theories to family life.

As in earlier chapters, applying sociology's three major theoretical approaches offers a range of insights about families. The Applying Theory table on page 422 summarizes what we can learn from each approach.

Family	Structural-Functional Theory	Social-Conflict and Feminist Theories	Symbolic-Interaction and Social-Exchange Theories
What is the level of analysis?	Macro-level	Macro-level	Micro-level
What is the importance of the family for society?	The family performs vital tasks, including socializing the young and providing emotional and financial support for members. The family helps regulate sexual activity.	The family perpetuates social inequality by handing down wealth from one generation to the next. The family supports patriarchy as well as racial and ethnic inequality.	Symbolic-interaction theory explains that the reality of family life is constructed by members in their interaction. Social-exchange theory shows that courtship typically brings together people who offer the same level of advantages.

Functions of the Family: Structural-Functional Theory

According to the structural-functional approach, the family performs many vital tasks. For this reason, the family is sometimes called the "backbone of society."

1. **Socialization.** As noted in Chapter 3 ("Socialization: From Infancy to Old Age"), the family is the first and most important setting for child rearing. Ideally, parents help children develop into well-integrated and contributing members of society. Of course, family socialization continues throughout the life cycle. Adults change within marriage, and as any parent knows, mothers and fathers learn as much from their children as their children learn from them.

2. **Regulation of sexual activity.** Every culture regulates sexual activity in the interest of maintaining kinship organization and property rights. As discussed in Chapter 6 ("Sexuality and Society"), the incest taboo is a norm forbidding sexual relations or marriage between certain relatives. Although the incest taboo exists in every society, exactly which relatives cannot marry varies from one culture to another The matrilineal Navajo, for example, forbid marrying any relative of one's mother. Our bilateral society applies the incest taboo to both sides of the family but limits it to close relatives, including siblings, parents, aunts and uncles, and grandparents. In the United States, half the states allow first cousin marriages (sometimes with age restrictions), and half the states forbid such marriages.

Why does some form of incest taboo exist in every society? Part of the reason is rooted in biology: Reproduction between close relatives of any species raises the odds of producing offspring with mental or physical damage. But why, of all living species, do only humans observe an incest taboo? The answer is that controlling reproduction among close relatives is necessary for social organization. For one thing, the incest taboo limits sexual competition in families by restricting sex to spouses. Second, because family ties define people's rights and obligations toward one another, reproduction between close relatives would hopelessly confuse kinship ties and threaten social order. Third, by requiring people to marry outside their immediate families, the incest taboo serves to tie together the larger society as people look beyond close kin when seeking to form new families.

BananaStock/Thinkstock/Getty Images

Often, we experience modern society as cold and impersonal. In this context, the family can be a haven in a heartless world. Not every family lives up to this promise, of course, but people in families tend to be happier and live longer than those who live alone.

3. **Social placement.** Families are not needed for people to reproduce, but families do help maintain social organization. Parents pass on their own social identity—in terms of race, ethnicity, religion, and social class—to their children at birth.

4. **Material and emotional security.** Many people view the family as a "haven in a heartless world," offering physical protection, emotional support, and financial assistance. Perhaps this is why people living in families tend to be happier, healthier, and wealthier than people living alone (Goldstein & Kenney, 2001; Fustos, 2010).

EVALUATE Structural-functional theory explains why society, at least as we know it, is built on families. But this approach glosses over the diversity of Canadian family life and ignores how other social institutions (such as government) could meet at least some of the same human needs. Finally, structural-functionalism overlooks the negative aspects of family life, including patriarchy and family violence.

CHECK YOUR LEARNING What four important functions does the family provide for the operation of society?

Inequality and the Family: Social-Conflict and Feminist Theories

Like the structural-functional approach, the social-conflict approach, including feminist theory, considers the family central to our way of life. But instead of focusing on ways that kinship benefits society, this approach points out how the family perpetuates social inequality.

1. **Property and inheritance.** Friedrich Engels (1902, orig. 1884) traced the origin of the family to men's need (especially in the higher classes) to identify heirs so that they could hand down property to their sons. Families thus concentrate wealth and reproduce the class structure in each new generation.

2. **Patriarchy.** Feminists link the family to patriarchy. To know who their heirs are, men must control the sexuality of women. Families therefore transform women into the sexual and economic property of men. A century ago in Canada, most wives' earnings belonged to their husbands. Today, women still bear most of the responsibility for child rearing and housework (Stapinski, 1998; England, 2001; Benoit & Hallgrimsdottir, 2011).

3. **Race and ethnicity.** Racial and ethnic categories persist over generations only to the degree that people marry others like themselves. Endogamous marriage supports racial and ethnic inequality (Lynn & Todoroff, 1998; Mandell & Duffy, 2000, 2004).

EVALUATE Social-conflict and feminist theories show another side of family life: its role in social stratification. Friedrich Engels criticized the family as part and parcel of capitalism. But non-capitalist societies also have families (and family problems). The family may be linked to class inequality, as Engels argued, and to gender inequality, as feminist theory claims. But it carries out societal functions not easily accomplished by other means.

CHECK YOUR LEARNING Point to three ways in which the family supports social inequality.

Constructing Family Life: Micro-Level Theories

Both the structural-functional and social-conflict approaches view the family as a structural system. By contrast, micro-level analysis explores how individuals shape and experience family life.

Symbolic-Interaction Theory

Ideally, family living offers an opportunity for *intimacy*, a word with Latin roots that mean "sharing fear." As family members share many activities and establish trust, they build

According to social-exchange theory, people form relationships based on what each offers to the other. Generally, partners see the exchange as fair or "about even." *The Bachelor Canada* is a reality dating game show that follows a single bachelor who typically begins the show with 25 romantically interested women. By the end of the season, the bachelor is expected to select a wife by gradually eliminating the other women. How does this show reflect our society's views of romance?

emotional bonds. Of course, the fact that parents act as authority figures often limits their closeness with younger children. Only as young people approach adulthood do kinship ties open up to include sharing confidences with greater intimacy (Macionis, 1978).

Social-Exchange Theory

Social-exchange theory, another micro-level approach, describes courtship and marriage as forms of negotiation (Blau, 1964). Dating allows each person to assess the advantages and disadvantages of a potential spouse. In essence, exchange theory suggests, people "shop around" to make the best "deal" they can.

In patriarchal societies, gender roles dictate the elements of exchange: Men bring wealth and power to the marriage marketplace, and women bring beauty. The importance of beauty in this traditional system explains women's long-standing concern with their appearance and sensitivity about revealing their age. But as women have joined the labour force, they have become less dependent on men to support them, and so the terms of exchange for women and men are becoming more similar.

EVALUATE Micro-level theory balances structural-functional and social-conflict visions of the family as an institutional system. Both the symbolic-interaction and social-exchange approaches focus on the individual experience of family life. However, micro-level theories miss the bigger picture: The experience of family life is similar for people in the same social and economic categories.

CHECK YOUR LEARNING How does a micro-level approach to understanding the family differ from a macro-level approach? State the main ideas of symbolic-interaction theory and social-exchange theory.

Stages of Family Life

(13.3) Analyze changes in the family over the life course.

The family is a dynamic institution. Not only does the family itself change over time, but the way any of us *experiences* family changes as well as we move through the life course. A new family begins with the couple engaged in courtship and evolves as the new partners settle into the realities of married life. Next, for most couples at least, come the years spent developing careers and raising children, leading to the later years of marriage, after the children have left home to form families of their own. We will look briefly at each of these four stages.

Courtship and Romantic Love

November 17, Victoria, British Columbia. It is a typical late-autumn Saturday in the city. We are at the Interfaith Chapel attending the marriage of Jan and Nathan. Both are in their early twenties and beaming at their new status. On the surface, there is nothing at all unusual about the young couple. Their relationship is based on romantic love rather than an arrangement struck between their *parents or extended families, a practice still common in parts of the world. However, the new couple is different in at least one respect. Signifying the expanding role of the internet in both Canada and England (where Nathan comes from), the couple's courtship (which spanned several months) took place online. According to Jan, by the time she actually met Nathan in person, they were already planning their marriage.*

In rural areas of low- and middle-income countries throughout the world, most people consider courtship too important to be left to the young. *Arranged marriages* are alliances between two extended families of similar social standing and usually involve an exchange not just of children but also of wealth and favours. Romantic love has little to do with marriage, and parents may make such arrangements when their children are very young. A century ago in Sri Lanka and India, half of all girls married before age 15. As the Thinking Globally box on page 426 explains, child marriage still occurs in some parts of the world today. Currently, perhaps one in nine young women in low-income nations is married before the age of 15; about one in three is married before the age of 18 (Mayo, 1927; Mace & Mace, 1960; Population Reference Bureau, 2011).

Because traditional societies are more culturally homogeneous, almost all young men and women have been well socialized to be good spouses. Therefore, parents can arrange marriages with little thought about whether or not the two individuals involved are *personally* compatible because they know that the partners are being raised to be *culturally* compatible.

Industrialization both erodes the importance of extended families and weakens traditions. As young people begin the process of choosing their own mate, dating sharpens courtship skills and allows sexual experimentation. Marriage is delayed until young people complete their education, build financial security that will allow them to live apart from their parents, and gain the life experience needed to select a suitable partner.

Our culture celebrates *romantic love*—affection and sexual passion for another person—as the basis for marriage. We find it hard to imagine marriage without love, and popular culture, from fairy tales such as *Cinderella* to today's television sitcoms and dramas, portrays love as the key to a successful marriage.

Our society's emphasis on romance motivates young people to "leave the nest" to form families of their own; physical passion may also help a new couple through difficult adjustments in learning to live together (Goode, 1959). On the other hand, because feelings change over time, romantic love is a less stable foundation for marriage than social and economic considerations, one reason that the divorce rate is much higher in Canada than in nations where cultural traditions are a stronger guide in the choice of a partner. But even in our country, sociologists point out, society aims Cupid's arrow more than we like to think. Most people fall in love with others of the same race who are close in age and of similar social class. Our society "arranges" marriages by encouraging **homogamy** (literally, "like marrying like"), *marriage between people with the same social characteristics.* The extent of homogamy is greater for some categories of our population (such as older people and immigrants from traditional societies) than for others (younger people and those who live with less concern for cultural traditions).

homogamy marriage between people with the same social characteristics

Settling In: Ideal and Real Marriage

Our culture gives young people an idealized, "happily ever after" picture of marriage. Such optimism can lead to disappointment, especially for women, who have long been taught to view marriage as the key to personal happiness. Also, romantic love involves a lot of fantasy: We fall in love with others not always as they are but as we want them to be.

Sexuality, too, can be a source of disappointment. In the romantic haze of falling in love, people may see marriage as an endless sexual honeymoon, only to face the sobering realization that sex eventually becomes a less-than-all-consuming passion. Yet, as philosopher and sociologist Slavoj Žižek observes, fantasy, or the false perspective of the real

Thinking Globally

Early to Wed: A Report from Rural India

In a remote village in India's western state of Rajasthan, two families gather at midnight to celebrate a traditional wedding ritual. The ceremony will unite Sumitra Jogi, an 18-month-old bride, with her 7-year-old groom. It is May 2, in Hindu tradition an especially good day to marry. Sumitra's father smiles as the ceremony begins; her mother cradles the infant, who has fallen asleep. The groom, wearing a special costume and a red and gold turban on his head, gently reaches up and grasps the baby's hand. Then, as the ceremony ends, the young boy leads the child and mother around the wedding fire three-and-a-half times while the audience beams at the couple's first steps together as husband and wife.

Child weddings are illegal in India, but traditions are strong in rural regions, and laws against child marriage are hard to enforce. As a result, thousands of children marry each year. "In rural Rajasthan," explains one social worker, "all of the girls are married by age 14. These are poor, illiterate families, and they don't want to keep girls past their first menstrual cycle."

For now, Sumitra Jogi will remain with her parents. But in 8 or 10 years, a second ceremony will send her to live with her husband's family, and her married life will begin.

If the reality of marriage is years in the future, why do families push their children to marry at such an early age? Parents of girls know that the younger the bride, the smaller the dowry they must offer to the groom's family. Also, when girls marry this young, there is no question about their virginity, which raises their value on the marriage market. No one in these situations thinks about love or the fact that the children are too young to understand what is taking place (J.W. Anderson, 1995).

Although outlawed, arranged marriages involving children are still known to take place in traditional, remote areas of India. Depicted above is such a wedding ceremony held in a small village in the state of Rajasthan, India.

What Do You Think?

1. Why are arranged marriages common in very traditional communities?

2. List several advantages and disadvantages of arranged marriages from the point of view of the families involved.

3. Can you point to ways in which mate selection in Canada is "arranged" by society?

---

people in our lives, may even be required for marriages to work. Without fantasy, argues Žižek, sex would not be possible. Fantasy animates our desires and sex lives, as there is no purely sexual or physical relationship. Žižek helps us identify a paradox here: Fantasy, while necessary for sex, also undermines the very sex we can experience since the fantasy would end if it were ever fully satisfied (Žižek, 1997). It seems that sexuality and some disappointment are destined to go hand-in-hand, as there is no real marriage without its ideal counterpart.

Although the frequency of marital sex does decline over time, about two in three married people report that they are satisfied with the sexual dimension of their relationship. In general, couples with the best sexual relationships experience the most satisfaction in their marriages. Sex may not be the one key to marital happiness, but more often than not, good sex and good relationships go together (Laumann et al., 1994; T. W. Smith, 2006).

infidelity sexual activity outside one's marriage

Infidelity—*sexual activity outside one's marriage*—is another area where the reality of marriage does not match our cultural ideal. In a recent survey, 76 percent of Canadian adults said a married person having sex outside of marriage is "morally unacceptable." Even so, 12 percent of married, common-law, or living in a relationship Canadians indicated that they had been sexually unfaithful to their partners at least once (Forum Research, 2012; Pew Research Center, 2014).

Child Rearing

Despite the demands children make on us, many Canadians include at least one child in their vision of an ideal family. Today, however, few people in Canada, similar to their counterparts in a number of other countries, want more than a few children. This is a change from two centuries ago, when eight children was the Canadian average.

Big families pay off in pre-industrial societies because children supply needed labour. People therefore regard having children as a wife's duty, and in the absence of effective birth control, childbearing is a regular event. Of course, a high death rate in pre-industrial societies prevents many children from reaching adulthood; as late as 1900, one-third of children born in Canada died by age 10.

Economically speaking, industrialization transforms children from an asset to a liability. It now costs low-income parents more than $200 000 to raise one child, including university or college tuition; middle-class parents commonly spend about $300 000, and high-income families spend $500 000 and more (Lino, 2012). No wonder the Canadian average steadily dropped during the twentieth century to one child per family (Statistics Canada, 2007a)!

The trend toward smaller families is most pronounced in high-income nations. The picture differs in low-income regions in Latin America, Asia, and especially Africa, where many women have few alternatives to bearing children. In many African nations, as a glance back at Global Map 1–1 on page 6 shows, four or five children is still the norm.

"Son, you're all grown up now. You owe me two hundred and fourteen thousand dollars."

Parenting is a very expensive, lifelong commitment. As our society has given people greater choices about family life, more adults have decided to delay childbirth or remain childless. According to a report by Statistics Canada (2013a), since the data have been tracked in 1945, the fertility rate was higher for the first time in 2010 for women in their late thirties than in their early twenties. Canadians want to prioritize their families. About 85 percent claim that they would like to spend more time with their families (UBC News, 2012). For many families, including Rosa Yniguez's described in the opening to this chapter, having fewer children is an important step toward resolving the tension between work and parenting (Gilbert, 2005). The decline in fertility rate for Canadian women is not surprising given that young parents are raising families with less time and money than parents in the 1970s (UBC News, 2012).

Children of working parents spend most of the day at school or at daycare and many are *latchkey kids* who must fend for themselves (Child and Family Canada, 2003; Vandivere et al., 2003). Traditionalists in the "family values" debate charge that many mothers work at the expense of their children, who receive less parenting. Progressives reply that such criticism unfairly blames women for wanting the same opportunities men have long enjoyed.

Most Northern European countries provide generous family leaves and benefits, as well as public child care, to help ease the conflict between family and work (Baker, 1995). Changes in the Canadian Employment Insurance Act have brought the length of family leave (12 months as of January 2001) within the range of that found in the Nordic countries. However, the Canadian leave is accompanied by low benefits (55 percent of previous wages), compared to Nordic counties (Benoit, 2000). Even worse off are American parents. Congress took a small step toward easing the conflict between family and job responsibilities by passing the Family and Medical Leave Act in 1993. This law allows up to 90 days of unpaid leave from work for either parent to care for a new child or deal with a serious family emergency. Still, most adults in the United States have to juggle parental and job responsibilities.

Recent research shows that the countries with the highest participation rates of fathers in parental leave are those with non-transferable leave programs (i.e., if the father does not take the leave, the couple loses it) and high wage replacement rates, such as in the Nordic countries.

Sweden currently has a father's parental leave participation rate of 90 percent, while participation in Norway is 89 percent and in Iceland is 84 percent (Moss & O'Brien, 2006). One in five fathers claims parental leave benefits in Canada (Beaupré & Cloutier, 2007; Marshall, 2008). In 2006, Quebec introduced its own Parental Insurance Plan, which set aside a five-week non-transferable leave for fathers. Data show that 76 percent of eligible fathers in Quebec took some type of parental leave, compared with 26 percent of non-Quebec fathers (Findlay & Kohen, 2012). Reasons behind these cross-national and intra-country differences include the fact that males are generally higher earners than females, and families may be reluctant for the father to claim parental leave because of the greater financial load (Anxo et al., 2007).

The Family in Later Life

Increasing life expectancy in Canada means that couples who stay married do so for a longer time. By age 60, most have completed the task of raising children. At this point, marriage brings a return to living with only a spouse.

Like the birth of children, their departure—creating an "empty nest"—requires adjustments, although a marriage often becomes closer and more satisfying. Years of living together may lessen a couple's sexual passion, but understanding and commitment often increase.

Personal contact with children usually continues because most older adults live near at least one of their grown children. In 2011, there were about 7 million grandparents in Canada, with each having an average of 4.2 grandchildren. About 600 000 grandparents resided in the same household as their grandchildren. Of these co-residing grandparents, 12 percent lived in households where no parents or middle generation was present. A term often applied to these families is *skip-generation families* (Statistics Canada, 2015).

The other side of the coin is that adults in mid-life now provide more care for aging parents. The "empty nest" may not be filled by a parent coming to live in the home, but many adults find that caring for parents living to 80, 90, and beyond can be as taxing as raising young children. The oldest of the baby boomers—now reaching 65—are called the "sandwich generation" because many of them, especially women, will spend as many years caring for their aging parents as they did caring for their children (Lund, 1993).

The final and surely the most difficult transition in married life comes with the death of a spouse. Wives typically outlive husbands because of their greater life expectancy and the fact that women usually marry men several years older than themselves. Wives can thus expect to spend some years as widows. The challenge of living alone after the death of a

Andi Berger/Shutterstock

The experience of family life changes as we move through the life course. One important responsibility for many people as they move through middle age is caring for aging parents. In what ways does the process of aging change the relationship between parents and their sons and daughters?

spouse is especially great for men, who usually have fewer friends than widows and may lack housekeeping skills.

Increasingly, more married and common-law couples—including many same-sex couples—are not having children. They will also face the same problems associated with aging, but without the resources and support that caring children and grandchildren may provide.

Families in Canada: Class, Race, and Gender

(13.4) Explain how class, race, and gender shape family life.

D imensions of inequality—social class, ethnicity, race, and gender—are powerful forces that shape marriage and family life. This discussion addresses each of these factors in turn, but bear in mind that they overlap in our lives.

Social Class

Social class determines both a family's financial security and its range of opportunities. Interviewing working-class women, Lillian Rubin (1976) found that wives thought a good husband was a man who held a steady job, did not drink too much, and was not violent. Rubin's middle-class respondents, by contrast, never mentioned such things; these women simply *assumed* that a husband would provide a safe and secure home. Their ideal husband was someone they could talk to easily, sharing feelings and experiences.

Clearly, what women (and men) hope for in marriage—and what they end up with—is linked to their social class. Much the same holds for children: Boys and girls lucky enough to be born into more affluent families enjoy better mental and physical health, develop more self-confidence, and go on to greater achievement than children born to poor parents (McLeod & Shanahan, 1993; Duncan et al., 1998). A case in point is participating regularly in organized sport or lessons, with 17 to 25 percent of Canadian youth not doing so. Low household income is one of the strongest determinants of lack of participation (Brooker & Hyman, 2010).

Ethnicity and Race

As Chapter 11 ("Race and Ethnicity") discusses, ethnicity and race are powerful forces that shape family life. Keep in mind, however, that Aboriginal and visible minority families are diverse and do not fit any single generalization or stereotype.

Aboriginal Families in Canada

Over 1.4 million people, accounting for 4.3 percent of the Canadian population, identify themselves as Aboriginal (Statistics Canada, 2013b). This category is comprised of First Nations, Métis, and Inuit peoples who display a wide variety of family types. About half of all registered First Nations Indian status holders reside in one of Canada's 617 reserves. The total reserve population in 2011 was 360 620 people, with a majority of residents claiming some type of Aboriginal identity (McCue, 2011). Inuit and Métis people do not tend to reside on reserves, but in self-governing communities.

Generally, Aboriginal children under the age of 14 are less likely than non-Aboriginal children to live with both parents and more likely to live in non-traditional family arrangements. About half (49.6 percent) of all Aboriginal children, compared to three-quarters (76 percent) of non-Aboriginal children, live in families where both parents are present. Roughly one-third (34.4 percent), compared to one-sixth (17.4 percent) of non-Aboriginal children, reside with a single parent. A smaller number of Aboriginal children (2.7 percent) live in skip-generation families or with other relatives (1.2 percent). And about 4 percent of all Aboriginal children, compared to 0.3 percent of non-Aboriginal children, reside in foster care (Statistics Canada, 2013b).

Since the 1960s, the proportion of Aboriginal children placed in care by social agencies has increased dramatically. Currently, Aboriginal children account for 48.1 percent of all foster care children (Statistics Canada, 2013b). Their over-representation can be attributed to the decisions of judges to remove them from parents who cannot provide adequate care because of poverty, alcoholism, unemployment, inadequate housing, and other social conditions. Sometimes children are placed in foster care when social workers or police do not comprehend Aboriginal family practices (Sawchuk, 2011).

Recently, following the example of the Nisichawayasihk Cree Nation in Nelson House, the Misipawistik First Nation in northern Manitoba adopted a new approach in order to reverse the large number of Aboriginal children in foster care: Rather than removing the child from a dangerous or troubled home, they remove the parent—typically, a single mother. The child receives care from either the extended family or a respite worker, while the parents undergo counselling and treatment. The result is that most parents return within three months and children do not need to be apprehended (Mason, 2015).

When discussing Aboriginal family patterns, we have to also take into consideration the history and ongoing impact of colonialism. In 2015, the Truth and Reconciliation Commission (TRC) affirmed that the Canadian government committed cultural genocide against Aboriginal people. Throughout most of the history of this country, Canadian colonialism aimed at the "destruction of those structures and practices that allow the group to continue as a group" (Truth and Reconciliation Commission of Canada, 2015a:5). The TRC recognized that this was achieved through the seizure of Aboriginal lands, the forcible relocation of many Aboriginal peoples to reserves, the prohibition of Aboriginal languages and spiritual practices, and "most significantly" through the disruption of families "to prevent the transmission of cultural values and identity from one generation to the next" (Truth and Reconciliation Commission of Canada, 2015a:5). As is now well-known, the residential school system, aided by Christian missionaries, forcibly removed Aboriginal children from their families in order to assimilate them or, as Duncan Scott Campbell, Canadian Deputy Minister in charge of Indian Affairs from 1913 to 1932, maintained, "to kill the Indian in the child" (Truth and Reconciliation Commission of Canada, 2012).

Established around the 1880s, residential schools were home to tens of thousands of Aboriginal children until 1996, when the last school closed down. As described in Chapter 3 ("Socialization: From Infancy to Old Age"), the schools functioned as total institutions where children were subjected to involuntary resocialization through such techniques as forced confinement, harsh discipline, routine and regimentation, the suppression of cultural practices and Aboriginal languages, and even further family separation of brothers and sisters (Truth and Reconciliation Commission of Canada, 2015a). In addition, many of the children were neglected and abused and most were forced to subsist on inadequate diets and to live in poorly maintained buildings. The TRC estimates that at least 4000 children died while in the care of residential school staff.

The effects of this institution on Aboriginal families have been disastrous: With the separation of adults and children, traditional Aboriginal families began to erode. Upon return, many children could not communicate with their families due to the language policy of the schools. Having been exposed to a curriculum that undermined their Aboriginal identities and self-worth meant that the children were culturally dislocated. Furthermore, the abuse they suffered affected their ability to parent.

Given the legacy of cultural genocide in Canada, and the central role that family disruption played in it, it is not surprising that a number of TRC recommendations call for measures that are specific to children and families. Among its 94 recommendations are calls for such things as "culturally appropriate early childhood education programs for Aboriginal families"; the development of a "curriculum for all student clergy" that recognizes the role of Christian organizations in promoting "religious conflict in Aboriginal families"; and the requirement that "all child-welfare decision makers consider the impact of the residential school experience on children and their caregivers" (Truth and Reconciliation Commission of Canada, 2015b).

Visible Minority Families in Canada

Analysis of visible minority families must begin with the stark reality of economic disadvantage. The incidence of low income among families of visible minorities is significantly above the Canadian average (Statistics Canada, 2006). Immigrants who are members of visible minorities —even those who have been in Canada for an extended period of time—are at much greater risk of poverty than other immigrants. However, sociologist Peter Li observes that "over time, immigrants tend to improve their earnings and eventually reach a level equivalent to the average Canadian earnings" (2003:90). Current trends suggest that while an earning gap exists, family-class immigrants are expected to catch up in fewer years than did their predecessors.

Historically, Canada has attempted to secure a steady inflow of family-class immigrants. The recent changes to the family-class sponsorship program, a long-standing cornerstone of Canadian immigration policy, means that immigrant families are being divided. Currently, only 5000 parents or grandparents are admissible, and the minimum earning requirements for one to qualify as a sponsor have been raised. As some observers note, this reflects a shift to prioritizing the economic class of immigrants over the family class (Li, 2003; Go, 2013).

Visible minority families in Canada are varied. Indo-Canadian families tend to reside with extended family members, while this is no longer the case for Chinese families; families from Afghanistan insist on endogamous marriage for their children, while Japanese Canadians are more likely to marry non-Japanese Canadians (Ambert, 2012). And as some traditional immigrant community members attest, traditional values sometimes undergo negotiation when parental expectations clash with the more mainstream expectations of visible minority youth.

There is also another way in which visible minority families vary: As illustrated in Figure 13–1, the incidence of lone parenthood is higher among Aboriginal and black women than it is among Chinese women.

Visible minority families also experience various forms of racism. One example is in the housing market. Early immigrants to British Columbia, for example, faced hardships not only in finding work and maintaining their cultures, but also in obtaining property. Until the middle of the twentieth century, racially restrictive housing covenants kept Chinese, Japanese, Indian, and African immigrants from being able to purchase or rent real estate in a number of Victoria and Vancouver neighbourhoods (CBC News, 2014). Multi-family residences, constructed since the mid-1980s in the suburbs of Richmond and Surrey by Chinese and Indo-Canadian families, are currently igniting the racism of white neighbours who label these developments "monster homes." It is telling that this pejorative term has never been applied to mansions constructed by wealthy white families in North or West Vancouver. The so-called "monster home debate" has led to zoning-bylaw negotiations, linking families and property ownership to cultural and racial conflict (Madokoro, 2011).

Diversity Snapshot

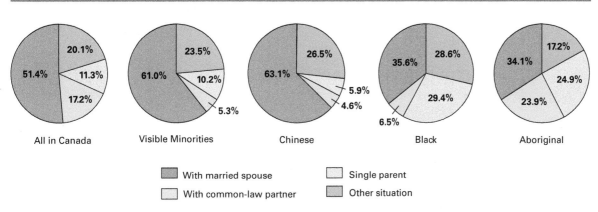

FIGURE 13–1 Living Situation of Females Aged 25 to 44 by Visible Minority and Aboriginal Status, Canada, 2006

Source: Statistics Canada (2011b). Population Groups (28), Age Groups (8), Sex (3) and Selected Demographic, Cultural, Labour Force, Educational and Income Characteristics (309), for the Total Population of Canada, Provinces, Territories, Census Metropolitan Areas and Census Agglomeration. [Electronic Data Base]. Catalogue no. 97-564-XCB2006009[1].IVT. 2011ag.] Reproduced and distributed on an "as is" basis with the permission of Statistics Canada.

Ethnically and Racially Mixed Marriages

Adrian Burke/Corbis

While interracial marriage has always been legal in Canada, values and norms ensured that such marriages were uncommon. Today, interracial marriages are less rare, but for most Canadians race and ethnicity continue to guide the process of courtship and marriage.

Most spouses have similar social backgrounds with regard to class and race. But over the course of the twentieth century, ethnicity came to matter less and less. Today, a woman of German or French ancestry might readily marry a man of Irish or English background without inviting disapproval from their families or from society in general.

As Chapter 11 ("Race and Ethnicity") shows, for the last 20 years, mixed-race unions have been on the rise. In 1991, couples in mixed-race unions accounted for 2.6 percent of all Canadian couples; in 2011, they represented 4.6 percent (Statistics Canada, 2014). Canadians are also more likely than their U.S. neighbours to endorse intermarriage. According to Reginald Bibby, 77 percent of Americans and 92 percent of Canadians approve of marriages between blacks and whites. Furthermore, in Canada blacks are actually more likely (43 percent) to form racially mixed unions than blacks in the United States (10 percent) (Bibby, 2007).

But while these are welcome developments, they still serve as reminders that race continues to divide and shape family life: The majority of Canadian couples, 95.4 percent, are in unions with someone of the same racial background, and black and white marriages still face prejudice in ways that Turkish and Polish marriages do not.

Gender

The sociologist Jessie Bernard (1982) says that every heterosexual marriage is actually two different relationships: the woman's marriage and the man's marriage. The reason is that few marriages have two equal partners. Although patriarchy has diminished, many people still expect husbands to be older and taller than their wives and to have more important, better-paid jobs.

Why, then, do many people think that marriage benefits women more than men? The positive stereotype of the carefree bachelor contrasts sharply with the negative image of the lonely spinster, suggesting that women are fulfilled only through being wives and mothers.

However, Bernard points out, married women actually have poorer mental health, less happiness, and more passive attitudes toward life than single women do. Married men, on the other hand, generally live longer, are mentally better off, and report being happier than single men (Fustos, 2010). These differences suggest why, after divorce, men are more eager than women to find a new partner.

Bernard concludes that there is no better assurance of long life, health, and happiness for a man than having a woman devote her life to taking care of him and providing the security of a well-ordered home. She is quick to add that marriage *could* be healthful for women if husbands did not dominate wives and expect them to do almost all the housework. Survey responses confirm that couples rank "sharing household chores" as one of the most important factors that contribute to a successful marriage (Pew Research Center, 2007, 2012a).

Transitions and Problems in Family Life

 13.5 Analyze the effects of divorce, remarriage, and violence on family life.

The newspaper columnist Ann Landers once remarked that 1 marriage in 20 is wonderful, 5 in 20 are good, 10 in 20 are tolerable, and the remaining 4 are "pure hell." Families can be a source of joy, but the reality of family life can also fall short of the ideal.

Divorce

Our society strongly supports marriage. A survey of Canadians found that getting married at some point in their lives is "very important" (47 percent) or "somewhat important"

(33 percent) to them (Bibby, 2004). In another survey, nearly all young people between ages 15 and 19 years planned to get married, and most of them said they expected to spend the rest of their lives with their future partner (Bibby, 2009).

Many of today's marriages, however, unravel. Figure 13–2 shows an increase in the Canadian divorce rate that started in the late 1960s (when the divorce laws were liberalized) and peaked in 1987 (when restrictions were eased on marital dissolutions). Demographers estimate that if the divorce rate remained as high as it was in 1987, 50.6 percent of marriages would end in divorce by the thirtieth wedding anniversary. The divorce rate gradually levelled off and the estimated number of marriages ending in divorce before the thirtieth anniversary decreased to 40 percent in 1995 and to 34.8 percent in 1997, but climbed to 37.7 percent in 2000. In 2008, the rate was 40.7 percent (Statistics Canada, 2006, 2011c; Kelly, 2012).

FIGURE 13–2 Divorces and Marriages in Canada, 1926–2008

Source: Statistics Canada, Health Statistics Division, Canadian Vital Statistics, Divorce Database and Marriage Database, http://statcan.gc.ca/pub/85-002-x/2012001/article/11634-eng.htm. Reproduced and distributed on an "as is" basis with the permission of Statistics Canada.

The United States has the fourth highest divorce rate in the world; it is about one-and-a-half times higher than in Canada. The high divorce rate of both societies has many causes (Furstenberg & Cherlin, 1991; Etzioni, 1993; Popenoe, 1999; Greenspan, 2001):

1. **Individualism is on the rise.** Today's family members spend less time together. We have become more individualistic and more concerned with our personal happiness and earning income than with the well-being of our partners and children.

2. **Romantic love fades.** Because our culture bases marriage on romantic love, relationships may fail as sexual passion fades. Many people end a marriage in favour of a new relationship that promises renewed excitement and romance.

3. **Women are less dependent on men.** Women's increasing participation in the labour force has reduced wives' financial dependency on their husbands. Thus women find it easier to leave unhappy marriages.

4. **Many of today's marriages are stressful.** With both partners working outside the home in most cases, people have less time and energy for family life. This makes raising children harder than ever. Children do stabilize some marriages, but divorce is most common during the early years of marriage when many couples have young children.

5. **Divorce has become socially acceptable.** Divorce no longer carries the powerful stigma it did just a few generations ago. Family and friends are now less likely to discourage couples in conflict from divorcing.

6. **Legally, a divorce is easier to get.** In the past, courts required divorcing couples to demonstrate that one or both were guilty of behaviour such as adultery or physical abuse. Today, all provinces allow divorce if a couple simply declares that the marriage has failed. Concern about easy divorce, voiced by many Canadians, has led some to advocate rewriting the marriage laws.

Who Divorces?

At greatest risk of divorce are young couples—especially those who marry after a brief courtship—who tend to lack money and emotional maturity. The chance of divorce also rises if a couple marries after an unexpected pregnancy or if one or both partners have substance abuse problems. People who are not religious are more likely to divorce than those who have strong religious beliefs. Finally, people whose parents divorced also have a higher divorce rate themselves. Researchers suggest that a role-modelling effect is at work: Children who see parents go through divorce are more likely to consider divorce themselves (Pew Research Center, 2008; Tavernise & Gebeloff, 2011; Copen et al., 2013).

Rates of divorce (and remarriage) have remained about the same among people with a college education and those with high-paying jobs. At the same time, divorce rates are increasing (and marriage rates have been declining) among those who do not attend college and among those with low-paying work. As the Power of Society section in Chapter 1 ("Sociology: Perspective, Theory, and Method") suggests, more disadvantaged members of our society appear to be turning away from marriage, not so much because they do not wish to be married, but because they lack the economic security needed for a stable family life (Cross & Mitchell, 2014). This trend shows how income inequality in Canada is affecting family life.

Furthermore, regional differences in divorce can be observed. In Canada, divorces are highest in Quebec and the Yukon and lowest in Nunavut and Newfoundland and Labrador. But the explanation is social rather than geographic: Regions with higher divorce rates tend to be ones where more social change occurs. Contributing factors are rural–urban migration, greater social mobility, decreasing religiosity, and the entry of women into the workforce.

Finally, men and women who have already divorced once are more likely to divorce than people who have married for the first time. Why? For many people the factors raising the odds of divorce follow them from one marriage to the next. Perhaps, too, having decided once to leave a marriage makes people more likely to reach the same conclusion again.

Divorce and Children

Because mothers usually gain custody of children but fathers typically earn more income, the well-being of many children depends on fathers making court-ordered child support payments called *alimony*. The majority, 97 percent, of alimony recipients are women, and the beneficiaries in 93 percent of all alimony cases are children. In 2010, the median monthly payment was $305. A study that evaluated alimony reported that across Canada, in March 2010, payment was received by 64 percent of recipients in full, 10 percent in part, while 26 percent did not receive any payment at all (Charron & Robinson, 2011).

In recent years courts have decreased the amount of sole custody they have historically awarded to mothers. In 2003, mothers were awarded sole custody of fewer than half (48 percent) of the dependent Canadian children for whom custody was determined through divorce proceedings. This is down from 75.8 percent in 1988. A similar downward trend also occurred with fathers. Custody of a child or dependant was awarded to the father in only 8 percent of cases in 2003, a drop from a peak of 15 percent in 1986. The other big change is that, in 2004, 46.5 percent of dependent children for whom custody was awarded had custody given jointly to the husband and wife, a continuation of a 15-year trend of steady increases in joint custody arrangements (Statistics Canada, 2008).

While all of the reasons may not be clear, recent research indicates that children living in post-divorce custodial households have higher incidences of behavioural or emotional problems than children living with both of their biological parents (C. Williams, 2002; Strohschein, 2005). Other research shows that children adapt better when their father remains an active parent, even if he is not residing in the same household (Allard et al., 2005). This involves non-residential fathers who are more than "Sunday daddies" and instead relate to their children as fully engaged parents who provide emotional and other support and take an active role in discipline (Ambert, 2009).

Divorce may be a solution for a couple in an unhappy marriage, but it can be a problem for children who experience the withdrawal of a parent from their social world. In what ways can divorce be harmful to children? Is there a positive side to divorce? How might separating parents better prepare their children for the transition of parental divorce?

Remarriage and Blended Families

More than half of all people who divorce remarry, most within five years. Nationwide, a substantial number of all marriages are now remarriages, at least for one partner. Men, who benefit more from wedlock, are more likely than women to remarry.

Remarriage often creates *blended families*, composed of children and some combination of biological parents and stepparents. With brothers, sisters, half-siblings, a stepparent—not to mention a biological parent who may live elsewhere and be married to someone else with other children—young people in blended families face the challenge of defining many new relationships and deciding just who is part of the nuclear family. Parents often have trouble defining responsibilities for household work among people unsure of their relationships to each other. When the custody of children is an issue, ex-spouses can be an unwelcome presence for people in a new marriage. Although blended families require a great deal of new adjustment, they also offer both young and old the chance to relax rigid family roles (Furstenberg & Cherlin, 2001; McLanahan, 2002).

Blended families are also formed when parents have children with more than one partner. As the rate of children in Canada born to unmarried parents rises (in 2006, it was 30 percent), the share of people who live in blended families is increasing (Ventura, 2009).

Family Violence

The ideal family is a source of pleasure and support. However, the disturbing reality of many homes is **family violence**, *emotional, physical, or sexual abuse of one family member by another*. With the exception of the police and the military, claims sociologist Richard J. Gelles, the family is "the most violent group in society" (quoted in Roesch, 1984:75).

family violence emotional, physical, or sexual abuse of one family member by another

Violence Against Women

In 2013, there were 87 820 victims of family violence and more than two-thirds (68 percent) of all family violence victims were female. The most common form of family brutality is intimate partner violence, in which women account for 8 out of 10 victims (Canadian Centre for Justice Statistics, 2015). Like most violent crime, intimate partner violence often goes unreported to police. Even so, as discussed in Chapter 7 ("Deviance"), the General Social Survey (GSS) measures people's experiences of violence regardless of whether it was reported to the police or not. According to the GSS, only 22 percent of incidences of intimate partner violence are reported to police (Brennan, 2011). The 2009 GSS findings estimate that 6.4 percent of women in Canada who are married, in common-law relationships, or in contact with their former partners were exposed to intimate partner violence over the five-year period predating the survey (Canadian Centre for Justice Statistics, 2011). The data, furthermore, revealed that victims and perpetrators were just as likely to be university or high school educated, upper or working class.

Historically, the law defined wives as the property of their husbands, so that no man could be charged with raping his wife. In the past, too, the law regarded domestic violence as a private family matter, giving victims few options. Now, even without separation or divorce, a woman can at least obtain court protection from an abusive spouse. Bill C-126, known as the Anti-Stalking Law, prohibits an ex-partner from following or otherwise threatening a woman (Statistics Canada, 1995). Further, communities across North America have established shelters to provide counselling and temporary housing for women and children driven from their homes by domestic violence. GSS data indicate that what we call "violence against women" is qualitatively and quantitatively different from violence against men, especially in family settings. Females are more likely than males to be victimized multiple times and to experience sexual assault, harassment, and murder by a family member. Overall, Canadian women are still more likely to be hurt by a family member than to be mugged or raped by a stranger or injured in an automobile accident. Also, the harm caused by domestic violence to women often goes beyond the physical injuries. Victims often lose their ability to trust others. One study found that women who had been physically or sexually abused were much less likely than non-victims to form stable relationships later on (Cherlin et al., 2004). Clearly, the idea that a family is a safe haven in a sometimes heartless and cruel world does not hold the same weight for women as it does for men.

Violence Against Children

Family violence also victimizes children. Because children have limited contact with the outside world, are dependent on their caretakers, and may fear reprisal from family members, the GSS also suspects that violence against children is even more underreported than violence against older victims. Keeping this in mind, 2013 police data reveal that 6700 children and youth were victims of family-related violence. About 4 out of 10 incidences resulted in injury, with physical assault being the most common type of family violence. Sexual assault was the next most common kind of violence committed against children, following other violent crimes, and kidnapping/abduction. While homicide tends to be rare (319 children and youth were victims of family-related homicide in 2013), 6 out of 10 children and youth were killed by a family member. Following the pattern of greater female victimization, female children were 1.5 times more likely to be victimized than boys, and were 4 times more likely in cases of sexual victimization (Canadian Centre for Justice Statistics, 2015).

Most child abusers are male; in 2010, males were the perpetrators of 79 percent of the reported incidences of family violence (Sinha, 2012). These men do not conform to a simple stereotype, but most abusers do share one trait: They were abused themselves as children. Researchers have found that violent behaviour in close relationships is learned (Levine, 2001).

Alternative Family Forms

(13.6) Describe the diversity of family life in Canada.

For the first time, since 2006, most families in Canada are composed of a married couple without children. In 2011, couples without children accounted for 44.5 percent of all families, while couples with children made up 39.2 percent of all families (Statistics Canada, 2012). Figure 13–3 shows the widening gap between these two family types. Furthermore, in recent decades, our society has displayed increasing diversity in family life.

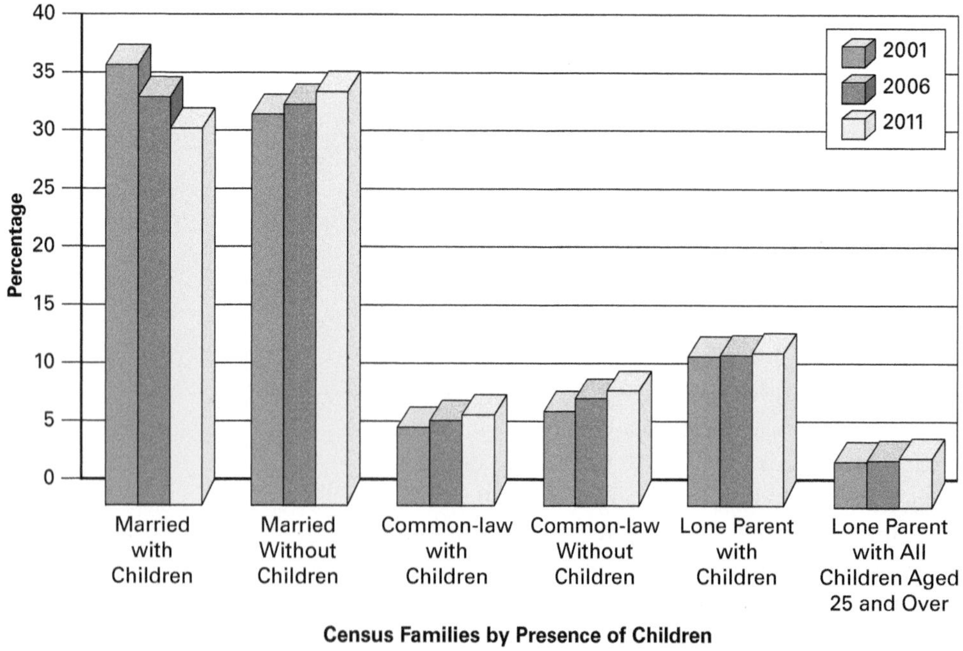

One-Parent Families

Lone parents represented 16.3 percent of all census families in 2011, which is just slightly higher than the 15.9 percent in 2006, suggesting a levelling out (Statistics Canada, 2012). Eight out of ten lone-parent families were headed by lone mothers. Female-headed one-parent families accounted for 12.8 percent of all census families in 2011. These families may result from divorce, death, or the decision of an unmarried woman to have a child. Men headed the remainder of the one-parent families (3.5 percent). One-parent families headed by men increased 16.2 percent between

FIGURE 13–3 Distribution of Families in Canada

In 2006, for the first time, there were more couples without children than couples with children. This pattern was maintained in 2011.

Source: Statistics Canada (2012). http://www12.statcan.ca/census-recensement/2011/as-sa/98-312-x/2011001/fig/fig1-eng.cfm. Reproduced and distributed on an "as is" basis with the permission of Statistics Canada.

2006 and 2011, more than double the growth of one-parent families headed by women (Statistics Canada, 2012).

Many one-parent families are multi-generational, with single parents (most of whom are mothers) turning to their own parents (again, often mothers) for support. In countries such as Canada and the United States, then, the rise in single parenting is tied to both a declining role for fathers and a growing importance for grandparents. By contrast, in countries such as Sweden and Finland, the increasing role of the welfare state in providing social services such as public child care significantly increases single parenthood but without an increased role for grandparents (Macionis & Plummer, 1997).

Research shows that growing up in a one-parent family usually puts children at a disadvantage. Some studies claim that because a father and a mother each make a distinctive contribution to a child's social development, one parent has a hard time doing as good a job alone. But the most serious problem for one-parent families, especially if that parent is a woman, is poverty. The Canadian Women's Foundation estimates that 21 percent of single mothers raise their children in poverty (2013). On average, children growing up in a single-parent family start out poorer, get less schooling, and end up with lower incomes as adults. Such children are also more likely to become single parents themselves (Popenoe, 1993; Blankenhorn, 1995; Kantrowitz & Wingert, 2001; McLanahan, 2002; Pew Research Center, 2007).

Cohabitation

Cohabitation is *the sharing of a household by an unmarried couple.* In global perspective, cohabitation as a long-term form of family life, with or without children, is especially common in Sweden and other Scandinavian countries and is gaining in popularity in other European nations. The prevalence of cohabiting couples in Canada increased substantially over the past three decades, from a low of 6 percent in 1981 to 16.7 percent in 2011 (Statistics Canada, 2007b, 2012). Setting a new record, the number of cohabiting families surpassed lone-parent families in 2011. Nearly half of such unions involve children, sometimes born within the common-law union itself or otherwise from a former relationship (Statistics Canada, 2012).

National Map 13–1 on page 438 illustrates the high proportion of cohabitation in Quebec, where 30 percent of all couples live in such a union, a rate similar to that in Sweden (Turcotte & Bélanger, 1998; Statistics Canada, 2002). Cohabitation is gaining in popularity in Canada, and as this trend continues it may influence the future number of one-parent families because common-law unions have a higher probability of dissolution than do formal marriages (Wu, 2000). According to one Statistics Canada study (2000), women whose first marriage ended in divorce tend to enter a new union, but are likely to opt for a common-law arrangement rather than marriage. The same holds true for women whose first union was common law: They are also likely to form a new relationship but tend to continue to live common law. So, while marriage may be less popular, conjugal unions continue to be popular among Canadians.

cohabitation the sharing of a household by an unmarried couple

Gay and Lesbian Couples

In 2001, the Netherlands became the first country to permit same-sex marriage. Since then, 19 countries have extended marriage—in name as well as in practice—to same-sex couples: Belgium (2003), Spain (2005), Canada (2005), South Africa (2006), Norway (2008), Sweden (2009), Portugal (2010), Iceland (2010), Argentina (2010), Denmark (2012), Brazil (2013), France (2013), Uruguay (2013), New Zealand (2013), Great Britain (2013), Luxembourg (2014), Finland (2014), Ireland (2015), and the United States (2015).

In the United States, Massachusetts became the first state to legalize same-sex marriage in 2004. Since then, 37 states and the District of Columbia had followed suit. In 2015, the United States Supreme Court ruled in favour of the right of gay and lesbian couples to marry.

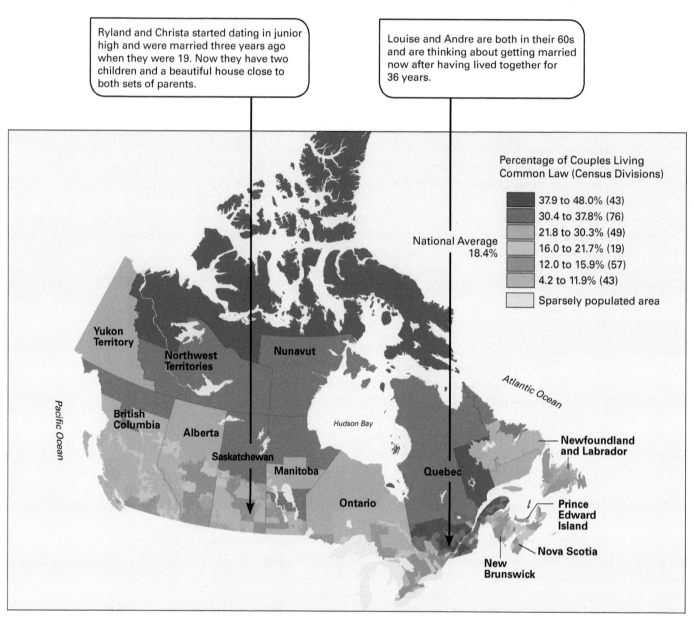

Ryland and Christa started dating in junior high and were married three years ago when they were 19. Now they have two children and a beautiful house close to both sets of parents.

Louise and Andre are both in their 60s and are thinking about getting married now after having lived together for 36 years.

Percentage of Couples Living Common Law (Census Divisions)

- 37.9 to 48.0% (43)
- 30.4 to 37.8% (76)
- 21.8 to 30.3% (49)
- 16.0 to 21.7% (19)
- 12.0 to 15.9% (57)
- 4.2 to 11.9% (43)
- Sparsely populated area

National Average 18.4%

NATIONAL MAP 13–1 Cohabitation Across Canada

Even though more than 18 percent of all couples live in common-law relationships in Canada, this percentage varies greatly across the country. One might think that it would be couples in urban areas leading the way in this trend. But as the map shows, it is Quebec and the rural areas in other parts of Canada that are at the forefront in this trend. The lowest rate of cohabitation, on the other hand, occurs in Southern Manitoba and in York, just outside of Toronto. What do you think explains the patterns you see in this map? Perhaps it is easier to explain why Quebec has a high rate than to explain the high rate in the rural areas.

Source: Estimated based on data in Statistics Canada (2011d).

In 1999, the Supreme Court of Canada held that same-sex couples must be granted essentially the same rights as married couples. In 2003, the Court of Appeal of Ontario held that homosexuals have a right to get married. The federal government decided not to appeal this and similar cases, and instead instituted legislation to the same effect. The federal government was forced to act after a series of court rulings struck down provincial marriage laws. Courts in Ontario, Quebec, and British Columbia have ruled that the exclusion of gays and lesbians unjustifiably violates equality rights. Gays and lesbians were allowed to marry immediately after the Ontario verdict, and did so, as a result of a new right denied to them throughout most of human history. Other changes have taken place as well. A bill in 2000 extended full federal tax and social benefits to same-sex couples, and some provincial benefit plans and employers have recognized same-sex unions in their private insurance plans. In 2000, British Columbia changed a variety of provincial statutes to grant same-sex couples the same rights and obligations as common-law couples. Meanwhile, the number of same-sex families has increased; between 2006 and 2011, their number grew by 42.4 percent, compared to a 4.8 percent increase for opposite-sex couples (Statistics Canada, 2012).

Some same-sex couples are conceiving using donated sperm (for lesbian couples) or a surrogate (for gay male couples), while others are raising offspring from previous heterosexual unions or taking the adoption route. Clearly, gay parenting challenges many traditional notions about the family. It also indicates that many gay and lesbian couples derive the same rewards from child rearing as heterosexuals do.

Gay couples can legally marry in Canada. Some are raising children from previous heterosexual unions, and some have adopted children.

Singlehood

While marriage is becoming less common, it still constitutes the most popular family structure. Married couples account for 67 percent of all families; cohabitation, which as has already been shown to be on the rise, is the second most popular family form, accounting for 16.7 percent of all families (Statistics Canada, 2012). As such, we tend to see singlehood as a transitory stage of life that ends with either marriage or cohabitation. In recent decades, however, more people have deliberately chosen to live alone. In the early 1950s, only 1 household in 12 consisted of a single person. This proportion had risen to one in four by 2001. In 2011, there were actually more unmarried Canadians than married Canadians: 46.4 percent of the Canadian population aged 15 and older was either married or cohabiting, while 53.6 percent were single (Milan, 2013).

The proportion of unmarried women in their late twenties has increased from 20 percent in 1981 to 67.4 percent in 2011. Similarly, the proportion of unmarried women in their early thirties has increased from 10.5 percent in 1981 to 43.4 percent in 2011 (Milan, 2013). Underlying this trend is the increasing number of women pursuing post-secondary education, which has pushed back the age at first marriage. Women who complete college or university are more likely to marry and marry later in life than women who do not (Kent, 2011).

By mid-life, many unmarried women sense a lack of available men. Because our society expects women to "marry up," the older a woman is, the more education she has, and the better her job, the more difficulty she has finding a suitable husband.

New Reproductive Technologies and Families

Medical advances involving new reproductive technologies are also changing families. In 1978, England's Louise Brown became the world's first "test-tube baby"; since then, tens of thousands of children have been conceived outside the womb.

Test-tube babies are the product of *in vitro fertilization*, in which doctors unite a woman's egg and a man's sperm "in glass" (usually not a test tube but a shallow dish) rather than in a woman's body. Doctors then either implant the resulting embryo in the womb of the woman who is to bear the child or freeze it for implantation at a later time.

Modern reproductive technologies allow some couples who cannot conceive normally to have children. These techniques may also eventually help reduce the incidence of birth defects. Genetic screening of sperm and eggs would allow medical specialists to increase the odds for the birth of a healthy baby. But new reproductive technologies also raise difficult and troubling questions: When one woman carries an embryo developed from the egg of another, who is the mother? When a couple divorces, which spouse is entitled to use, or destroy, their frozen embryos? Should parents use genetic screening to select the traits of their child such as sex or hair colour? Such questions remind us that technology changes faster than our ability to understand the consequences of its use. The Controversy & Debate box discusses the ethical dilemma surrounding a recent new reproductive technology: ectogenesis, or "genesis outside the womb."

Controversy & Debate

Ectogenesis and the Mother as Machine

Ectogenesis, sometimes referred to as "genesis outside the womb," refers to the process of fertilizing an ovum and then developing it in an artificial womb outside a woman's body (Colman, 2004). Direct ectogenesis on humans is not currently permitted but scientists have been testing the procedure on animals. Recent pioneering ectogenetic research by Dr. Helen Hung-Ching Liu at Cornell University in the United States and Dr. Yoshinori Kuwabara at Juntendo University in Japan suggests that Huxley's "brave new world" is close at hand. In 1997, Kuwabara developed an artificial womb made from a plastic box filled with amniotic fluid that was used to bring goat fetuses to term after they were taken from their mothers' wombs. The offspring developed complications due to respiratory problems and later died, but the experiment itself was deemed a major breakthrough. Liu has refined a procedure that allows an egg to be fertilized through in vitro fertilization and then implanted into an artificial uterus made of cells from a human uterus. Authorities intervened after six days of gestation because of legal restrictions, but had they not done so, it is highly likely that the fertilized eggs would have matured in the artificial womb and produced full-term newborns. Biomedical science thus promises a not-too-distant future when human ectogenesis will be a viable option.

Yet, as with other complex developments in new reproductive technologies, the social implications of ectogenesis have caused heated debate among ethicists and social scientists. One cause for concern has been its impact on reproductive rights for women and men. Ethicists, including Peter Singer and Deane Wells (2006), make their case in support of the procedure, arguing that ectogenesis could be regulated in the same way as other reproductive technologies and holds the possibility of sidestepping the abortion debate and enhancing reproductive equality between women and men. Radical feminists such as Shulamith Firestone (1970) have contended that ectogenesis could be a powerful tool to eliminate the fundamental biological inequality between women and men: physical pregnancy and childbirth. Firestone argued that eliminating biological differences between the genders was a fundamental prerequisite for gender equality in family life (Najand, 2010). Other researchers are less convinced that technological developments such as ectogenesis will have the desired long-range societal impact of gender equality in families. The evidence is clear that gender equality is premised not

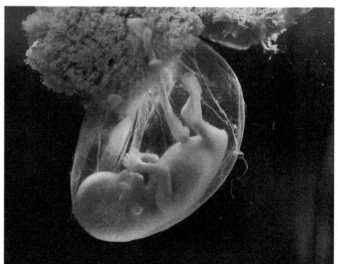

only on equal partnership in the home but also on the social context of other crucial factors, including access to postpartum support, child care, employment, wage equity, and health and social services (Saul, 2003). Irina Aristarkhova (2005) argues that feminist scholars need to challenge head-on the dichotomy between "mother" and "machine" that underlies the ectogenetic desire (the desire for reproduction external to the maternal body) among philosophers and scientists to enable a positive and ethical understanding of the maternal body within society.

What Do You Think?

1. What, exactly, are the social implications of ectogenesis?

2. How does this new technology apply differently to men and women?

3. Do you agree that "genesis outside the womb" is an ethical problem as well as a social problem? Why or why not?

4. In your opinion, should we support research on human ectogenesis?

Sources: Firestone (1970), Saul (2003), Colman (2004), Aristarkhova (2005), Singer and Wells (2006), and Najand (2010).

Families: Looking Ahead

Family life in Canada will continue to change in years to come, and with change comes controversy. Advocates of "traditional family values" line up against those who support greater personal choice. Sociologists cannot predict the outcome of this debate, but based on ongoing research on family patterns, we can suggest five likely future trends.

First, the divorce rate is likely to remain high, even in the face of evidence that marital breakups put children at higher risk of poverty. Today's marriages are about as durable as they were a century ago, when many were cut short by death. The difference is that now more couples *choose* to end marriages that fail to meet their expectations. Although the divorce rate has declined since 1980, it is unlikely that we will ever return to the low rates that marked the early decades of the twentieth century.

Second, family life in the future will be more diverse. Cohabiting couples, one-parent families, gay and lesbian families, and blended families are all on the rise. Most families are still based on marriage, and most married couples still have children. But the diversity of family forms reflects a trend toward more personal choice as well as people responding to economic challenges.

Third, men continue to play a limited role in child rearing. In the 1950s, a decade many people consider the "golden age" of families, men began to withdraw from active parenting (Snell, 1990; Stacey, 1990). In recent years, a countertrend has become evident with some older, highly educated fathers making the choice to stay at home with young children, many using computer technology to continue their work. In non-earner parent stay-at-home families (18 percent of all families) in 2009, 12 percent (or nearly one in eight) had stay-at-home dads, compared to just 1 percent in 1976 (Statistics Canada, 2010). But we should not overestimate the importance of this trend because the stay-at-home dad represents only a small minority of all fathers of young children. The bigger picture is that the high divorce rate in Canada, the continuing high rate of single motherhood, and the low involvement of fathers with their children after divorce are weakening children's ties to fathers and increasing children's risk of poverty.

Fourth, families will continue to feel the effects of economic changes. In many homes, both household partners work, increasing income but reducing marriage and family to the interaction of weary men and women trying to fit a little "quality time" with their children into an already full schedule. The long-term effects of the two-career couple on families as we have known them are likely to be mixed. In addition, in an era of low wages and decreased job security, more and more young people (many of whom continue to live with parents) do not feel that they have the economic stability necessary to marry and live on their own.

Fifth and finally, the importance of new reproductive technologies will increase. Ethical concerns about whether what *can* be done *should* be done will surely slow these developments, but new reproductive technologies will continue to alter the traditional experience of parenthood.

Despite the changes and controversies that have shaken the family in Canada, most people in our society still report being happy in their roles as partners and parents. Marriage and family life will likely remain a foundation of our society for generations to come, while family types become increasingly more diverse.

Religion: Concepts and Theories

13.7 Apply sociology's major theories to religion.

Like family, religion plays an important part in human society. Families have long used religious rituals to celebrate birth, recognize adulthood, and mourn the dead.

The French sociologist Emile Durkheim stated that religion emerges when human beings learn to distinguish the **profane** (from Latin, meaning "outside the temple"), *included as an*

religion a social institution involving beliefs and practices based on recognizing the sacred

ordinary part of everyday life, from the **sacred**, *set apart as extraordinary, inspiring awe and reverence.* Setting them apart is the essence of all religious belief. **Religion**, then, is *a social institution involving beliefs and practices based on recognizing the sacred.*

There is great diversity in matters of faith, and nothing is sacred to everyone. Although people regard most books as profane, Jews believe that the Torah (containing the first five books of the Hebrew Bible, also known as the Old Testament) is sacred, in the same way that Christians revere the Old and New Testaments of the Bible and Muslims exalt the Qur'an (Koran).

But no matter how a community of believers draws religious lines, Durkheim (1965:62, orig. 1915) explained, people understand profane things in terms of their everyday usefulness: We log on to the internet with our computer or turn a key to start our car. What is sacred we reverently set apart from daily life, giving it a "forbidden" or "holy" aura. For example, Muslims remove their shoes before entering a mosque to avoid defiling a sacred place with soles that have touched the profane ground outside.

The sacred is embodied in *ritual*, or formal, ceremonial behaviour. Holy Communion is the central ritual of Christianity; to the Christian faithful, the wafer and wine consumed during communion are treated not in a profane way as food but as the sacred symbols of the body and blood of Jesus Christ.

faith belief based on conviction rather than on scientific evidence

Religion, as a social activity, is a matter of **faith**, *belief based on conviction rather than on scientific evidence.* The New Testament of the Bible defines faith as "the conviction of things not seen" (Hebrews 11:1) and urges Christians to "walk by faith, not by sight" (2 Corinthians 5:7).

Some people with strong religious beliefs may be disturbed by the thought of sociologists turning a scientific eye on what they hold sacred. However, sociological study is not concerned with the truth or falsity of any religious doctrine. Sociologists study religion as a social institution, just as they study the family or the economy. Sociological analysis takes a worldly approach, seeking to understand what religions have in common and how they differ as well as how religious activity affects society as a whole.

Sociologists apply the major theoretical approaches to the study of religion just as they do to any other topic. Each provides distinctive insights about the ways religion shapes social life.

Functions of Religion: Structural-Functional Theory

According to Emile Durkheim (1965, orig. 1915), society has a life and power of its own beyond the life of any individual. In a sense, society itself is godlike, shaping the lives of its members and living on beyond them. Practising religion, people everywhere celebrate the awesome power of their society.

totem an object in the natural world collectively defined as sacred

No wonder people around the world transform everyday objects into sacred symbols of their collective life. Members of technologically simple societies do this with a **totem**, *an object in the natural world collectively defined as sacred.* The totem—perhaps an animal or an elaborate work of art—becomes the centrepiece of ritual and symbolizes the power of collective life over the individual. In our society, the flag is a quasi-religious totem that is not to be used in a profane way (say, as clothing or as a tablecloth) or allowed to touch the ground.

Similarly, the preamble in the Canadian constitution begins with the words "Whereas Canada is founded upon principles that recognize the supremacy of God." In addition, the line "God keep our land glorious and free" in the Canadian national anthem functions as a widely established totem that ties many members of Canadian society together.

Durkheim identified three major functions of religion that contribute to the operation of society:

profane included as an ordinary part of everyday life

sacred set apart as extraordinary, inspiring awe and reverence

1. **Establishing social cohesion.** Religion unites people through shared symbolism, values, and norms. Religious thought and ritual establish rules of fair play, organizing our social life.

2. **Providing social control.** Societies use religious ideas to promote conformity. By defining God as a "judge" of human behaviour, many religions encourage people to obey cultural norms. Religion can also be used to back up political systems. In medieval Europe, for example, monarchs claimed to rule by "divine right." Even today, our leaders publicly ask for God's blessing, implying that their efforts are right and just.

3. **Providing meaning and purpose.** Religious belief offers the comforting sense that our lives serve some greater purpose. Strengthened by such beliefs, people are less likely to despair in the face of change or even tragedy. For this reason, we mark major life transitions—including birth, marriage, and death—with religious observances.

EVALUATE In Durkheim's structural-functional theory, religion represents the collective life that helps hold society together. The major weakness of this approach is that it downplays religion's dysfunctions, especially the fact that strongly held beliefs can generate social conflict. Terrorists have claimed that God supports their actions, and nations march to war under the banner of their God. Social research might very well show that religious beliefs have provoked more violence in the world than differences of social class.

CHECK YOUR LEARNING What are Durkheim's three functions of religion for society?

Constructing the Sacred: Symbolic-Interaction Theory

From a symbolic-interaction point of view, religion (like all of society) is socially constructed. Through various rituals—from daily prayers to annual events such as Easter, Passover, or Ramadan—people sharpen the distinction between the sacred and the profane. Furthermore, says Peter Berger (1967:35–36), placing our small, brief lives within some "cosmic frame of reference" gives us the appearance of "ultimate security and permanence."

Marriage is a good example. If two people look on marriage as a simple contract, they can agree to split up whenever they want. Their bond makes much stronger claims on them when it is defined as holy matrimony, which is surely one reason for the lower divorce rate among people with strong religious beliefs. More generally, whenever faced with uncertainty or life-threatening situations—such as illness, natural disaster, terrorist attack, or war—many people find comfort in sacred symbols.

Religion is founded on the concept of the sacred—aspects of our existence that are set apart as extraordinary and demand our submission. Bowing, kneeling, or prostrating oneself are all ways of symbolically surrendering to a higher power. These Filipino Christians are practising self-flagellation in order to seek atonement for their sins in an annual Lenten ritual.

EVALUATE Using the symbolic-interaction approach, religion gives everyday life sacred meaning. Berger adds that the sacred's ability to give meaning and stability to society depends on ignoring the fact that it is socially constructed. After all, how much strength could believers gain from their sacred beliefs if they saw them merely as strategies for coping with tragedy? A major criticism of this micro-level view is that it ignores religion's link to social inequality, to which we turn next.

CHECK YOUR LEARNING How would Peter Berger explain the fact that deeply religious people have a low divorce rate?

Inequality and Religion: Social-Conflict Theory

The social-conflict approach highlights religion's support of social inequality. Religion, proclaimed Karl Marx, serves elites by legitimizing the status quo and diverting people's attention from social inequities.

Today, the British monarch is the formal head of the Church of England, illustrating the close ties between religious and political elites. In practical terms, working for political change may mean opposing the church and, by implication, opposing God. Religion also encourages people to accept the social problems of this world while they look hopefully to a "better world to come." In a well-known statement, Marx characterized religion as "the sigh of the oppressed creature, the sentiment of a heartless world, and the soul of soulless conditions. It is the opium of the people" (1964:27, orig. 1848).

Gender and Religion: Feminist Theory

Feminist theory explains that religion and social inequality are also linked through gender because virtually all the world's major religions are patriarchal. For example, the Qur'an, the sacred text of Islam, gives men social dominance over women by defining gender roles: "Men are in charge of women. . . . Hence good women are obedient. . . . As for those whose rebelliousness you fear, admonish them, banish them from your bed, and scourge [punish] them" (Qur'an 4:34, quoted in W. Kaufman, 1976:163).

Christianity, the major religion in the Western Hemisphere, has also supported patriarchy throughout history. Although Christians revere Mary, the mother of Jesus, the New Testament contains the following passages:

> A man . . . is the image and glory of God; but woman is the glory of man. For man was not made from woman, but woman from man. Neither was man created for woman, but woman for man. (1 Corinthians 11:7–9)

> As in all the churches of the saints, the women should keep silence in the churches. For they are not permitted to speak, but should be subordinate, as even the law says. If there is anything they desire to know, let them ask their husbands at home. For it is shameful for a woman to speak in church. (1 Corinthians 14:33–35)

> Wives, be subject to your husbands, as to the Lord. For the husband is the head of the wife as Christ is the head of the church. . . . As the church is subject to Christ, so let wives also be subject in everything to their husbands. (Ephesians 5:22–24)

Judaism has also traditionally supported patriarchy. Male Orthodox Jews recite the following prayer each day:

> Blessed art thou, O Lord our God, King of the Universe, that I was not born a gentile.
> Blessed art thou, O Lord our God, King of the Universe, that I was not born a slave.
> Blessed art thou, O Lord our God, King of the Universe, that I was not born a woman.

Despite patriarchal traditions, most religions now have women in leadership roles, and many are introducing more gender-neutral language in hymnals and prayer books. Such changes involve not just organizational patterns but also conceptions of God. The theologian Mary Daly puts the matter bluntly: "If God is male, then male is God" (cited in Woodward, 1989:58).

Mohamed al-Sayaghi/Reuters

Patriarchy is found in all of the world's major religions, including Christianity, Judaism, and Islam. Male dominance can be seen in restrictions that limit religious leadership to men and also in regulations that prohibit women from worshipping along with men.

EVALUATE Social-conflict and feminist theories emphasize the power of religion to support social inequality. Yet religion also promotes change toward equality. For example, nineteenth-century religious groups in North America played an important part in the movement to abolish slavery. In the 1950s and 1960s, religious organizations and their leaders were at the core of the civil rights movement. In the 1960s and 1970s, many clergy actively opposed the Vietnam War, and today some support any number of progressive causes such as feminism, the rights of migrants and refugees, and gay rights.

Applying Theory

	Structural-Functional Theory	Symbolic-Interaction Theory	Social-Conflict and Feminist Theories
What is the level of analysis?	Macro-level	Micro-level	Macro-level
What is the importance of religion for society?	Religion performs vital tasks, including uniting people and controlling behaviour. Religion gives life meaning and purpose.	Religion strengthens marriage by giving it (and family life) sacred meaning. People often turn to sacred symbols for comfort when facing danger and uncertainty.	Religion supports social inequality by claiming that the social order is just. Organized religion supports the domination of women by men. Religion turns attention from problems in this world to a "better world to come."

The Applying Theory table summarizes the three theoretical approaches to understanding religion.

CHECK YOUR LEARNING How does religion help maintain class inequality and gender stratification?

Religion and Social Change

(**13.8**) Analyze how religion encourages social change.

Religion can be the conservative force portrayed by Karl Marx. But at some points in history, as Max Weber (1958, orig. 1904–05) explained, religion has promoted dramatic social change.

Max Weber: Protestantism and Capitalism

Weber believed that particular religious ideas set into motion a wave of change that brought about the industrialization of Western Europe. The rise of industrial capitalism was encouraged by Calvinism, a movement within the Protestant Reformation.

Central to the religious thought of John Calvin (1509–1564) is the doctrine of *predestination*: An all-knowing, all-powerful God has selected some people for salvation while condemning most to eternal damnation. Each person's fate, sealed before birth and known only to God, is either eternal glory or endless hellfire.

Driven by anxiety over their fate, Calvinists understandably looked for evidence of God's favour in this world and came to see prosperity as a sign of divine blessing. Religious conviction and a rigid devotion to duty thus led Calvinists to work hard, and many amassed great wealth. But money was not for selfish spending or even for sharing with the poor, whose plight they saw as a mark of God's rejection. As agents for God's work on earth, Calvinists believed that they could best fulfill their "calling" by reinvesting profits and achieving ever-greater success in the process.

All the while, Calvinists practised self-denial by living thrifty lives. In addition, they eagerly embraced technological advances that promised to increase their workplace effectiveness. Together, these traits laid the groundwork for the rise of industrial capitalism. In time, the religious fervour that motivated early Calvinists weakened, resulting in a profane "Protestant work ethic." To Max Weber, the spirit that animated industrial capitalism was a "disenchanted" religion, further showing the power of religion to change the shape of society.

Liberation Theology

Historically, Christianity has reached out to suffering and oppressed people, urging all to strengthen their faith in a better life to come. In recent decades, however, some church leaders and theologians have taken a decidedly political approach and endorsed **liberation theology**, *the combining of Christian principles with political activism, often Marxist in character.*

liberation theology the combining of Christian principles with political activism, often Marxist in character

Liberation theology is a social movement that started in the late 1960s in Latin America's Roman Catholic Church. Today, Christian activists continue to help people in poor nations liberate themselves from abysmal poverty. Their message is simple: Social oppression runs counter to Christian morality, so as a matter of faith and justice, Christians must promote greater social equality.

Pope Francis has expressed support for the world's poor. He has also criticized global capitalism, calling it a "selfish ideal" that provides wealth by excluding large segments of the working poor (Cassidy, 2013). Perhaps the current pope will steer a different course than Pope Benedict XVI and Pope John Paul II, who condemned liberation theology for distorting traditional church doctrine with left-wing politics. In any case, the liberation theology movement has gained strength in the poorest countries of Latin America, where many people's Christian faith drives them to improve conditions for the world's poor (Neuhouser, 1989; J.E. Williams, 2002).

Types of Religious Organizations

13.9 Distinguish among church, sect, and cult.

Sociologists categorize the hundreds of different religious organizations in Canada along a continuum, with *churches* at one end and *sects* at the other, as shown in Figure 13–4. We can describe any religious organization in relation to these two ideal types by locating it on the church-sect continuum.

Church

Drawing on the ideas of his teacher, Max Weber, Ernst Troeltsch (1931) defined a **church** as *a religious organization that is well integrated into the larger society*. Churchlike organizations typically persist for centuries and include generations of the same families. Churches have well-established rules and regulations and expect leaders to be formally trained and ordained.

Though concerned with the sacred, a church accepts the ways of the profane world. Church members conceive of God in intellectual terms (say, as a force for good) and favour abstract moral standards ("Do unto others as you would have them do unto you"). By teaching morality in safely abstract terms, church leaders avoid social controversy. For example, many churches celebrate the unity of all peoples but say little about their own lack of social diversity. By downplaying this type of conflict, a church makes peace with the status quo (Troeltsch, 1931).

state church a church formally linked to the state

A church may operate with or apart from the state. A **state church** is *a church formally linked to the state*. For centuries, Roman Catholicism was the official religion of the Roman Empire, and Confucianism was the official religion in China until the early twentieth century. Today, the Anglican Church is the official church of England, and Islam is the official religion of Pakistan and Iran. State churches count everyone in the society as a member, which sharply limits tolerance of religious differences.

Churches ←————————————————————————→ **Sects**

Churches	Sects
• try to appeal to everyone	• hold rigid religious convictions
• have a highly formal style of worship	• have a spontaneous and emotional style of worship
• formally train and ordain leaders	• follow highly charismatic leaders
• are long-established and organizationally stable	• form as breakaway groups and are less stable
• attract members of high social standing	• attract members who are social outsiders

FIGURE 13–4 Church–Sect Continuum

Churches and sects are two opposing ideal types of religious organization. Any real-life religious organization will fall somewhere on the continuum between these two concepts.

church a religious organization that is well integrated into the larger society

sect a religious organization that stands apart from the larger society

cult a religious organization that is largely outside a society's cultural traditions

A **denomination** is *a church, independent of the state, that recognizes religious pluralism.* Denominations exist in nations, including Canada, that formally separate church and state. This country has dozens of Christian denominations, including Catholics, Baptists, Episcopalians, Methodists, and Lutherans, as well as various branches of Judaism, Islam, and other traditions. Although members of a denomination hold to their own beliefs, they recognize the right of others to have different beliefs.

denomination a church, independent of the state, that recognizes religious pluralism

Sect

Unlike a church, which tries to fit into the larger society, a **sect** is *a religious organization that stands apart from the larger society.* Sect members hold rigid religious convictions and deny the beliefs of others. Compared to churches, which try to appeal to everyone (the term "catholic" also means "universal"), a sect forms an exclusive group. To members of a sect, religion is not so much one aspect of life as it is a formal plan for living. In extreme cases, members of a sect may withdraw completely from society to practise their faith without interference. The Amish and Hutterite communities of Canada have long isolated themselves from modern life. Because our culture generally considers religious tolerance a virtue, members of sects are sometimes accused of being narrow-minded in insisting that they alone follow the true religion (Kraybill, 1994; P.W. Williams, 2002).

In organizational terms, sects are less formal than churches. Sect members may be highly spontaneous and emotional in worship, compared to members of churches, who tend to listen passively to their leaders. Sects also reject the intellectualized religion of churches, stressing instead the personal experience of divine power. Rodney Stark (1985:314) contrasts a church's vision of a distant God ("Our Father, who art in Heaven") with a sect's more immediate God ("Lord, bless this poor sinner kneeling before you now").

Churches and sects also have different patterns of leadership. The more churchlike an organization is, the more likely its leaders are formally trained and ordained. Sectlike organizations, which celebrate the personal presence of God, expect their leaders to show divine inspiration in the form of **charisma** (from Greek, meaning "divine favour"), *extraordinary personal qualities that can infuse people with emotion and turn them into followers.*

charisma extraordinary personal qualities that can infuse people with emotion and turn them into followers

Sects generally form as breakaway groups from established religious organizations (Stark & Bainbridge, 1979). Their psychic intensity and informal structure make them less stable than churches, and many sects form, only to disappear soon after. The sects that do endure typically become more like churches, with declining emphasis on charismatic leadership as they become more bureaucratic.

To sustain their membership, many sects actively recruit, or *proselytize*, new members. Sects value highly the experience of *conversion*, or religious rebirth. For example, Jehovah's Witnesses go door to door to share their faith with others in the hope of attracting new members.

Finally, churches and sects differ in their social composition. Because they are more closely tied to the world, well-established churches tend to include people of high social standing. Sects attract more disadvantaged people. A sect's openness to new members and its promise of salvation and personal fulfillment appeal to people who feel they are social outsiders.

Cult

A **cult** is *a religious organization that is largely outside a society's cultural traditions.* Most sects spin off from a conventional religious organization. However, a cult typically forms around a highly charismatic leader who offers a compelling message of a new and very different way of life. Researchers have counted as many as 5000 cults in North America (Marquand & Wood, 1997).

Because some cult principles or practices are unconventional, many people view cults as deviant or even evil. The suicides of 39 members of California's Heaven's Gate cult in 1997—people who claimed that dying was the doorway to a higher existence, perhaps in the company of aliens from outer space—confirmed the negative image the public holds of many cults. Also in 1997, the charred bodies of five people were found inside a house in Saint Casimir, Quebec. The three women and two men were members of the Solar Temple, an international cult professing the belief that such ritualized suicides lead to rebirth on a planet known as "Sirius." In short, say some scholars, calling a religious community a "cult" amounts to dismissing its members as crazy (Shupe, 1995; Gleick, 1997).

This charge is unfair because there is nothing basically wrong with this kind of religious organization. Many religions—Christianity, Islam, and Judaism included—began as cults. Of course, few cults exist for very long. One reason is that they are even more at odds with the larger society than sects. Many cults demand that members not only accept their teaching but also adopt a radically new lifestyle. This is why people sometimes accuse cults of brainwashing their members, although research suggests that most people who join cults suffer no psychological harm (Kilbourne, 1983; P.W. Williams, 2002).

In global perspective, the range of religious activity is truly astonishing. This woman in Ghana, celebrating the Kokuzahn voodoo festival, throws sand into her open eyes. What religious practices common in Canada might seem astonishing to people living in other countries?

animism the belief that elements of the natural world are conscious life forms that affect humanity

Religion in History

13.10 Contrast religious patterns in pre-industrial and industrial societies.

Like family, religion is a part of every known society. Also like family, religion shows marked variation over time and from place to place.

Early hunters and gatherers embraced **animism** (from the Latin, meaning "breath of life"), *the belief that elements of the natural world are conscious life forms that affect humanity.* Animists view forests, oceans, mountains, and the wind as spiritual forces. Many Native American societies are animistic, which explains their reverence for the natural environment.

Belief in a single divine power responsible for creating the world arose with pastoral and horticultural societies, which first appeared 10 000 to 12 000 years ago. The conception of God as a "shepherd" arose because Judaism, Christianity, and Islam all begun among pastoral peoples.

Religion becomes more important in agrarian societies. The huge cathedrals that dominated the towns of medieval Europe—many of which remain standing today—are evidence of the central role of religion in the social life of medieval agrarian society.

The Industrial Revolution introduced the growing importance of science to everyday life. More and more, people looked to physicians and scientists for the knowledge and comfort they used to get from priests. Did industrialism mean the end of religious life? As Durkheim saw it, "the old gods are growing old or already dead" (1965, orig. 1915:427). And yet, Durkheim also predicted that new gods would be born to replace the old. His theory maintains that religion persists in industrial societies because religion expresses the power of society itself. So long as human beings remain social creatures, we are likely to see religion represent the social world in symbolic form. Durkheim referred to the new religion of new industrial societies as "the cult of the individual."

Animism is widespread in traditional societies, whose members live respectfully within the natural world on which they depend for their survival. Animists see a divine presence not just in themselves but in everything around them. Their example has inspired "New Age" spirituality, described on pages 453 to 455.

Religion in Canada

(13.11) Analyze patterns of religiosity in Canada.

Compared to almost every other high-income nation in the world, as Figure 13–5 suggests, Canada is a relatively religious country (Inglehart & Welzel, 2010). But measuring the strength of religion in our society turns out to be difficult, as the following section explains.

Religious Affiliation

Not only do about 6 in 10 people in our society claim that religion is important in their lives, but as Table 13–1 shows, Protestants and Catholics are projected to remain the largest religious groups for the foreseeable future (Mata, 2010). At the national level, the largest religious group remains Catholic; 38.7 percent of Canadians identify with this religion and their membership has slightly increased over the decade. While Protestant denominations still comprised the second-largest major religious group in 2011, their numbers have declined along with their representation in the population, from 35 percent in 1991 to 26 percent in 2011.

Most of the decline in Protestant denominations during the last two decades took place within the largest six denominations, such as the Anglican Church and the United Church, with Baptists being the only group bucking this downward trend. The largest increases in religious affiliations occurred among faiths such as Islam, Hinduism, Sikhism, and Buddhism, reflecting the increasing numbers of immigrants from regions outside of Europe, in particular Asia and the Middle East.

By global standards, people in Canada and the United States are relatively religious; more so, for example, than Australians, Norwegians, Swedes, and Japanese. Just how religious we are, however, depends on precisely how one operationalizes this concept. Over 20 percent of Canadians in 2011 reported "no religion," a substantial increase from 1985, when the figure was 12 percent, and from 1971, when a mere 1 percent reported not having any religion (Clark & Schellenberg, 2006; Statistics Canada, 2013c).

Religiosity

Religiosity is *the importance of religion in a person's life.* According to the National Household Survey conducted in 2011, about 76 percent of Canadian adults identify with a particular religion.

However, the question "How religious are we?" has no easy answer, and it is likely that many people claim to be more religious than they really are. Overall, although most people in Canada claim to be at least somewhat religious, probably no more than a quarter actually are. Among those reporting a religious affiliation, an increasing number of Canadians report that they have not attended any religious services in the previous year. In 1986, 43 percent of Canadian adults attended religious services at least once a month; by 2010, that figure had fallen to 27 percent (Figure 13–6) (Pew Research Center, 2013). Further, there is a notable

religiosity the importance of religion in a person's life

Global Snapshot

- In general, people in higher-income countries, including Canada, are less religious than those in lower-income nations. The U.S. population is an important exception to this pattern.

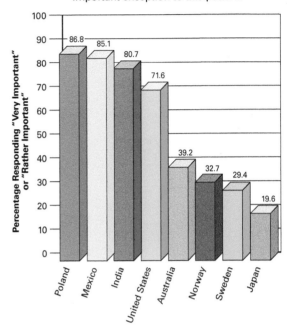

Survey Question: "How important is religion in your life?"

FIGURE 13–5 Religiosity in Global Perspective

Religion is stronger in the United States than in many other high-income nations. Canada holds a middling position. Sweden and Japan are comparatively unreligious.

Source: World Values Survey (2010).

Table 13–1 Religions in Canada, 2011 (percent)

Catholic	Other Christian	Muslim	Hindu	Sikh	Buddhist	Jewish	Other Religions	No Religion
38.7	28.6	3.2	1.5	1.4	1.1	1	0.6	23.9

Source: Statistics Canada (2013c)

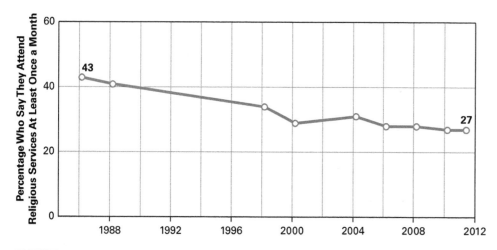

FIGURE 13–6 Religiosity in Canada, 1986–2012

Source: Pew Research Center (2013).

regional pattern regarding people who report a religious affiliation and/or attend religious services regularly. People from Quebec were the most likely to report religious affiliation, but also to report not attending religious services. People from British Columbia were most likely to not attend religious services, while residents of Atlantic Canada were least likely to not attend religious services (Clark & Schellenberg, 2006).

Keep in mind, too, that people probably claim to be more religious than they really are. One team of researchers, which recently tallied actual church attendance in Ashtabula County in northeast Ohio, concluded that twice as many people said they attended church on a given Sunday as really did so. Strong religious values in American society encouraged a "desirability" effect in the reporting of church attendance (Campbell & Curtis, 1994). In actuality, it is estimated that no more than 20 percent of the Canadian population actually attend worship services regularly, while another 58 percent attend at least once a year (Bibby, 2002). Finally, religiosity varies among denominations. In Canada, weekly attendance at religious services has declined significantly for both Catholics and Protestants since World War II, although in the past decade attendance has increased slightly among fundamentalist Protestant sects, a phenomenon that is much more pronounced in the United States.

Yet, in his book *Restless Gods: The Renaissance of Religion in Canada* (2002), well-known sociologist of religion Reginald Bibby maintains that there is a significant rejuvenation of religion currently under way in Canada, both inside and outside the churches. Bibby notes that the vast majority of Canadians are continuing to look to religion for answers to questions about the meaning of life, birth, suffering, and life after death. Sociologists of religion also note that the "nones," who claim no religious affiliation, are a diverse category that includes everyone from atheists and agnostics to non-observant Jews and Muslims. Social researcher Sarah Wilkins-Laflamme argues that we ought to consider that the nones might be "somes," engaging in spiritual practice and possibly in search for a religious identity. A fifth of the nones attend religious services once a year, and a third say that spiritual beliefs play an important role in their lives (Brean, 2014; Wilkins-Laflamme, 2014). Clearly, the question "How religious are we?" yields no easy answers.

Religion: Class, Ethnicity, and Race

Religious affiliation is related to a number of other factors. We shall consider three: social class, ethnicity, and visible minority status.

Social Class

In the nineteenth century, religion played a vital role in the Canadian economy. Religious membership established networks that affected job availability, income, and home ownership, ultimately shaping one's social class standing (Baskerville, 2001). Protestants of European background have traditionally occupied a privileged place in Canadian society, while Catholics—the majority from French backgrounds and residing in the poorer regions of the country, such as Quebec and the Atlantic provinces—have tended to be of more moderate social standing (Porter, 1965). Yet circumstances have changed recently: Quebec society has become more secularized and the population has experienced increased upward mobility, while at the same time the increasing religious diversity of Canadian society has challenged the once-dominant Protestant majority.

Furthermore, while most Canadians are religious, on average the non-religious have a slightly higher social standing. Those who have higher educational attainment are less likely to report religious affiliation. Research in the United States also confirms that atheists and agnostics have a higher social class standing (Statistics Canada, 2001; Pew Research Center, 2012b).

Ethnicity

Throughout the world, religion is tied to ethnicity, largely because one religion stands out in a single nation or geographic region. Islam predominates in the Arab societies of the Middle East, Hinduism is fused with the culture of India, and Confucianism runs deep in Chinese society. Christianity and Judaism do not follow this pattern; although these religions are mostly Western, Christians and Jews are found all over the world.

A dome-shaped hut serves as a sweat lodge in which prayer and purification are combined. Practised in a variety of ways by a number of Aboriginal peoples, the sweat lodge can be employed for such specific purposes as working out family problems, to cure illness or addiction, or to teach specific customs that allow for the strengthening of identity.

The link between religion and ethnicity also comes through in Canada. Our society encompasses Anglo-Saxon Protestants, Irish Catholics, Russian Jews, and people of Greek Orthodox heritage. This linking of nation and religious belief results from the arrival of immigrants from nations with a distinctive major religion. Still, nearly every ethnic category displays some religious diversity. For example, people of English ancestry may be Protestants, Roman Catholics, Jews, Hindus, Muslims, or followers of other religions.

Traditional Aboriginal spirituality is practised today only among 4.5 percent of all Aboriginal peoples (Statistics Canada, 2013d). Just as the major world's religions reflect ethnic and national differences, First Nations, Métis, and Inuit religions vary widely. Nonetheless, a few common themes can be identified. Many traditional Aboriginal beliefs feature, for example, creation and trickster myths. The trickster assumes a variety of forms (Coyote for Mohawks; a half-human-and-half-spirit being for the Cree, Blackfoot, and Ojibwa; and a spider for the Sioux) that represent a Great Spirit which steals an important resource. Creation myths are also varied, and account for the origins of the universe by, for example, representing the earth as being formed on the back of a turtle (Smith, 2012).

Race

Historically, the church has been central to the community and political needs of blacks living in Canada and the United States. Transported to the Western Hemisphere in slave ships, most Africans became Christians, the dominant religion in the Americas, sometimes blending Christian beliefs with elements of African religions they brought with them.

Slavery existed in New France, where in 1760 about 100 black people were held captive. The Catholic Church allowed black slaves participation in baptism, communion, and burial, while never objecting to, but rather facilitating, the institution of slavery (by, for example, baptizing the slaves with the last names of their white owners) (Winks, 1971).

By the 1870s, British Loyalists, resettling from the United States, arrived with thousands of free and enslaved blacks. Most free blacks chose Nova Scotia as a destination, where the racism of whites relegated them to sharecropping and low-pay menial jobs. The majority of the black Loyalist settlers were Anglican, Methodist, and Baptist. Finding themselves second-class members of these churches led them to establish their own religious organizations (Gillard, 1998). As black people migrated from the rural South to the industrial cities of the North, and some as far afield as eastern Canada, the church played a key role in addressing problems of dislocation, poverty, and prejudice. Further, black churches have provided an important avenue of achievement for talented men and women. In the United States, Ralph Abernathy, Martin Luther King, Jr., and Jesse Jackson have all achieved world recognition for their work as religious leaders.

Religiosity also varies by immigrant status. Compared with people born in Canada, recent immigrants have a higher degree of religiosity, offsetting somewhat the growing secular trend. Immigrants coming from South Asia (e.g., India and Pakistan), Southeast Asia (e.g., the Philippines), and the Caribbean and Central and South America report the highest religiosity while the lowest level of religiosity is found among immigrants from East Asia (e.g., China and Japan) and Western, Northern, and Eastern Europe (Clark & Schellenberg, 2006).

Religion in a Changing Society

(13.12) Discuss recent trends in religious life.

Like family life, religion is also changing in Canada. In the following sections, we look at two major aspects of change: changing affiliations over time and the process of secularization.

Changing Affiliation

A lot of change is going on in the world of religion. Membership in established mainstream churches such as the Episcopalian and Presbyterian denominations has fallen dramatically. At the same time, other religious categories, from the New Age spiritual movement, Hare Krishna, and Scientology to Hinduism, Islam, Sikhism, and Buddhism, have increased in popularity. Another dynamic aspect of religion is that people are moving from one religious organization to another. A survey in the United States by the Pew Forum on Religion and Public Life (2008) reveals that 44 percent of adults report having switched religious affiliation at some point in their lives. The pattern of being born and raised with a religious affiliation one keeps throughout one's life is no longer the case. When we add in those who have moved away from religion altogether, the pattern by which people are born and raised with a religious affiliation they keep throughout their lives is no longer the case for at least half of the U.S. population.

Such personal changes mean that religious organizations experience a pattern of people coming and going. For some time, for example, Catholics have represented almost one-fourth of the American adult population. But this fairly stable statistic hides the fact that about one-third of all people raised Catholic have left the church. At the same time, about the same number of people—including many immigrants—have joined this church. A more extreme example is the Jehovah's Witnesses: Two-thirds of the people raised in this church have left, but their numbers have been more than replaced by converts recruited by members who travel from door to door spreading their message.

secularization the historical decline in the importance of the supernatural and the sacred

Secularization

If people are less connected to the religious organization of their childhood, should we conclude that religion is getting weaker? Investigating this question brings us to the concept of **secularization**, *the historical decline in the importance of the supernatural and the sacred.* Secularization (from a Latin word for "worldly," meaning literally "of the present age") is commonly associated with modern, technologically advanced societies in which science is the major way of understanding.

Today, we are more likely to experience the transitions of birth, illness, and death in the presence of physicians (people with scientific knowledge) than church leaders (whose knowledge is based on faith). This shift alone suggests that

In the last 50 years, traditional "mainstream" religious organizations have lost about half their membership. But during this same period, non-Christian religions and new spiritual movements have increased their membership.

religion's importance for our everyday lives has declined. Harvey Cox (1971:3, orig. 1965) explains:

> The world looks less and less to religious rules and rituals for its morality or its meanings. For some [people] religion provides a hobby, for others a mark of national or ethnic identification, for still others an aesthetic delight. For fewer and fewer does it provide an inclusive and commanding system of personal and cosmic values and explanations.

If Cox is right, should we expect religion to disappear someday? Some analysts point to survey data that show that the share of our adult population claiming no religious affiliation has increased from about 10 percent in the 1980s to about 25 percent today. Cross-national surveys carried out in 30 nations show a similar pattern, documenting an increasing share of people who identify as atheists (those who claim no divine power exists) in 23 of the 30 nations (Pew Research Center, 2012b; Smith, 2012; Brean, 2014).

Other analysts point to the fact that some dimensions of religion (such as belief in life after death) may have declined, but others (such as religious affiliation) have increased, especially for certain minority groups (Bibby, 2002). We should also be attentive to variation over time and differences across age groups. While between 1985 and 1995 religious non-attendance rates of Canadians expressing a religious affiliation increased across all age groups, in 2004 there was a slight decrease in non-attendance across all age groups apart from those over 60 years (Clark & Schellenberg, 2006).

Everyone sees religious change; what people disagree about is whether this change is good or bad. Conservatives see any weakening of religion as a mark of moral decline. Progressives view secularization as liberation from the dictatorial beliefs of the past, giving people greater choice about what to believe. Secularization has also brought many traditional religious practices, such as ordaining only men, into line with modern social attitudes that support greater gender equality.

According to the secularization thesis, religion should weaken in high-income nations as people enjoy higher living standards and greater security. A global perspective shows that this thesis holds for the nations of Western Europe, where most measures of religiosity have declined and are now low. In Canada, religious affiliation has declined somewhat and at the same time become increasingly diversified. In contrast, the United States, the richest country of all, is an exception; religion remains quite strong there.

Civil Religion

One dimension of secularization is what Robert Bellah (1975) calls **civil religion**, *a quasi-religious loyalty binding individuals in a basically secular society.* In other words, formal religion may lose power, but citizenship has its own religious qualities. Most people in the United States consider their way of life a force for moral good in the world. Some Canadians express similar sentiments. Many people also find religious qualities in political movements, whether liberal or conservative (Williams & Demerath, 1991).

civil religion a quasi-religious loyalty linking individuals in a basically secular society

Civil religion involves a range of rituals, from standing to sing the national anthem at sporting events to waving the flag at public parades. At all such events, the Canadian flag serves as a sacred symbol of national identity, and most members of our society expect people to treat it with respect.

"New Age" Seekers: Spirituality Without Formal Religion

December 29, Machu Picchu, Peru. We are ending the first day exploring this magnificent city built by the Inca people at the top of the Andes Mountains. Lucas, a local shaman, or religious leader, is leading 12 members of our tour group in a ceremony of thanks. He kneels on the dirt floor of the small stone building and reverently places offerings—corn and beans, sugar, plants of all colours, and even bits of gold and

In recent decades, an increasing number of people have sought spiritual development outside of established religious organizations. This trend has led some analysts to conclude that Canada is becoming a *postdenominational society*. In simple terms, a small but increasing share of people seem to be spiritual seekers, believing in a vital spiritual dimension to human existence that they pursue more or less separately from any formal denomination.

What exactly is the difference between this so-called New Age focus on spirituality and a traditional concern with religion? As one analysis (Cimino & Lattin, 1999:62) puts it, spirituality is

> the search for . . . a religion of the heart, not the head. It . . . downplays doctrine and dogma, and revels in direct experience of the divine—whether it's called the "holy spirit" or "divine consciousness" or "true self." It's practical and personal, more about stress reduction than salvation, more therapeutic than theological. It's about feeling good rather than being good. It's as much about the body as the soul.

Millions of people across North America today take part in New Age spirituality. The following six core values define the New Age religious movement (Wesselman, 2001:39–42; Walsh, 2012):

1. **Seekers believe in a higher power.** There exists a higher power, a vital force that is within all things and all people. Each of us, then, is partly divine, just as the divine spirit exists everywhere in the world around us.

2. **Seekers believe we are all connected.** Because "spirit" is everywhere in the universe, everything and everyone are interconnected. As New Agers like to say, "We are all one."

3. **Seekers believe in a spirit world.** The physical world we perceive with our five senses is not all there is; more important is the existence of a spiritual reality or "spirit world."

4. **Seekers want to experience the spirit world.** Spiritual development means gaining the ability to experience the spirit world. Many seekers come to understand that helpers and teachers (in some traditions, called "angels") dwell in the spirit world and can touch their lives.

5. **Seekers pursue transcendence.** Various techniques (such as yoga, meditation, and prayer) give people an increasing ability to rise above the immediate physical world (the experience of "transcendence"), which seekers believe to be the larger purpose of life.

6. **Some seekers pursue political change.** While for some seekers spirituality means a turning from the ways of this world, for others spirituality demands seeking both political change to end the destruction of the natural environment and an economic system that is based on competition rather than co-operation.

From a traditional point of view, this New Age concern with spirituality may seem more like psychology than religion. Perhaps it would be fair to say that New Age spirituality combines elements of rationality (an emphasis on individualism as well as tolerance and pluralism)

Artist William Perehudoff as published in a Pictorial History of the Doukhobors (1969, copyright Modern Press) by Koozma Tarasoff

Terry McLean's *The Arms Burning of 1895* (1977) depicts the life-changing experience by which many people of Doukhobor ancestry publicly burned their weapons, effectively combining pacifism with Christianity. The burning of arms has been reenacted by Canadian Doukhobors as a reminder of this sect's nonviolent commitments.

with a spiritual focus (searching for meaning beyond our everyday concerns). It is this combination that makes New Age seeking particularly popular in the modern world (Tucker, 2002; Besecke, 2003, 2005).

Religious Revival: "Good Old-Time Religion"

At the same time as New Age spirituality is flourishing, a great deal of change has been going on in the world of organized religion. As noted earlier, membership in established, mainstream churches has plummeted. The largest decline occurred among Presbyterians, whose numbers fell 36 percent in the 1990s. Pentecostals recorded the second-largest drop in membership, falling 15 percent across the decade. The number of United Church adherents declined 8 percent, Anglicans declined 7 percent, and Lutherans declined 5 percent. During the same period, affiliation with other religious organizations (including Evangelical Missionary Church, Hutterites, Adventists, and Christian and Missionary Alliance) has risen just as dramatically. Since the 1950s, weekly attendance at conservative evangelical churches in Canada has increased from 700 000 to 1.5 million (Bibby, 2002).

These opposing trends suggest that secularization itself may be self-limiting: As churchlike organizations become more worldly, many people leave them in favour of sectlike communities offering a more intense religious experience (Roof & McKinney, 1987; Jacquet & Jones, 1991; Iannaccone, 1994; Hout, Greeley, & Wilde, 2001).

One striking religious trend today is the growth of **fundamentalism**, *a conservative religious doctrine that opposes intellectualism and worldly accommodation in favour of restoring traditional, otherworldly religion*. In the United States, fundamentalism has made the greatest gains among Protestants. Southern Baptists, for example, are the largest Protestant religious community in the United States. But fundamentalist groups have also grown among Roman Catholics, Jews, and Muslims.

Religious "fundamentalism" such as that of the Fundamentalist Church of Jesus Christ of Latter-day Saints has mainly emerged in parts of Alberta and British Columbia, reflecting the somewhat moralistic social values (for example, anti–gay rights, traditional gender roles) and conservative political views articulated more often in Alberta and British Columbia than in other provinces. Yet the flavour of conservative Protestantism found there tends to be less evangelical and all-encompassing than the religious fundamentalism south of the Canadian border (Dawson, 1998).

In response to what they see as the growing influence of science and the weakening of the conventional family, religious fundamentalists defend what they call "traditional values." As they see it, liberal churches are simply too open to compromise and change. Religious fundamentalism is distinctive in five ways (Hunter, 1983, 1985, 1987):

1. **Fundamentalists take the words of sacred texts literally.** Fundamentalists insist on a literal reading of sacred texts such as the Bible to counter what they see as excessive intellectualism among more liberal religious organizations. For example, fundamentalist Christians believe that God created the world in seven days precisely as described in the biblical book of Genesis.

2. **Fundamentalists reject religious pluralism.** Fundamentalists believe that tolerance and relativism water down personal faith. Therefore, they maintain that their religious beliefs are true and other beliefs are not.

3. **Fundamentalists pursue the personal experience of God's presence.** In contrast to the worldliness and intellectualism of other religious organizations, fundamentalists encourage a return to "good old-time religion" and spiritual revival. Among fundamentalist Christians, being "born again" and having a personal relationship with Jesus Christ should be evident in a person's everyday life.

4. **Fundamentalists oppose "secular humanism."** Fundamentalists think accommodation to the changing world weakens religious faith. They reject "secular humanism," our society's tendency to look to scientific experts rather than God for guidance about how to live. There is nothing new in this tension between science and religion, as the Controversy & Debate box on page 457 explains.

fundamentalism a conservative religious doctrine that opposes intellectualism and worldly accommodation in favour of restoring traditional, otherworldly religion

5. **Many fundamentalists endorse conservative political goals.** Although fundamentalism tends to back away from worldly concerns, some fundamentalist leaders have entered politics to oppose the "liberal agenda," including feminism and gay rights. Fundamentalists oppose abortion, same-sex marriage, high levels of immigration, and evolutionary science; they support the traditional two-parent family, seek a return of prayer in schools along with a teaching of creationism, and criticize the mass media for approaching stories from a liberal viewpoint. Christian fundamentalist elements could be found in the social conservatism of the former federal political party, the Canadian Alliance, which in 2003 merged with the Conservative Party of Canada.

Opponents regard fundamentalism as judgmental, rigid, and self-righteous. But many believers find in fundamentalism, with its greater religious certainty and emphasis on experiencing God's presence, an appealing alternative to the more intellectual, tolerant, and worldly "mainstream" denominations (Marquand, 1997).

Which religious organizations are fundamentalist? In recent years, the world has become aware of an extreme form of fundamentalist Islam that supports violence directed against Western culture. In North America, the term is most commonly applied to conservative Christian organizations in the evangelical tradition, including Pentecostals, Southern Baptists, Seventh-Day Adventists, and the Assemblies of God. Several national religious movements, including Promise Keepers (a men's organization) and Chosen Women, have a fundamentalist orientation. In national surveys, 25 percent of U.S. adults describe their religious upbringing as "fundamentalist," 40 percent claim a "moderate" religious upbringing, and 31 percent cite a "liberal" background (NORC, 2013:265). Canada differs from the United States in this regard, with just less than 3 percent of the population claiming membership in "other Christian" groups

In contrast to local congregations of years past, some religious organizations, especially fundamentalist ones, have become *electronic churches* dominated by "prime-time preachers" (Hadden & Swain, 1981). Electronic religion found in the United States has made James Dobson, Joel Osteen, Billy and Franklin Graham, Robert Schuller, and other "televangelists" more famous than all but a few clergy in the past. Perhaps 5 percent of the American television audience (about 10 million people) are regular viewers of religious television, and 20 percent (about 40 million) watch some religious programming every week (NORC, 2013:603). Again, the data from Canada show a different trend: Canadians appear to have much smaller appetites than do their southern neighbours for viewing evangelical services on television. One explanation is that aggressive marketing of religion by sectarian competitors is much more advanced in the United States than in other countries, including Canada and Britain (Bibby, 1987; Dawson, 1998).

Religion: Looking Ahead

The popularity of media ministries, the growth of religious fundamentalism, new forms of spirituality, and the connection of millions of people to mainstream churches show that religion will likely remain a major part of modern society for decades to come. Even as some people move away from organized religion, immigration from South Asia, Southeast Asia, the Middle East, and the Caribbean and Central and South America should intensify as well as diversify the religious character of Canadian society in the twenty-first century (Yang & Ebaugh, 2001; Clark & Schellenberg, 2006).

The world is becoming more complex, and social change seems to move at a faster pace than our capacity to make sense of it all. While weakening religion for some, this process also fires the religious imaginations of many. As new technology gives us the power to alter, sustain, and even create life, we face increasingly difficult moral questions. Against this backdrop of uncertainty, many people look to their faith for inspiration, guidance, and hope.

Controversy & Debate

Does Science Threaten Religion?

Sean: I think someday science will prove religion to be false.

Sophie: You better hope God doesn't prove *you* to be false.

Rasheed: Cool it, both of you. I don't think science and religion are talking about the same thing at all.

About 400 years ago, the Italian physicist and astronomer Galileo (1564–1642) helped launch the Scientific Revolution with a series of startling discoveries. Dropping objects from the Leaning Tower of Pisa, he discovered some of the laws of gravity; making his own telescope, he observed the solar system and found that earth orbited the sun, not the other way around.

For his trouble, Galileo was challenged by the Roman Catholic Church, which had preached for centuries that earth stood motionless at the centre of the universe. Galileo only made matters worse by responding that religious leaders had no business talking about matters of science. Before long, he found his work banned and himself under house arrest.

As Galileo's treatment shows, right from the start, science has had an uneasy relationship with religion. In the nineteenth century, the two clashed again over the issue of creation. Charles Darwin's masterwork, *On the Origin of Species*, states that humanity evolved from lower forms of life over the course of a billion years—a theory that seems to fly in the face of the biblical account of creation found in Genesis, which states that "God created the heavens and the earth," introducing living things on the third day and, on the fifth and sixth days, animals, including human beings fashioned in God's own image.

Today—almost four centuries after Galileo was silenced—many people still debate the apparently conflicting claims of science and religion. One-third of U.S. adults claim to believe that the Bible is the literal word of God, and many of them reject any scientific findings that run counter to it (NORC, 2013:303). In 2005, all eight members of the school board in

Dover, Pennsylvania, were voted out of office after they took a stand that many townspeople saw as weakening the teaching of evolution; at the same time, the Kansas state school board ordered the teaching of evolution to include its weaknesses and limitations from a religious point of view ("Much Ado about Evolution," 2005).

In 2008, the province of Quebec replaced religious education—specifically, Catholic Religious and Moral Instruction, Protestant Moral and Religious Education, and Moral Education programs—in private, religious, and public schools with the controversial "ERC" (Ethics, Religion and Culture) classes. The latter aims to reflect social changes by teaching about religion from a perspective that recognizes the social diversity of Quebec society. ERC courses have been challenged by Christian and Jewish organizations, as well as by parents. In 2015, the Supreme Court of Canada has ruled that Loyola High School, a Jesuit organization that has sought an exemption to ERC courses, must continue to teach them but can offer its own perspective.

Reflecting perhaps the potential for a new middle ground, 44 percent of U.S. adults (and also many church leaders) say the Bible is a book of truths *inspired* by God without being accurate in a literal, scientific sense. In addition, a recent survey of U.S. scientists found that half of them claimed to believe in God or some form of higher power (Pew Research Center, 2009). So it seems that some people are able to embrace science and religion at the same time. But scientists tend to be more skeptical. A survey on the religiosity of scientists in the United States found that on average scientists tend to be half as likely to believe in a god. Over 40 percent say they do not believe in God, while only 4 percent of the American population makes the same claim (Pew Research Center, 2009).

What Do You Think?

1. Why do you think scientifically minded people tend to reject religious accounts of human creation? Why do some religious people reject scientific accounts?

2. Does the sociological study of religion challenge anyone's faith? Why or why not?

3. Should some religious Quebec schools and parents be exempt from ERC courses? Should they be allowed to modify them to reflect their own perspective? Why or why not?

Sources: Gould (1981), Huchingson (1994), Applebome (1996), Greeley (2008), and Van Praagh (2015).

Seeing Sociology in Everyday Life

How do the mass media portray the family?

Many are familiar with the traditional families portrayed in popular television shows of the 1950s such as *The Adventures of Ozzie and Harriet* and *Leave It to Beaver*. Both of these shows had a working father, homemaker mother, and two (wonderful) sons. But, as the images below and on page 459 suggest, today's television shows present a far wider range of family types.

Ursula Coyote/AMC/Everett Collection

While television shows 50 years ago presented the family as a cultural ideal, today's shows are far more likely to present the reality of family life. This means not only a variety of family types but, as shown in the popular television show *Breaking Bad*, the struggles and conflicts within families.

In the sitcom *New Girl*, Jess Day is a twenty-something teacher who needs a place to live after ending a relationship. Responding to an ad seeking a roommate, she moves in with three young men. In what ways does this group resemble a family?

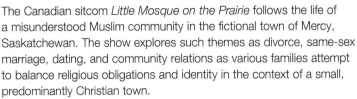

The Canadian sitcom *Little Mosque on the Prairie* follows the life of a misunderstood Muslim community in the fictional town of Mercy, Saskatchewan. The show explores such themes as divorce, same-sex marriage, dating, and community relations as various families attempt to balance religious obligations and identity in the context of a small, predominantly Christian town.

HINT The general pattern found in the mass media today is certainly different from that common in the 1950s, the so-called "golden age of families." Today's television shows emphasize that careers leave little time for families, provide fewer examples of stable marriages, and show the many ways in which people create family-like groups. Some people might say that Hollywood has an anti-family bias. Perhaps, but scriptwriters find that nonconventional family forms make for more interesting stories. To what extent do you agree with the view that most people today are capable of finding satisfying relationships, whether or not these relationships correspond to a traditional family form?

Seeing Sociology in *Your* Everyday Life

1. After reading through the photo essay, list your own favourite television shows and, in each case, evaluate the importance of family life in the show. Is family life included in the show? If so, what family forms are presented? Are families a source of happiness for people or not? Are the families forced to deal with any religious themes, and if so what are they?

2. Go to www.sociologyinfocus.com to access the Sociology in Focus blog, where you can read the latest posts by a team of young sociologists who apply the sociological perspective to topics of popular culture.

3. This chapter explains that family life in today's society is more and more about making choices. What are the underlying reasons that family life is more varied today than it was, say, a century ago?

Making the Grade

Andersen Ross/Getty Images

Families: Basic Concepts and Global Variations

13.1 Describe families and how they differ around the world. (pages 418–421)

All societies are built on *kinship*. The **family** varies across cultures and over time:

- In high-income nations, *marriage* is monogamous.
- Many lower-income nations permit *polygamy*, of which there are two types: *polygyny* and *polyandry*.
- In global perspective, *patrilocality* is most common, but industrial societies favour *neolocality*, and a few societies have *matrilocal residence*.
- Industrial societies use *bilateral descent*; pre-industrial societies are either *patrilineal* or *matrilineal*.

family a social institution found in all societies that unites people in co-operative groups to care for one another, including any children
kinship a social bond based on common ancestry, marriage, or adoption
marriage a legal relationship, usually involving economic co-operation, sexual activity, and childbearing
extended family a family composed of parents and children as well as other kin; also known as a *consanguine family*
nuclear family a family composed of one or two parents and their children; also known as a *conjugal family*
endogamy marriage between people of the same social category
exogamy marriage between people of different social categories
monogamy marriage that unites two partners
polygamy marriage that unites a person with two or more spouses
descent the system by which members of a society trace kinship over generations

Theoretical Analysis of Families

13.2 Apply sociology's major theories to family life. (pages 421–424)

- **Structural-functional theory** shows how families help society operate smoothly: socialization of the young, regulation of sexual activity, social placement, and providing material and emotional support.
- **Social-conflict theory** and **feminist theory** explore how the family perpetuates social inequality by transmitting divisions based on class, ethnicity, race, and gender.
- **Symbolic-interaction theory** and **social-exchange theory** highlight the variety of family life as experienced by various family members.

Stages of Family Life

13.3 Analyze changes in the family over the life course. (pages 424–429)

- Arranged marriages are common in pre-industrial societies; courtship based on romantic love is central to mate selection in Canada.
- Family size has decreased over time as industrialization increases the costs of raising children and as more women go to school and join the labour force.
- Many middle-aged couples care for aging parents; the final transition in marriage begins with the death of a spouse.

homogamy marriage between people with the same social characteristics
infidelity sexual activity outside one's marriage

Families in Canada: Class, Race, and Gender

13.4 Explain how class, race, and gender shape family life. (pages 429–432)

- **Social class** is a powerful force that shapes family life. Children born into rich families typically have better mental and physical health and go on to achieve more in life than children born into poor families.
- **Ethnicity and race** can affect a person's experience of family life, although no single generalization fits all families within a particular category.
- **Gender** affects family dynamics because husbands dominate in most marriages.

Transitions and Problems in Family Life

13.5 Analyze the effects of divorce, remarriage, and violence on family life. (pages 432–436)

- Nearly half of today's marriages will end in **divorce**.
- Remarriage creates blended families that include children from previous marriages.
- **Family violence** is a widespread problem. Most adults who abuse family members were themselves abused as children.

family violence emotional, physical, or sexual abuse of one family member by another

Alternative Family Forms

13.6 Describe the diversity of family life in Canada. (pages 436–441)

- One-parent families, cohabitation, gay and lesbian couples, and singlehood have become more common in recent years. Since 2006, married couples without children are the most common family type.
- Same-sex marriage has been legal in Canada since 2005. In 2015, it became legal in the United States.
- Although controversial, new reproductive technologies are changing conventional ideas of parenthood.

cohabitation the sharing of a household by an unmarried couple

Religion: Concepts and Theories

13.7 Apply sociology's major theories to religion. (pages 441–445)

- **Religion** is a major social institution based on setting the *sacred* apart from the *profane*.
- **Structural-functional theory** suggests that religion unites people, promotes social cohesion, and gives meaning and purpose to life (Emile Durkheim).
- **Symbolic-interaction theory** explains that we socially construct religious beliefs; we especially seek religious meaning when faced with life's uncertainties (Peter Berger).
- **Social-conflict theory** claims that religion justifies the status quo. In this way, religion supports inequality (Karl Marx).
- **Feminist theory** highlights the fact that major religions have traditionally been patriarchal.

profane included as an ordinary part of everyday life

sacred set apart as extraordinary, inspiring awe and reverence

religion a social institution involving beliefs and practices based on recognizing the sacred

faith belief based on conviction rather than on scientific evidence

totem an object in the natural world collectively defined as sacred

Religion and Social Change

13.8 Analyze how religion encourages social change. (pages 445–446)

- Max Weber showed how Calvinist beliefs promoted the rise of industrial capitalism.
- **Liberation theology**, a fusion of Christian principles and political activism, encourages social change.

liberation theology the combining of Christian principles with political activism, often Marxist in character

Types of Religious Organizations

13.9 Distinguish among church, sect, and cult. (pages 446–448)

- **Churches** are religious organizations that are well integrated into their society.
- **Sects** are the result of religious division and are marked by charismatic leadership and suspicion of the larger society.
- **Cults** are religious organizations based on new and unconventional beliefs and practices.

church a religious organization that is well integrated into the larger society

state church a church formally linked to the state

denomination a church, independent of the state, that recognizes religious pluralism

sect a religious organization that stands apart from the larger society

charisma extraordinary personal qualities that can infuse people with emotion and turn them into followers

cult a religious organization that is largely outside a society's cultural traditions

Religion in History

13.10 Contrast religious patterns in pre-industrial and industrial societies. (page 448)

- Early hunters and gatherers typically embraced animism; belief in a single divine power developed with horticultural and pastoral technology.
- The Industrial Revolution increased the importance of science in understanding the world.

animism the belief that elements of the natural world are conscious life forms that affect humanity

Religion in Canada

13.11 Analyze patterns of religiosity in Canada. (pages 449–452)

religiosity the importance of religion in a person's life

Canada is relatively religious and a religiously diverse nation.

- 6 in 10 people claim religion is important in their lives
- The largest religious category is Catholic, accounting for 38.7 percent of the population.
- The second-largest category are the "nones"—the non-religious who profess no religious affiliation and make up 23.9 percent of the population.
- Protestant denominations such as Anglican, United Church, and Baptist have been declining.
- Islam, Hinduism, Sikhism, and Buddhism have experienced growth.

Religious affiliation is tied to social class, ethnicity, and race.

- On average, Protestants tend to enjoy high social standing; Catholics and members of sects have lower standing.
- Religion is often linked to the ethnic background of immigrants who came from countries with a major religion.
- Brought here as slaves, and later arriving as freepersons, most Africans became Christians. The black church has served as an important community resource against racism.

Religion in a Changing Society

13.12 Discuss recent trends in religious life. (pages 452–457)

- In Canada, while some indicators of religiosity (like membership in mainstream churches) have declined, others (such as New Age spiritual movements) have increased.
- **Secularization** is a decline in the importance of the supernatural and sacred.
- Today, **civil religion** takes the form of a quasi-religious patriotism.
- The New Age movement pursues spiritual development outside conventional religious organizations.
- **Fundamentalism** opposes religious accommodation to the world, interprets religious texts literally, and rejects religious diversity.

secularization the historical decline in the importance of the supernatural and the sacred

civil religion a quasi-religious loyalty linking individuals in a basically secular society

fundamentalism a conservative religious doctrine that opposes intellectualism and worldly accommodation in favour of restoring traditional, otherworldly religion

14 Education, Health, and Medicine

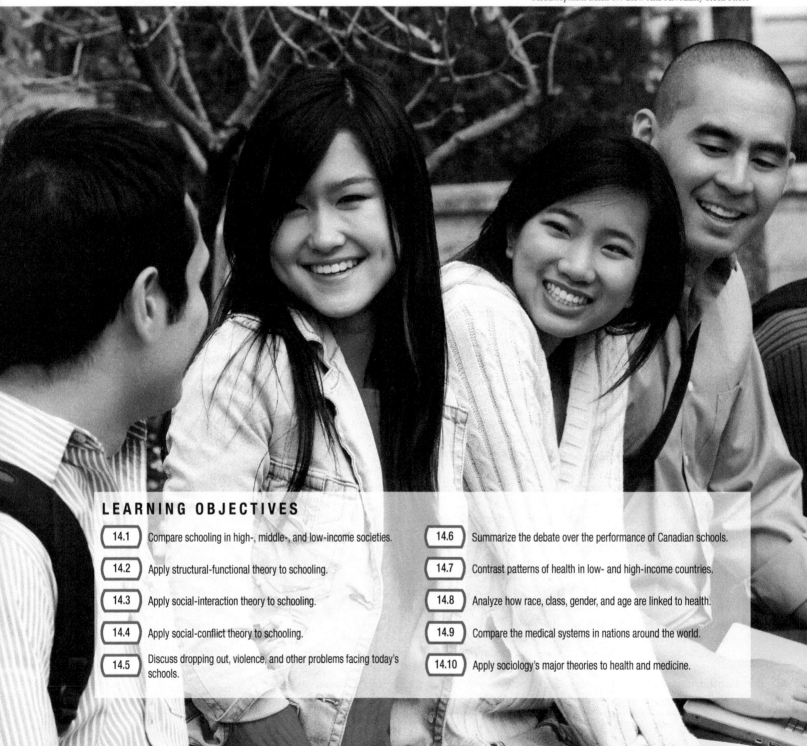

RedChopsticks Batch 17/Glow Asia RF/Alamy Stock Photo

LEARNING OBJECTIVES

14.1 Compare schooling in high-, middle-, and low-income societies.

14.2 Apply structural-functional theory to schooling.

14.3 Apply social-interaction theory to schooling.

14.4 Apply social-conflict theory to schooling.

14.5 Discuss dropping out, violence, and other problems facing today's schools.

14.6 Summarize the debate over the performance of Canadian schools.

14.7 Contrast patterns of health in low- and high-income countries.

14.8 Analyze how race, class, gender, and age are linked to health.

14.9 Compare the medical systems in nations around the world.

14.10 Apply sociology's major theories to health and medicine.

the Power of Society

to open the door to college

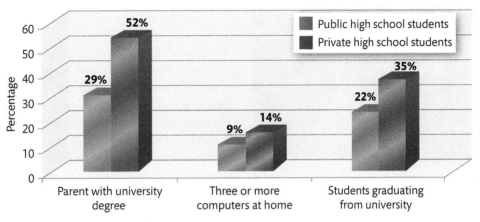

Source: Frenette and Chan (2015).

Do the odds of pursuing post-secondary education simply reflect a personal desire for more schooling? Research shows that our economic class shapes our educational experience. Students who attend private high schools tend to score higher on standardized tests and are more likely to complete post-secondary studies than students who attend public schools. What private school students also have in common is their economic class position: They tend to live in families with higher incomes (total parental income averaged $35 568 for families of public high school students and $44 628 for families of private high school students) and with parents who are also more likely to be university educated. In short, our society is organized in a way that opens the door to higher education far wider for some categories of people than for others.

Chapter Overview

This chapter explains the operation of education and health care, which are two major social institutions that emerge in modern societies. The discussion of both education and health includes a global perspective and a focus on Canada.

WavebreakMediaMicro/Fotolia

When Lisa Addison was growing up, she always smiled when her teachers said she was smart and encouraged her to go to college. "I liked hearing that," she recalls. "But I didn't know what to do about it. No one in my family had ever gone to college. I didn't know which courses to take in high school. I had no idea of how to apply to a college. How would I pay for it? What would college be like if I got there?"

Uncertain about her future, Addison found herself "kind of goofing off in school." After finishing high school, she spent the next 15 years working as a waitress in a restaurant and then as a kitchen helper in a catering company. Now, at the age of 38, Addison has decided to go back to school. "I don't want to do this kind of work for the rest of my life. I am smart. I can do better. At this point, I am ready for college."

Addison took a giant step through the door of her local community college and, with the help of counsellors, set her sights on an associate's degree in business. When she finishes this two-year program, she plans to transfer to a four-year university to complete a bachelor's degree. Then she hopes to go back into the food service industry—but this time as a manager at higher pay (Toppo & DeBarros, 2005).

Education is a social institution that has particular importance to people looking to advance their careers. This chapter explains *why* schooling is more important than ever for success in Canada today and also describes *who* benefits most from schooling. The second half of the chapter examines *health* and the social institution of *medicine*. Good health, like good schooling, is distributed unequally throughout our society's population. In addition, patterns involving both schooling and education reveal striking differences from society to society.

Education: A Global Survey

14.1 Compare schooling in high-, middle-, and low-income societies.

Education is *the social institution through which society provides its members with important knowledge, including basic facts, job skills, and cultural norms and values.* Education takes many forms, from informal family discussions around the dinner table to lectures and labs at large universities. In high-income nations, education depends largely on **schooling**, *formal instruction under the direction of specially trained teachers.*

Schooling and Economic Development

The extent of schooling in any society is tied to its level of economic development. In low- and middle-income countries, which are home to most of the world's people, families and local communities teach young people important knowledge and skills. Formal schooling, especially learning that is not directly connected to survival, is available mainly to wealthy people who can afford to pursue personal enrichment. The word *school* is from a Greek root that means "leisure." In ancient Greece, famous teachers such as Plato, Socrates, and Aristotle taught aristocratic, upper-class men who had plenty of spare time. The same was true in ancient China, where the famous philosopher K'ung Fu-tzu (Confucius) shared his wisdom with just a privileged few.

December 30, the Cuzco region, Peru. High in the Andes Mountains of Peru, families send their children to the local school. But "local" can mean five kilometres away or more, and there are no buses, so these children, almost all from poor families, walk an hour or more each way. Schooling is required by law, but in the rural highlands, some parents prefer to keep their children at home where they can help with the farming and livestock.

Today, schooling in low-income countries reflects the national culture. In Afghanistan, for example, secular education continues to be under threat. Similarly, schooling in Bangladesh (Asia), Zimbabwe (Africa), and Haiti (Latin America) has been shaped by the distinctive cultural traditions of these nations.

All low-income countries have one trait in common when it comes to schooling: There is not much of it. In the poorest nations (including several in Central Africa), about one-fourth of all children never get to school (World Bank, 2013a); worldwide, almost one-third of all children never make it as far as the secondary grades. As a result, about one-sixth of the world's people cannot read or write. Global Map 14–1 on page 466 shows the extent of illiteracy around the world, and the national comparisons in the text illustrate the link between schooling and economic development.

education the social institution through which society provides its members with important knowledge, including basic facts, job skills, and cultural norms and values

schooling formal instruction under the direction of specially trained teachers

Schooling in India

India has recently become a middle-income country, but people there still earn only about 7 percent of the average North American income, and most poor families depend on the earnings of children. Even though India has outlawed child labour, many children continue to work in factories—weaving rugs or making handicrafts—up to 60 hours per week, which greatly limits their opportunities for schooling.

Today, 92 percent of children in India complete primary school, typically in crowded schoolrooms where one teacher may face 40 or more children. In comparison, Canada has a ratio of 14 students per teacher in public elementary and secondary schools. In India, 63 percent of students go on to secondary school, but just 18 percent enter college. Currently, about one-third of India's people are unable to read and write (UNESCO, 2012; Statistics Canada, 2013a; World Bank, 2013a).

Patriarchy also shapes Indian education. Indian parents are joyful at the birth of a boy because he and his future wife will both contribute income to the family. But there are economic costs to raising a girl: Parents must provide a dowry (a gift of wealth to the groom's family), and after her marriage, a daughter's work benefits her husband's family. Therefore, some Indians see less reason to invest in the schooling of girls, so only 60 percent of girls (compared with 66 percent of boys) reach the secondary grades. So what do girls do if they are not in school? Most of the children working in Indian factories are girls—a family's way of benefiting from their daughters while they can (World Bank, 2013b).

In many low-income nations, children are as likely to work as to attend school, and girls receive less schooling than boys. But the doors to schooling are now opening to more girls and women. These young women are studying nursing at Somalia University in downtown Mogadishu.

Schooling in Japan

Schooling has not always been part of the Japanese way of life. Before industrialization brought mandatory education in 1872, only a privileged few attended school. Today, Japan's educational system is widely praised for training some of the world's highest achievers.

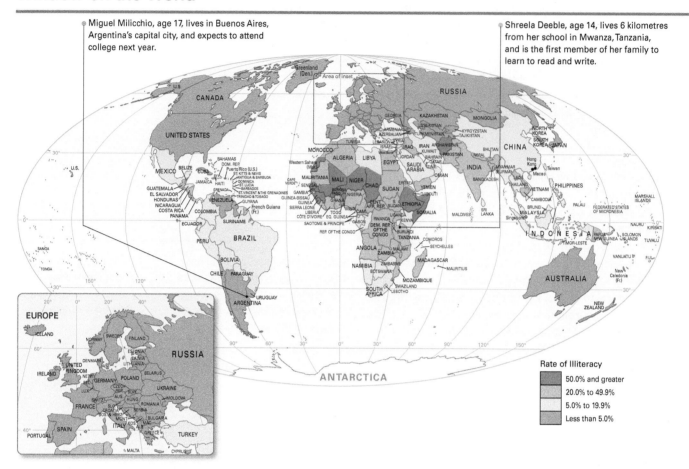

Miguel Milicchio, age 17, lives in Buenos Aires, Argentina's capital city, and expects to attend college next year.

Shreela Deeble, age 14, lives 6 kilometres from her school in Mwanza, Tanzania, and is the first member of her family to learn to read and write.

Rate of Illiteracy

- 50.0% and greater
- 20.0% to 49.9%
- 5.0% to 19.9%
- Less than 5.0%

GLOBAL MAP 14–1 Illiteracy in Global Perspective

Reading and writing skills are widespread in high-income countries, where illiteracy rates generally are below 5 percent. In much of Latin America, however, illiteracy is more common, one consequence of limited economic development. In 13 nations—most of them in Africa—illiteracy is the rule rather than the exception; there people rely on the oral tradition of face-to-face communication rather than the written word.

Sources: UNESCO (2012) and United Nations Development Programme (2012).

The early grades concentrate on transmitting Japanese traditions, especially a sense of obligation to family. Starting in their early teens, students take a series of rigorous and highly competitive examinations. These written tests, which are like the Scholastic Assessment Test (SAT) in the United States, decide the future of all Japanese students.

More students graduate from high school in Japan (93 percent) than in Canada (88 percent). But competitive examinations in Japan, among other factors, mean that fewer students complete a college or university degree when compared to many other high-income countries. In 2012, 53 percent of Canadians aged 25 to 64 had completed post-secondary education, surpassing all other Organisation for Economic Cooperation and Development (OECD) nations, including Japan, who is second at 47 percent (OECD, 2014). Understandably, Japanese students take these entrance examinations very seriously, and about half attend special "cram schools" to prepare for them. Japanese schooling produces impressive results. In a number of fields, notably mathematics, young Japanese students (who rank seventh in the world in mathematics) outperform students in most other high-income nations, including Canada (ranked thirteenth in mathematics) (OECD, 2014).

Schooling in the United States

The United States was among the first countries to set a goal of mass education. By 1850, about half of the young people between the ages of 5 and 19 were enrolled in school. By 1918, all states had passed *mandatory education laws* requiring children to attend school until the age of 16 or completion of grade 8. The country reached a milestone in the mid-1960s, when for the first time a majority of U.S. adults had high school diplomas. Today, 87.6 percent of adults 25 years of age or older have completed high school, and 30.9 percent have a four-year college degree (U.S. Census Bureau, 2012).

Schooling in the United States also tries to promote *equal opportunity*. National surveys show that most people think schooling is crucial to personal success, and a majority believe that everyone has the chance to get an education consistent with personal ability and talent (NORC, 2013:242, 2199). However, this opinion expresses cultural ideals rather than reality. A century ago, for example, women were all but excluded from higher education; even today, most people who attend college and university come from families with above-average incomes.

Schooling in Canada

As in the United States and Japan, the educational system in Canada has been shaped by past patriarchal traditions and cultural norms. The result is a mixture of public schools, elite private schools, and publicly funded separate Roman Catholic schools. At the same time, a strong belief in social equality in regard to literacy and basic schooling has prevailed—a tradition, in fact, that predates the emergence of the modern education system as we have come to know it (Harrigan, 1990). Yet throughout the twentieth century, educational participation was influenced by gender, geographic location, and social class. And to some extent, it can be argued that this remains the case even today.

Nevertheless, formal education for children of all social backgrounds has changed enormously since the mid-nineteenth century in our country. Prior to this time, education for most children—apart from those of the elite—was informal and unorganized (Prentice, 1977). Even by the turn of the twentieth century, school attendance remained sporadic, and most students—boys and girls in equal proportions—dropped out after grade 3 (Harrigan, 1990; Baldus & Kassam, 1996). This was especially true for rural children. Further, schoolteachers were often ill-trained and poorly paid, typically receiving lower wages than day labourers of the time. Prejudice restricted females from public teaching until the second half of the nineteenth century and, even thereafter, conditions were hardly equal between the sexes. For example, when Martha Hamm Lewis entered teachers' training school in the mid-nineteenth century in New Brunswick, her principal required that she "enter the classroom ten minutes before the male students, sit alone at the back of the room, always wear a veil, leave the classroom five minutes before the end of the lesson and leave the building without speaking to any of the young men" (MacLellan cited in Wilson, 1996:99).

The early public schools in Canada did not champion class equality despite proclaiming an egalitarian ideology. Rather, they served to reproduce the existing social class system and to teach its validity to students in order to minimize conflict between the social classes (Curtis, 1988:370–371). Likewise, the early school books of Upper Canada (later to be called Ontario) were "infused with a hefty dose of class interest" (Baldus & Kassam, 1996:328), with their authors aiming mainly to curtail insubordination stemming from the "lower orders."

As the twentieth century unfolded, women came to dominate the teaching profession, the quality of instruction greatly improved, and national legislation was passed requiring that children of both sexes across Canada remain in school until at least their mid-teens. Increasingly, most groups embraced publicly funded education as a minimum requirement for future success in a modern industrial society.

Today, with the exception of Aboriginal peoples, primary and secondary education are provincial responsibilities. Each province has its own ministry or department of education, which is responsible for determining funding and developing curriculum guidelines. At the local level, school boards implement these standards.

About 5 million students were enrolled in publicly funded elementary and secondary schools in Canada during the academic year 2010–11, a slight drop from the previous year

TABLE 14–1 Number and Proportion of the Population Aged 25 to 64 by Highest Level of Educational Attainment, 2011

Educational Attainment	Number	Percent
No certificate, diploma, or degree	2 330 575	12.7
High school diploma or equivalent	4 270 660	23.2
Post-secondary qualification	11 782 700	64.1
Trades certificate	2 218 800	12.1
Trades certificate or diploma (other than Registered Apprenticeship certificate)	1 314 095	7.1
Registered Apprenticeship certificate	904 710	4.9
College diploma	3 913 710	21.3
University certificate below bachelor level	894 750	4.9
University degree	4 755 420	25.9
Bachelor's degree	3 032 220	16.5
University certificate above bachelor level	495 810	2.7
Medical degree	127 365	0.7
Master's degree	938 220	5.1
Earned doctorate	161 805	0.9
Total	18 383 920	100.0

Source: Statistics Canada (2013c). Education in Canada: Attainment, Field of Study and Location of Study. Ottawa: Minister of Industry. Catalogue no: v99-012-X2011001. 2013c. Reproduced and distributed on an "as is" basis with the permission of Statistics Canada.

(Statistics Canada, 2013b). Many students continue their education: enrolment in Canadian universities for 2012–13 was 1.2 million students, and in colleges it was 739 959; Canada has approximately 95 public and private not-for-profit universities and university degree–level colleges and 80 community colleges (Statistics Canada, 2010a, 2014a). Table 14–1 shows the distribution in the adult population by educational attainment. Overall, Canadians continue to make great strides in post-secondary education, accelerating the trend that has slowly emerged over the last century or so. The increase for females is particularly impressive, as noted in Chapter 8 ("Social Stratification"). According to the 2011 census, 64.1 percent of Canadians aged 25 to 64 have acquired a post-secondary education certificate, diploma, or degree. Among 55- to 64-year-olds, women make up only 47.3 percent of those who have graduated from a university. Among 25- to 34-year-olds, however, women make up 59.1 percent of all those who have graduated (Statistics Canada, 2013c).

In 2011, Canadian provincial and federal governments spent an estimated 13 percent of their public expenditures on education. This amounts to 5.6 percent of the gross domestic product (GDP) spent on education, which is the average for OECD countries. However, Canadian post-secondary students pay some of the highest tuition fees among OECD countries. About 43 percent of their education was privately funded in 2011, higher than the OECD average of 31 percent (OECD, 2014).

The Functions of Schooling

14.2 Apply structural-functional theory to schooling.

Structural-functional theory focuses on ways in which schooling supports the operation and stability of society:

1. **Socialization.** Technologically simple societies look to families to transmit a way of life from one generation to the next. As societies gain complex technology, they turn to trained teachers to pass on specialized knowledge that adults will need in order to participate politically, economically, and socially.

2. **Cultural innovation.** Faculty at colleges and universities invent culture as well as pass it along to students. Especially at centres of higher education, scholars conduct research that leads to discoveries and changes our way of life.

3. **Social integration.** Schools mould a diverse population into one society sharing norms and values. This is one reason why provinces enacted mandatory education laws a century ago when immigration became very high. In light of the ethnic diversity of many urban areas today, schooling continues to serve this purpose.

4. **Social placement.** Schools identify talent and match instruction to ability. Schooling increases meritocracy by rewarding talent and hard work regardless of social background and provides a path to upward social mobility.

Graduation from college or university is an important event in the lives of an ever-increasing number of people in Canada. Look over the discussion of the functions of schooling. How many of these functions do you think people in post-secondary education are aware of? Can you think of other social consequences?

5. **Latent functions.** Schooling serves several less widely recognized functions. It provides child care for the growing number of parents who work outside the home. In addition, it occupies thousands of young people in their twenties who would otherwise be competing for limited opportunities in the job market. High schools, colleges, and universities also bring together people of marriageable age. Finally, school networks can be a valuable career resource throughout life.

EVALUATE Structural-functional theory stresses ways that formal education supports the operation of a modern society. However, this approach overlooks the fact that the classroom behaviour of teachers and students can vary from one setting to another, a focus of symbolic-interaction theory, which is discussed next. In addition, structural-functional theory says little about many problems of our educational system and how schooling helps reproduce the class structure in each generation, which is the focus of the social-conflict theory, covered in the final theoretical section on schooling.

CHECK YOUR LEARNING Identify five functions of schooling for the operation of society.

Schooling and Social Interaction

14.3 Apply social-interaction theory to schooling.

The basic idea of symbolic-interaction theory is that people create the reality they experience in their day-to-day interactions. We use this approach to explain how stereotypes can shape what goes on in the classroom.

The Self-Fulfilling Prophecy

Chapter 4 ("Social Interaction in Everyday Life") presented the Thomas theorem, which states that situations people define as real become real in their consequences. Put another way, people who expect others to act in certain ways often encourage that very behaviour. In doing so, people set up a *self-fulfilling prophecy.*

Jane Elliott, an elementary school teacher in the all-white community of Riceville, Iowa, carried out a simple experiment that showed how a self-fulfilling prophecy can take place in the classroom. In 1968, Elliott was teaching a grade 4 class when Martin Luther King, Jr. was murdered. Her students were puzzled and asked why a national hero had been brutally shot. Elliott responded by asking her white students what they thought about people of colour and was stunned to learn that they held many powerful negative stereotypes.

To show the class the harmful effects of such stereotypes, Elliott performed a classroom experiment. She found that almost all of the children in her class had either blue eyes or brown eyes. She told the class that children with brown eyes were smarter and worked harder than children with blue eyes. To be sure everyone could easily tell which category a child fell into, a piece of brown or blue cloth was pinned to each student's collar.

Elliott recalls the effect of this "lesson" on the way students behaved: "It was just horrifying how quickly they became what I told them they were." Within half an hour, Elliott continued, a blue-eyed girl named

How good are you as a student? The answer is that you are as good as you and your teachers think you are. The television show *Glee* demonstrates how the help of an inspiring teacher encourages students toward greater self-confidence and higher achievement.

Michael Yarish/Fox/Everett Collection

Carol had changed from a "brilliant, carefree, excited little girl to a frightened, timid, uncertain, almost-person." Not surprisingly, in the hours that followed, the brown-eyed students came to life, speaking up more and performing better than they had before. The prophecy had been fulfilled: Because the brown-eyed children thought they were superior, they became superior in their classroom performance; they also became "arrogant, ugly, and domineering" toward the blue-eyed children. For their part, the blue-eyed children began underperforming, becoming the inferior people they believed themselves to be.

At the end of the day, Elliott explained to the students what they had experienced. She applied the lesson to race, pointing out that if white children thought they were superior to black children, they would expect to do better in school, just as many children of colour who live in the shadow of the same stereotypes would underperform in school. The children also realized that the society that teaches these stereotypes, as well as the hate that often accompanies them, encourages the kind of violence that ended the life of Martin Luther King, Jr. (Kral, 2000).

EVALUATE Symbolic-interaction theory explains how we all build reality in our everyday interactions with others. When school officials define some students as "gifted," for example, we can expect teachers to treat them differently and expect the students themselves to behave differently as a result of having been labelled in this way. If students and teachers come to believe that one race is academically superior to another, the behaviour that follows may be a self-fulfilling prophecy.

One limitation of this approach is that people do not just make up such beliefs about superiority and inferiority. Rather, these beliefs are built into a society's system of social inequality, which brings us to social-conflict theory.

CHECK YOUR LEARNING How can the labels that schools place on some students affect the students' actual performance and the reactions of others?

Schooling and Social Inequality

14.4 Apply social-conflict theory to schooling.

Social-conflict theory challenges the structural-functional idea that schooling develops everyone's talents and abilities. Instead, this approach emphasizes three ways in which schooling causes and perpetuates social inequality:

1. **Social control.** As Samuel Bowles and Herbert Gintis (1976) see it, the demand for public education in the late nineteenth century was based on capitalist factory owners' need for an obedient and disciplined workforce. Once in school, immigrants learned not only the English language but also the importance of following orders. Today, social-conflict theorists consider how education is increasingly integrated into corporate models. Corresponding to the ongoing privatization of public education are new forms of social control that undermine critical thought and academic freedom (Côté, Day, & De Peuter, 2007).

   hidden curriculum the subtle presentations of political or cultural ideas in the classroom

   In schools, social control is established through what sociologists call the **hidden curriculum**, *the subtle presentations of political or cultural ideas in the classroom*. While students are expected to learn what is on the curriculum (for example, arithmetic and grammar), the hidden curriculum refers to lessons that are not explicitly acknowledged. For example, forming straight lines before entering the school teaches elementary students compliance, just as asking permission for a bathroom break communicates to students the fact that they must learn to regulate their bodily functions according to the rhythms of institutional life.

2. **Standardized testing.** Critics claim that the assessment tests widely used by schools reflect our society's dominant culture, placing minority students at a disadvantage. By defining majority students as smarter, standardized tests unfairly transform privilege into

Sociological research has documented the fact that young children living in low-income communities typically learn in classrooms like the one on the left, with large class sizes and low budgets that do not provide for high technology and other instructional materials. Children from high-income communities typically enjoy classroom experiences such as the one shown on the right, with small classes and the latest learning technology.

personal merit (Crouse & Trusheim, 1988; Putka, 1990). Scott McLean (1997) argues that even the very notion of an individual assessment measure, as well as our detailed statistical system for recording students' academic performance, holds little meaning among Inuit in the Canadian Arctic.

3. **Tracking.** Despite controversy over standardized tests, many North American schools use them for **tracking**, *assigning students to different types of educational programs*, such as college preparatory classes, general education, and vocational and technical training. Tracking supposedly helps teachers meet each student's individual abilities and interests. However, the education critic Jonathan Kozol (1991) considers tracking one of the "savage inequalities" in the North American school system. Most students from privileged backgrounds get into higher tracks, where they receive the best the school can offer. Students from disadvantaged backgrounds end up in lower tracks, where teachers stress memorization and put little focus on creativity (Bowles & Gintis, 1976; Kilgore, 1991; Gamoran, 1992). As a result of such criticisms, some Canadian schools have destreamed their educational programs in recent years. Yet a variety of groups have opposed destreaming—including school boards, teachers, and middle-class parents; the latter worry that, without different tracks, their university-bound children will not have the required skills to compete successfully at university.

tracking assigning students to different types of educational programs

Public and Private Education

Across Canada, virtually all elementary and secondary school students continue to attend public schools. Currently, only 6 percent of students attend a private educational institution (Frenette & Chan, 2015). According to the Canadian Council on Learning (2006), the growth of private schooling has continued to rise slightly across the country.

When examined over time, private school enrolment in Canada shows a very gradual climb, from an all-time low in 1971 of only 2.41 percent to 4 percent of elementary and secondary students in 1981–82. However, in the mid-1980s, private school enrolment dropped noticeably, owing in part to a decision by the Ontario government to publicly fund Catholic secondary education for students in grades 11, 12, and 13. Such students were subsequently excluded from private school student rolls. More recently, private school enrolment numbers have begun to climb slowly again, reflecting some Canadian parents' growing dissatisfaction with the quality of public school education for their children (Maxwell & Maxwell, 1995).

Canadian Accredited Independent Schools (CAIS) is an association for elite private schools across the country. Its membership comprises 93 "independent" (non-public) schools that enrol a little more than 10 percent of the total private school enrolment (CAIS, 2013). According to Mary Percival Maxwell and James Maxwell (1995:335), "[d]espite their small numbers these schools have played a crucial role in the social reproduction of the upper classes . . . [and] their graduates are disproportionately represented in the various institutional elites."

More than half of CAIS private schools were established prior to 1920; 22 of them were founded in the nineteenth century. The original-member CAIS schools were not only exclusive along class lines; most were open only to a single sex, a policy that was reinforced by the sponsoring religious denomination. Before World War I, upper-class Canadian families were likely to send both their daughters and sons to board at elite private schools. Worsening economic circumstances in subsequent decades meant that many could no longer afford private educations for both daughters and sons. Instead, families tended to commit their reduced resources to their sons' private school educations and send their daughters to less expensive local schools. As a result, by 1993, there remained only 16 private girls' schools (Maxwell & Maxwell, 1995). Yet even the single-sex private schools for boys have been forced to change with the times. During the 1970s, declining enrolment forced many of them to go "co-ed." At the same time, the ethnic makeup of these schools has become more diverse, reflecting the more heterogeneous ethnic makeup of the upper and upper-middle classes in present-day Canadian society. Despite their changing student populations, Canada's elite private schools continue to prepare their students for leadership positions in the various elites of the larger society, which does not differ significantly from what sociologists have observed in earlier generations (Porter, 1965; Clement, 1975; Newman, 1975).

Public school financing does not differ very much across Canada, owing to the country's relative success in redistributing wealth through income tax (Oreopoulos, 2006). Nevertheless, as the Thinking About Diversity box on page 474 shows, schools in many Aboriginal communities are understaffed and in need of repairs. In addition, in Canada, public schools are not all the same. Differences in funding between rich and poor communities result in unequal resources; this means that children in more affluent areas receive a better education than children in low-income communities. National Map 14–1 shows one key dimension of difference: Median teacher salaries vary by about $30 000 in regional comparisons.

Furthermore, Canadian data indicate that the provinces vary substantially in the educational attainment of the adult population. Among provinces and territories, the highest proportion of university degree holders can be found in Ontario (28.9 percent), British Columbia (27.3 percent), and the Yukon (25.8 percent). The greatest proportion of Registered Apprenticeship certificate holders are in Alberta (7.6 percent), Saskatchewan (7.0 percent), and the Yukon (6.9 percent). Provinces and territories with the highest proportion of no certificate, diploma, or degree holders are Nunavut (46.0 percent), the Northwest Territories (21.6 percent), and Newfoundland and Labrador (20.3 percent) (Statistics Canada, 2013c).

At the local level, differences in school funding can be dramatic. Blanshard Elementary is in one of Victoria's poorest neighbourhoods, where 37 percent of families earn less than $30 000 per year, and the school looks the part, with large classes and a building in obvious need of repair. Uplands Elementary, by contrast, is found in one of Victoria's most affluent communities, where only 12 percent of families earn less than $30 000 per year. The teachers are keen and the facilities are state-of-the-art.

Not everyone thinks that money is the key to good schooling. A classic report by a research team headed by James Coleman (1966) confirmed that schools in low-income communities and with mostly minority populations suffer problems ranging from larger class size to insufficient libraries and too few science labs. But the Coleman report cautioned that more money by itself will not magically improve schooling. More important are the co-operative efforts of teachers, parents, and the students themselves. In other words, even if school funding were exactly the same everywhere, students who benefit from more *cultural capital*—that is, those whose parents value schooling, read to their children, and

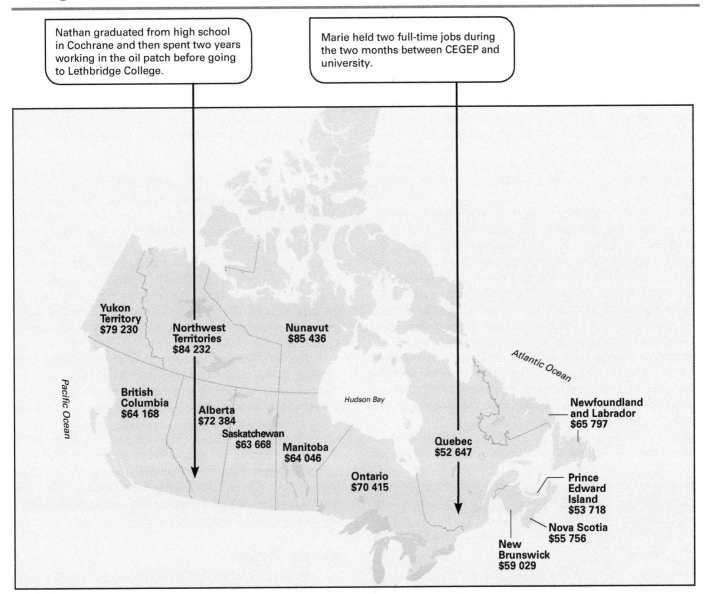

Nathan graduated from high school in Cochrane and then spent two years working in the oil patch before going to Lethbridge College.

Marie held two full-time jobs during the two months between CEGEP and university.

Yukon Territory $79 230

Northwest Territories $84 232

Nunavut $85 436

Atlantic Ocean

Pacific Ocean

British Columbia $64 168

Alberta $72 384

Saskatchewan $63 668

Hudson Bay

Newfoundland and Labrador $65 797

Manitoba $64 046

Quebec $52 647

Ontario $70 415

Prince Edward Island $53 718

Nova Scotia $55 756

New Brunswick $59 029

NATIONAL MAP 14–1   Teachers' Salaries Across Canada

In 2010, the median employment income for high school teachers in Canada who worked full time for the whole year was $62 533. The map shows the median income for all provinces and territories; incomes range from a high of $85 436 in Nunavut to a low of $52 647 in Quebec. Looking at the map, what pattern do you see? What do high-salary (and low-salary) regions have in common?

Source: Compiled by J. Burkowicz from Statistics Canada (2011a).

encourage the development of imagination (see Chapter 3 "Socialization: From Infancy to Old Age")—would still perform better. In short, we should not expect schools alone to overcome marked social inequality (Schneider et al., 1998; Israel, Beaulieu, & Hartless, 2001; Ornstein, 2010). Further research confirms the difference that the home environment makes in a student's school performance. A research team studied the rate at which school-age children gain skills in reading and mathematics (Downey, von Hippel, & Broh, 2004). Because Canadian children go to school six to seven hours a day, five days a week, and do not attend school during summer months, the researchers calculate that children spend only about 13 percent of their waking hours in school. During the school year, high-income children learn somewhat more quickly than low-income children, but the learning gap is far greater during the summer season when children are not in school. The researchers

Thinking About Diversity: Race, Class, and Gender

"A Time for Dreams": Aboriginal Education in Canada

In 2014, while teachers in British Columbia took province-wide job action in order to protest growing class sizes and program cuts, students in the remote Cree community of Attawapiskat, Ontario, faced a starkly different challenge to their education. Having seen their J.R. Nakogee Elementary School close down due to a massive diesel spill, the students were forced to attend classes, from 2000 to 2014, in a collection of portables that sat on top of the toxic site.

Studying in the portables meant receiving an inferior, if not dangerous, education. For starters, portables exposed students to environmental health hazards. An Attawapiskat Education Authority report noted the presence of "high levels of the contaminants benzene, toluene, ethyl benzene, and xylenes, some of which are carcinogenic agents" (Reimer, 2010:125). Numerous cases of nosebleeds, headaches, and nausea have been reported by students and teachers alike. The portables were also in rough shape. They "[were] so run-down that the windows do not close properly, the heat fails on a regular basis, and mice have infested the buildings" (King, Edwards, & Blackstock, 2013:95). Thus, in addition to health risks, students endured the hardship of studying during −40 degree winters by keeping their winter clothes on indoors. In Attawapiskat, it seems, students have learned to write with mitts on.

As some community leaders observe, Attawapiskat is not an isolated case. Across Canada, First Nations schools have historically been underfunded. Underfunding means that learning resources are lacking and that overcrowding, teacher scarcity, disrepair, and issues like mould infestation can be found in many on-reserve schools. Perhaps it is not surprising that a former teacher described the conditions at Attawapiskat as comparable to those of a Third World country.

But does the problem of Aboriginal education run even deeper than that? Sociologists and activists believe that underfunding alone is not the issue. Karl Reimer argues that "the twenty-first century seems to be bearing witness to a new colonial policy of neglect and educational apartheid through which Indigenous peoples in Canada are denied the same right to education as their non-Indigenous neighbours" (2010:127). Inadequate response to disasters and underfunding must be connected to the low social status of Aboriginal people and to a government which, as Reimer points out, would have never allowed the situation of Attawapiskat to occur elsewhere in Canada.

In the face of these challenges, a significant response to the situation at Attawapiskat has come from its students. The Cree youth Shannen Koostachin, along with her peers, pressured the government for a new school. Believing that "school should be a time for dreams, and every kid deserves this," Koostachin helped to mobilize students to launch their own social media campaign. Student activists met with Minister Strahl, who denied them a new school. In response, they submitted their own report to the United Nations. Their activism offers some hope. Although many First Nations schools continue to languish, at least in Attawapiskat a new school opened in August 2014.

CLS Design/Shutterstock

What Do You Think?

1. How does the educational experience of students in Attawapiskat compare to your own?

2. Have students at your school taken up activism to address an issue related to education?

3. Besides providing adequate funding, what other changes would our society have to make to eliminate the inferior education of Aboriginal students?

Sources: Adopted from Reimer (2010); Shannen's Dream Campaign (2011); King, Edwards, and Blackstock (2013).

---

conclude that when it comes to student performance, schools matter, but the home and local environment matter more. Put another way, schools close some of the learning gap that is created by differences in family resources, but they do not "level the playing field" between rich and poor children the way we like to think they do.

Access to Higher Education

Schooling is the main path to high-paying jobs, but 29.4 percent of young Canadians—known as "gappers"—delay their post-secondary studies for at least four months after graduating from high school (Canadian Council on Learning, 2008). By age 20, two in ten high school graduates had not enrolled in a college, university, or trade school (Tomkowicz & Bushnik, 2003). Young people often take time off between high school and post-secondary education for pragmatic reasons, such as the desire to have a break from school or to travel. However, the most important reason is the need to save up enough money to pay for their post-secondary studies. Aboriginal youth, Anglophones, youth from Ontario, and youth whose parents have lower levels of education take the longest time between completing high school and entering post-secondary education (Bozick & DeLuca, 2005; Hango, 2008, 2011). There are long-range consequences for taking time off before pursuing post-secondary education; once employed, gappers have higher incomes initially but non-gappers, once employed, catch up quickly and eventually make higher incomes (Canadian Council on Learning, 2008).

While more young people in Canada are accessing higher education today than ever before, those from less-privileged family backgrounds are not increasing their participation nearly to the extent that their more privileged counterparts are (Bouchard & Zhao, 2000; Lowe & Krahn, 2000; Statistics Canada, 2008). On average, undergraduate students in Canadian universities and colleges paid $5959 in tuition fees in 2014–15 compared with $5767 a year earlier (Statistics Canada, 2014b). Government funding as a portion of overall institutional revenues has declined steadily for the past 20 years, forcing universities and colleges to look for additional funding from student tuition fees and, to a lesser extent, from the private sector. In the 1960s and 1970s, government was responsible for 90 percent of post-secondary funding. Throughout the 1980s, 84 percent of university operating revenue came from government funding. By 2000–01, government's share of university funding had decreased to 61 percent, whereas revenues from student fees had grown to 34 percent (Robertson, 2003; Canadian Federation of Students, 2013). At the same time, however, post-secondary students have gained from increased public expenditure on scholarships and bursaries, including most recently the Millennium Scholarship Fund (MSF). However, while there was an increase in expenditure on scholarships and bursaries in the recent decades, federal government investment has now levelled out.

The amount owing by those who take out student loans is also increasing. Students from the graduating class of 1995 who received student loans owed on average $11 000 at graduation—a whopping 39 percent increase over the class of 1990 and 59 percent over the class of 1986 (Statistics Canada, 2003). Today, according to the Canadian Federation of Students, the average student debt is $27 000 (Sagan, 2014). It is little wonder that the financial burdens of higher education discourage many young people from less-privileged backgrounds from attending.

Over the past 25 years, educational attainment for Aboriginal people aged 25 to 64 has also generally improved. The fact remains, however, that Aboriginal people still lag behind other Canadians in regard to post-secondary degrees or diplomas (see Figure 14–1). In 2011, 22 percent of the non-reserve Aboriginal population stopped their education short of completing high school, compared to 11 percent of the non-Aboriginal population (Statistics Canada, 2013d). On a more positive note, new immigrants to Canada actually attain more education than do their Canadian-born counterparts. This is partly explained by the higher educational levels of recent immigrants when compared with those of the Canadian-born population (Statistics Canada, 2011b).

For those who do complete post-secondary education, rewards include not just intellectual and personal growth but also increased opportunities for secure employment and higher income. This is especially the case for women. In 2010, almost three-quarters of women (71.4 percent) but only about two-thirds of men (64.5 percent) aged 25 to

Diversity Snapshot

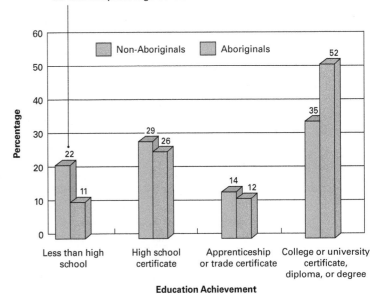

- Almost a quarter of off-reserve Aboriginal Canadians do not complete high school.

FIGURE 14–1 Off-Reserve Aboriginal Peoples and Non-Aboriginal Peoples, Aged 25 to 64, by Education Attainment, Canada, 2011

Source: Compiled by J. Burkowicz from Statistics Canada (2013d).

TABLE 14–2 Median Annual Earnings of Women and Men Employed Full Year, Full Time, by Educational Attainment, 2010

	Women dollars	Men dollars	Earning's Ratio percentage
No certificate, diploma, or degree	30 389	39 694	76.6
Graduated high school	37 405	45 039	83.1
Some post-secondary	42 263	54 823	77.1
Post-secondary certificate or diploma	49 231	61 383	80.2
University degree	62 739	74 642	84.1
TOTAL	44 341	54 132	81.9

Source: Calculated by J. Burkowicz based on Statistics Canada (2011a).

44 had completed post-secondary education. This is in contrast to the group age 65 and over, in which only 32.7 percent of women and 42.6 percent of men had completed post-secondary education (Statistics Canada, 2011b). In 2010, women with university degrees who worked full time, full year earned $53 400, an increase from $48 260 in 2000 and more than 10 percent since 1968. This was the largest increase in earnings across the educational groupings for both men and women. Earnings for women with some secondary school but who had not completed their high school education increased much more slowly—up 4.1 percent between 1980 and 2000 to $24 914.

Despite this dramatic increase in the earnings of women with university degrees who worked full time, full year, they still get a lower return on this investment than men. In 2011, based on median annual earnings, women earned only 82 cents for every $1 earned by their male counterparts. This figure is inflated because women have a higher level of education than men—59 percent of all associate and bachelor's degrees and first professional degrees are held by women. Looking at the differences in income by education level, the differences between the earnings of men and women exist at all education levels. Table 14–2 shows that additional years of education tend to increase women's earnings but do little to decrease the wage gap itself.

Greater Opportunity: Expanding Higher Education

With some 2 million people enrolled in colleges and universities, Canada is a world leader in providing education to its people. According to the OECD, Canada has one of the highest proportions (53 percent) of post-secondary educated adults among OECD members (who average 32 percent) (OECD, 2014). This country also enrols a significant amount of international students, with over 100 000 non-resident student permits issued in 2014 (Government of Canada, 2014).

One reason for this achievement is that there are 97 universities and 133 colleges in Canada. Some two-year colleges are private, but most are publicly funded community colleges that serve a local area and charge lower tuition.

Because higher education is a path to better jobs and higher income, the government makes money available to help certain categories of people pay the costs of college. The Canadian Armed Forces continue to offer post-secondary funding to enlistees; in addition, veterans continue to benefit from government grants and scholarships.

Privilege and Personal Merit

If attending college or university is a rite of passage for rich men and women, as social-conflict theory suggests, then *schooling transforms social privilege into personal merit*. Given our cultural emphasis on individualism, we tend to see credentials as badges of ability rather than as symbols of family affluence (Sennett & Cobb, 1973).

When we congratulate the new graduate, we rarely recognize the resources—in terms of both money and cultural capital—that made this achievement possible. Yet, in the United States, young people from families with incomes exceeding $200 000 average more than 400 points higher on the SAT exam than those whose families earn less than $20 000 a year (College Board, 2013). In Canada, a similar pattern prevails: Schools in which students score higher on standardized tests tend to be located in high-income areas (Alphonso & Grant, 2013). The richer students are thus more likely to get into college and university; once there, they are also more likely to complete their studies and get a degree. In a *credential society*—one that evaluates people on the basis of their schooling—companies hire job applicants with the best education. This process ends up helping people who are already advantaged and hurting those who are already disadvantaged (Collins, 1979).

Education			
	Structural-Functional Theory	**Symbolic-Interaction Theory**	**Social-Conflict Theory**
What is the level of analysis?	Macro-level	Micro-level	Macro-level
What is the importance of education for society?	Schooling performs many vital tasks for the operation of society, including socializing the young and encouraging discovery and invention to improve our lives. Schooling helps unite a diverse society by teaching shared norms and values.	How teachers define their students—as well as how students think of themselves—can become real to everyone and affect students' educational performance.	Schooling maintains social inequality through unequal schooling for rich and poor. Within individual schools, tracking provides privileged children with a better education than poor children.

EVALUATE Social-conflict theory links formal education to social inequality to show how schooling transforms privilege into personal worthiness and disadvantage into personal deficiency. However, the social-conflict approach overlooks the extent to which finishing a degree reflects plenty of hard work and the extent to which schooling provides upward mobility for talented women and men from all backgrounds. In addition, despite claims that schooling supports the status quo, today's college and university curricula challenge social inequality on many fronts.

CHECK YOUR LEARNING Explain several ways in which education is linked to social inequality.

The Applying Theory table sums up what the theoretical approaches show us about education.

Problems in the Schools

14.5 Discuss dropping out, violence, and other problems facing today's schools.

Intense debate revolves around schooling in Canada. Because we expect schools to do so much—equalize opportunity, instill discipline, and fire imagination—people are divided on whether public schools are doing their job. Although half of adults give their local schools a grade of A or B, just as many give a grade of C or below (Bushaw & Lopez, 2012).

Discipline and Violence

When many of today's older teachers think back to their own student days, school "problems" consisted of talking out of turn, chewing gum, breaking the dress code, or cutting class. Today's schools are grappling with drug and alcohol abuse, teenage pregnancy, and outright violence.

While Canadians are used to hearing about violence in the United States, our collective conscience was shocked by the 1999 fatal shooting at the W.R. Myers school in Taber, Alberta, as well as the 2006 Dawson College shooting in Montreal. We need to keep in mind, however, that not all school violence is so attention grabbing. Many acts of violence committed at schools—including verbal abuse, harassment, and bullying—are harder to detect.

These are Cree students attending the Lac la Ronge mission school in Saskatchewan. Several hundred thousand Aboriginal students attended schools run by the Anglican church between 1820 and 1969. In 1993, the Archbishop Michael Peers issued a formal apology for the physical, sexual, cultural, and emotional abuse many of the Aboriginal students suffered in these schools.

Student Passivity

If some schools are plagued by violence, many more are filled with students who are bored. Some of the blame for their passivity can be placed on the fact that electronic devices, from television to iPhones, now claim far more of young people's time than school, parents, and community activities. But schools must share the blame because the educational system itself encourages student passivity (Coleman, Hoffer, & Kilgore, 1981).

Bureaucracy

The small, personal schools that served local communities a century ago have evolved into huge education factories. Theodore Sizer (1984:207–09) identified five ways in which large, bureaucratic schools undermine education:

1. **Rigid uniformity.** Bureaucratic schools run by outside specialists (such as provincial education officials) generally ignore the cultural character of local communities and the personal needs of their children.

2. **Numerical ratings.** School officials define success in terms of numerical attendance rates and dropout rates, and teachers "teach to the tests," hoping to increase test scores. Overlooked in the process are dimensions of schooling that are difficult to quantify, such as creativity and enthusiasm.

3. **Rigid expectations.** Officials expect 15-year-olds to be in grade 10 and those in grade 11 to score at a certain level on a standardized verbal achievement test. Rarely are exceptionally bright and motivated students permitted to graduate early. Likewise, poor performers are pushed from grade to grade, doomed to fail year after year.

4. **Specialization.** High school students learn French from one teacher, receive guidance from another, and are coached in sports by still others. Students shuffle between 50-minute periods throughout the school day. As a result, no school official comes to know the child well.

5. **Little individual responsibility.** Highly bureaucratic schools do not empower students to learn on their own. Similarly, teachers have little say in how they teach their classes; any change in the pace of learning or other deviation from the set curriculum risks disrupting the system.

Of course, with 5.1 million schoolchildren in Canada, schools have to be bureaucratic to get the job done. But Sizer recommends that we "humanize" schools by eliminating rigid scheduling, reducing class size, and training teachers more broadly to make them more involved in the lives of their students. Overall, as James Coleman (1993) has suggested, schools need to be less "administratively driven" and more "output-driven." Perhaps this transformation could begin by ensuring that graduation from high school depends on what students have learned rather than on how many years they have spent in the building.

Higher Education: The Silent Classroom

Passivity is also common among college and university students. Sociologists rarely study the college or university classroom—a curious fact, considering how much time they spend there. One exception was a study of a coeducational university where David Karp and William Yoels (1976) found that even in small classes, only a few students speak up. Thus passivity is a classroom norm, and students even become irritated if one of their number is especially talkative.

According to Karp and Yoels, most students think that classroom passivity is their own fault. But as anyone who watches young people outside of class knows, they are usually active and vocal. It is clearly the schools that teach students to be passive and to view instructors as experts who serve up "knowledge" and "truth." Students see their proper role as quietly listening and taking notes. As a result, the researchers estimate, just 10 percent of college class time is used for discussion.

Faculty can bring students to life in their classrooms by making use of four teaching strategies: 1) calling on students by name when they volunteer; 2) positively reinforcing student participation; 3) asking analytical rather than factual questions and giving students time to answer; and 4) asking for student opinions even when no one volunteers a response (Auster & MacRone, 1994).

Dropping Out

If many students are passive in class, others are not there at all. The problem of *dropping out*—quitting before earning a high school diploma—leaves young people (many of whom are disadvantaged to begin with) unprepared for the world of work and at high risk of poverty.

There has been a notable reduction in the Canadian high school dropout rates in the last decade. Nevertheless, in 1999, 12 percent of 20-year-olds had not completed their secondary education and, equally disturbing, the boys' rate was 1.5 times higher than that of girls. By 2009–10, while the overall dropout rate had fallen to 8.5 percent, it was 10.3 percent for males but only 6.6 percent for females. Check out the Sociology in Everyday Life box on page 484 for further information about why males are less likely to be seen on university and college campuses.

Dropout rates for Aboriginal youth remain high (22.6 percent in 2009–10). Immigrant and visible minority youth have comparatively low dropout rates (6.2 percent in 2009–10) and also go on to attain more university education than Canadian-born youth. However, as noted in Chapter 11 ("Race and Ethnicity"), immigrant and visible minority youth get a lower return on education when trying to enter the labour market (Statistics Canada, 2010b).

Many of the problems students have during their high school years follow them to college and university. Those who had difficulty attending, passing, and attaining high grades in high school are much more likely to drop out of post-secondary school than their colleagues who did not have these difficulties in high school (Butlin, 2000; Bowlby, 2005; Canadian Council on Learning, 2006). In addition, data gathered by the Toronto District School Board indicates that 32 percent of LGBTQ students do not graduate high school, while the same applies to 22 percent of straight students (Toronto District School Board, 2014).

Academic Standards

In Canada, as in many other countries, fears have been growing about the standard of education. According to a Conference Board of Canada report in 2000, Canada's position as one of the strongest economic nations in the world is "at risk because of the high secondary-school dropout rate, as well as a short supply of skilled labour and high public debt" (Conference Board of Canada, 2000). A more recent report stated that, while our education system has

functional illiteracy a lack of the reading and writing skills needed for everyday living

improved to an "A" grade, with a ranking of second among 17 peer countries, and our graduation rate has significantly improved, we need to improve our master's and doctoral programs and our adult literacy rate (Conference Board of Canada, 2011). Similar fears surround the extent of **functional illiteracy**, *a lack of the reading and writing skills needed for everyday living* (Coulombe, Tremblay, & Marchand, 2004).

Results from the 2003 Adult Literacy and Life Skills Survey (Statistics Canada, 2005) confirmed earlier 1994 findings: Many older Canadians have difficulty coping with the unfamiliar literacy and numeracy demands of employment and daily living. Depending on the country surveyed, 33 to 66 percent of adults did not attain the third of five skill levels, the minimum that educators consider needed to deal with our post-industrial knowledge society. In Canada, 42 percent of adults aged 16 to 65 are functionally illiterate (Canadian Learning and Literacy Network, 2015). The Canadian Council

For all categories of people in Canada, dropping out of school greatly reduces the chances of getting a good job and earning a secure income. Why is the dropout rate particularly high among Aboriginal students?

Gene Krebs/Getty Images

on Learning predicts that the situation will get worse. According to the organization, the number of adults who are functionally illiterate will increase by 25 percent in the next two decades. By 2031, about 15 million adults will lack reading and writing skills (KGO Adult Literacy Program, 2015).

Those most at risk for functional illiteracy include low-income families, the unemployed, seniors, Aboriginal peoples, prisoners, people with disabilities, and visible minorities (KGO Adult Literacy Program, 2015).

Grade Inflation

Academic standards depend on the use of grades that have clear meaning and are awarded for work of appropriate quality. Yet recent decades have seen substantial *grade inflation,* the awarding of ever-higher grades for average work. Though not necessarily found in every school, grade inflation is evident in both secondary and post-secondary education.

In *Ivory Tower Blues* (2007), sociologists James Côté and Anton Allahar observe that in the 1960s, the average university student had a C grade. Between the 1960s and 1990s, the distribution of As and Cs reversed. While in the 1960s about 7 percent of students received As, by the 1990s the number jumped to 25 percent.

A few colleges and universities have enacted policies that limit the share of A grades (generally to one-third of all grades). But there is little evidence that grade inflation will be reversed anytime soon. As a result, the C grade (which used to mean "middle of the pack") may all but disappear, making just about every student "above average."

What accounts for grade inflation? In part, grade inflation in colleges and universities is exacerbated at the high school level, where teachers are pressured to keep students from dropping out and to steer them toward university education. For their part, colleges and universities have responded by requiring higher entrance grades, thus also contributing to grade inflation. As Côté and Allahar note, "in the 1980s, the average entering grade for Ontario universities was a mid-B; currently it is a low A" (2007:20-1). In addition, our credential society itself creates this phenomenon: College and university credentials are today increasingly expected for jobs that used to be filled by high school–educated baby boomers. How has this affected universities? As Côté and Allahar (2011) observe, about the same time as grade inflation started to occur, universities have undergone a shift from the teaching role (following the liberal tradition) to a training role (following the new corporate tradition).

Current Issues in Canadian Education

(**14.6**) Summarize the debate over the performance of Canadian schools.

Our society's schools continuously confront new challenges. This section explores several recent and important educational issues.

School Choice

Some analysts claim that our schools teach poorly because they have no competition. Giving parents options for schooling their children might force all schools to do a better job. This is the essence of a policy called *school choice.*

The goal of school choice is to create a market for education so that parents and students can shop for the best value. According to one proposal, the government would give vouchers to families with school-age children and allow them to spend that money at public or private schools. In recent years, a few U.S. cities have experimented with choice plans designed to make public schools perform better to win the confidence of families.

Supporters claim that giving parents a choice about where to enrol their children is the only sure way to improve all schools (Clemens et al., 2014). While in the United States supporters claim school choice will decrease racial segregation and improve test scores, Canadian supporters link school choice to middle-class values of choice and increasing parental involvement (Davies & Aurini, 2008). However, critics (including teachers' unions) charge that school choice amounts to giving up on Canada's commitment to public education and that it will increase class inequality (Morse, 2002; Hopkinson, 2011).

One school choice strategy involves *charter schools,* public schools that are given more freedom to try new policies and programs. Alberta is the only province with charter schools where currently 13 such schools exist. Charter schools have the freedom to pursue a special purpose—such as meeting the needs of gifted students, following traditional teaching models, or being run as art schools—while adhering to the provincial curriculum. Charter schools can thus be considered "semiautonomous" (Lawton & Brown, 2012). Charter schools differ from private schools in that they are non-profit organizations that depend on public funding.

Another development in the school choice movement is *schooling for profit.* Supporters of this plan say school systems can be operated more efficiently by private profit-making companies than by local governments. Private schooling is nothing new, of course; more than 1900 schools in Canada are currently run by private organizations and religious groups (Moneo, 2013).

Research confirms that many public school systems suffer from bureaucratic bloat, spending far too much and teaching far too little. And Canadian society has long looked to competition to improve quality. Evidence suggests that for-profit schools have greatly reduced administrative costs, but their ability to produce better academic outcomes is criticized by research. To be sure, as the Power of Society section at the beginning of the chapter notes, students who attend private (for-profit) schools tend to achieve higher standardized test scores and are more likely to attend college or university than students who attend public (not for-profit) schools. However, we should be cautious of quickly attributing these outcomes to the quality of education offered at private schools. Private schools are actually quite similar to public schools in terms of resources and practices (Frenette & Chan, 2015). It is more likely that private schools outperform public schools due to the kind of students that tend to attend private education—typically, wealthier students with university educated parents. In light of conflicting evidence about the performance of for-profit schools, emotions among both supporters and critics of this policy continue to run high, with each side claiming to speak for the well-being of the schoolchildren caught in the middle (Richburg, 2008; Mezzacappa, 2010).

Home Schooling

Home schooling is gaining popularity in Canada. In 2012, over 21 500 children received their formal schooling at home, representing a 29 percent increase over five years (Van Pelt, 2015).

Why do parents—especially mothers—undertake the enormous challenge of schooling their own children? A couple of decades ago, most of the parents who pioneered home schooling (which is legal in Canada) wanted to give their children a strongly religious upbringing. Today, however, many home-schooling families simply believe that public schools are not doing a good job and think they can do better. To benefit their children, many parents are willing to change work schedules and relearn algebra or other necessary subjects. Many belong to groups in which parents combine their efforts, specializing in what each knows best (Lois, 2013).

Advocates of home schooling allege that given the poor performance of many public schools, no one should be surprised that a growing number of

All provinces in Canada permit home schooling. In Europe, however, many nations outlaw this practice. This German family requested and received political asylum in the United States so that they could teach their children at home. Why do you think home schooling has been controversial?

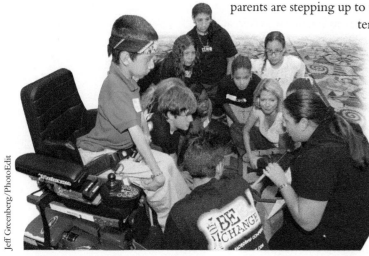

Jeff Greenberg/PhotoEdit

Educators have long debated the best way to teach children with disabilities. On one hand, such children may benefit from separate facilities staffed by specially trained teachers. On the other hand, children are less likely to be stigmatized as "different" if they are included in regular classrooms.

parents are stepping up to teach their own children. Even more impressive is that this system works—on average, students who learn at home, specifically in families who choose to home school for educational reasons, outperform those who learn in school (Van Pelt, 2015). Critics argue that home schooling reduces the amount of federal funding going to local public schools, which ends up hurting the majority of students. In addition, as one critic points out, home schooling "takes some of the most affluent and articulate parents out of the system. These are the parents who know how to get things done with administrators" (Chris Lubienski, quoted in Cloud & Morse, 2001:48).

Schooling People with Disabilities

According to the Learning Disabilities Association of Canada (2007), about 3 percent of children report some kind of learning disability, which is greater than the number of all other kinds of disabilities. Other research, such as the National Longitudinal Survey of Children and Youth (NLSCY), puts the number at almost 5 percent for children aged 6 to 15. The NLSCY reports that this number, however, varies from 1.6 percent for 6-year-olds to 7.2 percent for 10-year-olds (Learning Disabilities Association of Ontario, 2011).

Children with disabilities may have difficulty getting to and from school; once there, many with crutches or wheelchairs cannot negotiate stairs and other obstacles in school buildings. Those with learning disabilities such as hyperactivity or dyslexia need extensive personal attention from specially trained teachers. As a result, many children with mental and physical disabilities have won the right to a public education only after persistent efforts by parents and other concerned citizens (Horn & Tynan, 2001).

mainstreaming integrating students with disabilities or special needs into the overall educational program

About 95 percent of children with disabilities attend public schools (Brennan, 2009). This pattern reflects the principle of **mainstreaming**, which means *integrating students with disabilities or special needs into the overall educational program*. Mainstreaming is a form of *inclusive education* that works best for physically impaired students who have no difficulty keeping up academically with the rest of the class. A benefit of mixing children with and without disabilities in the same classrooms is allowing everyone to learn to interact with people who are different from each other.

Adult Education

According to one survey, between July 2007 and July 2008, approximately 10 million Canadian adults representing 47 percent of those aged 18 to 64 enrolled in some type of schooling or training. Adult education encompasses such broad activities as formal educational credit-based schooling, informal job-training, self-directed learning, and further education. The majority of adult learners, 34 percent, were involved in informal job-related training, while 18 percent participated in formal credit-based programs (Council of Ministers of Education, 2012). The likelihood of adult learners entering the classroom to seek further education (not training) depends on their age, level of education, and class. Generally, older adults are less likely to seek more education. And those with higher educational attainment are more likely to further pursue education, as are professional employees rather than industrial workers (Council of Ministers of Education, 2012; Livingstone & Raykov, 2013).

Why do adults return to the classroom? The most common reasons given are to advance a career or train for a new job, but many are simply seeking personal enrichment. During economic downturns, as we have experienced in recent years, the number of adults returning to the classroom (including many who are out of work) typically goes up. Regardless of the reason adults return to the classroom, support is lacking; about 4 million adults in Canada express an unmet need for education (Livingstone & Raykov, 2013).

The Turbulence of the Teaching Labour Market

A final challenge for Canadian schools is finding the right balance of teachers to fill the classrooms. From the 1970s to the 2000s, educational planners across Canada worried that a shortage of teachers would leave many schools understaffed. Ontario, for example, expected to lose 45 percent of its teachers due to retirement between 1998 and 2008. The province responded by funding more seats in teacher educational programs (Galway, 2015). Teaching jobs were in abundance and were difficult to fill. By the mid-2000s, the shortage had turned into an oversupply. The Ontario College of Teachers warned about a surplus of teachers in 2005, along with growing underemployment (Ontario College of Teachers, 2012). Teaching jobs were increasingly becoming scarce and easy to fill.

Across Canada, educational planners are suggesting that there is a surplus of recent graduates who want to but cannot find work as teachers. Nova Scotia reported a critical overabundance of new teachers in 2008 and 2012 (Tibbetts, 2008; Galway, 2015), and in British Columbia it is well known that finding work is quite difficult as "[t]here are roughly 3300 certified teachers for 900 teaching jobs in the province every year" (Hyslop, 2014). Many of these reports, however, also note shortages in certain areas. For example, French language teachers are in demand in British Columbia amid this surplus of teachers. Furthermore, the overabundance is more pronounced in the Atlantic provinces, Ontario, and British Columbia than in Alberta or in Aboriginal on-reserve communities.

What causes the turbulence in the teaching labour market? A number of social factors come into play, such as changes in student enrolment, government policy, school board funding, as well as population change due to immigration and migration patterns. In Ontario, fewer teachers retired than was expected, leading to a surplus of teachers that could not be absorbed by the labour market.

Recent reports indicate that the situation may be changing yet again. From a shortage from the 1970s to the mid-2000s, to a surplus from the mid-2000s to the mid-2010s, qualified teachers may be in demand again. The Canadian government maintains that the current job prospects for newly trained secondary school teachers are "fair" (Service Canada, 2014), and in its most current report, the Ontario College of Teachers reports "significant change in direction" (2014:4). With a renewed wave of retirements and fewer graduates, the surplus may be starting to recede. Whether this is going to be the case across Canada remains to be seen. What is certain, however, is that the teaching labour market is difficult to predict.

Debate about education in Canada extends beyond the issues noted here. The Seeing Sociology in Everyday Life box on page 484 highlights the declining share of college students who are men.

Schooling: Looking Ahead

Despite the facts that Canada leads the world in sending people to post-secondary schools and that the high school dropout rates have improved, the public school system still struggles with serious problems, including comparative lower success rates for males and Aboriginal students.

Many of the problems of schooling discussed in this chapter have their roots in the larger society. We cannot expect schools *by themselves* to provide high-quality education. Schools will improve only to the extent that students, teachers, parents, and local communities commit themselves to educational excellence. In short, educational problems are *social* problems for which there is no quick fix.

For much of the twentieth century, there were just two models for education in Canada: public schools run by the government and private schools operated by non-governmental organizations. In recent decades, however, many new ideas about schooling have emerged, including schooling for profit and a wide range of "school choice" programs. In the decades ahead, we will probably see some significant changes in mass education, guided in part by the results of social science research into the outcomes of different strategies.

Seeing Sociology in Everyday Life

The Twenty-First-Century Campus: Where Are the Men?

Meg: What's with this campus having so few men?

Tricia: Does it matter? I'd rather focus on my work.

Mark: I don't mind it at all!

A century ago, the campuses of colleges and universities across North America might as well have hung out a sign that read "Men Only." Almost all of the students and faculty were male. There were a small number of women's colleges, but many more schools—including some of the most prestigious universities such as University of Toronto, McGill, Yale, Harvard, and Princeton—barred women outright.

Since then, women have won greater social equality. By 1980, the number of women enrolled at North American universities and colleges finally matched the number of men.

In a surprising trend, however, the share of women on campus has continued to increase. As a result, in 2011, men accounted for only 40.9 percent of bachelor's degree holders aged 25 to 34 (Statistics Canada, 2013c). Meg DeLong noticed the gender imbalance right away when she moved into her dorm at her new university; she soon learned that just 39 percent of her first-year classmates were men. In some classes there were few men, and women usually dominated discussions. Out of class, DeLong and

Corbis/SuperStock

many other women soon complained that having so few men on campus hurt their social life. Not surprisingly, most of the men felt otherwise (Fonda, 2000).

What accounts for the shifting gender balance on North American campuses? One theory is that young men are drawn away from college or university by the lure of jobs, especially in high technology. This pattern is sometimes termed the "Bill Gates syndrome," after the Microsoft founder, who dropped out of higher education and soon became the world's richest person. In addition, analysts point to an anti-intellectual male culture. Young women are drawn to learning and seek to do well in school, but young men attach less importance to studying. Rightly or wrongly, more men seem to think they can get a good job without investing years of their lives and a considerable amount of money in pursuit of a university or college degree.

The gender gap is evident in all racial and ethnic categories and at all class levels. Among Canadian Aboriginal individuals aged 35 to 44, 13.6 percent of women and only 7.6 percent of men held a university degree in 2011 (Statistics Canada, 2013e). The lower the income level, the greater the gender gap in post-secondary attendance.

Many educators are concerned about a lack of men on campus. In an effort to attract more balanced enrolments, some North American academic institutions are adopting what amounts to affirmative action programs for males. But courts in several jurisdictions have already ruled such policies illegal. Many colleges and universities are therefore turning to more active recruitment; admissions officers are paying special attention to male applicants and stressing an institution's strength in mathematics and science—areas traditionally popular with men. In the same way that colleges and universities across the country are striving to increase their share of Aboriginal and visible minority students, the hope is that they can also succeed in attracting a larger share of men.

What Do You Think?

1. Why do you think women outnumber men on college and university campuses?

2. Is there a gender imbalance on your campus? Does it create problems? If so, what problems? For whom?

3. Should post-secondary institutions try to balance enrolments by sex? Is affirmative action for men a good or bad way to do this?

Another factor that will continue to reshape schools is information technology. Today, almost all primary and secondary schools use computers for instruction. Computers prompt students to be more active and allow them to progress at their own pace. Even so, computers will never bring to the educational process the personal insights or imagination of a motivated human teacher.

At the college level, online learning is now available at about three-fourths of all institutions, and about one-fourth of today's college students take one or more courses online.

An increasing share of textbooks is now electronic, and this digital format allows readers to become more active in their own learning (Parker, Lenhart, & Moore, 2011).

Technology will never solve all the problems that plague our schools, including violence and rigid bureaucracy. What we need is a broad plan for social change that will provide universal schooling of high quality—a goal that we have yet to achieve.

Health: A Global Survey

(14.7) Contrast patterns of health in low- and high-income countries.

Another institution that expands greatly in modern societies is **medicine**, *the social institution that focuses on fighting disease and improving health.* In ideal terms, according to the World Health Organization (1946:3), **health** is *a state of complete physical, mental, and social well-being.* This definition underscores the important fact that health is as much a social as a biological issue.

medicine the social institution that focuses on fighting disease and improving health

health a state of complete physical, mental, and social well-being

Health and Society

Society affects people's health in four major ways:

1. **Cultural patterns define health.** Standards of health vary from culture to culture. A century ago, yaws, a contagious skin disease, was so common in sub-Saharan Africa that people there considered it normal (Dubos, 1980). In many areas of Canada and the United States, a rich diet is so common that most adults consider overeating to be normal and are now overweight. "Health," therefore, is sometimes a matter of having the same conditions or diseases as one's neighbours (Pinhey, Rubinstein, & Colfax, 1997; CDC, 2011a).

   What people see as healthful also reflects what they think is morally good. Members of our society (especially men) think that a competitive way of life is "healthy" because it fits our cultural mores, but stress contributes to heart disease and many other illnesses. People who object to homosexuality on moral grounds call this sexual orientation "sick," even though it is natural from a biological point of view. Thus ideas about health act as a form of social control, encouraging conformity to cultural norms.

2. **Cultural standards of health change over time.** Early in the twentieth century, some physicians warned women not to go to college or university because higher education would strain the female brain. Others claimed that masturbation was a threat to health. We now know that both of these ideas are false. Fifty years ago, on the other hand, few physicians understood the dangers of cigarette smoking or too much sun exposure, practices that we now recognize as serious health risks. Even patterns of basic hygiene change over time. Today, most people in Canada bathe or shower every day; this is three times as often as 50 years ago (Gillespie, 2000).

3. **A society's technology affects people's health.** In poor nations, infectious diseases are widespread because of malnutrition and poor sanitation. As industrialization raises living standards, people become healthier. But industrial technology also creates new threats to health. As Chapter 15 ("Population, Urbanization, and Environment") explains, high-income ways of life endanger health by overtaxing the world's resources and creating pollution.

4. **Social inequality affects people's health.** Most societies distribute resources unequally. Overall, the rich have far better physical, mental, and emotional health than the poor.

Because health is closely linked to social life, human well-being has improved over the long course of history as societies developed more advanced technology. Differences in societal development are also the cause of striking differences in health around the world today.

Health in Low-Income Countries

Around the world, severe poverty cuts decades off the long life expectancy typical of rich countries. People living in sub-Saharan Africa have a life expectancy of barely 50 years, and in the poorest countries, nearly 1 in 10 newborns dies within a year and almost 1 in 4 people dies before reaching the age of 30 (Population Reference Bureau, 2012; World Bank, 2013b).

The World Health Organization reports that 1 billion people around the world—one person in six—suffer from serious illness due to poverty. Most poverty-linked disease occurs in low-income countries, where poverty accounts for 70 percent of all illness. In rich countries, by contrast, poverty is the cause of just 7 percent of all illness (Bloom et al., 2011; Murray et al., 2012).

How does poverty threaten health? In simple terms, poor sanitation and malnutrition kill people of all ages. Poor people commonly lack safe drinking water, and bad water carries a number of infectious diseases, including influenza, pneumonia, and tuberculosis, which are widespread killers in poor societies today. To make matters worse, medical personnel are few and far between in low-income countries; as a result, the world's poorest people—many of whom live in Central Africa—never see a physician.

In a classic example of a vicious circle, poverty breeds disease, which reduces people's ability to work, increasing poverty. When medical technology does control infectious disease, the populations of poor nations soar. But without enough resources to provide for the current population, poor societies can ill afford population increases. Therefore, programs that lower death rates in poor countries will succeed only if they are coupled with programs that reduce birth rates.

Health in High-Income Countries

As the standard of living rises, health generally improves. But, looking back in time, this improvement did not take place immediately. By 1800, as the Industrial Revolution took hold, factory jobs in cities attracted people from the countryside. Cities quickly became overcrowded, causing serious sanitation problems. Factories fouled the air with smoke, and workplace accidents were common.

Gradually, industrialization raised living standards, providing better nutrition and safer housing for most people, so that after about 1850, health began to improve. Also around this time, medical advances began to control infectious diseases. In 1854, for example, a researcher named John Snow mapped the street addresses of London's cholera victims and found that they had all drunk water from the same well. Not long afterwards, scientists linked cholera to a specific bacterium and developed a vaccine against the deadly disease. Armed with scientific knowledge, early environmentalists campaigned against common practices such as discharging raw sewage into rivers used for drinking water. By the early twentieth century, death rates from infectious diseases had fallen sharply.

A glance at Table 14–3 shows that many of the leading killers in 1921–1925 were infectious diseases. Today, in all but the poorest nations of the world, such diseases account for just a small percentage of deaths. It is now chronic illnesses, such as heart disease, cancer, and stroke, that cause most deaths, usually in old age (Murray et al., 2012).

TABLE 14–3 Leading Causes of Death in Canada over Time

1921–1925	2011
1. Heart disease	1. Cancer
2. Influenza, bronchitis, and pneumonia	2. Heart disease
3. Disease of early infancy	3. Stroke
4. Tuberculosis	4. Chronic lower respiratory diseases
5. Cancer	5. Accidents
6. Gastritis, duodenitis, enteritis, and colitis	6. Diabetes
7. Accidents	7. Alzheimer's disease
8. Communicable diseases	8. Influenza and pneumonia

Sources: Information for 1921–1925 is from Katherine Arnup, "Death, Dying and Canadian Families." The Vanier Institute of the Family, 2013, p. 6; information for 2011 is from Statistics Canada (2014c).

Health in Canada

(**14.8**) Analyze how race, class, gender, and age are linked to health.

Because Canada is a rich nation, health is generally good by world standards. Still, some categories of people have much better health than others.

Who Is Healthy? Age, Gender, Class, and Race

Social epidemiology is *the study of how health and disease are distributed throughout a society's population.* Social epidemiologists examine the origin and spread of epidemic diseases and try to understand how people's health is tied to their physical and social environments. In Canada, a 4.7-year gap for men and 2.3-year gap for women in average life expectancy separates the richest and poorest communities (Greenberg & Normandin, 2011). This difference can be examined through the lens of age, gender, social class, and race.

social epidemiology the study of how health and disease are distributed throughout a society's population.

Age and Gender

In Canada, the death of a young person is a rare event that is typically viewed as unexpected and tragic. Still, young people do fall victim to accidents and, in recent decades, to acquired immune deficiency syndrome (AIDS).

Throughout the life course, women have better health than men. First, girls are less likely than boys to die before or immediately after birth. As socialization begins, males become more aggressive and individualistic than females, which contributes to young males having three times the risk of accidents, four times the rate of suicide, and five times the risk of dying from a homicide (CDC, 2012). Later in life, men are also more likely to die from heart disease. As the Thinking About Diversity box on page 488 explains, the combination of chronic impatience, uncontrolled ambition, and outbursts of hostility that physicians call "coronary-prone behaviour" is a fairly close match with our culture's definition of masculinity. This is one important way in which gender affects the "bottom line" of longevity, with women, on average, outliving men by about five years. Yet, women are twice as likely as men to be given a diagnosis of unipolar depression, anxiety, panic disorder, or agoraphobia, and three times as likely to be diagnosed as having a histrionic personality and borderline personality disorder. Research suggests that mental health problems are influenced by gender roles and, in fact, that certain diagnoses are gender specific (Benoit et al., 2009).

Social Class and Race

Government researchers tell us that higher income goes hand-in-hand with a longer life expectancy. By dividing Canadians into five equal groups by income (quintiles) based on neighbourhood income, researchers are able to determine that the poorest communities in Canada have a life expectancy of 78.7 years while the highest income-earning communities have a life expectancy of 82.2 years. Income thus accounts for a gap of 3.5 years. Poor health regions tend to have higher rates of obesity, smoking, and drinking, and are more likely to be remote or rural, with relatively more Aboriginal populations, and fewer high school and university graduates (Greenberg & Normandin, 2011).

Infant mortality—the death rate among children under one year of age—is twice as high for Aboriginal children in Canada as for other children born to privilege. Although the health of the richest children in this country is the best in the world, the poorest children in Canada are as vulnerable to disease as those in low-income nations such as Lebanon and Vietnam.

Health, race, and ethnicity are also linked. Because Aboriginal Canadians are much more likely than other Canadians to be poor, they are more likely to die in infancy and to have a shorter life expectancy, as Figure 14–2 shows. Sex complicates this picture because females outlive males in each racial category.

Cigarette Smoking

Cigarette smoking tops the list of preventable health hazards in Canada. More than 47 000 men and women die prematurely each year as a direct result of cigarette smoking, a figure that exceeds the death toll from alcohol, cocaine, heroin, homicide, suicide, automobile accidents, and AIDS combined. Put differently, about 20 percent of all deaths in the last decade have been caused by smoking (Janz, 2012). Smokers also suffer more often from minor illnesses such as the flu, and pregnant women who smoke increase the likelihood of spontaneous abortion, prenatal death, and low-birthweight babies. Even non-smokers exposed to cigarette smoke have

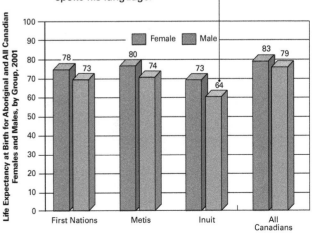

• Simon Pastori, 72, has only ever seen health professionals from the south. None of them spoke his language.

FIGURE 14–2 Projected Life Expectancy at Birth by Aboriginal Status, Canada, 2017

Source: Statistics Canada (2010c). Aboriginal Statistics at a Glance. Catalogue no. 89-645-XWE. 2010c. Reproduced and distributed on an "as is" basis with the permission of Statistics Canada.

Thinking About Diversity: Race, Class, and Gender

Masculinity: A Threat to Health?

Jeff: Cindy! If you don't get out of there in ten seconds, I'm gonna break the door down!

Cindy: Chill out! I have as much right to be in the bathroom as you do. I'll come out when I'm ready.

Jeff: Are you going to take *all day*?

Cindy: Why are you guys always in such a hurry?

Physicians call it "coronary-prone behaviour." Psychologists call it the "Type A personality." Sociologists recognize it as our culture's concept of masculinity. This combination of attitudes and behaviour, common among men in our society, includes chronic impatience ("Get outta my way!"), uncontrolled ambition ("I've gotta have it—I *need* that!"), and free-floating hostility ("Why are people *such idiots?*").

This pattern, although normal from a cultural point of view, is one major reason that men who are driven to succeed are at high risk of heart disease. By acting out the Type A personality, we may get the job done, but we set in motion complex biochemical processes that are very hard on the human heart.

Steve Prezant/Corbis

Here are a few questions to help you determine your own degree of risk (or that of someone important to you):

1. Do you believe you have to be aggressive to succeed? Do nice guys finish last? For your heart's sake, try to remove hostility from your life. Here's a place to start: Eliminate profanity from your speech. Try replacing aggression with compassion, which can be surprisingly effective in dealing with other people. Medically speaking, substituting compassion and humour for irritation and aggravation will improve your health.

2. How well do you handle uncertainty and opposition? Do you lose patience with other people ("Why won't the waiter take my order?" "This customer just doesn't get it!")? We all like to know what's going on, and we want others to agree with us. But the world often doesn't work that way. Accepting uncertainty and opposition makes us more mature and certainly healthier.

3. Are you uncomfortable showing positive emotions? Many men think giving and accepting love—from women, from children, and from other men—is a sign of weakness. But the medical truth is that love supports health and anger damages it.

As human beings, we have a great deal of choice about how we live. Think about the choices you make, and reflect on how our society's idea of masculinity often makes us hard on others (including those we love) and, just as important, hard on ourselves.

What Do You Think?

1. Do you think masculinity is harmful to health? Why or why not?

2. Have you had any experiences that cause you to link masculinity or femininity to health?

3. How might we try to modify our behaviour in the interest of better health?

Sources: Friedman and Rosenman (1974) and M.P. Levine (1990).

---

a high risk of smoking-related diseases; health officials estimate that second-hand smoke caused 831 deaths in adults in 2002, mostly from heart disease and lung cancer (Health Canada, 2011).

Only after World War I did smoking become popular in this country. The adult popularity of cigarettes peaked in 1960, when almost 45 percent of Canadian adults smoked. Despite growing evidence of its dangers, smoking remained fashionable until around a generation ago. By 2011, 22.3 percent of males and 17.5 percent of females aged 12 or older smoked cigarettes either daily or occasionally (Janz, 2012). Today, an increasing number of people consider smoking a mild form of social deviance, and all territories and provinces have banned smoking in public buildings.

Quitting tobacco is difficult because cigarette smoke contains nicotine, a physically addictive drug. In addition, many people smoke to cope with stress: Divorced and separated people, the unemployed, and people serving in the armed forces are likely to smoke. While more Canadian men than women smoke, cigarettes (the only form of tobacco use popular among women) have taken a toll on women's health. By the early 1990s, lung cancer surpassed breast cancer as a cause of death among Canadian women.

In 2013, tobacco companies reported over $30 billion in sales in Canada. With revenues like that, the tobacco industry is able to spend significant amounts every year employing lobbyists to influence tobacco policy. It is also able to finance efforts aimed at presenting the controversy over smoking in terms of the "antismoking lobby" versus people who choose to smoke and also funds campaigns to play down the ways that tobacco companies threaten public health (Eriksen, Mackay, & Ross, 2012).

In 1997, the tobacco industry admitted that cigarette smoking is harmful to health and agreed to stop marketing cigarettes to young people. Despite the antismoking trend in North America, research shows that 4 percent of middle school students, 16 percent of high school students, and 31 percent of college students smoke at least occasionally. E-cigarettes, whose effects on health remain unknown, have been tried by 20 percent of Canadians aged 15 to 19. In addition, chewing tobacco as well as using hookahs to smoke flavoured tobacco are gaining popularity among the young, and both practices are threats to health (CDC, 2011b; American College Health Association, 2012; National Conference of State Legislatures, 2012; Reid et al., 2015).

The tobacco industry has increased its sales abroad, especially in low- and middle-income countries where there is less regulation of tobacco products. In many countries, especially in Asia, a large majority of men smoke. Worldwide, more than 1 billion adults (about 25 percent of the total) smoke, consuming some 6 trillion cigarettes annually, and there is as yet no sign of the decline in smoking that we have seen in high-income countries. If the current global trends continue, 80 percent of tobacco-related deaths will occur in low- and middle-income nations and the death toll will increase to more than 8 million a year by 2030, which amounts to one smoking-related death in the world every four seconds (Horton, 2012).

The harm that can come from cigarette smoking is real. But the good news is that about 10 years after quitting, an ex-smoker's health is about as good as that of someone who never smoked at all.

Eating Disorders

An **eating disorder** is *a physical and mental disorder that involves intense dieting or other unhealthy method of weight control driven by the desire to be very thin.* Often, the desire to be thin is itself a symptom of some other underlying mental illness or condition. One eating disorder, *anorexia nervosa,* is characterized by dieting to the point of starvation; another is *bulimia,* which involves binge eating followed by induced vomiting to avoid weight gain.

Gender plays a part in eating disorders: Among teenagers, girls are about three times more likely than boys to be affected by these diseases. Among adults, women are three times more likely to suffer from anorexia nervosa and five times more likely to suffer from bulimia than are men. People with eating disorders come from all social backgrounds, although risk levels are highest among whites living in affluent families.

For Canadian women, culture equates slimness with being successful and attractive to men. Conversely, we tend to stereotype overweight women (and to a lesser extent, men) as lazy, sloppy, and even stupid (Levine, 1987; Becker, 1999; National Institute of Mental Health, 2012).

Research shows that most college- and university-age women believe that "guys like thin girls," that being thin is crucial to physical attractiveness, and that they are not as thin as men would like. In fact, most college-age women actually want to be thinner than most college-age men want them to be. Men typically express more satisfaction with their own body shapes (Fallon & Rozin, 1985), though some research into young men has related body image dissatisfaction to unhealthy body-building practices, including the use of anabolic steroids (Spurr, Barry, & Walker, 2013).

Because few women are able to meet our culture's unrealistic standards of beauty, many women develop a low self-image. Our idealized image of beauty leads many young women to diet to the point of risking their health and even their lives.

People with eating disorders contend with more than their illness. Research indicates that they are also viewed by others not as people with a disorder but as weak individuals who are seeking attention. In fact, the stigma attached to eating disorders was found to be more severe than the stigma attached to depression (Roehrig & McLean, 2010).

eating disorder a physical and mental disorder that involves intense dieting or other unhealthy method of weight control driven by the desire to be very thin

Obesity

Eating disorders such as anorexia nervosa and bulimia are serious, but they are not the biggest eating-related problem in Canada. In the population as a whole, obesity is rapidly on the rise.

The Canadian government reports that 41.3 percent of men and 26.9 percent of women are overweight compared to 12 percent for the entire world (Statistics Canada, 2012). Being overweight is defined as having a *body mass index* (BMI) of 25.0 to 29.9, or roughly 10 to 30 pounds over a healthy weight. Obesity is a more serious issue that is defined as having a BMI of 30 or higher, or being at least 30 pounds over a healthy weight. Of all adults in Canada, 24.8 percent are clinically obese. Researchers note a 17.5 percent increase in obesity rates across Canada since 2003 (Navaneelan & Janz, 2014). National Map 14–2 shows this trend.

Being overweight can limit physical activity and raises the risk of a number of serious diseases, including heart disease, stroke, and diabetes. According to a 2010 report, the cost of treating diseases caused by obesity is $6 billion, representing slightly over 4 percent of Canada's health care budget. Most seriously, from 1985 to 2000 some 57 000 people died in Canada from diseases related to being overweight (Katzmarzyk & Ardern, 2004; Canadian Obesity Network, 2015).

Seeing Ourselves

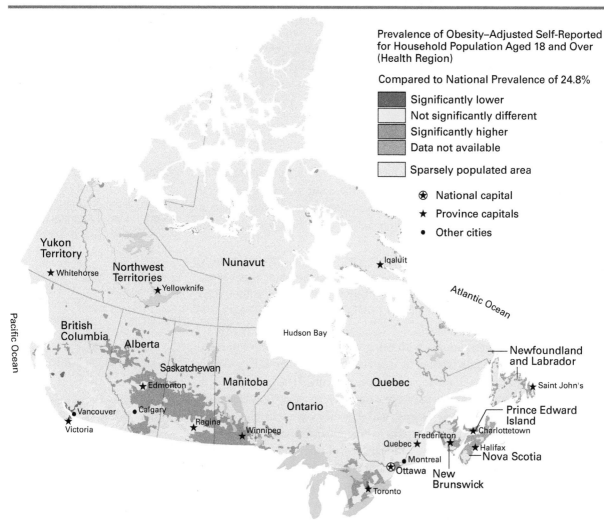

NATIONAL MAP 14–2   Obesity Across Canada, 2011–2012

The map shows the prevalence of obesity in each health region in Canada by comparing it to the national average of 24.8 percent. Obesity levels are lowest in Kelowna, British Columbia (17 percent), and highest in Saint John, New Brunswick (38.1 percent). What factors do you think are responsible for this distribution of obesity across Canada?

Source: Navaneelan and Janz (2014). http://www.statcan.gc.ca/pub/82-624-x/2014001/article/11922/c-g/fig01-eng.htm. Reproduced and distributed on an "as is" basis with the permission of Statistics Canada.

What are the social causes of obesity? One factor is that we live in a society in which more and more people have jobs that keep them sitting in front of computer screens rather than engaging in the type of physical labour that was common a century ago. Even when we are not on the job, most of the work around the house is done by machines (or other people). Children spend more of their time sitting as well, watching television or playing video games.

Then, of course, there is diet. The typical person in North America is eating more salty, sugary, and fatty food than ever before (Wells & Buzby, 2008). And as companies try to sell food for less money to gain efficiencies of scale, all meals are getting larger: The U.S. Department of Agriculture reported that in 2000, the typical U.S. adult consumed 64 more kilograms (140 more pounds) of food each year than was true a decade earlier. Comparing old and new editions of cookbooks, recipes that used to say they would feed six now say they will feed four. The odds of being overweight go up among people with lower incomes partly because they may lack the education to make healthy choices and partly because stores in low-income communities offer a greater selection of low-cost, high-fat snack foods and fewer healthful fruits and vegetables. As well, those with lower incomes may lack an affordable way to exercise (Hellmich, 2002).

Just as researchers have tracked a rising tide of obesity in Canada, they are also finding increasing prejudice directed against people who are overweight. Simply put, many people see being thin as embodying important cultural values such as personal discipline, trying hard, and ambition to succeed. Being overweight, by contrast, seems to imply the absence of these same traits.

Such attitudes are not only widespread but also can be quite harmful. Evidence suggests that physicians are likely to doubt the ability of overweight patients to follow "doctor's orders"; similarly, juries may be less likely to feel sympathy for an overweight person accused of a crime. Perhaps most important of all, employers tend to assess workers and job candidates who are overweight in less positive terms, even in the absence of any supporting evidence (Neporent, 2013).

Sexually Transmitted Infections

Sexual activity, though both pleasurable and vital to the continuation of our species, can transmit more than 50 types of *sexually transmitted infections* (STIs). Because our culture associates sex with sin, some people regard STIs not only as illnesses but also as marks of immorality.

STIs grabbed national attention during the "sexual revolution" of the 1960s, when infection rates rose dramatically as people became sexually active at younger ages and had a greater number of partners. This means that STIs are an exception to the general decline in infectious diseases over the course of the past century. By the late 1980s, the rising dangers of STIs, especially AIDS, generated a sexual counterrevolution as people moved away from casual sex (Kain, 1987; Laumann et al., 1994). The following sections briefly describe several common STIs.

Gonorrhea, Chlamydia, and Syphilis

Gonorrhea, chlamydia, and syphilis are caused by microscopic organisms that are almost always transmitted by sexual contact. Untreated, gonorrhea causes sterility, chlamydia can lead to infertility in women and prostate infection in men, and syphilis can damage major organs and result in blindness, mental disorders, and death.

After a steady and dramatic decline in gonorrhea rates since the early 1980s, an increase of 40.8 percent was reported between 2002 and 2011. The 2011 rate for gonorrhea was 33.1 per 100 000. Males (38.4 per 100 000) had higher rates than females (27.8 per 100 000) and the highest growth rate was found in the Northwest Territories. Chlamydia is the most prominent STI in Canada, with an increase of 61.8 percent between 2002 and 2011. Its 2011 rate was 290.4 per 100 000. Chlamydia continues to spread steadily among males and females, as well as all age groups. It is currently, however, more prominent among females (378.7 per 100 000) than males (200.1 per 100 000). The highest growth rates for chlamydia were observed in the Northwest Territories, the Yukon, Manitoba, and Saskatchewan. Syphilis rates have followed a similar pattern of significant decline over time, though the pattern has reversed in the recent period for both males and females and is especially noticeable among the country's poorer populations, such as residents of Vancouver's Downtown Eastside. Thus, the national rate had remained between 0.4 and 0.6 per 100 000 throughout the 1990s. From 2002 to 2011, syphilis rose by 231.8 percent. In 2011, the observed rate for syphilis was 5.1 per 100 000. Syphilis continued to affect males (9.6 per 100 000) more than females (0.7 per 100 000) and the highest growth rate was reported in Quebec and New Brunswick (Public Health Agency of Canada, 2011).

The three STIs discussed here can easily be cured with antibiotics such as penicillin. Thus, none is currently a major health problem in Canada.

Genital Herpes

Genital herpes is not a reportable STI in Canada. It is estimated, however, that the prevalence rate is about one in five in the adult population (Steben & Sacks, 1997). Though far less serious than gonorrhea and syphilis, herpes is incurable. People with genital herpes may not have any symptoms, or they may experience periodic, painful blisters on the genitals accompanied by fever and headache. Although it is not fatal to adults, women with active genital herpes can transmit the disease during a vaginal delivery, and it can be deadly to newborns. Therefore, infected women often give birth by Caesarean section (CDC, 2011c).

AIDS

The most serious of all STIs is acquired immune deficiency syndrome (AIDS). Identified in 1981, it is incurable and almost always fatal. AIDS is caused by the human immunodeficiency virus (HIV), which attacks white blood cells, weakening the immune system. AIDS thus makes a person vulnerable to a wide range of diseases that eventually cause death.

HIV deaths in Canada numbered 303 in 2011. In addition, officials recorded some 3175 new cases in Canada in 2011, raising the total number of cases on record to 78 511. Of these people, 18 275 have died (Public Health Agency of Canada, 2014). Globally, the number of HIV infections is no longer rapidly increasing. In 2011, about 2.5 million adults and children became infected, which represents a 20 percent drop from the annual number of new infections a decade earlier. At the same time, the number of infected people remains huge, about 34 million people. The global AIDS death toll now exceeds 25 million, with about 1 percent of the 2011 total of 1.7 million deaths occurring in the United States (UNAIDS, 2012). Global Map 14–2 on page 493 shows that Africa (especially south of the Sahara) has the highest HIV infection rate and accounts for 69 percent of all world cases. The good news is that many of the countries in this region of the world are making dramatic strides toward reducing the rate of infections, especially among children. The risk of infection remains higher for females than for males, not only because HIV is transmitted more easily from men to women but also because many African cultures encourage women to be submissive to men (UNAIDS, 2012).

Upon infection, people with HIV display no symptoms at all, so most are unaware of their condition. Symptoms of AIDS may not appear for a year or longer, during which time an infected person may infect others. Within five years, one-third of infected people who have gone untreated develop full-blown AIDS; half develop AIDS within 10 years; and almost all become sick within 20 years. In low-income countries, the progression of the illness is much more rapid, with many people dying within a few years of becoming infected.

HIV is infectious but not contagious. That means that HIV is transmitted from person to person through blood, semen, or breast milk but not through casual contact such as shaking hands, hugging, sharing towels or dishes, swimming together, or even coughing and sneezing. The risk of transmitting AIDS through saliva (as in kissing) is extremely low. The risk of transmitting HIV through sexual activity is greatly reduced by the use of latex condoms. However, abstinence or an exclusive relationship with an uninfected person is the only sure way to avoid infection.

Specific behaviours place people at high risk for HIV infection. *Anal sex* can cause rectal bleeding, allowing easy transmission of HIV from one person to another. The fact

Window on the World

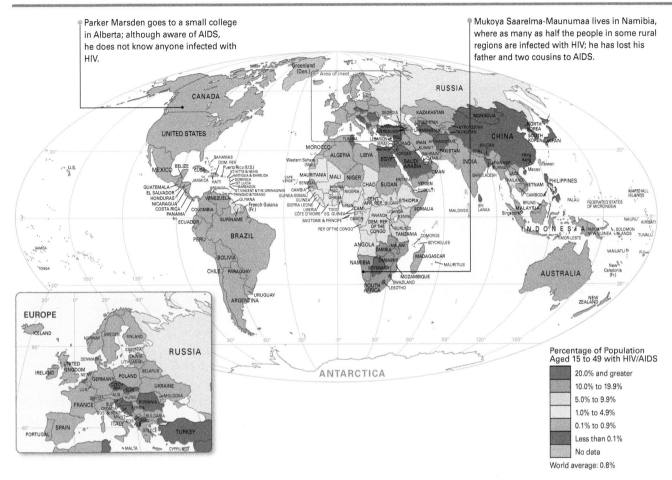

Parker Marsden goes to a small college in Alberta; although aware of AIDS, he does not know anyone infected with HIV.

Mukoya Saarelma-Maunumaa lives in Namibia, where as many as half the people in some rural regions are infected with HIV; he has lost his father and two cousins to AIDS.

Percentage of Population Aged 15 to 49 with HIV/AIDS

- 20.0% and greater
- 10.0% to 19.9%
- 5.0% to 9.9%
- 1.0% to 4.9%
- 0.1% to 0.9%
- Less than 0.1%
- No data

World average: 0.8%

GLOBAL MAP 14–2   HIV/AIDS Infection of Adults in Global Perspective

Sixty-nine percent of all global HIV infections are in sub-Saharan Africa. In Swaziland, one-fourth of people between the ages of 15 and 49 are infected with HIV/AIDS. This very high infection rate reflects the prevalence of other sexually transmitted diseases and infrequent use of condoms, two factors that promote transmission of HIV. South and Southeast Asia account for about 15 percent of global HIV infections; by contrast, North America and South America taken together account for 8 percent of global HIV infections. From another angle, in Thailand, 1 percent of people are now infected compared to 0.2 percent of people in Canada. The incidence of infection in Muslim nations is extremely low by world standards.

Sources: Population Reference Bureau (2012), UNAIDS (2012), and Public Health Agency of Canada (2014).

that many men who have sex with other men (MSM) engage in anal sex helps explain why this category accounted for 49.3 percent of HIV cases in Canada in 2013. This represents a decrease from 80 percent when HIV first became known in the mid-1980s (Public Health Agency of Canada, 2014).

Sharing needles to inject drugs is a second high-risk behaviour. At present, intravenous drug users account for 12.8 percent of people with HIV, so sex with an intravenous drug user is also very risky. Because intravenous drug use is more common among poor people and Aboriginal peoples in Canada, AIDS is now becoming a disease of the socially disadvantaged. The majority of HIV cases reported in 2013, 49.4 percent, were accounted for by whites. Fewer were reported by racial minorities. However, we should note that many racial minorities are overrepresented in HIV cases while whites, who make up approximately 80 percent of the population, are underrepresented: Black Canadians (2.9 percent of the population) account for 17.3 percent of people diagnosed with HIV, and Aboriginal Canadians (4.3 percent of the population) account for 15.9 percent of HIV cases. Among women,

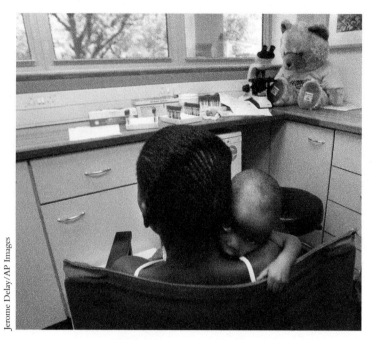

In the African nation of Botswana, about 25 percent of the population lives with HIV. In recent years, the spread of AIDS in sub-Saharan Africa has been greatly reduced. Even so, some 16 000 children under age 14 in Botswana are now living with HIV. This infant, who already has AIDS, is fighting for his life.

39.3 percent diagnosed were black, 32 percent Aboriginal, and 21.3 percent white. By contrast, Asian Canadians (15 percent of the population) account for only 6 percent of HIV cases (Public Health Agency of Canada, 2014).

Use of any drug, including alcohol, also increases the risk of being infected with HIV to the extent that it impairs judgment. In other words, even people who understand the risks may make bad choices regarding sexual activity or intravenous drug use when under the influence of alcohol, ecstasy, or some other drug.

As we already noted, 49.3 percent of people with AIDS became infected through MSM exposure, but heterosexual activity can transmit HIV, and the danger rises with the number of sexual partners one has, especially if they fall into high-risk categories. In Canada, heterosexual contact is the second highest reported category for HIV transmission, accounting for 29.6 percent of all cases in 2013 (Public Health Agency of Canada, 2014). Worldwide, heterosexual relations are the primary means of HIV transmission, accounting for two-thirds of all infections. In the 1980s, the Canadian government initially responded slowly to the AIDS crisis, largely because gays and intravenous drug users are widely viewed as deviant. But funding for AIDS research, including from the country's primary health funding agency (the Canadian Institutes of Health Research), has increased dramatically in recent years, and researchers have identified some drugs, including protease inhibitors, that suppress the symptoms of the disease. Canada has also approved a safe injection site in Vancouver, British Columbia. The facility opened its doors in 2003 and is the first of its kind in North America. A study published in the *New England Journal of Medicine* shows that drug users who use Vancouver's safe injection site are more likely to enter detox and other treatment facilities (Kerr et al., 2005). Other research has shown that the safe injection site has helped to increase public order, reduce needle sharing in Vancouver's Downtown Eastside (Wood et al., 2004), and reduce fatal overdoses in the vicinity by 35 percent, and by 9 percent in all of Vancouver (Marshall et al., 2011). However, educational programs remain the most effective weapon against AIDS because prevention is the only way to stop a disease that so far has no cure.

Ethical Issues Surrounding Death

Now that technological advances are giving human beings the power to draw the line separating life and death, we must decide how and when to do so. In other words, questions about the use of medical technology have added an ethical dimension to health and illness.

When Does Death Occur?

Common sense suggests that life ends when breathing and heartbeat stop. But the ability to revive or replace a heart and artificially sustain respiration makes this definition of death obsolete. So medical and legal experts now define death as an *irreversible* state involving no response to stimulation, no movement or breathing, no reflexes, and no indication of brain activity (Ladd, 1979; Wall, 1980; Jones, 1998).

Do People Have a Right to Die?

Today, medical personnel, family members, and patients themselves face the burden of deciding when the life of a terminally ill person should end. Among the most difficult cases are the thousands of people in Canada in a permanent vegetative state who cannot express their own desires about life and death.

Generally speaking, the first duty of physicians and hospitals is to protect a patient's life. Even so, a mentally competent person in the process of dying can refuse medical treatment or even nutrition either at the time or, in advance, through a document called a *living will* that states the extent of medical care a person would want or not want in the event of an illness or injury that leaves the person unable to make decisions.

Mercy killing is the common term for **euthanasia**, *assisting in the death of a person suffering from an incurable disease.* Euthanasia (from the Greek, meaning "a good death") poses for many an ethical dilemma, being at once an act of kindness and a form of killing.

euthanasia assisting in the death of a person suffering from an incurable disease; also known as *mercy killing*

Whether there is a "right to die" is one of today's most difficult issues. All people with incurable diseases have a right to refuse treatment that might prolong their lives. But whether a physician should be allowed to help bring about death is at the heart of today's debate. Supporters of *active* euthanasia—allowing a dying person to enlist the services of a physician to bring on a quick death—argue that there are circumstances (as when a dying person is suffering great pain) that make death preferable to life. Critics counter that permitting active euthanasia invites abuse. They fear that patients will feel pressure to end their lives to spare family members the burden of caring for them and avoid the high costs of hospitalization.

Many people in Canada are terminally ill, and some do express a wish for assistance to end their life. Such was the case for British Columbia resident Sue Rodriguez, who took her case all the way to the Supreme Court in 1993. The court did not rule in her favour, though Rodriguez ultimately got her wish through the assistance of an anonymous physician. In Saskatchewan, farmer Robert Latimer has been in and out of court for the carbon-monoxide poisoning of his disabled daughter, Tracy, in 1993. She had a severe case of cerebral palsy and Latimer maintains he acted "out of love" and that he had no choice but to kill her because she had had enough. The Saskatchewan Court of Appeal ruled in November 1998 that Latimer had to return to prison to serve his life sentence, with no opportunity for parole for 10 years. Latimer's lawyers appealed the case to the Supreme Court of Canada but lost. Latimer served his 10-year sentence for ending his daughter's life and was granted full parole on December 8, 2010.

A 2010 Angus Reid poll reported that 85 percent of Canadians believe that legalizing euthanasia would allow suffering people to ease their pain and establish clearer regulations for physicians regarding end-of-life decisions. In addition, two-thirds of Canadians agreed that legalizing euthanasia would not send the message that the lives of the sick or disabled are less valuable (Angus Reid Global Monitor, 2010).

Since the cases of Rodriguez and Latimer, the Supreme Court has in a recent ruling struck down the prohibition on assisted suicide. In 2015, with a unanimous vote, the court decided that protecting free will outweighs the duty to conserve human life.

The Medical Establishment

14.9 Compare the medical systems in nations around the world.

Throughout most of human history, health care was the responsibility of individuals and their families. Medicine emerges as a social institution only as societies become more productive and people take on specialized work.

Members of agrarian societies today still turn to traditional health practitioners, including acupuncturists and herbalists. In industrial societies, medical care falls to specially trained and licensed professionals, from anaesthesiologists to X-ray technicians. The medical establishment of modern, industrial societies took form over the past 200 years.

The Rise of Scientific Medicine

In pre-Confederation Canada, herbalists, druggists, barbers, midwives, and ministers practised the healing arts. But not all were effective: Unsanitary instruments, lack of anaesthesia, and simple ignorance made surgery a terrible ordeal, and physicians probably killed as many people as they saved.

In 1795, the first Medical Act attempted to regulate the practices of "physic and surgery" in Upper Canada by making it illegal for untrained healers to practise medicine without licences; only those with university degrees were exempted. The impracticality of the ruling soon became apparent, and the small degree-holding segment of the medical profession was left vulnerable to public critics. The original Medical Act was repealed in 1806, and traditional healers, including midwives, remained immune from the licensing laws of the Ontario Medical Board for the next half-century. In 1866, however, the government changed the law so that practitioners of midwifery and other healing arts, such as naturopathy, required medical degrees. That meant the predominantly male medical profession in the province enjoyed a legal monopoly over the birthing chamber by the time of Confederation in 1867 (Benoit, 1998). No female physicians were licensed in Ontario until the 1880s, and owing to continuing patriarchal traditions, few women entered this profession for many decades thereafter. Although some "traditionalist" physicians opposed this turn of events embraced by their "radical" colleagues and called instead for formal training and legalization of lay healers, their efforts proved unsuccessful (Biggs, 1983).

The Canadian Medical Association (CMA), founded in 1867, also symbolized the growing acceptance of a scientific model of medicine. The CMA widely publicized the successes of its members in identifying the causes of life-threatening diseases—bacteria and viruses—and developing vaccines to prevent them. Still, other approaches to health care, such as regulating nutrition, also had defenders. But the CMA responded boldly—some thought arrogantly—to these alternative approaches to health care, trumpeting the superiority of its practitioners.

The influential Flexner Report of 1910 highlighted the abysmal situation of Canadian medical education, reporting that 90 percent of all physicians at the time received their training from profit-making schools, which offered few or no resources for authentic clinical training. Abraham Flexner recommended the elimination of all "diploma mills" and the tightening of education and licensing standards for Canadian and U.S. physicians. Traditional healers, as well as black and female physicians, became easy targets for the reformed medical profession.

The Flexner Report effectively led to the closing down of schools teaching other methods of healing (herbal medicine, homeopathy, etc.), limiting the practice of medicine to those with medical science degrees. These developments awarded medical doctors the primary role in the health care of the population, and gave social legitimacy to *scientific medicine*—the social institution that focuses on combating disease and improving health. In the process, both the prestige and the income of physicians rose dramatically; today, physicians in Canada are among the highest-paid workers in the country.

Practitioners of other approaches (such as naturopathy, midwifery, and chiropractic medicine) for a time held on to their traditional practices, but these practitioners were relegated to the fringe of the medical profession. However, chiropractic services have in the past decade gained partial coverage under some provincial health care systems. More recently, midwifery has also gained coverage under most territorial and provincial health care systems and the process is under way in the other regions (DeVries et al., 2001; Bourgeault, Benoit, & Davis-Floyd, 2004; Wrede, Benoit, & Einarsdottir, 2008). Scientific medicine, taught in expensive, urban medical schools, also changed the social profile of physicians. As the CMA standards took hold, most physicians came from privileged backgrounds and practised in cities. Furthermore, as mentioned above, women had figured prominently in many fields of healing denigrated by the CMA. Some early medical schools did train women but, owing to the Flexner Report and declining

Prado, Madrid, Spain/Bridgeman Images

The profession of surgery has existed only for several centuries. Before that, barbers offered their services to the very sick, often cutting the skin to "bleed" a patient. Of course, this "treatment" was rarely effective, but it did produce plenty of bloody bandages, which practitioners hung out to dry. This practice identifies the origin of the red and white barber poles we see today.

financial resources, most of these schools soon closed. Only in recent decades have women increased their representation in the medical profession. In 1998, women accounted for 28 percent of Canada's practising physicians, up from 25 percent in 1993 (Canadian Institute for Health Information, 2000). In 2015, women made up 39.2 percent of all physicians in Canada (Canadian Medical Association, 2015).

Yet female physicians in Canada tend to remain clustered in the lower-ranking medical specialties. They account for 56.9 percent of specialists in pediatrics and only 7.9 percent of specialists in cardiac surgery (Canadian Medical Association, 2015). Furthermore, female physicians are also separated by a glass ceiling from their male colleagues in top administrative and specialty posts.

Holistic Medicine

The scientific model of medicine has been tempered by the introduction of **holistic medicine**, *an approach to health care that emphasizes prevention of illness and takes into account a person's entire physical and social environment*. Holistic practitioners agree on the need for drugs, surgery, artificial organs, and high technology, but they emphasize treating the whole person rather than just symptoms and focus on health rather than disease. There are three foundations of holistic health care (Gordon, 1980; Patterson, 1998):

holistic medicine an approach to health care that emphasizes prevention of illness and takes into account a person's entire physical and social environment

1. **Treat patients as people.** Holistic practitioners are concerned not only with symptoms but also with how people's environment and lifestyle affect health. Holistic practitioners extend the bounds of conventional medicine, taking an active role in fighting poverty, environmental pollution, and other dangers to public health.

2. **Encourage responsibility, not dependency.** A scientific approach to medicine puts physicians in charge of health, and patients are to follow the physician's orders. Holistic medicine tries to shift some responsibility for health from physician to patient by emphasizing health-promoting behaviour. Holistic medicine favours an *active approach to health* rather than a *reactive approach to illness.*

3. **Provide personal treatment.** Scientific medicine treats patients in impersonal offices and hospitals, both disease-centred settings. Holistic practitioners favour, as much as possible, a personal and relaxed environment such as the home.

In sum, holistic care does not oppose scientific medicine but shifts the emphasis from treating disease to achieving the greatest well-being for everyone. Recently, the College of Family Physicians of Canada (2009) issued a discussion paper that built on changes elsewhere and introduced the concept of "medical home" as part of its efforts to renew primary health care across the country. Underlying the concept of medical home is a patient-centred approach to care that draws on principles of holistic medicine.

Paying for Health Care: A Global Survey

As medicine has come to rely on advanced technology, the costs of medical care in industrial societies have skyrocketed. Countries throughout the world have adopted different strategies to meet these costs.

March 14, Vinales, Cuba. We have difficulty finding the hospital because there are no big signs on the modest whitewashed building. Finally, we enter the large open area and encounter a friendly, efficient nurse who beckons us into an examination room. Annika has felt weak ever since we left Victoria for Havana and was not able to ride her touring bike more than a few kilometres yesterday. We explain our story in English to the Spanish-speaking physician assigned to us; it's a challenge, but gestures and goodwill come to our aid. The hospital is spotless but crumbling. A slow leak has made a hole in the ceiling; water drops into a bucket. The X-ray machine looks as if it is hand-cranked. But, 90 minutes later, we walk out of the hospital with a firm diagnosis of pneumonia, an X-ray to take back home to our family physician, and prescriptions for two kinds of antibiotics. To our amazement, the Cuban physician attending our daughter declined any payment, shaking her head in seeming disbelief that we should even ask about the cost. After picking up the medicine in the local pharmacy we have spent the equivalent of $1.35! We wonder if we could have been helped so quickly and efficiently on a Saturday morning back in Canada and know that the cost of the medicine would have been much higher at home. Why did we bother to get travellers' health insurance?

People's Republic of China

This economically growing but still mostly agrarian nation faces the immense task of providing health care for more than 1.3 billion people. China continues to experiment with private medicine, but the government controls most health care.

China's "barefoot doctors," roughly comparable to Canadian paramedics, used to bring some modern methods of health care to peasants in rural villages. Today, a shift to a private-based medical-insurance system has eliminated the barefoot doctors. With their disappearance, diseases that had once been eradicated have made a comeback to the countryside, and China currently struggles to attract doctors to these regions (World Health Organization, 2008).

Traditional healing arts, involving acupuncture and medicinal herbs, are still widely practised. The Chinese approach to health is based on a holistic concern for the interplay of mind and body (Kaptchuk, 1985).

Russian Federation

The Russian Federation has transformed what was a state-dominated economy into more of a market system. For this reason, health care is in transition. But the state remains in charge of health care, and the government claims that everyone has a right to basic medical care.

People in the Russian Federation do not choose a physician but report to a local government health facility. Physicians have much lower incomes than physicians in Canada, earning about the same salary as skilled industrial workers (by contrast, Canadian physicians earn roughly five times as much as Canadian industrial workers). Also, about 72 percent of Russia's physicians are women, compared to 39.2 percent in Canada. As in our society, occupations dominated by women in the Russian Federation offer lower pay.

In recent years, the Russian Federation has suffered setbacks in health, due in part to a falling standard of living. Rising demand for medical care and cutbacks in government spending on health have strained a bureaucratic system that at best provides highly standardized and impersonal care. The optimistic view is that as living standards rise, the quality of medical service will improve. In Russia's uncertain times, what does seem clear is that inequalities in medical care will increase (Landsberg, 1998; Mason, 2004; Zuckerman, 2006).

Sweden

In 1891, Sweden began a mandatory, comprehensive system of government health care. Citizens pay for this program with their taxes, which are among the highest

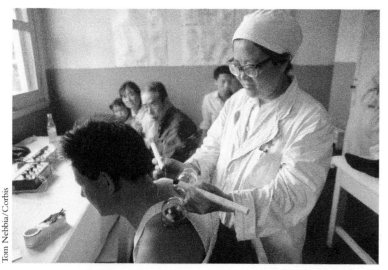

Tom Nebbia/Corbis

Traditional healers work to improve people's health throughout the world. This patient is receiving a traditional needle therapy in Suining, a city in China's Sichuan province. Do you think people in Canada are accepting of traditional healing practices? Why or why not?

in the world. Typically, physicians are government employees, and most hospitals are government managed. Sweden's system is called **socialized medicine**, *a medical care system in which the government owns and operates most medical facilities and employs most physicians.* Figure 14–3 shows the extent of socialized medicine in specific high-income countries.

Great Britain

In 1948, Great Britain also established socialized medicine by creating a dual system of health services. All British citizens are entitled to health care provided by the National Health Service, but those who can afford it may go to physicians and hospitals that operate privately.

The United States

Even after the historic passage of the new health care bill in 2010, the United States stands alone among high-income nations in having no universal, government-sponsored program of health care. The United States has a **direct-fee system**, *a medical care system in which patients pay directly for the services of physicians and hospitals.* Europeans look to government to fund 70 to nearly 90 percent of health care costs (paid for through taxation), but in the United States the federal, state, and local governments pay just 53 percent of all health care costs (U.S. Department of Health and Human Services, 2012).

In the United States, rich people can buy the best health care in the world, but poor people are worse off than their counterparts in Europe. This difference translates into relatively high death rates among both infants and adults in the United States compared with many European countries (Population Reference Bureau, 2012). In fact, in terms of infant mortality (the odds that an infant will die during the first year of life), the United States is ranked only forty-ninth among global nations and below many European countries. From another angle, researchers report that, despite spending more money per person than other high-income countries, the United States provides its people with higher rates of disease and injury and also a shorter life span (Population Reference Bureau, 2012; *The Lancet*, 2013).

Several states, including Maine, Vermont, and Massachusetts, have enacted programs that provide health care to everyone. Why does the United States have no national program that provides universal care? First, during World War II, the government took control of the economy and froze worker earnings. As a way to increase compensation during the wage freeze, more employers began providing health care benefits. Second, labour unions worked to expand health care from employers rather than going after government programs. Third, the public generally favours a private, worker-and-employer system because U.S. culture stresses individual self-reliance. Fourth, and finally, the AMA and the health insurance industry have strongly and consistently opposed national medical care.

There is no question that medical care in the United States is very expensive. The cost of medical care increased dramatically, from $12 billion in 1950 to $2.7 trillion in 2011 (U.S. Department of Health and Human Services, 2012). This amounts to $8700 per person, more than any other nation spends for health care, including Canada.

Japan

Physicians in Japan operate privately, but a combination of government programs and private insurance pays medical costs. As shown in Figure 14–3, the Japanese approach health care much like the Europeans, with most medical expenses paid through the government.

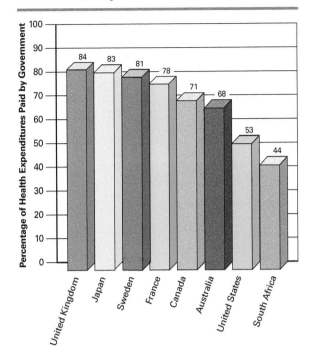

FIGURE 14–3 Extent of Socialized Medicine in Selected Countries

The governments of many high-income countries pay a greater share of their people's medical costs than the Canadian government does.

Source: World Bank (2013b).

socialized medicine a medical care system in which the government owns and operates most medical facilities and employs most physicians

direct-fee system a medical care system in which patients pay directly for the services of physicians and hospitals

The Canadian Health Care System

Since 1972, Canada has had a "single-payer" model of health care that provides care to all Canadians. Like a giant insurance company, the Canadian government pays physicians and hospitals according to a set schedule of fees. Canada's "medicare" system is predominantly a publicly financed, privately delivered health care system. The system provides access to universal comprehensive coverage for hospital and inpatient and outpatient services that are deemed necessary by a physician. While the administration and delivery of health services is the responsibility of each individual province or territory, the system is a national one to the extent that all areas of the country are expected to adhere to national principles. The federal government sets and administers national principles, or standards, for the health care system under the 1984 Canada Health Act (the standards are universality, accessibility, portability, comprehensive coverage, and public administration). The federal government also helps to finance provincial health care services through monetary transfers.

Therefore, Canada does not have a system of "socialized health care," such as that of Sweden, where the government is the principal employer of physicians. Most Canadian physicians are instead private practitioners who work in independent or group practices and enjoy a high degree of autonomy. Private physicians are mainly paid on a fee-for-service basis and submit their service claims directly to the provincial health insurance plan for payment (Blishen, 1991; Segall & Chappell, 2000; McGurran, 2013). Non-hospital dental care, many drugs, ambulance transport, private hospital beds, and other health services not covered by provincial health plans are either privately financed through employee benefit plans or paid for by individual Canadians. Total spending on health care in Canada was more than $211 billion in 2013, or 11.2 percent of the GDP. This means that the total health expenditure per capita in 2013 was approximately $5988 (CIHI, 2010, 2013).

In 2011, OECD countries spent an average of 9.6 percent of their GDPs, or $3410 per person, on health care, while Canada spent 11.2 percent of its GDP, or $4522 per person, including both private and public expenditures. As shown in Figure 14–3, non-insured private health costs made up 29 percent of total health care costs in Canada in 2013. The roughly 70 percent public and 30 percent private split has been fairly constant since the 1990s (CIHI, 2013).

In sum, despite the many benefits of the Canadian health care system, there are problems that need to be addressed. Compared with the systems of other countries, including that of our neighbour to the south, the Canadian health care system makes less use of state-of-the-art technology. Some critics also point out that it responds slowly to people's needs, often requiring those facing major surgery to wait months or even a year for attention (Grant, 1984; Vayda & Deber, 1984; Wait Time Alliance, 2014). Further, recent government cutbacks in health care funding have caused concern among Canadians that their much-admired health care system is in crisis. Despite these issues, public support for public health care remains strong in Canada. A Nanos Research poll reported that 94 percent of Canadians support a public health care model, as opposed to for-profit, private health care model (Canadian Health Coalition, 2011). Another Nanos poll (2013) reveals that 6 out of 10 Canadians support the idea of paying higher taxes for home care and drug coverage. One government-commissioned review of the health care system, established in 1994 and known as the National Forum on Health, solicited opinions from the public and health providers on the way forward for coming decades. The final report, *Canada Health Action: Building on the Legacy*, noted that the country is not confronting a health care crisis as such, yet the health care system is under significant stress. Though underfunding was not singled out as a main cause, the report noted the need for better strategies in spending public tax dollars on health care, as well as the need to focus attention on the underlying determinants of health.

A 2002 report—*Building on Values: The Future of Health Care in Canada*, by the Commission on the Future of Health Care in Canada headed by former premier of Saskatchewan

Roy Romanow—made similar recommendations. The Commission's mandate was to review the country's health care system, engage Canadians in a national dialogue on its future, and make recommendations to improve the system's quality and sustainability. The report was based on comprehensive, broad-based public consultations that included 21 days of public hearings, televised in-studio policy debates with health care experts, 12 policy dialogues at Canadian universities, a forum on Aboriginal health, and deliberative dialogue sessions with Canadian citizens in 12 cities across Canada. In addition, more than 30 000 Canadians took part in the Commission's two consultation surveys. The results reinforce the findings of early reports on health care in Canada, which found that Canadians want to keep the core principles of the medicare model that accorded with their strongly held values of universality, equal access, solidarity, and fairness. On the other hand, they also stated very strongly that the present employment of health care resources does not match their values of efficiency and accountability.

The proposal to create a national accountability system for Canadian health care was one recommendation to help solve such weaknesses. Some of the provinces, on the other hand, do not agree with this recommendation, because they would like more control over the health care in their province. This old battle between Ottawa and the provincial capitals is unlikely to be resolved in the near future given that the stakes are perceived to be very high due to the large proportion of governmental budgets spent on health care.

The Nursing Shortage

Another issue in health care is the shortage of nurses across Canada. In 2010, there were 287 344 registered nurses (people with the degree of R.N.), an increase of 4.8 percent since 2007. At the same time, Canada is dealing with a shortage of nurses. Looking ahead, if no changes in policy take place, the Canadian Nurses Association estimates that by 2022, Canada will be short 60 000 full-time RNs (Canadian Nurses Association, 2012, 2015).

The increasing demand for nurses is due to several factors. First, technological advances in medicine allow more illnesses to be treated. Second, there has been a rapid expansion

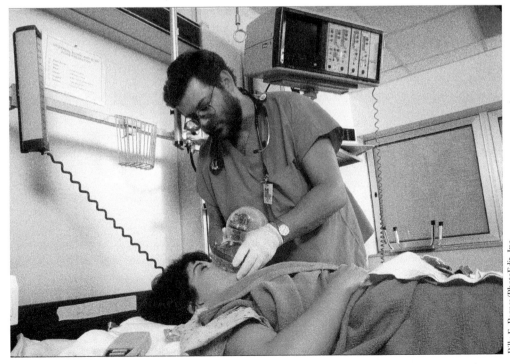

Billy E. Barnes/PhotoEdit, Inc.

Throughout Canada, there is a serious shortage of nurses. One strategy for filling the need is for nursing programs to recruit more men into this profession. In 2010, nearly all RNs (93.6 percent) in the Canadian workforce were female; this figure has not changed much in the last half-decade.

in hospital outpatient services, such as same-day surgery, rehabilitation, and chemotherapy. Third, an increasing focus on preventive care, rather than simply treating disease or accidents, means that more people than ever are receiving care. Fourth, and most important of all, the aging population of Canada is consuming more and more medical services. Another cause of the shortage is that today's young women have a wide range of job choices, and fewer are drawn to the traditionally female occupation of nursing. This fact is evident in the rising average age of working nurses, which is now 45.4 years (Canadian Nurses Association, 2012). Another is that many of today's nurses are unhappy with their working conditions, citing heavy patient loads, too much required overtime, a stressful working environment, and a lack of recognition and respect from supervisors, physicians, and hospital managers. In fact, one survey found that a majority of working nurses say they would not recommend the field to others, and more registered nurses are leaving the field for other jobs (Bourgeault & Wrede, 2008).

A positive sign is that the nursing shortage is bringing change to this profession. Salaries for certified nurse anaesthetists are rising, although slowly. Some hospitals and physicians are also offering signing bonuses in an effort to attract new nurses. In addition, nursing programs are trying harder to recruit a more diverse population, seeking more minorities (which are currently underrepresented) and, especially, more men (who currently make up only about 6.4 percent of registered nurses) (Canadian Nurses Association, 2012).

Theories of Health and Medicine

(14.10) Apply sociology's major theories to health and medicine.

Each of sociology's theoretical approaches—structural-functional theory, symbolic-interaction theory, and social-conflict and feminist theories—helps us organize and understand facts and issues concerning human health.

Structural-Functional Theory: Role Theory

Talcott Parsons (1951) viewed medicine as society's strategy to keep its members healthy. Parsons considered illness dysfunctional because it reduces people's abilities to perform their roles.

The Sick Role

Society responds to sickness not only by providing medical care but also by allowing people a **sick role**, *patterns of behaviour defined as appropriate for people who are ill.* According to Parsons, the sick role releases people from everyday obligations such as going to work or attending classes. However, people cannot simply claim to be ill; they must "look the part" and, in serious cases, get the help of a medical expert. After assuming the sick role, the patient must want to get better and must do whatever is needed to regain good health, including co-operating with health professionals.

sick role patterns of behaviour defined as appropriate for people who are ill

The Physician's Role

Physicians evaluate people's claims of sickness and help restore sick people to normal routines. To do this, physicians use their specialized knowledge and expect patients to follow "doctor's orders" in order to complete treatment.

> **EVALUATE** Parsons's analysis links illness and medicine to the broader organization of society. Others have extended the concept of the sick role to some non-sickness situations such as pregnancy (Myers & Grasmick, 1989).
>
> One limitation of the sick-role concept is that it applies to acute conditions (such as the flu or a broken leg) better than to chronic illnesses (such as heart disease), which may not be reversible. In addition, a sick person's ability to assume the sick role (to take time off from work to regain health) depends on the patient's resources. Finally, illness is not completely

dysfunctional; it can have some positive consequences: Many people who experience a serious illness consider it an opportunity to re-evaluate their lives and gain a better sense of what is truly important to them (D.G. Myers, 2000; Ehrenreich, 2001).

CHECK YOUR LEARNING Define the sick role. How does turning illness into a role in this way help society operate?

Symbolic-Interaction Theory: The Meaning of Health

Using the symbolic-interaction approach, society is less a grand system than a complex and changing reality. In this view, health and medical care are socially constructed by people in everyday interaction.

The Social Construction of Illness

If both health and illness are socially constructed, people in a poor society may view malnutrition as normal. Similarly, many members of our own society give little thought to the harmful effects of a rich diet.

Our response to illness is also based on social definitions that may or may not square with medical facts. People with AIDS may be forced to deal with prejudice that has no medical basis. Likewise, students may pay no attention to symptoms of real illness on the eve of a vacation but head for the infirmary hours before a mid-term examination with a case of the sniffles. In short, health is less an objective fact than a negotiated outcome.

How people define a medical situation may actually affect how they feel. Medical experts marvel at *psychosomatic* disorders (a fusion of the Greek words for "mind" and "body"), when state of mind guides physical sensations (Hamrick, Anspaugh, & Ezell, 1986). Applying the Thomas theorem (presented in Chapter 4, "Social Interaction in Everyday Life"), we can say that once health or illness is defined as real, it can become real in its consequences.

The Social Construction of Treatment

Also in Chapter 4, we used Erving Goffman's dramaturgical approach to explain how physicians tailor their physical surroundings (their office) and their behaviour (the "presentation of self") so that others see them as competent and in charge.

The sociologist Joan Emerson (1970) further illustrates this process of reality construction in her analysis of the gynecological examination carried out by a male physician. The situation could be seriously misinterpreted because a man touching a woman's genitals is conventionally viewed as a sexual act and possibly an assault.

To ensure that the situation is defined as impersonal and professional, medical personnel wear uniforms, and the examination room is furnished with nothing but medical equipment. The physician's manner is designed to make the patient feel that to him, examining the genital area is no different from treating any other part of the body. A female nurse is usually present during the examination, not only to assist the physician but also to avoid any impression that a man and woman are "alone together."

Managing situational definitions is rarely taught in medical schools. This oversight is unfortunate, because as Emerson's analysis shows, understanding how medical personnel construct reality in the examination room is as important as mastering the medical skills needed for treatment. One recent study found that physicians who were weak in social skills, even if they were well trained medically, were much more likely to be the targets of complaints and lawsuits filed by patients (Tamblyn et al., 2007).

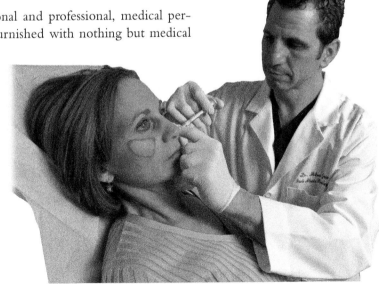

Definitions of health are based on cultural standards, including ideas about beauty. Every year, millions of people undergo cosmetic surgery to bring their appearance into line with societal definitions of how people ought to look.

The Social Construction of Personal Identity

A final insight provided by the symbolic-interaction approach is how surgery can affect people's self-image and social identity. The reason that medical procedures can have a major effect on how we think of ourselves is that our culture places great symbolic importance on some organs and other parts of our bodies. People who lose a limb (say, in military combat) typically experience serious doubts about being "as much of a person" as before. The effects of surgery can be important even when there is no obvious change in physical appearance. For example, Jean Elson (2004) points out that one out of three women in the United States eventually has her uterus surgically removed in a procedure known as a *hysterectomy*. In interviews with women who had undergone the procedure, Elson found that the typical woman faced serious self-doubt about gender identity—asking, in other words, "Am I still a woman?" Only 10 percent of hysterectomies are for cancer; most are performed in response to pain, bleeding, or cysts—conditions not dangerous enough to rule out less invasive treatments. Perhaps, Elson points out, physicians might be more willing to consider alternative treatment if they were aware of how symbolically important the loss of the uterus is to many women.

Many women who undergo breast surgery have much the same reaction, doubting their own feminine identity and worrying that men will no longer find them attractive. For men to understand the significance of such medical procedures, it is only necessary to imagine how a male might react to the surgical loss of any or all of his genitals.

EVALUATE Symbolic-interaction theory reveals that what people view as healthful or harmful depends on a host of factors that are not, strictly speaking, medical. This approach also shows that in any medical procedure, both patient and medical staff engage in a subtle process of reality construction. Finally, this approach has helped us understand the symbolic importance of limbs and other bodily organs; the loss of any part of the body—through accident or elective surgery—can have important consequences for personal identity.

By directing attention to the meanings people attach to health or illness, symbolic-interaction theory draws criticism for implying that there are no objective standards of well-being. Certain physical conditions do indeed cause specific changes in people, regardless of how we may view those conditions. People who lack sufficient nutrition and safe water, for example, suffer from their unhealthy environment, whether they define their surroundings as normal or not.

A recent study shows that the share of beginning college or university students who described their physical health as "above average" has declined from 74 percent of men and 54 percent of women in 1985 to 66 percent of men and 45 percent of women in 2012 (Astin et al., 2002; Pryor et al., 2013). While these changing perceptions may reflect a real decline in health (due, say, to eating more unhealthy food), might they also be due to changes in the ways students see the world? Can you offer possible explanations for this decline?

CHECK YOUR LEARNING Explain what it means to say that both health and the treatment of illness are socially constructed.

Social-Conflict and Feminist Theories: Inequality and Health

Social-conflict analysis points out the connection between health and social inequality, as shown in the Applying Theory table on page 505. Following the ideas of Karl Marx, we can link patterns of health to the operation of capitalism. In addition, feminist theory links health and medicine to gender stratification. Most attention has gone to three main issues: access to medical care, the effects of the profit motive, and the politics of medicine.

Applying Theory

Health			
	Structural-Functional Theory	**Symbolic-Interaction Theory**	**Social-Conflict and Feminist Theories**
What is the level of analysis?	Macro-level	Micro-level	Macro-level
How is health related to society?	Illness is dysfunctional for society because it prevents people from carrying out their daily roles.	Societies define "health" and "illness" differently according to their living standards.	Health is linked to social inequality, with rich people having more access to care than poor people.
	The sick role releases people who are ill from responsibilities while they try to get well.	How people define their own health affects how they actually feel (psycho-somatic conditions).	Capitalist medical care places the drive for profits over the needs of people.
			Scientific medicine downplays the social causes of illness, including poverty, racism, and sexism.

Access to Care

Health is important to everyone. But by requiring individuals to pay directly for medical care, capitalist societies allow the richest people to have the best health. The access problem is more serious in the United States than in most other high-income nations because that country does not have a universal medical care system.

Conflict theorists argue that capitalism provides excellent health care for the rich but at the expense of the rest of the population. Most of the 49 million people in the United States who lack health care coverage at present have moderate to low incomes. The same is the case in middle- and low-income countries around the globe without comprehensive health care systems.

The Profit Motive

Marxist theory goes further, arguing that the real problem goes beyond access to medical care to the capitalist economy that defines health and medicine. Under a capitalist system, the primary goal of medicine is not health but profit. The profit motive turns physicians, hospitals, and the pharmaceutical industry into multibillion-dollar corporations. The drive for higher profits encourages unnecessary tests and surgery and a reliance on expensive drugs rather than focusing on improving people's lifestyles and living conditions.

Of more than 25 million surgical operations performed in North America each year, three-fourths are elective, meaning that they are intended to promote long-term health and are not prompted by a medical emergency. Of course, any medical procedure or use of drugs is risky and harms between 5 and 10 percent of patients. Therefore a Marxist analysis suggests that medical procedures, including surgery, reflect not just the medical needs of patients but also the financial interests of surgeons and hospitals (Cowley, 1995; Nuland, 1999).

Finally, according to this approach, our society is too tolerant of physicians having a direct financial interest in the tests and procedures they order for their patients (Pear & Eckholm, 1991). Health care should be motivated by a concern for people, not profits.

Medicine as Politics

Although science claims to be politically neutral, feminist theory claims that scientific medicine often takes sides on significant social issues. For example, throughout most of the twentieth century, the Canadian medical establishment mounted a strong and sustained campaign against the legalization and public funding of midwives, although the World Health Organization recommends midwives as essential health care providers for women. Moreover, the history of medicine shows that not only has sexual and racial discrimination kept women and racial minorities out of medicine but also that

Controversy & Debate

The Genetic Crystal Ball: Do We Really Want to Look?

Felisha: Before I get married, I want my partner to have a genetic screening. It's like buying a house or a car—you should check it out before you sign on the line.

Eva: Do you expect to get a warranty, too?

The liquid in the laboratory test tube seems ordinary enough, like a syrupy form of water. But this liquid is one of the greatest medical breakthroughs of all time; it may even hold the key to life itself. The liquid is deoxyribonucleic acid, or DNA, the spiralling molecule that is found in cells of the human body and contains the blueprint for making each one of us human as well as different from every other person.

The human body is composed of roughly 100 trillion cells, most of which contain a nucleus of 23 pairs of chromosomes (one of each pair comes from each parent). Each chromosome is packed with DNA in segments called genes. Genes guide the production of protein, the building blocks of the human body.

If genetics sounds complicated (and it is), the social implications of genetic knowledge are even more complex. Scientists discovered the structure of the DNA molecule in 1952, and in recent years they have made great gains in "mapping" the human genome. Charting our genetic landscape will help us understand how each bit of DNA shapes our being.

Steve Murez/Black Star

Scientists are learning more and more about the genetic factors that prompt the eventual development of serious diseases. If offered the opportunity, would you want to undergo a genetic screening that would predict the long-term future of your own health?

But do we really want to turn the key to understanding life itself? And what do we do with this knowledge once we have it? Research has already identified genetic abnormalities that cause many diseases, including sickle-cell anemia, muscular dystrophy, Huntington's disease, cystic fibrosis, and some forms of cancer. Gazing into a person's genetic "crystal ball," physicians may be able to manipulate segments of DNA to prevent diseases before they appear.

But many people urge caution in such research, warning that genetic information can easily be abused. At its worst, genetic mapping opens the door to Nazi-like efforts to breed a "super race." In 1994, the People's Republic of China began to use genetic information to regulate marriage and childbirth with the purpose of avoiding "new births of inferior quality."

All over the world, many parents will want to use genetic testing to predict the health (or even the eye colour) of their future children. What if they want to abort a fetus because it falls short of their standards? When genetic manipulations become possible, should parents be able to create "designer children"?

Then there is the issue of "genetic privacy." Can a prospective spouse request a genetic evaluation of her fiancé before agreeing to marry? Can life insurance companies demand genetic testing before issuing a policy? Should employers be allowed to screen job applicants to weed out those whose future illnesses might drain their company's health care funds? Clearly, what is scientifically possible is not always morally desirable. Society is already struggling with questions about the proper use of our expanding knowledge of human genetics. Such ethical dilemmas will multiply as genetic research moves forward in the years to come.

What Do You Think?

1. Traditional wedding vows join couples "in sickness and in health." Do people have a right to know the future health of a partner before tying the knot? Why or why not?

2. Should parents be permitted to genetically "design" their children? Why or why not?

3. Is it right that private companies doing genetic research are able to patent their discoveries so that they can profit from the results, or should this information be made available to everyone? Explain your answer.

Sources: D. Thompson (1999) and Golden and Lemonick (2000).

---

discrimination has been supported by "scientific" opinions about, say, the inferiority of women and other minorities (Leavitt, 1984). Consider the diagnosis of "hysteria," a term that has its origins in the Greek word *hyster*, meaning "uterus." In choosing this word to describe a wild, emotional state, the medical profession suggested that being a woman is somehow the same as being irrational.

Even today, according to the social-conflict approach, scientific medicine explains illness in terms of bacteria and viruses, ignoring the damaging effects of poverty, racism, and sexism.

In effect, scientific medicine hides the bias in our medical system by transforming these social issues into simple biology.

EVALUATE Social-conflict analysis, including Marxist and feminist theory, provides still another view of the relationships among health, medicine, and society. According to this approach, social inequality is the main reason why some people have better health than others.

The most common objection to the social-conflict approach is that it minimizes the advances in health brought about by scientific medicine and higher living standards. Though there is plenty of room for improvement, health indicators for our population as a whole rose steadily over the course of the twentieth century, and they compare well with those in other high-income nations.

CHECK YOUR LEARNING How are health and medical care linked to social classes, capitalism, and gender stratification?

Sociology's three major theoretical approaches, summed up in the Applying Theory table on page 505, explain why health and medicine are social issues. The Controversy & Debate box on page 506 explains how advancing technology, far from solving our health problems, is raising new questions and concerns.

The famous French scientist Louis Pasteur (1822–1895), who spent much of his life studying how bacteria cause disease, said just before he died that health depends less on bacteria than on the social environment in which the bacteria are found (Gordon, 1980:7). Explaining Pasteur's insight is sociology's contribution to human health.

Health and Medicine: Looking Ahead

In the early 1900s, deaths from infectious diseases such as diphtheria and measles were widespread. Because scientists had yet to develop penicillin and other antibiotics, even a simple infection from a minor wound might have become life-threatening. Today, a century later, most members of our society take for granted good health and long life.

More people in Canada are taking personal responsibility for their health. Even so, there are some grounds for concern. Obesity is one major problem. If this trend continues, the younger generation may become the first to show a decline in life expectancy. Every one of us can live better and longer if we eat sensibly and in moderation, exercise regularly, and avoid tobacco.

Another health problem that our society faces, discussed throughout this chapter, is the changing social profile of people with AIDS, which increasingly afflicts youth, the poor, Aboriginals, women, and the marginalized and reminds us that Canada has much to do to improve the health of disadvantaged members of our society.

Finally, we find that health problems are far greater in low-income nations than in Canada. The good news is that life expectancy for the world as a whole has been rising— from 48 years in 1950 to 70 years today—and the biggest gains have been in poor-resourced countries (Population Reference Bureau, 2012). But in much of Latin America, Asia, and especially Africa, hundreds of millions of adults and children lack not only health care but adequate food and safe water as well. Improving the health of the world's poorest people is a critical challenge in the years to come.

Seeing Sociology in Everyday Life

CHAPTER 14 Education, Health, and Medicine

How does society affect patterns of health?

Certain occupations put people at higher-than-average risk of accident or death. One example is coal mining, which has long been one of the deadliest jobs. Although the death toll from mining accidents in Canada has gone down over time, even miners who manage to avoid mine collapses or explosions typically suffer harm from years of breathing coal dust. Look at the photos in this feature: How do they link health to a way of life?

Crews on fishing boats such as this one spend months at a time battling high seas and often frigid temperatures. As documented on the television show *The Deadliest Catch*, it is a rare and fortunate fishing season that brings no death or serious injury. What other jobs threaten the health and well-being of Canadian workers?

Although we may think that the work of law enforcement agents is dangerous, injury statistics indicate that workplace fatalities are much lower for police officers than for fishing crews, miners, loggers, and construction and transportation workers. In 2013, workplace fatalities claimed the lives of 6 police officers compared to 61 miners and oil-well workers and 221 construction workers (Association of Workers' Compensation Boards of Canada, 2013; Officer Down Memorial Page, 2015). Why do you think the public responds differently to the death of police officers than it does to the death of other workers?

About 80 workers died annually over a three-year period ending in 2009 in jobs that involve mining, quarrying, and petroleum production. What social patterns (think about class, gender, and other factors) can you see in the history of mining and health?

Lloyd Sutton/Alamy Stock Photo

HINT Among the most dangerous jobs in Canada are farming (dangers come from using power equipment), mining, timber cutting, truck driving, and constructing tall buildings. Many members of the military also face danger on a daily basis. In general, people in the working class are at greater risk than middle-class people, who typically work in offices; men also predominate in the most dangerous jobs. In Canada, about 1000 workplace fatalities and well over 300 000 lost-time workplace injuries occur annually.

Seeing Sociology in *Your* Everyday Life

1. Think about the effects of schooling on health. In what ways does getting a university or college degree (and perhaps a graduate or professional degree) improve a person's likelihood of leading a healthy life?

2. Go to www.sociologyinfocus.com to access the Sociology in Focus blog, where you can read the latest posts by a team of young sociologists who apply the sociological perspective to topics of popular culture.

3. Given the importance of sexuality in our thinking about women in Canada (and how they think about themselves), how do you think medical procedures such as mastectomy (surgical removal of part or all of a breast) affect women's personal and social identity? (To learn more about these experiences, see Elson, 2004.)

Maria Janicki/Alamy Stock Photo

Making the Grade

Education: A Global Survey

(14.1) Compare schooling in high-, middle-, and low-income societies. (pp. 464–468)

Education is the major social institution for transmitting knowledge and skills, as well as teaching cultural norms and values.
- In pre-industrial societies, education occurs informally within the family.
- Industrial societies develop formal systems of schooling to educate their children.

education the social institution through which society provides its members with important knowledge, including basic facts, job skills, and cultural norms and values
schooling formal instruction under the direction of specially trained teachers

The Functions of Schooling

(14.2) Apply structural-functional theory to schooling. (pp. 468–469)

Structural-functional theory highlights major functions of schooling, including socialization, cultural innovation, social integration, and the placement of people in the social hierarchy.
- Latent functions of schooling include providing child care and building social networks.

Schooling and Social Interaction

(14.3) Apply social-interaction theory to schooling. (pp. 469–470)

Symbolic-interaction theory shows us that stereotypes can have important consequences for how people act. Students who think they are academically superior are likely to perform better; those who think they are inferior are likely to perform less well.

Schooling and Social Inequality

(14.4) Apply social-conflict theory to schooling. (pp. 470–477)

Social-conflict theory links schooling to the hierarchy involving class, race, and gender.
- Formal education serves as a means of generating conformity to produce obedient adult workers.
- Standardized achievement tests have been criticized as culturally biased tools that lead to labelling less-privileged students as personally deficient; *tracking* has been criticized as a program that gives privileged youngsters a richer education.

hidden curriculum subtle presentations of political or cultural ideas in the classroom
tracking assigning students to different types of educational programs

Problems in the Schools

(14.5) Discuss dropping out, violence, and other problems facing today's schools. (pp. 477–480)

- *Violence* permeates many schools. It assumes various forms, such as verbal abuse, harassment, bullying, and school shootings.
- The bureaucratic character of schools fosters *high dropout rates* and *student passivity*.
- *Declining academic standards* are reflected in today's lower average scores on achievement tests and grade inflation.

functional illiteracy a lack of the reading and writing skills needed for everyday living

Current Issues in Canadian Education

(14.6) Summarize the debate over the performance of Canadian schools. (pp. 480–485)

- The *school choice movement* seeks to make schools more accountable to the public. Innovative school choice options include magnet schools, schooling for profit, and charter schools.
- The original pioneers of *home schooling* did not believe in public education because they wanted to give their children a strongly religious upbringing; home schooling advocates today believe that they can better meet the educational needs of their children.
- Children with mental or physical disabilities have historically been schooled in special classes; *mainstreaming* affords them broader opportunities and exposes all children to a more diverse student population.
- Adults represent a growing proportion of students in Canada; the majority of adult learners are involved in informal job-related training.
- The Canadian teaching market is turbulent. A number of factors—including changes in student enrolment, government policy, school board funding, immigration, and migration—have played a role in variously creating a shortage of teachers between the 1970s and the mid-2000s to creating a surplus from the mid-2000s to the mid-2010s.

mainstreaming integrating students with disabilities or special needs into the overall educational program

Health: A Global Survey

(**14.7**) Contrast patterns of health in low- and high-income countries. (pp. 485–486)

medicine the social institution that focuses on fighting disease and improving health

health a state of complete physical, mental, and social well-being

Health is a social issue because personal well-being depends on a society's level of technology and its distribution of resources. A society's culture shapes definitions of health.

- With industrialization, health improved dramatically in Western Europe and North America in the nineteenth century.
- In the 1920s, infectious diseases were among the leading killers; today, most people in Canada die in old age of chronic illnesses such as heart disease, cancer, or stroke.
- Poor nations suffer from inadequate sanitation, hunger, and other problems linked to poverty.
- Life expectancy in low-income nations is about 20 years less than in Canada; in the poorest nations, 10 percent of children die within a year of birth, and almost 25 percent die before the age of 30.

Health in Canada

(**14.8**) Analyze how race, class, gender, and age are linked to health. (pp. 486–495)

social epidemiology the study of how health and disease are distributed throughout a society's population

eating disorder a physical and mental disorder that involves intense dieting or other unhealthy method of weight control driven by the desire to be very thin

euthanasia assisting in the death of a person suffering from an incurable disease; also known as *mercy killing*

- Throughout the life course, women have better health than men.
- The poorest communities in Canada have a life expectancy of 78.7 years; the highest income-earning communities have a life expectancy of 82.2 years
- Current issues in Canadian health care include cigarette smoking, which is the greatest preventable cause of death; eating disorders and obesity; an increase in sexually transmitted diseases; and dilemmas associated with advancing medical technology and the right to die.

The Medical Establishment

(**14.9**) Compare the medical systems in nations around the world. (pp. 495–502)

holistic medicine an approach to health care that emphasizes prevention of illness and takes into account a person's entire physical and social environment

socialized medicine a medical care system in which the government owns and operates most medical facilities and employs most physicians

direct-fee system a medical care system in which patients pay directly for the services of physicians and hospitals

- Health care was historically a family concern but with industrialization became the responsibility of trained specialists.
- The model of scientific medicine is the foundation of the Canadian medical establishment.
- Socialist societies define medical care as a right and offer basic care equally to everyone.
- Capitalist societies view medical care as a commodity to be purchased, although most help pay for medical care through socialized medicine or national health insurance.
- In Canada, everyone has access to universal comprehensive coverage for hospital and inpatient and outpatient services that are deemed necessary by a physician.
- Women account for 39.2 percent of all physicians in Canada.

Theories of Health and Medicine

(**14.10**) Apply sociology's major theories to health and medicine. (pp. 502–507)

sick role patterns of behaviour defined as appropriate for people who are ill

Structural-functional theory considers illness to be dysfunctional because it reduces people's abilities to perform their roles (Talcott Parsons). Role analysis explains that society responds to illness by defining roles:

- The *sick role* excuses the ill person from routine social responsibilities.
- The *physician's role* is to use specialized knowledge to take charge of the patient's recovery.

Symbolic-interaction theory investigates the meanings that people attach to health, illness, and medical care. These meanings are socially constructed by people in everyday interaction:

- Our response to illness is not always based on medical facts.
- How people define a medical situation may affect how they feel.

Social-conflict theory focuses on the unequal distribution of health and medical care.

- Marxist theory criticizes the Canadian medical establishment for its overreliance on drugs and surgery, the dominance of the profit motive, and its overemphasis on the biological rather than the social causes of illness.
- **Feminist theory** criticizes the scientific establishment for "scientific" statements and policies that effectively allow men to dominate women.

15 Population, Urbanization, and Environment

Ken Cedeno/Corbis

LEARNING OBJECTIVES

15.1 Explain the concepts of fertility, mortality, and migration and how they affect population size.

15.2 Analyze population trends using Malthusian theory and demographic transition theory.

15.3 Summarize patterns of urbanization in Canada and around the world.

15.4 Identify the contributions of Tönnies, Durkheim, Simmel, Park, Wirth, and Marx to our understanding of urban life.

15.5 Describe the third urban revolution now under way in poor societies.

15.6 Analyze current environmental problems such as pollution and global warming.

15.7 Evaluate progress toward creating an ecologically sustainable culture.

the Power of Society

to shape our view of global warming

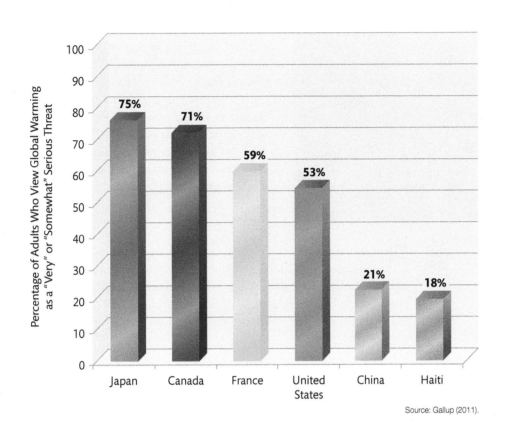

Source: Gallup (2011).

Are attitudes about global warming just our personal opinions? One way to answer this question is to look around the world. The majority of Canadians see global warming as a "somewhat serious" or "very serious" threat. In the United States, however, the population is almost evenly divided. The level of concern about global warming is typically far lower in low-income nations, where people are more concerned with their basic needs such as food and shelter. Clearly, society has the power to shape our view on environmental issues just as it shapes so many other aspects of our lives.

Chapter Overview

This chapter explores three dimensions of social change: population dynamics, urbanization, and increasing threats to the natural environment. Not only are all three important, but they are also closely linked.

Fox Photos/Getty Images

Two hundred years ago, Captain George Vancouver first charted the Burrard Inlet, home to such Coast Salish Indigenous people as the Squamish, Tsleil-Waututh, and Musqueam. One hundred years later, Vancouver was home to fewer than 50 000 people. Today, with a lower mainland population of more than 2.5 million, and as the city has expanded outward, commuting for an hour to work is commonplace.

Growth like this prompted experts to coin the term *urban sprawl*. Such uncontrolled growth is the result of more and more people, all of whom want bigger houses, as well as the conveniences offered by roads, schools, recreation facilities, and, of course, superstores and shopping malls. No doubt, most people in Canada see growth like this as good—the product of prosperity.

But is it that simple? This chapter examines three closely related processes: population increase, urbanization, and the state of the natural environment. As we shall see, population has soared during the past two centuries—in Canada and also around the world—and cities everywhere have grown rapidly. We shall consider how these changes have altered the shape of societies and what they mean for the future of the planet. We begin with population.

Demography: The Study of Population

(**15.1**) Explain the concepts of fertility, mortality, and migration, and how they affect population size.

When humans first began to cultivate plants some 12 000 years ago, Earth's entire *Homo sapiens* population was around 5 million, about the number of people living in just the province of British Columbia today. Very slow growth pushed the global total in 1 CE to perhaps 300 million, or about the current population of the United States.

Starting around 1750, world population began to spike upward. We now add more than 84 million people to the planet each year; today, the world now holds 7.1 billion people (Population Reference Bureau, 2012).

The causes and consequences of this drama are the basis of **demography**, *the study of human population*. Demography (from Greek, meaning "description of people") is a cousin of sociology that analyzes the size and composition of a population and studies how and why people move from place to place. Demographers not only collect statistics but also raise important questions about the effects of population growth and suggest how it might be controlled. The following sections present basic demographic concepts.

Fertility

The study of human population begins with how many people are born. **Fertility** is *the incidence of childbearing in a country's population*. During her childbearing years, from the onset of menstruation (typically in the early teens) to menopause (usually in the late forties), a woman is capable of bearing more than 20 children. But *fecundity*, or maximum possible childbearing, is sharply reduced by cultural norms, finances, and personal choice.

Demographers describe fertility using the **crude birth rate**, *the number of live births in a given year for every 1000 people in a population.* To calculate a crude birth rate, divide the number of live births in a year by a society's total population and multiply the result by 1000. In Canada, in 2010, there were 382 027 births in a population of 34 108 752, yielding a crude birth rate of 11.2 (Statistics Canada, 2011a, 2011b).

> January 18, Coshocton County, Ohio. Having just finished the mountains of meat and potatoes that make up a typical Amish meal, we have gathered in the living room of Jacob Raber, a member of this rural Amish community. Mrs. Raber, a mother of four, is telling us about Amish life. "Most of the women I know have 5 or 6 children," she says with a smile, "but certainly not everybody—some have 11 or 12!"

A country's birth rate is described as "crude" because it is based on the entire population, not just women in their childbearing years. In addition, this measure ignores differences among various categories of the population: Fertility among the Amish, for example, is quite high, and fertility among Asians Canadians is low. But the measure is easy to calculate and allows rough comparisons of the fertility of one country or region to others. Part (a) of Figure 15–1 shows that, compared to the rest of the world, the crude birth rate of North Americans is low.

Mortality

Population size also reflects **mortality**, *the incidence of death in a country's population.* To measure mortality, demographers use the **crude death rate**, *the number of deaths in a given year for every 1000 people in a population.* This time, we take the number of deaths in a year, divide by the total population, and multiply the result by 1000. In 2010, there were 250 810 deaths in the Canadian population of 34 108 752, yielding a crude death rate of 7.4 (Statistics Canada, 2011b, 2011c). Part (a) of Figure 15–1 shows that this rate is about average.

A third useful demographic measure is the **infant mortality rate**, *the number of deaths among infants under one year of age for each 1000 live births in a given year.* To compute infant mortality,

Global Snapshot

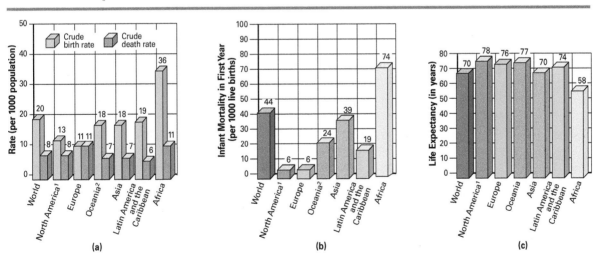

FIGURE 15–1 (a) Crude Birth Rates and Crude Death Rates, (b) Infant Mortality Rates, and (c) Life Expectancy Around the World, 2012

By world standards, North America has a low birth rate, an average death rate, a very low infant mortality rate, and high life expectancy.

[1]United States and Canada. [2]Australia, New Zealand, and South Pacific Islands.

Source: Population Reference Bureau (2012).

divide the number of deaths of children under one year of age by the number of live births during the same year, and multiply the result by 1000. In 2007, there were 1881 infant deaths and 367 864 live births in Canada (Statistics Canada, 2011d, 2011e). Dividing the first number by the second and multiplying the result by 1000 yields an infant mortality rate of 5.11. Part (b) of Figure 15–1 indicates that by world standards, North American infant mortality is very low.

But remember that differences exist among various categories of people. For example, Aboriginal peoples, who are twice as likely as non-Aboriginal peoples to live below the poverty line, have an infant mortality rate twice as high as the national rate. Within this category, Inuit rates are four times as high as the overall Canadian infant mortality rate (Smylie et al., 2010).

life expectancy the average life span of a country's population

Low infant mortality greatly raises **life expectancy**, *the average life span of a country's population*. Canadian males born between 2007 and 2009 can expect to live 78.8 years and females can look forward to 83.3 years (Statistics Canada, 2012a). As part (c) of Figure 15–1 shows, life expectancy in North America is 20 years greater than is typical of the low-income countries in Africa.

Migration

Population size is also affected by **migration**, *the movement of people into and out of a specified territory*. Migration can involve the crossing of national political boundaries (by immigrants or refugees, for example) as well as movement within a country (think rural to urban migration). Movement into a country, or *immigration*, is measured as an *immigration rate,* calculated as the number of people entering an area for every 1000 people in the population. Movement out of a country, or *emigration*, is measured in terms of an *emigration rate,* the number leaving for every 1000 people. Both types of migration usually occur at the same time; the difference between them is the *net migration rate.*

All nations also experience internal migration, movement within their borders from one region to another. We use the terms *in-migration* and *out-migration* to describe this movement. National Map 15–1 on page 517 shows population change across Canada, due in part to in- and out-migration, but also to immigration and regional fertility rates.

Migration is sometimes voluntary, as when people leave a small town to move to a larger city. In such cases, "push-pull" factors are typically at work: A lack of jobs "pushes" people to move, and more opportunity elsewhere "pulls" people elsewhere. The lack of jobs for Newfoundlanders in the last few decades stimulated out-migration to Fort McMurray, Alberta. It is estimated that Newfoundland migrants make up 16.5 percent of that city's population today, the largest groups after Albertans (Wittmeier, 2014). Migration can also be involuntary, as during the forced transport of 10 million Africans to the Western Hemisphere as slaves or when Hurricane Katrina forced tens of thousands of people to flee New Orleans.

Population Growth

Fertility, mortality, and migration all affect the size of a society's population. In general, rich nations (such as Canada) grow as much from immigration as from natural increase; poorer nations (such as Pakistan) grow almost entirely from natural increase.

To calculate a population's *natural growth rate*, demographers subtract the crude death rate from the crude birth rate. The natural growth rate of the Canadian population in 2010

demography the study of human population

fertility the incidence of childbearing in a country's population

crude birth rate the number of live births in a given year for every 1000 people in a population

mortality the incidence of death in a country's population

crude death rate the number of deaths in a given year for every 1000 people in a population

infant mortality rate the number of deaths among infants under one year of age for each 1000 live births in a given year

migration the movement of people into and out of a specified territory

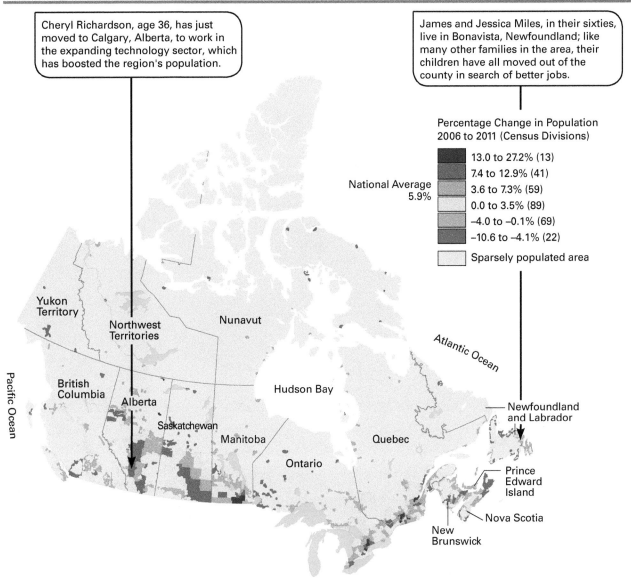

Cheryl Richardson, age 36, has just moved to Calgary, Alberta, to work in the expanding technology sector, which has boosted the region's population.

James and Jessica Miles, in their sixties, live in Bonavista, Newfoundland; like many other families in the area, their children have all moved out of the county in search of better jobs.

Percentage Change in Population 2006 to 2011 (Census Divisions)

	13.0 to 27.2% (13)
	7.4 to 12.9% (41)
National Average 5.9%	3.6 to 7.3% (59)
	0.0 to 3.5% (89)
	−4.0 to −0.1% (69)
	−10.6 to −4.1% (22)
	Sparsely populated area

NATIONAL MAP 15–1 Population Change, 2006 to 2011, Across Canadian Provinces and Territories

This map shows that, between 2006 and 2011, interprovincial migration was highest to western provinces and territories. During this period, Alberta and Yukon experienced growth at almost double the national average, while the Northwest Territories experienced zero growth, and Nova Scotia experienced the least growth. What factors do you think are behind internal migration? What categories of people do you think remain in areas that are losing population?

Source: Statistics Canada (2012b). https://www12.statcan.gc.ca/census-recensement/2011/geo/map-carte/ref/thematic_download-thematiques_telecharger-eng.cfm?SERIES=D. Reproduced and distributed on an "as is" basis with the permission of Statistics Canada.

was 3.8 per 1000 (the crude birth rate of 11.2 minus the crude death rate of 7.4), or about 0.4 percent annual growth.

Global Map 15–1 on page 518 shows that population growth in Canada and other high-income nations is well below the world average of 1.2 percent. Earth's low-growth continents are Europe (currently showing no growth) and North America (increasing by 0.5 percent). Close to the global average are Oceania (1.2 percent), Asia (1.1 percent), and Latin America (1.2 percent). The highest-growth region in the world is Africa (2.4 percent).

A handy rule of thumb for estimating a nation or region's growth is to divide the number 70 by the population growth rate; this yields the *doubling time* in years. Thus an annual growth

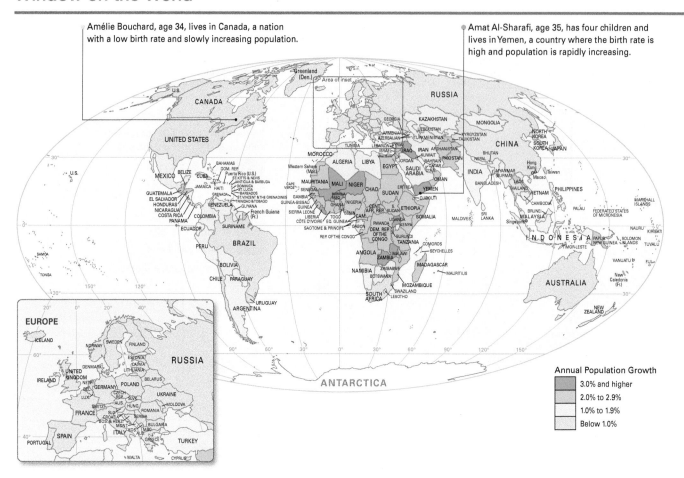

Amélie Bouchard, age 34, lives in Canada, a nation with a low birth rate and slowly increasing population.

Amat Al-Sharafi, age 35, has four children and lives in Yemen, a country where the birth rate is high and population is rapidly increasing.

Annual Population Growth
- 3.0% and higher
- 2.0% to 2.9%
- 1.0% to 1.9%
- Below 1.0%

GLOBAL MAP 15–1 Population Growth in Global Perspective

The richest countries of the world—including Canada, the United States, and the nations of Europe—have growth rates below 1 percent. The nations of Latin America and Asia typically have growth rates around 1.5 percent, a rate that doubles a population in 47 years. Africa has an overall growth rate of 2.4 percent (despite only small increases in countries with a high rate of AIDS), which cuts the doubling time to 29 years. In global perspective, we see that a society's standard of living is closely related to its rate of population growth: Population is rising fastest in the world regions that can least afford to support more people.

Source: U.S. Census Bureau (2013).

rate of 2 percent (found in the Latin American nations of Bolivia, Honduras, and Belize) doubles a population in 35 years, and a 3 percent growth rate (found in the African nations of Niger, Mali, and Gambia) drops the doubling time to just 23 years. The rapid population growth of the poorest countries is deeply troubling because these countries can barely support the populations they have now.

Population Composition

sex ratio the number of males for every 100 females in a nation's population

Demographers also study the makeup of a society's population at a given point in time. One variable is the **sex ratio**, *the number of males for every 100 females in a nation's population.* In 2014, the sex ratio in Canada was 99 (99 males for every 100 females). Sex ratios are usually below 100 because, on average, women outlive men. Because the area around Cape Breton, Nova Scotia, has an aging population, its sex ratio is 91, or 91 males for every 100 females. In India, however, the sex ratio is 108; not only is the population much younger, but also many parents value sons more than daughters and may either abort a female fetus or, after birth, give more care to their male children, raising the odds that a female child will die.

A more complex measure is the **age-sex pyramid**, *a graphic representation of the age and sex of a population.* Figure 15–2 presents the age-sex pyramids for Aboriginal and non-Aboriginal Canadians. Higher death rates as people age give these figures a rough pyramid shape. In the non-Aboriginal pyramid, the bulge near the middle reflects the high birth rates during the "baby boom" from the mid-1940s to the mid-1960s. The contraction for people in their twenties and thirties reflects the subsequent "baby bust" when the number of births declined from a high of 479 000 in 1959 to 343 000 in 1973.

Aboriginal Canadians, for whom 46 percent of individuals are under the age of 25, have a much younger age structure compared to non-Aboriginal Canadians, only 29 percent of whom are under the age of 25.

Comparison of the Aboriginal and non-Aboriginal age-sex pyramids shows different demographic trends. The age-sex pyramid for Aboriginal Canadians, comparable to that of nations with high fertility, is wider at the bottom because the number of births increases every year. Aboriginal Canadians, in short, are a much younger population. With a larger share of females still in their childbearing years, the Aboriginal crude birth rate is, understandably, considerably higher than the non-Aboriginal, and its annual rate of natural growth is higher than the non-Aboriginal Canadian rate. Between 1996 and 2001, the fertility rate for all Canadian women was 1.5 children; for Aboriginal women it was 2.6 children (O'Donnell & Wallace, 2011). Even if Aboriginal women should undergo a reduction in the number of children per family, they would still likely experience what demographers call *demographic momentum*—the tendency for a growing population to continue to grow due to the large number of people in their childbearing years.

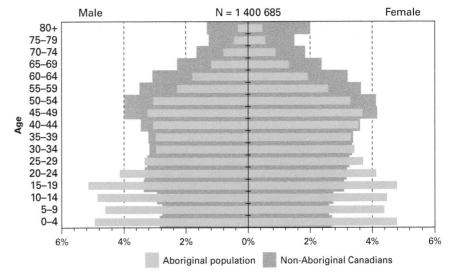

Aboriginal Canadians, for whom 46 percent of individuals are under the age of 25, have a much younger age structure compared to non-Aboriginal Canadians, only 29 percent of whom are under the age of 25.

FIGURE 15–2 Age-Sex Pyramid of Aboriginal and Non-Aboriginal Population, 2011

By looking at the shape of Canada's Aboriginal and non-Aboriginal population pyramid, you can predict future levels of population increase.

Source: Aboriginal Affairs and Northern Development Canada (2013). "Aboriginal Peoples (identity-based) - Age Pyramid of Aboriginal Population, 2011" Age-Sex pyramid available here: https://www.aadnc-aandc.gc.ca/eng/1370438978311/1370439050610. Used with permission.

age-sex pyramid a graphic representation of the age and sex of a population

History and Theory of Population Growth

15.2 Analyze population trends using Malthusian theory and demographic transition theory.

In the past, people wanted large families because human labour was the key to productivity. In addition, until rubber condoms were invented in the mid-1800s, prevention of pregnancy was uncertain at best. But high death rates from infectious diseases put a constant brake on population growth.

A major demographic shift began about 1750 as the world's population turned upward, reaching the 1 billion mark by 1800. This milestone (which took all of human history to reach) was repeated barely a century later in 1930, when a second billion people were added to the planet. In other words, not only was population increasing, but the *rate* of growth was accelerating as well. Global population reached 3 billion by 1962 (just 32 years later) and 4 billion by 1974 (only 12 years after that). The rate of world population increase has slowed recently, but the planet passed the 5 billion mark in 1987, the 6 billion mark in 1999, and the 7 billion mark early in 2012. In no previous century did the world's population even double; in the twentieth century, it *quadrupled*.

Currently, the world is gaining almost 84 million people each year; 98 percent of this increase is in poor countries. Experts predict that Earth's population will reach 8 billion

Marcia Chambers/dbimages/Alamy Stock Photo

This street scene in Madurai, India, conveys the vision of the future found in the work of Thomas Robert Malthus, who feared that population increase would overwhelm the world's resources. Can you explain why Malthus had such a serious concern about population? How is demographic transition theory a more hopeful analysis?

by 2025 and will climb more slowly to about 9.3 billion by 2050 (United Nations, Department of Economic and Social Affairs, 2011a). Given the world's troubles feeding the present population, such an increase is a matter of urgent concern.

Malthusian Theory

The sudden population spurt 250 years ago sparked the development of demography. Thomas Robert Malthus (1766–1834), an English economist and clergyman, warned that population increase would soon lead to social chaos. Malthus (1926, orig. 1798) calculated that population would increase in what mathematicians call a *geometric progression*, illustrated by the series of numbers 2, 4, 8, 16, 32, and so on. At such a rate, Malthus concluded, world population would soon soar out of control.

Food production would also increase, Malthus explained, but only in *arithmetic progression* (as in the series 2, 3, 4, 5, 6, and so on) because even with new agricultural technology, farmland is limited. Thus Malthus presented a distressing vision of the future: people reproducing beyond what the planet could feed, leading ultimately to widespread starvation and war over what resources were left.

Malthus recognized that artificial birth control or abstinence might change his prediction. But he considered one morally wrong and the other impractical. Famine and war therefore stalked humanity in Malthus's mind, and he was justly known as "the dismal parson."

EVALUATE Fortunately, Malthus's prediction was flawed. First, by 1850, the European birth rate began to drop, partly because children were becoming an economic liability rather than an asset and partly because people began using artificial birth control. Second, Malthus underestimated human ingenuity: Modern drip-irrigation techniques, advanced fertilizers, and effective pesticides have increased farm production and saved vital resources far more than he could have imagined (Yemma, 2011).

Some people criticized Malthus for ignoring the role of social inequality in world abundance and famine. For example, Karl Marx (1967, orig. 1867) objected to viewing suffering as a "law of nature" rather than the curse of capitalism. More recently, "critical demographers" have claimed that saying poverty is caused by high birth rates in low-income countries amounts to blaming the victims. On the contrary, they see global inequality as the real issue (Horton, 1999; Kuumba, 1999).

Still, Malthus offers an important lesson. Habitable land, clean water, and fresh air are limited resources, and greater economic productivity has taken a heavy toll on the natural environment. In addition, medical advances have lowered death rates, pushing up world population. In principle, of course, no level of population growth can go on forever. People everywhere must become aware of the dangers of population increase.

CHECK YOUR LEARNING What did Malthus predict about human population increase? About food production? What was his overall conclusion?

Demographic Transition Theory

A more complex analysis of population change is **demographic transition theory**, *a thesis that links population patterns to a society's level of technological development*. Figure 15–3 shows the demographic consequences at four levels of technological development.

Pre-industrial, agrarian societies (Stage 1) have high birth rates because of the economic value of children and the absence of birth control. Death rates are also high because of low living standards and limited medical technology. Deaths from outbreaks of disease cancel out births, so population rises and falls only slightly over time. This was the case for thousands of years in Europe before the Industrial Revolution.

Stage 2, the onset of industrialization, brings a demographic transition as death rates fall due to greater food supplies and scientific medicine. But birth rates remain high, resulting in rapid population growth. It was during Europe's Stage 2 that Malthus formulated his ideas, which accounts for his pessimistic view of the future. The world's poorest countries today are in this high-growth stage.

In Stage 3, a mature industrial economy, the birth rate drops, curbing population growth once again. Fertility falls because most children survive to adulthood and because high living standards make raising children expensive. In short, affluence transforms children from economic assets into economic liabilities. Smaller families, made possible by effective birth control, are also favoured by women working outside the home. As birth rates follow death rates downward, population growth slows further.

Stage 4 corresponds to a post-industrial economy in which the demographic transition is complete. The birth rate keeps falling, partly because dual-income couples gradually become the norm and partly because the cost of raising children continues to increase. This trend, linked to steady death rates, means that population grows only very slowly or even decreases. This is the case today in Japan, Europe, Canada, and the United States.

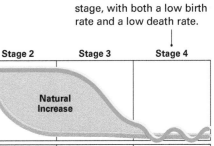

Canada is in this historical stage, with both a low birth rate and a low death rate.

	Stage 1	Stage 2	Stage 3	Stage 4
Birth Rate / Death Rate		Natural Increase		
Level of Technology	Pre-industrial	Early Industrial	Mature Industrial	Post-industrial
Population Growth	Very Slow	Rapid	Slowing	Very Slow

FIGURE 15–3 Demographic Transition Theory

Demographic transition theory links population change to a society's level of technological development.

demographic transition theory a thesis that links population patterns to a society's level of technological development

EVALUATE Demographic transition theory suggests that the key to population control lies in technology. Instead of the runaway population increase feared by Malthus, this theory sees technology slowing growth and spreading material plenty.

Demographic transition theory is linked to modernization theory, one approach to global development discussed in Chapter 9 ("Global Stratification"). Modernization theorists are optimistic that poor countries will solve their population problems as they industrialize. But critics, notably dependency theorists, strongly disagree. Unless there is a redistribution of global resources, they maintain, our planet will become increasingly divided into industrialized "haves," enjoying low population growth, and non-industrialized "have-nots," struggling in vain to feed more and more people.

CHECK YOUR LEARNING Explain the four stages of demographic transition theory.

Global Population Today: A Brief Survey

What can we say about population in today's world? Drawing on the discussion so far, we can identify important patterns and reach several conclusions.

The Low-Growth North

When the Industrial Revolution began in the Northern Hemisphere, the population increase in Western Europe and North America was a high 3 percent annually. But in the centuries since, the growth rate has steadily declined, and in 1970, it fell below 1 percent. As our

zero population growth the rate of reproduction that maintains population at a steady level

post-industrial society settles into Stage 4, the Canadian birth rate is below the replacement level of 2.1 children per woman, a point demographers term **zero population growth**, *the rate of reproduction that maintains population at a steady level.* In 2012, 81 nations, almost all of them high-income countries, were at or below the point of zero population growth.

Among the factors that serve to hold down population in these post-industrial societies are a high proportion of men and women in the labour force, rising costs of raising children, trends toward later marriage and singlehood, and widespread use of contraceptives and abortion.

In high-income nations, then, population increase is not the pressing problem that it is in poor countries. On the contrary, many governments in high-income countries, including Italy and Japan, are concerned about a future problem of *underpopulation* because declining population size may be difficult to reverse and also because the swelling ranks of the elderly can look to fewer and fewer young people for support (El Nasser & Overberg, 2011; Hamilton, Martin, & Ventura, 2012; Population Reference Bureau, 2012; United Nations Development Programme, 2012).

The High-Growth South

Population is a critical problem in poor nations of the Southern Hemisphere. No nation of the world lacks industrial technology entirely; demographic transition theory's Stage 1 applies today to remote rural areas of low-income nations. But much of Latin America, Africa, and Asia is at Stage 2, with a mix of agrarian and industrial economies. Advanced medical technology, supplied by rich countries, has sharply reduced death rates, but birth rates remain high. This is why low-income societies now account for 82 percent of Earth's people and 98 percent of global population increase.

In some of the world's poorest countries, such as the Democratic Republic of the Congo in Africa, women still have, on average, more than six children during their lifetimes. But in most poor countries, birth rates have fallen from about six children per woman (typical in 1950) to about three. But this level of fertility is still high enough to make global poverty much worse. This is why leaders in the battle against global poverty point to the importance of reducing fertility rates in low-income nations.

Notice, too, that a key element in controlling world population growth is improving the status of women. Why? Because of this simple truth: Give women more life choices and they will have fewer children. History has shown that women who are free to decide when and where to marry, bear children as a matter of choice, and have access to education and to good jobs will limit their own fertility (Axinn & Barber, 2001; Roudi-Fahimi & Kent, 2007; Population Reference Bureau, 2012).

The Demographic Divide

High- and low-income nations display very different population dynamics, a gap that is sometimes called the *demographic divide.* In Italy, a high-income nation with very low growth, women average just 1.4 children in their lifetimes. Such a low birth rate means that the number of annual births is less than the number of deaths. This means that at the moment, Italy is actually *losing* population. Looking ahead to 2050, and even assuming some gains from immigration, Italy's population is projected to be about the same as it is today. But the share of elderly people in Italy—now 21 percent—will only increase as time goes on.

How different the patterns are in a low-income nation such as the Democratic Republic of the Congo. There, women still average six to seven children, so

David Turnley/Corbis

Fertility in Canada has fallen during the past century and is now quite low. But some categories of the Canadian population have much higher fertility rates. One example is the Mennonites, a religious society living in rural areas of Ontario. It is common for Mennonite couples to have five, six, or more children. Why do you think the Mennonites favour large families?

even with a high mortality rate, this nation's population will more than double by 2050. The share of elderly people is extremely low—about 3 percent—and almost half that country's people are below the age of 16. With such a high growth rate, it is no surprise that the problem of poverty is bad and getting worse: About three-fourths of the people are undernourished (Population Reference Bureau, 2012).

In sum, a demographic divide now separates rich countries with low birth rates and aging populations from poor countries with high birth rates and very young populations. Just as humanity has devised ways to reduce deaths around the world, it must now bring down population growth, especially in poor countries where projections suggest a future as bleak as that imagined by Thomas Malthus centuries ago.

Today, China stands out as a nation that has taken a strong stand on reducing population increase. That country's controversial one-child policy, enacted back in the 1970s, has reduced China's population by about 250 million.

Urbanization: The Growth of Cities

(15.3) Summarize patterns of urbanization in Canada and around the world.

> October 8, Hong Kong. The cable train grinds to the top of Victoria Peak, where we behold one of the world's most spectacular vistas: the city of Hong Kong at night! A million bright, colourful lights ring the harbour as ships, ferries, and traditional Chinese junks slowly slip by. Day and night, few places match Hong Kong for sheer energy: This small city is as economically productive as British Columbia, Alberta, and Saskatchewan combined or as the entire nation of Finland. We could sit here for hours entranced by the spectacle of Hong Kong.

Throughout most of human history, the sights and sounds of great cities such as Hong Kong, Paris, and Toronto were simply unimaginable. Our distant ancestors lived in small, nomadic groups, moving as they depleted vegetation or hunted migratory game. The tiny settlements that marked the emergence of civilization in the Middle East some 12 000 years ago held only a small fraction of Earth's people. Today, the largest three or four cities of the world hold as many people as the entire planet did back then.

Urbanization is *the concentration of population into cities.* Urbanization redistributes population within a society and transforms many patterns of social life. We will trace these changes in terms of three urban revolutions: the emergence of cities beginning 10 000 years ago, the development of industrial cities after 1750, and the explosive growth of cities in poor countries today.

urbanization the concentration of population into cities

The Evolution of Cities

Cities are a relatively new development in human history. Only about 12 000 years ago did our ancestors begin living in permanent settlements, which set the stage for the *first urban revolution.*

The First Cities

As explained in Chapter 2 ("Culture"), hunting and gathering forced people to move all the time; however, once our ancestors discovered how to domesticate animals and cultivate crops, they were able to stay in one place. Raising their own food also created a material surplus, which freed some people from food production and allowed them to build shelters, make tools, weave cloth, and take part in religious rituals. The emergence of cities led to both higher living standards and job specialization.

The first city that we know of was Jericho, which lies to the north of the Dead Sea in what is now the West Bank. When first settled some 10 000 years ago, it was home to only 600 people. But as the centuries passed, cities grew to tens of thousands of people and became the centres of vast empires. By 3000 BCE, Egyptian cities flourished, as did cities in China about 2000 BCE and in Central and South America about 1500 BCE. In North America, however, only a few Native American societies formed settlements; widespread urbanization had to await the arrival of European settlers in the seventeenth century.

Pre-industrial European Cities

European cities date back some 5000 years to the Greeks and later the Romans, both of whom created great empires and founded cities across Europe, including Vienna, Paris, and London. With the fall of the Roman Empire, the so-called Dark Ages began as people withdrew into defensive walled settlements and warlords battled for territory. Only in the eleventh century did Europe become more peaceful; trade flourished once again, allowing cities to grow.

Medieval cities were quite different from those familiar to us today. Beneath towering cathedrals, the narrow and winding streets of London, Brussels, and Florence teemed with merchants, artisans, priests, peddlers, jugglers, nobles, and servants. Occupational groups such as bakers, carpenters, and metalworkers clustered together in distinct sections or "quarters." Ethnicity also defined communities as residents tried to keep out people who differed from themselves. The term "ghetto" (from the Italian word *borghetto*, meaning "outside the city walls") was first used to describe the neighbourhood in which the Jews of Venice were segregated.

Industrial European Cities

As the Middle Ages came to a close, steadily increasing commerce enriched a new urban middle class, or *bourgeoisie* (French, meaning "townspeople"). With more and more money, the bourgeoisie soon rivalled the hereditary nobility.

By about 1750, the Industrial Revolution triggered a *second urban revolution*, first in Europe and then in North America. Factories unleashed tremendous productive power, causing cities to grow bigger than ever before. London, the largest European city, reached 550 000 people by 1700 and exploded to 6.5 million by 1900 (A.F. Weber, 1963, orig. 1899; Chandler & Fox, 1974).

Cities not only grew but changed shape as well. Older winding streets gave way to broad, straight boulevards to handle the increasing flow of commercial traffic. Steam and electric trolleys soon crisscrossed the expanding cities. Because land was now a commodity to be bought and sold, developers divided cities into regular-sized lots (Mumford, 1961). The centre of the city was no longer the cathedral but a bustling central business district filled with banks, retail stores, and tall office buildings.

With a new focus on business, cities became ever more crowded and impersonal. Crime rates rose. Especially at the outset, a few industrialists lived in grand style, but most men, women, and children barely survived by working in factories.

Organized efforts by workers to improve their lives eventually brought changes to the workplace, such as better pay and benefits, safety and health regulations, and pension plans. Although it grew out of a concern to protect the rights of workers, the labour movement also played a significant role in stopping child labour, securing better housing, and the right to vote. Public services such as water, sewer systems, and electricity further improved urban living. Today, some urbanites still live in poverty, but a rising standard of living has partly fulfilled the city's historical promise of a better life.

The Growth of North American Cities

Most of the Native Americans who inhabited North America for thousands of years before the arrival of Europeans were migratory people who formed few permanent settlements. The spread of villages and towns came after European colonization.

Colonial Settlement: 1565–1800

In 1565, the Spanish built a settlement at Saint Augustine, Florida, and in 1607, the English founded Jamestown, Virginia. The first lasting settlement came in 1624, when the Dutch established New Amsterdam, later renamed New York. These settlements preceded those in Canada. For example, the first European did not reach the site that was to become Toronto until 1615.

The arrival of Europeans played a central role in the transformation, and often decline, of Aboriginal settlements. In the sixteenth century, the Iroquois homeland, known as the Haudenosaunee Confederacy, was made up of five Aboriginal nations and stretched from the Genesee River to what is today New York State. It consisted of seven to eight large agricultural towns in which one to two thousand people resided, surrounded by many smaller neighbourhood villages. The Iroquois also founded communities in present-day Ontario, Quebec, Pennsylvania, and Ohio (Jordan, 2013). By the eighteenth century, the Haudenosaunee Confederacy consisted of six self-governing nations. With encroaching European settlements and the emergence of Canadian Confederation, Aboriginal people in the Haudenosaunee Confederacy, and throughout North America, were subjected to forced resettlement.

New York, Boston (founded by the English in 1630), and Quebec City (where there was merely a trading post in 1608) started out as tiny villages in a vast wilderness. They resembled medieval towns in Europe, with narrow, winding streets that still curve through lower Manhattan, downtown Boston, and parts of Quebec City. But economic growth soon transformed these quiet villages into thriving towns with wide streets usually laid out in a grid pattern. Montreal (founded in 1642) had grown to about 18 000 by the end of the eighteenth century, while Captain Vancouver had in 1792 just explored and charted the Burrard Inlet, home of the Coast Salish peoples since at least 9000 BCE. As Table 15–1 shows, when the nineteenth century closed, Canada was still an overwhelmingly rural society.

Urban Expansion: 1800–1860

Early in the nineteenth century, as cities in Eastern Canada grew bigger, towns sprang up along the transportation routes that opened the Canadian West. First, the cities along the major waterways connected to the Great Lakes emerged. By 1851, Quebec City had a population of 52 000, whereas the younger city of Montreal had already grown to 57 000.

Progress was slow away from the waterways of the Great Lakes. It was only in 1860, for example, that New Westminster (now part of the Greater Vancouver Area) became the first incorporated municipality west of Ontario. It was not until the completion of the Canadian Pacific Railway in 1885 that urbanization spread to the western provinces.

The Metropolitan Era: 1860–1950

Industrialization also gave an enormous boost to urbanization, as factories strained to produce goods. Now waves of people fled the countryside for cities in hopes of obtaining better jobs. Joining them were tens of millions of immigrants, mostly from Europe, forming a culturally diverse urban mix.

At the time of Canadian Confederation in 1867, less than 20 percent of the population lived in urban areas. By 1951, this proportion had grown

TABLE 15–1 Urban Population of Canada, 1851–2011

	Population	Urban	Rural	Urban	Rural
		Number		% of total population	
Canada					
1851	2 436 297	318 079	2 118 218	13	87
1861	3 229 633	527 220	2 702 413	16	84
1871	3 737 257	722 343	3 014 914	19	81
1881	4 381 256	1 109 507	3 271 749	25	75
1891	4 932 206	1 537 098	3 395 108	31	69
1901	5 418 663	2 023 364	3 395 299	37	63
1911	7 221 662	3 276 812	3 944 850	45	55
1921	8 800 249	4 353 428	4 446 821	49	51
1931	10 376 379	5 572 058	4 804 321	54	46
1941	11 506 655	6 252 416	5 254 239	54	46
1951	14 009 429	8 628 253	5 381 176	62	38
1956	16 080 791	10 714 855	5 365 936	67	33
1961	18 238 247	12 700 390	5 537 857	70	30
1966	20 014 880	14 726 759	5 288 121	74	26
1971	21 568 305	16 410 785	5 157 520	76	24
1976	22 992 595	17 366 970	5 625 625	76	24
1981	24 343 177	18 435 923	5 907 254	76	24
1986	25 309 330	19 352 080	5 957 250	76	24
1991	27 296 856	20 906 872	6 389 984	77	23
1996	28 846 758	22 461 207	6 385 551	78	22
2001	30 007 094	23 908 211	6 098 883	80	20
2006	31 612 897	25 350 743	6 262 154	80	20
2011	33 476 688	27 147 274	6 329 414	81	19

Sources: Statistics Canada (2011f). http://www.statcan.gc.ca/tables-tableaux/sum-som/l01/cst01/demo62a-eng.htm. Reproduced and distributed on an "as is" basis with the permission of Statistics Canada.

to 62 percent. Individual cities grew accordingly. By 1911, the supremacy of Montreal and Toronto (with populations of 470 000 and 377 000, respectively) was well established. The next-largest cities were Winnipeg (136 000) and Vancouver (100 000). These were still small cities compared to New York, which had already passed the 4 million mark. Such growth marked the era of the **metropolis** (from Greek words meaning "mother city"), *a large city that socially and economically dominates an urban area*. Metropolises became the economic centres of Canada.

Industrial technology pushed the urban skyline ever higher. In the 1880s, steel girders and mechanical elevators allowed buildings to rise more than 10 stories high. Railroads and highways drew cities outward. By 1931, pushing upward and outward, cities were home to a majority of the Canadian population.

Urban Decentralization: 1950–Present

The industrial metropolis reached its peak about 1950. Since then, something of a turnaround—termed *urban decentralization*—has occurred as people have left downtown areas for outlying **suburbs**, *urban areas beyond the political boundaries of a city*. The centres of some long-established cities have stopped growing, and some lost considerable population in the decades after 1950. At the same time, suburban populations increased rapidly. The urban landscape of densely packed central cities evolved into sprawling suburban regions. Nevertheless, Canada remains a country dotted with population centres located in a vast expanse of sparsely populated land, as National Map 15–1 on page 517 illustrates.

Suburbs and Urban Decline

Imitating the European aristocracy, some of the rich had town houses in the city as well as large country homes beyond the city limits. But not until after World War II did ordinary people find a suburban home within their reach. With more and more cars in circulation, new four-lane highways, government-backed mortgages, and inexpensive tract homes, the suburbs grew rapidly. By 1981, most of the population in Canada's largest cities lived in suburbs outside the central city (McVey, Jr. & Kalbach, 1995).

Decentralization was not good news for everyone, however. Rapid suburban growth threw cities into financial chaos. Population decline meant reduced tax revenues. Further, cities that lost affluent people to the suburbs were left with the burden of providing expensive social programs to the poor who stayed behind. Soon the downtown core came to be synonymous with traffic congestion, crime, drugs, unemployment, and poverty. Vancouver's Downtown Eastside stands out as one of the most dramatic examples of this process; however, marginalized populations are not as concentrated in other Canadian cities as they are in the cities of the United States.

Canadian inner cities have fared better in large part because of early adoption of urban renewal policies. Under this program, provincial and local governments have paid for the rebuilding of many inner cities; Montreal started this as early as 1966 (Wolfe, 1992). Affordable housing and effective public transportation in Canada's large and middle-sized cities have recently emerged as major problems for city planners (Bunting, Filion, & Walks, 2004; Filion, McSpurren, & Appleby, 2006).

The urban critic Paul Goldberger (2002) points out that the decline of central cities has also led to a decline in the importance of public space. Historically, the heart of city life was played out on the streets. The French word for a sophisticated person is *boulevardier,* which literally means "street person"—a term that has a negative meaning in Canada today. The active life that once took place on public streets and in public squares now takes place in shopping malls, the lobbies of cineplex theatres, and gated residential communities—all privately owned spaces. Further reducing the vitality of today's urban places is the spread of television, the internet, and other media that people use without leaving home.

Neighbourhood Gentrification

gentrification the process by which working-class communities are displaced by an influx of middle-class property developers

Following urban decline, some city neighbourhoods underwent—and are still undergoing—**gentrification**, *the process by which working-class communities are displaced by an influx of middle-class property developers.* Beginning in Canada in the 1960s, gentrification is usually seen by urban developers as a worthwhile effort to "rejuvenate" or "modernize" cheap and unprofitable sections of cities. In Vancouver, for example, neighbourhoods like Kitsilano and Strathcona saw old apartments, student houses, and industrial sites redeveloped into condominiums and luxury homes (Macdonald & Chai, 2009). Today, Vancouver's Chinatown and the Downtown Eastside, Toronto's Parkdale and The Junction, as well as Montreal's Old Montreal and the downtown port area, are also seeing the appearance of new businesses and apartments.

According to R. Alan Walks and Richard Maaranen, gentrification takes place in three stages. The first, "pioneer" stage, involves the arrival of artists and those who favour a countercultural lifestyle to less-expensive, working-class neighbourhoods. Their influx introduces to the neighbourhood an aesthetic identity. In pursuit of that aesthetic, renters arrive, triggering the second stage. Their arrival spurs renovation, which drives up the price of rent, making the neighbourhood paradoxically too expensive for the artists as well as the original working-class members. In the third stage, professionals, retailers, and developers view the neighbourhood as a safe investment. They purchase property in order to redevelop and redesign it, thus completing the neighbourhood's transformation (Walks & Maaranen, 2008).

Some major cities in Canada are undergoing gentrification. The development of new condos and restaurants often displaces formerly well-established communities.

By replacing what are deemed as unfashionable areas with new business and living spaces, developers argue that crime and poverty decrease at the same time as the retail sector and municipal services grow (Sullivan, 2007). Gentrification is thus sometimes seen as a form of urban recycling. However, critics—often made up of long-time community members themselves—point out that with gentrification, social problems such as poverty and crime do not so much disappear as they are simply pushed out of view. What disappears, in these newly redeveloped areas, is affordable housing along with the original character of the communities.

Megalopolis: The Regional City

Another result of urban decentralization is urban regions. Statistics Canada recognizes 114 regional cities, which are called *census agglomerations* (CAs)—towns and surrounding areas where more than 10 000 people live in the urban core. The smallest CA is Bay Roberts, Newfoundland, which had a population of 10 871 in 2011 (Statistics Canada, 2012c). One-third of Canada's population lives in the three largest urban areas identified by Statistics Canada—the 33 *census metropolitan areas* (CMAs), which are cities and surrounding areas where more than 100 000 people live

Commuter traffic jams are a growing concern in Canada's large metropolitan areas.

in the urban core. These CMAs range in size from Toronto at 5.5 million to Peterborough at about 119 000 (Statistics Canada, 2012c).

As regional cities grow, they begin to overlap. The "Golden Horseshoe" is a continuous urban area encompassing the west end of Lake Ontario, where about 8.6 million people live. It represents a quarter of the population of Canada and over half of the population of Ontario (Statistics Canada, 2013a). On an even larger scale, along the U.S. east coast a 650-kilometre supercity stretches from New England to Virginia.

In the early 1960s, the French geographer Jean Gottmann (1961) coined the term **megalopolis** to designate *a vast urban region containing a number of cities and their surrounding suburbs.*

Edge Cities

Urban decentralization has also created *edge cities*, business centres some distance from the old downtowns. Edge cities—a mix of corporate office buildings, shopping malls, hotels, and entertainment complexes—differ from suburbs, which contain mostly homes. The population of suburbs peaks at night, but the population of edge cities peaks during the workday.

As part of expanding urban regions, most edge cities have no clear physical boundaries, although some do have names (including Oshawa outside Toronto and Surrey outside Vancouver).

Changes to Rural Areas

Most of Canada is rural. At the same time, most of the nation's people are urban: The 2011 census showed that 81 percent of the country's 33.4 million people were living in urban places.

As shown in Table 15–1 on page 525, the trend toward becoming an urban society has been under way over the course of Canadian history. Immigration has played a part in the process of urbanization because most newcomers settle in cities. In addition, there has been net migration from rural areas to urban places, typically by people seeking greater social, educational, and economic opportunity.

During the early 1990s, however, there developed a new trend, which analysts called the *rural rebound*. What this meant was that, instead of losing population to the urban areas, some rural counties actually gained population. These gains were due mostly to migration as more people moved to rural places than left them for cities. The biggest gains in this process were seen in rural counties with special beauty such as lakes or ski areas. People were drawn to such rural communities not only by their natural beauty and clean air but also by their slower pace of life with less traffic and less crime. Standing out is the whole area between Vancouver and Calgary, and also "cottage country" north of Toronto.

In the late 1990s, however, the rural rebound pattern faded, so that once again, most rural counties lost more people to migration than they gained. But the pattern was uneven. Rural counties that were highly scenic continued to increase in population due to migration, as did rural areas within commuting distance to large cities. By contrast, remote rural areas and those where the economy was largely based on farming saw little or no population gains or experienced declines.

Urbanism as a Way of Life

15.4 Identify the contributions of Tönnies, Durkheim, Simmel, Park, Wirth, and Marx to our understanding of urban life.

Early sociologists in Europe and North America focused their attention on the rise of cities and how urban life differed from rural life. We briefly examine their accounts of urbanism as a way of life.

Ferdinand Tönnies: *Gemeinschaft* and *Gesellschaft*

In the nineteenth century, the German sociologist Ferdinand Tönnies (1855–1937) studied how life in the new industrial metropolis differed from life in rural villages. From this contrast, he developed two concepts that have become a lasting part of sociology's terminology.

Peasant Dance (left, c. 1565), by Pieter Breughel the Elder, conveys the essential unity of rural life forged by generations of kinship and neighbourhood. By contrast, Lily Furedi's *Subway* (right) communicates the impersonality common to urban areas. Taken together, these paintings capture Tönnies's distinction between *Gemeinschaft* and *Gesellschaft*.

Pieter Breughel the Elder (c. 1525/30–1569), *Peasant Dance*, c. 1565, Kunsthistorisches Museum, Vienna/Superstock. Lily Furedi, American. *Subway*. Oil on canvas, 99 × 123 cm. National Collection of Fine Arts, Washington, D.C./Smithsonian Institute.

Tönnies (1963, orig. 1887) used the German word **Gemeinschaft** ("community") to refer to *a type of social organization in which people are closely tied by kinship and tradition*. The *Gemeinschaft* of the rural village joins people in what amounts to a single primary group.

By and large, argued Tönnies, *Gemeinschaft* is absent in the modern city. On the contrary, urbanization creates **Gesellschaft** ("association"), *a type of social organization in which people come together only on the basis of individual self-interest*. In the *Gesellschaft* way of life, individuals are motivated by their own needs rather than by a desire to help improve the well-being of everyone. By and large, city dwellers have little sense of community or common identity and look to others mainly when they need something. Tönnies saw in urbanization a weakening of close, long-lasting social relations in favour of the brief and impersonal ties or secondary relationships typical of business.

> **Gemeinschaft** a type of social organization in which people are closely tied by kinship and tradition
>
> **Gesellschaft** a type of social organization in which people come together only on the basis of individual self-interest

Emile Durkheim: Mechanical and Organic Solidarity

The French sociologist Emile Durkheim agreed with much of Tönnies's thinking about cities. However, Durkheim countered that urbanites do not lack social bonds; they simply organize social life differently than rural people.

Durkheim described traditional, rural life as *mechanical solidarity*, social bonds based on common sentiments and shared moral values. With its emphasis on tradition, Durkheim's concept of mechanical solidarity bears a striking similarity to Tönnies's *Gemeinschaft*. Urbanization erodes mechanical solidarity, Durkheim explained, but it also generates a new type of bonding, which he called *organic solidarity*, social bonds based on specialization and interdependence. This concept, which parallels Tönnies's *Gesellschaft*, reveals an important difference between the two thinkers. Both thought the growth of industrial cities weakened tradition, but Durkheim optimistically pointed to a new kind of solidarity. Where societies had been built on *likeness* (mechanical solidarity), Durkheim now saw social life based on *difference* (organic solidarity).

For Durkheim, urban society offered more individual choice, moral tolerance, and personal privacy than people find in rural villages. In sum, Durkheim thought that something is lost in the process of urbanization, but much is gained.

Georg Simmel: The Blasé Urbanite

The German sociologist Georg Simmel (1858–1918) offered a microanalysis of cities, studying how urban life shapes individual experience. According to Simmel, individuals perceive the city as a crush of people, objects, and events. To prevent being overwhelmed by all this stimulation, urbanites develop a *blasé attitude*, tuning out much of what goes on around them. Such detachment does not mean that city dwellers lack compassion for others; they simply keep their distance as a survival strategy so that they can focus their time and energy on the people and things that really matter to them.

The Chicago School: Robert Park and Louis Wirth

Sociologists in North America soon joined the study of rapidly growing cities. Robert Park (1864–1944), a leader of the first North American sociology program at the University of Chicago, sought to add perspective by getting out on the streets and studying cities. As he said of himself, "I suspect that I have actually covered more ground, tramping about in cities in different parts of the world, than any other living man" (1950:viii). Walking the streets, Park found the city to be an organized mosaic of distinctive ethnic communities, commercial centres, and industrial districts. Over time, he observed, these "natural areas" develop and change in relation to one another. To Park, the city was a living organism—a human kaleidoscope.

Another major figure in the Chicago School of urban sociology was Louis Wirth (1897–1952). Wirth (1938) is best known for blending the ideas of Tönnies, Durkheim, Simmel, and Park into a comprehensive theory of urban life.

Wirth began by defining the city as a setting with a large, dense, and socially diverse population. These traits result in an impersonal, superficial, and transitory way of life. Living among millions of others, urbanites come into contact with many more people than residents of rural areas. So when city people notice others at all, they usually know them not in terms of *who they are* but *what they do*—as, for instance, the bus driver, the florist, or the grocery store clerk. These specialized urban relationships are pleasant for all concerned, but we should remember that self-interest rather than friendship is the main reason behind the interaction.

The impersonal nature of urban relationships, together with the great social diversity found in cities today, makes city dwellers more tolerant than rural villagers. Rural communities often jealously enforce their narrow traditions, but the heterogeneous population of a city rarely shares any single code of moral conduct (T.C. Wilson, 1985, 1995).

EVALUATE In both Europe and North America, early sociologists presented a mixed view of urban living. Rapid urbanization troubled Tönnies, and Wirth saw personal ties and traditional morality lost in the anonymous rush of the city. Durkheim and Park emphasized urbanism's positive face, pointing to more personal freedom and greater personal choice.

One problem with all these views is that they paint urbanism in broad strokes that overlook the effects of class, race, and gender. There are many kinds of urbanites—rich and poor, black and white, Anglo and Aboriginal, women and men—all leading distinctive lives (Gans, 1968). Indeed, as the Thinking About Diversity box explains, the share of visible minorities in the largest Canadian cities is expected to continue growing sharply in the next decade. We see social diversity most clearly in cities where various categories of people are large enough to form distinct, visible communities (Macionis & Parrillo, 2013).

CHECK YOUR LEARNING Of these urban sociologists—Tönnies, Durkheim, Park, and Wirth—which were more positive about urban life? Which were more negative? In each case, explain why.

Urban Ecology

urban ecology the study of the link between the physical and social dimensions of cities

Sociologists (especially members of the Chicago School) developed **urban ecology**, *the study of the link between the physical and social dimensions of cities.* One issue of interest to urban ecologists is why cities are located where they are. Broadly speaking, the first cities emerged in fertile regions where the ecology favoured raising crops. Pre-industrial people, concerned with defence, built their cities on mountains (ancient Athens was perched on an outcropping of rock) or surrounded by water (Paris and Mexico City were founded on islands). With the

Thinking About Diversity: Race, Class, and Gender

Minorities Now a Majority in the Largest Canadian Cities

According to the results of the 2011 census, 20.6 percent of Canadians—about one in five—are foreign born. Many foreign-born residents reside in major Canadian cities: Toronto, Vancouver, and Montreal account for 63.4 percent of the immigrant population. It is predicted that, by 2031, just about a half (46 percent) will be foreign born or have a foreign-born parent. As well, by 2031, the prediction is that almost half (47 percent) of second-generation Canadians will belong to a visible minority group, which is more than double the 2011 proportion at 19.1 percent.

Why the change? By far, the most important reason is the increase in immigration and the large proportion of immigrants who are visible minorities. Since 1980, 8 of 10 immigrants to Canada have arrived from Asia. Contributing factors for the increase are the younger age structure of the visible minority population (younger populations have more children) and the slightly higher fertility rates.

There will be dramatic differences in the proportions of visible minorities in different parts of Canada. The greatest increase in the size and proportion of the visible minority population will be evident in Toronto, where visible minorities are expected to be a numerical majority by 2017—up from 47 percent of the population in 2011. Hamilton is an interesting contrast because, with only 14.3 percent, it has relatively few visible minority persons.

The differences in the proportions of visible minorities in rural and urban areas are reflected in provincial differences also. In 2011, 94.8 percent of all visible minorities resided in just four provinces: British Columbia, Alberta, Ontario, and Quebec.

Political officials and other policy-makers examine these figures closely. Clearly, the future vitality of the largest Canadian cities depends on meeting the needs and taking advantage of the contributions of the swelling minority—and especially immigrant—populations.

What Do You Think?

1. Why are the visible minority populations of large Canadian cities increasing?

2. What positive changes does a numerical majority of visible minorities bring to a city?

3. What challenges does a numerical majority of visible minorities bring to a city?

Source: Statistics Canada (2010, 2013b).

Total Population

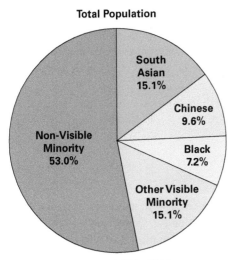

Top Visible Minorities, Toronto CMA, 2011

Visible minorities make up 47 percent of the population of Toronto, accounting for 79.2 percent of Ontario's visible minority population.

Source: Ontario Ministry of Finance (2013).

---

coming of the Industrial Revolution, economic considerations gained importance, which explains why all major North American cities were situated near rivers or natural harbours that facilitated trade.

Urban ecologists also study the physical design of cities. In 1925, Ernest W. Burgess, a student and colleague of Robert Park, described land use in Chicago in terms of *concentric zones*. City centres, Burgess observed, are business districts bordered by a ring of factories, followed by residential rings with housing that becomes more expensive the farther it is from the noise and pollution of the city's centre.

Homer Hoyt (1939) refined Burgess's observations, noting that distinctive districts sometimes form *wedge-shaped sectors*. For example, one fashionable area may develop next to another, or an industrial district may extend outward from a city's centre along a train or trolley line.

Chauncy Harris and Edward Ullman (1945) added yet another insight: As cities decentralize, they lose their single-centre form in favour of a *multi-centred model*. As cities grow, residential areas, industrial parks, and shopping districts typically push away from one another. Few people wish to live close to industrial areas, for example, so the city becomes a mosaic of distinct districts.

The Industrial Revolution created great cities across Canada. In recent decades, however, the movement of industry abroad has brought decline to a number of cities in Ontario and Quebec. Yet today's high levels of immigration are bringing new life to many cities as a new generation of young people joins the urban mix. In the Greater Toronto Area, much of a recent gain in population is due to surging South Asian immigration.

Social area analysis investigates what people in particular neighbourhoods have in common. Three factors seem to explain most of the variation: family patterns, social class, and race and ethnicity (Shevky & Bell, 1955; Johnston, 1976). Families with children look for areas with single-family homes or large apartments and good schools. The rich seek high-prestige neighbourhoods, often in the central city near cultural attractions. People with a common race or ethnic heritage tend to cluster in distinctive communities.

Brian Berry and Philip Rees (1969) tied together many of these insights. They explained that distinct family types tend to settle in the concentric zones described by Burgess. Specifically, households with many children tend to live in the outer areas of a city, while "young singles" cluster toward the city's centre. Social class differences are primarily responsible for the sector-shaped districts described by Hoyt—for instance, the rich occupy one "side of the tracks" and the poor the other. And racial and ethnic neighbourhoods are found at various points throughout the city, consistent with Harris and Ullman's multi-centred model.

Urban Political Economy

In the late 1960s, many large North American cities were rocked by riots. In the wake of this unrest, some analysts turned away from the ecological approach to a social-conflict understanding of city life. The *urban political economy model* applies Karl Marx's analysis of conflict in the workplace to conflict in the city (Lindstrom, 1995).

Political economists reject the ecological approach's view of the city as a natural organism with particular districts and neighbourhoods developing according to an internal logic. They claim that city life is defined by larger institutional structures, especially the economy. For political economists, the process of gentrification, described earlier, is a form of economic class conflict. Capitalism is the key to understanding urban life because this economic system transforms the city into real estate traded for profit and concentrates wealth and power in the hands of the few. From this point of view, for example, the development of the West Edmonton Mall and the resulting decline in downtown Edmonton can be understood only by an analysis that includes the close relationship that the developer (the Ghermezian family) had with provincial and municipal politicians.

EVALUATE The fact that many Canadian cities appear to be in crisis—with pockets of deep poverty, high crime rates, and homelessness—seems to favour the political economy model over the urban ecology approach. But one criticism applies to both: They focus on Canadian cities during a limited period of history. Much of what we know about industrial cities does not apply to pre-industrial towns in our own past or the rapidly growing cities in many poor nations today. It is unlikely that any single model of cities can account for the full range of urban diversity.

CHECK YOUR LEARNING In your own words, explain what the urban ecology theory and the urban political economy theory teach us about cities.

Urbanization in Low-Income Countries

(15.5) Describe the third urban revolution now under way in poor societies.

> *November 16, Cairo, Egypt. People call the vast Muslim cemetery in Old Cairo the "City of the Dead." In truth, it is very much alive: Tens of thousands of squatters have moved into the mausoleums, making this place an eerie mix of life and death. Children run across the stone floors, clotheslines stretch between the monuments, and an occasional television antenna protrudes from a tomb roof. With Cairo's population increasing at the rate of 1000 people a day, families live where they can.*

As noted earlier, twice in its history, the world has experienced a revolutionary expansion of cities. The first urban revolution began about 8000 BCE with the first urban settlements and continued until permanent settlements were in place on several continents. About 1750, the second urban revolution took off; it lasted for two centuries as the Industrial Revolution spurred rapid growth of cities in Europe and North America.

A third urban revolution is now under way. Today, approximately 78 percent of people in industrial societies are already city dwellers. But extreme urban growth is occurring in low-income nations. In 1950, about 25 percent of the people in poor countries lived in cities. In 2008, for the first time in history, the world became mostly urban for the first time in history, with more than half of humanity living in cities (Population Reference Bureau, 2012).

As the population of our planet continues to climb, the share of humanity living in urban places is also increasing. As noted earlier, global population is projected to reach 9.3 billion by 2050. Almost all of this increase will take place in cities, as the urban share of the world's population climbs to about 68 percent (United Nations, 2012).

Not only are more of the world's people living in cities, but also more of these cities are passing the 10 million mark. In 1975, only three cities in the world, Tokyo, New York, and Mexico City, had populations exceeding 10 million, and all these cities were in high-income nations. In 2011, 23 cities had passed this mark, and only 5 of them were in high-income nations. By 2025, 14 more "megacities" will be added to the list and only 2 of these 14 will be in a high-income nation (9 in Asia, 2 in Latin America, and 1 in Africa) (Brockerhoff, 2000; United Nations, 2012).

This third urban revolution is taking place in the developing world because many poor nations have entered the high-growth Stage 2 of the demographic transition. Falling death rates have fuelled population increases in Latin America, Asia, and especially Africa. For urban areas, the rate of increase is *twice as high* because in addition to natural increase, millions of people leave the countryside each year in search of jobs, health care, education, and conveniences such as running water and electricity.

Cities do offer more opportunities than rural areas, but they provide no quick fix for the massive problems of escalating population and grinding poverty. Many cities in less economically developed nations—including Mexico City, Egypt's Cairo, India's Kolkata (formerly Calcutta), and Manila in the Philippines—are simply unable to meet the basic needs of much of their population. All these cities are surrounded by wretched shantytowns—settlements of makeshift homes built from discarded materials. As noted in Chapter 9 ("Global Stratification"), even city dumps are home to thousands of poor people, who pick through the piles of waste hoping to find enough to eat or sell to make it through another day.

Environment and Society

(15.6) Analyze current environmental problems such as pollution and global warming.

The human species has prospered, rapidly expanding over the entire planet. An increasing share of the global population now lives in cities, complex settlements that offer the promise of a better life than that found in rural villages.

But these advances have come at a high price. Never before in history have human beings placed such demands on the planet. This disturbing development brings us to focus on the interplay between the natural environment and society. Like demography, **ecology** is another cousin of sociology, formally defined as *the study of the interaction of living organisms and the natural environment*. Ecology rests on the research of natural scientists as well as social scientists. This text focuses on the aspects of ecology that involve familiar sociological concepts and issues.

The **natural environment** is *Earth's surface and atmosphere, including living organisms, air, water, soil, and other resources necessary to sustain life*. Like every other species, humans depend on the natural environment to survive. Yet with our capacity for culture, humans stand apart from other species; we alone take deliberate action to remake the world according to our own interests and desires, for better and for worse.

Why is the environment of interest to sociologists? Environmental problems, from pollution to global warming, do not arise from the natural world operating on its own. Such problems result from the specific actions of human beings, which means that they are *social problems*.

The Global Dimension

The study of the natural environment requires a global perspective. The reason is simple: Regardless of political divisions among nations, the planet is a single **ecosystem**, *a system composed of the interaction of all living organisms and their natural environment*.

The Greek meaning of *eco* is "house," reminding us that this planet is our home and that all living things and their natural environment are interrelated. A change in any part of the natural environment ripples throughout the entire global ecosystem.

Consider, from an ecological point of view, the popularity of hamburgers. People in North America (and, increasingly, around the world) have created a huge demand for beef, which has greatly expanded the ranching industry in Brazil, Costa Rica, and other Latin American nations. To produce the lean meat sought by fast-food corporations, cattle in Latin America feed on grass, which uses a great deal of land. Latin American ranchers get the land for grazing by clearing thousands of square miles of forests each year. These tropical forests are vital to maintaining Earth's atmosphere. Deforestation ends up threatening everyone, including the people in North America who enjoy hamburgers (N. Myers, 1984a).

Technology and the Environmental Deficit

Sociologists point to a simple formula: $I = PAT$, where environmental impact (I) reflects a society's population (P), its level of affluence (A), and its level of technology (T). Members of societies with simple technology—the hunters and gatherers described in Chapter 2 ("Culture")—hardly affect the environment because they are few in number, are poor, and have only simple technology. On the contrary, nature affects all aspects of their lives as they follow the migration of game, watch the rhythm of the seasons, and suffer from natural catastrophes such as fires, floods, droughts, and storms.

Societies at intermediate stages of technological development, being both larger and richer, have a somewhat greater capacity to affect the environment. But the environmental impact of horticulture (small-scale farming), pastoralism (the herding of animals), and even agriculture (the use of animal-drawn plows) is limited because people still rely on muscle power for producing food and other goods.

---

ecology the study of the interaction of living organisms and the natural environment

natural environment Earth's surface and atmosphere, including living organisms, air, water, soil, and other resources necessary to sustain life

ecosystem a system composed of the interaction of all living organisms and their natural environment

Humans' ability to control the natural environment increased dramatically with the changes brought about by the Industrial Revolution. Muscle power gave way to engines that burn fossil fuels: coal at first and then oil. Such machinery affects the environment in two ways: We consume more natural resources, and we release more pollutants into the atmosphere. Even more important, armed with industrial technology, we are able to bend nature to our will, tunnelling through mountains, damming rivers, irrigating deserts, and drilling for oil in the arctic wilderness and on the ocean floor. This explains why people in rich nations, who represent just 23 percent of humanity, account for nearly half of the world's energy use (World Bank, 2012).

Not only do high-income societies use more energy, but they also produce 100 times more goods than agrarian societies do. Higher living standards in turn increase the problem of solid waste (because people ultimately throw away most of what they produce) and pollution (industrial production generates smoke and other toxic substances).

The most important insight sociology offers about our physical world is that environmental problems do not simply "happen." Rather, the state of the natural environment reflects the ways in which social life is organized—how people live and what they think is important. Moreover, the greater the technological power of a society, the greater that society's ability to threaten the natural environment.

From the start, people recognized the material benefits of industrial technology. But only a century later did they begin to see the long-term effects on the natural environment. Today, we realize that the technological power to make our lives better can also put the lives of future generations at risk, and there is a national debate about how to address this issue.

Evidence suggests that we are running up an **environmental deficit**, *profound long-term harm to the natural environment caused by humanity's focus on short-term material affluence* (Bormann, 1990). The concept of environmental deficit is important for three reasons. First, it reminds us that environmental concerns are *sociological*, reflecting societies' priorities about how people should live. Second, it suggests that much environmental damage—to the air, land, and water—is unintended, at least in the sense that most people do not realize all the consequences of cutting down forests, strip mining, or using throwaway packaging. Again, sociological analysis is helpful in making such consequences clearer. Third, in some respects, the environmental deficit is *reversible*. Inasmuch as societies have created environmental problems, societies can undo many of them.

environmental deficit
profound long-term harm to the natural environment caused by humanity's focus on short-term material affluence

Culture: Growth and Limits

Whether we recognize environmental dangers and decide to do something about them is a cultural matter. Thus along with technology, culture has powerful environmental consequences.

The Logic of Growth

When you turn on the television news, you might hear a story like this: "The government reported bad economic news today, with the economy growing by only half a percent during the first quarter of the year." If you stop to think about it, our culture defines an economy that isn't growing as "stagnant" (which is bad) and an economy that is getting smaller as a "recession" or a "depression" (which is *very* bad). What is "good" is *growth*—lots of it—which makes the economy get bigger and bigger. More cars, bigger homes, more income, more spending—the idea of *more* is at the heart of our cultural definition of living well (McKibben, 2007).

One of the reasons we define growth in positive terms is that we value *material comfort*, believing that money and the things it buys improve our lives. We also believe in the idea of *progress*, thinking the future will be better than the present. In addition, we look to *science* to make our lives easier and more rewarding. In simple terms, "having things is good," "life gets better," and "people are clever." Taken together, such cultural values form the *logic of growth*.

An optimistic view of the world, the logic of growth holds that powerful technology has improved our lives and new discoveries will continue to do so in the future. Throughout the history of Canada and other high-income nations, the logic of growth has been the driving force behind settling the wilderness, building towns and roads, and pursuing material affluence.

However, "progress" can lead to unexpected problems, including strain on the environment. The logic of growth responds by arguing that people (especially scientists and other technology experts) will find a way out of any problem that growth places in our path. For example, before the world runs short of oil, scientists will come up with new hybrid and electric cars, and eventually hydrogen, solar, or nuclear engines (or some yet unknown technology) will develop to meet the world's energy needs.

Environmentalists counter that the logic of growth is flawed because it assumes that natural resources such as oil, clean air, fresh water, and topsoil will always be plentiful. We can and will exhaust these *finite* resources if we continue to pursue growth at any cost. Echoing Malthus, environmentalists warn that if we call on Earth to support increasing numbers of people, we will surely deplete finite resources, destroying the environment—and ourselves—in the process.

The Limits to Growth

If we cannot invent our way out of the problems created by the logic of growth, perhaps we need another way of thinking about the world. Environmentalists therefore counter that growth must have limits. Stated simply, the *limits-to-growth thesis* is that humanity must put in place policies to control the growth of population, production, and use of resources in order to avoid environmental collapse.

In *The Limits to Growth*, a controversial book that was influential in launching the environmental movement, Donella Meadows and her colleagues (1972) used a computer model to calculate the planet's available resources, rates of population growth, amount of land available for cultivation, levels of industrial and food production, and amount of pollutants released into the atmosphere. The authors concede that any long-range predictions are speculative, and some critics think they are plain wrong (Simon, 1981). But right or wrong, the conclusions of the study call for serious consideration. First, the authors claim that we are quickly consuming Earth's finite resources. Supplies of oil, natural gas, and other energy sources are declining and will continue to drop, a little faster or slower depending on the conservation policies of rich nations and the speed with which other nations such as India and China continue to industrialize. Within the next 100 years, resources will run out, crippling industrial output and causing a decline in food production.

This limits-to-growth theory shares Malthus's pessimism about the future. People who accept it doubt that current patterns of life are sustainable for even another century. Perhaps we all can learn to live with less. This may not be as hard as you might think: Research shows, for example, that an increase in material consumption in recent decades has not brought an increase in levels of personal happiness (D.G. Myers, 2000). And yet, the Canadian economy is based on the promise of endless growth, encouraging us to consume more, not less. Can capitalism and environmentalism ever find a balance or is John Foster, author of *Ecology Against Capitalism*, right to call "infinite expansion within a finite environment" a contradiction in terms (Foster, 2002)? In the end, environmentalists warn, either we make fundamental changes in how we live, placing less strain on the natural environment, or widespread hunger and conflict will force change on us.

Solid Waste: The Disposable Society

Across Canada, people generate a massive amount of solid waste *each and every day*. Figure 15–4 shows the composition of Winnipeg's trash.

As a rich nation of people who value convenience, Canada has become a *disposable society*. We consume more products than virtually any other nation, and many of these products have

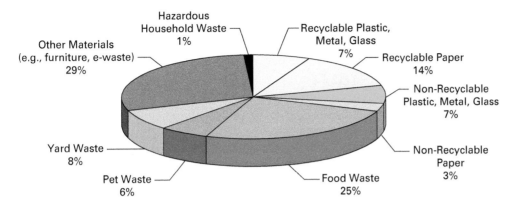

FIGURE 15–4 Composition of Winnipeg's Residential Waste

Source: Stantec Consulting Ltd. (2011).

throwaway packaging. For example, fast food is served with cardboard, plastic, and Styrofoam containers that we throw away within minutes. Countless other products, from film to fishhooks, are elaborately packaged to make the products more attractive to the customer and to discourage tampering and theft.

Manufacturers market soft drinks, beer, and fruit juices in aluminum cans, glass jars, and plastic containers, which not only consume finite resources but also generate mountains of solid waste. Then there are countless items intentionally designed to be disposable: pens, razors, flashlights, batteries, and even cameras. Other commodities, from light bulbs to automobiles, are designed to have a limited useful life and then become unwanted junk. As Paul Connett (1991) points out, even the words we use to describe what we throw away—*waste, litter, trash, refuse, garbage, rubbish*—show how little we value what we cannot immediately use. But this was not always the case, as the Seeing Sociology in Everyday Life box on page 538 explains.

Living in a rich society, the average person in North America consumes hundreds of times more energy, plastics, lumber, water, and other resources than someone living in a low-income country, such as Bangladesh or Tanzania, and nearly twice as much as people in some other high-income countries, such as Sweden and Japan. This high level of consumption means not only that we in Canada use a disproportionate share of the planet's natural resources but also that we generate most of the world's refuse.

We like to say that we throw things "away." But most of the 25 million tons of solid waste our society produced in 2012 never went away (Statistics Canada, 2015). Rather, it ended up in landfills, which are, literally, filling up. Material in landfills also can pollute underground water supplies. The city of Toronto is trying to deal with this issue. After running out of space in its own landfills, it tried to ship garbage 600 kilometres north by rail to the abandoned Adams Lake mine, close to the community of Kirkland Lake. Fierce opposition led to the garbage being shipped to the Green Lane landfill near St. Thomas, Ontario. However, the controversy erupts again whenever an accident occurs that involves one of the hundreds of trucks that daily drive back and forth. In addition, what goes into landfills all too often stays there, sometimes for centuries. Tens of millions of tires, diapers, and other items we bury in landfills each year do not decompose but will remain as an unwelcome legacy for future generations.

Environmentalists argue that we should address the problem of solid waste by doing what many of our grandparents did: use less and turn "waste" into a resource. Part of the solution is *recycling*, reusing resources we would otherwise discard. Recycling is an accepted practice in Japan and many other nations, and it is becoming more common in Canada, where, depending on the province or territory, we now reuse anywhere from 18 to 24 percent of waste materials (van der Werf & Cant, 2012). The share is increasing as more municipalities pass laws requiring reuse of certain materials such as glass bottles and aluminum cans and as the business of recycling becomes more profitable.

Seeing Sociology in Everyday Life

Why Grandma Macionis Had No Trash

Grandma Macionis, we always used to say, never threw anything away. Not food, not bottles or cans, not paper. Not even coffee grounds. Nothing.

Grandma was born and raised in Lithuania—the "old country"—where life in a poor village shaped her in ways that never changed, even after she came to the United States as a young woman and settled in Philadelphia.

In her later years, when I knew her, I can remember the family travelling together to her house to celebrate her birthday. We never knew what to get Grandma, because she never seemed to need anything. She lived a simple life and had simple clothes and showed little interest in "fancy things." She had no electric appliances. She used her simple tools until they wore out. Her kitchen knives, for example, were worn narrow from decades of sharpening. The food that was left over from meals was saved.

Grandma Macionis, in the 1970s, with the first author.

What could not be saved was recycled as compost for her vegetable garden.

After opening a birthday present, she would carefully save the box, refold the wrapping paper, and roll up the ribbon—all of these things meant as much to her as whatever gift they contained. We all knew her routines and we smiled together as we watched her put everything away, knowing she would find a way to use each item again and again.

As strange as Grandma sometimes seemed to her grandchildren, she was a product of her culture. A century ago, in fact, there was little "trash." If socks wore thin, people mended them, probably more than once. When they were beyond repair, they were used as rags for cleaning or sewn with bits of other old clothing into a quilt. Everything had value—if not in one way, then in another.

During the twentieth century, as women joined men in working outside the home, income went up. Families began buying more appliances and other "timesaving" products. Before long, few people cared about the kind of recycling that Grandma practised. Soon cities sent crews from block to block to pick up truckloads of discarded material. The era of "trash" had begun.

What Do You Think?

1. Just as Grandma Macionis was a product of her culture, so are we. Do you know people who have plenty but never seem to think they have enough?

2. What cultural values make people today demand timesaving products and "convenience" packaging?

3. Do you think recent decades have brought a turnaround so that people are now more aware of a need to recycle? How does today's recycling differ from that practised by Grandma Macionis?

So far, however, our appetite for consumption continues to outpace our efforts to curb our waste. When it comes to municipal waste, Canada received a "D" on its Conference Board of Canada–issued report card, which ranked it last out of 17 countries (2015). In 2009, this country produced 777 kilograms per capita of municipal waste, which is twice as much as the lowest producer, Japan.

Water and Air

Oceans, lakes, and streams are the lifeblood of the global ecosystem. Humans depend on water for drinking, bathing, cooking, cleaning, recreation, and a host of other activities.

According to what scientists call the *hydrologic cycle*, Earth naturally recycles water and refreshes the land. The process begins as heat from the sun causes Earth's water, 97 percent of which is in the oceans, to evaporate and form clouds. Because water evaporates at lower temperatures than most pollutants, the water vapour that rises from the seas is relatively pure, leaving various contaminants behind. Water then falls to the Earth as rain, which drains into streams and rivers and finally returns to the sea. Two major concerns about water, then, are supply and pollution.

Water Supply

Less than one-tenth of 1 percent of Earth's water is suitable for drinking. It is not surprising, then, that for thousands of years, water rights have figured prominently in laws around the world. Today, some regions of the world, especially the tropics, enjoy plentiful fresh water, using a small share of the available supply. However, high demand, coupled with modest reserves, makes water supply a matter of concern in much of North America and Asia, where people look to rivers rather than rainfall for their water. In China, aquifers are dropping rapidly. In the Middle East, water supply is reaching a critical level. Iran is rationing water in its capital city. In Egypt, the Nile River provides just one-sixth as much water per person as it did in 1900. Across northern Africa and the Middle East, as many as 1 billion people may lack the water they need for irrigation and drinking by 2030. From another angle, by this time the world will be able to provide 40 percent less water than the planet requires (United Nations Environment Programme, 2008; Walsh, 2009).

Rising population and the development of more complex technology have greatly increased the world's appetite for water. The global consumption of freshwater (now estimated at about 3800 cubic kilometres) has doubled since 1950 and is rising steadily. As a result, even in parts of the world that receive plenty of rainfall, people are using groundwater faster than it can be replenished naturally. In the Tamil Nadu region of southern India, for example, so much groundwater is being used that the water table has fallen 30 metres over the last several decades. Mexico City—which has sprawled to some 3600 square kilometres—has pumped so much water from its underground aquifer that the city has sunk nine metres in the past century and continues to drop about five centimetres per year. Closer to home, on January 2014, the Governor of California proclaimed a State of Emergency, ordering various agencies to take measures against drought and water shortages. In Canada, we have access to a disproportionate share of the world's fresh water. In some ways we seem to realize the importance of this resource, as whenever water exports have been proposed, Canadians were up in arms in opposition. We also, however, seem to take water for granted: Compared to other high-income countries, Canada has the lowest municipal water prices and some of the highest per capita water use. According to one

A majority of Canadian cities have water treatment facilities. Low-income, rural, and Aboriginal communities, however, are more likely to experience environmental problems. As of January 2015, 126 First Nations communities were subject to drinking water advisories.

Water is vital to life, and it is also in short supply. The state of Gujarat, in western India, has experienced a long drought. In the village of Natwarghad, people crowd together, lowering pots into the local well, taking what little water is left.

study, when it comes to water use, Canada ranks 15th out of 16 peer countries (Conference Board of Canada, 2015).

In light of such developments, we must face the reality that water is a valuable and finite resource. Greater conservation of water by individuals—the average person in Canada consumes about 250 litres of water a day—is part of the answer. However, households around the world account for just 11 percent of water use. It is even more crucial that we curb water consumption by industry, which uses 19 percent of the global total, and farming, which consumes 70 percent of the total for irrigation.

Perhaps new irrigation technology will reduce the future demand of water. But here again, we see how population increase, as well as economic growth, strains our ecosystem (Solomon, 2010; UNESCO World Water Assessment Programme, 2012).

Water Pollution

In large cities from Mexico City to Cairo to Shanghai, many people have no choice but to drink contaminated water. Infectious diseases such as typhoid, cholera, and dysentery, all caused by waterborne micro-organisms, spread rapidly through these populations. Besides ensuring ample *supplies* of water, we must protect the *quality* of water.

Water quality in Canada is generally good by global standards. However, even here the problem of water pollution is steadily growing, as in the case of the raw sewage from Halifax, St. John's, and Victoria that goes straight into the ocean. Decades of heavy pollution of the Great Lakes, and of countless streams and rivers across the country, has seriously threatened plant and fish life, and for some species has resulted in extinction.

A special problem is *acid rain*—falling precipitation made acidic by air pollution—which destroys plant and animal life. Acid rain begins with power plants burning fossil fuels (oil and coal) to generate electricity; this burning releases sulphuric and nitrous oxides into the air. As the wind sweeps these gases into the atmosphere, they react with the air to form sulphuric and nitric acids, which turns atmospheric moisture acidic.

This is a clear case of one type of pollution causing another: Air pollution (from smokestacks) ends up contaminating water (in lakes and streams that collect acid rain). Acid rain is truly a global phenomenon because the regions that suffer the harmful effects may be thousands of kilometres from the source of the original pollution. For instance, British power plants have caused acid rain that has devastated forests and fish in Norway and Sweden, up to 1600 kilometres to the northeast. Similarly, U.S. smokestacks have been accused of poisoning the forests in Eastern Canada.

Air Pollution

Because we are surrounded by air, most people in Canada are more aware of air pollution than contaminated water. One of the unexpected consequences of industrial technology, especially the factory and the motor vehicle, has been a decline in air quality. In 1950, exhaust fumes from automobiles shrouded cities such as Vancouver, where the air is trapped between the wind from the ocean and the postcard-pretty mountains. In London in the mid-twentieth century, factory smokestacks, automobiles, and coal fires used to heat homes all added up to the worst urban air quality the world has ever known. The fog that some British jokingly called "pea soup" was in reality a deadly mix of pollutants: In 1952, an especially thick haze that hung over London for five days killed 4000 people.

Air quality improved in the final decades of the twentieth century. Rich nations passed laws that banned high-pollution heating, including the coal fires that choked London. In addition, scientists devised ways to make factories and motor vehicles operate much more cleanly. In fact, today's vehicles produce only a fraction of the pollution that spewed from models of the 1950s and 1960s. And cleaner air has improved human health: Experts estimate that improvement in North America's air quality over the past several decades has added almost half a year to the average life span (Chang, 2009).

If high-income countries can breathe a bit more easily than they once did, the problem of air pollution in poor societies is becoming more serious. One reason is that people in low-income countries still rely on wood, coal, peat, and other "dirty" fuels to cook their food and heat their homes. In addition, nations eager to encourage short-term industrial development may pay little attention to the longer-term dangers of air pollution. As a result, many cities in Latin America, Eastern Europe, and Asia are plagued by air pollution as bad as London's "pea soup" back in the 1950s.

The Rainforests

Rainforests are *regions of dense forestation, most of which circle the globe close to the equator.* The largest tropical rainforests are in South America (notably Brazil), west-central Africa, and Southeast Asia. In all, the world's rainforests cover some 1.5 billion acres, or 5 percent of Earth's total land surface.

rainforests regions of dense forestation, most of which circle the globe close to the equator

Like other global resources, rainforests are falling victim to the needs and appetites of the surging world population. As noted earlier, to meet the demand for beef, ranchers in Latin America burn forested areas to increase their supply of grazing land. We are also losing rainforests to the hardwood trade. People in rich nations pay high prices for mahogany and other woods because, as environmentalist Norman Myers (1984b:88) puts it, they have "a penchant for parquet floors, fine furniture, fancy panelling, weekend yachts, and high-grade coffins." Under such economic pressure, the world's rainforests are now just half their original size, and they continue to shrink by about 1 percent (60 700 square kilometres) annually. Unless we stop this loss, the rainforests will vanish before the end of this century and with them will go protection for the Earth's biodiversity and climate (United Nations, Department of Economic and Social Affairs, 2011b).

Global Warming

Why are rainforests so important? One reason is that they cleanse the atmosphere of carbon dioxide (CO_2). Since the beginning of the Industrial Revolution, the amount of CO_2 produced by humans, mostly from factories and automobiles, has risen sharply. Much of this CO_2 is absorbed by the oceans. But plants also take in CO_2 and in the process expel oxygen. This is why rainforests are vital to maintaining the chemical balance of the atmosphere.

The problem is that production of CO_2 is rising while the amount of plant life on Earth is shrinking. To make matters worse, rainforests are being destroyed mostly by burning, which releases even more CO_2 into the atmosphere. Experts estimate that the atmospheric concentration of CO_2 is now 41 percent higher than it was 150 years ago and rising rapidly (Adam, 2008; U.S. Department of Commerce, National Oceanic & Atmospheric Administration, 2013).

High above Earth, CO_2 acts like the glass roof of a greenhouse, letting heat from the sun pass through to the surface while preventing much of it from radiating away from the planet. The result of this *greenhouse effect*, say ecologists, is **global warming**, *a rise in Earth's average temperature due to an increasing concentration of carbon dioxide in the atmosphere*. Since the Industrial Revolution, the global temperature has risen about 0.7°C (to an average of 14.4°C). Scientists continue to debate the numbers, but they warn that the planet's temperature could rise by 3°C to as much as 6°C during this century. Already, the polar ice caps are melting, and over the last century, the average level of the oceans has risen about six inches. Scientists predict that increasing average temperatures could melt so much ice that the sea level would rise enough to cover low-lying land all around the world: Water would cover all of the Maldive Islands in the Indian Ocean, most of Bangladesh, and much of the coasts of North America. Such a change would create perhaps 100 million "climate change refugees." On the other hand, this same process of rising temperatures will affect other regions of the world very differently. The U.S. Midwest, currently one of the most productive agricultural regions in the world, would likely become more arid. No wonder that, for more than a decade, government agencies throughout the world have been working to limit greenhouse gas emissions (Gillis, 2011; McMahon, 2011; Reed, 2011; Klinenberg, 2013).

Some scientists point out that we cannot be sure of the consequences of global warming. Others point to the fact that global temperature changes have been taking place throughout history, apparently having little or nothing to do with rainforests or human activity. But the majority of scientists, including 97 percent of all climate scientists, have now reached a clear consensus: Global warming over the past century has been likely caused by human activity and it is a serious problem that threatens the future for all of us (Kerr, 2005; Gore, 2006; International Panel on Climate Change, 2007; Singer, 2007; Ridley, 2012; NASA, 2015).

Declining Biodiversity

Our planet is home to as many as 30 million species of animals, plants, and micro-organisms. As rainforests are cleared and humans extend their control over nature, several dozen unique species of plants and animals cease to exist each day, reducing the planet's *biodiversity*.

But given the vast number of living species, why should we be concerned by the loss of a few? Environmentalists give four reasons. First, our planet's biodiversity provides a varied source of human food. Using agricultural high technology, scientists can "splice" familiar crops with more exotic plant life, making food more bountiful as well as more resistant to insects and disease. Certain species of life are even considered vital to the production of human food. Bees, for example, perform the work of pollination, a necessary stage in the growth of plants. The fact that the bee population has declined by one-third in North America and by two-thirds in the Middle East is cause for serious concern. Thus sustaining biodiversity helps feed our planet's rapidly increasing population.

Second, Earth's biodiversity is a vital genetic resource used by medical and pharmaceutical researchers to produce hundreds of new compounds each year that cure disease and improve our lives. For example, children in Canada now have a good chance of surviving leukemia, a disease that was almost a sure killer two generations ago, because of a compound derived from a tropical flower

Members of small, simple societies, such as the Mentawi in Indonesia, live in greater harmony with nature; they do not have the technological means to greatly affect the natural world. Although we tend to think of our complex societies as superior to the way of life of such people, the truth is that there is much we can—indeed, we must—learn from them.

called the rosy periwinkle. The oral birth control pill, used by tens of millions of women in this country, is another product of plant research involving the Mexican forest yam. Because biodiversity itself allows our ecosystem to control many types of diseases, it is likely that if biodiversity declines, the transmission of disease will increase.

Third, with the loss of any species of life—whether it is the ancient Kootenay River white sturgeon, the magnificent California condor, the famed Chinese panda, the spotted owl, or even a single species of ant—the beauty and complexity of the natural environment are diminished. There are clear warning signs of such loss: Three-fourths of the world's 10 000 species of birds are declining in number.

Finally, unlike pollution, the extinction of any species is irreversible and final. An important ethical question, then, is whether we who live today have the right to impoverish the world for those who will live tomorrow (E.O. Wilson, 1991; Keesing et al., 2010; Capella, 2011).

Environmental Racism

Conflict theory has given rise to the concept of **environmental racism**, *patterns of development that expose poor people, especially minorities, to environmental hazards*. Historically, factories that spew pollution have stood near neighbourhoods of the poor and people of colour. Why? In part, the poor themselves were drawn to factories in search of work, and their low incomes often meant they could afford housing only in undesirable neighbourhoods. Sometimes the only housing that fit their budgets stood in the very shadow of the plants and mills where they worked.

Nobody wants a factory or dump nearby, but the poor have little power to resist. Through the years, the most serious environmental hazards have been located in Nova Scotia's Africville (not in upscale Point Pleasant Park), in Ontario's Sarnia 45 Indian Reserve (not wealthy Sunnybrook), and in Northern Alberta's Athabasca tar sands, a 140 000-square-kilometre area (not in affluent Strathcona).

environmental racism patterns of development that expose poor people, especially minorities, to environmental hazards

Looking Ahead: Toward a Sustainable Society and World

(15.7) Evaluate progress toward creating an ecologically sustainable culture.

The demographic analysis presented in this chapter reveals some disturbing trends. We see, first, that Earth's population has reached record levels because birth rates remain high in poor nations and death rates have fallen just about everywhere. Reducing fertility will remain a pressing need throughout this century. Even with some recent decline in the rate of population increase, the nightmare Thomas Malthus described is still a real possibility, as the Controversy & Debate box on page 545 explains.

Further, population growth remains greatest in the poorest countries of the world, which cannot meet the needs of their present populations, much less future ones. Supporting 84 million additional people on our planet each year, 83 million of them in economically less developed countries, will require a global commitment to provide not just food but housing, schools, and employment as well. The well-being of the entire world may ultimately depend on resolving the economic and social problems of poor, overly populated countries and bridging the widening gulf between "have" and "have-not" nations.

Urbanization is continuing, especially in poor countries. For thousands of years, people have sought out cities in the hope of finding a better life. But the sheer numbers of people who live in today's megacities—including Mexico City, São Paulo (Brazil), Lagos (Nigeria), Mumbai (India), and Manila (Philippines)—have created urban problems on a massive scale.

Mark Blinch/Reuters

If human ingenuity created the threats to our environment that we now face, can humans also solve these problems? In recent years, a number of designs for small, environmentally friendly cars show the promise of new technology. But do such innovations go far enough? Will we have to make more basic changes to our way of life to ensure human survival in the centuries to come?

Around the world, humanity is facing a serious environmental challenge. Part of this problem is population increase, which is greatest in poor societies. But part of the problem is the high levels of consumption in rich nations such as our own. By increasing the planet's environmental deficit, our present way of life is borrowing against the well-being of our children and their children. Globally, members of rich societies, who currently consume so much of Earth's resources, are mortgaging the future security of the poor countries of the world.

ecologically sustainable culture a way of life that meets the needs of the present generation without threatening the environmental legacy of future generations

The answer, in principle, is to create an **ecologically sustainable culture**, *a way of life that meets the needs of the present generation without threatening the environmental legacy of future generations.* Sustainable living depends on three strategies.

First, the world needs to *bring population growth under control.* The current population of 7.1 billion is already straining the natural environment. Clearly, the higher the world's population climbs, the more difficult environmental problems will become. Even if the recent slowing of population growth continues, the world will have about 9.3 billion people by 2050. Few analysts think that the planet can support this many people; most argue that we must hold the line at about 7 billion, and some argue that we must *decrease* population in the coming decades (Smail, 2010).

A second strategy is to *conserve finite resources.* This means meeting our needs with a responsible eye toward the future by using resources efficiently, seeking alternative sources of energy, and in some cases, learning to live with less.

A third strategy is to *reduce waste.* Whenever possible, simply using less is the best solution. Learning to live with less is not likely to come easily, but keep in mind the research that suggests that as our society has consumed more and more, people have not become any happier (D.G. Myers, 2000). Recycling programs, too, are part of the answer, and recycling can make everyone part of the solution to our environmental problems.

In the end, making all these strategies work depends on a basic change in the way we think about ourselves and our world. Our *egocentric* outlook sets our own interests as standards for how to live, but a sustainable environment demands an *ecocentric* outlook that helps us see how the present is tied to the future and why everyone must work together.

Controversy & Debate

Apocalypse: Will People Overwhelm the Planet?

Sunita: I'm telling you, there are too many people already! Where is everyone going to live?

Tabitha: Have you ever been to Saskatchewan? Or the Yukon? There's plenty of empty space out there.

Marco: Maybe now. But I'm not so sure about our children—or their children . . .

Are you worried about the world's increasing population? Think about this: By the time you finish reading this feature, more than 1000 people will have been added to our planet. By this time tomorrow, global population will have risen by more than 230 000. Currently, as the table shows, there are more than four births for every two deaths on the planet, pushing the world's population upward by 84 million people annually. Put another way, global population growth amounts to adding another Germany to the world each year.

It is no wonder that many demographers and environmentalists are deeply concerned about the future. Earth has an unprecedented population of 7.1 billion: The 3 billion people we have added since 1974 alone roughly equals the planet's total in 1960. Might Thomas Malthus, who predicted that overpopulation would push the world into war and suffering, be right after all? If we do not change our ways, predict Lester Brown and other *neo-Malthusians*, we face a coming apocalypse. Brown admits that Malthus failed to imagine how much technology (especially the use of fertilizers and the ability to genetically modify plants) could boost the planet's agricultural output. But he maintains that Earth's rising population is rapidly outstripping its finite resources. Families in many poor countries can find little firewood, members of rich countries are depleting the oil reserves, and everyone is draining our supply of clean water and poisoning the planet with waste. Some analysts argue that we have already passed Earth's "carrying capacity" for population and we need to

	Births	Deaths	Net Increase
Per year	140 541 944	56 238 002	84 303 942
Per month	11 711 829	4 686 500	7 025 329
Per day	385 046	154 077	230 969
Per hour	16 020	6 420	9 600
Per minute	267	107	160
Per second	4.5	1.8	2.7

hold the line or even reduce global population to ensure humanity's long-term survival.

But other analysts, the *anti-Malthusians*, sharply disagree. Julian Simon points out that two centuries after Malthus predicted catastrophe, Earth supports almost six times as many people who, on average, live longer, healthier lives than ever before. With more advanced technology, people have devised ways to increase productivity and limit population increase. As Simon sees it, this is cause for celebration. Human ingenuity has consistently proved the doomsayers wrong, and Simon is betting it will continue to do so.

What Do You Think?

1. Where do you place your bet? Do you think Earth can support 8 or 10 billion people?

2. What, if anything, do you think should be done about global population increase?

3. Were Malthus alive today, would he feel relieved or would he say "I told you so!"? Explain.

Sources: Brown (1995), Simon (1995), Scanlon (2001), Smail (2010), Population Reference Bureau (2012), and U.S. Census Bureau (2013).

Most nations in the southern half of the world are *underdeveloped*, unable to meet the basic needs of their people. At the same time, most countries in the northern half of the world are *overdeveloped*, using more resources than the planet can sustain over time. The changes needed to create a sustainable ecosystem will not come easily, and they will be costly. But the price of *not* responding to the growing environmental deficit will certainly be greater (Kellert & Bormann, 1991; Brown et al., 1993; Population Action International, 2000; Barlow, 2013).

Finally, consider that the great dinosaurs dominated this planet for some 160 million years and then perished forever. Humanity is far younger, having existed for a mere 250 000 years. Compared to the rather dimwitted dinosaurs, our species has the gift of great intelligence. But how will we use this ability? What are the chances that our species will continue to flourish 160 million years—or even 160 years—from now? The answer depends on the choices that will be made by one of the 30 million species living on Earth: human beings.

Seeing Sociology in Everyday Life

CHAPTER 15 Population, Urbanization, and Environment

Why is the environment a social issue?

As this chapter explains, the state of the natural environment depends on how society is organized, especially the importance a culture attaches to consumption and economic growth.

Henny Ray Abrams/AP Images

We learn to see economic expansion as natural and good. When the economy stays the same for a number of months, we say we are experiencing "stagnation." How do we define a period when the economy gets smaller, as happened during the fall of 2008?

David Cooper/Toronto Star/ZUMAPRESS.com/Newscom

What would it take to convince members of our society that smaller (rather than bigger) might be better? Why do we seem to prefer not just bigger cars but also bigger homes and more and more material possessions?

HINT If expansion is "good times," then contraction is a "recession" or perhaps even a "depression." Such a worldview means that it is normal—or even desirable—to live in a way that increases stress on the natural environment. Sustainability, an idea that is especially important as world population increases, depends on learning to live with what we have or maybe even learning to live with less. Although many people seem to think so, it really doesn't require a 2700-kilogram SUV to move around urban areas. Actually, it might not require a car at all. This new way of thinking requires that we do not define social standing and personal success in terms of what we own and what we consume. Can you imagine a society like that? What would it be like?

Seeing Sociology in *Your* Everyday Life

1. Here is an illustration of the problem of runaway growth (Milbrath, 1989:10): "A pond has a single water lily growing on it. The lily doubles in size each day. In 30 days, it covers the entire pond. On which day does it cover half the pond?" When you realize the answer, discuss the implications of this example for population increase.

2. Go to www.sociologyinfocus.com to access the Sociology in Focus blog, where you can read the latest posts by a team of young sociologists who apply the sociological perspective to topics of popular culture.

3. Do you think that the world's increasing population is a problem or not? What about the state of our planet's natural environment?

Amit Dave/Reuters/Landov

Demography: The Study of Population

(15.1) Explain the concepts of fertility, mortality, and migration, and how they affect population size. (pages 514–519)

Demography analyzes the size and composition of a population and how and why people move from place to place.

- **Fertility** is the incidence of childbearing in a country's population. Demographers describe fertility using the **crude birth rate**.
- **Mortality** is the incidence of death in a country's population. Demographers measure mortality using both the **crude death rate** and the **infant mortality rate**.
- The **net migration rate** is the difference between the in-migration rate and the out-migration rate.
- In general, rich nations grow almost as much from immigration as from natural increase; poorer nations grow almost entirely from natural increase.
- Demographers use **age-sex pyramids** to show the composition of a population graphically and to project population trends.

demography the study of human population
fertility the incidence of childbearing in a country's population
crude birth rate the number of live births in a given year for every 1000 people in a population
mortality the incidence of death in a country's population
crude death rate the number of deaths in a given year for every 1000 people in a population
infant mortality rate the number of deaths among infants under one year of age for each 1000 live births in a given year
life expectancy the average life span of a country's population
migration the movement of people into and out of a specified territory
sex ratio the number of males for every 100 females in a nation's population
age-sex pyramid a graphic representation of the age and sex of a population

History and Theory of Population Growth

(15.2) Analyze population trends using Malthusian theory and demographic transition theory. (pages 519–523)

- Historically, world population grew slowly, as high birth rates were offset by high death rates.
- About 1750, world population rose sharply, mostly due to falling death rates.
- In the late 1700s, Thomas Robert Malthus warned that population growth would outpace food production, resulting in social calamity.
- **Demographic transition theory** claims that technological advances slow population increase.
- Currently, the world is gaining 84 million people each year, with 98 percent of this increase taking place in poor countries. World population is expected to reach about 9.3 billion by 2050.

demographic transition theory a thesis that links population patterns to a society's level of technological development
zero population growth the rate of reproduction that maintains population at a steady level

Urbanization: The Growth of Cities

(15.3) Summarize patterns of urbanization in Canada and around the world. (pages 523–528)

The **first urban revolution** began with the appearance of cities about 10 000 years ago.

- By about 2000 years ago, cities emerged in most regions of the world except North America.
- Pre-industrial cities have low-rise buildings; narrow, winding streets; and personal social ties.

A **second urban revolution** began about 1750 as the Industrial Revolution propelled rapid urban growth in Europe.

- Cities' physical form changed as planners created wide, regular streets to facilitate commerce.
- The emphasis on business, and the increasing size of cities, made urban life more impersonal.

A **third urban revolution** is now occurring in poor countries.

In Canada, urbanization has been going on for almost 300 years.

- Urbanization came to North America with European colonists who displaced most of the Aboriginal inhabitants.
- By 1850, hundreds of new cities had been founded from coast to coast.
- By 1931, a majority of the Canadian population lived in urban areas.
- Since 1950, the decentralization of cities has resulted in the growth of suburbs and edge cities.
- Since 1960, gentrification has been transforming working-class neighbourhoods in major Canadian cities.
- Although rural places that are near large cities, as well as those that are especially scenic, are attracting migrants, rural areas currently lose net population through migration to cities.

urbanization the concentration of population into cities
metropolis a large city that socially and economically dominates an urban area
suburbs urban areas beyond the political boundaries of a city
gentrification the process by which working-class communities are displaced by an influx of middle-class property developers
megalopolis a vast urban region containing a number of cities and their surrounding suburbs

Urbanism as a Way of Life

15.4 Identify the contributions of Tönnies, Durkheim, Simmel, Park, Wirth, and Marx to our understanding of urban life. (pages 528–532)

Rapid urbanization during the nineteenth century led early sociologists to study the differences between rural and urban life.

Ferdinand Tönnies built his analysis on the concepts of *Gemeinschaft* and *Gesellschaft*.

- *Gemeinschaft*, typical of the rural village, joins people in what amounts to a primary group.
- *Gesellschaft*, typical of the modern city, describes individuals motivated by their own needs rather than by a desire to help improve the well-being of the community.

Emile Durkheim agreed with much of Tönnies's thinking but claimed that urbanites do not lack social bonds; the basis of social solidarity simply differs in the two settings. He described

- **mechanical solidarity**—social bonds based on common sentiments and shared moral values. This type of social solidarity is typical of traditional, rural life.
- **organic solidarity**—social bonds based on specialization and interdependence. This type of social solidarity is typical of modern, urban life.

Georg Simmel claimed that the overstimulation of city life produced a blasé attitude in urbanites.

Robert Park, at the University of Chicago, claimed that cities permit greater social freedom.

Louis Wirth saw large, dense, heterogeneous populations creating an impersonal and self-interested, though tolerant, way of life.

Karl Marx's analysis of conflict in the city is echoed in the urban political economy model.

Gemeinschaft a type of social organization in which people are closely tied by kinship and tradition

Gesellschaft a type of social organization in which people come together only on the basis of individual self-interest

urban ecology the study of the link between the physical and social dimensions of cities

Urbanization in Low-Income Countries

15.5 Describe the third urban revolution now under way in poor societies. (page 533)

- The third urban revolution is taking place now in low-income nations.
- Almost all global population increase is taking place in cities. Of the 23 cities with population greater than 10 million, 18 are in poor nations.

Environment and Society

15.6 Analyze current environmental problems such as pollution and global warming. (pages 534–543)

The state of the **environment** is a social issue because it reflects how human beings organize social life.

- Societies increase the **environmental deficit** by focusing on short-term benefits and ignoring the long-term consequences brought on by their way of life.
- The more complex a society's technology, the greater its capacity to alter the natural environment.
- The *logic-of-growth thesis* supports economic development, claiming that people can solve environmental problems as they arise.
- The *limits-to-growth thesis* states that societies must curb development to prevent eventual environmental collapse.
- Much of the solid waste we throw away ends up in landfills, which are filling up and can pollute groundwater.
- The supply of clean water is already low in some parts of the world. Industrial technology has caused a decline in air quality.
- Rainforests help remove carbon dioxide from the atmosphere and are home to a large share of this planet's living species. Under pressure from development, the world's rainforests are now half their original size and are shrinking by about 1 percent annually.
- Conflict theory has drawn attention to **environmental racism**.

ecology the study of the interaction of living organisms and the natural environment

natural environment Earth's surface and atmosphere, including living organisms, air, water, soil, and other resources necessary to sustain life

ecosystem a system composed of the interaction of all living organisms and their natural environment

environmental deficit profound long-term harm to the natural environment caused by humanity's focus on short-term material affluence

rainforests regions of dense forestation, most of which circle the globe close to the equator

global warming a rise in Earth's average temperature due to an increasing concentration of carbon dioxide in the atmosphere

environmental racism patterns of development that expose poor people, especially minorities, to environmental hazards

Looking Ahead: Toward a Sustainable Society and World

15.7 Evaluate progress toward creating an ecologically sustainable culture. (pages 543–545)

- Our planet's population has reached record levels due to high fertility in low-income nations, coupled with declining mortality almost everywhere.
- As population increases, humanity faces environmental challenges that involve both greater consumption of resources and higher levels of pollution.

ecologically sustainable culture a way of life that meets the needs of the present generation without threatening the environmental legacy of future generations

16 Social Change: Modern and Postmodern Societies

LEARNING OBJECTIVES

16.1 State four defining characteristics of social change.

16.2 Explain how culture, conflict, ideas, population patterns, collective behaviour, and social movements direct social change.

16.3 Apply the ideas of Tönnies, Durkheim, Weber, and Marx to our understanding of modernity.

16.4 Apply structural-functional theory to modern social life.

16.5 Apply social-conflict theory to modern social life.

16.6 Apply sociological theory to understand how people experience modern social life.

16.7 Evaluate the positive and negative consequences of social change.

16.8 Discuss postmodernism as one type of social criticism.

16.9 Evaluate possible directions of future social change.

the Power of Society

to encourage or discourage participation in social movements

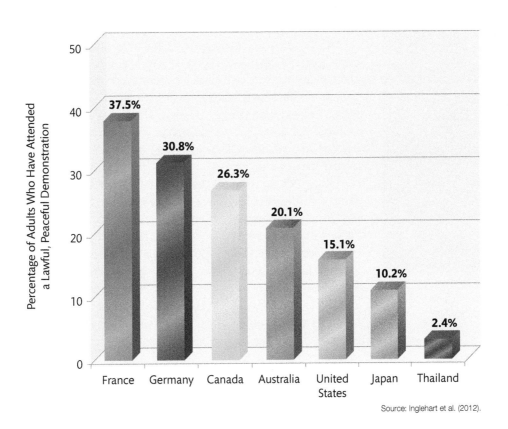

Percentage of Adults Who Have Attended a Lawful, Peaceful Demonstration

- France: 37.5%
- Germany: 30.8%
- Canada: 26.3%
- Australia: 20.1%
- United States: 15.1%
- Japan: 10.2%
- Thailand: 2.4%

Source: Inglehart et al. (2012).

Is being active in a social movement just a matter of personal choice? When asked if they had ever attended a lawful, peaceful demonstration in support of some social movement, about 25 percent of Canadian adults said "yes." In some nations, that share is lower: Just 15 percent of the U.S. population say they have engaged in a demonstration, 10 percent of the Japanese, and only 2 percent of adults in Thailand say the same. But 31 percent of Germans have engaged in a demonstration, as have 38 percent of the French. Whether people "take to the streets" to show their support for a cause depends on more than decisions made by individuals; it also reflects the culture of the larger society.

Chapter Overview

Society does not stay the same. This chapter explores social change, explaining how modern societies differ from earlier, traditional societies. The chapter discusses many causes of change, including collective behaviour, disasters, and social movements.

Nelson Hancock/Dorling Kindersley Limited

The five-storey red brick apartment building at 253 East Tenth Street has been standing for more than a century. In 1900, one of the 20 small apartments in the building was occupied by 39-year-old Julius Streicher; Christine Streicher, age 33; and their four young children. The Streichers were immigrants, both having come in 1885 from their native Germany.

The Streichers probably considered themselves successful. Julius operated a small clothing shop a few blocks from his apartment; Christine stayed at home, raised the children, and did housework. Like most people in the country at that time, neither Julius nor Christine had graduated from high school, and they worked for 10 to 12 hours a day, 6 days a week. Their income—average for that time—was about $35 a month, or about $425 per year. (In today's dollars, that would be slightly more than $11 000, which would put the family well below the poverty line.) They spent almost half of their income for food; most of the rest went for rent.

Today, Dorothy Sabo resides at 253 East Tenth Street, living alone in the same apartment where the Streichers spent much of their lives. Now 87, she is retired from a career teaching art at a nearby museum. In many respects, Sabo's life has been far easier than the life the Streichers knew. For one thing, when the Streichers lived there, the building had no electricity (people used kerosene lamps and candles) and no running water (Christine Streicher spent most of every Monday doing laundry using water she carried from a public fountain at the end of the block). There were no telephones, no television, and, of course, no computers. Today, Dorothy Sabo takes such conveniences for granted. Although she is hardly rich, her pension and social security amount to several times as much (in constant dollars) as the Streichers earned.

Sabo has her own worries. She is concerned about the environment and often speaks out about global warming. But a century ago, if the Streichers and their neighbours were concerned about "the environment," they probably would have meant the smell coming up from the street. At a time when motor vehicles were just beginning to appear in their city, carriages, trucks, and trolleys were all pulled by horses—thousands of them. These animals dumped 60 000 gallons of urine and 2.5 million pounds of manure on the streets each and every day—an offensive mixture churned and splashed by countless wheels onto everything and everyone within a stone's throw of the streets (Simon & Cannon, 2001).

I t is difficult for most people today to imagine how different life was a century ago. Not only was life much harder back then, but it was also much shorter. Statistical records show that life expectancy was just 46 years for U.S. men and 48 years for U.S. women, compared to about 76 and 81 years today, respectively (Hoyert & Xu, 2012). The figures for Canadian men and women at the turn of the twentieth century were similar: 50 years for women and 47 years for men (Martel & Bélanger, 2000). For Canadians born in 2007 to 2009, the life expectancy is now 83 years for females and 79 years for males (Statistics Canada, 2012a).

Over the past 100 years, much has changed for the better. Yet, as this chapter explains, social change is not all positive. Even change for the better can have negative consequences too, causing unexpected new problems. Early sociologists were mixed in their assessment of *modernity*, changes brought about by the Industrial Revolution. Likewise, today's sociologists point to both good and bad aspects of *postmodernity*, the transformations caused by the Information Revolution and the post-industrial economy. One thing is clear: For better or worse, the rate of change has never been faster than it is now.

What Is Social Change?

(16.1) State four defining characteristics of social change.

In earlier chapters, we examined relatively fixed or *static* social patterns, including status and role, social stratification, and social institutions. We also looked at the *dynamic* forces that have shaped our way of life, ranging from innovations in technology to the growth of bureaucracy and the expansion of cities. These are all dimensions of **social change**, *the transformation of culture and social institutions over time.* This process of social change has four major characteristics:

1. **Social change happens all the time.** "Nothing is constant except death and taxes" goes the old saying. Yet our thoughts about death have changed dramatically as life expectancy in Canada has nearly doubled in the past century. And back in the Streichers' day, Canadians paid little or no taxes on their earnings; taxation increased over the course of the twentieth century, along with the size and scope of government. In short, even the things that seem constant are subject to the twists and turns of change.

   Still, some societies change faster than others. As Chapter 2 ("Culture") explained, hunting and gathering societies change quite slowly; members of technologically complex societies, by contrast, can witness significant change within a single lifetime.

   It is also true that in any society, some cultural elements change faster than others. William Ogburn's theory of *cultural lag* (see Chapter 2, "Culture") asserts that material culture (that is, things) changes faster than nonmaterial culture (ideas and attitudes). For example, genetic technology that allows scientists to alter and perhaps even create life has developed more rapidly than our ethical standards for deciding when and how to use the technology.

2. **Social change is sometimes intentional but often unplanned.** Industrial societies actively promote many kinds of change. For example, auto manufacturers seek more efficient ways to power our cars, and advertisers try to convince us that life is not complete without a 4G cell phone or some other new electronic gadget. Yet rarely can anyone envision all the consequences of the changes that are set in motion.

   Back in 1900, when the country still relied on horses for transportation, people looked ahead to motor vehicles that would take a single day to carry them distances that used to take weeks or months. But no one could see how much the mobility provided by automobiles would alter everyday life in Canada and other industrial societies, scattering family members, threatening the environment, and reshaping cities and suburbs. Nor could automotive pioneers have predicted the more than 2000 deaths that occur as a result of car accidents each year in Canada alone (Statistics Canada, 2014).

3. **Social change is controversial.** The history of the automobile shows that social change brings both good and bad consequences. Cars brought an end to the muck of urine and manure on city streets, but they spewed carbon monoxide into the air. In the same contradictory way, capitalists benefited from greater production and profits made possible by the Industrial Revolution at the same time that workers pushed back against the machines that they feared would make their skills obsolete.

   Today, as in the past, people disagree about how we ought to live and what we should welcome as "progress." We see this disagreement every day in the changing patterns of social interaction between Aboriginal people and non–Aboriginal people, visible minorities and other Canadians, women and men, and homosexuals and heterosexuals that are welcomed by some people and opposed by others.

social change the transformation of culture and social institutions over time

These young men are performing in a hip-hop dance marathon in Hong Kong. Hip-hop music, dress style, and dancing have become popular in Asia, a clear case of cultural diffusion. Social change occurs as cultural patterns move from place to place, but people in different societies don't always have the same understanding of what these patterns mean. How might Chinese youth understand hip-hop differently from the young Black North Americans who originated it?

4. **Some changes matter more than others.** Some changes (like clothing fads) have only passing significance; others (like the invention of computers) have already changed the world. Will the Information Revolution turn out to be as important as the Industrial Revolution? Like the automobile and television, computers have both positive and negative effects, providing new kinds of jobs while eliminating old ones, linking people in global electronic networks while isolating people in offices, offering vast amounts of information while threatening personal privacy.

Causes of Social Change

16.2 Explain how culture, conflict, ideas, population patterns, collective behaviour, and social movements direct social change.

Social change has many causes. In a world linked by sophisticated communication and transportation technology, change in one place often sets off change elsewhere.

Culture and Change

Chapter 2 ("Culture") identified three important sources of cultural change. First, *invention* produces new objects, ideas, and social patterns. Rocket propulsion research, which began in the 1940s, has produced sophisticated spacecraft that reach toward the stars. Today we take such technology for granted; during this century, a significant number of people may well have an opportunity to travel in space.

Second, *discovery* occurs when people take notice of existing elements of the world. For example, medical advances offer a growing understanding of the human body. Beyond their direct effects on human health, medical discoveries have extended life expectancy, setting in motion the "greying" of Canadian society (see Chapter 3, "Socialization: From Infancy to Old Age").

Third, *diffusion* creates change as products, people, and information spread from one society to another. Ralph Linton (1937) recognized that many familiar aspects of our culture came from other lands. For example, the cloth used to make our clothing was developed in Asia, the clocks we see all around us were invented in Europe, and the coins we carry in our pockets were devised in what is now Turkey.

In general, material things change more quickly than cultural ideas. That is, breakthroughs such as the science of altering and perhaps even creating life are taking place faster than our understanding of when—and even whether—they are morally desirable.

Conflict and Change

Inequality and conflict within a society also produce change. Karl Marx saw class conflict as the engine that drives societies from one historical era to another. In industrial-capitalist societies, he maintained, the struggle between capitalists and workers pushes society toward a socialist system of production.

In the 130 years since Marx's death, this model has proved simplistic. Yet Marx correctly foresaw that social conflict arising from inequality (involving not just class but also race and gender) would force changes in every society, including our own, to improve the lives of working people.

Ideas and Change

Max Weber also contributed to our understanding of social change. Although Weber agreed that conflict could bring about change, he traced the roots of most social change to ideas. People with charisma (Martin Luther King, Jr is an example) can carry a message that changes the world.

Weber (1958, orig. 1904–1905) also highlighted the importance of ideas by revealing how the religious beliefs of early Protestants set the stage for the spread of industrial capitalism (see Chapter 13, "Family and Religion"). The fact that industrial capitalism developed primarily in areas of Western Europe where the Protestant work ethic was strong proved to Weber the power of ideas to bring about change.

Ideas also direct social movements. Social change occurs when people join together in the pursuit of a common goal, such as cleaning up the environment or improving the lives of oppressed people.

Demographic Change

Population patterns also play a part in social change. The typical Canadian household was twice as large in 1900 (5 people) as it is today (2.5 people) (Statistics Canada, 2011a). Women are having fewer children, and more people are living alone. Change is also taking place as our population grows older. By 2011, 14.4 percent of the Canadian population was over age 65, three times the proportion in 1900. By 2031, seniors will account for 22.8 percent of the country's total population (Statistics Canada, 2011b). Medical research and health care services already focus extensively on the elderly, and life will change in countless other ways as homes and household products are redesigned to meet the needs of older consumers.

Migration within and between societies is another demographic factor that promotes change. Between 1870 and 1930, millions of immigrants entered industrial cities. Thousands more from rural areas joined the rush. As a result, farm communities declined, cities expanded, and Canada for the first time became a predominantly urban nation. Similar changes are taking place today as people moving from Moncton to Prince George mix with new immigrants from Latin America, Asia, and India.

Where in Canada have demographic changes been greatest, and where have they been less pronounced? National Map 16–1 on page 556 provides one answer, showing areas of Canada that have grown and declined recently.

Collective Behaviour and Change

Sociologists study various types of collective behaviour that can bring about social change. **Collective behaviour** is *activity involving a large number of people that is unplanned, often controversial, and can bring about change*. Collective behaviour involves people in collectivities, which differ from social groups because many people may be involved without most having any direct interaction with others.

collective behaviour activity involving a large number of people that is unplanned, often controversial, and can bring about change

Crowds

One type of collective behaviour is the **crowd**, which is *a temporary gathering of people who share a common focus of attention and who influence one another*. Crowds are a fairly new development: Most of our ancestors never saw a large crowd. In medieval Europe, for example, about the only time large numbers of people gathered in one place was when armies faced off on the battlefield (Laslett, 1984). Today, however, crowds of 25 000 or more are common at rock concerts and sporting events, and even in the registration halls of large universities. Some political events and demonstrations, including the recent rallies in cities of the Middle East, reached 100 000 people or more. Estimates placed the size of the crowd at the SARS Benefit Concert in Toronto, Ontario, at about 450 000 people (CBC, 2003).

Given their large numbers, crowds have the power to bring about change. Political demonstrations and rallies, often based on networks supported by computer and cell phone technology, drew together tens of thousands of people in cities of the Arab world during 2011 to bring about unprecedented political change.

Mobs and Riots

Sometimes crowds can turn violent, transforming into a **mob**, which is *a highly emotional crowd that pursues a violent or destructive goal*. In the history of the United States, lynching was probably the most notorious example of mob behaviour. After the Civil War, so-called lynch

crowd a temporary gathering of people who share a common focus of attention and who influence one another

mob a highly emotional crowd that pursues a violent or destructive goal

riot a social eruption that is highly emotional, violent, and undirected

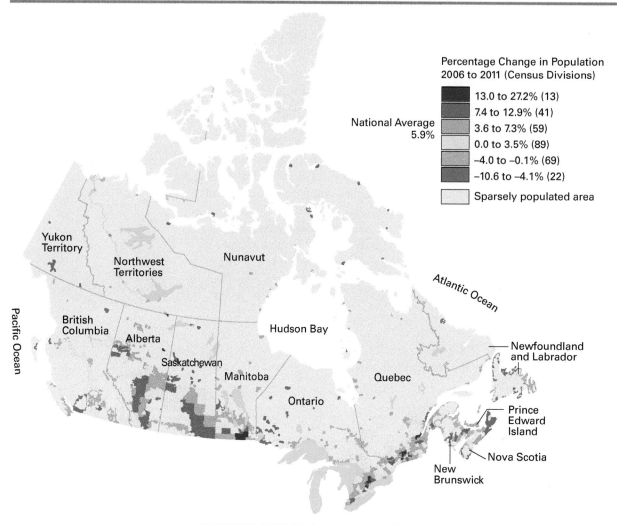

NATIONAL MAP 16–1   Population Change, Canada, 2006 to 2011

Between 2006 and 2011, the population in Canada grew by 5.9 percent. Although every province and most territories experienced growth, the high growth rates in central Alberta and around British Columbia, Saskatchewan, Yukon, and Manitoba stand out. How well do these changes reflect the moves you have made during your lifetime? How do you think these changes (and your moves) have affected the communities you moved to and from?

Source: Statistics Canada (2012b, 2012c).

mobs terrorized newly freed African Americans trying to prevent a breakdown of the race-based caste system that put whites in a position of privilege. Any person of colour who challenged white superiority risked death at the hands of hate-filled whites.

Similarly, a **riot** is *a social eruption that is highly emotional, violent, and undirected.* Riots are typically an expression of deep dissatisfaction on the part of people frustrated with the way society is operating. People riot in response to what they see as social injustice, as if to say, "We won't take it anymore!" Unlike the action of a mob, a riot usually has no clear goal, except perhaps to express dissatisfaction. The cause of most riots is some long-standing anger or grievance. As a "violent situation waiting to happen," a riot typically is ignited by some minor incident that causes people to start destroying property and harming other persons. Over the years, hockey fans have rioted over won and lost Stanley Cup finals, just as alter-globalization movement protestors have rioted in response to meetings of global economic leaders.

What does a riot accomplish? One answer is "power." As current events around the world show us, ordinary people can gain power when they act collectively. The power of the crowd to challenge the status quo and sometimes to force social change is one reason crowds are controversial. Throughout history, defenders of the status quo have feared "the mob" as a threat. By contrast, those seeking change have supported this type of collective action.

Rumour

Collective behaviour is sometimes guided by **rumour**, which refers to *unconfirmed information that people spread informally, by word of mouth or by using electronic devices*. Rumour thrives in a climate of uncertainty, when people care about some issue but are not sure of the facts. In a number of cities, for example, rumours about potential police action spread quickly among members of the Occupy Wall Street movement. Rumour is unstable, not only because people are not sure about the facts but also because individuals may give the rumour a "spin" as they pass it along. Rumour is also difficult to stop. The mass media and the internet can quickly spread local issues and events across the country and around the world. Because rumour can trigger the formation of crowds and direct their action, government officials as well as leaders of protest organizations establish rumour control centres during a crisis in order to manage information.

rumour unconfirmed information that people spread informally, by word of mouth or by using electronic devices

Fashions and Fads

A final way in which collective behaviour can influence the process of social change involves fashions and fads. Fashions and fads involve people spread over a large area. **Fashion** refers to *social patterns favoured by a large number of people*. People's tastes in clothing, music, and cars, as well as ideas about politics, change often, going in and out of fashion.

A **fad** refers to *an unconventional social pattern that people embrace briefly but enthusiastically*. Fads, sometimes called *crazes*, are common in high-income societies where many people have the money to spend on amusing, if often frivolous, things. From the Atkins Diet and drive-in theatres to water beds and hula hoops, fads generate an intense interest that fails to sustain itself. Pokémon cards are another example of the rise and fall of a fad. Justin Bieber probably hopes that he does not turn out to be a fad.

How do fads differ from fashions? Fads capture the public imagination but quickly burn out. Because fashions reflect basic cultural values like individuality and sexual attractiveness, they tend to stay around for a while. Therefore, a fashion—but rarely a fad—becomes a more lasting part of popular culture. Streaking, for instance, was a fad that came out of nowhere and soon vanished; denim clothing, however, is an example of fashion that originated in the rough mining camps of Gold Rush California in the 1870s and is still popular today.

fashion social patterns favoured by a large number of people

fad an unconventional social pattern that people embrace briefly but enthusiastically

Social Movements and Change

A final cause of social change lies in the efforts of people like us. People commonly band together to form a **social movement**, *an organized activity in which people set out to encourage or discourage social change*. Social movements, such as the political movements that swept across the Middle East in 2011, are common in the modern world. Canada's history includes all kinds of social movements, from Aboriginal people resisting colonization by Europeans and the drive for the vote for women and other minorities to today's organizations supporting or opposing abortion, higher wages and better working conditions for workers, gay rights, environmental protections, and the legalization of marijuana.

Social movements are about connecting people who share some political goal. Computer technology, including smartphones and social networking internet sites, has made it easier than ever before for large numbers of people to connect.

Types of Social Movements

Sociologists classify social movements according to several variables (Aberle, 1966; Cameron, 1966; Blumer, 1969). One variable asks: Who is changed? Some movements target selected people and others try to change everyone. A second variable asks: How much change? Some movements seek only limited change in our lives; others pursue a radical transformation of society. Combining these variables results in four types of social movements, shown in Figure 16–1 on page 558.

social movement an organized activity in which people set out to encourage or discourage social change

claims making the process of trying to convince the public and public officials of the importance of joining a social movement to address a particular issue

How Much Change?

	Limited	Radical
Specific Individuals	Alterative Social Movement	Redemptive Social Movement
Everyone	Reformative Social Movement	Revolutionary Social Movement

Who Is Changed?

FIGURE 16–1 Four Types of Social Movements

There are four types of social movements, reflecting who is changed and how great the change is.

Source: Based on Aberle (1966).

Alterative social movements are the least threatening to the status quo because they seek limited change in only part of the population. Their aim is to help certain people *alter* their lives. Mothers Against Drunk Drivers (MADD) is one example of an alterative social movement; it seeks to change public views and laws in order to stop impaired driving.

Redemptive social movements also target specific individuals, but they seek radical change. Their aim is to help certain people *redeem* their lives. For example, Alcoholics Anonymous is an organization that helps people with an alcohol addiction achieve a sober life.

Reformative social movements aim for only limited change but target everyone. The same-sex marriage movement sought to reform marriage laws. Similarly, the labour movement tends to be reformist in seeking higher wages, better working conditions, and benefits for workers. *Revolutionary social movements* are the most extreme of all, working for major transformation of an entire society. Sometimes pursuing specific goals, sometimes spinning utopian dreams, these social movements reject existing social institutions as flawed in favour of a radically new alternative. From left-wing communist, anarchist, feminist, Civil Rights, and anti-apartheid organizations to right-wing militia, neoliberal, fascist, and white supremacist groups, revolutionary social movements seek to radically change our way of life.

Claims Making

In 1981, the Centers for Disease Control and Prevention began to track a strange disease that was killing people, most of them homosexual men. The disease came to be known as AIDS (acquired immune deficiency syndrome). Although AIDS was clearly a deadly disease, it was given little public or media attention. It was only about five years later that the public became aware of the rising number of deaths and began to think of AIDS as a serious social threat.

The change in public thinking was the result of **claims making**, *the process of trying to convince the public and public officials of the importance of joining a social movement to address a particular issue.* In other words, for a social movement to form, some issue has to be defined as a problem that demands public attention. Usually, claims making begins with a small

Torontonian/Alamy Stock Photo

Claims making is the process of convincing others of the importance of some problem and the need for specific change. The Occupy movement has called attention to increasing economic inequality in Canada and many countries around the world. In your opinion, how much actual change has this movement caused?

number of people. In the case of AIDS, the gay community in large cities (notably Toronto, Vancouver, San Francisco, and New York) mobilized to convince people of the dangers posed by this deadly disease. Over time, if the mass media give the issue attention and public officials speak out on behalf of the problem, it is likely that the social movement will gain strength.

Considerable public attention has now been given to AIDS, and there is ongoing research aimed at finding a cure. The process of claims making goes on all the time for dozens of issues. Recently, for example, the Idle No More movement drew attention to the unequal status of Aboriginal people in Canada. By staging protests across the country that call for Indigenous sovereignty and draw attention to ongoing colonial relations, and by criticizing the lack of environmental protection in relationship to the mining, logging, fishing, and oil industries, Idle No More has ignited a national debate (Wotherspoon & Hansen, 2013; Barker, 2014).

Explaining Social Movements

Sociologists have developed several explanations of social movements. *Deprivation theory* holds that social movements arise among people who feel deprived of something, such as income, safe working conditions, or political rights. Whether you feel deprived or not, of course, depends on what you expect in life. Therefore, people band together when they experience **relative deprivation**, *a perceived disadvantage arising from some specific comparison.* This concept helps explain why movements for change surface in both good and bad times: It is not people's absolute standing that counts but how they perceive their situation in relation to the situations of specific other people (J.C. Davies, 1962; Merton, 1968).

Mass-society theory, a second explanation, argues that social movements attract socially isolated people who join a movement in order to gain a sense of belonging, identity, and purpose. From this point of view, social movements have a personal as well as a political agenda (Melucci, 1989).

Culture theory, a third theoretical scheme, points out that social movements depend not only on money and other material resources but also on cultural symbols. People must have a shared understanding of injustice in the world before they will mobilize to bring about change. In addition, specific symbols (such as photographs of the World Trade Center towers engulfed in flames after the September 11, 2001, terrorist attacks) helped mobilize people to support the military campaigns in Afghanistan and Iraq (McAdam, McCarthy, & Zald, 1996; J.E. Williams, 2002).

Fourth, *resource mobilization theory* points out that no social movement is likely to succeed—or even get off the ground—without substantial resources, including money, human labour, office and communications equipment, access to the mass media, and a positive public image. Because most social movements begin small, they must look beyond themselves to mobilize the resources required for success (Zhao, 1998; Passy & Giugni, 2001; Packer, 2003).

Fifth, *political-economy theory* is a Marxist approach that claims that social movements arise in opposition to the capitalist economic system, which fails to meet the needs of the majority of people. Despite record corporate profits, North American society is in crisis, with millions of people unable to find good jobs, living below the poverty line, and (in the United States) struggling to survive without health insurance. Social movements arise as workers organize to demand higher wages, citizens rally for a health policy that protects everyone, and people march in opposition to spending billions to fund wars while ignoring basic needs at home (Buechler, 2000). While resources are necessary for such activism, political-economy theory points out that on their own, resources are not enough; success, today, comes down to "unifying dissenting groups into a system of alliances" (Carroll & Ratner, 2010:8) and realizing the capacities of various segments of the wage-earning class (Gürcan & Peker, 2015).

Sixth and finally, *new social movements theory* points out the distinctive character of recent social movements in post-industrial societies. Instead of seeking unity on specific economic or political demands, these movements are often non-unified, leaderless (Burkowicz, 2014), and expressive, with the goal of "awareness-raising rather than monopolizing the control of power" (Vahabzadeh, 2003:10). In their diverse, multiple forms, contemporary movements address various types of oppression, paying attention to economic inequality as well as to social issues like racism, sexism, homophobia, animal rights, immigration, the environment, and ableism (Day, 2005). This broader scope of contemporary social movements results from closer ties between ordinary people around the world, who are now linked by the mass media and new information technology (Jenkins & Wallace, 1996; F. Rose, 1997).

relative deprivation a perceived disadvantage arising from some specific comparison

Stages in Social Movements

Social movements typically unfold in four stages: emergence, coalescence, bureaucratization, and decline. The *emergence* of social movements occurs as people begin to think that all is not well. Some, such as gay rights and women's movements, are born of widespread dissatisfaction. Others emerge as a small group tries to mobilize the population, as when gay activists raised public concern about AIDS.

Coalescence takes place when a social movement defines itself and develops a strategy for attracting new members and "going public." Movement participants or leaders determine policies and decide on tactics, which may include demonstrations or rallies to attract media attention.

As it gains members and resources, a social movement may undergo *bureaucratization*. As a movement becomes established, it depends less on the charisma and talents of a few leaders and more on a professional staff, which increases the chances for the movement's long-term survival.

Finally, social movements *decline* as resources dry up, the group faces overwhelming repression, the leadership is "bought off" by offers of money or power from within the "system," or when members finally achieve their goals. Some well-established organizations outlive their original causes and move on to new crusades; others lose touch with the idea of changing society and choose instead to become part of the "system" (Piven & Cloward, 1977; Miller, 1983).

Disasters: Unexpected Change

disaster an event, generally unexpected, that causes extensive harm to people and damage to property

Sometimes change results from events that are both unexpected and unwelcome. A **disaster** is *an event, generally unexpected, that causes extensive harm to people and damage to property.* Disasters are of three types. *Natural disasters* include floods, earthquakes, forest fires, and hurricanes (such as Hurricane Katrina, which devastated the Gulf Coast in 2005) (Erikson, 2005). A second type is the *technological disaster*, which is widely regarded as an *accident* but is more accurately the result of our inability to control technology (Erikson, 2005). The 2011 radiation leak at the Fukushima Daiichi nuclear plant is one recent example of a technological disaster. A third type is the *intentional disaster*, in which one or more organized groups deliberately harm others. War, terrorist attacks, and the genocide in places including Syria (2012–2013), Libya (2011), the Darfur region of Sudan (2003–2010), Yugoslavia (1992–1995), and Rwanda (1994) are examples of intentional disasters.

The full scope of the harm caused by disasters may become evident only many years after the event. The Thinking Globally box on page 561 describes a technological disaster that is still affecting people and their descendants more than 50 years after it took place.

Sociologists classify disasters into three types. The 2010 tsunami that brought massive flooding to Japan is an example of a natural disaster. The 2010 oil spill in the Gulf of Mexico was a technological disaster. The slaughter of hundreds of thousands of people and the displacement of millions more from their homes in the Darfur region of Sudan since 2003 is an example of an intentional disaster.

Thinking Globally

A Never-Ending Atomic Disaster

It was just after dawn on March 1, 1954, and the air was already warm on Utrik Island, a small bit of coral and volcanic rock in the South Pacific that is one of the Marshall Islands. The island was home to 159 people, who lived by fishing much as their ancestors had done for centuries. The population knew only a little about the outside world—a missionary from the United States taught the local children, and two dozen military personnel lived at a small U.S. weather station with an airstrip that received one plane each week.

At 6:45 A.M., the western sky suddenly lit up brighter than anyone had ever seen, and seconds later, a rumble like a massive earthquake rolled across the island. Some of the Utrik people thought the world was coming to an end. And truly, the world they had always known was about to change forever.

About 160 miles to the west, on Bikini Island, the United States military had just detonated an atomic bomb, a huge device with 1000 times the power of the bomb used at the end of World War II to destroy the Japanese city of Hiroshima. The enormous blast vaporized the island and sent a massive cloud of dust and radiation into the atmosphere. The military expected the winds to take the cloud north into an open area of the ocean, but the cloud blew east instead. By noon, the radiation cloud had engulfed a Japanese fishing boat ironically called the *Lucky Dragon*, exposing the 23 people on board to a dose of radiation that would eventually sicken or kill them all. By the end of the afternoon, the deadly cloud spilled across Utrik Island.

The cloud was made up of coral and rock dust, all that was left of Bikini Island. The dust fell softly on Utrik Island, and the children, who remembered pictures of snow shown to them by their missionary teacher, ran out to play in

Corbis

the white powder that was piling up everywhere. No one realized that it was contaminated with deadly radiation.

Three-and-one-half days later, the U.S. military landed planes on Utrik Island and informed all the people that they would have to leave immediately, taking nothing with them. For three months, the island people were held at another military base, and then they were returned home.

Many of the people who were on the island that fateful morning died young, typically from cancer or other diseases associated with radiation exposure. But even today, those who survived consider themselves and their island poisoned by the radiation, and they believe that the poison will never go away. The radiation may or may not still be in their bodies, but it has certainly worked its way deep into their culture. More than half a century after the bomb exploded, people still talked about the morning that "everything changed." The damage from this disaster turns out to be much more than medical—it was a social transformation that left the people with a deep belief that they are all sick, that life will never be the same, and that powerful people who live on the other side of the world could have prevented the disaster but did not.

What Do You Think?

1. In what sense is a disaster like the 2011 radiation leak in Japan never really over?

2. In what ways did the atomic bomb test change the culture of the Utrik people?

3. What does this account lead us to expect about the long-term consequences of other disasters, such as the 1982 sinking of the *Ocean Ranger* in the Grand Banks area of Newfoundland that caused 84 crew members to drown?

Source: Based on Erikson (2011).

Kai Erikson (1976, 1994, 2005) has investigated dozens of disasters of all types and has reached three major conclusions about the social consequences of disasters. First, disasters are *social disruptions*. We all know that disasters harm people and destroy property, but only recently have analysts begun to discuss disasters as threats to *human security* (Futamora, Hobson, & Turner, 2011). This concept points to the fact that disasters also damage human community. When a dam burst and sent a mountain of water down West Virginia's Buffalo Creek in 1972, it killed 125 people, destroyed 1000 homes, and left 4000 people homeless. After the waters had gone and help was streaming into the area, the people were paralyzed not only by the loss of family members and friends but also by the loss of their entire way of life. Even four decades later, they have never been able to rebuild the community life that they once knew. We can pinpoint when disasters start, Erikson explains, but we cannot know when they will end. The full consequences of the radiation leak in Japan have yet to be learned.

Second, Erikson explains that the social damage is more serious when an event involves some toxic substance, as is common with technological disasters. As the case of radiation falling on Utrik Island shows us, people feel "poisoned" when they have been exposed to a dangerous substance that they fear and over which they have no control.

Third, the social damage is most serious when the disaster is caused by the actions of other people. This can happen through negligence or carelessness (as in technological disasters) or through wilful action (intentional disasters). Our belief that "other people will do us no harm" is a foundation of social life, Erikson claims. But when others act carelessly (as when some Middle Eastern government leaders used deadly force to put down protests in 2011 and 2012), many who survive lose their trust in others to such a degree that it may never be restored.

Modernity

(16.3) Apply the ideas of Tönnies, Durkheim, Weber, and Marx to our understanding of modernity.

modernity changes brought about by the Industrial Revolution

modernization the process of social change begun by industrialization

A central concept in the study of social change is **modernity**, *changes brought about by the Industrial Revolution.* In everyday terms, *modernity* (its Latin root means "lately") refers to the present in relation to the past. Sociologists include in this catch-all concept all of the social patterns that were set in motion by the Industrial Revolution, which began in Western Europe in the 1750s. **Modernization**, then, is *the process of social change begun by industrialization.* Table 16–1 provides a summary of change in Canada over the course of the twentieth century.

Peter Berger (1977) identified four major characteristics of modernization:

1. **The decline of small, traditional communities.** Modernity involves "the progressive weakening, if not destruction, of the . . . relatively cohesive communities in which human beings have found solidarity and meaning throughout most of history" (1977:72). For thousands of years, in the camps of hunters and gatherers and in the rural villages of Europe and North America, people lived in small communities where life revolved around family and neighbourhood. Such traditional worlds gave each person a well-defined place that, although limiting range of choice, offered a strong sense of identity, belonging, and purpose.

   Small, isolated communities still exist in Canada, of course, but they are home to only a tiny percentage of this nation's people. These days, the isolation of most of these communities is only geographic: Except among those who are extremely poor or who reject modernity on religious grounds, cars, telephones, television, and computers give rural families the pulse of the larger society and connect them to the entire world.

2. **The expansion of personal choice.** People in traditional, pre-industrial societies view their lives as shaped by forces beyond human control—gods, spirits, fate. As the power of tradition weakens, people come to see their lives as an unending series of options, a process Berger calls *individualization.* For instance, many people in Canada choose a particular "lifestyle" (sometimes adopting one after another), showing an openness to change. Indeed, a common belief in our modern culture is that people *should* take control of their lives.

   Widespread support for greater personal choice has political consequences. A cultural orientation toward greater individualism means that modern, high-income societies (compared to traditional, low-income societies) are likely to be democratic (Inglehart & Welzel, 2010).

TABLE 16–1 Canada: A Century of Change

	1900	2000
National population	5 million	31 million
Share living in cities	40%	80%
Life expectancy	46 years (men), 48 years (women)	78 years (men), 83 years (women)
Median age	23	39
Average household income	$8000 (in 2000 dollars)	$60 000 (in 2000 dollars)
Share of income spent on food	43%	10%
Share of homes with flush toilets	10%	98%
Average number of cars	1 car for every 2000 households	1.5 cars/trucks for every household
Divorce rate	about 1 in 20 marriages	about 8 in 20 marriages
Average litres of petroleum products consumed	100 per person per year	4000 per person per year

3. **Increasing social diversity.** In pre-industrial societies, strong family ties and powerful religious beliefs enforce conformity and discourage diversity and change. Modernization promotes a more rational, scientific worldview as tradition loses its hold and people gain more and more individual choice. The growth of cities, the expansion of impersonal bureaucracy, and the social mix of people from various backgrounds combine to encourage diverse beliefs and behaviour.

4. **Orientation toward the future and a growing awareness of time.** Premodern people focus on the past; people in modern societies think more about the future. Modern people are not only forward-looking but also optimistic that new inventions and discoveries will improve their lives.

Traditional people organize their lives around sunlight and seasons. With the introduction of clocks in the late Middle Ages, Europeans began to organize their lives in terms of hours and minutes. Focused on personal gain, modern people demand precise measurement of time and are likely to agree that "time is money." Berger (inspired by Weber) points out that one good indicator of a society's degree of modernization is the share of people who keep track of time by continually glancing at their wristwatches (or, nowadays, their cell phones).

Recall that modernization touched off the development of sociology itself. As Chapter 1 ("Sociology: Perspective, Theory, and Method") explained, the discipline originated in the wake of the Industrial Revolution in Western Europe at a point when social change was proceeding rapidly. Early European and North American sociologists tried to analyze the rise of modern society and its consequences, both good and bad, for human beings.

Finally, in the process of comparing industrial societies with those that came before, we find it easy to assume that *everything* in our world is new. This is not the case, as the Seeing Sociology in Everyday Life box on page 564 explains with an historical look at a favourite type of modern clothing—jeans.

Ferdinand Tönnies: The Loss of Community

The German sociologist Ferdinand Tönnies produced a lasting account of modernization in his theory of *Gemeinschaft* and *Gesellschaft* (see Chapter 15, "Population, Urbanization, and Environment"). Like Peter Berger, whose work he influenced, Tönnies (1963, orig. 1887) viewed modernization as the progressive loss of *Gemeinschaft*, or human community. As Tönnies saw it, the Industrial Revolution weakened the social fabric of family and tradition by introducing a businesslike emphasis on facts, efficiency, and money. European and North American societies gradually became rootless and impersonal as people came to associate with one another mostly on the basis of self-interest—the state Tönnies termed *Gesellschaft*.

Early in the twentieth century, at least some parts of Canada could be described using Tönnies's concept of *Gemeinschaft*. Families that had lived for many generations in small villages and towns were bound together into a hardworking and slow-moving way of life. Telephones (invented in 1876) were rare; not until 1915 could one place a coast-to-coast call. Living without television (introduced commercially in 1933 and not widespread until after 1950), families entertained themselves, often gathering with friends in the evening to share stories, sorrows, or song. Lacking rapid transportation (Henry Ford's assembly line began in 1908, but cars became common only after World War II), many people knew little of the world beyond their hometown.

George Tooker's 1950 painting *The Subway* depicts a common problem of modern life: Weakening social ties and eroding traditions create a generic humanity in which everyone is alike yet each person is an anxious stranger in the midst of others.

Source: George Tooker, *The Subway*, 1950, egg tempera on gesso panel, 18¹⁄₈ × 36¹⁄₈ inches, Whitney Museum of American Art, New York. Purchased with funds from the Juliana Force Purchase Award, 50.23. Photograph © Whitney Museum of American Art

Tradition and Modernity: The History of Jeans

Sociologists like to contrast "tradition" and "modernity." Tönnies, Durkheim, Weber, and even Marx developed theories that contrasted social patterns that existed "then" with those that exist "now." Such theories are enlightening. But thinking in terms of "tradition versus modernity" encourages us to think that the past and the present have little in common.

All the thinkers discussed in this chapter saw past and present as strikingly different. But it is also true that countless elements of today's society—ranging from religion to warfare—have been part of human society for a very long time. It is also the case that many cultural elements that we think of as "modern" turn out to have been around much longer than many of us realize.

One element of culture that we think of as distinctly modern is jeans. This piece of clothing, common enough to be considered almost a "uniform" among young people, moved to the centre of popular culture when it swept college campuses in the late 1960s.

But many people would be surprised to learn that jeans have been worn for centuries. The term *dungarees*, a common name for jeans before the 1960s, is derived from the Hindi word *dungri*, a district of the Indian city Mumbai (formerly Bombay) where the coarse cloth is thought to have originated. From there, the fabric spread westward into Europe. The term *jeans* can be traced back to the name of the Italian city of Genoa, where the cotton fabric was widely worn in the 1650s. Another word for the fabric, *denim*, refers to the French city of Nîmes, reflecting the fact that, somewhat later, people described the cloth as being "de Nîmes."

Art historians have identified paintings from the sixteenth century that show people—typically the poor—wearing jeans. In the 1700s, British sailors used this fabric not only for making sails but also for constructing hammocks to sleep in and for fashioning shipboard clothing.

More than a century later, in 1853, U.S. clothing manufacturer Levi Strauss sold dungarees to miners who were digging for gold in the California gold rush. Strong and durable, jeans became the clothing of choice among people who had limited budgets and who did demanding physical labour.

Cowboys across the West quickly adopted the practical new style, and by the beginning of the twentieth century, jeans were worn by almost all working people. By the 1930s, most prisoners were also wearing denim.

This pattern made jeans a symbol of lower social standing, and many middle-class people looked down on them. As a result, especially in higher-income communities, public school officials banned the wearing of dungarees.

By the 1960s, however, a youth-based counterculture was emerging, that rejected the older pattern of "looking upward" and copying the styles of the rich and famous. Instead, fashion began "looking downward," adopting the look of working people and even the down and out. By the end of the 1960s, rock stars, Hollywood celebrities, and college students favoured jeans as a way to make a statement that they identified with working people—part of the era's more left-leaning political attitudes.

Of course, there was money to be made in this new trend. By the 1980s, the fashion industry was cashing in on the popularity of jeans by promoting "designer jeans" among more well-off people who probably had never entered a factory in their lives. A teenage Brooke Shields helped launch Calvin Klein jeans (1980) that became all the rage among people who were able to spend three and four times as much as the jeans worn by ordinary people.

By the beginning of this century, jeans had become an accepted form of dress not only in schools but also in the corporate world. Many CEOs of North American corporations—especially in the high-tech fields—now routinely wear jeans to work and even to public events.

As you can see, jeans turn out to have a very long history. The fact that jeans existed both "then" and "now," all the while taking on new and different meanings, reveals the limitation of characterizing cultural elements as either "traditional" or "modern" in a world in which societies invent and reinvent their way of life all the time.

What Do You Think?

1. Is your attitude toward jeans different from that of your parents? If so, how and why?

2. Do you think the changing trend in the popularity of jeans suggests broader changes in our society before and after the 1960s? Explain.

3. How popular is wearing jeans on your campus? What about among your professors? Can you explain these patterns?

Source: Based, in part, on Brazilian (2011).

In art from the 1500s, we see poor people wearing denim. In the 1800s, jeans became the uniform for the western cowboy, and by the 1960s, they were the clothing of choice on campus. More recently, corporate executives (especially in tech companies) have made jeans acceptable in the workplace.

Inevitable tensions and conflicts divided these communities of the past. But according to Tönnies, the traditional spirit of *Gemeinschaft* meant that people were "essentially united in spite of all separating factors" (1963:65, orig. 1887).

Modernity turns society inside out so that, as Tönnies put it, people are "essentially separated in spite of uniting factors" (1963:65, orig. 1887). This is the world of *Gesellschaft*, where, especially in large cities, most people live among strangers and ignore the people they pass on the street. Trust is hard to come by in a mobile and anonymous society in which people put their personal needs ahead of group loyalty and a majority of adults believe "you can't be too careful" in dealing with people (NORC, 2013:2386). No wonder researchers conclude that even as we become more affluent, the social health of modern societies has declined (Myers, 2000).

EVALUATE Tönnies's theory of *Gemeinschaft* and *Gesellschaft* is the most widely cited model of modernization. The theory's strength lies in its synthesis of various dimensions of change: growing population, the rise of cities, and increasingly impersonality in social interaction. But modern life, though often impersonal, still has some degree of *Gemeinschaft*. Even in a world of strangers, modern friendships can be strong and lasting. In addition, some analysts think that Tönnies favoured—perhaps even romanticized—traditional societies while overlooking bonds of family and friendship that continue to flourish in modern societies.

CHECK YOUR LEARNING As types of social organization, how do *Gemeinschaft* and *Gesellschaft* differ?

Emile Durkheim: The Division of Labour

The French sociologist Emile Durkheim shared Tönnies's interest in the important social changes that resulted from the Industrial Revolution. For Durkheim (1964, orig. 1893), modernization was marked by an increasing **division of labour**, or *specialized economic activity*. Every member of a traditional society performs more or less the same activities; modern societies function by having people perform highly specific jobs.

> **division of labour** specialized economic activity

Durkheim explained that pre-industrial societies are held together by *mechanical solidarity*, or shared moral sentiments. Members of such societies view everyone as basically alike, doing the same work and belonging together. Durkheim's concept of mechanical solidarity is virtually the same as Tönnies's *Gemeinschaft*.

With modernization, the division of labour (job specialization) becomes more and more pronounced. To Durkheim, this change means less mechanical solidarity but more of another kind of tie: *organic solidarity*, mutual dependency between people engaged in specialized work. Put simply, modern societies are held together not by likeness but by difference: All of us must depend on others to meet most of our needs. Organic solidarity corresponds to Tönnies's concept of *Gesellschaft*.

Despite obvious similarities in their thinking, Durkheim and Tönnies viewed modernity somewhat differently. To Tönnies, modern *Gesellschaft* amounted to the loss of social solidarity because people lose the "natural" and "organic" bonds of the rural village, leaving only the "artificial" and "mechanical" ties of the big city. Durkheim had a more positive view of modernity, even reversing Tönnies's language to bring home the point. Durkheim labelled modern society "organic," arguing that modern society is no less natural than any other, and he described traditional societies as "mechanical" because they are so regimented. Durkheim viewed modernization not so much as a loss of community as a change from community based on bonds of likeness (kinship and neighbourhood) to community based on economic interdependence (the division of labour). Durkheim's view of modernity is thus both more complex and more positive than Tönnies's view.

EVALUATE Durkheim's work, which resembles that of Tönnies, is a highly influential analysis of modernity. Of the two, Durkheim was more optimistic; still, he feared that modern societies might become so diverse that they would collapse into **anomie**, *a condition in which society provides little moral guidance to individuals*. Living with weak moral norms, modern people can become egocentric, placing their own needs above those of others and, in their social isolation, find little purpose in life.

> **anomie** a condition in which society provides little moral guidance to individuals

Supporting Durkheim's analysis, the vast majority of adults report that they see moral questions not in clear terms of right and wrong but as confusing "shades of gray" (NORC, 2013:607). In addition, the suicide rate, which Durkheim considered a good index of anomie, did in fact increase in North America over the course of the twentieth century. Yet shared norms and values seem strong enough to give most people a sense of meaning and purpose. Whatever the hazards of anomie, most people value the personal freedom modern society gives us.

CHECK YOUR LEARNING Define mechanical solidarity and organic solidarity. In his view of the modern world, what makes Durkheim more optimistic than Tönnies?

Max Weber: Rationalization

For Max Weber, modernity meant replacing a traditional worldview with a rational way of thinking. In pre-industrial societies, tradition acts as a constant brake on social change. To traditional people, "truth" is roughly the same as "what has always been" (1978:36, orig. 1921). To modern people, however, "truth" is the result of rational calculation. Because they value efficiency and have little reverence for the past, modern people readily adopt new social patterns that allow them to achieve their goals.

Echoing Tönnies's and Durkheim's claim that industrialization weakens tradition, Weber characterized modern society as "disenchanted." The unquestioned truths of an earlier time had been challenged by rational thinking. In short, said Weber, modern society turns away from the gods just as it turns away from the past. Throughout his life, Weber studied various modern "types"—the scientist, the capitalist, the bureaucrat—all of whom share the forward-looking, rational, and detached worldview that he believed was coming to dominate humanity.

EVALUATE Compared with Tönnies and especially Durkheim, Weber was very critical of modern society. He knew that science could produce technological and organizational wonders, yet he worried that science was turning us away from more basic questions about the meaning and purpose of human existence. Weber feared that rationalization, especially in bureaucracies, would erode the human spirit with endless rules and regulations.

CHECK YOUR LEARNING How did Weber understand modernity? What does it mean to say that the modern world (think of the scientists, capitalists, and bureaucrats) is "disenchanted"?

Pearson Education

Max Weber maintained that the distinctive character of modern society was its rational worldview. Virtually all of Weber's work on modernity centred on types of people he considered typical of their age: the scientist, the capitalist, and the bureaucrat. Each is rational to the core: The scientist is committed to the orderly discovery of truth, the capitalist to the orderly pursuit of profit, and the bureaucrat to orderly conformity to a system of rules.

Some of Weber's critics think that the alienation Weber attributed to bureaucracy actually stemmed from social inequality. This criticism leads us to the ideas of Karl Marx.

Karl Marx: Capitalism

For Karl Marx, modern society was synonymous with capitalism; he saw the Industrial Revolution as primarily a *capitalist* revolution. Marx traced the emergence of the bourgeoisie in medieval Europe to the expansion of commerce. The bourgeoisie gradually displaced the feudal aristocracy as the Industrial Revolution gave it control of a powerful new productive system.

Marx agreed that modernity weakened small communities (as described by Tönnies), increased the division of labour (as noted by Durkheim), and encouraged a rational worldview (as Weber claimed). But he saw these simply as triggered by, and occurring simultaneously with, capitalism. According to Marx, capitalism draws population away from farms and small towns into an ever-expanding market system centred in the cities; specialization is needed for efficient factories; and rationality is illustrated by the capitalists' endless pursuit of profit.

Earlier chapters have painted Marx as a spirited critic of capitalist society, but his vision of modernity also includes a good bit of optimism. Unlike Weber, who viewed modern society as an "iron cage" of bureaucracy from which there was no escape, Marx believed that social conflict in capitalist societies would sow the seeds of revolutionary change, leading to an egalitarian socialism. Such a society, as he saw it, would harness the wonders of industrial technology to enrich people's lives and rid the world of social classes, the source of conflict, inequality, and exploitation. Although Marx's evaluation of modern capitalist society was highly negative, he imagined a future of human freedom, creativity, and community.

EVALUATE Marx's theory of modernization is a complex theory of capitalism. But he underestimated the dominance of bureaucracy in modern societies. Furthermore, we should also consider if Marx's views on history and class inequality are still relevant today. Marx argued that the profit-seeking nature of capitalism would drive workers into greater poverty and polarize capitalist society into two hostile camps—the bourgeoisie and proletariat. While in Canada we have witnessed the polarization of wealth, it is not the case that a clear class line divides a destitute, and increasingly revolutionary, working class from the capitalist class.

CHECK YOUR LEARNING Of the four theorists just discussed—Tönnies, Durkheim, Weber, and Marx—who comes across as the most optimistic about modern society? Who was the most pessimistic? Explain your choices.

Structural-Functional Analysis: Modernity as Mass Society

(16.4) Apply structural-functional theory to modern social life.

June 16, on Shelbourne Street at McKenzie Avenue. From the car window, we see CIBC, Shell, and Petro-Canada gas stations, Home Depot, Canadian Tire, Safeway, Boston Pizza, and Tim Hortons—all big organizations. And it's the same everywhere.

This intersection happens to be in Victoria, British Columbia. But it could be in Kingston, Halifax, Montreal, Surrey, or almost anywhere else in Canada. The rise of modernity is a complex process involving many dimensions of change, described in earlier chapters and reviewed here in the Summing Up table on page 569. How can we make sense of so many changes going on at once? Sociologists have two broad explanations of modern society, one guided by the structural-functional approach and the other based on social-conflict theory.

The first explanation, guided by the structural-functional approach and drawing on the ideas of Tönnies, Durkheim, and Weber, understands modernity as the emergence of a *mass society* (Kornhauser, 1959; Nisbet, 1969; Berger, Berger, & Kellner, 1974; Pearson, 1993). A **mass society** is *a society in which prosperity and expanding bureaucracy have weakened traditional social ties.* A mass society is highly productive; on average, people have more income than ever. At the same time, it is marked by weak kinship and impersonal neighbourhoods, leaving individuals feeling socially isolated. Although many people have material plenty, they are spiritually weak and often experience moral uncertainty about how to live.

The Mass Scale of Modern Life

Mass-society theory argues, first, that the scale of modern life has greatly increased. Before the Industrial Revolution, Europe and North America formed a mosaic of rural villages and small towns. In these local communities, which inspired Tönnies's concept of *Gemeinschaft*, people lived out their lives surrounded by kin and guided by a shared heritage. Gossip was an informal yet highly effective way of ensuring conformity to community standards. Such small communities tolerated little social diversity—the state of mechanical solidarity described by Durkheim.

For example, before 1690, English law demanded that everyone participate regularly in the Christian ritual of Holy Communion (Laslett, 1984). On the North American continent, only Rhode Island among the New England colonies tolerated any religious dissent. Because social differences were repressed in favour of conformity to established norms, subcultures and countercultures were few, and change proceeded slowly.

Increasing population, the growth of cities, and specialized economic activity driven by the Industrial Revolution gradually altered this pattern. People came to know one another by their jobs (for example, as "the doctor" or "the bank clerk") rather than by their kinship group or hometown. People looked on most others simply as strangers. The face-to-face communication of the village was eventually replaced by the impersonal mass media: newspapers, radio, television, and the computer-based social media that link people throughout the world. Large organizations steadily assumed more and more responsibility for the daily tasks that had once been carried out by family, friends, and neighbours; public education drew more and more people to schools; police, lawyers, and courts supervised a formal criminal justice system. Even charity became the work of faceless bureaucrats working for various large social welfare organizations.

Geographic mobility, mass communication, and exposure to diverse ways of life all weaken traditional values. People become more tolerant of social diversity, defending individual rights and freedom of choice. Treating people differently because of their race, sex, or religion comes to be defined as backward and unjust. In the process, minorities at the margins of society gain greater power and broader participation in public life. The appointment of Michaëlle Jean, a refugee from Haiti, as governor general of Canada and the election of Barack Obama, an African American, to the highest office in the United States are surely indicators that ours is now a modern society (West, 2008).

The mass media give rise to a national culture that washes over the traditional differences that used to set off one region from another. As one analyst put it, "Even in Baton Rouge, Louisiana, the local kids don't say 'y'all' anymore; they say 'you guys' just like on TV" (Gibbs, 2000:42). Mass-society theorists fear that the transformation of people of various backgrounds into a generic mass provides greater moral freedom but it may also end up dehumanizing everyone.

The Ever-Expanding State

In the small-scale pre-industrial societies of Europe, government amounted to little more than a local noble. A royal family formally reigned over an entire nation, but in the absence of swift transportation and efficient communication, even absolute monarchs had far less power than today's political leaders.

As technological innovation allowed government to expand, the centralized state grew in size and importance. At the time of Confederation, the Canadian government was a tiny organization, its primary function being national defence. Since then, government has assumed responsibility for more and more areas of social life: schooling; regulating wages and working conditions; establishing standards for products of all sorts; providing financial assistance to the elderly, the ill, and the unemployed; providing loans to students; and recently, bailing out corporations facing financial ruin. To pay for such programs, taxes have soared. According to the Canadian Centre for Policy Alternatives, today's average family in Canada pays 35 percent in taxes (Ivanova, 2013); according to the Fraser Institute, the average family pays 42 percent in taxes (Lammam & Palacios, 2014) to support the broad array of services that government provides.

In a mass society, power resides in large bureaucracies, leaving people in local communities with little control over their lives. For example, government officials mandate that local schools must have a standardized educational program, local products must be government-certified, and every citizen must maintain extensive tax records. Although such regulations may protect people and enhance social equality, they also force us to deal more and more with nameless officials in distant and often unresponsive bureaucracies, and they undermine the autonomy of families and local communities.

mass society a society in which prosperity and expanding bureaucracy have weakened traditional social ties

class society a capitalist society with pronounced social stratification

Summing Up

Traditional and Modern Societies: The Big Picture

Elements of Society	Traditional Societies	Modern Societies
Cultural Patterns		
Values	Homogeneous; sacred character; few subcultures and countercultures	Heterogeneous; secular character; many subcultures and countercultures
Norms	Great moral significance; little tolerance of diversity	Variable moral significance; high tolerance of diversity
Time orientation	Present linked to past	Present linked to future
Technology	Pre-industrial; human and animal energy	Industrial; advanced energy sources
Social Structure		
Status and role	Few statuses, most ascribed; few specialized roles	Many statuses, some ascribed and some achieved; many specialized roles
Relationships	Typically primary; little anonymity or privacy	Typically secondary; much anonymity and privacy
Communication	Face to face	Face-to-face communication supplemented by mass media
Social control	Informal gossip	Formal police and legal system
Social stratification	Rigid patterns of social inequality; little mobility	Fluid patterns of social inequality; high mobility
Gender patterns	Pronounced patriarchy; women's lives centred on the home	Declining patriarchy; increasing share of women in the paid labour force
Settlement patterns	Small-scale; population typically small and widely dispersed in rural villages and small towns	Large-scale; population typically large and concentrated in cities
Social Institutions		
Economy	Based on agriculture; much manufacturing in the home; little white-collar work	Based on industrial mass production; factories become centres of production; increasing white-collar work
State	Small-scale government; little state intervention in society	Large-scale government; much state intervention in society
Family	Extended family as the primary means of socialization and economic production	Nuclear family still has some socialization functions but is more a unit of consumption than of production
Religion	Religion guides worldview; little religious pluralism	Religion weakens with the rise of science; extensive religious pluralism
Education	Formal schooling limited to elites	Basic schooling becomes universal, with growing share of people receiving advanced education
Health	High birth and death rates; short life expectancy because of low standard of living and simple medical technology	Low birth and death rates; longer life expectancy because of higher standard of living and sophisticated medical technology
Social Change	Slow; change evident over many generations	Rapid; change evident within a single generation

EVALUATE The growing scale of modern life certainly has positive aspects but only at the price of losing some of our cultural heritage. Modern societies increase individual rights, have greater tolerance of social differences, and raise living standards (Inglehart & Baker, 2000). But they are prone to what Weber feared most—excessive bureaucracy—as well as to Tönnies's self-centredness and Durkheim's anomie. The size, complexity, and tolerance of diversity of modern societies all but doom traditional values and family patterns, leaving individuals isolated, powerless, and materialistic. As Chapter 12 ("Economics and Politics") noted, Canadians are increasingly disenchanted with voting and the political process. But should we be surprised that individuals in vast, impersonal societies such as ours end up thinking that no one person can make much of a difference?

Critics sometimes say that mass-society theory romanticizes the past. They remind us that many people in the small towns of our past were eager to set out for a better standard of living in cities. This approach also ignores problems of social inequality. Critics claim this theory attracts social and economic conservatives who defend conventional morality and are indifferent to the historical inequality of women and other minorities.

CHECK YOUR LEARNING

In your own words, state the mass-society analysis of modernity. What are two criticisms of it?

Social-Conflict Analysis: Modernity as Class Society

(**16.5**) Apply social-conflict theory to modern social life.

The second explanation of modernity derives mostly from the ideas of Karl Marx. From a social-conflict perspective, modernity takes the form of a **class society**, *a capitalist society with pronounced social stratification*. While agreeing that modern societies have expanded to a mass scale, this approach views the heart of modernization as an expanding capitalist economy, marked by inequality (Habermas, 1970; Harrington, 1984; Buechler, 2000).

Social-conflict theory sees modernity not as an impersonal mass society but as an unequal class society in which some categories of people are second-class citizens. In December 2011, the United Nations special envoy for Aboriginal peoples criticized the federal government for its failure to respond to the terrible housing conditions in the Aboriginal community of Attawapiskat in northern Ontario.

Capitalism

Class-society theory follows Marx in claiming that the increasing scale of social life in modern society has resulted from the growth and greed unleashed by capitalism. Because a capitalist economy pursues ever-greater profits, both production and consumption steadily increase.

According to Marx, capitalism rests on "naked self-interest" (Marx & Engels, 1972:337, orig. 1848). This self-centredness weakens the social ties that once united small communities. Under capitalism people are transformed into commodities: a source of labour and a market for capitalist products.

Capitalism supports science not just as the key to greater productivity but also as an ideology that justifies the status quo. Modern societies encourage people to view human well-being as a technical puzzle to be solved by engineers and other scientific experts rather than through the pursuit of social justice. For example, a capitalist culture seeks to improve health through advances in scientific medicine rather than by eliminating poverty, despite the fact that poverty is a core cause of poor health.

Businesses also raise the banner of scientific logic, trying to increase profits through greater efficiency. As Chapter 12 ("Economics and Politics") explained, capitalist corporations have reached enormous size and control unimaginable wealth as a result of global expansion. From the class-society point of view, the expanding scale of life is less a function of *Gesellschaft* than the inevitable and destructive consequence of capitalism.

Persistent Inequality

Modernity has gradually worn away some of the rigid categories that set nobles apart from commoners in pre-industrial societies. But class-society theory maintains that elites are still with us, not as the nobles of an earlier era, but in the form of capitalist millionaires. In Canada, we may have no hereditary monarchy, but the richest 20 percent of the population receives 40 percent of after-tax income after transfers and taxes (Grabb & Guppy, 2009).

What of the state? Mass-society theorists argue that the state works to increase equality and fight social problems. Marx disagreed; he doubted that the state could accomplish more than minor reforms because, as he saw it, real power lies in the hands of the capitalists who control the economy. Other class-society theorists add that to the extent that working people and minorities do enjoy greater political rights and a higher standard of living today, these changes were the result of political struggle, not government goodwill. Despite our pretensions of democracy, they conclude, most people are powerless in the face of wealthy elites.

EVALUATE Class-society theory dismisses Durkheim's argument that people in modern societies suffer from anomie, claiming instead that they suffer from alienation and powerlessness. Not surprisingly, the class-society interpretation of modernity enjoys widespread support among liberals and radicals who favour greater equality and seek extensive regulation (or abolition) of the capitalist marketplace.

A basic criticism of class-society theory is that it overlooks the increasing prosperity of modern societies and the fact that discrimination based on race, ethnicity, religion, and gender is now illegal and is widely regarded as a social problem. In addition, many people in Canada do not want an egalitarian society; they prefer a system of unequal rewards that reflects personal differences in talent and effort.

Based on socialism's inability to catch up to the standard of living of capitalist economies, some observers are skeptical about a centralized economy's ability to cure the ills of modernity. Many other problems in Canada—including industrial pollution, lack of economic democracy, and government corruption—are also found in socialist nations.

CHECK YOUR LEARNING In your own words, state the class-society theory of modernity. What are several criticisms of it?

The Summing Up table contrasts the two interpretations of modernity. Mass-society theory focuses on the increasing impersonality of social life and the growth of government; class-society theory stresses the expansion of capitalism and the persistence of inequality.

Summing Up

Two Interpretations of Modernity

	Mass Society	Class Society
Process of modernization	Industrialization; growth of bureaucracy	Rise of capitalism
Effects of modernization	Increasing scale of life; rise of the state and other formal organizations	Expansion of the capitalist economy; persistence of social inequality

Modernity and the Individual

(16.6) Apply sociological theory to understand how people experience modern social life.

Both mass- and class-society theories look at the broad patterns of change since the Industrial Revolution. But from these macro-level approaches, we can also draw micro-level insights into how modernity shapes individual lives.

Mass Society: Problems of Identity

Modernity freed individuals from the small, tightly knit communities of the past. Most people in modern societies have the privacy and freedom to express their individuality. However, mass-society theory suggests that so much social diversity, widespread isolation, and rapid social change make it difficult for many people to establish any coherent identity at all (Wheelis, 1958; Berger, Berger, & Kellner, 1974).

As Chapter 3 ("Socialization: From Infancy to Old Age") explains, people's personalities are mostly a product of their social experiences. The small, homogeneous, and slowly changing societies of the past provided a firm, if narrow, foundation for building a personal identity. Even today, Amish and Mennonite communities that flourish in Canada and the United States teach young men and women "correct" ways to think and behave. Not everyone born into an Amish community can tolerate such rigid demands for conformity, but most members establish a well-integrated and satisfying personal identity (Kraybill & Olshan, 1994; Kraybill & Hurd, 2006).

Mass societies are quite another story. Socially diverse and rapidly changing, they offer only shifting sands on which to build a personal identity. Left to make many life decisions on their own, people—especially those with greater wealth—face a bewildering array of options. The freedom to choose has little value without standards to guide the selection process, and in a tolerant mass society, people may find little reason to choose one path over another. As a result, some people may experience what novelist Douglas Coupland called "option paralysis" (1991) and give up making a choice altogether, while many others shuttle from one identity to another, changing their lifestyles, relationships, and even religions in search of an elusive "true self." Given the widespread "relativism" of modern societies, people without a moral compass lack the security and certainty once provided by tradition.

To David Riesman (1970, orig. 1950), modernization brings changes in **social character**, *personality patterns common to members of a particular society*. Pre-industrial societies promote what Riesman calls **tradition-directedness**, *rigid conformity to time-honoured ways of living*. Members

Mass-society theory relates feelings of anxiety and lack of meaning in the modern world to rapid social change that washes away tradition. This notion of modern emptiness and isolation is captured in the photo on the left. Class-society theory, by contrast, ties such feelings to social inequality, by which some categories of people are made into second-class citizens (or not made citizens at all), an idea expressed in the photo on the right.

of traditional societies model their lives on those of their ancestors, so that "living a good life" amounts to "doing what people have always done."

Tradition-directedness corresponds to Tönnies's *Gemeinschaft* and Durkheim's mechanical solidarity. Culturally conservative, tradition-directed people think and act alike. Unlike the conformity often found in modern societies, the uniformity of tradition-directedness is not an effort to imitate a popular celebrity or follow the latest fashions. Instead, people are alike because they all draw on the same solid cultural foundation. Amish women and men exemplify tradition-directedness; in the Amish culture, tradition ties everyone to ancestors and descendants in an unbroken chain of righteous living.

Today, members of diverse and rapidly changing societies are likely to view a tradition-directed personality as deviant because it seems so rigid. Modern people prize personal flexibility, the capacity to adapt, and sensitivity to others. Riesman calls this type of social character **other-directedness**, *openness to the latest trends and fashions, often expressed by imitating others.* Because their socialization occurs in societies that are continuously in flux, other-directed people develop fluid identities marked by superficiality, inconsistency, and change. They try on different "selves" almost like new clothing, seek out role models, and engage in varied performances as they move from setting to setting (Goffman, 1959). In a traditional society, such "shiftiness" marks a person as untrustworthy, but in a changing, modern society, the ability to fit in virtually anywhere—like a chameleon changing its colours to match its environment—is very useful.

In societies that value the up-to-date rather than the traditional, people look to others for approval, using members of their own generation rather than elders as role models. Peer pressure can be irresistible to people without strong standards to guide them. Our society urges people to be true to themselves, but when social surroundings change so rapidly, how can people develop the self to which they should be true? This problem lies at the root of the identity crisis so widespread in industrial societies today. "Who am I?" is a nagging question that many of us struggle to answer. In truth, this problem is not so much concerned with us as with the inherently unstable mass society in which we live.

social character personality patterns common to members of a particular society

tradition-directedness rigid conformity to time-honoured ways of living

other-directedness openness to the latest trends and fashions, often expressed by imitating others

Class Society: Problems of Powerlessness

Class-society theory paints a different picture of modernity's effects on individuals. This approach maintains that persistent inequality undermines modern society's promise of individual freedom. For some people, modernity serves up great privilege, but for many others, everyday life means coping with economic uncertainty and a growing sense of powerlessness (K.S. Newman, 1993; Ehrenreich, 2001).

For racial and ethnic minorities, the problem of relative disadvantage looms even larger. Similarly, although women participate more broadly in modern societies, they continue to run up against traditional barriers of sexism. This approach rejects mass-society theory's claim that people suffer from too much freedom; according to class-society theory, our society still denies a majority of people full participation in social life.

As Chapter 9 ("Global Stratification") explains, the expanding scope of world capitalism has placed more of Earth's population under the influence of multinational corporations. As a result, 75 percent of the world's income is concentrated in high-income nations, where just 23 percent of its people live. Is it any wonder, class-society theorists ask, that people in poor nations seek greater power to shape their own lives?

The problem of widespread powerlessness led Herbert Marcuse (1964) to challenge Max Weber's claim that modern society is rational. Marcuse condemned modern society as irrational for failing to meet the needs of so many people. Although modern capitalist societies produce unparalleled wealth, poverty remains the daily plight of more than 1 billion people. Marcuse added that technological advances further reduce people's control over their own lives. High technology gives a great deal of power to a small core of specialists—not the majority of people—who now dominate discussion of when to go to war, what our energy policy should be, and how people should pay for health care. Countering the popular view that technology *solves* the world's problems, Marcuse believed that science *causes* them. In sum, class-society theory asserts that people suffer because modern societies concentrate knowledge, wealth, and power in the hands of a privileged few.

Modernity and Progress

(16.7) Evaluate the positive and negative consequences of social change.

In modern societies, most people expect and applaud social change. We link modernity to the idea of *progress* (from the Latin, meaning "moving forward"), a state of continual improvement. We see stability as stagnation.

Given our bias in favour of change, members of our society tend to regard traditional cultures as backward. But change, particularly toward material affluence, is a mixed blessing. As the Thinking Globally box on page 575 shows, social change is too complex simply to equate with progress.

Even getting rich has both advantages and disadvantages, as the cases of the Kaiapo and Gullah show in the Thinking Globally box. Historically, among people in countries such as Canada and the United States, a rising standard of living has made lives longer and more comfortable. At the same time, many people wonder whether today's routines are too stressful, with families often having little time to relax or to spend time together. It is interesting in this respect that measures of happiness have declined in the United States but not Canada; Canadians are the second happiest category in the world, after Australians (Inglehart, Welzel, & Foa, 2010; Myers, 2000).

Science, too, has its pluses and minuses. People in North America are more confident than people living in most other industrial societies that science improves our everyday lives (Inglehart et al., 2012). But surveys also show that many adults feel that science "makes our way of life change too fast" (NORC, 2013:1329).

New technology has always sparked controversy. Just over a century ago, the introduction of automobiles and telephones allowed more rapid transportation and more efficient communication, improving people's lives. At the same time, such technology also weakened traditional attachments to hometowns and even to families. Today, people might wonder whether computer technology will do the same thing: giving us access to people around the world but shielding us from the community right outside our doors; providing more information than ever before but in the process threatening personal privacy. In short, we all realize that social change comes faster all the time, but we may disagree about whether a particular change is good or bad for society.

Modernity: Global Variation

October 1, Kobe, Japan. Riding the computer-controlled monorail high above the streets of Kobe or the 320-kilometre-per-hour bullet train to Tokyo, we see Japan as the society of the future, in love with high technology. Yet the Japanese remain strikingly traditional in other respects: Few corporate executives and almost no politicians are women, young people still show seniors great respect, and public orderliness contrasts with the relative chaos of many North American cities.

Japan is a nation at once traditional and modern. This contradiction reminds us that although it is useful to contrast traditional and modern societies, the old and the new often coexist in unexpected ways. In the People's Republic of China, ancient Confucian principles are mixed with contemporary socialist thinking. In Saudi Arabia and Qatar, the embrace of the latest modern technology is mixed with respect for the ancient principles of Islam. Likewise, in Mexico and much of Latin America, people observe centuries-old Christian rituals even as they struggle to move ahead economically. In short, although we may think of tradition and modernity as opposites, combinations of traditional and modern are far from unusual, and they are found throughout the world.

Thinking Globally

Does "Modernity" Mean "Progress"? The Kaiapo of the Amazon and the Gullah of Georgia

The firelight flickers in the gathering darkness. Chief Kanhonk sits, as he has done at the end of the day for decades, and gathers his thoughts for an evening of animated storytelling (Simons, 2007). This is the hour when the Kaiapo, a small society in Brazil's lush Amazon region, celebrate their heritage. Because the Kaiapo are a traditional people with no written language, the elders rely on evenings by the fire to pass along their culture to their children and grandchildren. In the past, evenings like this have been filled with tales of brave Kaiapo warriors fighting off Portuguese traders in pursuit of slaves and gold.

But as the minutes pass, only a few older villagers assemble for the evening ritual. "It is the Big Ghost," one man grumbles, explaining the poor turnout. The "Big Ghost" has indeed descended on them; its bluish glow spills from windows throughout the village. The Kaiapo children—and many adults as well—are watching reality shows on television. The installation of a satellite dish in the village several years ago has had consequences far greater than anyone imagined. In the end, what their enemies failed to do with guns, the Kaiapo may well do to themselves with prime-time programming.

The Kaiapo are among the 230 000 native peoples who inhabit Brazil. They stand out because of their striking body paint and ornate ceremonial dress. During the 1980s, they became rich from gold mining and harvesting mahogany trees. Now they must decide if the recent affluence is a blessing or a curse.

To some, material wealth means the opportunity to learn about the outside world through travel and television. Others, like Chief Kanhonk, are not so sure. Bathed in the firelight, he thinks aloud: "I have been saying that people must buy useful things like knives and fishing hooks. Television does not fill the stomach. It only shows our children and grandchildren white people's things." Bebtopup, the oldest priest, nods in agreement: "The night is the time the old people teach the young people. Television has stolen the night" (Simons, 2007:522).

Far to the north, in the United States, half an hour by ferry from the coast of Georgia, lies the island community of Hog Hammock on swampy Sapelo Island. The 70 African-American residents of the island today trace their ancestry back to the first slaves who settled there in 1802.

Raukari, Mauri

Walking past the brightly painted houses nestled among yellow pine trees draped with Spanish moss, visitors feel transported back in time. The local people, known as Gullahs (or in some places, Geechees), speak *creole*, a mixture of English and West African languages. They fish, living much as they have for hundreds of years in a region that is an important environmental ecosystem (Dewan, 2010).

But the future of this way of life is now in doubt. The young people who grow up in Hog Hammock can find no work other than fishing and making traditional crafts. "We have been here nine generations and we are still here," says one local. Then, referring to the island's 19 children, she adds, "It's not that they don't want to be here; it's that there's nothing here for them—they need to have jobs" (Curry, 2001:41).

Just as important, with people on the mainland looking for waterside homes for vacations or year-round living, the island has become prime real estate. Not long ago, one larger house went up for sale, and the community was shocked to learn of an asking price over $1 million. The locals know only too well that their property taxes have gone sky high. Edna Holmes, whose family has lived on Hog Hammock for four generations, had long paid about $200 a year in taxes on her house; in recent years, the bill shot up to $2000. Says Holmes, "The county is trying to tax us out" (Brown, 2013). If this pattern continues, the natural beauty of Hog Hammock is likely to be paved over so that the area becomes another Hilton Head, once a Gullah community on the South Carolina coast that is now home to well-to-do people from the mainland.

It is probably only a matter of time until the people of Hog Hammock sell their homes and move inland. But Edna Holmes and most other residents are unhappy at the thought of selling out, even for a good price. After all, moving away will mean the end of their cultural heritage.

The stories of the Kaiapo and the people of Hog Hammock show us that change is not a simple path toward "progress." These people may be moving toward modernity, but this process will have both positive and negative consequences. In the end, both groups of people may enjoy a higher standard of living with better homes, more clothing, and new technology. But their newfound affluence will come at the price of their traditions. The drama of these people is now being played out around the world as more and more traditional cultures are being lured away from their heritage by the affluence and materialism of rich societies.

What Do You Think?

1. Why is social change both a winning and a losing proposition for traditional peoples?

2. Do the changes described here improve the lives of the Kaiapo? What about the Gullah community?

3. Do traditional people have any choice about becoming modern? Explain your answer.

Postmodernity

(16.8) Discuss postmodernism as one type of social criticism.

postmodernity social patterns characteristic of post-industrial societies

If modernity was the product of the Industrial Revolution, could the Information Revolution be creating a postmodern era? A number of scholars think so, and they use the term **postmodernity** to refer to *social patterns characteristic of post-industrial societies*.

Precisely what postmodernism is remains a matter of debate. The term has been used for decades in literary, philosophical, and even architectural circles. It has moved into sociology on a wave of social criticism that has been building since the spread of left-leaning politics in the 1960s. Although there are many variations of postmodern thinking, all share the following five themes (Hall & Neitz, 1993; Inglehart, 1997; Rudel & Gerson, 1999):

1. **In important respects, modernity has failed.** The promise of modernity was a life free from want. As postmodernist critics see it, however, the twentieth century was unsuccessful in solving social problems such as poverty. This fact is evident in today's high rates of unemployment and poverty, as well as the widespread sense of financial insecurity.

2. **The bright light of "progress" is fading.** Modern people look to the future expecting their lives to improve in significant ways. Members (and even leaders) of a postmodern society are less confident about what the future holds. The strong optimism that carried society into the modern era more than a century ago has given way to widespread pessimism; a recent poll indicates that 55 percent of Canadians are concerned that the economy is in decline, while 85 percent say that the cost of living is outpacing their earnings (Bensimon Byrne, 2015).

3. **Science no longer holds the answers.** The defining trait of the modern era was a scientific outlook and a confident belief that technology would make life better. But postmodern critics argue that science has failed to solve many old problems (such as poor health) and has even created new problems (such as pollution and global warming).

   Postmodernist thinkers discredit science, claiming that it implies a singular truth along with the possibility of objective knowledge. On the contrary, they maintain science is a social institution that is located in a broader social context which, in turn, rules out any objective interpretations of "truth."

4. **Cultural debates are intensifying.** Now that the world is capable of producing material abundance, ideas are taking on more importance. This creates a space for ideas to take on greater importance. In this sense, postmodernity is also a postmaterialistic era in which issues such as social justice, the state of the natural environment, and animal rights command more and more public attention.

5. **Social institutions are changing.** Just as industrialization brought sweeping transformation to social institutions, the rise of post-industrial society is remaking society all over again. For example, the Industrial Revolution placed *material things* at the centre of productive life; the Information Revolution emphasizes *ideas*. Similarly, the postmodern family no longer conforms to any one pattern; on the contrary, individuals are choosing among many family forms.

EVALUATE Analysts who claim that Canada and other high-income nations are entering a postmodern era criticize modernity for failing to meet human needs. In defence of modernity, there have been marked increases in longevity and living standards over the past century. If we take the postmodernist view and reject science as bankrupt and progress as a sham, what are the alternatives?

CHECK YOUR LEARNING In your own words, state the defining characteristics of a postmodern society.

Modernization and Our Global Future

(**16.9**) Evaluate possible directions of future social change.

Imagine the entire world's population reduced to a single village of 1000 people. About 90 residents of this "global village" earn half of all the income. Another 125 people are so poor that their lives are at risk.

The tragic plight of the world's poor shows that some desperately needed change has not yet occurred. Chapter 9 ("Global Stratification") presented two competing views of why 1 billion people around the world are so poor. *Modernization theory* claims that in the past, the entire world was poor and that technological change, especially the Industrial Revolution, enhanced human productivity and raised living standards in many nations. From this point of view, the solution to global poverty is to promote technological development and market economies around the world.

For reasons suggested earlier, however, global modernization may be difficult. Recall that David Riesman portrayed pre-industrial people as *tradition-directed* and likely to resist change. So, if rich nations are to help poor countries grow economically as suggested by modernization theorists, they must develop strategies to overcome this resistance. Industrial nations can speed development by exporting technology to poor regions, welcoming students from these countries, and providing foreign aid to stimulate economic growth.

The review of modernization theory in Chapter 9 points to some success for these policies in Latin America and more dramatic results in the small Asian countries of Taiwan, South Korea, and Singapore, and in Hong Kong (part of the People's Republic of China). But jump-starting development in the poorest countries of the world poses greater challenges. Even where dramatic change has occurred, modernization involves a trade-off. Traditional people, such as Brazil's Kaiapo, may gain wealth through economic development, but only at the cost of losing their traditional identity and values as they are drawn into a global "McCulture" based on Western materialism, pop music, trendy clothes, and fast food. One Brazilian anthropologist expressed optimism about the future of the Kaiapo: "At least they quickly understood the consequences of watching television. . . . Now [they] can make a choice" (Simons, 2007:523).

But not everyone thinks that modernization is really an option. According to a second approach to global stratification, *dependency theory*, today's poor societies have little ability to modernize, even if they want to. From this point of view, the major barrier to economic development is not traditionalism but global domination by rich capitalist societies.

Dependency theory asserts that rich nations achieved their modernization at the expense of poor ones, by taking their valuable natural resources and exploiting their human labour. Even today, the world's poorest countries remain locked in a disadvantageous economic relationship with rich nations, dependent on wealthy countries to buy their raw materials and in return provide them with whatever manufactured products they can afford. According to this view, continuing ties with rich societies will only perpetuate current patterns of global inequality.

Whichever approach you find more convincing, keep in mind that change in Canada is no longer separate from change in the rest of the world. At the beginning of the twentieth century, most people in today's high-income countries lived in relatively small settlements with limited awareness of the larger world. Today, the world has become one huge village because the lives of all people are increasingly interconnected.

The twentieth century witnessed unprecedented human achievement. Yet solutions to many problems of human existence—including finding meaning in life, resolving conflicts between nations, and eliminating poverty—have eluded us. To this list of pressing matters new concerns have been added, such as controlling population growth and establishing an environmentally sustainable society. In the coming years, we must be prepared to tackle such problems with imagination, compassion, and determination. Our growing understanding of human society gives us reason to be hopeful that we can get the job done.

Seeing Sociology in Everyday Life

CHAPTER 16 Social Change: Modern and Postmodern Societies

Is tradition the opposite of modernity?

Conceptually, this may be true. But as this chapter explains, traditional and modern social patterns combine in all sorts of interesting ways in our everyday lives. Look at the photographs below and on page 579, and identify elements of tradition and modernity. Do they seem to go together, or are they in conflict? Why?

These young girls live in the city of Istanbul in Turkey, a country that has long debated the merits of traditional and modern life. What sets off traditional and modern ways of dressing? Do you think such differences are likely to affect patterns of friendship? Would the same be true in Canada?

Paul Prescott/Alamy Stock Photo

Efrem Lukatsky/AP Images

When the first McDonald's restaurant opened in the city of Kiev in Ukraine, many people stopped by to taste a hamburger and see what "fast food" was all about. As large corporations expand their operations around the world, do they tip the balance away from tradition in favour of modernity? If so, how?

Shawn Baldwin/The New York Times/Redux

In Riyadh, Saudi Arabia, these young men are shopping for the latest in cell phones. Does such modern technology threaten a society's traditions?

HINT Although sociologists analyze tradition and modernity as conceptual opposites, every society combines these elements in various ways. People may debate the virtues of traditional and modern life, but the two patterns are found almost everywhere. Technological change always has social consequences—for example, the use of cell phones changes people's social networks and economic opportunities; similarly, the spread of McDonald's changes not only what people eat but also where and with whom they share meals.

Seeing Sociology in *Your* Everyday Life

1. How do tradition and modernity combine in your life? Point to several ways in which you are traditional and several ways in which you are thoroughly modern.

2. Go to www.sociologyinfocus.com to access the Sociology in Focus blog, where you can read the latest posts by a team of young sociologists who apply the sociological perspective to topics of popular culture.

3. What do you see as the advantages of living in a modern society? What are the drawbacks?

Nelson Hancock/Dorling
Kindersley, Ltd.

Making the Grade

What Is Social Change?

16.1 State four defining characteristics of social change. (pages 553–554)

Social change is the transformation of culture and social institutions over time. Societies change all the time, sometimes faster, sometimes more slowly. Social change often generates controversy.

social change the transformation of culture and social institutions over time

Causes of Social Change

16.2 Explain how culture, conflict, ideas, population patterns, collective behaviour, and social movements direct social change. (pages 554–562)

- **Culture:** *Invention* produces new objects, ideas, and social patterns. *Discovery* occurs when people take notice of existing elements of the world. *Diffusion* creates change as products, people, and information spread from one society to another.
- **Conflict:** Karl Marx claimed that class conflict between capitalists and workers pushes society toward a socialist system of production. Social conflict arising from class, race, and gender inequality has resulted in social changes that have improved the lives of working people.
- **Ideas:** Max Weber claimed that the fact that industrial capitalism developed first in Europe where the Protestant work ethic was strong shows the power of ideas to bring about change.
- **Population Patterns:** The aging of Canadian society has resulted in changes to family life and the development of consumer products to meet the needs of the elderly. Migration within and between societies promotes change.
- **Collective Behaviour: Crowds**, in the form of political demonstrations and protest rallies, can bring about political change. **Mobs** and **riots** are types of crowds that are highly emotional and often violent; by threatening the status quo, they often result in social change. **Rumour** thrives in a climate of uncertainty and can trigger the formation of crowds and direct their action. **Fashion**, which reflects changes in cultural values, guides people's tastes in clothing, music, and automobiles, as well as their political attitudes. **Fads** are social patterns that people embrace enthusiastically but for a very short period of time.
- **Types of Social Movements:** *Alterative social movements* seek limited change in specific individuals (e.g., MADD). *Redemptive social movements* seek radical change in specific individuals (e.g., Alcoholics Anonymous). *Reformative social movements* seek limited change in the whole society (e.g., the environmental movement). *Revolutionary social movements* seek radical change in the whole society (e.g., the Communist party).
- **Explanations of Social Movements:** *Deprivation theory:* Social movements arise among people who feel deprived of something, such as income, safe working conditions, or political rights. *Mass-society theory:* Social movements attract socially isolated people seeking a sense of identity and purpose. *Culture theory:* Social movements depend not only on money and resources but also on cultural symbols that motivate people. *Resource mobilization theory:* A moment's success is linked to available resources, including money, labour, and the mass media. *Political-economy theory:* Social movements arise in opposition to the capitalist economic system, which fails to meet the needs of the majority of people. *New social movements theory:* Social movements in post-industrial societies are typically leaderless and expressive, addressing a wide range of political, economic, and social issues.

collective behaviour activity involving a large number of people that is unplanned, often controversial, and can bring about change

crowd a temporary gathering of people who share a common focus of attention and who influence one another

mob a highly emotional crowd that pursues a violent or destructive goal

riot a social eruption that is highly emotional, violent, and undirected

rumour unconfirmed information that people spread informally, by word of mouth or by using electronic devices

fashion social patterns favoured by a large number of people

fad an unconventional social pattern that people embrace briefly but enthusiastically

social movement an organized activity in which people set out to encourage or discourage social change

claims making the process of trying to convince the public and public officials of the importance of joining a social movement to address a particular issue

relative deprivation a perceived disadvantage arising from some specific comparison

disaster an event, generally unexpected, that causes extensive harm to people and damage to property

Modernity

16.3 Apply the ideas of Tönnies, Durkheim, Weber, and Marx to our understanding of modernity. (pages 562–567)

Modernity refers to the social consequences of industrialization: the decline of traditional communities, the expansion of personal choice, increasing social diversity, and a focus on the future.

modernity changes brought about by the Industrial Revolution

modernization the process of social change begun by industrialization

- **Ferdinand Tönnies** described modernization as the transition from *Gemeinschaft* to *Gesellschaft*, characterized by the loss of traditional community and the rise of individualism.
- **Emile Durkheim** saw modernization as a society's expanding division of labour. *Mechanical solidarity*, based on shared activities and beliefs, is gradually replaced by *organic solidarity*, in which specialization makes people interdependent.
- **Max Weber** saw modernity as the decline of a traditional worldview and the rise of rationality. Weber feared the dehumanizing effects of modern rational organization.
- **Karl Marx** saw modernity as the triumph of capitalism over feudalism.

> **division of labour** specialized economic activity
>
> **anomie** Durkheim's term for a condition in which society provides little moral guidance to individuals

Structural-Functional Analysis: Modernity as Mass Society

(**16.4**) Apply structural-functional theory to modern social life. (pages 567–570)

- According to **mass-society theory**, modernity increases the scale of life, enlarging the role of government and other formal organizations in carrying out tasks previously performed by families in local communities.
- Cultural diversity and rapid social change make it difficult for people in modern societies to develop stable identities and to find meaning in their lives.

> **mass society** a society in which prosperity and expanding bureaucracy have weakened traditional social ties

Social-Conflict Analysis: Modernity as Class Society

(**16.5**) Apply social-conflict theory to modern social life. (pages 570–571)

- According to **class-society theory**, modernity involves the rise of capitalism into a global economic system resulting in persistent social inequality. By concentrating wealth in the hands of a few, modern capitalist societies generate widespread feelings of alienation and powerlessness.

> **class society** a capitalist society with pronounced social stratification

Modernity and the Individual

(**16.6**) Apply sociological theory to understand how people experience modern social life. (pages 572–574)

- **Mass Society: Problems of Identity** According to David Riesman, pre-industrial societies exhibit **tradition-directedness:** Everyone in society draws on the same solid cultural foundation, and people model their lives on those of their ancestors. Modern societies exhibit **other-directedness:** Because their socialization occurs in societies that are continuously in flux, other-directed people develop fluid identities marked by superficiality, inconsistency, and change.
- **Class Society: Problems of Powerlessness** According to Herbert Marcuse, modern society is irrational because it fails to meet the needs of so many people. Technological advances further reduce people's control over their own lives. People suffer because modern societies concentrate both wealth and power in the hands of a privileged few.

> **social character** personality patterns common to members of a particular society
>
> **tradition-directedness** rigid conformity to time-honoured ways of living
>
> **other-directedness** openness to the latest trends and fashions, often expressed by imitating others

Modernity and Progress

(**16.7**) Evaluate the positive and negative consequences of social change. (pages 574–575)

- A rising standard of living has made lives longer, and the conveniences brought to us by developments in science and technology have made our everyday lives more comfortable.
- Many people are stressed and have little time to relax; advancements in transportation and communications technology have weakened traditional attachments to hometowns and families; there have been no increases in measures of personal happiness over recent decades.

Postmodernity

(**16.8**) Discuss postmodernism as one type of social criticism. (page 576)

Postmodernity refers to the cultural traits of post-industrial societies. Postmodern criticism of society centres on the failure of modernity, and specifically science, to fulfill its promise of prosperity and well-being.

> **postmodernity** the transformations caused by the Information Revolution and the post-industrial economy

Modernization and Our Global Future

(**16.9**) Evaluate possible directions of future social change. (page 577)

- *Modernization theory* links global poverty to the power of tradition. Rich nations can help poor countries develop their economies.
- *Dependency theory* explains global poverty as the product of the world economic system. The operation of multinational corporations makes poor nations economically dependent on rich nations.

Glossary

abortion   the deliberate termination of a pregnancy

absolute poverty   a lack of resources that is life-threatening

achieved status   a social position a person takes on voluntarily that reflects personal ability and effort

ageism   prejudice and discrimination on the basis of age.

age-sex pyramid   a graphic representation of the age and sex of a population

agriculture   large-scale cultivation using plows harnessed to animals or more powerful energy sources

alienation   the experience of isolation and misery resulting from powerlessness

animism   the belief that elements of the natural world are conscious life forms that affect humanity

anomie   a condition in which society provides little moral guidance to individuals

anticipatory socialization   learning that helps a person achieve a desired position

ascribed status   a social position a person receives at birth or takes on involuntarily later in life

asexuality   a lack of sexual attraction to people of either sex

assimilation   the process by which minorities gradually adopt patterns of the dominant culture

authoritarianism   a political system that denies the people participation in government

authority   power that people perceive as legitimate rather than coercive

beliefs   specific thoughts or ideas that people hold to be true

bisexuality   sexual attraction to people of both sexes

blue-collar occupations   lower-prestige jobs that involve mostly manual labour

bureaucracy   an organizational model rationally designed to perform tasks efficiently

bureaucratic inertia   the tendency of bureaucratic organizations to perpetuate themselves

bureaucratic ritualism   a focus on rules and regulations to the point of undermining an organization's goals

capitalism   an economic system in which natural resources and the means of producing goods and services are privately owned

capitalists   people who own and operate factories and other businesses in pursuit of profits

caste system   social stratification based on ascription, or birth

cause and effect   a relationship in which change in one variable (the independent variable) causes change in another (the dependent variable)

charisma   extraordinary personal qualities that can infuse people with emotion and turn them into followers

charismatic authority   power legitimized by extraordinary personal abilities that inspire devotion and obedience

church   a religious organization that is well integrated into the larger society

civil religion   a quasi-religious loyalty linking individuals in a basically secular society

claims making   the process of trying to convince the public and public officials of the importance of joining a social movement to address a particular issue

class society   a capitalist society with pronounced social stratification

class system   social stratification based on both birth and individual achievement

cohabitation   the sharing of a household by an unmarried couple

cohort   a category of people with something in common, usually their age

collective behaviour   activity involving a large number of people that is unplanned, often controversial, and can bring about change

colonialism   the process by which some nations enrich themselves through political and economic control of other nations

community-based corrections   correctional programs operating within society at large rather than behind prison walls

concept   a mental construct that represents some part of the world in a simplified form

concrete operational stage   the level of human development at which individuals first see causal connections in their surroundings

conglomerates   giant corporations composed of many smaller corporations

conspicuous consumption   buying and using products because of the "statement" they make about social position

corporate crime   the illegal actions of a corporation or people acting on its behalf

corporation   an organization with a legal existence, including rights and liabilities, separate from that of its members

correlation   a relationship in which two (or more) variables change together

counterculture   cultural patterns that strongly oppose those widely accepted within a society

crime   the violation of a society's formally enacted criminal law

crimes against property   (property crimes) crimes that involve theft of money or property belonging to others

crimes against the person   (violent crimes) crimes that direct violence or the threat of violence against others

criminal justice system   the organizations—police, courts, and prison officials—that respond to alleged violations of the law

criminal recidivism   later offences by people previously convicted of crimes

critical sociology   the study of society that focuses on the need for social change

crowd   a temporary gathering of people who share a common focus of attention and who influence one another

crude birth rate   the number of live births in a given year for every 1000 people in a population

crude death rate   the number of deaths in a given year for every 1000 people in a population

cult   a religious organization that is largely outside a society's cultural traditions

cultural capital   material objects, values, and knowledge acquired by members of the elite culture

cultural integration   the close relationships among various elements of a cultural system

cultural lag   the fact that some cultural elements change more quickly than others, disrupting a cultural system

cultural relativism   the practice of judging a culture by its own standards

cultural transmission   the process by which one generation passes culture to the next

cultural universals   traits that are part of every known culture

culture   the ways of thinking, the ways of acting, and the material objects that together form a people's way of life

culture shock   personal disorientation when experiencing an unfamiliar way of life

Davis-Moore thesis   the functional analysis claiming that social stratification has beneficial consequences for the operation of society

democracy   a political system that derives its legitimacy from the people as a whole

demographic transition theory   a thesis that links population patterns to a society's level of technological development

demography   the study of human population

denomination   a church, independent of the state, that recognizes religious pluralism

dependency theory   a model of economic and social development that explains global inequality in terms of the historical exploitation of poor nations by rich ones

dependent variable   the variable that changes

descent   the system by which members of a society trace kinship over generations

deterrence   the attempt to discourage criminality through the use of punishment

deviance   the recognized violation of cultural norms

direct-fee system   a medical care system in which patients pay directly for the services of physicians and hospitals

disaster   an event, generally unexpected, that causes extensive harm to people and damage to property

discrimination   unequal treatment of various categories of people

division of labour   specialized economic activity

dramaturgical analysis   Erving Goffman's term for the study of social interaction in terms of theatrical performance

dyad   a social group with two members

eating disorder   a physical and mental disorder that involves intense dieting or other unhealthy method of weight control driven by the desire to be very thin

ecologically sustainable culture   a way of life that meets the needs of the present generation without threatening the environmental legacy of future generations

ecology   the study of the interaction of living organisms and the natural environment

economy the social institution that organizes a society's production, distribution, and consumption of goods and services

ecosystem a system composed of the interaction of all living organisms and their natural environment

education the social institution through which society provides its members with important knowledge, including basic facts, job skills, and cultural norms and values

ego a person's conscious efforts to balance innate pleasure-seeking drives with the demands of society

emotional labour suppressed or induced feelings produced by an employee in accordance with the rules of an organization

empirical evidence information we can verify with our senses

endogamy marriage between people of the same social category

environmental deficit profound long-term harm to the natural environment caused by humanity's focus on short-term material affluence

environmental racism patterns of development that expose poor people, especially minorities, to environmental hazards

ethnicity a shared cultural heritage

ethnocentrism the practice of judging another culture by the standards of one's own culture

ethnomethodology Harold Garfinkel's term for the study of the way people make sense of their everyday surroundings

Eurocentrism the dominance of European (especially English) cultural patterns

euthanasia assisting in the death of a person suffering from an incurable disease; also known as *mercy killing*

exogamy marriage between people of different social categories

experiment a research method for investigating cause and effect under highly controlled conditions

expressive leadership group leadership that focuses on the group's well-being

extended family a family composed of parents and children as well as other kin; also known as a *consanguine family*

fad an unconventional social pattern that people embrace briefly but enthusiastically

faith belief based on conviction rather than on scientific evidence

family a social institution found in all societies that unites people in co-operative groups to care for one another, including any children

family violence emotional, physical, or sexual abuse of one family member by another

fashion social patterns favoured by a large number of people

feminism support of social equality for women and men

feminization of poverty the trend of women making up an increasing proportion of the poor

fertility the incidence of childbearing in a country's population

folkways norms for routine or casual interaction

formal operational stage the level of human development at which individuals think abstractly and critically

formal organization a large secondary group organized to achieve its goals efficiently

functional illiteracy a lack of the reading and writing skills needed for everyday living.

fundamentalism a conservative religious doctrine that opposes intellectualism and worldly accommodation in favour of restoring traditional, otherworldly religion

Gemeinschaft a type of social organization in which people are closely tied by kinship and tradition

gender the personal traits and social positions that members of a society attach to being female or male

gender roles (also known as **sex roles**) attitudes and activities that a society links to each sex

gender stratification the unequal distribution of wealth, power, and privilege between men and women

gender-conflict theory (feminist theory) the study of society that focuses on inequality and conflict between women and men

generalized other widespread cultural norms and values we use as references in evaluating ourselves

genocide the systematic killing of one category of people by another

gentrification the process by which working-class communities are displaced by an influx of middle-class property developers

gerontocracy a form of social organization in which the elderly have the most wealth, power, and prestige

gerontology the study of aging and the elderly

Gesellschaft a type of social organization in which people come together only on the basis of individual self-interest

global economy economic activity that crosses national borders

global perspective the study of the larger world and our society's place in it

global stratification patterns of social inequality in the world as a whole

global warming a rise in Earth's average temperature due to an increasing concentration of carbon dioxide in the atmosphere

government a formal organization that directs the political life of a society

groupthink the tendency of group members to conform, resulting in a narrow view of some issue

hate crime a criminal act against a person or a person's property by an offender motivated by racial or other bias

health a state of complete physical, mental, and social well-being

heterosexism prejudice or discrimination against non-heterosexuals

heterosexuality sexual attraction to someone of the other sex

hidden curriculum the subtle presentations of political or cultural ideas in the classroom

high culture cultural patterns that distinguish a society's elite

high-income countries nations with the highest overall standards of living

holistic medicine an approach to health care that emphasizes prevention of illness and takes into account a person's entire physical and social environment

homogamy marriage between people with the same social characteristics

homophobia discomfort over close personal interaction with people thought to be gay, lesbian, or bisexual

homosexuality sexual attraction to someone of the same sex

horticulture the use of hand tools to raise crops

hunting and gathering the use of simple tools to hunt animals and gather vegetation for food

hypothesis a statement of a possible relationship between two (or more) variables

id the human being's basic drives

ideology cultural beliefs that justify particular social arrangements, including patterns of inequality

incest taboo a norm forbidding sexual relations or marriage between certain relatives

income earnings from work or investments

independent variable the variable that causes the change

industry the production of goods using advanced sources of energy to drive large machinery

infant mortality rate the number of deaths among infants under one year of age for each 1000 live births in a given year

infidelity sexual activity outside one's marriage

in-group a social group toward which a member feels respect and loyalty

institutional prejudice and discrimination bias built into the operation of society's institutions

instrumental leadership group leadership that focuses on the completion of tasks

intergenerational social mobility upward or downward social mobility of children in relation to their parents

interpretive sociology the study of society that focuses on discovering the meanings people attach to their social world

intersection theory analysis of the interplay of race, class, and gender, which often results in multiple dimensions of disadvantage

intersexual people people whose bodies (including genitals) have both female and male characteristics

intragenerational social mobility a change in social position occurring during a person's lifetime

kinship a social bond based on common ancestry, marriage, or adoption

labelling theory the idea that deviance and conformity result not so much from what people do as from how others respond to those actions

labour unions organizations that seek to improve wages and working conditions through various strategies, including negotiations and strikes

language a system of symbols that allows people to communicate with one another

latent functions the unrecognized and unintended consequences of any social pattern

laws systems of rules recognized and enforced by governing institutions

liberation theology the combining of Christian principles with political activism, often Marxist in character

life expectancy the average life span of a country's population

looking-glass self Cooley's term for a self-image based on how we think others see us

low-income countries   nations with a low standard of living, in which most people are poor

macro-level orientation   a broad focus on social structures that shape society as a whole

mainstreaming   integrating students with disabilities or special needs into the overall educational program

manifest functions   the recognized and intended consequences of any social pattern

marriage   a legal relationship, usually involving economic co-operation, sexual activity, and childbearing

Marxist political-economy model   an analysis that explains politics in terms of the operation of a society's economic system

mass media   the means for delivering impersonal communications to a vast audience

mass society   a society in which prosperity and expanding bureaucracy have weakened traditional social ties

master status   a status that has special importance for social identity, often shaping a person's entire life

material culture   the physical things created by members of a society

matriarchy   a form of social organization in which females dominate males

measurement   a procedure for determining the value of a variable in a specific case

medicalization of deviance   the transformation of moral and legal deviance into a medical condition

medicine   the social institution that focuses on fighting disease and improving health

megalopolis   a vast urban region containing a number of cities and their surrounding suburbs

meritocracy   social stratification based on personal merit

Metaphysical Stage   the Enlightenment and the ideas of Hobbes, Locke, and Rousseau

metropolis   a large city that socially and economically dominates an urban area

micro-level orientation   a close-up focus on social interaction in specific situations

middle-income countries   nations with a standard of living about average for the world as a whole

migration   the movement of people into and out of a specified territory

military-industrial complex   the close association of the federal government, the military, and defence industries

minority   any category of people distinguished by physical or cultural difference that a society sets apart and subordinates

miscegenation   biological reproduction by partners of different racial categories

mob   a highly emotional crowd that pursues a violent or destructive goal

modernity   changes brought about by the Industrial Revolution

modernization   the process of social change begun by industrialization

modernization theory   a model of economic and social development that explains global inequality in terms of technological and cultural differences between nations

monarchy   a political system in which a single family rules from generation to generation

monogamy   marriage that unites two partners

monopoly   the domination of a market by a single producer

mores   norms that are widely observed and have great moral significance

mortality   the incidence of death in a country's population

multiculturalism   a perspective recognizing the cultural diversity of Canada and promoting equal standing for all cultural traditions

multinational corporation   a large business that operates in many countries

natural environment   Earth's surface and atmosphere, including living organisms, air, water, soil, and other resources necessary to sustain life

neocolonialism   a new form of global power relationships that involves not direct political control but economic exploitation by multinational corporations

network   a web of weak social ties

nonmaterial culture   the ideas created by members of a society

nonverbal communication   communication using body movements, gestures, and facial expressions rather than speech

norms   rules and expectations by which a society guides the behaviour of its members

nuclear family   a family composed of one or two parents and their children; also known as a *conjugal family*

nuclear proliferation   the acquisition of nuclear weapons technology by more and more nations

objectivity   personal neutrality in conducting research

oligarchy   the rule of the many by the few

oligopoly   the domination of a market by a few producers

operationalize a variable   specify exactly what is to be measured before assigning a value to a variable

organizational environment   factors outside an organization that affect its operation

organized crime   a business supplying illegal goods or services

other-directedness   openness to the latest trends and fashions, often expressed by imitating others

out-group   a social group toward which a person feels a sense of competition or opposition

participant observation   a research method in which investigators systematically observe people while joining them in their routine activities

pastoralism   the domestication of animals

patriarchy   a form of social organization in which males dominate females

peer group   a social group whose members have interests, social position, and age in common

personal space   the surrounding area over which a person makes some claim to privacy

personality   a person's fairly consistent patterns of acting, thinking, and feeling

plea bargaining   a legal negotiation in which a prosecutor reduces a charge in exchange for a defendant's guilty plea

pluralism   a state in which people of all races and ethnicities are distinct but have equal social standing

pluralist model   an analysis of politics that sees power as spread among many competing interest groups

political revolution   the overthrow of one political system in order to establish another

politics   the social institution that distributes power, sets a society's goals, and makes decisions

polygamy   marriage that unites a person with two or more spouses

popular culture   cultural patterns that are widespread among a society's population

pornography   sexually explicit material intended to cause sexual arousal

positivism   a scientific approach to knowledge based on "positive" facts as opposed to mere speculation

positivist sociology   the study of society based on scientific observation of social behaviour

post-industrial economy   a productive system based on service work and computer technology

post-industrialism   the production of information using computer technology

postmodernity   social patterns characteristic of post-industrial societies

power   the ability to achieve desired ends despite resistance from others

power-elite model   an analysis of politics that sees power as concentrated among the rich

prejudice   a rigid and unfair generalization about an entire category of people

preoperational stage   the level of human development at which individuals first use language and other symbols

presentation of self   Erving Goffman's term for a person's efforts to create specific impressions in the minds of others

primary group   a small social group whose members share personal and lasting relationships

primary sector   the part of the economy that draws raw materials from the natural environment

primary sex characteristics   the genitals, organs used for reproduction

profane   included as an ordinary element of everyday life

profession   a prestigious white-collar occupation that requires extensive formal education

proletarians   people who sell their labour for wages

prostitution   the selling of sexual services

queer theory   a body of research findings that challenges the heterosexual bias in Canadian society

race   a socially constructed category of people who share biologically transmitted traits that members of a society consider important

race-conflict theory   the study of society that focuses on inequality and conflict between people of different racial and ethnic categories

racism   the belief that one racial category is innately superior or inferior to another

rainforests   regions of dense forestation, most of which circle the globe close to the equator

rationality   a way of thinking that emphasizes deliberate, matter-of-fact calculation of the most efficient way to accomplish a particular task

rationalization of society   the historical change from tradition to rationality as the main type of human thought

rational-legal authority   power legitimized by legally enacted rules and regulations (also known as *bureaucratic authority*)

reference group a social group that serves as a point of reference in making evaluations and decisions

rehabilitation a program for reforming the offender to prevent later offences

relative deprivation a perceived disadvantage arising from some specific comparison

relative poverty the lack of resources of some people in relation to those who have more

reliability consistency in measurement

religion a social institution involving beliefs and practices based on recognizing the sacred

religiosity the importance of religion in a person's life

research method a systematic plan for doing research

resocialization radically changing an inmate's personality by carefully controlling the environment

retribution an act of moral vengeance by which society makes the offender suffer as much as the suffering caused by the crime

riot a social eruption that is highly emotional, violent, and undirected

role behaviour expected of someone who holds a particular status

role conflict conflict among the roles connected to two or more statuses

role set a number of roles attached to a single status

role strain tension among the roles connected to a single status

routinization of charisma the transformation of charismatic authority into some combination of traditional and bureaucratic authority

rumour unconfirmed information that people spread informally, by word of mouth or by using electronic devices

sacred set apart as extraordinary, inspiring awe and reverence

Sapir-Whorf thesis the idea that people see and understand the world through the cultural lens of language

scapegoat a person or category of people, typically with little power, whom people unfairly blame for their own troubles

schooling formal instruction under the direction of specially trained teachers

science a logical system that develops knowledge from direct, systematic observation

scientific management the application of scientific principles to the operation of a business or other large organization

Scientific Stage modern physics, chemistry, sociology

secondary group a large and impersonal social group whose members pursue a specific goal or activity

secondary sector the part of the economy that transforms raw materials into manufactured goods

secondary sex characteristics bodily development, apart from the genitals, that distinguishes biologically mature females and males

sect a religious organization that stands apart from the larger society

secularization the historical decline in the importance of the supernatural and the sacred

segregation the physical and social separation of categories of people

self George Herbert Mead's term for the part of an individual's personality composed of self-awareness and self-image

sensorimotor stage the level of human development at which individuals experience the world only through their senses

sex the biological distinction between females and males

sex ratio the number of males for every 100 females in a nation's population

sex roles see *gender roles*

sexism the belief that one sex is innately superior to the other

sexual harassment comments, gestures, or physical contacts of a sexual nature that are deliberate, repeated, and unwelcome

sexual orientation a person's romantic and emotional attraction to another person

sick role patterns of behaviour defined as appropriate for people who are ill

significant others people, such as parents, who have special importance for socialization

social change the transformation of culture and social institutions over time

social character personality patterns common to members of a particular society

social construction of reality the process by which people creatively shape reality through social interaction

social control attempts by society to regulate people's thoughts and behaviour

social dysfunction any social pattern that may disrupt the operation of society

social epidemiology the study of how health and disease are distributed throughout a society's population.

social functions the consequences of a social pattern for the operation of society as a whole

social group two or more people who identify with and interact with one another

social institution a major sphere of social life, or societal subsystem, organized to meet human needs

social interaction the process by which people act and react in relation to others

social media technology that links people in social activity

social mobility a change in position within the social hierarchy

social movement an organized activity in which people set out to encourage or discourage social change

social stratification a system by which a society ranks categories of people in a hierarchy

social structure any relatively stable pattern of social behaviour

social-conflict approach a framework for building theory that sees society as an arena of inequality that generates conflict and change

socialism an economic system in which natural resources and the means of producing goods and services are collectively owned

socialization the lifelong social experience by which people develop their human potential and learn culture

socialized medicine a medical care system in which the government owns and operates most medical facilities and employs most physicians

societal protection rendering an offender incapable of further offences temporarily through imprisonment or permanently by execution

society people who interact in a defined territory and share a culture

socio-economic status (SES) a composite ranking based on various dimensions of social inequality

sociological perspective the special point of view of sociology that sees general patterns of society in the lives of particular people

sociology the systematic study of human society

special-interest group people organized to address some economic or social issue

spurious correlation an apparent but false relationship between two (or more) variables that is caused by some other variable

state capitalism an economic and political system in which companies are privately owned but co-operate closely with the government

state church a church formally linked to the state

status a social position that a person holds

status consistency the degree of uniformity in a person's social standing across various dimensions of social inequality

status set all the statuses a person holds at a given time

stereotype a simplified description applied to every person in some category

stigma a powerfully negative label that greatly changes a person's self-concept and social identity

structural social mobility a shift in the social position of large numbers of people due more to changes in society itself than to individual efforts

structural-functional approach a framework for building theory that sees society as a complex system whose parts work together to promote solidarity and stability

subculture cultural patterns that set apart some segment of a society's population

suburbs urban areas beyond the political boundaries of a city

superego the cultural values and norms internalized by an individual

survey a research method in which subjects respond to a series of statements or questions on a questionnaire or in an interview

symbol anything that carries a particular meaning recognized by people who share a culture

symbolic-interaction approach a framework for building theory that sees society as the product of the everyday interactions of individuals

technology knowledge that people use to make a way of life in their surroundings

terrorism acts of violence or the threat of violence used as a political strategy by an individual or a group

tertiary sector the part of the economy that involves services rather than goods

Theological Stage the Church in the Middle Ages

theoretical approach a basic image of society that guides thinking and research

theory a statement of how and why specific facts are related

Thomas theorem W.I. Thomas's claim that situations defined as real are real in their consequences

total institution a setting in which people are isolated from the rest of society and controlled by an administrative staff

totalitarianism a highly centralized political system that extensively regulates people's lives

totem an object in the natural world collectively defined as sacred

tracking assigning students to different types of educational programs

tradition behaviour, values, and beliefs passed from generation to generation

traditional authority power legitimized by respect for long-established cultural patterns

tradition-directedness rigid conformity to time-honoured ways of living

transgender appearing or behaving in ways that challenge conventional cultural norms concerning how females and males should look and act

transsexuals people who feel they are one sex even though biologically they are the other

triad a social group with three members

urban ecology the study of the link between the physical and social dimensions of cities

urbanization the concentration of population into cities

use of existing sources a research method in which a researcher uses data already collected by others

validity actually measuring exactly what you intend to measure

values culturally defined standards that people use to decide what is desirable, good, and beautiful and that serve as broad guidelines for social living

variable a concept whose value changes from case to case

victimless crimes violations of law in which there are no obvious victims

visible minority persons, other than Aboriginal peoples, who are non-Caucasian in race or non-white in colour

war organized, armed conflict among the people of two or more nations, directed by their governments

wealth the total value of money and other assets, minus outstanding debts

welfare capitalism an economic and political system that combines a mostly market-based economy with extensive social welfare programs

welfare state a system of government agencies and programs that provide benefits to the population

white-collar crime crime committed by people of high social position in the course of their occupations

white-collar occupations higher-prestige jobs that involve mostly mental activity

zero population growth the rate of reproduction that maintains population at a steady level

References

Blue type denotes reference citations new to this sixth edition.

Chapter 1

BAGLEY, ROBIN. *Sexual Offences Against Children: Report of the Committee on Sexual Offences Against Children and Youth.* Ottawa: Canadian Government Publishing, 1984.

BALTZELL, E. DIGBY. "Introduction to the 1967 Edition." In W.E.B. Du Bois, ed., *The Philadelphia Negro: A Social Study.* New York: Schocken Books, 1967.

BENOIT, CECILIA, and ALISON MILLAR. *Dispelling Myths and Understanding Realities: Working Conditions, Health Status, and Exiting Experiences of Sex Workers.* Sponsored by Prostitutes Empowerment, Education and Resource Society (PEERS). Funded by BC Health Research Foundation, Capital Health District, and BC Centre of Excellence on Women's Health, 2001.

BERGER, PETER L. *Invitation to Sociology.* New York: Anchor Books, 1963.

BLACK, CASSANDRA. "Survey Reports More Women Are Having Extramarital Affairs." *Associated Content* (May 4, 2007). [Online] Available April 19, 2009, at http://www.associatedcontent.com/article/231316/survey_reports_more_women_are_having.html

BOWLES, SAMUEL, and HERBERT GINTIS. *Schooling in Capitalist America: Educational Reform and the Contradictions of Economic Life.* New York: Basic Books, 1976.

CAIN, PATRICK. "Who filled out the National Household Survey? (and why did Statscan cut its census standards in half?)" *Global News.* 2013. http://globalnews.ca/news/873012/who-filled-out-the-national-household-survey-and-why-did-statscan-cut-its-census-standards-in-half/#statscan

CANADIAN SOCIOLOGICAL ASSOCIATION. "Statement of Professional Ethics." 2012. [Online] https://www.csa-scs.ca/code-of-ethics

CIHR (CANADIAN INSTITUTES OF HEALTH RESEARCH), NSERC (NATURAL SCIENCES and ENGINEERING RESEARCH COUNCIL OF CANADA), and SSHRC (SOCIAL SCIENCES AND HUMANITIES RESEARCH COUNCIL OF CANADA). *Tri-Council Policy Statement: Ethical Conduct for Research Involving Humans.* Ottawa: Her Majesty the Queen in Right of Canada, 2014. [Online] http://www.pre.ethics.gc.ca/eng/policy-politique/initiatives/tcps2-eptc2/Default/

CIHR (CANADIAN INSTITUTES OF HEALTH RESEARCH). *CIHR Guidelines for Health Research Involving Aboriginal People.* 2007. [Online] www.cihr-irsc.gc.ca/e/29134.html

COMTE, AUGUSTE. *Auguste Comte and Positivism: The Essential Writings.* Gertrud Lenzer, ed. New York: Harper Torchbooks, 1975; orig. 1851–54.

CONFERENCE BOARD OF CANADA. "Suicides." 2015. [Online] Available at http://www.conferenceboard.ca/hcp/provincial/health/suicide.aspx

CROSS, PHILIP, and PETER MITCHELL. *The Marriage Gap Between Poor and Rich Canadians: How Canadians are split into haves and have-nots along marriage lines.* Institute of Marriage and Family Canada. February 2014. [Online] http://www.imfcanada.org/canadian-marriage-gap

CROSS, PHILIP. "The post-recession recovery of Canadian exports, 2009–2011." *Canadian Economic Observer.* Vol. 24, No. 9 (2011). Statistics Canada Catalogue no. 11-010-X. http://www.statcan.gc.ca/pub/11-010-x/2011009/part-partie3-eng.htm

DEPARTMENT OF JUSTICE CANADA. *Canadian Charter of Rights and Freedoms.* 1982. [Online] http://laws-lois.justice.gc.ca/eng/charter/

DEUTSCHER, IRWIN. *Making a Difference: The Practice of Sociology.* New Brunswick, NJ: Transaction, 1999.

DU BOIS, W.E.B. *The Philadelphia Negro: A Social Study.* New York: Schocken Books, 1967; orig. 1899.

DURKHEIM, EMILE. *Suicide.* New York: Free Press, 1966; orig. 1897.

EICHLER, MARGRIT. *Nonsexist Research Methods: A Practical Guide.* Winchester, MA: Unwin Hyman, 1988.

FEAGIN, JOE R., and VERA HERNÁN. *Liberation Sociology.* Boulder, CO: Westview Press, 2001.

GIOVANNINI, MAUREEN. "Female Anthropologist and Male Informant: Gender Conflict in a Sicilian Town." In John J. Macionis and Nijole V. Benokraitis, eds., *Seeing Ourselves: Classic, Contemporary, and Cross-Cultural Readings in Sociology.* 2nd ed. Englewood Cliffs, NJ: Prentice Hall, 1992:27–32.

HALL, STUART M. *Policing the Crisis: Mugging, the State, and Law and Order.* London: Macmillan. 1978.

Hallgrimsdottir, H., R. Phillips, and C. Benoit. "Fallen Women and Rescued Girls: Social Stigma and Media Narratives of the Sex Industry in Victoria, BC, from 1980 to 2005." *Canadian Review of Sociology and Anthropology.* Special Issue, Vol. 43, No. 3 (2006):265–80.

HANEY, CRAIG, W. CURTIS BANKS, and PHILIP G. ZIMBARDO. "Interpersonal Dynamics in a Simulated Prison." *International Journal of Criminology and Penology.* Vol. 1 (1973):69–97.

HECKATHORN, DOUGLAS. "Respondent-Driven Sampling: A New Approach to the Study of Hidden Populations." *Social Problems.* Vol. 44, No. 2 (1997):174–99.

HESS, BETH B. "Breaking and Entering the Establishment: Committing Social Change and Confronting the Backlash." *Social Problems.* Vol. 46, No. 1 (February 1999):1–12.

KITZINGER, JENNY. "Media Templates: Patterns of Association and the (Re) Construction of Meaning Over Time." *Media, Culture, and Society.* Vol. 22 (2000): 61–84.

LAPCHICK, RICHARD, WITH ANGELICA GUIAO. "The 2015 Racial and Gender Report Card: National Basketball Association" Orlando: The Institute for Diversity and Ethics in Sport (TIDES), University of Central Florida. April 15, 2015c. [Online] http://www.tidesport.org/Ammended%20-%20The%202015%20MLB%20Racial%20&%20Gender%20Report%20Card.pdf

LAPCHICK, RICHARD, WITH DIEGO SALAS. "The 2015 Racial and Gender Report Card: Major League Baseball." Orlando: The Institute for Diversity and Ethics in Sport (TIDES), University of Central Florida. April 15, 2015a. [Online] http://www.tidesport.org/Ammended%20-%20The%202015%20MLB%20Racial%20&%20Gender%20Report%20Card.pdf

LAPCHICK, RICHARD, WITH LEROY ROBINSON. "The 2015 Racial and Gender Report Card: National Football League." Orlando: The Institute for Diversity and Ethics in Sport (TIDES), University of Central Florida. April 15, 2015b. [Online] http://www.tidesport.org/The%202015%20NFL%20Racial%20and%20Gender%20Report%20Card.pdf

LOWMAN, JOHN. "Taking Young Prostitutes Seriously." *Canadian Review of Sociology and Anthropology.* Vol. 24, No. 1 (1987):99–116.

MILLS, C. WRIGHT. *The Sociological Imagination.* New York: Oxford University Press, 1959.

OAKES, JEANNIE. "Classroom Social Relationships: Exploring the Bowles and Gintis Hypothesis." *Sociology of Education.* Vol. 55, No. 4 (October 1982):197–212.

———. *Keeping Track: How High Schools Structure Inequality.* New Haven, CT: Yale University Press, 1985.

PARKER-POPE, TARA. "Love, Sex, and the Changing Landscape of Infidelity." *New York Times* (October 27, 2008). www.nytimes.com/2008/10/28/health/28.well.html?_r=1

PATEMAN, CAROLE. *The Sexual Contract.* Cambridge, UK: Polity Press, 1988.

PERRUCCI, ROBERT. "Inventing Social Justice: SSSP and the Twenty-First Century." *Social Problems.* Vol. 48, No. 2 (May 2001):159–67.

POPULATION REFERENCE BUREAU. "Datafinder." 2012. [Online] Available at http://www.prb.org/DataFinder.aspx

RUBIN, LILLIAN BRESLOW. *Worlds of Pain: Life in the Working-Class Family.* New York: Basic Books, 1976.

SACKS, VALERIE. "Women and AIDS: An Analysis of Media Misrepresentations." *Social Science and Medicine.* Vol. 42, No. 1 (1996):59–73.

SEALE, CLIVE. "Health and Media: An Overview." *Sociology of Health and Illness* 25 (2003):513–31.

SMITH, TOM W. *American Sexual Behavior: Trends, Sociodemographic Differences, and Risk Behavior.* Chicago: National Opinion Research Center, March 2006. www.norc.org/NR/rdonlyres/2663F09F-2E74-436E-AC81-6FFBF288E183/0/AmericanSexualBehavior2006.pdf

SPREEN, MARIUS, and RONALD ZWAAGSTRA. "Personal Network Sampling, Outdegree Analysis and Multilevel Analysis: Introducing the Network Concept in Studies of Hidden Populations." *International Sociology.* Vol. 9 (1994):475–91.

STATISTICS CANADA. CANSIM Table 051-0001—Estimates of population, by age group and sex for July 1, Canada, provinces and territories. [Electronic Data File]. 2012a.

———. CANSIM Table 102-0551—Deaths and mortality rate, by selected grouped causes, age group and sex, Canada. [Electronic Data File]. 2014.

———. *Final Report on 2016 Census Options: Proposed Content Determination Framework and Methodology Options.* Ottawa: Statistics Canada, 2012b.

TOCQUEVILLE, ALEXIS DE. *The Old Regime and the French Revolution.* Stuart Gilbert, trans. Garden City, NY: Anchor/Doubleday, 1955; orig. 1856.

TRAVERS, ANN. "Thinking the Unthinkable: Imagining an 'Un-American,' Girl-friendly, Women- and Trans-Inclusive Alternative for Baseball." *Journal of Sport and Social Issues.* Vol. 72, No. 1 (2013):78–96.

Ungerleider, C.S. "Media, Minorities and Misconceptions: The Portrayal of Minorities in Canadian News Media." *Canadian Ethnic Studies.* Vol. 23, No. 3 (1991):158–64.

UNITED NATIONS, FOOD AND AGRICULTURE ORGANIZATION. "Food Security Statistics." Updated 10/9/2012. Available at http://www.fao.org/economic/ess/food-security-statistics/en/

UPTHEGROVE, TAYNA R., VINCENT J. ROSCIGNO, and CAMILLE ZUBRINSKY CHARLES. "Big Money Collegiate Sports: Racial Concentration, Contradictory Pressures, and Academic Performance." *Social Science Quarterly.* Vol. 80, No. 4 (December 1999):718–37.

WATKINS, S. CRAIG, and RANA EMERSON. "Feminist Media Practices and Feminist Media Criticism." *Annals of the American Academy of Political and Social Science.* 571 (2000):151–66.

WHYTE, WILLIAM FOOTE. *Street Corner Society.* 3rd ed. Chicago: University of Chicago Press, 1981; orig. 1943.

WORLD BANK. "World DataBank: Education Statistics." 2012. Available at http://databank.worldbank.org/data/views/variableselection/selectvariables.aspx?source=education-statistics#

———. "World DataBank: World Development Indicators." 2012. Available at http://databank.worldbank.org/data/views/variableSelection/selectvariables.aspx?source=world-development-indicators

WRIGHT, EARL, II. "The Atlanta Sociological Laboratory, 1896–1924: A Historical Account of the First American School of Sociology." *Western Journal of Black Studies.* Vol. 26, No. 3 (2002a):165–74.

———. "Why Black People Tend to Shout! An Earnest Attempt to Explain the Sociological Negation of the Atlanta Sociological Laboratory Despite Its Possible Unpleasantness." *Sociological Spectrum.* Vol. 22, No. 3 (2002b):325–61.

ZIMBARDO, PHILIP G. "Pathology of Imprisonment." *Society.* Vol. 9, No. 1 (April 1972):4–8.

ZIRIN, DAVE. *A Peoples History of Sports in the United States: 250 Years of Politics, Protest, People, and Play.* New York: New Press, distributed by W.W. Norton & Co., 2008.

Chapter 2

ADAMS, MICHAEL. *Sex in the Snow: Canadian Social Values at the End of the Millennium.* Toronto: Penguin Canada, 1997.

———. *Unlikely Utopia: The Surprising Triumph of Canadian Pluralism.* Toronto: Viking, 2007.

ANGUS REID PUBLIC OPINION. *Canadians Review What Is Morally Acceptable.* 2007. www.angus-reid.com/polls/29842/canadians_review_what_is_morally_acceptable/

APTN NATIONAL NEWS. "Aboriginal groups labelled 'adversaries' by federal government: document." *Aboriginal People's Television Network* (January 26, 2012). http://aptn.ca/news/2012/01/26/aboriginal-groups-labelled-adversaries-by-federal-government-document/

ASANTE, MOLEFI KETE. *Afrocentricity.* Trenton, NJ: Africa World Press, 1988.

ATKINSON, MICHAEL. *Tattooed: The Sociogenesis of a Body Art.* Toronto: The University of Toronto Press, 2003.

BAILEY, PATRICIA G., J.J. TUINMAN, STAN JONES. "Literacy." *Historica Canada* (February 2012). http://www.thecanadianencyclopedia.ca/en/article/literacy/

BALAKRISHNAN, T.R., E. LAPIERRE-ADAMCYK, and K.J. KROTKI. *Family and Childbearing in Canada: A Demographic Analysis.* Toronto: University of Toronto Press, 1993.

BANNERJI, HIMANI. *The Dark Side of the Nation: Essays on Multiculturalism, Nationalism and Gender.* Toronto: Canadian Scholars' Press, 2000.

BANTING, K., T. COURCHENE, and L. SEIDLE, eds. *Belonging? Diversity, Recognition and Shared Citizenship in Canada.* Montreal: Institute for Research on Public Policy, 2007.

BARON, STEPHEN. "General Strain, Street Youth, and Crime: Testing Agnew's Revised Theory," *Criminology.* Vol. 42 (2004):57–483.

BAROVICK, HARRIET. "Tongues That Go Out of Style." *Time* (June 10, 2002):22.

BEAMAN, L., and P. BEYER. *Religion and Diversity in Canada.* Boston: Brill, 2008.

BELL, DAVID, and LORNE TEPPERMAN. *The Roots of Disunity: A Look at Canadian Political Culture.* Toronto: McClelland & Stewart, 1979.

BENNETT, CAROLYN. "Dear Harper, It's Time to Reset Your Relationship with Aboriginals." *HuffPost Politics Canada* (December 14, 2013). http://www.huffingtonpost.ca/hon-carolyn-bennett/aboriginals-harper-relationship_b_4440473.html

BENOIT, CECILIA, and H. HALLGRIMSDOTTIR, eds. *Valuing Care Work: Comparative Perspectives.* Toronto: University of Toronto Press, 2011.

BENOIT, CECILIA, M. JANSSON, H. HALLGRIMSDOTTIR, and E. ROTH. "Street Youth's Life Course Transitions." *Comparative Social Research.* Vol. 25 (2008):329–57.

BROADBENT INSTITUTE. *Canadian Values are Progressive Values: A Snapshot of the Views of New and Canadian-Born Urban/Suburban Canadians, 2013.* 2013. https://www.broadbentinstitute.ca/sites/default/files/documents/polling-en-web.pdf

CANADIAN AUTOMOBILE ASSOCIATION "CAA survey takes a sober look at drinking and driving." 2010. http://www.caasco.com/~/media/about-us/documents/news-releases/drinking-and-driving-120810.ashx

CHAGNON, NAPOLEON A. *Yanomamö: The Fierce People.* 4th ed. Austin, TX: Holt, Rinehart and Winston, 1992.

CLARK, W. "Delayed Transitions of Young Adults." *Canadian Social Trends.* No. 84 (2007):14–22.

CRYSTAL, DAVID. *The Cambridge Encyclopedia of the English Language.* 3rd ed. Cambridge, MA: Cambridge University Press, 2010.

CURTIS, JAMES E., EDWARD G. GRABB, and NEIL GUPPY. *Social Inequality in Canada.* Scarborough, ON: Prentice Hall, 1999.

DAY, RICHARD J.F. *Multiculturalism and the History of Canadian Diversity.* Toronto: University of Toronto Press, 2000.

DICKASON, OLIVE PATRICIA. *Canada's First Nations: A History of Founding Peoples from Earliest Times.* Toronto: McClelland and Stewart, 1992.

ENCYCLOPEDIA OF MUSIC IN CANADA. "Rock 'n' roll and rock music, Anglo-Canadian." 2011. www.thecanadianencyclopedia.com/index.cfm?PgNm=tce&Params=U1ARTU0003007

ENVIRONICS RESEARCH GROUP. "Canadians continue to voice strong support for actions to address climate change, including an international treaty and carbon taxes." 2011a. http://www.environics.ca/reference-library?news_id=109

———. "Canadians feel improving the health care system lies with addressing inefficient management over expanding funding." 2011b. http://www.environics.ca/news-and-insights?news_id=110

European Union. "Europeans and Their Languages." 2012. Available at http://ec.europa.eu/languages/languages-of-europe/eurobarometer-surveyen.htm

FISHER, ELIZABETH. *Woman's Creation: Sexual Evolution and the Shaping of Society.* Garden City, NY: Anchor/Doubleday, 1979.

GAIRDNER, WILLIAM D. *The Trouble With Canada. . . Still! A Citizen Speaks Out.* Toronto: Key Porter Books, 2010.

GAUTNEY, HEATHER. *Protest and Organization in the Alternative Globalization Era: NGOs, Anti-authoritarian Movements, and Political Parties.* New York: Palgrave Macmillan, 2010.

GHOSH, RATNA. *Redefining Multicultural Education.* Toronto: Harcourt Brace Canada, 1996.

HARRIS, MARVIN. *Cultural Anthropology.* 2nd ed. New York: Harper & Row, 1987.

HAYDEN, THOMAS. "Losing Our Voices." *U.S. News & World Report* (May 26, 2003):42.

HELIN, DAVID W. "When Slogans Go Wrong." *American Demographics.* Vol. 14, No. 2 (February 1992):14.

IBM. "Web site by country/region and language." 2012. Available at http://www.ibm.com/planetwide/select/selector.htm

INGELHART, RONALD ET AL. "World Values Survey." 2012. http://www.worldvaluessurvey.com/

INGLEHART, RONALD AND CHRISTIAN WELZEL. "World Values Survey: Inglehart-Welzel Cultural Map of the World." 2010. www.worldvaluessurvey.com

INTER-PARLIAMENTARY UNION. "Women in National Parliaments." 2011. www.ipu.org/wmn-e/world.htm

KAY, PAUL, and WILLETT KEMPTON. "What Is the Sapir-Whorf Hypothesis?" *American Anthropologist.* Vol. 86, No. 1 (March 1984):65–79.

KELLER, HELEN. *The Story of My Life.* New York: Doubleday Page, 1903.

KRAYBILL, DONALD B. *The Riddle of Amish Culture.* Baltimore: Johns Hopkins University Press, 1989.

———. "The Amish Encounter with Modernity." In Donald B. Kraybill and Marc A. Olshan, eds., *The Amish Struggle with Modernity.* Hanover, NH: University Press of New England, 1994:21–33.

LEACOCK, ELEANOR. "Women's Status in Egalitarian Societies: Implications for Social Evolution." *Current Anthropology.* Vol. 19, No. 2 (June 1978):247–75.

LEWIS, M. PAUL, ED. *Ethnologue: Languages of the World.* 16th ed. Dallas, TX: SIL International, 2009.

LINTON, RALPH. "One Hundred Percent American." *American Mercury.* Vol. 40, No. 160 (April 1937):427–29.

LIPSET, SEYMOUR MARTIN. "Canada and the United States: The Cultural Dimension." In Charles F. Donan and John H. Sigler, eds., *Canada and the United States.* Englewood Cliffs, NJ: Prentice Hall, 1985.

MARX, KARL, and FRIEDRICH ENGELS. *The Marx-Engels Reader.* 2nd ed. In Robert C. Tucker, ed. New York: Norton, 1978; orig. 1859.

MORELL, VIRGINIA. "Minds of Their Own: Animals Are Smarter than You Think." *National Geographic.* Vol. 213, No. 3 (March 2008):36–61.

MURDOCK, GEORGE PETER. "The Common Denominator of Cultures." In Ralph Linton, ed., *The Science of Man in World Crisis.* New York: Columbia University Press, 1945:123–42.

NANOS, NIK. "Charter Values Don't Equal Canadian Values: Strong Support for Same-Sex and Property Rights." *Policy Options.* (February 2007):50–55.

NOLAN, PATRICK, and GERHARD E. LENSKI. *Human Societies: An Introduction to Macrosociology.* 11th ed. Boulder, CO: Paradigm, 2010.

OGBURN, WILLIAM F. *On Culture and Social Change.* Chicago: University of Chicago Press, 1964.

OGMUNDSON, R., and J. McLAUGHLIN. "Changes in An Intellectual Elite 1960–1990: The Royal Society Revisited." *Canadian Review of Sociology & Anthropology.* Vol. 31, No. 1 (February 1994):1–13.

PARSONS, TALCOTT. *Societies: Evolutionary and Comparative Perspectives.* Englewood Cliffs, NJ: Prentice Hall, 1966.

PINKER, STEVEN. *The Language Instinct.* New York: Morrow, 1994.

PORTER, JOHN. *The Vertical Mosaic.* Toronto: University of Toronto Press, 1965.

QIN, AMY. "Chinese City Defends Dog Meat Festival, Despite Scorn" *New York Times* (June 23, 2015). http://www.nytimes.com/2015/06/24/world/asia/dog-eaters-in-yulin-china-unbowed-by-global-derision.html?_r=0

REITZ, JEFFREY G. *The Survival of Ethnic Groups.* Toronto: McGraw-Hill Ryerson, 1980.

RILEY, S., C. GRIFFIN, and Y. MOREY. "The Case for 'Everyday Politics': Evaluating Neo-tribal Theory as a Way to Understand Alternative Forms of Political Participation, Using Electronic Dance Music Culture as an Example." *Sociology.* Vol. 44 (2010):345–63.

ROCHER, GUY. "The Quiet Revolution in Quebec." In James Curtis and Lorne Tepperman, eds., *Images of Canada: The Sociological Tradition.* Scarborough, ON: Prentice Hall, 1990:22–29.

SAWCHUCK, JOE. "Social Conditions of Aboriginal People." *Historica Canada.* 2011. http://www.thecanadianencyclopedia.ca/en/article/native-people-social-conditions/

SAPIR, EDWARD. "The Status of Linguistics as a Science." *Language.* Vol. 5, No. 4 (1929):207–14.

———. *Selected Writings of Edward Sapir in Language, Culture, and Personality.* David G. Mandelbaum, ed. Berkeley: University of California Press, 1949.

SRIVASTAVA, SARITA. "Troubles with 'Anti-racist Multiculturalism': The Challenges of Anti-racist and Feminist Activism." In Sean Hier and Singh Bolaria, eds., *Race and Racism in 21st Century Canada: Continuity, Complexity, and Change.* Peterborough, ON: Broadview Press, 2007:291–312.

STATISTICS CANADA. *Profile of Language, Immigration, Citizenship, Mobility and Migration for Canada, Provinces, Territories, Census Divisions and Census Subdivisions, 2006 Census.* 2007. [Online] www12.statcan.gc.ca/census-recensement/2006/dp-pd/prof/rel/Rp-eng.cfm?LANG=E&APATH=3&DETAIL=0&DIM=0&FL=A&FREE=0&GC=0&GID=0&GK=0&GRP=1&PID=89770&PRID=0&PTYPE=89103&S=0&SHOWALL=0&SUB=0&Temporal=2006&THEME=70&VID=0&VNAMEE=&VNAMEF=

———. *Place of Birth for the Immigrant Population by Period of Immigration, 2006 Counts and Percentage Distribution, for Canada, Provinces and Territories—20% Sample Data.* 2011. [Online] www12.statcan.gc.ca/census-recensement/2006/dp-pd/hlt/97-557/T404-eng.cfm?Lang=E&T=404&GH=4&GF=1&SC=1&S=1&O=D

———. *Linguistic Characteristics of Canadians: Analytical Document.* Ottawa: Statistics Canada. Catalogue no. 98-314-X2011001, 2012a.

———. *Aboriginal Languages in Canada.* 2012b. Statistics Canada Catalogue no. 98-314-X2011003. [Online] http://www12.statcan.gc.ca/census-recensement/2011/as-sa/98-314-x/98-314-x2011003_3-eng.cfm

———. *Immigration and Ethnocultural Diversity in Canada.* Ottawa: Minister of Industry. Catalogue no. 99-010-X2011001, 2013.

STEYN, MARK. "Is Canada's Economy a Model for America?" *Imprimis.* Vol. 37, No. 1 (January 2008):1–7.

STUESSY, JOE, and SCOTT LIPSCOMB. *Rock and Roll: Its History and Stylistic Development.* 6th ed. Upper Saddle River, NJ: Prentice Hall, 2009.

SUMNER, WILLIAM GRAHAM. *Folkways.* New York: Dover, 1959; orig. 1906.

TANNER, JULIAN, HARVEY KRAHN, and TIMOTHY F. HARTNAGEL. *Fractured Transitions from School to Work: Revisiting the Dropout Problem.* Toronto: Oxford University Press, 1995.

TODD, D. "B.C. Residents Ready to Combat a Decade of High Poverty: Poll." *The Vancouver Sun.* 2011.

[Online] http://communities.canada.com/vancouversun/blogs/thesearch/archive/2011/03/07/b-c-residents-ready-to-combat-a-decade-of-high-poverty.aspx

TOEWS, MIRIAM. *A Complicated Kindness.* New York: Counterpoint Press, 2005.

UNESCO. Data reported in "Tower of Babel Is Tumbling Down—Slowly." *U.S. News & World Report* (July 2, 2001):9.

———. "Toronto (Canada)." *Learning to Live Together.* 2014. [Online] http://www.unesco.org/new/en/social-and-human-sciences/themes/fight-against-discrimination/coalition-of-cities/good-practices/toronto/

WHORF, BENJAMIN LEE. "The Relation of Habitual Thought and Behavior to Language." In *Language, Thought, and Reality.* Cambridge, MA: Technology Press of MIT; New York: Wiley, 1956:134–59; orig. 1941.

WILLIAMS, ROBIN M., JR. *American Society: A Sociological Interpretation.* 3rd ed. New York: Knopf, 1970.

WORKPLACE DIVERSITY UPDATE. "Ernst & Young: Recognized Diversity Pioneer." Vol. 12, No. 4 (April 2004):1–2.

WORLD BANK. "World DataBank: Education Statistics." 2012. Available at http://databank.worldbank.org/data/views/variableselection/selectvariables.aspx?source=education-statistics

WU, ZHENG. "Premarital Cohabitation and the Timing of First Marriage." *Canadian Review of Sociology and Anthropology.* Vol. 36, No. 1 (February 1999):109–27.

YAMADA, M. "Meanings of Tattoos in the Context of Identity-Construction: A Study of Japanese Students in Canada." *Japan Studies Review.* Vol. XII (2008):3–21.

Chapter 3

AMERICAN PSYCHOLOGICAL ASSOCIATION. *Violence and Youth: Psychology's Response.* Washington, DC: American Psychological Association, 1993.

ARIES, PHILIPPE. *Centuries of Childhood: A Social History of Family Life.* New York: Vintage, 1962.

ARNETT, J. "The Developmental Context of Substance Abuse in Emerging Adulthood." *Journal of Drug Issues* (Spring 2005):235–54.

———. "Emerging Adulthood in Europe: A Response to Bynner." *Journal of Youth Studies.* Vol. 9, No. 1 (2006):111–23.

ARTZ, SIBYLLE. *Sex, Power, & the Violent School Girl.* Toronto: Trifolium Books, 1998.

ASPINALL, P. "The Conceptualisation and Categorisation of Mixed Race/Ethnicity in Britain and North America: Identity Options and the Role of the State." *International Journal of Intercultural Relations.* Vol. 27, No. 3 (2003):269–96.

BAKER, MAUREEN. *Canadian Family Policies: Cross-National Comparisons.* Toronto: University of Toronto Press, 1995.

BALDUS, BERND, and VERNA TRIBE. "Children's Perceptions of Inequality." In Lorne Tepperman and James Curtis, eds., *Everyday Life: A Reader.* Toronto: McGraw-Hill Ryerson, 1992:88–97.

BEGLEY, SHARON. "Gray Matters." *Newsweek* (March 7, 1995):48–54.

BENOIT, CECILIA, and H. HALLGRIMSDOTTIR, eds. *Valuing Care Work: Comparative Perspectives.* Toronto: University of Toronto Press, 2011.

BENOIT, CECILIA, M. JANSSON, and M. ANDERSON. "Understanding Health Disparities among Female Street Youth." In B. Leadbeater and N. Way, eds., *Urban Girls Revisited: Building Strengths.* New York: New York University Press, 2007:321–37.

BENOIT, CECILIA, M. JANSSON, H. HALLGRIMSDOTTIR, and E. ROTH. "Street Youth's Life Course Transitions." *Comparative Social Research.* Vol. 25 (2008):329–57.

BERGER, PETER L. *Invitation to Sociology.* New York: Anchor Books, 1963.

BERTRAND, JANE, MARGARET MCCAIN, J. FRASER MUSTARD, and J. DOUGLAS WILLIAMS. "A First Tier for Canadian Children: Findings from the Early Years Study in Ontario." *Atlantic Centre for Policy Research.* Fredericton, NB: University of New Brunswick. No. 6 (July 1999):1–4.

BEST, RAPHAELA. *We've All Got Scars: What Boys and Girls Learn in Elementary School.* Bloomington: Indiana University Press, 1983.

BOURDIEU, PIERRE. "The Forms of Capital." In J. Richardson, ed., *Handbook of Theory and Research for the Sociology of Education.* New York: Greenwood, 1986:241–58.

CANADIAN RADIO-TELEVISION AND TELECOMMUNICATIONS COMMISSION. "Communications Monitoring Report 2013: Broadband availability and adoption of digital technologies." 2013. http://www.crtc.gc.ca/eng/publications/reports/policymonitoring/2013/cmr6.htm

CHAPPELL, N.L. "Aging in Canada." In E. Palmore, ed., *International Handbook on Aging.* Westport, CT: Praeger Publishers, 2009.

CHAPPELL, NEENA, LYNN MACDONALD, and MICHAEL STONES. *Aging in Contemporary Canada.* 2nd ed. Toronto: Prentice Hall, 2005.

CHODOROW, NANCY. *Femininities, Masculinities, Sexualities: Freud and Beyond.* Lexington, KY: University of Kentucky Press, 1994.

CITIZENS FOR PUBLIC JUSTICE. *Poverty Trends Scorecard.* 2012. www.cpj.ca/files/docs/poverty-trends-scorecard.pdf

COOLEY, CHARLES HORTON. *Human Nature and the Social Order.* New York: Schocken Books, 1964; orig. 1902.

CURTISS, SUSAN. *Genie: A Psycholinguistic Study of a Modern-Day "Wild Child."* New York: Academic Press, 1977.

DAUVERGNE, MIA. "Adult correctional statistics in Canada, 2010/2011." *Juristat* (October 11, 2012). Catalogue no. 85-002-X. [Online] http://www.statcan.gc.ca/pub/85-002-x/2012001/article/11715-eng.htm

DAVIES, MARK, and DENISE B. KANDEL. "Parental and Peer Influences on Adolescents' Educational Plans: Some Further Evidence." *American Journal of Sociology.* Vol. 87, No. 2 (September 1981):363–87.

DAVIS, KINGSLEY. "Extreme Social Isolation of a Child." *American Journal of Sociology.* Vol. 45, No. 4 (January 1940):554–65.

———. "Final Note on a Case of Extreme Isolation." *American Journal of Sociology.* Vol. 52, No. 5 (March 1947):432–37.

DELEUZE, GILLES, and FELIX GUATTARI. *Anti-Oedipus: Capitalism and Schizophrenia.* Minneapolis: University of Minnesota Press, 1983.

DICKASON, OLIVE PATRICIA. *Canada's First Nations: A History of Founding Peoples from Earliest Times.* Toronto: McClelland and Stewart, 1992.

DONOVAN, VIRGINIA K., and RONNIE LITTENBERG. "Psychology of Women: Feminist Therapy." In Barbara Haber, ed., *The Women's Annual, 1981: The Year in Review.* Boston: Hall, 1982:211–35.

DUFF, CAMERON, AJAY K. PURI, and CLIFTON CHOW. "Ethno-Cultural Differences in the Use of Alcohol and Other Drugs: Evidence from the Vancouver Youth Drug Reporting System." *Journal of Ethnicity in Substance Abuse.* Vol. 10, No. 1 (March 2011):2–23.

EICHLER, MARGRIT. *Family Shifts: Families, Policies, and Gender Equality.* Toronto: Oxford University Press, 1997.

ELLISON, CHRISTOPHER G., JOHN P. BARTKOWSKI, and MICHELLE L. SEGAL. "Do Conservative Protestant Parents Spank More Often? Further Evidence from the National Survey of Families and Households." *Social Science Quarterly.* Vol. 77, No. 3 (September 1996):663–73.

ENSIGN, JOSEPHINE, and MICHELLE BELL. "Illness Experiences of Homeless Youth." *Qualitative Health Research.* Vol. 14, No. 9 (2004):1239–54.

ERIKSON, ERIK H. *Childhood and Society.* New York: Norton, 1963; orig. 1950.

FELLMAN, BRUCE. "Taking the Measure of Children's TV." *Yale Alumni Magazine* (April 1995):46–51.

FERNALD, ANNE, VIRGINIA A. MARCHMAN, and ADRIANA WEISLEDER. "SES differences in language processing skill and vocabulary are evident at 18 months." *Developmental Science.* Vol. 16, No. 2 (December 8, 2013):234–248. doi: 10.1111/desc.12019

FETTO, JOHN. "Me Gusta TV." *American Demographics.* Vol. 24, No. 11 (January 2003):14–15.

FRANCIS, M. "The 'Civilizing' of Indigenous People in Nineteenth-Century Canada." *World History.* Vol. 9, No. 1 (1998):51–87.

GIBBS, NANCY. "What Kids (Really) Need." *Time* (April 30, 2001):48–49.

GILLIGAN, CAROL. *In a Different Voice: Psychological Theory and Women's Development.* Cambridge, MA: Harvard University Press, 1982.

———. *Making Connections: The Relational Worlds of Adolescent Girls at Emma Willard School.* Cambridge, MA: Harvard University Press, 1990.

GOFFMAN, ERVING. *Asylums: Essays on the Social Situation of Mental Patients and Other Inmates.* Garden City, NY: Anchor Books, 1961.

GOLDBERG, BERNARD. *Bias: A CBS Insider Exposes How the Media Distort the News.* Washington, DC: Regnery, 2002.

GOLDSMITH, H.H. "Genetic Influences on Personality from Infancy." *Child Development.* Vol. 54, No. 2 (April 1983):331–35.

GORMAN, CHRISTINE. "Stressed-Out Kids." *Time* (December 25, 2000):168.

HARLOW, HARRY F., and MARGARET KUENNE HARLOW. "Social Deprivation in Monkeys." *Scientific American* (November 1962):137–46.

HERTZMAN, C. "Framework for the Social Determinants of Early Child Development." In R.E. Tremblay, R.G. Barr, R.D. Peters, and M. Boivin, eds., *Encyclopedia on Early Childhood Development.* Montreal: Centre of Excellence for Early Childhood Development, 2010:1–9. [Online] www.child-encyclopedia.com/documents/HertzmanANGxp.pdf

HERTZMAN, C., C. POWER, S. MATTHEWS, and O. MANOR. "Using an Interactive Framework of Society and Lifecourse to Explain Self-Rated Health in Early Adulthood." *Social Science & Medicine.* Vol. 53 (2001):1575–85.

HOFFMAN, JAN. "Masculinity in a Spray Can." *New York Times.* January 29, 2010. [Online] Available at http://www.nytimes.com/2010/01/31/fashion/31smell.html

HUMAN RIGHTS WATCH. "Children's Rights: Child Labor." 2006. [Online] Available April 9, 2006, at http://www.hrw.org/children/labor.htm

HYMEL, S., N. ROCKE HENDERSON, and R. BONANNO. "Moral Disengagement: A Framework for Understanding Bullying among Adolescents." *Journal of Social Sciences.* Vol. 8 (2005):1–11.

HYMOWITZ, KAY S. "Kids Today Are Growing Up Way Too Fast." *Wall Street Journal* (October 28, 1998):A22.

INTERNATIONAL LABOUR ORGANIZATION, INTERNATIONAL PROGRAMME ON THE ELIMINATION OF CHILD LABOUR (ILO-IPEC). "Children in Hazardous Work—What We Know, What We Need to Do." 2011. [Online] Available at http://www.ilo.org/ipecinfo/product/viewProduct.do?productId=17035

INTERNATIONAL TELECOMMUNICATIONS UNION. "ICT Indicators Database." 2012. Available at http://www.itu.int/ITU-D/ICTEYE/Indicators/Indicators.aspx

JORDAN, ELLEN, and ANGELA COWAN. "Warrior Narratives in the Kindergarten Classroom: Renegotiating the Social Contract?" *Gender and Society.* Vol. 9, No. 6 (December 1995):727–43.

KOBAYASHI, K.M. "Midlife Crises: Understanding the Changing Nature of Relationships in Middle Age Canadian Families." In D. Cheal, ed., *Canadian Families Today.* 2nd ed. Don Mills, ON: Oxford University Press, 2010:84–97.

KOBAYASHI, K.M., D. CLOUTIER-FISHER, and M. ROTH. "The Link Between Social Isolation and Health Among Older Adults in Small City and Small Town, British Columbia." *Journal of Aging and Health.* Vol. 21 (2009):374–97.

KOHLBERG, LAWRENCE, and CAROL GILLIGAN. "The Adolescent as Philosopher: The Discovery of Self in a Postconventional World." *Daedalus.* No. 100 (Fall 1971):1051–86.

KOHLBERG, LAWRENCE. *The Psychology of Moral Development: The Nature and Validity of Moral Stages.* New York: Harper & Row, 1981.

KOHN, MELVIN L. *Class and Conformity: A Study in Values.* 2nd ed. Homewood, IL: Dorsey Press, 1977.

KONIGSBERG, RUTH DAVIS. "New Ways to Think About Grief." *Time* [Online] Available January 29, 2011, at http://www.time.com/time/magazine/article/0,9171,2042372-2,00.html

KÜBLER-ROSS, ELISABETH. *On Death and Dying.* New York: Macmillan, 1969.

LAREAU, ANNETTE. "Invisible Inequality: Social Class and Childrearing in Black Families and White Families." *American Sociological Review*. Vol. 67, No. 5 (October 2002):747–76.

LAROSSA, RALPH, and DONALD C. REITZES. "Two? Two and One-Half? Thirty Months? Chronometrical Childhood in Early Twentieth-Century America." *Sociological Forum*. Vol. 166, No. 3 (September 2001):385–407.

LICHTER, S. ROBERT, and DANIEL R. AMUNDSON. "Distorted Reality: Hispanic Characters in TV Entertainment." In Clara E. Rodriguez, ed., *Latin Looks: Images of Latinas and Latinos in the U.S. Media*. Boulder, CO: Westview Press, 1997:57–79.

MEAD, GEORGE HERBERT. *Mind, Self, and Society*. Charles W. Morris, ed. Chicago: University of Chicago Press, 1962; orig. 1934.

MELTZER, BERNARD N. "Mead's Social Psychology." In Jerome G. Manis and Bernard N. Meltzer, eds., *Symbolic Interaction: A Reader in Social Psychology*. 3rd ed. Needham Heights, MA: Allyn & Bacon, 1978.

METZ, MICHAEL E., and MICHAEL H. MINER. "Psychosexual and Psychosocial Aspects of Male Aging and Sexual Health." *Canadian Journal of Human Sexuality*. Vol. 7, No. 3 (Summer 1998):245–60.

MILLIGAN, K. "The Evolution of Elderly Poverty in Canada." Social and Economic Dimensions of an Aging Population (SEDAP) Research Paper 170. Hamilton, ON: McMaster University, 2007.

MITCHELL, BARBARA A. *The Boomerang Age: Transitions to Adulthood in Families*. New Brunswick, NJ: Aldine Transaction, 2006.

MORETTI, M., M. JACKSON, and C. ODGERS, eds. *Girls and Aggression: Contributing Factors and Intervention Principles*. New York: Kluwer Academic Publishers, 2004.

NELSON, L., and C. BARRY. "Distinguishing Features of Emerging Adulthood: The Role of Self-Classification as an Adult." *Journal of Adolescent Research*. Vol. 20 (2005):242–62.

NORC. *General Social Surveys, 1972–2010: Cumulative Codebook*. Chicago: National Opinion Research Center, 2011. Available at http://www.norc.org/GSS+Website

ORNELAS, I., K. PERREIRA, and G. AYALA. "Parental Influences on Adolescent Physical Activity: A Longitudinal Study." *International Journal of Behavioral Nutrition and Physical Activity*. Vol. 4, No. 3 (2007). doi:10.1186/1479-5868-4-3 [Online] www.ijbnpa.org/content/4/1/3

PUBLIC HEALTH AGENCY OF CANADA. 2009. Analyses performed using Health Canada's DAIS edition of anonymized microdata from the *Canadian Community Health Survey 2009: Healthy Aging*, prepared by Statistics Canada.

RIDEOUT, VICTORIA. "Parents, Children, and Media: A Kaiser Family Foundation Survey." June 2007. www.kff.org/entmedia/upload/7638.pdf

ROTHMAN, STANLEY, STEPHEN POWERS, and DAVID ROTHMAN. "Feminism in Films." *Society*. Vol. 30, No. 3 (March/April 1993):66–72.

RYMER, RUSS. *Genie*. New York: HarperPerennial, 1994.

SCHULENBERG, J.E., A.C. MERLINE, L. JOHNSTON, P. O'MALLEY, and J. BACHMAN. "Trajectories of Marijuana Use During the Transition to Adulthood: The Big Picture Based on National Panel Data." *Journal of Drug Issues*. Vol. 35, No. 2 (2005):255–79.

SINGER, J.L. and D.G. SINGER. "Psychologists Look at Television: Cognitive, Developmental, Personality, and Social Policy Implications." *American Psychologist*. Vol. 38, No. 7 (July 1983):826–34.

SMITH, TOM W. "Are We Grown Up Yet? U.S. Study Says Not 'til 26." *Yahoo! News* (May 23, 2003). http://news.yahoo.com

SPENCER STUART. "Leading CEOs: A Statistical Snapshot of S&P 500 Leaders." December 2008. www.spencerstuart.com/research/articles/975

STATISTICS CANADA. *Women in Canada 2000: A Gender-based Statistical Report*. Ottawa: Housing, Family and Social Statistics Division. Catalogue no. 89-503XPE. Ottawa: Ministry of Industry, 2000.

———. *Earnings and Incomes of Canadians over the Past Quarter Century, 2006 Census*. 2008a. [Online] www.statcan.gc.ca/bsolc/olc-cel/olc-cel?catno=97-563-XIE2006001&lang=eng

———. *Estimates of population, by age group and sex for July 1, Canada, provinces and territories, annual*. CANSIM table 051-0001. Ottawa: Statistics Canada, 2010. http://www23.statcan.gc.ca/imdb/p2SV.pl?Function =getSurvey&SDDS=3604.

———. *Figure 15, More Young Adults in Their Twenties Live in the Parental Home in 2006*. 2011. [Online] www12.statcan.ca/census-recensement/2006/as-sa/97-553/figures/c15-eng.cfm.

———. *Census metropolitan areas and census agglomerations, 2011*. Produced by the Geography Division, Statistics Canada, 2012a. http://www12.statcan.ca/census-recensement/2011/geo/map-carte/ref/thematic_download_as-thematiques_telecharger_as-eng.cfm? SERIES=B&MAPCODE=01

———. *The Canadian Population in 2011: Age and Sex: Analytical Document*. Ottawa: Statistics Canada. Catalogue no. 98-311-X2011001, 2012b.

———. *Life expectancy, at birth and at age 65, by sex, Canada, provinces and territories*. CANSIM Table 102-0512 [Electronic Data Base]. 2012c.

———. *Ethnic Origin (264), Single and Multiple Ethnic Origin Responses (3), Generation Status (4), Age Groups (10) and Sex (3) for the Population in Private Households of Canada, Provinces, Territories, Census Metropolitan Areas and Census Agglomerations, 2011 National Household Survey*. Catalogue no. 99-010-X2011028. 2013a.

———. "Canadian Internet Use Survey, 2012" *The Daily* (November 26, 2013b). http://www.statcan.gc.ca/daily-quotidien/131126/dq131126d-eng.htm

STEVENSON, KATHRYN. "Family Characteristics of Problem Kids." *Canadian Social Trends*. Vol. 55 (Winter 1999):2–6.

TANNER, JULIAN, HARVEY KRAHN, and TIMOTHY F. HARTNAGEL. *Fractured Transitions from School to Work: Revisiting the Dropout Problem*. Toronto: Oxford University Press, 1995.

TELEVISION BUREAU OF CANADA. "Television Basics: 2013-2014." 2013. http://www.tvb.ca/pages/tvbasics

THRUPKAEW, NOY. "No Minor Issue." *National Geographic*. Vol. 218, No. 5 (November 2010):18.

TREAS, JUDITH. "Older Americans in the 1990s and Beyond." *Population Bulletin*. Vol. 50, No. 2 (May 1995).

TVB. "TV Basics." August 2012. Available at http://www.tvb.org/trends/95487=U.S. Census Bureau. "Age and Sex Composition: 2010." 2011. Available at http://www.census.gov/prod/cen2010/briefs/c2010br-03.pdf

UNICEF. "ChildInfo Statistics by Area: Child Survival and Health." 2012. Available at http://www.childinfo.org/

U.S. DEPARTMENT OF LABOR. "List of Goods Produced by Child Labor or Forced Labor, 2012." 2012. Available at http://www.dol.gov/ilab/programs/ocft/2012TVPRA.pdf

WEITZMAN, LENORE J. *The Divorce Revolution: The Unexpected Social and Economic Consequences for Women and Children in America*. New York: Free Press, 1985.

———. "The Economic Consequences of Divorce Are Still Unequal: Comment on Peterson." *American Sociological Review*. Vol. 61, No. 3 (June 1996):537–38.

WHITE, JENNIFER and MICHAEL J. KRAL. "Re-Thinking Youth Suicide: Language, Culture, and Power." *Journal for Social Action in Counseling and Psychology*. Vol. 6, No. 1 (Summer 2014):122-42.

WILSON, CLINT C., II, and FELIX GUTIERREZ. *Minorities and Media: Diversity and the End of Mass Communication*. Beverly Hills, CA: Sage, 1985.

Chapter 4

BAKALAR, NICHOLAS. "Reactions: Go On, Laugh Your Heart Out." *New York Times* (March 8, 2005). www.nytimes.com/2005/03/08/health/08reac.html

BAKER, PATRICIA S., WILLIAM C. YOELS, JEFFREY M. CLAIR, and RICHARD M. ALLMAN. "Laughter in the Triadic Geriatric Encounters: A Transcript-Based Analysis." In Rebecca J. Erikson and Beverly Cuthbertson-Johnson, eds., *Social Perspectives on Emotion*. Vol. 4. Greenwich, CT: JAI Press, 1997:179–207.

BENOKRAITIS, NIJOLE, and JOE R. FEAGIN. *Modern Sexism: Blatant, Subtle, and Overt Discrimination*. 2nd ed. Englewood Cliffs, NJ: Prentice Hall, 1995.

BERGER, PETER L., and THOMAS LUCKMANN. *The Social Construction of Reality: A Treatise in the Sociology of Knowledge*. Toronto: Penguin, 1966.

BOURDIEU, P. *Language and Symbolic Power*. Cambridge, UK: Polity Press, 1993.

BRODY, L. *Gender, Emotion, and Family*. Cambridge, MA: Harvard University Press, 1999.

BUTLER, JUDITH. *Excitable Speech: A Politics of the Performative*. London: Routledge, 1997.

DARLING, ROSALYN, and BENJAMIN BRYANT. "Stigma of Disability." In D. Clifton, ed., *Encyclopedia of Criminology and Deviant Behavior*. Philadelphia, PA: Brunner-Routledge, 2001:482–85.

DAVIES, CHRISTIE. *Ethnic Humor around the World: A Comparative Analysis*. Bloomington: Indiana University Press, 1990.

EBAUGH, HELEN ROSE FUCHS. *Becoming an Ex: The Process of Role Exit*. Chicago: University of Chicago Press, 1988.

EKMAN, PAUL. "Biological and Cultural Contributions to Body and Facial Movements in the Expression of Emotions." In A. Rorty, ed., *Explaining Emotions*. Berkeley: University of California Press, 1980a:73–101.

———. *Face of Man: Universal Expression in a New Guinea Village*. New York: Garland Press, 1980b.

FARRELL, MICHAEL B. "Cambridge Becoming Social Media Research Hub." *Boston Globe* (July 28, 2012). Available at http://www.bostonglobe.com/business/2012/07/27/cambridge-becoming-hub-for-social-media-research-from-mit-Microsoft/eG9s355T8Tg5YIJWuulqXN/story.html

FARRIS, COREEN, TERESA A. TREAT, RICHARD J. VIKEN, and RICHARD M. MCFALL. "Perceptual Mechanisms That Characterize Gender Differences in Decoding Women's Sexual Intent." *Psychological Science*. Vol. 19, No. 4 (2008):348–54.

FLAHERTY, MICHAEL G. "A Formal Approach to the Study of Amusement in Social Interaction." *Studies in Symbolic Interaction*. Vol. 5. New York: JAI Press, 1984:71–82.

———. "Two Conceptions of the Social Situation: Some Implications of Humor." *Sociological Quarterly*. Vol. 31, No. 1 (Spring 1990):93–106.

FLOWERS, PAUL, MARK DAVIS, GRAHAM HART, MARSHA ROSENGARTEN, JAMIE FRANKIS, and JOHN IMRIE. "Diagnosis and Stigma and Identity amongst HIV Positive Black Africans Living in the UK." *Psychology & Health*. Vol. 21, No. 1 (2006):109–22.

FOX, B. *When Couples Become Parents: The Creation of Gender in the Transition to Parenthood*. Toronto: University of Toronto Press, 2009.

GARFINKEL, HAROLD. *Studies in Ethnomethodology*. Cambridge, UK: Polity Press, 1967.

GOFFMAN, ERVING. *The Presentation of Self in Everyday Life*. Garden City, NY: Anchor Books, 1959.

———. *Interactional Ritual: Essays on Face to Face Behavior*. Garden City, NY: Anchor Books, 1967.

HENLEY, NANCY, MYKOL HAMILTON, and BARRIE THORNE. "Womanspeak and Manspeak: Sex Differences in Communication, Verbal and Nonverbal." In John J. Macionis and Nijole V. Benokraitis, eds., *Seeing Ourselves: Classic, Contemporary, and Cross-Cultural Readings in Sociology*. 2nd ed. Englewood Cliffs, NJ: Prentice Hall, 1992.

HOCHSCHILD, ARLIE RUSSELL. "Emotion Work, Feeling Rules, and Social Structure." *American Journal of Sociology*. Vol. 85, No. 3 (November 1979):551–75.

———. *The Managed Heart*. Berkeley: University of California Press, 1983.

JOHNSON, CATHRYN. "Gender, Legitimate Authority, and Leader-Subordinate Conversations." *American Sociological Review*. Vol. 59, No. 1 (February 1994):122–35.

KEYS, JENNIFER. "Running the Gauntlet: Women's Use of Emotional Management Techniques in the Abortion Experience," *Symbolic Interaction*, Vol. 33, No. 1 (Winter 2010): 41–70. http://www.jstor.org/stable/10.1525/si.2010.33.1.41

LEE, Z. "Korean Culture and Sense of Shame." *Transcultural Psychiatry*. Vol. 36 (1999):181–94.

LINK, BRUCE, and JO PHELAN. "Social Conditions as Fundamental Causes of Disease." *Journal of Health and Social Behavior*. Extra Issue, 1995:80–94.

LINTON, RALPH. *The Study of Man.* New York: Appleton-Century, 1937.

MACIONIS, JOHN J. "A Sociological Analysis of Humor." Presentation to the Texas Junior College Teachers Association, Houston, 1987.

MCCREATH, G. *The Politics of Blindness: From Charity to Parity.* Vancouver: Granville Island Publishing, 2011.

MCDANIEL, SUSAN A. "Women's Changing Relations to the State and Citizenship: Caring and Intergenerational Relations in Globalizing Western Democracies." *Canadian Review of Sociology and Anthropology.* Vol. 39, No. 2 (2002):1–26.

MERTON, ROBERT K. *Social Theory and Social Structure.* New York: Free Press, 1968.

NACK, ADINA. "Bad Girls and Fallen Women: Chronic STD Diagnoses as Gateways to Tribal Stigma." *Symbolic Interaction.* Vol. 25 (2002):463–85.

NANCARROW CLARKE, JUANNE, and LAUREN NANCARROW CLARKE. *Finding Strength. A Mother and Daughter's Story of Childhood Cancer.* Toronto: Oxford University Press, 1999.

NIPPERT-ENG, CHRISTENA E. *Home and Work: Negotiating Boundaries through Everyday Life.* Chicago: The University of Chicago Press, 1995.

NOSEK, MARGARET A., ROSEMARY B. HUGHES, NANCY SWEDLUND, HEATHER B. TAYLOR, and PAUL SWANK. "Self-Esteem and Women with Disabilities." *Social Science & Medicine.* Vol. 56 (2003):1737–47.

ORLANSKY, MICHAEL D., and WILLIAM L. HEWARD. *Voices: Interviews with Handicapped People.* Columbus, OH: Merrill, 1981.

PIRANDELLO, LUIGI. "The Pleasure of Honesty" (1917). In *To Clothe the Naked and Two Other Plays.* New York: Dutton, 1962:143–98.

POWELL, CHRIS, and GEORGE E.C. PATON, eds. *Humor in Society: Resistance and Control.* New York: St. Martin's Press, 1988.

PRIMEGGIA, SALVATORE, and JOSEPH A. VARACALLI. "Southern Italian Comedy: Old to New World." In Joseph V. Scelsa, Salvatore J. La Gumina, and Lydio Tomasi, eds., *Italian Americans in Transition.* New York: American Italian Historical Association, 1990:241–52.

SANSOM, WILLIAM. *A Contest of Ladies.* London: Hogarth, 1956.

SAUNDERS, T. "Becoming an Ex-Sex Worker: Making Transitions Out of a Deviant Career." *Feminist Criminology.* Vol. 2, No. 1 (2007):74–95.

SHIVELY, JOELLEN. "Cowboys and Indians: Perceptions of Western Films among American Indians and Anglos." *American Sociological Review.* Vol. 57, No. 6 (December 1992):725–34.

SIMMEL, GEORG. *The Sociology of Georg Simmel.* Kurt Wolff, ed. New York: Free Press, 1950; orig. 1902.

SMITH-LOVIN, LYNN, and CHARLES BRODY. "Interruptions in Group Discussions: The Effects of Gender and Group Composition." *American Journal of Sociology.* Vol. 54, No. 3 (June 1989):424–35.

SPEIER, HANS. "Wit and Politics: An Essay on Laughter and Power." Robert Jackall, ed. and trans. *American Journal of Sociology.* Vol. 103, No. 5 (March 1998): 1352–401.

STEPANIKOVA, IRENA, QIAN ZHANG, DARRYL WIELAND, G. PAUL ELEAZER, and THOMAS STEWART. "Non-Verbal Communication between Primary Care Physicians and Older Patients: How Does Race Matter?" *Journal of General Internal Medicine* (December 6, 2011). Available at http://www.springerlink.com/content/d84k724x813755g1/fulltext.html

SVEBAK, SVEN. Cited in Marilyn Elias, "Study Links Sense of Humor, Survival." [Online] Available March 14, 2007, at http://www.usatoday.com

TAUB, DIANE E., PENELOPE A. MCLORG, and PATRICIA L. FANFLIK. "Stigma Management Strategies among Women with Physical Disabilities: Contrasting Approaches of Downplaying or Claiming a Disability Status." *Deviant Behavior.* Vol. 25, No. 2 (2004):169–90.

THOMAS, PIRI. *Down These Mean Streets.* New York: Signet, 1967.

THOMAS, W.I. "The Relation of Research to the Social Process." In Morris Janowitz, ed., *W.I. Thomas on Social Organization and Social Personality.* Chicago: University of Chicago Press, 1966:289–305; orig. 1931.

THOMAS, W.I., and DOROTHY SWAINE THOMAS. *The Child in America: Behavior Problems and Programs.* New York: Knopf, 1928.

THORNE, BARRIE, CHERIS KRAMARAE, and NANCY HENLEY, eds. *Language, Gender, and Society.* Rowley, MA: Newbury House, 1983.

TREVIÑO, JAVIER, ed. *Goffman's Legacy.* Lanham, MD: Rowman & Littlefield Publishers, Inc., 2003.

TURKLE, SHERRY. *Alone Together: Why We Expect More from Technology and Less from Each Other.* New York: Basic Books, 2012.

TURNER, JONATHAN. *On the Origins of Human Emotions: A Sociological Inquiry into the Evolution of Human Emotions.* Stanford, CA: Stanford University Press, 2000.

UNITED NATIONS. "The World's Women 2010: Trends and Statistics." 2010. Available at http://unstats.un.org/unsd/demographic/products/Worldswomen/wwwork2010.htm

VAN STERKENBURG, J., and A. KNOPPERS. "Dominant Discourses about Race/Ethnicity and Gender in Sport Practice and Performance." *International Review for the Sociology of Sport.* Vol. 39, No. 3 (2004):301–21.

VEENHOF, BEN, and PETER TIMUSK. "Online activities of Canadian boomers and seniors." *Canadian Social Trends,* Statistics Canada, Catalogue no. 11-008. 2009.

WALLACE, JEAN. "Social Relationships, Well-Being, and Career Commitment: Exploring Cross-Domain Effects of Social Relationships." *Canadian Review of Sociology.* Vol. 50, No. 2 (2013):135–153.

WTULICH, JOESPHINE. *American Xenophobia and the Slav Immigrant.* New York: East European Monographs, 1994.

YOELS, WILLIAM C., and JEFFREY MICHAEL CLAIR. "Laughter in the Clinic: Humor in Social Organization." *Symbolic Interaction.* Vol. 18, No. 1 (1995):39–58.

Chapter 5

ALLEN, THOMAS B., AND CHARLES O. HYMAN. *We Americans: Celebrating a Nation, Its People, and Its Past.* Washington, DC: National Geographic Society, 1999.

ARMSTRONG, PAT, AND HUGH ARMSTRONG. *Wasting Away: The Undermining of Canadian Health Care.* Toronto: Oxford University Press, 1996.

———. *Wasting Away: The Undermining of Canadian Health Care.* 2nd ed. Toronto: Oxford University Press, 2002.

"Army Apologizes" (January 7, 2009). www.reuters.com/article/idUSTRE50674G20090107

ASCH, SOLOMON. *Social Psychology.* Englewood Cliffs, NJ: Prentice Hall, 1952.

BALL, KIRSTIE. "Workplace Surveillance: An Overview." *Labor History.* Vol. 51, No. 1 (February 2010):87–106.

BARKER, ADAM. "'A Direct Act of Resurgence, a Direct Act of Sovereignty': Reflections on Idle No More, Indigenous Activism, and Canadian Settler Colonialism." *Globalizations* (2014). doi: 10.1080/14747731.2014.971531

BARON, JAMES N., MICHAEL T. HANNAN, AND M. DIANE BURTON. "Building the Iron Cage: Determinants of Managerial Intensity in the Early Years of Organizations." *American Sociological Review.* Vol. 64, No. 4 (August 1999):527–47.

BENOIT, CECILIA. *Women, Work and Social Rights: Canada in Historical and Comparative Perspective.* Scarborough, ON: Prentice Hall Canada, 2000.

BLAU, PETER M. *Inequality and Heterogeneity: A Primitive Theory of Social Structure.* New York: Free Press, 1977.

BLAU, PETER M., TERRY C. BLUM, AND JOSEPH E. SCHWARTZ. "Heterogeneity and Intermarriage." *American Sociological Review.* Vol. 47, No. 1 (February 1982):45–62.

BOBO, LAWRENCE, AND VINCENT L. HUTCHINGS. "Perceptions of Racial Group Competition: Extending Blumer's Theory of Group Position to a Multiracial Social Context." *American Sociological Review.* Vol. 61, No. 6 (December 1996):951–72.

BROOKS, DAVID. *Bobos in Paradise: The New Upper Class and How They Got There.* New York: Simon & Schuster, 2000.

CANADIAN BANKERS ASSOCIATION. "Credit Cards: Statistics and Facts." (May 2014). [Online] http://www.cba.ca/en/media-room/50-backgrounders-on-banking-issues/123-credit-cards

CASTILLA, EMILIO J. "Gender, Race, and Meritocracy in Organizational Careers." *American Journal of Sociology.* Vol. 113, No. 6 (May 2008):1479–526.

CHEN, W., AND BARRY WELLMAN. "Net and Jet: The Internet Use, Travel and Social Networks of Chinese Canadian Entrepreneurs." *Information, Communication and Society.* Vol. 12, No. 4 (2009):525–47.

CHRISTIE, NANCY. *Engendering the State: Family, Work, and Welfare in Canada.* Toronto: University of Toronto Press, 2000.

DREW, S., M. MILLS, and B. GASSAWAY. *Dirty Work: The Social Construction of Taint.* Waco, TX: Baylor University Press, 2007.

EAGLY, A., and M. JOHANNESEN-SCHMIDT. "The Leadership Styles of Women and Men." *Journal of Social Issues.* Vol. 57, No. 4 (2001):781–97.

EAGLY, ALICE H., MARY C. JOHANNESEN-SCHMIDT, and MARLOES L. VAN ENGEN. "Transformational, Transactional, and Laissez-Faire Leadership Styles: A Meta-Analysis Comparing Women and Men." *Psychological Bulletin.* Vol. 129, No. 4 (July 2003):569–91.

ETZIONI, AMITAI. *A Comparative Analysis of Complex Organization: On Power, Involvement, and Their Correlates.* Rev. and enlarged ed. New York: Free Press, 1975.

FERNANDEZ, ROBERTO M., and NANCY WEINBERG. "Sifting and Sorting: Personal Contacts and Hiring in a Retail Bank." *American Sociological Review.* Vol. 62, No. 6 (December 1997):883–902.

GOODNIGHT, RONALD. "Laissez-faire leadership." *The Economic Journal* 98, no. 392 (2004): 755–771.

GREEN, GARY PAUL, LEANN M. TIGGES, and DANIEL DIAZ. "Racial and Ethnic Differences in Job-Search Strategies in Atlanta, Boston, and Los Angeles." *Social Science Quarterly.* Vol. 80, No. 2 (June 1999):263–90.

GWYNNE, S.C., and JOHN F. DICKERSON. "Lost in the E-mail." *Time* (April 21, 1997):88–90.

HAGAN, JACQUELINE MARIA. "Social Networks, Gender, and Immigrant Incorporation: Resources and Restraints." *American Sociological Review.* Vol. 63, No. 1 (February 1998):55–67.

HALBERSTAM, DAVID. *The Reckoning.* New York: Avon Books, 1986.

HARRISON, D. "The Role of Military Culture in Military Organizations Responses to Woman Abuse in Military Families." *The Sociological Review.* Vol. 54, No. 3 (2006):546–574.

HARRISON, DEBORAH, and LUCIE LALIBERTÉ. *No Life Like It: Military Wives in Canada.* Toronto: James Lorimer & Company, 1994.

HELGESEN, SALLY. *The Female Advantage: Women's Ways of Leadership.* New York: Doubleday, 1990.

HEYMANN, PHILIP B. "Civil Liberties and Human Rights in the Aftermath of September 11." *Harvard Journal of Law and Public Policy.* Vol. 25, No. 2 (Spring 2002):441–57.

HIER, SEAN. *Panoptic Dreams: Streetscape Video Surveillance in Canada.* Vancouver: UBC Press, 2010.

HUI, SYLVIA. "Bloomberg Takes Cues from London's Security-Obsessed Security." *The Huffington Post.* [Online] Available May 11, 2010, at http://www.huffingtonpost.com/2010/05/11/bloomberg-taking-cues-fro_n_571359.html

IDE, THOMAS R., and ARTHUR J. CORDELL. "Automating Work." *Society.* Vol. 31, No. 6 (September/October 1994):65–71.

INTERNATIONAL TELECOMMUNICATIONS UNION. "ICT Indicators Database." 2012 Available at http://www.itu.int/ITU-D/ict/publications/

JANIS, IRVING L. *Victims of Groupthink.* Boston: Houghton Mifflin, 1972.

———. *Crucial Decisions: Leadership in Policymaking and Crisis Management.* New York: Free Press, 1989.

KAMINER, WENDY. "Volunteers: Who Knows What's in It for Them?" *Ms.* (December 1984):93–96, 126–28.

KANTER, ROSABETH MOSS, and BARRY A. STEIN. "The Gender Pioneers: Women in an Industrial Sales Force." In Rosabeth Moss Kanter and Barry A. Stein, eds., *Life in Organizations.* New York: Basic Books, 1979:134–60.

KANTER, ROSABETH MOSS. *Men and Women of the Corporation.* New York: Basic Books, 1977.

KAPLAN-MYRTH, N. "Sorry Mates: Reconciliation and Self-Determination in Australian Aboriginal Health." *Human Rights Review*. Vol. 6, No. 4 (2005):69–83.

KISS, SIMON and VINCENT MOSCO. "Negotiating Electronic Surveillance in the Workplace: A Study of Collective Agreements in Canada." *Canadian Journal of Communication*. Vol. 30, No. 4 (2005):549–564.

LIN, NAN, KAREN COOK, and RONALD S. BURT, EDS. *Social Capital: Theory and Research*. Hawthorne, NY: Aldine de Gruyter, 2001.

MADDOX, SETMA. "Organizational Culture and Leadership Style: Factors Affecting Self-Managed Work Team Performance." Paper presented at the annual meeting of the Southwest Social Science Association, Dallas, February 1994.

McDONALD'S CORPORATION. "Company Profile." 2012. Available at http://www.aboutmcdonalds.com/mcd/investors/company_profile.html

MEIER, FRED. "Toyota All but Locks Sales Crown for 2012, Dumping GM." *USA Today* (July 25, 2012). Available at http://content.usatoday.com/communities/driveon/post/2012/07/toyota-all-but-locks-sales-crown-for-2012-dumping-gm/1#.UX_AwLXCaSp

MERTON, ROBERT K. *Social Theory and Social Structure*. New York: Free Press, 1968.

MICHELS, ROBERT. *Political Parties*. Glencoe, IL: Free Press, 1949; orig. 1911.

MILGRAM, STANLEY. "Behavioral Study of Obedience." *Journal of Abnormal and Social Psychology*. Vol. 67, No. 4 (November 1963):371–78.

———. "Group Pressure and Action Against a Person." *Journal of Abnormal and Social Psychology*. Vol. 69, No. 2 (August 1964):137–43.

———. "Some Conditions of Obedience and Disobedience to Authority." *Human Relations*. Vol. 18, No. 1 (February 1965):57–76.

———. "The Small World Problem." *Psychology Today* (May 1967):60–67.

MILLER, ARTHUR G. *The Obedience Experiments: A Case of Controversy in Social Science*. New York: Praeger, 1986.

MORRISETTE, RENE, GRANT SCHELLENBERG, and ANICK JOHNSON. "Diverging Trends in Unionization." *Perspectives on Labour and Income*. Vol. 6, No. 4 (April 2005):5–12.

MULLIGAN-FERRY, LIZ, ANDREW MALORDY, and ASHLEY PETER. *2012 Catalyst Census: Financial Post 500 Women Senior Officers and Top Earners*. 2013. [Online] http://www.catalyst.org/knowledge/2012-catalyst-census-financial-post-500-women-senior-officers-and-top-earners

O'HARROW, ROBERT, JR. "ID Theft Scam Hits D.C. Area Residents." *Yahoo! News* (February 21, 2005). http://news.yahoo.com

"Online Privacy: It's Time for Rules in Wonderland." *Business Week* (March 20, 2000):82–96.

OUCHI, WILLIAM. *Theory Z: How American Business Can Meet the Japanese Challenge*. Reading, MA: Addison-Wesley, 1981.

PETERSEN, TROND, ISHAK SAPORTA, and MARC-DAVID L. SEIDEL. "Offering a Job: Meritocracy and Social Networks." *American Journal of Sociology*. Vol. 106, No. 3 (November 2000):763–816.

PHILADELPHIA, DESA. "Tastier, Plusher—and Fast." *Time* (September 30, 2002):57.

PINCHOT, GIFFORD, and ELIZABETH PINCHOT. *The End of Bureaucracy and the Rise of the Intelligent Organization*. San Francisco: Berrett-Koehler, 1993

PODOLNY, JOEL M., and JAMES N. BARON. "Resources and Relationships: Social Networks and Mobility in the Workplace." *American Sociological Review*. Vol. 62, No. 5 (October 1997):673–93.

RESKIN, BARBARA F., and DEBRA BRANCH MCBRIER. "Why Not Ascription? Organizations' Employment of Male and Female Managers." *American Sociological Review*. Vol. 65, No. 2 (April 2000):210–33.

RIDGEWAY, CECILIA L. *The Dynamics of Small Groups*. New York: St. Martin's Press, 1983.

RITZER, GEORGE. *The McDonaldization of Society: An Investigation into the Changing Character of Contemporary Social Life*. Thousand Oaks, CA: Pine Forge Press, 1993

ROSSEN, JEFF., and TRACY CONNOR. "NYC has 'smart' camera network to thwart terror attacks." *NBC News*. April 25, 2013. http://usnews.nbcnews.com/_news/2013/04/25/17916487-nyc-has-smart-camera-network-to-thwart-terror-attacks

SAPORITO, BILL. "Spotlight: Toyota's Recall." *Time* (February 15, 2010):17.

SCHLOSSER, ERIC. *Fast-Food Nation: The Dark Side of the All-American Meal*. New York: Perennial, 2002.

SEGALL, A., and C. FRIES. *Pursuing Health and Wellness Healthy Societies, Healthy People*. New York: Oxford University Press, 2011.

SHIPLEY, JOSEPH T. *Dictionary of Word Origins*. Totowa, NJ: Rowman & Allanheld, 1985.

SIMMEL, GEORG. *The Sociology of Georg Simmel*. Kurt Wolff, ed. New York: Free Press, 1950; orig. 1902.

SOUTH, SCOTT J., and STEVEN F. MESSNER. "Structural Determinants of Intergroup Association: Interracial Marriage and Crime." *American Journal of Sociology*. Vol. 91, No. 6 (May 1986):1409–30.

STATISTICS CANADA. *Women in Canada: A Gender-based Statistical Report*. 2011. http://www.statcan.gc.ca/pub/89-503-x/89-503-x2010001-eng.htm

———. "Residential Telephone Service Survey, 2013." *The Daily* (June 23, 2014). [Online] http://www.statcan.gc.ca/daily-quotidien/140623/dq140623a-eng.htm

STEIN, JOEL. "Your Data, Yourself." *Time*. Vol. 177, No. 11 (March 21, 2011):40–46.

STOUFFER, SAMUEL A., et al. *The American Soldier: Adjustment during Army Life*. Princeton, NJ: Princeton University Press, 1949.

SULLIVAN, BARBARA. "McDonald's Sees India as Golden Opportunity." *Chicago Tribune* (April 5, 1995):B1.

TAJFEL, HENRI. "Social Psychology of Intergroup Relations." *Annual Review of Psychology*. Palo Alto, CA: Annual Reviews, 1982:1–39.

TANNEN, DEBORAH. *Talking from 9 to 5: How Women's and Men's Conversational Styles Affect Who Gets Heard, Who Gets Credit, and What Gets Done at Work*. New York: Morrow, 1994.

TAYLOR, FREDERICK WINSLOW. *The Principles of Scientific Management*. New York: Harper & Brothers, 1911.

TINGWALL, ERIC. "Auto Insurance Gets Cheaper but Potentially More Invasive." *Automobile* (December 2008):74.

TOLSON, JAY. "The Trouble with Elites." *Wilson Quarterly*. Vol. 19, No. 1 (Winter 1995):6–8.

TORRES, LISA, and MATT L. HUFFMAN. "Social Networks and Job Search Outcomes among Male and Female Professional, Technical, and Managerial Workers." *Sociological Focus*. Vol. 35, No. 1 (February 2002):25–42.

UPPAL, SHARANJI. "Unionization 2010." *Perspectives on Labour and Income*. Vol. 11, No. 10 (2010):18–27.

VÉZINA, MIREILLE and SUSAN CROMPTON. "Volunteering in Canada." *Canadian Social Trends*. Statistics Canada Catalogue no. 11-008-X. 2012. http://www.statcan.gc.ca/pub/11-008-x/2012001/article/11638-eng.pdf

WALBY, KEVIN. "Open-Street Camera Surveillance and Governance in Canada." *Canadian Journal of Criminology and Criminal Justice*. Vol. 47, No. 4 (October 2005):655–83.

WATTS, DUNCAN J. "Networks, Dynamics, and the Small-World Phenomenon." *American Journal of Sociology*. Vol. 105, No. 2 (September 1999):493–527.

WEBER, MAX. *Economy and Society: An Outline of Interpretive Sociology*. Guenther Roth and Claus Wittich, eds. Berkeley: University of California Press, 1978; orig. 1921.

WELCH, MARY AGNES. "A crippling case of red tape." *Winnipeg Free Press* (March 21, 2014):A3.

WELLMAN, BARRY, ED. *Networks in the Global Village*. Boulder, CO: Westview Press, 1999.

WERTH, CHRISTOPHER. "To Watch the Watchers." *Newsweek* (October 20, 2008):E4.

WHITE, RALPH, and RONALD LIPPITT. "Leader Behavior and Member Reaction in Three 'Social Climates.'" In Dorwin Cartwright and Alvin Zander, eds., *Group Dynamics*. Evanston, IL: Row & Peterson, 1953:586–611.

WILDAVSKY, BEN. "Small World, Isn't It?" *U.S. News & World Report* (April 1, 2002):68.

YEATTS, DALE E. "Creating the High Performance Self-Managed Work Team: A Review of Theoretical Perspectives." Paper presented at the annual meeting of the Southwest Social Science Association, Dallas, February 1994.

Chapter 6

ABEL, G., L. FITZGERALD, and C. HEALY, eds. *Taking the Crime out of Sex Work: New Zealand Sex Workers' Fight for Decriminalisation*. Bristol, UK: Policy Press, 2010.

ALAN GUTTMACHER INSTITUTE. "U.S. Teenage Pregnancies, Births, and Abortions, 2008: National Trends by Race and Ethnicity." February 2012. Available at http://www.guttmacher.org/pubs/USTPtrends08.pdf

ANGUS REID GROUP INC. *Let's Talk About Sex, Tables*. Public release (March 3, 1998a). [Online] www.ipsos-reid.com/media/content/pdf/pr030398tb.pdf

ANGUS REID GLOBAL. *Gender split reveals deep divide between men, women on issues surrounding the sex trade*. Public release (June 10, 2014). [Online] http://www.angusreidglobal.com/wp-content/uploads/2014/06/ARG-C-36-Prostitution-June-2014.pdf

ANGUS REID. *Americans More Morally Conservative Than Canadians and Britons*. 2013. http://www.angusreidglobal.com/wp-content/uploads/2013/01/2013.01.31_Morality.pdf

ASTIN, ALEXANDER W., LETICIA OSEGUERA, LINDA J. SAX, and WILLIAM S. KORN. *The American Freshman: Thirty-Five-Year Trends*. Los Angeles: UCLA Higher Education Research Institute, 2002.

BEARMAN, PETER S., JAMES MOODY, and KATHERINE STOVEL. "Chains of Affection." *American Journal of Sociology*. Vol. 110, No. 1 (July 2004):44–91.

BENEDICT, RUTH. "Continuities and Discontinuities in Cultural Conditioning." *Psychiatry*. Vol. 1, No. 2 (May 1938):161–67.

BENOIT, CECILIA, and ALISON MILLAR. *Dispelling Myths and Understanding Realities: Working Conditions, Health Status, and Exiting Experiences of Sex Workers*. Sponsored by Prostitutes Empowerment, Education and Resource Society (PEERS). Funded by BC Health Research Foundation, Capital Health District, and BC Centre of Excellence on Women's Health, 2001.

BENOIT, CECILIA, and F. SHAVER. "Critical Issues and New Directions in Sex Work Research." *The Canadian Review of Sociology and Anthropology*. Vol. 43 (2006):243–52.

BLACKWOOD, EVELYN, and SASKIA WIERINGA, eds. *Female Desires: Same-Sex Relations and Transgender Practices across Cultures*. New York: Columbia University Press, 1999.

BOETHUS, MARIA-PIA. "The End of Prostitution in Sweden?" Stockholm: Swedish Institute. No. 426 (October 1999). [Online] www.si.se/eng/esverige/cs426.html

BORITCH, HELEN. *Fallen Women: Female Crime and the Criminal Justice System in Canada*. Toronto: ITP Nelson, 1997.

BOYCE, W. *Young People in Canada, Their Health and Well-Being*. Ottawa: Health Canada, 2004.

BOYCE, W., M. DOHERTY, C. FORTIN, and D. MACKINNON. *Canadian Youth, Sexual Health and HIV/AIDS Study: Factors Influencing Knowledge, Attitudes and Behaviours*. Toronto: Council of Ministers of Education, Canada, 2003.

BOYER, DEBRA. "Male Prostitution and Homosexual Identity." *Journal of Homosexuality*. Vol. 17, Nos. 1, 2 (1989):151–84.

BRENNAN, S., and A. TAYLOR-BUTTS. *Sexual Assault in Canada: 2004 and 2007*. Ottawa: Statistics Canada, 2008.

BROCK, DEBORAH. *Making Work, Making Trouble: Prostitution as a Social Problem*. Toronto: University of Toronto Press, 1998.

CENTERS FOR DISEASE CONTROL AND PREVENTION. "Deaths: Final Data for 2010, Tables." 2012. Available at http://www.cdc.gov/nchs/data/dvs/deaths_2010_release.pdf

———. "Understanding Teen Dating Violence." 2012. Available at http://www.cdc.gov/ViolencePrevention/pdf/TeenDatingViolence2012-a.pdf

CHANDRA, ANJANI, WILLIAM D. MOSHER, CASEY COPEN, and CATLAINN SIONEAN. "Sexual Behavior, Sexual Attraction, and Sexual Identity in the United States: Data from the 2006–2008 National Survey of Family Growth." *National Health Statistics Reports*. No 36. Hyattsville, MD: National Center for Health

Statistics. 2011. Available at http://www.cdc.gov/nchs/data/nhsr/nhsr036.pdf

CHAPKIS, WENDY. *Live Sex Acts: Women Performing Erotic Labor*. New York: Routledge, 1997.

CHURCH, S., and M. HENDERSON. "Violence by Clients towards Female Prostitutes in Different Work Settings." *British Medical Journal*. Vol. 322 (2001):524–25.

COLTON, HELEN. *The Gift of Touch: How Physical Contact Improves Communication, Pleasure, and Health*. New York: Seaview/Putnam, 1983.

CRACY, DAVID. "Psychologists Repudiate Gay-to-Straight Therapy." *Yahoo News*. [Online] Available August 5, 2009, at http://news.yahoo.com/s/ap/20090805/ap_on_re_us/us_psychologists_gays

CROSSETTE, BARBARA. "Female Genital Mutilation by Immigrants Is Becoming Cause for Concern in the U.S." *New York Times International* (December 10, 1995):11.

DAVIDSON, JULIA O'CONNELL. *Prostitution, Power, and Freedom*. Ann Arbor: University of Michigan Press, 1998.

DAVIS, KINGSLEY. "Sexual Behavior." In Robert K. Merton and Robert Nisbet, eds., *Contemporary Social Problems*. 3rd ed. New York: Harcourt Brace Jovanovich, 1971:313–60.

DEANGELLIS, TORI. "Is Technology Ruining Our Kids?" *Monitor on Psychology APA*. Vol. 42, No. 9 (October 2011):62. Available at http://www.apa.org/monitor/2011/10/technology.aspx

DELUCA, MATTHEW. "Debate on celibacy for Catholic priests is old but welcome, experts say." *NBC News*. 2013. http://www.nbcnews.com/news/other/debate-celibacy-catholic-priests-old-welcome-experts-say-f8C11133098

DICKINSON, AMY. "When Dating Is Dangerous." *Time* (August 27, 2001):76.

DU MONT, J., and M.J. MCGREGOR. "Sexual Assault in the Lives of Urban Sex Workers: A Descriptive and Comparative Analysis." *Women & Health*. Vol. 39 (2004):79–96.

DWORKIN, ANDREA. *Intercourse*. New York: Free Press, 1987.

ELIAS, JAMES, VERN BULLOUGH, VERONICA ELIAS, and JOYCELYN ELDERS, eds. *Prostitution: On Whores, Hustlers, and Johns*. New York: Prometheus Books, 1998.

ENVIRONICS INSTITUTE. *Focus Canada 2010 Final Report*. 2010. https://www.google.ca/url?sa=t&rct=j&q=&esrc=s&source=web&cd=1&cad=rja&uact=8&ved=0CB0QFjAA&url=http%3A%2F%2Fwww.queensu.ca%2Fcora%2F_files%2Ffc2010report.pdf&ei=GeT4VN6XEMXuoATau4LYDg&usg=AFQjCNHTqmgjtFp_FtyVLYOidVgpWKRPIg

ESTES, RICHARD J. "The Commercial Sexual Exploitation of Children in the U.S., Canada, and Mexico." Reported in "Study Explores Sexual Exploitation." [Online] Available September 10, 2001, at http://dailynews.yahoo.com.

FARLEY, MELISSA, JACQUELINE LYNNE, and ANN J. COTTON. "Prostitution in Vancouver: Violence and the colonization of First Nations women." *Transcultural Psychiatry*. Vol. 42, No. 2 (June 2005): 242–271.

FORD, CLELLAN S., and FRANK A. BEACH. *Patterns of Sexual Behavior*. New York: Harper Bros., 1951.

FORUM RESEARCH. *More than one tenth of married Canadians admit to adultery*. 2012a. https://www.forumresearch.com/forms/News%20Archives/News%20Releases/47950_Canada-wide_-_Infidelity_Poll_%28Forum_Research%29_%2820121116%29.pdf

———. *One twentieth of Canadians claim to be LGBT*. 2012b. http://www.forumresearch.com/forms/News%20Archives/News%20Releases/67741_Canada-wide_-_Federal_LGBT_(Forum_Research)_(20120628).pdf

———. *Just one eighth admit to viewing pornography*. 2014. http://poll.forumresearch.com/post/98/just-one-eighth-admit-to-viewing-pornography/

FOUCAULT, MICHEL. *The History of Sexuality: An Introduction*. Vol. 1. Robert Hurley, trans. New York: Vintage, 1990; orig. 1978.

GAGNÉ, PATRICIA, RICHARD TEWKSBURY, and DEANNA MCGAUGHEY. "Coming Out and Crossing Over: Identity Formation and Proclamation in a Transgender Community." *Gender and Society*. Vol. 11, No. 4 (August 1997):478–508.

GATES, GARY. "How Many People Are Lesbian, Gay, Bisexual, and Transgender?" The Williams Institute. April 2011. Available at http://williamsinstitute.law.ucla.edu/wp-content/uploads/Gates-How-Many-People-LGBT-Apr-2011.pdf

GAVE, ELENI N. "In the Indigenous Muxe Culture of Mexico's Oaxaca State, Alternative Notions of Sexuality Are Not Only Accepted, They're Celebrated." *Travel and Leisure* (November 2005. [Online] Available June 15, 2009, at http://travelandleisure.com/articles/stepping-out/page/2/print

GEERTZ, CLIFFORD. "Common Sense as a Cultural System." *Antioch Review*. Vol. 33, No. 1 (Spring 1975):5–26.

GIDDENS, ANTHONY. *The Transformation of Intimacy*. Cambridge, UK: Polity Press, 1992.

GLOBE AND MAIL, THE. "Judge Decriminalizes Prostitution in Ontario, but Ottawa Mulls Appeal." September 28, 2010. www.theglobeandmail.com/news/national/ontario/judge-decriminalizesprostitution-in-ontario/article1730433/?cmpid=rss1

GREENBERG, DAVID F. *The Construction of Homosexuality*. Chicago: University of Chicago Press, 1988.

HACKLER, JIM. "Criminalizing Sex." In Jim Hackler, ed., *Canadian Criminology: Strategies and Perspectives*. Scarborough, ON: Prentice Hall Canada, 1999:254–67.

HAMER, DEAN, and PETER COPELAND. *The Science of Desire: The Search for the Gay Gene and the Biology of Behavior*. New York: Simon & Schuster, 1994.

HUFFMAN, KAREN. *Psychology in Action*. New York: Wiley, 2000.

KESSLER, SUZANNE, and WENDY MCKENNA. "Who Put the 'Trans' in Transgender? Gender Theory and Everyday Life." *The International Journal of Transgenderism*. Vol. 4, No. 3 (2000). Available at http://iiav.nl/ezines/web/IJT/97-03/numbers/symposion/kessler.htm

KINSEY, ALFRED, WARDELL BAXTER POMEROY, and CLYDE E. MARTIN. *Sexual Behavior in the Human Male*. Philadelphia, PA: Saunders, 1948.

KINSEY, ALFRED, WARDELL BAXTER POMEROY, CLYDE E. MARTIN, and PAUL H. GEBHARD. *Sexual Behavior in the Human Female*. Philadelphia, PA: Saunders, 1953.

KLUCKHOHN, CLYDE. "As an Anthropologist Views It." In Albert Deutsch, ed., *Sex Habits of American Men*. New York: Prentice Hall, 1948.

KRUKS, GABRIEL N. "Gay and Lesbian Homeless/Street Youth: Special Issues and Concerns." *Journal of Adolescent Health*. Special Issue, No. 12 (1991):515–18.

KUNKEL, DALE, et al. *Sex on TV, 2005*. Menlo Park, CA: Henry J. Kaiser Family Foundation, 2005. www.kff.org/entmedia/entmedia110905pkg.cfm

LACEY, MARC. "A Distinct Lifestyle: The Muxe of Mexico." *New York Times* (December 7, 2008):4.

LAND, VICTORIA, and CELIA KITZINGER. "Speaking as a Lesbian: Correcting the Heterosexist Presumption." *Research on Language and Social Interaction*. Vol. 38, No. 4 (2005):371–416.

LAUMANN, EDWARD O., JOHN H. GAGNON, ROBERT T. MICHAEL, and STUART MICHAELS. *The Social Organization of Sexuality: Sexual Practices in the United States*. Chicago: University of Chicago Press, 1994.

LELAND, JOHN. "Bisexuality." *Newsweek* (July 17, 1995):44–49.

LEVAY, SIMON. *The Sexual Brain*. Cambridge, MA: MIT Press, 1993.

LEWIS, J., and E. MATICKA-TYNDALE. *Escort Services in a Border Town: Methodological Challenges Conducting Research Related to Sex Work*. Health Canada, Ottawa: Division of STD Prevention and Control, 1999.

LEWIS, J., E. MATICKA-TYNDALE, F. SHAVER, and H. SCHRAMM. "Managing Risk and Safety on the Job." *Journal of Psychology and Human Sexuality*. Vol. 17 (2005): 147–67.

LOWMAN, J. "Prostitution Law Reform in Canada." In Institute of Comparative Law in Japan, ed., *Toward Comparative Law in the 21st Century*. Tokyo: Chuo University Press, 1998:919–46.

———. "Violence and the Outlaw Status of (Street) Prostitution in Canada." *Violence Against Women*. Vol. 6 (2000):987–1011.

LOWMAN, JOHN, and CHRIS ATCHISON. "Men Who Buy Sex: A Survey in the Greater Vancouver Regional District." *Canadian Review of Sociology and Anthropology*. Vol. 43, No. 3 (2006):281–96.

LOWMAN, JOHN, and LAURA FRASER. *Violence Against Persons Who Prostitute: The Experience in British Columbia*. Technical Report No. TR1996-14e. Ottawa: Department of Justice Canada, 1995. [Online] http://mypage.uniserve.ca/~lowman/violence/title.htm

MACKINNON, C.A. *Feminism Unmodified: Discourses on Life and Law*. Cambridge, MA: Harvard University Press, 1987.

MARQUARDT, ELIZABETH, and NORVAL GLENN. *Hooking Up, Hanging Out, and Hoping for Mr. Right*. New York: Institute for American Values, 2001.

MARTINEZ, GLADYS, CASEY COPEN, and JOYCE ABMA. "Teenagers in the United States: Sexual Activity, Contraceptive Use, and Childbearing, 2006–2010 National Survey of Family Growth." National Center for Health Statistics. *Vital Health Stat*. Vol. 23. No. 31. (2011). Available at http://www.cdc.gov/nchs/data/series/sr_23/sr23_031.pdf

MATICKA-TYNDALE, E. "Sexuality and Sexual Health of Canadian Adolescents: Yesterday, Today and Tomorrow." *Canadian Journal of Human Sexuality*. Vol. 17, No. 3 (2008):85–95.

MCCARGAR, MARILLA. "Canada's long struggle for reproductive rights." *The Star*. 2014. [Online] http://www.thestar.com/opinion/commentary/2014/06/02/canadas_long_struggle_for_reproductive_rights.html

MCCARTHY, BILL, and TERESA CASEY. "Love, Sex and Crime: Adolescent Romantic Relationships and Offending." *American Sociological Review*. Vol. 73, No. 6 (2008):944–69.

MCCREARY CENTRE SOCIETY. *Healthy Youth Development: Highlights from the 2003 Adolescent Health Survey III*. Vancouver: Author, 2004.

MCKAY, ALEXANDER. "Trends in Canadian National and Provincial/Territorial Teen Pregnancy Rates: 2001-2010." *Canadian Journal of Human Sexuality*. Vol. 21, No. 3–4 (2012):161–175.

MCKAY, ALEXANDER, and MICHAEL BARRETT. "Trends in Teen Pregnancy Rates from 1996–2006: A Comparison of Canada, Sweden, U.S.A., and England/Wales." *Canadian Journal of Human Sexuality*. Vol. 19, No. 1–2 (2010):43–52.

MCLAREN, ANGUS, and ARLENE TIGAR MCLAREN. *The Bedroom and the State: The Changing Practices and Politics of Contraception and Abortion in Canada 1880–1980*. Toronto: McClelland and Stewart, 1986.

MIRACLE, TINA S., ANDREW W. MIRACLE, and ROY F. BAUMEISTER. *Human Sexuality: Meeting Your Basic Needs*. Upper Saddle River, NJ: Prentice Hall, 2003.

MUGYENYI, BIANCA. "From abortion rights to reproductive justice." *Briarpatch*. January/February 2013. Available at http://briarpatchmagazine.com/articles/view/from-abortion-rights-to-reproductive-justice

MURDOCK, GEORGE PETER. *Social Structure*. New York: Free Press, 1965; orig. 1949.

MURRAY, STEPHEN O., and WILL ROSCOE, eds. *Boy-Wives and Female-Husbands: Studies of African Homosexualities*. New York: St. Martin's Press, 1998.

NATIONAL CONFERENCE OF STATE LEGISLATURES. "Marriages." 2012. Available at http://www.ncsl.org/programs/cyf/cousins.htm

NORC. *General Social Surveys, 1972–2012*. Chicago: National Opinion Research Center. March 2013. Available at http://www.norc.org/GSS+Website/

OLYSLAGER, FEMKE, and LYNN CONWAY. "On the Calculation of the Prevalence of Transsexualism." 2007. http://ai.eecs.umich.edu/people/conway/TS/Prevalence/Reports/Prevalence%20of%20Transsexualism.pdf

PARIS, MAX. "Should the prostitution law debate hear from johns?" *CBC News*. 2014. [Online] http://www.cbc.ca/news/politics/should-the-prostitution-law-debate-hear-from-johns-1.2675048

PEAT MARWICK AND PARTNERS. "Canadians' Attitudes toward and Perceptions of Pornography and Prostitution." *Working Papers on Pornography and Prostitution #6*. Ottawa: Department of Justice, 1984.

PEW RESEARCH CENTER. "What's morally acceptable? It depends on where in the world you live." April 2014. http://www.pewresearch.org/fact-tank/2014/04/15/whats-morally-acceptable-it-depends-on-where-in-the-world-you-live/

PHILLIPS, RACHEL, and CECILIA BENOIT. "Social Determinants of Health Care Access among Sex Industry Workers in Canada." *Sociology of Health Care.* Vol. 23 (2005):79–104.

POPULATION REFERENCE BUREAU. " Datafinder." 2011. [Online] Available at http://www.prb.org/DataFinder.aspx

POPULATION REFERENCE BUREAU. "DataFinder: Reproductive Health Variables." 2012. Available at http://www.prb.org/DataFinder.aspx

PRYOR, JOHN H., et al. "The American Freshman: National Norms Fall 2012 (Expanded Edition)." Cooperative Institutional Research Program at the Higher Education Research Institute at UCLA. 2013. Available at http://www.heri.ucla.edu/monographs/TheAmericanFreshman2012-Expanded.pdf

REECE, MICHAEL, DEBBY HERBENICK, J. DENNIS FORTENBERRY, STEPHANIE SANDERS, VANESSA SCHICK, BRIAN DODGE, and SUSAN MIDDLESTADT. "National Survey of Sexual Health and Behavior (NSSHB)." 2010. [Online] Available at http://www.nationalsexstudy.indiana.edu

ROSENBERG, MICA. "Mexican Transvestite Fiesta Rocks Indigenous Town." Reuters (November 23, 2008). www.reuters.com/article/lifestyleMolt/idUSTRE4AM1PB20081123

ROTERMANN, M. "Trends in Teen Sexual Behaviour and Condom Use." *Health Reports.* Vol. 19, No. 3 (2008):1–5. Catalogue no. 82-003-XWE2008003; http://www.statcan.gc.ca/bsolc/olc-cel/olc-cel?lang=eng&catno=82-003-X

———. "Sexual behaviour and condom use of 15- to 24-year-olds in 2003 and 2009/2010." *Health Reports.* Vol. 23, No. 1 (2012):1–5. Catalogue no. 82-003-X; http://www.statcan.gc.ca/pub/82-003-x/2012001/article/11632-eng.htm

SAINT JAMES, MARGO, and PRISCILLA ALEXANDER. "What Is Coyote?" 2004. www.coyotela.org/what-is.html

SCAMBLER, GRAHAM, and ANNETTE SCAMBLER. *Rethinking Prostitution: Purchasing in the 1990s.* London and New York: Routledge, 1997.

SEDGH, GILDA., S. SINGH, S.K. HENSHAW, A. BANKOLE, I.H. SHAW, AND E. AHMAN. "Induced Abortion: Incidence and Trends Worldwide from 1995 to 2008." *The Lancet.* Vol. 379, No. 9816 (February 18, 2012):625–32.

SHAVER, FRANCES. "Prostitution: A Female Crime?" In Ellen Adelberg and Claudia Currie, eds., *In Conflict with the Law: Women and the Canadian Justice System.* Vancouver: Press Gang Publishers, 1993.

SHOVELLER, J., J. JOHNSON, M. PRKACHIN, and D. PATRICK. "Around Here, They Roll Up the Sidewalks at Night': A Qualitative Study of Youth Living in a Rural Canadian Community." *Health and Place.* Vol. 13 (2007):826–38.

SKIM HEALTHCARE. *Global Erectile Dysfunction Poll. Country report - Canada August 2011.* Sponsored by Eli Lilly Canada, 2011.

SMITH, TOM W. "American Sexual Risk Behavior: Trends, Socio-Demographic Differences, and Behavior." March 2006. [Online] Available January 29, 2009, at http://www.norc.org/NR/rdonlyres/2663F09F-2E74-436E-AC81-6FFBF288E183/0/AmericanSexualBehavior2006.pdf

SNYDER, HOWARD N. "Sexual Assault of Young Children as Reported to Law Enforcement: Victim, Incident, and Offender Characteristics." U.S. Department of Justice. 2000. http://bjs.ojp.usdoj.gov/index.cfm?ty=pbdetail&iid=1147

STATISTICS CANADA. CANSIM II Database Retrieval Output. Series v14225267. Ottawa: Statistics Canada, 2011a.

———. CANSIM II Database Retrieval Output. Series v14225271. Ottawa: Statistics Canada, 2011b.

———. CANSIM II Database Retrieval Output. Series v14225269. Ottawa: Statistics Canada, 2011c.

———. *Fifty years of families in Canada: 1961 to 2011.* Statistics Canada catalogue no. 98-312-X2011003, 2012a.

———. *Portrait of Families and Living Arrangements in Canada.* Statistics Canada catalogue no. 98-312-X2011001, September 2012b.

———. *Crude Birth Rate, Age-Specific and Total Fertility Rates (Live Births), Canada, Provinces and Territories.* [Electronic Data File]. CANSIM table 102-4505. 2013.

STORMS, MICHAEL D. "Theories of Sexual Orientation." *Journal of Personality and Social Psychology.* Vol. 38, No. 5 (May 1980):783–92.

SURRATT, H.L., J.A. INCIARDI, S.P. KURTZ, and M.C. KILEY. "Sex Work and Drug Use in a Subculture of Violence." *Crime & Delinquency.* Vol. 50 (2004):43–59.

TRAVERS, ANN. "Thinking the Unthinkable: Imagining an 'Un-American,' Girl-friendly, Women- and Trans-Inclusive Alternative for Baseball." *Journal of Sport and Social Issues.* Vol. 72, No. 1 (2013):78-96.

UNITED NATIONS. UN World Contraceptive Use 2007. 2008. [Online] Available at http://www.un.org/esa/population/publications/contraceptive2007/contraceptive2007.htm

VAILLANCOURT, R. Gender Differences in Police-Reported Violent Crime in Canada, 2008. Catalogue no. 85F0033M, no. 24. Ottawa: Statistics Canada, 2010.

VENTURA, STEPHANIE J., SALLY C. CURTIN, JOYCE C. ABMA, and STANLEY K. HENSHAW. "Estimated Pregnancy Rates and Rate of Pregnancy Outcomes for the United States, 1990–2008." National Vital Statistics Reports. Vol. 60, No. 7. Hyattsville, MD: National Center for Health Statistics. June 20, 2012. Available at http://www.cdc.gov/nchs/data/nvsr/nvsr60/nvsr60_07.pdf

WATTS, C., and C. ZIMMERMAN. "Violence against Women." *Lancet.* Vol. 359 (2002):1232–37.

WEINBERG, GEORGE. *Society and the Healthy Homosexual.* Garden City, NY: Anchor Books, 1973.

WEINBERG, MARTIN, FRANCES SHAVER, and COLIN WILLIAMS. "Gendered Sex Work in the San Francisco Tenderloin." *Archives of Sexual Behaviour,* 2000.

WEISBERG, D. KELLY. *Children of the Night: A Study of Adolescent Prostitution.* Lexington, MA: DC Heath, 1985.

Chapter 7

AKERS, RONALD L., MARVIN D. KROHN, LONN LANZA-KADUCE, and MARCIA RADOSEVICH. "Social Learning and Deviant Behavior." *American Sociological Review.* Vol. 44, No. 4 (August 1979):636–55.

ALLAN, EMILIE ANDERSEN, and DARRELL J. STEFFENSMEIER. "Youth, Underemployment, and Property Crime: Differential Effects of Job Availability and Job Quality on Juvenile and Young Adult Arrest Rates." *American Sociological Review.* Vol. 54, No. 1 (February 1989):107–23.

AMNESTY INTERNATIONAL. "Death Penalty in 2012." 2012. Available at http://www.amnesty.org/en/death-penalty

ANDERSON, ELIJAH. "The Code of the Streets." *Atlantic Monthly.* Vol. 273 (May 1994):81–94.

———. "The Ideologically Driven Critique." *American Journal of Sociology.* Vol. 197, No. 6 (May 2002):1533–50.

ASSOCIATION OF WORKERS' COMPENSATION BOARDS OF CANADA. "Fatality Statistics." 2013. http://awcbc.org/?page_id=14

BBC. "Sudan 'Trousers Woman' Released." *BBC Mobile News.* [Online] Available September 8, 2009, at http://news.bbc.co.uk/2/hi/8244339.stm

BECKER, HOWARD S. *Outside: Studies in the Sociology of Deviance.* New York: Free Press, 1966.

BELTRAME, JULIAN, and BRENDA BRANSWELL. "The Enemy Within." *Maclean's.* Vol. 113, No. 43 (October 23, 2000):36–38.

BLAU, JUDITH R., and PETER M. BLAU. "The Cost of Inequality: Metropolitan Structure and Violent Crime." *American Sociological Review.* Vol. 47, No. 1 (February 1982):114–29.

BOYCE, JILLIAN, and ADAM COTTER. "Homicide in Canada, 2012." *Juristat* (December 19, 2013). Catalogue no. 85-002-X. [Online] http://www.statcan.gc.ca/pub/85-002-x/2013001/article/11882-eng.htm

BOYCE, JILLIAN, ADAM COTTER, and SAMUEL PERREAULT. "Police-reported crime statistics in Canada, 2013." *Juristat* (July 23, 2013). Catalogue no. 85-002-X. [Online] http://www.statcan.gc.ca/pub/85-002-x/2014001/article/14040-eng.htm

BRADY CAMPAIGN TO PREVENT GUN VIOLENCE. 2012. Available at http://www.bradycampaign.org/

CANADA, DEPARTMENT OF JUSTICE. "Victim Participation in the Plea Negotiation Process in Canada." 2015.

[Online] http://www.justice.gc.ca/eng/rp-pr/cj-jp/victim/rr02_5/p0.html

CANADIAN PRESS. "List of some e-cigarette rules in Canada." *The Vancouver Sun* (MAY 13, 2015). http://www.theprovince.com/health/List+some+ecigarette+rules+Canada/11049995/story.html

CANADIAN PRESS NEWSWIRE. *Reporter Recovering from Murder Attempt Says Tougher Biker Laws Needed.* October 21, 2000.

CARLSON, NORMAN A. "Corrections in the United States Today: A Balance Has Been Struck." *American Criminal Law Review.* Vol. 13, No. 4 (Spring 1976):615–47.

CBC NEWS. *Canadians Split on Pot, Death Penalty: Poll.* 2010. www.cbc.ca/news/canada/story/2010/03/18/ekos-poll018.html

CHAN, WENDY, and DOROTHY CHUNN. *Racialization, Crime, and Criminal Justice in Canada.* Toronto: University of Toronto Press, 2014.

CHIRICOS, TED, RANEE McENTIRE, and MARC GERTZ. "Perceived Racial and Ethnic Composition of Neighborhood and Perceived Risk of Crime." *Social Problems.* Vol. 48, No. 3 (August 2001):322–40.

CHOPRA, ANUJ. "Iranian Rap Music Bedevils the Authorities." *U.S. News & World Report* (March 24, 2008):33.

CLOSS, WILLIAM J., and PAUL F. McKENNA. "Profiling a Problem in Canadian Police Leadership: The Kingston Police Data Collection Project." *Canadian Public Administration.* Vol. 49, No. 2 (2006):143–60.

CLOWARD, RICHARD A., and LLOYD E. OHLIN. *Delinquency and Opportunity: A Theory of Delinquent Gangs.* New York: Free Press, 1966.

COHEN, ALBERT K. *Delinquent Boys: The Culture of the Gang.* New York: Free Press, 1971; orig. 1955.

COHEN, PATRICIA. "Genetic Basis for Crime: A New Look." *The New York Times* (June 19, 2011).

COTTER, ADAM. "Firearms and violent crime in Canada, 2012." *Juristat* (April 23, 2014). Catalogue no. 85-002-X. [Online] http://www.statcan.gc.ca/pub/85-002-x/2014001/article/11925-eng.htm

CTV NEWS. "Six-month sentence for man convicted in cross-burning." January 10, 2011. http://www.ctvnews.ca/six-month-sentence-for-man-convicted-in-cross-burning-1.594331

CURRIE, ELLIOTT. *Confronting Crime: An American Challenge.* New York: Pantheon Books, 1985.

DAUVERGNE, M., and S. TURNER. "Police-Reported Crime Statistics in Canada, 2009." *Juristat.* Vol. 20, No. 2 (2010). Catalogue no. 85-002-X. [Online] www.statcan.gc.ca/pub/85-002-x/2010002/article/11292-eng.pdf

DAUVERGNE, MIA. "Adult correctional statistics in Canada, 2010/2011." *Juristat* (October 11, 2012). Catalogue no. 85-002-X. [Online] http://www.statcan.gc.ca/pub/85-002-x/2012001/article/11715-eng.htm

DEATH PENALTY INFORMATION CENTER. "Innocence and the Death Penalty." 2012. Available at http://www.deathpenaltyinfo.org/innocence-and-death-penalty#inn-yr-rc

DEMUTH, STEPHEN, and DARRELL STEFFENSMEIER. "The Impact of Gender and Race-Ethnicity on the Pretrial Release Process." *Social Problems.* Vol. 51, No. 2 (May 2004):222–42.

DERBER, CHARLES. *The Wilding of America: Money, Mayhem, and the New American Dream.* 3rd ed. New York: Worth, 2004.

DURKHEIM, EMILE. *The Division of Labor in Society.* New York: Free Press, 1964a; orig. 1893.

———. *The Rules of Sociological Method.* New York: Free Press, 1964b; orig. 1895.

DWYER, JIM. "Dizzying Price for Seeking the Death Penalty." *The New York Times* (June 2, 2011).

EBOH, CAMILLUS. "Nigerian Woman Loses Appeal against Stoning Death." *Yahoo! News* (August 19, 2002). http://news.yahoo.com

ELIAS, ROBERT. *The Politics of Victimization: Victims, Victimology, and Human Rights.* New York: Oxford University Press, 1986.

ELLIOTT, DELBERT S., and SUZANNE S. AGETON. "Reconciling Race and Class Differences in Self-Reported and Official Estimates of Delinquency." *American Sociological Review.* Vol. 45, No. 1 (February 1980):95–110.

ENVIRONMENT CANADA. "Spill results in $125,000 penalty for Canadian Natural Resources Limited."Enforcement Notifications (March 18, 2015). http://www.ec.gc.ca/alef-ewe/default.asp?lang=En&n=97069692-1

ERIKSON, KAI T. *Wayward Puritans: A Study in the Sociology of Deviance.* New York: Wiley, 2005; orig. 1966.

FENNARIO, TOM. "Quebec eyes move against Kahnawake-hosted online gambling sites." *APTN National News* (April 24, 2015). http://aptn.ca/news/2015/04/24/quebec-eyes-move-kahnawake-hosted-online-gambling-sites/

GARFINKEL, HAROLD. "Conditions of Successful Degradation Ceremonies." *American Journal of Sociology.* Vol. 61, No. 2 (March 1956):420–24.

GLUECK, SHELDON, and ELEANOR GLUECK. *Unraveling Juvenile Delinquency.* New York: Commonwealth Fund, 1950.

GOFFMAN, ERVING. *Stigma: Notes on the Management of Spoiled Identity.* Englewood Cliffs, NJ: Prentice Hall, 1963.

GOODWIN, LIZ. "Gun Deaths Set to Outstrip Car Fatalities for First Time in 2015." *The Lookout.* December 19, 2012. Available at http://news.yahoo.com/blogs/lookout/gun-deaths-set-outstrip-car-fatalities-first-time-152632492.html

GOTTFREDSON, MICHAEL R., and TRAVIS HIRSCHI. "National Crime Control Policies." *Society.* Vol. 32, No. 2 (January/February 1995):30–36.

GRIFFITHS, CURT T., YVON DANDURAND, and DANIELLE MURDOCH. "The Social Reintegration of Offenders and Crime Prevention." 2007. http://www.publicsafety.gc.ca/cnt/rsrcs/pblctns/scl-rntgrtn/index-eng.aspx#s2

HARRIES, KEITH D. *Serious Violence: Patterns of Homicide and Assault in America.* Springfield, IL: Thomas, 1990.

HARTOCOLLIS, ANEMONA. "Man Is Convicted of Attempted Murder as Hate Crime in Village Rampage." *New York Times* (March 2, 2007):B6.

HEALTH CANADA. "Medical Use of Marijuana." December 2014. http://www.hc-sc.gc.ca/dhp-mps/marihuana/index-eng.php

HERPERTZ, SABINE C., and HENNING SASS. "Emotional Deficiency and Psychopathy." *Behavioral Sciences and the Law.* Vol. 18, No. 5 (September/October 2000):567–80.

HEYDARY HAMILTON PC. "An Overview of Online Gaming in Canada." (January 2006). http://www.heydary.com/publications/gaming_lawyers_canada.html

HIRSCHI, TRAVIS. *Causes of Delinquency.* Berkeley: University of California Press, 1969.

HIV/AIDS LEGAL NETWORK. *Sex, Work, Rights: Reforming Canadian Criminal Laws On Prostitution.* Toronto: Author, 2005.

HOPE, TRINA L., HAROLD G. GRASMICK, and LAURA J. POINTON. "The Family in Gottfredson and Hirschi's General Theory of Crime: Structure, Parenting, and Self-Control." *Sociological Focus.* Vol. 36, No. 4 (November 2003):291–311.

HUTCHINS, HOPE. "Police resources in Canada, 2013." *Juristat* (March 27, 2014). Catalogue no. 85-002-X. [Online] http://www.statcan.gc.ca/pub/85-002-x/2014001/article/11914-eng.htm#a7

INCIARDI, JAMES A. *Elements of Criminal Justice.* 2nd ed. New York: Oxford University Press, 2000.

JONES, CHARISSE. "Upon Release from Prison, Some Can Feel Lost."*USA Today* (December 14, 2007):5A.

JUSTICE EDUCATION SOCIETY. "Aboriginal Restorative Justice Remedies." 2015. http://www.justiceeducation.ca/research/aboriginal-sentencing/restorative-justice

KING, KATHLEEN PIKER, and DENNIS E. CLAYSON. "The Differential Perceptions of Male and Female Deviants." *Sociological Focus.* Vol. 21, No. 2 (April 1988):153–64.

KITTRIE, NICHOLAS N. *The Right to Be Different: Deviance and Enforced Therapy.* Baltimore, MD: Johns Hopkins University Press, 1971.

KOCHANEK, KENNETH D., JIAQUAN XU, SHERRY L. MURPHY, ARIALDI M. MINIÑO, and HSIANG-CHING KUNG. "Deaths: Final Data for 2009." National Vital Statistics Reports. Vol. 60, No. 3. 2011. Available at http://www.cdc.gov/nchs/data/nvsr/nvsr60/nvsr60_03.pdf

KUBRIN, CHARLES E. "Gangstas, Thugs, and Hustlas: Identity and the Code of the Street in Rap Music." *Social Problems.* Vol. 52, No. 3 (2005):360–78.

LANGBEIN, LAURA I., and ROSEANA BESS. "Sports in School: Source of Amity or Antipathy?" *Social Science Quarterly.* Vol. 83, No. 2 (June 2002):436–54.

LEMERT, EDWIN M. *Social Pathology: A Systematic Approach to the Theory of Sociopathic Behavior.* New York: McGraw-Hill, 1951.

———. *Human Deviance, Social Problems, and Social Control.* 2nd ed. Englewood Cliffs, NJ: Prentice Hall, 1972.

LEMONICK, MICHAEL D. "The Search for a Murder Gene." *Time* (January 20, 2003):100.

LEONARD, EILEEN B. *Women, Crime, and Society: A Critique of Theoretical Criminology.* White Plains, NY: Longman, 1982.

LIAZOS, ALEXANDER. "The Poverty of the Sociology of Deviance: Nuts, Sluts, and Perverts." *Social Problems.* Vol. 20, No. 1 (Summer 1972):103–20.

LISKA, ALLEN E., and BARBARA D. WARNER. "Functions of Crime: A Paradoxical Process." *American Journal of Sociology.* Vol. 96, No. 6 (May 1991):1441–63.

LITTLE, CRAIG, and ANDREA RANKIN. "Why Do They Start It? Explaining Reported Early-Teen Sexual Activity." *Sociological Forum.* Vol. 16, No. 4 (December 2001):703–29.

MAHONY, TINA H. "Women and the Criminal Justice System." *Women in Canada: A Gender-based Statistical Report.* Catalogue no. 89-503X. Ottawa: Ministry of Industry, 2011.

MARTIN, JOHN M., and ANNE T. ROMANO. *Multinational Crime: Terrorism, Espionage, Drug and Arms Trafficking.* Newbury Park, CA: Sage, 1992.

MARTINEZ, RAMIRO, JR. "Latinos and Lethal Violence: The Impact of Poverty and Inequality." *Social Problems.* Vol. 43, No. 2 (May 1996):131–46.

MERTON, ROBERT K. "Social Structure and Anomie." *American Sociological Review.* Vol. 3, No. 6 (October 1938):672–82.

———. *Social Theory and Social Structure.* New York: Free Press, 1968.

MILLAR, PAUL, and AKWASI OWUSU-BEMPAH. "Whitewashing Criminal Justice in Canada: Preventing Research through Data Suppression." *Canadian Journal of Law and Society.* Vol. 26, No. 3 (2011):653-661

MILLER, WALTER B. "Lower-Class Culture as a Generating Milieu of Gang Delinquency." In Marvin E. Wolfgang, Leonard Savitz, and Norman Johnston, eds., *The Sociology of Crime and Delinquency.* 2nd ed. New York: Wiley, 1970:351–63; orig. 1958.

MILLER, WILLIAM J., and RICK A. MATTHEWS. "Youth Employment, Differential Association, and Juvenile Delinquency." *Sociological Focus.* Vol. 34, No. 3 (August 2001):251–68.

MOFFITT, TERRIE E., et al. "A Gradient of Childhood Self-Control Predicts Health, Wealth, and Public Safety." *Proceedings of the National Academy of Sciences of the United States of America.* [Online] Available January 30, 2011, at http://www.pnas.org/content/early/2011/01/20/1010076108

MUNROE, SUSAN. "Abolition of Capital Punishment in Canada." About.com: Canada Online. July 2007. http://canadaonline.about.com/od/crime/a/abolitioncappun.htm

NORC. *General Social Surveys, 1972–2012.* Chicago: National Opinion Research Center. March 2013. Available at http://www.norc.org/GSS+Website/

"Our Cheating Hearts." Editorial. *U.S. News & World Report* (May 6, 2002):4.

PAROLE BOARD OF CANADA. "Performance Monitoring Report, 2013-2014." 2013/14. http://pbc-clcc.gc.ca/rprts/pmr/pmr_2013_2014/index-eng.shtml#a1

PERREAULT, S. *Violent Victimization of Aboriginal People in the Canadian Provinces, 2009.* Ottawa: Statistics Canada, 2011. Catalogue no. 85-002-X. [Online] www.statcan.gc.ca/pub/85-002-x/2011001/article/11415-eng.pdf

PERREAULT, SAMUEL, and SHANNON BRENNAN. "Criminal victimization in Canada, 2009." *Juristat* (September 28, 2010). Catalogue no. 85-002-X. [Online] http://www.statcan.gc.ca/pub/85-002-x/2010002/article/11340-eng.htm

PEW RESEARCH CENTER FOR THE PEOPLE AND THE PRESS. 2012. Available at http://www.people-press.org/question-search/?qid=1814733&pid=51&ccid=50#top

PINKER, STEVEN. "Are Your Genes to Blame?" *Time* (January 20, 2003):98–100.

PRYOR, JOHN H., KEVIN EGAN, LAURA PALUCKI BLAKE, SYLVIA HURTADO, JENNIFER BERDAN, and MATTHEW CASE. "The American Freshman: National Norms Fall 2012 (Expanded Edition)." Cooperative Institutional Research Program at the Higher Education Research Institute at UCLA. 2013. Available at http://www.heri.ucla.edu/monographs/TheAmericanFreshman2012-Expanded.pdf

QUILLIAN, LINCOLN, and DEVAH PAGER. "Black Neighbors, Higher Crime? The Role of Racial Stereotypes in Evaluations of Neighborhood Crime." *American Journal of Sociology.* Vol. 107, No. 3 (November 2001):717–67.

QUINNEY, RICHARD. *Class, State and Crime: On the Theory and Practice of Criminal Justice.* New York: McKay, 1977.

RECKLESS, WALTER C., and SIMON DINITZ. "Pioneering with Self-Concept as a Vulnerability Factor in Delinquency." *Journal of Criminal Law, Criminology, and Police Science.* Vol. 58, No. 4 (December 1967):515–23.

ROGERS, RICHARD G., REBECCA ROSENBLATT, ROBERT A. HUMMER, and PATRICK M. KRUEGER. "Black-White Differentials in Adult Homicide Mortality in the United States." *Social Science Quarterly.* Vol. 82, No. 3 (September 2001):435–52.

SCHEFF, THOMAS J. *Being Mentally Ill: A Sociological Theory.* 2nd ed. New York: Aldine, 1984.

SHANKS, PETE. "Promoting a Genetic Basic for Crime." *Psychology Today* and the Center for Genetics and Society (June 27, 2011). Available at http://www.psychologytoday.com/blog/genetic-crossroads/201106/promoting-genetic-basis-crime

SHELDON, WILLIAM H., EMIL M. HARTL, and EUGENE MCDERMOTT. *Varieties of Delinquent Youth.* New York: Harper Bros., 1949.

SHERMAN, LAWRENCE W., and DOUGLAS A. SMITH. "Crime, Punishment, and Stake in Conformity: Legal and Informal Control of Domestic Violence." *American Sociological Review.* Vol. 57, No. 5 (October 1992):680–90.

SHOVER, NEAL, and ANDREW HOCHSTETLER. *Choosing White-Collar Crime.* New York: Cambridge University Press, 2006.

SMITH, DOUGLAS A. "Police Response to Interpersonal Violence: Defining the Parameters of Legal Control." *Social Forces.* Vol. 65, No. 3 (March 1987):767–82.

SMITH, DOUGLAS A., and CHRISTY A. VISHER. "Street-Level Justice: Situational Determinants of Police Arrest Decisions." *Social Problems.* Vol. 29, No. 2 (December 1981):167–77.

SMITH, DOUGLAS A., and PATRICK R. GARTIN. "Specifying Specific Deterrence: The Influence of Arrest on Future Criminal Activity." *American Sociological Review.* Vol. 54, No. 1 (February 1989):94–105.

SNIDER, LAUREEN. *About Canada: Corporate Crime.* Halifax & Winnipeg: Fernwood, 2015.

SPITZER, STEVEN. "Toward a Marxian Theory of Deviance." In Delos H. Kelly, ed., *Criminal Behavior: Readings in Criminology.* New York: St. Martin's Press, 1980:175–91.

STACK, STEVEN, IRA WASSERMAN, and ROGER KERN. "Adult Social Bonds and the Use of Internet Pornography." *Social Science Quarterly.* Vol. 85, No. 1 (March 2004):75–88.

STASTNA, KAZI. "What's behind Canada's improving crime stats?" *CBC News* (July 26, 2013). http://www.cbc.ca/news/canada/what-s-behind-canada-s-improving-crime-stats-1.1315377

STATE OF OREGON. "Governor Kitzhaber Issues Reprieve—Calls for Action on Capital Punishment." November 22, 2011. Available at http://www.oregon.gov/gov/media_room/pages/press_releasesp2011/press_112211.aspx

STATISTICS CANADA. "Street Prostitution in Canada." *Juristat.* Catalogue no. 85-002XPE. Vol. 17, No. 2 (February 1997):1–12.

———. *Police-Reported Crime Statistics 2009.* 2010. [Online] www.statcan.gc.ca/daily-quotidien/100720/dq100720a-eng.htm

————. Ethnic Origin (264), Single and Multiple Ethnic Origin Responses (3), Generation Status (4), Age Groups (10) and Sex (3) for the Population in Private Households of Canada, Provinces, Territories, Census Metropolitan Areas and Census Agglomerations, 2011 National Household Survey. (2011). [Electronic Data File] Catalogue no. 99-010-X2011028.

————. "Police-reported hate crimes, 2012." *The Daily* (June 26, 2014a). http://www.statcan.gc.ca/daily-quotidien/140626/dq140626b-eng.htm

————. "Homicide in Canada, 2013." *The Daily* (December 1, 2014b). http://www.statcan.gc.ca/daily-quotidien/141201/dq141201a-eng.htm

————. "Canada's crime rate: Two decades of decline." *Canadian Megatrends* (January 27, 2015). http://www.statcan.gc.ca/pub/11-630-x/11-630-x2015001-eng.htm

STEWART, HAMISH. *Fundamental Justice: Section 7 of the Canadian Charter of Rights and Freedoms*. Toronto: Faculty of Law, University of Toronto, 2012.

SULLIVAN, ANDREW. Lecture delivered at Kenyon College, April 4, 2002.

SUTHERLAND, EDWIN H. "White Collar Criminality." *American Sociological Review*. Vol. 5, No. 1 (February 1940):1–12.

SZASZ, THOMAS S. *The Myth of Mental Illness: Foundations of a Theory of Personal Conduct*. New York: Dell, 1961.

————. *The Manufacturer of Madness: A Comparative Study of the Inquisition and the Mental Health Movement*. New York: Harper & Row, 1970.

————. "Cleansing the Modern Heart." *Society*. Vol. 40, No. 4 (May/June 2003):52–59.

————. "Protecting Patients against Psychiatric Intervention." *Society*. Vol. 41, No. 3 (March/April 2004):7–10.

TERRY, DON. "In Crackdown on Bias, a New Tool." *New York Times* (June 12, 1993):8.

THOMAS, JENNIFER. "Adult Correctional Services in Canada, 1998–99." *Juristat*. Statistics Canada Catalogue no. 85-002-XIE. Vol. 20, No 3 (June 2000):1–16.

THORNBERRY, TERRANCE, and MARGARET FARNSWORTH. "Social Correlates of Criminal Involvement: Further Evidence on the Relationship between Social Status and Criminal Behavior." *American Sociological Review*. Vol. 47, No. 4 (August 1982):505–18.

TITTLE, CHARLES R., WAYNE J. VILLEMEZ, and DOUGLAS A. SMITH. "The Myth of Social Class and Criminality: An Empirical Assessment of the Empirical Evidence." *American Sociological Review*. Vol. 43, No. 5 (October 1978):643–56.

UGGEN, CHRISTOPHER. "Ex-Offenders and the Conformist Alternative: A Job-Quality Model of Work and Crime." *Social Problems*. Vol. 46, No. 1 (February 1999): 127–51.

U.S. DEPARTMENT OF JUSTICE, BUREAU OF JUSTICE STATISTICS. "Prisoners in 2010." 2011. Available at http://bjs.ojp.usdoj.gov/content/pub/pdf/p10.pdf

U.S. DEPARTMENT OF JUSTICE, FEDERAL BUREAU OF INVESTIGATION. "Crime in the United States 2011." 2012. Available at http://www.fbi.gov/about-us/cjis/ucr/crime-in-the.u.s/2011/crime-in-the-u.s.-2011

VALDEZ, A. "In the Hood: Street Gangs Discover White-Collar Crime." *Police*. Vol. 21, No. 5 (May 1997):49–50, 56.

VOLD, GEORGE B., and THOMAS J. BERNARD. *Theoretical Criminology*. 3rd ed. New York: Oxford University Press, 1986.

WARR, MARK, and CHRISTOPHER G. ELLISON. "Rethinking Social Reactions to Crime: Personal and Altruistic Fear in Family Households." *American Journal of Sociology*. Vol. 106, No. 3 (November 2000):551–78.

WEBB, KATE. "Crack use in Vancouver has declined since free crackpipe distribution began." *Metro*. 2013. Available at http://metronews.ca/news/vancouver/719151/crack-use-in-vancouver-has-declined-since-free-crackpipe-distribution-began/

WILSON, REID. "FBI: Chicago passes New York as murder capital of U.S." *The Washington Post*. 2013. http://www.washingtonpost.com/blogs/govbeat/wp/2013/09/18/fbi-chicago-passes-new-york-as-murder-capital-of-u-s/

WOLFGANG, MARVIN E., ROBERT M. FIGLIO, and THORSTEN SELLIN. *Delinquency in a Birth Cohort*. Chicago: University of Chicago Press, 1972.

WOLFGANG, MARVIN E., TERRENCE P. THORNBERRY, and ROBERT M. FIGLIO. *From Boy to Man, from Delinquency to Crime*. Chicago: University of Chicago Press, 1987.

WORTLEY, SCOT, and AKWASI OWUSU-BEMPAH. "The usual suspects: police stop and search practices in Canada." *Policing & Society*. Vol. 21, No. 4 (December 2011):395–407

WORTLEY, SCOT, and LYSANDRA MARSHALL. *Race and Police Stops in Kingston, Ontario: Results of a Pilot Project*. Kingston, ON: Kingston Police Services Board, 2005.

WRIGHT, JAMES D. "Ten Essential Observations on Guns in America." *Society*. Vol. 32, No. 3 (March/April 1995):63–68.

WRIGHT, RICHARD A. *In Defense of Prisons*. Westport, CT: Greenwood Press, 1994.

Chapter 8

ABORIGINAL AFFAIRS AND NORTHERN DEVELOPMENT CANADA. "Aboriginal Income Disparity in Canada." 2013. https://www.aadnc-aandc.gc.ca/eng/1378411773537/1378411859280

ADBUSTERS. "#OCCUPYWALLSTREET: A shift in revolutionary tactics." 2011. https://www.adbusters.org/blogs/adbusters-blog/occupywallstreet.html

ANGUS REID GROUP INC. *Public Support for the Federal Gun Control Legislation*. Public release (December 23, 1996). [Online] www.angusreid.com/pressrel/gun-control.html

————. *Canadians' Views on Including Sexual Orientation in Human Rights Legislation*. Public release (May 10, 1998). [Online] www.angusreid.com/pressrel/pr100598.html

BAINBRIDGE, JAY, MARCIA K. MEYERS, and JANE WALDFOGEL. "Childcare Reform and the Employment of Single Mothers." *Social Science Quarterly*. Vol. 84, No. 4 (December 2003):771–91.

BALTZELL, E. DIGBY. *The Protestant Establishment: Aristocracy and Caste in America*. New York: Vintage Books, 1964.

BASSUK, ELLEN J. "The Homelessness Problem." *Scientific American*. Vol. 251, No. 1 (July 1984):40–45.

BEECH, HANNAH. "Murder, Lies, Abuse of Power and Other Crimes of the Chinese Century." *Time*. May 14, 2012. Available at http://www.time.com/time/magazine/article/0,9171,2113802-3,00.html

BEEGHLEY, LEONARD. *The Structure of Social Stratification in the United States*. Needham Heights, MA: Allyn & Bacon, 1989.

BELLER, EMILY, and MICHAEL HOUT. "Intergenerational Social Mobility: The United States in Comparative Perspective." *The Future of Children*. Vol. 16, No. 2 (Fall 2006). www.futureofchildren.org/information2826/information_show.htm?doc_id=389282

BIAN, YANJIE. "Chinese Social Stratification and Social Mobility." *Annual Review of Sociology*. Vol. 28 (2002):91–116.

BOHANNAN, CECIL. "The Economic Correlates of Homelessness in Sixty Cities." *Social Science Quarterly*. Vol. 72, No. 4 (December 1991):817–25.

BOTT, ELIZABETH. *Family and Social Network*. New York: Free Press, 1971; orig. 1957.

BRADBURY, BRUCE, MILES CORAK, JANE WALDFOGEL, and ELIZABETH WASHBROOK. "Inequality in Early Childhood Outcomes." In John Ermisch, Markus Jantti, and Timothy M. Smeeding, eds., *From Parents to Children: The Intergenerational Transmission of Advantage*. New York: Russell Sage Foundation, 2012:87–119.

BROWN, MARK, and DAVID HODGES. "The All-Canadian Wealth Test 2015 charts." *Money Sense*. 2014. http://www.moneysense.ca/planning/the-all-canadian-wealth-test-2015-charts/

BROWN, MARK. "The real cost of raising kids." 2015. *Money Sense*. http://www.moneysense.ca/planning/the-real-cost-of-raising-a-child/

BRYM, ROBERT J., and BONNIE J. FOX. *From Culture to Power: The Sociology of English Canada*. Toronto: Oxford University Press, 1989.

CASAVANT, LYNE. "Composition of the Homeless Population." Government of Canada Publications. Parliamentary Research Branch. 1999. http://publications.gc.ca/Collection-R/LoPBdP/modules/prb99-1-homelessness/composition-e.htm

CBC NEWS. "Who are Canada's top 1%?" 2013. http://www.cbc.ca/news/canada/who-are-canada-s-top-1-1.1703321

CENTRAL INTELLIGENCE AGENCY. "CIA World Factbook." 2012. Available at #https://www.cia.gov/library/publications/the-world-factbook/index.html#

CHANG, LESLIE T. *Factory Girls: From Village to City in a Changing China*. New York: Spiegel & Grau, 2008.

CITIZENS FOR PUBLIC JUSTICE. "Poverty Trends Score-card: Canada 2012." 2012. http://www.cpj.ca/poverty-trends-scorecard

CLARK, MARGARET S., ED. *Prosocial Behavior*. Newbury Park, CA: Sage, 1991.

CLEMENT, WALLACE. *The Canadian Corporate Elite*. Toronto: McClelland and Stewart, 1975.

COLEMAN, RICHARD P., and LEE RAINWATER. *Social Standing in America*. New York: Basic Books, 1978.

COLLIN, C., and H. JENSEN. *A Statistical Profile of Poverty in Canada*. Ottawa: Parliamentary Information and Research Service Library of Parliament Publication, 2009. Catalogue no. PRB 09-17E. [Online] www.parl.gc.ca/Content/LOP/ResearchPublications/prb0917-e.htm#a8

CONFERENCE BOARD OF CANADA. "High-School Attainment." 2015a. http://www.conferenceboard.ca/hcp/provincial/education/highschool.aspx

————. "Canadian Income Inequality." 2015b. http://www.conferenceboard.ca/hcp/hot-topics/caninequality.aspx

CORAK, MILES. "Equality of Opportunity and Inequality across the Generations: Challenges Ahead." *Horizons: Policy Research Initiative*. Vol. 8, No. 3 (April 2006a):43–50.

DAHRENDORF, RALF. *Class and Class Conflict in Industrial Society*. Stanford, CA: Stanford University Press, 1959.

DANIELS, ROBERT V. "Revolution, Modernization and the Paradox of Twentieth- Century Russia." *Canadian Slavonic Papers: Revue Canadienne des Slavistes*. Vol. 42, No. 3 (2000):249-268.

DAVIS, KINGSLEY, and WILBERT MOORE. "Some Principles of Stratification." *American Sociological Review*. Vol. 10, No. 2 (April 1945):242–49.

DIDERICHSEN, F., M. WHITEHEAD, B. BURSTROM, and M. ABERG. "Sweden and Britain: The Impact of Policy Context on Inequities in Health." In T. Evans, M. Whitehead, F. Diderichsen, A. Bhuya, and M. Wirth, eds., *Challenging Inequities in Health: From Ethics to Action*. New York: Oxford University Press, 2001:241–55.

DOMHOFF, G. WILLIAM. *Who Rules America Now? A View of the '80s*. Englewood Cliffs, NJ: Prentice Hall, 1983.

EKOS RESEARCH. "So What's Really Bothering You Canada?" 2013. http://www.ekospolitics.com/index.php/2013/10/so-whats-really-bothering-you-canada/

EMPLOYMENT AND SOCIAL DEVELOPMENT CANADA. "Financial Security - Family Income." Date modified 2015a. http://well-being.esdc.gc.ca/misme-iowb/.3ndic.1t.4r@-eng.jsp?iid=21#M_1

————. "Calculation of the financial ability of the employer(s)." Date modified 2015b. http://www.esdc.gc.ca/eng/jobs/foreign_workers/caregiver/autocal.shtml

————. "Financial Security - Low Income Incidence." Date modified 2015c. http://well-being.esdc.gc.ca/misme-iowb/.3ndic.1t.4r@-eng.jsp?iid=23#M_8

FEDERAL RESERVE BOARD. "2010 Survey of Consumer Finances." 2012. Available at http://www.federalreserve.gov/econresdata/scf/files/2010_SCF_Chartbook.pdf

FLAVELLE, DANA. "Canada's inequality growing: Stats Can." *Toronto Star*. 2014. http://www.thestar.com/business/personal_finance/investing/2014/09/11/rich_gaining_more_wealth_study_shows.html

FORBES. "The World's Billionaires." 2015. http://www.forbes.com/billionaires/list/#version:static_country:Canada

FOROOHAR, RANA. "Your Incredible Shrinking Paycheck." *Time*. Vol. 177, No. 8 (February 28, 2011):24.

FOX, JUSTIN. "Pay Them Less? Hell, Yes." *Time* (March 2, 2009):30.

GAETZ, STEPHEN, JESSE DONALDSON, TIM RICHTER, and TANYA GULLIVER. "The State of Homelessness in Canada 2013." Toronto: Canadian Homelessness Research Network Press, 2013.

GERBER, THEODORE P., and MICHAEL HOUT. "More Shock than Therapy: Market Transition, Employment, and Income in Russia, 1991–1995." *American Journal of Sociology.* Vol. 104, No. 1 (July 1998):1–50.

GOYDER, J. *The Prestige Squeeze.* Montreal: McGill-Queen's University Press, 2009, Table 4-1, pp. 106-10.

GRAVES, FRANK. "From the End of History to the End of Progress: The Shifting Meaning of the Middle Class." Presentation to the Queen's 2014 International Institute on Social Policy, Kingston, Ontario, 2014. http://www.ekospolitics.com/index.php/2014/08/from-the-end-of-history-to-the-end-of-progress/

GREENBERG, LAWSON, and CLAUDE NORMANDIN. "Disparities in life expectancy at birth." *Health at a Glance.* Ottawa: Statistics Canada, 2011.

GROSSMAN, LEV. "2010 Person of the Year: Mark Zuckerberg." *Time.* Vol. 176, No. 26 (December 27, 2010):44–75.

HALSETH, GREG, and LAURA RYSER. "A Primer For Understanding Issues Around Rural Poverty." *The Community Development Institute at the University of Northern British Columbia.* Prince George: UNBC, 2010.

HARFORD, TIM. "The American Dream: Getting to the Starting Line." [Online] Available October 9, 2007, at http://www.forbes.com/entrepreneurs/2007/10/09/income-mobility-opportunity-ent-dream1007-cx_th_1009harford.html

HELMAN, CHRISTOPHER. "America's 25 Highest-Paid CEOs." *Forbes.* October 12, 2011. Available at http://www.forbes.com/sites/christopherhelman/2011/10/12/americas-25-highest-paid-ceos/

HOUT, MICHAEL, CLEM BROOKS, and JEFF MANZA. "The Persistence of Classes in Post-Industrial Societies." *International Sociology.* Vol. 8, No. 3 (September 1993):259–77.

HOUT, MICHAEL. "More Universalism, Less Structural Mobility: The American Occupational Structure in the 1980s." *American Journal of Sociology.* Vol. 95, No. 6 (May 1998):1358–400.

IPSOS-REID. "Same-Sex Marriage: The Debate Enjoined." Public release (August 8, 2003). [Online] www.ipsos-reid.com/media/dsp_displaypr_cdn.cfm?id_to_view=1877

IVANOVA, IGLIKA. "What is a middle class income these days?" *Canadian Centre for Policy Alternatives.* 2011. http://www.policynote.ca/what-is-a-middle-class-income-these-days/

———. "BC minimum wage increase leaves workers in poverty." *Canadian Centre for Policy Alternatives.* 2015. http://www.policynote.ca/bc-minimum-wage-increase-leaves-workers-in-poverty/#comments

JOHNSON, IAN. "China's Aristocratic Class Wields Its Influence to Shape Politics." *New York Times* (November 13, 2012).

KAISER, EMILY. "Special Report: The Haves, the Have-Nots and the Dreamless Dead." [Online] October 22, 2010. Available at http://finance.yahoo.com/news/Special-Report-The-havesthe-rb-736053606.html?x=0

KAUFMAN, LESLIE. "Surge in Homeless Families Sets Off Debate on Cause." *New York Times* (July 29, 2004). [Online] Available May 4, 2009, at http://www.nytimes.com/2004/06/29/us/surge-in-homeless-families-sets-off-debate-oncause.html?fta=y

KEISTER, LISA A. *Wealth in America: Trends in Wealth Inequality.* Cambridge, MA: Cambridge University Press, 2000.

KOHN, MELVIN L. *Class and Conformity: A Study in Values.* 2nd ed. Homewood, IL: Dorsey Press, 1977.

KOZOL, JONATHAN. *Rachel and Her Children: Homeless Families in America.* New York: Crown, 1988.

KUZNETS, SIMON. "Economic Growth and Income Inequality." *American Economic Review.* Vol. 14, No. 1 (March 1955):1–28.

———. *Modern Economic Growth: Rate, Structure, and Spread.* New Haven, CT: Yale University Press, 1966.

LAREAU, ANNETTE. "Invisible Inequality: Social Class and Childrearing in Black Families and White Families." *American Sociological Review.* Vol. 67, No. 5 (October 2002):747–76.

LENSKI, GERHARD E. *Power and Privilege: A Theory of Social Stratification.* New York: McGraw-Hill, 1966.

LEWIS, OSCAR. *Children of Sachez.* New York: Random House, 1961.

LIN, NAN, and WEN XIE. "Occupational Prestige in Urban China." *American Journal of Sociology.* Vol. 93, No. 4 (January 1988):793–832.

LIU, MELINDA, and DUNCAN HEWITT. "The Rise of the Sea Turtles." *Newsweek* (August 18, 2008):29–31.

LORD, WALTER. *A Night to Remember.* Rev. ed. New York: Holt, Rinehart and Winston, 1976.

LOWE, GRAHAM S. *The Quality of Work: A People-Centred Agenda.* Toronto: Oxford University Press, 2000.

MABRY, MARCUS, and TOM MASLAND. "The Man after Mandela." *Newsweek* (June 7, 1999):54–55.

MACIONIS, J. JOHN., and LINDA M. GERBER. *Sociology,* eighth Canadian edition. Toronto: Pearson, 2014.

MACKENZIE, HUGH. "Canada's CEO Elite 100: The 0.01%" Ottawa: Canadian Centre for Policy Alternatives, 2012. www.policyalternatives.ca

MACLEAN'S. "The highest-paid Canadians in major league sports." 2014. http://www.macleans.ca/economy/money-economy/highest-paid-canadians-in-major-league-sports-in-2014-15/

MARX, KARL, and FRIEDRICH ENGELS. "Manifesto of the Communist Party." In Robert C. Tucker, ed., *The Marx-Engels Reader.* New York: Norton, 1972:331–62; orig. 1848.

MASON, DAVID S. "Fairness Matters: Equity and the Transition to Democracy." *World Policy Journal.* Vol. 20, No. 4 (Winter 2003–04). 2004. www.worldpolicy.org/journal/articles/wpj03-4/mason.htm

MCGROARTY, PATRICK, and DEVON MAYLIE. "Zuma Renews Push for Power." *Wall Street Journal.* (June 27, 2012):A13.

MCKEE, VICTORIA. "Blue Blood and the Color of Money." *New York Times* (June 9, 1996):49–50.

MCLEOD, JAY. *Ain't No Makin' It: Aspirations and Attainment in a Low-Income Neighborhood.* Boulder, CO: Westview Press, 1995.

MILBOURNE, P., and P. CLOKE. "The hidden faces of rural homelessness." In P. Milbourne and P. Cloke, eds., *International Perspectives on Rural Homelessness.* Abingdon, Oxfordshire: Routledge, 2006.

MOORE, MICHAEL J. "Wall Street Bonuses Cut." *Bloomberg Businessweek.* (November 15, 2012). Available at http://www.businessweek.com/articles/2012-11-15/wall-street-bonuses-cut

MORISSETTE, RENÉ, GARNETT PICOT, and YUQIAN LU. *The Evolution of Canadian Wages over the Last Three Decades.* Analytical Studies Branch Research Paper Series No. 347. (2013). Statistics Canada Catalogue no. 11F0019M. [Online] http://www.statcan.gc.ca/pub/11f0019m/11f0019m2013347-eng.htm

MOUW, TED. "Job Relocation and the Racial Gap in Unemployment in Detroit and Chicago, 1980 to 1990." *American Sociological Review.* Vol. 65, No. 5 (October 2000):730–53.

MURPHY, JOHN. "Some Rise but Most Sink in Soweto's Sea of Slums." *Baltimore Sun* (October 6, 2002). [Online] Available November 15, 2008, at http://www.baltimoresun.com/news/health/balte.soweto06oct06,0,1833961.story

NATIONAL COUNCIL OF WELFARE. "Poverty Profile: Special Edition." 2012. https://www.google.ca/url?sa=t&rct=j&q=&esrc=s&source=web&cd=3&cad=rja&uact=8&ved=0CCoQFjACahUKEwiZvKLG5dvHAhWDnIgKHV8yCrA&url=http%3A%2F%2Fwww.esdc.gc.ca%2Feng%2Fcommunities%2Freports%2Fpoverty_profile%2Fsnapshot.pdf&usg=AFQjCNG-bxB8TqTcKRSbaH0LiRu7lFtWsg&sig2=J1QvOabRpyiiMIkrFrKJrg&bvm=bv.102022582,d.cGU

NELSON, AMY L. "The Effect of Economic Restructuring on Family Poverty in the Industrial Heartland, 1970–1990." *Sociological Focus.* Vol. 31, No. 2 (May 1998):201–16.

NEW YORK TIMES. "The Pay at the Top." April 9, 2011. Available at http://projects.nytimes.com/executive_compensation

NORC. *General Social Surveys, 1972–2010: Cumulative Codebook.* Chicago: National Opinion Research Center, 2011. [Online] Available at http://www.norc.org/GSS+Website

OECD (ORGANISATION FOR ECONOMIC CO-OPERATION AND DEVELOPMENT). "A Family Affair: Intergenerational Social Mobility across OECD Countries. Economic Policy Reforms Going for Growth." 2010. www.oecd.org/dataoecd/3/62/44582910.pdf

———. *Pensions at a Glance 2013 OECD and G20 Indicators.* 2013. http://www.oecd-ilibrary.org/finance-and-investment/pensions-at-a-glance-2013_pension_glance-2013-en

OLSEN, DENIS. *The State Elite.* Toronto: McClelland and Stewart, 1980.

OSTRANDER, SUSAN A. "Upper-Class Women: The Feminine Side of Privilege." *Qualitative Sociology.* Vol. 3, No. 1 (Spring 1980):23–44.

———. *Women of the Upper Class.* Philadelphia, PA: Temple University Press, 1984.

PACKARD, MARK. Personal communication (2002).

PENDAKUR, KRISHNA, and RAVI PENDAKUR. "The colour of money: earnings differentials among ethnic groups in Canada." *Canadian Journal of Economics.* Vol. 31, No. 3 (August 1998):518-548.

———. "The Colour of Money Redux: Immigrant/Ethnic Earnings Disparity in Canada 1991–2006." Forthcoming in Li and Teixiera, eds., *Economic and Housing Experience of Immigrants.* Montreal-Kingston: McGill-Queens University Press, 2015.

PERRY, ALEX. "South Africa Looks for a Leader." *Time* (April 27, 2009):38–41.

PEW RESEARCH CENTER. 2012. Available at http://www.people-press.org/question-search/?qid=1814733&pid=51&ccid=50#top

PORTER, JOHN. *The Vertical Mosaic.* Toronto: University of Toronto Press, 1965.

POWELL, BILL. "Postcard: Dongguan." *Time* (December 15, 2008):4.

RAPOSA, ANDREW. "Why Marx Matters." *New Politics* (April 26, 2015). http://newpol.org/content/why-marx-matters

REID, ANGUS. *How the New Economy Is Changing Our Lives.* Toronto: Doubleday Canada, 1996.

RICHBURG, KEITH B. "China's Communist Rulers Find Newly Rich a Headache." *The Richmond Times-Dispatch.* September 14, 2011:A2.

ROTH, ZACHARY. "Labor: Lavish CEO Pay Still Rising." *The Lookout,* April 20, 2011. Available at http://news.yahoo.com/s/yblog_thelookout/20110420/tsyblog_thelookout/labor-lavish-ceo-pay-still-rising

SALVATION ARMY. *The Dignity Project: Debunking Myths About Poverty in Canada.* 2011a. http://www.salvationarmy.ca/

———. "Canada Speaks: The Dignity Project." 2011b. http://intraspec.ca/CanadaSpeaks_report_May2011.pdf

SENNETT, RICHARD. *The Corrosion of Character: The Personal Consequences of Work in the New Capitalism.* New York: Norton, 1998.

SERVICE CANADA. "Firefighters." Date modified 2014. http://www.servicecanada.gc.ca/eng/qc/job_futures/statistics/6262.shtml#consider

STATISTICS CANADA. Selected Income Characteristics (35), Aboriginal Identity (8), Age Groups (6) and Sex (3) for Population, for Canada, Provinces, Territories and Census Metropolitan Areas, 2001 Census—20% Sample Data (2003a). [Electronic Data File] Catalogue no. 97F0011XIE2001047.

———. Income Status (4) and Census Family Structure for Census Families, Sex, Age Groups and Household Living Arrangements for Non-family Persons 15 Years and Over and Sex and Age Groups for Persons in Private Households (87), for Canada, Provinces, Census Metropolitan Areas and Census Agglomerations, 1995 and 2000—20% Sample Data. (2003b) [Electronic Data File] Catalogue no. 97F0020XCB01006.

———. *2006 Census: Earnings, Income and Shelter Costs.* 2008. www.statcan.gc.ca/daily-quotidien/080501/dq080501a-eng.htm

———. *Aboriginal Peoples of Canada, 2006 Census.* Catalogue no. 92-593-XCB2006001. 2009a. [Online] www.statcan.gc.ca/bsolc/olc-cel/olc-cel?catno=92-593-XCB2006001&lang=eng&issnote=1

———. *Earnings and Incomes of Canadians over the Past Quarter Century, 2006 Census: Earnings.* 2009b. [Online] www12.statcan.ca/census-recensement/2006/as-sa/97-563/p5-eng.cfm

———. *2006 Community Profiles*. 2010. [Online] www12. statcan.ca/census%E2%80%90recensement/2006/ dp%E2%80%90pd/prof/92%E2%80%90591/search-recherche/lst/page.cfm?Lang=E&GeoCode=35

———. *Selected Demographic, Sociocultural, Education and Labour Characteristics (322), Sex (3) and Income Status in 2010 (6) for the Population in Private Households of Canada, Provinces, Census Metropolitan Areas and Census Agglomerations, 2011 National Household Survey*. 2011a. http://www12.statcan.gc.ca/nhs-enm/ 2011/dp-pd/dt-td/Rp-eng.cfm?LANG=E&APATH= 3&DETAIL=0&DIM=0&FL=A&FREE=0&GC=0& GID=0&GK=0&GRP=1&PID=106715&PRID=0& PTYPE=105277&S=0&SHOWALL=0&SUB=0& Temporal=2013&THEME=98&VID=0&VNAMEE= &VNAMEF=

———. *Income and Earnings Statistics in 2010 (16), Age Groups (8C), Sex (3), Work activity in 2010 (3), Highest Certificate, Diploma or Degree (6) and Selected Sociocultural Characteristics (60) for the Population Aged 15 Years and Over in Private Households of Canada, Provinces, Territories and Census Metropolitan Areas, 2011 National Household Survey*. Statistics Canada. Catalogue no. 99-014-X2011041. 2011b.

———. *Canada Year Book 2011*. Ottawa: Minister of Industry, 2011c.

———. *Selected Demographic, Sociocultural, Education and Labour Characteristics (322), Sex (3) and Income Status in 2010 (6) for the Population in Private Households of Canada, Provinces, Census Metropolitan Areas and Census Agglomerations, 2011 National Household Survey*. Statistics Canada. Catalogue no. 99-014-X2011043. 2011d.

———. *Income Status after Tax (3A) and Economic Family Structure (4) for the Economic Families in Private Households of Canada, Provinces, Census Divisions and Census Subdivisions, 2005—20% Sample Data*. [Electronic Data File]. Catalogue no. 97-563-XCB2006040[1].IVT. 2011e.

———. *Education in Canada: Attainment, Field of Study and Location of Study*. Ottawa: Minister of Industry. Catalogue no. v99-012-X2011001. 2013a.

———. *Table 202-0605 Median after-tax income, by economic family type, 2011 constant dollars*. CANSIM table 202-0605. Date modified 2013b.

———. *Modified Table 202-0703—Market, Total and After-Tax Income, by Economic Family Type and After-Tax Income Quintiles, 2007 Constant Dollars, Annual*. Catalogue no. 703[1].ivt. Date modified 2013c.

———. "Survey of Financial Security, 2012." *The Daily* (February 25, 2014a). http://www.statcan.gc.ca/ daily-quotidien/140225/dq140225b-eng.htm?HPA

———. "Canadian Income Survey, 2012." *The Daily* (December 10, 2014b). http://www.statcan.gc.ca/ daily-quotidien/141210/dq141210a-eng.htm

———. *Table 111-0012 Family characteristics, by family type, age of older adult, and family income*. Catalogue no. 111-0012. Date modified 2015a.

———. "Study: Employment patterns of families with children, 1976 to 2014." *The Daily* (June 24, 2015b). http://www.statcan.gc.ca/daily-quotidien/150624/ dq150624a-eng.htm

TEDESCO, THERESA. "Where's the public outrage over sky-high CEO pay?" *Financial Post*. March 28, 2013. http://business.financialpost.com/executive/ leadership/say-on-pay-gets-vote-of-approval

TENCER, DANIEL. "Highest Paid CEOs In Canada: CCPA Study Says Top Execs Taking Home Ever Greater Share of the Pie." *Huffington Post*. January 2, 2013. http://www.huffingtonpost.ca/2013/01/02/canadian-ceo-earnings-2011-ccpa_n_2397251.html

TUMIN, MELVIN M. "Some Principles of Stratification: A Critical Analysis." *American Sociological Review*. Vol. 18, No. 4 (August 1953):387–94.

U.S. HOUSE OF REPRESENTATIVES. *1991 Green Book*. Washington, DC: U.S. Government Printing Office, 1991.

UNICEF. "Measuring child poverty." 2012. http://www. unicef-irc.org/publications/series/16/

UNITED NATIONS DEVELOPMENT PROGRAMME. *Human Development Report 2011*. Statistical Tables. [Online] Available at http://hdr.undp.org/en/statistics/data/

UPPAL, SHARANJIT, and SÉBASTIEN LAROCHELLE-CÔTÉ. *Factors associated with voting*. Ottawa: Statistics Canada Catalogue no. 75-001-X. 2012.

———. *Changes in wealth across the income distribution, 1999 to 2012*. Ottawa: Statistics Canada. Catalogue no. 75-006-X. 2015.

VEALL, MICHAEL R. "Top income shares in Canada: recent trends and policy implications." *The Canadian Journal of Economics/Revue Canadienne D'Economique*. Vol. 45, No. 4 (2012):1247-1272. doi:10.1111/j.1540-5982.2012.01744.x.

WALKER, KAREN. "'Always There for Me': Friendship Patterns and Expectations among Middle- and Working-Class Men and Women." *Sociological Forum*. Vol. 10, No. 2 (June 1995):273–96.

WARNER, W. LLOYD, and PAUL S. LUNT. *The Social Life of a Modern Community*. New Haven, CT: Yale University Press, 1941.

WEITZMAN, LENORE J. "The Economic Consequences of Divorce Are Still Unequal: Comment on Peterson."*American Sociological Review*. Vol. 61, No. 3 (June 1996):537–38.

WILKINSON, R. *The Impact of Inequality: How to Make Sick Societies Healthier*. New York: The New Press, 2005.

WILLIAMSON, JEFFREY G., and PETER H. LINDERT. *American Inequality: A Macroeconomic History*. New York: Academic Press, 1980.

WILLIAMSON, SAMUEL H. "Six Ways to Compute the Relative Value of a U.S. Dollar Amount, 1790 to Present." Measuring Worth. 2012. Available at http://www. measuringworth.com/index.html

WILSON, WILLIAM JULIUS. *When Work Disappears: The World of the New Urban Poor*. New York: Knopf, 1996a.

———. "Work." *New York Times Magazine* (August 18, 1996b):26ff.

WINES, MICHAEL, and IAN JOHNSON. "After a Horrific Crash, a Stark Depiction of Injustice in China." *The New York Times Online*. November 18, 2011. Available at http://www.nytimes. com/2011/11/19/world/asia/a-horrific-crash-sets-off-online-anger-inchina.html?ref=china

WOLFF, EDWARD N. "Recent Trends in Household Wealth in the United States: Rising Debt and the Middle-Class Squeeze." Levy Economics Institute of Bard College. June 2007. www.levy.org/pubs/wp_502.pdf

WORLD BANK. "Russian Economic Report #26." September 25, 2011a. [Online] Available at http://docu-ments.worldbank.org/curated/en/2011/09/15115904/ growing-risks

———. "Russian Federation Partnership, Country Program Snapshot." September 2011b. [Online] Available at http://siteresources.worldbank.org/INTRUSSIAN-FEDERATION/Resources/Russia_Snapshot.pdf

———. "World DataBank: World Development Indicators." 2012. Available at http://data.worldbank.org/ data-catalog/world-development-indicators

WORLD WEALTH REPORT. "Regional View." 2015. https:// www.worldwealthreport.com/reports/population/ north_america/canada

WU, XIAOGANG, and DONALD G. TREIMAN. "Inequality and Equality under Chinese Socialism: The Hukou System and Intergenerational Occupational Mobility." *American Journal of Sociology*. Vol. 113, No. 2 (September 2007):415–45.

YARDLEY, WILLIAM. "The Branding of the Occupy Movement." *New York Times*. November 27, 2011. http://www.nytimes.com/2011/11/28/business/ media/the-branding-of-the-occupy-movement.html? pagewanted=all&_r=1

YEN, HOPE. "Census Shows 1 in 2 People are Poor or Low-Income." Associated Press. December 15, 2011. Available at http://finance.yahoo.com/news/census-shows-1-2-people-103940568.html

ZAGORSKY, JAY. "Divorce Drops a Person's Wealth by 77 Percent." Press release, January 18, 2006. www. eurekalert.org/pub_releases/2006-01/osu-dda011806. php

ZUCKERMAN, MORTIMER B. "The Russian Conundrum." *U.S. News & World Report* (March 13, 2006):64.

Chapter 9

ANTI-SLAVERY INTERNATIONAL. 2012. Available at http:// www.antislavery.org/english/default.aspx

BANGLADESH GARMENT MANUFACTURERS & EXPORTERS ASSOCIATION. 2012. Available at http://www.bgmea. com.bd/home/pages/aboutus

BAUER, P.T. *Equality, the Third World, and Economic Delusion*. Cambridge, MA: Harvard University Press, 1981.

BEARAK, BARRY. "Lives Held Cheap in Bangladesh Sweatshops." *New York Times* (April 15, 2001):A1, A12.

BERGER, PETER L. *The Capitalist Revolution: Fifty Propositions about Prosperity, Equality, and Liberty*. New York: Basic Books, 1986.

BERGESEN, ALBERT, ed. *Crises in the World-System*. Beverly Hills, CA: Sage, 1983.

BONANNO, ALESSANDRO, DOUGLAS H. CONSTANCE, and HEATHER LORENZ. "Powers and Limits of Transnational Corporations: The Case of ADM." *Rural Sociology*. Vol. 65, No. 3 (September 2000):440–60.

BURKETT, ELINOR. "God Created Me to Be a Slave." *New York Times Magazine* (October 12, 1997):56–60.

BUSSOLO, MAURIZIO, RAFAEL DE HOYOS, DENIS MEDVEDEV, and VICTOR SULLA. "Demographic Change, Economic Growth, and Income Distribution: An Empirical Analysis Using Ex-Ante Microsimulations." Paper prepared for Global Economic Prospects, 2007.

CHEN, SHAOHUA, and MARTIN RAVALLION. "An Update to the World Bank's Estimates of Consumption Poverty in the Developing World." World Bank. 2012. Available at http://siteresources.worldbank.org/ INTPOVCALNET/Resources/Global_Poverty_ Update_2012_02-29-12.pdf

CONSORTIUM FOR STREET CHILDREN. "Street Children Statistics." 2011. Available at http://www.streetchildren. org.uk/_uploads/resources/Street_Children_Stats_ FINAL.pdf

DAVIES, JAMES B., SUSANNA SANDSTRÖM, ANTHONY SHORROCKS, and EDWARD N. WOLFF. *The World Distribution of Household Wealth*. Discussion Paper No. 2008/03. Helsinki: United Nations University–World Institute for Development Economics Research. February 2008. www.wider.unu.edu/publications/ working-papers/discussion-papers/2008/en_GB/ dp2008-03/

DAVIES, JAMES, RODRIGO LLUBERAS, and ANTHONY SHORROCKS. "Credit Suisse Global World Databook, 2012." 2012. Available at https://infocus.credit-suisse.com/data/_product_documents/_shop/369553/ 2012_global_wealth_databook.pdf

DELACROIX, JACQUES, and CHARLES C. RAGIN. "Structural Blockage: A Cross-National Study of Economic Dependency, State Efficacy, and Underdevelopment." *American Journal of Sociology*. Vol. 86, No. 6 (May 1981):1311–47.

DIXON, WILLIAM J., and TERRY BOSWELL. "Dependency, Disarticulation, and Denominator Effects: Another Look at Foreign Capital Penetration." *American Journal of Sociology*. Vol. 102, No. 2 (September 1996):543–62.

ECONOMIST, THE. "Paving the Way." [Online] Available January 27, 2011, at http://www.economist.com/ node/18013822?story_id=18013822&fsrc=rss

FIREBAUGH, GLENN. "Growth Effects of Foreign and Domestic Investment." *American Journal of Sociology*. Vol. 98, No. 1 (July 1992):105–30.

———. "Does Foreign Capital Harm Poor Nations? New Estimates Based on Dixon and Boswell's Measures of Capital Penetration." *American Journal of Sociology*. Vol. 102, No. 2 (September 1996):563–75.

FIREBAUGH, GLENN, and DUMITRU SANDU. "Who Supports Marketization and Democratization in Post-Communist Romania?" *Sociological Forum*. Vol. 13, No. 3 (September 1998):521–41.

FIREBAUGH, GLENN, and FRANK D. BECK. "Does Economic Growth Benefit the Masses? Growth, Dependence, and Welfare in the Third World." *American Sociological Review*. Vol. 59, No. 5 (October 1994):631–53.

FISHER, MAX. "The Country Where Slavery Is Still Normal." *The Atlantic* (June 28, 2011). Available at http://www. theatlantic.com/international/archive/2011/06/the-country-where-slavery-is-still-normal/241148/

FORBES. "World's Billionaires." 2012. Available at http:// www.forbes.com/wealth/billionaires

FOREIGN AFFAIRS, TRADE, AND DEVELOPMENT CANADA. *Statistical Report on International Assistance, Fiscal Year 2013-2014*. 2015. [Online] http:// international.gc.ca/development-developpement/dev-results-resultats/reports-rapports/sria-rsai-2013-14. aspx?lang=eng

FRANK, ANDRÉ GUNDER. *On Capitalist Underdevelopment.* Bombay: Oxford University Press, 1975.

————. *Crisis in the World Economy.* New York: Holmes & Meier, 1980.

————. *Reflections on the World Economic Crisis.* New York: Monthly Review Press, 1981.

FRAYSSINET, FABIANA. "Agribusiness Driving Land Concentration." Inter Press Service News Agency. [Online] Available October 5, 2009, at http://ipsnews.net/news.asp?idnews=48734

GALANO, ANA MARIA. "Land Hungry in Brazil." *Courier* (July/August 1998). www.unesco.org/courier/1998_08/uk/somm/intro.htm

GOESLING, BRIAN. "Changing Income Inequalities within and between Nations: New Evidence." *American Sociological Review.* Vol. 66, No. 5 (October 2001):745–61.

HOSSAIN, NAOMI. "Exports, Equity, and Empowerment: The Effects of Readymade Garments Manufacturing Employment on Gender Equality in Bangladesh." World Bank. 2011. Available at http://siteresources.worldbank.org/INTWDR2012/Resources/7778105-1299699968583/7786210-1322671773271/Hossain-Export-Equity-employment.pdf

HWANG, STEPHEN W. "Homelessness and Health." *Canadian Medical Association Journal.* Vol. 164, No. 2 (January 2001):229–33.

IBGE (INSTITUTO BRASILEIRO DE GEOGRAFIA E ESTATÍSTICA). Census of Agriculture, 2006. [Online] Available at http://www.ibge.gov.br/english/presidencia/noticias/noticia_visualiza.php?id_noticia=1464&id_pagina=1

INTERNATIONAL LABOUR ORGANIZATION. "Forced Labour." 2012. Available at http://www.ilo.org/global/topics/forced-labour/lang-en/index.htm

KENTOR, JEFFREY. "The Long-Term Effects of Foreign Investment Dependence on Economic Growth, 1940–1990." *American Journal of Sociology.* Vol. 103, No. 4 (January 1998):1024–46

————. "The Long-Term Effects of Globalization on Income Inequality, Population Growth, and Economic Development." *Social Problems.* Vol. 48, No. 4 (November 2001):435–55.

KIHIKA, MAUREEN. "Ghosts and Shadows: A History of Racism in Canada." *Canadian Graduate Journal of Sociology and Criminology.* Vol. 2, No. 1 (Spring 2013):35–44.

LANDSEA CENTER FOR WOMEN'S LAND RIGHTS. 2011. Available at http://www.landesa.org/women-and-land

LAPPÉ, FRANCES MOORE, and JOSEPH COLLINS. *World Hunger: Twelve Myths.* New York: Grove Press/Food First Books, 1986.

LAPPÉ, FRANCES MOORE, JOSEPH COLLINS, and PETER ROSSET. *World Hunger: Twelve Myths.* 2nd ed. New York: Grove Press, 1998.

LEOPOLD, EVELYN. "Sudan's Young Endure 'Unspeakable' Abuse: Report." *Yahoo! News* (April 19, 2007). http://news.yahoo.com

LEVINSON, F. JAMES, and LUCY BASSETT. "Malnutrition Is Still a Major Contributor to Child Deaths." Population Reference Bureau. 2007. www.prb.org/pdf07/Nutrition2007.pdf

LINDAUER, DAVID L., and AKILA WEERAPANA. "Relief for Poor Nations." *Society.* Vol. 39, No. 3 (March/April 2002):54–58.

MILANOVIC, BRANKO. "Global Inequality Recalculated: The Effect of New 2005 PPP Estimates on Global Inequality." World Bank. August 2009. http://siteresources.worldbank.org/INTDECINEQ/Resources/Global_Inequality_Recalculated.pdf

————. "Global Income Inequality: New Results and Implications for 21st Century Policy." World Bank. 2011. Available at http://siteresources.worldbank.org/EXTABCDE/Resources/7455676-1292528456380/7626791-1303141641402/7878676-1306699356046/Parallel-Sesssion-6-Branko-Milanovic.pdf

MOORE, WILBERT E. "Modernization as Rationalization: Processes and Restraints." In Manning Nash, ed., *Essays on Economic Development and Cultural Change in Honor of Bert F. Hoselitz.* Chicago: University of Chicago Press, 1977:29–42.

————. *World Modernization: The Limits of Convergence.* New York: Elsevier, 1979.

ORGANISATION FOR ECONOMIC CO-OPERATION AND DEVELOPMENT. *Charts, Tables, and Databases.* 2015. Available at http://www.oecd.org/dac/stats/data.htm

ORHANT, MELANIE. "Human Trafficking Exposed." *Population Today.* Vol. 30, No. 1 (January 2002):1, 4.

PARSONS, TALCOTT. *Societies: Evolutionary and Comparative Perspectives.* Englewood Cliffs, NJ: Prentice Hall, 1966.

PERRY, ALEX. "Africa Rising." *Time.* Vol. 180, No. 23 (December 3, 2012):48–52.

POPULATION REFERENCE BUREAU. "World Population Data Sheet." 2012a. Available at http://www.prb.org/pdf12/2012-population-data-sheet_eng.pdf

————. "World Population Data Sheet." 2012b. Available at http://www.prb.org/pdf12/2012-population-data-sheet_eng.pdf

————. "Contraceptive Use Among Married Women Ages 15–49, by Method Type." 2015. Available at http://www.prb.org/DataFinder/Topic/Rankings.aspx?ind=42

ROSTOW, WALT W. *The Stages of Economic Growth: A Non-Communist Manifesto.* Cambridge, MA: Cambridge University Press, 1960.

————. *The World Economy: History and Prospect.* Austin: University of Texas Press, 1978.

SALA-I-MARTIN, XAVIER. *The World Distribution of Income.* Working Paper No. 8933. Cambridge, MA: National Bureau of Economic Research, 2002.

SCHAFFER, MICHAEL. "American Dreamers." *U.S. News & World Report* (August 26, 2002):12–16.

STATISTICS CANADA. "Survey of Financial Security, 2012." *The Daily* (February 25, 2014). [Online] http://www.statcan.gc.ca/daily-quotidien/140225/dq140225b-eng.htm

U.S. AGENCY FOR INTERNATIONAL DEVELOPMENT (USAID). "U.S. Overseas Loans and Grants." 2012. Available at http://gbk.eads.usaidallnet.gov/

U.S. CENSUS BUREAU, FOREIGN TRADE DIVISION. "Foreign Trade Statistics." 2012. Available at http://www.census.gov/foreign-trade/index.html

U.S. DEPARTMENT OF LABOR. "List of Goods Produced by Child Labor or Forced Labor, 2012." 2012. Available at http://www.dol.gov/ilab/programs/ocft/2012TVPRA.pdf

UN IGME. "Levels and Trends in Child Mortality." 2014. Available at http://www.childmortality.org/

UNITED NATIONS. "Millennium Development Goals." 2011. [Online] Available at http://www.un.org/millenniumgoals

UNITED NATIONS DEVELOPMENT PROGRAMME. "Human Development Indices: A Statistical Update." December 18, 2008. http://hdr.undp.org/en/statistics/data/

————. "International Human Development Indicators." 2012. Available at http://hdrstats.undp.org/en/indicators/default.html

UNITED NATIONS STATISTICS DIVISION. "The World's Women 2010: Trends and Statistics." Chapter 8: Poverty. 2010. Available at http://unstats.un.org/unsd/demographic/products/Worldswomen/WW2010pub.htm

UNITED NATIONS WORLD FOOD PROGRAMME. "Undernutrition: Women and Children Paying the Price." 2008. Available at http://www.wfp.org/english/?n=37

UNITED NATIONS, DEPARTMENT OF ECONOMIC AND SOCIAL AFFAIRS. "World Population Prospects: The 2010 Revision." 2011. Available at http://esa.un.org/unpd/wpp/index.htm

UNITED NATIONS, FOOD AND AGRICULTURE ORGANIZATION (FAO). The State of Food Insecurity in the World 2012." 2012. Available at http://www.fao.org/fileadmin/user_upload/newsroom/docs/sofi-faqs.pdf

VOGEL, EZRA F. *The Four Little Dragons: The Spread of Industrialization in East Asia.* Cambridge, MA: Harvard University Press, 1991.

WALLERSTEIN, IMMANUEL. *The Modern World-System: Capitalist Agriculture and the Origins of the European World-Economy in the Sixteenth Century.* New York: Academic Press, 1974.

————. *The Capitalist World-Economy.* New York: Cambridge University Press, 1979.

————. "Crises: The World Economy, the Movements, and the Ideologies." In Albert Bergesen, ed., *Crises in the World-System.* Beverly Hills, CA: Sage, 1983:21–36.

————. *The Politics of the World Economy: The States, the Movements, and the Civilizations.* Cambridge: Cambridge University Press, 1984.

WEBER, MAX. *The Protestant Ethic and the Spirit of Capitalism.* New York: Scribner, 1958; orig. 1904–05.

WORLD BANK. *2008 World Development Indicators.* Washington, DC: World Bank, 2008.

————. "World DataBank: Health, Nutrition, and Population Statistics." 2012a. Available at http://data.worldbank.org/data-catalog/health-nutrition-and-population-statistics

————. "World DataBank: World Development Indicators." 2012b. Available at http://data.worldbank.org/data-catalog/world-development-indicators

WORSLEY, PETER. "Models of the World System." In Mike Featherstone, ed., *Global Culture: Nationalism, Globalization, and Modernity.* Newbury Park, CA: Sage, 1990:83–95.

Chapter 10

ARMSTRONG, ELISABETH. *The Retreat from Organization: U.S. Feminism Reconceptualized.* Albany: State University of New York Press, 2002.

AUCC (ASSOCIATION OF UNIVERSITIES AND COLLEGES OF CANADA). "Speaking Notes. Speech by Claire Morris, President Association of Universities and Colleges of Canada." 2008. www.aucc.ca/_pdf/english/speeches/2008/swaac_speech_claire_morris_05_02_bil.pdf

BAYDAR, NAZLI, and JEANNE BROOKS-GUNN. "Effect of Maternal Employment and Child-Care Arrangements on Preschoolers' Cognitive and Behavioral Outcomes: Evidence from Children from the National Longitudinal Survey of Youth." *Developmental Psychology.* Vol. 27, No. 6 (November 1991):932–35.

BEAUJOT, RODERIC. "Gender Models of Family and Work." *Horizons Policy Research Initiative.* Vol. 8, No. 3 (April 2006):24–26.

BEM, SANDRA LIPSITZ. *The Lenses of Gender: Transforming the Debate on Sexual Inequality.* New Haven, CT: Yale University Press, 1993.

BENOIT, CECILIA, L. SHUMKA, et al. "Explaining the Health Gap Between Girls and Women in Canada." *Sociological Research Online.* Vol. 14, No. 5 (2009). www.socresonline.org.uk/14/5/9.html

BENOIT, CECILIA. *Women, Work and Social Rights: Canada in Historical and Comparative Perspective.* Scarborough, ON: Prentice Hall Canada, 2000a.

————. "Variation within Post-Fordist and Liberal Welfare State Countries: Women's Work and Social Rights in Canada and the United States." In Thomas Boje and Arnlaug Leira, eds., *Gender, Welfare State and the Market: Towards a New Division of Labour.* London: Routledge, 2000b:71–88.

BERNARD, JESSIE. *The Female World.* New York: Free Press, 1981.

BONNER, JANE. Research presented in the Public Broadcast System telecast *The Brain #6: The Two Brains.* Videocassette VHS 339. Newark, NJ: WNET-13 Films, 1984.

BOYLE, ELIZABETH HEGER, FORTUNATA SONGORA, and GAIL FOSS. "International Discourse and Local Politics: Anti-Female-Genital-Cutting Laws in Egypt, Tanzania, and the United States." *Social Problems.* Vol. 48, No. 4 (November 2001):524–44.

BUTLER, JUDITH. *Gender Trouble: Feminism and the Subversion of Identity.* New York: Routledge, 2006.

CANADIAN HUMAN RIGHTS COMMISSION. "Voting Rights." Accessed June 19, 2015. [Online] http://www.chrc-ccdp.ca/en/browseSubjects/votingRights.asp

CATALYST. "*Fortune* 500 Board Seats Held by Women." 2012. Available at http://www.catalyst.org/knowledge/fortune-500-board-seats-held-women

CBC NEWS. "Women now hold 8.5% of Canada's top jobs." 2015a. http://www.cbc.ca/news/business/women-now-hold-8-5-of-canada-s-top-jobs-1.3001744

————. "Harassment in Canada's military tolerated by leadership, former justice finds." 2015b. http://www.cbc.ca/news/politics/harassment-in-canada-s-military-tolerated-by-leadership-former-justice-finds-1.3055493

CBS NEWS POLLS. "Poll: Women's Movement Worthwhile." [Online] Available October 23, 2005, at http://www.cbsnews.com/stories/2005/10/22/opinion/polls/main965224.shtml

CECI, STEPHEN J., and WENDY M. WILLIAMS. "Understanding Current Causes of Women's Underrepresentation in Science." *The Proceedings of the National Academy of Sciences*. 2011. [Online] Available at http://www.human.cornell.edu/hd/loader.cfm?csModule=security/getfile&PageID=60893

CENTERS FOR DISEASE CONTROL AND PREVENTION. "Deaths: Final Data for 2010, Tables." 2012. Available at http://www.cdc.gov/nchs/data/dvs/deaths_2010_release.pdf

CHARLES, MARIA. "Cross-National Variation in Occupational Segregation." *American Sociological Review*. Vol. 57, No. 4 (August 1992):483–502.

COHEN, PHILIP N., and MATT L. HUFFMAN. "Individuals, Jobs, and Labor Markets: The Devaluation of Women's Work." *American Sociological Review*. Vol. 68, No. 3 (June 2003):443–63.

COLLEGE BOARD, THE. "2012 College-Bound Seniors: Total Group Profile Report." [Online] 2012. Available at http://research.collegeboard.org/programs/sat/data/cb-seniors-2012

COLLINS, PATRICIA HILL. *Black Feminist Thought: Knowledge, Consciousness, and the Politics of Empowerment*. 2nd ed. New York: Routledge, 2000.

COLTRANE, SCOTT, and MELINDA MESSINEO. "Mass Mediated Inequality: Images of Race and Gender in 1990s' Television Advertising." *Sex Roles*. Vol. 42, No. 5/6 (2000):363–89.

CORRELL, SHELLEY J. "Gender and the Career Choice Process: The Role of Biased Self-Assessment." *American Journal of Sociology*. Vol. 106, No. 6 (May 2001):1691–730.

CORTESE, ANTHONY J. *Provocateur: Images of Women and Minorities in Advertising*. Lanham, MD: Rowman & Littlefield, 1999.

CRENSHAW, KIMBERLÉ WILLIAMS. "Mapping the Margins: Intersectionality, Identity Politics, and Violence against Women of Color." *Stanford Law Review*. Vol. 43, No. 6 (1991):1241–99.

CROSSETTE, BARBARA. "Female Genital Mutilation by Immigrants Is Becoming Cause for Concern in the U.S." *New York Times International* (December 10, 1995):11.

DAVIS, ANGELA. *Women, Race and Class*. New York: Random House, 1981.

DAVIS, DONALD M., cited in "TV Is a Blonde, Blonde World." *American Demographics*, special issue: *Women Change Places*. 1993.

DOYLE, JAMES A. *The Male Experience*. Dubuque, IA: Brown, 1983.

DROLET, MARIE. "The Persistent Gap: New Evidence of the Canadian Gender Wage Gap." Ottawa: Statistics Canada, Business and Labour Market Analysis Division. Catalogue no. 11F0019MPE, No. 157. 2001. [Online] www.statcan.ca/english/research/11F0019MIE/11F0019MIE2001157.pdf

DWORKIN, ANDREA. *Intercourse*. New York: Free Press, 1987.

EHRENREICH, BARBARA. *The Hearts of Men: American Dreams and the Flight from Commitment*. Garden City, NY: Anchor Books, 1983.

———. "The Real Truth about the Female Body." *Time* (March 15, 1999):56–65.

ENGELS, FRIEDRICH. *The Origin of the Family*. Chicago: Kerr, 1902; orig. 1884.

ENGLAND, PAULA, JOAN M. HERMSEN, and DAVID A. COTTER. "The Devaluation of Women's Work: A Comment on Tam." *American Journal of Sociology*. Vol. 105, No. 6 (May 2000):1741–60.

ERICKSON, LYNDA, and BRENDA O'NEILL. "The Gender Gap and the Changing Woman Voter in Canada." *International Political Science Review*. Vol. 23, No. 4 (2002):373-92.

FERREE, MYRA MARX, and BETH B. HESS. *Controversy and Coalition: The New Feminist Movement across Four Decades of Change*. 3rd ed. New York: Routledge, 1995.

FORBES. "*Forbes* 400." 2012. Available at http://www.forbes.com/forbes-400/

FOROOHAR, RANA. "The 100% Solution." *Time*. Vol. 177, No. 21 (May 23, 2011):22.

FORUM RESEARCH. *Just one eight admit to viewing pornography*. 2014. http://poll.forumresearch.com/post/98/just-one-eighth-admit-to-viewing-pornography/

FREEDMAN, ESTELLE B. *No Turning Back: The History of Feminism and the Future of Women*. New York: Ballantine Books, 2002.

FRENCH, MARILYN. *Beyond Power: On Women, Men, and Morals*. New York: Summit Books, 1985.

FULLER, REX, and RICHARD SCHOENBERGER. "The Gender Salary Gap: Do Academic Achievement, Intern Experience, and College Major Make a Difference?" *Social Science Quarterly*. Vol. 72, No. 4 (December 1991):715–26.

GEWERTZ, DEBORAH. "A Historical Reconsideration of Female Dominance among the Chambri of Papua New Guinea." *American Ethnologist*. Vol. 8, No. 1 (1981):94–106.

GIBBS, NANCY. "What Kids (Really) Need." *Time* (April 30, 2001):48–49.

GIDENGIL, ELISABETH, ANDRÉ BLAIS, JOANNA EVERITT, PATRICK FOURNIER, and NEIL NEVITTE. "Back to the Future? Making Sense of the 2004 Canadian Election Outside Quebec." *Canadian Journal of Political Science*. Vol. 39, No. 1 (2006):1-25

GILLIGAN, CAROL. *In a Different Voice: Psychological Theory and Women's Development*. Cambridge, MA: Harvard University Press, 1982.

GOFFMAN, ERVING. *Gender Advertisements*. New York: Harper Colophon, 1979.

GOLDBERG, STEVEN. *The Inevitability of Patriarchy*. New York: Morrow, 1974.

GRAYBOW, MARTHA. "Women Directors Help Boost the Bottom Line." *Yahoo! News* (October 1, 2007). http://news.yahoo.com

GREENSPOON, EDWARD. "Pay-Equity Costs Too High: Chrétien." *Globe and Mail* (August 18, 1998):A3.

HANEY, LYNNE. "After the Fall: East European Women since the Collapse of State Socialism." *Contexts*. Vol. 1, No. 3 (Fall 2002):27–36.

HARPSTER, PAULA, and ELIZABETH MONK-TURNER. "Why Men Do Housework: A Test of Gender Production and the Relative Resources Model." *Sociological Focus*. Vol. 31, No. 1 (February 1998):45–59.

HEALTH CANADA. *Federal Interdepartmental Working Group on Female Genital Mutilation: Female Genital Mutilation and Health Care—An Exploration of the Needs and Roles of Affected Communities and Health Care Providers in Canada*. Ottawa: Author, 1999.

HEATH, JULIA A., and W. DAVID BOURNE. "Husbands and Housework: Parity or Parody?" *Social Science Quarterly*. Vol. 76, No. 1 (March 1995):195–202.

HENLEY, NANCY, MYKOL HAMILTON, and BARRIE THORNE. "Womanspeak and Manspeak: Sex Differences in Communication, Verbal and Nonverbal." In John J. Macionis and Nijole V. Hertz, *More Equal Than Others: Women and Men in Dual-Career Marriages*. Berkeley: University of California Press, 1986.

HERMAN, DIANNE. "The Rape Culture." In John J. Macionis and Nijole V. Benokraitis, eds., *Seeing Ourselves: Classic, Contemporary, and Cross-Cultural Readings in Sociology*. 5th ed. Upper Saddle River, NJ: Prentice Hall, 2001.

HERTZ, R. *More Equal Than Others: Women and Men in Dual-Career Marriages*. Berkeley: University of California Press, 1986.

HEWLETT, SYLVIA ANN, and CAROLYN BUCK LUCE. "Off-Ramps and On-Ramps: Keeping Talented Women on the Road to Success." *Harvard Business Review*. Vol. 83, No. 3 (March 2005):43–54.

HEWLETT, SYLVIA ANN. "As Careers Paths Change, Make On-Ramping Easy." [Online] Available July 8, 2010, at http://blogs.hbr.org/hbr/hewlett/2010/07/as_careers_paths_change_make_o.html

HOOKS, BELL. *Feminist Theory: From Margin to Center*. 2nd ed. London: Pluto Press, 2000.

INTER-PARLIAMENTARY UNION. "Women in National Parliaments." 2012. Available at http://www.ipu.org/wmn-e/classif.htm

IPSOS. "Can Men Be Feminists Too? Half (48%) of Men in 15 Country Survey Seem to Think So." (May 23, 2014). [Online] http://www.ipsos-na.com/news-polls/pressrelease.aspx?id=6511

JOHNSON, J., and L. GREAVES. *Better Science with Sex and Gender: A Primer for Health Research*. Vancouver: Women's Health Research Network, 2007.

KRAHN, HARVEY J., and GRAHAM S. LOWE. *Work, Industry, and Canadian Society*. 3rd ed. Toronto: ITP Nelson, 1998.

KRIEGER, N. "Genders, Sexes, and Health: What Are the Connections—and Why Does It Matter?" *International Journal of Epidemiology*. Vol. 32 (2003):652–57.

KRISTOF, NICHOLAS, and SHERYL WU DUNN. *Half the Sky: Turning Oppression into Opportunity for Women Worldwide*. New York: Vintage Books, 2010.

LEIRA, ARNLAUG. "Combining Work and Family: Nordic Policy Reforms in the 1990s." In Thomas Boje and Arnlaug Leira, eds., *Gender, Welfare State and the Market: Towards a New Division of Labour*. London: Routledge, 2000:157–74.

LENGERMANN, PATRICIA MADOO, and RUTH A. WALLACE. *Gender in America: Social Control and Social Change*. Englewood Cliffs, NJ: Prentice Hall, 1985.

LEVER, JANET. "Sex Differences in the Complexity of Children's Play and Games." *American Sociological Review*. Vol. 43, No. 4 (August 1978):471–83.

LEWIN, TAMAR. "Girls' Gains Have Not Cost Boys, Report Says." *New York Times* (May 20, 2008). www.nytimes.com/2008/05/20/education/20girls.html?partner=permalink&exprod=permalink

LIBRARY OF PARLIAMENT. "International Women's Day: Canadian Women as Leaders." 2012. [Online] Available at http://www.parl.gc.ca/Content/LOP/ResearchPublications/2012-09-e.htm

MANITOBA WOMEN'S DIRECTORATE. "About Women." Vol. 9, No. 1 (January/February 1984). http://www.gov.mb.ca/msw/index.html

MARATHONGUIDE.COM. "Marathon Records." 2012. Available at http://www.marathonguide.com/history/records/index.cfm

MARSHALL, SUSAN E. "Ladies against Women: Mobilization Dilemmas of Antifeminist Movements." *Social Problems*. Vol. 32, No. 4 (April 1985):348–62.

MARTIN, CAROL LYNN, and RICHARD A. FABES. "The Stability and Consequences of Young Children's Same-Sex Peer Interactions." *Developmental Psychology*. Vol. 37, No. 3 (May 2001):431–46.

MASON, MARY ANN, and MARC GOULDEN. "Do Babies Matter (Part II)? Closing the Baby Gap." *Academe* (November–December 2004) [Online] http://www.aaup.org/publications/Academe/2004/04nd/04ndmaso.htm

MCCALL, LESLIE. "The Complexity of Intersectionality." *Signs: Journal of Women in Culture and Society*. Vol. 30, No. 3 (2005):1771-1800.

MCELROY, WENDY. *XXX: a woman's right to pornography*. New York: St. Martin's Press, 1995.

MEAD, MARGARET. *Sex and Temperament in Three Primitive Societies*. New York: Morrow, 1963; orig. 1935.

MESSINEO, MELINDA. "Does Advertising on Black Entertainment Television Portray More Positive Gender Representations Compared to Broadcast Networks?" *Sex Roles*. Vol. 59, No. 9/10 (2008):752–64.

MILAN, ANNE, LESLIE-ANNE KEOWN, and COVADONGA ROBLES URQUIJO. "Families, Living Arrangements and Unpaid Work." *Women in Canada: A Gender-Based Statistical Report*, 6th ed. Catalogue no. 89-503-X. 2011. [Online] http://www.statcan.gc.ca/pub/89-503-x/2010001/article/11546-eng.htm

MORISSETTE, RENÉ, GARNETT PICOT, and YUQIAN LU. *The Evolution of Canadian Wages over the Last Three Decades*. Analytical Studies Branch Research Paper Series No. 347. (2013). Statistics Canada Catalogue no. 11F0019M. [Online] http://www.statcan.gc.ca/pub/11f0019m/11f0019m2013347-eng.htm

MORRA, NORMAN, and MICHAEL D. SMITH. "Men in Feminism: Reinterpreting Masculinity and Femininity." In Nancy Mandell, ed., *Feminist Issues: Race, Class, and Sexuality*. 2nd ed. Scarborough, ON: Prentice Hall Allyn and Bacon Canada, 1998:160–78.

MURDOCK, GEORGE PETER. "Comparative Data on the Division of Labor by Sex." *Social Forces*. Vol. 15, No. 4 (May 1937):551–53.

NATIONAL DEFENCE AND THE CANADIAN ARMED FORCES. "Canadian Armed Forces – Historical milestones of women." March 6, 2014a. http://www.forces.gc.ca/en/news/article.page?doc=canadian-armed-forces-historical-milestones-of-women/hie8w7rl

———. "Women in the Canadian Armed Forces." March 6, 2014b. http://www.forces.gc.ca/en/news/article.page?doc=women-in-the-canadian-armed-forces/hie8w7rm

NELLIE MCCLUNG FOUNDATION. "Women's Firsts – Canada." Accessed June 19, 2015. [Online] http://www.ournellie.com/womens-suffrage/womens-firsts-canada/

NOLAN, PATRICK, and GERHARD E. LENSKI. Human Societies: An Introduction to Macrosociology. 11th ed. Boulder, CO: Paradigm, 2010.

NORC. General Social Surveys, 1972–2012. Chicago: National Opinion Research Center. March 2013. Available at http://www.norc.org/GSS+Website

OECD (ORGANISATION FOR ECONOMIC CO-OPERATION AND DEVELOPMENT). Closing the Gender Gap: Act Now. 2012. http://dx.doi.org/10.1787/9789264179370-en

OVADIA, SETH. "Race, Class, and Gender Differences in High School Seniors' Values: Applying Intersection Theory in Empirical Analysis." Social Science Quarterly. Vol. 82, No. 2 (June 2001):341–56.

PAPPAS, STEPHANIE. "Americans Like Baby Boys Best." Live Science. June 24, 2011. Available at http://news.yahoo.com/s/livescience/20110624/sc_livescience/americanslikebabyboysbest

PARSONS, TALCOTT. "Age and Sex in the Social Structure of the United States." American Sociological Review. Vol. 7, No. 4 (August 1942):604–16.

———. The Social System. New York: Free Press, 1951.

———. Essays in Sociological Theory. New York: Free Press, 1954.

PAXTON, PAMELA, MELANIE M. HUGHES, and JENNIFER L. GREEN. "The International Women's Movement and Women's Political Participation, 1893–2003." American Sociological Review. Vol. 71, No. 6 (December 2006):898–920.

PAYSCALE. "Floral Designer Salary (Canada)." 2015a. http://www.payscale.com/research/CA/Job=Floral_Designer/Hourly_Rate

———. "Truck Driver, Light or Delivery Services Salary (Canada)." 2015b. http://www.payscale.com/research/CA/Job=Truck_Driver%2c_Light_Or_Delivery_Services/Hourly_Rate

PLAN INTERNATIONAL. "Because I am a Girl: The State of the World's Girls 2011 - So, what about boys?" 2011. https://plan-international.org/about-plan/resources/publications/campaigns/because-i-am-a-girl-so-what-about-boys

POPENOE, DAVID. "Parental Androgyny." Society. Vol. 30, No. 6 (September/October 1993):5–11.

POPULATION REFERENCE BUREAU. "Datafinder." 2012. Available at http://www.prb.org/DataFinder.aspx

———. "Female Genital Mutilation/Cutting: Data and Trends: Update 2010." 2010. Available at http://www.prb.org/pdf10/fgm-wallchart2010.pdf

PRENTICE, ALISON, PAULA BOURNE, GAIL CUTHBERT BRANDT, BETH LIGHT, WENDY MITCHINSON, and NAOMI BLACK. Canadian Women: A History. 2nd ed. Toronto: Harcourt Brace & Company, 1996.

RAPHAEL, RAY. The Men from the Boys: Rites of Passage in Male America. Lincoln: University of Nebraska Press, 1988.

RIDGEWAY, CECILIA L., and LYNN SMITH-LOVIN. "The Gender System and Interaction." Annual Review of Sociology. Vol. 25 (August 1999):191–216.

ROSENDAHL, MONA. Inside the Revolution: Everyday Life in Socialist Cuba. Ithaca, NY: Cornell University Press, 1997.

ROSSI, ALICE S. "Gender and Parenthood." In Alice S. Rossi, ed., Gender and the Life Course. New York: Aldine, 1985:161–91.

SABATINI, JOSHUA. "San Francisco Circumcision Ban Headed for November Ballot." The Examiner. [Online] Available February, 18, 2011, at http://www.sfexaminer.com/local/2011/02/san-francisco-circumcision-ban-headednovember-ballot

SAINT JEAN, YANICK, and JOE R. FEAGIN. Double Burden: Black Women and Everyday Racism. Armonk, NY: Sharpe, 1998.

SHEA, RACHEL HARTIGAN. "The New Insecurity." U.S. News & World Report (March 25, 2002):40.

SHELLENBARGER, SUE. "The Name Change Dilemma." The Wall Street Journal (May 13, 2011). Available at http://finance.yahoo.com/family-home/article/112736/name-change-dilemma-women-marriage-wsj?mod=family-love_money

SINHA, MAIRE. "Measuring violence against women: Statistical trends." Juristat. Statistics Canada Catalogue no. 85-002-X. (February 25, 2013):1–120.

STACEY, JUDITH. Patriarchy and Socialist Revolution in China. Berkeley: University of California Press, 1983.

STATISTICS CANADA. Education in Canada, 1999. Statistics Canada Catalogue no. 81229-XIE, May 2000.

———. "University Degrees, Diplomas and Certificates Awarded." The Daily, 2003. [Online] www.statcan.ca/Daily/English/030708/d030708a.htm

———. "The Teaching Profession: Trends from 1999 to 2005." Education Matters. Vol. 3, No. 4 (2006a). [Online] www.statcan.gc.ca/pub/81-004-x/81-004-x2006004-eng.htm

———. Employment Income Statistics in 2010 (7), Sex (3), Work Activity in 2010 (3), Highest Certificate, Diploma or Degree (6) and Occupation - National Occupational Classification (NOC) 2011 (693) for the Population Aged 15 Years and Over in Private Households of Canada, Provinces and Territories, 2011 National Household Survey. [Electronic Data File.] Catalogue no. 99-014-X2011042. 2011a.

———. Income and Earnings Statistics in 2010 (16), Age Groups (8C), Sex (3), Work activity in 2010 (3), Highest Certificate, Diploma or Degree (6) and Selected Sociocultural Characteristics (60) for the Population Aged 15 Years and Over in Private Households of Canada, Provinces, Territories and Census Metropolitan Areas, 2011 National Household Survey. Statistics Canada. Catalogue no. 99-014-X2011041. 2011b.

———. Education in Canada: Attainment, Field of Study and Location of Study. Analytical Document Catalogue no. 99-012-X2011001. 2013a. http://www12.statcan.gc.ca/nhs-enm/2011/as-sa/99-012-x/99-012-x2011001-eng.cfm

———. Portrait of Canada's Labour Force. Analytical Document Catalogue no. 99-012-X2011002. 2013b. http://www12.statcan.gc.ca/nhs-enm/2011/as-sa/99-012-x/99-012-x2011002-eng.cfm#a5

———. Average Earnings by Sex and Work Pattern. CANSIM Table 202-0102 [Electronic Database]. 2013c.

———. "Back to school...by the numbers." The Daily (August 25, 2014). [Online] http://www.statcan.gc.ca/eng/dai/smr08/2014/smr08_190_2014

———. Labour Force Survey Estimates (LFS), by Sex and Age Group, Seasonally Adjusted and Unadjusted. CANSIM Table 282-0087 [Electronic Database]. 2015a.

———. Full-Time and Part-Time Employment by Sex and Age Group. CANSIM Table 282-0002 [Electronic Database]. 2015b.

———. Labour Force Survey Estimates (LFS), by National Occupational Classification for Statistics (NOC-S) And Sex, Unadjusted for Seasonality. CANSIM Table 282-0009 [Electronic Database]. 2015c.

———. Labour Force Characteristics by Age and Sex. CANSIM Table 282-0002 [Electronic Database]. 2015d.

STIER, HAYA. "Continuity and Change in Women's Occupations following First Childbirth." Social Science Quarterly. Vol. 77, No. 1 (March 1996):60–75.

STRATTON, LESLIE S. "Why Does More Housework Lower Women's Wages? Testing Hypotheses Involving Job Effort and Hours Flexibility." Social Sciences Quarterly. Vol. 82, No. 1 (March 2001):67–76.

SUSSMAN, DEBORAH, and LAHOUARIA YSSAAD. "The Rising Profile of Women Academics." Perspectives on Labour and Income. Catalogue no. 75-001-XIE. Ottawa: Statistics Canada, 2005.

TALLICHET, SUZANNE E. "Barriers to Women's Advancement in Underground Coal Mining." Rural Sociology. Vol. 65, No. 2 (June 2000):234–52.

TANNEN, DEBORAH. You Just Don't Understand: Women and Men in Conversation. New York: Morrow, 1990.

———. Talking from 9 to 5: How Women's and Men's Conversational Styles Affect Who Gets Heard, Who Gets Credit, and What Gets Done at Work. New York: Morrow, 1994.

TAVRIS, CAROL, and CAROL WADE. Psychology in Perspective. 3rd ed. Upper Saddle River, NJ: Prentice Hall, 2001.

TONG, ROSEMARIE. Feminist Thought: A More Comprehensive Introduction. 3rd ed. Boulder, CO: Westview, 2009.

TRIVENTI, M. "Something Changes, Something Not: Long-Term Trends in Gender Segregation of Fields of Study in Italy." Italian Journal of Sociology of Education. No. 2 (2010). www.ijse.eu/index.php/ijse/article/viewFile/71/76

UDRY, J. RICHARD. "Biological Limitations of Gender Construction." American Sociological Review. Vol. 65, No. 3 (June 2000):443–57.

UNITED NATIONS DEVELOPMENT PROGRAMME. "Human Development Report 2014." Statistical Tables. 2014. [Online] Available at http://hdr.undp.org/en/content/table-4-gender-inequality-index

U.S. DEPARTMENT OF LABOR, BUREAU OF LABOR STATISTICS. "Highlights of Women's Earnings." 2012. Available at http://www.bls.gov/cps/cpswom2011.pdf

VOGEL, LISE. Marxism and the Oppression of Women: Toward a Unitary Theory. New Brunswick, NJ: Rutgers University Press, 1983.

WILLIAMS, CARA. "Economic Well-being." Statistics Canada. Catalogue no. 89-503-X, 2010. http://www.statcan.gc.ca/pub/89-503-x/2010001/article/11388-eng.htm

WOLF, NAOMI. The Beauty Myth: How Images of Beauty Are Used against Women. New York: Morrow, 1990.

WORLD HEALTH ORGANIZATION. "Prevalence of Female Genital Mutilation." 2012. Available at http://www.who.int/reproductivehealth/topics/fgm/prevalence/en/index.html

———. Canada: WHO statistical profile. 2015. http://www.who.int/countries/can/en/

Chapter 11

ADORNO, THEODORE W., ELSE FRENKEL-BRUNSWIK, DANIEL J. LEVINSON, AND R. NEVITT SANFORD. The Authoritarian Personality. New York: Harper, 1950.

AMERICAN SOCIOLOGICAL ASSOCIATION. The Importance of Collecting Data and Doing Social Scientific Research on Race. Washington, DC: American Sociological Association, 2003.

BALAKRISHNAN, T.R., and FENG HOU. The Changing Patterns of Spatial Concentration and Residential Segregation of Ethnic Groups in Canada's Major Metropolitan Areas 1981–1991. Discussion Paper No. 95-2. London, ON: University of Western Ontario, Population Studies Centre, 1995.

BENJAMIN, LOIS. The Black Elite: Facing the Color Line in the Twilight of the Twentieth Century. Chicago: Nelson-Hall, 1991.

BENOIT, CECILIA, and DENA CARROLL. "Aboriginal Midwifery in British Columbia: A Narrative Still Untold." Western Geographic Series. Vol. 30 (1995):221–46.

BIOGRAPHY.COM. "Drake Biography." 2014. http://www.biography.com/people/drake-596834

BLANTON, KIMBERLY. "Borrowers Sue Subprime Lender, Allege Race Bias." Boston Globe. July 13, 2007. www.boston.com/business/personalfinance/articles/2007/07/13/borrowers_sue_subprime_lender_allege_race_bias/

BOGARDUS, EMORY S. "Social Distance and Its Origins." Sociology and Social Research. Vol. 9 (July/August 1925):216–25.

———. A Forty-Year Racial Distance Study. Los Angeles: University of Southern California Press, 1967.

BONILLA-SILVA, EDUARDO. Racism Without Racists: Color-Blind Racism and the Persistence of Racial Inequality in the United States. 2nd ed. Toronto: Rowman & Littlefield, 2006.

BRAND, DIONNE. No Burden to Carry: Narrative of Black Working Women in Ontario, 1920s to 1950s. Toronto: Women's Press, 1992.

BRODKIN, KAREN B. "How Did Jews Become White Folks?" In John J. Macionis and Nijole V. Benokraitis, eds., Seeing Ourselves: Classic, Contemporary, and Cross-Cultural Readings in Sociology. 7th ed. Upper Saddle River, NJ: Prentice Hall, 2007.

BURKOWICZ, JAKUB. "Were the Slavs White?" Congress 2013 @ the Edge: Canadian Association of Slavists Annual Conference. June 2013.

———. "In Defense of Counterposed Strategic Orientations: Anarchism and Antiracism." In P.J. Lilley and Jeff Shantz, eds., *New Developments in Anarchist Studies*. Brooklyn, NY: Thought Crimes, 2015:97–144.

CALIFORNIA NEWSREEL. "Race: The Power of an Illusion: Genetic Diversity Quiz." 2003. www.pbs.org/race/000_About/002_04_a-godeeper.htm

CAMARA, EVANDRO. Personal communication, 2000.

CANADIAN COUNCIL FOR REFUGEES. "Increase in Temporary Foreign Worker Numbers." 2012. http://ccrweb.ca/en/increase-temporary-foreign-worker-numbers

CARMICHAEL, STOKELY, AND CHARLES V. HAMILTON. *Black Power: The Politics of Liberation in America*. New York: Vintage Books, 1967.

CHAN, WENDY, and DOROTHY CHUNN. *Racialization, Crime, and Criminal Justice in Canada*. Toronto: University of Toronto Press, 2014.

COHEN, MARK NATHAN. *Health and the Rise of Civilization*. New Haven, CT: Yale University Press, 1989.

COMMONS, JOHN R. *Races and Immigrants in America*. New York: The Macmillan Company, 1907.

CUMMINGS, SCOTT, and THOMAS LAMBERT. "Anti-Hispanic and Anti-Asian Sentiments among African Americans." *Social Science Quarterly*. Vol. 78, No. 2 (June 1997):338–53.

DICKASON, OLIVE PATRICIA. *Canada's First Nations: A History of Founding Peoples from Earliest Times*. Toronto: McClelland and Stewart, 1992.

DOBYNS, HENRY F. "An Appraisal of Techniques with a New Hemispheric Estimate." *Current Anthropology*. Vol. 7, No. 4 (October 1966):395–446.

DOLLARD, JOHN, et al. *Frustration and Aggression*. New Haven, CT: Yale University Press, 1939.

EMERSON, MICHAEL O., GEORGE YANCEY, and KAREN J. CHAI. "Does Race Matter in Residential Segregation? Exploring the Preferences of White Americans." *American Sociological Review*. Vol. 66, No. 6 (December 2001):922–35.

ETOWA, J., J. WIENS, W.T. BERNARD, and B. CLOW. "Determinants of Black Women's Health in Rural and Remote Communities." *Canadian Journal of Nursing Research*. Vol. 39 (2007):56–76.

FRAGER, RUTH A. *Sweatshop Strife: Class, Ethnicity, and Gender in the Jewish Labour Movement in Toronto, 1900–1939*. Toronto: University of Toronto Press, 1992.

FREDRICKSON, GEORGE M. "The Historical Origins and Development of Racism." 2003. http://www.pbs.org/race/000_About/002_04-background-02-01.htm

GEE, ELLEN. "Population." In Robert Hagedorn, ed., *Sociology*. 4th ed. Toronto: Holt, Rinehart & Winston, 1990:195–226.

GESCHWENDER, JAMES A. *Racial Stratification in America*. Dubuque, IA: Brown, 1978.

GILMOUR, RJ, DAVINA BHANDAR, JEET HEER, and MICHAEL C.K. MA, eds. *"Too Asian?" Racism, Privilege, and Post-Secondary Education*. Toronto: Between the Lines. 2012.

GIONET, LINDA, and SHIRIN ROSHANAFSHAR. "Select health indicators of First Nations people living off reserve, Métis and Inuit." Ottawa: Statistics Canada, Health Statistics Division. Catalogue no. 82-624-X. 2013. http://www.statcan.gc.ca/pub/82-624-x/2013001/article/11763-eng.pdf

GOTHAM, KEVIN FOX. "Race, Mortgage Lending, and Loan Rejections in a U.S. City." *Sociological Focus*. Vol. 31, No. 4 (October 1998):391–405.

GUINDON, HUBERT. "Quebec and the Canadian Question." In James Curtis and Lorne Tepperman, eds., *Images of Canada: The Sociological Tradition*. Scarborough, ON: Prentice-Hall Inc., 1990:30–41.

HARRIS, DAVID R., and JEREMIAH JOSEPH SIM. "Who Is Multiracial? Assessing the Complexity of Lived Race." *American Sociological Review*. Vol. 67, No. 4 (August 2002):614–27.

HEALTH CANADA. *A Statistical Profile on the Health of First Nations in Canada: Self-Rated Health and Selected Conditions, 2002 to 2005*. Ottawa: Author, 2009. www.hc-sc.gc.ca/fniah-spnia/pubs/aborig-autoch/2009-stats-profil-vol3/index-eng.php#a2

HERRNSTEIN, RICHARD J., and CHARLES MURRAY. *The Bell Curve: Intelligence and Class Structure in American Life*. New York: Free Press, 1994.

HILL, MARK E. "Race of the Interviewer and Perception of Skin Color: Evidence from the Multi-City Study of Urban Inequality." *American Sociological Review*. Vol. 67, No. 1 (February 2002):99–108.

HSU, FRANCIS L.K. *The Challenge of the American Dream: The Chinese in the United States*. Belmont, CA: Wadsworth, 1971.

IACOVETTA, FRANCA. *Such Hardworking People: Italian Immigrants in Postwar Toronto*. Montreal: McGill-Queen's University Press, 1992.

———. "Remaking Their Lives: Immigrants, Survivors, and Refugees." In Joy Parr, ed., *A Diversity of Women: Ontario, 1945–1980*. Toronto: University of Toronto Press, 1995:135–67.

ICELAND, JOHN, et al. "Racial and Ethnic Residential Segregation and Household Structure: A Research Note." *Social Science Research*. Vol. 39, No. 1 (2010): 39–47.

INCIARDI, JAMES A., HILARY L. SURRATT, and PAULO R. TELLES. *Sex, Drugs, and HIV/AIDS in Brazil*. Boulder, CO: Westview Press, 2000.

INDIAN AND NORTHERN AFFAIRS CANADA. *Nisga'a Final Agreement—Issues and Responses*. 2008. www.ainc-inac.gc.ca/al/ldc/ccl/fagr/nsga/nfa/snr-eng.asp

JACKSON, ANDREW. "Racial discrimination and the economic downturn." *The Broadbent Blog* (June 26, 2013). https://www.broadbentinstitute.ca/en/blog/racial-discrimination-and-economic-downturn

JAFFE, A.J. *The First Immigrants from Asia: A Population History of the North American Indians*. New York and London: Plenum Press, 1992.

JAMIESON, KATHLEEN. "Sex Discrimination and the *Indian Act*." In J. Rick Ponting, ed., *Arduous Journey: Canadian Indians and Decolonialization*. Toronto: McClelland & Stewart, 1986:112–36.

JEFFRIES, T. "Sechelt Women and Self-Government." In G. Creese and V. Strong-Boag, eds., *British Columbia Reconsidered: Essays on Women*. Vancouver: Press Gang Publishers, 1992:90–95.

JOSEPHY, ALVIN M., JR. *Now That the Buffalo's Gone: A Study of Today's American Indians*. New York: Knopf. 1982.

KALBACH, WARREN E., and WAYNE W. MCVEY. *The Demographic Basis of Canadian Society*. 2nd ed. Toronto: McGraw-Hill, 1979.

KAUFMAN, ROBERT L. "Assessing Alternative Perspectives on Race and Sex Employment Segregation." *American Sociological Review*. Vol. 67, No. 4 (August 2002):547–72.

KIHIKA, MAUREEN. "Ghosts and Shadows: A History of Racism in Canada." *Canadian Graduate Journal of Sociology and Criminology*. Vol. 2, No. 1 (Spring 2013):35–44.

KOGAWA, JOY. *Obasan*. Markham, ON: Penguin Books, 1981.

KRYSAN, MARIA. "Community Undesirability in Black and White: Examining Racial Residential Preferences through Community Perceptions." *Social Problems*. Vol. 49, No. 4 (November 2002):521–43.

LAI, H.M. "Chinese." In *Harvard Encyclopedia of American Ethnic Groups*. Cambridge, MA: Harvard University Press, 1980:217–33.

LEITCH, KELLIE. *Employment Equity Act: Annual Report 2012*. Ottawa: Her Majesty the Queen in Right of Canada, 2013. http://www.labour.gc.ca/eng/standards_equity/eq/pubs_eq/annual_reports/2012/index.shtml

LI, PETER. *Destination Canada: Immigration Debates and Issues*. Toronto: Oxford University Press, 2003.

LOVEMAN, MARA. "Is 'Race' Essential?" *American Sociological Review*. Vol. 64, No. 6 (December 1999):890–98.

LUCIUK, LUBOMYR Y. *A Time for Atonement: Canada's first national internment operations and the Ukrainian Canadians, 1914–1920*. Kingston, ON: Limestone Press, 1988.

MALIK, KENAN. *The Meaning of Race: Race, History and Culture in Western Society*. London: Macmillan, 1996.

MASSEY, DOUGLAS S., and NANCY A. DENTON. "Hypersegregation in U.S. Metropolitan Areas: Black and Hispanic Segregation along Five Dimensions." *Demography*. Vol. 26, No. 3 (August 1989):373–91.

MATAS, ROBERT, and CRAIG MCINNES. "Critics of Nisga'a Treaty Demand Referendum." *Globe and Mail* (July 23, 1998):A1, A5.

MATTHIESSEN, PETER. *Indian Country*. New York: Viking Press, 1984.

NAGEL, JOANE. "Constructing Ethnicity: Creating and Recreating Ethnic Identity and Culture." *Social Problems*. Vol. 41, No. 1 (February 1994):152–76.

NG, ROXANNE. "Racism, Sexism and Immigrant Women." In Sandra Burt, Lorraine Code, and Lindsay Dorney, eds., *Changing Patterns: Women in Canada*. 2nd ed. Toronto: McClelland and Stewart, 1993:279–307.

NG, ROXANNE, and TANIA DAS GUPTA. "Nation Builders? The Captive Labour Force of Non-English Speaking Immigrant Women." *Canadian Women's Studies*. Vol. 3, No. 1 (1993):83–85.

OLZAK, SUSAN. "Labor Unrest, Immigration, and Ethnic Conflict in Urban America, 1880–1914." *American Journal of Sociology*. Vol. 94, No. 6 (May 1989):1303–33.

OMATSU, MARYKA. *Bittersweet Passage: Redress and the Japanese Canadian Experience*. Toronto: Between the Lines, 1992.

OREOPOULOS, PHILIP. "Why Do Skilled Immigrants Struggle in the Labor Market? A Field Experiment with Thirteen Thousand Resumes." *American Economic Journal: Economic Policy 3*. Vol. 3, No. 4 (November 2011):148–171.

OWEN, CAROLYN A., HOWARD C. ELSNER, and THOMAS R. MCFAUL. "A Half-Century of Social Distance Research: National Replication of the Bogardus Studies." *Sociology and Social Research*. Vol. 66, No. 1 (1977):80–98.

PARRILLO, VINCENT, and CHRISTOPHER DONOGHUE. "Updating the Bogardus Social Distance Studies: A New National Survey." *Social Science Journal*. Vol. 42, No. 2 (April 2005):257–71.

PERLMUTTER, PHILIP. "Minority Group Prejudice." *Society*. Vol. 39, No. 3 (March/April 2002):59–65.

PONTING, J. RICK. "Racial Conflict: Turning Up the Heat." In Dan Glenday and Ann Duffy, eds., *Canadian Society: Understanding and Surviving the 1990s*. Toronto: McClelland and Stewart, 1994:86–118.

PONTING, J. RICK, and JERILYNN KIELY. "Disempowerment: 'Justice,' Racism, and Public Opinion." In J. Rick Ponting, ed., *First Nations in Canada: Perspectives on Opportunity, Empowerment, and Self-Determination*. Whitby, ON: McGraw-Hill Ryerson, 1997.

PRENTICE, ALISON, PAULA BOURNE, GAIL CUTHBERT BRANDT, BETH LIGHT, WENDY MITCHINSON, and NAOMI BLACK. *Canadian Women: A History*. 2nd ed. Toronto: Harcourt Brace & Company, 1996.

ROCHER, GUY. "The Quiet Revolution in Quebec." In James Curtis and Lorne Tepperman, eds., *Images of Canada: The Sociological Tradition*. Scarborough, ON: Prentice Hall, 1990:22–29.

ROSENBERG, LOUIS. *Canada's Jews: A Social and Economic Study of Jews in Canada in the 1930s*. Montreal: McGill-Queen's University Press, 1993; orig. 1939.

ROTHENBERG, PAULA. *White Privilege*. 3rd ed. New York: Worth, 2008.

SALE, KIRKPATRICK. *The Conquest of Paradise: Christopher Columbus and the Columbian Legacy*. New York: Knopf, 1990.

SATZEWICH, VICTOR. "Whiteness Limited: Racialization and the Social Construction of 'Peripheral Europeans.'" *Social History*. Vol. 33, No. 66 (2000):271–290.

SHIELDS, M., and S. WHEATLEY PRICE. "Racial Harassment, Job Satisfaction and Intentions to Quit: Evidence from the British Nursing Profession." 2000. http://netec.mcc.ac.uk/WoPEc/data/Papers/izaiza-dpsdp164.html

SKELTON, CHAD. "How much money do people just like you make? (online calculator)" *Vancouver Sun* (September 12, 2013). http://blogs.vancouversun.com/2013/09/12/how-much-money-do-people-just-like-you-make-2/

SMITH, TOM W. "Anti-Semitism Decreases but Persists." *Society*. Vol. 33, No. 3 (March/April 1996):2

SOWELL, THOMAS. *Race and Culture*. New York: Basic Books, 1994.

———. "Ethnicity and IQ." In Steven Fraser, ed., *The Bell Curve Wars: Race, Intelligence, and the Future of America*. New York: Basic Books, 1995:70–79.

SPENCER, MARTIN E. "Multiculturalism, 'Political Correctness,' and the Politics of Identity." *Sociological Forum*. Vol. 9, No. 4 (December 1994):547–67.

STATISTICS CANADA. *National Population Health Survey Overview, 1994–95.* Ottawa: Minister of Industry, 1995.

———. *Projections of the Diversity of the Canadian Population, 2006 to 2031.* Ottawa: Minister of Industry. Catalogue no. 91-551-X. 2010.

———. *Visible Minority Groups (15), Immigrant Status and Period of Immigration (9), Age Groups (10) and Sex (3) for the Population of Canada, Provinces, Territories, Census Divisions and Census Subdivisions, 2006 Census—20% Sample Data.* [Electronic Data File]. Catalogue no. 97-562-XCB2006016[1].IVT. 2011a.

———. *Income and Earnings Statistics in 2010 (16), Age Groups (8C), Sex (3), Work activity in 2010 (3), Highest Certificate, Diploma or Degree (6) and Selected Sociocultural Characteristics (60) for the Population Aged 15 Years and Over in Private Households of Canada, Provinces, Territories and Census Metropolitan Areas, 2011 National Household Survey.* Statistics Canada. Catalogue no. 99-014-X2011041. 2011b.

———. *Immigration and Ethnocultural Diversity in Canada, National Household Survey, 2011.* Ottawa: Minister of Industry. Catalogue no. 99-010-X2011001. 2013a.

———. *Ethnic Origin (264), Single and Multiple Ethnic Origin Responses (3), Generation Status (4), Age Groups (10) and Sex (3) for the Population in Private Households of Canada, Provinces, Territories, Census Metropolitan Areas and Census Agglomerations, 2011 National Household Survey.* Catalogue no. 99-010-X2011028. 2013b.

———. *National Household Survey: Immigration and Ethnocultural Diversity – Visible Minority (15), Generation Status (4), Age Groups (10) and Sex (3) for the Population in Private Households of Canada, Provinces, Territories, Census Metropolitan Areas and Census Agglomerations, 2011 National Household Survey, National Household Survey Year 2011.* Catalogue no. 99-010-X2011029. 2013c.

———. "Aboriginal Peoples in Canada: First Nations People, Métis and Inuit." Ottawa: Minister of Industry. Catalogue no. 99-011-X2011001. 2013d.

———. "Mixed Unions in Canada, National Household Survey (NHS), 2011." *NHS in Brief.* Ottawa: Minister of Industry. Catalogue no. 99-010-X2011003. 2014.

STEELE, SHELBY. *The Content of Our Character: A New Vision of Race in America.* New York: St. Martin's Press, 1990.

SUNG, BETTY LEE. *Mountains of Gold: The Story of the Chinese in America.* New York: Macmillan, 1967.

THOMAS, W.I. "The Relation of Research to the Social Process." In Morris Janowitz, ed., *W.I. Thomas on Social Organization and Social Personality.* Chicago: University of Chicago Press, 1966:289–305; orig. 1931.

THOMAS, W.I., and DOROTHY SWAINE THOMAS. *The Child in America: Behavior Problems and Programs.* New York: Knopf, 1928

TODOROVA, MIGLENA S. "Imagining 'In-between' Peoples across the Atlantic." *Journal of Historical Sociology.* Vol. 19, No. 4 (December 2006):397–418.

TYLER, S. LYMAN. *A History of Indian Policy.* Washington, DC: U.S. Department of the Interior, Bureau of Indian Affairs, 1973.

WALIA, HARSHA. "Why Everyone Should Care About the Temporary Foreign Worker Program," in *The Mainlander* (June 23, 2014). http://themainlander.com/2014/06/23/why-everyone-should-care-about-the-temporary-foreign-worker-program/

WILKES, RIMA, and JOHN ICELAND. "Hypersegregation in the Twenty-First Century." *Demography.* Vol. 41, No. 1 (February 9, 2004):23–36.

WILLIAMS, D.R., H.W. NEIGHBORS, and J.S. JACKSON. "Racial/Ethnic Discrimination and Health: Findings from Community Studies." *American Journal of Public Health.* Vol. 93, No. 2 (2003):200–08.

WONG, LLOYD, and RICARDO TRUMPER. "Canada's Guestworkers: Racialized, Gendered and Flexible," *Race and Racism in 21st Century Canada: Continuity, Complexity, and Change.* Peterborough, ON: Broadview Press, 2007:151–70.

YEE, M. "Chinese Canadian Women: Our Common Struggle." In G. Creese and V. Strong-Boag, eds., *British Columbia Reconsidered: Essays on Women.* Vancouver: Press Gang Publishers, 1992.

ZUCCHI, J. *A History of Ethnic Enclaves in Canada.* Ottawa: Canadian Historical Association, 2007. www.collectionscanada.gc.ca/obj/008004/f2/E-31_en.pdf

Chapter 12

ALLEN, MIKE. "Card Check Battle Starts Tomorrow." *Politico* (March 9, 2009). www.politico.com/news/stories/0309/19786.html

ALLIANCE FOR BOARD DIVERSITY. "Alliance for Board Diversity Data Sheet, 2011 Update." 2011. Available at http://theabd.org/

ANDERSON, CAMERON D., and LAURA B. STEPHENSON, eds. *Voting Behaviour in Canada.* Vancouver: UBC Press, 2010.

ASTIN, ALEXANDER W., LETICIA OSEGUERA, LINDA J. SAX, and WILLIAM S. KORN. *The American Freshman: Thirty-Five-Year Trends.* Los Angeles: UCLA Higher Education Research Institute, 2002.

BARNES, JULIAN E. "War Profiteering." *U.S. News & World Report* (May 13, 2002):20–24.

BARTLETT, DONALD L., and JAMES B. STEELE. "How the Little Guy Gets Crunched." *Time* (February 7, 2000):38–41.

BELL, JIM. "Will Enthusiasm for Democracy Endure in Egypt and Elsewhere?" Pew Research Center. [Online] Available March 8, 2011, at http://pewresearch.org/pubs/1918/enthusiasm-for-democracy-in-egypt-tunisiafragile-eastern-europe-experience-shows?src=prc-latest&proj=peoplepress

BERGER, PETER L. *The Capitalist Revolution: Fifty Propositions about Prosperity, Equality, and Liberty.* New York: Basic Books, 1986.

BOWLBY, GEOFF. "The Labour Market Review." Perspectives on Labour and Income. Statistics Canada Catalogue no. 75-001-XIE. Vol. 2, No. 1 (January 2001):5–35.

BURKOWICZ, JAKUB. "Camping at the Crossroads: Introductory Essay to a Special Issue on Antiracism and Anarchism." *Affinities: A Journal of Radical Theory, Culture, and Action.* Vol. 8, No. 1 (Summer 2014):1-22.

CANADIAN BUSINESS. "Map: Canadian unemployment rates by province and region." 2013. http://www.canadianbusiness.com/economy/gallery/canada-unemployment-rates/

CANADIAN UNION OF PUBLIC EMPLOYEES. "Fact Sheet: Bill C-525 - Employees' Voting Rights Act." 2013. http://cupe.ca/fact-sheet-bill-c-525-employees-voting-rights-act

CENTRAL INTELLIGENCE AGENCY. "A Comparison of the US and Soviet Economies: Evaluating the Performance of the Soviet System." 1985. http://www.foia.cia.gov/document/0000497165

———. "CIA World Factbook." 2012. https://www.cia.gov/library/publications/the-world-factbook/index.html

CHANCE, DAVID, and JACK KIM. "North Korea Mourns Dead Leader, Son is 'Great Successor'." Reuters. December 19, 2011. Available at http://news.yahoo.com/north-koreastate-tv-says-kim-jong-il-031257363.html

CHOMSKY, NOAM. "On the U.S. Human Rights Record." *The New Statesman.* July 1994. http://www.chomsky.info/articles/199407—.htm

CLARK, KIM. "Bankrupt Lives." *U.S. News & World Report* (September 16, 2002):52–54.

CLEMENT, WALLACE. *The Canadian Corporate Elite.* Toronto: McClelland and Stewart, 1975.

DAHL, ROBERT A. *Who Governs?* New Haven, CT: Yale University Press, 1961.

———. *Dilemmas of Pluralist Democracy: Autonomy vs. Control.* New Haven, CT: Yale University Press, 1982.

DALMIA, SHIKRA. "Obama and Big Labor." *Forbes* (October 29, 2008). www.forbes.com/2008/10/28/obama-card-check-oped-cx_sd_1029dalmia.html

DECARLO, SCOTT, ed. "*Forbes:* The Global 2000." 2012. http://www.forbes.com/global2000/list/

DEDRICK, DENNIS K., and RICHARD E. YINGER. "MAD, SDI, and the Nuclear Arms Race." Unpublished manuscript. Georgetown, KY: Georgetown College, 1990.

DIXON, WILLIAM J., and TERRY BOSWELL. "Dependency, Disarticulation, and Denominator Effects: Another Look at Foreign Capital Penetration." *American Journal of Sociology.* Vol. 102, No. 2 (September 1996):543–62.

ÉCOLE NATIONALE D'ADMINISTRATION PUBLIQUE. "Canadian Governments Compared." January 2013. http://etatscanadiens-canadiangovernments.enap.ca/en/nav.aspx?sortcode=2.0.2.0

ECONOMIST, THE. "Daily Chart: War deaths in Iraq." 2010. http://theeconomist.tumblr.com/post/1400841788/daily-chart-war-deaths-in-iraq-wikileaks

EKOS RESEARCH. "Looking Backward, Looking Forward: Five Big Forces Shaping Our Society." January 2013. www.eikospolitics.ca

———. "Midsummer Haze Clouds Voter Outlook." 2015. http://www.ekospolitics.com/index.php/2015/07/midsummer-haze-clouds-voter-outlook/

ELECTIONS CANADA. *Map of official results for the 41st general election (2011).* 2011. http://www.elections.ca/res/cir/maps/map.asp?map=ERMap_41&lang=e

ENGDAHL, F. WILLIAM. *Full Spectrum Dominance: Totalitarian Democracy in the New World Order.* Boxboro, MA: Third Millennium Press, 2009.

"Female Opinion and Defense since September 11th." *Society.* Vol. 39, No. 3 (March/April 2002):2.

FIREBAUGH, GLENN, and DUMITRU SANDU. "Who Supports Marketization and Democratization in Post-Communist Romania?" *Sociological Forum.* Vol. 13, No. 3 (September 1998):521–41.

FIREBAUGH, GLENN, and FRANK D. BECK. "Does Economic Growth Benefit the Masses? Growth, Dependence, and Welfare in the Third World." *American Sociological Review.* Vol. 59, No. 5 (October 1994):631–53.

FISHER, ROGER, and WILLIAM URY. "Getting to Yes." In William M. Evan and Stephen Hilgartner, eds., *The Arms Race and Nuclear War.* Englewood Cliffs, NJ: Prentice Hall, 1988:261–68.

FORUM RESEARCH. *Federal Conservatives rebound.* July 2015. http://poll.forumresearch.com/post/327/tied-with-ndp/

FOX, JUSTIN. "Why Denmark Loves Globalization." *Time* (November 15, 2007). www.time.com/time/magazine/article/0,9171,1684528,00.html

FREEDOM HOUSE. "Freedom in the World Comparative and Historical Data." 2013. Available at http://www.freedomhouse.org/report-types/freedom-world

GELLMAN, BARTON. "Julian Assange." *Time.* Vol. 176, No. 26 (December 27, 2010–January 3, 2011):90–94.

GENERAL MOTORS. "Corporate Strategy." 2012. Available at http://www.gm.com/company/investors/corporate-strategy.html

GERLACH, MICHAEL L. *The Social Organization of Japanese Business.* Berkeley: University of California Press, 1992.

GOODE, WILLIAM J. "Encroachment, Charlatanism, and the Emerging Profession: Psychology, Sociology, and Medicine." *American Sociological Review.* Vol. 25, No. 6 (December 1960):902–14.

GREENHOUSE, STEVEN. "Many Entry-Level Workers Find Pinch of Rough Market." *New York Times* (September 4, 2006). www.nytimes.com/2006/09/04/us/04labor.html

GUTIERREZ, CARL. "Bear Stearns Announces More Job Cuts." *Forbes* (October 3, 2007). www.forbes.com/markets/2007/10/03/bear-stearns-layoffs-markets-equitycx_cg_1003markets23.html

HOLTSLANDER, CATHY. *Losing Our Grip | 2015 Update: How Corporate Farmland Buy-up, Rising Farm Debt, and Agribusiness Financing of Inputs Threaten Family Farms and Food Sovereignty.* National Farmers Union. March 2015. http://www.nfu.ca/issues/losing-our-grip-2015-update

HUMAN RESOURCES AND SKILLS DEVELOPMENT CANADA. *Work—Unemployment Rate.* 2011. www4.hrsdc.gc.ca/.3ndic.1t.4r$$$$$-eng.jsp?iid=16

IGNATIUS, ADI. "A Tsar Is Born." *Time* (December 31, 2007):46–62.

INDUSTRY CANADA. *Key Small Business Statistics—July 2010: How Many People Are Self-Employed?* 2011a. www.ic.gc.ca/eic/site/sbrp-rppe.nsf/eng/rd02501.html

———. *What Are the Characteristics of the Self-Employed?* 2011b. www.ic.gc.ca/eic/site/sbrp-rppe.nsf/eng/rd02354.html

INTERNAL REVENUE SERVICE. "SOI Tax Stats—Business Tax Statistics." 2012. Available at http://www.irs.gov/uac/SOI-Tax-Stats—Business-Tax-Statistics

INTERNATIONAL LABOUR ORGANIZATION. Key Indicators of the Labour Market. 7th ed. 2014. http://www.ilo.org/empelm/what/WCMS_114240/lang—en/index.htm

IPSOS-REID. 2011 Exit Poll. 2011. http://www.ipsos-na.com/news-polls/canada/

———. With Writ Drop on Horizon, Two Front Running Parties Tied: Harper Conservatives (33%, +5) Close Gap on Mulcair NDP (34%, −1) as Trudeau Liberals Tumble (25%, −4). July 2015. http://www.ipsos-na.com/news-polls/pressrelease.aspx?id=6925

IRAQ BODY COUNT. "The War in Iraq: 10 years and counting." 2013. https://www.iraqbodycount.org/analysis/numbers/ten-years/

JENKINS, J. CRAIG. Images of Terror: What We Can and Can't Know about Terrorism. Hawthorne, NY: Aldine de Gruyter, 2003.

JOHNSON, PAUL. "The Seven Deadly Sins of Terrorism." In Benjamin Netanyahu, ed., International Terrorism. New Brunswick, NJ: Transaction Books, 1981:12–22.

KALLEBERG, ARNE L., BARBARA F. RESKIN, and KEN HUDSON. "Bad Jobs in America: Standard and Nonstandard Employment Relations and Job Quality in the United States." American Sociological Review. Vol. 65, No 2 (April 2000):256–78.

KAPLAN, DAVID E., and MICHAEL SCHAFFER. "Losing the Psywar." U.S. News & World Report (October 8, 2001):46.

KARATNYCKY, ADRIAN. "The 2001–2002 Freedom House Survey of Freedom: The Democracy Gap." In Freedom in the World: The Annual Survey of Political Rights and Civil Liberties, 2001–2002. New York: Freedom House, 2002:7–18.

KENTOR, JEFFREY. "The Long-Term Effects of Foreign Investment Dependence on Economic Growth, 1940–1990." American Journal of Sociology. Vol. 103, No. 4 (January 1998):1024–46.

KIVANT, BARBARA. "Reassessing Risk." Time (November 17, 2008):Global 1–4.

KOHUT, ANDY. "Public and Occupy Wall Street Movement Agree on Key Issues." Pew Research Center. October 19, 2011. Available at http://www.people-press.org/2011/10/19/haves-and-have-nots/

KONO, CLIFFORD, DONALD PALMER, ROGER FRIEDLAND, and MATTHEW ZAFONTE. "Lost in Space: The Geography of Corporate Interlocking Directorates." American Journal of Sociology. Vol. 103, No. 4 (January 1998):863–911.

LEACY, F.H. Historical Statistics of Canada. 2nd ed., electronic ed. Statistics Canada Catalogue no. 11-516-XIE. Ottawa: Statistics Canada, 1999.

LEITCH, KELLIE. Employment Equity Act: Annual Report 2012. Ottawa: Her Majesty the Queen in Right of Canada, 2013. http://www.labour.gc.ca/eng/standards_equity/eq/pubs_eq/annual_reports/2012/index.shtml

LIAZOS, ALEXANDER. People First: An Introduction to Social Problems. Needham Heights, MA: Allyn & Bacon, 1982.

LYND, ROBERT S., and HELEN MERRELL LYND. Middletown in Transition. New York: Harcourt, Brace & World, 1937.

MARCUSE, HERBERT. One Dimensional Man: studies in the ideology of advanced industrial society. Boston: Beacon Press, 1966.

MARSHALL, KATHERINE. "Part-time by Choice." Perspectives on Labour and Income. Statistics Canada Catalogue no. 75-001-XIE. Vol. 1, No. 2 (November 2000):5–12.

MARULLO, SAM. "The Functions and Dysfunctions of Preparations for Fighting Nuclear War." Sociological Focus. Vol. 20, No. 2 (April 1987):135–53.

MCGEEHAN, PATRICK, and MATHEW R. WARREN. "Adding to Recession's Pain, Thousands to Lose Job Benefits." New York Times (January 11, 2009). www.nytimes.com/2009/01/12/nyregion/12benefits.html

MCNALLY, DAVID. Another World is Possible: Globalization and Anti-Capitalism. Winnipeg, MN: Arbeiter Ring Publishing, 2006.

MILLER, TERRY, KIM HOLMES, and EDWIN FEULNER. "2012 Index of Economic Freedom." 2012. http://www.heritage.org/index/Default.aspx

MILLS, C. WRIGHT. The Power Elite. New York: Oxford University Press, 1956.

MINISTRY OF INDUSTRY. A Guide to Research on the New Economy. 2003. http://dsp-psd.pwgsc.gc.ca/Collection/Statcan/11-622-M/11-622-MIE2003001.pdf

———. Women in Canada: Work Chapter Updates. Catalogue no. 89F0133XIE. 2007. www.statcan.gc.ca/cgi-bin/af-fdr.cgi?l=eng&loc=89f0133x2006000-eng.pdf

MONTAIGNE, FEN. "Russia Rising." National Geographic. Vol. 200, No. 5 (September 2001):2–31.

MOORE, GWEN, ET AL. "Elite Interlocks in Three U.S. Sectors: Nonprofit, Corporate, and Government." Social Science Quarterly. Vol. 83, No. 3 (September 2002):726–44.

NORC. General Social Surveys, 1972–2012. Chicago: National Opinion Research Center. March 2013. Available at http://www.norc.org/GSS+Website/

OECD (ORGANISATION FOR ECONOMIC CO-OPERATION AND DEVELOPMENT). "Harmonised Unemployment Rates." 2011a. www.oecd.org/dataoecd/60/12/46861245.pdf

———. "OECD Statistics (GDP, Unemployment, Income, Population, Labour, Education, Trade, Finance, Prices...)." 2011b. http://stats.oecd.org/Index.aspx

———. "Incidence of Involuntary Part Time Workers." 2011c. http://stats.oecd.org/Index.aspx?DataSetCode=INVPT_I

———. "Country Statistical Profile: Denmark." 2012. http://www.oecd-ilibrary.org/economics/country-statistical-profile-denmark_20752288-table-dnk

———. "Trade Union Density." 2015. https://stats.oecd.org/Index.aspx?DataSetCode=UN_DEN

OFFICE OF THE COMMISSIONER OF LOBBYING OF CANADA. Administering the Lobbying Act. December 2011. http://www.ocl-cal.gc.ca/eic/site/012.nsf/eng/h_00436.html

O'HAGAN, ELLIE MAE. "Evo Morales has proved that socialism doesn't damage economies." The Guardian. October 14, 2014. http://www.theguardian.com/commentisfree/2014/oct/14/evo-morales-reelected-socialism-doesnt-damage-economies-bolivia

PAMMET, JON H., and LAWRENCE LEDUC. "Explaining the Turnout Decline in Canadian Federal Elections: A New Survey of Non-Voters." Ottawa: Elections Canada, 2003. [Online] www.elections.ca/loi/tur/tud/TurnoutDecline.pdf

PEW RESEARCH CENTER. "Confidence in Democracy and Capitalism Wanes in Former Soviet Union." December 5, 2011. http://pewresearch.org/pubs/2139/russia-lithuania-ukraine-former-soviet-union-democracy-capitalism-individualism economic-conditions?src=prc-newsletter

PEW RESEARCH CENTER, FORUM ON RELIGION AND PUBLIC LIFE. "The Global Religious Landscape: A Report on the Size and Distribution of the World's Major Religious Groups as of 2010." December 2012. Available at http://www.pewforum.org/global-religious-landscape.aspx

POLSBY, NELSON W. "Three Problems in the Analysis of Community Power." American Sociological Review. Vol. 24, No. 6 (December 1959):796–803.

PRYOR, JOHN H., KEVIN EGAN, LAURA PALUCKI BLAKE, SYLVIA HURTADO, JENNIFER BERDAN, and MATTHEW CASE. "The American Freshman: National Norms Fall 2012 (Expanded Edition)." Cooperative Institutional Research Program at the Higher Education Research Institute at UCLA. 2013. Available at http://www.heri.ucla.edu/monographs/TheAmericanFreshman2012-Expanded.pdf

PUBLIC SERVICE ALLIANCE OF CANADA. "Senate passes bill making it harder to unionize, despite its errors." 2014. http://psacunion.ca/senate-passes-bill-making-it-harder-unionize

RITZER, GEORGE, and DAVID WALCZAK. Working: Conflict and Change. 4th ed. Englewood Cliffs, NJ: Prentice Hall, 1990.

ROGERS, MARTIN. "In Memory of Kim Jong-Il: Dear Leader, G.O.A.T." The Daily Take. December 21, 2011. Available at http://www.thepostgame.com/blog/daily-take/201112/memory-kim-jong-il-dear-leader-and-goa

ROTHMAN, STANLEY, and AMY E. BLACK. "Who Rules Now? American Elites in the 1990s." Society. Vol. 35, No. 6 (September/October 1998):17–20.

RULE, JAMES, and PETER BRANTLEY. "Computerized Surveillance in the Workplace: Forms and Delusions." Sociological Forum. Vol. 7, No. 3 (September 1992):405–23.

SACHS, JEFFREY D. "The Case for Bigger Government." Time (January 19, 2009):34–36.

SAFINA, CARL. "Occupied Economy: A brief history of the first corporate century." Adbusters. February 2012. https://www.adbusters.org/magazine/100/occupied-economy.html

SAPORITO, BILL. "Can Wal-Mart Get Any Bigger?" Time (January 13, 2003):38–43.

SAX, LINDA J., ET AL. The American Freshman: National Norms for Fall 2003. Los Angeles: UCLA Higher Education Research Institute, 2003.

SCHELL, ORVILLE. "How Walmart Is Changing China." The Atlantic. December 2011. http://www.theatlantic.com/magazine/archive/2011/12/how-walmart-is-changing-china/8709/3/

SENTENCING PROJECT. "Felony Disenfranchisement Laws in the United States." 2012. Available at http://www.sentencingproject.org/Admin%5CDocuments%5Cpublications%5Cfd_bs_fdlawsinus.pdf

SHAW, HOLLIE. "Quebec ruling against Wal-Mart Canada closing unionized store hollow victory for labour." Financial Post. June 27, 2014. http://business.financialpost.com/news/retail-marketing/wal-mart-violated-quebecs-labour-code-by-closing-store-after-worker-unionization-attempt-court-rules

SIVARD, RUTH LEGER. World Military and Social Expenditures, 1987–88. 12th ed. Washington, DC: World Priorities, 1988.

SKOCPOL, THEDA. States and Social Revolutions: A Comparative Analysis of France, Russia, and China. Cambridge, MA: Cambridge University Press, 1979.

SMITH, ADAM. An Inquiry into the Nature and Causes of the Wealth of Nations. New York: Modern Library, 1937; orig. 1776.

STATISTICS CANADA. Projections of the Diversity of the Canadian Population. Catalogue no. 91-551-X. Ottawa: Minister of Industry, 2010.

———. CANSIM II: Canadian Socio-Economic Information Management System [Computer File]. Series v2522952. Ottawa: Statistics Canada, 2011a.

———. CANSIM II: Canadian Socio-Economic Information Management System [Computer File]. Series v2522972. Ottawa: Statistics Canada, 2011b.

———. CANSIM II: Canadian Socio-Economic Information Management System [Computer File]. Series v2522982. Ottawa: Statistics Canada, 2011c.

———. CANSIM II: Canadian Socio-Economic Information Management System [Computer File]. Series v2522992. Ottawa: Statistics Canada, 2011d.

———. CANSIM II: Canadian Socio-Economic Information Management System [Computer File]. Series v2523002. Ottawa: Statistics Canada, 2011e.

———. CANSIM II: Canadian Socio-Economic Information Management System [Computer File]. Series v2523012. Ottawa: Statistics Canada, 2011f.

———. CANSIM II: Canadian Socio-Economic Information Management System [Computer File]. Series v2523022. Ottawa: Statistics Canada, 2011g.

———. 2011 National Household Survey, Catalogue Number 99-010-X2011038, 2011h.

———. "Reasons for not voting in the May 2, 2011 federal election." The Daily (July 5, 2011h). http://www.statcan.gc.ca/daily-quotidien/110705/dq110705a-eng.htm

———. CANSIM Table 183-0002—Public sector employment, wages and salaries, seasonally unadjusted and adjusted, ★Terminated★ monthly. [Electronic Data File]. Last updated May 30, 2012.

———. Portrait of Canada's Labour Force. 2013. Ottawa: Minister of Industry. Catalogue no. 99-012-X2011002.

———. Visible Minority (15), Age Groups (10), Sex (3) and Selected Demographic, Cultural, Labour Force, Educational and Income Characteristics (315) for the Population in Private Households of Canada,

Provinces, Territories, Census Metropolitan Areas and Census Agglomerations, 2011 National Household Survey. Last updated March 4, 2014. [Electronic Data File]. Catalogue no. 99-010-X2011038.

———. CANSIM Table 282-0008—Employment by Industry. [Electronic Data File]. 2015a.

———. CANSIM Table 282-0089—Labour force survey estimates (LFS), employment by class of worker and sex, seasonally adjusted and unadjusted. [Electronic Data File]. 2015b.

———. CANSIM Table 282-0087—Labour force survey estimates (LFS), by sex and age group, seasonally adjusted and unadjusted monthly (persons unless otherwise noted). [Electronic Data File]. 2015c.

———. *Average hourly wages of employees by selected characteristics and occupation, unadjusted data, by province (monthly) (Canada).* Last updated July 10, 2015d. http://www.statcan.gc.ca/tables-tableaux/sum-som/l01/cst01/labr69a-eng.htm

STEVENS, ANDREW J.R. *Call Centers and the Global Division of Labor: A Political Economy of Post-Industrial Employment and Union Organizing.* New York: Routledge, 2014.

STOCKHOLM INTERNATIONAL PEACE RESEARCH INSTITUTE. "SIPRI Yearbook." 2012. Available at http://www.sipri.org/yearbook

TALMON, JACOB LEIB. *The Rise of Totalitarian Democracy.* Boston: Beacon Press, 1952.

THOMPSON, MARK, and DOUGLAS WALLER. "Shield of Dreams." *Time* (May 8, 2001):45–47.

TILLY, CHARLES. "Does Modernization Breed Revolution?" In Jack A. Goldstone, ed., *Revolutions: Theoretical, Comparative, and Historical Studies.* New York: Harcourt Brace Jovanovich, 1986:47–57.

TOCQUEVILLE, ALEXIS DE. *The Old Regime and the French Revolution.* Stuart Gilbert, trans. Garden City, NY: Anchor/Doubleday, 1955; orig. 1856.

UGGEN, CHRISTOPHER, and JEFF MANZA. "Democratic Contraction? Political Consequences of Felon Disenfranchisement in the United States." *American Sociological Review.* Vol. 67, No. 6 (December 2002):777–803.

UNITED NATIONS DEVELOPMENT PROGRAMME. *Human Development Report 1990.* New York: Oxford University Press, 1990.

UPPAL, SHARANJIT, and SÉBASTIEN LAROCHELLE-CÔTÉ. "Factors associated with voting." *Perspectives on Labour and Income.* Vol. 24, No. 1 (Spring 2012). Statistics Canada Catalogue no. 75-001-XIE.

U.S. DEPARTMENT OF LABOR, BUREAU OF LABOR STATISTICS. "Current Employment Statistics—CES (National)." 2012. http://www.bls.gov/ces/home.htm

———. "International Labor Comparisons." 2013. http://www.bls.gov/fls/

U.S. OFFICE OF MANAGEMENT AND BUDGET. "The Budget for Fiscal Year 2013." 2012. Available at http://www.gpo.gov/fdsys/browse/collectionGPO.action?collectionCode=BUDGET

VALLAS, STEPHEN P., and JOHN P. BECK. "The Transformation of Work Revisited: The Limits of Flexibility in American Manufacturing." *Social Problems.* Vol. 43, No. 3 (August 1996):339–61.

WAIT, T. *Canadian Demographic and Social Values at a Glance: Impact on Strategic HR Planning.* Ottawa: Department of National Defence, 2002.

WALLERSTEIN, IMMANUEL. *The Capitalist World-Economy.* New York: Cambridge University Press, 1979.

WALMART. "Corporate and Financial Facts." 2012. http://news.walmart.com/walmart-facts/corporate-financial-fact-sheet

———. "Our Locations." 2014. http://corporate.walmart.com/our-story/locations/canada

WALSH, BRYAN. "How Business Saw the Light." *Time* (January 15, 2007):56–57.

WEBER, MAX. *Economy and Society: An Outline of Interpretive Sociology.* Guenther Roth and Claus Wittich, eds. Berkeley: University of California Press, 1978; orig. 1921.

WEIDENBAUM, MURRAY. "The Evolving Corporate Board." *Society.* Vol. 32, No. 3 (March/April 1995):9–20.

WHITAKER, MARK. "Ten Ways to Fight Terrorism." *Newsweek* (July 1, 1985):26–29.

WILES, P.J.D. *Economic Institutions Compared.* New York: Halstead Press, 1977.

WORLD BANK. "Countries and Regions." 2012. http://go.worldbank.org/9FV1KFE8P0

———. "World DataBank: World Development Indicators." 2012. http://data.worldbank.org/data-catalog/world-development-indicators

WRIGHT, QUINCY. "Causes of War in the Atomic Age." In William M. Evan and Stephen Hilgartner, eds., *The Arms Race and Nuclear War.* Englewood Cliffs, NJ: Prentice Hall, 1987:7–10.

Chapter 13

ALLARD, F.L., et al. "Maintien de l'engagement paternel après une rupture conjugale: point de vue des pères vivant en contexte de pauvreté. *Enfances, familles, générations.* Vol. 3 (2005):1–42.

AMBERT, A. *Divorce: Facts, Causes & Consequences.* Ottawa: Vanier Institute of the Family, 2009. www.vifamily.ca/sites/default/files/divorce_facts_causes_consequences.pdf

AMBERT, ANNE-MARIE. *Changing Families: Relationships in Context.* 2nd ed. Toronto: Pearson, 2012.

ANDERSON, JOHN WARD. "Early to Wed: The Child Brides of India." *Washington Post* (May 24, 1995):A27, A30.

ANGUS REID INSTITUTE. *Religion and faith in Canada today: strong belief, ambivalence and rejection define our views.* March 26, 2015. http://angusreid.org/faith-in-canada/

ANXO, DOMINIQUE, et al. *Parental Leave in European Companies.* Luxembourg, Belgium: European Foundation for the Improvement of Living and Working Conditions. Office for Official Publications of the European Communities, 2007.

APPLEBOME, PETER. "70 Years after Scopes Trial, Creation Debate Lives." *New York Times* (March 10, 1996):1, 10.

ARISTARKHOVA, I. "Ectogenesis and Mother as Machine." *Body and Society.* Vol. 11, No. 3 (2005):43–59.

ASHLEY, SEAN MATTHEW. "Sincere but Naive: Methodological Queries Concerning the British Columbia Polygamy Reference Trial." *Canadian Review of Sociology.* Vol. 51, No. 4 (November 2014):325–342.

BAKER, MAUREEN. *Canadian Family Policies: Cross-National Comparisons.* Toronto: University of Toronto Press, 1995.

BASKERVILLE, PETER. "Did Religion Matter? Religion and Wealth in Urban Canada at the Turn of the Twentieth Century: An Exploratory Study." *Social History.* Vol. 34, No. 67 (2001):61–95.

BEAUJOT, R. *Earning and Caring in Canadian Families.* Toronto: Broadview, 2000.

BEAUPRÉ, PASCALE, and ELISABETH CLOUTIER. *Navigating Family Transitions: Evidence from the General Social Survey—2006.* Statistics Canada Catalogue no. 89-625-XIE, No. 002. 2007.

BELLAH, ROBERT N. *The Broken Covenant.* New York: Seabury Press, 1975.

BENOIT, CECILIA, and H. HALLGRIMSDOTTIR, eds. *Valuing Care Work: Comparative Perspectives.* Toronto: University of Toronto Press, 2011.

BENOIT, CECILIA. *Women, Work and Social Rights: Canada in Historical and Comparative Perspective.* Scarborough, ON: Prentice Hall Canada, 2000.

BERGER, PETER L. *The Sacred Canopy: Elements of a Sociological Theory of Religion.* Garden City, NY: Doubleday, 1967.

BERNARD, JESSIE. *The Future of Marriage.* 2nd ed. New Haven, CT: Yale University Press, 1982.

BESECKE, KELLY. "Speaking of Meaning in Modernity: Reflexive Spirituality as a Cultural Resource." *Sociology of Religion.* Vol. 62, No. 3 (2003):365–81.

———. "Seeing Invisible Religion: Religion as a Societal Conversation about Transcendent Meaning." *Sociological Theory.* Vol. 23, No. 2 (June 2005):179–96.

BIANCHI, SUZANNE M., and DAPHNE SPAIN. "Women, Work, and Family in America." *Population Bulletin.* Vol. 51, No. 3 (December 1996).

BIBBY, REGINALD W. *Fragmented Gods: The Poverty and Potential of Religion in Canada.* Toronto: Irwin, 1987.

———. *Restless Gods: The Renaissance of Religion in Canada.* Toronto: Stoddart, 2002.

———. *A Survey of Canadian Hopes and Dreams.* Ottawa: The Vanier Institute of the Family, 2004. www.vifamily.ca/library/publications/futured.html

———. "Racial Intermarriage: Canada & the U.S." Project Canada Press Release #9, University of Lethbridge. 2007.

———. *The Emerging Millennials: How Canada's Newest Generation Is Responding to Change and Choice.* Lethbridge, AB: Project Canada Books, 2009.

BLANKENHORN, DAVID. *Fatherless America: Confronting Our Most Urgent Social Problem.* New York: HarperCollins, 1995.

BLAU, PETER M. *Exchange and Power in Social Life.* New York: Wiley, 1964.

BREAN, JOSEPH. "One in four Canadians declare affiliation to no religion, but why are so many 'nones' surprisingly religious?" *National Post.* May 26, 2014. http://news.nationalpost.com/holy-post/one-in-four-canadians-declare-affiliation-to-no-religion-but-why-are-so-many-nones-surprisingly-religious

BRENNAN, S. "Self-reported spousal violence, 2009." *Family Violence in Canada: A Statistical Profile.* Statistics Canada Catalogue no. 85-224-X. 2011.

BROOKER, A., and I. HYMAN. "Time Use." *Canadian Index of Wellbeing.* 2010. www.ciw.ca/Libraries/Documents/Time_Use-Report_Highlights.sflb.ashx.

CAMPBELL, ROBERT A., and JAMES E. CURTIS. "Religious Involvement Across Societies." *Journal for the Scientific Study of Religion.* Vol. 33, No. 3 (September 1994):217–29.

CANADIAN CENTRE FOR JUSTICE STATISTICS. *Family Violence in Canada: A Statistical Profile.* Catalogue no. 85-224-XIE. Ottawa: Minister of Industry, 2011.

———. *Family violence in Canada: A statistical profile, 2013.* Catalogue no. 85-002-X. 2015. http://www.statcan.gc.ca/pub/85-002-x/2014001/article/14114-eng.htm

CANADIAN WOMEN'S FOUNDATION. "The Facts About Women and Poverty." 2013. http://www.canadianwomen.org/facts-about-poverty#5

CASSIDY, JOHN. "Pope Francis's Challenge to Global Capitalism." *The New Yorker.* December 3, 2013. http://www.newyorker.com/news/john-cassidy/pope-franciss-challenge-to-global-capitalism

CBC NEWS. "Vancouver real estate titles reveal city's racist history." (August 26, 2014). http://www.cbc.ca/news/canada/british-columbia/vancouver-real-estate-titles-reveal-city-s-racist-history-1.2747924

CHARRON, MATHIEU, and PAUL ROBINSON. "Child and spousal support in metropolitan and non-metropolitan areas 2009/2010." *Juristat.* Component of Statistics Canada Catalogue no. 85-002-X (2011). http://www.statcan.gc.ca/pub/85-002-x/2011001/article/11424-eng.htm

CHERLIN, ANDREW J., LINDA M. BURTON, TERA R. HART, and DIANE M. PURVIN. "The Influence of Physical and Sexual Abuse on Marriage and Cohabitation." *American Sociological Review.* Vol. 69, No. 6 (December 2004):768–89.

CHILD AND FAMILY CANADA. How Families Are Doing in the '90s. (2003). [Online] www.cfc-efc.ca/docs/vocfc/00001083.htm

CIMINO, RICHARD, and DON LATTIN. "Choosing My Religion." *American Demographics.* Vol. 21, No. 4 (April 1999):60–65.

CLARK, W., and G. SCHELLENBERG. "Who's Religious?" *Canadian Social Trends* (Summer 2006). Statistics Canada Catalogue no. 11-008. www.statcan.gc.ca/pub/11-008-x/2006001/pdf/9181-eng.pdf

COLMAN, S. *The Ethics of Artificial Uteruses: Implications for Reproduction and Abortion.* Burlington, VT: Ashgate Publishing Company, 2004.

COPEN, CASEY E., KIMBERLY DANIELS, JONATHAN VESPA, and WILLIAM D. MOSHER. "First Marriages in the United States: Data from the 2006–2010 National Survey of Family Growth." National Health Statistics Reports, No. 49. 2012. Available at http://www.cdc.gov/nchs/data/nhsr/nhsr049.pdf

COX, HARVEY. *The Secular City.* Rev. ed. New York: Macmillan, 1971; orig. 1965.

CROSS, PHILIP, and PETER MITCHELL. *The Marriage Gap Between Poor and Rich Canadians: How Canadians are split into haves and have-nots along marriage lines.* Institute of Marriage and Family Canada. February 2014. http://www.imfcanada.org/canadian-marriage-gap

DAWSON, LORNE. *Comprehending Cults: The Sociology of New Religious Movements*. Toronto: University of Toronto Press, 1998.

DUNCAN, GREG J., W. JEAN YEUNG, JEANNE BROOKS-GUNN, and JUDITH R. SMITH. "How Much Does Childhood Poverty Affect the Life Chances of Children?" *American Sociological Review*. Vol. 63, No. 3 (June 1998):406–23.

DURKHEIM, EMILE. *The Elementary Forms of Religious Life*. New York: Free Press, 1965; orig. 1915.

ENGELS, FRIEDRICH. *The Origin of the Family, Private Property and the State*. Chicago: Kerr, 1902; orig. 1884.

ENGLAND, PAULA. "Three Reviews on Marriage." *Contemporary Sociology*. Vol. 30, No. 6 (November 2001):564–65.

ETZIONI, AMITAI. "How to Make Marriage Matter." *Time*. Vol. 142, No. 10 (September 6, 1993):76.

FINDLAY, LEANNE C., and DAFNA E. KOHEN. "Leave practices of parents after the birth or adoption of young children." *Canadian Social Trends* (July 30, 2012). Statistics Canada Catalogue no. 11-008-X. http://www.statcan.gc.ca/pub/11-008-x/2012002/article/11697-eng.pdf

FIRESTONE, S. *The Dialectic of Sex*. New York: William Morrow and Co., 1970.

FORUM RESEARCH. *More than one tenth of married Canadians admit to adultery*. 2012. https://www.forumresearch.com/forms/News%20Archives/News%20Releases/47950_Canada-wide_-_Infidelity_Poll_%28Forum_Research%29_%2820121116%29.pdf

FOX, BONNIE, and MEG LUXTON. "Conceptualizing Family." In Bonnie Fox, ed., *Family Patterns/Gender Relations*. Toronto: Oxford University Press, 2001:22–33.

FURSTENBERG, FRANK F., JR., and ANDREW CHERLIN. *Divided Families: What Happens to Children When Parents Part*. Cambridge, MA: Harvard University Press, 1991.

———. "Children's Adjustment to Divorce." In Bonnie J. Fox, ed., *Family Patterns, Gender Relations*. 2nd ed. New York: Oxford University Press, 2001.

FUSTOS, KATA. "Marriage Benefits Men's Health." Population Reference Bureau. September 2010. Available at http://www.prb.org/Articles/2010/usmarriage-menshealth.aspx

GILBERT, NEIL. "Family Life: Sold on Work." *Society*. Vol. 42, No. 3 (2005):12–17.

GILLARD, DENISE. "The Black Church in Canada." *McMaster Journal of Theology and Ministry*. Vol. 1 (1998). http://www.mcmaster.ca/mjtm/1-5.htm

GLEICK, ELIZABETH. "The Marker We've Been Waiting For." *Time* (April 7, 1997):28–42.

GO, AVVY YAO-YAO. "What happened to family values in immigration?" *The Star* (May 28, 2013). http://www.thestar.com/opinion/commentary/2013/05/28/what_happened_to_family_values_in_immigration.html

GOLDSTEIN, JOSHUA R., and CATHERINE T. KENNEY. "Marriage Delayed or Marriage Forgone? New Cohort Forecasts of First Marriage for U.S. Women." *American Sociological Review*. Vol. 66, No. 4 (August 2001):506–19.

GOODE, WILLIAM J. "The Theoretical Importance of Love." *American Sociological Review*. Vol. 24, No. 1 (February 1959):38–47.

GOULD, STEPHEN J. "Evolution as Fact and Theory." *Discover* (May 1981):35–37.

GREELEY, ANDREW M. *Religious Change in America*. Cambridge, MA: Harvard University Press, 1989.

GREENSPAN, STANLEY I. *The Four-Thirds Solution: Solving the Child-Care Crisis in America*. Cambridge, MA: Perseus, 2001.

HADDEN, JEFFREY K., and CHARLES E. SWAIN. *Prime-Time Preachers: The Rising Power of Televangelism*. Reading, MA: Addison-Wesley, 1981.

HOUT, MICHAEL, ANDREW M. GREELEY, and MELISSA J. WILDE. "The Demographic Imperative in Religious Change in the United States." *American Journal of Sociology*. Vol. 107, No. 2 (September 2001):468–500.

HUCHINGSON, JAMES E. "Science and Religion." *Miami* (Florida) *Herald* (December 25, 1994):1M, 6M.

HUNTER, JAMES DAVISON. *American Evangelicalism: Conservative Religion and the Quandary of Modernity*. New Brunswick, NJ: Rutgers University Press, 1983.

———. "Conservative Protestantism." In Philip E. Hammond, ed., *The Sacred in a Secular Age*. Berkeley: University of California Press, 1985:50–66.

———. *Evangelicalism: The Coming Generation*. Chicago: University of Chicago Press, 1987.

IANNACCONE, LAURENCE R. "Why Strict Churches Are Strong." *American Journal of Sociology*. Vol. 99, No. 5 (March 1994):1180–211.

INGLEHART, RONALD, and CHRISTIAN WELZEL. "World Values Survey: Inglehart-Welzel Cultural Map of the World." 2010. www.worldvaluessurvey.com

JACQUET, CONSTANT H., and ALICE M. JONES. *Yearbook of American and Canadian Churches, 1991*. Nashville, TN: Abingdon Press, 1991.

JENSON, J. "Changing the Paradigm: Family Responsibility or Investing in Children." *Canadian Journal of Sociology*. Vol. 29, No. 2 (2004):169–92.

KANTROWITZ, BARBARA, and PAT WINGERT. "Unmarried with Children." *Newsweek* (May 28, 2001):46–52.

KAUFMAN, WALTER. *Religions in Four Dimensions: Existential, Aesthetic, Historical, and Comparative*. Pleasantville, NY: Reader's Digest Press, 1976.

KELLY, MARY BESS. "Divorce cases in civil court, 2010/2011." *Juristat*. Component of Statistics Canada Catalogue no. 85-002-X (2012). http://statcan.gc.ca/pub/85-002-x/2012001/article/11634-eng.htm

KENT, MARY MEDERIOS. "U.S. Women Delay Marriage and Children for College." Population Reference Bureau. January 2011. [Online] Available at http://www.prb.org/Articles/2011/usmarriageandchildbirth.aspx

KILBOURNE, BROCK K. "The Conway and Siegelman Claims against Religious Cults: An Assessment of Their Data." *Journal for the Scientific Study of Religion*. Vol. 22, No. 4 (December 1983):380–85.

KRAYBILL, DONALD B. "The Amish Encounter with Modernity." In Donald B. Kraybill and Marc A. Olshan, eds., *The Amish Struggle with Modernity*. Hanover, NH: University Press of New England, 1994:21–33.

LAUMANN, EDWARD O., JOHN H. GAGNON, ROBERT T. MICHAEL, and STUART MICHAELS. *The Social Organization of Sexuality: Sexual Practices in the United States*. Chicago: University of Chicago Press, 1994.

LEVINE, SAMANTHA. "The Price of Child Abuse." *U.S. News & World Report* (April 9, 2001):58.

LI, PETER S. *Destination Canada: Immigration Debates and Issues*. Toronto: Oxford University Press, 2003.

LINO, MARK. "Expenditures on Children by Families, 2011." Miscellaneous Publication Number 1528-2011. U.S. Department of Agriculture, Center for Nutrition Policy and Promotion. 2012. Available at http://www.cnpp.usda.gov/Publications/CRC/crc2011.pdf

LUND, DALE A. "Caregiving." *Encyclopedia of Adult Development*. Phoenix, AZ: Oryx Press, 1993:57–63.

LYNN, MARION, and MILANA TODOROFF. "Women's Work and Family Lives." In Nancy Mandell, ed., *Feminist Issues: Race, Class, and Sexuality*. 2nd ed. Scarborough, ON: Prentice Hall Allyn and Bacon Canada, 1998:208–32.

MACE, DAVID, and VERA MACE. *Marriage East and West*. Garden City, NY: Doubleday/Dolphin, 1960.

MACIONIS, JOHN J. "Intimacy: Structure and Process in Interpersonal Relationships." *Alternative Lifestyles*. Vol. 1, No. 1 (February 1978):113–30.

MACIONIS, JOHN J., and KEN PLUMMER. *Sociology: A Global Introduction*. New York: Prentice Hall Europe, 1997.

MADOKORO, LAURA. "Chinatown and Monster Homes: The Splintered Chinese Diaspora in Vancouver." *Urban History Review*. Vol. 39, No. 2 (2011):17–24.

MANDELL, NANCY, and ANN DUFFY, eds. *Canadian Families: Diversity, Conflict, and Change*. 2nd ed. Scarborough, ON: ITP Nelson, 2000.

———, eds. *Canadian Families: Race, Class, Gender and Sexuality*. 3rd ed. Toronto: Harcourt, Brace & Co., 2004.

MARQUAND, ROBERT, and DANIEL B. WOOD. "Rise in Cults as Millennium Approaches." *Christian Science Monitor* (March 28, 1997):1, 18.

MARQUAND, ROBERT. "Worship Shift: Americans Seek Feeling of 'Awe.'" *Christian Science Monitor* (May 28, 1997):1, 8.

MARSHALL, K. "Fathers' Use of Paid Parental Leave." *Perspectives on Labour and Income*. Catalogue no. 75-001-X. 2008. www.statcan.gc.ca/pub/75-001-x/75-001-x2008106-eng.pdf

MARX, KARL. *Karl Marx: Early Writings*. T.B. Bottomore, ed. New York: McGraw-Hill, 1964; orig. 1848.

MASON, GARY. "Remove the parent, not the child." *Globe and Mail* (April 10, 2015). http://www.theglobeandmail.com/globe-debate/remove-the-parent-not-the-child/article23875303/

MATA, F. *Religion-Mix Growth in Canadian Cities: A Look at 2006–2031 Projections Data*. Report Prepared for Department of Canadian Heritage. 2010. [Online] www.ssc.uwo.ca/MER/MERcentre/conference%20presentations/Mata,Fernando.pdf

MAYO, KATHERINE. *Mother India*. New York: Harcourt, Brace, 1927.

MCCUE, HARVEY. "Reserves." *Historica Canada* (May 31, 2011). http://www.thecanadianencyclopedia.ca/en/article/aboriginal-reserves/

MCLANAHAN, SARA. "Life without Father: What Happens to the Children?" *Contexts*. Vol. 1, No. 1 (Spring 2002):35–44.

MCLEOD, JANE D., and MICHAEL J. SHANAHAN. "Poverty, Parenting, and Children's Mental Health." *American Sociological Review*. Vol. 58, No. 3 (June 1993):351–66.

MILAN, ANNE. "Marital Status: Overview, 2011." Statistics Canada Catalogue no. 91-209-X (July 2013). http://www.statcan.gc.ca/pub/91-209-x/2013001/article/11788-eng.htm

MOSS, PETER, and MARGARET O'BRIEN, eds. *International Review of Leave Policies and Related Research 2006*. Employment Relations Research Series No. 57. London: Department of Trade and Industry, 2006.

"Much Ado about Evolution." *Time* (November 21, 2005):23.

MURDOCK, GEORGE PETER. *Social Structure*. New York: Free Press, 1965; orig. 1949.

NAJAND, N. "Ectogenesis: The Ethical Implications of a New Reproductive Technology." Unpublished Master thesis. Victoria, BC: University of Victoria, 2010.

NEUHOUSER, KEVIN. "The Radicalization of the Brazilian Catholic Church in Comparative Perspective." *American Sociological Review*. Vol. 54, No. 2 (April 1989):233–44.

NORC. *General Social Surveys, 1972–2012*. Chicago: National Opinion Research Center. March 2013. Available at http://www.norc.org/GSS+Website

Peters Atlas of the World. New York: Harper & Row, 1990.

PEW FORUM ON RELIGION & PUBLIC LIFE. "U.S. Religious Landscape Survey." February 2008. http://religions.pewforum.org/reports

PEW RESEARCH CENTER. "As Marriage and Parenthood Drift Apart, Public Is Concerned about Social Impact." July 1, 2007. http://pewsocialtrends.org/pubs/526/marriage-parenthood

———. "Social and Demographic Trends: Reports." 2008. http://pewsocialtrends.org/pubs

———. "Religion and Science in the United States: Scientists and Belief." 2009. Available at http://www.pewforum.org/2009/11/05/scientists-and-belief/

———. "American Values Survey Question Database." 2012a. Available at http://www.people-press.org/values-questions/

———. "'Nones' on the Rise: Demographics." 2012b. Available at http://www.pewforum.org/2012/10/09/nones-on-the-rise-demographics/

———. "Canada's Changing Religious Landscape." 2013. Available at http://www.pewforum.org/2013/06/27/canadas-changing-religious-landscape/

———. "What's morally acceptable? It depends on where in the world you live." April 2014. http://www.pewresearch.org/fact-tank/2014/04/15/whats-morally-acceptable-it-depends-on-where-in-the-world-you-live/

POPENOE, DAVID. "American Family Decline, 1960–1990: A Review and Appraisal." *Journal of Marriage and the Family.* Vol. 55, No. 3 (August 1993):527–55.

———. "Can the Nuclear Family Be Revived?" *Society.* Vol. 36, No. 5 (July/August 1999):28–30.

POPULATION REFERENCE BUREAU. "Who Speaks for Me? Ending Child Marriage Fact Sheet." May 2011. [Online] Available at http://www.prb.org/pdf11/child-marriagefact-sheet.pdf

PORTER, JOHN. *The Vertical Mosaic.* Toronto: University of Toronto Press, 1965.

ROESCH, ROBERTA. "Violent Families." *Parents.* Vol. 59, No. 9 (September 1984):74–76, 150–52.

ROOF, WADE CLARK, and WILLIAM MCKINNEY. *American Mainline Religion: Its Changing Shape and Future.* New Brunswick, NJ: Rutgers University Press, 1987.

RUBIN, LILLIAN BRESLOW. *Worlds of Pain: Life in the Working-Class Family.* New York: Basic Books, 1976.

SAUL, S. *Feminism Issues and Arguments.* New York: Oxford University Press, 2003.

SAWCHUK, JOE. "Social Conditions of Aboriginal People." *Historica Canada* (October 31, 2011). http://www.thecanadianencyclopedia.ca/en/article/native-people-social-conditions/

SHUPE, ANSON. *In the Name of All That's Holy: A Theory of Clergy Malfeasance.* Westport, CT: Praeger, 1995.

SINGER, P., and D. WELLS. "Ectogenesis." In Scott Gelfand and John R. Shook, eds., *Ectogenesis: Artificial Womb Technology and the Future of Human Reproduction.* Amsterdam: Rodopi, 2006.

SINHA, MAIRE. *Family violence in Canada: A statistical profile, 2010.* Statistics Canada Catalogue no. 85-002-X. Ottawa: Minister of Industry, 2012.

SMITH, TOM W. *American Sexual Behavior: Trends, Sociodemographic Differences, and Risk Behavior.* Chicago: National Opinion Research Center, March 2006. www.norc.org/NR/rdonlyres/2663F09F-2E74-436E-AC81-6FFBF288E183/0/AmericanSexualBehavior2006.pdf

———. *Beliefs about God across Time and Countries.* Chicago: NORC/University of Chicago, 2012.

SNELL, MARILYN BERLIN. "The Purge of Nurture." *New Perspectives Quarterly.* Vol. 7, No. 1 (Winter 1990):1–2.

STACEY, JUDITH. *Brave New Families: Stories of Domestic Upheaval in Late-Twentieth-Century America.* New York: Basic Books, 1990.

STAPINSKI, HELENE. "Let's Talk Dirty." *American Demographics.* Vol. 20, No. 11 (November 1998):50–56.

STARK, RODNEY. *Sociology.* Belmont, CA: Wadsworth, 1985.

STARK, RODNEY, and WILLIAM SIMS BAINBRIDGE. "Of Churches, Sects, and Cults: Preliminary Concepts for a Theory of Religious Movements." *Journal for the Scientific Study of Religion.* Vol. 18, No. 2 (June 1979):117–31.

STATISTICS CANADA. *Women in Canada: A Statistical Report.* 3rd ed. Ottawa: Minister of Industry, 1995.

———. *The Daily* (March 16, 2000). [Online] www.statcan.ca/Daily/English/000316/d000316.pdf

———. *Religious Groups in Canada.* Ottawa: Minister of Industry, 2001. Catalogue No. 85F0033MIE.

———. "2001 Census: Marital Status, Common-law Status, Families, Dwellings and Households." *The Daily* (October 22, 2002) [Online] www.statcan.ca/Daily/English/021022/td021022a.htm

———. *Women in Canada: A Gender-Based Statistical Analysis.* 5th ed. Ottawa: Statistics Canada. Catalogue no. 89-503-XIE, 2006.

———. *Census Families by Number of Children at Home, by Province and Territory (2006 Census).* 2007a. [Online] www40.statcan.ca/l01/cst01/famil50a-eng.htm

———. *Family Portrait: Continuity and Change in Canadian Families and Households in 2006, 2006 Census.* Catalogue no. 97-553-XIE. 2007b. [Online] http://dsp-psd.pwgsc.gc.ca/collection_2007/statcan/97-553-X/97-553-XIE2006001.pdf

———. *Report on the Demographic Situation in Canada 2005 and 2006.* Catalogue no. 91-209-X. 2008. [Online] http://dsp-psd.pwgsc.gc.ca/collection_2008/statcan/91-209-X/91-209-XIE2004000.pdf

———. *Father's Day By the Numbers.* 2010. [Online] www42.statcan.gc.ca/smr08/2010/smr08_143_2010-eng.htm

———. *Estimates of Census Families for Canada, Provinces and Territories.* 2011a. [Online] www.statcan.gc.ca/cgi-bin/imdb/p2SV.pl?Function=getSurvey&SDDS=3606&lang=en&db=imdb&adm=8&dis=2#a2.

———. *Population Groups (28), Age Groups (8), Sex (3) and Selected Demographic, Cultural, Labour Force, Educational and Income Characteristics (309), for the Total Population of Canada, Provinces, Territories, Census Metropolitan Areas and Census Agglomeration.* [Electronic Data Base]. Catalogue no. 97-564-XCB2006009[1]. IVT. 2011b.

———. *Divorces and Crude Divorce Rates.* CANSIM Table 101-6501, v42136127 [Electronic Database]. 2011c.

———. *Census Family Status (6), Age Groups (20) and Sex (3) for the Population in Private Households of Canada, Provinces, Territories, Census Divisions and Census Subdivisions, 2006 Census—20% Sample Data.* [Electronic Data File]. Catalogue no. 97-553-XCB2006015[1]. IVT. 2011d.

———. *Portrait of Families and Living Arrangements in Canada.* Statistics Canada Catalogue no. 98-312-X2011001, September 2012.

———. "Report on the Demographic Situation in Canada, 2008 to 2012." *The Daily* (July 9, 2013a). [Online] http://www.statcan.gc.ca/daily-quotidien/130709/dq130709a-eng.htm

———. *Aboriginal Peoples in Canada: First Nations People, Métis and Inuit.* Statistics Canada Catalogue no. 99-011-X2011001. Ottawa: Minister of Industry, 2013b.

———. "2011 National Household Survey: Immigration, place of birth, citizenship, ethnic origin, visible minorities, language and religion" *The Daily* (May 8, 2013c). [Online] http://www.statcan.gc.ca/daily-quotidien/130508/dq130508b-eng.htm?HPA

———. *Immigration and Ethnocultural Diversity in Canada.* Statistics Canada Catalogue no. 99-010-X2011001. Ottawa: Minister of Industry, 2013d.

———. "Mixed Unions in Canada, National Household Survey (NHS), 2011." *NHS in Brief.* Ottawa: Minister of Industry. Catalogue no. 99-010-X2011003. 2014.

———. "Study: Grandparents living with their grandchildren, 2011." *The Daily* (April 14, 2015). [Online] http://www.statcan.gc.ca/daily-quotidien/150414/dq150414a-eng.htm

STROHSCHEIN, LISA A. "Parental Divorce and Child Mental Health Trajectories." *Journal of Marriage and Family.* Vol. 67 (2005):1286–300.

TAVERNISE, SABRINA, and ROBERT GEBELOFF. "Once Rare in Rural America, Divorce Is Changing the Face of Its Families." *The New York Times.* [Online] Available March 23, 2011, at http://www.nytimes.com/2011/03/24/us/24divorce.html?_r=1&ref=sabrinatavernise

TROELTSCH, ERNST. *The Social Teaching of the Christian Churches.* New York: Macmillan, 1931.

TRUTH AND RECONCILIATION COMMISSION OF CANADA. *They Came for the Children: Canada, Aboriginal Peoples, and Residential Schools.* Winnipeg: Truth and Reconciliation Commission of Canada, 2012.

———. *What We Have Learned: Principles of Truth and Reconciliation.* 2015a. Available at http://www.trc.ca/websites/trcinstitution/index.php?p=890

———. *Truth and Reconciliation Commission of Canada: Calls to Action.* 2015b. Available at http://www.trc.ca/websites/trcinstitution/index.php?p=890

TUCKER, JAMES. "New Age Religion and the Cult of the Self." *Society.* Vol. 39, No. 2 (February 2002):46–51.

TURCOTTE, PIERRE, and ALAIN BÉLANGER. *The Dynamics of Formation and Dissolution of First Common-Law Unions in Canada.* Research report. Ottawa: Statistics Canada, 1998.

UBC NEWS. "New poll shows Canadians want to make family a priority." (February 7, 2012). http://news.ubc.ca/2012/02/07/new-poll-shows-canadians-want-to-make-family-a-priority/

UBELACKER, SHERYL. "Two-child families becoming the norm in Canada." *Globe and Mail* (February 8, 2012). http://www.theglobeandmail.com/news/national/two-child-families-becoming-the-norm-in-canada/article544511/

U.S. CENSUS BUREAU. "Fertility." 2012. Available at http://www.census.gov/hhes/fertility/data/cps/supplemental.html

VAN PRAAGH, SHAUNA. "Why not take the Supreme Court's religious-studies ruling into the classroom?" *Globe and Mail* (March 19, 2015). http://www.theglobeandmail.com/globe-debate/why-not-take-the-supreme-courts-religious-studies-ruling-into-the-classroom/article23536103/

VANDIVERE, S., K. TOUT, J. CAPIZZANO, and M. ZASLOW. "Left Unsupervised: A Look at the Most Vulnerable Children." *Child Trends Research Brief* (2003):1–8.

VENTURA, STEPHANIE J. "Changing Patterns of Nonmarital Childbearing in the United States." *Centers for Disease Control and Prevention* (May 2009). http://www.cdc.gov/nchs/pressroom/09newsreleases/unmarriedbirths.htm

WALSH, NEALE DONALD. "The Overhaul of Humanity." *Light of Consciousness: Journal of Spiritual Awareness.* Vol. 24, No. 4 (Winter 2012):23–25.

WEBER, MAX. *The Protestant Ethic and the Spirit of Capitalism.* New York: Scribner, 1958; orig. 1904–05.

WESSELMAN, HANK. *Visionseeker: Shared Wisdom from the Place of Refuge.* Carlsbad, CA: Hay House, 2001.

WILKINS-LAFLAMME, SARAH. "Toward Religious Polarization? Time Effects on Religious Commitment in U.S., UK, and Canadian Regions." *Sociology of Religion.* Vol. 75, No. 2 (2014):284–308. doi:10.1093/socrel/sru001

WILLIAMS, CARA. "Family Disruptions and Childhood Happiness." *Canadian Social Trends.* No. 62 (Autumn 2002):2–4. Statistics Canada Catalogue no. 11-008-XPE.

WILLIAMS, JOHNNY E. "Linking Beliefs to Collective Action: Politicized Religious Beliefs and the Civil Rights Movement." *Sociological Forum.* Vol. 17, No. 2 (June 2002):203–22.

WILLIAMS, PETER W. *America's Religions: From Their Origins to the Twenty-First Century.* Urbana: University of Illinois Press, 2002.

WILLIAMS, RHYS H., and N.J. DEMERATH III. "Religion and Political Process in an American City." *American Sociological Review.* Vol. 56, No. 4 (August 1991):417–31.

WINKS, ROBIN W. *The Blacks in Canada: A History.* New Haven, London: Yale University Press, 1971.

WOODWARD, KENNETH L. "Feminism and the Churches." *Newsweek* (February 13, 1989):58–61.

WU, ZHENG. *Cohabitation: An Alternative Form of Living.* Don Mills, ON: Oxford University Press, 2000.

YANG, FENGGANG, and HELEN ROSE FUCHS EBAUGH. "Transformations in New Immigrant Religions and Their Global Implications." *American Sociological Review.* Vol. 66, No. 2 (April 2001):269–88.

ŽIŽEK, SLAVOJ. "Desire: Drive = Truth: Knowledge." *UMBR(a): On the Drive* (1997). http://www.lacan.com/zizek-desire.htm

Chapter 14

ALPHONSO, CAROLINE, and TAVIA GRANT. "A tale of two schools: The correlation between income and education in Toronto." *Globe and Mail* (November 16, 2013). http://www.theglobeandmail.com/news/national/time-to-lead/a-tale-of-two-schools-the-correlation-between-income-and-education/article15463950/?page=all

AMERICAN COLLEGE HEALTH ASSOCIATION. "National College Health Assessment Reference Group Data Report." Baltimore: American College Health Association. 2012. Available at http://www.acha-ncha.org/pubs_rpts.html

ANGUS REID GLOBAL MONITOR. *Most Canadians Generally Agree with Euthanasia.* 2010. www.angus-reid.com/polls/38352/most_canadians_generally_agree_with_euthanasia/

ARNUP, KATHERINE. "Death, Dying and Canadian Families." The Vanier Institute of the Family. 2013. http://www.vanierinstitute.ca/modules/news/newsitem.php?ItemId=550

ASSOCIATION OF WORKERS' COMPENSATION BOARDS OF CANADA. *Table 36 Number of Fatalities, by Industry and Jurisdiction, 2011-2013.* 2013. http://awcbc.org/?page_id=14

ASTIN, ALEXANDER W., LETICIA OSEGUERA, LINDA J. SAX, and WILLIAM S. KORN. *The American Freshman: Thirty-Five-Year Trends.* Los Angeles: UCLA Higher Education Research Institute, 2002.

AUSTER, CAROL J., and MINDY MACRONE. "The Classroom as a Negotiated Social Setting: An Empirical Study of the Effects of Faculty Members' Behavior on Students' Participation." *Teaching Sociology*. Vol. 22, No. 4 (October 1994):289–300.

BALDUS, BERND, and MEENAZ KASSAM. "'Making Me Truthful and Mild:' Values in Nineteenth-Century Ontario Schoolbooks." *Canadian Journal of Sociology*. Vol. 21, No. 3 (1996):327–57.

BECKER, ANNE E. "The Association of Television Exposure with Disordered Eating among Ethnic Fijian Adolescent Girls." Paper presented at the annual meeting of the American Psychiatric Association, Washington, DC, May 19, 1999.

BENOIT, CECILIA, et al. "Explaining the Health Gap Between Girls and Women in Canada." *Sociological Research Online*. Vol. 14, No. 5 (2009). www.socresonline.org.uk/14/5/9.html

BENOIT, CECILIA. "Rediscovering Appropriate Care: Maternity Traditions and Contemporary Issues in Canada." In David Coburn et al., eds., *Health and Canadian Society*. 3rd ed. Toronto: University of Toronto Press, 1998.

BIGGS, LESLEY. "The Case of the Missing Midwives: A History of Midwifery in Ontario from 1795–1900." *Ontario History*. Vol. 75 (1983):21–35.

BLISHEN, BERNARD. *Doctors in Canada*. Toronto: University of Toronto Press, 1991.

BLOOM, D.E., E.T. CAFIERO, E. JANÉ-LLOPIS, S. ABRAHAMS-GESSEL, L.R. BLOOM, S. FATHIMA, A.B. FEIGL, T. GAZIANO, M. MOWAFI, A. PANDYA, K. PRETTNER, L. ROSENBERG, B. SELIGMAN, A.Z. STEIN, and C. WEINSTEIN. *The Global Economic Burden of Non-Communicable Diseases*. September 2011. Geneva: World Economic Forum.

BOUCHARD, BRIGITTE, and JOHN ZHAO. "University Education: Recent Trends in Participation." *Education Quarterly Review*. Vol. 6, No. 4 (August 2000):24–32

BOURGEAULT, I.L., and S. WREDE. *Caring Beyond Borders: Comparing the Relationship between Work and Migration Patterns in Canada and Finland*. Special Issue of *The Canadian Journal of Public Health* on "Finding Dignity in Health Care and Health Care Work." C. Benoit and H. Hallgrimsdottir, eds. Vol. 99 (Suppl. 2, 2008): S22–S26.

BOURGEAULT, IVY, CECILIA BENOIT, and ROBBIE DAVIS-FLOYD, eds. *Reconceiving Midwifery*. Montreal-Kingston: McGill-Queen's University Press, 2004.

BOWLBY, G. "Provincial Dropout Rates—Trends and Consequences." *Education Matters*. Statistics Canada Catalogue no. 81-004-XIE, Vol. 2, No. 4 (2005).

BOWLES, SAMUEL, and HERBERT GINTIS. *Schooling in Capitalist America: Educational Reform and the Contradictions of Economic Life*. New York: Basic Books, 1976.

BOZICK, R., and S. DELUCA "Better Late Than Never? Delayed Enrollment in the High School to College Transition." *Social Forces*. Vol. 84 (2005):531–54.

BRENNAN, SHANNON. "Participation and Activity Limitation Survey 2006: Facts on Learning Limitations." Statistics Canada Catalogue no. 89-628-X 2009014. Ottawa: Minister of Industry, 2009.

BUSHAW, WILLIAM J., and SHANE J. LOPEZ. "Public Education in the United States: A Nation Divided." *Phi Delta Kappan*. Vol. 94, No. 1 (September 2012).

BUTLIN, GEORGE. "Determinants of University and Community College Leaving." *Education Quarterly Review*. Statistics Canada Catalogue no. 81-003-XIE. Vol. 6, No. 4 (August 2000):8–23.

CAIS. *Strategic Directions for 2013/14 to 2016/17*. 2013. http://www.cais.ca/page.cfm?p=618

CANADIAN COUNCIL ON LEARNING. *The State of Post-secondary Education in Canada*. 2006. www.ccl-cca.ca/ccl/Reports/PostSecondaryEducation/Archives2006/index.html

———. *Gappers: Taking Time Off between High School and Post-Secondary Studies*. 2008. www.ccl-cca.ca/pdfs/LessonsInLearning/Jun-26-08-Gappers-Taking-time-off.pdf

CANADIAN FEDERATION OF STUDENTS. *Funding for Post-Secondary Education*. 2013. http://cfs-fcee.ca/

CANADIAN HEALTH COALITION. "Canadians' Views on Public Health Care Solutions." 2011. http://healthcoalition.ca/canadians-want-future-budget-surpluses-invested-in-healthcare-want-secure-federal-funding-not-tied-to-the-economy/

CANADIAN INSTITUTE FOR HEALTH INFORMATION. *Health Care in Canada: A First Annual Report*. Ottawa: Statistics Canada, 2000.

CANADIAN LEARNING AND LITERACY NETWORK. "Literacy Statistics." 2015. http://www.literacy.ca/literacy/literacy-sub/

CANADIAN MEDICAL ASSOCIATION. "Canadian physician statistics." 2015. https://www.cma.ca/En/Pages/canadian-physician-statistics.aspx

CANADIAN NURSES ASSOCIATION. "2010 Workforce Profile of Registered Nurses in Canada." 2012. https://www.cna-aiic.ca/en/download-buy/nursing-statistics

———. "Health Human Resources." 2015. https://www.cna-aiic.ca/en/on-the-issues/better-value/health-human-resources

CANADIAN OBESITY NETWORK. "Obesity in Canada." 2015. http://www.obesitynetwork.ca/obesity-in-canada

CDC (CENTERS FOR DISEASE CONTROL AND PREVENTION). "Overweight and Obesity." 2011a. [Online] Available at http://www.cdc.gov/obesity/data/adult.html

———. "Smoking and Tobacco Use." 2011b. [Online] Available at http://www.cdc.gov/tobacco/index.htm

———. "2010 Sexually Transmitted Diseases Surveillance." 2011c. [Online] Available at http://www.cdc.gov/std/stats10/tables.htm

———. "Behavioral Risk Factor Surveillance System: Prevalence and Trends Data." 2012. Available at http://apps.nccd.cdc.gov/BRFSS/

CIHI (CANADIAN INSTITUTE FOR HEALTH INFORMATION). "National Health Expenditure Trends, 1975 to 2010." 2010. http://secure.cihi.ca/cihiweb/products/NHEX_Trends_Report_2010_final_ENG_web.pdf

———. "Health Spending in Canada 2013." 2013. https://www.cihi.ca/en/spending-and-health-workforce/health-spending/health-spending-in-canada-2013

CLEMENS, JASON, MILAGROS PALACIOS, JANE LOYER, and FRAZIER FATHERS. "Measuring Choice and Competition in Canadian Education: An Update on School Choice in Canada." Fraser Institute. 2014. http://www.fraserinstitute.org/research-news/display.aspx?id=20887

CLEMENT, WALLACE. *The Canadian Corporate Elite*. Toronto: McClelland and Stewart, 1975.

CLOUD, JOHN, and JODIE MORSE. "Home Sweet School." *Time* (August 27, 2001):46–54.

COLEMAN, JAMES S. "The Design of Organizations and the Right to Act." *Sociological Forum*. Vol. 8, No. 4 (December 1993):527–46.

COLEMAN, JAMES S., et al. *Equality of Educational Opportunity*. Washington, DC: U.S. Government Printing Office, 1966.

COLEMAN, JAMES S., THOMAS HOFFER, and SALLY KILGORE. *Public and Private Schools: An Analysis of Public Schools and Beyond*. Washington, DC: National Center for Education Statistics, 1981.

COLLEGE BOARD, THE. "Trends in Higher Education: Average Published Undergraduate Charges by Sector, 2012–13." 2013. Available at http://trends.collegeboard.org/college-pricing/figures-tables/average-published-undergraduate-charges-sector-2012-13

COLLEGE OF FAMILY PHYSICIANS OF CANADA. "Patient-Centred Primary Care in Canada: Bring It on Home." Discussion paper. 2009. www.cfpc.ca/ProjectAssets/Templates/Resource.aspx?id=890

COLLINS, RANDALL. *The Credential Society: A Historical Sociology of Education and Stratification*. New York: Academic Press, 1979.

CONFERENCE BOARD OF CANADA. *Performance and Potential, 2000–2001*. Ottawa: The Conference Board of Canada, 2000. [Online] www.conferenceboard.ca/pdfs/pp_00kf.pdf

———. *Hot Topic: Advanced Skills & Innovation: How Much Do Advanced Skills Affect Innovation?* 2011. http://sso.conferenceboard.ca/hcp/hot-topics/innovation.aspx

CÔTÉ, JAMES E., and ANTON L. ALLAHAR. *Ivory Tower Blues: A University System in Crisis*. Toronto: University of Toronto Press, 2007.

———. *Lowering Higher Education: The Rise of Corporate Universities and the Fall of Liberal Education*. Toronto: University of Toronto Press, 2011.

CÔTÉ, MARK, RICHARD J.F. DAY, and GREIG DE PEUTER, eds. *Utopian Pedagogy: Radical Experiments against Neoliberal Globalization*. Toronto: University of Toronto Press, 2007.

COULOMBE, S., J.F. TREMBLAY, and S. MARCHAND. *Literacy Scores, Human Capital and Growth Across 14 OECD Countries*. Ottawa: Statistics Canada, 2004.

COUNCIL OF MINISTERS OF EDUCATION. "Adult Learning and Education – Canada progress report for the UNESCO Global Report on Adult Learning and Education (GRALE) and the end of the United Nations Literacy Decade." 2012. http://www.cmec.ca/9/publications/?searchCat=4

COWLEY, GEOFFREY. "The Prescription That Kills." *Newsweek* (July 17, 1995):54.

CROUSE, JAMES, and DALE TRUSHEIM. *The Case against the SAT*. Chicago: University of Chicago Press, 1988.

CURTIS, BRUCE. *Building the Educational State: Canada West, 1831–1871*. London, ON: Althouse Press, 1988.

DAVIES, SCOTT, and JANICE D. AURINI. "School Choice as Concerted Cultivation: The Case of Canada." In Martin Forsey, Scott Davies, and Geoffrey Walford, eds., *The Globalisation of School Choice?* Didcot, Oxford: Syposium Books, 2008.

DEVRIES, R., C. BENOIT, E. VAN TEIJLINGEN, and SIRPA WREDE, eds. *Birth by Design: The Social Shaping of Maternity Care in Northern Europe and North America*. London: Routledge, 2001.

DOWNEY, DOUGLAS B., PAUL T. VON HIPPEL, and BECKETT A. BROH. "Are Schools the Great Equalizer? Cognitive Inequality during the Summer Months and School Year." *American Sociological Review*. Vol. 59, No. 5 (October 2004):613–35.

DUBOS, RENÉ. *Man Adapting*. Enlarged ed. New Haven, CT: Yale University Press, 1980.

EHRENREICH, BARBARA. *Nickel and Dimed: On (Not) Getting By in America*. New York: Henry Holt, 2001.

ELSON, JEAN. *Am I Still a Woman? Hysterectomy and Gender Identity*. Philadelphia, PA: Temple University Press, 2004.

EMERSON, JOAN P. "Behavior in Private Places: Sustaining Definitions of Reality in Gynecological Examinations." In H.P. Dreitzel, ed., *Recent Sociology*. Vol. 2. New York: Collier, 1970:74–97.

ERIKSEN, MICHAEL, JUDITH MACKAY, and HANA ROSS. "The Tobacco Atlas, Fourth Ed." Atlanta, GA: American Cancer Society; New York: World Lung Foundation. 2012. Available at http://www.TobaccoAtlas.org

FALLON, A.E., and P. ROZIN. "Sex Differences in Perception of Desirable Body Shape." *Journal of Abnormal Psychology*. Vol. 94, No. 1 (1985):100–05.

FONDA, DAREN. "The Male Minority." *Time* (December 11, 2000):58–60.

FRENETTE, MARC, and PING CHING WINNIE CHAN. "Academic Outcomes of Public and Private High School Students: What Lies Behind the Differences?" Statistics Canada Catalogue no. 11F0019M — No. 367. Ottawa: Minister of Industry, 2015.

FRIEDMAN, MEYER, and RAY H. ROSENMAN. *Type A Behavior and Your Heart*. New York: Fawcett Crest, 1974.

GALWAY, GERALD. "Is Education Still a Viable Career Option in Atlantic Canada?" In Nancy Maynes and Blaine E. Hatt, eds., *The Complexity of Hiring, Supporting, and Retaining New Teachers Across Canada*. Polygraph Series: Canadian Association for Teacher Education (CATE). 2015. https://sites.google.com/site/cssecate/polygraph-book-series

GAMORAN, ADAM. "The Variable Effects of High-School Tracking." *American Sociological Review*. Vol. 57, No. 6 (December 1992):812–28.

GILLESPIE, MARK. "Trends Show Bathing and Exercise Up, TV Watching Down." Gallup.com. January 2000. www.gallup.com/poll/3352/Trends-Show-BathingExercise-Up-Watching-Down.aspx

GOLDEN, FREDERIC, and MICHAEL D. LEMONICK. "The Race Is Over." *Time* (July 3, 2000):18–23.

GORDON, JAMES S. "The Paradigm of Holistic Medicine." In Arthur C. Hastings et al., eds., *Health for the Whole Person: The Complete Guide to Holistic Medicine*. Boulder, CO: Westview Press, 1980:3–27.

GOVERNMENT OF CANADA. "More International Students are Choosing Canada." *News Release* (November 7, 2014). http://news.gc.ca/web/article-en.do?nid=901549

GRANT, KAREN R. "The Inverse Care Law in the Context of Universal Free Health Insurance in Canada: Toward Meeting Health Needs through Public Policy." *Sociological Focus*. Vol. 17, No. 2 (April 1984):137–55.

GREENBERG, LAWSON, and CLAUDE NORMANDIN. "Disparities in life expectancy at birth." *Health at a Glance*. Ottawa: Statistics Canada, 2011.

HAMRICK, MICHAEL H., DAVID J. ANSPAUGH, and GENE EZELL. *Health*. Columbus, OH: Merrill, 1986.

HANGO, D. *Taking Time Off between High School and Postsecondary Education: Determinants and Early Labour Market Outcomes*. Statistics Canada Catalogue no. 81-004-XIE 2008. Ottawa: Culture, Tourism and the Centre for Education Statistics, 2008.

———. *Delaying Post-secondary Education: Who Delays and for How Long?* Statistics Canada Catalogue no. 81-595-M. Ottawa: Minister of Industry, 2011.

HARRIGAN, PATRICK J. "The Schooling of Boys and Girls in Canada." *Journal of Social History*. Vol. 23, No. 4 (Summer 1990):803–26.

HEALTH CANADA. "Smoking and Mortality." Date modified 2011. http://www.hc-sc.gc.ca/hc-ps/tobac-tabac/legislation/label-etiquette/mortal-eng.php

HELLMICH, NANCI. "Environment, Economics Partly to Blame." *USA Today* (October 9, 2002):9D.

HOPKINSON, NATALIE. "Why School Choice Fails." *The New York Times* (December 4, 2011). Available at http://www.nytimes.com/2011/12/05/opinion/why-school-choicefails.html

HORN, WADE F., and DOUGLAS TYNAN. "Revamping Special Education." *Public Interest*. No. 144 (Summer 2001):36–53.

HORTON, RICHARD. "GBD 2010: Understanding Disease, Injury, and Risk." *The Lancet*. Vol. 380, No. 9859 (December 15, 2012):2053–54. Available at http://www.thelancet.com/journals/lancet/article/PIIS0140-6736(12)62133-3/fulltext

HYSLOP, KATIE. "Too Many Teachers?" *The Tyee* (October 28, 2014). http://thetyee.ca/News/2014/10/28/Too-Many-Teachers-in-BC/

ISRAEL, GLENN D., LIONEL J. BEAULIEU, and GLEN HARTLESS. "The Influence of Family and Community Social Capital on Educational Achievement." *Rural Sociology*. Vol. 66, No. 1 (March 2001):43–68.

JANZ, TERESA. "Current Smoking Trends." Statistics Canada Catalogue no. 82-624-X. Ottawa: Statistics Canada, 2012.

JONES, D. GARETH. "Brain Death." *Journal of Medical Ethics*. Vol. 24, No. 4 (August 1998):237–43.

KAIN, EDWARD L. "A Note on the Integration of AIDS into the Sociology of Human Sexuality." *Teaching Sociology*. Vol. 15, No. 4 (July 1987):320–23.

KAPTCHUK, TED. "The Holistic Logic of Chinese Medicine." In Berkeley Holistic Health Center, *The New Holistic Health Handbook: Living Well in a New Age*. Shepard Bliss et al., eds. Lexington, MA: Steven Greene Press, 1985:41.

KARP, DAVID A., and WILLIAM C. YOELS. "The College Classroom: Some Observations on the Meaning of Student Participation." *Sociology and Social Research*. Vol. 60, No. 4 (July 1976):421–39.

KATZMARZYK, P.T., and C.I. ARDERN. "Overweight and obesity mortality trends in Canada 1985-2000." *Canadian Journal of Public Health*. Vol. 95, No. 1 (2004):16–20.

KERR, THOMAS, MARK TYNDALL, KATHY LI, JULIO S.G. MONTANER, and EVAN WOOD. "Safer Injection Facility Use and Syringe Sharing in Injection Drug Users." *Lancet*. Vol. 366 (2005):316–18.

KGO ADULT LITERACY PROGRAM. *Facts*. 2015. http://www.kgoadultliteracy.com/index.php/adult-literacy/facts

KILGORE, SALLY B. "The Organizational Context of Tracking in Schools." *American Sociological Review*. Vol. 56, No. 2 (April 1991):189–203.

KING, JENNIFER, CHELSEA EDWARDS, and CINDY BLACKSTOCK. "A Time for Dreams: The Right to Education for First Nations Children and Youth Living On-Reserve." In Kate Tilleczek and H. Bruce Ferguson, eds., *Youth, Education, and Marginality: Local and Global Expressions*. Waterloo, ON: Wilfrid Laurier University Press, 2013.

KOZOL, JONATHAN. *Savage Inequalities: Children in America's Schools*. New York: Crown Publishers, a division of Random House, Inc., 1991.

KRAL, BRIGITTA. "The Eyes of Jane Elliott." *Horizon Magazine*. 2000. www.horizonmag.com/4/jane-elliott.asp

LADD, JOHN. "The Definition of Death and the Right to Die." In John Ladd, ed., *Ethical Issues Relating to Life and Death*. New York: Oxford University Press, 1979:118–45.

LANDSBERG, MITCHELL. "Health Disaster Brings Early Death in Russia." *Washington Times* (March 15, 1998):A8.

LAUMANN, EDWARD O., JOHN H. GAGNON, ROBERT T. MICHAEL, and STUART MICHAELS. *The Social Organization of Sexuality: Sexual Practices in the United States*. Chicago: University of Chicago Press, 1994.

LAWTON, STEPHEN B., and DANIEL J. BROWN. "Charter Schools." *Historica Canada* (April 11, 2012). http://www.thecanadianencyclopedia.ca/en/article/charter-schools/

LEARNING DISABILITIES ASSOCIATION OF CANADA. "Prevalence of Learning Disabilities." 2007. http://ldac-acta.ca/learn-more/ld-basics/prevalence-of-lds

LEARNING DISABILITIES ASSOCIATION OF ONTARIO. "Learning Disabilities Statistics." 2011. http://www.ldao.ca/introduction-to-ldsadhd/ldsadhs-in-depth/articles/about-lds/learning-disabilities-statistics/

LEAVITT, JUDITH WALZER. "Women and Health in America: An Overview." In Judith Walzer Leavitt, ed., *Women and Health in America*. Madison: University of Wisconsin Press, 1984:3–7.

LEVINE, MICHAEL P. "Reducing Hostility Can Prevent Heart Disease." *Mount Vernon (Ohio) News* (August 7, 1990):4A.

LEVINE, MICHAEL. *Student Eating Disorders: Anorexia Nervosa and Bulimia*. Washington, DC: National Educational Association, 1987.

LIVINGSTONE, D.W., and MILOSH RAYKOV. "Adult Learning Trends in Canada: Basic Findings of the WALL 1998, 2004 and 2010 Surveys." Centre for the Study of Education and Work Ontario Institute for Studies in Education. Toronto: University of Toronto, 2013.

LOIS, JENNIFER. *Home Is Where the School Is: The Logic of Homeschooling and the Emotional Labor of Mothering*. New York: New York University Press, 2013.

LOWE, GRAHAM, and HARVEY KRAHN. "Work Aspirations and Attitudes in an Era of Labour Market Restructuring: A Comparison of Two Canadian Youth Cohorts." *Work, Employment and Society*. Vol. 14, No. 1 (2000):1–22.

MARSHALL, BRANDON D.L., et al. "Reduction in overdose mortality after the opening of North America's first medically supervised safer injecting facility: a retrospective population-based study." *The Lancet* (2011). doi:10.1016/S0140-6736(10)62353-7

MASON, DAVID S. "Fairness Matters: Equity and the Transition to Democracy." *World Policy Journal*. Vol. 20, No. 4 (Winter 2003–04). 2004. www.worldpolicy.org/journal/articles/wpj03-4/mason.htm

MAXWELL, MARY PERCIVAL, and JAMES MAXWELL. "Going Co-Ed: Elite Private Schools in Canada." *Canadian Journal of Sociology*. Vol. 20, No. 3 (Summer 1995): 333–57.

MCGURRIN, JOHN J. "Canada." In Luigi Siciliani, Michael Borowitz, Valerie Moran, eds., *Waiting Time Policies in the Health Sector: What Works?* OECD Health Policy Studies, OECD Publishing, Paris, 2013. doi: http://dx.doi.org/10.1787/9789264179080-en

MCLEAN, SCOTT. "Objectifying and Naturalizing Individuality: A Study of Adult Education in the Canadian Arctic." *Canadian Journal of Sociology*. Vol. 22, No. 1 (Winter 1997):1–30.

MEZZACAPPA, DALE. "Only Six Providers Approved for 'Turnaround'" *Philadephia Public Schools Notebook*. 2010. [Online] Available at http://www.thenotebook.org/blog/102296/six-providers-approved-turnaround

MONEO, SHANNON. "The ABCs of private education." *Globe and Mail* (September 26, 2013). http://www.theglobeandmail.com/news/national/education/the-abcs-of-private-education/article14530589/

MORSE, JODIE. "A Victory for Vouchers." *Time* (July 8, 2002):32–34.

MURRAY, CHRISTOPHER, et al. "Disability-Adjusted Life Years (DALYs) for 291 Diseases and Injuries in 21 Regions, 1990–2010: A Systematic Analysis for the Global Burden of Disease Study 2010." *The Lancet*. Vol. 380, No. 9859 (December 15, 2012):2197–223. Available at http://www.thelancet.com/journals/lancet/article/PIIS0140-6736(12)61689-4/fulltext

MYERS, DAVID G. *The American Paradox: Spiritual Hunger in an Age of Plenty*. New Haven, CT: Yale University Press, 2000.

MYERS, SHEILA, and HAROLD G. GRASMICK. "The Social Rights and Responsibilities of Pregnant Women: An Application of Parsons' Sick Role Model." Paper presented to the Southwestern Sociological Association, Little Rock, AR, March 1989.

NANOS RESEARCH. "Canadians want future budget surpluses invested in healthcare, want secure federal funding not tied to the economy." 2013. http://www.nanosresearch.com/library/opinion_2013.html

NATIONAL CONFERENCE OF STATE LEGISLATURES. "State Smoke-Free Laws and Health." 2012. Available at http://www.ncsl.org/default.aspx?tabid=19911

NATIONAL INSTITUTE OF MENTAL HEALTH. "Eating Disorders." 2012. Available at http://www.nimh.nih.gov/health/publications/eating-disorders/complete-publication.shtml

NAVANEELAN, TANYA, and TERESA JANZ. "Adjusting the scales: Obesity in the Canadian population after correcting for respondent bias." *Health at a Glance*. Statistics Canada, Catalogue no. 82-624-X. 2014.

NEPORENT, LIZ. "Stigma Against Fat People the Last Acceptable Prejudice, Studies Find." ABC News. January 22, 2013. Available at http://abcnews.go.com/Health/stigma-obese-acceptable-prejudice/story?id=18276788

NEWMAN, PETER. *The Canadian Establishment*. Vol. 1. Toronto: McClelland & Stewart, 1975.

NORC. *General Social Surveys, 1972–2012*. Chicago: National Opinion Research Center. March 2013. Available at http://www.norc.org/GSS+Website/

NULAND, SHERWIN B. "The Hazards of Hospitalization." *Wall Street Journal* (December 2, 1999):A22.

OECD. *Education at a Glance: OECD Indicators*. 2014. http://www.oecd.org/education/eag.htm

ONTARIO COLLEGE OF TEACHERS. "Transition to Teaching 2012." 2012. http://www.oct.ca/becoming-a-teacher/transition-to-teaching/previous-reports

———. "Transition to Teaching 2014." 2014. http://www.oct.ca/becoming-a-teacher/transition-to-teaching

OREOPOULOS, PHILIP. "The Compelling Effects of Compulsory Schooling: Evidence from Canada." *Canadian Journal of Economics*. Vol. 39, No. 1 (2006):22–52.

ORNSTEIN, ALLAN C. "Achievement Gaps in Education." *Society*. Vol. 47, No. 5 (September/October 2010):424–29.

PARKER, KIM, AMANDA LENHART, and KATHLEEN MOORE. "The Digital Revolution and Higher Education." Pew Research: Social & Demographic Trends (August 28, 2011). Available at http://www.pewsocialtrends.org/2011/08/28/the-digital-revolution-and-higher-education/

PARSONS, TALCOTT. *The Social System*. New York: Free Press, 1951.

PATTERSON, ELISSA F. "The Philosophy and Physics of Holistic Health Care: Spiritual Healing as a Workable Interpretation." *Journal of Advanced Nursing*. Vol. 27, No. 2 (February 1998):287–93.

PEAR, ROBERT, and ERIK ECKHOLM. "When Healers Are Entrepreneurs: A Debate over Costs and Ethics." *New York Times* (June 2, 1991):1, 17.

PINHEY, THOMAS K., DONALD H. RUBINSTEIN, and RICHARD S. COLFAX. "Overweight and Happiness: The Reflected Self-Appraisal Hypothesis Reconsidered." *Social Science Quarterly*. Vol. 78, No. 3 (September 1997):747–55.

POPULATION REFERENCE BUREAU. "Datafinder." 2012. Available at http://www.prb.org/DataFinder.aspx

PORTER, JOHN. *The Vertical Mosaic*. Toronto: University of Toronto Press, 1965.

PRENTICE, ALISON. *The School Promoters*. Toronto: McClelland and Stewart, 1977.

Pryor, John H., Kevin Egan, Laura Palucki Blake, Sylvia Hurtado, Jennifer Berdan, and Matthew Case. "The American Freshman: National Norms Fall 2012 (Expanded Edition)." Cooperative Institutional Research Program at the Higher Education Research Institute at UCLA. 2013. Available at http://www.heri.ucla.edu/monographs/TheAmericanFreshman2012-Expanded.pdf

Public Health Agency of Canada. "Executive Summary - Report on Sexually Transmitted Infections in Canada: 2011." 2011. http://www.phac-aspc.gc.ca/sti-its-surv-epi/rep-rap-2011/index-eng.php

———. "HIV and AIDS in Canada: Surveillance Report to December 31, 2013." Minister of Public Works and Government Services Canada, 2014.

Putka, Gary. "SAT to Become a Better Gauge." *Wall Street Journal* (November 1, 1990):B1.

Reid, Jessica, David Hammond, Vicki Rynard, and Robin Burkhalter. *Tobacco Use in Canada: Patterns and Trends, 2015 Edition.* Waterloo, ON: Propel Centre for Population Health Impact, University of Waterloo, 2015.

Reimer, Karl. "What Other Canadian Kids Have: The Fight for a New School in Attawapiskat." *Native Studies Review.* Vol. 19, No. 1 (2010):119-136.

Richburg, Keith B. "School Privatization Plan Sputters." *Washington Post* (June 29, 2008). [Online] Available February 3, 2009, at http://www.boston.com/news/education/k_12/articles/2008/06/29/school_privatization_plan_sputters

Robertson, Todd. "Changing Patterns of University Finance." *Education Quarterly Review.* Vol. 9, No. 2. Catalogue no. 81-003-XIE (June 2003):9–17.

Roehrig, James P., and Carmen P. McLean. "A Comparison of Stigma Toward Eating Disorders Versus Depression." *International Journal of Eating Disorders.* Vol. 43, No. 7 (November 2010):671–74.

Sagan, Aleksandra. "Average student debt difficult to pay off, delays life milestones." *CBC News* (March 11, 2014). http://www.cbc.ca/news/canada/average-student-debt-difficult-to-pay-off-delays-life-milestones-1.2534974

Schneider, Mark, Melissa Marschall, Paul Teske, and Christine Roch. "School Choice and Culture Wars in the Classroom: What Different Parents Seek from Education." *Social Science Quarterly.* Vol. 79, No. 3 (September 1998):489–501.

Segall, Alexander, and Neena Chappell. *Health and Health Care in Canada.* Toronto: Prentice Hall, 2000.

Sennett, Richard, and Jonathan Cobb. *The Hidden Injuries of Class.* New York: Vintage Books, 1973.

Service Canada. "Secondary School Teachers." Date modified 2014. http://www.servicecanada.gc.ca/eng/qc/job_futures/statistics/4141.shtml

Shannen's Dream Campaign. *Our Dreams Matter Too: First Nations children's rights, lives, and education: An alternate report from the Shannen's Dream Campaign to the United Nations Committee on the Rights of the Child on the occasion of Canada's 3rd and 4th periodic reviews.* 2011. [Online] http://www.fncaringsociety.com/sites/default/files/docs/OurDreams-June2011.pdf

Sizer, Theodore R. *Horace's Compromise: The Dilemma of the American High School.* Boston: Houghton Mifflin, 1984.

Spurr, S., L. Barry, and K. Walker. "Exploring adolescent views of body image: The influence of media." *Issues in Comprehensive Pediatric Nursing.* Vol. 36 (2013):17-36.

Statistics Canada. *The People: Student Indebtedness.* (2003) [Online] http://142.206.72.67/02/02c/02c_007b_e.htm

———. *Learning a Living: First Results of the Adult Literacy and Life Skills Survey.* Catalogue no. 89-603-XWE. Ottawa: Minister of Industry, Canada, and Organization for Economic Cooperation and Development (OECD), 2005.

———. *Educational Portrait of Canada, Census 2006.* Catalogue no. 97-560-X2006001. 2008.

———. *University Enrolments by Registration Status and Sex, by Province.* 2010a. [Online] www40.statcan.ca/l01/cst01/educ53a-eng.htm

———. "Trends in Dropout Rates and the Labour Market Outcomes of Young Dropouts." *Education*

Matters: Insights on Education, Learning and Training in Canada. 2010b. [Online] www.statcan.gc.ca/pub/81-004-x/2010004/article/11339-eng.htm

———. *Aboriginal Statistics at a Glance.* Catalogue no. 89-645-XWE. 2010c.

———. *Employment Income Statistics in 2010 (7), Sex (3), Work Activity in 2010 (3), Highest Certificate, Diploma or Degree (6) and Occupation - National Occupational Classification (NOC) 2011 (693) for the Population Aged 15 Years and Over in Private Households of Canada, Provinces and Territories, 2011 National Household Survey.* 2011a. http://www12.statcan.gc.ca/nhs-enm/2011/dp-pd/dt-td/Rp-eng.cfm?TABID=2&LANG=E&APATH=3&DETAIL=0&DIM=0&FL=A&FREE=0&GC=0&GK=0&GRP=1&PID=106738&PRID=0&PTYPE=105277&S=0&SHOWALL=0&SUB=0&Temporal=2013&THEME=98&VID=0&VNAMEE=&VNAMEF=

———. *Learning—Educational Attainment.* 2011b. www4.hrsdc.gc.ca/.3ndic.1t.4r$$$$$-eng.jsp?iid=29#M_4

———. *Overweight and obese adults (self-reported), 2012.* 2012. http://www.statcan.gc.ca/pub/82-625-x/2013001/article/11840-eng.htm

———. *Table C.2.3 Student-educator ratio in public elementary and secondary schools, Canada, provinces and territories, 2001/2002 to 2010/2011.* [Electronic Data File]. Catalogue no. 81-582-X. 2013a.

———. *Summary Elementary and Secondary School Indicators for Canada, the Provinces and Territories, 2006/2007 to 2010/2011.* [Electronic Data File]. Catalogue no. 81-595-M. 2013b.

———. *Education in Canada: Attainment, Field of Study and Location of Study.* Ottawa: Minister of Industry. Catalogue no. v99-012-X2011001. 2013c.

———. *Table D.6.3 Educational attainment of the population aged 25 to 64, off-reserve Aboriginal, non-Aboriginal, and total population, Canada, provinces and territories, 2009, 2010 and 2011.* [Electronic Data File]. Catalogue no. 81-599-X. 2013d.

———. *The educational attainment of Aboriginal peoples in Canada.* Ottawa: Minister of Industry. Catalogue no. 99-012-X2011003. 2013e.

———. *Postsecondary enrolments, by registration status, Pan-Canadian Standard Classification of Education (PCSCE), Classification of Instructional Programs, Primary Grouping (CIP_PG), sex and immigration status.* Cansim Table 477-0019 [Electronic Database]. Date modified 2014a.

———. "University tuition fees, 2014/2015." *The Daily* (September 11, 2014b). http://www.statcan.gc.ca/daily-quotidien/140911/dq140911b-eng.htm

———. *Leading causes of death, total population, by age group and sex, Canada.* CANSIM table 102-0561 [Electronic Data File]. Date modified 2014c.

Steben, Marc, and Stephen L. Sacks. "Genital Herpes: The Epidemiology and Control of a Common Sexually Transmitted Disease." *Canadian Journal of Human Sexuality.* Vol. 6, No. 2 (1997):127–34.

Tamblyn, R., M. Abrahamowicz, D. Dauphinee, and D. Klass. "Physician Scores on a National Clinical Skills Examination as Predictors of Complaints to Medical Regulatory Authorities." *Journal of the American Medical Association.* Vol. 298, No. 9 (September 2007):993–1001.

The Lancet. "Wealth But Not Health in the USA." Vol. 381, Issue 9862 (January 19, 2013). Available at http://www.thelancet.com/journals/lancet/article/PIIS0140-6736(13)60069-0/fulltext

The Officer Down Memorial Page. "Honoring Officers Killed in the Year 2013." 2015. http://canada.odmp.org/year.php?year=2013

Thompson, Dick. "Gene Maverick." *Time* (January 11, 1999):54–55.

Tibbetts, Janice. "Teacher shortage turning into oversupply." *National Post* (January 31, 2008). http://www.nationalpost.com/news/story.html?id=277562

Tomkowicz, Joanna, and Tracey Bushnik. *Who Goes to Post-Secondary Education and When: Pathways Chosen by 20-Year-Olds.* Education Skills and Learning—Research Papers. Statistics Canada Catalogue no. 81-595-MIE. Ottawa: Statistics Canada, 2003 [Online] www.statcan.ca/english/research/81-595-MIE/81-595-MIE2003006.pdf

Toppo, Greg, and Anthony Debarros. "Reality Weighs Down Dreams of College." *USA Today* (February 2, 2005):A1.

Toronto District School Board. *Parent and Student Census.* 2014. http://www.tdsb.on.ca/AboutUs/Research/ParentandStudentCensus.aspx

UNAIDS. "2012 Report on the Global AIDS Eepidemic." 2012. Available at http://www.unaids.org/en/media/unaids/contentassets/documents/epidemiology/2012/gr2012/20121120_UNAIDS_Global_Report_2012_with_annexes_en.pdf

UNESCO Institute of Statistics. "Data Centre." 2012. Available at http://stats.uis.unesco.org/unesco/tableviewer/document.aspx?ReportId=143

United Nations Development Programme. "International Human Development Indicators." 2012. Available at http://hdrstats.undp.org/en/indicators/default.html

U.S. Census Bureau. "Educational Attainment." 2012. Available at http://www.census.gov/hhes/socdemo/education/data/cps/2012/tables.html

U.S. Department of Health and Human Services, Substance Abuse and Mental Health Services Administration (SAMHSA). "Results from the 2011 National Survey on Drug Use and Health: National Findings." 2012. Available at http://www.samhsa.gov/data/NSDUH/2011SummNatFindDetTables/

Van Pelt, Deani Neven. "Home Schooling in Canada: The Current Picture - 2015 Edition." Fraser Institute. 2015. http://www.fraserinstitute.org/research-news/news/display.aspx?id=22984

Vayda, Eugene, and Raisa B. Deber. "The Canadian Health Care System: An Overview." *Social Science and Medicine.* Vol. 18, No. 3 (1984):191–97.

Wait Time Alliance. "Time to Close the Gap: Report Card on Wait Times in Canada June 2014." 2014. http://www.waittimealliance.ca/wp-content/uploads/2014/06/FINAL-EN-WTA-Report-Card.pdf

Wall, Thomas F. *Medical Ethics: Basic Moral Issues.* Washington, DC: University Press of America, 1980.

Wells, Hodan Farah, and Jean C. Buzby. *Dietary Assessment of Major Trends in U.S. Food Consumption, 1970–2005.* Economic Information Bulletin No. (EIB 33). Washington, DC: U.S. Department of Agriculture, March 2008.

Wilson, S.J. *Women, Families and Work.* 4th ed. Toronto: McGraw-Hill Ryerson, 1996.

Wood, Evan, Thomas Kerr, Will Small, Kathy Li, David C. Marsh, Julio S.G. Montaner, and Mark W. Tyndall. "Changes in Public Order After the Opening of a Medically Supervised Safer Injecting Facility for Illicit Injection Drug Users." *Canadian Medical Association Journal.* Vol. 170, No. 10 (May 2004):1551–56.

World Bank. "World DataBank: Education Statistics." 2013a. Available at http://data.worldbank.org/data-catalog/ed-stats

———. "World DataBank: World Development Indicators." 2013b. Available at http://data.worldbank.org/data-catalog/world-development-indicators

World Health Organization. "China's village doctors take great strides." *Bulletin of the World Health Organization,* Vol. 86, No. 12 (December 2008).

Wrede, S., C. Benoit, and T. Einarsdottir. "Equity and Dignity in Maternity Care Provision in Canada, Finland and Iceland: Finding Dignity in Health Care and Health Care Work." *Canadian Journal of Public Health.* Vol. 99 (Suppl. 2, 2008):16–21.

Zuckerman, Mortimer B. "The Russian Conundrum." *U.S. News & World Report* (March 13, 2006):64.

Chapter 15

Aboriginal Affairs and Northern Development Canada. *Aboriginal Demographics from the 2011 National Household Survey.* 2013. https://www.aadnc-aandc.gc.ca/eng/1370438978311/1370439050610#toc

Adam, David. "World CO2 Levels at Record High, Scientists Warn." *Guardian* (May 12, 2008). [Online] Available July 16, 2008, at http://www.guardian.co.uk/environment/2008/may/12/climatechange.carbonemissions

Axinn, William G., and Jennifer S. Barber. "Mass Education and Fertility Transition." *American Sociological Review.* Vol. 66, No. 4 (August 2001):481–505.

BARLOW, MAUDE. *Blue Future: Protecting Water for People and the Planet Forever*. Toronto: House of Anansi, 2013.

BERRY, BRIAN L., and PHILIP H. REES. "The Factorial Ecology of Calcutta." *American Journal of Sociology*. Vol. 74, No. 5 (March 1969):445–91.

BORMANN, F. HERBERT. "The Global Environmental Deficit." *BioScience*. Vol. 40, No. 2 (1990):74.

BROCKERHOFF, MARTIN P. "An Urbanizing World." *Population Bulletin*. Vol. 55, No. 3 (September 2000):1–44.

BROWN, LESTER R. "Reassessing the Earth's Population." *Society*. Vol. 32, No. 4 (May/June 1995):7–10.

BROWN, LESTER R., et al., eds. *State of the World 1993: A Worldwatch Institute Report on Progress toward a Sustainable Society*. New York: Norton, 1993.

BUNTING, T., P. FILION, and A. WALKS. "The Uneven Geography of Housing Affordability Stress in Canadian Metropolitan Areas." *Housing Studies*. Vol. 19 (2004):361–93.

CAPELLA, PETER. "UN Alarmed at Huge Decline in Bee Numbers." Yahoo.com [Online] Available March 10, 2011, at http://news.yahoo.com/s/afp/20110310/sc_afp/unenvironmentspeciesanimalfarmbee_20110310124832

CHANDLER, TERTIUS, and GERALD FOX. *3000 Years of Urban History*. New York: Academic Press, 1974.

CHANG, ALICIA. "Study: Cleaner Air Adds 5 Months to U.S. Life Span." *Yahoo News* (January 21, 2009). [Online] Available April 10, 2009, at http://www.newsvine.com/_news/2009/01/21/2339450-study-cleaner-air-adds-5-months-to-us-life-span

CONFERENCE BOARD OF CANADA. "Municipal Waste Generation." 2015. http://www.conferenceboard.ca/hcp/details/environment/municipal-waste-generation.aspx

CONNETT, PAUL H. "The Disposable Society." In F. Herbert Bormann and Stephen R. Kellert, eds., *Ecology, Economics, and Ethics: The Broken Circle*. New Haven, CT: Yale University Press, 1991:99–122.

EL NASSER, HAYA, and PAUL OVERBERG. "U.S. Growth Slows, Still Envied." *USA Today* (January 7–9, 2011):1A.

FILION, P., K. MCSPURREN, and B. APPLEBY. "Wasted Density? The Impact of Toronto's Residential Density Distribution Policies on Transit Use and Walking." *Environment and Planning A*. Vol. 38 (2006):1367–92.

FOSTER, JOHN BELLAMY. *Ecology Against Capitalism*. New York: Monthly Review Press, 2002.

GALLUP. "Fewer Americans, Europeans View Global Warming as a Threat." April 20, 2011. Available at http://www.gallup.com/poll/147203/Fewer-Americans-Europeans-View-Global-Warming-Threat.aspx#2

GANS, HERBERT J. *People and Plans: Essays on Urban Problems and Solutions*. New York: Basic Books, 1968.

GILLIS, JUSTIN. "Sea-Level Science." *Conservation*. Vol. 12, No. 1 (Spring 2011):44–45.

GOLDBERGER, PAUL. Lecture delivered at Kenyon College, September 22, 2002.

GORE, AL. *An Inconvenient Truth: The Crisis of Global Warming*. Emmaus, PA: Rodale Books, 2006.

GOTTMANN, JEAN. *Megalopolis*. New York: Twentieth Century Fund, 1961.

HAMILTON, BRADY E., JOYCE A. MARTIN, and STEPHANIE J. VENTURA. "Births: Preliminary Data for 2011." *National Vital Statistics Reports*. Vol. 61, No. 5 (2012). Available at http://www.cdc.gov/nchs/data/nvsr/nvsr61/nvsr61_05.pdf

HARRIS, CHAUNCY D., and EDWARD L. ULLMAN. "The Nature of Cities." *Annals of the American Academy of Political and Social Sciences*. Vol. 242, No. 1 (November 1945):7–17.

HORTON, HAYWARD DERRICK. "Critical Demography: The Paradigm of the Future?" *Sociological Forum*. Vol. 14, No. 3 (September 1999):363–67.

HOYT, HOMER. *The Structure and Growth of Residential Neighborhoods in American Cities*. Washington, DC: Federal Housing Administration, 1939.

INTERNATIONAL PANEL ON CLIMATE CHANGE. *Climate Change, 2007*. New York: United Nations, 2007.

JOHNSTON, R.J. "Residential Area Characteristics." In D.T. Herbert and R.J. Johnston, eds., *Social Areas in Cities. Vol. 1: Spatial Processes and Form*. New York: Wiley, 1976:193–235.

JORDAN, KURT A. "Incorporation and Colonization: Postcolumbian Iroquois Satellite Communities and Processes of Indigenous Autonomy." *American Anthropologist*. Vol. 115, No. 1 (March 2013):29–43.

KEESING, FELICIA, et al. "Impacts of Biodiversity on the Emergence and Transmission of Infectious Disease." *Nature: International Weekly Journal of Science*. Vol. 468, No. 7324. [Online] Available December 2, 2010, at http://www.nature.com/nature/journal/v468/n7324/full/nature09575.html

KELLERT, STEPHEN R., and F. HERBERT BORMANN. "Closing the Circle: Weaving Strands among Ecology, Economics, and Ethics." In F. Herbert Bormann and Stephen R. Kellert, eds., *Ecology, Economics, and Ethics: The Broken Circle*. New Haven, CT: Yale University Press, 1991:205–10.

KERR, RICHARD A. "Climate Models Heat Up." *Science Now* (January 26, 2005):1–3.

KLINENBERG, ERIC. "Adaptation." *The New Yorker* (January 7, 2013):32–37.

KUUMBA, M. BAHATI. "A Cross-Cultural Race/Class/Gender Critique of Contemporary Population Policy: The Impact of Globalization." *Sociological Forum*. Vol. 14, No. 3 (March 1999):447–63.

LINDSTROM, BONNIE. "Chicago's Post-Industrial Suburbs." *Sociological Focus*. Vol. 28, No. 4 (October 1995):399–412.

MACDONALD, AMY and STEPHANIE CHAI. "The Effects of Gentrification on Artists in Two Vancouver Neighbourhoods." *Western Geography*. Vol. 19 (2009):61–77.

MACIONIS, JOHN J., and VINCENT N. PARRILLO. *Cities and Urban Life*. 6th ed. Upper Saddle River, NJ: Pearson, 2013.

MALTHUS, THOMAS ROBERT. *First Essay on Population 1798*. London: Macmillan, 1926; orig. 1798.

MARX, KARL. *Capital*. Friedrich Engels, ed. New York: International Publishers, 1967; orig. 1867.

MCKIBBEN, BILL. *Deep Economy: The Wealth of Communities and the Durable Future*. New York: Times Books, 2007.

MCMAHON, BUCKY. "Vanishing Point." *Conservation*. Vol. 12, No. 1 (Spring 2011):40–48.

MCVEY JR., WAYNE W., and WARREN E. KALBACH. *The Demographic Basis of Canadian Society*. 2nd ed. Toronto: McGraw-Hill, 1979.

MEADOWS, DONELLA H., DENNIS L. MEADOWS, JORGAN RANDERS, and WILLIAM W. BEHRENS III. *The Limits to Growth: A Report on the Club of Rome's Project on the Predicament of Mankind*. New York: Universe, 1972.

MILBRATH, LESTER W. *Envisioning a Sustainable Society: Learning Our Way Out*. Albany: State University of New York Press, 1989.

MUMFORD, LEWIS. *The City in History: Its Origins, Its Transformations, and Its Prospects*. New York: Harcourt, Brace & World, 1961.

MYERS, DAVID G. *The American Paradox: Spiritual Hunger in an Age of Plenty*. New Haven, CT: Yale University Press, 2000.

MYERS, NORMAN. "Humanity's Growth." In Edmund Hillary, ed., *Ecology 2000: The Changing Face of the Earth*. New York: Beaufort Books, 1984a:16–35.

———. "The Mega-Extinction of Animals and Plants." In Sir Edmund Hillary, ed., *Ecology 2000: The Changing Face of the Earth*. New York: Beaufort Books, 1984b:82–107.

NASA. "Consensus: 97% of climate scientists agree." July 2, 2015. http://climate.nasa.gov/scientific-consensus/

O'DONNELL, VIVIAN, and SUSAN WALLACE. "First Nations, Métis and Inuit Women." *Women in Canada: A Gender-Based Statistical Report*. Catalogue no. 89-503-X. 2011. [Online] http://www.statcan.gc.ca/pub/89-503-x/2010001/article/11442-eng.htm

ONTARIO MINISTRY OF FINANCE. "2011 National Household Survey Highlights: Factsheet 2." June 2013. http://www.fin.gov.on.ca/en/economy/demographics/census/nhshi11-2.html

PARK, ROBERT E. *Race and Culture*. Glencoe, IL: Free Press, 1950.

POPULATION ACTION INTERNATIONAL. *People in the Balance: Population and Resources at the Turn of the Millennium*. Washington, DC: Population Action International, 2000.

POPULATION REFERENCE BUREAU. "Datafinder." 2011, 2012. Available at http://www.prb.org/DataFinder.aspx

———. "World Population Data Sheet." 2012. Available at http://www.prb.org/pdf12/2012-population-data-sheet_eng.pdf

REED, BRIAN. "Could People from Kiribati Be 'Climate Change Refugees'?" *The Two-Way*. National Public Radio news blog. [Online] Available February 17, 2011, at http://www.npr.org/templates/archives/archive.php?thingId=131216964

RIDLEY, MATT. "Cooling Down the Fears of Climate Change." *Wall Street Journal*. (December 19, 2012):A19.

ROUDI-FAHIMI, FARZANEH, and MARY MEDERIOS KENT. "Challenges and Opportunities: The Population of the Middle East and North Africa." *Population Bulletin*. Vol. 65, No. 2 (June 2007). Washington, DC: Population Reference Bureau, 2007.

SCANLON, STEPHAN J. "Food Availability and Access in Less Industrialized Societies: A Test and Interpretation of Neo-Malthusian and Technoecological Theories." *Sociological Forum*. Vol. 16, No. 2 (June 2001):231–62.

SHEVKY, ESHREF, and WENDELL BELL. *Social Area Analysis*. Palo Alto, CA: Stanford University Press, 1955.

SIMON, JULIAN. *The Ultimate Resource*. Princeton, NJ: Princeton University Press, 1981.

———. "More People, Greater Wealth, More Resources, Healthier Environment." In Theodore D. Goldfarb, ed., *Taking Sides: Clashing Views on Controversial Environmental Issues*. 6th ed. Guilford, CT: Dushkin, 1995.

SINGER, S. FRED. "Global Warming: Man-Made or Natural?" *Imprimis*. Vol. 36, No. 8 (2007):1–5.

SMAIL, J. KENNETH. "Let's *Reduce* Global Population!" In John J. Macionis and Nijole V. Benokraitis, eds., *Seeing Ourselves: Classic, Contemporary, and Cross-Cultural Readings in Sociology*. 8th ed. Upper Saddle River, NJ: Prentice Hall, 2010:413–17.

SMYLIE, JANET, DESHAYNE FELL, ARNE OHLSSON, and THE JOINT WORKING GROUP ON FIRST NATIONS, INDIAN, INUIT, AND MÉTIS INFANT MORTALITY OF THE CANADIAN PERINATAL SURVEILLANCE SYSTEM. "A Review of Aboriginal Infant Mortality Rates in Canada: Striking and Persistent Aboriginal/Non-Aboriginal Inequities." *Canadian Journal of Public Health*, Vol. 101, No. 2 (March/April 2010):143-148.

SOLOMON, STEVEN. *Water: The Epic Struggle for Wealth, Power, and Civilization*. New York:HarperCollins, 2010.

STANTEC CONSULTING LTD. "Comprehensive Integrated Waste Management Plan." Final Project Report prepared for The City of Winnipeg. September 2011. [Online] http://www.winnipeg.ca/finance/findata/matmgt/documents//2012/153-2012//153-2012_Appendix_E-Comprehensive_Integrated_Waste_Management_Plan.pdf

STATISTICS CANADA. *2006 Census: Portrait of the Canadian Population in 2006: Findings*. 2010. [Online] www12.statcan.gc.ca/census-recensement/2006/as-sa/97-550/index-eng.cfm?CFID=3674780&CFTOKEN=64671080

———. *Estimates of Births, Deaths and Marriages, Canada, Provinces and Territories, Quarterly (Number)*. CANSIM Table 530001, v62 [Electronic Data Base]. 2011a.

———. *Estimates of Population, by Age Group and Sex for July 1, Canada, Provinces and Territories, Annually (Persons Unless Specified)*. Cansim Table 510001, v466668 [Electronic Database]. 2011b.

———. *Estimates of Births, Deaths and Marriages, Canada, Provinces and Territories, Quarterly (Number)*. Cansim Table 530001, v77 [Electronic Database]. 2011c.

———. *Infant Mortality, by Sex and Birth Weight*. Cansim Table 102-0030, v5939542 [Electronic Database]. 2011d.

———. *Canada, Place of Residence of Mother; Total, Month of Birth; Number of Live Births*. CANSIM Table 102-4502, v21400536 [Electronic Database]. 2011e.

———. *Population, urban and rural, by province and territory (Canada)*. Population estimates and projections, 2011 Census. 2011f. http://www.statcan.gc.ca/tables-tableaux/sum-som/l01/cst01/demo62a-eng.htm

———. *Life expectancy, at birth and at age 65, by sex, Canada, provinces and territories*. CANSIM Table 102-0512 [Electronic Data Base]. 2012a.

———. *Canada - Population change, 2006 to 2011 by 2011 census division.* Produced by the Geography Division, Statistics Canada, 2012b. https://www12.statcan.gc.ca/census-recensement/2011/geo/map-carte/ref/thematic_download-thematiques_telecharger-eng.cfm?SERIES=D#DESC_D

———. *Population and dwelling counts, for census metropolitan areas and census agglomerations, 2011 and 2006 censuses.* Population and Dwelling Count Highlight Tables, 2011 Census. 2012c. http://www12.statcan.gc.ca/census-recensement/2011/dp-pd/hlt-fst/pd-pl/Table-Tableau.cfm?LANG=Eng&T=201&SR=1&RPP=150&S=3&O=D

———. "Population, Greater Golden Horseshoe, 1971, 2001 and 2011." *Human Activity and the Environment: Measuring ecosystem goods and services in Canada.* Ottawa: Minister of Industry, 2013a.

———. *Immigration and Ethnocultural Diversity in Canada, National Household Survey, 2011.* Ottawa: Minister of Industry. Catalogue no. 99-010-X2011001. 2013b.

———. *Disposal of waste, by source, Canada, provinces and territories.* CANSIM Table 153-0041 [Electronic Data Base]. 2015.

SULLIVAN, DANIEL MONROE. "Reassessing Gentrification Measuring Residents' Opinions Using Survey Data." *Urban Affairs Review.* Vol. 42, No. 4 (March 2007):583–592.

TÖNNIES, FERDINAND. *Community and Society (Gemeinschaft und Gesellschaft).* New York: Harper & Row, 1963; orig. 1887.

UNESCO WORLD WATER ASSESSMENT PROGRAMME. "World Water Development Report 4: Managing Water Under Uncertainty and Risk." March 2012. Available at http://www.unesco.org/new/en/natural-sciences/environment/water/wwap/wwdr/wwdr4-2012/

UNITED NATIONS DEVELOPMENT PROGRAMME. "International Human Development Indicators." 2012. Available at http://hdrstats.undp.org/en/indicators/default.html

UNITED NATIONS ENVIRONMENT PROGRAMME (UNEP). *Vital Water Graphics—An Overview of the State of the World's Fresh and Marine Waters.* 2nd ed. Nairobi, Kenya, 2008. [Online] Available at http://www.unep.org/dewa/vitalwater/index.html

UNITED NATIONS, DEPARTMENT OF ECONOMIC AND SOCIAL AFFAIRS. "World Population Prospects: The 2010 Revision." May 2011a. Available at http://esa.un.org/unpd/wpp/index.htm

———. "The State of Forests in the Amazon Basin, Congo Basin and Southeast Asia." June 2011b. Available at http://www.fao.org/forestry/fra/70893/en/

U.S. CENSUS BUREAU. "International Data Base." 2013. Available at http://www.census.gov/population/international/

U.S. DEPARTMENT OF COMMERCE, NATIONAL OCEANIC AND ATMOSPHERIC ADMINISTRATION. "Trends in Atmospheric Carbon Dioxide, Mauna Loa." January 2013. Available at http://www.esrl.noaa.gov/gmd/ccgg/trends/

VAN DER WERF, PAUL, and MICHAEL CANT. "Growing Waste, Stalled Diversion: The state of waste in Canada." *Solid Waste & Recycling* (June 1, 2012). http://www.solidwastemag.com/features/growing-waste-stalled-diversion/

WALKS, R. ALAN, and RICHARD MAARANEN. "The Timing, Patterning, & Forms of Gentrification & Neighbourhood Upgrading in Montreal, Toronto, & Vancouver, 1961 to 2001." Research Paper 211. Centre for Urban and Community Studies, University of Toronto, 2008.

WALSH, BRYAN. "A River Ran Through It." *Time.* Vol. 174, No. 23 (December 14, 2009):56–63.

WEBER, ADNA FERRIN. *The Growth of Cities.* New York: Columbia University Press, 1963; orig. 1899.

WILSON, EDWARD O. "Biodiversity, Prosperity, and Value." In F. Herbert Bormann and Stephen R. Kellert, eds., *Ecology, Economics, and Ethics: The Broken Circle.* New Haven, CT: Yale University Press, 1991:3–10.

WILSON, THOMAS C. "Urbanism and Tolerance: A Test of Some Hypotheses Drawn from Wirth and Stouffer." *American Sociological Review.* Vol. 50, No. 1 (February 1985):117–23.

———. "Urbanism and Unconventionality: The Case of Sexual Behavior." *Social Science Quarterly.* Vol. 76, No. 2 (June 1995):346–63.

WIRTH, LOUIS. "Urbanism as a Way of Life." *American Journal of Sociology.* Vol. 44, No. 1 (July 1938):1–24.

WITTMEIER, BRENT. "Go west, young Easterner. Fort McMurray is where the money is." *Edmonton Journal* (January 7, 2014). http://www.edmontonjournal.com/business/west+young+Easterner+Fort+McMurray+where+money/9219801/story.html

WOLFE, JEANNE M. "Canada's Liveable Cities." *Social Policy.* Vol. 23, No. 1 (Summer 1992):56–65.

WORLD BANK. "World DataBank: World Development Indicators." 2012. Available at http://data.worldbank.org/data-catalog/world-development-indicators

YEMMA, JOHN. "As the World's Population Heads Toward a Peak, Malthusian Worries Reemerge. "*The Christian Science Monitor.* [Online] Available February 7, 2011, at http://www.csmonitor.com/Commentary/editors-blog/2011/0207/Asworld-population-heads-toward-a-peak-Malthusian-worries-reemerge

Chapter 16

ABERLE, DAVID F. *The Peyote Religion among the Navaho.* Chicago: Aldine, 1966.

BARKER, ADAM. "'A Direct Act of Resurgence, a Direct Act of Sovereignty': Reflections on Idle No More, Indigenous Activism, and Canadian Settler Colonialism." *Globalizations* (2014). doi:10.1080/14747731.2014.971531

BENSIMON BYRNE. "Economic Update." *The Consumerology Report* (February 2015). [Online] http://consumerology.ca/

BERGER, PETER L. *Facing Up to Modernity: Excursions in Society, Politics, and Religion.* New York: Basic Books, 1977.

BERGER, PETER L., BRIGITTE BERGER, and HANSFRIED KELLNER. *The Homeless Mind: Modernization and Consciousness.* New York: Vintage Books, 1974.

BLUMER, HERBERT G. "Collective Behavior." In Alfred McClung Lee, ed., *Principles of Sociology.* 3rd ed. New York: Barnes & Noble Books, 1969:65–121.

BRAZILIAN, ALEXA. "Forever in Blue Jeans." *Wall Street Journal.* January 8, 2011. Available at http://online.wsj.com/article/SB10001424052748704111504576060150008236490.html

BROWN, ROBBIE. "History-Rich Georgia Island Wins Second Look at Taxes." *New York Times.* Available January 29, 2013, at http://www.nytimes.com/2013/01/30/us/history-rich-georgia-island-wins-second-look-on-taxes.html

BUECHLER, STEVEN M. *Social Movements in Advanced Capitalism: The Political Economy and Cultural Construction of Social Activism.* New York: Oxford University Press, 2000.

BURKOWICZ, JAKUB. "In Defense of Counterposed Strategic Orientations: Anarchism and Antiracism." *Affinities: A Journal of Radical Theory, Culture, and Action.* Vol. 8, No. 1 (Summer 2014):1–22.

CAMERON, WILLIAM BRUCE. *Modern Social Movements: A Sociological Outline.* New York: Random House, 1966.

CAROLL, WILLIAM K., and ROBERT S. RATNER. "Social Movements and Counter-Hegemony: Lessons from the Field." *New Proposals: Journal of Marxism and Interdisciplinary Inquiry.* Vol. 4, No. 1 (October 2010):7–22.

CBC NEWS. *Toronto Rocked.* 2003. http://www.cbc.ca/news2/background/sarsbenefit/

COUPLAND, DOUGLAS. *Generation X: tales for an accelerated culture.* New York: St. Martin's Press, 1991.

CURRY, ANDREW. "The Gullahs' Last Stand?" *U.S. News & World Report* (June 18, 2001):40–41.

DAVIES, JAMES C. "Toward a Theory of Revolution." *American Sociological Review.* Vol. 27, No. 1 (February 1962):5–19.

DAY, RICHARD J.F. *Gramsci Is Dead: Anarchist Currents in the Newest Social Movements.* Toronto: Between the Lines, 2005.

DEWAN, SHAILA. "Ecosystem vs. an Endangered Culture." *New York Times.* [Online] Available July 1, 2010, at http://green.blogs.nytimes.com/2010/07/01/ecosystem-vs-an-endangered-culture/?scp=1&sq=Gullah&st=cse

DURKHEIM, EMILE. *The Division of Labor in Society.* New York: Free Press, 1964; orig. 1893.

EHRENREICH, BARBARA. *Nickel and Dimed: On (Not) Getting By in America.* New York: Henry Holt, 2001.

ERIKSON, KAI T. *Everything in Its Path: Destruction of Community in the Buffalo Creek Flood.* New York: Simon & Schuster, 1976.

———. *A New Species of Trouble: Explorations in Disaster, Trauma, and Community.* New York: Norton, 1994.

———. Lecture at Kenyon College, February 7, 2005.

———. "The Day the World Turned Red: A Report on the People of Utrik." *The Yale Review,* Vol. 99, No. 1 (2011).

FUTAMORA, MADOKA, CHRISTOPHER HOBSON, and NICHOLAS TURNER. "Natural Disasters and Human Security." United Nations University, April 29, 2011. Available at http://unu.edu/publications/articles/natural-disasters-and-human-security.html

GIBBS, NANCY. "The Pulse of America along the River." *Time* (July 10, 2000):42–46.

GOFFMAN, ERVING. *The Presentation of Self in Everyday Life.* Garden City, NY: Anchor Books, 1959.

GRABB, E., and N. GUPPY. *Social Inequality in Canada: Patterns, Problems & Policies.* 5th ed. Don Mills, ON: Pearson Education Canada, 2009.

GÜRCAN, EFE CAN, and EFE PEKER. *Challenging Neoliberalism at Turkey's Gezi Park: From Private Discontent to Collective Class Action.* New York: Palgrave Macmillan, 2015.

HABERMAS, JÜRGEN. *Toward a Rational Society: Student Protest, Science, and Politics.* Jeremy J. Shapiro, trans. Boston: Beacon Press, 1970.

HALL, JOHN R., and MARY JO NEITZ. *Culture: Sociological Perspectives.* Englewood Cliffs, NJ: Prentice Hall, 1993.

HARRINGTON, MICHAEL. *The New American Poverty.* New York: Penguin Books, 1984.

HOYERT, DONNA, and JIAQUAN XU. "Deaths: Preliminary Data for 2011." National Vital Statistics Reports. Vol. 61, No. 6. Hyattsville, MD: National Center for Health Statistics. October 10, 2012. Available at http://www.cdc.gov/nchs/data/nvsr/nvsr61/nvsr61_06.pdf

INGLEHART, RONALD, and CHRISTIAN WELZEL. "The WVS Cultural Map of the World." 2010. Available at http://www.worldvaluessurvey.org/wvs/articles/folder_published/article_base_54

INGLEHART, RONALD, et al. "World Values Survey." 2012. Available at http://www.worldvaluessurvey.com/

INGLEHART, RONALD, and WAYNE E. BAKER. "Modernization, Cultural Change, and the Persistence of Traditional Values." *American Sociological Review.* Vol. 65, No. 1 (February 2000):19–51.

INGLEHART, RONALD, CHRISTIAN WELZEL, and ROBERTO FOA. "Happiness Trends in 24 Countries, 1946–2006." 2010. www.worldvaluessurvey.org/wvs/articles/folder_published/article_base_106

INGLEHART, RONALD. *Modernization and Postmodernization: Cultural, Economic, and Political Change in 43 Societies.* Princeton, NJ: Princeton University Press, 1997.

IVANOVA, IGLICA. "Are average Canadians paying too much in taxes?" Canadian Centre for Policy Alternatives – Policy Note. 2013. http://www.policynote.ca/are-average-canadians-paying-too-much-in-taxes/

JENKINS, J. CRAIG, and MICHAEL WALLACE. "The Generalized Action Potential of Protest Movements: The New Class, Social Trends, and Political Exclusion Explanations." *Sociological Forum.* Vol. 11, No. 2 (June 1996):183–207.

KORNHAUSER, WILLIAM. *The Politics of Mass Society.* New York: Free Press, 1959.

KRAYBILL, DONALD B., and JAMES P. HURD. *Horse-and-Buggy Mennonites: Hoofbeats of Humility in a Postmodern World.* University Park: Pennsylvania State University Press, 2006.

KRAYBILL, DONALD B., and MARC A. OLSHAN, EDS. *The Amish Struggle with Modernity.* Hanover, NH: University Press of New England, 1994.

LAMMAM, CHARLES, and MILAGROS PALACIOS. "Taxes versus the Necessities of Life: The Canadian Consumer Tax Index, 2014." Fraser Institute. 2014. http://www.fraserinstitute.org/research-news/research/publications/Taxes-versus-the-Necessities-of-Life---The-Canadian-Consumer-Tax-Index,-2014/

LASLETT, PETER. *The World We Have Lost: England before the Industrial Age.* 3rd ed. New York: Scribner, 1984.

LINTON, RALPH. "One Hundred Percent American." *American Mercury*. Vol. 40, No. 160 (April 1937):427–29.

MARCUSE, HERBERT. *One-Dimensional Man*. Boston: Beacon Press, 1964.

MARTEL, L., and A. BÉLANGER. *An Analysis of the Change in Dependence-Free Life Expectancy in Canada between 1986 and 1996: Report on the Demographic Situation in Canada, 1998-1999*. Statistics Canada Catalogue no. 91-209-XPE. 2000.

MARX, KARL, and FRIEDRICH ENGELS. "Manifesto of the Communist Party." In Robert C. Tucker, ed., *The Marx-Engels Reader*. New York: Norton, 1972:331–62; orig. 1848.

MCADAM, DOUG, JOHN D. MCCARTHY, and MAYER N. ZALD. "Introduction: Opportunities, Mobilizing Structures, and Framing Processes—Toward a Synthetic, Comparative Perspective on Social Movements." In Doug McAdam, John D. McCarthy, and Mayer N. Zald, eds., *Comparative Perspectives on Social Movements: Political Opportunities, Mobilizing Structures, and Cultural Framings*. New York: Cambridge University Press, 1996:1–19.

MELUCCI, ALBERTO. *Nomads of the Present: Social Movements and Individual Needs in Contemporary Society*. Philadelphia, PA: Temple University Press, 1989.

MERTON, ROBERT K. *Social Theory and Social Structure*. New York: Free Press, 1968.

MILLER, FREDERICK D. "The End of SDS and the Emergence of Weatherman: Demise through Success." In Jo Freeman, ed., *Social Movements of the Sixties and Seventies*. White Plains, NY: Longman, 1983:279–97.

MYERS, DAVID G. *The American Paradox: Spiritual Hunger in an Age of Plenty*. New Haven, CT: Yale University Press, 2000.

NEWMAN, KATHERINE S. *Declining Fortunes: The Withering of the American Dream*. New York: Basic Books, 1993.

NISBET, ROBERT A. *The Quest for Community*. New York: Oxford University Press, 1969.

NORC. *General Social Surveys, 1972–2012*. Chicago: National Opinion Research Center. March 2013. Available at http://www.norc.org/GSS+Website/

PACKER, GEORGE. "Smart-Mobbing the War." *New York Times Magazine* (March 9, 2003):46–49.

PASSY, FLORENCE, and MARCO GIUGNI. "Social Networks and Individual Perceptions: Explaining Differential Participation in Social Movements." *Sociological Forum*. Vol. 16, No. 1 (March 2001):123–53.

PEARSON, DAVID E. "Post-Mass Culture." *Society*. Vol. 30, No. 5 (July/August 1993):17–22.

PIVEN, FRANCES FOX, and RICHARD A. CLOWARD. *Poor People's Movements: Why They Succeed, How They Fail*. New York: Pantheon Books, 1977.

RIESMAN, DAVID. *The Lonely Crowd: A Study of the Changing American Character*. New Haven, CT: Yale University Press, 1970; orig. 1950.

ROSE, FRED. "Toward a Class-Cultural Theory of Social Movements: Reinterpreting New Social Movements." *Sociological Forum*. Vol. 12, No. 3 (September 1997):461–94.

RUDEL, THOMAS K., and JUDITH M. GERSON. "Postmodernism, Institutional Change, and Academic Workers: A Sociology of Knowledge." *Social Science Quarterly*. Vol. 80, No. 2 (June 1999):213–28.

SIMON, ROGER, and ANGIE CANNON. "An Amazing Journey." *U.S. News & World Report* (August 6, 2001):10–19.

SIMONS, MARLISE. "The Price of Modernization: The Case of Brazil's Kaiapo Indians." In John J. Macionis and Nijole V. Benokraitis, eds., *Seeing Ourselves: Classic, Contemporary, and Cross-Cultural Readings in Sociology*. 7th ed. Upper Saddle River, NJ: Prentice Hall, 2007.

STATISTICS CANADA. *Household size, by province and territory (2011 Census) (Newfoundland and Labrador, Prince Edward Island, Nova Scotia)*. 2011a http://www.statcan.gc.ca/tables-tableaux/sum-som/l01/cst01/famil53a-eng.htm

———. *Canadians in Context—Aging Population*. 2011b. http://www4.hrsdc.gc.ca/.3ndic.1t.4r@-eng.jsp?iid=33

———. *Table 102-0512—Life expectancy at birth, by sex, by province*. 2012a http://www.statcan.gc.ca/tables-tableaux/sum-som/l01/cst01/health26-eng.htm

———. *Canada - Population change, 2006 to 2011 by 2011 census division*. 2012b http://www12.statcan.gc.ca/census-recensement/2011/geo/map-carte/ref/thematic_download-thematiques_telecharger-eng.cfm?SERIES=D

———. *The Canadian Population in 2011: Population Counts and Growth*. Catalogue no. 98-310-X2011001. Ottawa: Minister of Industry, 2012c.

———. *Table 102-0551—Motor vehicle accidents causing death, by sex and by age group (Both sexes no.)*. 2014. http://www.statcan.gc.ca/tables-tableaux/sum-som/l01/cst01/health112a-eng.htm

TÖNNIES, FERDINAND. *Community and Society (Gemeinschaft und Gesellschaft)*. New York: Harper & Row, 1963; orig. 1887.

VAHABZADEH, PEYMAN. *Articulated Experiences: Toward a Radical Phenomenology of Contemporary Social Movements*. New York: State University of New York Press, 2003.

WEBER, MAX. *The Protestant Ethic and the Spirit of Capitalism*. New York: Scribner, 1958; orig. 1904–05.

———. *Economy and Society: An Outline of Interpretive Sociology*. Guenther Roth and Claus Wittich, eds. Berkeley: University of California Press, 1978; orig. 1921.

WEST, CORNEL. "The Obama Moment." *U.S. News & World Report* (November 17, 2008):29.

WHEELIS, ALLEN. *The Quest for Identity*. New York: Norton, 1958

WILLIAMS, JOHNNY E. "Linking Beliefs to Collective Action: Politicized Religious Beliefs and the Civil Rights Movement." *Sociological Forum*. Vol. 17, No. 2 (June 2002):203–22.

WOTHERSPOON, TERRY, and JOHN HANSEN. "The 'Idle No More' Movement: Paradoxes of First Nations Inclusion in the Canadian Context." *Social Inclusion*. Vol. 1, No. 1 (July 2013):21–36.

ZHAO, DINGXIN. "Ecologies of Social Movements: Student Mobilization during the 1989 Prodemocracy Movement in Beijing." *American Journal of Sociology*. Vol. 103, No. 6 (May 1998):1493–529.

Author Index

614

Subject Index

Bono, Chas, 166
"Bountiful," 421
Bourgeoisie, 248, 524
Brand, Dionne, 9
Brazeau, Patrick, 211
Brazil, 345
Bre-X, 211–212
British Canadians, 360
Broadbent Institute, 54
Buddhists and Buddhism, 301, 346, 449, 452
Buffett, Warren, 283
Bundchen, Gisele, 237
Bureaucratization, 560
Bureaucracy. *see also* Formal organizations
    characteristics of, 147–148
    defined, 147
    inefficiency, 149–150
    informal side of, 148–149
    and oligarchy, 150–151
    problems of, 149–151
Bureaucratic alienation, 149
Bureaucratic inertia, 150
Bureaucratic ritualism, 150
Bush, George W., 407

Calvin, John, 445
Campbell, Kim, 323
Canada
    abortion in, 191
    aging in, 98
    armed forces, 324
    automobile ownership, 57
    bilingualism, 63
    British Canadians, 360
    Canadian culture, 67
    the Canadian Dream, 267
    and capital punishment, 226, 227
    capitalism in, 249–250, 377
    censuses, 35
    changing workplace, 382*f*
    Charter of Rights and Freedoms. *see* Canadian
        Charter of Rights and Freedoms
    childbearing statistics, 5
    circumcision in, 188
    common-law marriage in, 168*m*
    crime rates in, 217–218
    crime severity in, 216*m*
    Criminal Code of Canada. *see* Criminal Code
        of Canada
    criminal justice system. *see* Criminal justice
        system
    cultural change in, 65
    death, causes of, 486*t*
    democracy in, 393
    deviance in, 201
    divorce in, 433
    dropping out of school, 479
    economic inequality in, 245*f*, 253, 254–258
    economy of, 9–10
    education in, 256, 471–474, 480–483
    election 2015, 400*m*
    ethnicity in, 90
    extramarital sex in, 173
    family in, 429–432, 435–436, 436–439
    feminists in, 336
    fertility rate in, 427, 522
    French Canadians, 360–362
    gender equality, 53, 313
    and the global economy, 267–268
    global interconnection, 8–11

and guns, 220
happiness in, 574
health care in, 500–501
health in, 486–495
higher education in, 476
history, 360
Human Rights Act, 214
immigration in, 9, 53, 63, 362–363, 431
income in, 255, 265*f*, 266*f*
income status, 284
Indian Act, 354–355, 361
inequality in, 276–277
internet usage, 109
internment in, 363, 364
language in, 63, 64*m*
life span in, 261
literacy rates in, 51
living arrangements in, 65, 66*f*, 92
and marijuana, 208
marriage in, 25, 167, 177*f*, 432–433
medical establishment, 496
migrant life in, 349
minorities in, 348*t*
multiculturalism, 46, 49–50, 59–60, 61–63
Nisga'a treaty, 361
nursing shortage in, 501–502
obesity in, 490*m*
occupational prestige, 256, 257*t*
Official Languages Act, 63
and oligarchy, 151
organized crime in, 213
pay equity in, 320
pluralism in, 356
police in, 222–223
political spectrum, 398–399
politics in, 396–401
population change, 516–517, 555, 556*m*
pornography in, 181
post-industrial economy, 381–388
poverty in, 235, 248, 268–273, 270*m*, 289–290
premarital sex, attitudes on, 167, 172
prison population, 226
privacy in, 156
prostitution in, 181–182, 183, 184, 218
race and ethnicity in, 256–258, 346, 347*t*,
    358–365, 366–367
racism in, 352
religions in, 346
religiosity in, 449–450
same-sex marriage, 438–439
schooling in, 467–468
segregation in, 357
senate scandal, 211
sex, frequency of, 173
sexual attitudes in, 169–174
sexual orientation in, 177
singlehood in, 438–439
social change in, 562*t*
social class in, 258–261
social mobility in, 264–265
social problems in, 10
suicide rates in, 7*f*, 15*f*
teen pregnancy in, 179–180
telephone ownership in, 147
television ownership in, 93
television watching in, 93–94
and underground economy, 206
unemployment in, 381, 384–386
union membership in, 146*f*, 382
United States culture, compared to, 73

urban population in, 525*t*
values in, 53–54
visible minorities in, 363–365, 431, 531
voter abstention in, 401
water in, 539–540
wealth in, 22, 283
welfare state, 396–397
women in managerial positions, 152
Canada Health Act, 500
Canadian Accredited Independent Schools
    (CAIS), 472
Canadian Association of Broadcasters, 94
Canadian Association of Police Chiefs has, 400
Canadian Bill of Rights, 221
Canadian Charter of Rights and Freedoms, 13, 53,
    54, 214, 221
Canadian Community Health Survey, 99
Canadian culture, 67
Canadian Employment Insurance Act, 427
Canadian Federation of the Blind, 112
Canadian Human Rights Act, 214, 334
Canadian Human Rights Tribunal, 320
Canadian Institutes of Health Research, 29
Canadian Intellectual Property Office, 66
Canadian Medical Association, 496
Canadian Natural Resources Ltd., 212
Canadian Sociological Association, 28
Cancer, 488
Cape Verde, 287
Capital punishment, 221, 222*m*, 226–228
Capitalism
    changes in, 380–381
    defined, 376, 377
    and democratic freedom, 393–394
    and deviance, 211
    features of, 376–377
    and feminism, 335
    and justice, 210
    and modernity, 567, 570–571
    and poverty, 300
    and religion, 445
    socialism, compared to, 377–380
    state capitalism, 377
    survival of, 249–250
    welfare capitalism, 377
Capitalists, 248
Capone, Al, 204
Captain Canuck, 75
Care and responsibility perspective, 86
Careers, 12, 384*f*. *see also* Work and workplace
Carnegie, Andrew, 248, 249
Carrey, Jim, 237
Caste systems, 237–246
Catalyst Census, 152
Category, 137
Catholics and Catholicism
    liberation theology, 445–446
    membership size, 449
    numbers of, 346
    and sexual abuse scandals, 206
    and sexuality, 188
    and social class, 450
    and suicide rates, 5
Cause and effect, 25
Celibacy, 188
Census, 35
Census agglomerations, 527
Censuses, 35
Chagnon, Napoleon, 47
Change, importance of, 26–27

and the military, 324, 407–408
and moral development, 86
and networks, 145
and occupations, 317–319
and peer group, 315
and performances, 121
and personal space, 121
and politics, 322–324, 399
and pornography, 328
and poverty, 269, 294
and reality construction, 330–331
and religion, 444–445
and research, 28
and schooling, 315
and social class, 263
and social groups, 143
and social mobility, 266
social-conflict theory, 329, 331–332
and socialization, 91, 314
and street crime, 218
structural-functional theory, 328–330
and suicide rates, 5–6, 7f
symbolic-interaction theory, 329, 330–331
theories of, 328–333
and unemployment, 319
and union membership, 146f
and voting, 401
and wage gap, 309
Gender blindness, 28
Gender gap, 324
Gender reassignment, 166
Gender roles, 314
Gender stratification
defined, 310
and inequality, 310–314
and social stratification, 317–328
and socialization, 314–317
summary, 340–341
theories of gender, 328–333
Gender-conflict/feminist theory
and deviance, 210, 214–215
discussion of, 72
explained, 17–18
and family, 422, 423
and health and medicine, 504–507
level of analysis, 20
and religion, 444–445
and sexuality, 187, 189–191
and sports, 20
summary, 20, 71
General assemblies, 65
General Social Survey (GSS) on Victimization, 215–216
Generalizations, 39
Generalized other, 87
Generation gap, 92
Genetics, 175, 506
Genital herpes, 492
Genocide, 357, 358
Gentleman's Agreement, 363
Gentrification, 526–527
Geometric progression, 520
Gerontocracy, 99
Gerontology, 99
Gesellschaft, 529, 563, 565
Gestures, 50
Gilligan, Carol, 86, 87
Glass ceiling, 319
Global communications, 69
Global culture, 69–70

Global economy, 9–10, 69, 375–376
Global feminism, 336
Global migration, 70
Global perspective, 8–11
Global stratification
defined, 282
dependency theory, 298–302
distribution of income and wealth, 283f
future of, 302–303
high-income countries, 285–286
low-income countries, 288
middle-income countries, 286–288
modernization theory, 295–298
overview, 283–288
and poverty, 288–294
summary, 306–307
terminology, 283–284
theories of, 295–302
and wealth, 289
wealth and well-being, 290t
Global warming, 513, 541–542
Goal orientation, 138
Goddard, Nicola, 324
Goffman, Erving, 21, 118
Goldman Sachs, 247
Gonorrhea, 491
Gorbachev, Mikhail, 243
Government, 391, 397f
Grade inflation, 480
Green Revolution, 300
Greying of Canada, 98
Groups and organizations, 135, 148, 160–161.
see also Formal organizations; Social groups
Groupthink, 140–141
Guest workers, 304–305
Guilt, 56
Gullah people, 575
Guns, 73, 220, 400
Gynocentricity, 28

Haiti, 285
Hamer people, 104
Hammergren, John, 275
Harb, Mac, 211
Harper, Stephen, 189
Hate crime, 213–214
Head tax, 364
Health and medicine
access to care, 505
and age, 487
in Canada, 486–495
eating disorders, 489
feminist theory, 504–507
and gender, 487
global perspective, 485–486
health, defined, 485
health care, 53, 497–501, 505
in high-income countries, 486
holistic medicine, 497
looking ahead, 507
in low-income countries, 486
medical establishment, 495–502
medicine, defined, 485
nursing shortage, 501–502
and obesity, 490–491
and politics, 505–507
profit motive, 505
and race and ethnicity, 487
scientific medicine, rise of, 495–496
sexually transmitted infections, 491–494

and smoking, 487–489
and social class, 261, 487
and social inequality, 485
social-conflict theory, 504–507
socialized medicine, 499
and society, 485
structural-functional theory, 502–503, 505
summary, 511
symbolic-interaction theory, 503–504, 505
and technology, 485
theories of, 502–507
Helman, Rose, 112
Helú, Carlos Slim, 283
Hermaphrodite, 166
Heroes, 230–231
Heterosexism, 190
Heterosexuality, 174
Hewlett-Packard, 154
Hidden curriculum, 91, 470
Hidden populations, 31–32
Hierarchy of positions, 147
High culture, 60
High-income countries
cultural differences in, 55, 285
defined, 8, 284
and global economic development, 297, 300
and global stratification, 285–286
and health, 486
Hill, Daniel Grafton, 18
Himel, Susan, 183, 184
Hindus and Hinduism, 238, 346, 449, 451, 452
Hip-hop music, 62, 553
Hirschi, Travis, 209
HIV/AIDS, 492–494, 558
Hobbes, Thomas, 13, 14, 405
Holistic medicine, 497
Holmes, Edna, 575
The Holocaust, 357
Homans, George, 21
Home schooling, 481–482
Homelessness, 100, 272–273
Homicide, 220
Homo sapiens, 49
Homogamy, 425
Homophobia, 179
Homosexuality, 174, 175–177. see also Sexual
orientation
Honduras, 5
Hooking up, 186
Horticulture, 58, 59, 252
Housework, 114m, 321
Human development, 80–81, 88–89
Human freedom, 73
Human intelligence. see Intelligence
Human nature, 22–23, 47
Human needs, 83
Human Research Ethics Committee, 29
Human rights, 53, 294
Human trafficking, 293–294
Humour
and conflict, 129
dynamics of, 127
foundation of, 126–127
functions of, 128
social construction of, 126–129
topics of, 127–128
Humphries, Mary, 214
Hunger, 290, 300
Hunting and gathering, 57–58, 59, 252
Hussein, Saddam, 406, 407

Navajo people, 422
Ndebele people, 57
Negotiation, 101
Neocolonialism, 294
Nepal, 67
Net migration rate, 516
Net worth, 255f
Networks, 143–145
New Age seekers, 453–455
New Guinea
   and gender, 311–312
   homosexuality in, 174
   sexuality in, 188
New social movements theory, 559
New World, 61
New Zealand, 182
Newton, Isaac, 14
Nicaragua, 287
Niger, 5
Nigeria, 215
Nisga'a treaty, 361
Nisichawayasihk Cree Nation, 430
Non-governmental organizations, 396
Nonmaterial culture, 46
Non-religious, 451
Nonverbal communication, 119–120
Normative organizations, 146
Norms, 55, 56, 201–202, 210. *see also* Values
North American Free Trade Agreement
   (NAFTA), 302
North Atlantic Treaty Organization (NATO), 150
North Korea
   economic activity in, 379
   slavery in, 292
   totalitarianism in, 395–396
Northern hemisphere, 521–522
Nuclear family, 418
Nuclear proliferation, 409
Nursing shortage, 501–502
Nurture, 80–81, 90

Obesity, 490–491
Objectivity, 25
O'Bryant, Aaron Jerald (AJ), 62
Occupations
   and gender, 317–319
   occupational prestige, 256, 257t
Occupy movement, 65, 71, 223, 254, 275, 558
Official Languages Act, 63
Old age. *see also* Aging
   defined, 89
   and family, 428–429
   and poverty, 268–269
   socialization in, 98–99
Old Order Mennonites, 70
Oligarchy, 150–151
Oligopolies, 389
One-parent families, 436–437
Online learning, 484–485
Open systems, 237
Operationalize a variable, 23
Opportunity, 209
Oral cultural tradition, 51
O'Ree, William, 21
Organic solidarity, 529, 565
Organizational environment, 148
Organized crime, 212, 213
On the Origin of Species (Darwin), 457
Other-directedness, 573
Out-groups, 141–142

Outsiders, 7
Overgeneralizing, 28
Ownership of property, 376, 377

Parental influence, 92–93
Parental leave, 320
Park, Robert, 530
Parole, 228
Parsons, Talcott, 329–330
Participant observation, 32–35, 37
Pascal, Blaise, 206
Passivity, 478–479
Pasteur, Louis, 507
Pastoralism, 58, 59, 252
Patriarchy, 312–314, 423, 444, 465
Patrilineal descent, 421
Patrilocality, 421
Patterns, 5–6
Pay equity, 320
Peace, 409–411
Pearce, Jeremy, 230
Peer group
   and criminality, 208–209
   defined, 91
   and gender, 315
   and socialization, 91–93
Peers, Michael, 477
Perestroika, 243
Performances, 119, 121
Personal freedom, 379–380
Personal growth, 11
Personal liberty, 13
Personal merit, 476
Personal profit, 377
Personal space, 121
Personality
   defined, 80
   development of, 84
   and deviance, 200–201
   Freud's model of, 83–84
Peters, Russell, 274
The Philadelphia Negro: A Social Study
   (Du Bois), 19
Physical disability, 112
Physician's role, 502
Piaget, Jean, 84–85
Pickton, Robert, 184
Pirandello, Luigi, 115
Plato, 13–14, 245
Play, 87
Plea bargaining, 223
The Pleasure of Honesty, 115
Pluralism, 356, 357
Pluralist model, 402, 403
Police, 222–223, 229
Political change, 13
Political revolution, 404–405
Political-economy theory, 559
Politics
   authoritarianism, 395
   in Canada, 396–401
   and class, 398
   defined, 391
   democracy. *see* Democracy
   and gender, 322–324, 399
   global perspective, 392
   global system, 396
   and health and medicine, 505–507
   looking ahead, 411
   Marxist political-economy model, 402, 403

monarchy, 392–393
and organizational environment, 148
party identification, 399
peace, pursuit of, 409–411
pluralist model, 402, 403
political freedom, 394m
political spectrum, 398–399
and power, theories of, 402–404
power-elite model, 402–403
and race, 399
and religion, 399
revolution, 404–405
and social class, 261–263
socialism. *see* Socialism
sociology as, 27
special-interest groups, 400–401
student snapshot, 399f
summary, 415
and television, 94
and terrorism, 405–406
totalitarianism, 395–396
voting, 401
and war, 406–409
welfare state, 396–397
Polyandry, 420
Polygamy, 419, 420, 421
Pope Francis, 446
Popular culture, 60, 62
Population
   composition of, 518–519
   demographic divide, 522–523
   demographic transition theory, 521
   demography, 514–519
   edge cities, 528
   and fertility, 514–515
   global perspective, 518m
   global population, 519, 521–523
   history and theory of population growth,
      519–523
   Malthusian theory, 520
   and migration, 516
   and minorities, 531
   and modernization theory, 297
   and mortality, 515–516
   overpopulation, 545
   population change, 517m, 555, 556m
   population growth, 516–518
   and poverty, 294
   rural areas, change to, 528
   and social change, 555
   summary, 548
   in survey research, 31
   and sustainability, 544
Population patterns, 148
Pornography, 180–181, 189, 328
Positivism, 14
Positivist sociology
   concepts in, 23
   defined, 22
   and meaning, 26
   measurement in, 23
   and scientific evidence, 22–23
   statistics in, 23
   and structural-functional approach, 27
   summary, 27
   variables in, 23
Postconventional level, 86
Post-industrial economy
   changing workplace, 381, 382f
   defined, 374